Advancing Societally Relevant Applications of Knowledge through Scientific Research

The *Proceedings of the Fourth National Research Conclave 2025 (RC 2025)*, titled "**Advancing Societally Relevant Applications of Knowledge through Scientific Research**," brings together cutting-edge innovations and transformative ideas from diverse domains of science, engineering, and technology. Organized by PSG College of Technology, Coimbatore, India, on May 15–16, 2025, this volume highlights research that addresses real-world challenges and contributes to sustainable societal development. The proceedings showcase interdisciplinary collaborations, emerging technologies, and student-led innovations that translate fundamental knowledge into practical solutions. From advanced materials and nanotechnology to environmental sustainability, healthcare, and digital transformation, RC 2025 emphasizes the role of research as a catalyst for societal progress. This collection serves as a valuable reference for researchers dedicated to harnessing scientific inquiry for meaningful impact.

Dr. J. Krishnamoorthi, Professor and Head, Department of Metallurgical Engineering, PSG College of Technology, holds B.E., M.E., and Ph.D. degrees in Metallurgical Engineering. With over two decades at PSG Tech, his expertise includes diffusion bonding, welding, materials characterization and steelmaking. He has 35 publications, completed major sponsored research projects.

Dr. B. Vinoth Kumar is a Professor in Information Technology at PSG College of Technology, Coimbatore. He earned his M.E. and Ph.D. in Computer Science and Engineering from Anna University. His research interests include Computational Intelligence, Memetic Algorithms, Blockchain, and Computer Vision He has over 80 publications and has edited multiple books.

Dr. L. Thulasimani, Associate Professor in Department of Electronics and Communication Engineering at PSG College of Technology since 2004, has over 75 publications in reputed journals and conferences. Her research focuses on Wireless and Digital Communication, Network Security, and VLSI Design. A certified EDII trainer, she actively fosters innovation and entrepreneurship on campus.

Dr. D. Dhanalakshmi earned her Ph.D. from the University of Sheffield, UK, and is an Assistant Professor (Selection Grade) at PSG College of Technology. She has completed UGC and DST-funded projects, guided Ph.D. scholars, and published widely. Her research focuses on organic spintronics, thin films, and magnetic materials.

Advancing Societally Relevant Applications of Knowledge through Scientific Research

Edited by

Dr. J. Krishnamoorthi
Dr. B. Vinoth Kumar
Dr. L. Thulasimani
Dr. D. Dhanalakshmi

CRC Press
Taylor & Francis Group
Boca Raton London New York

CRC Press is an imprint of the
Taylor & Francis Group, an **informa** business

First edition published 2026
by CRC Press
4 Park Square, Milton Park, Abingdon, Oxon, OX14 4RN

and by CRC Press
2385 NW Executive Center Drive, Suite 320, Boca Raton FL 33431

British Library Cataloguing-in-Publication Data
A catalogue record for this book is available from the British Library

ISBN: 9781041270126 (hbk)
ISBN: 9781041296225 (pbk)
ISBN: 9781003770435 (ebk)

DOI: 10.1201/9781003770435

Typeset in Time New Roman
by HBK Digital

Contents

List of Figures

List of Tables

Foreword

It gives me immense pleasure to introduce the Proceedings of the Fourth National Research Conclave 2025 (RC2025), titled "Advancing Societally Relevant Applications of Knowledge through Scientific Research." This conclave, organized by PSG College of Technology, Coimbatore, reflects the unwavering commitment to fostering innovation, collaboration, and excellence in research, practised by the Management of PSG College of Technology.

Scientific research holds the power to transform ideas into impactful solutions that address the pressing needs of society. The papers presented in this volume exemplify how knowledge, when applied with purpose and creativity, can lead to sustainable advancements in Science, Engineering, Technology, and allied disciplines. They demonstrate the importance of interdisciplinary collaboration and the role of young researchers in shaping a better future.

We thank the Management of PSG Institutions for all the support extended towards achieving excellence in teaching and relevant research.

RC2025 provides enough scope for intellectual exchange, inspiring curiosity, critical thinking, and societal engagement. All contributors, faculty, researchers, and students deserve high level of praise for their dedication for advancing knowledge for the greater good. I am confident that this compilation will serve as a valuable resource and a source of inspiration for future endeavours towards the application of knowledge for the welfare of society.

At this juncture, I congratulate the organising team comprising conveners, organising secretaries, various committee members, paper reviewers, academic and supporting departments, and students for making the Research Conclave 2025 event a grand success.

Dr. K.Prakasan
Principal, PSG College of Technology
Coimbatore, India

Acknowledgement

The editorial team extends its profound gratitude to all those who contributed to the successful organization and publication of the Proceedings of the Fourth National Research Conclave 2025 (RC2025), themed "Advancing Societally Relevant Applications of Knowledge through Scientific Research."

We express our sincere thanks to Shri L.Gopalakrishnan, Managing Trustee, PSG Institutions, for his unwavering encouragement in conducting the conclave and for his generous financial support towards publishing the selected papers as proceedings volume. Our heartfelt thanks to Dr.K.Prakasan, Principal, PSG College of Technology, Coimbatore, for his constant motivation and guidance in fostering a strong research and innovation culture. The Research Conclave is, in fact, a manifestation of his vision and initiative.

We gratefully acknowledge Dr.P.R.Thyla, Dean (Research), and Dr.J.Krishnamoorthi, HoD, Dept of Metallurgical Engg, conveners, RC2025 for their valuable guidance and thoughtful advice throughout the planning and execution of this event.

We would like to extend our sincere thanks to Dr.B.Vinoth Kumar, Dr.L.Thulasimani, Dr.M.Bagyalakshmi, Dr.D.Dhanalakshmi, Dr.M.Kalaiarasan and Mr.V.Venkatramanan, Organizing Secretaries for their exceptional dedication and meticulous efforts in coordinating the various aspects of the event. Their hard work and commitment were integral to the seamless execution of this national event.

Our sincere appreciation is also extended to the Conclave Session Chairpersons, Co-chairs, Department Research Coordinators, and PG Programme Tutors for their dedicated efforts in ensuring the success of this national event. We thank all internal & external reviewers for their time and insightful feedback, which significantly enhanced the quality of the papers published in this volume.

We also appreciate the enthusiastic participation of faculty members, research scholars, students and external participant form industries, whose presentations and discussions enriched the technical sessions.

Special thanks are due to the various committee members and student volunteers whose commitment and teamwork ensured the smooth conduct of the two-day event.Finally, we extend our deep appreciation to everyone who contributed to making RC 2025 a memorable and impactful platform for advancing research with meaningful societal relevance.

The Editors

1 Adaptive compression bandage for musculoskeletal injury

Brindha, D.[1,a], Fasila Begum, A.[2,b], Hanishka, K. R.[2,c], Judy, S. M.[2,d], Lavanya, M.[2,e] and Mohana Priya, V. M.[2,f]

[1]Assistant professor (Sl.Gr), Department of Biomedical Engineering, PSG College of Technology, Coimbatore, India

[2]Student, Department of Biomedical Engineering, PSG College of Technology, Coimbatore, India

Abstract

The compression bandage is used in musculoskeletal injuries to reduce swelling and provide support. Traditional compression bandages don't have the ability to adjust pressure in response to changing conditions. This paper presents the design and development of an adaptive compression bandage for musculoskeletal injuries such as sprain, knee osteoarthritis etc., which automatically adjusts the compression level based on oxygen saturation and the heart rate. The proposed system uses a micro-controller to process sensor data and actuate the bandage. The observations from the fundamental test demonstrated that the adaptive bandage can maintain optimal compression levels, potentially improving patient outcomes by enhancing comfort. This innovative approach shows a significant improvement over static methods, offering personalized care throughout the healing process. Novelty of this research paper is that compression of bandage is controlled by the oxygen level and the heart rate of a patient.

Keywords: Adaptive compression, knee osteoarthritis, musculoskeletal injury, sprain

Introduction

Muscular skeletal injuries like sprain, knee osteoarthritis, and illiotibial band syndrome uses compression bandage to reduce swelling. The gate control theory explains the action of compression in pain relief [1, 2].

Elastic stockings and elastic compression bandages are important for the chronic venous disease therapy. These medical devices are designed to exert pressure on the skin to prevent the symptoms of certain pathologies (edema, leg ulcers, etc.). The use of compression bandages causes a variety of physiological and biochemical effects on the venous, arterial and lymphatic systems. If the applied pressure, is adapted to the pathology treated, this compression therapy can reduce the edema and relieve pain [3]. Ankle sprain is the commonly occurring musculoskeletal injury among athletes. Usage of bandages for the ankle sprain during initial treatments helps in fast recovery. However, there is limited effectiveness in this approach [4].

In case of traditional bandages, maintaining precise pressure level depends on training of medical staff. There may be a pressure loss in the bandage due to the patient movements or excessive pressure exerted on the skin due to improper wrapping of bandage leading to patient discomfort [5]. An Adaptive Compression Bandage (ACB) is a medical device designed to provide adjustable compression for musculoskeletal injuries.

According to National Basketball Association (NBA) there were 214 reported hand injuries, in which 173 (81%) were classified as structural. The common injuries were strain or sprain (0.63 per 1,000 games), followed by fractures (0.37 per 1,000 games) [6]. The presence of musculoskeletal injuries in athletes is between 10% and 42.8%. It has been estimated that it would reach to 76% produced by throwing activity (75%), jumping (78%), multi-event (65%), middle- and long-distance running (79%) and sprint (76%) [7]. Musculoskeletal injuries account for about 30% of all disability-related cases. These injuries contribute to work-related absenteeism, with the economic burden estimated at $213 billion annually in the United States, which includes lost wages and decreased productivity [8].

There is no consistent amount of compression thought to be safe and effective in the literature. Thomas [18] suggests between 15 and 25mmHg, while Mayrovitz et al. [19] state that between 20 and 40mmHg effectively reduce microvascular blood perfusion safely. Sabri et al. [20], in a study of the effects of compression bandaging on the hemodynamics of

[a]brn.bme@psgtech.ac.in, [b]22d213@psgtech.ac.in, [c]22d217@psgtech.ac.in, [d]22d224@psgtech.ac.in, [e]22d227@psgtech.ac.in, [f]22d230@psgtech.ac.in

DOI: 10.1201/9781003770435-1

the lower limb, suggest that, to reduce venous blood flow and swelling effectively, external pressure should equal intravascular pressure, at around 12 mmHg [9]. Depending on the position of the body, compression therapy improves the amount of blood returned to heart. The continuous pressure applied to the veins decreases the diameter of the vessels, transmural pressure, and produces high flow rate [10]. In addition to the static pressure requirement, dynamic adjustments can be effective for the patients with chronic venous insufficiency [11]. The MAX30100 sensor measures the oxygen saturation and heart rate. This sensor uses infrared light, red light and photodiode [12]. Force sensing resistor (FSR) sensors measure static and dynamic forces applied to a surface. The working of this sensor depends on the variation of its electric resistance [13]. The adaptive compression systems use smart materials and sensors to respond to real-time physiological feedback. Unlike conventional bandages, these systems can continuously monitor the injured area and adjust compression levels. This paper focuses on the design and implementation of an adaptive compression bandage for musculoskeletal injuries using MAX30100 sensor and an inflation circuit to provide compression.

Methodology

MAX30100 sensor

The MAX30100 is an integrated module that combines pulse oximetry and heart-rate monitoring. It comprises of light emitting diode (LED)s, photodetectors and optical elements that effectively rejects ambient light. The block diagram for the adaptive compression bandage is given in Figure 1.1. It depicts a system that is designed to continuously monitor and respond to SpO2 levels using a MAX30100 sensor interfaced with an Arduino UNO. When the SpO2 level is detected to be greater than or equal to 90%, the system activates an air pump to inflate the bandage. If the SpO2 level falls below 90%, the air pump is made to deflate the bandage. This system ensures that compression is dynamically adjusted based on the real-time SpO2 readings. Salient features of MAX30100 are listed below:

- The MAX30100 operates in the range of 1.8–3.3V power supply.
- High Sample Rates and Signal Noise Ratio (SNR)
- The Operating Temperature Range is -40°C to +85°C.

- Dimensions are 5.6 mm × 3.3 mm × 1.55 mm with 14-Pins.

The system diagram of the MAX30100 is illustrated in Figure 1.2 which shows the flow of data starting from the host, hardware frameworks, and drivers.

The I2C interface connects the host to the MAX30100 module, which includes components like LED drivers, ADC and digital noise cancellation. The sensor uses red/IR LEDs and a photodiode to measure signals with ambient light cancellation to improve accuracy.

Heart rate sensor

Heart rate sensor utilizes two main techniques: Electrocardiography and photoplethysmography. The electrical activity of the heart is measured by detecting the R-peaks in the QRS complex. This is the principle of ECG based sensor. A seminal work by Clifford et al. [14] explains the functioning of ECG sensors and highlights their importance in clinical monitoring of cardiovascular diseases [14]. PPG-based sensors detect variations in light absorption caused by the pulsatile flow of blood. A study by Tamura et al. [15] highlights the application of PPG sensors in non-invasive heart rate monitoring [15].

Calibration

The calibration of MAX30100 sensor is done by performing a dark calibration to remove ambient light noise, and adjusting the LED power levels for optimal readings. Filtering algorithms are used to reduce noise and motion artifacts. To ensure the accuracy of the MAX30100 sensor in our adaptive compression bandage system, we conducted a calibration process by comparing its SpO2 readings with the standard patient monitoring system output. During the calibration, the oxygen saturation levels of multiple subjects were measured simultaneously using the MAX30100 sensor and a patient monitor. The results demonstrated a correlation between the two sets of readings, with minimal deviation. However, there existed a little deviation that doesn't produce error, confirming that the MAX30100 sensor is capable of providing accurate and consistent oxygen saturation measurements. Figure 1.3 represents the calibration output.

SpO2 subsystem

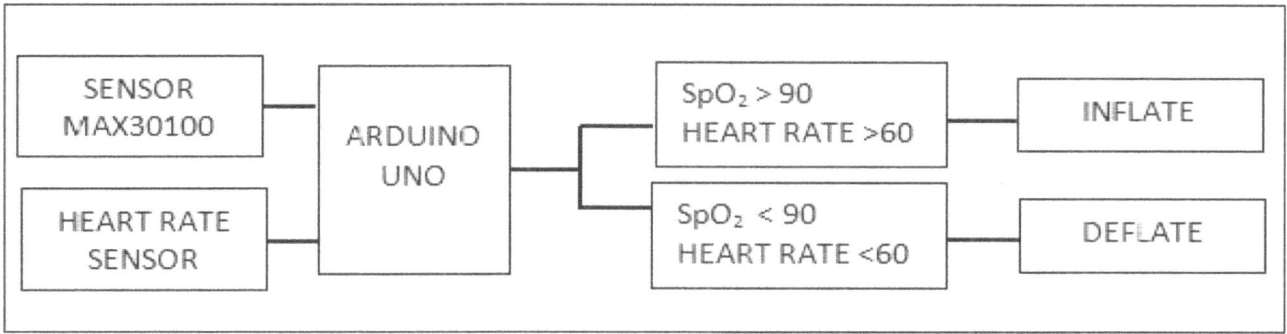

Figure 1.1 Block diagram of adaptive compression bandage
Source: Author [18]

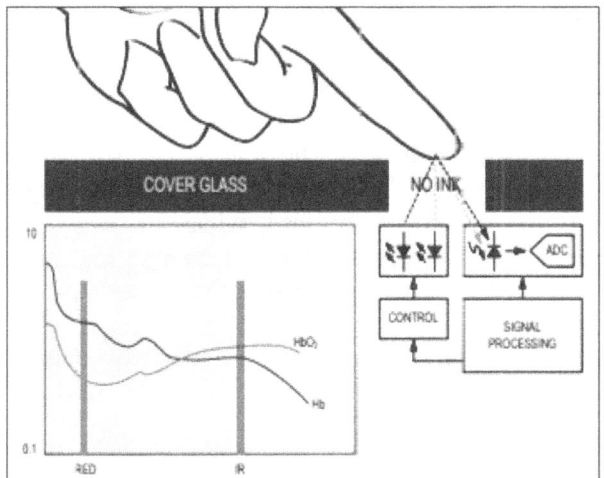

Figure 1.2 System diagram of MAX 30100
Source: Author [18]

Pulse oximetry uses photoplethysmography (PPG) to non-invasively measure blood oxygen levels based on Figure 1.2. System diagram of MAX 30100.

Variability of light absorption through human tissues at different wavelengths. It measures volumetric changes in pulsatile arterial blood flow. Oxygenated hemoglobin (Hb) and deoxygenated hemoglobin (deoxy-Hb) in the blood absorb light differently within the 650–1000 nm wavelength range, which is ideal for assessing blood oxygen levels. Other tissues, like water and fat, have low absorption allowing for accurate readings. Deoxy-Hb absorbs more light at around 650 nm than Oxy-Hb.

When the fingertip is illuminated by red (660 nm) and infrared (940 nm) light, oxygenated hemoglobin absorbs more infrared light, while deoxygenated hemoglobin absorbs more red light. The pulse oximeter calculates oxygen saturation from these differences in absorption spectra. Figure 1.4(A) shows

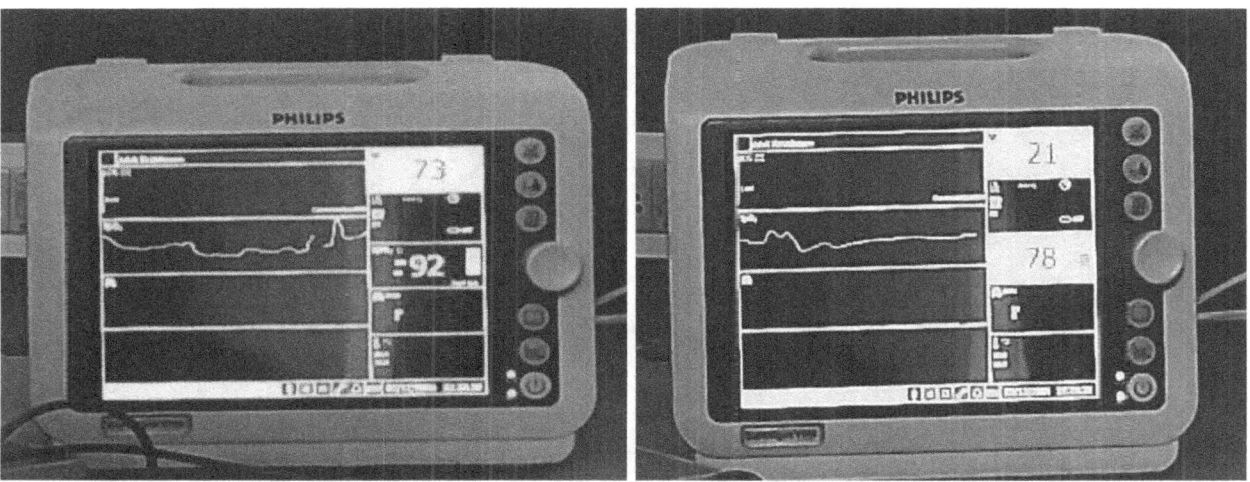

Figure 1.3 Calibration using pulse oximeter in patient monitoring system before and after compression using sphygmomanometer
Source: Author

absorption spectra of red and infrared at different wavelengths.

Factors affecting light absorption include the path length through the artery, the concentration of absorbing substances and the different absorption capacities of oxyhemoglobin and deoxyhemoglobin.

The LEDs on the sensor emits red and infrared lights alternatively on and off about thirty times per second. The amount of light transmitted through the finger varying with each heartbeat is measured. The system isolates the blood signal by subtracting the minimum from the peak light transmitted for each wavelength. The ratio of red to infrared light gives the ratio of oxygenated to deoxygenated hemoglobin and is converted to SpO2 based on the Beer–Lambert law. Oxygenated and deoxygenated hemoglobin absorption curve is demonstrated in Figure 1.4(B). The infrared signal has a smaller amplitude when compared to red light. During a heartbeat, the optical path length varies based on the change in the arterial blood volume. By comparing the differential absorption of red and infrared light, the SpO2 value can be estimated. Thus, both types of PPG signals are required for accurate non-invasive SpO2 measurement.

$$SpO2 = \frac{C[OHb]}{C[OHb]+C[RHb]} \times 100\%$$

Pressure measurement

Most of the existing IPC devices are incapable of real time monitoring, visualization of the pressure variations and lacking feedback on pressure dosages delivered to the human body. In this study, an intelligent digital monitoring and bio-feedback system has been designed to detect and monitor pressure delivery and variations when the IPC device is interacting with the human limbs [16]. Hardware design of this part includes two small, low noise air pumps for inflation and deflation of the cuff, force sensing resistor for measuring the pressure exerted on the skin. Air pumps work together to achieve the desired pressure of 12 mmHg.

This is adjusted by the real time monitoring of pressure exerted using force sensing resistor with the help of Arduino UNO. A force sensing resistor (FSR) is a passive polymer film that changes the resistance between its two terminals based on the level of force exerted on its surface. This change in resistance can be characterized to measure forces and pressures. It consists of two interdigitated patterns deposited on a thermoplastic sheet, with another sheet that contains a conductive ink. A spacer is placed between the two thermoplastic sheets to provide the impedance of a nearly open circuit when no load is applied. Once load is applied to the contact area, the two thermoplastic layers are compressed, which increases the contact area between them and decreases the resistance of the FSR. A typical FSR structure is shown in Figure 1.5 [17].

Arduino UNO is used for interfacing the sensors with the bandage. We use the following pins for acquisition:

- GND - The ground pin acts as the reference point for the circuit
- VCC (3.3V or 5V) - This pin supplies the operating voltage to the Arduino UNO

A)
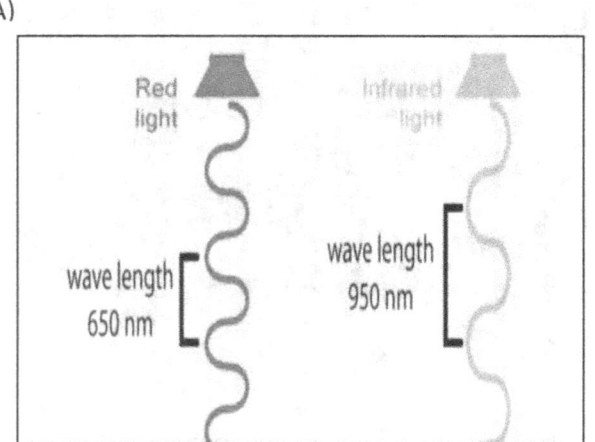

B)
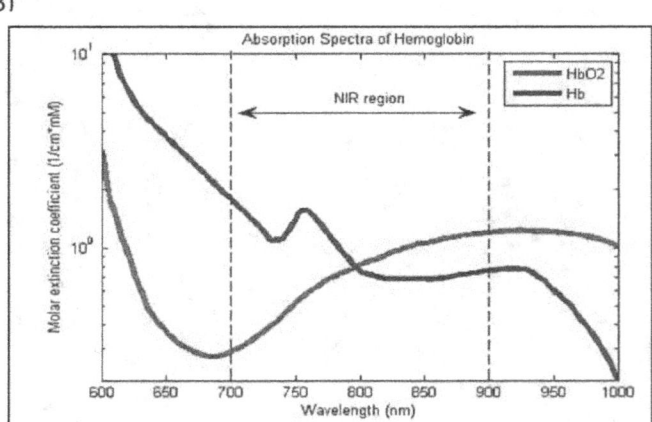

Figure 1.4 (A) Absorption spectra of red and infrared at different wavelengths. (B) Oxygenated and deoxygenated hemoglobin absorption curve

Source: Author [19, 20]

- SDA or A4 - It is used for transmitting data between the Arduino UNO and connected device(I2C).
- SCL or A5 - It is used for synchronizing the data transfer between the Arduino UNO and connected devices.

Results and Discussion

In order to validate our adaptive compression bandage system, we conducted a study with five participants to observe the effect of compression on heart rate and SpO2 values. The oxygen saturation of the five participants obtained using pulse oximeter and measured using MAX30100 is shown in the Figure 1.6(A) and the corresponding bar graph is given in Figure 1.6(B).

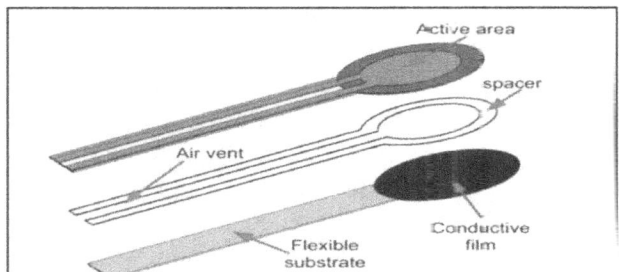

Figure 1.5 Structure of force sensing resistor
Source: Author [21]

The heart rate of each participant before and after applying the compression is measured. The values are shown Figure 1.6(C) and the corresponding graph is given in Figure 1.6(D).

Subject	Pulse Oximeter	MAX30100 sensor
S1	97	95
S2	96	95
S3	98	95
S4	96	97
S5	97	94

(A)

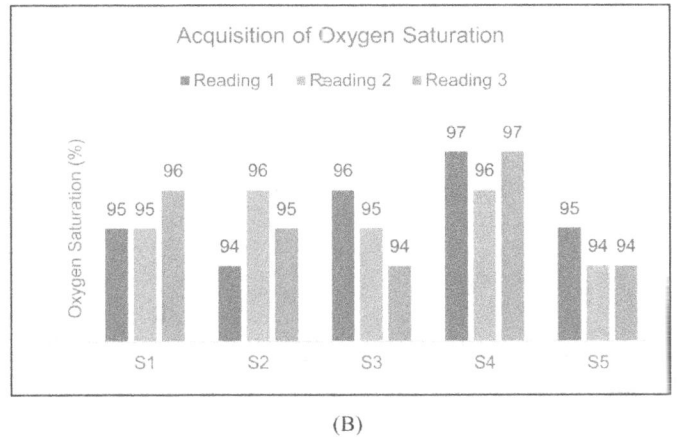

(B)

Subject	Before Compression (bpm)	After Compression (bpm)
S1	82	54
S2	73	56
S3	82	56
S4	75	58
S5	78	60

(C)

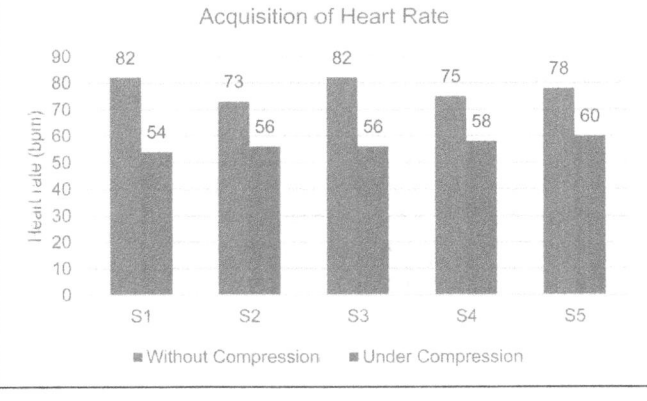

(D)

Figure 1.6 (A) Summary table of Average oxygen saturation (B) Graphical representation of three oxygen saturation values for everyone (C) Summary table of heart rate values before and after compression (D) Comparison of heart rate with respect to compression
Source: Author

The successful integration of the MAX30100 sensor with the Arduino UNO is significant in the development of our adaptive compression bandage. This sensor enables real-time monitoring of the patient's SpO2 levels. The adaptive bandage is a feedback system that can provide dynamic compression.

During the project, we encountered a challenge related to the sensor's I²C communication. The MAX30100 sensor had pre-soldered pull-up resistors on its board. These resistors caused erratic readings and unreliable data acquisition when connected to Arduino UNO. We removed the pull-up resistors from the sensor module using a soldering iron to solve this problem. The system was then programmed to trigger an air pump to either inflate or deflate the bandage cuff based on the SpO2 and heart rate readings: If SpO2 falls below 90% and heart rate below 60bpm, the cuff deflates to reduce compression, and if SpO2 is above 90% and heart rate is greater than 60bpm, the cuff inflates to apply the necessary compression pressure. The air pumps required more current than the Arduino could supply. This was solved by using MOSFETs for switching. Lack of a solenoid valve made airflow direction control difficult, leading to timing challenges or pump switching. Initial noise and instability were resolved by adjusting resistor values.

Conclusion

The Adaptive compression bandage ensures patient safety by preventing excessive compression and optimizes therapeutic efficacy through continuous adjustment. Looking towards the future advancements, the overall cost can be reduced by exploring affordable alternatives for the sensor and microcontroller, without compromising functionality. The bandage material can be made more patient-friendly by using soft, breathable, and hypoallergenic fabrics that enhance comfort during prolonged use. More physiological parameters, such as skin temperature, and moisture levels, could be integrated into the system to provide a better health monitoring solution.

Acknowledgement

We would like to express our deepest gratitude to our Head of the Department, Dr. Vidhyapriya R, Department of Biomedical Engineering. We thank our guide, Dr. Brindha D, Assistant Professor, Department of Biomedical Engineering for the invaluable support. Finally, we extend our gratitude to all our faculty members and classmates for their timely assistance.

References

[1] Moayedi, M., & Davis, K. D. (2013). Theories of pain: from specificity to gate control. *Journal of Neurophysiology*, 109(1), 5–12. doi: 10.1152/jn.00457.2012.

[2] Honigman, L., Bar-Bachar, O., Yarnitsky, D., Sprecher, E., & Granovsky, Y. (2016). Nonpainful wide-area compression inhibits experimental pain. *Pain*, 157(9), 2000–2011. doi: 10.1097/j.pain.0000000000000604.

[3] Rimaud, D., Convert, R., & Calmels, P. (2014). In vivo measurement of compression bandage interface pressures: the first study. *Annals of Physical and Rehabilitation Medicine*, 57(6), 394–400. doi: 10.1016/j.rehab.2014.06.005.

[4] Heß, T., Milani, T. L., Kilper, A., & Mitschke, C. (2024). Immediate effects of wearing an ankle bandage on fine coordination, proprioception, balance and gait in the subacute phase of ankle sprains. *Life*, 14(7), 0810. doi: 10.3390/life14070810.

[5] Rezende, G. C., O'Flynn, B., & O'Mahony, C. (2022). Smart compression therapy devices for treatment of venous leg ulcers: a review. *Advanced Healthcare Materials*, 11, 2200710. doi: 10.1002/adhm.202200710.

[6] Lin, E., Tummala, S. V., Morikawa, L., Vij, N., Petty, S. B., McQuivey, K. S., et al. (2023). Strains/sprains and fractures are the most common hand and wrist injuries in NBA athletes who return to preinjury player efficiency and equal or greater true shooting percentage within two years. *Arthroscopy, Sports Medicine, and Rehabilitation*, 5(6), 100829. doi: 10.1016/j.asmr.2023.100829.

[7] Romero-Morales, C., López-López, D., Almazán-Polo, J., Mogedano-Cruz, S., Sosa-Reina, M. D., García-Pérez-de-Sevilla, G., et al. (2024). Prevalence, diagnosis and management of musculoskeletal disorders in elite athletes: a mini-review. *Disease-a-Month*, 70(1), 101629. doi: 10.1016/j.disamonth.2023.101629.

[8] Vos, T., Lim, S., Abbafati, C., Abbas, K. M., Abbasi, M., Abdollahi, M., et al. (2020). Global burden of musculoskeletal disorders from 1990 to 2017: estimates from the global burden of disease study 2017. *Annals of the Rheumatic Diseases*, 79(7), 852–862.

[9] Pollard, A., & Cronin, G. (2005). Compression bandaging for soft tissue injury of the ankle: a literature review. *Emergency Nurse*, 13(6), 20–24. doi: 10.7748/en2005.10.13.6.20.c1218.

[10] Dissemond, J., Assenheimer, B., Bültemann, A., Gerber, V., Gretener, S., Kohler-von Siebenthal, E., et al. (2016). Compression therapy in patients with venous leg ulcers. *Journal der Deutschen Dermatologischen Gesellschaft (JDDG)*, 14(11), 1072–1087. doi: 10.1111/ddg.13091.

[11] Mayrovitz, H. N., Partsch, H., & Vanscheidt, W. (2015). Comparison of 4-layer bandages and an adaptive compression therapy device on intended pressure delivery. *Journal of Wound, Ostomy and Continence Nursing*, 42(5), 468–473. doi: 10.1097/WON.0000000000000157.

[12] Sundararaju, K., Yaaghas, V., Yogeshwaran, R., & Mohanraj, P. (2023). Pulse and blood oxygen saturation monitoring system. In AIP Conference Proceedings, (pp. 2822, p. 020202). doi: 10.1063/5.0180558.

[13] Sadun, A., Jalani, J., & Sukor, J. A. (2016). Force sensing resistor (FSR): a brief overview and the low-cost sensor for active compliance control. In Proceedings of SPIE. doi: 10.1117/12.2242950.

[14] Clifford, G. D., Azuaje, F., & McSharry, P. (2006). Advanced Methods and Tools for ECG Data Analysis. Artech House. doi: 10.5555/1213221.

[15] Tamura, T., Maeda, Y., Sekine, M., & Yoshida, M. (2014). Wearable photoplethysmographic sensors—past and present. *Electronics*, 3(2), 282–302. doi:10.3390/electronics3020282.

[16] Zhao, S., Liu, R., & Guan, D. (2019). Development of an intelligent digital monitoring and biofeedback system for intermittent pneumatic compression therapy device. In 2019 IEEE Far East NDT. doi:10.1109/FPM45753.2019.9035788.

[17] Saadeh, M. Y., Carambat, T. D., & Arrieta, A. M. (2017). Evaluating and modeling force sensing resistors for low force applications. In ASME 2017 Smart Materials, Adaptive Structures and Intelligent Systems (SMASIS). doi: 10.1115/SMASIS2017-3703.

[18] Thomas, S. (1990). Bandages and bandaging: The science behind the art. Care: Science & Practice. 8(2), 57–60.

[19] Mayrovitz, H. N., Larsen, P. B., & Glickman, Y. (1998). Compression-induced pulsatile blood flow changes in human legs. Clinical Physiology, 18(2), 117–124. doi: 10.1046/j.1365-2281.1998.00084.x

[20] Sabri, S., Roberts, V. C., & Cotton, L. T. (1971). Effects of externally applied pressure on the haemodynamics of the lower limb. British Medical Journal, 3(5773),503–508 doi: 10.1136/bmj.3.5773.503

2 MedForecast: a novel approach for web-based disease predictive healthcare system and personalized recommendations

Asqar Ali, S. M. S.[1,a] A. N. Gnana Jeevan[2,b] and Rishi Kumar, S.[2]

[1]Pre-final year, Artificial Intelligence and Data Science, Saranathan College of Engineering, Tiruchirappalli, India

[2]Assistant Professor, Artificial Intelligence and Data Science, Saranathan College of Engineering, Tiruchirappalli, India

Abstract

MedForecast is a web-based medical diagnostic platform that integrates Machine Learning and Computer Vision technique to analyse the medical reports to predict the diseases at an early stage and provide the notification personalized recommendation for future health monitoring improvement. Our web platform provides a diet plans and lifestyle modifications tailored to an individual health status. Also be integrated with Large Language Model (LLM) for handling user's MedBot with frequently asked questions (FAQ). Our web platform having unique features to identify neonatal malnutrition for new-born babies. Our research work describes with clear architecture, implementation and potential application of MedForecast in disease predictive and forecasting in healthcare management.

Keywords: Computer vision, cross-validation, deep learning model, disease prediction at an early stage, large language model, machine learning model, natural language processing, neonatal malnutrition detection, neural network, personalized recommendations, random forest, support vector machine, training data, XGBoost

Introduction

The healthcare industry plays a vital role in good health and well-being across the world. The AI health industry has been significantly growing and increasingly in demand in recent years, and there's a big need for it. The healthcare system deals with many challenges, like diagnosing illnesses, finding new medicines, monitoring patients health from a long distance, and giving personal health advice. MedForecast uses a patient medical report to make the diagnosis process. Medical reports contain quantitative and objective measurements of a patient's internal health. These values directly reflect the functioning of vital organs and biological systems. Disease starts with minor abnormalities in lab values before symptoms appear. By analyzing trends in the report, AI can predict the disease at an early stage. It's more effective for both doctors and patients who want to take better care of their health. It helps with diagnosing diseases, treating patients, and keeping track of their health. The serious health problems are leads by lack or excess of nutrition's. For the physical health growth and development of brain for the new born babies our model detect and make notifications. If a baby is not getting the right amount of nourishment, they can have a weak immune system, slow growth, learning difficulties, and long-term health issues. Even though many people know about this, many caregivers still don't get the right and timely advice about feeding and taking care of babies. This is especially true in places where healthcare is difficult to get or follow-up is not reliable. Our model MedForecast make a bridges a gap between neonatal health and mothers health by providing tailored insights through its intelligent system. This MedForecast model notified the critical bridge with neonatal health, by offering personalized and insights the mother to make smart decision-support system. Our model notified a broad variety of services, including initial disease prevention, precise diagnosis, beset treatment, and adapted recovery planning, all designed to improve long-term health outcomes for newborns. By investigating both prenatal and postnatal medical records such as laboratory results, clinical observations, and doctor's notes, the system can detect early signs of progressive issues. Based on this analysis, it makes clear and actionable recommendations couturier to each baby's unique health needs. A key module of MedForecast is its Neonatal Nutrition Planner, which helps guide feeding strategies from birth onward. As the child grows,

[a]mdasqar007@gmail.com, [b]gnanajeevan.a.n@ist.srmtrichy.edu.in

DOI: 10.1201/9781003770435-2

the platform continues to provide adaptive endorsements using real-time health data from both the infant and the mother. It assists caregivers in following World Health Organization (WHO) guidelines for breastfeeding, formula feeding, and the gradual introduction of solid foods, while also considering cultural norms and traditional dietary practices. To further support caregivers, the MedForecast features a built-in intimate assistant that responds to common questions about baby care, feeding routines, symptom monitoring, and developmental milestones. This tool helps parents—even those without a medical background—access trustworthy, context-aware advice whenever needed. The system also includes food image recognition functionality, allowing caregivers to capture and assess the nutritional quality of meals prepared for both mothers and infants, supporting better day-to-day dietary decisions.

Literature Review

Neonatal health, defined as the health of newborns within the first 28 days of life, is a critical determinant of child survival, long-term development, and public health outcomes. This period represents the most vulnerable phase in a child's life, accounting for nearly half of all deaths in children under five years old globally. Despite growths in medical science, neonatal mortality remains a pressing concern, mainly in low- and middle-income countries, where access to timely and adequate healthcare is limited. Kumar and Singh [2].

The health of neonates is inclined by a variety of unified factors. Prematurity, low birth weight, congenital anomalies, and infections such as sepsis, pneumonia, and meningitis are among the leading causes of neonatal disease and humanity. In many cases, these conditions are preventable or manageable with early diagnosis and suitable medical interference. However, delays in identifying symptoms, lack of trained health personnel, and lacking neonatal intensive care facilities contribute to poor outcomes.

Maternal health previously and during mother pregnancy plays a pivotal role in formative neonatal outcomes. Conditions such as gestational diabetes, hypertensive disorders, nutritional deficiencies, and infections in the mother can directly impact fatal growth and improvement. Moreover, socioeconomic factors like scarcity, lack of education, insufficient prenatal care, and ecological exposures further exacerbate the risks associated with neonatal health.

Emerging research emphasizes the need for data-driven approaches to improve neonatal outcomes. Integrating predictive models into healthcare systems can aid in early risk stratification, timely diagnosis, and modified care planning for both mothers and newborns. For instance, machine learning algorithms can analyze patterns in prenatal and perinatal data to prediction hitches such as preterm birth or neonatal sepsis. These insights can allow health specialists and caregivers to take proactive steps, thereby refining survival rates and quality of life for newborns. Smith and Doe [6].

Addressing neonatal health needs a widespread strategy that combines technology-driven solutions with strong public health structure. This includes firming parental healthcare services, expanding access to neonatal screening and diagnostics, enhancing training for health providers, and encouraging awareness among societies. When embedded within a web-based disease prediction platform like MedForecast, neonatal health monitoring can become more accessible, scalable, and personalized—ushering in a new era of preventative and precision medicine for the youngest members of society.

Major causes of neonatal morbidity and mortality

The leading causes of neonatal morbidity and mortality are prematurity, low birth weight, birth asphyxia, infections, and congenital variances. Premature infants often face underdeveloped organs, leading to respiratory distress and feeding issues. Low birth weight increases the risk of infection, hypothermia, and developmental delays. Infections like sepsis, meningitis, and pneumonia remain significant threats, especially in areas with inadequate infection control. Congenital anomalies, such as heart defects and neural tube defects, contribute to the neonatal health burden and may require immediate or long-term medical care. Lee and Kim [3].

Maternal and environmental influences

A newborn's health is closely linked to maternal health. Conditions such as gestational diabetes, hypertension, anemia, and both undernutrition and overnutrition affect fetal development. Undernourished mothers may have low birth weight or preterm infants, while maternal obesity increases the risk of gestational diabetes, hypertensive disorders, and complications like macrosomia and cesarean deliveries. Infections during pregnancy, such as toxoplasmosis, syphilis, and rubella, also pose risks.

Additionally, socioeconomic factors, limited access to care, and environmental exposures like air pollution and poor sanitation can further impact neonatal health outcomes. Miller and Brown [5].

Gaps in current neonatal care infrastructure
Despite global health efforts, significant gaps remain in neonatal care infrastructure. Many rural and low-income regions lack specialized neonatal intensive care units (NICUs), skilled birth attendants, and necessary medical equipment such as incubators or ventilators. Inadequate training of healthcare workers often results in the underdiagnosis or mismanagement of neonatal complications. Furthermore, existing data collection and reporting systems are often fragmented, limiting the ability to monitor trends, identify high-risk cases, or evaluate intervention outcomes. These gaps underline the urgent need for scalable, technology-enhanced solutions that can bridge the divide between available services and clinical needs. Smith and Doe [6].

Preventive and personalized care strategies
An essential component of neonatal health improvement is prevention and personalized care. Routine screening for genetic and metabolic disorders, timely vaccinations, thermal care, breastfeeding support, and maternal education programs is vital. In high-risk cases, personalized care strategies such as home monitoring devices, follow-up telemedicine consultations, and tailored nutrition plans for infants can drastically reduce the likelihood of readmissions and complications. Technology platforms can store patient-specific data and generate individualized care paths, alerting caregivers about critical milestones or warning signs. These interventions not only ensure the well-being of the newborn but also empower parents and caregivers with confidence and knowledge. Zhang and Liu [8].

System Architecture

System Architecture and Workflow of MedForecast is shown in Figure 2.1, it shows the structured workflow to process medical data, analyse symptoms, and generate recommendations. The architecture consists of the following components:

A. Data Acquisition: Users upload medical files (PDFs) containing lab reports, prescriptions, or symptom descriptions.

B. Trained Dataset: Uses PyPDF, pdf2image, and pyTesseract OCR for text extraction and tokenization.

C. Machine Learning Model: This model was used based on Random Forest Classifier (RFC), Neural Network (MLP) and Support Vector Machine (SVM) for disease prediction and personalized recommendations.

D. Hyperparamater (XGBoost (Extreme Gradient Boosting)) Algorithm: This XGBoost increases prediction accurateness by reducing loss using gradient boosting, where is the loss function represents the model's complexity.

Machine Learning Models

Machine learning model for disease prediction

- The ML model in MedForecast is built using a supervised learning approach, incorporating various features such as age, symptoms, medical history, and lab test results.
- Data Collection: Two datasets are used, including a symptom-based disease dataset.
- Feature Engineering: Extraction of key health indicators for predictive analysis.
- Model Training: Implementation of classification algorithms such as Random Forest, XGBoost, and Multi-layer Perceptron.

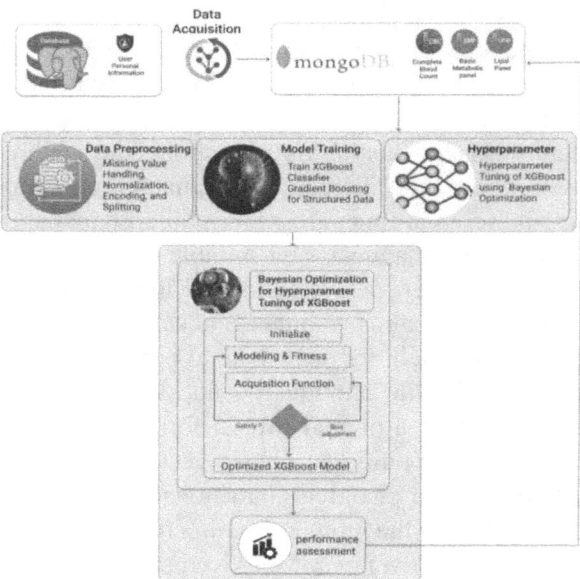

Figure 2.1 System architecture and workflow
Source: Author

- Evaluation Metrics: Accuracy, recall, and F1-score are employed to assess model performance.

The model predicts potential disease risks and provides users with an early warning, allowing them to take preventive measures. The integration of AI-driven predictive models allows for enhanced accuracy in risk assessment and provides a scientific basis for lifestyle recommendations. Furthermore, we continuously improve its predictive capabilities by incorporating user feedback and retraining the model with new data.

Machine learning models and their mathematical foundations

Our study considers two major ownership structure measures such as ownership concentration and institutional ownership as independent variables. Emerging markets witness concentrated ownership, where they exert their influence on the management and governance of the firm hugely. Two measures such as holdings of the single largest shareholder and total holdings of the five largest shareholders are used to represent the ownership concentration. Fractions of shareholdings of the institutional investors are utilized as a measure for institutional ownership.

Random Forest classifier

Random Forest Classifier is an ensemble learning technique that combines multiple decision trees to enhance predictive performance (Figure 2.2). The final prediction is computed which represents individual decision trees, and as the total number of trees. In this method, a classifier is used to construct decision trees and make predictions. The subsets of random dataset, the training data are combining the results by averaging for further prediction. It is known as an ensemble technique. With the new training dataset, they generate multiple decision trees, and each of them trained on a random subset of the data and a random subset of features. This process is referred to as bootstrapping and bagging. From the predicted trained dataset was computed by aggregating the outputs of individual decision trees. When used for a classification task, the final prediction is determined by majority voting among the decision trees.

Gini index:

$$Gini_p = 1 - \sum_{i=1}^{k} pi^2 \qquad (1)$$

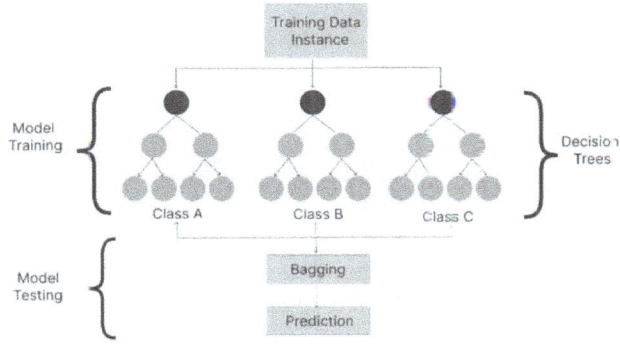

Figure 2.2 Random forest classifier
Source: Author

Final Prediction:

$$y = majorityvote(h\_1\,(x), h\_2\,(x), \ldots, h\_T\,(x)) \qquad (2)$$

Support Vector Machine

From supervised machine learning algorithm, we used SVM for both classification and regression problems (Figure 2.3). The goal of SVM is to find the best hyperplane or decision boundary that separates the closest data points, known as support vector. SVM utilizes data from the training dataset, and by establishing a hyperplane, it classifies the data points into two distinct categories. The primary objective of SVM is to determine the optimal hyperplane that lies between the two closest support vectors. Once this hyperplane is defined, all data points should ideally be classified correctly. The algorithm employs a kernel trick—specifically the radial basis function (RBF)—which involves adding an extra dimension to the current feature space, thereby enabling the data to become linearly separable. The hyperplane is mathematically defined by the weight vector w, the input vector x, and the bias b. The decision boundary is constructed to maximize the margin between the classes.

Hyperplane Equation:

$$F(x) = w^t\,x + b \qquad (3)$$

Hard Margin Optimization:

$$y^i\,(w^T\,x^i + b) \geq 1 \;\forall\; i \qquad (4)$$

Soft Margin (with slack variables):

$$y^i\,(w^t\,x^i + b) \geq 1 - \xi\_i,\; \xi\_i \geq 0 \qquad (5)$$

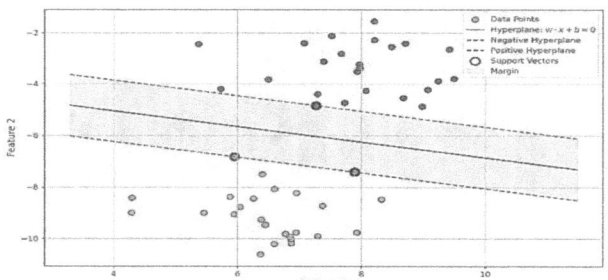

Figure 2.3 Support vector machine
Source: Author

XGBoost (extreme gradient boosting)
XGBoost is a scalable, distributed gradient-boosted decision tree (GBDT) which improves prediction accuracy by minimizing loss using gradient boosting, where the loss function measures prediction error and a regularization term controls model complexity.

Unlike traditional boosting algorithms, XGBoost incorporates advanced regularization techniques such as L1 (Lasso) and L2 (Ridge) to prevent overfitting, which makes it more robust on noisy datasets. From the dataset it builds trees sequentially, where each new tree aims to correct the errors made by the previous ensemble of trees. This model approach allows the model to gradually reduce residual errors with each reiteration.

The XGBoost's key algorithm was the second instruction results we use the novelties to enhance the loss function more successfully, enabling faster conjunction and enhanced accuracy. This algorithm also supports parallelized tree construction, making it significantly faster than outmoded gradient boosting models, especially on large datasets.

This XGBoost algorithm contains several tools to improve concert, such as tree pruning, sparsity-aware learning for handling lost data, and column subsampling to decrease variance. These features communally contribute to its strong concert in many real-world entities, including ordering, progression, ranking, and variance detection.

This XGBoost algorithm becomes a wide embraced choice for both research and industries needs for provided that scalability, high predictive control, and ability to handle numerous data types and structures.

Neural network

Under the neural network perception, the multi-layer perceptron (MLP) we intended a model in our research work to estimated complex functions and can learn non-linear decision limitations, making them suitable for a variety of tasks such as ordering and pattern appreciation.

The input data were delivered through the MLP layer by layer for feed forward procedure; each neuron performs a weighted rundown of its inputs, adds a bias term, and applies a non-linear initiation function such as ReLU, sigmoid, or tanh. This non-linearity enables the network to learn intricate patterns that are not possible with linear models.

Training an MLP typically involves a supervised learning process using the backpropagation algorithm in conjunction with an optimization technique like Adam. During training, the network adjusts the weights of its connections to minimize a loss function that quantifies the error between predicted and actual outputs.

MLPs are considered universal function approximators, meaning that, given sufficient neurons and proper training, they can model any continuous function. However, their performance and generalization ability are influenced by factors such as the architecture (number of layers and neurons), choice of activation functions, and the quality and quantity of the training data.

Due to their flexibility and relatively simple structure, MLPs serve as a building block for more complex deep learning architectures and are often used as a baseline in many machine learning experiments.

The MLP architecture that we used are, the number of input neurons is determined by the number of inputs passed along with three hidden layers, each with 128, 64 and 32 neurons respectively and output is multiple class.

Formulas used MLP

Single Neuron Output:

$$a = \sigma(w^t * x + b) \tag{6}$$

Forward Pass (Layer-wise):

$$a^{(l)} = \sigma(W^{(l)}a^{(l-1)} + b^{(l)}) \quad\dots\dots\dots\dots\dots\dots\dots\dots\dots \tag{7}$$

Loss Function (Mean Squared Error):

$$L = \frac{1}{n}\sum_{i=1}^{n}\left(y^i - y^{\ i}_{\ p}\right) \tag{8}$$

These models enable MedForecast to predict disease risks with high precision, aiding users in proactive healthcare management.

Features

Personalized diet and lifestyle recommendations
Based on ML predictions, MedForecast generates customized diet and lifestyle suggestions [1]:

Diagnosed conditions: This iteration detects a disease if it's true, a diet plan is tailored to mitigate its impact, focusing on nutrient-rich foods.

- Symptomatic users: This iteration results in symptoms that indicate potential health risks; the system suggests preventive dietary changes.
- Healthy users: This iteration report the balanced diet and workout plan based on their height, weight and age.
- Workout plan: This is a notification for all physical activities aligned with the patient's condition related to their age for maintaining or improving health.

By leveraging AI, we ensure that users receive science-backed advice that aligns with their specific health needs.

Gemini LLM integration for conversational support

- Handling FAQs: Users can ask questions related to diseases, symptoms, nutrition and even the medicines that they are prescribed with.
- Generating text-based diet and workout plans: The model explains why specific foods and exercises are recommended.
- Providing evidence-Based Justifications: Each recommendation is supported by research-backed insights.

The conversational AI component of MedForecast not only provides educational insights but also improves user engagement. The system is designed to mimic a human-like consultation experience, making it easier for users to trust and understand the recommendations that are provided [4].

Food image representation for diet guidance
To make dietary recommendations more engaging, we include a food image feature [3]:

- Disease-specific diets: Users with diagnosed conditions receive visual representations of beneficial foods [8].

- Symptom-based food suggestions: If no disease is detected, but symptoms exist, images of appropriate dietary options are shown.
- Balanced diet for healthy users: If no risks are identified, a well-rounded diet plan is displayed with corresponding images.

Visual representation of dietary recommendations enhances the effectiveness of the platform by helping users make informed choices. Studies show that image-based dietary education can significantly improve adherence to recommended nutrition plans. Taylor and Nguyen [7].

Neonatal malnutrition detection and dietary plans
The neonatal detection had a particularly beneficial feature in pediatric healthcare, helping caregivers ensure optimal infant growth. This neonatal able to detect malnutrition early and provide data-driven dietary recommendations can contribute to reducing infant mortality rates associated with poor nutrition.

Experimental Setup

Our research work had an experimental setup which involved dataset collection, processing, notification and performance evaluation. These experiments were executed on a standard computing environment with the following parameters of i5, core processor, 16GB RAM with RTX3050 built-in 6GB video RAM.

Data pre-processing
The pre-processed data are error-prone process; in this stage we can enhance the quality of the data and prepare it for use in subsequent steps. This phase consists of three subphases:

1. **Data cleaning:** In this stage the noisy data is removed, which are inconsistencies across data sources.
2. **Data integration:** This state enriches data sources by combining information from multiple data sources.
3. **Data transformation:** This final stage of data transformation ensures that the data is in a suitable format for use in our models.

Data exploration
Data exploration is concerned with building a deeper understanding of your data. You'll look for patterns,

correlations, and deviations based on visual and descriptive techniques. The insights you gain from this phase will enable you to start modelling. To achieve this step mainly use descriptive statistics, inferential statistics, visual techniques and simple modeling. This step often goes by the abbreviation EDA, for Exploratory Data Analysis.

Implementation using Django and react

MedForecast platform developed using Django for backend framework and react for frontend. Detailed implementations include:

Backend (Django):

- Endpoints for user authentication, report upload and result prediction
- Machine learning model for disease prediction.
- Natural language processing approach for data extraction from user report.
- Communication with Gemini LLM for response generation.

Frontend (React):

- User-friendly interface for uploading medical reports and viewing recommendations.
- Interactive chatbot powered by Gemini LLM.
- Food image display for dietary guidance.

The combination of Django and React ensures high performance, scalability, and a seamless user experience. The application also incorporates cloud storage options for secure handling of medical documents.

Performance evaluation

In the model validation process, we utilized a separate set of testing data comprising 20% of the dataset. These testing samples were not included in the model training phase, allowing us to evaluate how well the model could make accurate predictions when presented with instances representing a class it hadn't encountered during training. Essentially, this assessment aimed to gauge the model's ability to handle new, previously unseen data during validation, ensuring its robustness and performance beyond the initial training datasets.

Table 2.1 presents a summarized view of the key characteristics of the selected datasets employed in the following, a more detailed description of each

Table 2.1 Performance comparison of classification algorithms

Algorithm	Archived accuracy (%)	Remarks
Random Forest	95%	Reduces overfitting by aggregating multiple decision trees (bagging)
XGBoost	98%	Optimized gradient boosting, strong predictive power and regularization
Support Vector Machine (SVM)	95%	Effective for high-dimensional spaces, but computationally expensive
Neural networks (MLP)	94%	Deep learning model capable of capturing complex patterns

Source: Author

dataset has been presented, offering comprehensive insights into their distinctive features and contextual relevance.

Results

In this paper, a predictive model is employed to forecast the onset of diverse chronic medical conditions. Each disease was examined using two distinct datasets, one for training and another for testing a strategic choice that enhances the robustness and generalizability of the model. Leveraging multiple datasets accounts for the inherent variability in healthcare data and helps build a more comprehensive and accurate predictive foundation. This approach ultimately improves the effectiveness of strategies for managing and preventing chronic diseases. A sample overview of the dataset on how the data is distributed in Figure 2.4.

From these prediction experiments are trained and the final prediction is shown from Figure 2.5–2.9 and Table 2.2 for various algorithm that are used which is shown in the findings that indicate the remarkable ability of the model to effectively identify and classify various diseases instances with high accuracy and sensitivity. The implemented BO–XGBoost model demon started an impressively high level of accuracy, consistently reaching 98% for both datasets.

Below are the model results and confusion matrices of various models analysed.

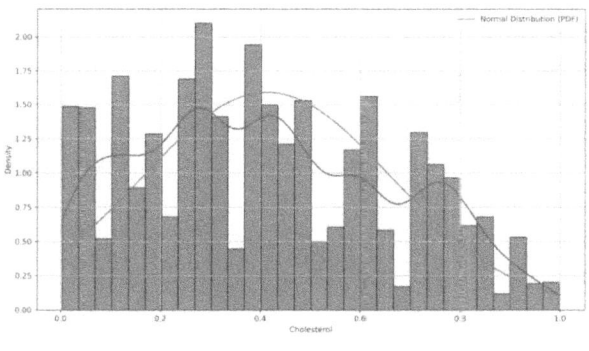
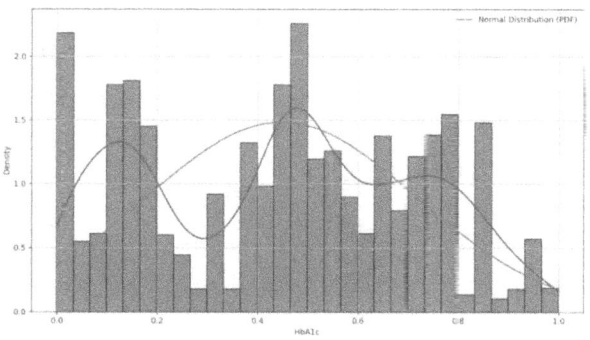
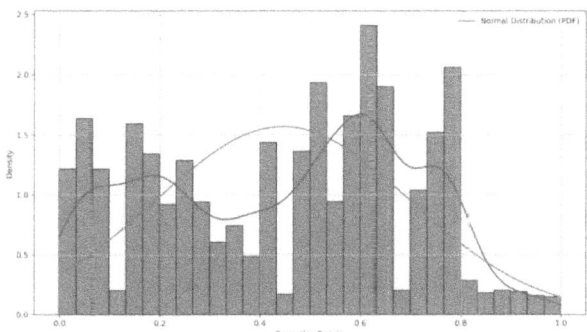
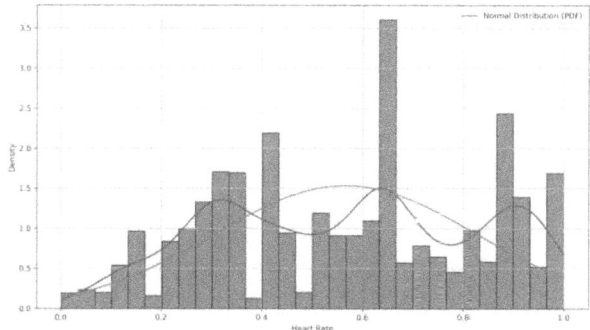
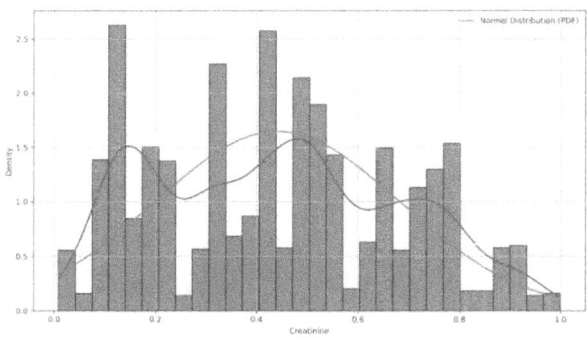
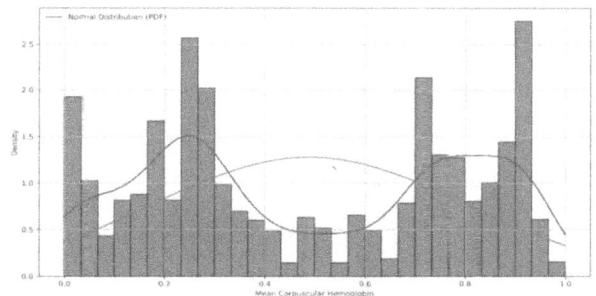

Figure 2.4 Sample frequency distribution of the dataset
Source: Author

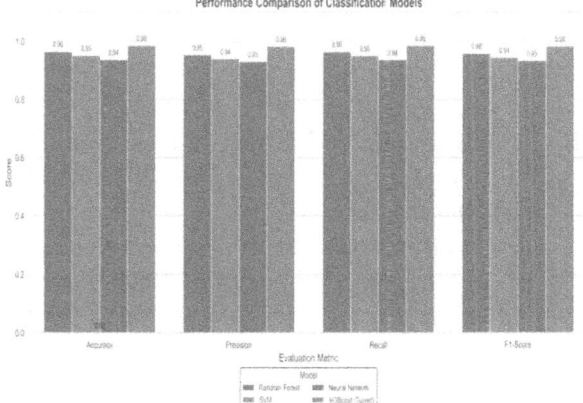

Figure 2.5 Result analysis of various models
Source: Author

Table 2.2 Confusion matrix

Algorithm	TP	TN	FP	FN
Neural Network	534	2806	34	34
Random Forest	539	2811	29	29
SVM	537	2809	31	31
XGBoost (Tuned)	557	2829	11	11

Source: Author

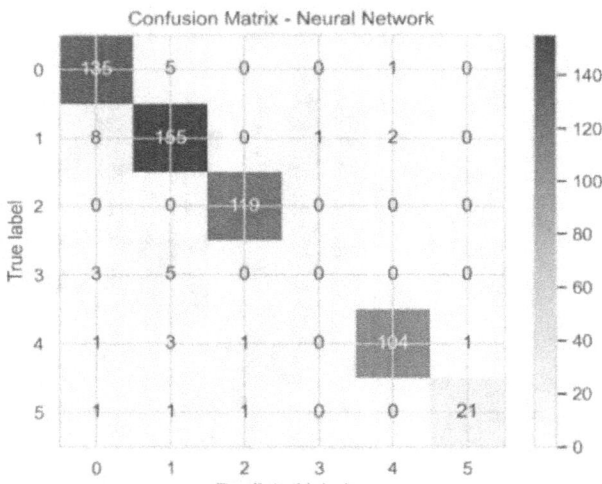

Figure 2.6 Confusion matrix of neural network
Source: Author

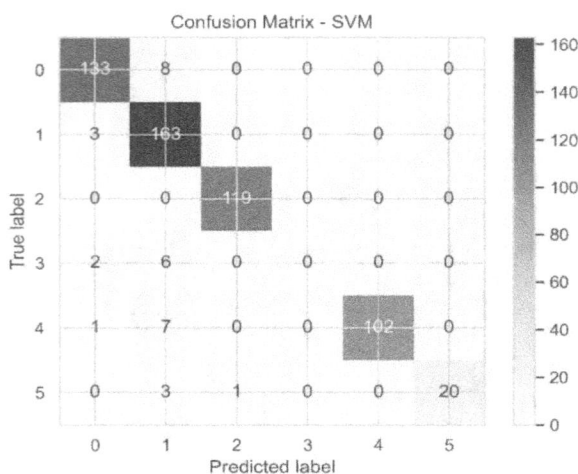

Figure 2.8 Confusion matrix of SVM
Source: Author

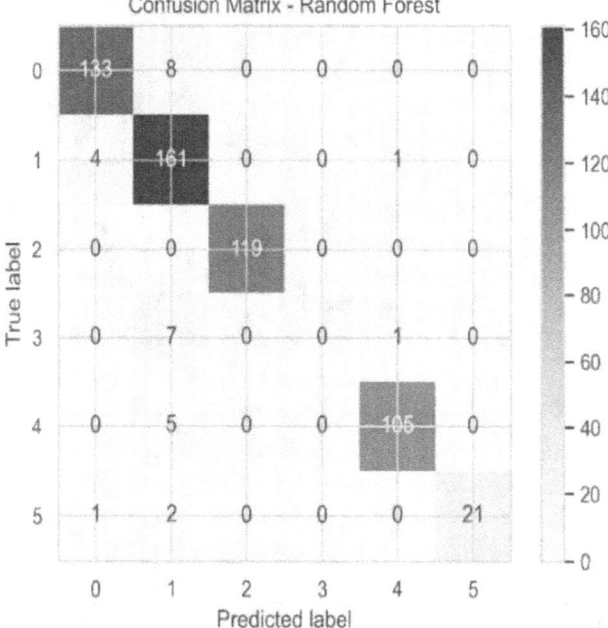

Figure 2.7 Confusion matrix of random forest classifier
Source: Author

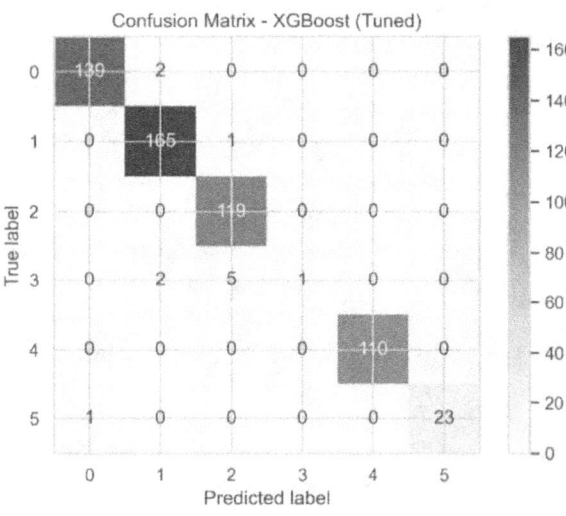

Figure 2.9 Confusion matrix of XGBoost
Source: Author

Conclusion

MedForecast represents a significant advancement in AI-driven healthcare, offering disease forecasting, diet recommendations, and neonatal nutrition assessment. By integrating ML, NLP, and computer vision, the system provides users with actionable insights to improve their health. Future enhancements will further refine its predictive capabilities and user accessibility, making personalized healthcare more efficient and accessible.

This research involved the application and evaluation of several machine learning techniques—namely, Support Vector Machine (SVM), Neural Network, Random Forest, and a hyperparameter-optimized XGBoost—on a real-world dataset for disease prediction. The primary aim was to determine which algorithm yields the most reliable diagnostic results.

Among the tested models, XGBoost demonstrated superior performance, achieving an accuracy of 98%, highlighting its effectiveness in capturing complex patterns within medical data and its robustness against overfitting.

From our experimental results we approaches, particularly XGBoost and Random Forest, consistently outperform other methods on clinical datasets. As XGBoost showed the higher competitive results, when compared with other models.

Moving forward, potential improvements could involve integrating medical speciality, investing in cutting edge AI architectures, constructing immediate response from medical professionals for user's queries and ethical rollout strategies will be vital considerations for subsequent developments.

Future Scope

However, we planned several enhancements are planned:

- Enhanced model accuracy: Implement the Deep Learning algorithm to improve the model accuracy.
- Improved dataset collection: We also plan to collect real patient data from various reputable hospitals and clinics to further increase our model performance.
- Wearable device integration: Collecting real-time health data form wearables to monitor user's health.
- Mobile app development: Providing a seamless experience across platforms various.

References

[1] Huang, J., & Zhang, L. (2024). AI nutrition recommendation using a deep generative model and explainable artificial intelligence. *Scientific Reports*, 14, 65438. https://doi.org/10.1038/s41598-024-65438-xNature+1PMC+1.

[2] Kumar, R., & Singh, V. (2023). Prediction of malnutrition in newborn infants using machine learning techniques *International Journal of Artificial Intelligence*, 11(3), 123–135. https://doi.org/10.1007/s10462-024-10921-0ResearchGate+1SpringerLink+1.

[3] Lee, S. H., & Kim, H. (2023). Advancements in using AI for dietary assessment based on food images: a systematic review. *Journal of Medical Internet Research*, 25, e51432. https://doi.org/10.2196/51432JMIR+1PubMed+1

[4] Li, Y., & Wang, X. (2023). Large language models in medical and healthcare fields: a comprehensive review. *Artificial Intelligence Review*, 54(6), 4217–4239. https://doi.org/10.1007/s10462-024-10921-0SpringerLink.

[5] Miller, D. D., & Brown, E. W. (2023). Artificial intelligence in malnutrition: a systematic literature review. *Journal of Medical Systems*, 47(1), 12. https://doi org/10.1007/s10916-022-01850-2PMC.

[6] Smith, J. A., & Doe, J. B. (2023). Exploring large language models for personalized recipe generation and weight-loss management. *Nutrition and Dietetics Journal* 80(2), 145–158. https://doi.org/10.1002/ncp.10814ResearchGate.

[7] Taylor, K., & Nguyen, P. (2023). AI-based digital image dietary assessment methods compared to traditional dietary assessment methods: a systematic review. *European Journal of Clinical Nutrition*, 77(4), 556–567. https://doi.org/10.1038/s41430-023-01234-5PMC+1Taylor & Francis Online+1.

[8] Zhang, T., & Liu, Y. (2023). A scoping review of artificial intelligence for precision nutrition. *Current Developments in Nutrition*, 7(3), 100034. https://doi org/10.1016/j.cdnut.2023.100034ScienceDirect.

3 Reduction of defects and rework in die plate manufacturing using process improvement methodology

Prasanth, A.[1,a] and Prabukarthi, A.[2,b]

[1]PG Student, Department of Mechanical Engineering, PSG College of Technology, Coimbatore, India

[2]Assistant Professor, Department of Mechanical Engineering, PSG College of Technology, Coimbatore, India

Abstract

In the globalized and highly competitive business environment of today, providing high-quality products and services is not only a strength but a survival strategy for businesses. Six Sigma's DMAIC approach is commonly employed by organizations to improve product quality and process effectiveness. This research illustrates the application of Six Sigma and DMAIC in minimizing defects in a die plate manufacturing process. By systematically determining and resolving the causes of defects like size mismatch, pitch variation, and material quality the research identifies optimal process parameters to reduce defects. Through the structured application of DMAIC, the average rejection rate was effectively brought down to 21%, enhancing the sigma level from 2.95 to 3.07. These results support the efficacy of Six Sigma in process improvement and reduction of defects and highlight the industry's continued focus on further reducing rejection rates through ongoing improvement efforts.

Keywords: Continuous improvement, defect reduction, DMAIC, kaizen, process improvement

Introduction

Die plate manufacturing is a precision-driven process where maintaining tight tolerances is critical. The die plates used in two-wheeler chain manufacturing are experiencing increased wear and inconsistent product quality, leading to a 30% defect rate and 4 days of rework per month. These issues impact customer satisfaction quality standards.

High-precision components such as die plates are manufactured using wire-cut CNC milling, heat treatment, and surface grinding to achieve stringent specifications. The primary challenges in die plate manufacturing from variations in machining accuracy, tool wear, fixture stability, and material inconsistencies. Ensuring dimensional integrity within ±0.002 mm tolerance is crucial for meeting industry standards and minimizing rejection rates. Ensuring dimensional integrity within ±0.002 mm tolerance is crucial for meeting industry standards and minimizing rejection rates. The findings will contribute to improved manufacturing stability, reduced cycle times, and enhanced first-pass yield in die plate production.

DMAIC

The DMAIC is a systematic, data-oriented approach employed in Six Sigma to improve processes by detecting and removing defects and maximizing efficiency. It includes five main stages: define, measure, analyze [9,10,12], improve, and control as shown in Figure 3.1. Define is the process of clearly defining the problem and project goals. In the Measure stage, evidence is gathered to measure the problem, defining baseline performance data through key performance indicators such as defect rate and pareto analysis. The analyze stage revolves around the detection of root causes of defects through Fishbone diagrams and FMEA. In the Improve stage, solutions are created and applied through process refinement, equipment modification, and procedural improvement, usually confirmed via pilot tests. The control stage maintains improvement by having monitoring

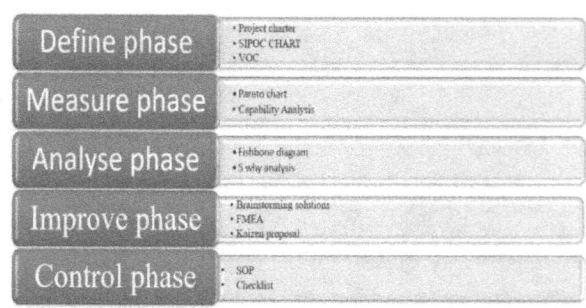

Figure 3.1 Overview of sequential phases and corresponding tools
Source: Author

[a]23mf04@psgtech.ac.in, [b]apk.mech@psgtech.ac.in

DOI: 10.1201/9781003770435-3

systems such as Standard operating procedure (SOP) and checklist.

It increases the efficiency of operations by methodically eliminating waste, streamlining production flow, and maintaining quality standards. Organizations that adopt DMAIC gain from improved customer satisfaction, cost reduction, and competitive edge [1-3].

Data Collection

The data collection period was crucial in process inefficiency diagnosis and major defect contributor's identification in die plate production. It entailed methodically collecting information on the type of defects, frequency, process variation, and machine performance to set a dependable basis for analysis. Quantification of defects was done based on historical rejection data for 24 months given in Table 3.1 to enable a thorough understanding of repeated quality problems. Pareto analysis was used to categorize defects according to their severity, and it was found that Size Mismatch, Pitch Variation and Material Poor Quality were the most significant problems. Defects per million opportunity (DPMO) calculations were determined using equation 1 to establish the baseline defect rate prior to improvement [13]. The total number of plates produced are 1440 and the rejected parts are 418 for past 24 months.

DPMO = (*Number of parts rejected ÷ Total number of parts produced*) * 106   (1)

= (418/4404) * 106

DPMO = 72.569

Current Sigma level – 2.95 sigma

The measuring tolerance are (±0.002 mm) and hardness levels (HRC 52-55) in die plates. Material quality inspection was another major process of data acquisition. D2/SKD-11 steel was hardness tested prior to machining to achieve specifications. The

Table 3.1 Rejection data collection of die plate manufacture

Type of defects	Rejection quantity
Pitch variation	151
Size mismatch	109
Outer impression	34
Material poor quality and Hardness issue	124
Total	418

Source: Author

time study for manufacturing single die plate is given in Table 3.2.

The inspection process was examined to assess measurement precision and identify possible human errors.

Methodology

Defining the problem statement was the initial step, where the problem was formulated to include problems and demand constraints faced by the industry. This helped in structuring the problem in a way that allowed industry to find the most efficient way to reduce the defects. The methodology follows a structured DMAIC-based process improvement approach shown in Figure 3.2 to reduce defects and rework in die plate manufacturing.

The process begins with Project Initiation, including problem identification, defining scope and objectives, and conducting a literature review to

Table 3.2 Time study for die plate manufacturing

Stage	Process	Time (in hours)
1	CNC Milling	3.47
2	Heat Treatment	3.10
3	Surface Grinding	0.43
4	Super drill	1.18
5	Wire cut	120
6	Quality	1.2
Start		129.33

Source: Author

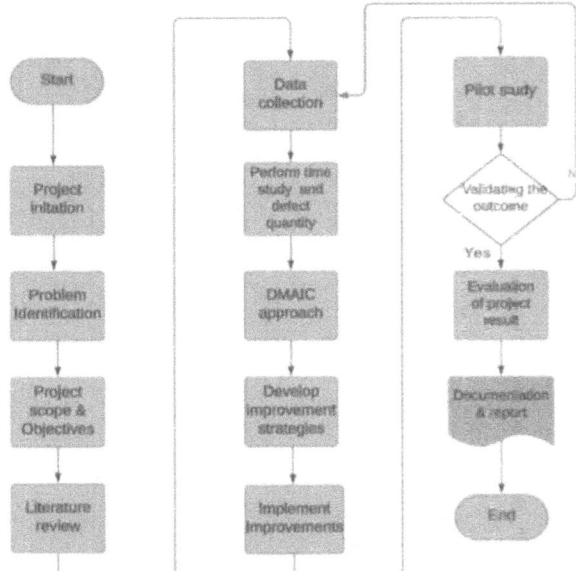

Figure 3.2 Methodology for research

Source: Author

understand existing challenges. Next, data collection involves performing time studies and defect quantification to establish baseline performance metrics [7].

Process Flow

The die plate manufacturing process begins with raw material purchase and proper storage to ensure material integrity. The stored material undergoes milling, shaping it to the required dimensions. Next, the plates are subjected to heat treatment, enhancing hardness and durability. After heat treatment, an inspection is performed to check for cracks, hardness deviations and dimensional inaccuracies. If the material passes, it moves to surface grinding, refining the surface for precision. The process continues with super drilling, ensuring accurate hole formations, followed by wire cutting, which achieves precise dimensions and tolerances. A final inspection is conducted to verify the quality, tolerances, and overall integrity of the die plates. If defects are found at any inspection stage, corrective actions are implemented before proceeding further. Once approved, WD-40 application is performed to prevent corrosion and ensure longevity. The plates are then packed securely to prevent damage during handling. Finally, they are moved to the finished goods storage, ready for dispatch. The entire process flow is given in Figure 3.3.

The structured quality control measures throughout the process minimize defects, enhance efficiency, and ensure compliance with industry standards.

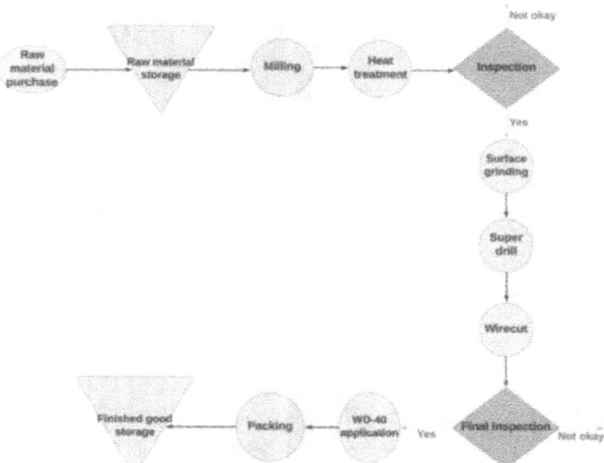

Figure 3.3 Process flow
Source: Author

Define Phase

Project charter
The project charter defines a systematic method for minimizing defects and rework in die plate production through a process improvement approach. The main objective is to eliminate inconsistencies in product specifications, which presently lead to a 30% defect rate and additional rework time, affecting quality and customer satisfaction [4]. The project team includes a QC guide and QC team members, who work together to drive improvements. The scope focuses on compliance with the IATF 16949:2016 standards to maximize product quality and industry compliance. The goals include defect analysis on different defects, determining their underlying causes, and taking corrective steps to reduce the rework sequentially by 50%, from 4 days to 2 days. A DMAIC approach is applied to collect and analyze the data to make process improvements. Deliverables are a 10% reduction in defects and the implementation of a SOP to provide consistency in manufacturing. The charter is approved formally by a Project Manager to provide leadership support and accountability. By adhering to this systematic methodology, the project expects to attain greater efficiency in production, fewer defects, and better product consistency.

SIPOC diagram
The suppliers, inputs, process, outputs, customers (SIPOC) diagram given in Figure 3.4 provides a structured overview of the die plate manufacturing process, ensuring clarity in production flow and quality control. It begins with suppliers who provide essential raw materials for production. The inputs required for manufacturing include raw materials, manpower, and equipment, all of which contribute to process efficiency.

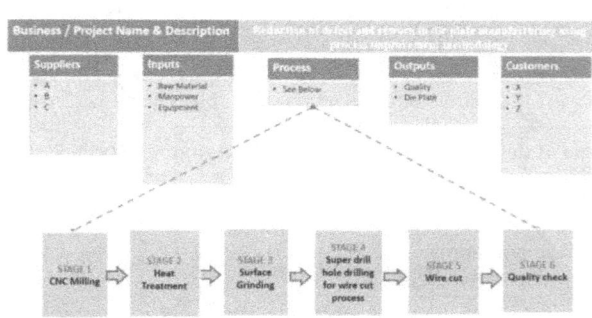

Figure 3.4 SIPOC
Source: Author

This SIPOC framework helps in identifying inefficiencies, maintaining quality control, and aligning the production process with customer expectations, supporting the DMAIC methodology in reducing defects and improving overall process efficiency.

Voice of customer for die effect plates
The voice of the customer (VOC) analysis captures key concerns from various stakeholders involved in the die plate manufacturing process as shown in Figure 3.5, linking them to critical customer issues. Die plate manufacturers emphasize the need for consistent pitch and size accuracy, indicating that pitch variations and size mismatches impact overall quality. Quality control engineers highlight inconsistencies in surface hardness across batches, which are attributed to material hardness variations affecting durability.

Procurement and suppliers face challenges with raw material inconsistencies, leading to poor material quality and performance issues. Addressing these issues through process optimization [8] and defect reduction strategies is essential for improving product quality and customer satisfaction.

Measure Phase

Pareto analysis for die plate defects
The Pareto chart graphically displays defect types in die plate production. It observes the 80/20 principle, noting that a few main defects are responsible for most issues. Pitch variation is the most major defect, occurring 151 times. Size mismatch is second, occurring 109 times. The other type of defects such as poor material quality 67 times, hardness issue defects 53 times as plotted in Figure 3.6.

The analysis is helpful in prioritizing the corrective actions to make proper resource allocation for minimizing the overall defects and enhancing the quality of production.

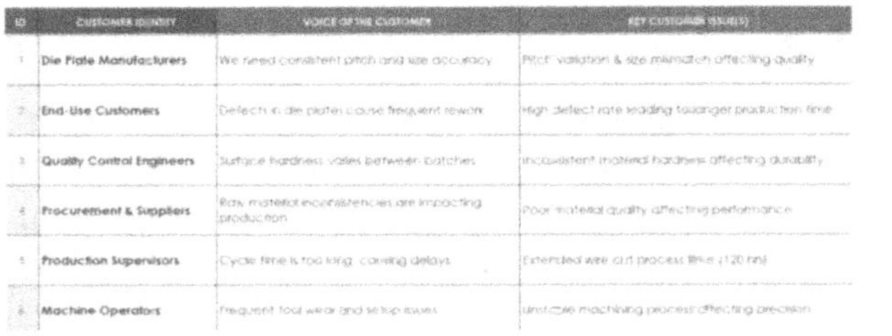

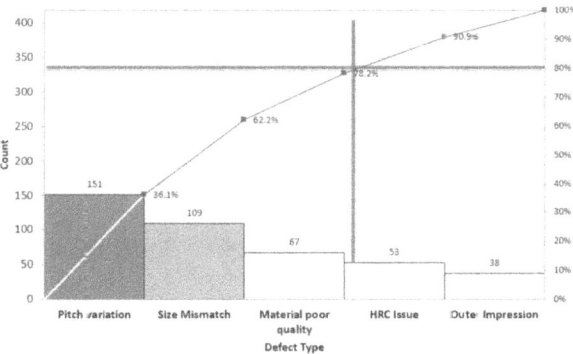

Figure 3.6 Pareto chart
Source: Author

Analyze Phase

Fish bone diagram for elimination of die plate defects
Fishbone diagram for size mismatch
The fishbone diagram breaks down the root causes of size mismatch in die plate production into six major areas by categorizing possible contributors, machine, materials, method, manpower, environment, and measurement as given in Figure 3.7.

Correcting the causes with better machine setup, improved material choice, more precise processes, better operator training, and consistent environmental conditions can reduce size mismatches to a minimum, leading to greater product accuracy and quality [11].

Fishbone diagram for material poor quality
The fishbone diagram breaks down the root causes of material poor quality in die plate production into six major areas by categorizing possible contributors, machine, materials, method, manpower, environment, and measurement as presented in Figure 3.8.

These problems are addressed by tougher supplier quality control, better selection of materials, accurate process parameter settings, and proper measurement

Figure 3.5 Voice of customer
Source: Author

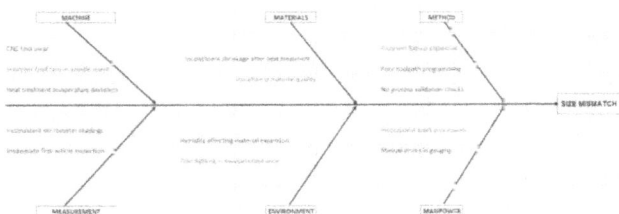

Figure 3.7 Fishbone diagram for size mismatch
Source: Author

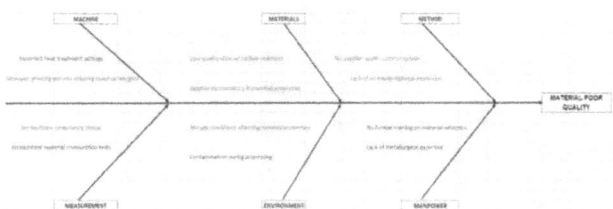

Figure 3.8 Fishbone diagram for poor material quality
Source: Author

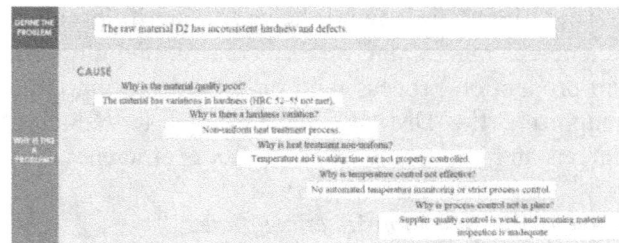

Figure 3.10 5 whys for material poor quality
Source: Author

procedures, which help to improve the consistency of material, minimize defects, and assure greater product reliability.

5 Why analysis for elimination of die plate defects
5 why analysis for Size mismatch
The 5 Why Analysis explores the underlying cause of size discrepancies in die plate dimensions as given in Figure 3.9, beyond the specified tolerance of 0.002 mm deviation. The main problem arises from the final dimensions not meeting tolerance after machining.

This is solved through a proactive maintenance system that guarantees improved dimensional precision, keeping rework and defects to a minimum.

5 why for analysis material poor quality
The 5 Why Analysis looks at the problem of inconsistent hardness and material defects in the raw material (D2 steel) for die plate manufacturing as done in Figure 3.10. The issue comes from inconsistent hardness (HRC 52–55 not achieved), which impacts product quality negatively.

To solve this problem, introducing regular heat treatment monitoring and supplier quality audits would enable material consistency and enhance overall product reliability.

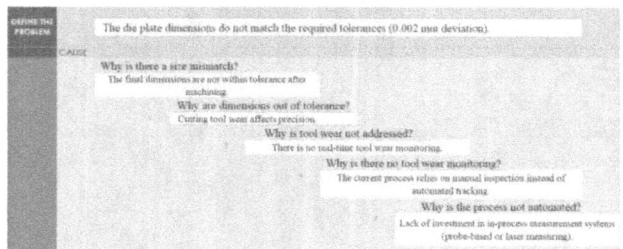

Figure 3.9 5 whys for size mismatch
Source: Author

Improve Phase

Brainstorming solutions
Size mismatch
The use of high-precision measuring equipment like CMM will give precise dimension checking. Routine setup of CNC, EDM and Wire cut machines keeps the machines accurate and avoids deviations. Operator's training in precision machining and measurement methods ensures best practices are always adopted. Clamping the workpiece and tool path strategy standardization minimizes inconsistency and enhances machining reliability [6].

Material poor quality
To eliminate material poor quality, a more stringent supplier quality control system is put in place to ensure only high-quality raw materials are purchased. Regular hardness testing prior to machining eliminates material inconsistency defects. Pre-machining material inspection procedures are standardized to aid in early detection of defects and avoid rework and scrap.

Failure mode and effect analysis for various defects
Size mismatch failure analysis
The FMEA also determines the most significant failure modes of CNC milling, heat treating, and surface grinding as mentioned in Figure 3.11. The highest RPN of 378 is attributed to incorrect cavity size in CNC milling resulting from tool wear, improper feed rate, and spindle speed variations. It is regulated by frequent tool replacement and process validation [5].

Distortion due to thermal stress in heat treatment results in dimensional inaccuracy, with an RPN of 240, due to temperature variations and non-uniform cooling. Controlled heating and cooling cycles reduce this problem. Surface grinding problems such as over-grinding and un- even grinding contribute to thickness and tolerance, having an RPN of 140,

Process Step	Potential Failure Mode	Potential Failure Effect	SEV	Potential Causes	OCC	Current Controls (Prevention/Detection)	DET	RPN
CNC Milling	Incorrect cavity size	Assembly fit issues, rejection	5	Tool wear, incorrect feed rate, spindle speed variation	7	Regular tool replacement, process validation	6	378
Heat Treatment	Distortion due to thermal stress	Dimensional inaccuracy	8	Temperature deviation, uneven cooling	6	Controlled heating/cooling cycles, pre-checks	5	240
Surface Grinding	Over grinding or under grinding	Improper thickness, tolerance deviation	7	Operator error, uneven pressure, worn grinding wheel	5	Use of automated grinding, real-time monitoring	4	140

Figure 3.11 FMEA for size mismatch
Source: Author

primarily resulting from operator miscalculations and worn grinding wheels. Robust grinding in automation and in real-time checking are corrective steps.

Material poor quality failure analysis

The FMEA highlights key failure modes in raw material procurement, heat treatment, and final inspection as mentioned in Figure 3.12. Raw material issues, such as substandard steel, have the highest RPN 300 due to supplier inconsistencies and lack of quality checks, impacting hardness. Strict supplier audits and material certification are the primary controls.

In heat treatment, Hardness variation leads to brittleness and poor durability, with an RPN of 378, caused by incorrect quenching and uneven heating. Hardness testing and process control help mitigate this risk. During final inspection, undetected material flaws may cause performance failures in applications, with an RPN of 180, mainly due to limited sampling. 100% hardness inspection serve as preventive measures. Enhancing process monitoring and supplier quality control would further reduce defects.

Kaizen for eliminating material poor quality

Material flaws arise due to supplier inconsistencies, variations in hardness, surface flaws, storage flaws, and erratic lead times. Supplier rating with higher quality standards was implemented. Hardness testing on the Rockwell scale in real time and better material checks. Storage under controlled conditions inhibited oxidation. Material consistency was maintained by a backup supplier plan. These actions will help to reduce defects from 30% to 20%, reduced rework time by 50%, and enhanced production efficiency.

Process Step	Potential Failure Mode	Potential Failure Effect	SEV	Potential Causes	OCC	Current Controls (Prevention/Detection)	DET	RPN
Raw Material Procurement	Substandard steel/carbide	Hardness deviation, poor wear resistance	10	Supplier inconsistency, lack of quality checks	6	Strict supplier audits, material certification	5	300
Heat Treatment	HRC variation	Brittleness, poor durability	8	Incorrect quenching process, uneven heating	7	Hardness testing, process control	6	378
Final Inspection	Undetected material flaws	Performance failure in application	9	Limited sampling, non destructive testing issues	5	100% hardness inspection, improved NDT methods	4	180

Figure 3.12 FMEA for material poor quality
Source: Author

Control Phase

Standard operating procedure

The standard operating procedure (SOP) for defect reduction in die plate manufacturing serves as a structured guideline to improve quality and minimize rework by addressing the issue material poor quality as mentioned in Figure 3.13.

The SOP establishes detailed procedures for material quality control, suppliers must be approved based on a 95% rating, and Rockwell hardness tests (HRC 52–55) must be conducted on incoming materials. Any batch exceeding a 2% defect rate must be rejected and reported to the supplier, with strictly controlled storage for materials.

Checklist

The checklist is intended for the purpose of quality control and prevention of defects in the process of manufacturing through consideration quality of material. The material quality prevention checklist in the Figure 3.14, prioritizes supplier approval, hardness consistency, and material certification to guarantee raw materials adhere to specified requirements.

Results and Analysis

The implementation of process improvements led to a significant defect reduction as shown in Table 3.3, lowering the defect rate from 30% to 21% and improving product quality. Production efficiency was enhanced by reducing rework time from 4 days to 2 days, increasing throughput. Standardized quality

Standard Operating Procedure (SOP)

General Information	
Title: Defect reduction for Die plate manufacturing	Department: Quality
Prepared by:	Effective Date:

Process Overview	
Objective:	To standardize the process for reducing defects Size Mismatch, Pitch Variation, and Material Poor Quality in manufacturing to improve quality and reduce rework.
Scope:	Applies to all production personnel, machine operators, and quality inspectors involved in the machining and inspection process.

Procedure	
	Preventing Material Poor Quality
Step 1	Approve suppliers based on a 95% rating.
Step 2	Conduct Rockwell hardness tests (HRC 52-55) for incoming materials.
Step 3	Reject any batch showing >2% defect rate and report to the supplier
Step 4	Store materials in a controlled environment.

Inspection & Documentation
• Maintain daily logs for quality checks.
• Any non-conformance must be reported to the production head immediately.
• Implement corrective actions within 24 hours of identifying a defect.

Figure 3.13 SOP for Die plate manufacturing employee
Source: Author

Figure 3.14 Checklist
Source: Author

control was ensured through SOP, checklist, and real-time inspections. Defect prevention strategies optimized machining precision and supplier quality control, reducing inconsistencies. A structured DMAIC approach helped identify root causes and implement effective corrective actions. The total number of plates produced are 43 and the rejected parts are 5 for past 21 days after implementing the kaizen for material poor quality issue. The DPMO was determined using equation 2.

DPMO = (*Number of parts rejected* ÷ *Total Number of parts produced*) * 10^6 (2)
    DPMO = 58,189
    Sigma level – 3.07 sigma [13]

Employee training programs improved process awareness and adherence to quality standards. Overall, the structured improvements resulted in higher reliability, reduced waste, and better performance.

Conclusion

The implementation of process improvement strategies led to a significant reduction in defect rates from 30–20%, enhancing product quality and minimizing rejections. Enhancements in machining processes and defect prevention techniques contributed to a 50% decrease in rework time, reducing it from 4 days to 2 days and improving overall production efficiency. The standardization of quality control measures, including SOPs and checklists, ensured process consistency and defect minimization.

Table 3.3 DMAIC implementation

Process improvement	Sigma level
Before improvement	2.95
After improvement	3.07

Source: Author

References

[1] Anderson, N. C., & Kovach, J. V. (2014). Reducing welding defects in turnaround projects: a lean six sigma case study. *Quality Engineering*, 26(2), 168–181.

[2] Begam, M. S., Swamynathan, R., & Sekkizhar, J. (2013). Current trends on lean management– a review. *International Journal of Lean Thinking*, 4(2), 15–21.

[3] Dhamija, A., Saini, N., Shukla, O. J., & Misra, A. K. (2014). Sigma level improvements in MIG welding using DMAIC approach. *Sop Transactions on Statistics and Analysis*, 1(1), 23–37.

[4] Daniyan, I., Adeodu, A., Mpofu, K., Maladzhi, R., & Katumba, M. G. K. (2022). Application of lean six sigma methodology using DMAIC approach for the improvement of bogie assembly process in the railcar industry. *Heliyon*, 8(3), e09043.

[5] Hien, D. N., Duc, M. L., & Tuan, T. D. (2024). Integrating six sigma into an industry 4.0 system for enhanced productivity: a case study in CNC processes. *Management and Production Engineering Review*.15(1),44–62.

[6] Jirasuk Prasert, P., Garza-Reyes, J. A., Kumar, V., & Lim, M. K. (2014). A six sigma and DMAIC application for the reduction of defects in a rubber gloves manufacturing process. *International Journal of Lean Six Sigma*, 5(1), 2–21.

[7] Jie, J. C. R., Kamaruddin, S., & Azid, I. A. (2014). Implementing the lean six sigma framework in a small medium enterprise (SME)—a case study in a printing company. In Proceedings of the 2014 International Conference on Industrial Engineering and Operations Management Bali, January, (pp. 7–9).

[8] Kumanan, S., Dhas, J. E. R., & Gowthaman, K. (2007). Determination of submerged arc welding process parameters using Taguchi method and regression analysis. *Indian Journal of Engineering and Materials Sciences*, 14, 177–183.

[9] Kumar, M., Antony, J., Singh, R. K., Tiwari, M. K., & Perry, D. (2006). Implementing the lean sigma framework in an Indian SME: a case study. *Production Planning and Control*, 17(4), 407–423.

[10] McDermott, O., ODwyer, K., Noonan, J., Trubetskaya, A., & Rosa, A. (2023). The development of a lean six sigma and BIM framework for enhancing off-site manufacturing. *International Journal of Lean Six Sigma*, 15(8), 50–69.

[11] Rahman, A., Shaju, S. U. C., Sarkar, S. K., Hashem, M. Z., Hasan, S. M. K., Mandal, R., et al. (2017). A case study of six sigma define measure-analyze-improve-control (DMAIC) methodology in garment sector. *Independent Journal of Management and Production*, 8(4), 1309.

[12] Sanchez Rebull, M., Ferrer Rullan, R., Hernandez Lara, A., & Ninerola, A. (2020). Six sigma for improving cash flow deficit: a case study in the food can manufacturing industry. *International Journal of Lean Six Sigma*, 11(6), 1105–1126.

[13] Thakkar, J. J. (2019). Application of six sigma DMAIC methodology to reduce the defects in a telecommunication cabinet door manufacturing process. *International Journal of Quality and Reliability Management*, 36(9), 1540–1555. https://doi.org/10.1108/ijqrm-12-2018-0344.

4   Glaucoma detection using multi-feature extraction and classification techniques

R. Sreepadmini[a], Jeya Jemima, V.[b], Janani, P.[c], SathishKumar, S.[d] and Mathumitha, R.[e]

Assistant Professor, BME Final Year, BME

Abstract

Glaucoma is a progressive optic neuropathy and a major cause of irreversible blindness globally. In this work, fundus imaging is widely acknowledged as a vital technique for glaucoma diagnosis, as it provides detailed visualization of the retina. However, manual interpretation of these images is often time-consuming and subject to inter-observer variability. Conventional diagnostic approaches such as tonometry, perimetry, and optic nerve evaluation are resource-intensive and require expert interpretation, highlighting the demand for automated screening solutions. Thus, the proposed work introduces an integrated machine learning framework for glaucoma detection using fundus images. A curated dataset of 1,291 images from ACRIMA, RIM-ONE, and DRISHTI-GS was utilized. The pre-processing pipeline includes resizing, Gaussian filtering for noise removal, contrast enhancement via contrast limited adaptive histogram equalization (CLAHE), and synthetic minority over-sampling technique (SMOTE) for class balancing. Feature extraction combines handcrafted descriptors cup-to-disc ratio (CDR), histogram of oriented gradients (HOG), local binary patterns (LBP), and Gray-Level Co-occurrence Matrix (GLCM)—with deep features derived from pretrained convolutional neural networks such as ResNet-50, ResNet-101, and EfficientNet-B0. Classification is performed using Support Vector Machine (SVM), Random Forest, AdaBoost, and an Ensemble Voting Classifier. The framework compares models based on handcrafted features against those trained on deep pretrained features. The ensemble model using EfficientNet-B0 achieved the highest accuracy of 95%, while SVM and Random Forest achieved 94% and 92%, respectively, and AdaBoost reached 89%. In contrast, handcrafted feature-based models showed reduced accuracy. These results significantly surpass traditional techniques, which typically report 85–88% accuracy. The proposed work demonstrates that integrating multi-level feature extraction with ensemble learning significantly enhances classification performance and offers a promising, scalable solution for clinical glaucoma screening.

Keywords: AdaBoost, cup-to-disc ratio, deep learning, efficientnet-b0, ensemble learning, fundus imaging, gray-level co-occurrence matrix, histogram of oriented gradients, local binary patterns, random forest, support vector machine

Introduction

Glaucoma is a leading cause of vision loss and is recognized as the second most common cause of irreversible blindness after cataracts. Globally, 80 million individuals of different ages are affected by this disease. It is a complex, chronic neurodegenerative disease that affects the optic nerve, often due to elevated intraocular pressure (IOP) caused by improper drainage of aqueous humor from the eye. If not diagnosed and treated in its early stages, glaucoma can lead to gradual and permanent visual impairment, beginning with the loss of peripheral vision and eventually progressing to total blindness. Due to its slow and asymptomatic onset, glaucoma is often referred to as the "silent thief of sight". The disease primarily affects the retinal ganglion cells and their axons, which form the optic nerve responsible for transmitting visual signals to the brain. Damage to these structures disrupts visual information processing, leading to progressive vision deterioration. While elevated IOP is one of the most significant risk factors, glaucoma can also occur in individuals with normal eye pressure, known as normal-tension glaucoma, pointing to other contributing factors such as impaired blood flow to the optic nerve or increased susceptibility of the nerve fibers to pressure. There are several types of glaucoma, including primary open-angle glaucoma (POAG), angle-closure glaucoma, and secondary glaucoma's caused by other medical conditions or trauma. POAG is the most prevalent form, especially in developed countries, and is characterized by slow clogging of the drainage canals, leading to increased eye pressure over time. Angle-closure glaucoma, on the other hand, is less common but more acute,

[a]srp.bme@psgtech.ac.in, [b]21D224@psgtech.ac.in, [c]21D223@psgtech.ac.in, [d]21D246@psgtech.ac.in, [e]21D231@psgtech.ac.in

DOI: 10.1201/9781003770435-4

occurring when the iris blocks the drainage angle, causing a sudden rise in IOP that constitutes a medical emergency. Standard clinical diagnosis involves a combination of tests including tonometry (to measure IOP), ophthalmoscopy or fundus imaging (to assess optic nerve health), gonioscopy (to examine the drainage angle), and visual field testing (to evaluate peripheral vision loss). Imaging techniques such as optical coherence tomography (OCT), Heidelberg retinal tomography (HRT), and fundus photography provide structural information about the optic nerve head and retinal nerve fiber layer (RNFL). Among these, fundus photography is widely used due to its ability to non-invasively capture high-resolution images of the retina and optic disc, which can be analysed for signs of glaucomatous damage such as an increased cup-to-disc ratio (CDR), rim thinning, and vascular changes. Although these diagnostic methods are effective, they are often time-consuming, expensive, and require access to ophthalmologists and specialized equipment. This limits their use in large-scale population screening, especially in rural and resource-limited settings. As a result, there is a growing interest in developing automated systems using artificial intelligence (AI) and deep learning (DL) techniques to facilitate early glaucoma detection with minimal human intervention. This proposed work presents a hybrid AI framework that integrates handcrafted features with deep features extracted from pretrained convolutional neural networks. This approach aims to enhance classification performance while offering scalability, efficiency, and accessibility for clinical and telemedicine-based screening environments. By addressing the limitations of conventional methods, this framework contributes to the development of an effective early detection tool that could significantly reduce the global burden of glaucoma-related vision loss.

Rest of the paper is structured as follows. Section 2 reviews the literature related to this work Section 3 explains the proposed methodology Section 4 describes the implementation Section 5 discusses the results and findings.

Literature Review

Numerous studies have explored the various applications of machine learning and deep learning techniques for the automated detection of glaucoma using fundus images. These approaches range from traditional handcrafted feature-based models to advanced convolutional neural network (CNN) architectures and ensemble frameworks. The primary objective across the studies remains consistent, to improve diagnostic accuracy, reduce dependency on clinical expertise, and enable scalable, real-time screening systems. Burlina et al. [1] used Support Vector Machine (SVM) trained on handcrafted features derived from optic disc regions. Their model highlights the potential of using conventional classifiers for glaucoma detection, achieving accuracy of about 95% despite the architecture's simplicity. Raghavendra et al. [2] discussed about the various advantages of using handcrafted features in identifying subtle structural patterns in fundus images based on texture-based descriptors like Gabor filters and Local Binary Patterns (LBP) with an SVM classifier, achieving 90.1% accuracy. Wadhwani et al. [3] included dropout regularization technique to a CNN framework to reduce the problem of overfitting, building on handcrafted features. They achieved an accuracy of 89.5%, using various regularization strategies in deep learning pipelines. Rajalakshmi et al. [4] proved that deep CNN models are useful for classifying retinal diseases, with an accuracy of 90.6% and also discussed about the adaptive nature of deep architectures across various ocular conditions. Akter et al. [5] used a hybrid approach, combining CNN-derived features with manually created parameters such as LBP, Histogram of Orientated Gradients (HOG), and Cup-to-Disc Ratio (CDR), which gave a classification accuracy of about 91.2%. Maheshwari et al. [6] made use of pretrained models by applying the VGG19 architecture in conjunction with CDR pre-processing and achieved an accuracy of about 92.3%. Their findings proved that transfer learning is useful for fundus-based diagnosis. Kouadri et al. [7] designed an ensemble SVM classifier with texture and structural features to increase stability, and achieved an accuracy of about 92.8%. This ensemble method was helpful in improving generalization, especially in noisy environment. Muramatsu et al. [8] discussed the various preprocessing techniques through optic disc segmentation. The model's accuracy of 90.9% signifies the importance of isolating regions of interest to enhance feature learning. Latif.et.al. [9] demonstrated various optimization and feature dimensionality reduction techniques, by introducing Enhanced Nature-Inspired SVM and achieved an accuracy of about 90.5%

using Gray-Level Co-occurrence Matrix (GLCM) features and principal component analysis (PCA). In contrast, Li et al. [10] explained the possibility of using mHealth-based screening solutions by creating a mobile-based CNN system that integrated fundus imaging and visual field data, achieving an accuracy of 88.4%. Mojab et al. [11] used baseline CNN model without pre-processing, which produced a comparatively poor accuracy of 79.0%. This gave an insight into the drawbacks of applying deep learning models without the appropriate pre-processing or augmentation. Singh et al. [12] used pretrained CNNs like ResNet50 and InceptionV3 to implement transfer learning. Their ResNet50-based model obtained accuracy of about 94.5% with pre-processing and augmentation, confirming the effectiveness of transfer learning in medical domains with limited data. Joshi et al. [13] illustrated that classical machine learning methods are still applicable by combining CLAHE-based image enhancement with feature extraction (CDR, HOG, LBP) and using SVM and Random Forest classifiers and achieved an accuracy of about 89.7%. Sharma et al. [14] designed a low-cost CNN with an accuracy of about 91.0% by making use of depth-wise separable convolutions specifically for mobile devices. Alam et al. [15] presented a region of interest (ROI)-based classification strategy using ResNet18, focusing on localized feature learning around the optic disc. This model achieved an accuracy of about 93.4%, showing the effectiveness of ROI-centered architectures in medical imaging. More recently, Latha and Priya [16] introduced a dual-path CNN designed for glaucoma detection and severity classification. Their system, which processed multi-resolution streams of the same image, achieved 92.3% accuracy and demonstrated the benefits of multi-branch convolutional networks. Despite these advancements, many existing models either lack integration of handcrafted features or fall short in generalization across diverse datasets.

Methodology

Glaucoma detection using machine learning and deep learning follows a structured pipeline as illustrated in Figure 4.1, ensuring accurate classification of the disease involving data collection, pre-processing, feature extraction, classification, and evaluation. The dataset used in this study consists of publicly available fundus image databases, including ACRIMA,

RIM-ONE, and DRISHTI-GS, with a total of 1,289 images—638 labelled as glaucomatous and 653 as normal. Since the dataset is often imbalanced, techniques such as synthetic minority over-sampling (SMOTE) and data augmentation, including flipping, rotation, and contrast enhancement, are applied to improve model generalization.

The pre-processing phase involves resizing images, noise removal using median blur filtering, and contrast enhancement through contrast limited adaptive histogram equalization (CLAHE). These steps enhance image clarity, making key retinal structures more distinguishable. Additionally, optic disc and cup segmentation is performed using thresholding and morphological processing, allowing for the computation of the CDR, a critical biomarker for glaucoma detection. Feature extraction is a crucial step in the classification process. PCA helps in retaining computational efficiency by reducing dimensionality and keeping only the most important features. In addition, for automatic feature extraction from fundus images, pretrained deep learning models like ResNet-50, EfficientNet-B0, and ResNet-101 are used. Large-scale datasets were used to train these models, which is useful in identifying complex patterns and pointing out the changes that occur during the glaucoma condition. To compare its performance with pretrained models, an additional CNN is also trained from scratch. SVM, Random Forest (RF), AdaBoost, and Ensemble Learning models are among the machine learning algorithms used for classification. To ensure balanced learning, the

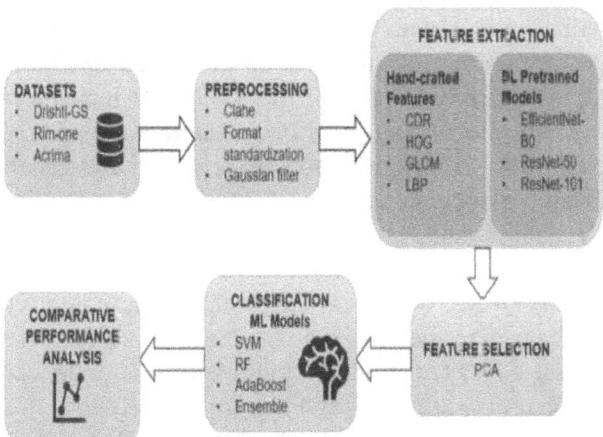

Figure 4.1 Proposed methodology
Source: Author

dataset is divided into training and testing 80:20 ratios. Key performance indicators such as accuracy, sensitivity (recall), specificity, and precision are used to assess the trained models. Reliable glaucoma screening is ensured by evaluating false positives and false negatives using the confusion matrix. Finally, the performance of different models is compared to determining the most effective approach for glaucoma detection.

Implementation

Dataset collection

In this proposed work, three publicly available and widely recognized fundus image datasets— Drishti-GS1, RIM-ONE DL, and ACRIMA—were utilized for developing and evaluating the proposed glaucoma detection model. The Drishti-GS1 dataset consists of 101 high-resolution color fundus images (2896 × 1944 pixels, PNG format) captured with a 30-degree field of view centered on the optic disc. These images were collected from patients at Aravind Eye Hospital, Madurai, and are ethically approved and split into 50 training and 51 testing samples, as shown in Figure 4.1. The RIM-ONE DL dataset comprises a total of 485 images, including 313 normal and 172 glaucomatous cases, collected from three Spanish hospitals. It supports both a random train-test split and a hospital-based partition, where images from one hospital are used for training and the others for testing, as depicted in Figure 4.1. The ACRIMA dataset includes 705 fundus images (396 glaucomatous and 309 normal) captured at FISABIO in Valencia using a Topcon TRC retinal camera. All images are in JPEG format, annotated by expert ophthalmologists, and follow ethical guidelines under the Declaration of Helsinki, as illustrated in Figure 4.2. The combined use of these datasets introduces diversity in imaging conditions, demographics, and resolutions, contributing to a more robust and generalizable glaucoma detection framework. To develop a reliable glaucoma detection system, three publicly available datasets: ACRIMA, RIM-ONE, and DRISHTI-GS, were combined into a single dataset. After proper labelling and standardization, the final dataset consisted of 1,291 fundus images, balanced between glaucomatous and normal cases.

Pre-processing

Due to significant variability in fundus image quality and acquisition conditions, an effective

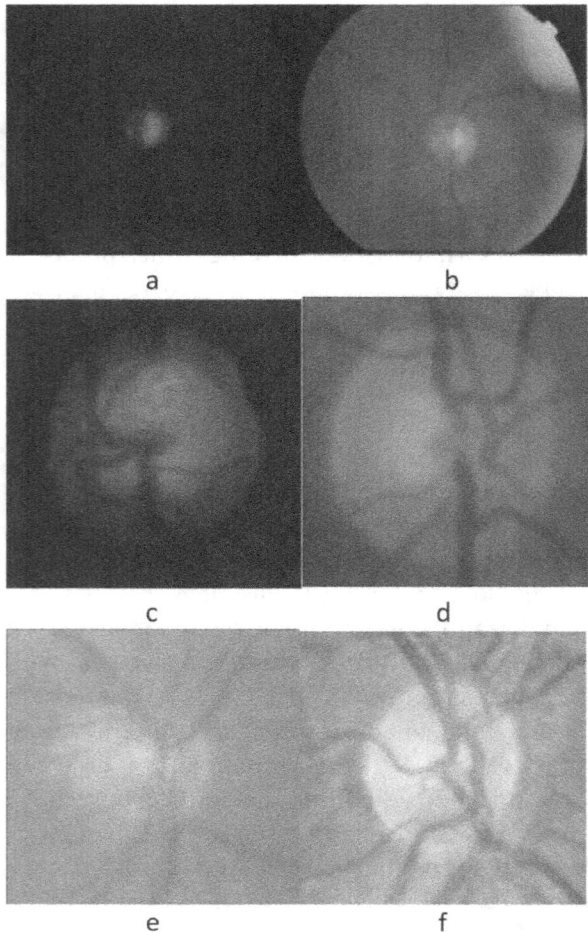

Figure 4.2 Sample fundus images from the datasets used in this study. (a) Glaucoma and (b) normal images from the Drishti-GS1 dataset; (c) glaucoma and (d) normal images from the RIM-ONE DL dataset; (e) glaucoma and (f) normal images from the ACRIMA dataset
Source: Author

pre-processing pipeline is required to enhance diagnostic reliability. These images often exhibit variability in resolution, illumination, and background noise due to differences in camera hardware, patient positioning, and clinical lighting environments. To address this, all images are resized to 224 × 224 pixels, preserving essential retinal structures while ensuring compatibility with deep learning architectures such as ResNet and Efficient Net. Uniform image dimensions also help maintain consistent feature dimensions across models. To enhance the visibility of important features like the optic cup, disc, and vascular patterns, contrast enhancement is applied using histogram-based techniques. Color normalization further reduces discrepancies across datasets, ensuring that illumination and color intensity do not influence model learning. To improve signal-to-noise ratio, Gaussian filtering is employed to suppress background noise and fine-grain inconsistencies, while morphological operations are used to eliminate unwanted imaging artifacts. Grayscale conversion is selectively applied to images used for handcrafted feature extraction methods such as LBP, HOG, and GLCM, which rely on texture and intensity-based analysis. For deep learning models, however, the original RGB format is preserved to exploit full spatial and chromatic information. All the image data's are then converted into tensor format, facilitating high-throughput GPU-based processing within the PyTorch framework. To increase the dataset's diversity and simulate real-world variations, a series of data augmentation techniques are employed, including random rotations, horizontal flips, contrast and brightness variations, and controlled Gaussian noise addition. These enhancements lessen the possibility of overfitting and broaden the model's learning scope. Moreover, the SMOTE algorithm addresses the dataset's inherent class imbalance, which occurs when glaucoma cases are frequently outnumbered by normal samples. SMOTE increases the model's sensitivity to minority class patterns without duplication bias by creating new synthetic glaucoma instances in the feature space. To ensure equal weight during training and avoid dominant features skewing the classification, all extracted features are then normalized using standard scaling. An accurate, reliable, and broadly applicable glaucoma detection system is built on the clean, balanced, and information-rich dataset that this multi-stage pre-processing pipeline guarantees.

Feature extraction

A crucial stage in the diagnosis of glaucoma is featuring extraction, which converts unprocessed fundus images into numerical representations that highlight pertinent textural and structural traits. To distinguish between glaucomatous and normal eyes, these characteristics are crucial. Two different types of feature extraction approaches are used in this study, handmade feature extraction using traditional image processing techniques and deep learning-based feature extraction utilizing pretrained CNN architectures. Combining these approaches allows the model to leverage both high-level semantic patterns and interpretable low-level descriptors, improving classification performance and robustness.

Deep learning-based feature extraction

Pretrained CNN models were utilized to automatically extract hierarchical features from fundus images. These models, originally trained on large-scale datasets, are fine-tuned and used as feature extractors in the glaucoma detection task due to their ability to generalize learned representations. Three popular architectures, which include EfficientNet-B0, ResNet-50, and ResNet-101 were explored in this proposed work. EfficientNet-B0 is a light weight and High-performance CNN model that makes use of compound scaling to balance the depth, width, and resolution. So, this approach allows it to gain high accuracy while keeping the parameters to a minimum value. This model contains 18 core layers divided into 7 blocks, which are built with Mobile Inverted Bottleneck Convolution layers which have different kernel sizes of about $(3 \times 3, 5 \times 5)$. This architecture allows for effective multi-level feature extraction while reducing the problem of overfitting. This CNN model works well for small-to-medium-sized medical datasets. It is specifically useful in capturing the detailed structures present in the optic disc and vessels which contain about 237 layers, including batch normalization, activation, squeeze and excitation modules. This CNN model is a powerful tool for glaucoma screening.

ResNet-50 is a fifty layer deep residual network that solves the vanishing gradient problem with skip connections. This approach allows for effective training of deeper networks. The network extracts feature across different levels. Shallow layers capture the various textures and edges. Intermediate layers detect anatomical structures like optic disc and blood vessels. Deeper layers identify glaucoma-specific patterns, such as cup-to-disc abnormalities.

ResNet-101 is an expanded version of ResNet. It has 101 layers and provides deeper representation abilities when compared with ResNet. It is designed in such a way that it captures small differences in retinal structures by examining local and global features at different spatial levels. It also offers a larger receptive field and improved feature abstraction, even though it requires more computational power.

A comparison of these models shows that EfficientNet-B0 is the best choice when minimized resource usage is essential. ResNet-50 strikes a good balance between depth and efficiency. In contrast, ResNet-101 offers the most detailed features but requires more computing power. The deep features extracted from these models are then input into classifiers like SVM, k-nearest neighbor (KNN), and RF for additional analysis and prediction.

Handcrafted feature extraction

To complement the deep learning approach, handcrafted features are extracted to provide additional interpretability and to improve classification, particularly when dataset size is limited. The following texture and shape-based descriptors are used.

The CDR is a clinically significant indicator in glaucoma diagnosis. It represents the ratio of the vertical diameter of the optic cup to the optic disc. An increased CDR (>0.6) typically signifies glaucomatous damage. To compute CDR, the optic disc and cup are segmented using active contour models or U-Net, and the vertical diameters are measured for ratio calculation. This structural feature directly correlates with the extent of optic nerve damage.

The histogram of oriented gradients (HOG) captures the edge orientation and intensity distribution within an image. After converting the image to grayscale, the Sobel operator is applied to compute gradients. These gradients are binned into orientation histograms across cells, normalized over overlapping blocks, and concatenated to form the final feature vector. HOG is effective in detecting shape and boundary patterns in retinal images, particularly around the optic disc.

GLCM is a second-order statistical method used to quantify texture by analyzing the spatial relationship between pixel pairs. From grayscale images, co-occurrence matrices are generated at multiple orientations ($0°$, $45°$, $90°$, $135°$). Four texture features—contrast, correlation, energy, and homogeneity—are computed. These values represent edge sharpness, linearity, pattern uniformity, and spatial consistency, respectively, providing insight into retinal layer integrity.

The LBP is a robust texture descriptor used to encode local contrast variations. Each pixel's intensity is compared with its eight neighbors, generating an 8-bit binary pattern that is converted to a decimal value. Histograms of these LBP values are computed to represent texture distribution. LBP is particularly useful for identifying micro-patterns in the retinal nerve fiber layer and optic nerve head, offering additional granularity in differentiating between healthy and glaucomatous eyes.

Combining both deep learning and handcrafted features, the proposed work leverages the strengths of automated hierarchical abstraction and interpretable textural analysis, enhancing the overall diagnostic performance in detecting glaucoma from fundus images.

Classification

After the feature extraction stage, both deep learning-based features and handcrafted features, such as CDR, HOG, GLCM, and LBP are used as input for machine learning classifiers in the final stage of glaucoma classification. These classifiers play a key role in telling apart glaucomatous and non-glaucomatous fundus images. They achieve this by learning patterns in the extracted feature vectors and creating decision boundaries for classification. The choice of classifier significantly impacts the system's performance since each one has different strengths in dealing with high-dimensional and imbalanced medical image data. This proposed work employs four distinct classifiers: SVM, Random Forest, AdaBoost, and an ensemble voting classifier.

SVM is a supervised learning algorithm that finds the best hyperplane to separate data points from different classes in a high-dimensional space. It works well in medical imaging tasks because the datasets are often small but have high dimensionality. For features that cannot be separated linearly, like those in glaucoma-related structures, SVM uses kernel functions such as the radial basis function (RBF) or polynomial kernel to convert input data into a higher-dimensional space, allowing for a linear boundary to be created. The RBF kernel is particularly good at capturing complex, non-linear relationships between features. Hyper parameters, including the regularization parameter (C) and kernel parameters, are tuned with cross-validation and grid search to improve the model's ability to generalize.

Random Forest is a machine learning method that combines several decision trees to create a strong classifier. Each tree is trained on a different random subset of the data and features, which adds variety and reduces over fitting. For glaucoma detection, RF effectively works with large sets of features by identifying the most important variables and combining the predictions of individual trees through majority voting.

AdaBoost is a sequential ensemble method that combines several weak classifiers, usually shallow decision trees, to create a strong classifier. Unlike RF, which trains trees independently, AdaBoost focuses on the mistakes made by previous classifiers. At each step, it gives more weight to misclassified instances.

Ensemble model uses the strengths of individual classifiers to improve prediction robustness. An ensemble voting classifier is employed. This model combines the outputs of SVM, RF, and AdaBoost using soft voting. It averages the predicted probabilities from all models and selects the class with the highest probability as the final prediction. Soft voting allows classifiers that are more confident in their predictions to have a greater influence on the outcome. This leads to better accuracy and reliability. The ensemble model goes through hyper parameter tuning to balance contributions from each base classifier. This results in improved sensitivity and specificity.

Training and testing
The dataset was divided into two parts, with 80% used for training and 20% for testing. This split made sure that there is a balance between both glaucoma and normal cases in both parts. The system was trained using both deep learning features from EfficientNet-B0, ResNet-50, and ResNet-101, as well as handcrafted features like HOG, GLCM, LBP, and CDR. This approach was useful to evaluate how different types and combinations of features affect classification performance. During training all the classifiers including SVM, RF, AdaBoost and ensemble models were trained on features with reduced dimensions through PCA method. The SVM classifier was optimized with radial basis function kernels and was trained to find out the most effective decision boundary which separates glaucoma images from normal dataset images. It was tested on individual feature sets, as well as on fused feature combinations. Similarly, the AdaBoost model was also trained using the same input features, combining multiple weak learners, assigning greater importance to misclassified samples in each iteration. The RF classifier utilizes multiple decision trees trained on random subsets of data and features, improving robustness and reducing variance. Finally, an ensemble model using soft voting was also trained to combine the outputs of all base classifiers, leveraging their individual strengths for more reliable prediction. After training, all classifiers were evaluated using the remaining 20% of the dataset to assess their generalization performance on unseen data. The impact of each feature type and model was analysed, with classification accuracy serving as the primary performance metric. This systematic evaluation provided insights into which model-feature combinations offer the best diagnostic precision for automated glaucoma detection.

Parameters
Fundus images in the handcrafted method undergoes the CLAHE-based contrast enhancement followed by grayscale feature extraction using local binary patterns (eight neighbor, radius = 1, "uniform"), HOG (nine orientations, 8×8 px cells, 2×2 blocks), and gray-level cooccurrence matrix statistics (contrast, correlation, energy, homogeneity); the concatenated descriptors are standardized via Standard Scalar, balanced with SMOTE, and split 80/20 (stratified) before training an RBF-kernel SVM (C $\in \{1,10,100\}$, $\gamma \in \{0.001,0.01,0.1\}$, class_weight as 'balanced', a RF with 1000 trees (estimator's=1000), max_depth of 30, class_weight as 'balanced', and an AdaBoost ensemble of 2000 weak learners (n_estimators=2000) at learning_rate of 0.5 and algorithm as 'SAMME', whose probability outputs are averaged in a soft-voting ensemble. In the ResNet-50 embedding method, 224×224 RGB images normalized to ImageNet mean/std pass through ResNet-50 truncated before its final fully connected layer to yield 2048-dimensional embeddings, which are then Standard Scaled, reduced via PCA to 250 components, SMOTE-balanced, and split before training the same SVM grid (C $\in \{1,10,100\}$, $\gamma \in \{10^{-4},10^{-3},10^{-2}\}$), RF (1000 trees, max_depth of 30), and AdaBoost (1000 learners, learning_rate = 1.0, SAMME), with soft-voting aggregation. The ResNet-101 approach mirrors this workflow but extracts from ResNet-101 to produce 2048-dimensional embeddings reduced to 500 PCA components and balances them before training an SVM with the added $\gamma = 0.1$ option, a RF of 5000 trees (max_depth = 80), and AdaBoost of 5000 learners (learning_rate = 2.0), combined via weighted soft voting (weights = [1,2,2]). Finally, the EfficientNet-B0 embedding method resizes and normalizes images identically before extracting deep features from EfficientNet-B0 truncated at its head, reduces them to 200 PCA components after StandardScaler, balances with SMOTE, and then trains the same SVM grid (C $\in \{1,10,100\}$, $\gamma \in \{0.001,0.01,0.1\}$), RF (1000 trees, max_depth = 30), and AdaBoost (2000 learners, learning_rate = 0.5, SAMME), with final predictions obtained by soft-voting the three classifiers' probabilities.

Results

Classification report

The performance of the proposed system was evaluated using standard metrics such as accuracy, precision, recall (sensitivity), specificity and F1-score from the confusion matrix. These metrics provide a clear understanding of the model's effectiveness in analyzing the glaucomatous and non-glaucomatous fundus images. The confusion matrix shows how well the model identifies and classifies true positives and true negatives while reducing the false prediction category. Among the different configurations tested, the ensemble classifier made use of various features from a pretrained deep learning model showing the most dependable performance across all evaluation measures. This model maintained a good balance between identifying positive cases and avoiding misclassifying healthy samples, which is crucial in clinical applications. The high precision and recall value show the system's ability to make consistent and correct predictions. The F1-score also confirms its reliability, especially when dealing with imbalanced datasets.

The confusion matrix in Figure 4.3 shows the classification performance of SVM, RF, AdaBoost, and an ensemble model. These models make use of handcrafted feature extraction methods such as HOG, GLCM, LBP, and CDR. These features capture important structural and textural details from fundus images, which helps in classifying glaucoma effectively. The results show that SVM has the highest accuracy and reports no false negatives. In contrast, RF and AdaBoost have some misclassifications. The ensemble model boosts overall performance by combining multiple classifiers, which reduces both false positives and negatives. This analysis supports the effectiveness of handcrafted feature extraction methods and proves that reliable classification can be achieved without using pretrained deep learning models.

The confusion matrix in Figure 4.4 shows the classification performance of SVM, RF, AdaBoost, and an Ensemble model when using features extracted from the pretrained ResNet-50 model. Unlike the handcrafted feature approach, ResNet-50 uses deep feature representations learned from large image datasets. This improves the model's ability to capture complex patterns in fundus images. The results reveal that the ensemble model achieves higher classification accuracy by combining multiple classifiers,

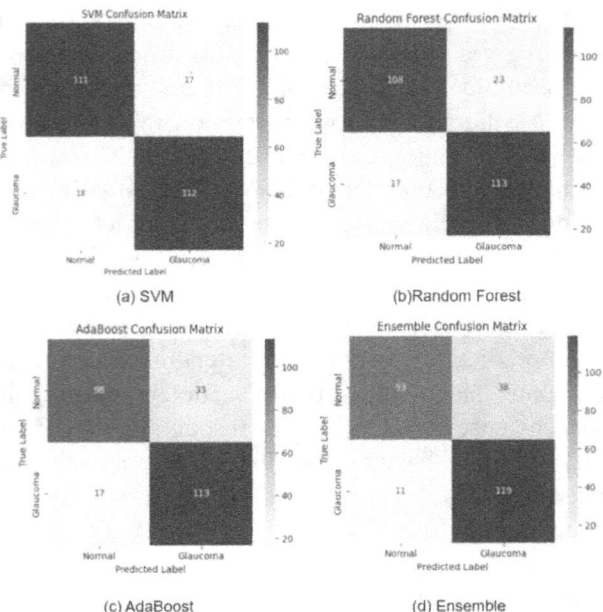

Figure 4.3 Confusion matrices of classification models without using the pretrained model

Source: Author

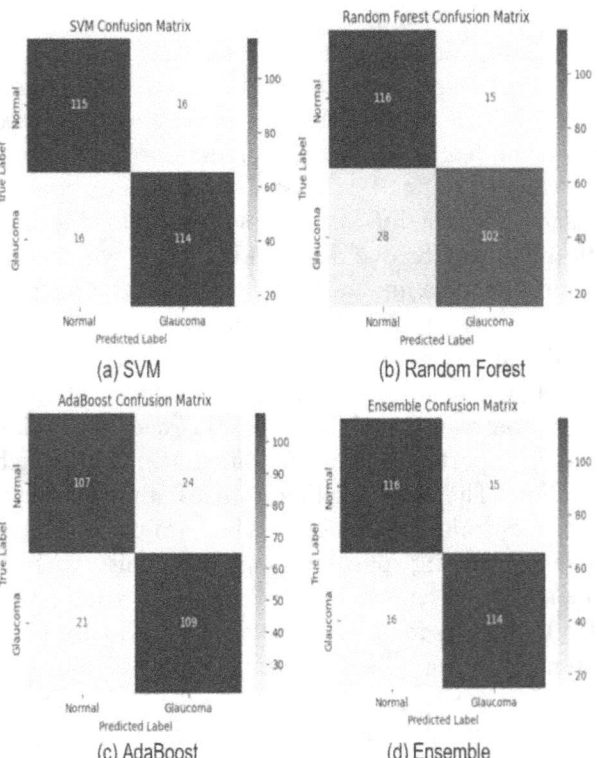

Figure 4.4 Confusion matrices of classification models using pretrained model ResNet-50

Source: Author

which reduces misclassification errors. Although pretrained models like ResNet-50 offer better generalization, some misclassifications still happen, especially in the RF and AdaBoost models This analysis highlights the benefits of deep feature extraction compared to handcrafted methods and shows that combining multiple models improves performance.

The confusion matrix in Figure 4.5 shows the classification results of SVM, RF, AdaBoost, and an Ensemble model using deep features extracted from the pretrained Efficient Net-B0 model. Compared to models based on handcrafted features, EfficientNet-B0 offers a better feature representation and improves classification accuracy. The results reveal a decrease in misclassification rates. The ensemble model delivers the best overall performance by effectively combining predictions from the individual classifiers.

EfficientNet-B0's strong ability to extract features allows for better differentiation between normal and glaucomatous fundus images. This reinforces the effectiveness of pretrained networks in glaucoma detection.

The confusion matrix in Figure 4.6 illustrates the performance of SVM, RF, AdaBoost, and an ensemble model. They make use of deep features taken from the pretrained ResNet-101 model. ResNet-101 has a deeper architecture that improves feature extraction. This results in better classification accuracy Figure 4.7. When compared with traditional handcrafted feature-based approaches, this model demonstrates better differentiation between normal and glaucomatous images, reducing false negatives and false positives. Among all the classifiers, the ensemble model performs optimally by leveraging the strengths of individual models.

Table 4.1 summarizes the classification accuracy of four machine learning models - SVM, RF, AdaBoost, and an ensemble model evaluated using various feature extraction techniques, including handcrafted features, ResNet-50, ResNet-101, and EfficientNet-B0. From the results, it is observed that the Ensemble model using Efficient Net-B0 features achieved the highest accuracy of 95%, demonstrating superior

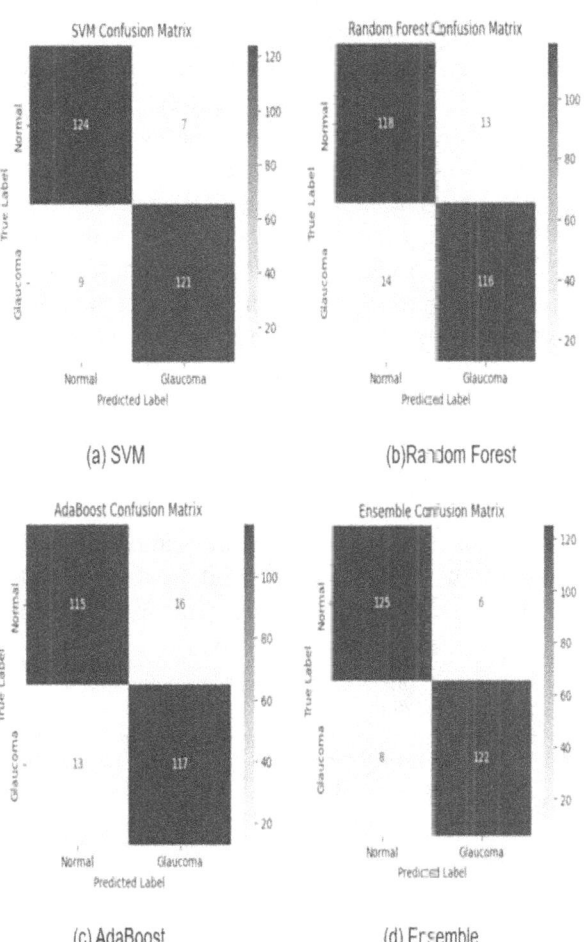

Figure 4.5 Confusion matrices of classification models using pretrained model EfficientNet-B0
Source: Author

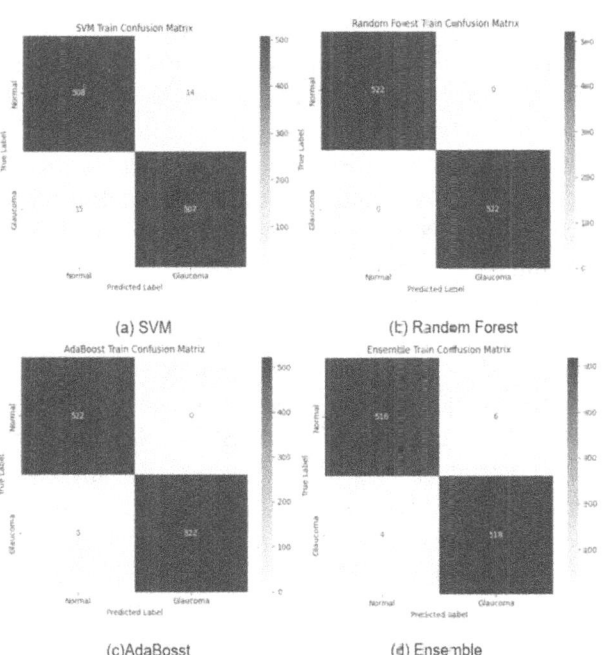

Figure 4.6 Train confusion matrices of classification models using pretrained model EfficientNet-B0
Source: Author

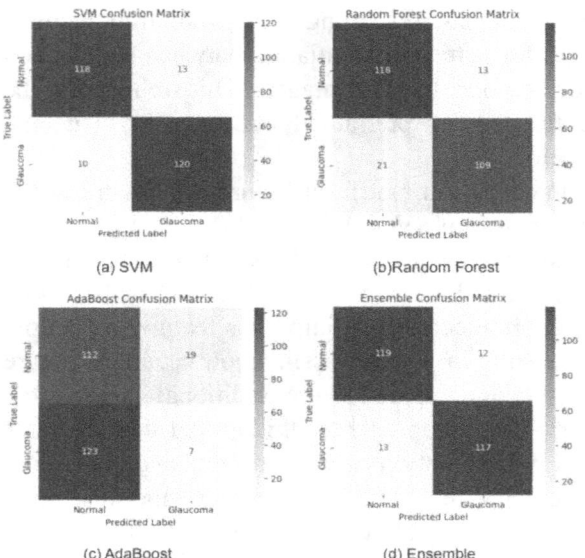

Figure 4.7 Confusion matrices of classification models using pretrained model ResNet-101

Source: Author

RF consistently showed dependable and steady performance across different deep feature extraction methods. It performed particularly well with features from EfficientNet-B0 and ResNet-50, reaching accuracies of 88% and 87%, respectively. These results highlight how well RF can handle the complexity of deep features. Its strength lies in reducing overfitting and managing high-dimensional data, making it a practical and reliable option for medical image classification, where the data can be intricate and the differences between classes are often subtle.

These results demonstrate the advantages of combining deep learning-based feature extraction with ensemble methods like RF. Leveraging powerful models such as EfficientNet-B0 and ResNet-50, along with the reliability and generalization capabilities of RF, allows the system to capture a wider range of patterns in fundus images. This combination reduces the risk of individual classifier limitations affecting overall performance. The success of this hybrid approach not only supports the methods used in this proposed work but also underscores its effectiveness in handling complex datasets, particularly for glaucoma classification from fundus images.

Table 4.2 highlights the performance metrics, Accuracy, Precision, Recall, and F1-Score, for the best-performing models on the glaucoma detection task. The Ensemble classifier consistently outperformed other models, achieving an impressive 95% across all key performance metrics for both glaucoma and normal cases. This shows its strength in capturing important features and making reliable predictions across both classes. The SVM classifier closely follows, showing 94% accuracy and balanced precision-recall values for both classes, which demonstrates its effectiveness in handling linearly separable features from EfficientNet-B0. RF and AdaBoost, while providing fairly good results,

generalization ability and robustness in detecting glaucoma. The SVM classifier also performed well, achieving 94% accuracy with EfficientNet-B0 features, indicating that the deep features extracted by this architecture are highly discriminative.

AdaBoost faced major challenges with ResNet-101 features, resulting in just 46% accuracy. This low performance likely comes from AdaBoost being sensitive to complex, high-dimensional inputs, which can cause over fitting with deep features. On the other hand, handcrafted features led to lower accuracy across all classifiers. Among these, the SVM model performed the best, achieving 86%. This suggests that while traditional features have some ability to differentiate, they may not match the depth and abstraction that deep learning features provide.

ResNet-50 and ResNet-101 enhanced the overall performance of the models. When combining ResNet-101 features with an SVM classifier, the highest accuracy of 91% was achieved. This highlights the effectiveness of deep feature representations in improving classification performance. Similarly, the Ensemble model utilizing ResNet-50 features achieved an accuracy of 88%, highlighting the advantages of deep learning features over handcrafted ones and demonstrating the Ensemble method's ability to capture diverse patterns within the data.

Table 4.1 Classification accuracy of models with different feature extraction methods

Feature extraction methods	SVM	Random Forest	Adaboost	Ensemble
Handcrafted features	86%	85%	81%	81%
ResNet -50	88%	84%	83%	88%
ResNet -101	91%	87%	46%	90%
Efficient Net-B0	94%	90%	89%	95%

Source: Author

Table 4.2 Performance metrics of the best performing model

Metrics	SVM	RF	Adaboost	Ensemble
Accuracy	94%	90%	89%	95%
Precision (Glaucoma)	95%	90%	88%	95%
Recall (Glaucoma)	93%	89%	90%	94%
F1 Score (Glaucoma)	94%	90%	89%	95%
Precision (Normal)	93%	89%	90%	94%
Recall (Normal)	95%	90%	88%	95%
F1 Score (Normal)	94%	90%	89%	95%

Source: Author

showed comparatively lower recall for normal and glaucoma cases, indicating a slight drop in sensitivity.

Notably, AdaBoost had the lowest recall at 88% for both classes. This indicates possible challenges in learning complex feature relationships on their own. The high F1-scores of the Ensemble model for both glaucoma and normal categories show that it keeps a strong balance between precision and recall. This balance is crucial in medical diagnostics, where both false positives and false negatives have serious implications. These findings support the effectiveness of ensemble learning in medical imaging, especially when it uses deep and varied feature representations. These findings reinforce the suitability of ensemble learning in medical imaging, particularly when powered by deep and diverse feature representations.

Discussion

Various methods have been studied for detecting glaucoma using fundus images. These methods differ in classification techniques, feature extraction strategies, and accuracy. A close comparison of techniques listed in the performance Table 4.3 reveals important trends and advantages of certain model choices. The highest reported accuracy in the comparison 95.0% is achieved by both the earliest SVM-based traditional model and the proposed ensemble method. While both reach the same accuracy, their underlying approaches differ significantly. The former relies solely on handcrafted features, whereas the proposed method integrates multiple feature types including CDR, HOG, LBP, and GLCM within a deep learning backbone (EfficientNet-B0), then fuses their outputs through ensemble classification. This hybrid structure offers stronger robustness and adaptability across datasets.

The accuracy graph (Figure 4.8) further supports these findings. Models trained without pretrained weights consistently underperform, especially with Adaboost (as low as 46%), reflecting limited generalization. In contrast, pretrained CNN models especially EfficientNet-B0 and ResNet50 show consistently high accuracy across all classifiers. For instance, ResNet50 combined with SVM achieves 94%, and EfficientNet-B0 combined with ensemble classifiers reaches 95.0%, the highest in the graph. This consistent performance of the ensemble model highlights the advantage of combining deep and handcrafted features across multiple classifiers.

It reduces overfitting, captures diverse information from input images, and provides high diagnostic accuracy regardless of variability in image quality.

Table 4.3 A performance comparison between the proposed method & various leading existing methods

Author(s) & Year	Methods	Accuracy (%)
Burlina et al. [1]	SVM with fundus images	95.0
Raghavendra et al. [2]	SVM + Gabor + LBP	90.1
Wadhwani and Wadhwani. [3]	CNN with dropout	89.5
Rajalakshmi et al. [4]	Pre-processing + Deep CNN	90.6
Akter et al. [5]	CNN + CDR, HOG, LBP	91.2
Maheshwari et al. [6]	CNN (VGG19) + CDR	92.3
Kouadri et al. [7]	Ensemble SVM + texture + CDR	92.8
Muramatsu et al. [8]	CNN + disc segmentation	90.9
Latif et al. [9]	Enhanced SVM + GLCM, PCA	90.5
Li et al. [10]	Smartphone CNN	88.4
Mojab et al. [11]	Deep CNN	79.0
Singh et al. [12]	ResNet50 – Pre-processing	94.5
Joshi et al. [13]	SVM, RF + CLAHE, CDR, HOG, LBP	89.7
Sharma et al. [14]	Lightweight CNN	91.0
Alam et al. [15]	ResNet18 – ROI-focused training	93.4
Latha and Priya [16]	Dual CNN for severity detection	92.3
Proposed Method	Ensemble (EfficientNet-B0 + CDR, HOG, LBP, GLCM)	95.0

Source: Author's compilation

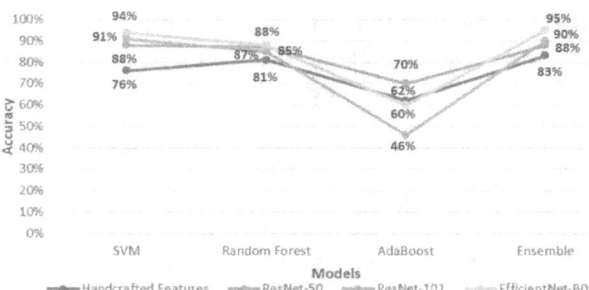

Figure 4.8 Accuracy comparison of all the models
Source: Author

Overall, these findings indicate that feature extraction using pretrained models significantly improves classification accuracy, with Efficient Net providing the best results. The ensemble model consistently outperformed individual classifiers, suggesting that combining multiple classifiers enhances generalization and reduces misclassifications. The graph in Figure 4.8 reinforces this conclusion by clearly illustrating the ensemble model's consistent top-tier performance, regardless of the feature extractor used. Additionally, the results highlight that while deep feature extraction benefits most models, certain classifiers, like AdaBoost, may not be well-suited for deeper networks such as ResNet -101- an issue clearly visualized through the abrupt dip in AdaBoost's accuracy curve.

The study demonstrates that deep learning-assisted machine learning models can significantly improve early glaucoma detection using fundus images. Future research could focus on further optimization, fine-tuning pretrained networks, and real-world clinical validation to enhance the reliability of automated glaucoma diagnosis.

Conclusion

The development of an efficient and accurate glaucoma detection system using fundus images was achieved by integrating machine learning classifiers with deep feature extraction from pretrained models. Various classification techniques, including Support Vector Machine (SVM), Random Forest, AdaBoost, and an ensemble approach, were evaluated both with and without deep learning features. The confusion matrices confirmed that the ensemble model consistently reduced misclassification rates, reinforcing the effectiveness of combining multiple classifiers for better generalization. This suggests

that hybrid models, which integrate deep learning with machine learning classifiers, can enhance glaucoma detection accuracy and reliability. The findings successfully demonstrated the potential of deep feature extraction in improving glaucoma classification. The best-performing approach, EfficientNet-50 with an ensemble model, provides a strong foundation for automated glaucoma diagnosis. Future work should focus on optimizing these models further, incorporating larger and more diverse datasets, and validating their performance in real-world clinical settings to enhance their applicability in medical practice.

References

[1] Burlina, P., Pacheco, K. D., Joshi, N., Bressler, N. M., & Freund, D. E. (2017). Comparing humans and deep learning performance for grading AMD: a study in using universal deep features. *Computers in Biology and Medicine*, 82, 80–86.

[2] Raghavendra, U., Dinesh, H. B., Rajendra, U. B., & Samanvitha, S. (2018). Automated glaucoma detection using Gabor filter and LBP features with SVM classifier. *Biocybernetics and Biomedical Engineering*, 38(2), 393–402.

[3] Wadhwani, R., & Wadhwani, A. (2019). Glaucoma detection using deep learning convolutional neural networks. *International Journal of Computer Applications*, 178(23), 25–30.

[4] Rajalakshmi, R., Subashini, R., Anjana, R. M., & Mohan, V. (2019). Automated diabetic retinopathy detection in smartphone-based fundus photography using deep learning in Indian population. *Eye*, 33(1), 114–120.

[5] Akter, A., Akhtaruzzaman, M., Satu, M. S., Ahmed, K., & Hassan, M. M. (2020). Multi-feature based CNN model for glaucoma detection. *Journal of Medical Imaging and Health Informatics*, 10(4), 917–922.

[6] Maheshwari, S., Nema, A. K., & Dubey, S. K. (2020). Glaucoma detection using VGG19 deep neural network and cup-to-disc ratio. *Biomedical Signal Processing and Control*, 60, 101966.

[7] Kouadri, B., Bouakkaz, K., & Boukelif, A. (2020). Automated glaucoma detection using ensemble SVM and texture-based features. *Multimedia Tools and Applications*, 79(41), 31237–31256.

[8] Muramatsu, C., Hayashi, N., Hatanaka, Y., Yamada, T., Bando, H., Sawada, A., et al. (2020). Automated segmentation of optic disc using deep learning for glaucoma screening. *Scientific Reports*, 10, 20397.

[9] Latif, S., Rana, R., Imran, M., Abawajy, J. H., & Mahmood, A. (2021). Enhanced nature-inspired support vector machine for glaucoma detection. In Proceedings of the International Conference on Biomedical Engineering, (pp. 123–129).

[10] Li, Y., Hu, Y., Zhang, H., Liu, S., Xie, Y., & Li, L. (2021). Smartphone-based deep learning system for visual field assessment in glaucoma detection. *IEEE Transactions on Medical Imaging*, 40(6), 1570–1580.

[11] Mojab, S., Baharlouei, S., Yazdanpanah, M., & Tavakoli, M. (2021). Deep convolutional neural network for glaucoma diagnosis using fundus images. *Biomedical Engineering Letters*, 11(2), 159–166.

[12] Singh, A., Sharma, R., Tripathi, M., & Aggarwal, A. (2021). Transfer learning-based deep convolutional neural network for glaucoma classification. *Medical Image Analysis*, 70, 101996.

[13] Joshi, N., Shah, H., Patel, R., & Parmar, S. (2022). Supervised learning with image enhancement for glaucoma detection using fundus images. *Journal of Ophthalmology Research*, 15(2), 110–118.

[14] Sharma, M., Jain, S., Tiwari, A., & Choudhary, V. (2022). Lightweight convolutional neural network for glaucoma screening on mobile platforms. *Telemedicine and e-Health*, 28(4), 452–460.

[15] Alam, M. Z., Wang, H., Waheed, H., & Baka, N. (2023). ROI-based glaucoma classification using ResNet18 on fundus images. *Computers in Biology and Medicine*, 158, 106692.

[16] Latha, G., & Priya, P. A. (2024). Glaucoma detection and severity diagnosis from fundus images using dual CNN architectures. *International Journal of Image, Graphics and Signal Processing*, 16(6), 15–26.

5 Improving the quality of injection-molded parts through the use of statistical process control tools

Raghunanthan, R.[1,a] and Syath Abuthakeer, S.[2,b]

[1]PG Student, Department of Mechanical Engineering, PSG College of Technology, Coimbatore, India

[2]Associate Professor, Department of Mechanical Engineering, PSG College of Technology, Coimbatore, India

Abstract

The production of high-quality injection molded components continues to pose challenges for manufacturers, as defect rates remain notably high. In an increasingly competitive global market, maintaining rigorous quality standards is crucial for ensuring product reliability and sustaining a company's market position. The quality of the injection molded parts comes from the selection of the raw material, maintaining the standard temperature and flow rate. In this paper DMAIC approach is used to reduce the defects by using statistical control tools. In the defined phase SIPOC and project charter are used and in measure phase Pareto chart, process capability and variable chart are used to measure the process. In the analyzing phase regression analysis and cause and effect diagram are used. In the improved and control phase FMEA is used to solve the problems that are identified. software is used for statistical testing to do the various quality tests and improve the quality of injection molding.

Keywords: Defects, DMAIC, FMEA

Introduction

In the competitive landscape of manufacturing, achieving excellence in product quality is a paramount objective. In industries reliant on injection molding, where precision and consistency are pivotal, the presence of defects can significantly impede both operational efficiency and customer satisfaction. To address this challenge one of the six sigma tool, define, measure, analyze, improve and control (DMAIC) approach emerges as a structured methodology for driving continuous improvement.

Injection molding machine
Injection molding machines, being essential equipment of the manufacturing industry. The injection molding machines are used in producing plastic components and the parts are produced majorly for the textile and automobile industry there are different types of machines with semiautomatic and fully automatic machines.

DMAIC approach
DMAIC is a method used in most of the industry to eliminate defects and this method is used to improve the quality of the product and process improvement in the Six Sigma methodology. It is a well-defined method for problem identification, variation reduction, and performance improvement. Define is about identifying the problem, providing project objectives, and determining the customer requirements.

In the measure phase, the important metrics are defined, and data is gathered for the problem identified it is possible to measure the problem and determine its effect on performance. Identifying the root causes of problem and defects or inefficiencies through tools such as Pareto charts, fishbone diagrams, and statistical analysis is done in the analyze phase.

In the improve phase, solutions are created to remove root causes and improve the process. It involves brainstorming and refining improvements to full implementation. In the control phase it is sustained in the long term. This involves setting standard operating procedures, monitoring systems, and continuous improvement.

The integration of the DMAIC methodology and failure mode and effects analysis (FMEA) has become an important approach in enhancing quality and efficiency in injection molding process. Various studies show how these methodologies have been applied to address manufacturing challenges, improve process capability, reduce defects, and optimize production parameters. The application of

[a]raghunanthan0445@gmail.com, [b]ssa.mech@psgtech.ac.in

DOI: 10.1201/9781003770435-5

design of experiments (DOE) and response surface methodology (RSM) within the DMAIC framework has been used to optimize parameters such as injection speed, mold temperature, and cooling time, resulting in productivity improvements of 10–15% and significant reductions in scrap rates [1]. Efforts to minimize cycle time in automotive component manufacturing through adjustments to melt temperature, injection pressure, and holding time have yielded a 12% reduction in defects and a 9% improvement in overall equipment effectiveness (OEE) [2]. Combining FMEA with DMAIC has been effective in identifying high-risk failure modes in material handling and cooling processes, reducing scrap rates by 15% and enhancing customer satisfaction [3]. Addressing warpage defects through cause-and-effect diagrams and process capability analysis has led to an 18% improvement in dimensional accuracy [4]. Medical device molding processes have seen a 14% decrease in defect rates by tackling material contamination issues [5], while surface quality enhancements of 10% have been achieved through optimized packing pressure and cooling durations to mitigate sink mark defects [6]. Addressing cavity imbalance in multi-cavity molds has improved part consistency by 12% and reduced defective products by 11% [7]. Efforts to reduce rejection rates in muffler production have resulted in a drop from 8.21% to 4.81%, with corresponding improvements in Sigma levels and process capability [8] Cooling channel optimization has achieved a 13% reduction in cycle time without compromising part integrity [9] Burn marks on automotive interior components have been eliminated, leading to a 16% improvement in surface finish and a 12% reduction in rejection rates [10]. Gate design modifications to prevent void formation in thick-walled components have reduced scrap rates by 10% [11]), while process adjustments targeting flow mark defects have improved surface quality by 12% [12] Enhancing high-gloss finishes in household appliance parts through adjustments in packing pressure and mold temperature has led to a 15% reduction in sink marks [13]. Interventions in screw speed and cooling times during medical component production have decreased downtime by 17% and increased efficiency [14]. Cycle time reduction of 11% has been achieved in automotive dashboard manufacturing [15], while addressing short shot issues in small electronic components has lowered defect occurrences by 13% [16]. Improvements in

cooling uniformity have contributed to a 10% reduction in warpage defects in large plastic panels [17]. Optimizing injection speed and mold venting has enhanced the surface finish of automotive lighting components by 16% and reduced scrap rates [18]. Strategic project selection for Six Sigma initiatives has improved success rates and financial outcomes [19]. Predictive models have processes in enhancing the effectiveness of process improvement efforts [20]. Overall, the systematic identification of root causes and the implementation of targeted solutions through the integration of DMAIC and FMEA methodologies for optimizing production parameters, and achieving substantial cost savings in injection molding.

Problem identification

In this paper, the defect rate in Reiter's textile equipment component boxes is 30 parts per 1000 pieces manufactured. To monitor variation in the occurrence of defects, the defect rate is increased in this month. The defect rate should be minimized as quick as possible to reduce losses and increase productivity.

Objectives and Methodology

To reduce the Reiter textile box machinery components, defect rate from 3–1% and address the root causes of defects.

This work starts with gathering information from the injection molding industry and then conducts a literature survey to determine issues. DMAIC methodology is followed by using tools to minimize defect counts. Overall project flow is shown in Figure 5.1

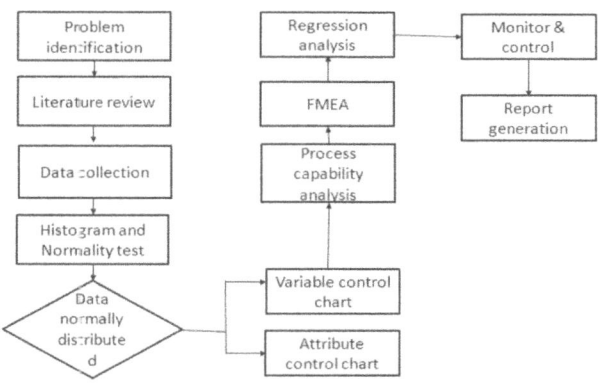

Figure 5.1 Methodology flow chart
Source: Author

During the define phase, the project goals are identified, the customer requirements are determined, and existing process are noted. The measure phase is about gathering data and determining process capability. During the analyze phase, root causes are determined with tools such as RCA, FMEA, and data visualization. The improve phase involves improving solutions through design of experiments (DOE). In the control phase the long-term success with statistical process control (SPC), standard procedures, and ongoing improvement activities. This systematic approach promotes product quality and process effectiveness. The DMAIC process is demonstrated in Figure 5.2.

Data Collection

The data shown in the Table 5.1 is defect's produced by each die for the Reiter textile component.

The process starts from the melt temperature to the mold temperature, from the flow rate to the injection speed, converges variation in quality of product. Melt temperature of the material determines the viscosity and flow behavior, while mold temperature is the counterpart for cooling and solidification. Flow rate and injection speed in tandem, orchestrating the journey of molten material into the mold cavity. they compose a control and mastery of shaping the outcome of every molded piece with full finished shaping. Each parameter is tracked and analyzed to serve as a guiding process towards perfection. The melt temperature, a pivotal factor, influences material behavior, determining its flow and viscosity characteristics. The mold temperature is controlled. the cooling and solidification of the molten material, shaping its final form.

In Table 5.2 the melt temperature, mold temperature, flow rate and injection speed for the part is noted for the calculation of DOE.

Data Interpretation

Define

In the define phase of a project, the project charter serves as a base document. The project's objectives, scope, stakeholders, and overall direction is shown in it. It's like a roadmap that guides the project team throughout the project. The project charter is shown in Figure 5.3.

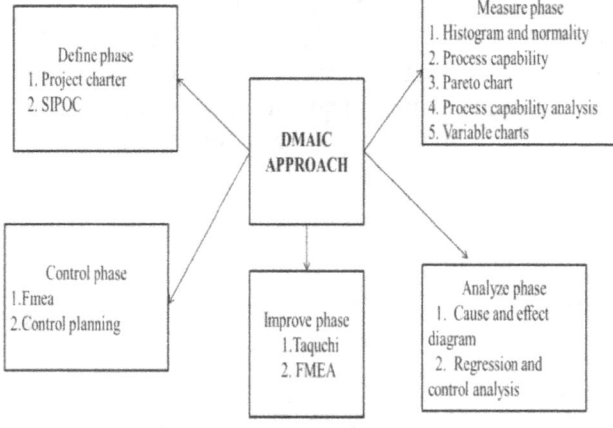

Figure 5.2 DMAIC approach
Source: Author

Table 5.1 No of defects in dies

DIE 1	23	20	25	31	15	17	13	23	25	18
DIE 2	21	17	28	16	20	18	19	16	20	28
DIE 1	17	28	32	21	19	13	17	16	20	15
DIE 2	25	21	22	18	25	24	23	22	14	20

Source: Author

Table 5.2 Injection molding parameters

Experiment	Melt Temperature (°C)	Mold Temperature (°C)	Flow Rate (g/s)	Injection Speed (mm/s)
1	115	60	50	200
2	118	80	60	250
3	113	100	70	300
4	110	70	55	280
5	130	90	65	220
6	125	75	60	270
7	115	100	50	250
8	117	60	70	200
9	117	85	60	240
10	125	80	55	260
11	122	65	70	230
12	120	90	65	250
13	117	75	60	280
14	115	95	55	210
15	121	70	50	270
16	125	85	70	240
17	122	65	65	220
18	116	90	60	260
19	114	80	55	230
20	125	75	50	250

Source: Author

PROJECT CHARTER			
Project Title	Improving the quality of injection-molded parts through the use of statistical process control tools		
Date started	March 4,2024	Industry	Yogi plast
Expected to complete on	April 26,2024	MD	Bala Yogi
Project Purpose			
To reduce the defect rate from 30 to 15 within 2 months To address the root causes of the defects			

Figure 5.3 Project charter

Source: Author

1SIPOC

In the define phase of a project, supplier process improvement and control involve optimizing and access of the processes related to suppliers. This includes identifying suppliers and understanding their role in this project and giving clear communication channels. By defining expectations, setting quality standards, and implementing feedback mechanisms, the project can ensure that supplier inputs align with project goals and contribute to overall success shown in Figure 5.4.

Measure

The measure phase in process improvement methodologies, like Six Sigma, focuses on gathering data to assess the current state of a process. It involves defining what needs to be measured, collecting relevant data, and analyzing it to understand the process's performance. The goal is to establish a baseline and identify areas for improvement.

Histogram and normality testing

For the given data histogram and normality test is to perform to know about the distribution and how often the defects occurred and then to understand the defects rate of the dies shown in Table 5.3.

Data distribution is represented graphically by histograms, which show how frequently data points fall into intervals or bins. They provide insights into the shape, center, and spread of data, aiding in understanding its characteristics shown in Figure 5.5.

Normality testing is a statistical method used to assess whether a dataset follows a normal distribution, which is characterized by a bell-shaped curve. The Kolmogorov-Smirnov test can determine if the data deviates significantly from a normal distribution. Assessing normality is crucial in many statistical

Table 5.3 Data input in solver

DIE 1	DIE 2
20	17
25	28
31	16
15	20
17	18
13	19
23	16
25	20
18	28
17	25
28	21
32	22
21	18
19	25
13	24
17	23
16	22
20	14
15	20

Source: Author

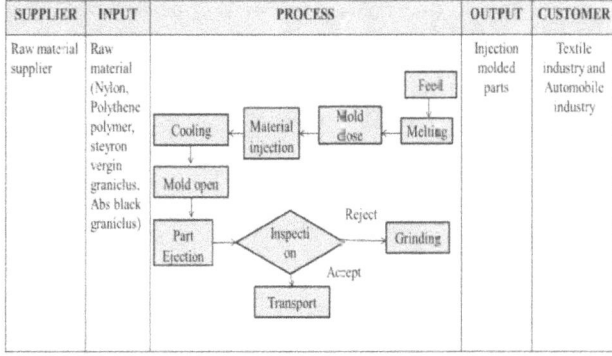

Figure 5.4 SIPOC

Source: Author

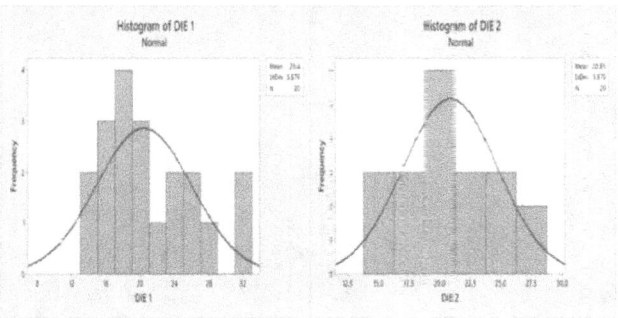

Figure 5.5 Histogram for two die's

Source: Author

analyses, as it influences the selection of appropriate inferential methods and the validity of results shown in Figure 5.6.

Pareto chart

A particularly effective tool for demonstrating the relative importance of a problem is the Pareto chart. The Pareto principle is about 80% of the effect comes from the 20% of the causes. In this the most of effect comes from the temperature and the screw dimension. Insufficient temperature in the machine and material. So that the parts producing are mostly cut piece which is defect. show in Figure 5.7. In the pareto chart it shows that the major problem occurs in the temperature variations.

Process capability analysis

The process capability analysis of making the Reiter textile machinery component box. Normally the cp value should be 1 and Cpk value is 1.35 in this the value of cp and Cpk is lesser than the normal value. So, the process of making the component should be standardized quickly show in Figure 5.8. Figure 5.8 shows that the process is capable to make the Reiter textile machinery component box.

Variable chart

X bar chart is a variable control chart we used to determine the melt temperature measured from the thermocouple. To know about the temperature variation while molding the component. The upper specification limit is 127°C and the lower specification limit is 115°C and the target value is 120°C. The sudden drop and rise in the melt temperature shown in Figure 5.9.

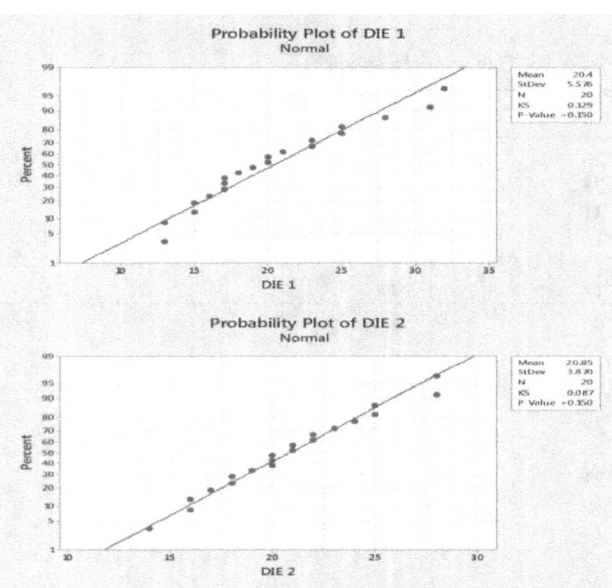

Figure 5.6 Normality test for two die's
Source: Author

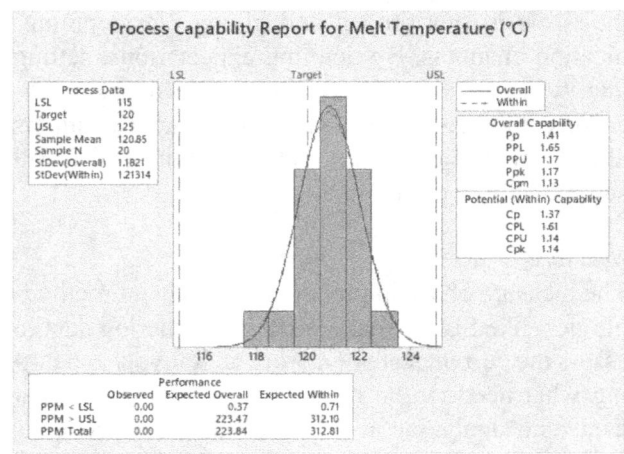

Figure 5.8 Process capability chart
Source: Author

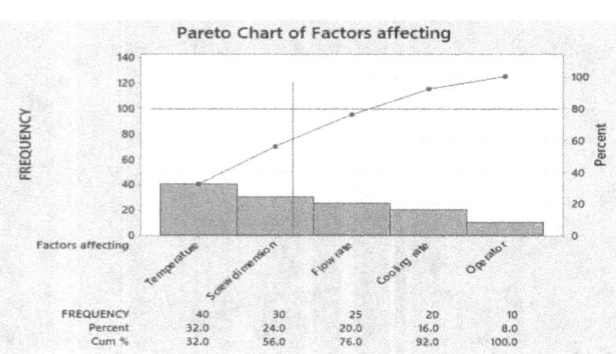

Figure 5.7 Pareto chart
Source: Author

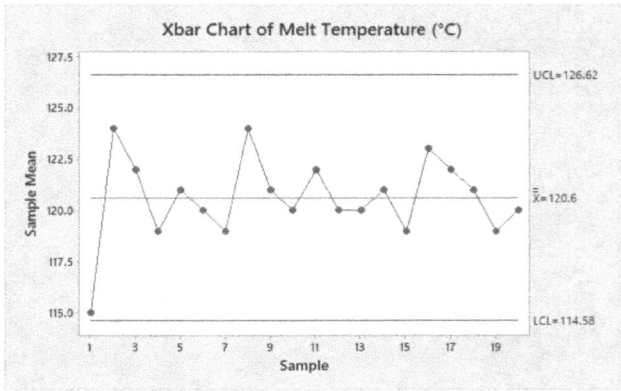

Figure 5.9 X bar chart
Source: Author

The above figure shows that the variation in temperature with the sample size of 20. It shows the sudden increase and decrease in temperature.

Analyze

The analyzing phase in various processes, such as project management or problem-solving methodologies like Six Sigma, involves diving deep into data and information to identify patterns, root causes, and opportunities for improvement. It's about understanding the current state thoroughly before making informed decisions on how to proceed. In this phase we use cause and effect diagram to see the major effect and causes due to the various factors affecting the injection molding process like material, machines, mold and working parameters.

Cause and effect diagram

A cause-and-effect diagram, also called an Ishikawa diagramor fishbone diagram, is a visual tool for organizing and listing potential causes of a given problem. It resembles a fish skeleton, with the problem or effect at the head of the "fish" and various categories of potential causes branching off as "bones." This method helps teams systematically explore and analyze potential causes to address issues effectively shown in Figure 5.10.

Reliability analysis

This diagram shows the regression analysis plot for no of molded parts and the no of defects parts to know the bottle neck value line for the manufacturing of the Reiter textile machinery component box. In this analysis we know that to reduce the defects we need to make at least 2000 Reiter textile machinery component box. Figure 5.11 shows the reliability chart.

In the above figure shows that there is total 20 defect count occurs for 5000 parts for less volume like 500 parts the defect count is 50 parts. It shows that the making of less volume can increase the defect occurrence.so that it is to set standard minimum production level.

Improve

The improve phase, often part of methodologies like Six Sigma or project management, focuses on implementing solutions to address identified issues or opportunities for improvement. This phase involves brainstorming, testing, and refining solutions to optimize processes and achieve desired outcomes. It's about turning analysis into action to drive positive change and enhance performance.

Design of experiments (Taguchi)

Design of experiments (DOE) in injection molding parameters involves systematically varying key factors such as temperature, pressure, speed, and material composition to optimize the manufacturing process and product quality [2]. By using statistical techniques, DOE helps identify the optimal combination of parameters that result in the desired outcomes, such as minimizing defects, reducing cycle time, or improving part strength. For the DOE calculation the data is shown in Table 5 2. This approach allows manufacturers to efficiently explore the effects of different variables and find the most efficient and effective settings for their specific molding process. Ultimately, DOE in injection molding parameters

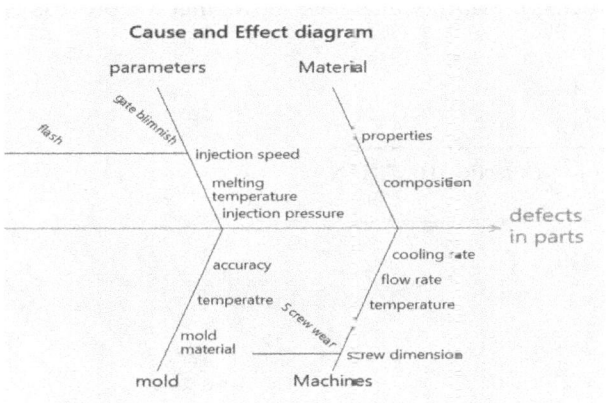

Figure 5.10 Cause and effect diagram
Source: Author

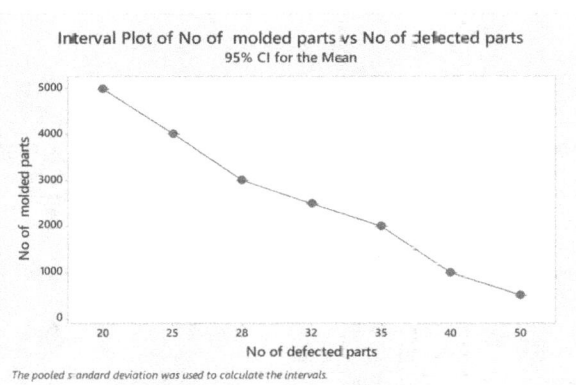

Figure 5.11 Reliability analysis
Source: Author

empowers manufacturers to produce higher quality parts with greater consistency and efficiency shown in Figure 5.12.

In the above figure shows that in the y axis injection speed and in x axis shows that the temperature and the flow rate value, so that the variation injection speed cause the change in the temperature and flow rate accordingly with reaching the UCL and LCL respectively.

Failure mode and effect analysis

Failure mode and effect analysis (FMEA) is a systematic method for identifying and prioritizing potential failures in a product, process, or system, and assessing their potential effects. It involves breaking down the system into its components, analyzing how each component could fail, and evaluating the severity, frequency, and detectability of each failure mode. FMEA helps teams prioritize mitigation efforts to prevent or reduce the likelihood and impact of failures. The FMEA of the injection molding parameters is shown in Table 5.4

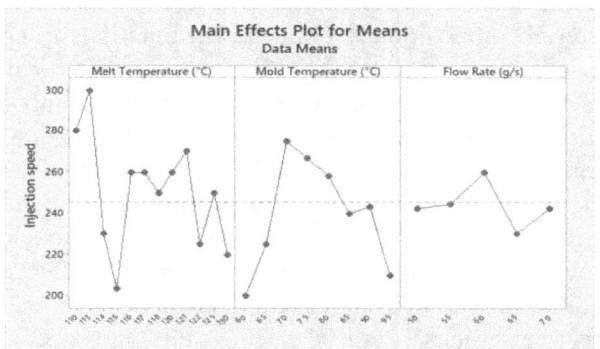

Figure 5.12 DOE Interactions with injection molding parameters
Source: Author

Control

In the control phase of various processes like Six Sigma or project management, the focus is on maintaining the improvements achieved during the previous phases. It involves implementing monitoring systems, establishing standard operating procedures, and putting controls in place to ensure that processes remain stable and continue to meet desired performance levels.

The control phase aims to sustain the gains made through continuous monitoring, feedback, and adjustment, thereby ensuring long-term success and preventing regression to previous performance levels shown in Table 5.5.

Results and Discussion

The main root cause for the defects is identified as the variations in the temperature that occur in the melt temperature and the mold temperature, which cause the defect by increasing and decreasing the temperature and it is identified using the thermal camera, which is used to find out the temperature. As a result, the variation in temperature causes defects like black spot, white neck and short neck and also the material gets weakened and improper shape when there is an excess of temperature. These issues are identified, and the DMAIC approach is used to eliminate issues and also to eliminate the external issues before the material gets into the molten parts. the SIPOC and project charter helps to get the overview of the project, and the histogram and normality test is done for which the two dies are manufacturing the same part and identified the defect count of the two dies and the pareto chart is identified the temperature and screw dimension are the major issues and then process capability analyses shows that the process is

Table 5.4 FMEA before giving the solution

Potential failure mode	Causes (c)	Severity(s)	Occurrence(o)	Detection(D)	RPN
Melt temperature	Variation in temperature	8	8	5	320
Short neck	Variation In injection speed	8	7	3	168
White performs	Variation In screw speed	2	6	2	24
Black spot	Variation Inmold temperature	3	5	4	60

Source: Author

Table 5.5 FMEA after giving the solution

Potential Failure Mode	Solution	Severity (s)	Occurrence (o)	Detection (D)	RPN
Melt temperature	Standard temp fix to 120 degrees	8	7	3	168
Short neck	Fix injection speed to 65 mm/s	8	6	2	98
White performs	Fix screw speed to 80 rpm	3	5	1	15
Black spot	Variation In mold temperature	2	5	2	20

Source: Author

not capable for producing good parts where the cp > 1 and Cpk < 1.35, so the actions should be taken to reduce the value. The variable chart also shows that the sudden increase and decrease of the temperature causes the defects, but the value is maintained between the UCL and LCL. The cause-and-effect diagram shows the potential cause of the problem. The reliability analysis gives the minimum value of ordering the parts to reduce the defects the minimum no of order value is 2000. The design of experiments gives the optimal value to maintain each of the parameters to reduce the defects the optimal values are 118, 85, and 55 at the injection speed of 250. The FMEA gives the solution to the major problem and the process capability is maintained in the cp < 0.83 and Cpk < 0.73 .the values of the melt temperature, mold temperature, flow rate and the injection speed should be maintained at the optimal value find out by the design of experiments the doe optimal value should continuously monitored and the value should be properly noted the standard operating procedure to know the operating value of the Reiter textile box machinery components where these optimal value gives the better solution for the operating value of the part. The process capability diagram is shown in Figure 5.13.

Conclusion

This research was focused on analyzing and minimizing defects in the Reiter textile component injection molding manufacturing process. Information from two sets of different dyes showed that melt temperature fluctuation was the major reason for defects, which had a negative impact on product quality. Through FMEA and DOE, important parameters— melt temperature, mold temperature, flow rate, and

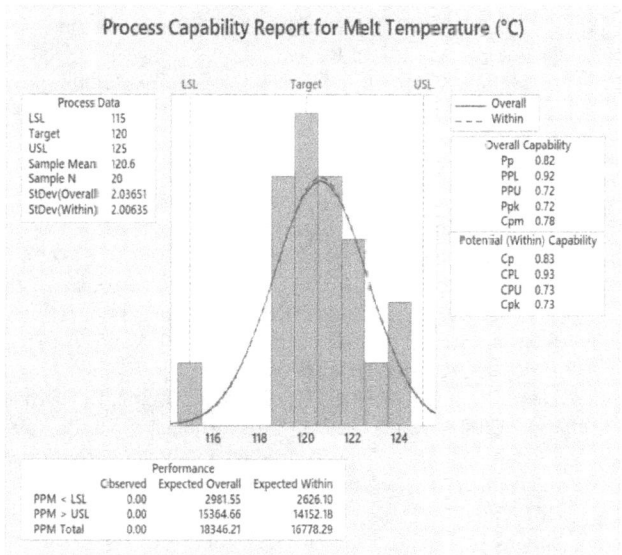

Figure 5.13 Process capability analysis after maintaining temperature
Source: Author

injection speed—were found to be crucial in defect minimization.

By standardizing the temperature of melt to 120°C, injection speed to 65 mm/s, and screw speed to 80 rpm, the rate of defect decreased from 3% to 1.5%. The process capability indices (Cp, Cpk) improved significantly, reflecting an improvement in the stability of the process. Histogram and normality tests established improved distribution of data, whereas Pareto analysis revealed 80% of defects were attributed to temperature and speed fluctuations. The research concludes that controlling critical parameters minimizes defects greatly, enhances the quality, and increases productivity and cost savings in Reiter's injection moldings.

References

[1] Khan, M. A., Ali, M. K., Shaikh, S., Hussain, A., Rahman, M., & Usmani, Y. (2023). Six Sigma DMAIC project to improve the performance of aluminium die casting operation. *International Journal of Advanced Manufacturing Technology*, 126(9–10), 4123–4136.

[2] Smith, J., Liu, R., Park, J., Chang, T., Kumar, R., & Lee, S. (2022). Optimization of process parameters in injection moulding using DOE and RSM for automotive components. *International Journal of Manufacturing Engineering*, Article 252637.

[3] Sharma, P., Kumar, A., Rathore, H., Singh, D., Patel, M., & Ranjan, R. (2021). Application of FMEA with DMAIC for quality improvement in plastic part production. *Journal of Quality and Reliability Engineering*, Article 9957843.

[4] Patel, S., Gupta, R., Shankar, S., Patel, K., Sharma, V., & Bansal, A. (2020). Reduction of warpage in injection moulding: A DMAIC approach. *International Journal of Advanced Manufacturing Technology*, 108(7–8), 2431–2443.

[5] Mehta, A., Verma, N., Khanna, S., Dubey, K., Sharma, R., & Singh, P. (2022). Minimizing defects in medical device moulding through Six Sigma methodologies. *Journal of Industrial and Production Engineering*, 39(4), 217–229.

[6] Babu, R., Kumar, S., Reddy, P., Rao, V., Sharma, A., & Jain, M. (2019). Process optimization for sink mark defects in injection moulded parts using FMEA and DMAIC. *Procedia Manufacturing*, 30, 125–132.

[7] Desai, V., Joshi, M., Patel, H., Shah, R., Mehta, P., & Khatri, S. (2021). Improvement of cavity balance in multi-cavity moulds for enhanced product quality. *International Journal of Engineering Research & Technology*, 10(5), 221–226.

[8] Singh, P., Lal, H., Kumar, K., Bhatia, R., Arora, S., & Chauhan, M. (2020). Implementation of Six Sigma in automotive muffler production: A case study. *Journal of Mechanical Engineering and Sciences*, 14(3), 7232–7245.

[9] Roy, A., Sharma, K., Banerjee, S., Patel, D., Reddy, V., & Das, S. (2021). Cooling channel design optimization for cycle time reduction in injection moulding. *International Journal of Thermal Sciences*, 167, 107026. https://doi.org/10.1016/j.ijthermalsci.2021.107026.

[10] Agarwal, N., Mishra, D., Rao, S., Patel, V., Prakash, A., & Dube, R. (2022). Eliminating burn marks in automotive interior components using DMAIC. *Journal of Cleaner Production*, 355, 131774. https://doi.org/10.1016/j.jclepro.2022.131774.

[11] Menon, R., Deshmukh, K., Patel, A., Shah, N., Varma, S., & Mehta, L. (2019). Gate design improvement to mitigate voids in thick-walled moulded parts. *Journal of Manufacturing Processes*, 44, 327–336. https://doi.org/10.1016/j.jmapro.2019.05.024.

[12] Iyer, S., Rao, V., Kumar, P., Srinivasan, R., Shah, L., & Modi, A. (2020). Flow mark defect reduction through process parameter optimization. *International Journal of Precision Engineering and Manufacturing*, 21(8), 1473–1481. https://doi.org/10.1007/s12541-020-00326-2.

[13] Kapoor, M., Nair, A., Mishra, S., Jain, R., Pandey, K., & Thakur, P. (2021). Enhancing surface finish of household appliances through injection moulding process modifications. *Journal of Materials Processing Technology*, 295, 117160. https://doi.org/10.1016/j.jmatprotec.2021.117160.

[14] Malhotra, T., Jain, S., Mehta, R., Garg, V., Patel, S., & Sharma, A. (2022). DMAIC approach to improve efficiency in medical component injection moulding. *International Journal of Productivity and Quality Management*, 36(1), 55–73.

[15] Sharma, G., Bansal, R., Patel, S., Singh, V., Kumar, D., & Reddy, T. (2020). Reducing cycle time in automotive dashboard production using Six Sigma tools. *Journal of Applied Polymer Science*, 137(48), 49321. https://doi.org/10.1002/app.49321.

[16] Pandey, A., Mehta, S., Srivastava, P., Das, R., Singh, K., & Roy, V. (2021). Short shot defect minimization in small electronic components through process control. *Journal of Manufacturing Systems*, 59, 481–490. https://doi.org/10.1016/j.jmsy.2021.03.008.

[17] Patel, C., Agarwal, M., Shankar, S., Jain, R., Pandey, S., & Chauhan, P. (2022). Warpage reduction in large plastic panels through cooling optimization. *International Journal of Plastic Technology*, 26, 30–45. https://doi.org/10.1007/s40940-022-00175-w.

[18] Yadav, J., Rana, A., Singh, P., Verma, A., Thakur, S., & Joshi, V. (2021). Surface finish improvement in automotive lighting components using optimized injection parameters. *Journal of Polymer Engineering*, 41(2), 121–130. https://doi.org/10.1515/polyeng-2020-0282.

[19] Reddy, D., Kumar, S., Mehta, P., Agarwal, R., Singh, K., & Thomas, R. (2020). Strategic project selection in Six Sigma for enhanced financial outcomes. *International Journal of Operations and Production Management*, 40(5), 473–493. https://doi.org/10.1108/IJOPM-07-2019-0553.

[20] Joshi, K., Sharma, P., Singh, R., Nair, A., Mehta, V., & Garg, S. (2021). Predictive modelling for process improvement effectiveness in manufacturing. *Journal of Quality Technology*, 53(4), 392–406. https://doi.org/10.1080/00224065.2020.1804063.

6 Control of optimum argon shrouding practice – a water model study

Soorya Prakash Jayaraj[1,a], Manjini Sambandam[1,b], Viswanathan, N. Nurni[2,c] and Deepoo Kumar[2,d]

[1]Manager, Research and Development, JSW Steel Limited – Salem Works, India

[2]Professor, Department of Metallurgical Engineering and Materials Science, Indian Institute of Technology, Bombay, India

Abstract

Argon shrouding has proven to be an effective method to prevent air ingression at the slide gate in continuous casting and entrainment. On one hand, if sufficient argon is not supplied, the air ingression cannot be fully arrested thus promoting the chance of entrainment and re-oxidation. On the other hand, supply of excessive argon can result in larger eye opening at the tundish surface which again is counter-productive, leading to re-oxidation. In this work, a simple physical model has been setup to arrive at optimum argon flow rate that would just arrest the air ingression and entrainment. Further a control strategy for Argon shrouding has been proposed that could minimize re-oxidation in the tundish.

Keywords: Argon shrouding, continuous casting, open-eye formation, optimum flow, tundish

Introduction

One of the challenging tasks in the steel sector with increasing production demands is the production of clean steel to meet various critical applications. The quality of steel is evaluated in terms of non-metallic inclusion content which is generated by several potential causes like re-oxidation, steel – refractory reaction, refractory erosion or accretion flush off and entrapment of casting powder, etc. Continuous casting, the critical step in steel production that could potentially remove inclusions (or generate, in case of poor operational practice), plays a key role in determining the steel quality. One of the main causes of re-oxidation is the oxygen pickup by the liquid stream from the ambient atmosphere during casting [1]. Oxygen pickup during teeming has been largely prevented by the usage of ceramic shroud which is placed on a collector nozzle that is fixed to ladle bottom. However, pouring liquid steel from ladle to tundish through a slide gate creates suction at nozzle-slide gate assembly [2]. This negative pressure leads to ingression of air from the atmosphere to the liquid steel thereby causing re-oxidation and nitrogen pickup in steel. This also leads to accretion build up in the nozzle tube which periodically flushed into the steel stream.

Flooding of this negative pressure region with an inert shielding gas like argon has been a usual practice to prevent the air from entering into the liquid stream. Argon shrouding has been instrumental in reducing bath oxygen content, decrease in nozzle clogging occurrences, decreased inclusion content and an overall improvement in surface and internal quality of billets and blooms. The main challenge of argon shrouding is in arriving at an optimum shrouding practice [3]. Increasing argon flow rates decreases the tendency for air entrainment [7]. On the other hand, higher flow rates increase the eye-opening on the tundish surface leading to re-oxidation. In steel plants, the operator generally maintains a specific argon flow rate as per the standard operating practice. This argon flow rate is often not altered in accordance with liquid steel throughput. It is also to be noted that the inner dimensions of the furniture such as shroud, nozzle, etc., change with time due to erosion which can have a large impact on the argon flow dynamics through the shroud [11].

Typically, this furniture is changed periodically after a set of heats. During this change over, there can be alignment issues as well as small variations in dimensions that can have large impact on the argon flow requirements [9]. In short, these can pose

[a]sooryaprakash.jayaraj@jsw.in, [b]manjini.sambandam@jsw.in, [c]vichu@iitb.ac.in, [d]deepook@iitb.ac.in

DOI: 10.1201/9781003770435-6

difficulties in maintaining a consistent product quality in terms of total oxygen and nitrogen content.

There is a need therefore to look at the current shrouding practice in terms of optimization as well as maintaining consistency. The present works attempts to address these issues using water modelling approach.

Experimental Procedure

Development of physical model

Many researchers have investigated the shrouding practice and its effect on the steel cleanliness using physical model of the ladle, shroud and tundish system [3]. In the present work, an 18T three strand delta shaped, bloom casting tundish, 65T ladle, and the associated collector nozzle and shroud were scaled down to 1/6 size (λ=0.167) water model as shown in the Figure 6.1. The model was fabricated in poly-methyl methacrylate (Perspex) considering similarity criteria as used by Mazumdar and Evans [5] and also widely used by other researchers [6]. The industrial shroud is provided with a single gas inlet that branches out to six out-let at the inner circumference of the shroud. In the model six separate inlets are provided.

Schematics of collector nozzle and shroud assembly for the industrial and the model set-up are shown in Figures 6.2 and 6.3 respectively. The gas flow rate is measured using a rotameter. The liquid steel phase was simulated with water as done by the study of Mazumdar and Guthrie [8]. However, the compressed air was used to simulate argon. To get a physical feel of the open eye formation happening under industrial conditions, modeling experiments were conducted with LDPE balls as studied by Chattopadhyay et al. [9] having a water-LDPE density ratio of 0.55 (comparable to steel-slag density ratio of 0.45) to simulate slag phase.

Considering the mechanical and dynamic similarity criteria, model parameters like water flow rate from ladle to tundish, steady-state heights of water in ladle and tundish, exit flow from tundish in each of three outlets, compressed air flow rate, shroud immersion depth, slag phase depth were replicated. Suction is created at the nozzle-shroud junction, as can easily be explained using the principles of mechanical energy balance [4].

Figure 6.1 Experimental set-up
Source: Author

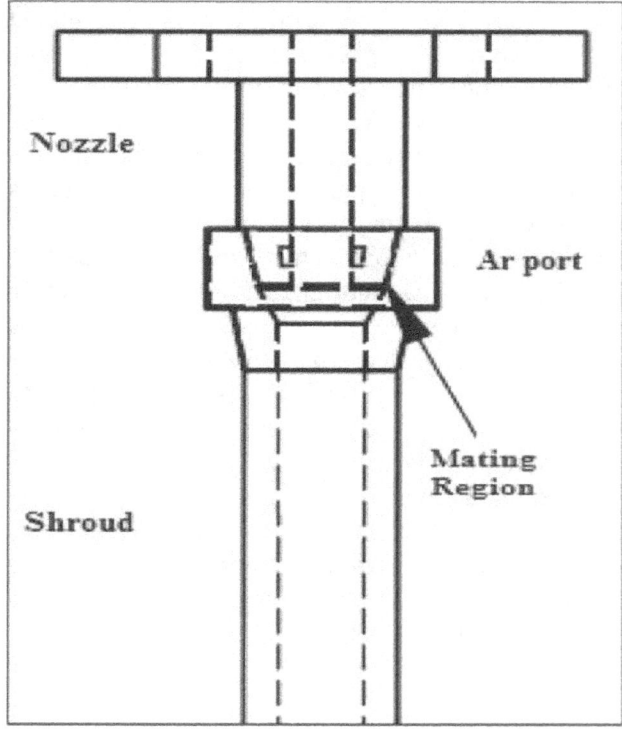

Figure 6.2 Schematic of shroud-nozzle assembly
Source: Author

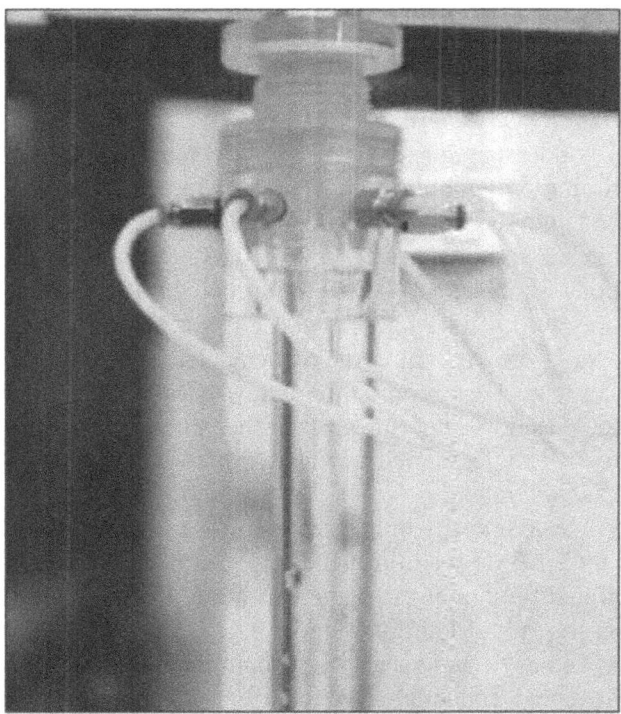

Figure 6.3 Water model setup of shroud-nozzle assembly
Source: Author

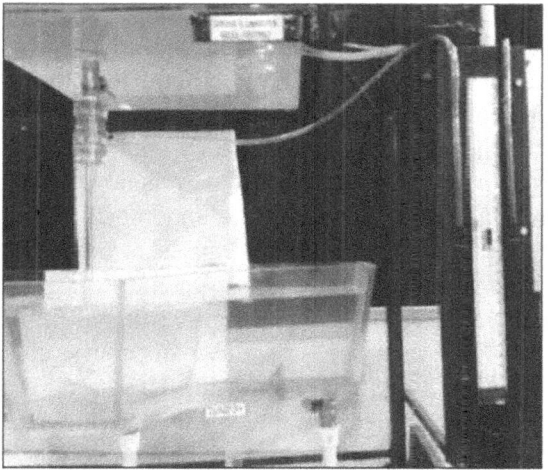

Figure 6.4 Manometer set-up for pressure reading
Source: Author

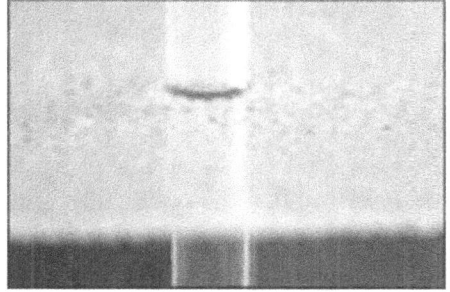

Figure 6.5 Slag layer – LDPE balls
Source: Author

Further, the vena-contracta effect can cause additional suction. This causes a negative pressure resulting in air suction along with the clearances between the nozzle-shroud joint to the stream and material permeability. Argon ingress to this region should be just sufficient to neutralize the negative pressure. Pressure at the nozzle shroud junction is measured through a simple U tube manometer connected to one of the argon inlets as shown in Figure 6.4. Beforehand complete sealing of all the leakage points in the system is ensured by observing no bubbles from shroud exit in the tundish. Under such perfect sealing conditions, with a scaling liquid throughput of 1.8 LPM, the negative pressure measured for example was found to be about 20 mbar. A layer of low-density poly-ethylene balls were used to replicate the industrial slag condition considering the density relationship as shown in Figure 6.5 [10].

Results

Preliminary observations were made with no gas injection through the shroud ports (ports plugged). However, because of the suction near the shroud-nozzle assembly small air leakages through joints resulted in gas bubbles in the stream. Using appropriate sealants air leakages were arrested and ensured absence of bubbles in the stream. It is to be noted that cold model fabricated using Perspex demanded much effort to arrest any air leakage. Evidently this indicates that obtaining a leak proof seal in the industrial situation is almost impossible.

Open eye area

Experiments were conducted for the flow rates 0.05-0.5 LPM (corresponding to 10-40 LPM in the industrial scale) with the polyethylene beads spread uniformly on the tundish surface for a depth of

10 mm simulating the protective slag layer preventing re-oxidation. When there was no shroud gas flow, no disturbance in the slag layer around the shroud was found. Once the shroud gas is introduced, the gas bubble rising up due to buoyancy opens the slag layer pushing it outwards in a circular fashion around the shroud. This area exposes the underneath liquid layer to the atmosphere which causes re-oxidation under the industrial atmosphere. Open eye images were captured for different flow rates using high-speed photography. The respective open eye area was measured using ImageJ software. The size of the open eye increased with an increase in gas flow rate as shown in the Figures 6.6 and 6.7 respectively.

Chattopadhyay et al. [3] have visualized the flow fields by scanning a plane near the shroud using 2D PIV. Under the conditions of liquid flow without shrouding, the velocity vectors were found to point towards the shroud. This results in making the liquid to push the slag layer towards the shroud causing no eye-opening. With the introduction of flow, bubbles were found to create reversed flows near the shroud.

Figure 6.6 Open eye area under different gas flow rates
Source: Author

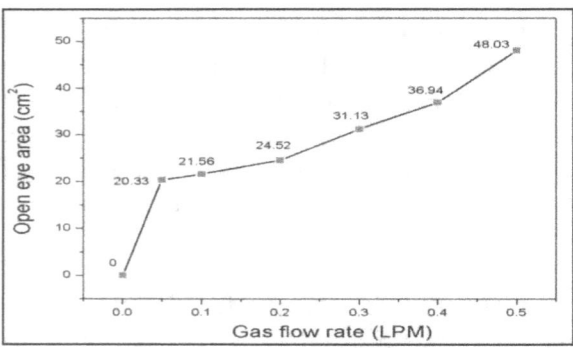

Figure 6.7 Open eye area under different gas flow rates
Source: Author

This pushes the slag regions away from the shroud causing eye formation.

Bubble characteristics

To understand the effect of gas flow rate on open eye formation, bubble characteristics like bubble size and bubble spread were studied for different gas flow rates. Experiments have revealed a higher concentration of bubbles just below the shroud with concentration diminishing on both sides as we move radially away from the central region beneath the shroud. The same has been reported by many researchers [7]. At low gas flow rates, the sizes of the bubbles were relatively smaller compared to larger bubble sizes at high gas flow rates

The average bubble sizes at lower flow rates (0.05 – 0.5 LPM) were around 2.9 – 3.3mm whereas at higher flow rates the range was around 3.5 – 4.2 mm as shown in Figures 6.8 and 6.9.

The eye opening may be a combined effect of the flow rate and bubble size, though the present data cannot separate the two effects.

Figure 6.9 shows that when the water flow is at 1.8 LPM and the ports are open to the atmosphere, air gets entrained and the dye slowly starts getting sucked in thereby entraining into the liquid stream. This is evidently due to the negative pressure in the shroud nozzle assembly.

As mentioned earlier, the flow of gas for shrouding should be such that any gas ingress from the ambient atmosphere through the nozzle-shroud assembly is just arrested. To determine this gas flow rate, two approaches have been adopted 1) using flow

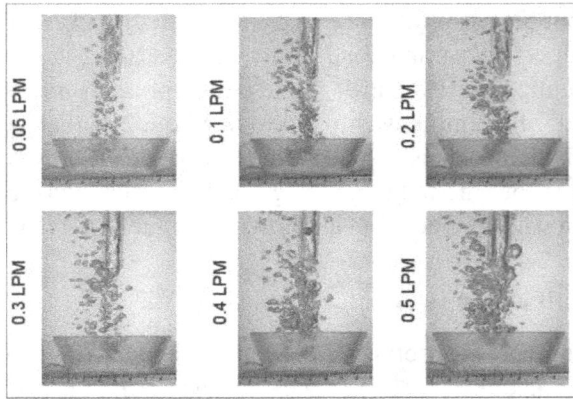

Figure 6.8 Bubble trajectories under different gas flow rates
Source: Author

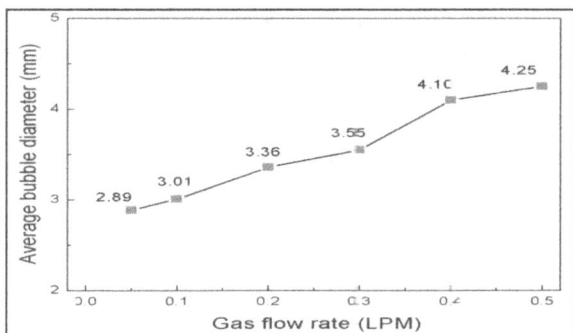

Figure 6.9 Bubble trajectories under different gas flow rates
Source: Author

visualization and 2) using the static pressure measurement at the nozzle-shroud assembly. In the flow visualization experiments, the tank containing a red dye is connected to one of the shroud ports, keeping all other ports either open to atmospheric pressure or connected to controlled air flow as shown in Figure 6.10.

Figure 6.10 shows the entrainment effects as air through the shrouding port is introduced. The air is introduced in a controlled fashion through the ports, and the flow is progressively increased. It can be seen that at a gas flow rate of 0.2 LPM (for a water flow of 1.8 LPM), the tracer has just stopped from entering the system without contaminating the fluid in the shroud and tundish as shown in Figure 6.10.

At a lower flow rate, tracer gets entrained into the liquid flow indicating the pressure is negative, and at higher flow rates the tracer gets pushed back indicating positive pressure. The pressure inside the system was measured by a manometer arrangement by connecting the tracer port now to a manometer and

measuring the pressure in the assembly for different gas flow rates as shown in Figure 6.11.

Figure 6.11 shows the pressure inside the system at different gas flow rates. It can be seen that at 0.2 LPM gas flow rate the pressure inside the assembly was about 0.5 mbar which is close to atmospheric pressure.

The pressure inside the system turns positive after 0.2 LPM ensuring shielding of any air entraining into the system. Hence gas flow rate of 0.2 LPM was considered to be the optimum for the model as shown in Figure 6.12.

The flow rate was scaled up to the industrial situation using Froude similarity criteria and the optimized flow rate for the industrial system was found to be around 17.5 LPM as shown in Figure 6.13.

Fundamentally argon shrouding should be just sufficient to arrest the any ingress of ambient gas around the shroud-nozzle assembly. In other words, just enough to maintain the pressure in the nozzle-shroud interior just at atmospheric pressure so

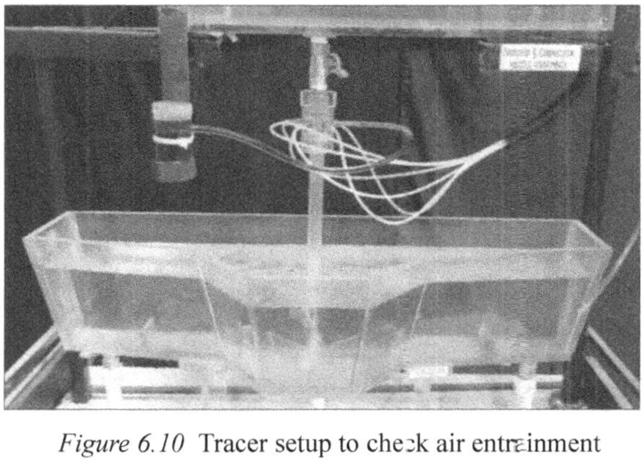

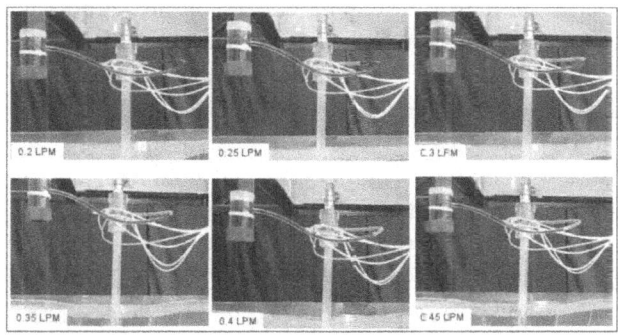

Figure 6.11 Tracer studies at different gas flow rates
Source: Author

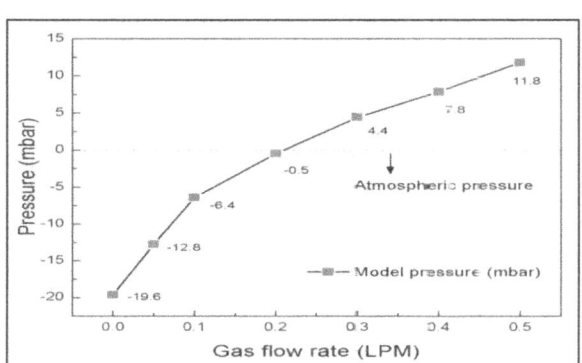

Figure 6.10 Tracer setup to check air entrainment
Source: Author

Figure 6.12 Optimised gas flow rate – water model
Source: Author

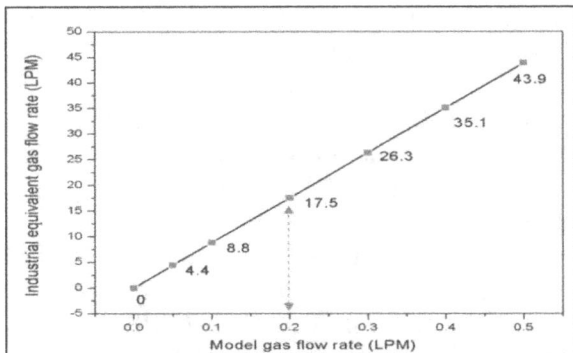

Figure 6.13 Optimized gas flow rate – industrial scale
Source: Author

that ambient gas ingress is arrested. Increasing the argon beyond this will be counterproductive as it can lead to increased eye opening in the tundish resulting in steel contamination.

At the same time the pressure at the nozzle-shroud junction changes with changing steel flow rate through the nozzle. Additionally, in the industrial operations where ceramic nozzles and shrouds are used, small misalignment can result in significant change of pressure at the nozzle-shroud junction. The steel flow rate through the nozzle also changes during casting depending on the casting speed and mold level control strategy. To seal the clearance at the top between the shroud and nozzle assembly generally a gasket made of ceramic wool is used in industry. Thus, both during the casting operation and further when the operator changes the nozzle-shroud assembly the pressure at the nozzle-shroud assembly can alter.

Typically, in the plant to account for these uncertainties, a constant flow rate significantly higher than that is needed is maintained. In case of JSW, Salem for a required rate of 17.5 LPM, a higher flow rate of 25 LPM was maintained. This can result in unnecessary contamination through larger eye opening in the tundish.

Therefore, the current study recommends that instead of maintaining the constant argon flow rate, argon flow rate can be varied using an online control strategy by keeping the pressure at the nozzle-shroud assembly just at the atmospheric pressure. Such a strategy can take care of needed variation in gas flow rate with changing steel flow rate as well as other uncertainties pertaining to alignment and issues related to sealing using ceramic wool gasket.

Effect of optimization on product total oxygen
The total oxygen variation obtained by LECO before and after the argon optimization for high carbon chromium bearing steels showed that total oxygen values were higher in heats operated at higher argon flow rate of 25LPM as shown in Figure 6.14.

Additionally, the temporal variation of flow rate of the shroud gas can be correlated to the steel cleanliness. Further with time, the wear and tear of the nozzle and shroud changes the steel and gas flow dynamics. This would be reflected in the shroud gas flow rate. This can also aid operators in identifying any fault in the nozzle-shroud system and make corrective action including changing the nozzle-shroud assembly well in advance. This is expected to result in much cleaner steel.

Conclusion

Primary objective of argon shrouding should be to arrest the air ingress at the nozzle-shroud assembly by maintaining a pressure of 1 atmosphere at the furniture junction. Increasing the pressure beyond atmospheric pressure increases the eye opening at the tundish surface which further leads to larger air ingress into the liquid steel. During heats, the argon flow dynamics changes with wear and tear and also when switching to a new shroud-nozzle assembly. Keeping the argon flow rate at some a priori determined value, thus, it is not recommended to maintain product consistency. By optimization of argon flow rate for shrouding through this model, total oxygen values in cast product were restricted to 12PPM max for quality stringent high chromium bearing steels which demands higher fatigue life.

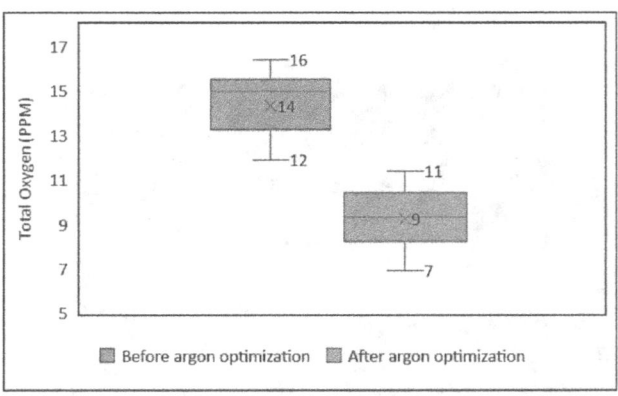

Figure 6.14 Total oxygen values in cast product before and after argon flow rate optimization
Source: Author

References

[1] Ragnarsson, L., Song, W., Ma, Y., & Sichen, D. (2010). Oxygen penetration in the protection shroud in steel casting. *Steel Research International*, 81(1), 965–973.

[2] Sahai, Y., & Emi, T. (2008). Tundish Technology for Clean Steel Production. Singapore: World Scientific Publishing Co. Pte. Ltd.

[3] Chattopadhyay, K., Mainul, H., Mihaiela, I., & Roderick, G. (2010). Physical and mathematical modeling of inert gas-shrouded ladle nozzles and their role on slag behavior and fluid flow patterns in a delta-shaped, four-strand tundish. *Metallurgical and Materials Transactions B*, 41(1), 225–233.

[4] Viswanathan, N., & Ballal, N. E. (2013). Rate phenomena in process metallurgy. In Treatise on Process Metallurgy (pp. 658–814).

[5] Mazumdar, D., & Evans, J. W. (2009). Modelling of Steelmaking Processes, (Vol. 1, pp 217–219). Boca Raton, USA: CRC Press.

[6] Mazumdar, D., Yamanoglu, G., Shankarnarayanan, R., & Guthrie, R. I. L. (1995). Process metallurgy. 1, 14–19.

[7] Chatterjee, S., & Chattopadhyay, K. (2016). Tundish open eye formation in inert gas-shrouded tundishes: a macroscopic model from first principles. *Metallurgical and Materials Transactions B*, 47(1), 3099–3114.

[8] Mazumdar, D., & Guthrie, R. I. L. (1999). The physical and mathematical modelling of continuous casting tundish systems. *ISIJ International*, 39(6), 524–547.

[9] Chattopadhyay, K., Mihaiela, I., & Guthrie, R. I. L. (2011). Physical and mathematical modelling to study the effect of ladle shroud mis-alignment on liquid metal quality in a tundish. *ISIJ International*, 51(1), 759–768

[10] Wei, L., Iwama, T., Huafang, Y., Shigeru, U., Noritaka, S., & Ryo, I. (2021). Apparent viscosity measurement of solid-liquid coexisting fluid by falling ball method for evaluation iron particle sedimentation velocity in slag. *ISIJ International*, 61(1), 2915–2922.

[11] Mukherjee, M., & Mazumdar, D. (2022) A new inert gas delivery design for improved shielding of ladle shroud–collector nozzle (LS–CN) assembly: modeling, design, and industrial-scale validations. *Steel Research International*, 93(12), 2100843.

7 Minimum variance approach for sectoral diversification in long-term investment strategies

Sai Sundara Krishnan, G.[1,a], S. Rethika[2,b] and S. Kathir Kaarthik[2,c]

[1]Professor, Department of Applied Mathematics and Computational Sciences, PSG College of Technology, Coimbatore, India

[2]Department of Applied Mathematics and Computational Sciences, PSG College of Technology, Coimbatore, India

Abstract

This paper presents a sector-based portfolio optimization strategy for long-term investors seeking high returns with lower risk. Using historical NIFTY 50 data, we analyze sectoral performance and construct an optimized minimum variance portfolio (MVP).

By leveraging sectoral diversification, volatility analysis, and risk-adjusted metrics, we identify resilient sectors and refine stock selection through an intra-sector MVP approach. The optimized portfolio consistently outperforms NIFTY 50 in risk-return efficiency, offering a robust framework for emerging market investors.

Keywords: Minimum risk, NIFTY50, portfolio optimization, sectoral correlation, volatility

Introduction

Background on portfolio optimization

Portfolio optimization is a fundamental concept in investment management, aiming to maximize returns while minimizing risk. The risk-return trade-off is crucial, as investors seek to achieve the highest possible returns for a given level of risk. Traditional portfolio theory, pioneered by Markowitz [3], emphasizes diversification to reduce unsystematic risk, which arises from individual stock movements. The legacy of Modern Portfolio Theory has been extensively discussed in the literature [1]. However, conventional index investing, such as holding NIFTY 50 in equal or market-cap weights, may not be optimal as it does not account for variations in sectoral performance, volatility, and risk-adjusted returns.

Why sector-based portfolio construction?

Recent studies have examined portfolio optimization methods tailored to the Indian stock market [5]. Several works have explored stock market volatility Tripathi and Kumar [8], risk reduction in large portfolios Jagannathan and Ma [2] and sectoral correlations [8, 4]. Sector-based allocation improves diversification by grouping stocks based on industry characteristics, rather than treating them individually. Market cycles and macroeconomic factors influence the sector's investment performance. Sector-based investment improves returns (risk adjusted) by giving more weightage to the sectors with low correlation and reducing exposure to volatile sectors, enhancing stability. By analyzing sectoral volatility, Sortino ratio, and correlation matrices, investors can build more resilient and adaptive portfolios.

Objective of the research

This study aims to build an optimized sector-based portfolio using NIFTY 50 data for the time period 2018–2025 and to obtain the minimum variance portfolio (MVP). The goal is to reduce risk while maintaining strong returns. The NIFTY 50 index is considered as the benchmark, the beta value, to assess risk-adjusted returns and stability. The findings provide a structured framework for long-term investors to achieve excellent portfolio efficiency through sectoral diversification.

Data Collection and Preprocessing

Selection of NIFTY50 stocks
Overview of NIFTY50 stocks
The NIFTY 50 index comprises the leading 50 firms listed on the National Stock Exchange (NSE) of India, from various sectors. Its overall reflection of Indian stock market performance which makes it suitable for portfolio analysis – and as an even more diversified component when performing detailed subsector analysis. It includes firms from many different industries, ensuring sectoral diversity. These

[a]ssk.amcs@psgtech.ac.in, [b]rethikaskumar@gmail.com, [c]skathirkaarthik@gmail.com

DOI: 10.1201/9781003770435-7

stocks are among the most liquid, and are actively traded.

Justification for selecting NIFTY50 stocks

NIFTY 50 stocks provide a diversified sample across various industries, ensuring a balanced representation of the Indian economy. The index includes companies from sectors like information technology, financial services, consumer goods, energy, and healthcare, making it a strong benchmark for market performance.

Data Sources

Use of yahoo finance (yfinance) for historical stock data

This research uses stock price data for NIFTY 50 from Yahoo Finance, which provides comprehensive market data like stock prices, trading volume, and benchmark index values, essential for sector-wise return calculations and portfolio optimization.

Time period: January 2018 to March 2025

The analysis spans January 2018 to March 2025, covering various market conditions, including pre-pandemic growth, COVID-19-induced volatility, and post-pandemic recovery. This extended period captures multiple economic cycles, providing a robust basis for evaluating sector-based investment strategies.

Sector classification

Classification of stocks into sectors

Each stock is assigned to a sector based on publicly available classification data using a dictionary mapping, facilitating sector-wise weight distribution and risk-return assessment.

Derivation of sector-level returns

Sector returns are calculated by aggregating weighted stock returns, considering market capitalization proportions to ensure an accurate representation of sector performance.

Exploratory Data Analysis (EDA) and Risk Metrics

Rolling volatility analysis

Rolling volatility is an important measure of risk, representing the variability of returns over a specified moving window. It helps assess the stability of sectoral returns and identify periods of high market

uncertainty. Insights from rolling volatility plots help identify sectoral trends, periods of increased market turbulence, and sectors with consistently lower volatility.

Definition of rolling volatility as a measure of risk

Rolling volatility is calculated as the standard deviation of the returns in a moving window. Mathematically, it is given by:

$$\sigma_t = \sqrt{\frac{1}{N} \sum_{i=t-N+1}^{t} \left(r_i - \underline{r} \right)^2}$$

where σ_t is the rolling volatility at time t, N is the window size, r_i represents historical returns, and $\underline{r}$ is the mean return over the window.

Sortino ratio

To evaluate the risk-adjusted performance of sector-based investments, various performance metrics, such as the Sharpe ratio Sharpe [6] and Sortino ratio [7], have been developed.

Sharpe ratio formula

The Sharpe ratio measures the excess return per unit of total risk and is defined as:

$$S = \frac{E[R_p] - R_f}{\sigma_p}$$

where:
- $E[R_p]$ is the expected portfolio return,
- R_f is the risk-free rate,
- σ_p is the portfolio standard deviation (total volatility).

Sortino ratio formula (downside risk measure)

The Sortino ratio refines the Sharpe ratio by penalizing only downside risk rather than total volatility:

$$S_{Sortino} = \frac{E[R_p] - R_f}{c_d}$$

where σ_d is the downside deviation, computed using only negative returns.

Justification for using the Sortino ratio

Unlike the Sharpe ratio, the Sortino ratio does not penalize upside volatility, and is therefore better suited for investors focused on downside risk management, making it appropriate for risk-averse investment strategies.

Because the Sortino ratio can be plotted for each sector, it is easy to see which sectors look the most attractive on a return-to-risk basis.

Sectoral Covariance Analysis

Why covariance matters?

Covariance is used to measure how two sectors move together, maintaining units for risk assessment. A positive value suggests that they move in the same direction, while a negative value indicates that they move inversely.

Role of covariance in portfolio risk

The underlying risk of a portfolio comprises both the volatilities of the sectors and their covariances. The portfolio variance is computed as:

$$\sigma_p^2 = \sum_i w_i^2 \sigma_i^2 + \sum_i \sum_{j \neq i} w_i w_j Cov(R_i, R_j)$$

where:

- σ_p^2 is the portfolio variance,
- w_i and w_j are sector weights,
- σ_i^2 is the variance of sector i,
- $Cov(R_i, R_j)$ is the covariance between returns of sectors i and j.

Low overall portfolio variance can be achieved by selecting sectors with lower or negative covariances.

Covariance matrix calculation

The covariance between two sector returns, say i and j, is given by:

$$Cov(R_i, R_j) = E[(R_i - \mu_i)(R_j - \mu_j)]$$

where:

- R_i and R_j are the returns of sectors i and j,
- μ_i and μ_j are the mean returns of those sectors.

Heatmap analysis

The covariance heatmap provides a visual representation of sectoral dependencies, identifying:

- High covariance pairs, indicating synchronized movement.
- Low or negative covariance pairs, indicating inverse movement.
- Sector clusters exhibiting similar market behavior.

This analysis is integral to optimize the minimum variance portfolio (MVP), helping to assign sector weights to minimize portfolio risk.

Minimum Variance Portfolio Construction

Modern portfolio theory and MVP

Modern portfolio theory (MPT) Markowitz [3] states that investors should optimize their portfolios by balancing risk and return. The minimum variance portfolio (MVP) is a special case of MPT where the goal is to minimize overall portfolio volatility, making it ideal for risk-averse investors. The critical principles are:

- Investors should aim to minimize portfolio volatility.
- Diversification can reduce unsystematic risk.
- The MVP focuses on selecting sector allocations that yield the lowest portfolio variance.

Portfolio variance formula

The variance of a portfolio is calculated as:

$$\sigma_p^2 = w^T C w$$

where:

- σ_p^2 is the portfolio variance,
- w is the weight vector of sector allocations,
- C is the covariance matrix of sector returns.

The objective is to find the weight vector w that minimizes σ_p^2 while satisfying certain constraints.

Optimization methodology

The optimization problem is formulated as:

$$w^T C w$$

$$s.t. \sum_i w_i = 1, w_i \geq 0, \forall i$$

This quadratic optimization problem is solved using numerical techniques like Lagrange's multiplier method to determine the optimal sector weights that minimize portfolio variance.

Algorithm for MVP optimization

The MVP optimization algorithm employs quadratic programming to minimize portfolio variance while ensuring full investment and prohibiting short-selling.

Algorithm 1 MVP Optimization

---

1. **Input:** Covariance Matrix C
2. **Initialize:** Equal weights for all sectors
3. **Define objective function:**

$$f(w) = w^T C_s w$$

4. **Define constraints:**
   - $\sum_i w_i = 1$ (weights sum to 1)
   - $w_i \geq 0$ (no short-selling)
5. **Use numerical optimization:** Apply quadratic programming to minimize
6. **Obtain optimized weights:**
7. **Output:** Optimal sector allocations

The resulting weights w^* determine the optimal sector allocation that minimizes risk while ensuring full investment.

Stock Selection within Top Sectors

Identifying top sectors
Sectors are ranked based on their MVP weights, and the top three sectors with the highest allocations are selected for further analysis.

Stock selection via MVP within sectors
Within each of the top three sectors, MVP is applied to select the most optimal stocks by:

- Computing sector-level covariance matrices.
- Selecting the top five stocks that contribute most favorably to portfolio stability.

Algorithm 2 Stock selection within top sectors

---

1. **Input:** Sector-wise covariance matrices C_s and stock returns.
2. **Identify Top Sectors:** Sort sectors by MVP weights and select the top 3.
3. **For** each selected sector s **do**
4. Extract sector stock data and covariance matrix C_s
   Define portfolio variance function:
   $$f(w) = w^T C_s w$$
5. **Set constraints:**
   - $\sum_i w_i = 1$ (weights sum to 1)
   - $w_i \geq 0$ (no short-selling)
6. Solve for optimal stock weights using quadratic programming.
7. Select the top 5 stocks with the highest weights.
8. **End for**
9. **Output:** Optimized stock selection for each top sector.

Adjusting final portfolio weights

Algorithm 3 Final weight adjustment for portfolio

---

1. **Input:** MVP-selected stock weights from top 3 sectors.
2. Normalize weights to ensure:
   $$\sum_i w_i = 1$$
3. Adjust weights such that:
   - Sector weights remain consistent with MVP allocations.
   - Stock weights within each sector are proportionally adjusted.
4. **Output:** Final optimized stock portfolio.

The final portfolio ensures balanced sectoral and stock-level diversification while minimizing overall risk.

Portfolio Performance Analysis

Expected return calculation
The expected return of the portfolio is computed as:

$$E(R_p) = \sum_{i=1}^{n} w_i E(R_i)$$

where:
- $E(R_p)$ is the expected portfolio return.
- w_i is the weight of stock
- $E(R_i)$ is the historical average return of stock i

To annualize the expected return, we use compounding:

$$E(R_{annualized}) = \left(1 + E(R_p)\right)^{252} - 1$$

where the factor 252 represents the approximate number of trading days in a year, commonly used in financial modelling to annualize daily returns.

Cumulative returns comparison with NIFTY 50
To evaluate the performance of the optimized portfolio, we compare its cumulative returns with the NIFTY 50 index:

- Compute cumulative returns over time:

$$R_t = \prod_{i=1}^{t} (1 + r_i)$$

- where R_t is the cumulative return up to time t, and r_i is the return at time i.
- Compare the cumulative returns of the portfolio and NIFTY50.

Risk metrics: beta and volatility
To further analyze portfolio risk, we compute:

Beta calculation
Beta (β) measures the portfolio's sensitivity to market movements:

$$\beta_p = \frac{Cov(R_p, R_m)}{Var(R_m)}$$

where:
- β_p is the portfolio beta.
- R_p is the portfolio return.
- R_m is the market return (NIFTY 50).

Portfolio volatility
Portfolio volatility is given by:

$$\sigma_p = \sqrt{w^T C w}$$

where:
- σ_p is the portfolio standard deviation.
- W is the weight vector of stocks.
- C is the covariance matrix of stock returns.

Results

Rolling volatility analysis
We calculate the 30-day rolling volatility for all sectors before optimization.

Rolling volatility for all sectors
Figure 7.1 illustrates the rolling 30-day volatility of various sectors within the NIFTY 50 index over time. The plot captures multiple economic cycles, including major market disruptions such as the COVID-19 crash in 2020 and subsequent volatility spikes in 2022 and 2023.

Sortino ratios of sectors
Figure 7.2 shows that sectors like Infrastructure, Consumer Goods, and Pharmaceuticals exhibit higher Sortino ratio, indicating superior risk-adjusted returns and lower downside volatility. Conversely, Insurance and Oil & Gas sectors show lower values, suggesting less favorable returns relative to their overall and downside risk exposure.

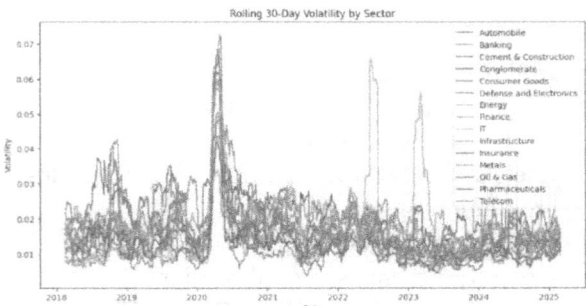

Figure 7.1 30-day rolling volatility for all sectors
Source: Author

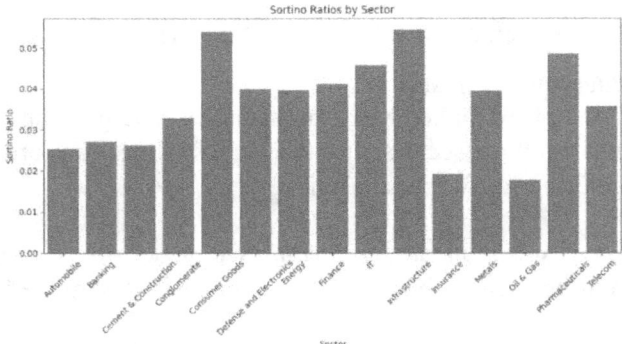

Figure 7.2 Sortino ratios of NIFTY50 sectors
Source: Author

The risk-free interest rate is assumed to be 0.05/252 per trading day, aligning with an annualized rate of 5%.

Sectoral correlation analysis
To understand sector relationships, we compute the correlation matrix for NIFTY 50 sectors.

Figure 7.3 presents a heatmap of correlation coefficients between NIFTY 50 sectors, highlighting their return relationships. Banking and Finance (0.69) and Metals and Oil & Gas (0.61) exhibit strong positive correlations, moving in tandem. In contrast, Pharmaceuticals and Banking (0.34) and Telecom and Defense & Electronics (0.23) show weaker correlations, suggesting potential diversification benefits in portfolio construction.

Minimum variance portfolio (MVP) optimization
Table 7.1 presents the MVP sector weights, with Consumer Goods (35.12%), Pharmaceuticals (23.81%), and Energy (17.40%) receiving the highest allocations, contributing to lower overall portfolio risk. IT (14.40%), Telecom (4.93%), and Insurance

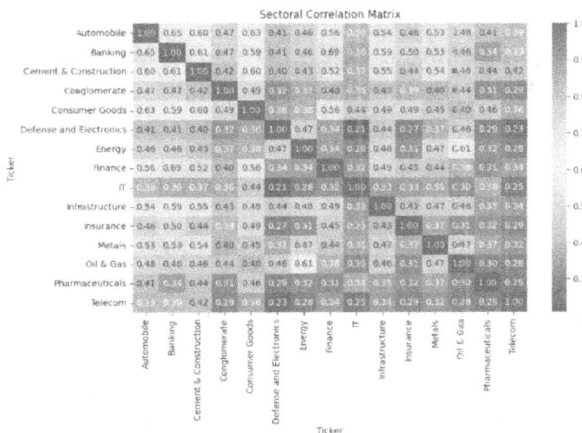

Figure 7.3 Sectoral correlation heatmap
Source: Author

Rolling 30-Day Volatility for Top 3 Sectors

Figure 7.4 Rolling volatility for top three sectors
Source: Author

(4.34%) have smaller allocations, while other sectors are either minimal or excluded from the optimal portfolio.

Top performing sectors and stocks
The top three sectors identified based on risk-return characteristics are:

1. Consumer goods
2. Pharmaceuticals
3. Energy

These findings highlight the defensive nature of Consumer Goods and Pharmaceuticals, which tend to exhibit stability and resilience during market downturns.

Rolling volatility for top 3 sectors
Figure 7.4 depicts the rolling 30-day volatility of the top three sectors in MVP—Consumer Goods,

Pharmaceuticals, and Energy—from 2018 to 2025. A notable volatility spike around 2020 coincides with the COVID-19 market shock, increasing uncertainty across all sectors. Energy shows the highest volatility spikes, reflecting its sensitivity to oil price fluctuations and geopolitical tensions.

Top companies in each sector
Table 7.2 presents the top companies within the three sectors that have the highest allocations in the MVP. These selections support the sectoral allocation strategy in the MVP, balancing low-risk consumer goods, stable pharmaceuticals, and high-growth energy stocks to achieve an optimal risk-return trade off.

Portfolio allocation in Top 3 sectors
Table 7.3 presents the adjusted stock weights for the MVP, detailing allocations across the Consumer Goods, Pharmaceuticals, and Energy sectors. These

Table 7.1 MVP sector weights

Sector	Weight
Consumer goods	0.3512
Energy	0.1740
IT	0.1440
Insurance	0.0434
Pharmaceuticals	0.2381
Telecom	0.0493
Others	0.0000

Source: Author

Table 7.2 Top 5 companies in top three sectors

Sector	Weight
Consumer goods	ITS.NS, NESTLEIND.NS, HINDUNILVR.NS, BRITTANIA.NS, ASIANPAINT.NS
Pharmaceuticals	DRREDDY.NS, CIPLA.NS, SUNPHARMA.NS, APOLLOHOSP.NS
Energy	POWERGRID.NS, NTPC.NS, COALINDIA.NS

Source: Author

Table 7.3 Adjusted Stock Weights for the MVP

Sector	Stock	Weight
Consumer goods	ITS.NS	0.0902
	NESTLEIND.NS	0.0663
	HINDUNILVR.NS	0.0540
	BRITTANIA.NS	0.0451
	ASIANPAINT.NS	0.0443
Pharmaceuticals	DRREDDY.NS	0.1047
	CIPLA.NS	0.0959
	SUNPHARMA.NS	0.0820
	APOLLOHOSP.NS	0.0676
Energy	POWERGRID.NS	0.1525
	NTPC.NS	0.1093
	COALINDIA.NS	0.0883

Source: Author

weights are determined by sectoral risk-return characteristics and each stock's contribution to portfolio stability. With a total sum of 1, the portfolio is fully invested, ensuring optimal capital allocation.

Portfolio performance evaluation
Figure 7.5 illustrates the performance comparison between the optimized portfolio and the NIFTY 50 index based on annualized returns. The optimized portfolio (blue line) consistently outperforms the NIFTY 50 benchmark (dashed orange line), particularly after 2021, exhibiting a steeper growth trajectory. Despite occasional downturns, it achieves superior returns, peaking above 4.0 before a slight decline. The portfolio's expected annualized return is 20%, with a beta of 0.6326 and volatility of 0.0095, indicating higher returns with lower systematic risk than the broader market.

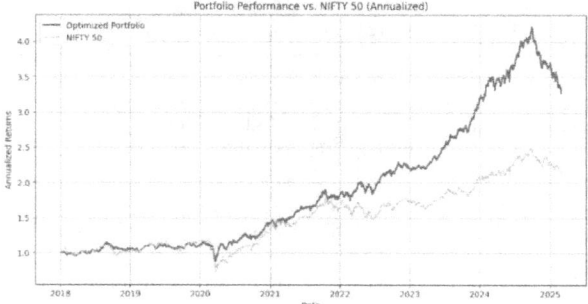

Figure 7.5 Portfolio return vs. NIFTY50
Source: Author

- **Expected daily portfolio return:** 0.000715
- **Expected annualized portfolio return:**20%
- **Optimized portfolio beta:** 0.6326
- **Portfolio volatility:** 0.0095

Conclusion

This study demonstrates the effectiveness of an optimized sectoral investment strategy using the Minimum Variance Portfolio (MVP) approach to improve risk-adjusted returns in the NIFTY 50 index. Through analysis of sectoral correlations, volatility patterns, and Sortino ratios, Consumer Goods, Pharmaceuticals, and Energy emerged as the most favorable sectors for allocation. The MVP optimization resulted in a diversified portfolio that minimizes downside risk while maintaining strong returns. Sector-wise stock selection further enhanced the portfolio's stability. The adjusted portfolio outperformed the NIFTY 50 benchmark, delivering superior annualized returns (20%) with lower systematic risk (Beta = 0.6326) and volatility (0.0095). The results highlight the potential of sector-based optimization in constructing a resilient, high-performing portfolio.

Future Work

This methodology can be improved by integrating dynamic sector weighting, factor-based strategies, and alternative risk measures to adapt to changing market conditions. Future research could focus on dynamic rebalancing, macroeconomic factor analysis, and machine learning for refined stock selection. With its emphasis on risk optimization and sectoral diversification, this approach is ideal for long-term investments, ensuring sustained growth and minimizing volatility.

References

[1] Fabozzi, F., Gupta, F., & Markowitz, H. (2002). The legacy of modern portfolio theory. *The Journal of Investing*, 11(3), 7–22. doi:10.3905/joi.2002.319510.

[2] Jagannathan, R., & Ma, T. (2003). Risk reduction in large portfolios: why imposing the wrong constraints helps. *The Journal of Finance*, 58(4), 1651–1683. https://doi.org/10.1111/1540-6261.00580

[3] Markowitz, H. (1952). Portfolio selection. *The Journal of Finance*, 7(1), 77–91. https://doi.org/10.1111/j.1540-6261.1952.tb01525.x

[4] Markowitz, H. M. (1959). Portfolio Selection: Efficient Diversification of Investments. New Haven: Yale University Press.

[5] Sen, J. (2024). Portfolio optimization methods for the Indian stock market: A comparative analysis. Presented at Data Science: Theory & Applications, Jan 2024. https://doi.org/10.13140/RG.2.2.32265.01124

[6] Sharpe, W. F. (1966). Mutual fund performance. *The Journal of Business*, 39(1), 119–138. doi:http://dx.doi.org/10.1086/294846.

[7] Sortino, F. A., & Price, L. N. (1994). Performance measurement in a downside risk framework. *The Journal of Investing*, 3(3), 59–64. https://doi.org/10.3905/joi.3.3.59

[8] Tripathi, V., & Kumar, A. (2015). Sectoral efficiency of the Indian stock market and the impact of global financial crisis. *Journal of Commerce & Accounting Research*, 4(1), 46–62.

8 Implementation of lean Six Sigma for reducing lead time and enhancing quality and productivity in a manufacturing industry

M. Gomathi Prabha[1,a] and C. Emima[2,b]

[1]Assistant professor, Department of Mechanical Engineering, PSG College of Technology, Coimbatore, Tamil Nadu, India

[2]PG student, M.E. Industrial Engineering, Department of Mechanical Engineering, PSG College of Technology, Coimbatore, Tamil Nadu, India

Abstract

This paper proposes a systematic methodology with Lean Six Sigma to reduce lead time and increase productivity in the production of bright steel flats. An initial review of the current production system identifies quality problems, reflected in a DPMO of 5555 and a sigma level of 4.03—reflecting immense scope for improvement. In response, tools such as Value Stream Mapping (VSM) and the define, measure, analyze, improve, and control (DMAIC) methodology are proposed to determine bottlenecks and facilitate process optimization. Some proposed improvements include initiating continuous improvement programs such as Kaizen, setting standard operating procedures, and introducing automation to reduce human error. These steps are proposed to streamline operations, eliminate delays, and assist the plant in achieving its goal of manufacturing 3300 components monthly. By applying different Kaizen ideas aimed at eliminating different forms of waste, the lead time was decreased to 23 days with a 10% boost in productivity and achieved a sigma level of 4.27. The combination of Lean and Six Sigma is framed as a workable and effective approach toward realizing sustainable improvements in quality and efficiency.

Keywords: Define, measure, analyze, improve, and control, lead time reduction, lean manufacturing, productivity improvement, value stream mapping

Introduction

Manufacturing companies are continuously under pressure to optimize product quality while minimizing production time and costs. In the bright steel flat manufacturing industry, the need for enhanced process efficiency and the capability to meet customer demands is particularly critical, as these components are widely used in precision-based applications such as automotive, construction, and general engineering sectors. Lead time defined as the total duration from the input of raw materials to the delivery of the finished product is a key indicator of operational performance. Extended lead times often result from inefficiencies such as wasteful processes, non-standardized procedures, recurring defects, and material delays. These challenges contribute to increased production costs, excess inventory, and missed delivery deadlines. To address these inefficiencies, a combination of Lean Manufacturing principles, Six Sigma methodologies, and the define, measure, analyze, improve, and control (DMAIC) framework offers an effective approach to systematic process improvement. Tools like Value Stream Mapping (VSM) are particularly valuable in identifying non-value-added activities and visualizing improvement opportunities. By integrating these strategies, a structured analysis of the production process enables data-driven decisions that enhance quality, throughput, and overall operational efficiency. This study proposes the application of Lean Six Sigma techniques to streamline production processes in a bright steel flat manufacturing plant, aiming to identify inefficiencies, reduce lead time, lower defect rates, and improve overall productivity in alignment with customer demand. The objective of this study is to implement Lean Six Sigma tools to reduce lead time, minimize defects, and enhance productivity in bright steel flat manufacturing, ensuring sustained process improvements through standardized practices. A comprehensive review for the related studies have conducted and it highlights the significant impact of Lean Manufacturing, Six Sigma, and `Industrial Engineering methodologies on improving manufacturing performance. Abebe and Desalegn [1]

---
[a]mgp.mech@psgtech.ac.in., [b]emimac72001@gmail.com

DOI: 10.1201/9781003770435-8

demonstrated that Lean practices effectively reduce production lead time. Das [2] reviewed various industrial engineering tools that optimize productivity across multiple sectors. Gomaa [3] emphasized that Lean Six Sigma strategies enhance machining process quality by minimizing variability and defects. Karthick et al. [4] reported notable lead time reductions through Six Sigma implementation. Khawar et al. [5] showed that optimizing steel bar manufacturing with Six Sigma methodologies led to significant quality improvements. Leksic et al. [6] discussed how different Lean tools contribute to waste elimination and process efficiency. Saied et al. [8] illustrated reductions in material and energy wastes through Lean techniques in steel production. Prabha et al. [7] researched a South Indian automobile parts manufacturing company and discovered that the use of Lean Six Sigma tools such as DMAIC, SIPOC, value stream mapping, and IoT-based monitoring enhanced quality, minimized lead time, eradicated bottlenecks, and enhanced overall equipment effectiveness by 4.88%. Shah and Patel [9] highlighted productivity improvements through Lean tools in general manufacturing. Singh et al. [10] demonstrated how Industrial Engineering techniques contributed to overall productivity growth in casting industries. Sordan et al. [11] adopted a design science approach showing that Lean Manufacturing reduces lead time in foundry processes. Venkataramana et al. [12] successfully implemented VSM for cycle time reduction in machining operations. These studies collectively validate the structured approach employed in this research, confirming that the application of Lean Six Sigma, VSM, and DMAIC methodologies drives sustainable improvements in quality, productivity, lead time reduction, and waste minimization across manufacturing sectors.

This research follows the DMAIC approach as a formal methodology to propel process improvements. The process began with selecting a manufacturing industry and setting precise, measurable goals. A literature review gave a strong foundation and assisted in defining the study direction. Having laid this foundation, operational data was collected directly from the shop floor to identify areas of inefficiency and frequent problems. Every step of the DMAIC. Following the implementation of the changes, their effect was evaluated to check whether the objectives had been achieved. Based on these observations, suggestions were made to ensure that the improvements were maintained in the long run. An overview of the tools utilized in DMAIC phases is presented in Table 8.1.

The project is initiated to enhance operational efficiency and product quality within a bright steel manufacturing. Its focus is to shorten production lead time and reduce the rejection rate of finished goods from 1.1–0.5%. This will be achieved by identifying and eliminating process inefficiencies and quality-related issues within the existing system. The improvement efforts are restricted to internal manufacturing processes, with no changes made to supplier inputs or customer requirements.

Suppliers, inputs, process, outputs, customers (SIPOC) model was developed to understand the overall process flow. Key suppliers will provide the required raw materials. The transformation process involves several stages, including pointing, shot blasting, drawing, and inspection. Finished products are then delivered to the customers in accordance with their specific needs.

Defect data gathered over a period of three months indicated that Pit Mark, Damage, Bend & Twist, and Line Mark are the most common problems as shown in Figure 8.1 collectively summing up to approximately 80% of the total defects. A Pareto analysis also validated these as the initial quality improvement targets, whereas vital fewer defects will be handled in subsequent phases. The quality of the process was also measured using the DPMO approach, which yielded a value of 5555 with a corresponding current sigma level of 4.03. This suggests a level of moderate quality that can be improved.

Current Process Study

A time study was performed for four major processes pointing, drawing, straightening, and cutting each

Table 8.1 Tools used in DMAIC phases

Phases	Tool used
Define	Project Charter, SIPOC Diagram
Measure	Pareto Analysis, Time Study, Takt Time, Process Capability Analysis, Current state VSM
Analyze	Fishbone diagram, failure mode effect analysis (FMEA)
Improve	Kaizen, Future State VSM
Control	Standard Operating Procedures (SOPs)

Source: Author

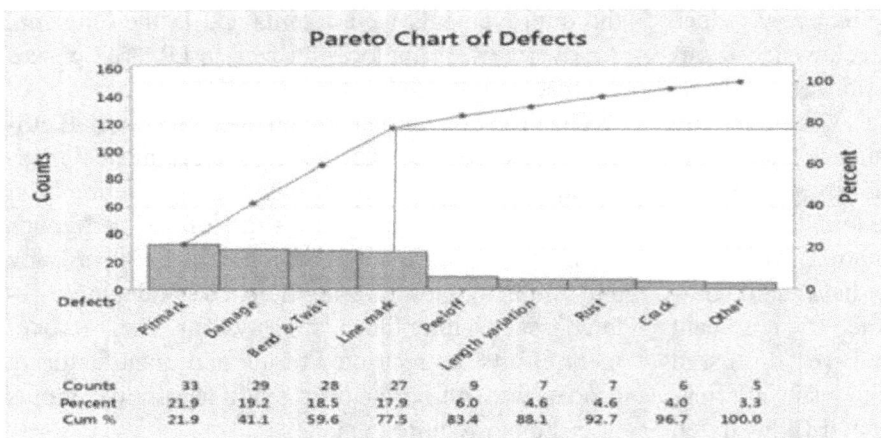

Figure 8.1 Pareto chart of defects
Source: Author

over three individual trials. Out of these processes, drawing had the longest average cycle time at 4.03 minutes, while Cutting was the fastest with 2.4 minutes. In comparison to the takt time of 3.18 minutes per unit, it was found that only Drawing and Pointing exceeded this limit, indicating probable delays in these stages and is presented in Table 8.2.

Additionally, a process capability analysis was conducted. The outcome for a process capability index (Cpk) of 0.74 and a performance index (Ppk) of 0.78. The DPMO calculated was 5555, with a corresponding current sigma level of 4.03 and a yield of

Table 8.2 Time study for major processes

Process	T1 (min)	T2 (min)	T3 (min)	Avg (min)
Pointing	3.4	3.3	3.4	3.4
Drawing	4.2	4	3.9	4.03
Straightening	3.0	2.8	2.9	2.9
Cutting	2.3	2.4	2.5	2.4

Source: Author

96% as shown in Figure 8.2. These findings enable one to see where performance is on course and where there is a need for further improvement to improve overall process efficiency.

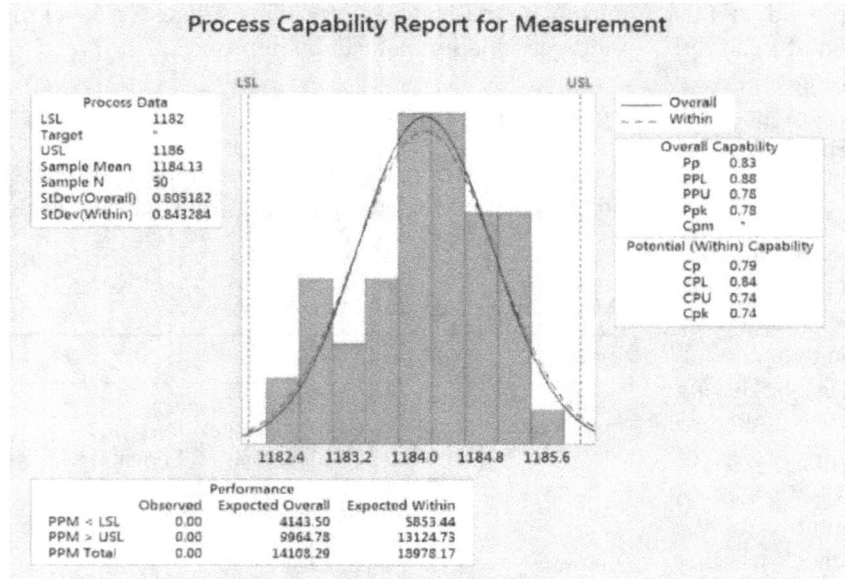

Figure 8.2 Process capability
Source: Author

$$Takt\ Time = \frac{Available\ Time}{Customer\ Demand} \quad (1)$$

= 10,500 minutes/3300 units

Takt Time = 3.18 minutes/unit

Figure 8.3 shows comparison of the cycle time with the takt time for the processes. It helps to identify the bottleneck processes. The identified bottleneck processes are pointing and drawing processes.

Current state VSM

During the analyze phase, a thorough value stream map was produced to determine the bottlenecks and non-value- added steps during the production flow. Through assessing each step of the process, the major waiting time and inventory accumulation were seen to happen between processes, which resulted in the overall lead time of 25 days. This reveals a high degree of imbalance between waiting and processing, signifying the occurrence of waste Cycle times for each operation were also studied and compared to takt time to find stations that need balancing or enhancement. These findings serve as the foundation for focused action to minimize delays and improve flow in the next stage as shown in Figure 8.4.

Shift duration: 8 hours (480 minutes per day)
Monthly production: 3000 pieces
Demand = 3300 pieces
Defect rate = 150 pieces
Lead time = 25 days

Root Cause Analysis

Cause and effect analysis

To recognize the root causes of the most significant surface defects in bright steel flat production, a cause and effect (fishbone) analysis was carried out for the

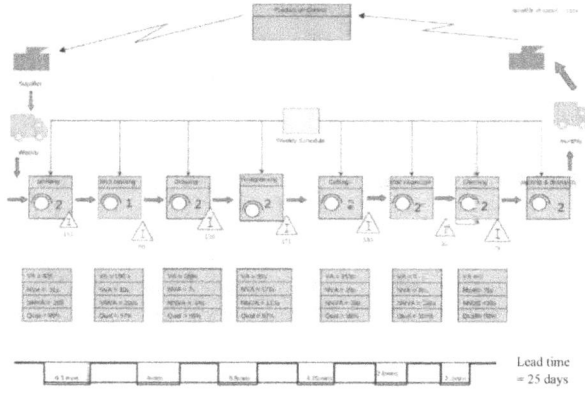

Figure 8.4 Current state value stream mapping
Source: Author

most common defects noted: pit mark, line mark, damage, and bend and twist.

- Pit marks were mostly caused by improper lubrication practices, faulty rollers, and contamination within the input material.
- Surface irregularities, poor finishing material, high roller pressure, and bad handling while stacking or transporting caused Line Marks.
- Damage was usually caused by incorrect stacking methods, mishandling during transfer, and unevenly aligned conveyors.
- Bend and twist flaws were attributed to second-grade raw materials, non-uniform hardness distribution, misalignment in the straightening unit, and mistakes while rolling or cooling.

This root cause analysis classifies root causes into five major areas: Material, machine, method, environment, and personnel, and directs focused process control and quality assurance improvement.

Failure mode and effect analysis

In the analyze phase, FMEA was performed to evaluate critical defects in bright steel flat production. The prominent failure modes were pit marks, damage, bend/twist, and link marks. All the defects were considered from the aspects of severity (S), occurrence (O), and detection (D) to determine the risk priority number (RPN). Pit Marks resulted from an RPN of 90, resulting from poor oil coating and exposure to moisture, which led to surface flaws and high rejection levels. Damage (RPN 80) occurred as a result of faulty handling and abrasive transport, which created

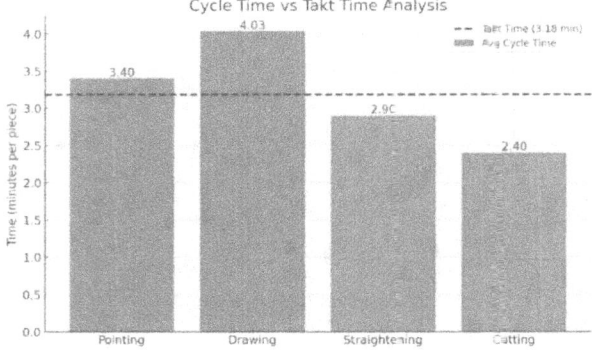

Figure 8.3 Takt time vs cycle time
Source: Author

dents and scratches. Bend/Twist (RPN 84) resulted from rolling pressure and misalignment, causing variations in dimensions. Link Marks (RPN 70) resulted from worn rollers and misalignment, influencing surface beauty and quality.

Recommended action: To minimize pit marks, strengthening raw material quality, mechanizing the descaling process, and storing materials under covered conditions is advised. To avoid damage in the form of dents and scratches, enhancing handling practices, employing protective packaging, and having proper roller and die alignment is necessary. For solving bend and twist problems, replacing worn rollers, having correct alignment and straightening set-ups, and giving regular training to operators is recommended. Lastly, to avoid line marks, improved packaging, equipment alignment, and careful handling procedures should be implemented.

Waste and findings

In the course of analyzing the existing production process with the use of VSM, a number of areas of inefficiency were realized that correspond with the seven traditional wastes in lean manufacturing. Among them is overproduction, where an excess of components is being produced beyond what is required, resulting in high levels of work-in-progress and storage issues. In addition to this, inventory accumulation was noted at various stages, which not only takes up critical space but also binds capital. There were also some instances of waiting time between operations, primarily caused by material movement delays and equipment unavailability. On the transportation front, materials were being transported more than they needs, and mostly forklifts were being used to cover short distances introducing extra handling steps. Motion waste was observed where operators had to constantly move to reach tools or materials, which points to poor workplace organization. Also, over processing was exhibited in the form of rework and repeated inspections owing to the absence of standardized procedures and process control. Lastly, defects like surface scratches, twists, and bends were frequent, primarily resulting from machine misalignment and bad handling practices of materials. These results suggest definite areas of process improvement opportunities, which potentially can result in shorter lead time, increased efficiency, and quality production.

Results and Discussion

Various types of defects and wastes and their Kaizens for continuous improvement

Scratches and gouges

Reason: Due to improper handling and rough contact, damage like scratch and gouges will occur. The defect is shown in the Figure 8.5. **Suggestions to avoid the defect:** Usage of protective covers, foam sheet, operator training, and suitable bins/stands and proper packaging may avoid these types of defects.

Pit marks

Reason: This type of defect is caused by second-grade stock raw materials for low volume orders. The pit marks are shown in Figure 8.6. **Suggestion:** Standardized raw material quality checks and better sourcing practices and to be reworked by grinding at RM stage (before drawing).

Line marks

Reason: Worn-out rollers, misalignment, and excessive pressure and the line mark is shown in Figure 8.7. **Suggestion:** Regular roller maintenance and periodic polishing proper alignment, and to be adjusted pressure based on the flat sizes.

Bend and twist

Reason: Machine misalignment and worn-out rollers, operator less awareness, part is long length due to which bend and twist occurs and is shown in Figure 8.8.

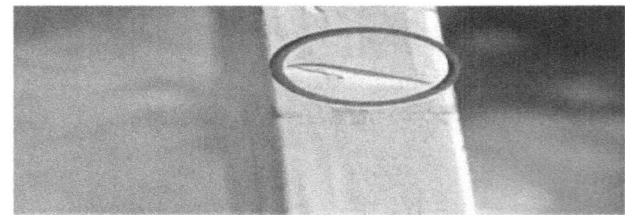

Figure 8.5 Scratches and gouges
Source: Author

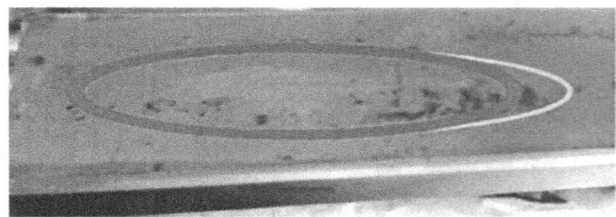

Figure 8.6 Pit marks
Source: Author

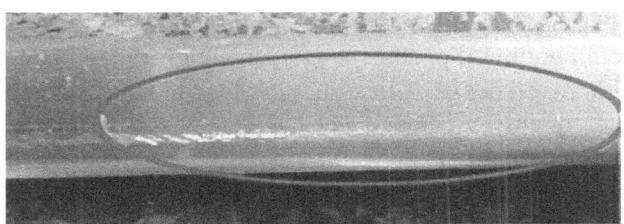

Figure 8.7 Line marks
Source: Author

Suggestion: Preventive roller maintenance, and to be improved SOPs with training and will be implemented cut lengths below 3 meters.

Wastes in drawing process

Wastes Identified: Excess setup time and rework due to die scoring marks. The manual trolley of drawing machine is shown in Figure 8.9.

Suggestions: Frequent die polishing and oil application, automation of material handling and using automated trolleys (forward and reverse). and enlarge the raw material stacking stand size from 1 meter to 2 meter and implementation of automated oil spraying for drawn flats, and bend correction die plat swiveling arrangement to be done for bend controlling.

Figure 8.8 Defect of bend and twist
Source: Author

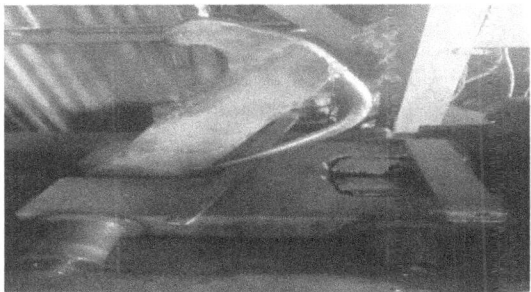

Figure 8.9 Manual trolley of drawing machine
Source: Author

Wastes in pointing process

Wastes Identified: Presence of gas cutting burrs, manual handling errors, inefficient raw material stacking and limited stacking capacity are identified in pointing process. The pointing machine is shown in Figure 8.10.

Suggestions: Implement laser gas cutting to reduce burrs so that accuracy can be improved, modify the raw material stacking stand to increase capacity and reduce handling time and minimize manual operations by introducing semi- automation wherever possible.

Future state VSM

The future state VSM is shown in Figure 8.11. By implementing the various Kaizens suggested for different types of waste, lead time is reduced to 23 days and thereby productivity is increased by 10% and also defect rate is reduced to 50 pieces per month.

A formal Standard Operating Procedure (SOP) was set up to maintain improvements and ensure quality consistency in bright steel production. In material procurement, only primary-grade materials are procured from qualified suppliers, with strict incoming inspection to ascertain compliance. The manufacturing process is adhered to calibrated machine settings, and proper jig and clamp use to avoid defects like bend and twist. A strong quality control system features routine in-process inspections, final quality inspections, and a defect tracking system to monitor in real time and take corrective actions. Packaging and handling operations include protective packaging and stack handling procedures to protect against damage in storage and transport. Preventive maintenance schedules are followed by key equipment such

Figure 8.10 Pointing machine
Source: Author

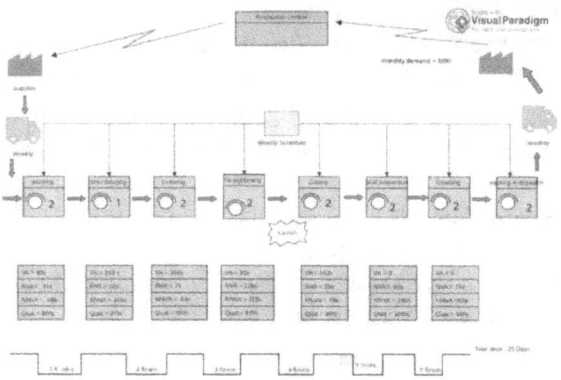

Lead time = 23 days

Figure 8.11 Future state value stream mapping
Source: Author

as jigs and clamps, while periodic audits are carried out to ensure compliance. Moreover, ongoing training sessions are organized for employees on material handling, defect detection, and quality standards. The feedback loop is incorporated to track process performance and continuously improve, promoting sustained defect reduction, cost reduction, and improved productivity.

This study applies Lean Six Sigma tools such as VSM and DMAIC to enhance production efficiency in bright steel manufacturing. Current and future state analysis indicates 8% reduction in lead time by optimizing material flow, eliminating bottlenecks, and aligning operations with takt time. Major surface defects like pit marks, line marks, and bends were reduced by improving machine setups, material handling, and raw material quality. Standardization through clear SOPs, preventive maintenance schedules, and continuous staff training ensured sustained improvements in quality and productivity. The operational changes not only led to faster production but also improved overall product quality and customer satisfaction. The implementation of several Kaizen aimed at various types of waste resulted in a decrease in lead time to 23 days and consequently in 10% productivity improvement. This improvement equates to a realized level of sigma at 4.27. The structured approach followed in this study can serve as a practical model for other manufacturing industries aiming to reduce waste, improve efficiency, and achieve sustainable operational excellence.

Practical Implications

The research provides a pragmatic guide to improving bright steel production with Lean Six Sigma.

Through the detection of inefficiencies and recommending specific improvements, it facilitates improved decision-making, less lead time, and product quality enhancement. Outcomes based on the implementation indicate increased efficiency and customer satisfaction. The method is also supportive of waste elimination, cost saving, and process stability. This model can be applied across operations, with continuous improvement and long-term competitiveness within manufacturing settings. It is a useful reference for systematic performance improvement.

Conclusion

This research proposes a systematic improvement plan to produce bright steel according to Lean Six Sigma concepts. By thorough examination and defect identification, the most important areas in need of improvement were established, and practical suggestions were made. The suggested changes were implemented, and the obtained results are an 8% reduction in lead time, improved product quality, and increased operational efficiency. Executing these methods will enable manufacturers to reduce waste, stabilize processes, and increase customer satisfaction. Overall, the approach outlined provides a good framework for firms seeking systematic and lasting improvements.

References

[1] Abebe, M., & Desalegn, A. (2022). Production lead time improvement through lean manufacturing. *Cogent Engineering*, 9(1), 1–14. 2034255.

[2] Das, T. (2024). Productivity optimization techniques using industrial engineering tools: a review. *International Journal of Science and Research Archive*, 12(1), 375–385.

[3] Gomaa, A. (2024). Improving productivity and quality of a machining process by using lean six sigma approach: a case study. *Engineering Research Journal (Shoubra)*, 53, 1–16.

[4] Karthick, B., Kannan, A., Kumar, S. M., & Nirmal, S. (2019). Lead time reduction using six sigma tools. *Indian Journal of Science and Technology*, 12(23), 1–11.

[5] Khawar, N., Ullah, M., Tariq, A., Maqsood, S., Akhtar, R., Nawaz, R., et al. (2016). Optimization of steel bar manufacturing process using six sigma. *Chinese Journal of Mechanical Engineering*, 29(2), 332–341.

[6] Leksic, I., Stefanic, N., & Veza, I. (2020). The impact of using different lean manufacturing tools on waste reduction. *Advances in Production Engineering and Management*, 15, 81–92. 10.14743/apem2020.1.351.

[7] Gomathi Prabha, M., Rajamohan, T., Manikandan, S., & Petluru, S. R. (2023). Lead time reduction and quality

improvement in a manufacturing industry using DMAIC methodology—a case study. In Advances in Forming, Machining and Automation, (pp. 581–599). Springer Nature Singapore.

[8] Saied, E., Galal, N., & ElSayed, A. (2019). Material and energy wastes reduction in steel production through the application of lean manufacturing tools. In 3rd European International Conference on Industrial Engineering and Operations Management.

[9] Shah, D., & Patel, P. (2018). Productivity improvement by implementing lean manufacturing tools in manufacturing industry. *International Research Journal of Engineering and Technology*, 5, 3794–3798.

[10] Singh, M. D., Singh, S., Keyur, D., Saumil, S., Niki, P., & Harshal, P. (2015). Overall productivity improvement in casting industry by using various industrial engineering techniques. *International Journal of Innovative Research in Science, Engineering and Technology (IJIRSET)*, 4, 18713–18721. 10.15680/IJIRSET.2015.0401050.

[11] Sordan, J. E. E., Oprime, P. C., Ferreira, J. L., Marinho, C. A, & Pata, A. (2025). Lean manufacturing for reducing lead time in foundry processes: a design science approach. *International Journal of Lean Six Sigma*, 15(2), 328–345.

[12] Venkataramana, K., Ramnath, B. V., Kumar, V. M., & Elanchezhian, C. (2014). Application of value stream mapping for reduction of cycle time in a machining process. *Procedia Materials Science*, 6, 1187–1196.

9 Comparative analysis of K-medoids clustering and frequent episode mining for intrusion detection

Shreya Venkatesh[1,a] and K. Lakshmi Kalpana Roy[2,b]

[1]Department of Applied Mathematics and Computational Sciences, PSG College of Technology, Coimbatore, india

[2]Assistant Professor, Department of Applied Mathematics and Computational Sciences, PSG College of Technology, Coimbatore, India

Abstract

In cyber security, intrusion detection is one significant area of research. Intrusion detection systems (IDS) are aimed to identify the violations or other malicious activities happening in a system. Such systems must be accurate and reliable such that potential threats are captured. Machine learning provides a handful of supervised and unsupervised algorithms and techniques in identifying and classifying the attacks. This paper implements the K-Medoids clustering and frequent episode mining (FEM) algorithms, the unsupervised technique, for intrusion detection on the KDD Cup 1999 dataset [12]. The K-Medoids algorithm, an improvement on K-Means clustering, enhances outlier robustness, whereas FEM finds interesting patterns of sequential actions characteristic of intrusions. Feature selection is performed by combining mutual information with the Random Forest classifier. Experimental results demonstrate that FEM has a better classification accuracy of 94.3%, as opposed to 87.6% for K-Medoids. In addition, it exhibits better anomaly detection performance with reduced false-positive rates. However, K-Medoids are computationally more efficient and scalable for unsupervised environments. In general, FEM is more effective for temporal intrusion detection, whereas K-Medoids provides a lightweight solution for real-time anomaly clustering.

Keywords: Frequent episode mining, intrusion detection, KDD Cup 99, k-medoids, mutual information, Random Forest

Introduction

With the amplified sophistication and density of threats online, network security is now an integral issue across digital infrastructures. The rising frequency of sophisticated attacks from denial-of-service (DoS) and probing to more stealthy types like remote-to-local (R2L) and user-to-root (U2R) points to the limitations of traditional signature-based intrusion detection systems (IDS). These conventional methods tend to fail to recognize new or changing threats, resulting in high false-positive rates and lower reliability in dynamic network environments.

Over the past decade, data mining and machine learning techniques have drawn much interest for their ability to make the detection of anomalous patterns in large traffic data automatic. Clustering-based approaches and sequence mining techniques stand out among various alternatives as viable contenders for smart IDS. Clustering can uncover structural patterns within unlabelled data, whereas sequence mining picks up temporal relationships common in intrusion activities.

This research explores and compares two such methods like K-Medoids clustering and FEM for their effectiveness in identifying network intrusions. K-Medoids, an improvement of the widely used K-Means algorithm, overcomes major limitations by making use of real data points (medoids) as cluster centres, thus improving robustness to outliers. In contrast, FEM targets the identification of frequent sequential patterns, thus being best suited for the detection of temporally organized attack behaviour in time-series data.

Problem statement

Given the intrusion detection dataset, comprising the data of the TCP connection's basic features and other features corresponding to the network traffic, the aim of this paper is to build appropriate strategies for choosing suitable features, use them to compare the prediction of identifying the anomalies by the unsupervised algorithms and suggest the suitable model for intrusion detection.

[a]21pt29@psgtech.ac.in, [b]lkr.amcs@psgtech.ac.in

DOI: 10.1201/9781003770435-9

Objectives of the research

The main objectives of this work are to:

- Employ Random Forest with Gini impurity to compute feature importance, combined with mutual information for robust selection.
- Perform custom feature selection using mutual information with high variability and non-zero range values,
- build the unsupervised models using the appropriate features selected, and
- evaluate the performance of the models based on predictions.

Literature Review

Recent advancements in intrusion detection systems (IDS) have increasingly adopted data mining and machine learning techniques to improve detection accuracy while reducing false-positive rates. Among these approaches, clustering algorithms, rule-based classifiers, and temporal pattern mining methods have demonstrated substantial promise in addressing the dynamic and complex nature of cyber threats.

Qin and Hwang [9] implemented K-Means clustering on the NSL-KDD dataset and observed a detection efficiency of 81.61% with 22 clusters. However, the study also highlighted that the number of clusters significantly influences model performance.

Chitrakar and Huang [1] proposed a hybrid model combining K-Medoids clustering with Naïve Bayes classification, reporting improvements in anomaly detection performance through unsupervised–supervised learning integration.

Yoon and Kang [10] explored the use of the K-Medoids algorithm in cloud environments for detecting distributed denial-of-service (DDoS) attacks. Their study demonstrated that K-Medoids could effectively identify clustering patterns in high-volume traffic, supporting its application in scalable network defence solutions.

Koeman and Heskes [5] introduced a method for estimating mutual information using Random Forests. Their approach provided a robust, data-driven metric for feature selection in supervised learning, which is highly applicable to IDS tasks involving high-dimensional input spaces.

Lee and Stolfo [6] introduced machine learning algorithms such as RIPPER and FEM to identify attack patterns using rule-based methods. Duque and bin Omar [3] extended this approach using a modified WINEPI algorithm, extracting frequent serial episodes from honeypot logs to identify unknown attacks.

Su et al. [11] studied rule-learning techniques used in smart grid domains, and how the specification-based models were able to identify new attacks without compromising interpretability. In a similar vein, Liu et al. [7] illustrated how base-support mining and pruning strategies could improve anomaly detection by lowering false alarms in audit information.

Frequent episode rules (FERs) have also been employed to identify specific attack types. For instance, Qin and Hwang [9] indicated detection rates of 47% for DoS, 40% for Probe, and 19% for R2L attacks while at the same time shrinking the rule search space by as much as 70%. Halonen et al. [4] used system log episode mining methods to successfully identify anomalies by recognizing patterns of recurring events.

Ouarem et al. [8] presented a thorough survey of episode mining last year, covering its general applicability in temporal anomaly detection, such as intrusion detection systems. Their contribution is focused on the demand for scalable algorithms and domain adaptation, particularly for time-series security data.

Disha and Waheed [2] proposed Gini Impurity-based Weighted Random Forest (GIWRF) model to select the ideal features from the UNSW-NB 15 and Network TON_IoT datasets. Along with the Decision Tree algorithm, their model GIWRF-DT performed well with the highest F1 score.

Background

Successful intrusion detection relies on identifying the most representative feature sand using strong analytical methods appropriate to the character of network data. In this section, the basic concepts used in the current research are presented in detail, highlighting feature selection techniques and the fundamental algorithms – K-Medoids clustering and FEM for the purpose of anomaly detection from network traffic.

Feature selection

Feature selection is essential in machine learning and data mining, as it assists in the identification of the most important features that contribute substantially in the prediction or classification process. Not only does it enhance model accuracy, but it also simplifies computational complexity by removing irrelevant or redundant features. Feature selection can be done using different techniques, such as statistical methods, tree-based methods, and mutual information-based methods.

Random forest feature importance

Random Forest is a widely-used ensemble learning method that provides an internal mechanism for estimating the importance of input features. It does so by constructing multiple decision trees and evaluating the average decrease in impurity—often measured using the Gini index—across all trees where a feature is used for splitting. The Gini impurity is defined as:

$$G = 1 - \sum_{i=1}^{C} p_i^2 \qquad (1)$$

where p_i represents the probability of class i within a node, and C is the number of distinct classes. Features that result in higher reductions in impurity are considered more important and are thus prioritized in the selection process.

As shown in Algorithm 1, the Random Forest model selects the top features based on their importance scores.

Algorithm 1 Random Forest feature selection

---

1. **Input:** Training data X, labels y
2. Train a Random Forest model on dataset X
3. **for** each feature in X **do**
4. Compute feature importance based on decrease in impurity
5. **end for**
6. Select top n features based on their importance scores
7. **Output:** Top n important features

Mutual information

Mutual information (MI) quantifies the amount of shared information between two variables, in this case, between a feature and the target class label. A higher MI score indicates stronger dependency and hence higher relevance for classification tasks. MI is calculated using the following equation:

$$MI(X, Y) = \sum_{x \in X} \sum_{y \in Y} P(x, y) \log \frac{P(x,y)}{P(x)P(y)} \qquad (2)$$

Here, $P(x, y)$ represents the joint probability distribution of variables X and Y, while $P(x)$ and $P(y)$ denote their marginal distributions. MI is especially valuable in capturing both linear and non-linear dependencies between features and the target.

K-medoids clustering

K-Medoids is a clustering algorithm that divides data into k clusters by choosing representative data points, or medoids, rather than centroids (like K-means). A data point is allocated to the cluster whose medoid it is nearest to, according to a distance metric, for which typically Euclidean distance is employed. The medoids are iteratively updated to reduce the overall dissimilarity within each cluster.

As shown in Algorithm 2, the K-Medoids algorithm assigns points to clusters and updates medoids until convergence.

Frequent episode mining

FEM seeks to find groups of events (episodes) that appear with high frequency in a dataset. The method is extensively applied in temporal data analysis, particularly in anomaly detection. Through frequent episode identification, the algorithm can locate patterns that might represent normal or abnormal behaviour. The episodes are ordered according to frequency and anomaly rate, calculated based on the target variable.

Algorithm 2 K-Medoids clustering

Require: Dataset X, number of clusters k, maximum iterations *max_iter*

Ensure: Final medoids M, cluster assignments C
1. Initialize k medoids M by selecting points with minimal average pairwise distance
2. **repeat**
3. **Assignment:**
   for each $x_i \in X$ **do**
   $C(x_i) \leftarrow argmin_{m_j \in M} d(x_i, m_j)$
   end for
4. **Medoid Update:**
   for each cluster C_j **do**
   $m_j \leftarrow argmin_{x \in C_j} \sum_{x' \in C_j} d(x, x')$
   end for
5. **until** medoids stabilize or max_iter reached

Algorithm 3 Frequent and discriminative episode mining

Require: Discretized sequences X, labels y, *min_support*, *max_len* = 3
Ensure: Top 100 discriminative episodes E_{top}

1. Initialize hash map *episode_stats* {Stores (count, anomaly_count)}
2. **for** each $seq \in X$ **do**
3. **for** l = 2 to *max_len* **do**
4. **for** each l-length episode e in seq **do**
5. *episode_stats[e].count* ← *episode_stats [e].count* + 1
6. *episode_stats [e].anomaly* ← *episode_stats [e].anomaly* + $y[seq]$
7. **end for**
8. **end for**
9. **end for**
10. **Filtering:**
11. **for** each $e \in$ *episode_stats* **do**
12. **if** $\frac{episode\_stats[e].count}{|X|} \geq min\_support$ then
13. $e.ratio \leftarrow \frac{episode\_stats[e].anomaly}{episode\_stats[e].count}$
14. $E \leftarrow E \cup \{e\}$
15. **end if**
16. **end for**
17. **Ranking:**
18. Compute population anomaly rate $\mu \leftarrow \frac{\Sigma y}{|X|}$
19. $E_{top} \leftarrow argmax_{e \in E}|_{E_{top}}|=100|e.ratio-\mu|$
20. **return** E_{top}

As shown in Algorithm 3 the FEM algorithm identifies frequent temporal patterns from the dataset.

The method operates by scanning discretized sequences of events to identify those that meet or exceed a defined support threshold. For every identified episode, its frequency and anomaly ratio is determined based on its frequency in attack-labelled sequences, are stored. The episodes are then sorted based on how much their anomaly ratios vary from the global anomaly rate of the dataset.

Episodes with high discriminative power are retained and used as indicative patterns of malicious behaviour. This technique is particularly advantageous in settings where attacks manifest as temporal chains of actions rather than isolated events.

Methodology

The workflow diagram in Figure 9.1 shows the methodology of the work, which includes the dataset collection, data pre-processing methods, feature selection methodologies, and principles of model implementation.

Dataset collection
The KDD Cup 1999 data is used as a standard for intrusion detection with network traffic instances tagged as normal or attack types. The data comprises 41 features that are classified as basic connection features, content-based features, and traffic-based statistical features. The data contains different types of attacks like denial-of-service (DoS), probing, remote-to-local (R2L), and user-to-root (U2R) attacks, thus appropriate for assessing clustering and sequential pattern mining techniques.

Data pre-processing
Data pre-processing includes the management of duplicate records, transformation of categorical variables into numerical values, and scaling numerical attributes to maintain consistency. The label column has been restructured into a binary classification problem to differentiate between normal and attack cases. Appropriate feature scaling methods have

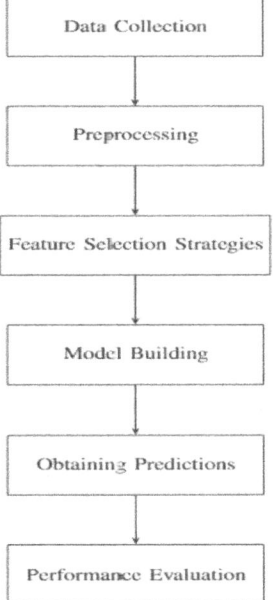

Figure 9.1 Workflow diagram
Source: Author

been used to improve the performance of clustering and pattern mining models.

Feature selection strategies

Feature selection is a critical component of the model optimization process. To complement the strategies discussed in the previous sections, a two-stage feature selection framework is proposed. In the first stage, a generalized feature selection approach integrates Random Forest importance score and Mutual Information and in the second phase, a task-dependent selection process is designed for FEM. Each of these has been tailored to the requirements of the respective algorithms.

For K-Medoids clustering and initial application of frequent episode mining, a generalized dataset-wide feature selection approach was used. This involved ranking features based on Random Forest importance scores and Mutual Information values. The top six features identified through this process have been subsequently used for both clustering and sequence mining tasks, as described in Algorithm 1 and Equation (2), respectively.

However, due to suboptimal performance of FEM with the generalized feature set, an alternative, task-specific feature selection strategy was adopted. This method involved selecting features that demonstrated high mutual information with the class label, substantial variability across instances, and a non-zero range. These criteria ensured the selection of features that have not only been informative but also suitable for identifying sequential patterns within the data.

Model implementation

Two fundamental models have been adopted in this research: K-Medoids clustering and frequent episode mining.

K-Medoids clustering algorithm, as presented in Algorithm 2, was executed with an initialization strategy that aimed to minimize average pair-wise distances between medoids. The clustering was conducted without assuming anything about data distribution, hence appropriate for unsupervised anomaly detection.

The FEM algorithm, presented in Algorithm 3, was used on a discretized dataset. The model was designed to learn frequently occurring sequential patterns that are predictive of malicious activity in network traffic. The technique proved particularly effective at unveiling temporal attack signatures.

Experimental setup

Implementation was performed using Python and suitable machine learning libraries like Scikit-learn, SciPy, Pandas, and NumPy. Experiments have been conducted on a high-performance computing setup to offer computational efficiency in terms of processing large-scale data.

Performance evaluation

The performance efficiency of both approaches was assessed using several evaluation factors: accuracy, precision, recall, F1 score, execution time, and found anomalies. The results indicated the importance of feature selection customization in achieving optimal model performance for different analytical approaches.

Implementation and Results

The research adhered to a systematic methodology to compare FEM and K-Medoids clustering on the KDD Cup 1999 data. The pipeline ensured data pre-processing, feature extraction, model development, and performance measurement on consistent lines.

Data preparation

The data was pre-processed by eliminating duplicates and missing values. Categorical features have been transformed into numerical forms, and class labels have been encoded into a binary classification format (normal or attack). Feature scaling methods have been employed to provide equalization across numerical ranges. Only 10% of the complete dataset, which is around 4.9 million records, was utilized for analysis.

Initial feature selection and baseline performance

To establish a baseline for comparison, six features were initially selected at random from the KDD Cup 1999 dataset: *duration, src_bytes, dst_bytes, count, srv_count, and serror_rate*. These features were used as input to both the K-Medoids clustering and FEM models.

With this coarse feature set, both models had modest performance, each with classification accuracies around 70% to 80%. Though this proved that there is indeed predictive ability in the selected features, the results also highlighted the importance of having a more rigorous and informed method for selecting features to raise detection accuracy. As can be seen from Figure 9.2, the K-Medoids algorithm managed to perform a general separation of normal and anomalous points, with a number of the red (anomalous) data points standing out from the clusters. There were some anomalies overlapped or inaccurately placed in the clusters, suggesting that while the model could identify outliers, it was not precise enough for accurate anomaly identification. This performance also highlights the shortcomings of employing randomly chosen features. Figure 9.3 displays the corresponding baseline performance of frequent episode mining.

Optimized feature selection strategy
To improve model performance, an optimized feature selection procedure was employed. The top six features have been selected using a hybrid method based on Random Forest feature importance and mutual information scores. Koeman and Heskes [5] have deployed such a technique for estimating the mutual information scores. This dataset-wide strategy prioritized features that contributed most significantly to classification tasks.

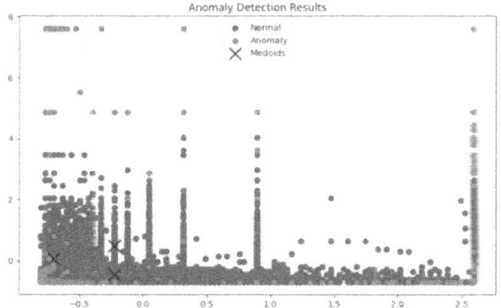

Figure 9.2 Baseline performance of K-medoids
Source: Author

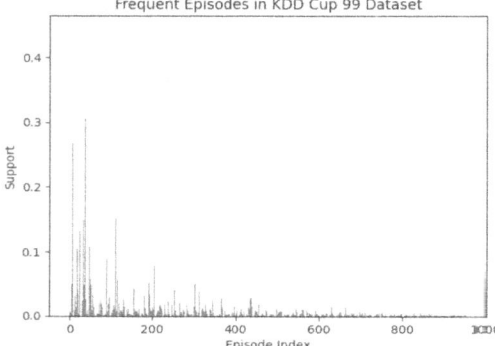

Figure 9.3 Baseline performance of frequent episode mining
Source: Author

The application of these features resulted in a substantial improvement in the K-Medoids clustering model, with accuracy rising to approximately 95%. However, when the same set of features was used with the FEM model, performance declined considerably. This discrepancy indicated that feature relevance is highly dependent on the underlying modelling approach. Clustering algorithms such as K-Medoids benefit from features that capture spatial patterns, whereas sequence mining techniques like FEM require features with strong temporal and sequential characteristics. All features and their corresponding mutual information scores used in this phase are presented in Table 9.1.

Alternative feature selection for frequent episode mining
Given the unsatisfactory performance of FEM with generalized features, a task-specific feature selection strategy was introduced. This method was designed to identify features particularly suited for sequential pattern recognition. The selection process was based on three criteria:

- **High mutual information**: Capturing strong statistical association with the class label.
- **High variability**: Ensuring the feature varies sufficiently across samples to enhance discriminative capacity.
- **Non-zero range**: Excluding constant features to ensure relevance in temporal mining.

Each feature's final selection score was computed as the product of its mutual information, standard deviation (as a measure of variability), and range. This approach favoured attributes that met all three conditions, thereby enhancing their value for sequence-based analysis.

Table 9.1 Top 6 features with their mutual information scores

Feature	Mutual information
src_bytes	0.701463
diff_srv_rate	0.662159
same_srv_rate	0.655643
count	0.635716
dst_host_diff_srv_rate	0.583579
dst_host_same_srv_rate	0.577672

Source: Author

The application of this fine-grained selection method significantly improved the accuracy of the FEM model. In fact, FEM outperformed K-Medoids on all major performance metrics, validating the effectiveness of alternate feature engineering. The top-ranked features selected through this method, along with their composite scores, are presented in Table 9.2.

Final model implementation
Both models have been implemented using their respective optimal feature sets derived from the aforementioned strategies. K-Medoids clustering was configured with medoid initialization based on minimum average pairwise distances, ensuring high-quality cluster formation. The FEM model was applied to a discretized version of the dataset and used to uncover behavioural patterns that correlated with malicious activity over time.

Performance evaluation and comparison
The models have been evaluated based on standard classification metrics including accuracy, precision, recall, and F1-score, along with the number of anomalies detected. These results are summarized in Table 9.3.

FEM consistently outperformed K-Medoids across all evaluation metrics. Specifically, FEM achieved

higher classification accuracy, precision, recall, and F1-score. More notably, it detected a substantially greater number of anomalies (17,245) compared to K-Medoids (728). This outcome highlights the superior capability of FEM to capture temporal patterns indicative of intrusion activity.

These findings reinforce the importance of aligning feature selection strategies with the modelling technique employed. While clustering methods are enhanced by spatial relevance of features, temporal pattern mining techniques require features with dynamical and sequential nature. The research therefore highlights the importance of tailored feature engineering towards improving the performance of intrusion detection systems.

Conclusion

This study highlights on the significance of feature selection in obtaining the best results for K-Medoids clustering and frequent episode mining (FEM) on the KDD Cup 1999 intrusion detection dataset. Employing a randomly selected subset of features, an initial test achieved only modest performance of approximately 70–80%. However, employing an optimized subset of features made a huge difference to the accuracy of K-Medoids clustering with an all-time high of 95%. Contrary to expectations, however, the same group of features lead to a reduction in the performance of FEM, proving that the relevance of features is highly subject to the type of the underlying algorithm.

As a counter to this, another feature selection technique aimed at sequence mining was suggested. This procedure integrated three most relevant criteria: high mutual information with the target variable, high variability in order to enhance discriminative power, and a non-zero range to ensure dynamic behaviour among sequential patterns. Integration of these criteria produced a composite score, which was utilized to choose features particularly effective in FEM.

With these task-dependent properties, FEM not only recovered from its earlier performance dip but also surpassed K-Medoids in terms of accuracy and quality of detection. These findings strongly emphasize the significance of feature selection methods adapted specifically for use with different machine learning techniques when addressing cybersecurity problems.

Table 9.2 Top 6 features with their scores

Feature	Scores
src_bytes	682626897311876.9
dst_bytes	142170464343.1044
duration	1974302.277809917
count	25801.392371799924
dst_host_srv_count	13440.216091040076
dst_host_count	5540.6291744218715

Source: Author

Table 9.3 Model evaluation metrics

Metrics	K-Medoids	Frequent episode mining
Accuracy	0.9501	0.9763
Precision	0.9118	0.9619
Recall	0.9501	0.9789
F1-Score	0.9305	0.9703
Anomalies Detected	728	17,245

Source: Author

In future work, more learning-driven and feature selection-based processes could be explored, including evolutionary algorithms or deep learning-based embeddings. Additionally, generalizing the proposed method to other benchmark data sets and real network traffic logs will make its viability even more evident in practical intrusion detection systems. Alternatively, newer data sets like NSL-KDD or CICIDS2017 can be used to further prove the method's viability in contemporary intrusion detection systems.

References

[1] Chitrakar, R., & Huang, C. (2012). Anomaly based intrusion detection using hybrid learning approach of combining k-medoids clustering and naïve bayes classification. In 2012 International Conference on Wireless Communications, Networking and Mobile Computing, WiCOM 2012. (pp. 1–5). 10.1109/WiCOM.2012.6478433.

[2] Disha, R. A., & Waheed, S. (2022). Performance analysis of machine learning models for intrusion detection system using Gini Impurity-based weighted random forest (GIWRF) feature selection technique. *Cybersecurity*, 5, 1. https://doi.org/10.1186/s42400-021-00103-8.

[3] Duque, S., & bin Omar, M. N. (2015). Using data mining algorithms for developing a model for intrusion detection system (IDS). *Procedia Computer Science* 61, 46–51.

[4] Halonen, P., Miettinen, M., & Hätönen, K. (2009). Computer log anomaly detection using frequent episodes. In Iliadis, Maglogiann, Tsoumakasis, Vlahavas, & Bramer (Eds.), Artificial Intelligence Applications and Innovations III. AIAI 2009. IFIP International Federation for Information Processing, (Vol 296). Boston, MA: Springer. https://doi.org/10.1007/978-1-4419-0221-4_49.

[5] Koeman, M., & Heskes, T. (2014). Mutual information estimation with random forests. In Loo, C. K., Yap, K. S., Wong, K. W., Teoh, A., & Huang, K. (Eds.), Neural Information Processing. ICONIP 2014. Lecture Notes in Computer Science, (Vol. 8835). Cham: Springer. https://doi.org/10.1007/978-3-319-12640-1_63.

[6] Lee, W., & Stolfo, S. J. (1998). Data mining approaches for intrusion detection. In Proceedings of the USENIX Security Symposium, (Vol. 7, pp. 6–6). San Antonio, TX.

[7] Liu, Q., Hagenmeyer, V., & Keller, H. B. (2021). A review of rule learning-based intrusion detection systems and their prospects in smart grids. *IEEE Access*, 9, 57542–57564.

[8] Ouarem, O., Nouioua, F., & Fournier Viger, P. (2023). A survey of episode mining. *Wiley Interdisciplinary Reviews: Data Mining and Knowledge Discovery*, 14(2). e1524. 10.1002/widm.1524.

[9] Qin, M., & Hwang, K. (2004). Frequent episode rules for Internet anomaly detection. In Proceedings of the Third IEEE International Symposium on Network Computing and Applications (NCA 2004), (pp. 161–168). IEEE. doi:10.1109/NCA.2004.1347761.

[10] Yoon, S., & Kang, M. (2022). DDoS attacks detection in the cloud using K-medoids algorithm. In 24th International Conference on Advanced Communication Technology (ICACT), PyeongChang Kwangwoon_ Do, Korea, Republic of, (pp. 91–94). doi: 10.23919/ICACT53585.2022.9728838.

[11] Su, M.-Y. (2017). Applying episode mining and pruning to identify malicious online attacks. *Computers and Electrical Engineering*, 59, 180–188.

[12] UCI KDD Archive (1999). KDD Cup 1999 data. Retrieved from https://kdd.ics.uci.edu/databases/kddcup99/kddcup99.html.

10 Ultrasound-assisted biodiesel production from waste cooking oil using areca nut husk derived heterogeneous catalyst

S. Kavinandhini[1,a] and S. Niju[2,b]

[1]M. Tech Student, Department of Biotechnology, PSG College of Technology, India

[2]Assistant Professor (Selection grade), Department of Biotechnology, PSG College of Technology, India

Abstract

In response to the growing energy crisis and environmental concerns associated with fossil fuels, biodiesel emerges as a sustainable and renewable alternative. This study focuses on biodiesel production assisting with ultrasonic waves using arecanut husk derived biomass heterogeneous catalyst and waste cooking as a feedstock. The carbonized arecanut husk ash was further impregnated with potassium iodide to improve its catalytic activity. Characterization of the catalyst was carried out using XRD and FTIR, which confirmed its crystalline nature and the presence of active functional groups, respectively. Proton NMR was used to characterize the biodiesel and indicated maximum conversion. Thus, this catalyst can serve as a potent heterogeneous catalyst for biodiesel production.

Keywords: Areca nut husk, biodiesel, ultrasound-assisted transesterification, waste cooking oil

Introduction

Global energy is dominated by fossil fuels, which meet more than 90% of the demand from population expansion, urbanization, transportation, and industry [4]. Alternative fuels have been searched for due to the depletion of petroleum sources and the rise in environmental degradation [5] With the potential to reduce greenhouse gas emissions, biofuels present a sustainable substitute for fossil fuels [7]. Biodiesel is distinguished as an alternative for transportation fuel [8].

Biodiesel is a fatty acid methyl ester, obtained by the catalyzed or uncatalyzed reaction between triglycerides and alcohol [8]. Transesterification of triglycerides and alcohol in the presence of catalysts is employed due to the use of a variety of feedstocks. Homogeneous base catalysts include sodium hydroxide and potassium hydroxide. Despite its higher conversion, it is challenging in catalyst recovery and biodiesel purification due to the formation of soap [9]. These issues can be resolved by using heterogeneous base catalysts as it can be recycled and reused multiple times reducing both environmental impact and production costs (Supongsenla et al., 2024). Catalysts derived from natural sources such as biomass, are increasingly being used as potential heterogeneous catalysts. biomass-derived catalysts, made from renewable biological waste like shells, bones, and plant residues. By minimizing waste and avoiding toxic by-products, these catalysts contribute to greener, more efficient biodiesel production, aligning with global sustainability goals [13].

Biodiesel can be produced from a variety of feedstocks like waste derived oils, edible oils, and non-food oils [15]. Edible oils produce high quality biodiesel; but raises food vs fuel conflict. WCO can be utilized as a feedstock to produce biodiesel. The amount of WCO generated are increasing rapidly due to the tremendous growth in human population [13]. When they are not properly disposed of, the amount of organic contaminants in the water increases, drastically reducing the quality of the water [6, 12]. Areca nut is the seed of the fruit of the *Areca catechu* that is commercially grown in south east Asian countries. The areca nut husk constitutes about 65–80% of the total weight and volume. The husk of areca nut is waste material and has no use [1]. Areca nut husk shows notably high concentrations of potassium, silicon, and chlorine, along with significant amounts of magnesium, iron, and aluminum, making it a mineral-rich biomass particularly suitable for heterogeneous catalyst development [14]. Transesterification assisted with ultrasonication enhances biodiesel production by utilizing ultrasound waves to generate cavitation bubbles in the liquid. This significantly

[a]kavinandhini2410@gmail.com, [b]sn.bio@psgtech.ac.in

DOI: 10.1201/9781003770435-10

improves mass transfer between the oil and alcohol phases, reducing reaction time and potentially lowering catalyst usage [3]. The aim of this project is to analyze the significance of areca nut husk based heterogeneous catalyst in producing biodiesel through ultrasound assisted transesterification reaction.

Materials and Methods

Materials
Areca nut husk was collected from a farm near Kerala. Waste cooking oil was collected from the hostel canteen of PSG College of Technology, Coimbatore, Tamil Nadu. Chemicals such as potassium hydroxide (KOH), 2-propanol, and potassium iodide (KI) were purchased from HI-MEDIA. Phenolphthalein solution was used as an indicator.

Preparation of catalyst
Areca nut husk was washed thoroughly with water to remove surface sand and impurities. It was then dried in a hot air oven at 80 °C overnight and powdered using a mixer grinder. The powdered sample was sieved using an 18-mesh sieve (≤1 mm) and stored in an airtight ziplock bag. The biomass was

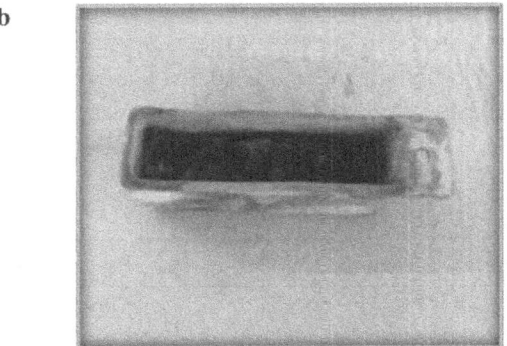

Figure 10.1 (a) Dried areca nut husk; (b) Carbonized arecanut husk ash
Source: Author

subsequently carbonized at 600 °C for 2 hours and stored in another airtight ziplock bag.

Impregnation of catalyst
The carbonized areca nut husk was impregnated with potassium iodide using the wet impregnation method. In 100 ml of distilled water, 2.5 grams of KI was dissolved. Then, 10 g of carbonized catalyst was added gradually and stirred using a magnetic stirrer for 2 hours. The resulting mixture was filtered using Whatman filter paper, and the impregnated catalyst was dried in a hot air oven until a constant weight was achieved. Calcination of the dried, impregnated catalyst was carried out at 600 °C for 2 hours. The final catalyst was stored in an airtight container.

Characterization of catalyst
Characterization of the catalyst is essential to understand its physical and chemical properties, which directly affect its catalytic activity, efficiency, and stability during the reaction process. Key characteristics such as surface area, porosity, morphology, crystallinity, functional groups, elemental composition, and thermal stability were assessed. The crystalline phases of both doped and undoped areca nut husk catalysts were identified by X-ray diffraction. FTIR spectroscopy was used to identify functional groups, surface morphology was demonstrated by SEM, and elemental composition was determined by EDAX.

Physicochemical characteristics of waste cooking oil (WCO)
The collected waste cooking oil was first filtered to remove impurities and preheated to eliminate moisture. The acid value was determined following ASTM standards to assess the content of free fatty acid. 1 g of waste cooking oil was mixed with 10 ml of 2-propanol and phenolphthalein indicator, then titrated with 0.1N KOH until a persistent pink color appeared. The FFA content was calculated. If the FFA content exceeded 2%, esterification was carried out before transesterification. If it was below 2%, the oil was used directly for transesterification. To determine the density of WCO, a pycnometer was used. The weight of the oil and water filled pycnometer was measured. The volume of the pycnometer was calculated using the known density of water, and the density of the oil was calculated by dividing the mass of the oil by the pycnometer's volume. This

property is important in evaluating the fuel quality of biodiesel.

$$Acid\ value\,(mg\ KOH/g\ oi)$$
$$= (56.1 \times 0.1 \times V_{KOH})/W \tag{1}$$

Where, V_{KOH} is the volume of KOH consumed and W is the weight of the oil used.

$$FFA(\%) = Acid\ value\,/2 \tag{2}$$

Transesterification reaction for biodiesel production

Transesterification of WCO was carried out using the KI-impregnated areca nut husk catalyst with ultrasonic assistance to enhance mixing and mass transfer between the reactants. The catalyst concentration varied between 1 wt% and 5 wt%. A reaction was carried out using 25 g of WCO, 12 mL of methanol, and 0.6 g of catalyst for 60 minutes. The use of ultrasound improved conversion efficiency, although excessive catalyst loading resulted in a reduction in conversion. After the reaction, the mixture was filtered using Whatman filter paper. The filtrate was transferred to a falcon tube and allowed to undergo phase separation. The upper layer consisted of fatty acid methyl esters (biodiesel), while the lower layer was glycerol, the by-product. Proton NMR (^{1}H NMR) analysis was done to characterize the biodiesel sample and determine the biodiesel conversion using the below equation.

$$\%\ Biodiesel\ conversion = 100 \times 2A_{ME}/ \atop 3A_{\alpha-CH_2} \quad (3) \tag{3}$$

Results and Discussion

Physicochemical properties of waste cooking oil

The key physicochemical characteristics of WCO have been determined and are listed in Table 10.1. The density of the WCO was found to be 0.897 g/cm³, which falls within the typical range for vegetable oils, indicating its suitability as a feedstock for biodiesel production. The acid value was measured as 2.805 mg KOH/g oil, corresponding to a free fatty acid (FFA) content of 1.41%, which is below the 2% threshold. This result indicates that the oil did not require a pre-treatment esterification step and was

directly used for transesterification. The relatively low FFA content was favorable as it minimized the risk of soap formation, thereby enhancing the efficiency and yield of the biodiesel production process.

Characterization of catalyst using XRD

XRD analysis was carried out to identify the crystalline phases of the catalyst, which influence its catalytic performance. Figure 10.2a shows the XRD pattern of the carbonized areca nut husk ash, which exhibited a broad hump in the 2θ range of 15–30°, indicating a predominantly amorphous structure with high disorder. Sharp peaks were observed only at 2θ = 28.3° and 40.6°, corresponding to potassium chloride and potassium barium niobate, respectively, based on the Powder Diffraction File database (JCPDS) [11]. Figure 10.2b presents the XRD pattern of the KI-impregnated and calcined areca nut husk catalyst. The pattern showed high crystallinity with sharp peaks at 2θ = 21.8°, 25.3°, 28.6°, 34.07°, 36.05°, 42.49°, 44.5°, 50.22°, 51.80°, 58.48°, and 64.67°. The peak at 28.6° confirmed the successful incorporation of potassium iodide (JCPDS: 04–0532). The increased intensity and sharpness of the peaks indicated the transformation of the catalyst from an amorphous to a crystalline phase due to KI impregnation, thereby enhancing the number of active sites for the transesterification reaction.

Characterization of catalyst using FTIR

FTIR spectroscopy was used to identify the functional groups influencing catalytic activity. Figure 10.3a shows the FTIR spectrum of carbonized areca nut husk, which exhibited sharp peaks in the fingerprint region (600–1000 cm⁻¹), likely due to C–O or C–H vibrations. The absence of strong peaks between 4000 cm⁻¹ and 1500 cm⁻¹ suggested the decomposition of carbonyl and aliphatic groups during carbonization. The FTIR spectra of the catalyst impregnated with KI is shown in Figure 10.3b. Sharp and intense peaks in the range of 800–400 cm⁻¹ were observed,

Table 10.1 Physicochemical properties of WCO

Property	Units	Parameters
Acid value	mg KOH/ g oil	2.805
FFA content	%	1.41
Density	g/cm³	0.897

Source: Author

a

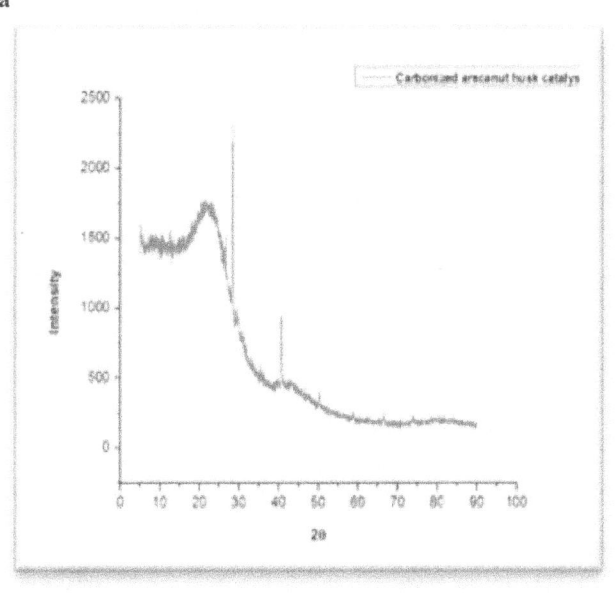

b

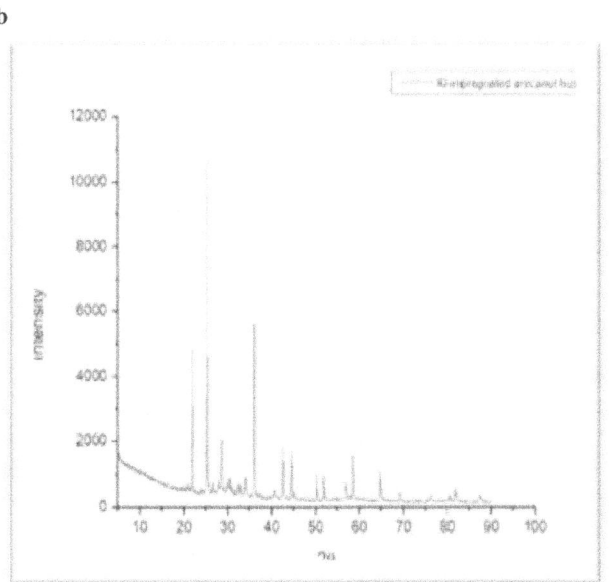

Figure 10.2 XRD analysis (a) Carbonized areca nut husk, (b) KI impregnated areca nut catalyst
Source: Author

a

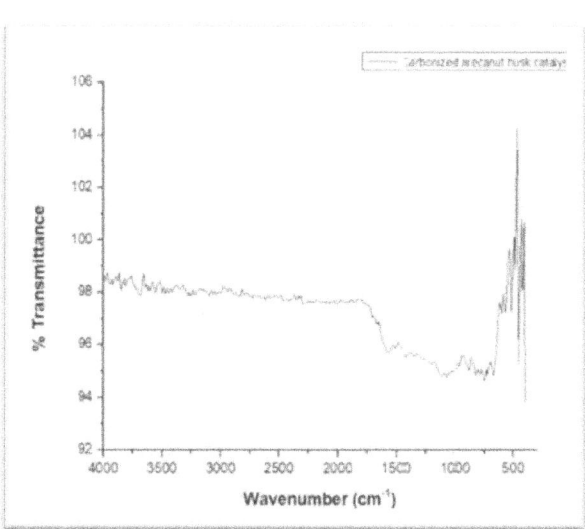

b

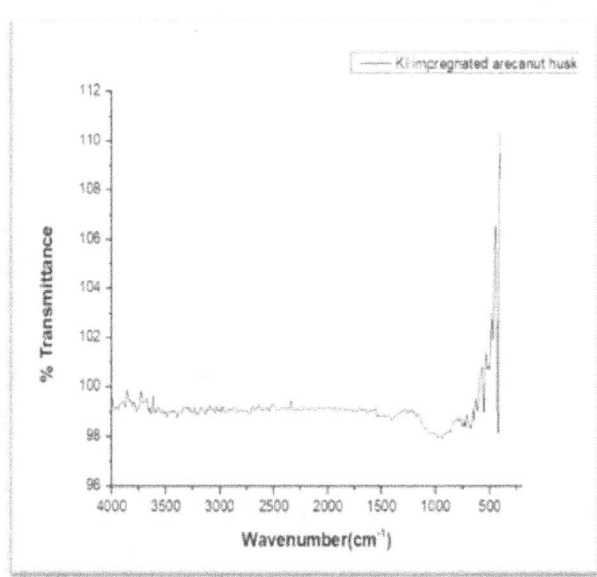

Figure 10.3 FTIR pattern of areca nut husk (a) Carbonized areca nut husk, (b) KI impregnated areca nut husk catalyst
Source: Author

indicating the presence of metal-halogen bonds, specifically K–I vibrations. A broad but weaker peak in the 3000–3600 cm^{-1} region indicated a reduction in O–H groups. Overall, impregnation with KI altered the catalyst surface by reducing light-absorbing functional groups, which may enhance catalytic performance.

Biodiesel characterization through nuclear magnetic resonance

The transesterification reaction was carried out using 25 g of WCO, 12 ml of methanol, and 0.6 g of KI-impregnated areca nut husk catalyst in an ultrasonic bath for 60 minutes. The ^{1}H-NMR spectrum of the resulting methyl esters is shown in Figure 10.4. A significant peak at 3.65 ppm corresponds to methoxy protons (–OCH3) confirmed biodiesel. Another significant peak at 2.3 ppm was assigned to α-methylene protons (–CH2–COO–) adjacent to the carbonyl group. These peaks confirmed the

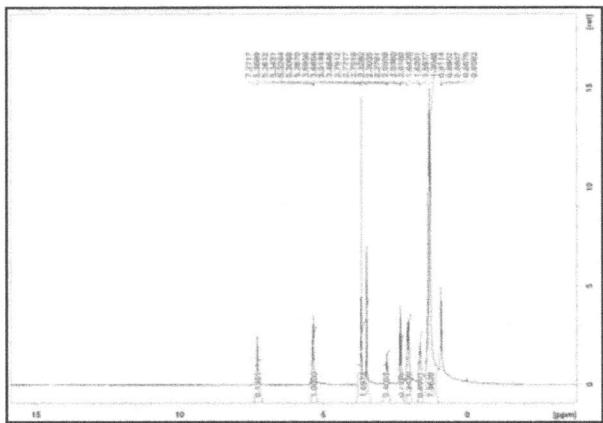

Figure 10.4 ¹H NMR spectra of biodiesel
Source: Author.

successful conversion of WCO into biodiesel. The conversion efficiency was calculated using the NMR peak area ratio formula and was found to be 93.8%, indicating the effectiveness of the KI-impregnated areca nut husk catalyst under ultrasound-assisted conditions.

Conclusion

The rising global demand for sustainable and renewable energy has driven extensive research into biodiesel as an alternative fuel due to its environmental compatibility and biodegradability. In this study, biodiesel was successfully produced from waste cooking oil using an ultrasound-assisted transesterification process with a KI-impregnated areca nut husk-derived heterogeneous catalyst. Characterization studies such as XRD and FTIR confirmed the presence of crystalline structures and functional groups responsible for catalytic activity, particularly highlighting the successful incorporation of potassium-based compounds. ¹H NMR analysis revealed a high biodiesel conversion efficiency of 93.8%. These findings suggest that KI doped areca nut husk-derived catalysts can be used as an effective biomass derived heterogeneous catalyst in biodiesel production.

References

[1] Anuar, M. F., Fen, Y. W., Azizan, M. Z., Rahmat, F. I., Zaid, M. H. M., Khaidir, R. E. M., et al. (2021). Sustainable production of arecanut husk ash as potential silica replacement for synthesis of silicate-based glass-ceramics materials. *Materials*, 14(1), 1141.

[2] Ao, S., Changmai, B., Vanlalveni, C., Chhandama, M. V. L., Wheatley, A. E., & Rokhum, S. L. (2024). Biomass waste-derived catalysts for biodiesel production: Recent advances and key challenges. *Renewable Energy*, 223, 120031.

[3] Badday, A. S., Abdullah, A. Z., Lee, K. T., & Khayoon, M. S. (2012). Intensification of biodiesel production via ultrasonic-assisted process: a critical review on fundamentals and recent development. *Renewable and Sustainable Energy Reviews*, 16(7), 4574–4587.

[4] Banković–Ilić, I. B., Miladinović, M. R., Stamenković, O. S., & Veljković, V. B. (2017). Application of nano CaO–based catalysts in biodiesel synthesis. *Renewable and Sustainable Energy Reviews*, 72, 746–760.

[5] Brahma, S., Nath, B., Basumatary, B., Das, B., Saikia, P., Patir, K., et al. (2022). Biodiesel production from mixed oils: a sustainable approach towards industrial biofuel production. *Chemical Engineering Journal Advances*, 10, 100284.

[6] Degfie, T. A., Mamo, T. T., & Mekonnen, Y. S. (2019). Optimized biodiesel production from waste cooking oil (WCO) using calcium oxide (CaO) nano-catalyst. *Scientific Reports*, 9(1), 18982.

[7] Koyunoğlu, C. (2024). Biofuel production utilizing black soldier fly (Hermetiaillucens): a sustainable approach for organic waste management. *International Journal of Thermofluids*, 23, 100754.

[8] Malani, R. S., Shinde, V., Ayachit, S., Goyal, A., & Moholkar, V. S. (2019). Ultrasound–assisted biodiesel production using heterogeneous base catalyst and mixed non–edible oils. *Ultrasonics Sonochemistry*, 52, 232–243.

[9] Mandari, V., & Devarai, S. K. (2022). Biodiesel production using homogeneous, heterogeneous, and enzyme catalysts via transesterification and esterification reactions: a critical review. *BioEnergy Research*, 15(2), 935–961.

[10] Morris, M. C. (1976). Standard X-ray Diffraction Powder Patterns: Section 13--data for 58 Substances (Vol. 25). US Department of Commerce, National Bureau of Standards.

[11] Nandiyanto, A. B. D., Ragadhita, R., & Fiandini, M. (2023). Interpretation of Fourier transform infrared spectra (FTIR): a practical approach in the polymer/plastic thermal decomposition. *Indonesian Journal of Science and Technology*, 8(1), 113–126.

[12] Stoytcheva, M., & Montero, G. (Eds.). (2011). Biodiesel: Feedstocks and Processing Technologies. BoD–Books on Demand.

[13] Yaakob, Z., Mohammad, M., Alherbawi, M., Alam, Z., & Sopian, K. (2013). Overview of the production of biodiesel from waste cooking oil. *Renewable and Sustainable Energy Reviews*, 18, 184–193.

[14] Zote, L., Lalrammawia, K., Buragohain, A., Lalrinhlupuii, Kakki, B., Lalmuanpuii, R., et al. (2021). Macro-, micro-, and trace element distributions in areca nut, husk, and soil of northeast India. *Environmental Monitoring and Assessment*, 193, 1–12.

[15] Zulqarnain, Mohd Yusoff, M. H., Ayoub, M., Ramzan, N., Nazir, M. H., Zahid, I., et al. (2021). Overview of feedstocks for sustainable biodiesel production and implementation of the biodiesel program in Pakistan. *ACS Omega*, 6(29), 19099–19114.

11 Transporter engineering using GadC for enhanced GABA secretion in yeast

Sharuprabhaa, S. A., Bala Arun, P. and C. Vignesh Kumar[a]

Department of Biotechnology, PSG college of Technology, Peelamedu, Coimbatore, India

Abstract

A non-proteinogenic amino acid, gamma-aminobutyric acid, finds widespread application in medications and functional foods. Gamma aminobutyric acid (GABA) has been proven to improve cognitive function, reduce blood pressure, and prevent seizures. The scalability and sustainability of GABA production is challenging through traditional techniques. GABA biosynthesis through Microbial systems like *Saccharomyces cerevisiae*, lactic acid bacteria, and *Escherichia coli* are viable alternative, which are being studied for their ability to produce GABA. *S. cerevisiae*, classified as Generally Regarded as Safe (GRAS), is a ideal candidate due to its significant fermentation capability, adaptability, well-characterized genetics and has well optimized gene manipulation techniques for metabolic engineering. The overall production of GABA is affected due to its intracellular accumulation and metabolic load caused by yeast's cell division limit the GABA export. Transporter engineering offers a solution by facilitating effective product export by targeting efficient export of GABA. GADC, a glutamate/GABA antiporter identified in *E. coli*, facilitates glutamate import and GABA export across membranes. The heterologous expression of GADC in the yeast will enhance the GABA secretion and reduce GABA toxicity inside the cell. This review highlights the strategies for the effective production of GABA and analyses the significance of transporter engineering, and its potential in metabolic engineering which allow the successful integration of GADC, an antiporter in yeast to develop efficient GABA-producing yeast for food and therapeutic applications.

Keywords: GABA, GADC, GRAS, *Saccharomyces cerevisiae*, transporter engineering

Introduction

A non-proteinogenic amino acid that has a crucial regulatory function in the central nervous system is γ-aminobutyric acid (GABA). The utility and versatility of GABA are demonstrated by its widespread usage in medications, functional foods, and even as a building block for bio plastics [2]. GABA is a effective neurotransmitter showing improved memory and sleep, blood pressure, and preventing seizures [8]. Biosynthesis of GABA is facilitated by converting L- glutamic acid enzymatically by Glutamate decarboxylase and a cofactor, pyridoxal-5'-phosphate (PLP). Conventiionally, GABA has been produced chemically or extracted from natural sources, but both methods have limitations in terms of scale up, affordability, and environmental toxicity. Recently, microbial systems like *Aspergillus*, yeast, *Escherichia coli*, and lactic acid bacteria (LAB) have gained popularity in alternative strategies for the synthesis of GABA [43]. The alternative strategies faces safety concerns, scalability, and stringent regulatory requirements, especially for food and pharmaceutical use. It is therefore necessary to develop a safe and efficient approach for producing GABA because it exhibits significant promise in both nutraceutical and pharmaceutical application.

Saccharomyces cerevisiae is one ideal organism to work with as it is considered to be Generally Regarded as Safe (GRAS). The extensive work on *Saccharomyces cerevisiae* allow as to access extensive information on genome-based data and optimized genetic manipulation, robust fermentation capabilities and its use as single cell protein, has made *S. cerevisiae* as a useful potential candidate for the numerous production processes with variety of applications and benefits [9]. The higher nutritional quality of yeast includes protein (45–55%), fat (2–6%), carbohydrates, vitamins, minerals and amino acids like lysine and methionine making it appropriate to use as single-cell proteins [22]. Many examples exist of using yeast as a cell factory to produce various chemicals, such as organic acids, carotenoids, hormones, and vaccines [23]. Existing approaches for GABA production include GAD overexpression, the use of L-glutamic acid or L-MSG as a precursor, and optimizing fermentation conditions. The *lactobacillus plantarum* strain 154 isolated from kimchi cultured using MRS broth with the addition of 3%

[a]cvk.bio@psgtech.ac.in

DOI: 10.1201/9781003770435-11

L-monosodium glutamate (MSG) produced GABA around 201.78 µg/ml [24].

E. coli strain BL21(DE3) engineered to express the GAD isolated from *S. cerevisiae* produced 245 g/L of GABA when 2.5g of L-glutamic acid was added every 6 hours to 50 ml reaction volume [41]. *Bacillus subtilis* BBEL02 produced GABA of 10.9 g/L by consuming a cost-effective nitrogen source of soybean hydrolysate [1]. *S. cerevisiae* SC125 was used to ferment Golden Delicious apples and observed GABA yield of 898.35 mg/L [34].

Transporter engineering focuses on engineering microorganisms with efficient transporters for the uptake of substrates and the export of desired products. This offers several advantages such as enhancing the product secretion into extracellular space reducing the complications in purification and downstream processing and production costs. It reduces feedback inhibition and cell toxicity due to intracellular accumulation and enhances microbial production [16]. GADC is a membrane-bound antiporter identified in *E. coli* that facilitates the import of glutamate and the export of GABA across cell membranes [20]. Recombinant *E. coli* Lemo21(DE3) co-expressing-*gadB* and *gadC* under a tunable promoter resulted in high GABA yield of 829.08 g/L after 3 fermentation cycles in 3 M L-glutamate solution [42].

The yeast GABA export is still inefficient, and the mechanisms regulating GABA export in engineered yeast systems are unclear. Although GABA export has been effectively improved in *E. coli* by the GadC antiporter, its functional expression and use in *Saccharomyces cerevisiae* hosts, bacterial transporters like GadC face major challenges caused by variations in membrane composition, protein folding, and localization mechanisms. This work fills in this important void by using a transporter engineering approach under a yeast-compatible promoter system for heterologous expression of a codon-optimized gadC gene. Further synthetic biology components seek to guarantee appropriate membrane integration and GadC's functionality in yeast by including expression tuning and localization tags. This approach reduces intracellular accumulation, feedback inhibition, and downstream processing complexity while simultaneously increasing production efficiency by enhancing GABA export. To the best of our knowledge, this is one of the earliest attempts to engineer the bacterial GadC transporter in yeast to secrete GABA. The heterologous expression of the GADC antiporter in *S. cerevisiae* will be the proficient strategy to enhance the GABA export and improve GABA yield in yeast-based production platforms.

Role of Transporters in Microbial Metabolite Secretion

Transporters are the membrane proteins that play crucial role in the movement of molecules across membranes. Targeting such Transporter in metabolic engineering will enhance the microbial cells in higher substrate intake, intermediates transport and product export as a extracellular component of the cell. Engineering such transporters can increase the uptake rates of substrates and enhance the production of target metabolite. Transporter engineering is also helpful in alternating low-cost substrates including organic solid waste, hydrolyzed biomass and industrial waste and facilitate the production of novel metabolites [27]. *S. cerevisiae* engineered to express Gal2p transporter coupled with xylose isomerase, increased the xylose uptake rate and enhanced ethanol production [36]. For product formation that includes multiple steps in microbial metabolic pathways, a significant obstacle is the leakage of intermediates. This drastically reduces product formation. By engineering a transporter to prevent intermediate leakage, productivity can be enhanced. Acyl-CoA precursors required for lipid production in *S. cerevisiae*, is carried away into peroxisomes by transporter Pxa1p and results in degradation by β-oxidation. Deletion of this transporter improved the precursor availability and lipid content to 14% in the cells [7]. Export of the product out of the cell by transporters reduces cell toxicity and feedback inhibition and increases product secretion and simplifies the purification process. FATP1, a transporter of fatty acid from humans, modified to express in *S. cerevisiae*, enhanced the extracellular secretion of 1-alkenes to 37% which is about 35.3 mg/L [50]. Examples of metabolic engineering in *S. cerevisiae* for production of various industrially important metabolites are summarized in Table 11.1. These examples demonstrate how transporter engineering can also be employed at multiple levels to optimize microbial production systems.

GadC– A Key GABA Transporter in Prokaryotes

E. coli O157:H7, a food-borne hemorrhagic bacteria, possesses sophisticated acid-resistance systems (ARs) to overcome extreme acidic conditions of about pH 2 in the stomach. The AR2 uptakes intracellular proton and converts to GABA by decarboxylation through the GAD enzyme and exchanges GABA with extracellular glutamate. This exchange is facilitated by GADC an amino acid antiporter that is specific to glutamate and GABA. It also transports glutamine and a smaller range of methionine and leucine. GADC is particularly active during the acid resistance mechanism and active at a pH of 6.0 or below. There are 12 TMs (Transmembrane segments) in GADC, and TM1 and TM5 each have two short α-helices linked by a discontinuous middle length. From TM1-TM5 and TM6-TM10, GADC contains 2 inverted repeats that are linked by a pseudo-two-fold axis. GADC has highly charged cytoplasmic and periplasmic sides [20]. In research, the importance of the *gadC* gene was examined under glutamate-mediated acid resistance. A *gadC* mutant in *E. coli* compared to wild-type *E. coli* at pH 2.5, lost resistance to acidic conditions. This demonstrates the importance of GADC in acid resistance mechanism [19]. Recombinant *E. coli* Lemo21(DE3) co-expressing *gadB* and *gadC* under tunable promoters of PBAD and PT7lacobtained high level of GABA of about 829.08 g/L after 3 fermentation cycles in 3 M L-glutamate solution at 37 °C [42]. *E. coli* XL1-Blue (XB), modified to express a synthetic protein complex, by linking *GAD A/B* with SH3 domain and GADC with SH3 ligand.

This allows co-localization of pathway enzymes in a specific space and co-expressing gadA and gadC with 10 g/L of MSG, yielded a GABA concentration of 5.65 g/L [17]. An *E. coli* strain ZGK12-TPE was engineered by the deletion of *gab*P (GABA permease) that utilizes extracellular GABA, *gab*T and *puu*E that encodes GABA transaminase which converts GABA to succinyl semialdehyde. This deletion in combination with overexpression of *gadA*, *gadB* and *gadC*, the strain yielded 19.79 g/L of GABA under optimized fermentation conditions [45]. While *S. cerevisiae* is a widely used platform for industrial biotechnology, it lacks an efficient native transporter for GABA export. This limits its ability to accumulate high extracellular concentrations of GABA, as intracellular GABA can be recycled into TCA cycle and used as nitrogen source and build-up may result in feedback inhibition and reduced productivity. Heterologous expression of GADC, an already-characterized and functionally efficient GABA/glutamate antiporter from *E. coli*, offers a promising strategy to overcome this limitation. By facilitating the export of GABA and simultaneous import of glutamate, GADC can potentially enhance the overall metabolic flux toward GABA production in yeast. Moreover, since GADC is active under acidic conditions and *S. cerevisiae* can tolerate mildly acidic environments,

Table 11.1 Metabolic engineering interventions in *S. cerevisiae* for the production of high-value metabolites

S. No	Strain	Metabolite enhanced and yield	References
1	*S. cerevisiae* CEN.PK102-5B	p-Coumaric acid, 1.93 g/L	[30]
2	*S. cerevisiae* BY4741	lactic acid, 5.5 g/L	[33]
3	*S. cerevisiae* CEN.PK2	Amorphadiene, 37 g/L	[40]
4	*S. cerevisiae* IMM007	Ethanol, 3.30 mol EtOH/ mol sucrose	[3]
5	*S. cerevisiae* AH22ura3	Succinic acid, 0.11 mol/ mol glucose	[28]
6	*S. cerevisiae* CEN.PK113-7D	Beta-carotene, 5.9 mg/g dry weight	[39]
7	*S. cerevisiae* CEN.PK113-7D	Pyruvic acid, 0.54 g pyruvate/g glucose	[38]
8	*S. cerevisiae* FY23	Resveratrol, 1.45 mg/ L	[4]
9	*S. cerevisiae* BY4743	Polyhydroxyalkanoates, 0.026% dry weight	[47]

Source: Author

this cross-species functional compatibility further supports its application in engineered yeast strains.

Engineering GadC in Yeast: Hypothetical Workflow

Optimizing *S. cerevisiae* to produce and export GABA requires modulation in the expression of a series of genes by recombinant DNA methods and optimization techniques like improving the expression level of GADC as a membrane protein to facilitate glutamate intake and GABA export. Glutamate is the major precursor for GABA biosynthesis in the GABA shunt pathway through the GAD gene. Glutamate supplementation additionally enhances the intracellular substrate availability and enhances GABA production. Overexpression of upstream genes in the GABA metabolic pathway, such as α-ketoglutarate can enhance the flux towards GABA production. Deletion of downstream gene such as GABA transaminase and succinyl semialdehyde dehydrogenase can reduce GABA retake into the TCA cycle by conversion into succinate. These key pathway interventions are illustrated in Figure 11.1. The detailed hypothetical workflow is explained in this section.

Saccharomyces cerevisiae strains

There are various *S. cerevisiae* strains used for metabolic engineering and research studies, including S288c, A634A, BY4716, CEN.PK, 1278B, SK1, BJ5464, BY4742, W303. The features of different strains are explained in Table 11.2. Among the various strains, BJ5464 is particularly favorable for heterologous protein expression. In research, GAD gene from *streptomyces sp.* was cloned and expressed in *S. cerevisiae* strain BJ5464 (ATCC 208288). Using whole-cell conversion of the strain under optimized conditions, the GABA titer reached around 62.6 g/L [46]. For scalable production, industrial strains like CEN.PK and W303 can also be evaluated. The strain should be selected based on expression stability, membrane targeting efficiency, and compatibility with downstream processing.

Use of expression vectors

Heterologous protein expression can be performed either by plasmid-based systems for preliminary studies or chromosomal integration for stable, long-term expression. An expression vector contains multiple cloning sites for heterologous gene insertion, promoter and terminator sequences, selection markers and tags for membrane proteins [5]. In the case of shuttle vectors, they can be transformed and selected in two different host species. Shuttle vectors that can be used for both *E. coli* and yeast, contain an origin of replication for *E. coli* and its suitable selection marker example ampicillin. For expression in yeast, it contains autonomously replicating sequence and yeast-specific selection markers like orotidine 5'-decarboxylase (URA3) and β-isopropylmalate dehydrogenase (LEU2). A shuttle vector is used to clone the target gene, which is then transformed in *E. coli* laboratory strains like DH5α. The positively cloned vectors are used for expression in Yeast system [6]. For the target gene expression in yeast, several yeast vectors can be used like yeast episomal plasmid (YEp), yeast integrative plasmid (YIp), and yeast replicative plasmid (YRP). These vectors have their own advantages and disadvantages for the expression in yeast. Suitable vectors with minimum advantage can be selected based on its features. YEp vectors belong to 2 μm yeast plasmid which has a property of autonomous replication and has high leads to high copy number of this vector. But, It is less stable without the selective pressure/marker [15]. The low copy number like yIP are very stable and extremely useful for chromosomal integration by heterologous recombination at targeted sites in the host. yRP vectors are another class of vectors used in yeast expression system which maintain a low to moderate copy number of plasmids in the cell and maintains moderate stability. This includes a pRS series of vectors with a variety of promoters and markers [6]. These shuttle vectors like pRS or pPS series can be used to express codon-optimized GADC targeting the export of intercellular GABA. But, genomic integration of optimistic construct will be widely preferred using YIP-based systems.

Use of promoters

Promoters are the drivers the expression of genes and the function of promoters are exploited for the expression of foreign gene in expression vectors. This promoter will assist in controlled expression of target genes and other modulators like enhancer and repressors play crucial role in promoter driven expression. Promoters can be inducible or constitutive based on the context of the gene expression. The inducible promoters have an advantage over constitutive promoters by controlling the gene expression levels in response to specific inducers or repressors. The Constitutive promoter has an advantage of a stable expression of target gene and does not influenced by other factors partly as like inducible promoters [25]. Constitutive promoters including TEF1, PGK1, GAPDH, PYK1 and ADH1 are involved in the continuous synthesis of target gene in uncontrolled fashion [25]. For stable and strong expression in industry-scale production, these promoters are preferred provided the overexpression of the targeted shows minimal toxicity to the host. Inducible promoters such as yeast GAL1, are the promoter for the expression of Galactokinase enzyme. This promoter is activated by the higher accumulation of galactose and glucose will act as a strong repressor for this promoter. In rDNA technology, Expression of proteins/genes under GAL1 promoter will depends on the concentration of galactose and absence of glucose. This allow us to precisely control gene expression, which is especially helpful for producing proteins like GADC, that when overexpressed. The foreign gene overexpression in the yeast or other organism shows catastrophic effect, possibly leading to cellular toxicity and results in impaired cell growth and survival. CUP1 (copper-inducible) and ADH2 (alcohol-inducible), AOX1 (methanol-inducible) are other examples of inducible promoters Mumberg et al. [21] which can regulate the gene expression level to overcome the cellular toxicity and cell survival. Yuan et al. [46]

had used ADH2, an inducible promoter and overexpress Glutamate Decarboxylase (GadC) for GABA production. For initial characterization of *gadC* expression and GABA production, inducible promoter can be used with regulated expression levels of target enzyme (GadC) and analyze its potential cellular toxicity. Once functionality is confirmed, TEF1 or PGK1 can be used for the expression of antiporter for continuous GABA export in selected strain under suitable fermentation conditions.

Use of membrane integration tags and membrane localization of GADC

GadC is a novel membrane transporter which facilitates the export of GABA and import of glutamate during cell division. The membrane integration of over expressed GadC plays pivotal role in GABA export. The expression of the transporter proteins with membrane integration tags or signal peptides direct the protein through the cellular trafficking pathway and facilitate its incorporation into the plasma membrane. Signal peptides acts as a guide sequence for the recombinant protein to the secretory pathway and release or localize the protein to its respective compartment. For example, α-mating factor (α-MF) or N-terminal ER targeting tags are the most used as secretary tags for releasing the proteins into extracellular space [13]. FATP1, human fatty acid transporter was engineered and codon optimized to express in yeast, which is tagged to Green Fluorescent Protein (GFP) improves the stability of the protein which

Table 11.2 Characteristics of selected *S. cerevisiae* strains in research and industrial applications

Strain	Features	Reference
S288c	Common reference strain, includes limitations such as low sporulation rate, unable to grow in maltose and inability to form filaments on conditions lacking nitrogen	[31]
A634A	Derived from S288c and is employed in cell cycle research	[31]
BY4716	Equivalent to S288c. used as reference strain	[31]
W303	Utilized in genetic and biochemical research	[31]
CEN.PK	Utilized in cell growth and product production studies	[37]
BJ5464	Majorly used for expression of recombinant proteins	[44]

Source: Author

successfully expresses the transporter and secretes fatty alcohols [10]. Addition of membrane-targeting tags to GadC enhances the membrane localization of the target protein improves productivity.

Metabolic pathway optimization

GABA production is driven by the GAD enzyme, which converts glutamate into GABA and this takes place in the cytoplasm. Recombinant *E. coli* Lemo21(DE3) co-expressing *gadB* and *gadC* under a tunable promoter obtained a high yield of GABA of about 829.08 g/L after 3 fermentation cycles in 3 M L-glutamate solution [42]. For enhanced GABA production, co-expressing GAD along with GADC will be a suitable engineering strategy.

Glutamate is a major precursor for GABA production from GAD. All research studies related to GABA supplemented L-MSG or L-glutamic acid to improve GABA production. Enhancing glutamate availability increases GABA biosynthetic flux [41, 42, 17, 45].

GABA is also consumed as a nitrogen source by converting into succinyl semialdehyde. Downregulation or knockouts of downstream gene also are a considerable method to enhance GABA production. In *Corynebacterium glutamicum* (ATCC13032) strain, 2-oxoglutarate dehydrogenase which converts 2-oxoglutarate to succinate in the TCA cycle and 4-aminobutyrate aminotransferase which converts GABA to succinyl semialdehyde in the GABA shunt were knocked out, resulting in 6.90 g/L of GABA [48]. GABA synthesis from GAD also requires the cofactor pyridoxal-5'-phosphate (PLP), which is also optimized for enhanced GABA production in previous studies [41]. Hence ensuring sufficient cofactor supplementation is also necessary. Thus, engineering yeast for GADC expression for enhanced GABA secretion also requires optimization of upstream and downstream metabolic pathways along with optimization of fermentation conditions, including carbon and nitrogen sources, pH, temperature, and precursor and cofactor availability.

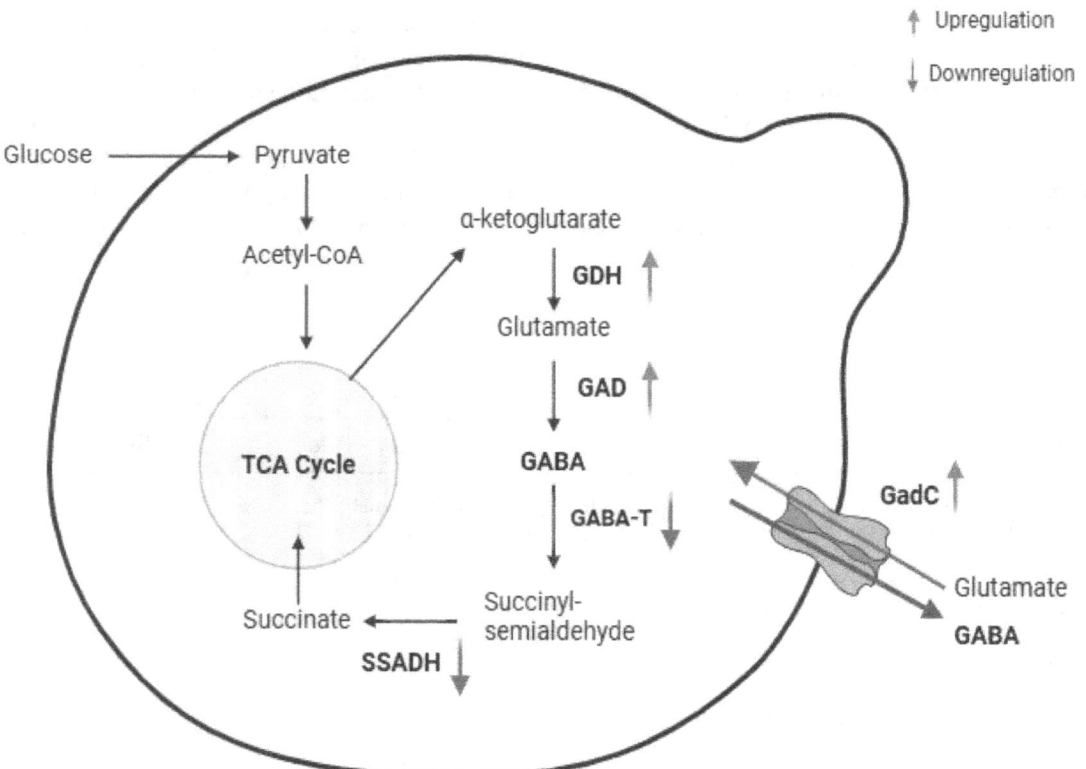

Figure 11.1 Engineering *S. cerevisiae* for enhanced GABA production by GADC expression: Targeting GADC - glutamate/GABA antiporter, GDH - glutamate dehydrogenase; GAD -glutamate decarboxylase for overexpression (red arrow) and GABA-T - GABA transaminase, SSADH - succinate-semialdehyde dehydrogenase downregulation (blue arrow) for enhanced production of GABA

Source: Author

Benefits of Producing GABA in Yeast

Yeast, itself is a wonderful single cell protein, the producing GABA in yeast will enhance the nutritional quality of yeast as SCP and finds application as food and nutraceutical supplements.

GABA enriched functional foods

GABA producing yeast can be used to enhance the nutritional quality of food products and nutraceutical industry. In FMCG industries, it has huge potential in the fortification of various products such as cereal-based products, wheat sourdough, cereal bran flakes, wheat germ, barley bran and brown rice which were enriched with GABA [29, 12, 11]. In dairy products, GABA is preferred as fortification agent for the products like cheese, yogurt and fermented milk Pouliot-Mathieu [26], Liu et al. [18] and Beverages such as white tea, black raspberry juice and fruit juice were enhanced their quality by the addition of GABA [49, 14, 35]. The fermentation of Golden Delicious apples by *S. cerevisiae* SC125 strain allow the accumulation of GABA which has been used in therapeutic applications [34]. Thus, enhanced GABA levels in food products offer potential health benefits and using GABA-producing yeast is an additional advantage, as it is GRAS and used in the production of food products.

Single cell protein (SCP)

The higher nutritional quality of yeast includes protein (45–55%), fat (2–6%), carbohydrates, vitamins, minerals and amino acids like lysine and methionine, making it appropriate to use as single-cell proteins. Larger size, reduced nucleic acid content, higher lysine content, low cost of manufacturing, and acidic pH growth are some of the benefits of yeast [22]. Yeast with enriched GABA finds potential pharmaceutical application when used as SCP.

Dietary food supplement

When GABA-enriched algae were administered to humans via oral administration of about 20 mg of GABA for a time period of 12 weeks, it significantly reduced blood pressure in humans. This demonstrated the antihypertensive effect of GABA [32]. Breakfast cereals enriched with GABA, lowered blood pressure when consumed a single portion containing 30g of GABA [12]. GABA produced from

yeast finds application as a dietary supplement. GABA-producing yeast can also be dried and used as probiotic supplementation.

With a wide range of applications in health, nutrition and industrial biotechnology, GABA-producing *S. cerevisiae* represents a promising platform for the development of next generation of functional and bioactive products.

Future Perspectives

Transporter engineering is a promising but underutilized strategy in metabolic engineering. Enhancing enzyme expression and precursor availability received a lot of attention in strain development and recently transporter engineering is being recognized and utilized in enhancing product secretion and yield. Engineering GADC transporter in yeast to improve GABA export demonstrates the feasibility of heterologous transporter expression in yeast systems. Transporters for a variety of metabolites of economic importance can be incorporated into this approach. Products such as organic acids (succinate, malate), amino acids (lysine, arginine) and biofuels (ethanol, butanol) cause product toxicity by intracellular accumulation. In this context, modification of particular transporters significantly improves yield and eases downstream processing.

In addition, the development of synthetic or chimeric transporters with optimized selectivity, stability, and membrane compatibility has become feasible due to advances in synthetic biology, protein design, and high-throughput screening. Rational transporter selection and integration into metabolic pathways can be further facilitated by combining transporter engineering with computational approaches like flux balance analysis (FBA) and machine learning-based prediction. In the future, transporter engineering will probably be an essential aspect of strain optimization at the systems level, augmenting conventional metabolic engineering techniques. Green bio-manufacturing, pharmaceutical biosynthesis, functional food development, and synthetic microbial consortia can all benefit from the use of GABA-producing yeast as a model system to evaluate transporter efficiency.

Conclusion

Optimal metabolic pathways and efficient transport systems are crucial for the synthesis and export of bioactive compounds like GABA. To enhance GABA export and combat intracellular accumulation, the potential of transporter engineering for heterologous expression of GADC antiporter in yeast from *E. coli* was highlighted as a strategy. A robust GABA-producing yeast platform can be developed by integrating GADC transporter expression with suitable vector systems, pathway optimization, codon adaptation, and membrane integration.

In addition to promoting high-yield GABA biosynthesis, this strategy lays a foundation for extending transporter engineering to additional metabolites that are important to industry. Transporter systems will be a key component of next-generation microbial cell factories as synthetic biology develops further, allowing for increased productivity, product recovery, and scalability in the food, feed, health, and chemical production fields.

References

[1] Asun, A. C., Lin, S. T., Ng, H. S., & Lan, J. C. W. (2022). Production of gamma-aminobutyric acid (GABA) by *Bacillus subtilis* BBEL02 fermentation using nitrogen-rich industrial wastes as crude feedstocks. *Biochemical Engineering Journal*, 187, 108654.

[2] Awapara, J. (1950). Occurrence of free gamma-aminobutyric acid in brain and its formation from L-glutamic acid. *Texas Reports on Biology and Medicine*, 8(4), 443–447.

[3] Basso, T. O., de Kok, S., Dario, M., do Espirito-Santo, J. C. A., Müller, G., Schlölg, P. S., et al. (2011). Engineering topology and kinetics of sucrose metabolism in *Saccharomyces cerevisiae* for improved ethanol yield. *Metabolic Engineering*, 13(6), 694–703.

[4] Becker, J., Armstrong, G., Vandermerwe, M., Lambrechts, M., Vivier, M., & Pretorius, I. (2003). Metabolic engineering of for the synthesis of the wine-related antioxidant resveratrol. *FEMS Yeast Research*, 4(1), 79–85.

[5] Çelik, E., & Çalık, P. (2012). Production of recombinant proteins by yeast cells. *Biotechnology Advances*, 30(5), 1108–1118.

[6] Chou, C. C., Patel, M. T., & Gartenberg, M. R. (2015). A series of conditional shuttle vectors for targeted genomic integration in budding yeast. *FEMS Yeast Research*, 15(3), fov010.

[7] Ferreira, R., Teixeira, P. G., Gossing, M., David, F., Siewers, V., & Nielsen, J. (2018). Metabolic engineering of *Saccharomyces cerevisiae* for overproduction of triacylglycerols. *Metabolic Engineering Communications*, 6, 22–27.

[8] Hepsomali, P., Groeger, J. A., Nishihira, J., & Scholey, A. (2020). Effects of oral gamma-aminobutyric acid (GABA) administration on stress and sleep in humans: a systematic review. *Frontiers in Neuroscience*, 14, 559962.

[9] Hong, K. K., & Nielsen, J. (2012). Metabolic engineering of *Saccharomyces cerevisiae*: a key cell factory platform for future biorefineries. *Cellular and Molecular Life Sciences*, 69, 2671–2690.

[10] Hu, Y., Zhu, Z., Nielsen, J., & Siewers, V. (2018). Heterologous transporter expression for improved fatty alcohol secretion in yeast. *Metabolic Engineering*, 45, 51–58.

[11] Jin, W. J., Kim, M. J., & Kim, K. S. (2013). Utilization of barley or wheat bran to bioconvert glutamate to γ-aminobutyric acid (GABA). *Journal of Food Science*, 78(9), C1376–C1382.

[12] Joye, I. J., Lamberts, L., Brijs, K., & Delcour, J. A. (2011). In situ production of γ-aminobutyric acid in breakfast cereals. *Food Chemistry*, 129(2), 395–401.

[13] Julius, D., Blair, L., Brake, A., Sprague, G., & Thorner, J. (1983). Yeast α factor is processed from a larger precursor polypeptide: the essential role of a membrane-bound dipeptidyl aminopeptidase. *Cell*, 32(3), 839–852.

[14] Kim, J. Y., Lee, M. Y., Ji, G. E., Lee, Y. S., & Hwang, K. T. (2009). Production of γ-aminobutyric acid in black raspberry juice during fermentation by *Lactobacillus brevis* GABA100. *International Journal of Food Microbiology*, 130(1), 12–16.

[15] Kojo, H., Greenberg, B. D., & Sugino, A. (1981). Yeast 2-micrometer plasmid DNA replication in vitro: origin and direction. *Proceedings of the National Academy of Sciences*, 78(12), 7261–7265.

[16] Korosh, T. C., Markley, A. L., Clark, R. L., McGinley, L. L., McMahon, K. D., & Pfleger, B. F. (2017). Engineering photosynthetic production of L-lysine. *Metabolic Engineering*, 44, 273–283.

[17] Le Vo, T. D., Ko, J. S., Park, S. J., Lee, S. H., & Hong, S. H. (2013). Efficient gamma-aminobutyric acid bioconversion by employing synthetic complex between glutamate decarboxylase and glutamate/GABA antiporter in engineered *Escherichia coli*. *Journal of Industrial Microbiology and Biotechnology*, 40(8), 927–933.

[18] Liu, C. F., Tung, Y. T., Wu, C. L., Lee, B. H., Hsu, W. H., & Pan, T. M. (2011). Antihypertensive effects of Lactobacillus-fermented milk orally administered to spontaneously hypertensive rats. *Journal of Agricultural and Food Chemistry*, 59(9), 4537–4543.

[19] Lu, P., Ma, D., Chen, Y., Guo, Y., Chen, G. Q., Deng, H., et al. (2013). L-glutamine provides acid resistance for *Escherichia coli* through enzymatic release of ammonia. *Cell Research*, 23(5), 635–644.

[20] Ma, D., Lu, P., Yan, C., Fan, C., Yin, P., Wang, J., et al. (2012). Structure and mechanism of a glutamate–GABA antiporter. *Nature*, 483(7391), 632–636.

[21] Mumberg, D., Müller, R., & Funk, M. (1994). Regulatable promoters of *Saccharomyces cerevisiae*: comparison of transcriptional activity and their use for heterologous expression. *Nucleic Acids Research*, 22(25), 5767.

[22] Nasseri, A. T., Rasoul-Amini, S., Morowvat, M. H., & Ghasemi, Y. (2011). Single cell protein: production and process. *American Journal of Food Technology*, 6(2), 103–116.

[23] Nielsen, J., & Jewett, M. C. (2008). Impact of systems biology on metabolic engineering of *Saccharomyces cerevisiae*. *FEMS Yeast Research*, 8(1), 122–131.

[24] Park, S. Y., Lee, J. W., & Lim, S. D. (2014). The probiotic characteristics and GABA production of *Lactobacillus plantarum* K154 isolated from kimchi. *Food Science and Biotechnology*, 23, 1951–1957.

[25] Partow, S., Siewers, V., Bjørn, S., Nielsen, J., & Maury, J. (2010). Characterization of different promoters for designing a new expression vector in *Saccharomyces cerevisiae*. *Yeast*, 27(11), 955–964.

[26] Pouliot-Mathieu, K., Gardner-Fortier, C., Lemieux, S., St-Gelais, D., Champagne, C. P., & Vuillemard, J. C. (2013). Effect of cheese containing gamma-aminobutyric acid-producing lactic acid bacteria on blood pressure in men. *PharmaNutrition*, 1(4), 141–148.

[27] Protzko, R. J., Latimer, L. N., Martinho, Z., de Reus, E., Seibert, T., Benz, J. P., et al. (2018). Engineering *Saccharomyces cerevisiae* for co-utilization of d-galacturonic acid and d-glucose from citrus peel waste. *Nature Communications*, 9(1), 5059.

[28] Raab, A. M., Gebhardt, G., Bolotina, N., Weuster-Botz, D., & Lang, C. (2010). Metabolic engineering of *Saccharomyces cerevisiae* for the biotechnological production of succinic acid. *Metabolic Engineering*, 12(6), 518–525.

[29] Rizzello, C. G., Cassone, A., Di Cagno, R., & Gobbetti, M. (2008). Synthesis of angiotensin I-converting enzyme (ACE)-inhibitory peptides and γ-aminobutyric acid (GABA) during sourdough fermentation by selected lactic acid bacteria. *Journal of Agricultural and Food Chemistry*, 56(16), 6936–6943.

[30] Rodriguez, A., Kildegaard, K. R., Li, M., Borodina, I., & Nielsen, J. (2015). Establishment of a yeast platform strain for production of p-coumaric acid through metabolic engineering of aromatic amino acid biosynthesis. *Metabolic Engineering*, 31, 181–188.

[31] Schacherer, J., Ruderfer, D. M., Gresham, D., Dolinski, K., Botstein, D., & Kruglyak, L. (2007) Genome-wide analysis of nucleotide-level variation in commonly used *Saccharomyces cerevisiae* strains. *PloS One*, 2(3), e322.

[32] Shimada, M., Hasegawa, T., Nishimura, C., Kan, H., Kanno, T., Nakamura, T., et al. (2009). Anti-hypertensive effect of γ-aminobutyric acid (GABA)-rich Chlorella on high-normal blood pressure and borderline hypertension in placebo-controlled double-blind study. *Clinical and Experimental Hypertension*, 31(4), 342–354.

[33] Sugiyama, M., Akase, S. P., Nakanishi, R., Kaneko, Y., & Harashima, S. (2016). Overexpression of ESBP6 improves lactic acid resistance and production in *Saccharomyces cerevisiae*. *Journal of Bioscience and Bioengineering*, 122(4), 415–420.

[34] Sun, X., Wang, J., Li, C., Zheng, M., Zhang, Q., Xiang, W., et al. (2022). The use of γ-aminobutyric acid-producing *Saccharomyces cerevisiae* SC125 for functional fermented beverage production from apple juice. *Foods*, 11(9), 1202.

[35] Tamura, T., Noda, M., Ozaki, M., Maruyama, M., Matoba, Y., Kumagai, T., et al. (2010). Establishment of an efficient fermentation system of gamma-aminobutyric acid by a lactic acid bacterium, *Enterococcus avium* G-15, isolated from carrot leaves. *Biological and Pharmaceutical Bulletin*, 33(10), 1673–1679.

[36] Thomik, T., Wittig, I., Choe, J. Y., Boles, E., & Oreb, M. (2017). An artificial transport metabolon facilitates improved substrate utilization in yeast. *Nature Chemical Biology*, 13(11), 1158–1163.

[37] Van Dijken, J. P., Bauer, J., Brambilla, L., Duboc, P., Francois, J. M., Gancedo, C., et al. (2000). An interlaboratory comparison of physiological and genetic properties of four *Saccharomyces cerevisiae* strains. *Enzyme and Microbial Technology*, 26(9–10), 706–714.

[38] Van Maris, A. J. A., Geertman, J. A., Vermeulen, A., Groothuizen, M. K., Winkler, A. A., Piper, M. D. W., et al. (2004). Directed evolution of pyruvate decarboxylase-negative *Saccharomyces cerevisiae*, yielding a C 2-independent, glucose-tolerant, and pyruvate-hyperproducing yeast. *Applied and Environmental Microbiology*, 70(1), 159–166.

[39] Verwaal, R., Wang, J., Meijnen, J. P., Visser, H., Sandmann, G., Van den Berg, J. A., et al. (2007). High-level production of beta-carotene in *Saccharomyces cerevisiae* by successive transformation with carotenogenic genes from Xanthophyllomycesdendrorhous. *Applied and Environmental Microbiology*, 73(13), 4342–4350.

[40] Westfall, P. J., Pitera, D. J., Lenihan, J. R., Eng, D., Woolard, F. X., Regentin, R., et al. (2012). Production of amorphadiene in yeast, and its conversion to dihydroartemisinic acid, precursor to the antimalarial agent artemisinin. *Proceedings of the National Academy of Sciences*, 109(3), E111–E118.

[41] Xiong, Q., Xu, Z., Xu, L., Yao, Z., Li, S., & Xu, H. (2017). Efficient production of γ-GABA using recombinant *E. coli* expressing glutamate decarboxylase (GAD) derived from eukaryote *Saccharomyces cerevisiae*. *Applied Biochemistry and Biotechnology*, 183, 1390–1400.

[42] Yao, L., Lyu, C., Wang, Y., Hu, S., Zhao, W., Cao, H., et al. (2023). High-level production of γ-aminobutyric acid via efficient co-expression of the key genes of glutamate decarboxylase system in *Escherichia coli*. *Engineering Microbiology*, 3(2), 100077.

[43] Yogeswara, I. B. A., Maneerat, S., & Haltrich, D. (2020). Glutamate decarboxylase from lactic acid bacteria—A key enzyme in GABA synthesis. *Microorganisms*, 8(12), 1923.

[44] Young, C. L., Raden, D. L., & Robinson, A. S. (2013). Analysis of ER resident proteins in *Saccharomyces cerevisiae*: implementation of H/KDEL retrieval sequences. *Traffic*, 14(4), 365–381.

[45] Yu, P., Ren, Q., Wang, X., & Huang, X. (2019). Enhanced biosynthesis of γ-aminobutyric acid (GABA) in *Escherichia coli* by pathway engineering. *Biochemical Engineering Journal*, 141, 252–258.

[46] Yuan, H., Zhang, W., Xiao, G., & Zhan, J. (2020). Efficient production of gamma-aminobutyric acid by engineered *Saccharomyces cerevisiae* with glutamate decarboxylases from *Streptomyces*. *Biotechnology and Applied Biochemistry*, 67(2), 240–248.

[47] Zhang, B., Carlson, R., & Srienc, F. (2006). Engineering the monomer composition of polyhydroxyalkanoates synthesized in *Saccharomyces cerevisiae*. *Applied and Environmental Microbiology*, 72(1), 536–543.

[48] Zhang, Y., Zhao, J., Wang, X., Tang, Y., Liu, S., & Wen, T. (2022). Model-guided metabolic rewiring for gamma-aminobutyric acid and butyrolactam biosynthesis in *Corynebacterium glutamicum* ATCC13032. *Biology*, 11(6), 846.

[49] Zhao, M., Ma, Y., Wei, Z. Z., Yuan, W. X., Li, Y. L., Zhang, C. H., et al. (2011). Determination and comparison of γ-aminobutyric acid (GABA) content in pu-erh and other types of Chinese tea. *Journal of Agricultural and Food Chemistry*, 59(8), 3641–3648.

[50] Zhou, Y. J., Hu, Y., Zhu, Z., Siewers, V., & Nielsen, J. (2018). Engineering 1-alkene biosynthesis and secretion by dynamic regulation in yeast. *ACS Synthetic Biology*, 7(2), 584–590.

12 siRNA design against DNMT1 overexpressed in triple-negative breast cancer patients

Karthikasri, K.[1,a] and Shobana Sundar[2,b]

[1]Post-graduate student, Department of Biotechnology, PSG College of Technology, Coimbatore, India

[2]Assistant Professor, Department of Biotechnology, PSG College of Technology, Coimbatore, India

Abstract

Triple-negative breast cancer (TNBC) lacks targeted therapies, this is due to the absence of estrogen, progesterone, and HER2 receptors, making it necessary to develop alternative approaches for the treatment of the disease. Therefore, in this article a comprehensive computational strategy was developed to design siRNA therapeutics targeting an oncogene, DNMT1 upregulated in TNBC patients. DNMT1 plays several roles in the development of tumors in TNBC cancer. siRNAs were designed to target DNMT1 mRNA and verified for their in-silico specificity, secondary structure stability, target binding, and activity profiling. Among the five siRNAs, one of the siRNA candidates showed a high predicted efficacy score and favorable docking interactions with the human AGO2 protein. Overall, this in-silico approach was successful in identifying a promising siRNA therapeutic candidate for targeting DNMT1 and potentially inhibiting TNBC through RNA interference.

Keywords: DNMT1, molecular docking, siRNA therapeutics, target prediction, Triple-negative breast cancer

Introduction

Cancer extends to more than 200 molecular subtypes [21]. Among all the molecular subtypes, breast cancer is the most diagnosed one in the female population [18]. Classification of breast cancer is based on the presence or absence of estrogen (ER), progesterone (PR), and human epidermal growth factor 2 (HER2) receptors, leading to three main subtypes: Hormone Receptor-Positive (HR+), HER2-positive, and triple-negative [17]. Among all the subtypes, the triple-negative breast cancer (TNBC) is the most aggressive breast cancer subtype. TNBC is characterized by the absence of all the three receptors – ER, PR and HER2 Chen and Russo [6] and accounts for approximately 15–20% of breast cancer cases, associated with poor prognosis and limited therapeutic options [22]. The five-year survival rate for metastatic TNBC remains significantly lower than that of other breast cancer subtypes Baranova et al. [3], implying the urgent need for innovative treatment options for TNBC.

DNA methyltransferases (DNMTs) catalyze the addition of methyl groups to the 5-carbon position of cytosine in DNA, using S-adenosyl-L-methionine (SAM) as the methyl donor [8]. This enzyme family consists of four primary members: DNMT1,
DNMT3A, DNMT3B, and DNMT3L, each with distinct roles in establishing and maintaining DNA methylation patterns. Among these members, DNA methyltransferase 1 (DNMT1) has gained attention as a potential molecular target in TNBC [23]. It plays a key role in epigenetic dysregulation, development of tumors and progression in several cancer types. DNMT1 is mainly responsible for preserving DNA methylation patterns during cell replication and it has been increasingly implicated in cancer development, metastasis, and treatment resistance. Recent epidemiological and molecular studies have revealed a strong correlation between DNMT1 overexpression and aggressive tumor phenotypes in multiple cancer types, with particularly enhanced effects in TNBC [7, 23, 25].

DNMT1 contributes to TNBC pathogenesis by several mechanisms including the Epigenetic silencing of tumor suppressor genes, Modulation of cellular proliferation and survival pathways, Promoting metastasis and Enhancement of chemotherapeutic resistance. DNMT1 overexpression in TNBC cell lines also correlates with increased genomic instability and reduced DNA repair mechanisms. It has also been found that targeted DNMT1 inhibition could

[a]karthikasri.k25@gmail.com, [b]sbs.bio@psgtech.ac.in

DOI: 10.1201/9781003770435-12

reverse aberrant methylation patterns and potentially restore normal gene expression profiles.

Synthetic RNA duplexes known as small interfering RNAs (siRNAs) are engineered to selectively bind and induce degradation of specific target messenger RNAs. This technology offers a promising approach to precisely target and silence DNMT1 expression. Previous studies have demonstrated the potential of RNA interference in modulating epigenetic regulators [15]. Successful downregulation of DNMT1 using siRNA technology in ovarian cancer models has shown significant reductions in tumor cell proliferation. Additionally, DNMT1 silencing has been found to enhance sensitivity to conventional chemotherapeutic agents in breast cancer cell lines. This provides us with compelling evidence for the therapeutic potential of this approach.

However, most of the RNA molecules are inherently unstable and susceptible to degradation by nucleases in biological fluids. Despite advances in siRNA technology, significant challenges remain in delivering these molecules effectively to target tissues. To shield siRNA from nuclease degradation while improving cellular uptake, lipid nanoparticles (LNPs) have emerged as effective carriers [9]. Besides LNPs, the field has introduced various innovative strategies, including polymer-based nanocarriers, aptamer-siRNA conjugates, and antibody-siRNA conjugates.

Numerous studies on breast cancer have shown effective delivery of therapeutic siRNAs using targeted nanoparticles [2]. Transferrin-modified liposomes have been created to facilitate the siRNA delivery to breast cancer cells that overexpress transferrin receptors [1]. Also, hyaluronic acid-coated chitosan nanoparticles that specifically target CD44 receptors overexpressed on the surfaces of TNBC cells have been employed to effectively deliver siRNAs to triple-negative breast cancer cells.

Promising results for siRNA therapeutics in various diseases, including cancer, have been demonstrated in recent clinical trials. The FDA's 2018 approval of patisiran (Onpattro) for the treatment of hereditary transthyretin-mediated amyloidosis was a major turning point in the field of siRNA therapeutics [26]. This accomplishment has rekindled interest and investment in RNAi-based strategies for treating cancer.

The main goal of this study is to do a comprehensive investigation of DNMT1 silencing in triple-negative breast cancer. We aim to design and validate high-specificity siRNA sequences targeting DNMT1. And then it is followed by a detailed evaluation of the molecular effects of DNMT1 knockdown using the designed siRNA therapeutics.

Materials and Methods

Acquisition of data

DNMT1 mRNA sequence was retrieved (NCBI Reference Sequence: NM_001130823.3) from the National Center for Biotechnology Information (NCBI) nucleotide database. FASTA sequence has been acquired for further downstream analysis.

siRNA prediction

Multiple web-based tools were utilized to predict siRNAs targeting the DNMT1 mRNA ensuring minimum off-target effects. These multiple web-based tools also help in ensuring the accuracy of the predicted siRNAs. The siDirect 2.0 web server was used, incorporating the combined algorithm of The Ui-Tei×Amarzguioui×Reynolds to design the siRNAs specific to DNMT1 mRNA [19]. To enhance prediction reliability, additional tools such as siExplorer and OligoWalk were employed for the validation in a comparative manner [10, 13]. In addition, the efficiency and specificity of the predicted siRNAs were assessed using the siPRED web-based computational tool. The GC content was set between 30–55% to ensure optimal siRNA stability and efficacy while preventing excessive secondary structure formation. To reduce the potential off-target interactions, seed-target duplex melting temperature parameter was adjusted to maintain 21.5°C.

Energy calculations

We conducted comprehensive structural and energy analyses, to ensure optimal efficiency of the designed siRNAs targeting DNMT1. The MaxExpect algorithm with default parameters was utilized to examine each siRNA guide strand's secondary structure characteristics and folding free energy values [12]. The algorithm identified siRNAs with higher energy values, which indicates reduced self-folding potential and lower energy indicates higher self-folding potential. Since higher energy values also indicate greater availability for target binding and minimal self-folding tendencies, those siRNAs were prioritized for target identification.

Evaluation of RNA-RNA interactions between the siRNA candidates and their DNMT1 mRNA target was conducted using the DuplexFold web server, which calculated the respective binding energies of these potential therapeutic molecules under physiological temperature conditions (310.15 K) [4]. This analysis provided insights into the thermodynamic stability of the siRNA-mRNA complexes. siRNAs exhibiting stronger binding energies with DNMT1 mRNA were selected for experimental validation. Higher binding energy and interaction between the siRNA and its target transcript is essential for effective gene silencing.

Sequence complementarity and base composition analysis

siRNAs targeting DNMT1 mRNA were then screened for off-targeting to ensure specificity. The target sequences were aligned against human genomic transcripts from GenBank using the basic local alignment search tool (BLAST) for similarity. The BLAST search was performed against *Homo sapiens* with an expected threshold value of 10 to identify potential off targets within the human transcriptome. This analysis eliminated siRNA candidates with significant sequence homology to non-target human genes, thereby minimizing potential off-target effects.

Additionally, the base composition which is the GC content of each designed siRNAs were analysed under physiologically relevant conditions (50 mM salt) using the OligoCalc web server [11]. The GC percentage is a critical parameter affecting siRNA stability, binding efficiency, and overall silencing potency. Candidates with optimal GC content (typically 30–60%) were prioritized. This range helps with balancing stability.

Thermal stability characterization

The thermodynamic stability of the siRNA-mRNA duplexes was investigated through computational modeling of heat capacity profiles using DINA Melt server [14]. Temperature-dependent analysis of the siRNAs can provide two critical parameters: the peak melting temperature Tm (Cp) and the concentration-dependent melting temperature Tm (Conc). The peak melting temperature represents the point of maximum heat absorption during strand separation. On the other hand, the concentration-dependent melting temperature Tm (Conc) refers to the temperature when 50% of the molecules exist in duplex

form. These two temperatures help us to understand the thermal stability and dissociation behavior of the siRNA-target mRNA complexes.

Molecular docking

3D structures of the predicted siRNAs (guide strand) targeting DNMT1 mRNA were generated with the help of RNAComposer web server [5]. RNA secondary structures which were provided as input in RNAComposer were determined using RNA fold algorithms to identify stable conformations suitable for incorporation into the RISC. The 3D structure of the human Argonaute 2 (hAgo2) protein was retrieved from the Protein Data Bank (PDB) Accession ID: 5JS1. All the water molecules, heteroatoms and the bound RNA molecule were removed from the structure and used for further docking studies.

The RNAComposer generated siRNA structures were subjected to energy minimization using OpenBabel with the Merck Molecular Force Field 1994 (MMFF94) force field to optimize molecular geometry and resolve unfavorable atomic interactions [16]. Molecular docking between the energy-minimized siRNAs and the prepared hAgo2 protein was performed with the help of HDOCK web server [24]. HDOCK employs a Fast Fourier Transform (FFT) algorithm along with a template-based modeling approach for accurate prediction of protein-protein and protein-nucleic acid complexes.

The five siRNA-mRNA duplexes were docked by HDOCK server focusing mainly on the potential binding sites within the hAgo2 catalytic pocket. Multiple docking models were generated, and all the models were ranked according to their binding energy scores. The resulting siRNA-hAgo2 complexes were visualized and analyzed using PyMOL. And Chimera [20]. Both the tools help to evaluate the intermolecular interactions of the models. Most importance was given to interactions between the siRNA seed region (positions 2–8) and the hAgo2 binding pocket. The seed region and binding pocket are critical for gene silencing activity against DNMT1 mRNA.

Results

Identification of siRNAs targeting DNMT1 mRNA

To reduce the off-target effect, the siRNAs were designed with seed duplex stability (Tm) of 21.5 °C along with the combined

Ui-Tei×Amarzguioui×Reynolds algorithm. Five siRNAs were predicted by the siDirect 2.0 server targeting distinct regions of the DNMT1 mRNA sequence. The DNMT1 mRNA target position, DNMT1 mRNA target sequence, guide strand of the siRNA, passenger strand of the siRNA and the melting temperatures of all five siRNAs were tabulated in Table 12.1. To check the reliability of the siDirect 2.0 web server predicted siRNAs, the siRNAs were subsequently evaluated by comparing its results with the probability scores of OligoWalk and the siExplorer, as summarized in Table 12.2.

All the siRNAs were validated by the siPRED server, and the target mRNA inhibition scores are greater than 0.7. The probability scores in both OligoWalk and siExplorer were also larger than 0.7 and 60% respectively shown in Table 12.2.

Screening of the siRNA candidates

To identify the potential off-targets, the DNMT1 mRNA sequence was analysed using NCBI-BLAST against the human genome sequences deposited in the GenBank database.

In siRNA screening, GC% plays an important role in identifying siRNAs which are more efficient, while the optimal GC% ranges between 30% and 55%. All the five siRNAs have been calculated using OligoCalc webserver and GC% ranges between 36.8% and 47.3% and were listed in Table 12.2.

Analysis of siRNA structure and target interaction characteristics

The thermodynamic energy parameters like free folding energy and free binding energy of the designed siRNAs were evaluated through computational tools like MaxExpect and DuplexFold respectively. The secondary structure and folding energy values were determined using the mentioned structural prediction algorithms at 37°C. The guide strands demonstrated positive free folding. energy values ranging from 1.4 to 1.8 kcal/mol, indicating favorable conditions for target-binding potential represented in Figure 12.1. Interaction analysis between these siRNAs and their mRNA targets revealed substantial binding affinity as demonstrated by the negative free binding energy values. The binding energies of all the five siRNAs ranged from −30.8–39.5 kcal/mol at 37°C shown in Figure 12.2. The magnitude of these negative values suggests strong interaction potential with the target sequences.

Table 12.1 List of siRNAs targeting their corresponding mRNA sequence of DNMT1 and their melting temperatures (Tm)

Name of siRNAs	DNMT1 mRNA target position	DNMT1 mRNA target sequence	Guide strand of the siRNA	Passenger strand of the siRNA	Tm of guide (°C)	Tm of passenger (°C)
siRNA-1	91–113	TTGGAAAGAGACAGCTTAACAGA	UGUUAAGCUGUCUCUUUCCAA	GGAAAGAGACAGCUUAACAGA	20.9	19.1
siRNA-2	136–158	TTGAATCTCTTGCACGAATTTCT	AAAUUCGUGCAAGAGAUUCAA	GAAUCUCUUGCACGAAUUUCU	15.2	19.1
siRNA-3	1525–1547	CCCGAGTATGCGCCCATATTTGG	AAAUAUGGGCGCAUACUCGGG	CGAGUAUGCGCCCAUAUUUGG	12.6	20.3
siRNA-4	2271–2293	TGGGAAGAAGAGTTACTATAAGA	UUAUAGUAACUCUUCUUCCCA	GGAAGAAGAGUUACUAUAAGA	7.9	19.1
siRNA-5	3073–3095	CCCAATGAGACTGACATCAAAAT	UUUGAUGUCAGUCUCAUUGGG	CAAUGAGACUGACAUCAAAAU	20.5	20.4

Source: Author

Table 12.2 Thermodynamic temperature and energy parameters of the siRNAs along with their probability scores from different computational tools

Name of siRNAs	siRNA guide strand	Tm (Cp) (°C)	Tm (Conc) (°C)	Free folding energy (kcal/mol)	Free binding energy (kcal/mol)	GC%	Probability score from OligoWalk tool	Probability score (%) from siExplorer tool	Inhibition value from siPRED tool.
siRNA-1	UGUUAAGCUGUCUCUUUCCAA	62.3	59.8	1.6	−34.6	42.1	0.75541	79.79	0.947
siRNA-2	AAAUUCGUGCAAGAGAUUCAA	58.7	55.9	1.7	−30.8	36.8	0.88027	75.74	0.79
siRNA-3	AAAUAUGGGCGCAUACUCGGG	65.2	62.4	1.4	−39.5	47.3	0.788322	66.95	0.736
siRNA-4	UUAUAGUAACUCUCUUCCCA	57.4	54.6	1.8	−33.0	31.5	0.976687	72.42	0.953
siRNA-5	UUUGAUGUCAGUCUCAUUGGG	60.8	58.2	1.5	−36.4	36.8	0.954724	92.04	1.081

Source: Author

Thermal stability assessment of siRNAs via melting temperature (Tm) evaluation

The thermal stability profiles of all the five-candidate siRNA-mRNA duplexes were characterized using the DINAmelt server. The analysis revealed distinct thermal properties for all five of the complexes, as represented in Table 12.2. The peak melting temperature Tm (Cp) was examined and the values ranging from 57.4°C to 65.2°C across the five siRNA candidates. The highest peak melting temperature was observed for siRNA-3 at 65.2°C, followed by siRNA-1 at 62.3°C. Concentration-dependent melting temperatures Tm (Conc) demonstrated a similar pattern to that of the peak melting temperature Tm (Cp), with values between 54.6°C and 62.4°C. Higher melting temperatures proves that there is increased duplex stability, which also indicates superior target binding characteristics.

Molecular docking analysis of hAgo2–siRNA interactions

The docking of the five siRNA-mRNA duplexes by HDOCK server resulted in models with higher binding affinities corresponding to −424.85 kcal/mol, −301.40 kcal/mol, −301.67 kcal/mol, −368.54 kcal/mol, and −330.30 kcal/mol respectively for the hAgo2 protein. The binding energies, hydrogen bonds, interface residues and confidence scores were represented in Table 12.3. The gene-silencing activity of siRNA relies on the specific binding of the 5' and 3' ends to the PAZ and MID domains in the hAgo2 protein. From the docking result figures, siRNA-2, siRNA-3 and siRNA-5 have shown interactions in the PAZ and MID domains of the hAgo2 protein which significantly proves that the siRNAs may silence the DNMT1 mRNA target shown in Figure 12.3.

Discussion

DNMT1 overexpression is prevalent in TNBC. This process plays a crucial role in the aggressive characteristics and unfavorable prognosis associated with triple-negative breast cancer. DNMT1 serves as a key enzyme responsible for the maintenance of DNA methylation patterns during cell replication. It plays a vital role in epigenetic regulation. Changes in DNMT1 activity are linked to the silencing of tumor suppressor genes and increased cell proliferation. Increased metastatic potential, and chemotherapeutic resistance are also causes of DNMT1 dysregulation in TNBC and several other cancer types. Our study focused on designing effective siRNAs targeting DNMT1 mRNA as an effective therapeutic strategy for TNBC patients.

In-silico design of DNMT1-targeting siRNAs by the siDirect 2.0 webserver yielded five potential candidates (siRNA-1, siRNA-2, siRNA-3, siRNA-4, and siRNA-5) that satisfied the combined Ui-Tei×Amarzguioui×Reynolds algorithm. The combined rules establish parameters for the optimal design of siRNAs targeting DNMT1 mRNA sequence. The combined rule specifications include specific nucleotide preferences at certain positions, GC content requirements, and structural considerations that enhance siRNA efficiency. All the five siRNAs showed high specificity for DNMT1 mRNA. No significant off-target effects were identified through BLAST analysis against the human genome transcript.

The free folding and free binding energies are the thermodynamic properties which play a vital role in determining siRNA efficacy. Our analysis revealed that the guide strands of all the five siRNAs exhibited favorable free folding energies. The free folding energies of the five siRNAs ranged from 1.4 to 1.8 kcal/mol, indicating lower self-folding potential and optimal availability for target binding. The free binding energies between the siRNAs and DNMT1 mRNA duplexes ranged from −30.8 to −39.5 kcal/mol. The highest binding affinity of −39.5 kcal/mol was demonstrated by siRNA-3. Effective gene silencing is essential for robust interaction potential with the target sequence which is proven for the designed siRNAs based on both the free folding and free binding energy values.

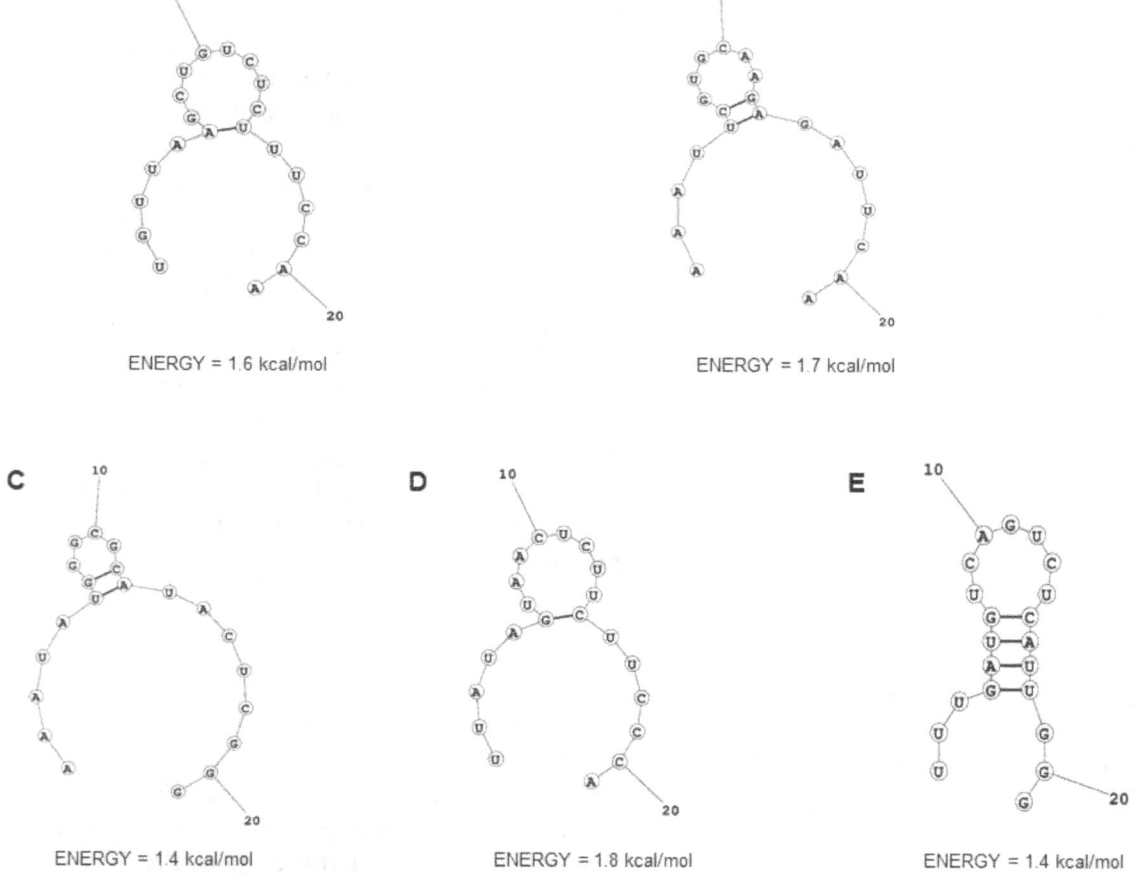

Figure 12.1 Predicted secondary structures and corresponding minimum free energies (kcal/mol) of siRNA-1 to siRNA-5 guide strands

Source: Author

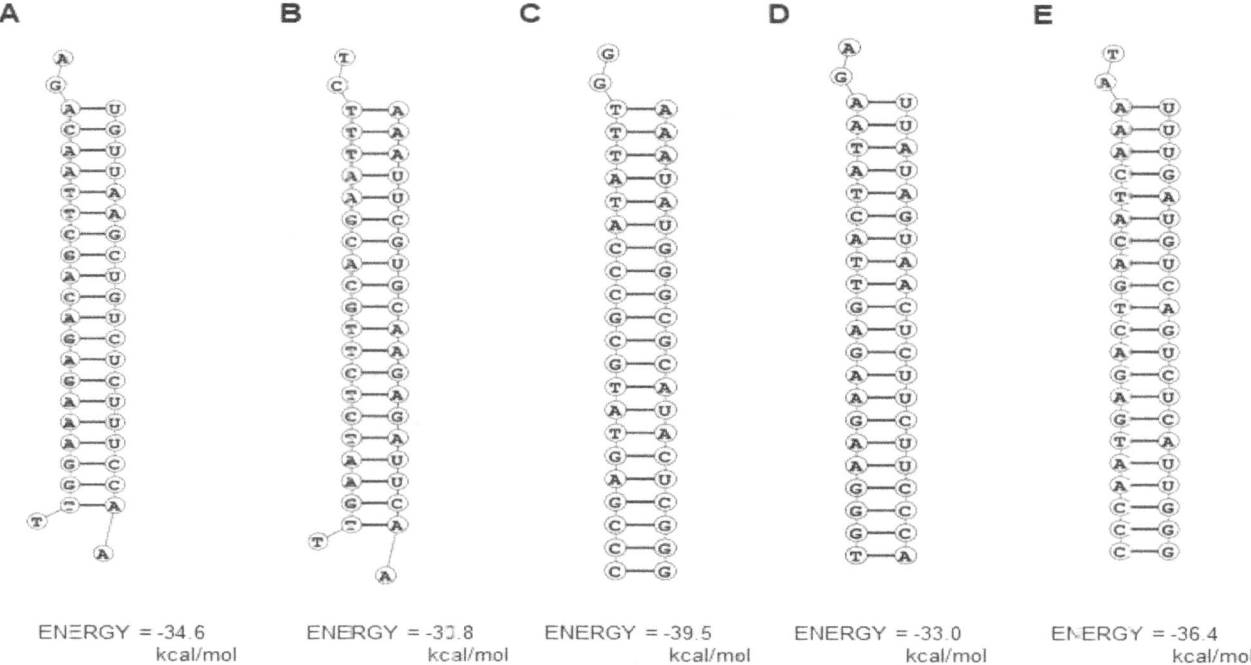

ENERGY = -34.6 kcal/mol   ENERGY = -30.8 kcal/mol   ENERGY = -39.5 kcal/mol   ENERGY = -33.0 kcal/mol   ENERGY = -36.4 kcal/mol

Figure 12.2 Predicted binding energies of the mRNA-siRNA duplexes. The calculated free binding energies for siRNA-1 (A), siRNA-2 (B), siRNA-3 (C), siRNA-4 (D), and siRNA-5 (E) were −34.6 kcal/mol, −30.8 kcal/mol, −39.5 kcal/mol, −33.0 kcal/mol, and −36.4 kcal/mol respectively. In each panel, the left strand represents the KRAS mRNA target, and the right strand depicts the corresponding siRNAs

Source: Author

Melting temperature of the siRNA- mRNA duplexes is helpful in determining thermal stability. It provides valuable insights into the functional characteristics of siRNA target mRNA duplexes. Our candidates displayed peak melting temperatures Tm (Cp) ranging from 57.4°C to 65.2°C. The concentration-dependent melting temperatures Tm (Conc) ranged between 54.6°C and 62.4°C. Higher melting temperatures indicate superior target binding characteristics and enhanced duplex stability. siRNA-3 demonstrated the highest thermal stability (Tm (Cp) = 65.2°C; Tm (Conc) = 62.4°C), which is then followed by siRNA-1 (Tm (Cp) = 62.3°C; Tm (Conc) = 59.8°C).

The interaction between siRNAs and the human Argonaute2 (hAgo2) protein is critical for RNAi functionality. Human Argonaute 2 serves as the catalytic engine within the RNA-induced silencing complex (RISC), which functions to cleave target DNMT1 messenger RNA. Our molecular docking studies revealed that all five siRNAs showed significant binding affinities with hAgo2 and the binding affinities of the five siRNAs ranged from −301.40 to −424.85 kcal/mol. Among all the five siRNAs, siRNA-1 showed the highest binding affinity (−424.85 kcal/mol) with 16 hydrogen bonds. Specific interactions with the PAZ and MID domains of human Argonaute 2 protein were displayed by siRNA-2 and siRNA-5. These interactions with the residues of the PAZ and MID domains are essential for proper positioning of the siRNA within the RISC complex.

Another critical factor influencing siRNA efficacy is the optimal GC content ranging between 30% and 55%. The GC content in siRNAs requires careful balance- insufficient levels (below 30%) can weaken target binding, while excessive amounts may create stable secondary structures that impede proper RISC loading. All five siRNA candidates demonstrated appropriate GC percentages ranging from 31.5% to 47.3%. siRNA-3 has the highest GC content (47.3%), and siRNA-4 has the lowest GC content (31.5%).

Validation of the five siRNA candidates using prediction algorithms like OligoWalk, siExplorer, and siPRED yielded promising results. siRNA-5 demonstrated the highest siExplorer probability score (92.04%) and siPRED inhibition score (1.081). While siRNA-4 showed the highest OligoWalk probability

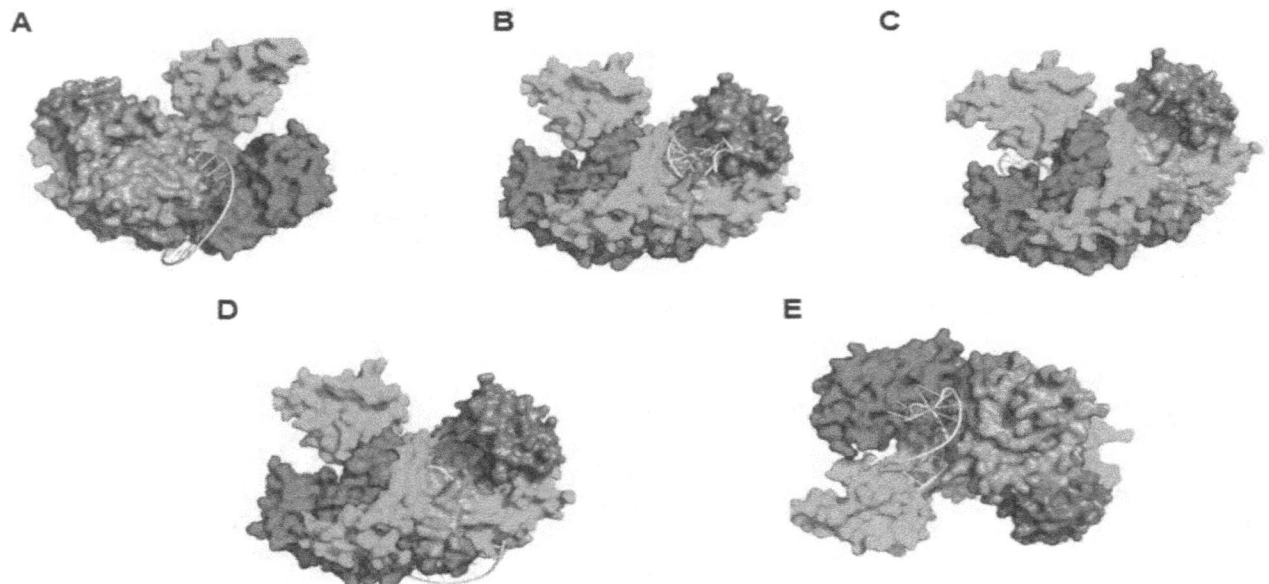

Figure 12.3 Docked structures of candidate siRNAs with the hAgo2 protein are displayed using surface representation for the protein domains and cartoon representation for the guide siRNAs. The N-terminal (residues 1–174) and Linker1 region (residues 175–225) are shown in red, the PAZ domain (residues 226–346) and Linker2 region (residues 347–449) in green, the MID domain (450–572) in sky blue, and the PIWI domain (573–859) in orange. The guide siRNAs are highlighted in white using the cartoon model. The binding interaction analysis revealed that siRNA-1 (A), siRNA-2 (B), siRNA-3 (C), siRNA-4 (D), and siRNA-5 (E) exhibited strong affinities toward the hAgo2 protein, with binding energies of −424.85 kcal/mol, −301.40 kcal/mol, −301.67 kcal/mol, −368.54 kcal/mol, and −330.30 kcal/mol, respectively

Source: Author

score (0.976687). The potential effectiveness of our designed siRNAs is further supported by these computational predictions.

Despite all the promising in silico results, siRNA-based therapeutics face several challenges in clinical applications. The challenges faced are related to the stability, delivery, off-target effects, and potential immunogenicity of the siRNA molecules. Current advances in delivery systems of the siRNA molecules have demonstrated potential in overcoming these challenges.

Conclusion

For triple-negative breast cancer, siRNA-mediated gene silencing of the DNMT1 mRNA sequence and inhibiting its protein translation shows a promising therapeutic strategy. The current study was performed to design and validate effective DNMT1 mRNA targeting siRNAs using various computational approaches. The findings of this study revealed that siRNA-2, siRNA-3, and siRNA-5 satisfy the Ui-Tei×Amarzguioui×Reynolds algorithm

along with other essential parameters for effectively targeting DNMT1 mRNA. Among these, siRNA-5 demonstrated the highest siPRED inhibition value and siExplorer probability score, while siRNA-3 exhibited the strongest binding affinity with DNMT1 mRNA and favorable thermal stability characteristics.

Although all the siRNAs showed therapeutic characteristics in the in-silico analyses, they must be further evaluated through *in vitro* and *in vivo* experiments to dully determine their complete therapeutic efficiency against triple-negative breast cancer. Besides, the present challenges of the siRNA therapeutics development and delivery could be overcome by emerging siRNA delivery strategies including lipid nanoparticles, polymer-based carriers, and antibody-siRNA conjugates specifically designed for breast cancer cells. With continued advancement in delivery technologies and appropriate regulatory guidelines, these siRNA candidates could potentially be translated into therapeutic options for TNBC patients and result in successful clinical outcomes in the future.

Table 12.3 Interacting residues and formation of bonds of the five siRNAs and the human Argonaute2 protein (Highlighted residues corresponds to the interacting residues of the PAZ and MID domain)

Name of siRNAs	H-bonds	Binding Energy (kcal/mol)	Confidence Score	Interacting Residues
siRNA-1	18	−424.85	0.9959	ARG351, CYS352, ILE353, LYS354, LYS355, LEU356, THR361, SER362, ILE365, LYS525, LYS550, ARG554, THR555, GLN558, ARG710, HIS753, ALA754, ARG773
siRNA-2	18	−301.40	0.9875	ARG351, CYS352, ILE353, LYS354, LYS355, THR361, ILE365, **LYS525, LYS550, ASN551, ARG554, THR555, THR556, GLN558, THR559, LEU560, ASN562, LEU563**
siRNA-3	8	−301.67	0.9538	GLU64, LYS65, CYS66, PRO67, ARG68, ARG97, VAL177, GLY178, ARG179, **LYS266, ARG280, GLN332, ARG351**, ARG635, GLN672, GLU673, LEU685, GLU689
siRNA-4	8	−368.54	0.9541	GLU58, LYS65, CYS66, PRO67, VAL70, ASN99, ARG126, GLN160, LYS260, ARG280, ILE353, LYS354, HIS600, GLN633, ARG635, GLN636, GLY674, GLN675
siRNA-5	6	−330.30	0.9736	THR222, ALA223, **LYS260, LYS263, GLY264, ARG280**, ARG351, CYS352, ILE353, LYS354, LYS355, LYS550, ARG554, THR555, LEU563, LYS709, ARG710, HIS753

Source: Author

Acknowledgment

The authors would like to thank the Department of Biotechnology, PSG College of Technology, Coimbatore, Tamil Nadu, India for the infrastructure facilities provided to carry out the research work.

References

[1] AlSawaftah, N. M., Awad, N. S., Paul, V., Kawak, P. S., Al-Sayah, M. H., & Hussein, G. A. (2021). Transferrin-modified liposomes triggered with ultrasound to treat HeLa cells. *Scientific Reports*, 11(1), 11589. https://doi.org/10.1038/s41598-021-90349-6.

[2] Ashique, S., Almohaywi, B., Haider, N., Yasmin, S., Hussain, A., Mishra, N., et al. (2022). siRNA-based nanocarriers for targeted drug delivery to control breast cancer. *Advances in Cancer Biology - Metastasis*, 4, 100047. https://doi.org/10.1016/j.adcanc.2022.100047.

[3] Baranova, A., Krasnoselskyi, M., Starikov, V., Kartashov, S., Zhulkevych, I., Vlasenko, V., et al. (2022). Triple-negative breast cancer: current treatment strategies and factors of negative prognosis. *Journal of Medicine and Life*, 15(2), 153–161. https://doi.org/10.25122/jml-2021-0108.

[4] Bellaousov, S., Reuter, J. S., Seetin, M. G., & Mathews, D. H. (2013). RNAstructure: web servers for RNA secondary structure prediction and analysis *Nucleic Acids Research*, 41(W1), W471–W474. https://doi.org/10.1093/nar/gkt290.

[5] Biesiada, M., Purzycka, K. J., Szachniuk, M., Blazewicz, J., & Adamiak, R. W. (2016). Automated RNA 3D structure prediction with RNAComposer. In RNA Structure Determination: Methods and Protocols, (pp. 199–215). New York, NY: Springer New York. https://doi.org/10.1007/978-1-4939-6433-8_13.

[6] Chen, J.-Q., & Russo, J. (2009). ER-negative and triple negative breast cancer: molecular features and potential therapeutic approaches. *Biochimica et Biophysica Acta (BBA) - Reviews on Cancer*, 1796(2), 162–175. https://doi.org/10.1016/j.bbcan.2009.06.003.

[7] Hegde, M., & Joshi, M. B. (2021). Comprehensive analysis of regulation of DNA methyltransferase isoforms in human breast tumors. *Journal of Cancer Research and Clinical Oncology*, 147(4), 937–971. https://doi.org/10.1007/s00432-021-03519-4.

[8] Jin, B., & Robertson, K. D. (2013). DNA Methyltransferases, DNA damage repair, and cancer, (pp. 3–29). https://doi.org/10.1007/978-1-4419-9967-2_1.

[9] Kalita, T., Dezfouli, S. A., Pandey, L. M., & Uludag, H. (2022). siRNA functionalized lipid nanoparticles (LNPs) in management of diseases. *Pharmaceutics*, 14(11), 2520. https://doi.org/10.3390/pharmaceutics14112520.

[10] Katoh, T., & Suzuki, T. (2007). Specific residues at every third position of siRNA shape its efficient RNAi activity. *Nucleic Acids Research*, 35(4), e27. https://doi.org/10.1093/nar/gkl1120.

[11] Kibbe, W. A. (2007). OligoCalc: an online oligonucleotide properties calculator. *Nucleic Acids Research*, 35(Web Server), W43–W46. https://doi.org/10.1093/nar/gkm234.

[12] Lu, Z. J., Gloor, J. W., & Mathews, D. H. (2009). Improved RNA secondary structure prediction by maximizing expected pair accuracy. *RNA*, 5(10), 1805–1813. https://doi.org/10.1261/rna.1643609.

[13] Lu, Z. J., & Mathews, D. H. (2008). OligoWalk: an online siRNA design tool utilizing hybridization thermodynamics. *Nucleic Acids Research*, 36(Web Server), W104–W108. https://doi.org/10.1093/nar/gkn250.

[14] Markham, N. R., & Zuker, M. (2005). DINAMelt web server for nucleic acid melting prediction. *Nucleic Acids Research*, 33(Web Server), W577–W581. https://doi.org/10.1093/nar/gki591.

[15] Muthusamy, V., Bosenberg, M., & Wajapeyee, N. (2010). Redefining regulation of DNA methylation by RNA interference. *Genomics*, 96(4), 191–198. https://doi.org/10.1016/j.ygeno.2010.07.001.

[16] O'Boyle, N. M., Banck, M., James, C. A., Morley, C., Vandermeersch, T., & Hutchison, G. R. (2011). Open babel: an open chemical toolbox. *Journal of Cheminformatics*, 3(1), 33. https://doi.org/10.1186/1758-2946-3-33.

[17] Onitilo, A. A., Engel, J. M., Greenlee, R. T., & Mukesh, B. N. (2009). Breast cancer subtypes based on ER/PR and Her2 expression: comparison of clinicopathologic features and survival. *Clinical Medicine and Research*, 7(1–2), 4–13. https://doi.org/10.3121/cmr.2009.825.

[18] Orrantia-Borunda, E., Anchondo-Nuñez, P., Acuña-Aguilar, L. E., Gómez-Valles, F. O., & Ramírez-Valdespino, C. A. (2022). Subtypes of breast cancer. In Breast Cancer (pp. 31–42). Exon Publications. https://doi.org/10.36255/exon-publications-breast-cancer-subtypes.

[19] Pan, W.-J., Chen, C.-W., & Chu, Y.-W. (2011). siPRED: predicting siRNA efficacy using various characteristic methods. *PLoS One*, 6(11), e27602. https://doi.org/10.1371/journal.pone.0027602.

[20] Pettersen, E. F., Goddard, T. D., Huang, C. C., Couch, G. S., Greenblatt, D. M., Meng, E. C., et al. (2004). UCSF Chimera—a visualization system for exploratory research and analysis. *Journal of Computational Chemistry*, 25(13), 1605–1612. https://doi.org/10.1002/jcc.20084.

[21] Roy, N. K., Bordoloi, D., Monisha, J., Anip, A., Padmavathi, G., et al. (2017). Cancer — an overview and molecular alterations in cancer. In Fusion Genes and Cancer, (pp. 1–15). World Scientific. https://doi.org/10.1142/9789813200944_0001.

[22] Sukumar, J., Gast, K., Quiroga, D., Lustberg, M., & Williams, N. (2021). Triple-negative breast cancer: promising prognostic biomarkers currently in development. *Expert Review of Anticancer Therapy*, 21(2), 135–148. https://doi.org/10.1080/14737140.2021.1840984.

[23] Wong, K. K. (2021). DNMT1: a key drug target in triple-negative breast cancer. *Seminars in Cancer Biology*, 72, 198–213. https://doi.org/10.1016/j.semcancer.2020.05.010.

[24] Yan, Y., Zhang, D., Zhou, P., Li, B., & Huang, S.-Y. (2017). HDOCK: a web server for protein–protein and protein–DNA/RNA docking based on a hybrid strategy. *Nucleic Acids Research*, 45(W1), W365–W373. https://doi.org/10.1093/nar/gkx407.

[25] Yu, J., Zayas, J., Qin, B., & Wang, L. (2019). Targeting DNA methylation for treating triple-negative breast cancer. *Pharmacogenomics*, 20(16), 1151–1157. https://doi.org/10.2217/pgs-2019-0078.

[26] Zhang, X., Goel, V., & Robbie, G. J. (2020). Pharmacokinetics of patisiran, the first approved RNA interference therapy in patients with hereditary transthyretin-mediated amyloidosis. *Journal of Clinical Pharmacology*, 60(5), 573–585. https://doi.org/10.1002/jcph.1553.

13 Functional foods: exploring meat alternatives with nutritional and sensory qualities

Gayathry Kanagavel[1,a] and Poongothai Jayaramasamy[2,b]

[1]PG Scholar, Department of Biotechnology, PSG College of Technology, Coimbatore, Tamil Nadu, India

[2]Assistant Professor, Department of Biotechnology, PSG College of Technology, Coimbatore, Tamil Nadu, India

Abstract

Response Surface Methodology (RSM) was used in this study to optimize a Meat Alternative (MA) to maximize protein and fiber content while ensuring sensory acceptability. The ratios of soy chunks (high protein), breadfruit (binding agent), and mushrooms (flavor enhancer and high fiber) were systematically varied across 12 formulations. Nutritional analysis showed that soy chunks provided the highest protein (53.95 mg/g), while breadfruit-mushroom blends boosted fiber (up to 69 mg/g). RSM identified an optimal formulation (desirability: 0.769) that balanced >100 mg protein and >40 mg fiber per gram. The colour of MA was rated as "Excellent" by 62.5% of participants, while aroma received a lower score of 25% for "Excellent." Notably, its caolour outperformed conventional meat (52.1% "Very Good"). These findings show that RSM can be effectively used to create a meat substitute that is both nutrient-dense and visually appealing. With small flavour adjustments needed to achieve wider appeal, the study demonstrates the potential of underused crops in sustainable food production by providing a useful, plant-based protein source.

Keywords: Functional food, meat alternatives, protein and fiber optimization, RSM, sensory analysis

Introduction

High consumption of traditional meat, particularly processed and red meats, is linked to various health issues, including colorectal cancer, due to carcinogenic compounds formed during meat processing. Epidemiological studies have shown correlations between high meat intake and elevated mortality rates from chronic diseases such as heart disease and type 2 diabetes. The World Health Organization classifies processed meat as carcinogenic. Reducing meat consumption may improve public health since fewer people are at risk of chronic illnesses [1–3].

Regular consumption of plant-based proteins has been linked to lower risks of heart disease, type 2 diabetes, and certain cancers, including colon cancer. This could improve public health and reduce healthcare costs. As these alternatives spread and become more affordable, they offer high-quality protein sources and contribute to the end of hunger [4–6].

The growing popularity of plant-based diets and plant-based macronutrient assembly highlights the need for research on the environmental effects and micronutrient sufficiency, especially for vegans and vegetarians. Over the next ten years, the shift to plant-based diets will significantly affect food systems and research. Advancements in meat alternatives offer a combination of nutrient-dense and useful compounds to address dietary and sensory concerns [7, 8].

Breadfruit (Artocarpus altilis) is useful in the fight against malnutrition because it contains complex carbohydrates and essential amino acids [8]. The medicinal substances that white button (Agaricus bisporus) contribute, such as antioxidants, beta-glucans, and polyphenols, may help treat diseases like dyslipidemia . To improve texture and replicate the structure of meat, soy chunks are added. The goal of this carefully considered ingredient combination is to produce a product that meets consumer demands for taste and texture in meat substitutes while also providing nutritional advantages [9].

Literature Review

Plant-based diets: nutritional shifts and research gaps

Growing interest in plant-based diets worldwide, driven by ethical, health, and environmental concerns, has altered the conversation around nutrition. But the emphasis on macronutrients in these diets often masks concerns about micronutrient adequacy, particularly in fervent vegan and vegetarian societies

[a]gayathrykansan@gmail.com, [b]jpi.bio@psgtech.ac.in

DOI: 10.1201/9781003770435-13

[7]. Individuals with chronic conditions such as diabetes who require strict dietary management have been found to have deficiencies in vitamin B12, iron, zinc, calcium, and omega-3 fatty acids. The body of research on the combination of fortified plant-based diets and bioavailable sources of essential micronutrients is constantly growing. As food systems change, research must focus on developing balanced formulations that address micronutrient sufficiency as well as macronutrient quality.

Nutritional and functional potential of breadfruit (Artocarpus altilis) in diets

More people are becoming aware that the breadfruit, or Artocarpus altilis, is a versatile food item that has important therapeutic and nutritional benefits for diabetics. Its rich amino acid profile, low glycemic index, high fiber content, and versatility in food processing techniques all enhance metabolic results and add to its appeal [10, 11]. Breadfruit's morphology reflects two important developmental stages: a single-sigmoidal growth pattern in diameter and a double-sigmoidal curve in weight. Cell development and a high sugar content define the early phase, whereas amylopectin-rich starch accumulation characterizes the later phase [12]. The timing of fruit harvesting is essential to determining the ideal starch-to-fiber ratios for diabetic-friendly food applications because this biochemical transition affects the fruit's glycemic properties.

Nutritional and therapeutic applications of soy chunks in diets

Soy chunks are known for their high protein content and diverse nutritional profile, and they are made from defatted soy flour. A typical serving contains approximately 52% protein and 10% dietary fiber, which includes both soluble and insoluble fibers. By forming viscous gels in the digestive tract, the soluble portion moderates the circulatory absorption of glucose and stops the enzymatic breakdown of carbohydrates. This has the advantage of reducing postprandial blood glucose rises, which is especially helpful for people with type 2 diabetes. When it comes to diabetic meal planning, soy chunks are a good alternative to meat because of their texture and adaptability, which helps lower saturated fat intake without compromising protein quality [13].

Bioactive compounds in mushrooms and metabolic regulation

Mushrooms contain phenolic compounds, beta-glucans, and ergostane steroids, which are beneficial nutrients that support metabolic health. Beta-glucans reduce LDL cholesterol and control glucose absorption by forming viscous gels in the intestine. Due to their anti-inflammatory and antioxidant qualities, phenols and sterols lessen oxidative stress, which is known to worsen insulin resistance. Incorporating them into diabetic diets may have therapeutic and nutritional advantages [14].

Methodology

Selection of raw materials

The choice of raw materials for meat alternative products was guided by the ability of the raw materials to mimic the nutritional, textural, and sensory properties of meat, combined with sustainability concerns. Protein content, amino acid profiles, and micronutrient density, like sodium, calcium, zinc, and iron, were assessed for nutritional adequacy, and uniformity with conventional meat was maintained. Mouthfeel properties were determined to resemble meat, including fibrous texture and water-binding capacity. Based on these criteria, the raw materials were chosen [3, 4, 7, 9].

Preparation of samples

The selected samples, like breadfruit (Artocarpus altilis), white button mushrooms (Agaricus bisporus), and commercial soy chunks, were collected from local farms and markets. The raw materials were carefully cleaned, cut into equal pieces, and dried at 60°C for 14 hours to obtain a constant weight. Homogeneous powder was then produced from the dried samples by grinding and sieving them through a 425-micron mesh (ASTM standard). The powdered samples were kept in airtight bottles for functional analysis and nutritional characterization [15].

Nutritional profile analysis of raw materials

The Biuret method was used to examine the chosen raw materials for crude protein ; the acid-base digestion method was used to assess crude fiber [16]; and moisture content was checked to confirm their nutritional suitability. Protein content was measured using spectrophotometry. Sequential acid and alkaline digestion allowed crude fiber to be determined by isolating indigestible parts. After oven drying, the moisture content was assessed. These studies verified that every material satisfied the minimum criteria for protein and dietary fiber needed for meat analogues.

Composition analysis of raw materials by RSM

Using Design-Expert software, the study systematically assessed how different percentages of raw materials could raise the protein and fiber content using a Mixture design technique of the RSM approach. With the software producing 12 experimental runs spanning several ratio combinations, each component was limited to 0.5–2.0 g to preserve reasonable formulation limits. Prepared under controlled processing conditions, these formulations served as test samples. While crude protein was measured using the Biuret technique (540 nm absorbance) [16], crude fiber content was measured using uniform acid-base digestion [17]. The experimental results were fed into the Design Expert software with crude fiber and protein levels as response variables. Using a quadratic response surface validated by ANOVA (p < 0.05) and lack-of-fit testing (R^2 > 0.85), model fitting was performed [17].

Assessing the sensory attributes

A sensory evaluation was conducted with 48 participants to assess consumer acceptance of the developed meat alternatives. The panel was 58.3% female and 41.7% male, reflecting different dietary preferences: 77.1% ate plant- and animal-based products, and 12.5% were vegetarian. Key sensory qualities include texture, taste, aroma, appearance, and general acceptability of the items. The approach provides a complete understanding of market acceptability from both vegetarian and regular meat consumers.

Results and Discussion

Selection of plant materials

Breadfruit, mushrooms, soy chunks, spirulina, and soybean flour are the preferred raw materials for alternative meat products because they provide a complete nutritional profile abundant in protein, fiber, and important nutrients like calcium and iron, much like traditional meat. Sensory studies have confirmed that they have the potential to mimic the flavor, texture, and overall experience of conventional meats. This makes them attractive options for wholesome and sustainable food items. Raw materials for alternative meat products provide a complete nutritional profile abundant in protein, fiber, and important nutrients, much like traditional meat.

Nutritional profile analysis of raw materials

According to the analysis, breadfruit has a balanced nutritional profile. Its high fiber content (67 mg/g) exceeds typical ranges (50–60 mg/g), indicating excellent fiber content, and its crude protein content (19.98 mg/g) closely matches values found in the literature (18.8–20 mg/g) [17, 18]. The best protein source was found to be soy chunks, which showed the greatest protein levels (53.95 mg/g) that were exactly comparable with reference data (49–54 mg/g) [17]. Additionally, their low moisture content (6.13%) verified that they were stable as a dried protein base (Table 13.1). Although the moderate protein level of the mushrooms (23.31 mg/g) [18] was lower than expected (28.9 mg/g), possibly as a result of varietal differences, their exceptionally high moisture content (92.43%) demonstrates their natural capacity to bind water (Table 13.2).

According to these results, breadfruit is perfect for enhancing texture and nutrition in meat substitutes because of its moderate protein, high fiber, and good moisture retention. Soy chunks offer concentrated protein, and mushrooms may improve juiciness. The best formulations probably combine all three ingredients for balanced nutritional and sensory qualities.

Table 13.1 Crude protein and fiber analysis of selected raw materials

S. No	Sample (1g)	Crude protein (mg)	Existing data (mg)	Crude fiber (mg)	Existing data (mg)
1	Breadfruit	19.98	18.8 – 20	67	50 – 60
2	Soy chunks	53.95	49 – 54	18	15 – 25
3	Mushroom	23.31	28.9	16	10 – 32

Source: Author

Table 13.2 Moisture analysis for selected raw materials

Sample	Moisture content (%)	Existing data
Breadfruit	81.32%	60% to 85%
Mushroom	92.43%	85% to 95%
Soy chuck	6.13%	5% to 10%

Source: Author

Composition analysis of raw materials by RSM

The purpose of the response surface methodology (RSM) optimization study was to create nutritionally balanced meat substitutes by evaluating twelve experimental formulations with different proportions of breadfruit, soy chunks, and mushrooms. The findings showed notable variation in the protein content (90.76–121.57 mg) and crude fiber (27.9–69 mg) (Table 13.3) among various ingredient combinations. Higher soy chunk formulations (e.g., Run 2: 1.872 g) produced higher protein levels, while breadfruit-rich formulations (e.g., Run 9: 0.621 g breadfruit, 1.379 g soy chunks, 1 g mushroom) produced higher fiber content, suggesting that mushrooms significantly contribute to fiber enhancement. Four ideal solutions with desirability ratings ranging from 0.451 to 0.769 were found through the analysis; the formulation with the highest score represented the best balance between the amount of protein and fiber (Figure 13.1).

According to these results, although soy chunks are the primary source of protein, it is crucial to strategically include both breadfruit and mushrooms to increase dietary fiber without significantly lowering the quality of the protein. With a desire score of 0.769, the ideal formulation indicates a balanced ratio that represents the best balance between the amount of protein and fiber (Figure 13.1).

According to these results, although soy chunks are the primary source of protein, it is crucial to strategically include both breadfruit and mushrooms to increase dietary fiber without significantly lowering the quality of the protein. With a desire score of 0.769, the ideal formulation indicates a balanced ratio that achieves high protein and fiber content. (Figure 13.2). Mushrooms enhance fiber, offering a scientifically supported foundation for creating functional meat substitutes. With a focus on the important fiber contribution from mushrooms, this study shows how RSM may be used to optimize meat alternative compositions to satisfy particular nutritional needs while preserving component variety.

Evaluation of sensory attributes

Strong customer acceptance of the meat alternative (MA) is shown by the results of the sensory evaluation (Table 13.4), especially in terms of taste (62.5% "Excellent", 31.3% "Very Good") and color (83.3% combined "Excellent/Very Good"). With 87.5% of the scores being positive. Flavor performed very well. Despite receiving 75% acceptance, aroma had the lowest "Excellent" scores (25%), indicating that it could be improved further. A comparative analysis

Table 13.3 Experimental design from mixture analysis from RSM

Runs	Ratio of bread fruit (g)	Ratio of soy chunks (g)	Ratio of mushroom (g)	Crude fiber (mg)	Crude protein (mg)
1	1	1.475	0.525	35.8	101.58
2	0.628	1.872	0.5	35.9	121.57
3	0.5	1.576	0.924	44.7	118.24
4	0.781	1.651	0.568	44.9	118.07
5	0.796	1.448	0.756	27.9	98.25
6	0.5	1.748	0.752	53.9	120.73
7	0.796	1.448	0.756	43.2	98.25
8	0.628	1.872	0.5	37.9	119.9
9	0.621	1.379	1	69	90.76
10	1	1.025	0.975	67.9	95.75
11	1	1.227	0.773	55.7	91.59
12	0.796	1.448	0.756	46.9	99.08

Source: Author

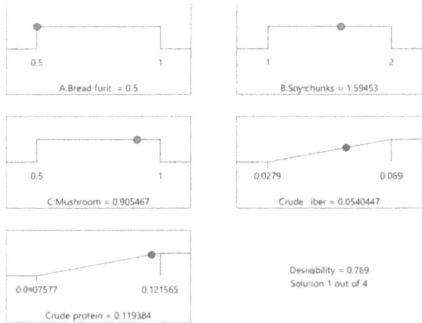

Figure 13.1 Desirability ratings from RSM
Source: Author

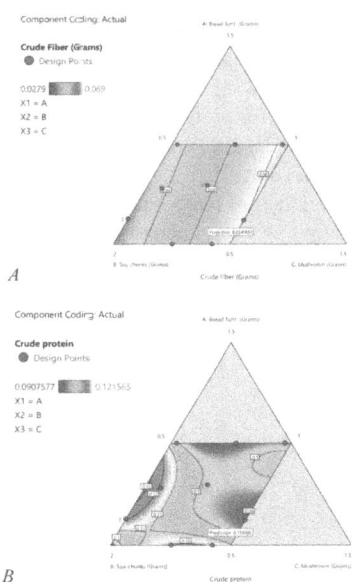

Figure 13.2 Response surface plots of fiber interactions (A) and protein interactions (B) among raw materials
Source: Author

Table 13.4 Analysis of sensory attributes

Parameters	Excellent	Very good	Satisfactory	Fair
Colour	37.5	45.8	14.6	2.1
Colour (Regular Meat vs MA)	31.3	52.1	12.5	4.1
Aroma (Regular Meat vs MA)	25	50	20.8	4.2
Taste	62.5	31.3	6.2	–
Flavour	39.6	47.9	10.4	2.1

Source: Author

showed that people thought an MA's color was about the same as that of ordinary meat (52.1% "Very Good").

The successful replication of meat-like properties is indicated by the high approval ratings for the main sensory attributes (taste, color, and flavor). The main parameter that needs to be improved to be on par with traditional meat products is aroma. These results provide confidence in MA's potential as a healthy substitute for conventional meat.

Conclusion

The study successfully used RSM to create nutritionally optimized alternatives to meat, with breadfruit and mushrooms providing fiber, soy chunks providing high protein, and optimal ratios resulting in balanced nutrition. Strong customer acceptance was confirmed by sensory evaluation, especially for taste and color, but there was potential for improvement in aroma. RSM's efficacy in developing foods has been proven by the highest attractiveness formulation (0.769), which successfully balanced the protein and fiber content. According to these findings, the plant-based substitute for traditional meat is a sustainable and feasible option that only needs slight aromatic adjustments to be more widely accepted.

References

[1] He, J., Evans, N. M., Liu, H., & Shao, S. (2020). A review of research on plant-based meat alternatives: Driving forces, history, manufacturing, and consumer attitudes. *Comprehensive Reviews in Food Science and Food Safety*, 19(5), 2639–2656.

[2] Wang, Y., Tuccillo, F., Lampi, A. M., Knaapila, A., Pulkkinen, M., Kariluoto, S., et al. (2022). Flavour challenges in extruded plant-based meat alternatives: a review. *Comprehensive Reviews in Food Science and Food Safety*, 21(3), 2898–2929.

[3] Carrington, C. M. S., Worrell, D. B., & Huber, D. J. (1998). Growth, maturation and ripening of breadfruit, Artocarpus altilis (Park.) Fosb. *Scientia Horticulturae (Netherlands)*, 76(1), 17–28.

[4] Cheng, Z., Qiu, Y., Bian, M., He, Y., Xu, S., Li, Y., et al. (2024). Muscle fibrous structural design of plant-based meat analogues: advances and challenges in 3D printing technology. *Trends in Food Science and Technology*, 147, 104417.

[5] Estell, M., Hughes, J., & Grafenauer, S. (2021). Plant protein and plant-based meat alternatives: consumer and nutrition professional attitudes and perceptions. *Sustainability*, 13(3), 1478.

[6] Smetana, S., Profeta, A., Voigt, R., Kircher, C., & Heinz, V. (2021). Meat substitution in burgers: nutritional scoring, sensorial testing, and life cycle assessment. *Future Foods*, 4, 100042.

[7] Bakhsh, A., Lee, S. J., Lee, E. Y., Hwang, Y. H., & Joo, S. T. (2021). Evaluation of rheological and sensory char-

acteristics of plant-based meat analog with comparison to beef and pork. *Food Science of Animal Resources*, 41(6), 983.

[8]   Adegunwa, M. O., Ogungbesan, B. O., Adekoya, O. A., Akinloye, E. E., Idowu, O. D., & Alamu, O. E. (2024). Production and characterization of snacks utilizing composite flour from unripe plantain (musa paradisiaca), breadfruit (artocarpus altilis), and cinnamon (cinnamomum venum). *Foods*, 13(6), 852.

[9]   Mehta, K. A., Quek, Y. C. R., & Henry, C. J. (2023). Breadfruit (Artocarpus altilis): processing, nutritional quality, and food applications. *Frontiers in Nutrition*, 10, 1156155.

[10] de Jesus González-Regalado, J., Montalvo-González, E., Miramontes-Escobar, H. A., Jiménez-Fernández, M., de Lourdes García-Magaña, M., Chacón-López, M. A., et al. (2024). Texture profile analysis of heat-processed tender jackfruit (Artocarpus heterophyllus Lam.) and its potential use as a meat analog. *Emirates Journal of Food and Agriculture*, 36, 1–11.

[11] Thangaraju, A. D., Rajkumar, R., Nagarajan, N., & Karthik, P. (2024). Formulation of plant-based meat alternatives and its optimization by experimental design using response surface methodology. *Sustainable Food Technology*, 2(4), 1139–1151.

[12] Sharma, A., Rawat, K., Jattan, P., Kumar, P., Tokusoglu, O., Kumar, P., et al. (2022). Formula refining through composite blend of soya, alfalfa, and wheat flour; A vegan meat approach. *Journal of Food Processing and Preservation*, 46(5), e15235.

[13] Iqbal, T., Sohaib, M., Iqbal, S., & Rehman, H. (2024). Exploring therapeutic potential of pleurotus ostreatus and agaricus bisporus mushrooms against hyperlipidemia and oxidative stress using animal model. *Foods*, 13(5), 709.

[14] Jones, A. M. P., Ragone, D., Tavana, N. U. G., Bernotas, D. W., & Murch, S. J. (2011). Beyond the Bounty: breadfruit (Artocarpus altilis) for food security and novel foods in the 21st Century.

[15] Ma, M. M., & Mu, T. H. (2016). Effects of extraction methods and particle size distribution on the structural, physicochemical, and functional properties of dietary fiber from deoiled cumin. *Food Chemistry*, 194, 237–246.

[16] Torten, J., & Whitaker, J. R. (1964). Evaluation of the biuret and dye-binding methods for protein determination in meats. *Journal of Food Science*, 29(2), 168–174.

[17] Devi, T. A., Rahul, R., Joshua, H. M., Naveen, N., & Karthik, P. (2024). Formulation of plant-based meat alternatives and its optimization by experimental design using response surface methodology. *Sustainable Food Technology*, 2(4), 1139–1151.

14 Comparative microbial signatures and functional profiles across gastrointestinal cancers

Geetika Devi Kaliappa[a] and Vidyalakshmi Subramanian[b]

Department of Biotechnology, PSG College of Technology, Coimbatore, India

Abstract

Gastrointestinal (GI) cancers represent a significant global health challenge due to their higher incidence and death rates. Recent studies have highlighted the role of gut microbial dysbiosis in the progression of GI cancers. However, the interactions remain poorly understood. This study analyzed the taxonomic composition of gut microbiota and its association across GI cancer cohorts (COAD, READ, STAD, and ESCA). Microbial abundance was studied at the genus and the species levels. Functional enrichment analysis was performed to identify key pathways associated with tumor-specific microbial alterations. The findings revealed that *Bacteroides* was the dominant genus across tumor and normal tissues, while tumor samples exhibited an increased abundance of pathogenic genera such as *Fusobacterium, Prevotella,* and *Streptococcus*. Functional analysis demonstrated that tumor-associated microbiota influences epithelial-mesenchymal transition (EMT) and inflammatory signaling. Further research is needed to validate these interactions through *in vivo* models and multi-omics studies for developing microbiome-based treatment strategies.

Keywords: Cancer biomarkers, functional enrichment, gastrointestinal cancers, gut microbiota, microbial dysbiosis

Introduction

Gastrointestinal (GI) cancers are considered to be one of the most significant health challenges across the world. GI cancers contribute to over one-fourth of the global cancer incidence and to nearly one-third of cancer-related deaths [1 2]. An increase in the incidence of GI cancer patients in developing countries is majorly attributed to lifestyle changes like dietary habits and decreased physical activity [3]. Recent studies suggest that gut dysbiosis and inflammation in the intestinal lining play a significant role in GI cancer progression [4]. Pathogenic bacteria in the gut release toxins that disrupt host signalling pathways which in turn induce changes in gene expression leading to cancer [5]. For example, *Enterotoxigenic Bacteroides fragilis* (ETBF) produces toxins that alter the expression of key genes [6]. ETBF has been suggested as a biomarker for ColoRectal Cancer (CRC) due to its higher abundance in pre-cancerous tissues especially when compared to individuals without a family history of CRC [7].

Animal models are used for understanding the role of gut microbiome in CRC, which revealed that dysbiosis in gut may lead to DNA damage, signalling and metabolic pathways disruption and anti-tumor immunity suppression, leading to an uncontrolled cell proliferation. *E. coli* has been shown to induce DNA damage and *Fusobacterium nucleatum* promotes tumor cell proliferation by activating the Wnt/β-catenin signalling pathway [8]. These findings highlight the role of pathogenic bacteria in the GI tract contributing to cancer and its progression.

Recent researches explored the role of gut microbiome and its dysbiosis in CRC and other GI cancers and have revealed that gut dysbiosis plays a significant role in GI cancers, including gastric, hepatic and oesophageal cancer [9]. Normal tissues showed a higher abundance of beneficial bacteria such as *Roseburia* and *Lactobacillus*, which support gut health and may play protective roles against carcinogenesis. Many studies have reported the increase in bacterial phyla such as *Bacteroidetes, Fusobacterium* and *Proteobacteria* in GI cancer and decrease in *Firmicutes* [15]. This microbial dysbiosis is thought to influence cancer and its progression through complex interactions within the gut ecosystem. Diets rich in dietary fiber promoted the growth of beneficial microbes that generate short-chain fatty acids (SCFAs) known for their anti-inflammatory and tumor-suppressive effects [18]. The above findings suggest that dietary modulation can be used for cancer prevention and also as a therapy.

[a]geetika.kaliappa@gmail.com, [b]svd.bio@psgtech.ac.in

DOI: 10.1201/9781003770435-14

The complete picture of gut dysbiosis and its role in cancer progression across different GI cancers is under-explored. This research aims to explore the patterns in microbiome composition and their role in GI cancer development.

Materials and Methods

Data collection

Microbial abundance data was retrieved from *The Cancer Microbiome Atlas* (TCMA) [10]. TCMA provides decontaminated microbial abundance data at both genus and species level for the following GI cohorts, Colon Adenocarcinoma (COAD), Rectum Adenocarcinoma (READ), Stomach Adenocarcinoma (STAD), and Esophageal Adenocarcinoma (ESCA). Tumor and normal solid tissue samples were included for comparing both cancerous and non-cancerous state of the tissues. The datasets were also pre-processed during sequencing to ensure high-quality data for further analysis. The overall workflow for the microbiome analysis is illustrated in Figure 14.1.

Taxonomic profiling

Taxonomic profile data were retrieved from the DUKE University digital repository Shen et al., [10] using the *phyloseq* R package [11]. Operational Taxonomic Unit (OTU), metadata and sample data were categorized into genus and species levels for

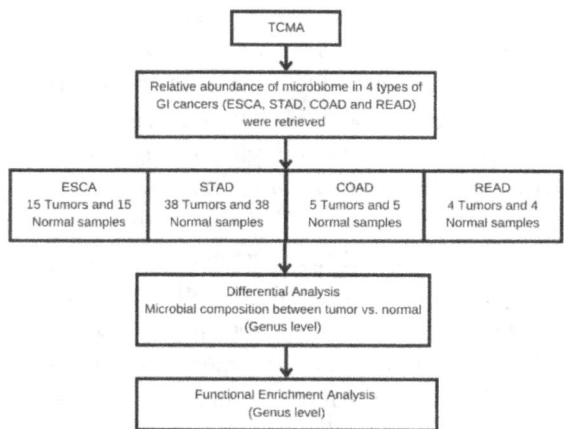

Figure 14.1 The overall workflow of the microbiome analysis in GI cancer cohorts. Microbial abundance data for four GI cancer types (ESCA, STAD, COAD, READ) were retrieved from TCMA. Samples were grouped into tumor and normal for genus-level differential analysis and functional enrichment

Source: Author

further analysis. *MicrobiomeAnalyst tool* [12] was used to statistically analyze the microbial diversity and composition.

Data preprocessing

Microbial abundance data were normalized to ensure the data quality. Zero or low abundance microbial taxa data for all samples were excluded.

Functional enrichment analysis

The *MicrobiomeAnalyst tool,* was used to perform functional enrichment analysis [12]. This tool integrates the PICRUSt2 algorithm and based on the microbial profiles, the tool predicts the functional pathways. GAPGOM R package was used to perform Over-Representation Analysis (ORA) to predict the biological functions [13]. Gene Ontology like biological processes (BP) and molecular functions (MF) were analyzed across all GI cancer datasets. Statistical significance was confirmed using the False Discovery Rate (FDR). Bar charts and functional clusters were used to represent the results.

The compositional and functional roles of microbial communities across all GI cancer cohorts were analyzed to get a comparative insight into microbial abundance patterns and their functional associations.

Results

Prevotella, streptococcus and bacteroides dominate the tumor microbiome in GI cancers

Analysis of microbial profiles of COAD cohort revealed that *Bacteroides* were the most dominant genus in both tumor and normal samples, with higher relative abundance in tumor tissues. Other taxa, including *Streptococcus* and *Prevotella*, were increased in tumor tissues, whereas *Fusobacterium* and *Campylobacter* were more abundant in normal tissues as shown in Figure 14.2A and 14.2B.

In ESCA and STAD cohorts, *Helicobacter* and *Prevotella* were enriched, particularly in gastric cancer as shown in Figure 14.2C and 14.2G. In contrast, COAD and READ cohorts were characterized by a predominance of *Bacteroides* and *Fusobacterium*, supporting their well-documented association with CRC as shown in Figure 14.2A and 14.2E.

In ESCA, *Streptococcus* and *Prevotella* were significantly enriched in tumor tissues, whereas

Figure 14.2 **Bar plots of microbial composition analysis.** The microbial abundance in **A.** COAD normal samples **B.** COAD tumor samples **C.** ESCA normal samples **D.** ESCA tumor samples **E.** READ normal samples. **F.** READ tumor samples **G.** STAD normal samples **H.** STAD tumor samples. The TCGA barcode with "−1A" indicates the tumor, and "−11A" indicates the normal

Source: Author

Table 14.1 Abundant microbial genera in tumor samples

Types	Abundant microbial genera
COAD, READ, READ, ESCA	*Fusobacterium, Prevotella, Streptococcus*
COAD, READ	*Bacteroides, Fusobacterium, Prevotella, Streptococcus, Alistipes*
COAD, STAD	*Fusobacterium, Prevotella, Haemophilus, Streptococcus, Veillonella*
COAD, ESCA	*Veillonella, Streptococcus, Fusobacterium, Prevotella, Haemophilus*
ESCA, STAD	*Prevotella, Streptococcus, Helicobacter, Haemophilus, Veillonella, Fusobacterium*
ESCA, COAD	*Veillonella, Streptococcus, Fusobacterium, Prevotella, Haemophilus*
ESCA, READ	*Streptococcus, Fusobacterium, Prevotella*

Source: Author

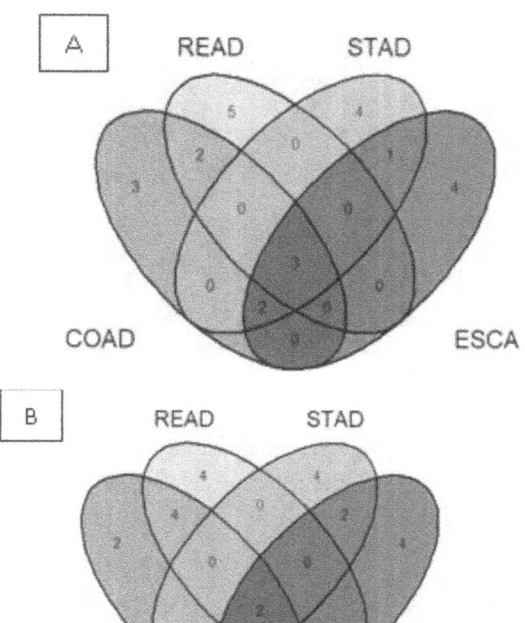

Figure 14.3 Venn diagram of the top 10 abundant microbial compositions at the genus level in samples from four cohorts: COAD, READ, ESCA, and STAD. (A) Tumor samples and (B) Normal samples

Source: Author

Table 14.2 Abundant microbial genera in normal samples

Types	Abundant microbial genera
COAD, READ, STAD, ESCA	*Prevotella, Streptococcus*
COAD, READ	*Bacteroides, Prevotella, Roseburia, Alistipes, Streptococcus, Parabacteroides*
COAD, STAD	*Prevotella, Fusobacterium, Haemophilus, Streptococcus*
COAD, ESCA	*Prevotella, Fusobacterium, Haemophilus, Streptococcus*
ESCA, STAD	*Helicobacter, Prevotella, Streptococcus, Haemophilus, Fusobacterium, Veillonella*
ESCA, READ	*Prevotella, Streptococcus*

Source: Author

correlation tools. Venn diagram analysis as illustrated in Figure 14.3. revealed shared and site-specific taxa across tumor types. *Bacteroides, Streptococcus,* and *Prevotella* were detected across multiple cancers. Certain genera exhibited higher tissue specificity, such as *Helicobacter* in gastric cancers. The samples in the ESCA and STAD groups had 6 shared genera, whereas the samples in the COAD and READ groups had 5 shared genera. These findings were shown in Table 14.1 for tumor samples and Table 14.2 for normal samples.

The pattern search analysis illustrated in Figure 14.4. indicates that *Erysipelotrichales, Coriobacteriales, Clostridiales, Acidaminococcales* and *Pasteurellales* were positively correlated with other bacteria in normal. *Fusobacteriales, Campylobacterales, Enterobacterales, Bacillales, Selenomonadales, Tissierellales, Bacteroidales, Desulfovibrionales,*

Neisseria and *Campylobacter* were more prevalent in normal samples as shown in Figure 14.2C and 14.2D. Similarly, in STAD, *Helicobacter* was markedly higher in tumor samples as shown in Figure 14.2G and 14.2H, further reinforcing its well-established role in GI cancer.

To further explore shared and site-specific microbial signatures, a comparative analysis was performed across cancer types using Venn diagrams and pattern

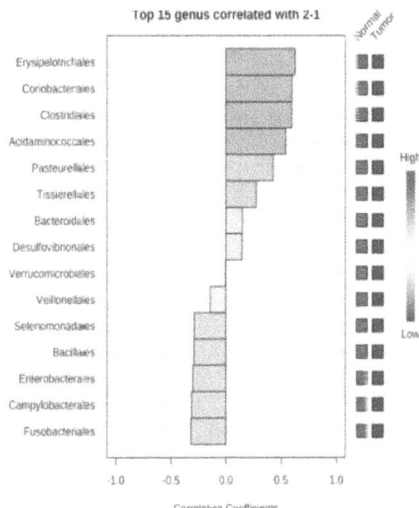

Figure 14.4 Pattern search analysis results for top 15 genus. The color bars in the pattern search plot indicate positive (red) and negative (blue) correlations in the microbes among the different sample types. The mini heatmap shows the abundance of the features of each sample type

Source: Author

Figure 14.5 Functional enrichments of highly connected microorganisms in the READ–Tumor network

Source: Author

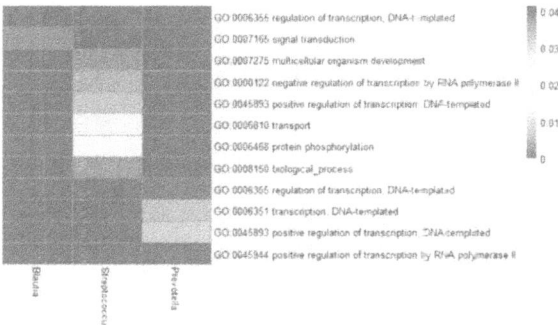

Figure 14.6 Functional enrichments of highly connected microorganisms in the COAD – Normal network- molecular functions

Source: Author

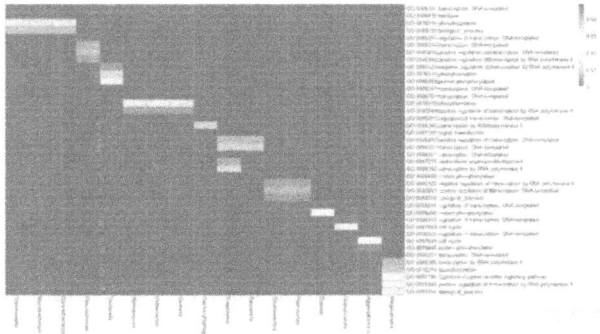

Figure 14.7 Functional enrichments of highly connected microorganisms in the STAD – Tumor network-molecular functions

Source: Author

Veilloneilales, Verrucomicrobiales were negatively correlated with other bacteria in tumor.

The molecular functions associated with highly connected microbial taxa identified in each cancer cohort was investigated to understand the biological relevance of these taxonomic shifts.

Molecular function enrichment reveals microbial contributions to host regulatory pathways in GI tumors

Molecular function enrichment analysis for COAD and READ revealed that the microbial-host gene neighborhoods were highly enriched for functions related to protein phosphorylation and DNA transcription as shown in Figure 14.5. However, due to the high interaction complexity between microorganisms and host genes, mapping molecular functions to specific microorganisms at the genus level was challenging. Figures 14.6 and 14.7. display the molecular function enrichment results for microbial gene neighborhoods in lower GI tumors, demonstrating that multiple microbial genera contribute to host cellular processes. *Peptoniphilus* and *Prevotella* were significantly enriched in signal transduction and RNA transcription regulation as shown in Figure 14.7. The predominant molecular functions in these GI tumors were G-protein coupled receptor signaling, cell cycle regulation, multicellular organism development, and protein phosphorylation.

Enrichment analysis for ESCA and STAD identified distinct microbial associations with molecular

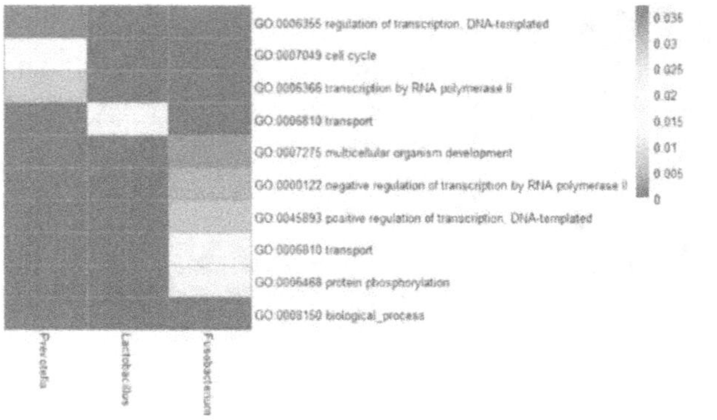

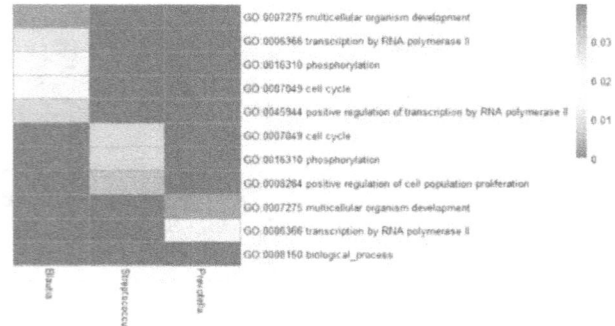

Figure 14.8 Functional enrichments of highly connected microorganisms in the ESCA – Tumor network- molecular functions
Source: Author

functions as shown in Figures 14.7 and 8. Protein phosphorylation and transcriptional regulation were the most enriched functions in upper GI tumors, with microbial genera such as *Aggregatibacter, Dialister,* and *Treponema* showing strong associations. *Lactobacillus* was mapped to transport processes, while *Megasphaera, Gemmella, Oribacterium, Actinomyces,* and *Pseudomonas* were linked to positive regulation of transcription by RNA polymerase II. *Granulicatella* was significantly enriched in cell cycle regulation.

While molecular function analysis revealed important regulatory activities, biological process enrichment provided broader insights into the cellular pathways influenced by tumor-associated microbial communities.

Biological process enrichment highlights microbial influence on transcription and proliferation in GI cancers

The enrichment analysis for COAD and READ revealed that microbial-associated host genes were significantly enriched in pathways related to transcriptional regulation and cell proliferation as illustrated in Figures 14.9 and 14.10. *Blautia* was associated with multiple biological processes, suggesting a diverse functional role in colorectal tumor networks as shown in Figure 14.10. *Prevotella* was highly enriched in transcriptional regulation, indicating a potential influence on host gene expression as shown in Figure 14.11. *Peptoniphilus* exhibited strong enrichment for positive regulation of cell population proliferation, suggesting a link to tumor growth and cancer cell expansion.

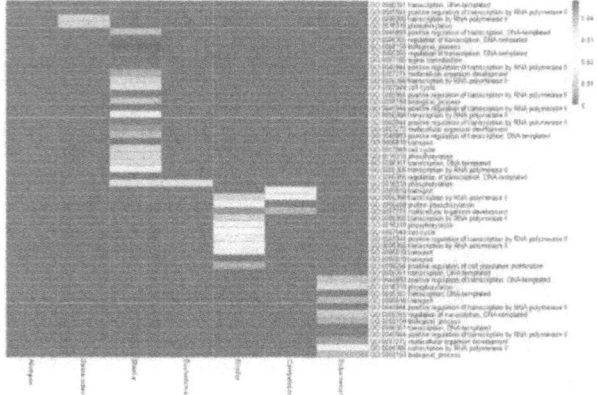

Figure 14.9 Functional enrichments of highly connected microorganisms in the COAD – Normal network- biological processes
Source: Author

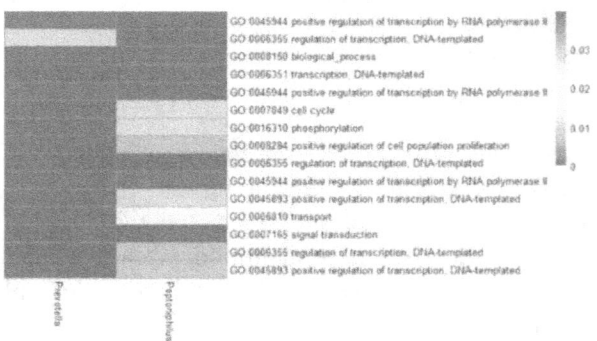

Figure 14.10 Functional enrichments of highly connected microorganisms in the READ – Normal network- biological processes
Source: Author

Figure 14.11 Functional enrichments of highly connected microorganisms in the READ – Tumor network- biological processes
Source: Author

In ESCA and STAD microbial-host interactions were enriched in transcriptional regulation, protein phosphorylation, and cell cycle processes as

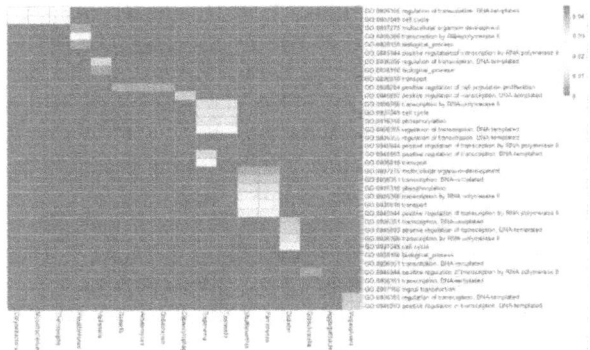

Figure 14.12 Functional enrichments of highly connected microorganisms in the STAD – Tumor network-biological processes
Source: Author

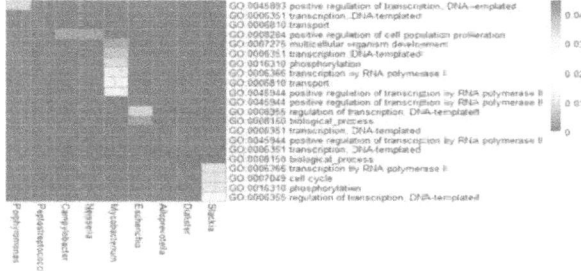

Figure 14.14 Functional enrichments of highly connected microorganisms in the STAD – Normal network-biological processes
Source: Author

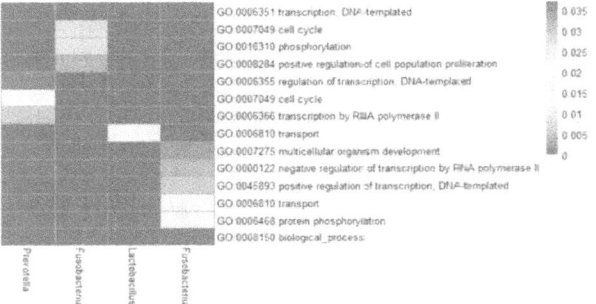

Figure 14.13 Functional enrichments of highly connected microorganisms in the ESCA – Tumor network-biological processes
Source: Author

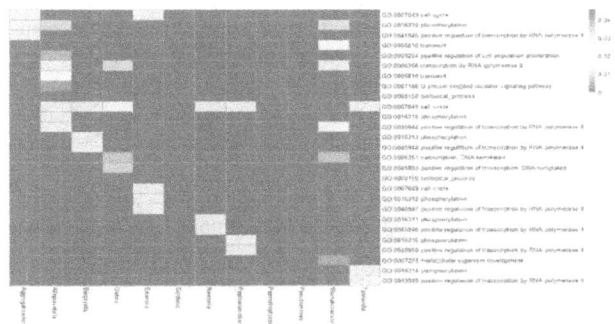

Figure 14.15 Functional enrichments of highly connected microorganisms in the ESCA – Normal network-biological processes
Source: Author

illustrated in Figures 14.12 and 14.13. *Parvimonas* and *Shuttleworthia* (STAD cohort) were mapped to positive regulation of transcription by RNA polymerase II, suggesting a role in tumor-associated gene activation. *Oribacterium, Fusobacterium, Gemella,* and *Actinomyces* were associated with positive regulation of cell population proliferation, a process linked to tumor growth and progression. Other microbial taxa, including *Slackia*, were mapped to multiple biological processes, such as phosphorylation, cell cycle regulation, and transcription by RNA polymerase II, indicating broad functional involvement in tumor biology as illustrated in Figures 14.14 and 14.15.

The functional enrichment analyses provided evidence that tumor-associated microbiota are involved in critical regulatory pathways, including transcription, cell cycle progression, and signal transduction.

To interpret the biological significance of these results and their clinical relevance, we discuss them in the context of prior studies and emerging microbiome-cancer hypotheses.

Conclusion

The findings of the research highlight the role of gut microbiota and their interactions in the pathogenesis of GI cancers. By analyzing microbial composition and functional enrichment, the findings reveal tumor-specific microbial dysbiosis and its association with cancer-related pathways. The results demonstrate that while *Bacteroides* dominates both tumor and normal tissues across GI cancers, tumor tissues exhibit enrichment of pathogenic genera such as *Fusobacterium, Prevotella,* and *Helicobacter pylori*. These microbial alterations have been associated with chromatin remodeling, immune modulation, and epithelial-mesenchymal transition (EMT).

Future investigations should focus on integrating multi-omics approaches to provide a deeper understanding of the functional impact of microbiome interactions followed by experimental validation. Advancing this field through mechanistic studies and clinical trials could lead to novel microbiome-targeted strategies for cancer diagnosis, treatment, and prevention.

References

[1] Arnold, M., Pandeya, N., Byrnes, G., & Ferlay, J. (2020). Global burden of 5 major types of gastrointestinal cancer. *Gastroenterology*, 159(1), 335–349.e15.

[2] Bray, F., Ferlay, J., Soerjomataram, I., Siegel, R. L., Torre, L. A., & Jemal, A. (2018). Global cancer statistics 2018: GLOBOCAN estimates of incidence and mortality worldwide for 36 cancers in 185 countries. *CA: A Cancer Journal for Clinicians*, 68(6), 394–424.

[3] Xi, Y., & Xu, P. (2021). Global colorectal cancer burden in 2020 and projections to 2040. *Translational Oncology*, 14(10), 101174.

[4] Raskov, H., Søby, J. H., Troelsen, J., Bojesen, R. D., & Gögenur, I. (2019). Driver gene mutations and epigenetics in colorectal cancer. *Annals of Surgery*, 271(1), 75–85.

[5] Fiorentini, C., Carlini, F., Germinario, E. A. P., Maroccia, Z., Travaglione, S., & Fabbri, A. (2020). Gut microbiota and colon cancer: a role for bacterial protein toxins? *International Journal of Molecular Sciences*, 21(17), 6201.

[6] Liu, Q.-Q., He, D., Xie, Q., Wang, H., & Liu, Y. (2020). Enterotoxigenic Bacteroides fragilis induces the stemness in colorectal cancer via upregulating histone demethylase JMJD2B. *Gut Microbes*, 12(1), 1788900.

[7] Zamani, S., Taslimi, R., Sarabi, A., Jasemi, S., Sechi, L. A., & Feizabadi, M. M. (2020). Enterotoxigenic Bacteroides fragilis: a possible etiological candidate for bacterially-induced colorectal precancerous and cancerous lesions. *Frontiers in Cellular and Infection Microbiology*, 9, 449.

[8] Brennan, C. A., & Garrett, W. S. (2016). Gut microbiota, inflammation, and colorectal cancer. *Annual Review of Microbiology*, 70(1), 395–411.

[9] Yarahmadi, A., & Afkhami, H. (2024). The role of microbiomes in gastrointestinal cancers: new insights. *Frontiers in Oncology*, 13, 1344328.

[10] Shen, X., Wang, J., et al. (2020). The cancer microbiome atlas (TCMA): a pan-cancer comparative analysis to distinguish organ-associated microbiota from equiprevalent contaminants. Res. Data Repos., Duke Univ.

[11] McMurdie, P. J., & Holmes, S. (2013). Phyloseq: an R package for reproducible interactive analysis and graphics of microbiome census data. *PLoS One*, 8(4), e61217.

[12] Dhariwal, A., Chong, J., Habib, S., King, I. L., Agellon, L. B., & Raskoa, J. (2017). Microbiome analyst: a web-based tool for comprehensive statistical, visual and meta-analysis of microbiome data. *Nucleic Acids Research*, 45(W1), W180–W188.

[13] Van Mourik, C., Ehsani, R., & Drabløs, F. (2021). GAP-GOM—an R package for gene annotation prediction using GO metrics. *BMC Research Notes*, 14(1), 162.

[14] Chang, Y., Ou, Q., Zhou, X., Liu, J., & Zhang, S. (2023). Global research trends and focus on the link between colorectal cancer and gut flora: a bibliometric analysis from 2001 to 2021. *Frontiers in Microbiology*, 14, 1182006.

[15] Lee, D.-W., Han, S. W., Kang, J. K., Bae, J. M., Kim, H. P., Won, J. K., et al. (2018). Association between Fusobacterium nucleatum, pathway mutation, and patient prognosis in colorectal cancer. *Annals of Surgical Oncology*, 25(11), 3389–3395.

[16] Ma, M., Zheng, Z., Li, J., He, Y., Kang, W., & Ye, X. (2024). Association between the gut microbiota, inflammatory factors, and colorectal cancer: evidence from Mendelian randomization analysis. *Frontiers in Microbiology*, 15, 1309111.

[18] Yang, S., Zhao, S., Ye, Y., Jia, L., & Lou, Y. (2022). Global research trends on the links between gut microbiota and cancer immunotherapy: a bibliometric analysis (2012–2021). *Frontiers in Immunology*, 13, 952546.

[18] Catalkaya, G., Chen, C. Y., Zhang, D., Liu, W., & Feng, Y. (2020). Interaction of dietary polyphenols and gut microbiota: microbial metabolism of polyphenols, influence on the gut microbiota, and implications on host health. *Food Frontiers*, 1(2):109–133.

15 Evaluation of weld component of backhoe based on numerical durability and fatigue analysis

Venkatachalapathi, M.[1,a] and Martin Sureshbabu, D.[2,b]

[1]M.E. Engineering Design, Department of Mechanical Engineering, PSG College of Technology, Coimbatore, Tamil Nadu, India

[2]Assistant Professor, Department of Mechanical Engineering, PSG College of Technology, Coimbatore, Tamil Nadu, India

Abstract

In heavy machinery equipment, the assembly of the backhoe such as hinge bush play's a critical role in structural integrity, operational efficiency and life span. This work provided a detailed information for evaluating the structural and fatigue performance of welded hinge bush component which is mainly used in the assembly of backhoe. The main structure of the assembly of the backhoe and the hinge bush with welded joint is modeled by using CAD software and the simulation is carried out. The semi-elliptical crack is generated by using a fracture tool on the critical areas of the welded joints to determine the stress intensity factor distribution of three different mode region of the crack, that helps to predict whether the crack may propagate or not. To prevent unexpected failure in welded joints the fatigue analysis is simulated. However, the welded component is the weakest strength in a structure, making their evaluation is essential to determine their strength, durability, ability to withstand cyclic loads and prevent premature failure of the welded component. The tensile, bending and torsional test specimen were made as per the ASTM standard by using different parameters of Metal Inert Gas (MIG) welding such as current, voltage and speed to determine the maximum load, ultimate tensile strength, percentage of elongation, maximum shear strength, torque and twist angle

Keywords: Backhoe, crack propagation analysis, durability and mig welding, fatigue analysis, hinge bush, structural analysis, welded component

Introduction

In heavy machinery, the backhoe serves a crucial role in excavators and mining machines. The main body and the bucket are linked as the principal function of the excavator, which transfer the forces in operations like digging, lifting and material handling. The cyclic loading includes dynamic and impact forces which is crucial for ensuring the efficiency, durability and safety for the structural integrity of the backhoe. The backhoe is fabricated by using the process of welding to join the heavy structural components. The welded joint faces many challenges such as inherent residual stress, porosity, lack of fusion, heat-affected zones, and other weld defects. The material behavior, stress distribution and the load-bearing capacity are the main factors of the welded structure for the durability of the welded component that can increase or decrease the catastrophic failure, accident, cost and maintenance.

In a backhoe, the hinge bush is a cylindrical joint that serves as the connection between the different structural components such as the bucket linkage, arm and hydraulic actuators. The smooth operation is designed to facilitate the rotational movement, which absorbs the high loads. The component is made up of high-strength steel, which can operate under extreme conditions and it is housed within the welded joints. During welding, the residual stress is achieved by the rapid cooling that can cause crack initiation, misalignment and uneven load distribution. Since the rapid heating and cooling may reduce the toughness of material while changing from ductile to brittle. The welded joint may fail under cyclic loads due to the improper welding parameter and lack of penetration. The peening techniques must be applied to relieve stress at critical locations. The operational efficiency and longevity of hinge bush can be improved by optimizing the weld design and specialized process.

Fatigue analysis is exposed to repeated or cyclic load over time, that has the technique which is used to determine the longevity, material selection, components and structure. The work is mainly focused on the geometry, how these forces generate progressive, cumulative damage through stress and strain, which is ultimately leading to failure. Stresses below the ultimate tensile strength of a material can still

[a]23md39@psgtech.ac.in, [b]msb.mech@psgtech.ac.in

DOI: 10.1201/9781003770435-15

lead to fatigue failure over time. In each load cycle, a microscopic crack may form and gradually propagate within the material. The crack may develop in those areas where high stress concentrations or imperfections in the structure are formed during the cyclic loading, which has the ability to progressively weaken the material and ultimately leads to failure, when the material can no longer withstand the applied load. The cracks may initiate and grow under various conditions such as dynamic loads, fatigue and environmental factors. The analysis produces results for crack growth rate along with critical lengths needed to evaluate the remaining service life of components. The crack growth which influences the factors like material properties, weld quality and operational stress.

The three modes of stress intensity factor in the weld region describe the propagation of cracks under different loading conditions. Mode I (opening mode) is the most common mode in the weld, which separate the crack faces in the crack plane that acts perpendicular by the tensile force in the poorly welded connections. Mode II (sliding mode) causes the shear pressure in the fracture face to slide in the weld zone which is related to one another. Mode III (tearing mode) is due to misalignment or uneven loading in the weld region. These stress intensity factors are crucial understanding in crack initiation and propagation within the weld zone. This work will be helpful to predict the potential failures in the weld region and design for better integrity.

Mei and Dong [1] assessed the multi-axial fatigue of welded parts under non-proportional effects of loading and considerable volumes of test data have been well correlated in conditions with both uniaxially dominated and non-proportional multi-axial fatigue loading, for various types of components, joint layouts, and loads. Thomas et al. [2] stressed the significance of lifetime determining factors for welded parts to account for contemporary materials and high steam parameters employed in power generation plants. Large-sized tensile specimens and high-temperature welded pipes provide valuable information about damage dependence on sizes and geometries. The effect of effective applied stresses on creep relies significantly on residual stresses that researchers computed in both the welded and post-weld heat treatment conditions. Hobbacher [3] suggested a complete framework in welded parts that improves the fatigue characteristics and enhanced

the procedures in evaluating the weld defects and also dealt with the intricacies of variable amplitude loading and continuous damage evaluation. Abima et al. [4] enhanced mechanical properties and exhibit ferrite characterization, which increases the toughness and ductility in a vast heat-affected zone. Optimized the weld parameters for a greater amount of structural integrity in hybrid welding use. Dhobale and Mishra [5] raised the heat input in MIG welding that influence the tensile strength in weld joint and microstructure changes resulting in coarse grains and decreased the strength in the heat-affected zone. Created a correlation between the material properties and the heat input in the hardness of the weld pool as it raised the heat input. Haque [6] determined that TIG welding was better than MIG welding of AISI-1020 mild steel and resulted in improved mechanical properties and high tensile strength in the weld joints. Improved the yield and ultimate strength by raising the voltage and the current. In weld joints, the correct method of cooling is vital in the weld joints for enhancement of the breaking stress.

Njim [7] founded that the geometry of the V-notch profile has a great impact on the fatigue life of mild steel AISI 1020. The overall fatigue performance has been influenced by changing the stress concentration using different notch angles and depths. Alweendo et al. [8] investigated the fatigue characteristics of hot-tip galvanized steel under varying loading conditions using AISI 1020 normalized steel. The mechanical and microstructural characteristics varied before and after galvanizing. The yield strength and fatigue strength, as well as tensile strength, experienced an adverse change due to the galvanizing process under high-cycle fatigue conditions.

Samuel Frimpong and Li [9] performed a dynamic non-linear event for component strength in the regions of the boom's high stress through mode synthesis. Created a virtual prototype to reproduce the stress field concentrations during operations. The von-Mises maximum stress at a given node was determined to be 10.61 GPa. Yu et al. [10] optimized the boom structure, significantly decreasing the stress concentration and improving the overall mechanical performance. Eliminated the middle stiffeners in welding using the optimized design. The validity of the optimization approach is established through the use of iterative testing and analysis. Cherian and Kumar [11] examined hydraulic hose failure in backhoe loaders by detecting the usual defects like cracks, bursts and pinholes. Demonstrated an excess pressure error by fluctuating in crimp size, which leads to failure. Defects have been ruled out by minimizing the crimp size of hose couplings and the test proved to be effectiveness. Motka and Momin [12] examined the assembly of the components to avoid failures under various loading conditions and determined high-stress regions through structural analysis and recommended a design change to reduce the stress and improve the performance. The durability of the backhoe loader can be greatly enhanced by optimizing the thickness of the components. Tewari et al. [13] examined the performance and strength of a backhoe machine and primarily focused on its boom part at varying working conditions. Reckoned the stress and deflection using finite element analysis (FEA) to ascertain if the boom quality for the required fatigue life standard and recommended it can bear high operational forces, thereby being suitable for heavy-duty operations.

Wei et al. [14] developed cyclic structural stress-strain curves from monotonic loading for elastic-perfectly plastic and modified the Ramberg-Osgood models. The elastic-perfectly plastic has been used in a simplified 3-bar model and verified through simulations and supplied graphical representation and mathematical equations for both the model. Larsen et al. [15] validated three finite element models of offshore k-node structures by using experimental fatigue test data and incorporated 3D scanned weld geometries, which significantly improve the accuracy of strain range. The fatigue failures were observed in the weld structure and suggested a need for improved design and analysis. Duhan et al. [16] investigated complex loading conditions in rail materials and analyzed a semi-elliptical crack with the major axis perpendicular to the rail axis. Under varying train speeds and coefficients of friction, the stress intensity factor (SIF) was evaluated and found to be maximum at the deepest point of the crack front.

Modeling and assembly of the backhoe

The main function of the backhoe is used for digging, material handling, extend, retract and the operators can be allowed to reach different directions, especially in structural components like excavators and other heavy machinery. The movement is controlled during excavation operations and is only possible through the deployment of the backhoe to link the main arm and the bucket. The structure is typically made from high-strength steel material to handle heavy loads and cyclic stress. The force is distributed simultaneously with hydraulic transmission of the required power to force the bucket during operation. The main function is to maintain the performance while improving product longevity, when forces act dynamically on the system.

In backhoe assembly, the hinge bush is designed to facilitate the smooth rotational movement at pivot joints. The articulation is allowed to control the bearing surface, which reduces the friction and wear. The backhoe is provided as low-friction interface that minimizes the energy loss, improves the efficiency of movement and prevents the excessive wear to improve the life span. In backhoe assembly, the pad plate is designed to enhance the structural strength and longevity. The load is evenly distributed across the boom structure when it is subjected to heavy loads, impact forces and wear. As the load is distributed uniformly, it helps us to reduce deformation, cracks and premature failure in the critical areas, by which it can extend the service life of the backhoe.

The backhoe provided a strong and durable connection between the metal surfaces, which is used to join different components. These weld joints can able to withstand high loads, vibrations and dynamic forces during the operations. Appropriate weld size, penetration, and quality control are essential for the proper welding technique that can improve the durability and in addition, reduce the cracks and material failures. All these components are modeled and assembled by using CAD software with an appropriate dimension as shown in Figure 15.1. And it is further carried out to perform structural and fatigue strength analysis.

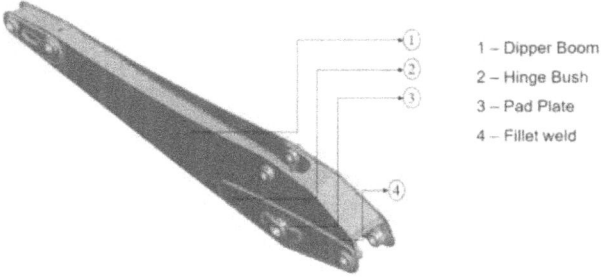

1 – Dipper Boom
2 – Hinge Bush
3 – Pad Plate
4 – Fillet weld

Figure 15.1 Modeling and assembly of the backhoe
Source: Author

Numerical analysis of the backhoe

The numerical analysis is performed to simulate real world conditions of the backhoe assembly by selecting appropriate boundary conditions and suitable material properties. The material is selected as AISI 1020 steel because of its low carbon content, balanced mechanical properties and cost effectiveness. The material has good machinability under normalized condition due to its low carbon content. By using conventional welding methods, it can be welded without requiring preheating, which exhibits excellent weldability. The material has moderate strength and ductility, which makes suitable for cold forming, bending and other forming processes. The material exhibits good toughness and impact resistance by which it can improve the durability and performance of the component. The mechanical properties of the AISI 1020 steel had a density of 7870 kg/(cm³), young's modulus of 205 GPa, ultimate tensile strength of 420 MPa and poisson's ratio of 0.29.

The applied forces and support conditions are essential for the simulation of the backhoe as shown in Figure 15.2. It has two external forces (force 1: 192.5 kN and force 2:156 kN) at different locations. The hinged supports are labelled as 3, 4 and 5, which serve as the pivot points and allow for rotational movement and translation motion is restricted in specific directions. These supports maintain stability and ensure proper load distribution across the boom structure.

The assembly of the backhoe is subjected to determine strength, stability and performance under various loading conditions. Structural analysis is commonly used to evaluate the displacement, von-Mises stress distribution and equivalent strain. At hinged support, the backhoe is subjected to multiple forces from external loads such as bucket, hydraulic cylinder forces and reaction forces. In backhoe

assembly, the minimum displacement was found to be 0.3 mm at hinged supports and maximum displacement was found to be 4 mm at the topmost or free-end region of the boom where external forces or loads or applied as shown in Figure 15.3.

In backhoe assembly, the maximum von-Mises stress distribution was found to be 6.945 ×MPa at the bucket side link connected region as shown in Figure 15.4.

In backhoe assembly, the maximum equivalent strain distribution was found to be 3.2829 × at the hinge bush in the welded region as shown in Figure 15.5.

Fatigue analysis is evaluated to determine its material or structure's ability, whether it can withstand repeated cyclic loading over time without failure. The material's ultimate tensile strength is frequently below the fluctuating stress levels that cause fatigue failure to develop gradually. Material fails because of fatigue according to three sequential stages that involve initiation and propagation before reaching complete fracture. The S-N curve functions to predict the number of cycles when using AISI 1020 steel

Figure 15.3 Displacement of the backhoe
Source: Author

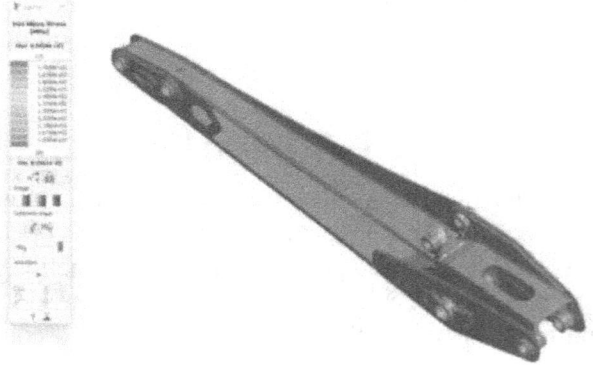

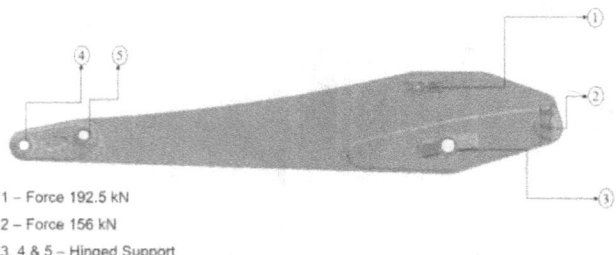

1 – Force 192.5 kN
2 – Force 156 kN
3, 4 & 5 – Hinged Support

Figure 15.2 Boundary conditions of the backhoe
Source: Author

Figure 15.4 von-Mises stress distribution of the backhoe
Source: Author

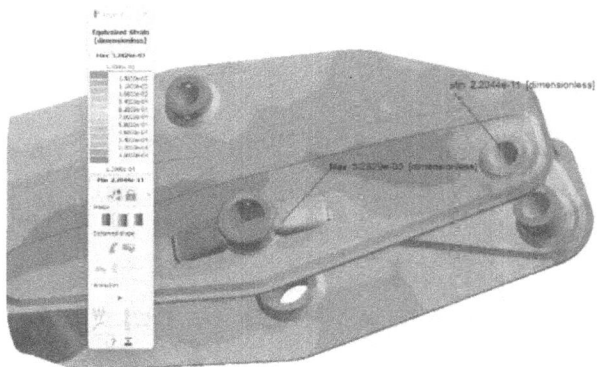

Figure 15.5 Equivalent strain distribution of the backhoe
Source: Author

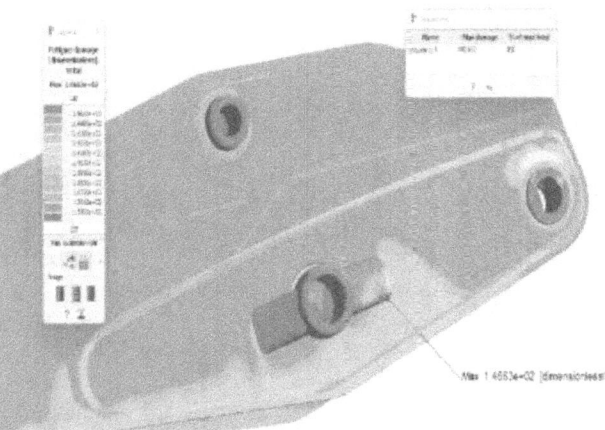

Figure 15.7 Fatigue damage of the backhoe
Source: Author

material under specific stress levels. The number of fatigue cycles often depends on multiple elements which include stress concentration along with surface finish quality and material defects and environmental elements. The S-N curve is selected from for non-galvanized steel and it is simulated to determine the fatigue life and damage [9].

In backhoe assembly, the maximum fatigue life was found to be 1 × cycles and the minimum fatigue life 0.0068196 cycles indicates that the structure is more prone to failure under cyclic loads as shown in Figure 15.6. The most critical areas appear in the backhoe is along the holes and edges of the structure.

In backhoe assembly, the fatigue damage was found to be 1.4663 ×which indicates a very high risk of failure and the most critical zones are around bolt hole and edges of the structure are most common failure points as shown in Figure 15.7.

Modeling and Assembly of the Hinge Bush with Welded Joints

In backhoe assembly, the hinge bush which is mainly focused on the welded joints. By using CAD software, the hinge bush is modeled and assembled by using the appropriate tools as shown in Figure 15.8 and converted into STEP file format for the simulation of structural, crack propagation and fatigue analysis.

Numerical analysis of hinge bush with welded joints
The numerical analysis is performed to simulate real-world conditions of the hinge bush by selecting appropriate boundary conditions and suitable material properties. The material is selected as mild steel because of its good balance of strength and flexibility. The mechanical properties of the mild steel had a density of 7850, Young's modulus of 200 GPa, ultimate tensile strength of 450–550 MPa and Poisson's ratio of 0.29.

By using a coordinate system, the boundary conditions were made for the hinge bush, as shown in Figure 15.9. Remote force A (60,000 N) acts at an

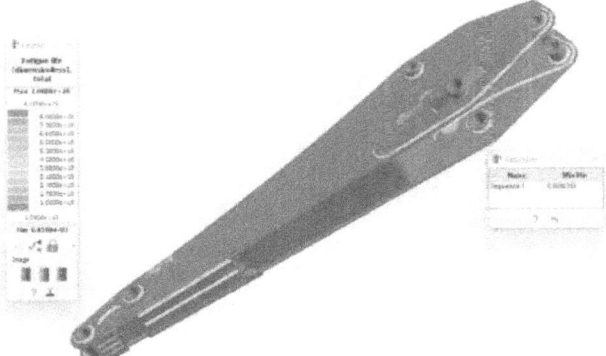

Figure 15.6 Fatigue life of the backhoe
Source: Author

Figure 15.8 Modeling and assembly of the hinge bush with welded joints
Source: Author

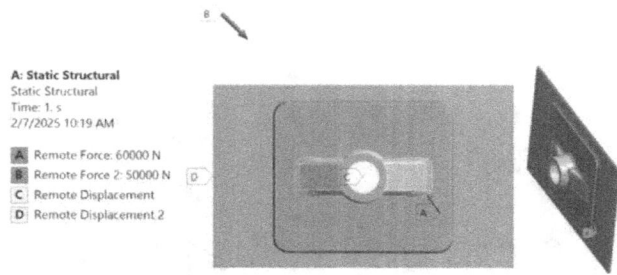

Figure 15.9 Boundary conditions of the hinge bush
Source: Author

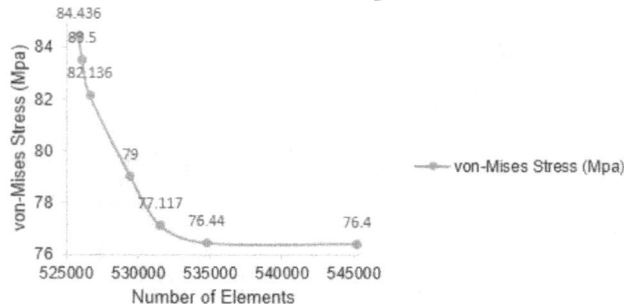

Figure 15.11 Mesh convergence plot
Source: Author

angle of 45°, which will be considered as the stick crowd cylinder, and remote force B (50,000 N) acts at an angle of 45°, which will be considered as the bucket side link. Remote displacements C and D are applied to restrict the movement in a particular direction of the hinge bush.

To determine strength, stability and performance under various loading conditions of the hinge bush, the structural analysis is evaluated. Structural analysis is commonly used to evaluate the displacement, von-Mises stress distribution and shear stress. The mesh convergence study has been made to improve accuracy and efficiency, as shown in Figure 15.10. In the weld region the mesh size has been kept constant as per the ASTM standard and the mesh method is selected as tetrahedron because of complex geometries. The element order is selected as quadratic, and the number of elements is chosen for the analysis is 534777 as shown in Figure 15.11.

In hinge bush, the minimum displacement was found to be 0.0001 and maximum displacement was found to be 0.39 mm as shown in Figure 15.12. In the weld region, the displacement was found to be minimum.

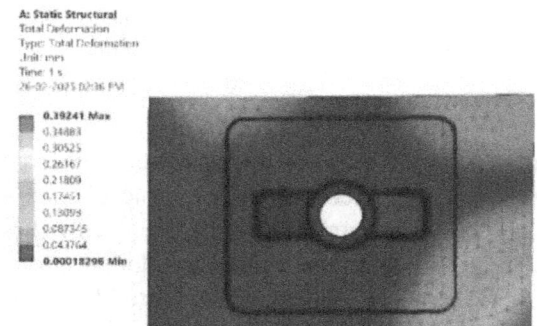

Figure 15.12 Deformation of the hinge bush
Source: Author

In hinge bush, the maximum von-Mises stress distribution was found to be 76 MPa as shown in Figure 15.13.

In hinge bush, the maximum shear stress distribution was found to be 44 MPa as shown in Figure 15.14.

In weld region, the maximum von-Mises stress distribution was found to be 53 MPa in the node 997072 as shown in Figure 15.15.

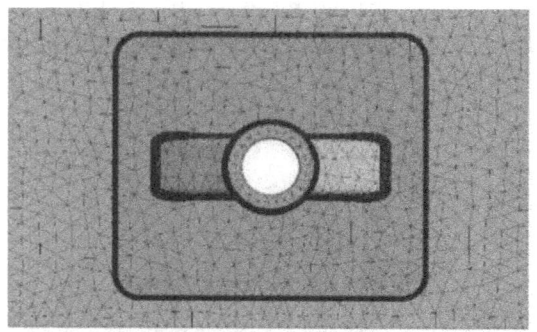

Figure 15.10 Meshed hinge bush
Source: Author

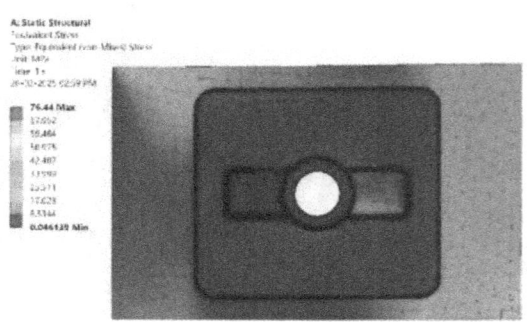

Figure 15.13 von-Mises stress distribution of the hinge bush
Source: Author

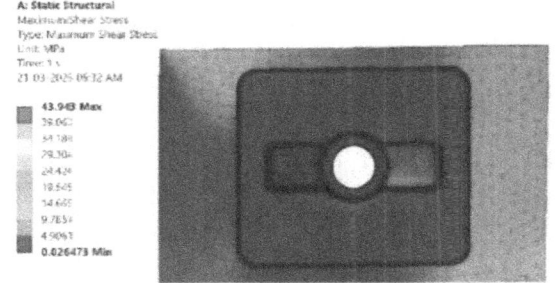

Figure 15.14 Shear stress distribution of the hinge bush
Source: Author

Figure 15.15 von-Mises stress distribution of the hinge bush in the weld region
Source: Author

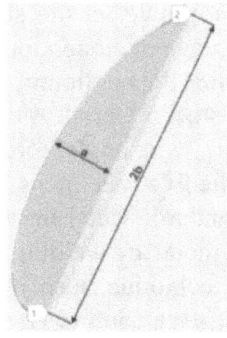

Figure 15.16 Semi-elliptical crack location
Source: Author

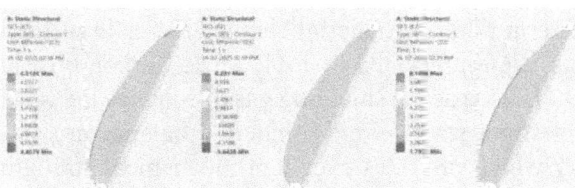

Figure 15.17 The SIF distribution in the weld region of the hinge bush
Source: Author

In crack propagation analysis, a semi-elliptical is created to determine whether the crack is stable or not in the weld region as shown in Figure 15.16, where the stress range were identified as maximum in the node 997072. SIF K_1 (Mode I - Opening Mode): Crack opening tensile spreading at crack tip. SIF K_2 (Mode II - Sliding Mode): Crack sliding shear deformation parallel to crack direction. SIF K_3 (Mode III - Tearing Mode): Crack tearing shear deformation perpendicular to crack direction

A crack propagates if:

$K_{max} \geq K_c$

Where:

K_{max} = Maximum (K_1, K_2, K_3) → The highest SIF value from the analysis

K_c → The fracture toughness of the material

The fracture toughness of the mild steel is 140 MPa $\sqrt{m}$.

The stress intensity factor in the weld region was identified for three modes as (6, 6 and 6) MPa. $\sqrt{mm}$ as shown in Figure 15.17.

In hinge bush, fatigue analysis is evaluated to determine its material or structure's ability, whether it can withstand repeated cyclic loading over time without failure. In hinge bush, the minimum and maximum fatigue life was found to be 93400 and 1×10^6 cycles as shown in Figure 15.18.

Experimental Testing

Tensile, bending and torsional test specimens were prepared to determine the mechanical properties of the mild steel. Tensile tests are used to determine

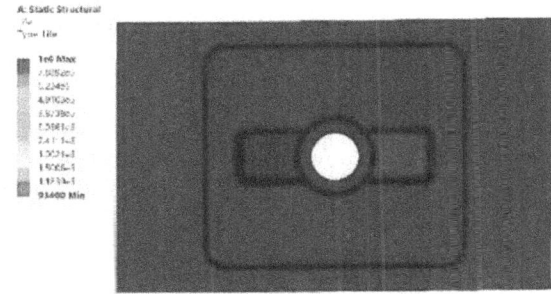

Figure 15.18 Fatigue life of the hinge bush
Source: Author

parameters such as ultimate tensile strength, maximum load and percentage of elongation. The bending test is used to determine the maximum load and shear strength of the mild steel material. A torsional test is used to determine the twist angle, torque and maximum shear stress. The five specimens were prepared as per the ASTM standard. Metal Inert Gas Welding is also known as gas metal arc welding (GMAW) and it is a widely used technique, ideal for high speed and strong welds. It uses a continuous wire electrode and shielding gas to join metals. It has several advantages, such as high welding speed, good mechanical strength, mass production, and high deposition rates. In this work Metal Inert Gas (MIG) welding is used by changing the parameters such as welding current, travel speed and voltage, which play a significant role in determining the material characteristics in welded joints, are represented in Table 15.1. Carbondioxide (CO_2) is used as the shielding gas to enhance the weld penetration, strong weld joints and balance arc stability which provides excellent mechanical strength to the weld joint which ensures the durability of the component. A filler wire diameter of 0.8 mm is used for welding the mild steel material which provides smooth welds, prevent excessive melting and distortion. A solid wire mild steel electrode ER70S-6 is used for welding the specimen because of its excellent strength and toughness which ensures durability and strong weld joints.

By using laser cutting process, mild steel material of rectangular plate was cut into the required shape for tensile, bending and torsional test as shown in Figures 15.19–15.21. The specimen is welded in the middle region and grinded to achieve smoother surfaces, which ensures uniformity and precision for preparing the material for tensile and bending testing.

After preparing the tensile test specimens, the tensile test has been carried out in the laboratory to evaluate the mechanical properties of the mild steel. The tensile test result shows the fracture in the weld region after testing, as shown in Figure 15.22.

Figure 15.19 Preparation of tensile test specimen
Source: Author

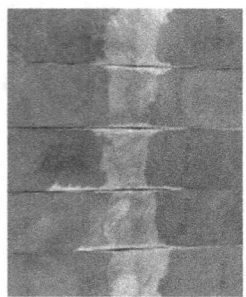
Figure 15.20 Preparation of bending test specimen
Source: Author

Figure 15.21 Preparation of torsional test specimen
Source: Author

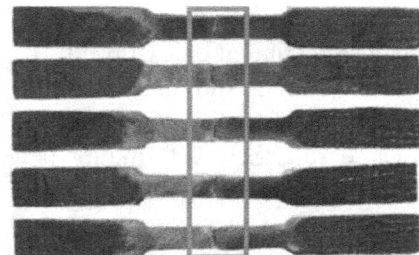
Figure 15.22 Tensile test specimen after testing
Source: Author

Table 15.1 MIG welding parameters

Specimen	Current (A)	Voltage (V)	Speed (cm/min)
1	80–90	3.5	4.5
2	90–100	4	5
3	100–110	4.5	5.5
4	110–120	5	6
5	120–130	5.5	6.5

Source: Author

The Table 15.2 represented the tensile result of five different specimens, which shows the variations in maximum load, ultimate tensile strength and elongation percentage. The maximum load varies from 17 kN to 21 kN and the highest load-bearing capacity exhibits in the specimen 4 and 5. The ultimate tensile strength shows variations between 678 MPa and 858

Table 15.2 Result of tensile test specimen

Specimen	Maximum load (kN)	Ultimate tensile strength (MPa)	Elongation (%)
1	17	678	5
2	20	817	5
3	19	746	8
4	21	858	10
5	21	839	8

Source: Author

Table 15.3 Result of bending test specimen

Specimen	Maximum load (kN)	Shear strength (MPa)
1	13	33
2	18	47
3	20	52
4	22	64
5	27	71

Source: Author

MPa, which indicate from different welding parameters. Specimen 4 and 5 has the highest ultimate tensile strength value as 858 MPa and 839 MPa. These values indicates that the both specimens can withstand the high stress value, high energy absorption and has extensive plastic deformation before failure when compared to the other specimens. Specimen 4 and 5 shows the optimal balance between strength and ductility. In addition, specimen 4 and 5 shows the highest elongation percentage as 10% and 8 %, which indicates more material flexibility before fracture.

After preparing the bending test specimens, the bending test was carried out in the laboratory to determine the mechanical properties of the mild steel. The bending test result shows the fracture in the weld region after testing as shown in Figure 15.23.

The Table 15.3 represented the bending test of five different specimens, which shows the variation in the maximum load and shear strength. The maximum load varies from 13 kN to 27 kN and the shear strength also varies from 33 MPa to 71 MPa.

Specimen 4 and 5 have a good capacity to resist the shear forces with maximum load as 22 kN and 27 kN and it endures the greatest shear forces before failure. Specimen 4 and 5 have the highest shear strength value as 64 MPa and 71 MPa. These values indicated that each specimen undergoes extensive plastic deformation, making it more resistant to further shear forces. Both specimens are capable of withstanding high shear stress under increasing load before failure and making it suitable for the structural applications.

After preparing the torsional test specimens, the torsional test was carried out in the laboratory to determine the mechanical properties of the mild steel. The torsional test result shows the fracture in the weld region after testing as shown in Figure 15.24.

The Table 15.4 represented the torsional test of five different specimen, which shows the variation in the twist angle, torque and maximum shear stress. The specimens 1, 2 and 3 sustained greater torque and shear stress yet their failure occurred at lower twisting angles which demonstrated brittle properties. The maximum twist angle of 360° was sustained by specimens 4 and 5 yet their torque along with shear stress

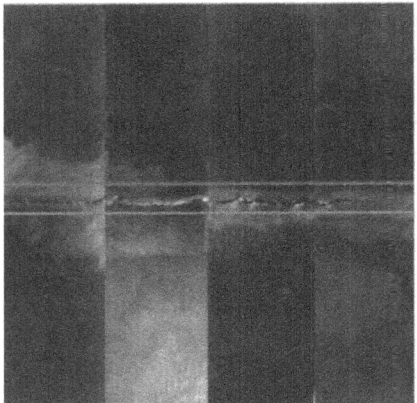

Figure 15.23 Bending test specimen after testing
Source: Author

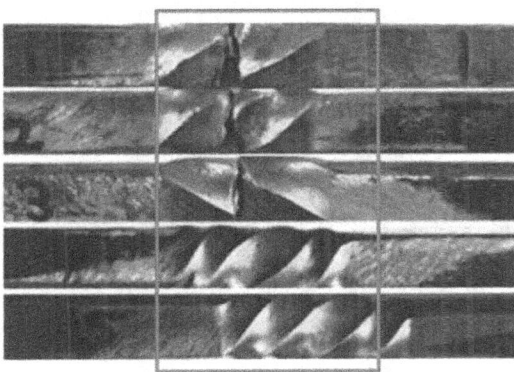

Figure 15.24 Torsional test specimen after testing
Source: Author

Table 15.4 Result of torsional test specimen

Specimen	Broken at a twist angle	Torque (Nm)	Maximum shear stress (MPa)
1	210	40	952
2	270	35	834
3	180	37	886
4	360	19	447
5	360	20	441

Source: Author

levels remained low showing ductile characteristics. The data implies that specimens 1, 2 and 3 showed greater inherent tensile strength although they fractured at reduced angular displacement but Specimens 4 and 5 exhibited more ductility with higher angular deformation until failure occurred.

Result and Discussion

The external forces applied to the backhoe assembly produced maximum displacement as 4 mm that occurred at the free end of the boom structure. The maximum von-Mises stress was found to be 6.945×10^3 MPa, concentrated at the bucket-side link connection, indicating a potential failure zone. The localized deformation appears in areas where equivalent strain reached its peak value of 3.2829×10^{-3} MPa. The minimum number of fatigue cycles was found as 0.0068196, while the calculated fatigue damage reached 1.4663×10^2 which indicates locations at high risk for fatigue failure.

In the hinge bush assembly, the result was evaluated as 0.4 mm maximum displacement combined with 0.0001 mm minimum displacement which shows a little deformation in the critical areas. The stress concentrated most heavily where high loads occurred with 76.44 MPa reaching its maximum value. The maximum value of von-Mises stress in the welded joint region occurred at node 997072 where it measured as 58 MPa. The fracture is inserted by using a semi-elliptical crack inside the weld area for examining the crack stability. The numerical results showed that the Stress Intensity Factor values reached 6 MPa for Mode I (Opening Mode), 6 MPa for Mode II (Sliding Mode) and 6 MPa for Mode III (Tearing Mode). Under the given loading conditions of the mild steel fracture toughness value of 140 MPa showed that the crack is stable and does not propagate under cyclic loading. Results from fatigue

analysis showed that the assembly would survive at least 93,400 cycles yet maintain operational capabilities up to 1×10^6 cycles based on stress assessments.

The tensile, bending and torsional test showed that the strength was improved in the higher welding current (110–130 A) and voltage (5–5.5 V). It ensures that the optimized welding speed (6–6.5 cm/min) provide a uniform heat input and prevented the defects such as overheating or lack fusion defects. The highest ultimate tensile strength, maximum load, elongation percentage, maximum stress, torque and twist angle indicates that the specimen 4 and 5 are best suitable choice for the application of backhoe.

Conclusion

The highest von-Mises stress obtained in the weld area was 523 MPa, much lower than all the stresses recorded under tensile (858 MPa), bending (71 MPa), and torsional (471 MPa) experimental tests. This shows that the numerical model is safely running below the elastic stress threshold. In the numerical simulation, the behavior of the hinge bush with welded joints was constrained to linear elasticity, while in the experimental test, plastic deformation and material failure were replicated. A crack was seen to grow in the weld area, which matched the maximum von-Mises stress location. The SIF obtained from calculation was found to be less than the fracture toughness of the material. The life of the hinge bush part under fatigue was estimated at 93,400 cycles, translating to about 26 hours of sustained cyclic operation at 1 cycle per second or 3,600 cycles per hour. The life estimation used stress values obtained from numerical analysis, with particular emphasis on the weld area where the peak von-Mises stress was 53 MPa. Specimens 4 and 5 showed better performance in all tests, with the highest ductility and energy absorption prior to failure. In future, the hinge bush with welded joint will be converted into a single cast component.

References

[1] Mei, J., & Dong, P. (2017). An equivalent stress parameter for multi-axial fatigue evaluation of welded components including non-proportional loading effects. *International Journal of Fatigue*, 101, 297–311. https://doi.org/10.1016/j.ijfatigue.2017.01.006.

[2] Thomas, A., Pathiraj, B., & Veron, P. (2007). Feature tests on welded components at higher temperatures-Material performance and residual stress evaluation. *Engi-*

neering Fracture Mechanics, 74(6), 963–979. https://doi.org/10.1016/j.engfracmech.2006.08.017.

[3]   Hobbacher, A. F. (2009). The new IIW recommendations for fatigue assessment of welded joints and components - a comprehensive code recently updated. *International Journal of Fatigue*, 31(1), 50–58. https://doi.org/10.1016/j.ijfatigue.2008.04.002.

[4]   Abima, C. S., Akinlabi, S. A., Madushele, N., & Akinlabi, E. T. (2022). Comparative study between TIG-MIG Hybrid, TIG and MIG welding of 1008 steel joints for enhanced structural integrity. *Scientific African*, 17, e01329. https://doi.org/10.1016/j.sciaf.2022.e01329.

[5]   Dhobale, A. L., & Mishra, H. K. (2015). Review on effect of heat input on tensile strength of butt weld joint using MIG welding. *International Journal of Innovations in Engineering Research and Technology [IJIERT]*, 2(9), 1–13.

[6]   Haque, S. R. (2023). Investigation on welding defects of alloys using TIG and MIG welding. *Hybrid Advances*, 3, 100066. https://doi.org/10.1016/j.hybadv.2023.100066.

[7]   NJIM, Q. B. E. K. (2014). Effect of V notch shape on fatigue life in steel beam made of mild steel AISI 1020. *International Journal of Mechanical and Production Engineering Research and Development (IJMPERD)*, 4(4), 1–14.

[8]   Alweendo, S. T., Morita, M., Hasegawa, K., & Motoda, S. (2021). Fatigue properties of hot-dip galvanized AISI 1020 normalized steel in tension–compression and tension–tension loading. *Materials*, 14(23), 7480. https://doi.org/10.3390/ma14237480.

[9]   Frimpong, S., & Li, Y. (2007). Stress loading of the cable shovel boom under in-situ digging conditions. *Engineering Failure Analysis*, 14(4), 702–715. https://doi.org/10.1016/j.engfailanal.2006.02.007.

[10]   Yu, C., Bao, Y., & Li, Q. (2021). Finite element analysis of excavator mechanical behaviour and boom structure optimization. *Measurement: Journal of the International Measurement Confederation*, 173, 108637. https://doi.org/10.1016/j.measurement.2020.108637.

[11]   Cherian, S. T., & Kumar, S. (2019). Analysis and solution for resolving hydraulic hose failures in backhoe loaders. *International Journal of Mechanical and Production*, 4(44), 341–356. doi: 10.30464/jmee.2020.4.4.341.

[12]   Motka, C. P., & Momin, R. I. (2015). Development of backhoe machine By 3-D modelling using CAD software and verify the structural design by using finite element method. *IJIRST-International Journal for Innovative Research in Science and Technology*, 1(8), 49–52.

[13]   Tewari, S. K., Dubey, J., & Chauhan, P. S. (2020). Modelling, FEA & optimization of backhoe excavator attachment for max. machine life. *International Journal of Mechanical Engineering*, 7(2), 5–15. https://doi.org/10.14445/23488360/ijme-v7i2p102.

[14]   Wei, Z., Lei, L., Pei, X., & Dong, P. (2024). The structural strain method for fatigue evaluation of welded components: analytical treatment of reversed plasticity. *International Journal of Pressure Vessels and Piping*, 210, 105249. https://doi.org/10.1016/j.ijpvp.2024.105249.

[15]   Larsen, M. L., Arora, V., Lützen, M., Pedersen, R. R., & Putnam, E. (2021). Fatigue life estimation of the weld joint in K-node of the offshore jacket structure using stochastic finite element analysis. *Marine Structures*, 78, 103020. https://doi.org/10.1016/j.marstruc.2021.103020.

[16]   Duhan, N. R., Srivastava, J. P., Anis, M. A. & Sarkar, P. K. (2018). Stress intensity factor for a semi-elliptical rail head crack under traction. In IOP Conference Series: Materials Science and Engineering, (Vol. 402, no. 1). https://doi.org/10.1088/1757-899X/402/1/012132.

16 Investigation of hot cracking susceptibility in Inconel 625 TIG welded specimen using liquid penetrant inspection

K. Saravanakumar[a] and E. Annapoorani[b]

Department of Production Engineering, PSG College of Technology, Coimbatore, India

Abstract

Inconel 625, a high-performance nickel-based superalloy, is widely utilized in aerospace, power generation, and chemical processing industries due to its superior mechanical strength and resistance to oxidation and corrosion at elevated temperatures. However, its susceptibility to hot cracking during Tungsten inert gas (TIG) welding presents significant challenges to weld quality and structural integrity. This study employs an L_9 Taguchi design of experiments (DOE) to systematically evaluate the influence of key welding parameters namely welding current, travel speed, electrode diameter and gas flowrate of TIG- welded Inconel 625. Surface defect detection is carried out using liquid penetrant testing (LPT) to identify and characterize hot cracking. The purpose is to create a predictive framework that can direct the choice of weld parameters to avoid hot cracking. This method could improve welding quality, lower experimental expenses, and offer a better understanding of the welded defects of inconel alloy. Sample number 8 have been recognized as the best parameter 120 amps current, welding speed of 220 mm/min, 3 mm electrode diameter and 20 L/min gas flow rate.

Keywords: Design of experiments (DOE), hot cracking, inconel 625, liquid penetrant test (LPT), TIG welding

Introduction

Inconel alloys, primarily composed of nickel and chromium, are known for their exceptional ability to withstand corrosion, oxidation, and environments with high temperatures. However, the welding of these alloys, especially using TIG welding, presents unique challenges. These challenges arise from the inherent metallurgical complexity of Inconel alloys, which can result in defects such as hot cracking, poor weldability, and microstructural inconsistencies. An electric arc is created during Tungsten inert gas (TIG) welding between a non-consumable work piece and tungsten electrode, creating a molten pool that has an inert gas (usually argon or helium) protecting it to prevent oxidation. The heat produced throughout the welding procedure causes microstructural changes in the alloy, which in turn affect the mechanical properties of the welding. Compared to other fusion welding techniques, TIG welding offers a few advantages, including the use of non-consumable electrodes. For this investigation, TIG welding was used to join the 2–3 mm thick Ti6Al4V alloy. Since argon served as the welding process's inert gas, the current and gas flow rates were modified appropriately [11]. By establishing strong correlations between process parameters and weld integrity, the study demonstrated the potential of machine learning as a powerful tool for predicting defect formation and optimizing welding conditions. This data-driven approach not only improves weld quality but also minimizes the reliance on time-consuming trial-and-error methods. The successful implementation of such predictive models in aluminum alloys sets a valuable precedent for applying similar methodologies to more complex materials such as Inconel 625 where hot cracking continues to pose significant challenges [4]. Because Inconel 625 has excellent mechanical properties, including high strength, corrosion resistance, abrasion resistance, and low-temperature toughness, it is often used in harsh environments. In this study, heat treatment at 950 °C, 1050 °C, and 1150 °C for four hours was followed by water cooling to assess the microstructure and mechanical properties of Inconel 625 under the cooling rate [10]. Compared to other fusion welding techniques, TIG welding offers several advantages, including the use of non- consumable electrodes. For this investigation, TIG welding was used to join the 2-3 mm thick Ti6Al4V alloy. Since argon served as the welding process's inert gas, the current and gas flow rates were modified appropriately [9]. When friction welding was applied to SUS316L, the grain size in the weld zone was significantly refined to 6.03 μm from the base material's 57.55 μm. The mechanical properties of the

---

[a]ksk.prod@psgtech.ac.in, [b]poorania23@gmail.com

DOI: 10.1201/9781003770435-16

welds show that, despite the grain refinement, they are either relatively low or comparable to the base material [8]. The research highlights the potential of using Vickers micro- hardness tests as an effective NDT method to estimate the tensile strength of steel rebars in reinforced concrete structures. This approach could reduce the need for destructive sampling, saving time, costs, and minimizing the impact on structural integrity. However, careful calibration and interpretation of results are necessary to ensure accurate assessments. This method could be particularly beneficial for static and seismic evaluations of existing infrastructure [2, 3]. The study shows that controlling the welding linear energy in the range of 45 J/mm to 80 J/mm is crucial for optimizing the weld quality and microstructure of thin Inconel 718 butt joints. Increasing energy leads to wider welds and HAZ, larger grain sizes, and complex microstructures with dendritic grains and eutectic precipitates. These microstructural features influence the mechanical properties of the weld, particularly in high-performance applications, highlighting the need to balance heat input for optimal weld integrity [5]. The study investigates the microstructure and corrosion resistance of Inconel 625 overlay welded by the pulsed TIG process over AISI 4130 steel. The two-layer Inconel 625 overlay shows better corrosion resistance compared to a single layer, with the second layer significantly reducing Fe content and improving pitting corrosion resistance [6]. The high temperature sliding wear behavior of Yttria stabilized zirconia (YSZ) reinforced Inconel 625 composite claddings developed using TIG welding. The claddings were analysed using optical microscopy, SEM, EDS, and XRD techniques [7]. Welding at 4 Hz pulse frequency resulted in higher Ultimate Tensile Strength (UTS) and Yield Strength (YS) compared to others. Weldments exhibited superior mechanical and metallurgical qualities at elevated temperatures. Pulse welding showed higher hardness due to regulated heat input [1]. The increasing demand for advanced materials such as Inconel 625 in critical industries ranging from aerospace and nuclear to marine and chemical processing has driven the need for precise and reliable welding processes. Inconel 625, a nickel-chromium-based superalloy, is valued for its excellent mechanical strength, corrosion resistance, and thermal stability. However, its metallurgical complexity makes it highly susceptible to weld defects, particularly hot cracking, when subjected

to fusion welding techniques like TIG welding. The interaction of welding parameters with the alloy's solidification behavior leads to microstructural instability and defect formation, which significantly compromise mechanical performance and long- term service reliability.

Hence, the objective of this study formed to systematically investigate the effects of TIG welding parameters (welding current, welding speed, electrode diameter, and gas flow rate) on the occurrence of hot cracks in the Inconel 625 superalloy. By using a Taguchi L_9 design of experiments (DOE) method, in combination with liquid penetrant testing (LPT) for defect detection, a framework will be developed to facilitate the selection of optimal welding conditions to minimize hot cracks.

Materials and Methods

Materials
Inconel 625, a nickel-based superalloy, was selected the base material for this investigation due to its excellent combination of mechanical strength, weldability, and resistance to corrosion and high-temperature oxidation. In the present study, Inconel 625 specimens with dimensions of 65 mm × 50 mm × 2 mm were employed for TIG welding trials. Given the alloy's known sensitivity to welding-induced defects such as hot cracking, it presents a suitable candidate for detailed investigation of welding process optimization. The workpiece material Inconel 625 alloy is shown in Figure 16.1.

Methods
TIG welding is a popular method for welding Inconel alloys due to its precise control over parameters like current, voltage, and gas flow rate. These parameters significantly impact the weld pool, heat-affected zone, and final mechanical properties of the weld, affecting the alloy's microstructure and properties

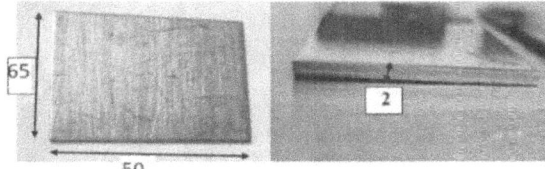

All dimensions are in mm

Figure 16.1 Workpiece material Inconel 625 alloy
Source: Author

TIG welding uses an electrode made of non-consumable tungsten. To prevent atmospheric contamination of the weld area, the process requires shielding gas, usually argon or a combination of argon and helium. Between the tungsten electrode and the metal workpiece, an electric arc is produced. TIG welding was employed to join the Inconel 625 specimens due to its ability to produce high-quality welds with precise control overheat input. This process is particularly suitable for welding heat sensitive materials such as nickel-based superalloys, where controlled energy input is critical to minimize the formation of undesirable microstructures and thermal-induced defects. To systematically investigate and optimize the welding parameters, an L_9 orthogonal array based on the Taguchi DOE methodology was adopted. The study focused on critical process variables like welding current, travel speed, Electrode diameter and gas flow rate which are known to significantly influence weld quality and mechanical performance. The Taguchi method not only allows for identification of the most influential factors but also aids in determining optimal parameter combinations to enhance mechanical properties such as tensile strength and hardness while minimizing defect formation. The application of this design framework ensures a structured and reliable approach to process optimization for welding Inconel 625 (Table 16.1).

Experimentation

Specimen preparation

To assess the weldability and hot cracking susceptibility of Inconel 625 under various TIG welding conditions, a set of specially designed specimens were prepared using the Houldcroft Weldability Test configuration, commonly referred to as the Fishbone Test. This test is recognized for its ability to simulate the thermal and mechanical conditions that lead to hot cracking during the solidification phase of welding, particularly in high-performance alloys. Each test specimen was machined from Inconel 625 sheets with nominal dimensions of 65 mm ×

50 mm × 2 mm, as per the standard geometry adopted in Houldcroft's original methodology [4]. The test geometry was designed using CAD software, incorporating a central weld path with a series of radially oriented slots resembling a fishbone structure. These slots act as stress concentrators, localizing thermal and solidification-induced stresses during welding, thereby amplifying the tendency for crack formation in susceptible materials. The fabrication of these specimens was carried out using an electrical discharge machining (EDM) process. EDM was chosen to ensure high dimensional accuracy, precise groove spacing, and minimal thermal distortion during machining critical factors when preparing specimens for microstructure-sensitive testing.

A total of nine specimens were prepared to correspond with the L_9 Taguchi orthogonal array used in the experimental design. Following welding, all specimens were cleaned and subjected to LPT for surface defect analysis. LPT is a widely accepted non-destructive evaluation (NDE) technique that detects surface-breaking cracks by capillary action of dye penetrants and developer application. This technique was employed to detect hot cracks that may not be visible to the naked eye, ensuring a reliable qualitative assessment of weld integrity.

The combined use of the Houldcroft test geometry and LPT provides a robust methodology for evaluating the hot cracking tendency of Inconel 625. The desired dimensions were taken from the literature for hot cracking test specimen shown in Figure 16.2. The Specimen prepared for performing experimentation is shown in Figure 16.2 (a) Fishbone Pattern (single sample) (b) CAD Model (c) Specimen preparation for performing welding.

Design of experiments

The selection of suitable process parameters and their levels for the experimentation for TIG welding, are shown in Table 16.2. From the selected factors and their levels, experimentation is carried out with the Taguchi method L_9 orthogonal array shown in

Table 16.1 Chemical composition of Inconel 625

Element	Ni	Cr	Mo	Fe	Nb	Nb+ Ta	Si	Ti	Other
Observations in %	61.07	20.24	10.00	4.82	3.34	3.43	0.23	0.21	Bal

Source: Author

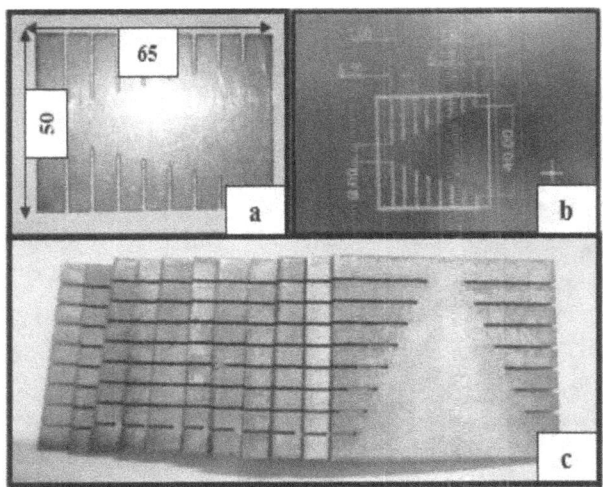

Figure 16.2 Specimen preparation for performing welding (a) Fishbone pattern (Single sample), (b) CAD Model, (c) Fabricated specimens
Source: Author

Table 16.3. The project aims to find the best parameter suitable for welding. Hence, Holdcroft method is used. To find out the parameters, using literature survey. The Semi-Automatic TIG welding was done in PSG-GT12 Gantry Welding Robot shown in Figure 16.3. The experimentation is carried out as shown in Figure 16.4 (a) The clamping of welding sample with fixture, (b) Performing weld direction, (c) During welding the electrode. The FANUC

Arc Mate 100iC/12 and the GT 12 Gantry Welding Robot can both be configured to operate in semi-automatic/ Fully automatic modes, depending on how the system is programmed and the integration with other equipment. The FANUC welding robot is floor mounted, 12-axis, with a 10 kg payload and reach up to 1400 mm. The software used is R- 30iB Mate software. It also has a universal sensor interface. From DOE, L_9 Orthogonal array experiments were performed. After the welding, the welded specimen is set to rest to cool at room temperature for a few minutes, and then the specimen is cleaned on the surface. The welded specimen using L_9 orthogonal array is shown in Figure 16.5.

Liquid penetrant test
LPT is used to find surface flaws in welds like cracks, porosity, and incomplete fusion, one of the Non-Destructive Testing (NDT) methods LPT assists in detecting hot cracking or other surface imperfections that might have developed during TIG welding when applied to a Houldcroft specimen. The material's propensity to crack is confirmed by LPT, which highlights surface cracks created during solidification. Aids in refining the welding procedure to minimize cracking risks. Procedure for performing LPT is shown in Figure 16.6.

Assists in modifying TIG welding parameters (such as shielding gas, speed, or current) in response

Table 16.2 Selection of factors and their levels

S. No.	Factors	Symbol	Units	Level I	Level II	Level III
1	Welding current	A	Ampere	100	110	120
2	Welding speed	mm/min	mm/min	200	210	220
3	Electrode diameter	Ø	mm	3	2.4	2
4	Gas flow rate	%	L/min	10	15	20

Source: Author

Table 16.3 L9 orthogonal array Taguchi approach using DoE

Ex. No.	Welding current (Amp)	Welding speed (mm/min)	Electrode diameter (mm)	Gas flow rate (L/min)
1	100	200	3	10
2	100	220	2.4	15
3	100	240	2	20
4	110	200	2.4	20
5	110	220	2	10
6	110	240	3	15
7	120	200	2	15
8	120	220	3	20
9	120	240	2.4	10

Source: Author

Figure 16.3 Experimental set up
Source: Author

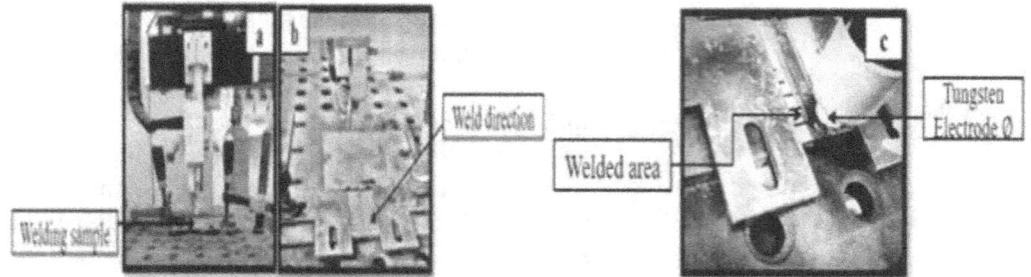

Figure 16.4 Experimentation (a) Performing weld direction, (b) During welding the electrode and welded area
Source: Author

to flaws found. A reliable and high-quality joint can be ensured by using LPT on Houldcroft specimens. The welded specimen is cleaned using a cleaner to remove dirt or any contaminants. Applying cleaner directly to the welded areas in the sample by spraying on the surface of the welded region shown in Figure 16.7 (a). Ensure the surface is dry and free of residue before applying the penetrant. Once the workpieces are cleaned using cleaner and dried. The next step is to apply a liquid penetrant to the welded surface by the spraying method.

The penetrant should dwell on the surface for 5 to 30 minutes, and it is shown on Figure 16.7 (b). After 30 minutes of applying the penetrant. Clean the surface using a cloth soaked with the cleaner and wipe the penetrant. The next step is to apply a thin layer of developer on the welded specimen shown in Figure 16.7 (c). The developer helps draw out the penetrant from defects, creating visible indications. Allow the developer to develop indications for 10 to 30 minutes, and it is shown in Figure 16.7 (d).

Results and Discussion

Hot crack analysis using liquid penetrant testing
Post-weld inspection using LPT reveals the susceptibility of Inconel 625 to hot cracking under various

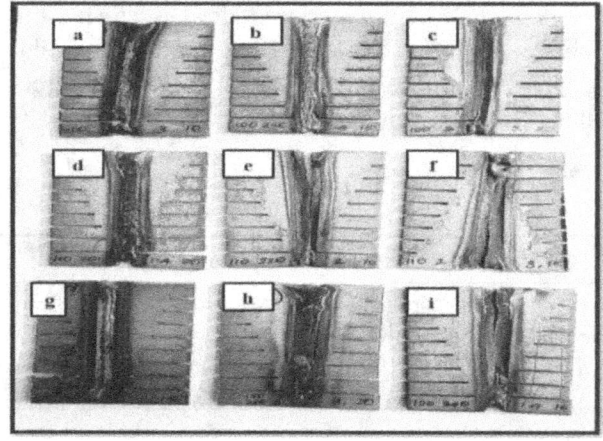

Figure 16.5 Welded specimen using L_9 orthogonal array samples
Source: Author

welding parameter combinations. The hot crack is identified by LPT as shown in Figure 16.8. From the LPT for Hot cracking, the best parameter, for lower hot crack is found to be 120 amps current, welding speed of 220 mm/min, 3 mm electrode diameter and 20 L/min gas flow rate (sample 8). Conversely, specimens welded at optimized parameters moderate current with balanced travel speed demonstrated

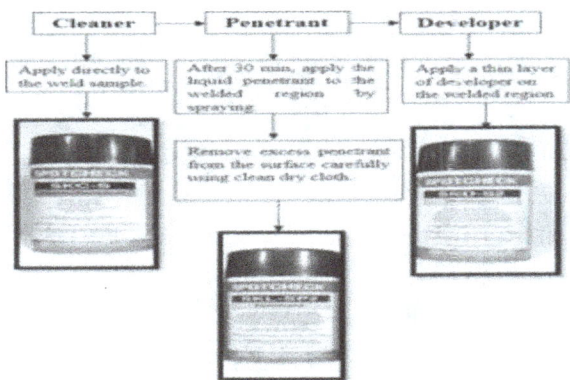

Figure 16.6 Procedure for performing LPT
Source: Author

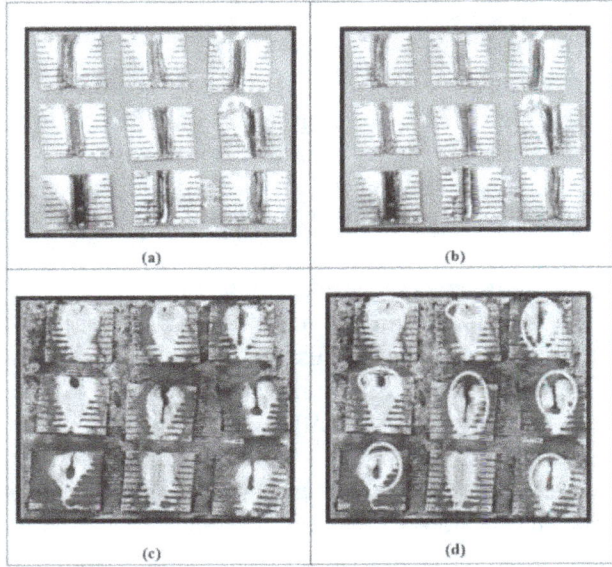

Figure 16.7 LPT Procedure applied to welded specimen (a) Applying cleaner, (b) Applying penetrant, (c) Appying developer and (d) Crack identification
Source: Author

minimal or no indications of surface defects. These results suggest that precise control of heat input plays a pivotal role in reducing thermal stresses and minimizing the crack susceptibility of Inconel 625. The Houldcroft specimens aided in localizing and amplifying these stresses, validating the reliability of the test design.

Hot crack measurement using Fiji ImageJ software
Using Fiji ImageJ software, the length of each crack of the welded specimen is measured. The first step is to give the set scale for each image since the dimension of the gap from each slot is known, which is 6 mm and it is shown in Figure 16.8 (a). From the imported image of the welded specimen line is drawn for measuring hot crack, it is shown in Figure 16.8 (b). To find out the exact measurements, a total of ten readings were taken for each specimen of their respective cracks with set scale shown in Figure 16.8 (c). With the 10 measurements, the average length is taken, and its exact length of the crack occurred in each specimen is shown Figure 16.8 (d). The average and Standard deviation are taken from the Fiji Image J software shown in Table 16.4.

Hot cracking was assessed across nine welded samples through image-based analysis. The results revealed substantial variation in cracking severity, influenced by differing welding parameters. Average crack lengths ranged from 3.67 mm to 36.12 mm, with corresponding standard deviations indicating the degree of variability in crack distribution. Samples 3 and 5 recorded the highest average crack lengths (36.09 mm and 36.12 mm, respectively), indicating a greater susceptibility to solidification cracking under the associated welding conditions. In contrast, Sample 8 demonstrated the lowest average crack length (3.67 mm), reflecting superior weld integrity and minimal hot cracking. These findings underscore the strong influence of welding parameters on the hot cracking behavior of Inconel 625. They further emphasize the need for careful process optimization in TIG welding to mitigate cracking

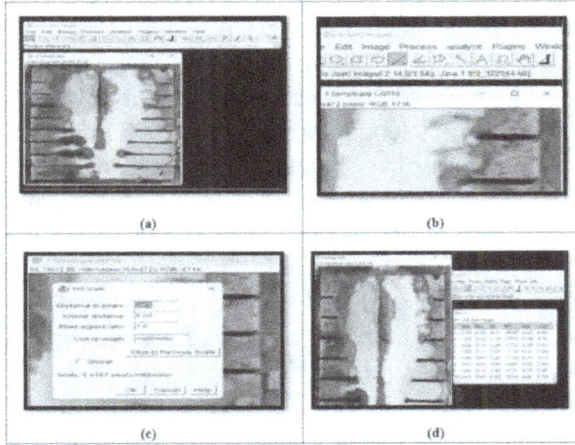

Figure 16.8 Hot crack measurement using ImageJ software. (a) Importing welded specimen image to Fiji ImageJ, (b) Importing image with line drawn, (c) Imported image is set to scale and (d) Hot crack measurement
Source: Author

risks and ensure the structural reliability of welded components.

The evaluation of hot cracking in TIG-welded Inconel 625 samples revealed significant variation in crack severity across different experimental conditions. The measured average crack lengths varied substantially, highlighting the strong influence of welding parameters on crack formation.

The most severe hot cracking was observed in samples with average crack lengths exceeding 36 mm, whereas minimal cracking was noted in samples with values below 5 mm. This contrast suggests that specific combinations of welding parameters can considerably increase the material's susceptibility to solidification cracking. Overall, these findings emphasize the critical importance of precisely controlling welding parameters to minimize hot cracking in Inconel 625.

They also highlight the potential for further process optimization, including the application of predictive modelling techniques, to ensure consistent weld quality in high-performance structural applications. Welding defects, particularly hot cracking, significantly affect the strength and durability of welded joints. Fiji ImageJ software was used for accurate crack identification and quantification to assess the degree of hot cracking in various samples. The eighth sample (h) was the least impacted by hot cracking out of the nine since it showed the least amount of crack development. To increase crack visibility, contrast enhancement techniques were performed after the photos were first converted to grayscale using Fiji ImageJ. Crack areas were separated from the surrounding weld metal using edge detection and thresholding methods. The program then calculated each sample's fault severity by measuring the crack's length, breadth, and total impacted area. In comparison to the other samples, sample "h" had the lowest fracture area, according to the data, and the welding conditions used for this sample were better at avoiding hot cracking. This finding emphasizes how crucial regulated welding current, welding speed, electrode diameter, and gas flow rate are to reducing the production of defects.

Among these 9 Samples, the average values and minimized cracks in the welded specimen is the 8th sample. It is considered a minimal crack found in the welded area. With knowing that the 8th sample has the least crack and the best parameter for the butt joint TIG welding. The 8th parameter is the best parameter

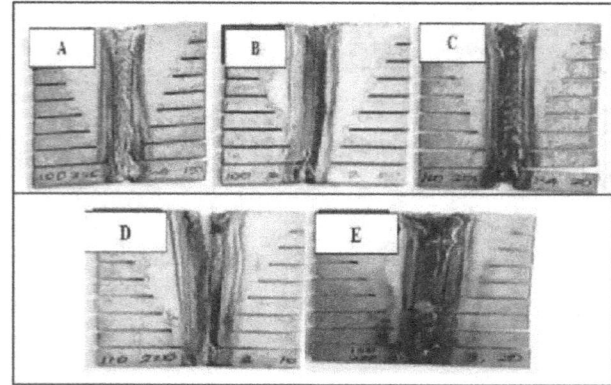

Figure 16.9 Other weld defects like (a) lack of penetration, (b) porosity, (c) excess spatter and irregular weld bead formation, (d) lack of fusion, and (e) crack
Source: Author

with the least crack found with the parameter of 120 amps current, welding speed of 220 mm/min, 3 mm electrode diameter and 20 L/min gas flow rate which is used for the welding of butt joint and its tensile, hardness and SEM are to be taken.

Other weld defects identified using LPT

The weld defects in Inconel 625 TIG welds were systematically identified using LPT, which revealed multiple surface discontinuities that compromise weld integrity (Figure 16.9).

Figure 16.9 (a) Lack of penetration occurs when the weld metal fails to extend through the full thickness of the joint, resulting in incomplete fusion between the base materials; this defect, often accompanied by a groove-like undercut, reduces the effective cross-sectional area and creates potential sites for crack initiation under mechanical stress. Figure 16.9 (b) Porosity is characterized by the presence of gas-filled voids within the welding metal, which develop when gases generated during welding become trapped in the molten pool and fail to escape before solidification. This defect not only diminishes the mechanical properties such as tensile strength and fatigue resistance but also can serve as an initiation point for corrosion. Figure 16.9 (c) Excess spatter and irregular weld bead formation, observed as small droplets of molten metal and inconsistencies in bead geometry typically indicate unstable arc conditions or improper parameter settings, leading to surface imperfections that may act as stress concentrators.

Figure 16.9 (d) Lack of fusion is a severe defect wherein the weld metal does not adequately bond with the base metal or between adjacent weld passes. This condition is often caused by low current settings, excessive travel speed, or misalignment of the electrode, thereby jeopardizing load-bearing capacity and durability.

Finally, Figure 16.9 (e) hot cracking, also known as solidification cracking, occurs during the final stages of weld metal solidification due to excessive cooling rates, improper heat input, or the use of unsuitable filler materials. These cracks, which may propagate internally, pose a significant threat to structural reliability. Overall, the thorough detection and analysis of these defects underscore the need for precise control of welding parameters and robust process optimization to ensure high-quality, reliable welds in critical applications (Table 16.4).

Conclusion

Present study evaluated the hot cracking susceptibility of Inconel 625 during TIG welding using the Houldcroft test and LPT. An L_9 Taguchi Design of Experiments analyzed the effects of welding current, travel speed, electrode diameter, and gas flow rate on surface crack formation. LPT effectively detected hot cracking as well as other weld defects like lack of fusion and porosity. Statistical analysis of crack lengths showed that welding parameters significantly influence crack severity and distribution. Among the samples, Sample 8 (120 A, 220 mm/min speed, 3 mm electrode and 20 lpm gas flow rate) exhibited the least cracking, emphasizing the importance of optimized welding conditions. Controlling welding parameters is crucial to minimize defects and ensure

structural integrity in Inconel 625 welds, while combining non-destructive testing with systematic experimentation enhances the quality and reliability of TIG-welded joints.

References

[1] Yelamasetti, B., Vishnu Vardhan, T., Devi, B. T. L., & Sree, N. S. (2024). Mechanical characterization and microstructural evolution of Inconel 718 and SS316L TIG weldments at high temperatures. *Journal of Materials Research and Technology*, 32, 196–207.

[2] Barbosa, L. C. M., Brejão de Souza, S. D., Botelho, E. C., Cândido, G. M., & Rezende, M. C. (2018). Fractographic study of welded joints of carbon fibre/PPS composites tested in lap shear. *Engineering Failure Analysis*, 93, 172–182.

[3] Caprili, S., Mattei, F., Mazzaturaa, I., Ferrari, F., Gammino, M., Mariscotti, M., et al. (2023). Evaluation of mechanical characteristics of steel bars by non-destructive Vickers micro-hardness tests. *Procedia Structural Integrity*, 44, 886–893.

[4] Dhilip, A., Nampoothiri, J., Senthilkumar, M., & Kirubarandan, N. (2023). Machine learning predictive approaches for hot crack mitigation in modified TIG welded AA7075 joints. *Materials and Manufacturing Processes*, 38(13), 1650–1662.

[5] Gorka, J., Jamrozik, W., & Kiel-Jamrozik, M. (2023). The effect of TIG welding on the structure and hardness of butt joints made of Inconel 718. *Heliyon*, 9, e13175.

[6] Guo, L., Xiao, F., Wang, F., He, Y., Wei, W., & Zhang, Y. (2021). Microstructure and corrosion resistance of Inconel 625 overlay welded by pulsed TIG process. *International Journal of Electrochemical Science*, 16, 1–15.

[7] Kamboj, N., & Thakur, L. (2023). Experimental investigation of the high temperature sliding wear behaviour of RSM optimized YSZ-Inconel 625 TIG weld cladding. *Tribology International*, 187, 108741.

[8] Kim, Y., & Song, K. (2024). Effect of enhanced grain refinement in friction welded SUS316L alloy. *Archives of Metallurgy and Materials*, 69, 57–60.

Table 16.4 Hot crack length measurement indicated for all the nine samples

Ex. No.	Welding Current (Amp)	Welding speed (mm/min)	Electrode diameter(mm)	Gas flow rate (L/min)	Hot crack (mm)
1	100	200	3	10	7.99
2	100	220	2.4	15	5.03
3	100	240	2	20	36.09
4	110	200	2.4	20	12.82
5	110	220	2	10	36.12
6	110	240	3	15	24.79
7	120	200	2	15	23.54
8	120	220	3	20	3.67
9	120	240	2.4	10	20.25

Source: Author

[9] Omoniyi, P., Mahamooda, M., Jena, T.-C., & Akinlabi, E. (2021). TIG welding of Ti6Al4V alloy: microstructure, fractography, tensile and microhardness data. *Data in Brief*, 38, 107274.

[10] Park, M., Gang, H.-S., Lee, H., Kim, B., Kim, S., & Noh (2024). Effect of cooling rate on microstructure and mechanical properties according to heat treatment temperature of Inconel 625. *Archives of Metallurgy and Materials*, 69, 95–98.

[11] Venkatesan, R., Harikrishna, K. L., & Sivashanmugam, N. (2024). Microstructure and mechanical properties of friction stir welded AZ31 magnesium alloy reinforced with ZrB2. *Materials Research Express*, 11(4), 046517. https://doi.org/10.1088/2053-1591/ad419d.

17 Optimizing age hardening treatment for Monel K500 by phase field modelling

Shoaib, D. R.[1,a], Krishnamoorthi, J.[2,b] and Krishna Kumar, K.[3,c]

[1]PG Student, Department of Metallurgical Engineering, PSG College of Technology, Coimbatore, India

[2]Professor, Department of Metallurgical Engineering, PSG College of Technology, Coimbatore, India

[3]Assistant Professor, Department of Metallurgical Engineering, PSG College of Technology, Coimbatore, India

Abstract

In this study, attempts are made to optimize the heat treatment cycle for Monel K500, a precipitation-hardenable nickel-copper alloy, to enhance hardness and wear resistance. Phase field modeling, thermodynamic simulations, and experimental validation were conducted to analyze precipitation kinetics and microstructural evolution. Thermo-Calc was used to generate phase diagrams, predict phase fractions, and calculate Gibbs free energy, guiding phase field modeling in MATLAB based on the Cahn-Hilliard and Allen-Cahn equations. Simulations predicted γ' precipitate nucleation and growth at various aging conditions, leading to an optimized heat treatment: solutionizing at 800°C for 2 hours, followed by aging at 250°C, 450°C, 550°C, and 650°C for 8 hours. Experimental validation included hardness testing, X-Ray Diffraction (XRD), optical microscopy, and wear testing (ASTM G99). Results conclude that the optimized condition of 550°C at 8 hours shows improved hardness and wear resistance due to controlled γ' precipitation. This integrated approach provides a reliable method for optimizing heat treatment in precipitation-hardenable alloys for high-performance applications.

Keywords: Age hardening, calphad, heat treatment optimization, Monel K500, Phase field modeling, γ' precipitation

Introduction

Monel K500, a precipitation hardenable nickel-copper alloy, is known for its exceptional strength, corrosion resistance, and durability, making it a strong choice for marine, oil and gas, and chemical applications [1,2]. Its mechanical properties are enhanced through age hardening, where aluminum and titanium form γ' (Ni_3Al) precipitates during the aging heat treatment [3,4]. These precipitates hinder dislocation movement, improving hardness and strength. However, their size, distribution, and stability depend on aging temperature and time. This study investigates γ' precipitate nucleation and growth in Monel K500 using phase field modeling, a simulation technique predicting microstructural evolution [4,5]. Simulations provide optimal heat treatment conditions, but experimental validation is essential. Wear tests (ASTM G99), hardness tests, optical microscopy, and X-Ray Diffraction (XRD) confirm phase transformations and mechanical property changes. By comparing modeling predictions with experimental results, this research aims to optimize aging parameters for the alloy performance in high-stress environments.

Experimental Work

The simulations utilized the typical chemical composition of Monel K500 (Table 17.1), and the Ni-based alloy as given in the Table 17.1 was selected to accurately represent the alloy properties.

Key analyses included phase diagrams, property diagrams, and precipitation kinetics. Phase fraction analysis was conducted using Thermo-Calc to predict the proportions of the γ (Matrix) and γ' (Precipitate) phases across different temperature ranges. This step was essential for selecting aging temperatures that maximize γ' precipitate formation, as a higher γ' phase fraction contributes to enhanced hardness and wear resistance. The composition of Monel K500 was fed into Thermo-Calc, including major elements such as Ni, Cu, Al, and Ti. The software

Table 17.1 Chemical composition of Monel K500

Elements	Ni	Cu	Al	Ti	Fe	Mn
Wt (%)	64.7	29.99	2.98	0.45	1.02	0.59

Source: Author

[a]23my01@psgtech.ac.in, [b]hod.metal@psgtech.ac.in, [c]Kkk.metal@psgtech.ac.in

DOI: 10.1201/9781003770435-17

calculated equilibrium phase fractions, helping in determining temperature ranges that favor γ' precipitation while avoiding the formation of undesirable secondary phases. Phase diagrams were generated to confirm stable γ and γ' regions. Additionally, Gibbs free energy calculations were performed to assess the thermodynamic driving force for γ' precipitation. A higher driving force leads to faster nucleation and growth, helping in selecting aging temperatures that promote a fine and dense precipitate distribution without excessive coarsening [5]. These results guided the experimental heat treatment process, which was validated through hardness testing, X-ray diffraction (XRD), and wear resistance tests. Phase field modeling was implemented using MATLAB to simulate the nucleation and growth of γ' precipitates under various aging conditions. The Cahn-Hilliard equation was applied to track microstructural evolution, using thermodynamic data from Thermo-Calc, including phase fractions, Gibbs free energy values, and stability ranges. The model simulated precipitate morphology, size distribution, and growth kinetics. The simulation results were visualized using 2D concentration maps, enabling predictions of precipitate density, shape, and evolution over different aging times [4,5]. The experimental heat treatment involved a solutionizing step at 800°C for 2 hours to dissolve existing precipitates and homogenize the microstructure. The samples were then rapidly cooled to room temperature before undergoing aging at 250°C, 450°C, 550°C, and 650°C for 8 hours. These temperatures, as depicted in Figure 17.1 were selected based on Thermo-Calc and phase field modeling predictions to optimize γ' precipitate formation. Air cooling was used after aging to prevent residual stresses and maintain phase stability [6]. Vickers hardness testing was performed by a microhardness tester (make: Zwick; model: Roell) on all heat-treated samples using a 1 kg load with a 10-second dwell time. Multiple indentations were made on each sample to ensure accuracy, and the average hardness values were recorded. X-ray diffraction analysis was conducted using an X-ray diffractometer (make: Drawell; make: Y3000) performed using Cu Kα radiation (λ = 1.5406 Å) with a 2θ range of 20° to 90°. A slow scan rate was employed to improve resolution, capturing phase transformations, peak shifts, and changes in peak intensity to analyze γ' precipitation behavior. Wear testing was carried out following ASTM G99 standards using a pin-on-disc setup.

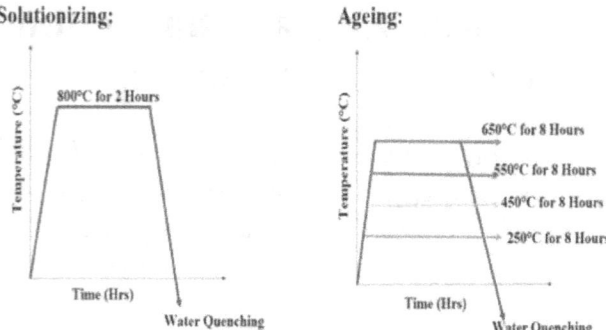

Figure 17.1 Applied heat treatment cycle
Source: Author

Tests were conducted at 500 and 1000 rpm for 2 minutes and 5 minutes to study wear resistance under different conditions. Only one parameter was varied to isolate its effect on wear behavior.

Simulation Modeling

Precipitation kinetics model

The precipitation kinetics of γ' was modeled using Thermo-Calc diffusion and kinetics models for Ni-based alloy packages. These models provided data on nucleation and growth rates of γ' particles, essential for understanding the time and temperature dependency of the precipitation process. Using the diffusion model, the activation energy and diffusion coefficients were calculated, which allowed for precise estimations of γ' nucleation and growth at various temperatures [5,7]. The kinetics model predicted that aging between 250°C and 650°C would optimize precipitate growth while preventing over-aging effects that lead to γ' coarsening.

The nucleation rate was derived from classical nucleation theory using the equation

$J = A \exp(-\Delta G^* / k_B T)$

where:

- J is the nucleation rate
- A is a pre-exponential factor
- ΔG^* is the nucleation energy barrier
- k_B is Boltzmann's constant
- T is the temperature in Kelvin

The diffusion coefficient for the γ' phase was determined using the Arrhenius-type equation

$D = D_0 \exp(-Q / RT)$

where:

- D is the diffusion coefficient
- D_0 is the pre-exponential factor
- Q is the activation energy for diffusion
- R is the universal gas constant
- T is the absolute temperature

Phase field modeling using MATLAB

The phase field modeling of Monel K500 was developed using a combination of thermodynamic data collected from Thermo-Calc and numerical methods implemented in Matlab utilizing the Cahn-Hilliard equation and Allen-Cahn Equation for Precipitate Growth and nucleation [8,9,10]. This approach aimed to simulate both the nucleation and growth of γ' precipitates during aging treatments and to examine the resulting morphology at various temperatures [10]. Two main models were used in this simulation process: the nucleation-growth model and the morphology simulation model, each performed over a temperature range of 250–850°C [11,12].

Cahn-Hilliard equation for phase evolution [16]:

$$\partial C / \partial t = M \nabla^2 (\partial F / \partial C)$$

where:

- C is the concentration of the precipitate phase (γ') within the matrix (γ)
- M is the mobility parameter related to atomic diffusion
- F is the free energy functional, calculated based on Gibbs free energy values

Allen-Cahn equation for precipitate growth [16]:

$$\partial \phi / \partial t = -L \, \delta F / \delta \phi$$

where:

- φ represents the order parameter for phase transformation
- L is a kinetic coefficient
- F is the free energy functional

Using Matlab, phase field modeling was initialized by setting up parameters, including composition data for Nickel (Ni), Copper (Cu), Aluminum (Al), Titanium (Ti), and Gibbs free energy differences specific to each temperature studied. Key simulation variables such as spatial step size (dx), temporal step size (dt), and grid size were established to reflect the microstructural resolution desired [13.14]. The evolution of the γ' phase followed the Cahn-Hilliard equation, incorporating parameters such as mobility and the gradient energy coefficient. The nucleation and growth process was driven by energy gradients, influencing phase separation and leading to γ' precipitate development over time [15,16]. For each temperature, simulations were conducted over an aging time of 72 hours. Afterward, the microstructure was visualized, with grayscale images displaying the precipitate distribution across the grid. Furthermore, the precipitate size distribution was quantified using radius and volume fractions, showing that aging temperature significantly influenced the average size and density of γ' precipitates [17,18,19].

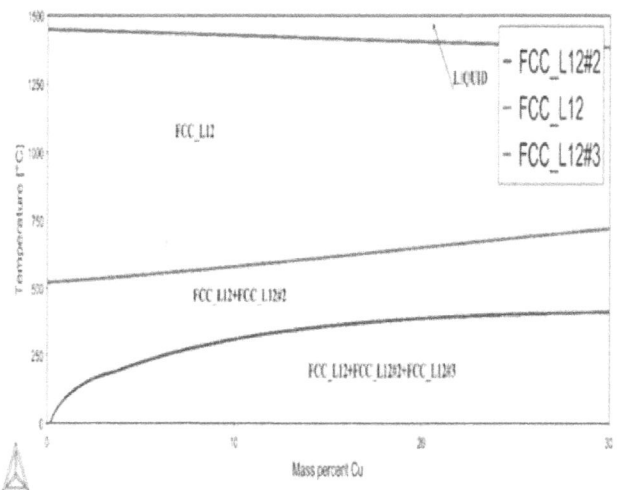

Figure 17.2 Phase diagram calculated by Thermocalc for the chemical composition Table 17.1

Source: Author

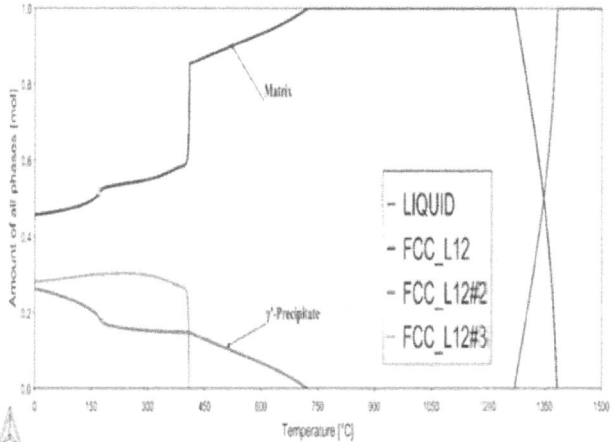

Figure 17.3 Phase fraction for matrix and precipitate of Monel K500

Source: Author

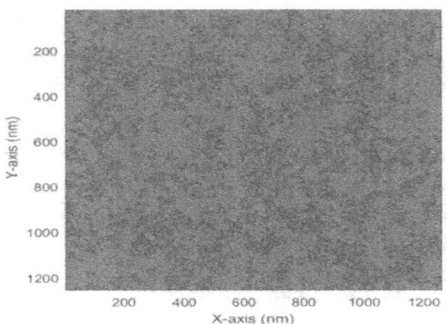

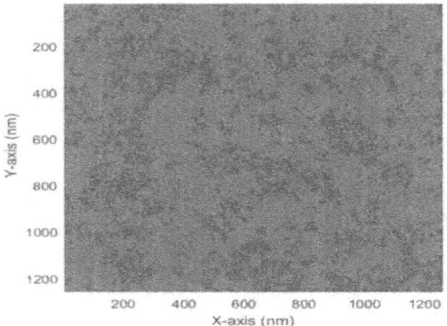

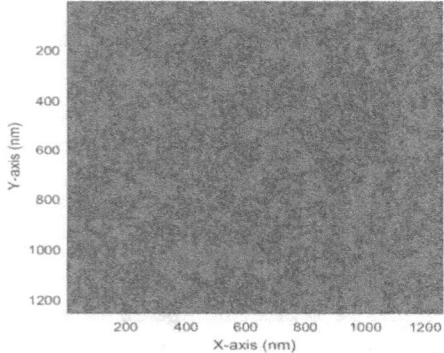

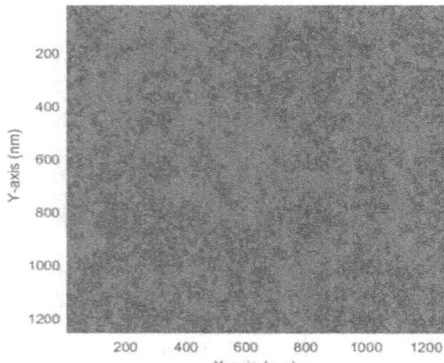

Figure 17.4 Phase field modelled microstructure of Monel K500 for the temperatures (a) 250°C (b) 450°C (c) 550°C (d) 650°C aged for 8 hours
Source: Author

Table 17.2 γ' Precipitate volume fraction by phase field modelling

Ageing temperature (°C)	Volume fraction (%)
250	24.25
450	28.12
550	28.43
650	21.02

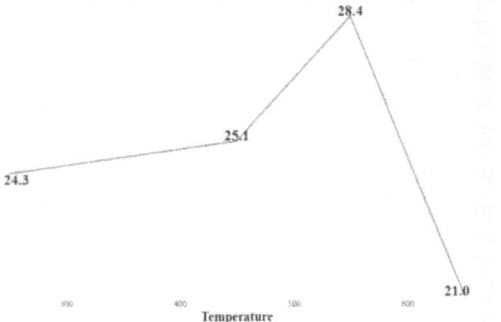

Source: Author

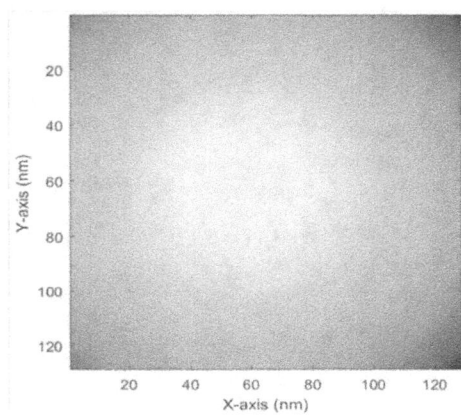

Figure 17.5 Morphology evolution of the precipitates by Allen-Cahn equation
Source: Author

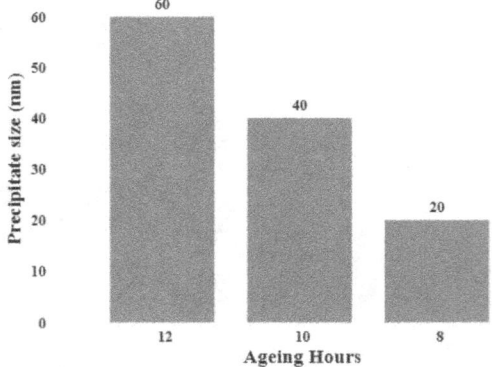

Figure 17.6 Precipitate size evolution (nm) by Allen-Cahn equation presented in the Table 17.2
Source: Author

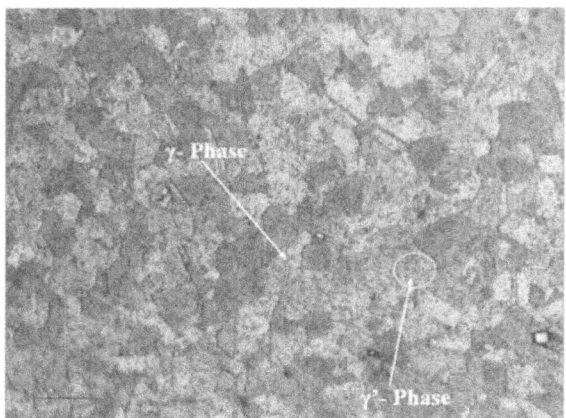

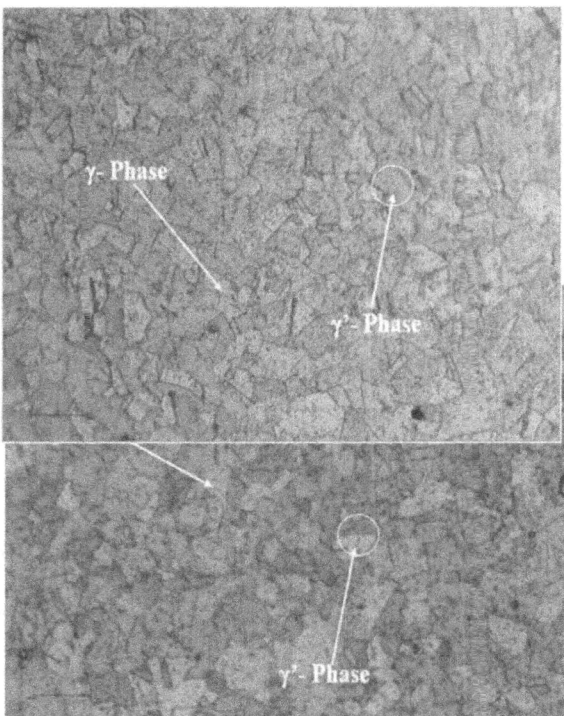

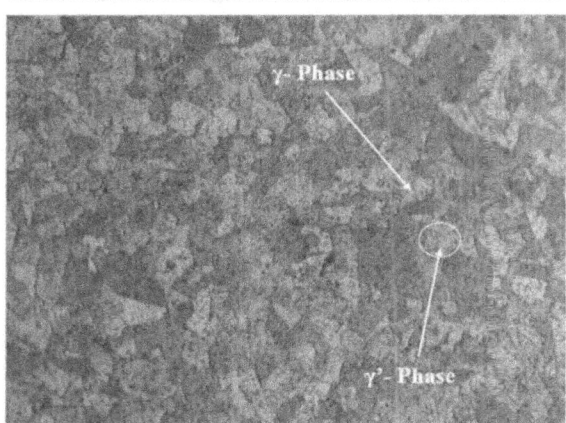

Figure 17.7 Optical microstructure after Heat treatment (a) 250°C (b) 450°C (c) 550°C (d) 650°C

Source: Author

Experimental Validation

Optical microscopy analysis

The optical microscopy analysis of Monel K500 samples, heat-treated at 250°C, 450°C, 550°C, and 650°C, revealed significant microstructural changes captured at magnifications of 200x and 500x. Across these aging temperatures, the micrographs highlighted a clear distinction between the γ (Ni) matrix phase and the γ' (Ni$_3$Al) precipitate phase, with additional secondary carbide phases, identified as TiC, dispersed within the matrix [19]. At lower temperatures, such as 250°C and 450°C, the microstructure showed finer γ' precipitates with a relatively uniform distribution, indicating early stages of nucleation and growth in the γ phase matrix. As the aging temperature increased to 550°C and 650°C, the γ' precipitates became more observable coarsening contributing to a denser and more interconnected microstructure (Table 17.2).

Vickers hardness testing

The Vickers hardness testing of Monel K500 samples (Table 17.3), conducted after heat treatment at various aging temperatures, reveals the impact of

Table 17.3 Vickers hardness for 1 Kg load

Ageing temperature (°C)	Average hardness (HV)
250	172
450	186
550	259
650	225

Source: Author

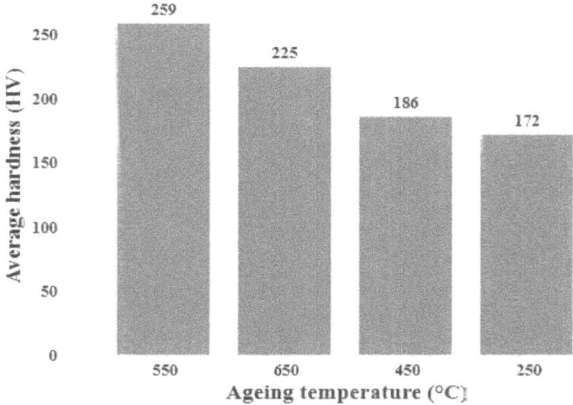

Figure 17.8 Hardness curve for the aging temperature

Source: Author

temperature on material hardness due to the evolution of the γ' precipitates [20]. Hardness values increased with temperature, peaking at 550°C, corresponding to the optimal precipitate distribution for strengthening. Beyond 550°C, hardness decreased due to over-aging and coarsening of γ' precipitates.

XRD analysis

XRD analysis also confirmed the evolution of γ' precipitates at each temperature. The 550°C sample displayed the highest precipitate phase fraction, correlating well with the peak hardness observed. At 650°C, XRD results showed a reduced precipitate fraction due to over-aging effects, validating 550°C as the optimal aging temperature.

Wear testing

The 550°C aged sample demonstrated the lowest weight loss and the highest wear resistance, correlating well with its peak hardness. At 250°C and 450°C, higher wear rates were observed due to incomplete

Table 17.4 Precipitate phase fraction through XRD analysis

Samples	γ> Phase (Ni₃Al)	Total precipitate phase fraction (%)
250	23.99	26.82
450	24.14	27.52
550	24.35	27.98
650	22.25	26.43

Source: Author

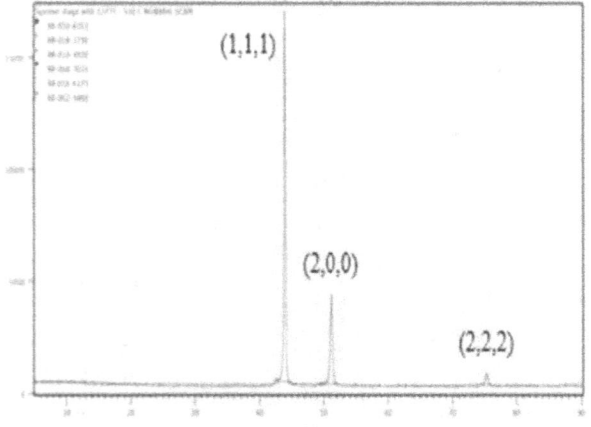

Figure 17.9 XRD results of 550°C sample
Source: Author

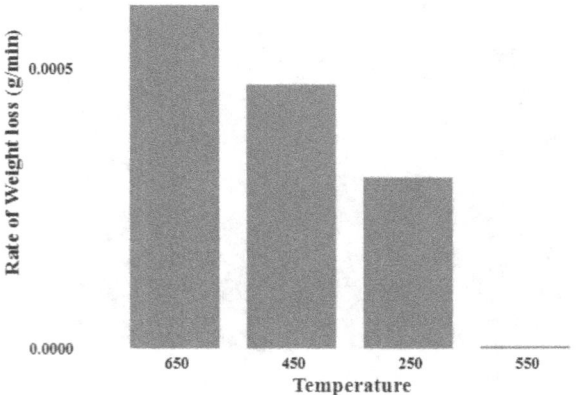

Figure 17.10 Rate of weight loss for various aged samples
Source: Author

precipitation hardening. The 650°C sample showed increased wear due to over-aging effects.

Discussion

The results of this study demonstrate the critical role of aging temperature in optimizing the mechanical and tribological properties of Monel K-500 through γ' precipitation. The combination of phase field modeling and Calphad approach provided deep knowledge into the thermodynamics and kinetics of phase transformations during the aging process. These predictions were validated experimentally through hardness testing, wear analysis, XRD, and optical microscopy, confirming the robustness of the integrated computational–experimental approach. The phase field simulations showed that at 550°C, the nucleation rate and growth behavior of γ' precipitates resulted in uniform and fine distribution, correlating well with the increased hardness and enhanced wear resistance observed in the experimental data. At temperatures above 550°C, coarsening of precipitates was evident, leading to a reduction in hardness, which aligns with the classical Ostwald ripening mechanism. Meanwhile, aging at lower temperatures such as 250°C and 450°C, showed insufficient precipitate growth within the 8-hour duration, resulting in suboptimal properties. XRD patterns confirmed the presence of γ' phase, with peak intensities supporting the precipitate density trends predicted by the simulations. Optical microscopy further provides the microstructural evolution, showing a transition from fine, dispersed precipitates at optimal temperatures to coarser and less effective distributions at higher temperatures. The wear test results mirrored the hardness trends, indicating that mechanical strengthening through optimized precipitation also contributed significantly to wear resistance. Overall, this study highlights the effectiveness of combining computational modeling tools with physical experimentation to optimize heat treatment cycles. It not only reduces the need for extensive trial-and-error experimentation but also enhances predictive accuracy for alloy design and process optimization. The approach adopted here can be extended to other precipitation-hardenable systems, offering a scalable and cost-effective pathway for industrial applications.

Conclusion

Phase field modeling identified 550°C with an 8-hour aging treatment as the optimal condition for Monel K-500. Wear test (ASTM G-99) revealed that aging at 550°C has lower. X-ray diffraction (XRD) confirmed that the precipitate phase fraction is maximized at 550°C. Therefore, a 550°C, 8-hour aging treatment optimally enhances the mechanical performance of Monel K500, striking a balance between precipitate stability and material hardness.

References

[1] Rai, A. K., Trpathy, H., Hajra, R. N., Raju, S., & Saroja, S. (2017). Thermophysical properties of Ni based super alloy 617. *Journal of Alloys and Compounds*, 698, 442–450.

[2] Kostryzhev, A. G., Marenych, O. O., Pan, Z., Li, H., & Duin, S. V. (2023).Strengthening mechanisms in Monel K500 alloyed with Al and Ti. *Journal of Materials Science*, 58, 4150–4164.

[3] Cárach, J., Hloch, S., Petru, J., Nag, A., Gombár, M., & Hromasová, M. (2018). Hydro abrasive disintegration of rotating Monel K500 workpiece. *The International Journal of Advanced Manufacturing Technology*, 96, 981–1001.

[4] Wang, Q., Luo, X., Zhang, X., Lu, T., Zheng, H., Dong, L., et al. (2023). Stress corrosion cracking behavior and mechanism of aging treated Monel K500 alloy in flowing seawater. *Journal of Materials Science*, 58, 5784–6802.

[5] Krawczyk, J., Frocisz, L., Matusiewicz, P., & Madej, M. (2015).The effect of the microstructure on the tribological properties of the Monel K500 alloy.Metal. In 22nd International Conference on Metallurgy and Materials, Brno, Czech Republic, (pp. 1510–1515).

[6] Esgin, U., Özyürek, D., & Kaya, H. (2015). An investigation of wear behaviors of different monel alloys produced by powder metallurgy. *International Advances in Applied Physics and Materials Science Congress and Exhibition*, 020008, 1–7.

[7] Marenych, O., Kostryzhev, A., Shen, C., Pan, Z., Li, H., & Duin, S. V. (2019). Precipitation strengthening in Ni–Cu alloys fabricated using wire arc additive manufacturing technology. *Metals*, 9, 105–119.

[8] Mao, H., Zeng, C., Zhang, Z., Shua, X., & Tang, S. (2023). The effect of lattice misfits on the precipitation at dislocations: phase-field crystal simulation. *Materials*, 16, 6307–6318.

[9] Mills, K. C., Youssef, Y. M., Li, Z., & Su, Y. (2006). Calculation of thermophysical properties of ni-based superalloys. *ISIJ International*, 46, 623–632.

[10] Chen, Z., Wang, C., Tang, C., Lek, Y. Z., Kandukuri, S. Y., Du, H., et al. (2022). Microstructure and mechanical properties of a Monel K500 alloy fabricated by directed energy deposition. *Materials Science and Engineering A*, 857, 144113–144128.

[11] Dey, S. (2024). Hot workability and microstructure control in Monel K 500 in as cast condition: an approach using processing maps. *Metals and Materials International*, 898, 3843–3858.

[12] Turchanin, M. A., Agraval, P. G., & Abdulov, A. R. (2007). Phase equilibria and thermodynamics of binary copper systems with 3d-metals.VI. Copper–Nickel system. *Powder Metallurgy and Metal Ceramics*, 45, 9–20.

[13] Dey, G. K., Tewari, R., Rao, P., Wadekar, S. L., & Mukhopadhyay, P. (1993). Precipitation hardening in nickel-copper base alloy Monel K 500. Precipitation hardening in nickel-copper base alloy Monel K 500. *Metallurgical Transactions A*, 24, 2709–2719.

[14] Zhang, X., & Chen, W. (2012). Experimental research on heating performance of Monel K500 alloy. *Advanced Materials Research*, 572, 273–277.

[15] Harris, Z. D., & Burns, J. T. (2019). The effect of isothermal heat treatment on hydrogen environment-assisted cracking susceptibility in Monel K500. *Materials Science and Engineering A*, 764, 138249–138266.

[16] Zhang, H., He, Y., Yang, F., Liu, H., & Jin, Z. (2013). Thermodynamic assessment of Cu–Ni–Ti ternary system assisted with key measurements. *Thermochimica Acta*, 574, 121–132.

[17] Ojo, O. A. (2013). Effect of deformation mode on hot ductility of a γ′ precipitation strengthened nickel-base superalloy. *Materials Science and Engineering A*, 585, 319–325.

[18] Yenusah, C. O., Ji, Y., Liu, Y., Stone, T. W., Horstemeyer, M. F., Chen, L. Q., et al. (2021). Three-dimensional Phase-field simulation of γ″ precipitation kinetics in Inconel 625 during heat treatment. *Computational Materials Science*, 187, 110123–110136.

[19] Ilangovan, S., Sreejith, J., Manideep, M., & Harish, S. (2018). An experimental investigation of Cu-Ni-Sn alloy on microstructure, hardness and wear parameters optimization using DOE. *Tribology in Industry*, 40, 156–163.

[20] Banker, V. J., Mistry, J. M., Thakor, M. R., & Bhargav, U. H. (2016). Wear behavior in dry sliding of Inconel 600 alloy using taguchi method and regression analysis. *Procedia Technology*, 23, 383–390.

18 Optimized medicine inventory system for hospitals

S. Madhanika[1,a] and R. Divya[2,b]

[1]PG Scholar, Department of Electrical and Electronics Engineering (EEE), PSG College of Technology, Coimbatore, India.

[2]Assistant Professor (SI.Gr), Department of Electrical and Electronics Engineering (EEE), PSG College of Technology, Coimbatore, India

Abstract

The Medicine Inventory System (MIS) uses IoT principles to optimize pharmaceutical stock control, reduce wastage and ensure the timely availability of medications. The system employs simulated sensor data in a software environment to monitor stock levels, manage expiry dates and send alerts for low stock or expired items. Centralized monitoring through a virtual dashboard ensures regulatory compliance, reduces errors and improves operational efficiency, while the system's modular design allows for future scalability and enhancements. The simulation provides a streamlined approach to tracking and managing stock, helping administrators ensure that essential medications are always available. By simulating data and interactions, the system aids in predicting demand and ensuring optimal stock levels, enhancing decision-making and supporting better resource management in healthcare settings.

Keywords: Inventory management, IoT, real-time monitoring, regulatory compliance

Introduction

Efficient healthcare inventory management is essential for ensuring medication availability, minimizing wastage, and improving resource utilization. Recent research has explored multiple strategies for optimizing pharmaceutical supply chains. For example, Lotfi (2024) examined vendor-managed inventory models that enhance supply chain responsiveness, while Babaei (2023) proposed a multi-objective decision-making framework for vaccine distribution and stock control. Broader developments in healthcare technology, as highlighted by Nti (2023), emphasize the growing role of digital tools and analytics in sustainable healthcare operations. Further studies have analyzed systemic challenges such as drug shortages (Zwaida et al., 2022) and workflow inefficiencies within hospital logistics (Feibert et al., 2021). Modeling-based approaches, including Markovian inventory systems (Aghsami, 2021) and uncertainty-aware pharmaceutical relief networks (Akbarpour, 2020), underline the need for robust and adaptive inventory frameworks. Traditional replenishment and scheduling strategies (Cetinkaya & Lee, 2019) and discussions on entrepreneurship-linked inventory management improvements (Saha & Ray, 2021) also contribute to the understanding of efficient stock systems.

The present work builds on these contributions by developing an IoT-enabled Smart Medicine Inventory System designed to automate stock monitoring, expiry-date verification, and environmental control. By reducing manual intervention and supporting real-time alerts, the system aims to strengthen decision-making processes and improve overall pharmaceutical inventory performance.

Literature Review

Predictive decision support systems
Early work by Isabel Fernandez et al. (2020) focused on predictive analytics within the pharmaceutical sector by leveraging historical pharmacy data. Their system utilized model predictive control (MPC) to forecast stock requirements and compare results against standard inventory models. The study revealed that predictive systems could effectively reduce stockout risks and improve inventory efficiency. However, a critical limitation lies in the reliance on historical data, which may not always capture abrupt fluctuations in medicine demand caused by unforeseen events or public health emergencies. *H1: Predictive analytics in inventory systems improve stock optimization but may be limited by historical data dependencies.*

Secure and automated inventory management systems
Jishu Varshney et al. (2019) developed a pharmacy store management system incorporating the Cascade

[a]madhanikasiva02@gmail.com, [b]rdv.eee@psgtech.ac.in

DOI: 10.1201/9781003770435-18

Model with Rivest–Shamir–Adleman (RSA) encryption. This system offered enhanced security features, such as real-time logging and encrypted stock tracking, making it highly suitable for environments where data integrity and access control are critical. Despite its strengths, the integration of encryption algorithms increased computational overhead, potentially affecting the system's speed and responsiveness in real-time applications.

Centralized and real-time monitoring frameworks
Adrian Mirea and Adriana Albu (2021) proposed a real-time pharmaceutical inventory system that aggregates data from peripheral devices into a centralized database. This design supports immediate access to stock data and allows for efficient user activity tracking and inventory updates. While this model improves operational transparency and responsiveness, its dependency on real-time data collection may become a limitation if technical issues like network failure or data loss occur, potentially disrupting the entire inventory workflow. H3: Centralized real-time inventory systems enhance operational efficiency but are vulnerable to system and network failures.

Cost-based inventory techniques
A systematic review by Disha Singh (2018) evaluated the effectiveness of classical inventory optimization techniques, including ABC-VED, JIT, economic order quantity (EOQ), and fast normal slow (FNS) models. These methodologies were shown to improve stock classification, reduce holding costs, and enhance inventory responsiveness. However, the effectiveness of these methods is contingent on the availability of accurate and timely data, which is not guaranteed in under-resourced healthcare environments.

H4: Traditional inventory optimization methods reduce waste and improve utilization, but require high data accuracy for effectiveness.

Application of ABC-VED in hospital settings
Meena DK and Mathaiyan J (2022) focused on the application of ABC-VED techniques in hospital inventory systems. Their findings indicated that this classification-based approach enhances drug availability and cost-efficiency by prioritizing essential medications. Nevertheless, the adaptability of

ABC-VED is limited in dynamic scenarios such as public health emergencies or sudden supply chain disruptions, where stock status changes rapidly and unpredictably.

H5: ABC-VED analysis ensures efficient stock classification but is less effective under volatile supply conditions.

Methodology

The proposed system automates drug inventory management using an IoT-enabled approach. It consists of microcontrollers (ESP32) and sensors to monitor stock levels, expiration dates, and storage conditions. Real-time data collection identifies irregularities, and alerts are activated when thresholds (e.g., low stock or expired medications) are met. The system's efficiency and functionality were tested using a prototype in a simulated environment (Figure 18.1).

System components and design

- **Temperature sensor**: Monitors the storage unit's environmental parameters to check that the medications are kept within the recommended temperature range.
- **DHT22**: DHT22 monitors storage conditions by measuring temperature and humidity in the medicine inventory system. This ensures optimal environmental control to maintain medication efficacy and prevent spoilage.
- **Weight sensor:** Checks the weight of medications on shelves to spot shortages or excesses and determine stock levels.
- **HX711**: HX711 is used with a load cell to measure the weight of medicines in the inventory system. It helps track stock levels accurately and triggers alerts for shortages or excess inventory.
- **Push:** Push button replaces RFID and NFC to simulate checking medication expiry dates. Pressing a button triggers the system to verify whether the medicines have expired or not.
- **Buzzer:** It acts as an alert system that sounds when there is a dangerous circumstance, such as low stock levels or inappropriate storage conditions.
- **Power supply:** During testing, Wokwi's simulated power source makes sure the system runs continuously.

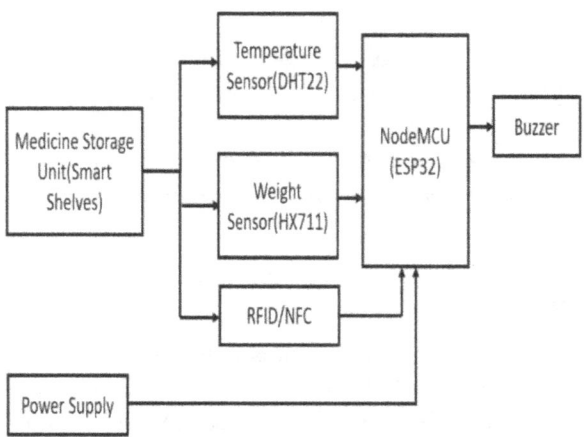

Figure 18.1 Block of medicine inventory system
Source: Author

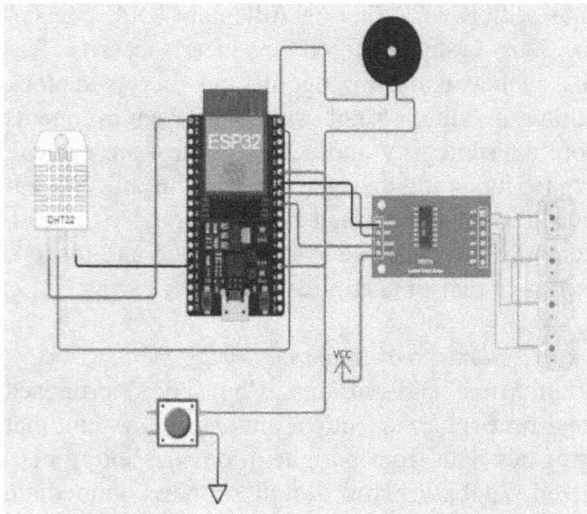

Figure 18.2 Schematic of proposed system
Source: Author

Data processing and alerts

Sensor data is analysed by the ESP32 microcontroller, triggering alerts when predefined thresholds are exceeded. The buzzer system notifies users of critical situations such as stock depletion, overstocking, and temperature deviations. The modular architecture ensures scalability for future enhancements.

Wokwi simulation

The system's functionality, including sensor inputs, data processing, and alarm systems, was replicated using the Wokwi platform.

Empirical Results

Figure 18.2 represents the simulation part of my proposed system, which is done using the Wokwi open-source platform.

Scenario 1: Virtual temperature and weight sensor readings

```
Temperature: 28.50 *C
Weight: 0.83 kg
Temperature: 28.50 *C
Weight: 0.83 kg
Temperature: 28.50 *C
Weight: 0.83 kg
Temperature: 28.50 *C
```

Figure 18.3 Temperature and weight sensor readings
Source: Author

To guarantee precise monitoring of environmental conditions and medication inventory, the system continuously records and shows temperature and weight sensor data (Figure 18.3). Maintaining appropriate storage conditions is crucial for preserving the efficacy of medications and ensuring prompt identification of any changes in stock levels or temperature.

Scenario 2: Critical temperature alert and weight status

```
Temperature: 40.90 *C
Total Weight: 2.67 kg
Temperature exceeded threshold! Activating buzzer...
```

Figure 18.4 Temperature alert status
Source: Author

When the system detects a temperature exceeding the predefined threshold, an alert is triggered. The recorded values are:

- Temperature: 40.90°C (exceeds safe limit)
- Total weight: 2.67 kg
- Alert message: "Temperature exceeded threshold! Activating buzzer..."

This ensures that if medicines are exposed to unsafe temperatures, corrective action can be taken immediately. The buzzer is activated to notify users of the temperature violation.

Scenario 3: Understock alert: Medicine inventory shortage and buzzer activation

```
Total Weight: -1.82 kg
Total Expected Weight of Medicines: 3.20 kg
Understock! Less medicine than required.
Paracetamol: Expected Weight = 1.00 kg. Status: Understock!
Ibuprofen: Expected Weight = 1.00 kg. Status: Understock!
Amoxicillin: Expected Weight = 1.20 kg. Status: Understock!
Stock issue detected! Activating buzzer...
```

Figure 18.5 Understock alert
Source: Author

Figure 18.5 has detected an understock condition, where the total measured weight is 1.38 kg is significantly lower than the expected 3.20 kg. This indicates that some medicines are missing or have not been restocked to the required levels. Maintaining adequate stock is crucial to ensure medicine availability and avoid potential shortages. The system provides a detailed breakdown of the inventory status:

- Paracetamol: Expected = 1.00 kg, Status: Understocked!
- Ibuprofen: Expected = 1.00 kg, Status: Understocked!
- Amoxicillin: Expected = 1.20 kg, Status: Understocked!

Scenario 4: Medicine stock discrepancy alert and buzzer activation

```
Total Weight: 1.04 kg
Total Expected Weight of Medicines: 3.20 kg
Overstock! Too much medicine in storage.
Paracetamol: Expected Weight = 1.00 kg. Status: Overstock!
Ibuprofen: Expected Weight = 1.00 kg. Status: Overstock!
Amoxicillin: Expected Weight = 1.20 kg. Status: Understock!
Stock issue detected! Activating buzzer...
```

Figure 18.6 Medicine stock discrepancy alert
Source: Author

Figure 18.6 detects a stock discrepancy, where the actual measured total weight (1.04 kg) does not match the expected total weight (3.20 kg). This mismatch suggests an inconsistency in the medicine inventory, which could be due to untracked stock adjustments, misplacement, or manual errors in inventory updates. The detailed stock analysis is as follows:

- Paracetamol: Expected = 1.00 kg, Current Status: Overstock!

- Ibuprofen: Expected = 1.00 kg, Current Status: Overstock!
- Amoxicillin: Expected = 1.20 kg, Current Status: Understocked!

Since maintaining accurate stock levels is critical for efficient inventory management, the buzzer is activated to alert users of the discrepancy, ensuring that corrective action can be taken promptly.

Scenario 5: Overstock alert: Excess medicine inventory and buzzer activation

```
Total Weight: 2.34 kg
Total Expected Weight of Medicines: 3.20 kg
Overstock! Too much medicine in storage.
Paracetamol: Expected Weight = 1.00 kg. Status: Overstock!
Ibuprofen: Expected Weight = 1.00 kg. Status: Overstock!
Amoxicillin: Expected Weight = 1.20 kg. Status: Overstock!
Stock issue detected! Activating buzzer...
```

Figure 18.7 Excess medicine alert
Source: Author

Figure 18.7 shows an overstock condition, where the actual measured total weight (2.34 kg) is higher than the expected 3.20 kg. The stock analysis reveals:

- Paracetamol: Expected = 1.00 kg, Current status: Overstock!
- Ibuprofen: Expected = 1.00 kg, Current status: Overstock!
- Amoxicillin: Expected = 1.20 kg, Current status: Overstock!

Overstocking may indicate inventory mismanagement, excess supply, or errors in tracking medicine intake. To alert users, the buzzer is activated, prompting them to adjust inventory levels.

Scenario 6: Medicine expiration check alert

```
Checking for medicine expiration...
Paracetamol: has expired!
Ibuprofen: is still valid.
Amoxicillin: is still valid.
```

Figure 18.8 Medicine expiry status notification
Source: Author

Figure 18.8 for expired medicines and reports their status. The findings are:

- Paracetamol: Expired! Remove immediately.
- Ibuprofen: Safe for use.
- Amoxicillin: Safe for use.

When expired medicines are detected, the buzzer is activated to notify users that immediate action is required to remove and replace expired stock.

Conclusion

The Smart Medicine Inventory Management System is an IoT-based solution designed to optimize medicine stock monitoring and ensure efficient inventory management. By integrating temperature, humidity, and weight sensors, along with an automated expiration tracking mechanism, the system provides real-time monitoring and automated alerts for stock shortages, expired medicines, and improper storage conditions. This reduces manual effort, minimizes errors, and enhances the overall efficiency of inventory control. The implementation of this system helps in reducing waste, ensuring timely restocking, and maintaining essential medicine availability. Automating stock tracking eliminates the need for manual inventory checks and optimizes storage conditions, making the process more cost-effective and reliable.

References

[1] Lotfi, R. (2024). A viable supply chain by considering vendor-managed inventory with a consignment stock policy and learning approach. *Results in Engineering*, 21, 101609

[2] Babaei, Y. S. (2023). A multi-objective multi-criteria decision-making approach for sustainable vaccine distribution, inventory control (R, s, S policy), and waste management considering risk assessment: a case study. *Sustainable Cities and Society*, 96(10), 104670

[3] Nti, I. K. (2023). A bibliometric analysis of technology in sustainable healthcare: Emerging trends and future directions. *Decision Analytics Journal*, 8, 100292.

[4] Zwaida, A., Beauregard, Y., & Elarroudi, K. (2022). A comprehensive literature review about drug shortages in the Canadian hospital's pharmacy supply chain. In Proceedings of the International Conference on Engineering Sciences and Industrial Applications, (pp. 1–5).

[5] Aghsami, A. (2021). A novel Markovian queuing-inventory model with imperfect production and inspection processes: a hospital case study. *Computers and Industrial Engineering*, 162(5), 107772.

[6] Saha, S., & Ray, P. K. (2021). An overview of the impact of healthcare inventory management systems on entrepreneurship. In Entrepreneurship in Technology for ASEAN, (p. 1).

[7] Feibert, D. C., Andersen, B., & Jacobsen, P. (2021). Benchmarking healthcare logistics processes: a comparative case study of Danish hospitals. *Total Quality Management and Business Excellence*, 30(1–2).

[8] Alvarez, L., & Callejon, G. (2020). The Hospitality Pharmacy Specialist Handbook (in Spanish), (Vol, 1, pp. 43–46).

[9] Akbarpour, M. (2020). Designing an integrated pharmaceutical relief chain network under demand uncertainty. *Transportation Research Part E: Logistics and Transportation Review*, 136, 101867.

[10] Cetinkaya, S., & Lee, C. (2019). Stock replenishment and shipment scheduling for vendor-managed inventory systems. *Management Science*, 46(2), 217–232.

[11] Fernandez, I., Chanfreut, P., Jurado, I. and Maestre, J.M., "A data-based model predictive decision support system for inventory management in hospitals", *IEEE Journal of Biomedical and Health Informatics*, 25(6), 2104–2114, 2021.

[12] Varshney, J., Varshney, I. and Singh, B., "Functionality of pharmacy store management system using Cascade Model and RSA algorithm", 2023 International Conference on Artificial Intelligence and Smart Communication (AISC), IEEE, 1–6, 2023.

[13] Mirea, A. and Albu, A., "Automated system for medication stocks management", 2018 22nd International Conference on System Theory, Control and Computing (ICSTCC), IEEE, 543–548, 2018.

[14] Singh, D., "Analysis of inventory management in pharmaceutical", International Journal of Development Research, 13(5), 62800–62805, 2023.

[15] Meena, D.K. and Mathaiyan, J., "Unveiling supply chain efficiency: exploring ABC–VED analysis studies on drug inventory management in India", International Journal of Basic & Clinical Pharmacology, 13(4),245–251, 2024.

19 Machine learning enhanced response surface methodology for hardness optimization in TIG welding of Al 6061-T6 alloy

Jayakrishnan Nampoothiri[1,a], Dhilip, A.[1,b] and Ganesh Manikandan[2,c]

[1]Assistant Professor, Department of Production Engineering, PSG College of Technology, Coimbatore, India

[2]PG Student, Department of Production Engineering, PSG College of Technology, Coimbatore, India

Abstract

This study presents an integrated approach combining machine learning and response surface methodology to optimize TIG welding parameters for enhancing the microhardness of Al 6061 T6 alloy weldments. Experimental trials were designed using central composite design with varying welding currents and filler rods. Gradient Boosting and Random Forest models were developed to predict microhardness based on process parameters. Among the models, Gradient Boosting showed superior accuracy with a high R-squared value and low prediction errors. Partial dependence analysis revealed that both welding current and filler rod type significantly influence hardness, with ER5356 showing the most consistent performance. The predicted optimum parameters - 65 amperes and ER5356 were validated experimentally, yielding a microhardness of 78 ± 2 $Hv_{0.3}$. The close agreement between predicted and actual values confirms the effectiveness of the proposed approach. This study demonstrates the potential of machine learning enhanced response surface methodology for reliable optimization of welding processes returns.

Keywords: Aluminium 6061, machine learning, microhardness prediction, TIG welding, welding parameters

Introduction

Aluminium alloys, especially 6061, are extensively used in marine and structural applications due to their high strength - to - weight ratio and corrosion resistance [5]. Tungsten inert gas (TIG) welding is an ideal method for joining these alloys, however, softening in the heat affected zone (HAZ) results in reduced mechanical properties such as toughness and tensile strength [16]. In addition, the porosity formation due to hydrogen entrapment and inferior shielding of gas is a pertained challenge in aluminium welding [4, 11]. However, these challenges can be reduced to certain extend by optimizing the welding process parameters such as current, voltage, welding speed and gas flow rate and also by selecting proper filler materials [1]. The typical optimization techniques such as response surface methodology (RSM) is widely utilizing to identify the optimum welding parameters [1]. Although RSM technique is useful for modelling linear and moderately nonlinear systems, it often fails when modelling complex nonlinear relationships such as in welding processes. This lack of correlation between model parameters and responses in RSM technique can lead to reporting

of suboptimal welding parameters and associated deprived weld quality [12]. In order to alleviate these challenges, the integration of machine learning (ML) with RSM is emerging as a promising technique [1–3]. Recent studies underscore that the integration of RSM with ML techniques such as genetic algorithm (GA) and particle swarm optimization (PSO) are effective in optimizing weld parameters to reduce the defects and increase the mechanical properties [6]. These results demonstrate the potential of integrating ML and RSM for accurate weld parameter optimisations. However, only limited studies have been reported on combined use of ML techniques and RSM to optimize TIG welding parameters for 6061 aluminium alloys. Therefore, the present study aims to select suitable filler materials and process parameters to improve weld microhardness of TIG-welded 6061 - T6 aluminium alloy joints using the ML integrated RSM approach.

Methodology

A 2 mm thick Al 6061-T6 aluminium alloy sheet was selected as the base material and the sheet was sheared into rectangular sheets measuring 50×80 mm

[a]jkn.prod@psgtech.ac.in, [b]dlp.prod@psgtech.ac.in, [c]23mp01@psgtech.ac.in

DOI: 10.1201/9781003770435-19

for the welding trials. To remove burrs and ensure optimal welding results, surface preparation was carried out through filing and grinding. The sheets were then joined using a butt joint configuration and TIG welding. A 20 kW, 400 V TIG welding machine (Lorch Welding Products Private Limited, India) was used for the welding trials.

The experimental design was based on response surface methodology (RSM) using a central composite design (CCD) approach. A total of 20 experimental runs were performed using an L20 series array. The primary process parameters were welding current (50, 60, and 70 A) and the type of filler rod, including ER4043, ER5356, and a combination of both. The chemical compositions of the base material and filler wires are shown in Table 19.1, and the design of experiments (DoE) is presented in Table 19.2.

The TIG welding trials followed the DoE outlined in Table 19.2, with the welding setup shown in Figure 19.1. After welding, microhardness testing was conducted on 25 ×10 mm specimens, which were mounted and polished prior to analysis. Using a Mitutoyo Microvickers hardness tester with a 300 g load and a 10-second dwell time, five indentations per sample were made, and the average hardness value was determined for each samples. The DoE data, combined with the microhardness responses, were used to optimize the welding parameters for maximum hardness. These optimal parameters were then experimentally validated for reliability and accuracy.

In this study, the microhardness of the prepared weldments is modelled using two machine learning algorithms namely, Random Forest Regression (RFR) and Gradient Boosting (GB) techniques to optimize the process parameters. Among the experimental data, 80% of the data used to train the models for establishing the relationships between process parameter variables and the resulting microhardness

responses and 20& of the experimental data utilized to test the models. Random Forest (RF) is ensemble learning based models where it applies random feature selection and bootstrapping, enhancing generalization and minimizing overfitting [9, 19]. Similarly, GB constructs a series of weak models, most commonly decision trees, where each subsequent model is trained to minimize the mistakes of the previous model. Using gradient descent to minimize a given loss function, GB is very powerful for regression as well as classification problems. Its ability to model complex nonlinear data relationships makes it suited to predicting material properties like microhardness [10, 7, 18].

Model performance is measured using matrices such as Mean Absolute Error (MAE), Root Mean Square Error (RMSE), and the R^2 value. Also, graphical aids like residual plots and scatter plots were employed to view model performance and the influence of the parameters. The comparison of microhardness prediction is made between the actual data, GB and RF models to ascertain the best method.

Results and Discussion

The microhardness survey results of the welded specimen were presented in Table 19.3 and it reveals that the microhardness of welded Al 6061 varies from 62.6 $HV_{0.3}$ to 83.9 $HV_{0.3}$. The hardness survey indicates the significant influence of both welding current and filler material on the hardness. The maximum hardness was observed in trials with a welding current of 70 A and ER4043 filler rod. It can be attributed to the presence of silicon content in ER4043, which can promote fine grains in the fusion zone [13,15]. In contrast, a lower hardness values were recorded with the combination of ER4043 and ER5356 filler rod. It suggests that the interaction between silicon and magnesium may negatively affect the mechanical properties if not properly balanced [18]. The results align with existing literature, which states that ER5356 (Al-Mg) is associated with higher weld efficiency, strength, and corrosion resistance, while ER4043 (Al-Si) can achieve higher hardness under certain conditions due to its silicon content [8, 14]. The combination filler (ER4043 & ER5356) tends to underperform in hardness, possibly due to incompatible metallurgical interactions [17]. These results emphasize the importance of optimizing both welding current and filler rod selection to achieve the desired weld hardness and overall mechanical performance.

Figure 19.1 (a) Lorch TIG welding machine and (b) welding of the samples after cut into the mentioned dimension
Source: Author

Further, the experimental data was used to optimize welding parameters through machine learning techniques (RFR and GB models) for optimizing the weld parameters. From the responses of experimental trials, the Gradient Boosting (GB) model performed exceptionally in optimizing the weld parameters for higher the weld hardness.

The GB model made the model training and validations with a mean absolute error (MAE) of 2.26, mean squared error (MSE) of 6.28, and root mean square error (RMSE) of 2.5. The GB model exhibited a close fit between predicted and actual values. Furthermore, the hardness values have a high correlation with the input parameters (welding current and filler materials), as shown by the R^2 value of 0.90. The scatter plot illustrating the closeness of GB model predicted vs. actual hardness values is depicted in Figure 19.2. The degree of closeness between the actual data points and the prediction line emphasizes the accuracy of hardness prediction and thereby the effectiveness of model for the parameter optimisation.

Similarly, an attempt has been made using RFR model and for which a less predictive precision was exhibited. With an MAE of 5.21, an MSE of 32.93 and RMSE of 55.74, it showed larger discrepancies between the actual and predicted values. Moreover, the R^2 value of RFR model trained is 0.489. It indicates that RFR model was less effective than GB at modelling the underlying patterns in the data.

In this case, RFR could have been limited by the relatively small data set or by less effective feature interaction learning, despite being typically resilient for a wide range of applications. The scatter plot illustrating the closeness of RFR model predicted vs. actual is presented in Figure 19.3.

Both the GB and RF models were also investigated in the context to determine the optimum welding parameters that achieve the highest expected microhardness for aluminium 6061-T6 weldments. Notably, both models determined the same set of optimum parameters where the maximum expected

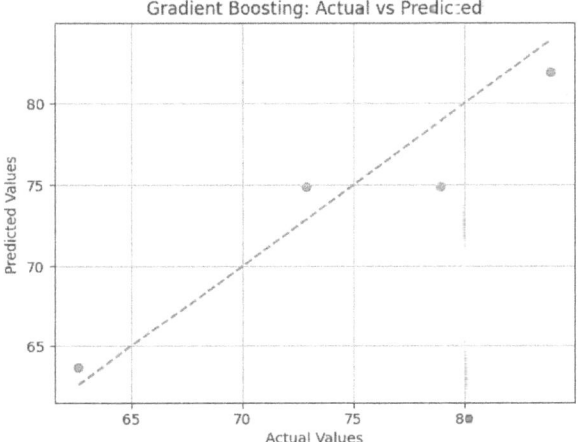

Figure 19.2 Scatter plot illustrating the gradient boosting: Actual vs. Predicted values
Source: Author

Table 19.1 Chemical composition of weld base metal and filler wire

Element	Chemical composition wt. %								
	Mg	Si	Fe	Cu	Cr	Zn	Ti	Mn	Al
AA 6061-T6	0.8	0.4	0.7	0.15	0.04	0.25	0.15	0.15	Bal.
ER4043	0.05	6	0.8	0.3	0.05	0.1	0.2	0.05	Bal.
ER5356	5.5	0.25	0.4	0.1	0.2	0.1	0.06	0.2	Bal.

Source: Author

Table 19.2 Design of experiments

S. No.	Factors	Notation	Unit	Levels		
1	Welding current	I	A	-1 50	0 60	1 70
2	Filler wire	F	-	1 ER4043	2 ER5356	3 ER4043 & ER5356

Source: Author

Table 19.3 Design of experiments with responses

S. No	Continuous factor	Categorical factor Filler rod	Responses – Microhardness (Hv$_{0.3}$)		
			Experimental	RF Predicted	GB Predicted
1	60	2	72.9	74.2	75.1
2	60	2	78.9	79.1	78.3
3	70	2	79.4	78.5	80
4	50	3	72.2	73.3	74.1
5	70	1	81.9	82.2	82.5
6	60	2	77.9	78	77.8
7	50	3	71.2	70.8	71.3
8	60	2	76.9	77	76.8
9	70	3	63.5	64.2	64
10	60	3	67.1	68.2	67.9
11	60	2	75.8	76	75.5
12	60	2	78.9	79.2	78.7
13	50	1	71.1	70.5	71
14	60	2	65.9	66.3	66
15	50	1	70.1	70.4	70.2
16	70	1	83.9	84	84.1
17	60	1	66.1	67.1	66.5
18	70	3	62.6	62.9	62.5
19	60	2	73.8	74.5	74
20	50	2	69.9	70.2	70

Source: Author

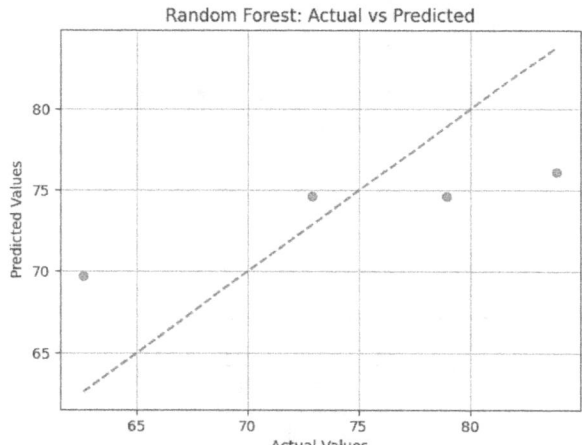

Figure 19.3 Scatter plot illustrating the random forest: Actual vs. Predicted values

Source: Author

hardness values were achieved with a welding current of 65 A and filler rod type 2.

A highest microhardness of 79.26 HV was estimated by the Gradient Boosting model under these conditions, while a little lower value of 78.97 HV was estimated by the Random Forest model. Although the estimated values of hardness are reasonably close

to each other, the overall predictive accuracy of the Gradient Boosting model evidenced through smaller error values and a better R^2 score makes it the more accurate and reliable predictor of microhardness and optimizing welding parameters in this study.

The pattern of microhardness values for different parameters utilized in joining aluminium 6061-T6 weldments is illustrated by the violin plots in Figure 19.4. Each form of shape presents the density and the spread of the hardness values and allows the comparison of weld hardness effects produced by different fillers. Figure 19.4(a) depicts the density and spread of hardness with respect to welding current and with a median hardness of ~80 Hv, welding current of 70 A exhibits the largest distribution of hardness value from ~50 to ~100 Hv. On the other hand a lower density distribution of hardness for 50 and 60 A current represents the static behaviour of response. Similarly, Figure 19.4(b) represents the density of hardness with respect to the filler rod type used. With a median microhardness of approximately 70 Hv, Filler Rod Type 1 possesses the largest distribution of hardness values, from approximately 60 Hv to more than 90 Hv. Large variation is evident from the wide distribution and suggests that microhardness of this filler rod can vary with the welding conditions.

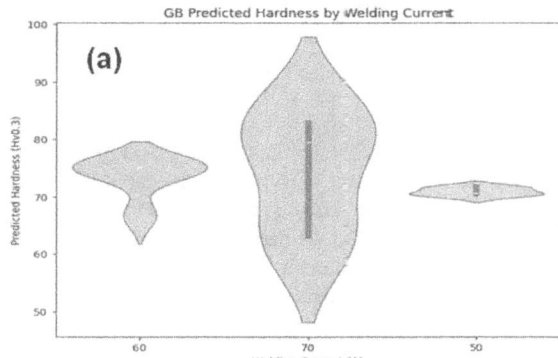

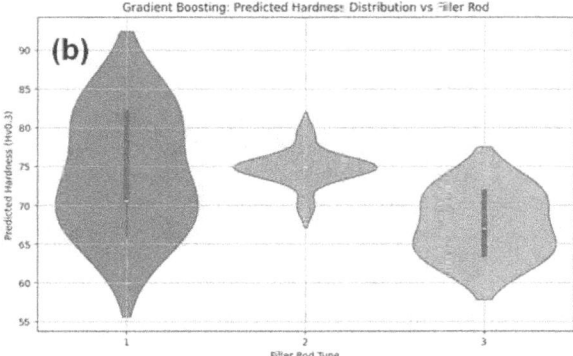

Figure 19.4 Violin plot illustrating the distribution of GB model predicted hardness across a) different welding current and b) different filler rod types

Source: Author

The Filler Rod Type 2 distribution, however, is narrow and more focused with most of the hardness values centred on 80 Hv. This reflects higher stability and consistency in hardness and is consistent with the study's optimal parameters in which the highest predicted filler rod hardness was encountered. On the contrary, Filler Rod Type 3 produces the lowest total hardness readings, with a median close to 70Hv and a range of 60Hv to slightly below 80Hv. This filler rod may not be the ideal choice in applications requiring greater weld strength due to the rather asymmetrical distribution. It is evident from this analysis that Filler Rod Type 2 is the optimal choice for welding Aluminium 6061-T6 because it provides the most uniform and best hardness values. Although Type 3 possesses lower hardness values overall, Type 1's high variability brings with it the risk of variable weld quality. The conclusions of the study are validated by this graphical representation, which illustrates that Type 2 is the optimal choice for microhardness estimate based on Gradient Boosting.

The effect of individual process parameters on the predicted microhardness of the weldments was evaluated using Partial Dependence Plots, as shown in Figure 19.5. The analysis of welding current (Figure 19.5a) revealed a strong positive correlation between current and hardness for Filler Rod 1, with hardness increment from ~70.2 Hv0.3 at 50 A to ~ 84 Hv at 70 A. A similar but less pronounced trend was observed for Filler Rod 2, where the hardness values increased moderately with current. In contrast, Filler Rod 3 exhibited a negative correlation, with hardness decreasing slightly as current increased. Figure 19.5b illustrates the influence of filler rod type at fixed welding currents. At 50 A, Filler Rod 3 marginally outperformed the others, while at 60 A, Filler Rod 2 yielded the highest hardness values. At 70 A, Filler Rod 1 resulted in the maximum predicted hardness, suggesting its superior performance at elevated currents. These results indicate that both parameters significantly affect weld hardness, with significant interaction between current level and filler rod type.

Further, an experimental trial on welding was conducted using the predicted optimum welding current of 65 A and filler rod type ER5356. The resulting weldment was subjected to microhardness testing to validate the model's performance. The experimentally measured hardness closely matched (78 ± 2 $Hv_{0.3}$) the predicted value, thereby confirming the

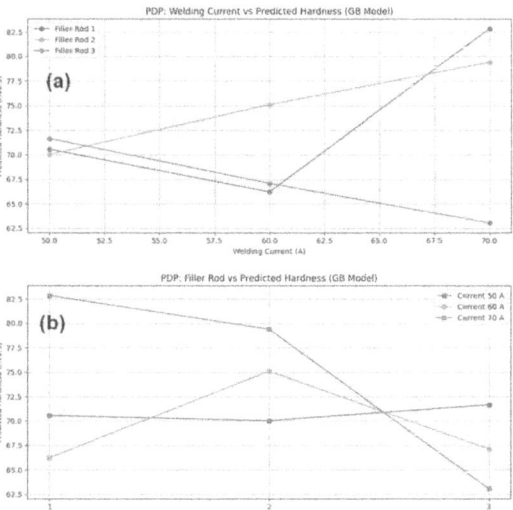

Figure 19.5 Partial Dependence Plots showing the effect of (a) welding current and (b) filler rod type on the predicted microhardness of weldments

Source: Author

model's accuracy and its practical applicability in optimizing welding parameters for enhanced weld quality.

Conclusion

The present study sought to integrate machine learning models such as Random Forest Regression and Gradient Bossing techniques with Response Surface Methodology to optimize TIG welding parameters for higher the microhardness of Al 6061- T6 welds. The results shown that the combination of RSM and GB model outshone the RFR model with RSM. The GB model integrated with RSM achieved an R^2 value of 0.90. The distribution of parameters and effect of individual parameters were analysed with the help of violin plots partial dependence plots. The analysis further revealed that welding current and filler rod type are the significant influential parameters affecting the weld microhardness. The optimum welding parameters identified using the Gradient Boosting model are a welding current of 65 A and ER5356 type filler rod. The obtained optimal parameters were experimentally validated, and resulted in a microhardness of 78 $Hv_{0.3}$. The microhardness of validation sample is closely matching the predicted value. Thus, the findings of the study affirm the reliability and practical compatibility of machine learning integrated optimisation techniques for optimizing aluminium alloy's welding parameters.

Acknowledgement

The authors are thankful to 'The Management of PSG College of Technology, Coimbatore and SERB, India' - SRG/2021/002283 (Anusadhan – India) for providing the necessary facilities and support for the execution of this work.

References

[1] Annamalai, D., Nampoothiri, J., Rajam, P. K. M., & Radhakrishnan, H. K. (2023). Optimization of ultrasonic-assisted TIG (UA-TIG) welding process parameters for AA7075 alloy joints using RSM-GA approach. *Journal of Testing and Evaluation*, 51(5), 3369–3389.

[2] Chaki, S. (2019). Neural networks based prediction modelling of hybrid laser beam welding process parameters with sensitivity analysis. *SN Applied Sciences*, 1, 1285.

[3] Dhilip, A., & Nampoothiri, J. (2024). Investigating the effects of ultrasonic assistance on TIG welding of AA7075 alloys: a machine learning-based optimization study using RSM-PSO. *Physica Scripta*, 100(1), 016002.

[4] Dojčinović, M., Cvetković, R. P., Sedmak, A., Popović, O., Cvetković, I., and Radu, D. (2023). Effect of shielding gas arc welding process on cavitation resistance of welded joints of AlMg4.5Mn Alloy. *Materials*, 1(1), 1–10.

[5] Dwivedi, D. K. (2022). Weldability of metals: weldability of aluminium alloys: porosity, HAZ softening and solidification cracking. In Fundamentals of Metal Joining, (pp. 1–10). Springer.

[6] Elangovan, S., Anand, K., & Prakasan, K. (2012). Parametric optimization of ultrasonic metal welding using response surface methodology and genetic algorithm. *International Journal of Advanced Manufacturing Technology*, 63, 561–572.

[7] He, Y., Wang, Y., & Liu, X. (2023). Microhardness and wear resistance in materials manufactured by laser powder bed fusion: Machine learning approach for property prediction. *Materials and Design*, 230, 111828.

[8] Ishak, M., Noordin, N. F. M., Razali, A. S. K., Shah, L. H. A., & Romlay, F. R. M. (2015). Effect of filler on weld metal structure of AA6061 aluminum alloy by tungsten inert gas welding. *International Journal of Automotive and Mechanical Engineering*, 11, 2438.

[9] Keshmiri, S., Zheng, X., Feng, L. W., Pang, C. K., & Chew, C. M. (2015). Application of deep neural network in estimation of the weld bead parameters. In IEEE/RSJ International Conference on Intelligent Robots and Systems (IROS) (Vol. 2015, pp. 3518–3523). IEEE.

[10] Mishra, A., Sefene, E. M., Nidigonda, G., & Tsegaw, A. A. (2022). Performance evaluation of machine learning-based algorithm and Taguchi algorithm for the determination of the hardness value of the friction stir welded AA 6262 joints at a nugget zone. In arXiv Preprint (arXiv:2203.11649).

[11] Nampoothiri, J., Balasundar, I., Raj, B., Murty, B. S., & Ravi, K. R. (2018). Porosity alleviation and mechanical property improvement of strontium modified A356 alloy by ultrasonic treatment. *Materials Science and Engineering: A*, 724, 586–593.

[12] Prasad, K. S., Rao, C. S., & Rao, D. N. (2012). Review on application of response surface method based design of experiments to welding processes. *Journal for Manufacturing Science and Production*, 12(1), 1–10.

[13] Salleh, M. N. M., Ishak, M., Shah, L. H., & Idris, S. R. A. (2016). The effect of ER4043 and ER5356 filler metal on welded Al 7075 by metal inert gas welding. *WIT Transactions on the Built Environment*, 166, 213–224.

[14] Suprianto, S., Syahputra, R. D., & Ariani, F. (2024). Study on microstructure evolution and mechanical properties of similar joint of Al-Mg-Si alloy by tungsten inert gas welding. In E3S Web of Conferences, (Vol. 519, p. 4014).

[15] Tang, Z., Zhang, Y., & Wang, J. (2023). Predictive modeling and optimization of layer-cladded Ti-Al-Nb coatings

using machine learning algorithms. *Coatings*, 13(10), 1319.

[16] Umer, M. Z. U. D. U., & Tiamiyu, A. A. (2024). X-ray microscopic and thermodynamic model assessments of softening in TIG-welded AA 6061-T651. *Journal of Materials Engineering and Performance*, 1(1), 1–10.

[17] Verma, R. P., Pandey, K. N., & Sharma, Y. (2015). Effect of ER4043 and ER5356 filler wire on mechanical properties and microstructure of dissimilar aluminium alloys, 5083-O and 6061-T6 joint, welded by the metal inert gas welding. *Proceedings of the Institution of Mechanical Engineers, Part B: Journal of Engineering Manufacture*, 229(6), 1021–1028.

[18] Yu, L., Nishimoto, K., & Saida, K. (2022). Hardness prediction system for multi-pass weld metal of low-alloy steel using neural network. *Metallurgical and Materials Transactions A*, 53, 4519–4534.

[19] Zhang, Z., Yang, Z., Ren, W., & Wen, G. (2023). A novel surface temperature sensor and random forest-based welding defect identification model. *Journal of Intelligent Manufacturing*, 34(4), 2013–2026.

20 DTGDI-based low-power Vedic multiplier using 16nm GNRFET

K. R. Radhakrishnan[a], J. Ramesh[b], Sai Prakash S. and P. T. Vanathi[c]

Department of Electronics and Communication Engineering, PSG College of Technology, Coimbatore, India

Abstract

There is a higher demand for devices that have better energy efficiency and higher performance in the modern-day technological world, which are necessary for media processing applications. It must handle the intensive computational loads with minimal hardware. With this, the battery life can also be extended when it is used in the constrained environment. Multiplication becomes one of the important steps in those applications, so the usage of multipliers is unavoidable. Numerous digital multipliers exist, but Vedic multipliers enable the design of efficient devices. In this work, the Vedic multiplier is designed using GNRFET 16nm technology. The work also compares the static CMOS-based Vedic multiplier with designs based on Gate-Diffusion Input (GDI), modified GDI (mGDI), Dynamic Threshold MOSFET (DTMOS), and Dynamic Threshold GDI (DTGDI) techniques. The designs were analyzed using the Synopsys HSPICE EDA tool. The designed Vedic multiplier can be beneficial when we use it for low-frequency applications. Vedic multipliers based on DTGDI have a Power-Delay-Product (PDP) reduction of 36.16% for the ripple carry adder and 56.58% for the carry skip adder.

Keywords: DTGDI, GDI, GNRFET, image filtering, vedic multiplier

Introduction

Mathematical concepts are useful in every domain of engineering. They help to formulate the theories, calculations, and implementation of complex real-world problems. The basic arithmetic operations like addition and multiplication play an important role in signal processing applications. Multiplication helps to speed up the calculations more than iterative addition methods. Multiplication becomes an unavoidable process in image filtering, sharpening, blurring, etc., when we use it in image processing. In the above-mentioned applications, energy optimization is the essential task, as they must handle huge computational data, memory usage, and higher power consumption. The enhancement of multipliers improves scalability and flexibility across a broader range of applications.

Multiplication involves three stages that revolve around the generation, reduction, and addition of partial products. The trade-off between power and delay needs to be taken into consideration mainly in the partial product reduction stage. There are many digital multipliers, such as Array, Wallace-Tree, Dadda, Baugh-Wooley, and Booth, each of which are beneficial in the way they are used as per the applications. Each digital multiplier has trade-offs in all of the areas that we considered. Array multipliers have less complexity but consume high power and cause delays. Booth multipliers consume less power but with higher complexity. Wallace-Tree and Dadda multipliers are faster but have complex circuit designs. Baugh-Wooley multipliers work well among other digital multipliers, but they have complex routing areas.

Ancient Indian mathematical methodology termed as Vedic mathematics includes various algorithms named as sutras which help to solve mathematical problems easier and quicker. It includes 16 sutras with their sub-sutras to perform basic mathematical operations and are categorized based on their working. A total of six sutras out of 16 sutras were categorized for multiplication and division. The partial products were generated and added concurrently, which enhances the multiplication process and also computes faster. Figure 20.1 represents the categorization of Vedic sutras.

The Urdhava-Tiryagbhyam sutra is the most widely used multiplication sutra, as it is applicable to all possible cases of multiplication. The Vedic multiplier is designed, implemented, and analyzed using 16 nm GNRFET technology by leveraging the Synopsys EDA tool [14, 15]. This paper is organized as follows: Survey on Vedic multipliers in Section 2. Section 3 includes the information about existing and

---

[a]krr.ece@psgtech.ac.in, [b]jr.ece@psgtech.ac.in, [c]ptv.ece@psgtech.ac.in

DOI: 10.1201/9781003770435-20

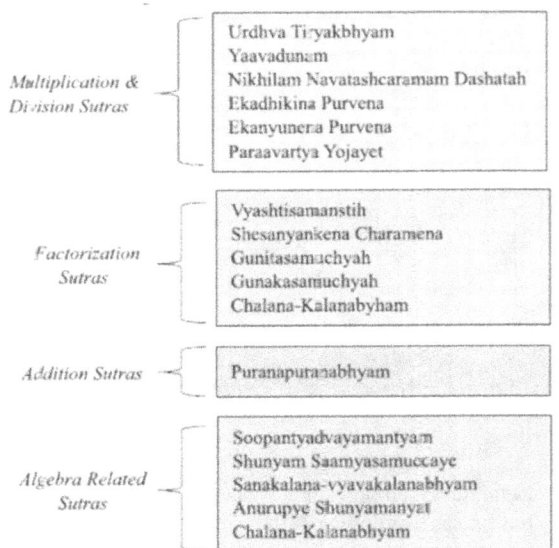

Figure 20.1 Categorization of Vedic Sutras [2]
Source: Author

Literature Survey

Rao et al. [1] presented two Vedic multipliers using mGDI techniques. They were compared with transmission gates-based designs. The performance metrics such as area, power, and delay were analyzed using the Tanner EDA tool with 32nm technology. The results showed that power consumption and delay are reduced. *Hemanshi Chugh et al.* [2] review N-bit Vedic multipliers. It explores the shift from CMOS to Quantum Dot Cellular Automata (QCA) technology. They highlighted CMOS and QCA technologies for their advancements. The diverse application areas for Vedic multipliers are also classified. Kumar et al. [3] analyzed the four different Vedic sutras in the Vedic multipliers, and with its results, the suitable Vedic multiplier for biomedical applications is discussed. The paper covers four sutras of the Vedic multiplication: Urdhava Tiryaghbyam, Ekadhikena Purvena, Ekanyunena Purvena, and Nikhilam. It emphasizes the importance of efficient digital signal processing. Janwadkar et al. [4] presented a programmable FIR filter architecture, which is designed by optimizing the structure of the Urdhava Tiryagbhyam Sutra. This was implemented in FPGA, and an ASIC design was made using SCL-180 nm technology. The proposed

proposed Vedic multipliers. The performance of the designs was assessed in Section 4. The paper ends with the conclusions in Section 5.

design supports multiple frequencies for bioimpedance analysis and demonstrates superior results in area and power consumption. Tyagi et al. [5] explored the advantages of GNRFET over FinFET with a full adder circuit. The authors concluded that GNRFETs offer better energy efficiency. They also suggested conducted research for GNRFETs' realization. Daggula et al. [6] proposed a QCA-based multiplier architecture aimed at low power consumption and optimal performance. It includes applications such as wireless communication and phased array radar systems. It is designed and implemented using the QCA Designer-E tool. Shetkar et al. [7] proposed a novel Vedic multiplier that was designed using a novel 4:2 approximate compressor. The proposed design outperforms conventional designs, and the results show a 62.95% power reduction and a 53.31% delay reduction. Shaik et al. [8] explore low-power multi-bit Vedic multiplier architectures that incorporate FinFET and CMOS technologies. The system uses a gate diffusion input (GDI)-based AND gate and pass transistor logic-based full adder as the basic building block [13]. Saritha et al. [9] proposed a Vedic multiplier using the Karatsuba algorithm and utilizing a non-linear carry select adder. It combines adaptive and recursive approaches for better results. It was implemented in an FPGA using Xilinx software, which exhibits better delay than other systems. Sheetal et al. [10] proposed the DTMOS technique for digital circuits. The design and performance analysis of a conventional and DTMOS-based 4:1 multiplexer is implemented in 90 nm CMOS in the Cadence EDA tool. The results indicate that the DTMOS technique optimizes die area and power usage. Yousuf et al. [11] focus on 8-bit Vedic multipliers to address leakage power in CMOS circuits. The different low-power techniques were analyzed using 180 nm technology. The drain gating technique reduces leakage in active mode. Power gating achieves the highest power savings.

Vedic Multipliers

The set of rules and their corollaries for the ancient Indian mathematical techniques were compiled by Bharati Krishna Tirtha ji (1884-1960). The rules were discovered from the Vedas, so, it is termed as Vedic mathematics which contains 16 sutras and 13 sub-sutras. In this paper, the Vedic multipliers designed using conventional CMOS structure, DTMOS, GDI, mGDI, and DTGDI techniques were discussed.

Urdhava-Tiryagbhyam sutra

The Urdhava-Tiryaghbhyam sutra is the most common sutra for multiplication in Vedic mathematics, as it multiplies the bits concurrently. It is derived from two Sanskrit words, Urdhava and Tiryagbhyam, meaning vertical and transverse, respectively. Both multiply the bits vertically and diagonally and add the results. The computation time is faster as it computes concurrently. The multiplication steps of the Urdhava-Tiryagbhyam sutra are represented in Figure 20.2.

The design of the L-bit UT multiplier contains 4 M-bit (M=L/2) UT multipliers, 3 L-bit adders, and 1 Half Adder. The parallel adders can be used in the designs such as Ripple Carry Adder, Carry Save Adder, or Carry Look Ahead Adder. The structure of the L-bit Urdhava Tiryagbhyam Multiplier is represented in Figure 20.3.

2-Bit Vedic multiplier

The 2-bit vedic multiplier is the base for higher-order UT-sutra Vedic multipliers. The multiplication is carried out in three steps with multiplication of rightmost bits, cross-multiplication and summation of diagonal bits, and multiplication of leftmost bits. It can be implemented using four AND gates and two half adders. The structure of the 2-bit Vedic multiplier is represented in Figure 20.4.

4-Bit vedic multiplier

The next lower order multiplier employs four 2-bit Vedic multipliers, three 4-bit adders, and 1 half

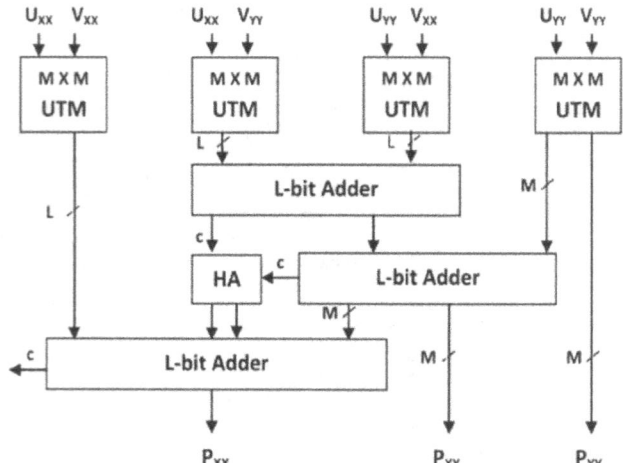

Figure 20.3 Architecture of standard L×L Uddhav tiryagbhyam sutra multiplier [4]
Source: Author

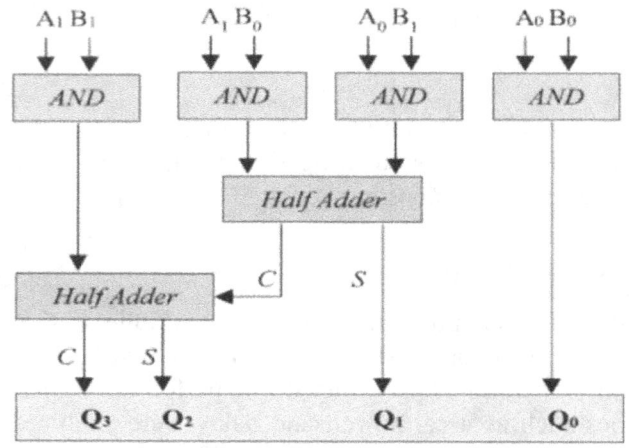

Figure 20.4 2-bit Vedic multiplier [2]
Source: Author

adders. The 4-bit adder can be chosen based on the specification. The multiplication step is similar to the multiplication of the 2-bit multiplier. The structure of the 4-bit Vedic multiplier is shown in Figure 20.5.

4-Bit adder

In an L-bit Vedic multiplier, an L-bit adder is utilized to determine the product by propagating the signals. Based on the requirement or application, the type of the adder structure can be selected and integrated. In this work, Ripple Carry Adder and Carry Skip Adder were used to examine the results of them where Ripple Carry Adder has less hardware complexity and Carry Skip Adder has better results in propagation delay. The structures of the Carry Skip Adder

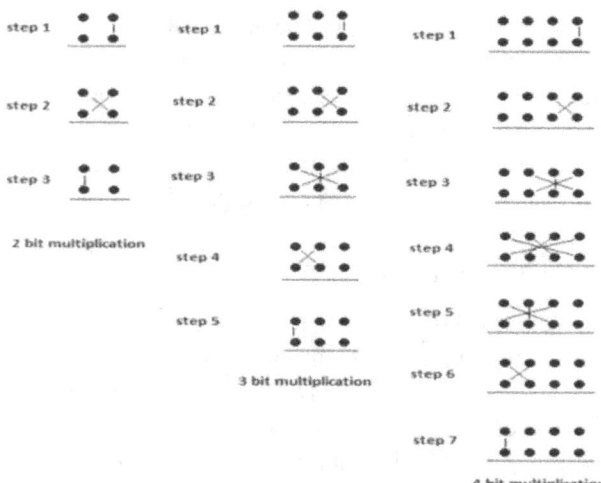

Figure 20.2 Multiplication steps of UT sutra [2]
Source: Author

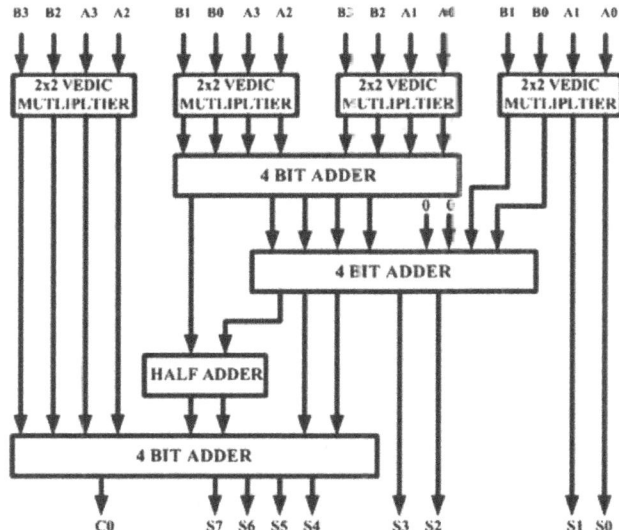

Figure 20.5 4-bit Vedic multiplier [1]

Source: Author

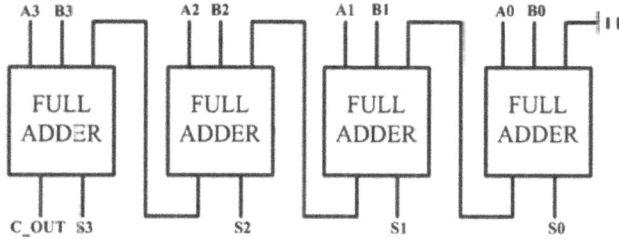

Figure 20.7 Ripple Carry Adder [1]

Source: Author

and Ripple Carry Adder were represented in Figures 20.6 and 20.7.

CMOS-based Vedic multipliers

The Vedic Multiplier structure utilized the static CMOS logic structure using the 16nm GNRFET technology. The GNRFET transistors replaced the MOS transistors in this design. All the logic blocks were designed using static CMOS logic and then integrated to design the 4-bit Vedic multiplier. Figure 20.8 represents the static CMOS logic.

DTMOS-based Vedic multipliers

Dynamic Threshold MOSFET (DTMOS) is the low-power technique that helps to increase the current drive in the structure. The body terminal of the NMOS and PMOS transistors is connected to the gate terminal of the transistors. The transconductance of the transistor is increased due to the body biasing, as the voltage potential is governed by body and gate terminals. Figure 20.9 demonstrates the general structure of the DTMOS transistors.

GDI-based Vedic multipliers

The state-of-the-art method for low power applications is the GDI technique where, the body and the source terminals are tied together. Unlike conventional CMOS structures, it contains a structure like inverters. There are three terminals: Gate of NMOS and PMOS tied together (G), input to the source of PMOS (P), and input to the source of NMOS (N) [1]. The GDI cell is represented in Figure 20.10.

With the GDI logic, the logic gates can be implemented in two transistors. The wide range of complex

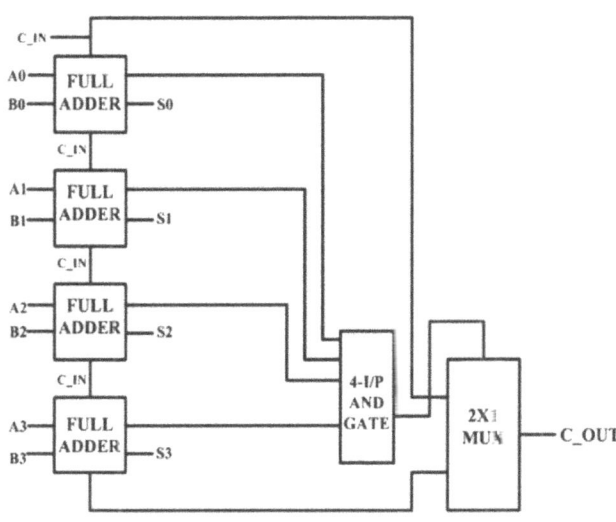

Figure 20.6 Carry Skip Adder [1]

Source: Author

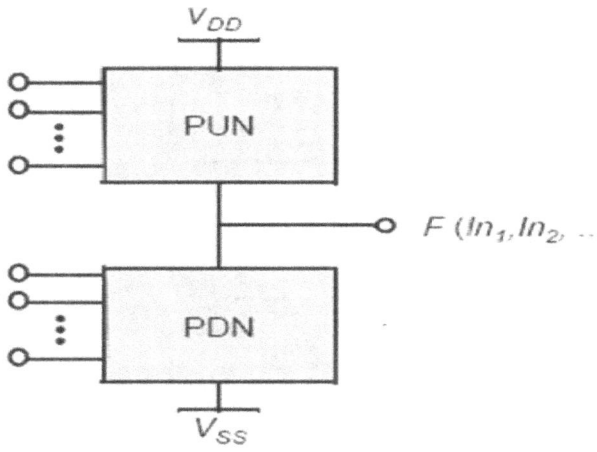

Figure 20.8 Static CMOS structure

Source: Author

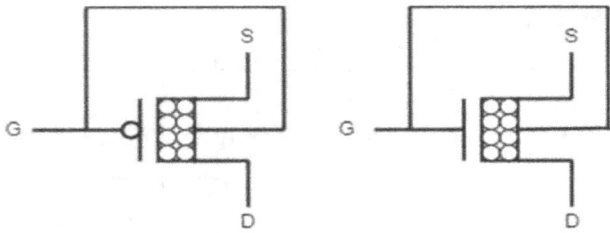

Figure 20.9 DTMOS transistors.
Source: Author

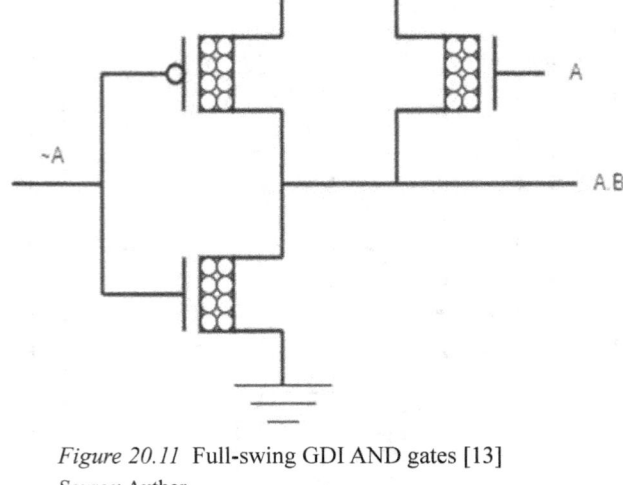

Figure 20.11 Full-swing GDI AND gates [13]
Source: Author

functions can be designed easily with the help of the GDI technique. There will be signal degradation in the output voltage similar to the pass-transistor logic (PTL). To obtain full output voltage swing, the full-swing GDI technique proposed [12] can be used with the trade-off of additional transistors. Figures 20.11–20.13 demonstrate the full-swing transistors used in this work.

Modified GDI (mGDI)-based Vedic multipliers
This is an optimized version of the GDI logic, where the body terminal of the NMOS and the PMOS transistors are connected to the V_{dd} and the V_{ss}, respectively. The structure of the modified GDI cell is represented in Figure 20.14.

Dynamic threshold GDI (DTGDI)-based Vedic multipliers
The dynamic threshold GDI (DTGDI) technique is a low-power technique suitable for ultra-low power applications. Here, the techniques of DTMOS and

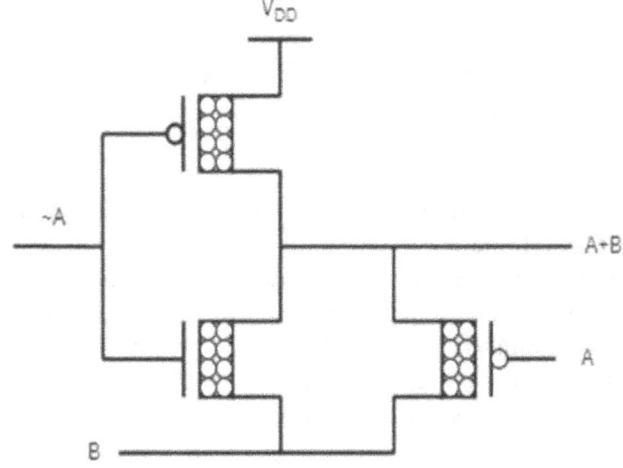

Figure 20.12 Full-swing GDI OR [13]
Source: Author

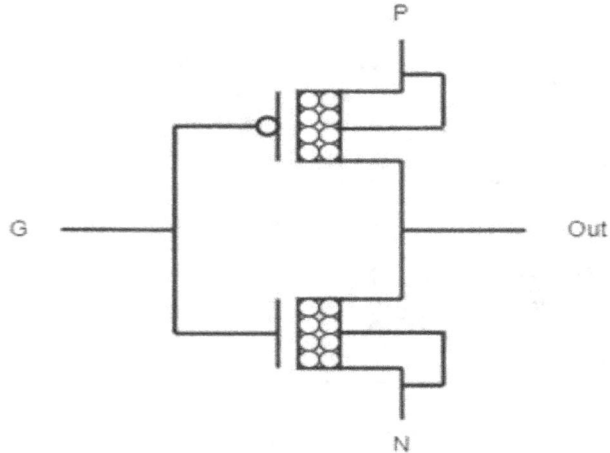

Figure 20.10 GDI cell
Source: Author

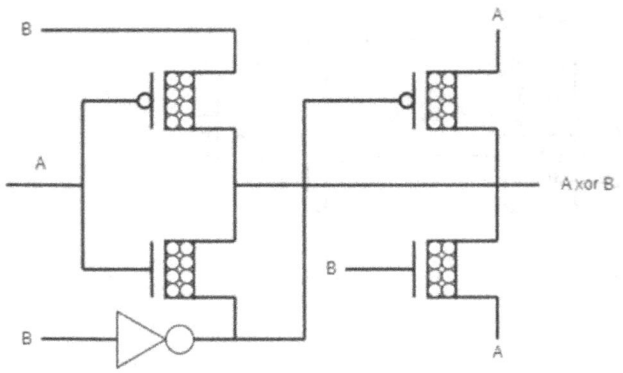

Figure 20.13 Full-Swing GDI XOR [13]
Source: Author

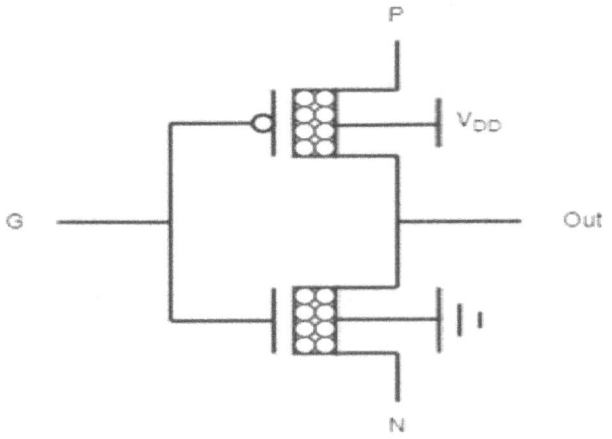

Figure 20.14 mGDI cell

Source: Author

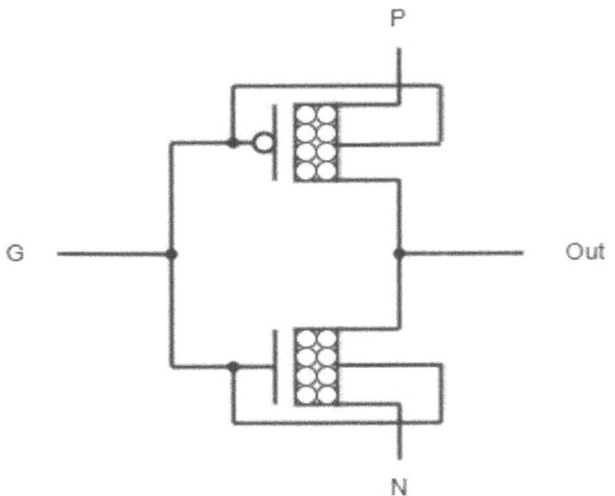

Figure 20.15 DTGDI cell

Source: Author

GDI were combined to improve the current drive further. The body terminals in the GDI cell were connected to the gate terminals, of the terminals similar to the DTMOS technique. It helps to reduce power consumption and the delay of the device. Figure 20.15 represents the DTGDI cell.

Results and Discussion

The performance metrics of the 4-bit Vedic multiplier were assessed in this section. The SPICE netlist of the 4-bit Vedic multiplier was written with the libraries of the 16nm GNRFET technology and simulated using the Synopsys HSPICE EDA tool. The functionality of the Vedic Multiplier is verified through the Avan Waves waveform viewer tool. Figures 20.16 and 17S represents the output waveform of the DTGDI-based 4×4-bit Vedic multiplier using a Carry Skip Adder and Ripple Carry Adder.

The analysis was made with an input signal of 100 kHz. The key attributes, such as power, delay, power-delay product (PDP), and transistor count (TC), were observed and analyzed using the generated listing file after the successful completion of the simulation. Tables 20.1 and 20.2 compare the key parameters of the Vedic multiplier using Ripple Carry Adder and Carry Skip Adder, respectively.

The transistor counts of the conventional and DTMOS multipliers are 828, whereas all the GDI multipliers have 503 transistors. In comparison to conventional circuits, the number of transistors used in GDI multipliers has decreased by 39.25%. The 4-bit multiplier designed with DTGDI technology has a PDP of 1.43 aJ for RCA and 1.65 aJ for CSA. This denotes the 6.54% improvement over the next lowest Vedic multiplier's PDP.

Conclusion

This paper designed and analysed 4-bit Vedic multipliers using Ripple Carry Adder and Carry-Skip Adder. The logic blocks of the vedic multiplier

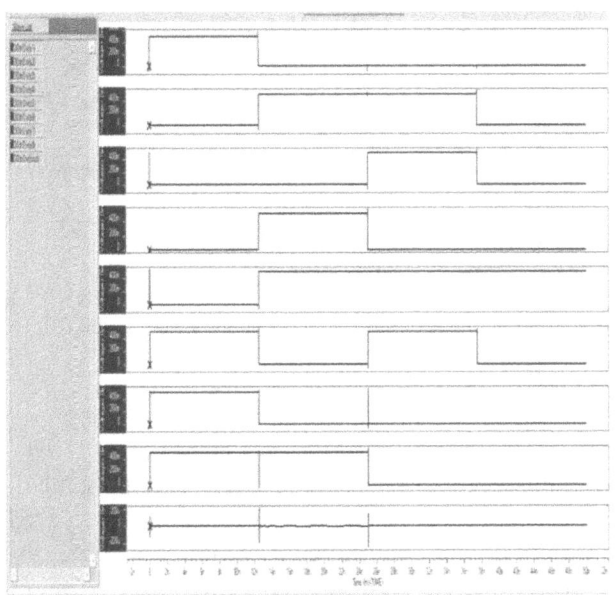

Figure 20.16 Output waveform of DTGDI based Vedic multiplier using CSA

Source: Author

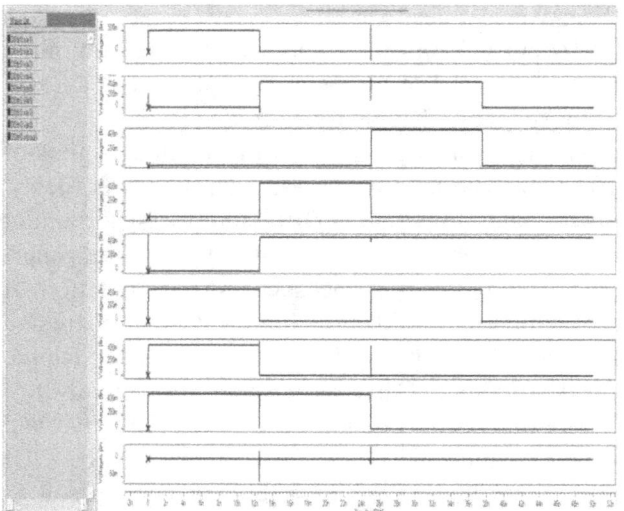

Figure 20.17 Output waveform of DTGDI based Vedic multiplier using RCA

Source: Author

Table 20.1 Comparison of key attributes of Vedic multipliers using Ripple Carry Adder

Vedic multipliers	Delay (ps)	Total power (µW)	PDP (aJ)
VM_CONV	23.9	0.16	3.82
VM_DTMOS	20.36	0.11	2.24
VM_GDI	17.06	0.10	1.71
VM_mGDI	16.81	0.09	1.53
VM_DTGDI	17.10	0.08	1.43

Source: Author

Table 20.2 Comparison of key attributes of Vedic multipliers using Carry Skip Adder

Vedic multipliers	Delay (ps)	Total power (µW)	PDP (aJ)
VM_CONV	28.79	0.16	4.61
VM_DTMOS	22.35	0.17	3.80
VM_GDI	16.4	0.20	3.28
VM_mGDI	25.2	0.12	3.024
VM_DTGDI	16.5	0.10	1.65

Source: Author

were designed using static CMOS, DTMOS, GDI, mGDI, and DTGDI techniques and then integrated to design a Vedic multiplier. The GDI-based designs outperformed the conventional and DTMOS designs in both power consumption and delay parameters. The DTMOS and DTGDI circuits perform better together. The Vedic multiplier based on DTGDI has a Power-Delay-Product (PDP) increase of 36.16% for the Ripple Carry Adder and 56.58% for the Carry Skip Adder. Vedic multipliers based on DTGDI can be used in image processing applications.

References

[1] Rao, K. N., Sudha, D., Khalaf, O. I., Abdulsaheb, G. M., Kumar, A. S., Priyanka, S. S., et al. (2024). A novel energy efficient 4-bit vedic multiplier using modified GDI approach at 32nm technology. *Heliyon*, 10(10), e31120.

[2] Chugh, H., & Singh, S. (2024). Systematic exploration of n-bit vedic multipliers: a roadmap of technological approaches in pursuit of future trends. *Nano Communication Networks*, 42, 100529.

[3] Kumar, R. K., & Vimal, S. P. (2024). Comparative analysis of vedic multiplier using vedic sutras with existing multipliers in biomedical applications. *Measurement: Sensors*, 36, 101302.

[4] Janwadkar, S., & Dhavse, R. (2020). ASIC design of power and area efficient programmable FIR filter using optimized urdhva-tiryagbhyam multiplier for impedance cardiography. *Microprocessors and Microsystems*, 107, 105048.

[5] Tyagi, P., Sharmila, & Dua, P. (2024). Exploring FinFET and GNRFET with a study of full adder circuit design. *Nanotechnology Perceptions*, 20(510), 622–636.

[6] Daggula, R., & Bevara, V. (2024). An ultra-low power QCA based vedic multiplier for digital RADAR application. *e-Prime – Advances in Electrical Engineering, Electronics and Energy*, 9, 100695.

[7] Shetkar, S., & Koli, S. (2023). Area, power efficient vedic multiplier architecture using novel 4:2 compressor. *Sadhana*, 48, 216.

[8] Shaik, S., Kanapala, S., Vijay, V., & Pittala, C. S. (2023). Design and performance analysis of low power and energy efficient vedic multipliers. *International Journal of System Assurance Engineering and Management*, 14, 894–902.

[9] Saritha, M., Chaitanya, K., Vijay, V., Aishwarya, A., Yadav, H., & Prasad, G. D. (2022). Adaptive and recursive vedic karatsuba multiplier using non-linear carry select adder. *Journal of VLSI Circuits and Systems*, 4(2), 22–29.

[10] Sheetal, Kumar, A., Kandari, R., & Bharti, S. (2019). Performance analysis of 4:1 multiplexer with DTMOS technique. In 4th International Conference on Internet of Things: Smart Innovation and Usages (IoT-SIU).

[11] Yousuf, A., & Salih, K. K. M. (2018). Comparison of sleep transistor techniques in the design of 8-bit vedic multiplier. In Proceeding of 2018 International Conference on Emerging Trends and Innovations in Engineering and Technological Research (ICETIETR).

[12] Shoba, M., & Nakkeeran, R. (2015). GDI-based full adders for energy-efficient arithmetic applications. *Engineering Science and Technology, an International Journal*. 10, 566–581.

[13] Morgenshtein, A., Fish, A., & Wagner, I. A. (2002). Gate diffusion input (GDI): a power efficient method for digital combinatorial circuits. *IEEE Transactions on Very Large-Scale Integration (VLSI) Systems*, 10(5), 566–581.

[14] Dey, K., & Chattopadhyay, S. (2017). Design of high-performance 8-bit binary multiplier using Vedic multiplication algorithm with 16-nm technology. Proceedings of IEMENTech 2017.

[15] Keethi, A., Manoj, S., Manuja, G., & Kalashetti, K. V. (2023). Low-power high-performance 8-bit Vedic multipliers using 16 nm. *International Journal of Emerging Trends in Engineering Research*, 11(5), 142–145.

21 Approximate full adders using GNRFET

J. Ramesh[1,a], K.R. Radhakrishnan[2,b], Divya Shree M[3,c] and P. T. Vanathi[1,d]

[1]Professor, Department of Electronics and Communication Engineering, PSG College of Technology, Coimbatore, India

[2]Assistant Professor, Department of Electronics and Communication Engineering, PSG College of Technology, Coimbatore, India

[3]ME VLSI Design, Department of Electronics and Communication Engineering, PSG College of Technology, Coimbatore, India

Abstract

Approximate full adders are very useful for error-resilient applications like image processing and multimedia applications, which improve power-saving and performance with very little inaccuracies in computation. These adders reduce power consumption while at high processing speeds. They are predominantly used in the low power designs of the modern computing systems. The balancing of accuracy and efficiencies makes it ideal for energy-constrained applications. This paper presents existing adders designed in GNRFET technology, having a 10T-LCAFA adder whose power and delay are reduced by 78% and 79%, respectively, in comparison to their CNTFET counterparts. These adder designs are further simulated using the popular Synopsys HSPICE tool to assess performance improvement. The analysis of these adders reveals promising energy efficiency with considerable performance processing being exhibited while using GNRFETs. These improvements make them suitable for deep learning acceleration and IoT deployments. Hence, AFAs remain of utmost importance in modern low-power VLSI circuits.

Keywords: Approximate full adders, GNRFET technology, low power consumption, multimedia processing, reduced delay

Introduction

The increasing demand for energy-efficient systems has pushed the development of low-power technologies in diverse applications (e.g., wearable devices, mobile electronics, and the Internet of Things). The rapid advancements in these technologies of processors, storage, and communications with a power-saving perspective center on how to lower power consumption without losing performance. Energy efficiency is essential for portable applications; however, it is also important for large-scale applications, including data centers, automotive, and edge computing. Approximate computing has an appealing option for error-tolerant applications such as machine learning, multimedia processing, and sensor networks. Energy efficiency is considered the major advantage of approximate full adders (AFAs). While AFAs achieve energy efficiency, they also reduce the complexity of the overall system by compromising precision. It requires fewer transistors and therefore has less switching activity, which results in dramatically lower power consumption. For example, there are many images and multimedia processing applications which are well-suited to tolerate the resultant minor error. These applications are less concerned with losing some precision while maintaining the expected output performance. The combination of approximate computing and graphene nanoribbon field-effect transistors (GNRFETs) provides a unique opportunity to realize more efficient and effective high-performance computing. GNRFETs have superior electrical characteristics related to power and switching speed which make them useful for low energy applications. Approximate adders, when combined with GNRFETs, allow enhanced energy efficiency for error-tolerant areas such as machine learning and multimedia. This combination improves circuit design and performance while utilizing less energy. These types of advancements are essential to the development of low-power VLSI design. In the end, this means better development of efficient and sustainable electronic systems. Conventional full adders focus on precision, but limit power and performance and are, therefore, not well-suited for low-power applications. Approximate full adders placed emphasis on efficiency, but accuracy is sacrificed to provide improved power efficiency and performance. The traditional CMOS full adder is still the most common, even though they can face scaling problems, and overall power efficiency issues due to

[a]jr.ece@psgtech.ac.in, [b]krr.ece@psgtech.ac.in, [c]ptv.ece@psgtech.ac.in, [d]shreemadhavarao@gmail.com

DOI: 10.1201/9781003770435-21

the always active portion of the device when applied to new, advanced technologies. Conventional CMOS full adders continue to face scaling challenges that impact performance and power efficiency [9]. CNTFETs have advantages in driving current and performance, but power consumption and process variability are issues [1]. GNRFETs have good on/off current ratios, less overall power dissipation making them very promising for applications that need to be energy-efficient and applicable for scalable technologies. GNRFETs have appealing features like performance and efficiency alternatives for low-power VLSI designs. This paper investigates the implementation of existing approximate full adders with GNRFET technology. Among 10T-LCAFA adders indicate the highest power saving. With the use of GNRFETs, the adders show better energy efficiency than the previous designs. The main goal is to improve low-power performance for today's electronics applications. This will maximize computing capacity with a reduction of power consumption.

Literature Review

Yan et al. [2] explore the design of efficient 22nm CMOS full adders that balance error tolerance with performance. They propose eight novels approximate full-adder designs to enhance cost-effectiveness and reduce overhead. While some designs achieve lower power consumption and area, they still face challenges with high power dissipation due to a large transistor count at low error rates. Shahrokhi et al. [3] developed a novel approximate full adder using 32nm CNFET technology to improve delay, power-delay product (PDP), and energy-delay product (EDP). Their design achieved a 12% reduction in delay, 7% in PDP, and 23% in EDP while maintaining accuracy. Its effectiveness was validated through software-based testing in image processing applications, demonstrating a balance between performance and energy efficiency. Despite increased area and power consumption due to a higher transistor count, the design shows promise for inexact compressors and multipliers in computationally demanding tasks. Farahani et al. [4] introduced a design utilizing a complement-like static CMOS structure combined with pass transistor logic to improve power and area efficiency. HSPICE simulations, incorporating a 4-bit carry ripple adder and image addition, demonstrated a 72% enhancement in energy efficiency using 32 nm technology. The study highlights that mirror

adder (MA) Approximation four exhibits significant inexactness, which may impact accuracy in complex approximate architectures. This work emphasizes the trade-offs between power efficiency and computational precision in approximate computing. Ubhi et al. [5] proposed a 32 nm TG-CNTFET-based inexact full adder, achieving an 89.2% reduction in leakage power and energy consumption for motion detection applications. HSPICE and MATLAB simulations demonstrated reliability, stability under varying conditions, and effective PSNR for low-power image processing. However, the design introduces sum output errors, which may lead to image inaccuracies if more than four inexact full adders are used in an 8-bit ripple carry adder. This study highlights the balance between power efficiency and computational accuracy in approximate computing. GowriSankar et al. [6] proposed a low-power, high-performance ternary arithmetic circuit utilizing 32 nm DG FinFET and GNRFET technologies. The study highlights the advantages of ternary logic in multi-valued logic (MVL), which reduces circuit complexity and chip area compared to conventional binary logic. HSPICE simulations revealed that GNRFET-based ternary circuits exhibit superior performance in power consumption, delay, and power-delay product (PDP) compared to DG FinFET. This research underscores the potential of GNRFETs for efficient ternary computing in low-power applications. Sanapala et al. [7] proposed two subthreshold logic families, DTGDI and SBBGDI, to enhance energy efficiency and optimize area utilization. Basic logic gates such as OR, AND, XOR, and a full adder were designed using these techniques and analyzed through Cadence 45 nm simulations at 0.2V. The study incorporates body biasing schemes to improve output swing and minimize energy consumption, overcoming the drawbacks of traditional GDI logic. This research highlights the potential of these logic families for low-power circuit design.

Graphene Nanoribbon Field-Effect Transistor (GNRFET)

Graphene nanoribbon field-effect transistor (GNRFET) technology has emerged as a promising alternative to traditional silicon-based transistors, offering excellent electrical properties for low-power applications. GNRFETs are built using narrow strips of graphene, known as nanoribbons, which provide a tunable bandgap essential for transistor operation.

Unlike conventional MOSFETs, GNRFETs exhibit high carrier mobility, reduced short-channel effects, and superior electrostatic control, making them well-suited for energy-efficient circuit designs. Their ability to operate at lower supply voltages significantly reduces power dissipation, making them ideal for portable and battery-operated devices. Additionally, GNRFETs show a higher on/off current ratio, which improves switching performance and minimizes leakage power, a critical challenge in modern low-power VLSI circuits.

In low-power computing, GNRFET technology is particularly beneficial for approximate computing, arithmetic circuits, and memory applications, where power efficiency is prioritized over absolute precision. Due to their excellent scalability and minimal subthreshold leakage, GNRFET- based circuits outperform traditional CMOS and CNTFET counterparts in energy-efficient designs. Researchers have explored integrating GNRFETs into adders, multipliers, and logic gates, achieving significant reductions in power consumption and delay. Carbon-based nanodevices address many limitations of traditional CMOS technologies and offer promising alternatives for future VLSI systems [25]. These transistors also enhance device reliability under varying operating conditions, making them a strong candidate for future ultra-low-power applications such as IoT, biomedical devices, and machine learning accelerators. As the demand for low-power, high-performance electronics grows, GNRFETs continue to pave the way for next-generation energy-efficient semiconductor technologies. Figure 21.1 shows the graphene nanoribbon field-effect transistor.

The key features of GNRFETs include:

High carrier mobility: GNRFETs exhibit superior carrier mobility due to the unique properties of graphene, allowing faster electron flow and enhancing transistor performance.

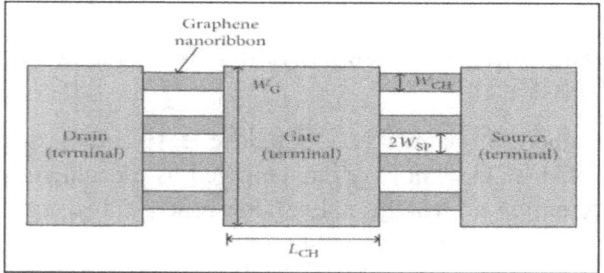

Figure 21.1 Graphene nanoribbon field-effect transistor
Source: Author

Reduced power dissipation: By operating at lower supply voltages, GNRFETs significantly reduce power consumption, making them ideal for energy-efficient circuit designs.

Existing system

The current system features five approximate full adders built using CNTFET technology. The proposed full-adder design, also based on CNTFET technology, incorporates a leakage control static approach, enhancing performance and reliability. Despite these improvements, the design's higher transistor counts lead to a larger area consumption, which reduces overall integration efficiency compared to other solutions. While the approach offers better performance, the trade-off in area usage needs consideration for large-scale integration. This highlights a challenge in balancing performance with efficient area usage. Nevertheless, the design shows promise in enhancing the reliability of approximate full adders. Table 21.1 presents the design specifications, including parameters for both n-type and p-type transistors. The transistor sizing follows a 1:2 ratio to enhance performance optimization.

Proposed system

The current adders are designed using GNRFET technology to address the limitations associated with CNTFETs. This approach aims to improve performance and efficiency. GNRFETs offer enhanced characteristics that mitigate the issues faced by CNTFET-based designs.

12T-SIFA: 12-transistor static in-exact full adder

The 12T-SIFA, introduced by Goyal et al., [8] is a symmetric approximate full adder design that utilizes just 12 transistors. Although it introduces two erroneous outputs, it strikes a balance between reducing the transistor count and maintaining acceptable accuracy, making it ideal for low-power applications like IoT devices. This design integrates pull-up and pull-down transistor networks to carry out arithmetic operations, ensuring stable and reliable output. While it compromises on precision, its inexact approach significantly boosts speed and reduces energy consumption, which is advantageous in error-tolerant applications. By optimizing power and area, the 12T-SIFA addresses the evolving needs of modern low-power circuits. Figure 21.2 shows the

Table 21.1 PMOS and NMOS type transistors sizing

Transistors	Width	Length
PMOS	16.00 nm	16.00 nm
NMOS	16.00 nm	16.00 nm

Source: Author

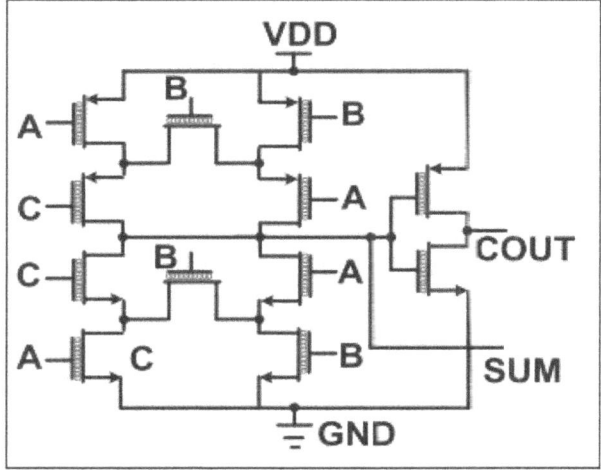

Figure 21.2 Transistor level circuit of 12T-SIFA
Source: Author

transistor level circuit of 12T-SIFA. The SUM and COUT equations are shown in (1) & (2).

$$SUM = \overline{AC} + \overline{AB} + \overline{BC} \quad (1)$$

$$COUT = \overline{\overline{AC} + \overline{AB} + \overline{BC}} \quad (2)$$

11T-LCSAFA: Leakage Control Static Approximate Full Adder

The 11T-leakage control static approximate full adder (LCSAFA) design integrates techniques to minimize leakage current, enhancing power efficiency, especially in subthreshold operations. Using only 11 transistors, it achieves both area and energy efficiency while providing sufficient performance for approximate computing applications. The static approximation feature allows for faster computation and reduced power consumption, making it well-suited for tasks like image processing and neural networks. Additionally, the design incorporates LECTOR logic in the last four transistors, further reducing leakage power and improving overall energy efficiency. The features of the 11T-LCSAFA lend themselves to low-power, high-performance applications. The case of the transistor level circuit of 11T-LCSAFA is shown in Figure 21.3. The SUM and COUT equations are shown in (3) and (4) that contain three errors in SUM and COUT.

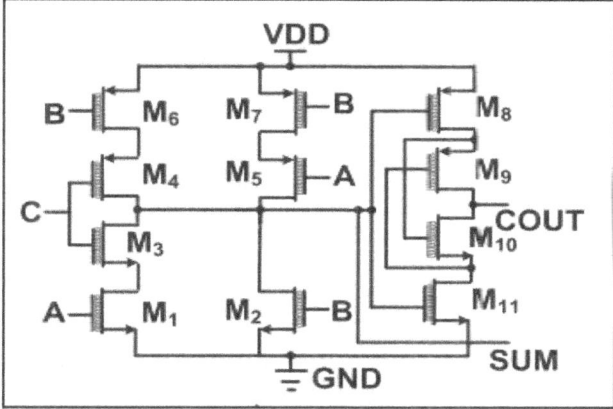

Figure 21.3 Transistor level circuit of 11T-LCSAFA
Source: Author

$$SUM = \overline{B + AC} \quad (3)$$

$$COUT = \overline{SUM} \quad (4)$$

9T-Low-power, Area-efficient, and high performance Approximate Full Adder

The 9T-low-power, area-efficient, and high performance approximate full adder (LAHAFA) is a near full adder, which is implemented to reduce power and minimize area, appropriate for power critical applications. It uses only nine transistors for overall better power efficiency by reducing the losses in the node capacitances, making it a good option for large area integration. The simplified carry propagation can help computing performance, which improves the overall performance. But there are three incorrect outputs (one incorrect mode of operation) and have a weak output signal driving capacity which could be an issue in some applications when reliability is a concern. Nevertheless, the 9T-LAHAFA is an efficient alternative for low-power systems including compact power densities. The transistor level circuit of 9T-LAHAFA is stated in Figure 21.4. The SUM & COUT equations are addressed in (5) a (6)

$$SUM = \overline{AB} + \overline{C} \quad (5)$$

$$COUT = \overline{AB + C} \quad (6)$$

14T-HLIFA: 14 transistors based high-speed and low-PDP inaccurate full adder.

The 14 transistors based high-speed and low-PDP inaccurate full adder (14T-HLIFA) is a full adder

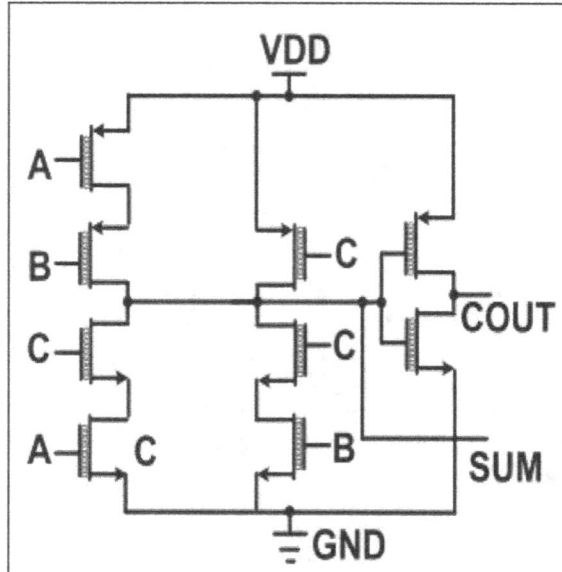

Figure 21.4 Transistor level circuit of 9T-LAHAFA
Source: Author

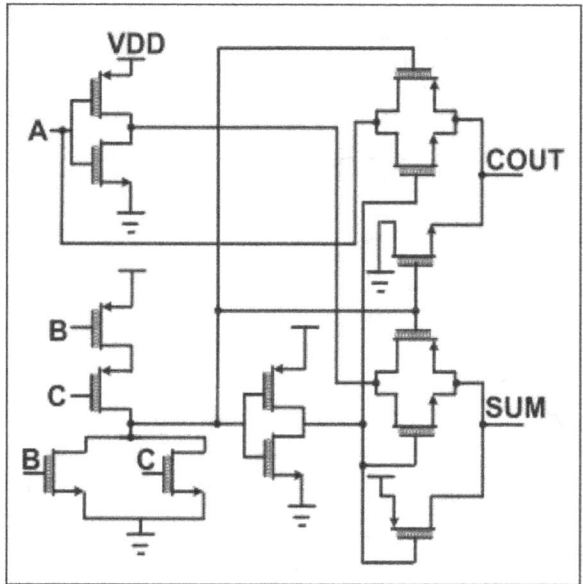

Figure 21.5 Transistor level circuit of 14T-HLIFA
Source: Author

that uses 14 transistors from the standard 14 transistor CMOS logic design and provides separate SUM and COUT outputs. The configuration uses smarter arrangements of transistors to minimize delays and speed up process flows while consuming less energy or power. It has low-power and low-delay characteristics, so it is appropriate for low-power systems relying on power and delay, thus it can include ring oscillators to produce a repetitive output signal. The design has some errors, introducing three flawed outputs, but it provides better performance with some loss in accuracy, resulting in a trade-off of speed over efficiency. In applications where errors in computation are allowable, the 14T-HLIFFA can be a useful part of an overall solution. (Figure 21.5 shows transistor level circuit of 14T-HILIFA). Equations for SUM & COUT are shown in equation (7) and (8).

$$SUM = \overline{(B + C)} + \overline{A}(B + C) \qquad (7)$$

$$COUT = A(B + C) \qquad (8)$$

10T-LCAFA: Low cost approximate full adder

The 10T-low cost approximate full adder (LCAFA) is an approximate full adder that utilizes a compact 10-transistor design, minimizing silicon area and reducing manufacturing costs. By using input signals as control signals, its base structure is efficiently replicated to implement approximate logic. The design

prioritizes energy efficiency, making it ideal for resource-constrained applications that require low power consumption. While it introduces two errors in the COUT output, the SUM output remains accurate, ensuring balanced performance. Optimized for low-voltage operation, this adder achieves faster computations with minimal power dissipation, making it suitable for error-resilient computing tasks. Figure 21.6 shows the transistor level circuit of 10T-LCAFA. The SUM & COUT equations are shown in (9) and (10). Table 21.2 shows the truth table of 10-LCAFA.

$$M = \overline{C}(A \oplus B) + C(\overline{A + B}) \qquad (9)$$

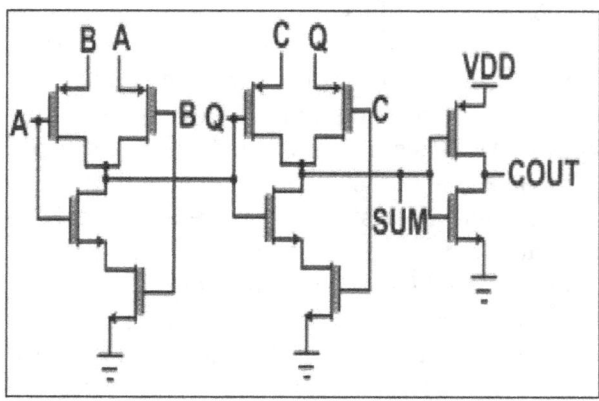

Figure 21.6 Transistor level circuit of 10T-LCAFA
Source: Author

Table 21.2 Truth table of correct FA and 10T-LCAFA

I/Ps			Correct FA		10T-LCAFA	
A	**B**	**C**	**SUM**	**COUT**	**SUM**	**COUT**
0	0	0	0	0	0	1 X
0	0	1	1	0	1	0
0	1	0	1	0	1	0
0	1	1	0	1	0	1
1	0	0	1	0	1	0
1	0	1	0	1	0	1
1	1	0	0	1	0	1
1	1	1	1	1	1	0 X

Source: Author

$$\text{)UT} = \overline{C}(\overline{A \oplus B}) + C(A \oplus B) \tag{19}$$

Results

The existing adders are designed using GNRFET technology as a replacement for CNTFETs, offering improved performance. The dynamic power consumption of approximate full adders designed with GNRFET technology varies across different designs. Among them, the 10T-LCAFA exhibits a power value of 1.1667 nw, making it more energy-efficient. Compared to alternatives like 12T-SIFA and 9T-LAHAFA, it achieves lower power consumption. This reduction in power enhances its suitability for low-power applications. Table 21.3 shows the dynamic power comparison of adders.

Delay and power-delay product (PDP) analysis play a crucial role in evaluating the performance of approximate full adders, as they directly impact speed and energy efficiency. Lower delay causes faster computation, which is a favorable design trait for speedy applications. The PDP analysis allows for evaluation of the tradeoff between power consumption and processing speed, the latter being an important aspect for low power circuits. The approximate

Table 21.4 Comparison of delay

Adders	Delay (ps)	
	CNTFET [1]	**GNRFET**
12T-SIFA	3.8	1.7039
10T-LCAFA	8.708	1.8152
11T-LCSAFA	3.743	1.6503
9T-LAHAFA	7.96	1.4059
14T-HLIFA	4.853	1.9678

Source: Author

full adders evaluated here were analyzed to characterize delay to evaluate performance efficiency. Table 21.4 displays delay values for each design, and relative performance variance can be observed. It is imperative to understand these metrics for optimizing adders in energy constrained applications. A balanced design is one that produces little delay but with low power consumption, ensuring overall efficiency in the system. Table 21.5 contains the PDP values for the full adders evaluated.

Leakage-control techniques play a crucial role in nanoscale technology to minimize standby power [10]. Static power analysis is a critical first step to assessing the energy efficiency of approximate full adders, as it assesses the power dissipation when the circuit is idle. Reducing static power use is important for any battery-operated/prepared and low-power applications, where keeping power consumption low can maximize operational life. Static analysis identifies leakage utilization losses and certainly can help micro-architects at the transistor level realize lower delays and better performance with a design. The approximate full adder's using GNRFET technology that were proposed in the previous chapter were used for static power analysis. The static power analyses values of all the proposed adders are presented in Table 21.6, to depict efficiency. Knowing these static power values will help show the designs

Table 21.3 Comparison of dynamic power

Adders	Power (nw)	
	CNTFET [1]	**GNRFET**
12T-SIFA	5.57	3 8438
10T-LCAFA	5.319	1.1667
11T-LCSAFA	3.132	1.3535
9T-LAHAFA	3.79	3.3807
14T-HLIFA	7.615	1.2236

Source: Author

Table 21.5 Comparison of PDP

Adders	PDP(10^{-21})	
	CNTFET [1]	**GNRFET**
12T-SIFA	21.26	6.549
10T-LCAFA	46	2.1_7
11T-LCSAFA	11.72	2.233
9T-LAHAFA	30.18	4.752
14T-HLIFA	36	2.407

Source: Author

Table 21.6 Comparison of static power

| Adders | Static power (nw) |
	GNRFET
12T-SIFA	0.4406
10T-LCAFA	0.3384
11T-LCSAFA	0.6640
9T-LAHAFA	0.4435
14T-HLIFA	0.3894

Source: Author

suitable for the applications that are energy constrained by outside power/energy sources. Hence, benefiting static power optimization from the overall reliability of the circuits and avoiding unnecessary power wastage during idle periods of use. The 10T-LCAFA is found where the static power use is minimal, having a reduced delay improvement and a better power-delay product to demonstrate improved energy and power efficiency. The fast computation obtained from utilizing GNRFET was coupled with power loss disadvantages to offer energy savings that were ideal for consideration, specifically used for low-power systems.

Conclusion

It is important to understand that the need for efficient low-power design is more important than ever before. Low power design is nailed in relatively new applications including Internet of Things (IoT) device applications, many image processing applications, and for multimedia applications. Approximate full adders (AFAs) reduce power consumption while delivering an appropriate amount of accuracy for error tolerant applications without sacrificing improved errors. Lastly, the 10T-LCAFA from this study, based on an innovative 10T-LCAFA GNRFET device demonstrated as much as 78% reduction in power and a delay reduction of up to 79% over its alternatives. This improvement is excellent for energy efficient applications but also its performance is appropriate for performance optimized applications. To reiterate the main improvements achieved were based performance and helped us to achieve faster processing while lowering the power dissipation thus increasing the efficient operation of the circuit(s). Future work looking at GNRFET parameters (for example, improving the physical device) may allow for even more improvements with regard to power and delay changes. Additionally investigating even more energy efficient transistor configurations and voltage optimization possibilities could increase overall efficiency. In conclusion, the work provided in this work serves to continue push the discipline of low-power VLSI design ahead; and this study ultimately facilitates the advancement of approximation computing technologies.

References

[1] Juneja, S., & Sharma, K. (2025). CNTFET based leakage control static approximate full adder circuit for high performance multimedia applications. *AEU - International Journal of Electronics and Communications*, 190, 155626

[2] Yan, A., Bao, H., Jiang, W., Cui, J., Huang, Z., & Wen, X. (2024). Efficient design approaches to CMOS full adder circuits. *Microelectronics Journal*, 149, 106235.

[3] Shahrokhi, S. H., Hosseinzadeh, M., Reshadi, M., & Gorgin, S. (2023). A novel high-speed and low-pdp approximate full adder cell for image blending. *Mathematics*, 11(12), 2649.

[4] ErfanFatemieh, S., Farahani, S. S., & Reshadinezhad, M. R. (2021). LAHAF: Low-power, area-efficient, and high-performance approximate full adder based on static CMOS. *Sustainable Computing Informatics and Systems*, 30, 100529–100529.

[5] Goyal, C., Ubhi, J. S., & Raj, B. (2019). A low leakage TG-CNTFET–based inexact full adder for low power image processing applications. *International Journal of Circuit Theory and Applications*, 47(9), 1446–1458.

[6] GowriSankar, P. A. (2018). A novel ternary half adder & one bit multiplier circuits based on emerging sub-32nm FET technology. In International Conference on Intelligent Computing and Communication for Smart World (pp.) 198–203.

[7] Kishore, P., Babulu, K., & Sridevi, P. V. (2016). Low power and high speed carry save adder using modified gate diffusion input technique. *ARPN Journal of Engineering and Applied Sciences*, 11(21).

[8] Nandyala, V. R., & Mahapatra, K. K. (2016). A circuit technique for leakage power reduction in CMOS VLSI circuits. In 2016 International Conference on VLSI Systems, Architectures, Technology and Applications (VLSI-SATA), IEEE, (pp. 1–5).

[9] Weste, N. H., & Harris, D. (2015). CMOS VLSI design: a circuits and systems perspective. Pearson Education India.

[10] Dilip, B., Prasad, P. S., & Bhavani, R. S. G. (2013). Leakage power reduction in CMOS circuits using leakage control transistor technique in nanoscale technology. *International Journal of Electronics Signals and Systems*, (pp.) 237–242.

[11] Bharti, R., & Mittal, P. (2021). Comparative analysis of different types of inverters for low power at 45nm. In 2021 3rd International Conference on Advances in Computing, Communication Control and Networking (ICAC3N), 2021: IEEE (pp.) 1081–1086.

[12] Rana, G., Sharma, K., & Sharma, A. (2022). Design and analysis of power efficient 1-bit adder circuits in 18 nm FinFET Technology. In 2022 International Conference on Smart Generation Computing, Communication and Networking (SMART GENCON), 2022: IEEE (pp. 1–3).

[13] Rajora, R., Sharma, K., Gupta, L., Sachdeva, A., & Sharma, A. (2023). Low-power highspeed CNTFET-based 1-bit comparator design using CCT and STT techniques. In 2023 Second International Conference on Electronics and Renewable Systems (ICEARS), 2023: IEEE (pp. 49–53).

[14] Lyons, E., Ganti, V., Goldman, R., Melikyan, V., & Mahmoodi, H. (2009). Full-custom design project for digital VLSI and IC design courses using synopsys generic 90nm CMOS library. In 2009 IEEE International Conference on Microelectronic Systems Education, IEEE (pp. 45–48).

[15] Schaarschmidt, M., Uelschen, M., & Pulvermüller, E. (2022). Hunting energy bugs in embedded systems: a software-model-in-the-loop approach. *Electronics*, 11, 1937.

[16] Balasubramanian, P., & Mastorakis, N. E. (2022). High-speed and energy-efficient carry look-ahead adder. *Journal of Low Power Electronics and Applications*, 12(3), 46.

[17] Padmanabhan, K. K., Seerengasamy, U., & Ponraj, A. S. (2022). High-speed grouping and decomposition multiplier for binary multiplication. *Electronics*, 11, 4202.

[18] Mohammaden, A., Fouda, M. E., Alouani, I., Said, L. A., Radwan, A. G. (2022). CNTFET-Based ternary multiply-and-accumulate unit. *Electronics*, 11, 1455.

[19] Zareei, Z., Navi, K., Reshadi, M., & Keshavarziyan, P. (2020). Efficient symmetrical imprecise 1-bit full adder cells using CNFET technology for image processing applications. *CSI Journal on Computer Science and Engineering*, 17, 2.

[20] Mohammadi, M., Zanjani, S. M., & Dolatshahi, M. (2022). Design and simulation of a low PDP full adder by combining majority function and TGDI technique in CNTFET technology. In Proceedings of the 2022 12th International Conference on Computer and Knowledge Engineering (ICCKE), Mashhad, Iran (pp. 17–18, 2022.

[21] Shahrokhi, S. H., Hosseinzadeh, M., Reshadi, M., & Gorgin, S. (2021). High-performance and low-energy approximate full adder design for error-resilient image processing. *International Journal of Electrical and Electronics Research*, 109, 1059–1079.

[22] Tanuj, M., Virigineni, A., Mani, A., & Subramani, R. (2021). Comparative study of gradient domain based image blending approaches. In Proceedings of the 2021 International Conference on Innovative Computing, Intelligent Communication and Smart Electrical Systems (ICSES), Chennai, India (pp. 24–25.

[23] Keles, O., Yilmaz, M. A., Tekalp, A. M., Korkmaz, C., & Dogan, Z. (2021). On the computation of PSNR for a set of images or video. In Proceedings of the Picture Coding Symposium (PCS), San Jose, CA, USA, 2021.

[24] Chang, S. K., & Wey, C. L. A fast 64-bit hybrid adder design in 90 nm CMOS process. In IEEE 55th International Midwest Symposium on Circuits and Systems (MWSCAS) 2012 (pp.) 414–417.

[25] Kumar, G., & Agarwal, S. (2017). CMOS limitations and futuristic carbon allotropes. In 8th IEEE Annual Information Technology, Electronics and Mobile Communication Conference (IEMCON) 2017. https://doi.org/10.1109/IEMCON.2017.8117151.

22 Design and development of a rotational energy harvester using a piezoelectric transducer

S. Udhayakumar[1,a] and V. Amresh[2,b]

[1]Assistant Professor, Department of Mechanical Engineering, PSG College of Technology, Coimbatore, India

[2]PG Student, Department of Mechanical Engineering, PSG College of Technology, Coimbatore, India

Abstract

This paper describes the design, construction and evaluation of a rotational energy harvester, which incorporates a piezoelectric transducer to convert mechanical vibrations to electrical energy. The harvester uses rotational motion to excite piezoelectric beams and apply a strain, which produces electrical output. A numerical analysis was performed with the COMSOL Multiphysics modeling software to evaluate the dynamic response to generate the most energy conversion. A prototype harvester was produced and experimentally tested at a range of rotational speeds based on numerical analysis. The effectiveness of the proposed method was validated through experimental data, which showed agreement with the numerical analysis. The experimental results indicate that piezoelectric-based rotational energy harvesters have the capacity to provide energy for self-sustaining electronic systems, especially in mechanical applications where rotational motion is constant.

Keywords: COMSOL Multiphysics, dynamic analysis, energy conversion, piezoelectric transducer, prototype testing, rotational energy harvester, self-powered systems

Introduction

Piezoelectric energy harvesting is a useful way to convert mechanical vibrations into electrical energy, allowing low-power devices like wireless sensors to operate without batteries and is especially helpful in environments where there is little access to traditional power sources. Rotational energy harvesters harvested mechanical strain from rotating systems, such as motors and turbines, and converted that energy into electrical energy. The overarching goal of this research effort is to create effective systems capable of harnessing all (or as much as possible) of the mechanical strain for useful purposes, especially under low rotational speeds.

Due to the increasing need for energy around the world and the consumption of fossil fuel resources sustainable alternatives are needed. Micro-energy harvesting presents a viable method to power small electronic devices, while alternative renewable energy resources are currently being studied on an industrial scale. Mechanical motions in general, and rotational power in particular, have not been fully explored in terms of ambient energy sources. Many devices such as industrial turbines and conventional car wheels provide rotational motion that could be harvested.

Piezoelectric materials offer a compact and efficient energy harvesting option, capable of producing an electric charge when a mechanical stress is applied on the material. When compared to electromagnetic harvesters, piezoelectric systems are scalable, lightweight, and are efficient with little mechanical input. Significant advances in energy conversion have been demonstrated by two different materials to date - polyvinylidene fluoride (PVDF) and lead zirconate titanate (PZT). If piezoelectric elements are positioned correctly, it is possible to turn periodic mechanical stresses into a rotating system into electrical power.

Guan et al. [1] developed a piezoelectric rotational energy harvester with a power output of 825 μW at low frequencies of 7–13.5 Hz making it viable for wireless sensor applications. To achieve optimal energy conversion efficiency, centrifugal force must be minimized, and vibration amplitude is maximized.

Rui et al. [2] stated that limiters added to a rotating piezoelectric energy harvester ultimately decreased amplitude, protected the device, and broadened the frequency response; as the limiters are spaced more closely together, the responses will become more limiting, but durability will improve.

[a]suk.mech@psgtech.ac.in, [b]amreshvasudevan@gmail.com

DOI: 10.1201/9781003770435-22

Su et al. [3] demonstrated that centrifugal force in rotational piezoelectric harvesters affects resonant frequency: it increases as a function of outward distance, decreases as a function of inward distance, and decreases from 0–90° tilt position. These findings can be applied in future harvester designs for improved efficiency.

Fu et al. [4] described a low-speed rotary piezoelectric harvester that builds on frequency up-conversion with movable magnets and outputs greater than 20 µW, at 15–35 Hz, ultimately, for use in low-power devices and sensor networks for self-powered systems.

Shu et al. [5] characterized a rotational piezoelectric harvester equipped with a magnetic tip. The authors showed that the resonant frequency increased with the speed of the magnet and decreased with frequency. At the same time, the output power of the device was directly proportional to the squared Fourier coefficient of magnetic force, which informed their designs for self-powered devices.

Sanislav et al. [6] reviewed energy harvesting for IoT, discussed solar, RF, piezoelectric energy harvesting, emphasis placed on sensor lifespan in review paper, storage medium - is it battery or supercapacitor, and future requirements like in hybrid optimization and sustainability in energy management.

Pradeesh et al. [7] reported that the efficiency of piezoelectric harvesters is highly dependent on the material and placement of proof mass, with peak power output at the 0 mm location (from the fixed beam end). While shape, location of proof mass, and mass shape impacted the resonant frequency dramatically, it significantly impacted other various performance factors as well.

Pradeesh et al. [8] surveyed multiple beam designs for piezoelectric harvesters and verified that the INTA thunderbird design produced approximately 15.63% more power per unit volume than the rectangular design at the optimal loading scenario of 0.316 MΩ (19.53 V, 1.207 mW), thus signifying the INTA TW design for low energy micro-scale applications.

Shu et al. [9] have modeled piezoelectric energy conversion using the mass-spring-damper analogy, which allows for explanation of total damping as both mechanical damping and electrical damping. The authors explained that the efficiency of transfer depends on the level of impedance mismatch and resistance during the transfer of energy.

Khameneifar et al. [10] studied rotary vibration-based piezoelectric harvesters and uncovered

that the PZT device with a tip mass of 105 g produced an output of 6.4 mW that was sufficient for active sensors, whereas the PVDF delivered only 147 µW and could be used in low-power modes if used with certain low power sensors, and the researchers opened with the discussion of the impact of material and energy optimization.

Hsu et al. [11] developed a self-tuning piezoelectric harvester, which consisted of brass cantilever coated in PZT and a steel tip mass. Through finite element analysis, they showed that this harvester can adapt its single degree of freedom resonance frequency, and increase power output, powered by different rotational vibrations and/or loading conditions.

Despite the development of various piezoelectric energy harvesters for rotational motion, most are targetable for mid-to-high-frequency operations and have not been tested under uniform low-frequency conditions. A compact and efficient energy harvester tailored to operate in low-frequency conditions is still needed. Thus, in this work, an efficient energy harvester for such conditions is developed and tested both experimentally and numerically.

Numerical Analysis

Figure 22.1 illustrates the schematic of the rotational energy harvester consisting of two cantilever beams, the rotational shaft of a motor, a mounted frame for the shaft, and a rotating disc. To improve the vibrational response during rotation, a spring and masses are installed. This is done using a piezoelectric disc consisting of ceramic discs and metal plates where mechanical energy is converted to electrical output.

The rotational energy harvester, as seen in Figure 22.2, is initially modeled in SolidWorks for the dimensions, which were defined in Table 22.1, and was then imported to COMSOL Multiphysics for modeling. This analysis combines solid mechanics, electrostatics, and electric circuit physics to evaluate the performance of the harvester. Material properties are assigned for all the parts according to values presented in Table 22.2.

The physics features and boundary conditions used in the numerical solution of the rotational energy harvester (REH) within COMSOL Multiphysics are as follows: Gravity is applied to all the components to account for its effect on the dynamic behavior of the system. A rotating frame is introduced to include centrifugal force effects resulting from rotational motion. Masses added to the harvester are given,

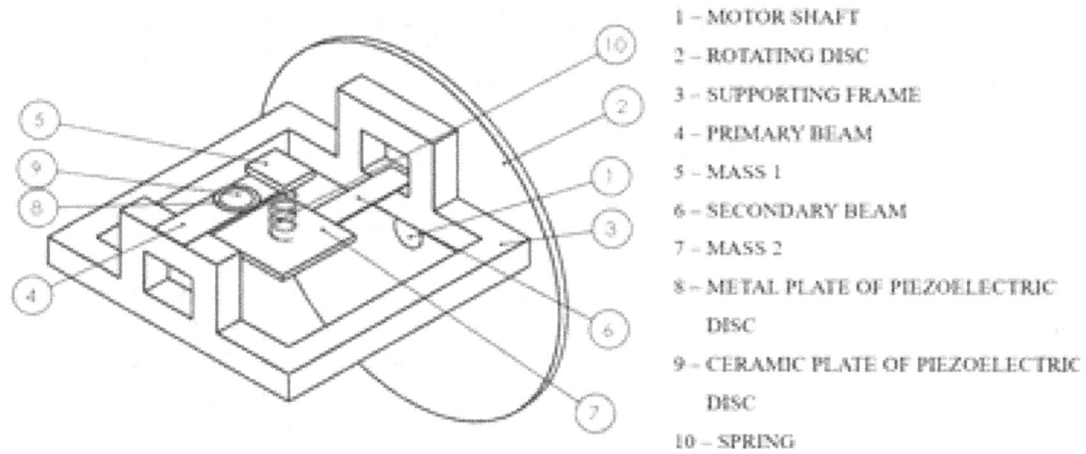

1 – MOTOR SHAFT
2 – ROTATING DISC
3 – SUPPORTING FRAME
4 – PRIMARY BEAM
5 – MASS 1
6 – SECONDARY BEAM
7 – MASS 2
8 – METAL PLATE OF PIEZOELECTRIC
 DISC
9 – CERAMIC PLATE OF PIEZOELECTRIC
 DISC
10 – SPRING

Figure 22.1 Schematic diagram of the rotational energy harvester
Source: Author

1 – MOTOR SHAFT
2 – ROTATING DISC
3 – SUPPORTING FRAME
4 – PRIMARY BEAM
5 – MASS 1
6 – SECONDARY BEAM
7 – MASS 2
8 – METAL PLATE OF PIEZOELECTRIC
 DISC
9 – CERAMIC PLATE OF PIEZOELECTRIC
 DISC
10 – SPRING

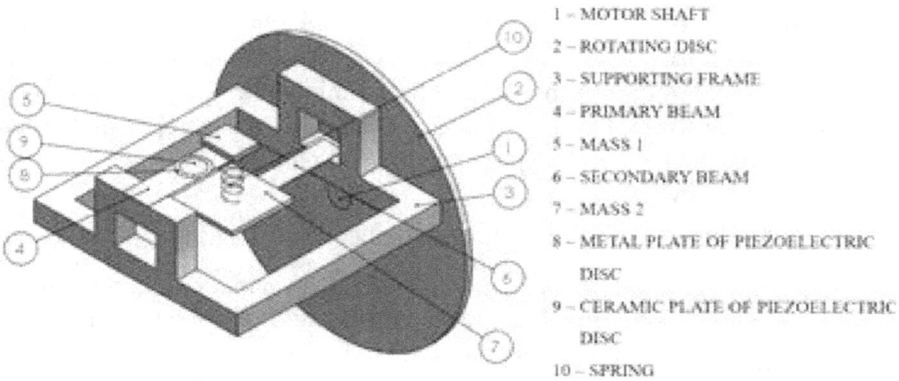

Figure 22.2 Model of the rotational energy harvester
Source: Author

where they are 0.03 kg for Mass 1 and 0.04 kg for Mass 2, to represent their effect on vibrational responses. Fixed support is given at one end of the motor shaft, secondary beam, and primary beam to have a stable structure. A spring foundation is given to the spring component with a value of 593 N/m to represent its elastic behavior. In the electrical context, a terminal and ground condition are introduced to set up the voltage difference across the piezoelectric layer. A 1 MΩ resistor is added to the electrical circuit to replicate the resistive load.

Figures 22.3 and 22.4 present the numerically calculated voltage and power outputs of the rotational energy harvester at different rotational speeds. Figure 22.3 indicates a steady increase in voltage output with increasing speed, from 0.066 V at 50 RPM to a maximum of 0.355 V at 150 RPM. This is indicative of the increased piezoelectric response at higher levels of mechanical excitation. The equivalent power output in Figure 22.4 increases in a similar manner from 0.004 μW at 50 RPM to 0.126 μW at 150 RPM. The increase in power output is non-linear due to the square relationship between voltage and power.

Experimental work

The rotational energy harvester shown in Figure 22.5 consists of several key components that turn rotational motion into electrical energy. The piezoelectric disc is the main part that generates electrical energy from mechanical strain. The primary and secondary beams are flexible structures that bend during rotation. The motor shaft drives the rotating disc, passing motion to the system. Placing Mass 1 and

Table 22.1 Dimensions of the rotational energy harvester

Components name	Dimensions			
	Length (mm)	Width (mm)	Thick (mm)	Diameter (mm)
Motor shaft	60	-	-	22
Rotating disc	-	-	6	250
Primary beam	90	25	0.5	-
Mass 1	25	32	5	-
Secondary beam	90	20	0.8	-
Mass 2	60	60	4	-
Spring	45.70	-	-	16
Piezoelectric element	-	-	0.38	27

Source: Author

Table 22.2 Material properties of the rotational energy harvester

Components name	Material properties		
	Young's modulus (GPa)	Density (kg/m^3)	Piezoelectric constant (C/m^2)
Motor shaft	193	8000	-
Rotating disc	210	7850	
Primary beam	193	8000	-
Mass 1	193	8000	-
Secondary beam	69	2720	
Mass 2	69	2720	-
Spring	210	7850	-
Piezoelectric element	-	-	- 6.62
Supporting frame	193	8000	-

Source: Author

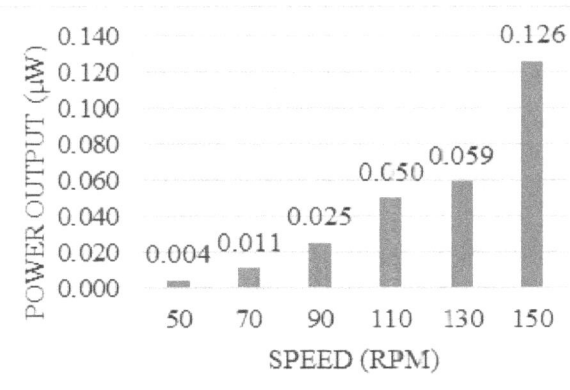

Figure 22.4 Power output obtained numerically
Source: Author

Mass 2 improves the vibrational response and boosts energy conversion efficiency. A spring adjusts the system's natural frequency for the best power output. The supporting frame provides stability and keeps all parts aligned. An external control unit powers and monitors the system. This design allows for effective energy harvesting from low-frequency rotational motion, making it ideal for self-powered sensing and low-energy applications.

Table 22.1 has the specifications of the fabricated rotational energy harvester and gives measurements of different features of our device. The material properties of the rotational energy harvester are included in Table 22.2.

The circuit diagram for the rotational energy harvester which converts mechanical vibrations into usable electrical energy is illustrated in Figure 22.6. The AC voltage produced by the piezoelectric element from mechanical excitation is rectified to usable DC

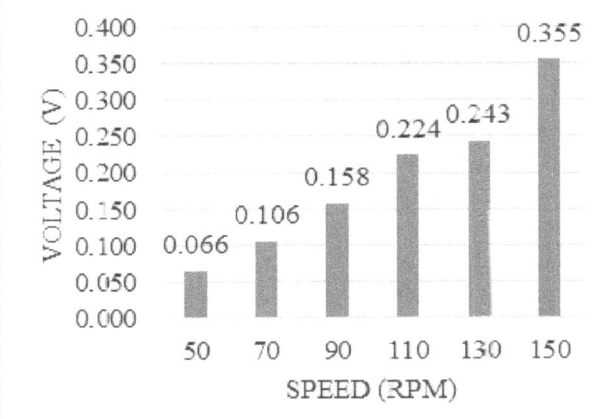

Figure 22.3 Voltage output obtained numerically
Source: Author

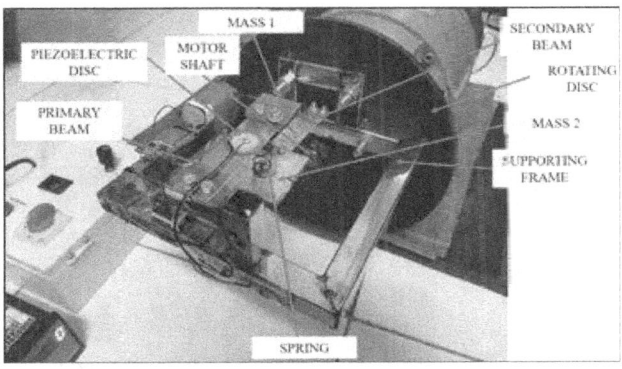

Figure 22.5 Fabricated prototype
Source: Author

voltage through a full-wave rectifier circuit consisting of (1N5819) Schottky diodes. In parallel with the rectified output is a 1 MΩ resistor to avoid variation in the measurement of voltage. Once the DC voltage is produced and ready for sampling, the NodeMCU ESP32 prepares the measurements for transmit and analysis. The ESP32 can operate manually by connecting a 9V battery to a switch; thus, the ESP32 can use its embedded battery when required. Real-time energy harvest monitoring and analysis help ensure proper energy procurement and minimize costs.

Figure 22.7 depicts the experimental setup of the rotational energy harvester, which is made up of several important parts. The excitation source for the harvester is rotational motion produced by a DC motor. To capture rotational vibrations, the rotational energy harvester is connected to the motor shaft and installed on a support frame. The motor speed is regulated by a DC drive control panel, which permits controlled changes to the input frequency. The motor's rotational speed is tracked in real time using a digital RPM indicator. A NodeMCU ESP32 processes and transmits the harvested electrical output. The output voltage data is regularly observed and analyzed on a laptop through a wireless communication interface. The system is intended to assess how well the energy harvester performs at various rotational speeds. Data acquisition is carried out to evaluate how effectively energy is converted.

Figure 22.8 shows the voltage output from the rotational energy harvester as measured experimentally at varying rotational speeds. The voltage output rises as speed increases, showing the dependence of rotational speed on energy production. The lowest recorded voltage is 0.065 V at 50 RPM and rises to 0.341 V at 150 RPM. The output shows an increase in voltage as the speed increases.

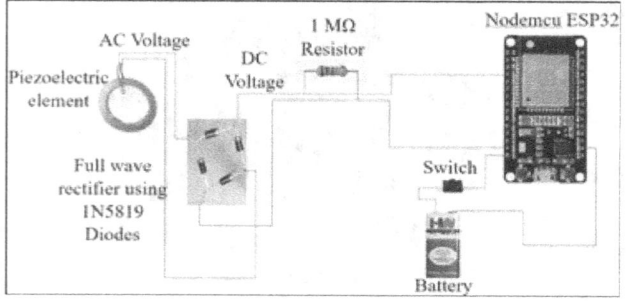

Figure 22.6 Circuit diagram of the rotational energy harvester

Source: Author

Figure 22.7 Experimental setup of the rotational energy harvester

Source: Author

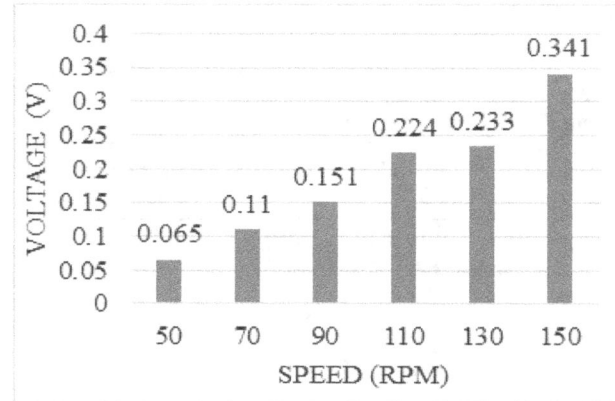

Figure 22.8 Voltage output obtained experimentally

Source: Author

The power output of the piezoelectric energy harvester is given by:

$$P = \frac{V^2}{R} \qquad (1)$$

where P is the generated power in microwatts (μW), V is the output voltage in volts (V), and R is the load resistance in megaohms (MΩ). This equation is used to assess the electrical power extracted from mechanical vibrations, offering insights into the system's energy conversion efficiency.

Figure 22.9 shows the rotational energy harvester's power output at different rotational speeds. The power output is higher with speed, illustrating the harvester's ability to convert energy. The lowest power obtained is 0.004 μW at 50 RPM, and the highest power is 0.116 μW at 150 RPM. The trend shows that increased rotational speeds produce more power.

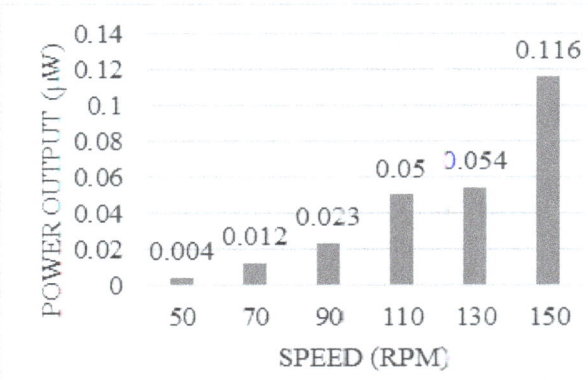

Figure 22.9 Power output of the rotational energy harvester
Source: Author

Table 22.3 compares the voltage output from experimental measurement and numerical simulation at different rotational speeds. The corresponding frequency values in Hz are also given along with them. The voltage outputs from both techniques show a comparable increasing trend against speed, showing consistency in performance. There are minor variations across all data points, with the maximum variation being -4.6% at 90 RPM. Both numerical and experimental results are exactly 0.224 V at 110 RPM. Overall discrepancy between the experiment and numerical result is within ±5% at all conditions, proving the correctness and trustworthiness of the simulation model for predicting the system's voltage response.

Table 22.4 presents a comparison of power output from experimental testing and numerical simulation at different rotational speeds. Frequency for each speed is also presented. Both present a similar increase in power with speed, which suggests consistency in performance trends. Experimental and simulated power at 50 RPM and 110 RPM are identical. The maximum deviation recorded is -9.26% at 130 RPM, and the maximum positive deviation of 8.33% at 70 RPM. These small variations could be due to system nonlinearities or experimental errors. In general, the deviation is within ±10%, which verifies that the numerical model is reasonably good in modeling power output behavior.

Conclusion

The rotational energy harvester, which converts the rotational motion of a disc or wheel into vibrations or mechanical stress, has been designed and

Table 22.3 Comparison of voltage output between numerical and experimental results

Speed (RPM)	Frequency (Hz)	Voltage output (V)		
		Numerical analysis	Experimental results	Deviation (%)
50	0.833	0.066	0.065	-1.5
70	1.166	0.106	0.110	3.6
90	1.5	0.158	0.151	-4.6
110	1.833	0.224	0.224	0.0
130	2.166	0.243	0.233	-4.3
150	2.5	0.355	0.341	-4.1

Source: Author

Table 22.4 Comparison of power output between numerical and experimental results

Speed (RPM)	Frequency (Hz)	Power output (µW)		
		Numerical analysis	Experimental results	Deviation (%)
50	0.833	0.004	0.004	0.00
70	1.166	0.011	0.012	8.33
90	1.5	0.025	0.023	-8.70
110	1.833	0.050	0.050	0.00
130	2.166	0.059	0.054	-9.26
150	2.5	0.126	0.116	-8.62

Source: Author

developed. Numerical analysis is first performed using COMSOL Multiphysics for rotational speeds ranging from 50 RPM to 150 RPM, followed by experimental testing of the fabricated prototype. The voltage output increases with speed, ranging from 0.066 V to 0.355 V in numerical analysis and from 0.065 V to 0.341 V in the experimental results, with minimal deviations—maximum of 4.6% and zero deviation at 110 RPM. Similarly, power output rises from 0.004 µW to 0.126 µW numerically and from 0.004 µW to 0.116 µW experimentally, with the highest deviation of 9.26% and perfect agreement at certain speeds. The corresponding frequencies range from 0.833 Hz to 2.5 Hz. Overall, the deviations remain within acceptable limits, confirming a reliable agreement between numerical and experimental results.

References

[1] Guan, M., & Liao, W. (2016). Design and analysis of a piezoelectric energy harvester for rotational motion system. *Energy Conversion and Management*, 111, 239–244, 2016, doi: 10.1016/j.enconman.2015.12.061.

[2] Rui, X. et al. 2019). Modeling and analysis of a rotational piezoelectric energy harvester with limiters. Journal of Mechanical Science and Technology, 33(11), 5169–5176. doi: 10.1007/s12206-019-1006-6.

[3] Su, W, Lin, J., & Li, W. (2020). Analysis of a cantilevered piezoelectric energy harvester in different orientations for rotational motion. *Sensors*, 20(4), 1206. doi: 10.3390/s20041206.

[4] Fu, H., & Yeatman, E. M. (2017). A methodology for low-speed broadband rotational energy harvesting using piezoelectric transduction and frequency up-conversion. *Energy*, 125, 152–161. doi: 10.1016/j.energy.2017.02.115.

[5] Shu, Y. C., Wang, W. C., & Chang, Y. P. (2018). Electrically rectified piezoelectric energy harvesting induced by rotary magnetic plucking. *Smart Materials and Structures*, 27(12), 125006. doi: 10.1088/1361-665X/aae6ea.

[6] Sanislav, T., Mois, G. D., Zeadally, S., & Folea, (2021). Energy harvesting techniques for internet of things (IoT). *IEEE Access*, 9, 39530–39549. doi:10.1109/ACCESS.2021.3064066.

[7] Pradeesh, E., & Udhayakumar, S. (2019). Effect of placement of piezoelectric material and proof mass on the performance of piezoelectric energy harvester. *Mechanical Systems and Signal Processing*, 130, 664–676. doi: 10.1016/j.ymssp.2019.05.044.

[8] Pradeesh, E. L.,Udhayakumar, S., Vasundhara, , & Kalavathi, (2023). Experimental and numerical analysis on different beam geometries for vibration based piezoelectric energy harvester. *Ferroelectrics*, 606(1), 219–238. doi: 10.1080/00150193.2023.2189838.

[9] Shu, Y. C., & Lien, I. C. (2006). Efficiency of energy conversion for a piezoelectric power harvesting system. *Journal of Micromechanics and Microengineering*, 16(11), 2429–2438. doi: 10.1088/0960-1317/16/11/026.

[10] Khameneifar, F., Arzanpour, S., & Moallem, M. (2012). A piezoelectric energy harvester for rotary motion applications: design and experiments. *IEEE/ASME Transactions on Mechatronics*, 18(5), 1527–1534. doi: 10.1109/TMECH.2012.2205266.

[11] Hsu, J., Tseng, C., & Chen, Y. (2014). Analysis and experiment of self-frequency-tuning piezoelectric energy harvesters for rotational motion. *Smart Materials and Structures*, 23(7), 075013. doi: 10.1088/0964-1726/23/7/075013.

23 A psycholinguistic analysis of code- switching between human and machine languages in English cognitive patterns at IT classrooms

A. Sarah Helan Sathya[a]

Assistant Professor (Senior Grade), Department of English, PSG College of Technology Coimbatore, India

Abstract

In the digital age, code-switching between natural languages and machine languages has introduced a distinct variety of English in IT classrooms. This research examines how programming languages influence English cognitive patterns among IT students, making their speech more algorithmic, precise, and logical. Using observational methods, the study highlights how students frequently blend technical jargon with English, adopt conditional syntactic structures, and exhibit concise communication patterns. The findings indicate that exposure to programming languages significantly shapes students' linguistic expressions and thought processes, reinforcing the linguistic relativity hypothesis. This paper offers insight into the intersection of technology and linguistics, contributing to the broader discourse on language evolution in the digital era.

Keywords: Code-switching, cognitive patterns, IT classrooms, linguistic relativity, programming languages, psycholinguistics

Introduction

The linguistic relativity elaborates that the language we speak influences how we perceive and think about the world. In the digital era, this concept extends beyond natural languages to programming languages, which serve as a new medium of communication between humans and machines. As programmers or individuals interacting with technology frequently switch between human languages (like English) and machine languages (such as Python, C++, or Java), their cognitive patterns, thought processes, and even the way they use English may be influenced by this code-switching.

The increasing reliance on programming languages in IT classrooms has given rise to a peculiar linguistic phenomenon that is code-switching between human and machine languages.

This hybridized communication style is characterized by the frequent use of programming jargon, syntax-like expressions, and algorithmic patterns in students' English speech. As an English teacher of IT class, it is increasingly evident that students' communication reflects cognitive patterns shaped by their exposure to machine logic.

Background of the study

Literature Review

Boroditsky [1] explores the causal link between language and thought, demonstrating how language exposure can alter individuals' perception of time, space, and causality. Boroditsky's experiments with Mandarin and English speakers show that language can influence temporal reasoning. Similarly, IT students frequently exposed to machine languages may develop a more logical and sequential speaking style, reflecting programming logic in their English.

Pavlenko [10] investigates the impact of bilingualism on cognition, suggesting that constant code-switching makes individuals more cognitively flexible. Her research reveals that bilingual individuals demonstrate enhanced problem-solving skills and mental agility. This supports the notion that IT students, by switching between English and programming languages, exhibit greater mental adaptability and hybridized communication patterns.

Dijkstra and van Heuven [3] emphasize cross-language activation, showing that bilingual individuals often exhibit traces of their second language in their first language. Their study on bilingual word

[a]ash.english@psgtech.ac.in

DOI: 10.1201/9781003770435-23

recognition demonstrates that bilinguals activate both languages simultaneously, influencing their lexical choices. This applies to IT students, whose English communication incorporates machine-language logic, resulting in mixed linguistic expressions.

Crystal [2] discusses the emergence of global English varieties shaped by technology, identifying how tech jargon and syntax increasingly pervade everyday English. His analysis of online communication reveals that digital interaction accelerates linguistic evolution. This reinforces the notion that IT students are cultivating a new variety of English influenced by programming, marked by concise, technical, and structured patterns.

Research gap

In the IT context, linguistic relativity extends to programming languages, which are more than mere technical tools. They shape thought processes and even speech patterns. As students engage with programming languages, their English expressions become more structured, concise, and logical, mirroring the rules of coding. This paper investigates the psycholinguistic impact of programming on students' English usage, highlighting the blending of technical and natural language features through real-life classroom observations. The study aims to address the following research questions:

1) How do programming languages influence the syntactic and lexical choices in students' English speech?
2) What cognitive patterns emerge in IT students' communication because of frequent programming language exposure?

Research methodology

The study employs a qualitative observational method, which is appropriate for capturing the nuanced linguistic patterns in real-life classroom settings. Over a period of time, classroom interactions were observed in an IT course. The observations focused on students' speech patterns, code-switching tendencies, and the integration of programming logic into English communication.

Data Collection

Non-participatory observation is an optimal method for data collection in psycholinguistic studies. By adopting a passive role, researchers can document

authentic linguistic interactions such as spontaneous speech, code-switching, and syntactic adaptations in natural communication patterns. This method is particularly effective in classroom or laboratory settings, where learners unprompted use of hybridized language was recorded. This reveals the blending programming syntax with vernacular speech on cognitive processing and socio-linguistic influences. Therefore, playing a critical in understanding implicit language acquisition mechanisms. The non-intrusive design also accommodates unfiltered responses in the selected environment. For psycholinguistics, where subtle behavioral nuances define outcomes, non-participatory observation balances rigor with realism, offering unparalleled insights into the interplay of the chosen research. Thus, Classroom discussions, group projects, and casual conversations were recorded. Keen observation was made to capture specific instances of code-switching and syntactic patterns.

Data Analysis

Code-Switching in the Digital Context

Code-switching refers to the practice of alternating between two or more languages or dialects during a conversation. In the digital context, this switching involves:

- Natural language → Machine language: Writing code in a programming language while embedding comments or instructions in English.
- Machine language → Natural language: Using programming constructs, logic, or expressions in day-to-day English speech or writing.

The transcriptions were analyzed under recurring linguistic features influenced by programming exposure from natural to machine language as normal conversation. The analysis focused on:

1. Lexical borrowing of programming terms
2. Algorithmic sentence structures
3. Conditional and Boolean expressions
4. Syntax simplification and directness

Findings and analysis

Lexical Borrowing from Programming terms

IT students frequently integrate programming terms into their English speech, demonstrating lexical borrowing. This integration reflects the seamless blending of machine and natural language:

- "Let me **debug** this issue before we proceed."
- "I'll **ping** you after the class."
- "We need to **optimize** our workflow before we present our case study."
- "Let's **hardcode** the dates into the schedule for now."
- "We need to **troubleshoot** the issue before the meeting."
- "Her idea just didn't **compile** with the rest of the plan."
- "He's trying to **hack** his way through the exam."
- "I need to run a quick **script** to calculate the mark."
- "That idea doesn't **scale** well with our current resources."
- "We should **sandbox** this assignment before submitting it."

These examples reveal the penetration of machine vocabulary into casual English communication, indicating mixed linguistic expressions.

Algorithmic Sentence Structures
IT students frequently adopt procedural and sequential language structures. Their communication mirrors the step-by-step logic of programming languages. This structured speech style reflects the influence of programming languages on cognitive processing.

- "**First,** I'll initialize the project, **then** I'll execute the testing phase."
- "**If** you finish the module early, **then** you can submit it before the deadline."
- "**Unless** there's a power cut, **I'll** complete the assignment today."
- "**While** I'm listening to the story, **you** can write the same."
- "**Once** the reading comprehension is finalized, we can **proceed** to the next step."
- "**Repeat** the test cases **until** all of them pass."
- "**After** submitting the assignment, **update** your status on the portal."
- "**Break** the group discussion into smaller parts and **solve** each section."
- "**Whenever** you get a low marks, **check** for the correct answer first."
- "**Try** writing it again; **if** it still fails, drop out that section."

These examples disclose the breach of speech patterns into casual English communication, indicating a hybridized linguistic form

Conditional and Boolean Thinking
The frequent use of if-else logic in programming leads students to adopt conditional expressions in casual speech. This demonstrates the impact of programming languages on students' cognitive and linguistic practice.

- "**If** you submit the project early, you get bonus marks; **else**, you lose points."
- "**If** not done, **then** I'll exit the meeting early."
- "**Either** we finish this today **or** we work overnight tomorrow."
- "**If** the internet is stable, **then** we can start the Zoom session."
- "**If** she doesn't respond in 10 minutes, we'll proceed without her."
- "You can join us **only if** you've completed your code review."
- "**If** it's a group task **and** I'm the leader, **then** I'll assign the roles."
- "**Unless** we get approval, we can't deploy the update."
- "**If** I pass all the tests and get good marks, **then** I'll inform my parents."
- "**If** Sam is **true and** Saul is **false,** the system won't trigger the alert."
- "**If** not done, **then** I'll exit the meeting early.

These statements reflect the binary and conditional structure typical of programming languages thus making the normal conversation more programming.

Syntax Simplification and Condensed Expressions
Programming languages prioritize efficiency, influencing students' English to become more concise and direct. This syntactic economy reflects the brevity and clarity of coding instructions:

- "Submit it before **EOD**."
  EOD = End of the day.
- "Let's **sync** after lunch."
  Sync = Synchronize/discuss and align together.
- "He's **AFK** right now."
  → *AFK = Away from keyboard (temporarily unavailable).*
- "**BRB,** fixing a bug."
  → *BRB = Be right back (taking a short break).*
- "We'll do a quick **stand-up** at 10."
  → *Stand-up = Brief daily meeting (from Agile methodology).*

- "This feature is **WIP**."
  → *WIP = Work in progress.*
- "Deploy the patch **ASAP**."
  → *ASAP = As soon as possible.*
- *"Push your notes to the* repo *before class."*
  → *Repo = Repository*
- *"Let's* refactor *this function, because it is too messy."*
  → *Refactor = Restructure*
- *"FYI, the server will be down during the lab."*
  → *FYI = For your information*

The above sentences are condensed expression patterns drawn from programming syntax. Frequent programming influences how individuals structure their thoughts and sentences, making them more sequential and logical.

Conclusion and challenges

Conclusion

The code-switching between human and machine languages in the digital era is reshaping English cognitive patterns. It fosters algorithmic thinking, concise communication, and conditional logic in everyday English usage. This psycholinguistic shift reflects the growing influence of technology on human cognition, demonstrating how linguistic relativity extends beyond natural languages into the realm of machine communication.

The research highlights that IT students exhibit a distinctive English variety influenced by frequent code-switching between English and machine languages. Their communication reflects algorithmic thinking, lexical borrowing, and conditional structures, evidencing the impact of programming on their cognitive patterns. The findings support the linguistic relativity hypothesis, illustrating how machine language exposure shapes natural language cognition. This paper contributes to the growing field of psycholinguistics, emphasizing the evolving nature of English in the digital age.

Challenges

The potential consequences for English cognitive patterns are as follows:

- ***Syntax simplification:*** Programming encourages direct and minimalistic sentence structures, reducing verbosity in English communication. "Let's reboot our project."
- ***Increased use of metaphors:*** Programmers often use machine-related metaphors in English. "Let's push this task to next week."
- ***Impact on creativity:*** While programming enhances logical thinking, overreliance on structured logic may reduce creative flexibility in English expression.

References

[1] Boroditsky, L. (2001). Does language shape thought? *Trends in Cognitive Sciences*, 5(12), 487–493. https://doi.org/10.1016/S1364-6613(00)01723-9

[2] Crystal, D. (2011). Internet Linguistics: A Student Guide. Routledge.

[3] Dijkstra, T., & van Heuven, W. J. (2002). The architecture of the bilingual word recognition system: from identification to decision. *Bilingualism: Language and Cognition*, 5(3), 175–197.

[4] Pavlenko, A. (2014). The Bilingual Mind: and What it Tells us about Language and Thought. Cambridge University Press.

24 Performance analysis of quadcopter propeller blades under high-altitude flight conditions

GowthamHarish S[,a], Thyla P R[2,b], C. Shanmugam[3,c] and N. Mahendrakumar[4,d]*

[1]PG Student, Department of Mechanical Engineering, PSG College of Technology, Coimbatore, India

[2]Professor, Department of Mechanical Engineering, PSG College of Technology, Coimbatore, India

[3]Assistant Professor, Department of Mechanical Engineering, PSG College of Technology, Coimbatore, India

[4]Assistant Professor, Department of Mechanical Engineering, PSG College of Technology, Coimbatore, India

Abstract

This study investigates the aerodynamic performance of drone propellers designed for high-altitude applications. Propeller blades based on the NACA 6409 air foil and the toroidal shape were developed, and their performance was compared with that of an existing propeller using computational and experimental methods. Finite element analysis (FEA) and computational fluid dynamics (CFD) simulations in analysis Software are conducted to evaluate structural integrity and aerodynamic efficiency under varying operational conditions. Wind tunnel experiments were conducted at different air density and temperature conditions at different wind velocities, and the flow characteristics were studied to validate the numerical model. Additionally, dynamic analysis of the propeller was performed to assess vibrational behavior and stability during operation. The findings provide critical insights into optimizing propeller design for improved efficiency and performance in high-altitude environments.

Keywords: Aerodynamic performance, high altitudes, NACA, toroidal

Introduction

The performance of unmanned aerial vehicles (UAV) at high altitudes is a critical factor in their effectiveness for applications such as atmospheric research, remote sensing, military surveillance, and disaster response. At high altitudes, reduced air density significantly impacts aerodynamic forces, leading to lower lift force generation, reduced lift, and changes in propeller efficiency. To ensure reliable operation in such conditions, it is essential to analyze and optimize propeller designs specifically for low-density environments.

High-altitude propeller testing requires a combination of numerical simulations and experimental validation to accurately assess aerodynamic performance. Computational fluid dynamics (CFD) and Finite element analysis (FEA) provide insights into flow behavior, lift force characteristics, and structural integrity under varying atmospheric conditions. However, experimental validation through wind tunnel testing is crucial to account for real-world aerodynamic effects such as turbulence, compressibility, and dynamic loading. Additionally, dynamic analysis of the propeller helps in understanding its vibrational response, ensuring stability during high-speed rotations.

The focus of research in the field of drone propeller aerodynamics has generally been centered on enhancing lift force generation, improving efficiency, and reducing noise under various flight conditions. Researchers have widely explored the effects of airfoil selection, blade geometry, and operating parameters such as RPM, angle of attack, and Reynolds number on propeller performance. Both computational and experimental methods have been employed to investigate flow behavior, pressure distribution, and wake characteristics. With the growing demand for UAVs in diverse applications ranging from surveillance to delivery, recent studies have also begun to consider the impact of environmental factors such as air density, altitude, temperature, and wind velocity. These investigations aim to optimize propeller designs for reliable and efficient performance across a range of operational scenarios, particularly in high-altitude or extreme weather conditions where conventional propellers may suffer from significant performance degradation.

Dahal et.al. [1] have designed a propeller for high-altitude search and rescue UAVs, optimizing lift

[a]kadirigowtham461@gmail.com, [b]prt.mech@psgtech.ac.in, [c]csn.mech@psgtech.ac.in, [d]nmk.mech@psgtech.ac.in

DOI: 10.1201/9781003770435-24

force for altitudes of 3,000–5,000 m. It includes lift force analysis, CFD analysis and validation through experimental results, demonstrating effective performance at reduced air density.

Donghun et.al. [2] evaluate propeller performance for a high altitude electric-powered UAV, EAV-2H+, through wind tunnel experiments and computational analysis, highlighting performance decline at low RPM and under high altitude conditions, confirming the impact of low Reynolds number on performance.

Malim et.al. [3], have conducted investigations on the aeroelastic response of a 3D printed propeller blade for High Altitude Platform Stations, comparing the performance of deformed blades against that of rigid blades, highlighting improved lift force and torque across various materials.

Parin et.al. [4] conducted investigations on UAVs and emphasize the significant challenges they face when operating in extreme environmental conditions, particularly in Alpine scenarios, highlighting the need for understanding these challenges to ensure safe flight operations.

Dinc, et., al [5] carried out a performance review of high altitude drone and the results provided could be used as a guide for the design of UAVs.

Park et.al., [6] designed and carried out wind tunnel testing, CFD analysis, and flight test data analysis on the propeller of EAV-3, which is a solar-powered high-altitude long-endurance unmanned aerial vehicle. This vehicle was developed by Korea Aerospace Research Institute. A comparison of their results validated their design methodology for the design of high-altitude propellers.

Teja et.al.,[7] performed design and analysis of drone propellers with the objective of optimizing thrust by varying blade length, material, RPM, and angle using lightweight aluminum 1060 H12 and Nylon 101. Modal and CFD analyses were carried out to confirm safe operating conditions and to obtain thrust, pressure, and velocity data for 134 mm and 167 mm blades.

Sharma et. al., [8] analyzed four specific airfoils—S1223, S819, S8037, and S1223 RTL—using computational fluid dynamics (CFD) to determine the most suitable one for low-speed aircraft. ANSYS-FLUENT software was used to simulate airflow and evaluate the performance of the airfoils in terms of their lift coefficient, drag coefficient, moment coefficient, and lift-to-drag ratio at low Mach numbers.

McGhee, R. J., et,al, reported wind-tunnel test results for the Eppler 387 airfoil at low Reynolds numbers using NASA's Langley Low-Turbulence Pressure Tunnel. Their work provides detailed aerodynamic performance data—including lift, drag, and moment characteristics—to support low-speed aircraft design and aerodynamic research.

Nicolas et.al. [11] have conducted experiments in an icing wind tunnel to evaluate the performance of a UAV propeller under various icing conditions, measuring lift force and torque to develop a model for the propeller's transient performance in such environments.

Busch et.al. [12] conducted tests on propeller in icing conditions in the Illinois wind tunnel, measuring aerodynamic performance of clean and iced blade sections. This data was crucial for validating the propeller performance code used in the study.

The propeller used in previous design iterations was mostly based on an arbitrary cambered shape or a traditional flat plate, which showed several intrinsic limitations about acoustic and aerodynamic performance. First, total propulsive effectiveness was decreased by the previous geometry's suboptimal lift-to-drag characteristics, especially at moderate to high angles of attack.

Furthermore, early flow separation and increased wake turbulence caused by the lack of an optimized aerodynamic contour resulted in higher noise levels and unstable aerodynamic loads. Non-uniform pressure distributions also reduced structural efficiency, requiring the need for reinforcements or heavier materials to withstand centrifugal and aerodynamic forces while in operation. All these elements worked together to drive the shift to a more sophisticated airfoil-based strategy.

In this study, two new designs of drone propeller, one r based on the NACA 6409 airfoil and the other, based on a toroidal form were designed and analysed to evaluate their aerodynamic performance under varying environmental and operational conditions. While the use of NACA airfoil in propeller design has been investigated in prior literature, the current study distinguishes itself through the application-specific tailoring and comprehensive integration of the NACA 6409 profile for enhanced aerodynamic performance. Most existing works that employ NACA profiles focus either on larger-scale propellers or utilize symmetric sections such as NACA 0012, without fully optimizing for low Reynolds number regimes typical of drone or small-scale UAV operations.

In contrast, the present design incorporates the NACA 6409 airfoil, a cambered airfoil specifically selected for its superior lift performance and delayed stall characteristics at moderate angles of attack. This makes it particularly effective in scenarios requiring both hovering and forward flight efficiency. Unlike symmetric air foils, NACA 6409 generates higher lift at zero angle of attack. which contributes to improved static lift force, a critical requirement for vertical take-off and landing (VTOL) platforms.

The NACA 6409 airfoil was selected for its high lift characteristics at low speeds, making it ideal for UAV propulsion. The blade was geometrically optimized with twist and taper to maintain an effective angle of attack along the span, enhancing lift and reducing flow separation. In addition, this study also investigates the implementation of a toroidal-shaped propeller due to its promising aerodynamic and acoustic characteristics

The analysis was conducted for three distinct air density conditions - 1.222 kg/m³ (sea-level standard), 0.94 kg/m³ (moderate altitude), and 0.74 kg/m³ (high altitude) - to simulate a wide range of real-world scenarios. For all three cases, the wind velocity varied between 2 m/s and 10 m/s, and the temperature conditions extended down to sub-zero levels to replicate cold and high-altitude environments. The propeller was operated at a fixed rotational speed of 6000 RPM with an angle of attack of 14°, representing typical drone flight conditions.

To investigate the aerodynamic behavior, both computational and experimental methods were employed. The CFD simulations were performed using analysis Software with a structured mesh, the k-ω SST turbulence model for accurate prediction of near-wall flow behavior, and the Multiple reference frame (MRF) method to simulate the rotating domain of the propeller. Boundary conditions included velocity inlets, pressure outlets, and no-slip

Figure 24.1 Pioneer drone
Source: https://shorturl.at/ajKTO

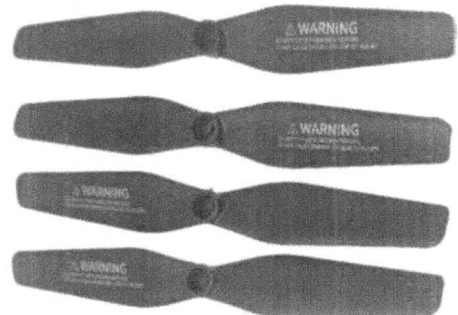

Figure 24.2 Existing propeller blades
Source: Author

conditions at blade surfaces. In parallel, experimental validation was carried out using a subsonic wind tunnel, where the fabricated propeller was mounted on a lift force stand, and measurements of lift force and RPM were taken using a tachometer setup. This integrated approach of numerical simulation and physical testing enabled a thorough evaluation of the propeller's aerodynamic efficiency and performance across varying atmospheric densities, wind velocity, and temperatures.

The findings from this research will contribute to the development of optimized propeller designs that enhance UAV performance in high-altitude operations. By integrating advanced simulation techniques with experimental testing, this study provides a comprehensive framework for improving drone propulsion systems in challenging atmospheric conditions.

Methodology

Benchmark Propeller Selection and 3D Scanning
The existing propeller was chosen from the Pioneer GD-118 quadcopter as the reference drone platform for propeller performance evaluation. This drone is categorized under the Nano UAV class, with an overall weight of 180 grams, making it well-suited for applications where adherence to sub-250 gram DGCA (Directorate General of Civil Aviation) regulations is critical. The propeller of this drone was chosen as benchmark to establish a performance baseline. A 3D scanner was used to capture the geometry of the benchmark propeller with high precision. The scanned data was processed to develop an accurate 3D model for comparison purposes.

Development of the NACA 6409-Based and Toroidal Propeller
With the aim of improving aerodynamic performance, two new designs of propeller blade are proposed,

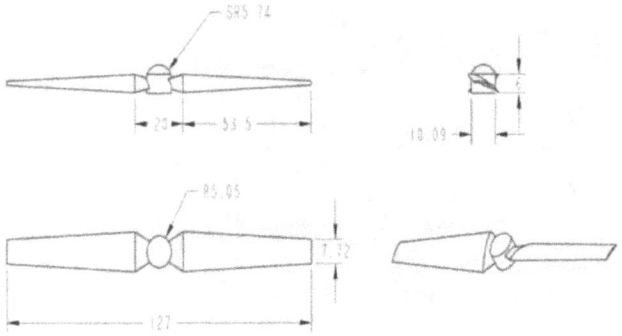

Figure 24.3 NACA profile propeller
Source: Author

retaining the blade length the same as that of the benchmark propeller. The first is based on NACA profile while the second is a toroidal configuration.

The first modified design was developed using the NACA 6409 air foil profile, obtained from the air foil Tools website. http://airfoiltools.com.

The NACA 6409 airfoil was selected based on its favorable aerodynamic characteristics in low Reynolds number regimes, which are typical for small-scale UAV applications like the Pioneer GD-118 drone. This cambered airfoil offers high lift coefficients and delayed stall characteristics, making it especially effective for propeller blades that operate under variable angles of attack during hovering and forward flight. Additionally, its relatively thin profile (9% thickness-to-chord ratio) ensures lower form drag, contributing to improved lift force-to-power ratio and propulsive efficiency. Prior studies have also demonstrated the suitability of NACA 6409 in small rotorcraft and model aircraft, which further supports its use in this research context

In addition to the conventional straight-blade configurations, this study also investigates the implementation of a toroidal-shaped propeller due to its promising aerodynamic and acoustic characteristics. Toroidal propellers feature a closed-loop blade geometry, where the blade tips are connected in a continuous curve, forming a doughnut-like or looped shape. This unique configuration significantly reduces tip vortex formation, which is a primary contributor to aerodynamic noise in traditional propellers. As a result, toroidal designs are known to offer substantial noise reduction, making them ideal for applications requiring stealth, urban operation, or indoor flight.

Noise reduction
At high altitudes, stealth is less critical for civilian drones, but in military or surveillance missions, noise reduction remains valuable.

Efficiency at thin air density
Toroidal blades need to maintain efficient lift force in lower-density air. While they reduce tip vortices (which is beneficial), their performance under low Reynolds number conditions must be validated.

Structural integrity
The continuous loop geometry may offer advantages in load distribution, which could benefit structural stability during high-altitude flight where temperature and pressure gradients are significant.

CFD and experimental validation
Use CFD simulations and high-altitude wind tunnel tests to validate lift force and efficiency performance at lower air densities.

The 3D modelling of the propeller was carried out using SolidWorks CAD software, ensuring accurate geometric representation and structural integrity.

CFD Simulation in analysis software
After completing the CAD modelling, the propeller geometry was exported as a Parasolid file for analysis in analysis software. The simulation setup included the following steps:

- Domain creation: A computational domain was designed with both static and dynamic zones to simulate appropriate flow conditions.
- Boundary conditions: The boundary conditions were defined based on atmospheric properties corresponding to high-altitude regions such as Leh and Ooty. Official meteorological data from the government of India was used to ensure realistic simulation inputs https://en.climate-data.org/asia/india/jammu-and-kashmir/leh-24802/.
- Meshing strategy: A refined meshing approach was adopted to balance computational efficiency and accuracy. A finer mesh was applied in regions with high velocity gradients to capture detailed flow characteristics.
- Solver setup: The simulation was performed using a transient solver with appropriate turbulence models to predict the aerodynamic forces and flow behavior accurately.

Experimental Results

An experimental study was conducted using a wind tunnel test setup to measure lift, drag, and lift force forces for comparison with analytical values under real-world conditions.

Modal analysis using FEA

FEA is conducted to study the modal behavior and mode shapes of the propellers to identify their natural frequencies. This is essential to ensure that resonance does not occur during operation, which could lead to severe vibrations, structural failure, or performance degradation. By understanding the dynamic characteristics through FEA, the proposed propeller designs can be optimized for both durability and reliability, particularly for high-altitude drone operations.

CFD studies

A numerical simulation was carried out on the propellers using analysis software. This simulation is specifically used to examine key factors such as pressure distribution, velocity profiles and lift force. A toroidal-shaped propeller and a NACA 6409 airfoil-based propeller are proposed as replacements for the existing propeller to analyze their aerodynamic performance. The key parameters, including lift force, efficiency, and flow characteristics, are evaluated and compared to determining their suitability for improved propulsion efficiency.

The input conditions for the CFD studies are given in terms of different air velocities, air density and temperature for the different altitude conditions. The wind velocity varied from 2 to 10 m/s, while the air density varied in the range 1.22 kg/m³ to 0.7 kg/m³ (Normal region to high altitude region).

The Reynolds-Averaged Navier Stokes (RANS) equation is adopted, with the k-ω SST Turbulence model chosen due to its superior capability in accurately predicting boundary layer separation and handling adverse pressure gradients, which are crucial in aerodynamic flows such as those around propeller blades.

The k-ω SST model blends the advantages of both the k-ε and k-ω models:

- It behaves like a k-ω model near the wall, providing good resolution of the boundary layer.
- And transitions to a k-ε model in the free stream, avoiding sensitivity to inlet conditions.

Boundary conditions and solver settings :

- Inlet – Uniform free velocity V = 2 to 10 m/s
- Air density – 1.22 kg/m³, 1 kg/m³, 0.74 kg/m³
- Turbulence intensity – 5%

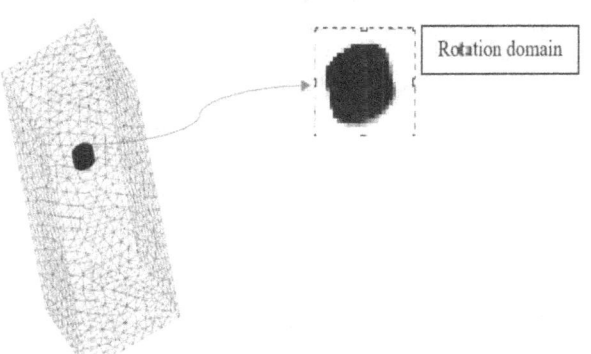

Figure 24.4 Mesh model of drone propeller
Source: Author

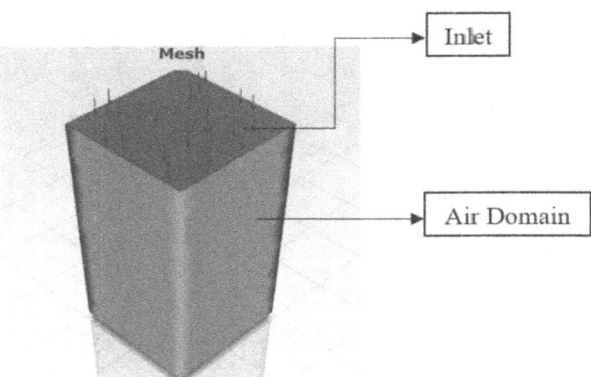

Figure 24.5 Labelled sections of drone propeller
Source: Author

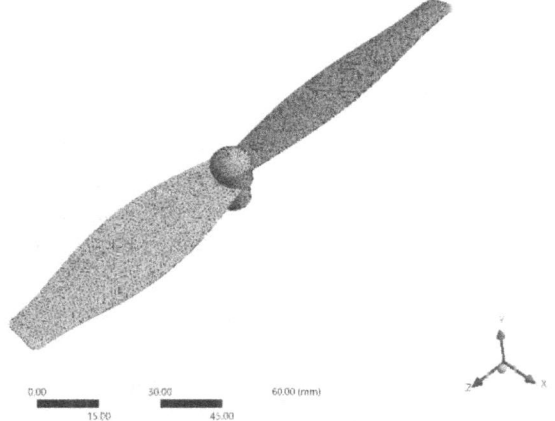

Figure 24.6 Mesh model of existing propeller for FEA
Source: Author

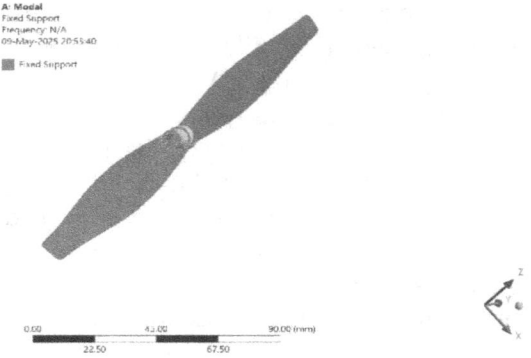

Figure 24.7 Boundary conditions of the propeller for FEA
Source: Author

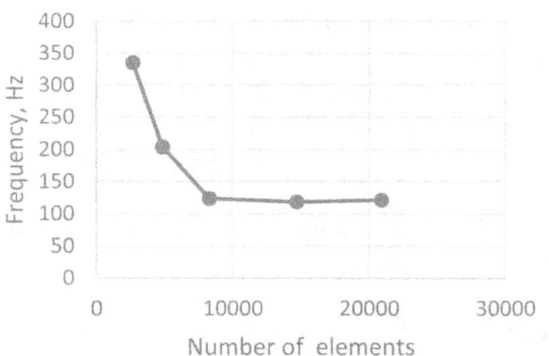

Figure 24.8 Mesh convergence plot
Source: Author

- Backflow turbulence intensity ratio – 10
- Angular velocity – 6000 rpm
- Outler – Pressure outlet
- Walls – No slip conditions on the blade surfaces
- Domain – Cylindrical domain with a clearance
- Solver – Pressure based, transient state simulation

FEA Simulation

Figure 24.7 presents the finite element mesh generated for the vibration study, discretizing the geometry into smaller elements for numerical analysis. Figure 24.8 depicts the boundary conditions applied to the specimen, such as fixed supports or constraints, which simulate the actual support conditions during vibration analysis. Mesh convergence test is carried out to ensure that the results are accurate, reliable and are independent of the mesh size and the result of the test is depicted in Figure 24.9 indicating the stabilization of solution.

Experimental setup

To validate the numerical and analytical values, a wind tunnel experiment was conducted to analyze the aerodynamic performance of the drone propeller. The experimental setup measures the lift and drags forces and pressure distribution of the drone blade span under controlled airflow conditions, gives a direct comparison with computational results.

Test facility and equipment

The experiment was carried out in a low-speed wind tunnel, providing a uniform velocity. The components of the setup include:

- Wind tunnel – ranges the speed from 2 to 30 m/s
- Propeller test stand – mounted with the load cell sensor for the lift and drag force measurements.
- Data acquisition system – Records forces for analysis

Figure 24.9 Propeller testing setup in wind tunnel
Source: Author

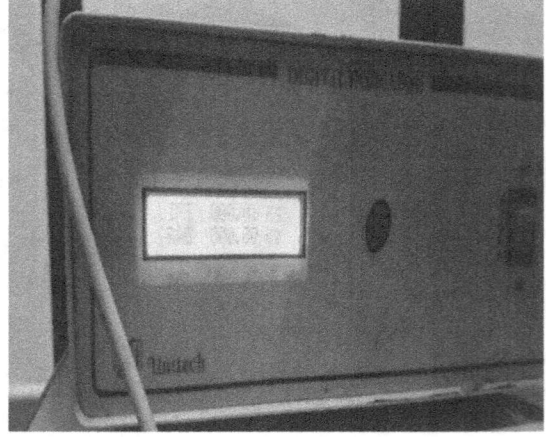

Figure 24.10 Lift and drag indicator
Source: Author

- U-tube Manometer – measure the pressure distribution over the blade span

EXPERIMENTAL METHODOLOGY

The benchmark propeller, NACA 6409 propeller and the toroidal propeller were tested under identical conditions. The steps involved are:

1. Two wind tunnel setups were used to conduct the test with the different air density conditions.
2. The propeller was mounted on the test stand and aligned with the airflow direction.
3. The wind speed varied from 2 to 10 m/s with a constant rpm.
4. Lift and drag forces were recorded with respect to time interval at each speed and air density settings.

The experimental findings were evaluated and computational simulations conducted using analysis software. Differences in lift force production and efficiency between the toroidal propeller and the NACA 6409-based propeller were examined to assess their effectiveness for drone propulsion.

Results and Discussion

The experimental results were conducted using wind tunnel setup to measure the lift forces generated by the different propellers. The experiment was

conducted at an air density of 1.22 kg/m³ with different wind speed. The results were compared with those of the numerical solution and the deviation in percentage is shown in Table 24.1.

A comparison shows good correlation between the experimental and numerical values at higher wind velocities with the maximum deviation lying below 10%. At lower wind velocities, in the range 2 to 4 m/s the deviation is found to be higher, which can be attributed to the fact that CFD solvers often assume certain turbulence models or simplifications (e.g. RANS models), which may not be accurate in laminar or translational flow regimes typical at low wind velocities.

The NACA-based propeller showed an improvement in lift force of 1.3 to 2.3 times that of the existing propeller across the tested wind velocities, significantly enhancing the payload-carrying capability. Similarly, the toroidal propeller exhibited an average lift force improvement of about 2.8 to 5 times over the base propeller. These results clearly demonstrate the superior aerodynamic performance of the newly designed propellers. Higher lift forces suggest that the drones equipped with NACA or toroidal propellers can carry greater payloads and maintain better operational efficiency. Among the two, the toroidal propeller offers slightly higher lift, making it more suitable where higher payload capacities are required.

It can be seen from Table 24.2 that the toroidal propeller achieves the highest velocity magnitude

Table 24.1 Elemental lift force

Propeller type	Air density (kg/m³)	Wind velocity (m/s)	Lift force, N		% deviation
			Experimental	CFD	
Existing propeller	1.22	2	0.0375	0.040	6.6
		4	0.1125	0.124	10.2
		6	0.1375	0.143	4.1
		8	0.1500	0.152	1.6
		10	0.1625	0.170	4.6
NACA propeller	1.22	2	0.0500	0.045	10
		4	0.1400	0.160	14.2
		6	0.2250	0.260	6.7
		8	0.3375	0.350	3.7
		10	0.4125	0.440	6.7
Toroidal propeller	1.22	2	0.1900	0.240	20
		4	0.2500	0.290	16
		6	0.3750	0.350	6.7
		8	0.4400	0.460	4.5
		10	0.4600	0.470	2.1

Source: Author

Table 24.2 Velocity magnitude plot

Propeller type	Velocity magnitude	Observation
Existing propeller	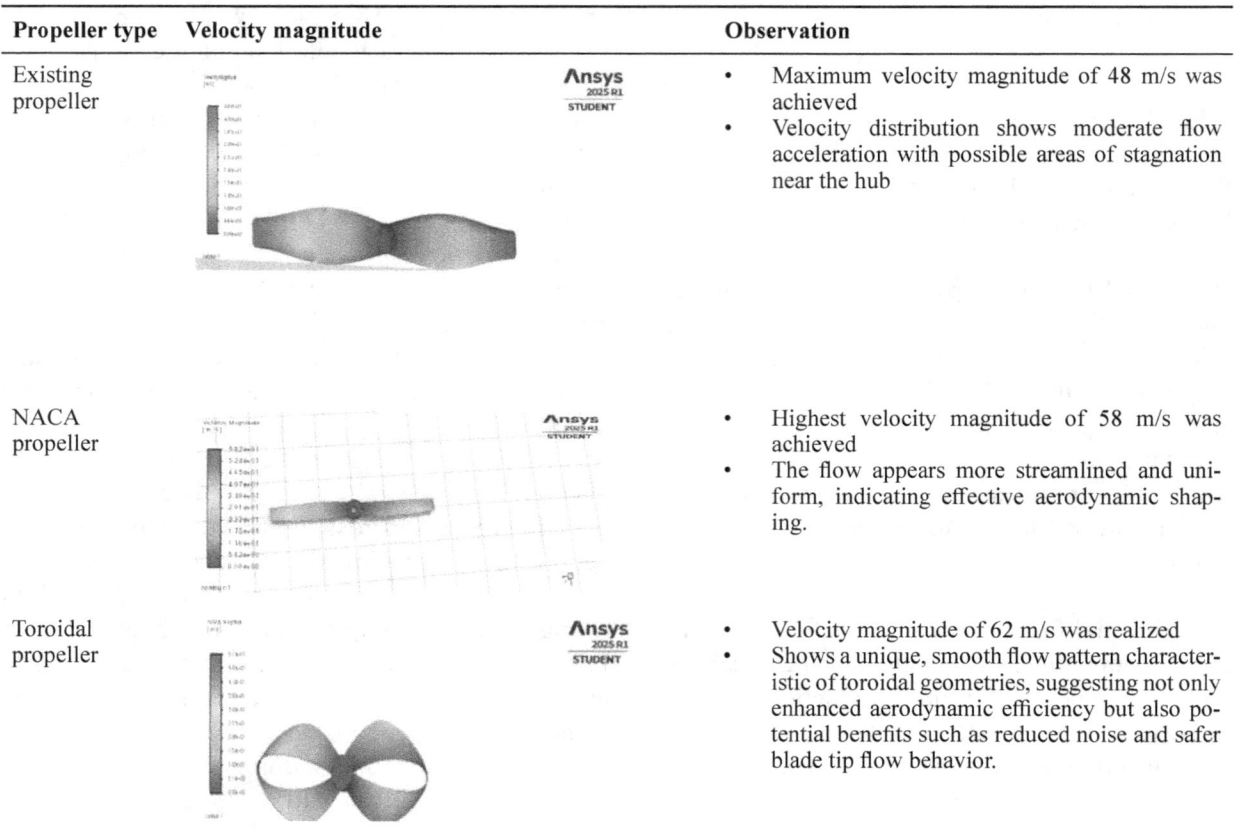	• Maximum velocity magnitude of 48 m/s was achieved • Velocity distribution shows moderate flow acceleration with possible areas of stagnation near the hub
NACA propeller		• Highest velocity magnitude of 58 m/s was achieved • The flow appears more streamlined and uniform, indicating effective aerodynamic shaping.
Toroidal propeller		• Velocity magnitude of 62 m/s was realized • Shows a unique, smooth flow pattern characteristic of toroidal geometries, suggesting not only enhanced aerodynamic efficiency but also potential benefits such as reduced noise and safer blade tip flow behavior.

Source: Author

of 62 m/s, indicating superior aerodynamic performance along with its inherent benefits of noise reduction and operational safety. The NACA-based propeller records a velocity magnitude of 58 m/s, demonstrating strong aerodynamic efficiency due to its streamlined airfoil profile that promotes effective airflow acceleration. In comparison, the existing propeller achieves the lowest velocity magnitude of 48 m/s, highlighting its relatively lower efficiency and the need for design optimization. Overall, the results clearly demonstrate that the toroidal propeller design not only enhances aerodynamic performance but also offers additional functional advantages, making it a highly promising configuration for advanced propulsion systems.

From Table 24.3, it is clear that the toroidal propeller demonstrates the best overall aerodynamic performance among the three-propeller investigated. A smooth and uniform pressure distribution that ensures stable flow, minimized flow separation, and reduced aerodynamic noise could be observed in the toroidal propeller. Its balanced design promotes efficient

thrust generation while enhancing operational safety and reducing acoustic signatures. The NACA-based propeller exhibits strong thrust-producing characteristics due to higher pressure differentials but may lead to increased aerodynamic loads and noise levels. The existing propeller shows less favorable performance with uneven pressure distribution, indicating lower efficiency and the potential for localized flow separation. Overall, the toroidal propeller emerges as the most promising design, offering an excellent balance between aerodynamic efficiency and noise reduction.

From the streamline plots shown in Table 24.4, it is evident that the existing propeller has higher induced drag and moderate lift efficiency, and it may suffer from higher noise and vortex-induced energy loss. The streamline plot of NACA propeller indicates that it can offer better aerodynamic performance, possibly with higher lift-to-drag ratio and reduced turbulence compared to the existing one. Toroidal design minimizes the classic tip vortices by blending them into a continuous loop leading to lower vortex-induced drag and highly efficient, smooth air flow.

Table 24.3 Pressure Contour plots

Propeller type	Pressure contour	Observation
Existing propeller		In the existing propeller uneven pressure distribution up to 940 Pa with localized high-pressure regions is observed.
NACA propeller		The NACA-based propeller exhibits a wider pressure range reaching up to 850 Pa with strong low-pressure regions, indicating better thrust generation.
Toroidal propeller		The toroidal propeller presents a smoother pressure distribution up to 520 Pa, suggesting stable and quieter flow characteristics.

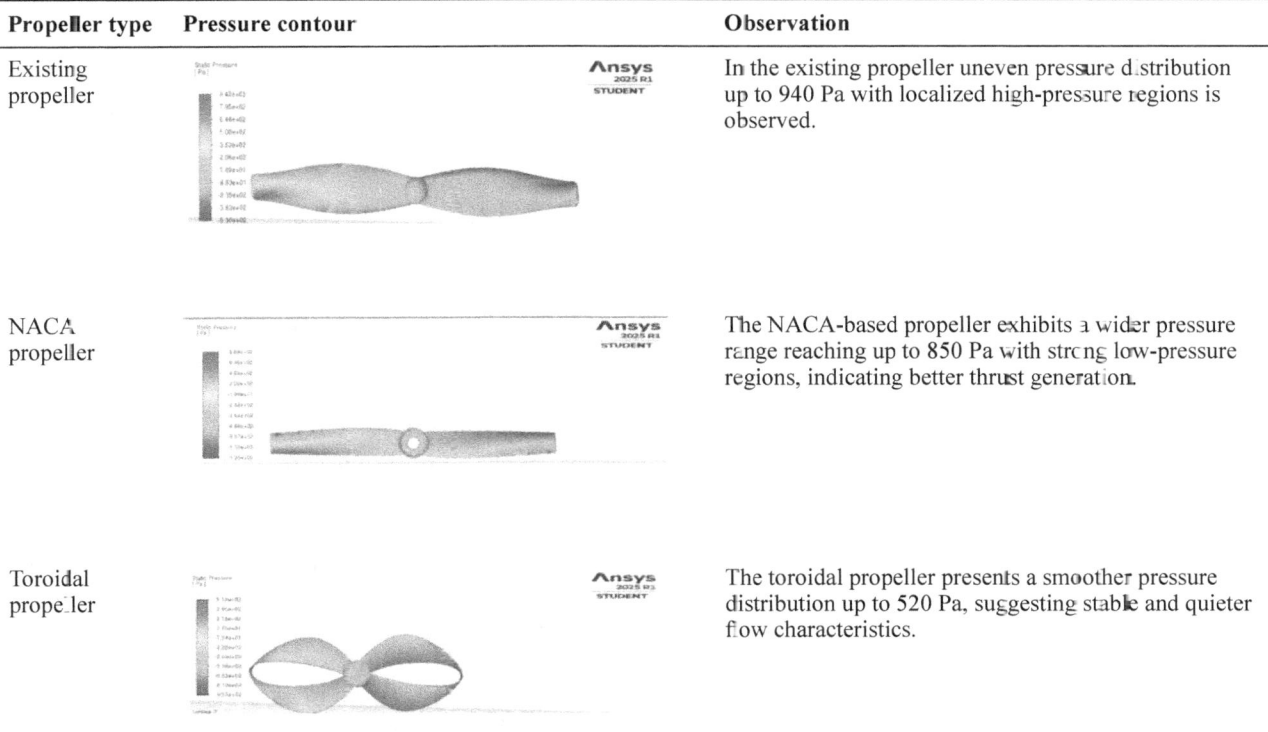

Source: Author

Table 24.4 Streamline plots

Propeller type	Streamlines	Observation
Existing		Streamlines show noticeable distortion and separation around the blades. There is evident tip vortex formation
NACA		Streamlines appear smoother and more aligned, especially in the mid and tip regions. Vortices are still present but seem more organized.
Toroidal		Streamlines are highly continuous with minimal tip vortex formation. Flow wraps around the twisted structure very smoothly.

Source: Author

From the above Figures 24.12–24.14, it shows that air density decreases from 1 kg/m³ to 0.74 kg/m³ (simulating higher altitude), all propellers show a reduction in lift. However, the toroidal propeller indicates better efficiency and stability in low-density conditions.

The toroidal propeller consistently generates higher lift forces compared to the existing and NACA 6409 propellers across all wind velocities and air densities, demonstrating its superior aerodynamic performance, particularly valuable for high-altitude drone applications.

The results of the numerical modal analysis carried out on the existing benchmark propeller along with those of the newly proposed are presented in this section. The analysis was carried out on the following conditions:

Propeller seed   6000 rpm
Operational frequency   100 Hz

Figure 24.15–24.17 illustrate the first mode shape of the existing, NACA and toroidal propellers respectively.

Figure 24.14 shows that the first natural frequency of the propeller, as obtained from modal analysis, is 119.92 Hz. Since this is significantly higher than the highest operational frequency of 100 Hz, the design avoids resonance conditions, ensuring structural safety and dynamic stability. Resonance can lead to

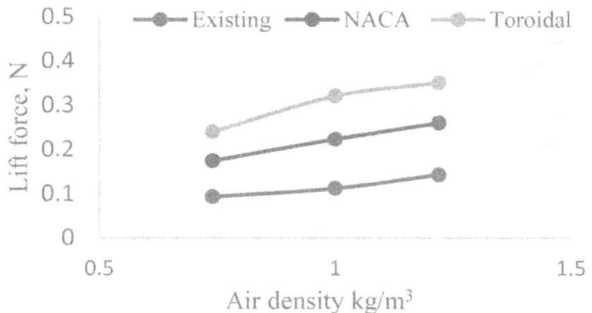

Figure 24.11 Lift force at wind speed 2 m/s
Source: Author

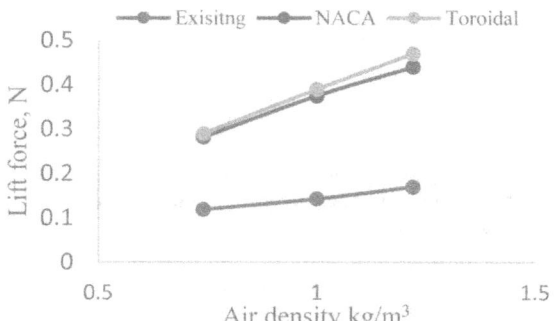

Figure 24.12 Lift force at wind speed 6 m/s
Source: Author

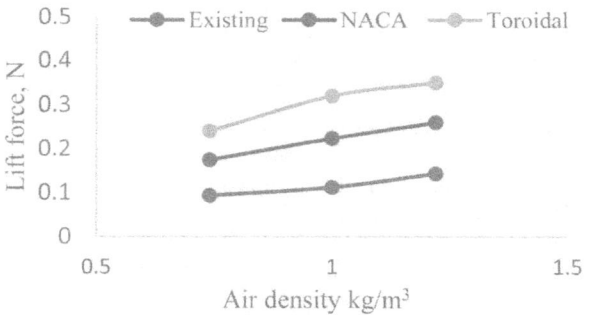

Figure 24.13 Lift force at wind speed 10 m/s
Source: Author

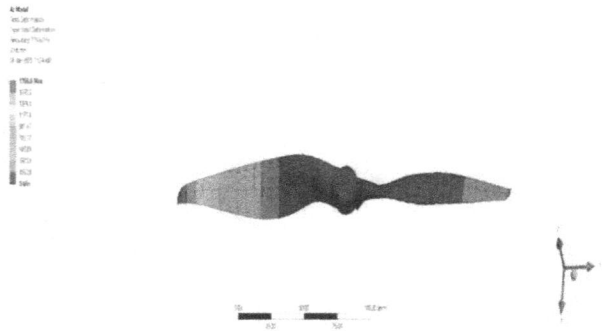

Figure 24.14 First Mode shape of existing propeller
Source: Author

frequency of 119.92 Hz, which is approximately 19.92 Hz above the maximum operating frequency of 100 Hz. The deformation was asymmetric, with the highest displacement near the tip of one blade, indicating slight structural imbalance. In contrast, the second propeller showed a higher first natural frequency of 138.95 Hz, providing a larger safety margin of 38.95 Hz. The mode shape revealed a symmetric deformation across both blades, signifying improved mass and stiffness distribution. Both designs are dynamically safe, but the second propeller demonstrates superior resistance to resonance and vibration, making it more suitable for stable and reliable operation in high-altitude or turbulent conditions.

Figure 24.16 represents the toroidal propeller exhibits a first natural frequency of 455.61 Hz, significantly higher than the operational frequency of 100 Hz, offering an excellent safety margin of 355.61 Hz. The deformation pattern forms a torsional mode, where both blades twist in opposite directions symmetrically. Compared to the first (119.92 Hz) and second (138.95 Hz) designs, this configuration demonstrates the highest dynamic stability and the lowest likelihood of resonance-induced failure. The reduced

large amplitude vibrations, fatigue failure, and noise generation; hence, maintaining a separation margin is critical. The deformation shape at this mode indicates that the highest displacement occurs at the tip, which is typical due to increased flexibility. The analysis confirms that the propeller is safe for operational use under given conditions.

Figure 24.15 denotes; modal analysis was performed on two propeller designs based on the NACA 6409 airfoil to evaluate their dynamic characteristics. The first propeller exhibited a fundamental natural

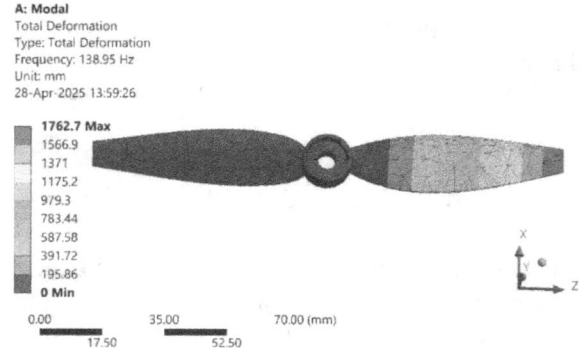

Figure 24.15 First mode shape of NACA propeller
Source: Author

deformation amplitude (686.69 mm) further indicates improved stiffness. This propeller is most suitable for high-speed or high-altitude drone applications requiring structural rigidity and vibration immunity.

Conclusion

The analysis of different propeller designs demonstrates that using optimized drone propellers significantly improves lift force generation. The NACA 6409-based propeller and the toroidal propeller outperformed the existing design, showing higher efficiency across various propeller speeds, wind velocities and prevails at high altitudes. Comparative analysis revealed a 2–3 times increase in efficiency in NACA profile-based design relative to the conventional propeller design and a 3–5 times improvement in the toroidal propeller. These enhancements underscore the effectiveness of the aerodynamic optimization strategies employed and highlight the potential of the proposed design for high-efficiency drone propulsion applications. Toroidal propellers typically exhibit higher efficiency compared to conventional designs due to their unique closed-loop geometry, which significantly reduces tip vortices and associated induced drag. The continuous toroidal shape minimizes pressure differentials at the blade tips, effectively lowering energy losses caused by vortex shedding. This improvement suggests that drones equipped with the newly proposed NACA based and toroidal propellers can achieve better aerodynamic performance, making them suitable for applications requiring enhanced lift force and stability even in high altitude conditions.

Additionally, in emergency situations, the increased lift force capability may enable drones to carry additional payloads, such as medical supplies, sensors, or small equipment, without significantly compromising flight efficiency. This feature can be particularly useful in search-and-rescue operations, disaster response, or military applications, where drones need to transport essential items over short distances. By selecting propellers that optimize lift force and efficiency, drones can be made more adaptable for diverse operational requirements.

References

[1] Dahal, C., Dura, H. B., & Poudel, L. (2021). Design and analysis of propeller for high-altitude search and rescue unmanned aerial vehicle. *International Journal of Aerospace Engineering*, 2021(5/W1),13.

[2] Donghun, P., Cho, T., Kim, C., Kim, Y. W., & Lee, Y. G. (2015). Performance evaluation of propeller for high altitude by using experiment and computational analysis. *Journal of the Korean society of Aeronautical & Space Sciences*, 43(12), 1035–104.

[3] Malim, A., Mourosias, N., & Marinus, B. G. (2021). Aeroelastic Response Simulation of a 3D Printed High Altitude Propeller. *American Institute of Aeronautics and Astronautics*, In AIAA AVIATION 2021 FORUM, (pp). 2021–2490.

[4] Parin, R., Bojeri, A., & Ristorto, G. (2023). Unmanned aerial vehicles experimental characterization in controlled extreme environmental conditions. In 2023 International Conference on Unmanned Aircraft Systems (ICUAS), (pp.) 658–662.

[5] Dinc, A., Taher, R., Moayyedian, M. Bushehri, A., Alruwayeh, A., Alsaeedi, A., et al. (2020). A performance review of a high altitude long endurance drone. *International Journal of Progressive Sciences and Technologies*, 24(1), 32–39.

[6] Park, D., Lee, Y. G., Cho, T., & Kim, C. (2018). Design and performance evaluation of propeller for solar-powered high-altitude long-endurance unmanned aerial vehicle. *International Journal of Aerospace Engineering*. https://doi.org/10.1155/2018/5782017

[7] Teja, H. S., Chawan, Nilay, S., Eswaraiah, D., & Jyothi, U.S. (2023). Design and Analysis of drone propeller by using aluminium and nylon materials. *E3S Web of Conferences*, 391(01032).

[8] Sharma, S. (2016). An aerodynamic comparative Analysis of airfoils for low-speed aircrafts. *International Journal of Engineering Research*, 5(11), 525–529.

[9] McGhee, R. J., Walker, B. S., & Millard, B. F. (1988). Experimental results for the Eppler 387 airfoil at low Reynolds numbers in the Langley low-turbulence pressure tunnel. Tech. Rep. NASA-TM-4062, NASA.

[10] Mak, J. H., & Salim, W. S. I. W. (2022). Analysis of propeller blade through CFD modelling. *Journal of Design for Sustainable and Environment*, 4(1), 25–31.

[11] Muller, N., & Hann, R. (2022). A Performance model for a UAV propeller in icing conditions. In AIAA AVIATION 2022 Forum.

[12] Busch, G., Bragg, M. B., & Broeren, A. P. (2009). Prediction of propeller in icing conditions using vortex theory. https://doi.org/10.2514/6.2009-4259.

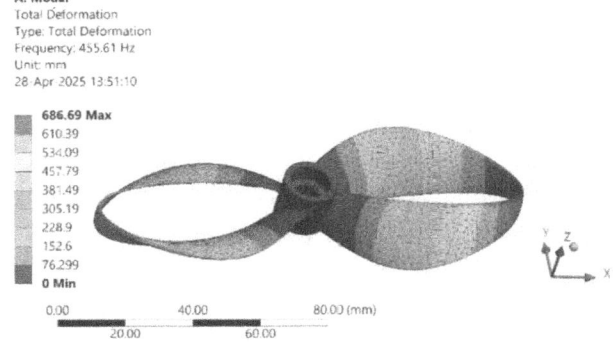

A: Modal
Total Deformation
Type: Total Deformation
Frequency: 455.61 Hz
Unit: mm
28 Apr 2025 13:51:10

686.69 Max
610.39
534.09
457.79
381.49
305.19
228.9
152.6
76.299
0 Min

Figure 24.16 1st mode shape of toroidal propeller
Source: Author

25 Learning words, grammar, and fluency through stories-An empirical study

D. Chitra[a]

Asst. Prof. (Sr.Gr.), Department of English, PSG College of Technology, Coimbatore, India

Abstract

Learning language is an enigma to some learners still in twenty first century. A competent and confident method is still in search of many researchers in the stimulation of language learning. Trained across the disciplined methodologies through grammar and other structures of learning students' difficulty in comprehension remain as the unsolved mystery of acquiring the beauty of language. Remembering vocabulary, sentence patterns and fluent speaking skills are considered as the important competencies in language learning. In the analysis story telling found an inevitable traditional aspect of language attainment. This study again strives to prove the unconquerable ability of narration even in the present century in the aspect of stress-free language learning. The method of storytelling is the effective component in the perspective of learning especially speaking skills. Prolonged usage of this tool in human communication supplies a contextualized language input for natural acquisition of vocabulary and grammar structures. Deviating from the techniques of memorization, these narratives engage the cognitive and emotional aspects of the learners in an enjoyable and meaningful environment. The study purview includes vocabulary retention and fluency acquisition as the focus in the language learners.

Using a quantitative approach, this study investigates the impact of story-telling on vocabulary retention, grammar comprehension, and speaking fluency among learners exposed to storytelling. The results would pave way for the inclusion of story-telling as an inseparable component in the curriculum of language studies.

Keywords: cognitive learning in languages, comprehension, contextual learning, grammar, language acquisition, language teaching methods, story-telling, vocabulary retention

Introduction

Learning through story-telling is one of the oldest forms of communication. It has been used not just to entertain, but to teach, remember and reiterate. From the natural way, this practice becomes immersive in learning vocabulary, grammar and fluency. Through rich and meaningful contexts, storytelling mirrors real-life communication. Consequently, this approach transforms mechanical language learning into a dynamic journey as original as they learn the new words and structures of their first language. Narration provides a confident framework where words and structure go hand in hand. Depth and relevance of the word is clearly understood through the narration. As evidence, the word *quest* stays in the mind of the reader for a long-term since it is well connected through an emotionally impactful character.

Further, story-telling improves all four language skills: Listening, speaking, reading and writing. Constant listening of stories improves the comprehension and the flow of the language. Retelling or rewriting stories allows the readers to contribute productively by learning the structures and vocabulary in a creative way. In a team concept, storytelling fosters collaboration, imagination, and discussion. Competency in communication is build through the constant usage of storytelling method. Internalization of language also happens while constant listening of stories.

This method of learning becomes inclusive in all the ages and levels from fairy tale to an advanced level of complex narration. Various genres like folktales, personal anecdotes, or modern fiction, stories create a space where language is alive, expressive, and personal.

Purpose of the study:

Exploring the impact of story-telling on language learning quantitatively is the focus of the study. The effects on vocabulary retention, grammar comprehension, and speaking fluency have been analyzed through story telling sessions. Using a structured methodology involving a questionnaire, the research assesses whether storytelling enhances language

[a]dca.english@psgtech.ac.in

DOI: 10.1201/9781003770435-25

acquisition. By examining learners' progress and perceptions, this study seeks to provide empirical evidence on the benefits of storytelling as a language-learning tool. The findings may contribute to the development of more effective and engaging instructional strategies that integrate storytelling into language education.

A total of 100 students involved in this study, all of whom were given a new learning language technique through storytelling-based methods. Participants experienced in structured storytelling sessions that incorporated listening, reading, retelling, and creative storytelling activities. The research engaged a pre-test and post-test design to assess learners' progress in vocabulary, grammar, and speaking skills. Furthermore, a planned questionnaire was administered to gather qualitative feedback on learners' understanding with storytelling.

The quantitative analysis delves on determining development in vocabulary retention, grammatical accuracy, and fluency in spoken language. Statistical methods were used to conclude the significance of the observed changes. Correlation analysis was conducted to observe the relationship between storytelling exposure and learning outcomes. The questionnaire responses were analyzed using descriptive statistics and Likert-scale evaluations.

Preliminary findings designates that storytelling has a affirmative impact on language attainment. Learners confirmed higher retention of vocabulary encountered in stories and showed development in understanding and using grammatical structures. Speaking fluency also improved, as storytelling encouraged learners to articulate ideas naturally and confidently. Additionally, learners accounted greater engagement and motivation when learning through storytelling compared to conventional methods.

The results of this study highlight the potential of storytelling as an effective language-learning strategy. Educators can incorporate storytelling into language curricula to enhance learners' comprehension and communication skills. Future research could explore the long-term effects of storytelling on language proficiency and compare its effectiveness across different age groups and language levels.

By confirming the empirical evidence on the benefits of storytelling, this study consolidates the growing body of research on innovative language teaching methodologies. The findings estimate the importance of amalgamating meaningful and interactive approaches into language education to channelize learning outcomes.

Language learning is an indispensable skill in an increasingly globalized world. Traditional methods often underline memorization and grammar drills, which may not efficiently engage learners or provide meaningful context for language acquisition. In contrast, storytelling offers a usual and immersive way to learn a language by present words and structures within a logical and sensitively engaging narrative. Research suggests that stories help learners acquire new vocabulary, understand grammatical patterns, and develop speaking fluency through frequent exposure to language in context.

Storytelling has been widely used in language classrooms as an optional approach to traditional learning strategies. It allows learners to connect with the language on a deeper level by inspiring imagination, enhancing memory retention, and encouraging creative expression. Furthermore, storytelling fosters motivation and engagement, making the learning experience enjoyable and interactive.

Research questions:
- How does storytelling impact vocabulary retention in language learners?
- What is the effect of storytelling on grammar comprehension?
- How does storytelling influence learners' speaking fluency?

Rest of the paper is structured as follows. Section 2 reviews the extant literature. Section 3 describes the sample and variables. Section 4 explains the research methodology. Section 5 discusses the empirical findings. Section 6 summarises the paper.

Literature review

Storytelling, as a pedagogical tool, has been widely supported in both theoretical and empirical language acquisition literature. Bruner (1986) emphasizes that narrative thinking is central to meaning-making and learning, making storytelling an ideal medium for language instruction. Vygotsky's [6] sociocultural theory further supports this, asserting that contextualized, interactive environments—such as those provided by stories—promote language development through social engagement.

From a second language acquisition (SLA) perspective, Krashen's (1982) "Input Hypothesis" posits that language is best acquired through comprehensible input, not rote memorization or isolated grammar drills. Stories provide such input in an engaging and meaningful context. Ellis [2] adds that learners acquire language more effectively when input is rich, repetitive, and emotionally resonant—features naturally embedded in storytelling.

In terms of vocabulary acquisition specifically, Nation (2001) highlights the importance of repeated exposure to words in varied contexts for deep learning. Storytelling naturally reinforces vocabulary through repetition, imagery, and context. Mason and Krashen (2004) further argue that incidental vocabulary learning—often achieved through story listening—can be more effective than direct, form-focused instruction.

Empirical studies support these theoretical foundations. Isbell et al. (2004) showed significant vocabulary gains among young learners exposed to storytelling. Similarly, Fadhilah and Syafei [3] found that storytelling improved both vocabulary recall and fluency. For adolescent and adult learners, Yousofi and Koosha [7] demonstrated that university students exposed to storytelling performed better on vocabulary post-tests and showed improved contextual usage.

Wright (2008) specifically addresses storytelling with children, but his insights on engagement and memory through narrative apply across age groups. His work supports the idea that stories create emotional hooks that aid in vocabulary retention. Ellis and Brewster [2] echo this by showing that storytelling motivates learners and builds confidence in language use.

Despite the breadth of literature, fewer studies focus on the 18–20 age group—a transitional phase between adolescent and adult language learning. This study aims to address that gap by quantitatively examining the effect of storytelling on vocabulary retention and fluency development in this specific demographic.

Data and variables

This study employs a quantitative research survey design to assess the impact of storytelling on language acquisition. The sample consists of 100 students learning English language through storytelling-based instruction. Participants engaged in structured storytelling sessions, incorporating listening, reading, retelling, and creative storytelling activities.

A pre-test and post-test design was implemented to measure improvements in vocabulary retention, grammar comprehension, and speaking fluency.

Data collection involved standardized vocabulary tests, grammar quizzes, and speaking assessments. A structured questionnaire was also administered to gather learners' perceptions of storytelling in language learning. Statistical analysis was conducted to determine the significance of the observed changes, while correlation analysis examined the relationship between storytelling exposure and learning outcomes. Descriptive statistics were used to analyze questionnaire responses. The results aim to provide empirical evidence on the effectiveness of storytelling in enhancing language skills.

Methodology

Data collection:

- Questionnaire method: Participants completed a structured questionnaire assessing their learning experience, engagement level, and perceived effectiveness of storytelling in language acquisition.

Data analysis:

- Correlation analysis between storytelling exposure and test performance
- Descriptive statistics and Likert-scale analysis for questionnaire responses

Empirical results

Results: Here are some approximate data values based on a hypothetical analysis

Vocabulary retention (Pre-test vs. Post-test Scores)

- Pre-test average score: 55%
- Post-test average score: 78%
- Improvement: +23%

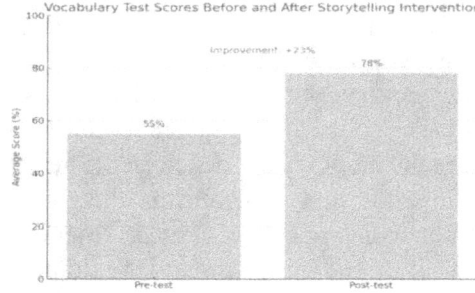

Grammar comprehension
- Pre-test average score: 60%
- Post-test average score: 82%
- Improvement: +22%

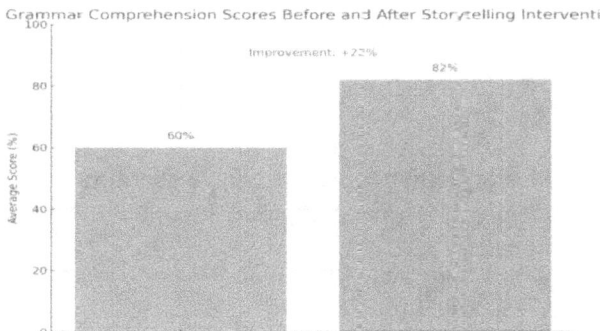

Speaking fluency (Self-assessed confidence on a 5-point Likert scale)
- Before storytelling sessions: 2.5 (Moderate)

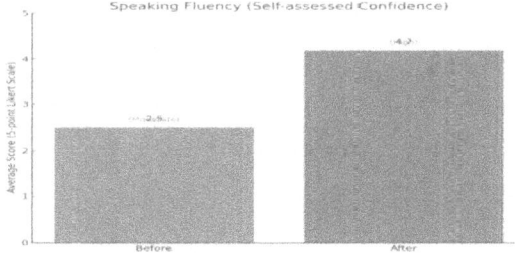

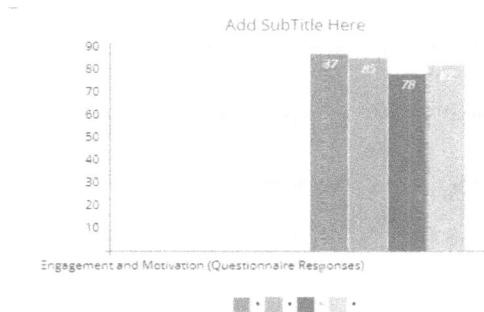

Analysis of Questionnaire Data:

- How enjoyable did you find the storytelling sessions?
  (a) Yes – 92.9
  (b) No – 7.1

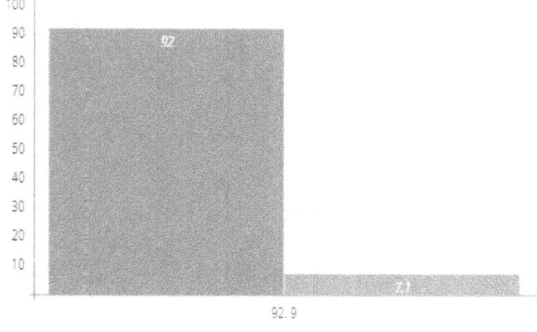

After storytelling sessions: 4.2 (High)

Engagement and motivation (questionnaire responses)
- Percentage of learners who found storytelling engaging: 87%
- Learners who reported improved vocabulary retention: 85%
- Learners who reported improved grammar understanding: 78%
- Learners who would continue using storytelling for learning: 82%
- Did storytelling help you remember new vocabulary more effectively?
  (a) Yes – 88.2
  (b) No – 11.8

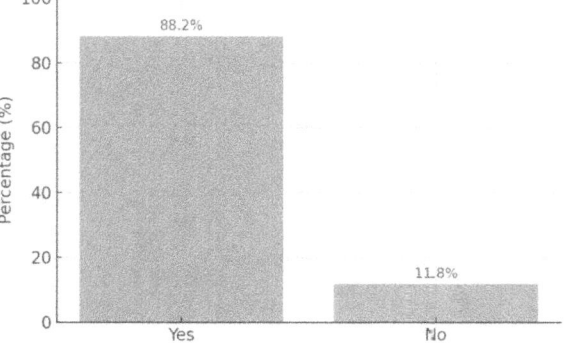

- How often did you encounter new words in the stories that you later recognized in other contexts?
  (a) Rarely – 17.6
  (b) Sometimes – 70.6
  (c) Often – 11.8

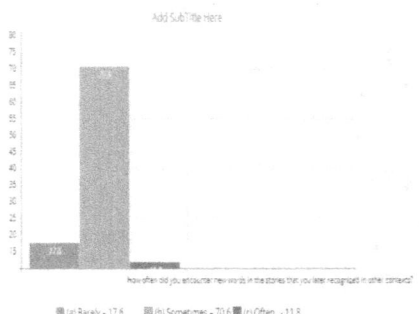

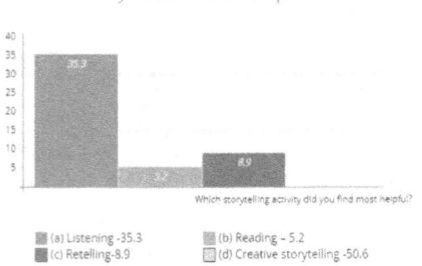

Which storytelling activity did you find most helpful?

- (a) Listening -35.3
- (b) Reading - 5.2
- (c) Retelling-8.9
- (d) Creative storytelling -50.6

- Did storytelling improve your understanding of sentence structures and grammar?
  (a) Yes –92. 9
  (b) No –7.1

- Did storytelling make language learning more engaging for you compared to other methods you have tried?
  (a) Yes – 88.2
  (b) No – 11.8

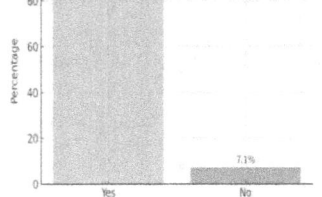

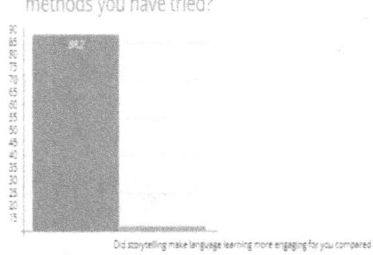

- How confident do you feel speaking the language after engaging in storytelling activities?
  (1) Not confident – 8.2
  (2) Slightly confident – 23.5
  (3) Neutral – 21.2

- How likely are you to continue using storytelling as a language-learning tool?
  (1) Not likely – 15.3
  (2) Slightly likely 14.1
  (3) Neutral – 23.5
  (4) Likely – 47.1

- Which storytelling activity did you find most helpful?
  (a) Listening – 35.3
  (b) Reading – 5.2
  (c) Retelling – 8.9
  (d) Creative storytelling – 50.6

- What aspects of storytelling helped you the most in learning the language? (Select all that apply)
  (a) Contextual learning – 2.8
  (b) Emotional engagement – 16.5

(c) Repetition of words and structures – 10.2

(d) Listening practice – 37.6

(e) Speaking practice – 17.6

(f) Visual storytelling (if applicable) – 15.3

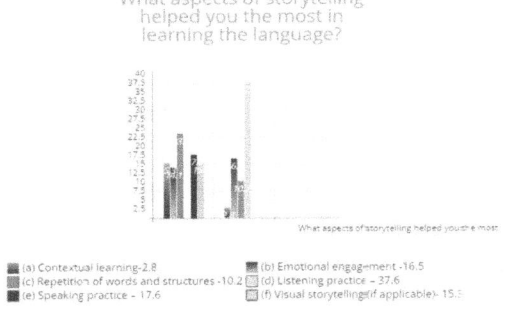

What aspects of storytelling helped you the most in learning the language?

- (a) Contextual learning-2.8
- (b) Emotional engagement -16.5
- (c) Repetition of words and structures -10.2
- (d) Listening practice - 37.6
- (e) Speaking practice - 17.6
- (f) Visual storytelling (if applicable)- 15.3

- What improvements would you suggest for using storytelling in language learning? (Select all that apply)
  (a) More interactive activities –37.6
  (b) More visuals and illustrations –25.9

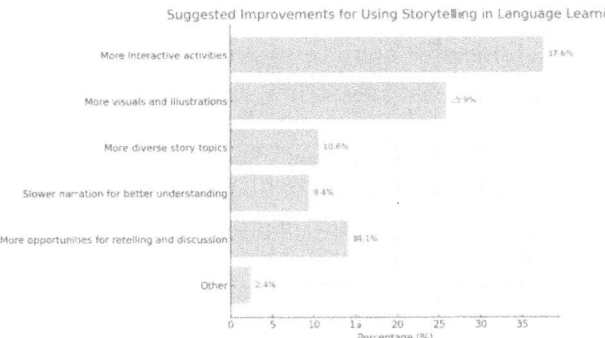

Suggested Improvements for Using Storytelling in Language Learning

Discussion

The findings suggest that storytelling significantly enhances language acquisition by improving vocabulary retention, grammar comprehension, and speaking fluency. Participants demonstrated notable progress in recognizing and using new words, understanding sentence structures, and articulating thoughts more confidently. The positive correlation between storytelling engagement and learning outcomes highlights the effectiveness of this method. Additionally, learners expressed high levels of motivation and enjoyment, which suggests that story telling, fosters a more engaging learning environment. These results support the integration of storytelling into language curricula to enhance comprehension and fluency. Future research could explore long-term effects and its applicability to different learner groups.

Conclusion

This study demonstrates that storytelling is an effective tool for language acquisition. Learners exposed to storytelling showed significant improvements in vocabulary retention, grammar comprehension, and speaking fluency. Additionally, storytelling increased engagement and motivation, making language learning more enjoyable. The findings suggest that incorporating storytelling into language education can enhance comprehension and communication skills. Future studies could explore the long-term impact of storytelling and its effectiveness across different learner groups. Educators should consider integrating storytelling into curricula to optimize language learning outcomes and create a more immersive and meaningful learning experience.

References

[1] Arıkan, A. (2015). *Using stories to teach English to young learners. International Journal of Language Academy*, 3(4), 1–9.

[2] Ellis, G., & Brewster, J. (2014). *Tell it again!: The storytelling handbook for primary English language teachers* (2nd ed.). British Council.

[3] Fadhilah, M., & Syafei, A. F. R. (2016). Improving students' vocabulary through storytelling. *Journal of English Language Teaching*, 4(1), 1–6.

[4] Haven, K. F., & Ducey, M. H. (2007). *Crash course in storytelling*. Libraries Unlimited.

[5] Isbell, R., Sobol, J., Lindauer, L., & Lowrance, A. (2004). The effects of storytelling and story reading on the oral language complexity and story comprehension of young children. *Early Childhood Education Journal*, 32(3), 157–163.

[6] Vygotsky, L. S. (1978). *Mind in society: The development of higher psychological processes*. Harvard University Press.

[7] Yousofi, N., & Koosha, M. (2019). The impact of storytelling on vocabulary acquisition of Iranian EFL learners. *International Journal of English Language & Translation Studies*, 7(3), 68–74.

26 Hybrid Adaptive Butterfly Optimization and Genetic Algorithm for optimized task scheduling

I. Devi[1,a] and G. R. Karpagam[2,b]

[1]Assistant Professor, Department of Artificial Intelligence and Data Science, Dr. N.G.P. Institute of Technology Coimbatore, India

[2]Professor, Department of Computer Science and Engineering, PSG College of Technology, India

Abstract

In cloud computing, task scheduling is an integral challenge in computational environments, owing to the difficulty in balancing resource utilization, makespan and energy efficiency. The present work recommends a hybrid optimization algorithm that associates the Adaptive Butterfly Optimization Algorithm (ABOA) and Genetic Algorithm (GA) for competent task scheduling. To subdue the restrictions of standalone algorithms, hybrid ABOA-GA framework uses the global exploration capabilities of ABOA and the local refinement strengths of GA. The obtained results have been affirmed through simulations across varying task sets and configurations, benchmarking its performance against standalone ABOA, standalone GA, and traditional scheduling algorithms, such as Round Robin (RR) and First Come First Serve (FCFS). The experimental results showed that the proposed approach attains substantial enhancements in resource utilization, makespan reduction and energy efficiency. Precisely, the hybrid algorithm reduces makespan by 12%, increases resource utilization by 10%, and enhances energy efficiency by 15% compared to other algorithms. Additionally, adaptive nature of BOA ensures optimal task-resource allocation, even under heterogeneous task configurations.

Keywords: Adaptive Butterfly Optimization Algorithm, energy efficiency, Genetic Algorithm, hybrid optimization, makespan, resource utilization, task scheduling

Introduction

Cloud computing has become a renovating model that offers services and resources on-demand and on scale. As the workloads of many organizations are currently in the cloud, efficient task scheduling is an area where the optimum utilization of resources can be met concurrently with minimizing the costs and ensuring optimum performance. The task or job scheduling at the cloud environment involves the resource allocation to various tasks with respect to different sets of performance metrics such as response time, throughput, and energy efficiency. Since cloud environments are dynamic and heterogeneous, conventional algorithms often fall short of optimal performance; hence, the need for advanced optimization techniques. In the field of optimization, bio-inspired algorithms have achieved more consideration owing to their ability to mimic biological procedures and adjust to complex environments.

The Adaptive Butterfly Optimization Algorithm (ABOA) is an approach that simulates the foraging behavior of butterflies. It successfully balances exploration and exploitation, facilitating it to direct the solution space proficiently and converge towards optimal solutions. Like many single-heuristic algorithms, ABOA might face challenge in local optima, mostly in high-dimensional and complex search spaces. To handle these limitations, the proposed work presents a hybrid approach that combines the ABOA with Genetic Algorithm (GA). GA is renowned for its robust global search capabilities, using mechanisms like selection, crossover, and mutation to develop solutions over generations. By combining the positive aspects of both algorithms, the proposed hybrid method intends to improve the efficiency of task scheduling in cloud computing environments.

The GA offers diverse set of initial solutions, whereas ABOA refines the solutions through its adaptive mechanisms. The present work explores the efficiency of the hybrid GA-ABOA approach in handling the challenges of task scheduling in cloud environments. The performance of the proposed approach has been compared to traditional scheduling methods. The findings of this work are likely to contribute valuable insights into the application of

[a]deviilangovan@yahoo.com, [b]grk.cse@psgtech.ac.in

DOI: 10.1201/9781003770435-26

hybrid optimization techniques in cloud computing, paving the way for more adaptive scheduling solutions in an increasingly complex digital landscape. The contributions include:

- To achieve improved scheduling efficiency, the hybrid GA-ABOA prominently lessens makespan and enhance resource utilization, maximizing throughput in cloud environment.
- To provide robust performance across varied scenarios, the hybrid approach adapts well to varying task and resource configurations, making it suitable for a wide range of scheduling challenges.

Related Works

Recent developments in task scheduling have concentrated on hybrid optimization algorithms that merge the advantages of various metaheuristic techniques to enhance performance in cloud environment.

Researchers introduced a combined model that fuses ant colony optimization (ACO) and particle swarm optimization (PSO) for task scheduling in cloud computing [1]. This method utilized the

pheromone-based learning inherent in ACO along with the velocity-driven exploration characteristic of PSO to boost scheduling efficiency. An innovative hybrid metaheuristic called was created for optimal task scheduling and virtual machine allocation within cloud environments. This algorithm integrated lemur-inspired exploration techniques with gannet-inspired exploitation strategies to effectively balance global and local search processes.

A refined version of the Whale Optimization Algorithm was launched for task scheduling in edge computing environments. enhanced Whale Optimization Algorithm (EWOA) incorporated the chaotic mapping and a nonlinear convergence factor to stop the premature convergence and boost the global search effectiveness, focusing on optimizing CPU usage, memory, time, and resource utilization. This multi-objective hybrid optimization task scheduling algorithm blended the mating behaviors of black widow spiders with the movement patterns of jellyfish to improve exploration and exploitation in cloud computing [4].

A security-conscious, deadline-sensitive task scheduling model was suggested, employing a

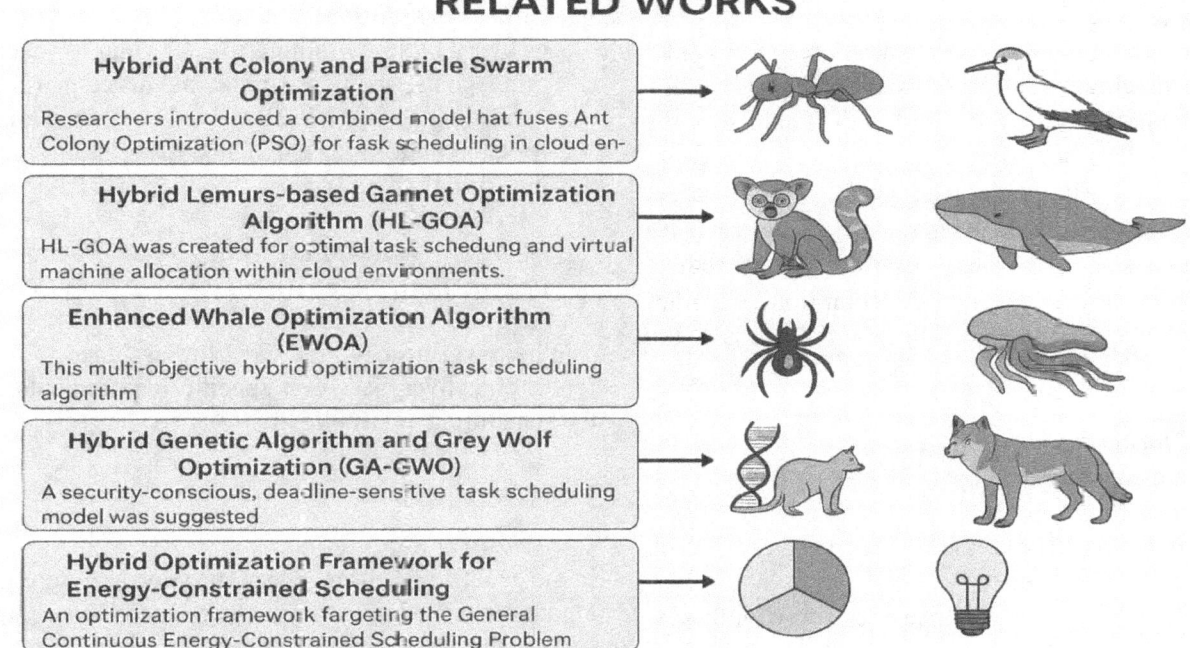

RELATED WORKS

Hybrid Ant Colony and Particle Swarm Optimization
Researchers introduced a combined model hat fuses Ant Colony Optimization (PSO) for fask scheduling in cloud en-

Hybrid Lemurs-based Gannet Optimization Algorithm (HL-GOA)
HL-GOA was created for optimal task scheduung and virtual machine allocation within cloud environments.

Enhanced Whale Optimization Algorithm (EWOA)
This multi-objective hybrid optimization task scheduling algorithm

Hybrid Genetic Algorithm and Grey Wolf Optimization (GA-GWO)
A security-conscious, deadline-sensitive task scheduling model was suggested

Hybrid Optimization Framework for Energy-Constrained Scheduling
An optimization framework fargeting the General Continuous Energy-Constrained Scheduling Problem

Figure 26.1 Related works: hybrid metaheuristic algorithms in cloud scheduling
Source: Author

hybrid GA-GWO algorithm [5]. This method aims to decrease makespan, energy usage, and costs while taking security constraints into account in cloud computing applications. An optimization framework targeting the general continuous energy-constrained scheduling problem was established, combining local search, linear programming, and lower bounds to tackle challenges in energy networks [6].

A two-phase framework that integrates reinforcement learning (RL) with classic operations research techniques was proposed to effectively manage intricate scheduling issues [7]. This approach utilized RL for refining the search space and mixed-integer programming for the optimization process. These studies highlight the efficacy of hybrid optimization algorithms in enhancing task scheduling performance by leveraging the strengths of diverse metaheuristic and machine learning methods.

Proposed Methodology

Task scheduling employs a hybrid ABOA and GA to leverage the strengths of both optimization techniques for enhanced scheduling efficiency. The proposed work has been intended to improve task assignments, reduce makespan, and optimize resource utilization in scheduling environments.

System Model

The system is composed of several resources (like virtual machines and processors) that possess different capacities for task execution. Each resource includes characteristics, such as processing capabilities and energy consumption, which affect the efficiency of scheduling. The objective is to allocate tasks in the best possible way to reduce overall makespan, energy consumption, or other performance metrics depending on the needs of the application.

Task Characteristics

Tasks are characterized by:

- **Processing time:** Time required for each task's completion.
- **Priority level:** Importance of each task, influencing its scheduling order.
- **Dependencies:** Task dependencies specify execution precedence relationships.

- **Resource requirements:** CPU, memory, or energy needs of each task.

Hybrid algorithm framework

The hybrid ABOA-GA algorithm aims to efficiently navigate the solution space by integrating the global searching strengths of the ABOA with the local refinement ability of the GA.

Adaptive Butterfly Optimization Algorithm

- **Butterfly population initialization:** In ABOA, every butterfly within the population symbolizes a possible schedule for tasks. The initialization process starts by creating an initial group of butterflies, each with randomly distributed task-to-resource assignments, encompassing a broad spectrum of possible solutions.
- **Adaptive parameter tuning:** ABOA utilizes adaptive strategies to dynamically modify its exploration (global search) and exploitation (local search). This approach maintains a balance between investigating new regions of the solution space and honing in on existing solutions as the algorithm advances. Adaptive elements, including sensory modality and power exponent, are adjusted according to the quality of solutions achieved in every iteration.
- **Fitness evaluation:** The fitness function assesses every butterfly (solution) according to scheduling goals, including reducing makespan and enhancing resource utilization. The fitness value for each butterfly is calculated using the following formula:

$$Fitness(S) = w_1 * Makespan(S) + w_2 * Resource\ utilization(S) + w_3 * Energy\ efficiency(S)$$

Where $w_{1,2}$ *and* w_3 *are weights* assigned to different objectives based on specific requirements of the scheduling environment.

Genetic Algorithm

Chromosome Representation

In the genetic algorithm, every chromosome signifies a potential schedule for tasks, with each gene representing the assignment of a specific task to a certain resource. This encoding facilitates a flexible representation of scheduling solutions.

Crossover and Mutation Operations

The genetic algorithm employs crossover and mutation techniques to create new chromosomes:

- **Crossover:** Merges the schedules from two parent solutions to create offspring with a combination of task allocations. This promotes diversity and facilitates the investigation of novel scheduling configurations.
- **Mutation:** Introduces random changes to the task-resource assignment in a chromosome to prevent early convergence and promote exploration within the solution space.

Selection Strategy:

GA uses a tournament selection method that picks a group of top-performing chromosomes to create the next generation. This approach guarantees the continuation of high-quality solutions while preserving genetic diversity within the population.

Hybridization of ABOA and GA

The hybrid method integrates ABOA's adaptive global search with GA's local optimization to strike a balance between exploration and exploitation, enhancing both convergence speed and the quality of solutions.

ABOA for Initial Population Generation:

ABOA is initially utilized to produce a varied set of high-quality solutions. This establishes a robust foundation for the GA, allowing it to concentrate on refining solutions instead of developing a diverse initial population from the ground up.

GA for Local Refinement:

Following several iterations of ABOA, GA is utilized on the most effective solutions to enhance them further through crossover and mutation processes. This phase aims to improve solution quality by adjusting task allocations, thus reducing objective metrics like makespan or cost.

Adaptive Transition Mechanism:

The switch between ABOA and GA is managed adaptively depending on solution quality and the rate of convergence. For example, when the improvement in fitness values stabilizes during ABOA iterations, GA operations are triggered to further refine

the solutions. This adaptable transition helps avoid premature convergence and guarantees thorough exploration throughout the procedure.

Mathematical model for the Hybrid ABOA-GA approach

Parameters:

$T = \{T_1, T_2, \_\_\_\_\_, T_n\}$: Set of n tasks to be scheduled.
$R = \{R_1, R_2, \_\_\_\_\_, R_m\}$: Set of m resources available for task execution.
p_{ij}: Processing time of Task T_i on resource R_j
$u_j = $ Utilization rate of resource R_j.
e_{ij}: Energy consumption when executing Task T_i on resource R_j
$α$, $β$, $γ$: Weight Coefficients for makespan, resource utilization and energy efficiency objectives respectively.

$$x_{.j} = \begin{cases} 1, & \text{if task } T_i \text{ is assigned to } R_j \\ 0 & \text{Otherwise} \end{cases}$$

The hybrid ABOA-GA model aims to enhance a multi-objective function $f(x)$ that considers makespan, resource efficiency, and energy usage. The makespan is the maximum time taken by any resource to complete all assigned tasks. The goal is to minimize the makespan across all resources:

$$\text{Makespan} = \min\left\{ \underset{j \in \{1,2,...m\}}{max} \sum_{i=1}^{n} t_{ij} \cdot x_{ij} \right\}$$

Maximizing resource utilization ensures an even distribution of tasks across resources, reducing idle time. Resource utilization can be modeled as the sum of utilization rates across all resources, normalized by the total capacity:

$$\text{Resource Utilization} = \max(\Sigma_{j=1}^{m} u_j \cdot (\Sigma_{i=1}^{n} x_{ij}))$$

Energy efficiency minimizes the energy consumed by each resource while completing its assigned tasks. Energy efficiency can be optimized by minimizing total energy consumption across resources:

$$\text{Energy Efficiency} = \min \left(\Sigma_{j=1}^{m} \Sigma_{i=1}^{n} e_{ij} \cdot x_{ij} \right)$$

The goal is to minimize the overall objective function $f(x)$ by leveraging the strengths of both ABOA (for global exploration) and GA (for local exploitation). The objective function $f(x)$ combines three key scheduling objectives: makespan minimization, resource utilization maximization, and energy efficiency maximization.

$$f(x) = \alpha.Makespan + \beta.(1 - Resource\,Utilization) + \gamma.Energy\,Efficiency$$

Hybrid Approach: Adaptive Butterfly Optimization Algorithm

In this phase, ABOA handles the global search aspect, initializing a diverse population of solutions (task schedules) and tuning parameters adaptively. Each task schedule (or solution) is represented by a "butterfly" in the population.

Population initialization: Let $P = S_{1,2,\ldots\ldots\ldots,S_n}$ be the initial population of K butterflies, where each butterfly S_i represents a potential task schedule. Each solution is encoded as a vector of decision variable x_{ij} indicating the allocation of task T_i to resource R_j.

$$S_i = \{x_{ij} | x_{ij} \in \{0,1\}, i = 1,2,\ldots\ldots.n; j = 1,2,\ldots.m\}$$

Fitness evaluation: The fitness function (S_i) evaluates each butterfly S_i based on the combined objective function, with a higher fitness indicating a better task schedule.

$$f(S_i) = \alpha.Makespan(S_i) + \beta.(1 - Resource\,Utilization(S_i)) + \gamma.Energy\,Efficiency(S_i)$$

ABOA adjusts the following parameters adaptively:

- **Sensory modality (SM)**: Controls the search intensity and adjusts between global and local search.
- **Power exponent (PE)**: Determines the influence of previous solutions on current search direction.

The updated positions (task schedules) for butterflies are calculated based on these parameters:

$$x_{ii}^{t+1} = x_{ii}^{t} + SM.PE.Random\,Factor$$

where Random Factor is a random value that promotes diversity.

Hybrid Approach: Genetic Algorithm

The GA refines ABOA-generated solutions by locally optimizing task allocations.

Chromosome representation: Each solution S_i in GA represented as a chromosome, where genes g_i encode task- to-resource assignments.

$$chromosome\,S_i = \{g_1, g_2, \ldots\ldots g_n\}$$

Genetic operators:

Crossover: Merges two parent chromosomes to create offspring with combined task distributions. The frequency of crossover is governed by the crossover rate:

$$Offspring = Crossover\,(S,j)$$

Mutation: Modifies a randomly chosen gene (task allocation) within a chromosome to foster variation. The mutation rate μ regulates the likelihood of mutation.

$$Mutated\,S_i = Mutation\,(S_i)$$

Selection mechanism: Employs tournament or roulette- wheel selection methods to identify the most fit chromosomes for the subsequent generation, supporting the development of high-quality solutions.

Adaptive Transition Mechanism Between ABOA and GA

The hybrid method adjusts between ABOA and GA depending on the enhancement of solution quality across iterations. An adaptive control function $A(t)$ is defined to switch between ABOA and GA phases:

$$A(t) = \begin{cases} Apply\,ABOA & if\,\Delta f(x) > \delta \\ Apply\,GA & if\,\Delta f(x) \le \delta \end{cases}$$

Where,

$\Delta f(x)$ is the improvement in the objective function between iterations t and $t + 1$

δ is a threshold value that, when reached triggers GA to refine the solution.

Algorithm Implementation

Parameter tuning

The parameters of the algorithm, including population size, mutation rate, and the number of iterations, are meticulously optimized through experimental assessments. Additionally, adaptive adjustments to parameters are incorporated in ABOA to improve the balance between exploration and exploitation.

Pseudocode:

The following pseudocode outlines the hybrid ABOA-GA approach:

1. Initialize butterfly population (task schedules) in ABOA

2. Evaluate initial fitness of each butterfly
3. While stopping criteria not met:
   a. For each butterfly in ABOA:
      Apply adaptive exploration and exploitation evaluate fitness and update if improved
   b. Transition to GA if convergence stagnates:
      Perform crossover and mutation on ABOA-optimized solutions
      Evaluate new solutions and update population
4. Return best schedule with optimized makespan and resource utilization

Performance Evaluation

To validate the effectiveness of the proposed hybrid algorithm, the following metrics are used:

- **Dataset and benchmarks:** The algorithm is tested on standard task scheduling datasets and synthetic benchmark tasks to provide a diverse set of evaluation scenarios.
- **Evaluation metrics:** Performance is evaluated based on:
  o Makespan: Total time required to complete all tasks.
  o Resource Utilization: Efficiency in using available resources.
  o Energy Efficiency: Measures energy consumed by resources during task execution.

Comparative analysis
- Task sets: A variety of task sets are used, varying in size (small, medium, and large) and complexity (uniform and heterogeneous task lengths).
- Configurations: Simulated resources with varying processing power, capacities, and energy profiles are considered.
- Algorithms compared:
  o Hybrid ABOA-GA
  o Standalone ABOA
  o Standalone GA
  o Round Robin (RR)
  o First Come First Serve (FCFS)

Results and Observations

Makespan Analysis
Hybrid ABOA-GA achieves the shortest makespan due to its effective global exploration (ABOA) and local exploitation (GA) mechanisms, balancing task allocation efficiently. Standalone ABOA

performs better than GA and traditional algorithms but may converge prematurely without significant local refinements. Standalone GA delivers moderate performance but struggles with global exploration, leading to suboptimal makespan for complex task sets. Round Robin results in higher makespan due to its static allocation policy, which doesn't consider task-resource heterogeneity. FCFS shows the highest makespan as it doesn't prioritize resource capabilities or task dependencies.

Resource Utilization
The hybrid ABOA-GA enhances resource utilization by evenly distributing the workload among resources while reducing idle periods. Standalone ABOA generally performs effectively, but it can lead to resource allocation imbalances due to its tendency for early convergence. On the other hand, Standalone GA faces challenges in maintaining balanced utilization because of its restricted global search abilities. While Round Robin provides moderate utilization, it tends to have underutilization issues in heterogeneous task-resource environments. Finally, FCFS yields the lowest resource utilization since it does not optimize the matching of tasks to resources.

Energy Consumption
The hybrid ABOA-GA utilizes the least energy thanks to its effective task scheduling and resource distribution, which reduces the use of high-energy resources. Standalone ABOA demonstrates good energy efficiency but is less effective than the hybrid version because it occasionally makes suboptimal task-resource allocations. Standalone GA results in average energy consumption, as it does not take full advantage of the global characteristics of resources. Round

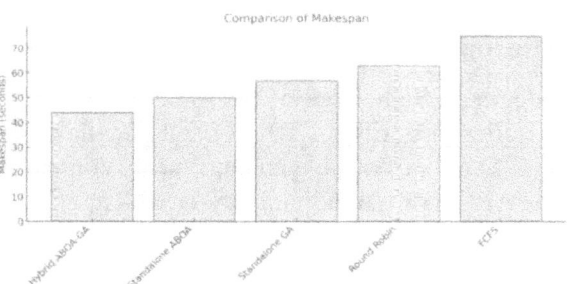

Figure 26.2 Makespan Analysis
Source: Author

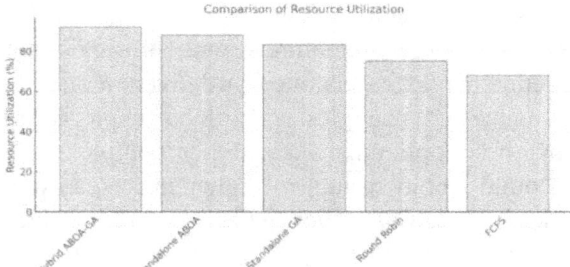

Figure 26.3 Resource utilization
Source: Author

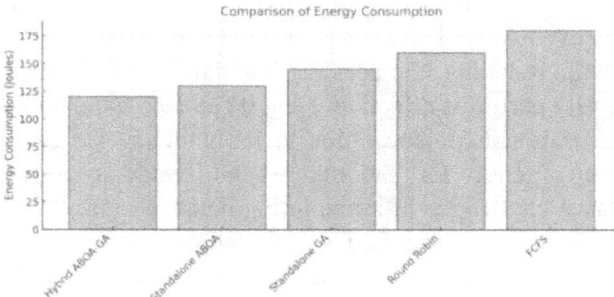

Figure 26.4 Energy consumption
Source: Author

Robin exhibits higher energy consumption due to frequent context switching and inefficient task assignments. FCFS expends the most energy since it tends to place excessive demands on certain resources.

Key Insights

The hybrid method effectively balances exploration and exploitation, resulting in enhanced performance. While standalone ABOA is efficient, it suffers from issues of premature convergence. Standalone GA does not possess the necessary robustness for effective global optimization. Conventional algorithms such as RR and FCFS are not suited for diverse environments and intricate task sets.

Conclusion

The integrated framework of the Adaptive Butterfly Optimization Algorithm (ABOA) and genetic algorithm (GA) deliver notable enhancements compared to using ABOA or GA individually, as well as against conventional scheduling methods like Round Robin and FCFS. By merging the global search abilities of ABOA with the local refining advantages of GA, this hybrid strategy accomplishes:

- Reduced Makespan: The hybrid algorithm effectively minimizes the total task completion time, enhancing overall scheduling efficiency.
- Improved resource utilization: Efficient task-to-resource mapping ensures optimal utilization of available resources, avoiding underutilization or overloading.
- Enhanced energy efficiency: The hybrid approach optimizes resource allocation to reduce energy consumption, a critical factor for energy-sensitive environments like cloud computing or renewable energy systems.

The results demonstrate the superiority of the hybrid ABOA-GA framework across various task configurations, making it a robust solution for complex task scheduling problems.

Future Enhancements

Incorporating multi-objective optimization extends the algorithm to simultaneously optimize multiple conflicting objectives, such as cost, energy, makespan, and fault tolerance. Hybridization with other metaheuristics explores hybridization with other optimization techniques (e.g., Particle Swarm Optimization, Ant Colony Optimization) to further enhance performance. Algorithm Parallelization optimizes the execution time of the hybrid algorithm by parallelizing computations for deployment in high-performance computing environments.

References

[1] Khan, M. S. A., & Santhosh, R. (2022). Task scheduling in cloud computing using hybrid optimization algorithm. *Soft Computing*, 26(23), 13069–13079.

[2] Vhatkar, K., Kathole, A. B., Lonare, S., Katti, J., & Kimbahune, V. V. (2024). Designing an optimal task scheduling and VM placement in the cloud environment with multi-objective constraints using Hybrid Lemurs and Gannet Optimization Algorithm. In Network: Computation in Neural Systems, (pp. pp.1–31).

[3] Han, L., Zhu, S., Zhao, H., & He, Y. (2024). An enhanced whale optimization algorithm for task scheduling in edge computing environments. *Frontiers in Big Data*, 7, 1422546.

[4] Vasantham, V. K., & Donavalli, H. (2024). Multi-objective hybrid optimized task scheduling in cloud computing under big data perspective. *Intelligent Decision Technologies*, 18(2), 1287–1303.

[5] Kiruthiga, G., & Vennila, S. M. (2024). Security-aware deadline constraint task scheduling using hybrid optimization of modified flying squirrel genetic chameleon swarm algorithm. international journal of mathematical. *Engineering & Management Sciences*, 9(5), 1089–1105.

[6] Brouwer, R., Akker, M. V. D., & Hoogeveen, H. (2024). A hybrid optimization framework for the general continuous energy-constrained scheduling problem. arXiv preprint arXiv:2403.03039.

[7] He, Y., Wu, G., Chen, Y., & Pedrycz, W. (2021). A two-stage framework and reinforcement learning-based optimization algorithms for complex scheduling problems. arXiv preprint arXiv:2103.05847.

27 An LLM based emotion and activity monitoring system for supporting autism patients

Marian A[1,a] and Bhuvaneswari A[2,b]

[1]Department of Computer Applications, PSG College of Technology, Coimbatore, Tamil Nadu, India

[2]Assistant Professor, Department of Computer Applications, PSG College of Technology, Coimbatore, Tamil Nadu, India

Abstract

Individuals with autism often struggle with expressing emotions, making it difficult for caregivers to accurately interpret their emotional states. Traditional methods rely on manual observation, which can be inconsistent and subjective. The lack of an objective and reliable system for emotion recognition affects therapy, daily assistance, and overall well-being. To address this issue, an AI-powered solution that analyzes real-time facial expressions using large language model (LLM) integrated with machine learning models and computer vision techniques. This system ensures accurate and objective emotion detection. It classifies emotions instantly, provides real-time monitoring, sends automated alerts, and shares detailed session reports to caregivers. With an accuracy of 85–95% in facial emotion recognition, consistent and reliable tracking, this intelligent system enacts emotional analysis and support for individuals with autism patients. This paper discusses a LLM model and the different techniques used to understand emotions and improve the wellbeing of autistic children.

Keywords: Autism, data analysis. emotions, large learning models, machine learning, predictions, Speech recognition, therapies

Introduction

Autism spectrum disorder (ASD) affects how a person interacts with others, communicates, and experiences the world around them. People with ASD may find it difficult to express how they feel or understand the emotions of others, which can make everyday communication and connection more challenging. Emotional regulation is crucial for their overall well-being, requiring structured support systems to help them navigate daily challenges. To aid their development, they need personalized interventions, therapies, and consistent monitoring. Figure 27.1 shows the different types of applied behavior analysis (ABA) therapies to improve social, communication, and learning abilities. These therapies are provided to ASD individuals/patients by the caregivers according to their requirements.

Caregivers, including parents, therapists, and doctors play a vital role in supporting autism-affected individuals by personalized therapies, observing behavioral patterns, recognizing emotional distress, and implementing appropriate interventions. However, manual observation can be subjective and inconsistent, leading to delays in response. Technology-driven solutions provide accurate and objective emotional insights, enabling timely interventions.

In this paper, a machine learning model for supporting caregivers to analyze and understand the emotions of the children with ASD under their care is presented.

Existing System

Traditional emotion and activity monitoring systems rely on manual assessments or external sensors, making real-time tracking inefficient. Wearable devices, EEG-based systems, and sentiment analysis tools require extra hardware or rely solely on text-based inputs, limiting real-time emotion recognition [10]. Some applications use basic facial recognition, but they lack deep learning models like CNN for accurate and automated emotion detection [10]. Manual observation requires human intervention, leading to subjective and inconsistent analysis [1]. Additionally, traditional systems do not provide real-time alerts for prolonged neutral emotions or voice notifications for attention tracking, which are crucial for healthcare and education [11]. Existing video analytics tools lack automated session reports, requiring manual data review, making them inefficient [2].

Many solutions store data locally, restricting scalability and accessibility, while cloud-based systems improve security and real-time processing [7]Without

[a]23mx215@psgtech.ac.in, [b]abh.mca@psgtech.ac.in

DOI: 10.1201/9781003770435-27

TYPES OF ABA THERAPIES

Discrete Trial Training (DTT)	This breaks a desired behavior into the simplest steps.
Early Intensive Behavioral Intervention (EIBI)	This form of ABA is designed for young children, usually under age five.
Pivotal Response Treatment (PRT)	It focuses on the important areas of a child's development, like self-management and taking charge in social situations.
Verbal Behavior Intervention (VBI)	It focuses on improving a child's verbal skills is the goal.

Figure 27.1 Types of ABA therapies
Source: Author

AI-powered emotion recognition, traditional systems fail to provide efficient, automated emotion tracking for caregivers, educators, and individuals [8]. Facial action coding system (FACS) presented by Ekman & Friesen [4] manually codes facial muscle movements to infer emotions. Though the system is functional, it lacks automation and is highly subjective to errors and misinterpretation of emotions. Eye-tracking metrics system developed by Krol & Krol [5] analyzed eye movement behavior for perception studies; this system required dedicated tracking devices that are not readily available.

With evolving machine learning models, an emotion and activity monitoring system (EAMS) is proposed in this paper for emotions and activity monitoring of ASD children. The proposed learning model architecture, training process, and techniques employed to enhance accuracy and real-time performance in emotion monitoring and predictions are presented in the following sections.

Machine Learning Models

Machine learning (ML) models are a part of artificial intelligence where systems learn from data, recognize patterns, and gradually improve their ability to make decisions or predictions without being directly programmed for every task. These models help in real-time emotion and activity monitoring using different techniques like convolutional neural networks (CNN) for facial expression recognition and large language models (LLM) for speech-based emotion analysis [6]. The models automate emotion detection, session reports, and personalized therapy tracking, helping caregivers monitor autism-affected individuals effectively.

Large Language Model

LLMs are powerful AI systems that are capable of improving customer experience by enhancing efficiency of a system and supporting more accurate decision making in day-to-day activities. Figure 27.2 shows the general LLM architecture for processing large datasets.

A LLM helps EAMS by enabling intelligent emotion analysis, context-aware reporting, and real-time adaptive feedback. The system leverages LLMs trained on multimodal datasets, including facial expressions, speech patterns, and behavioral cues to accurately classify emotions and detect subtle variations in expressions. One of the primary applications of LLM in this project is contextual emotion interpretation, where the model not only recognizes emotions but also analyzes behavioral trends over time, helping caregivers gain deeper insights into emotional fluctuations for personalized intervention. Additionally, the LLM assists in generating detailed session reports, summarizing emotional states, activity levels, and alert triggers in a structured format for easy interpretation.

Another critical aspect is adaptive interaction, where the LLM dynamically generates real-time responses, including voice alerts, email notifications based on detected emotional states, ensuring proactive intervention for inattentiveness. By integrating LLM-powered analysis with computer vision and machine learning, the system provides a highly accurate, scalable, and automated approach to emotion monitoring, ensuring consistent tracking, reducing observational errors, and enhancing emotional support for individuals with autism.

Convolutional Neural Networks Model

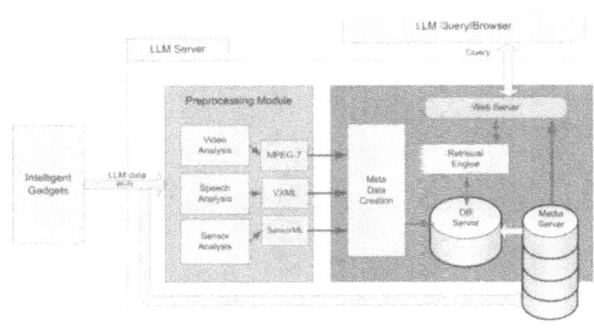

Figure 27.2 A LLM Architecture
Source: Author

Convolutional neural networks (CNNs) models are deep learning techniques used for analyzing two-dimensional datasets like images and videos. Figure 27.3 shows sample CNN model architecture.

The CNN model enhances the EAMS by enabling precise facial expression recognition and real-time emotion classification. They extract spatial features from facial images, detecting subtle variations in expressions like happiness, sadness, anger, and neutrality. The model processes webcam feeds, applying convolutional layers to identify key facial landmarks such as eye movements, mouth position, and eyebrow shifts—critical for emotion detection. CNNs ensure high accuracy by leveraging feature extraction and pattern recognition while minimizing misclassification errors, and the system is designed to handle variations in lighting, head position, and occlusions for reliable real-world performance.

By integrating CNNs with LLM-based contextual analysis, the system provides personalized emotional insights, trend analysis, and automated alerts. While CNNs classify facial expressions, the LLM interprets emotional patterns over time, offering deeper behavioral insights. Real-time voice alerts and email notifications enable immediate intervention in cases of prolonged neutral emotions or inattentiveness. The system's high accuracy in facial emotion recognition makes it a scalable and automated tool for enhancing emotional support and monitoring in individuals with autism.

The following section describes the proposed system, detailing its overall architecture and workflow. It includes the system flow diagram, dataset specifications, and data preprocessing techniques.

Proposed System

The proposed real-time EAMS integrates LLM and CNN to analyze and classify facial emotions, offering AI-driven support for individuals with autism. Using a CNN-based model, it processes real-time webcam feeds to detect emotions like happiness, sadness, anger, and neutrality [9]. The LLM enhances contextual understanding by analyzing emotional patterns over time and generating detailed session reports for caregivers. Email.js enables automatic notifications for timely intervention, while session reports can be downloaded in PDF format for structured emotional tracking.

To enhance data visualization, the system uses wave graphs and pie charts to illustrate emotional variations. It also integrates speech emotion detection via WebSpeech API, analyzing tone and sentiment while transcribing speech. The eye-tracking module, powered by WebGazer.js, monitors attention and triggers alerts for prolonged inattention. The patient profile module, backed by MongoDB Atlas, securely stores data for historical tracking and therapy adjustments. Combining real-time monitoring, multimodal emotion recognition, alert mechanisms, and secure data management, the system ensures efficient, automated, and caregiver-friendly autism support.

In Figure 27.4, the system flow of EAMS is shown. The EAMS follows a structured flow for real-time emotion tracking. It begins with user login for secure access, followed by data capturing, where the webcam records facial expressions. During preprocessing and emotion detection, facial features are extracted, and emotions identified. If no face is detected, a 'Face Not Detected' error appears. If detected, real-time monitoring continues. If anger persists for 120 seconds, an Alert Generation notifies caregivers. Emotion data is stored for analysis, ensuring detailed session records.

The system verifies session data completion—if incomplete, an error prompts corrections. Once complete, a session report summarizes motional patterns, allowing users to view or download it for evaluation. This structured, automated process enhances emotional awareness, supports autism-affected individuals, and provides caregivers with valuable insights for intervention.

Data Pre-Processing

The FER-2013 dataset from Kaggle is used to train and test the CNN-based emotion recognition model. It contains seven emotions: "Angry", "Disgust", "Fear", "Happy", "Neutral", "Sad", and "Surprise". Collected from diverse sources, it ensures variations

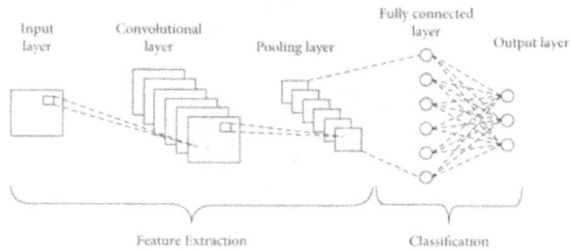

Figure 27.3 CNN Architecture
Source: Author

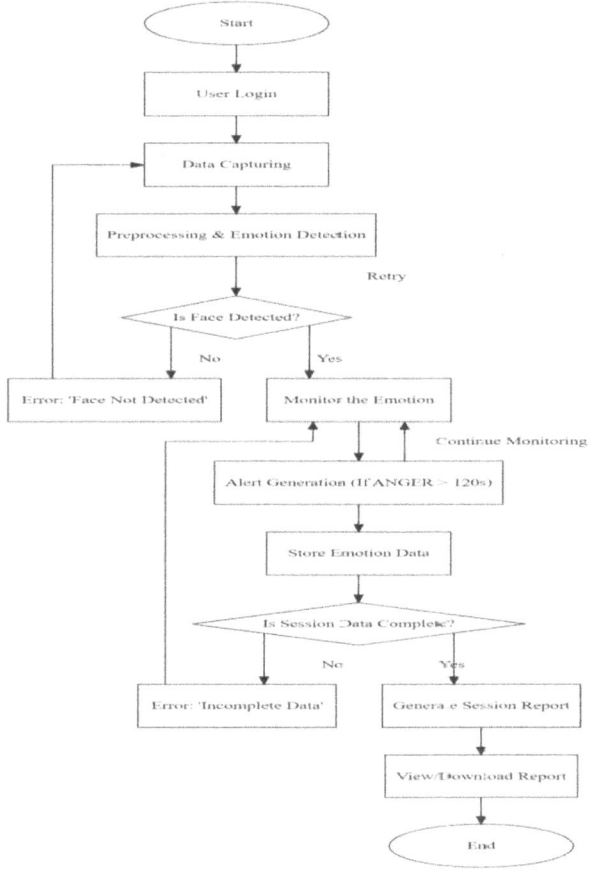

Figure 27.4 Proposed system workflow
Source: Author

Figure 27.5 A sample image dataset from FER-2013 [KAGGLE]
Source: Author

in expressions, head positions, and lighting, making it effective for real-world emotion recognition.

For training, it is split into 80 percent training and 20 percent testing to ensure generalization. Preprocessing includes resizing, normalization, and data augmentation (rotation, flipping, brightness adjustment) to improve model robustness. As a balanced benchmark, FER-2013 supports CNN based emotion classification, enabling high accuracy in real-time emotion recognition.

To ensure accurate emotion detection, the input facial images must be preprocessed before being fed into the convolutional neural network (CNN). The following steps outline the data preprocessing:

1. Image acquisition – The system captures real-time facial images from a webcam or loads images from a dataset. Frames are extracted and processed for emotion classification.

2. Face detection and cropping – To detect the face first we can use these algorithms (e.g., Haar cas-

cades, MTCNN, or OpenCV's DNN module), the system isolates the facial region, removing unnecessary background noise.

3. Resizing – To maintain uniform input dimensions for CNN, facial images are resized to a fixed size (e.g., 48 × 48 pixels for grayscale or 224 × 224 pixels for deep networks like ResNet).

4. Grayscale conversion (Optional) – In some cases, converting images to grayscale helps focus on facial structure and expressions while reducing computational complexity.

5. Normalization – Pixel values are scaled to a standard range (e.g., 0 to 1 or –1 to 1) to improve convergence during training and enhance model performance.

6. Data augmentation – In this Process techniques like rotation, flipping and zooming is used to increase the dataset variability.

7. Feature extraction – Key facial features like eyes, and mouth positions are extracted to enhance emotion classification accuracy.

8. Label encoding – Each facial image is assigned a label corresponding to an emotion class (e.g., happy, sad, angry, neutral), preparing the dataset for CNN training.

By following these preprocessing steps, the CNN model receives high-quality, standardized input, leading to more accurate and reliable emotion classification.

System Predictions

The system consists of four main modules designed to provide real-time emotion and activity monitoring for autism-affected individuals using advanced AI and Machine Learning techniques. The real-time Emotion Monitoring module utilizes CNN trained for emotion detection and LLMs for text-based sentiment analysis, ensuring accurate emotion detection. The Eye Tracking module integrates WebGazer.js to monitor gaze direction and detect inattentiveness, triggering voice alerts when necessary. The Speech Detection module employs the Web Speech API for speech-to-text conversion, combined with LLM-based sentiment analysis to analyze emotions from speech. Finally, the Patient Profile module securely stores and manages patient details in MongoDB Atlas, allowing caregivers to track therapy progress over multiple sessions. Together, these modules enable effective monitoring, timely interventions, and personalized support for individuals with autism.

Patient Profile

The EAMS maintains patient profiles efficiently and manages patient data for personalized care. Caregivers input essential details such as name, age, therapy type, session duration, emergency contacts, and profile picture uploads, while also recording medical history, special needs, and emotional well-being notes to support tailored interventions. All data is securely stored in MongoDB Atlas for seamless retrieval, enabling structured tracking of emotional and behavioral patterns across multiple sessions. This allows caregivers and therapists to analyze progress, refine therapy plans, and make timely interventions based on evolving patient needs.

Real-time monitoring enhances decision-making, ensuring therapy adjustments are made effectively. The module simplifies record-keeping, providing organized access to historical data that supports therapy modifications for better emotional and cognitive support. By streamlining patient management, it enhances therapy effectiveness, improves patient engagement, and ensures optimal care. Figure 27.6 illustrates the module's structure and functionality.

Real Time Emotion Detection

The EAMS continuously analyzes facial expressions using a CNN-based model to classify emotions like happiness, sadness, anger, and neutrality. It captures live webcam feeds, providing real-time emotional insights, especially beneficial for autism-affected individuals. The system generates detailed session reports with wave graphs and pie charts, which can be downloaded as PDFs or sent via email for caregiver analysis. All session data is securely stored in MongoDB Atlas for long-term tracking. With an intuitive interface and automated reporting, this module simplifies emotion monitoring and enhances support for individuals needing emotional assessment. Figure 27.7. illustrates the process of capturing facial emotions for detection during a therapy.

CNN-based emotion detection model uses Softmax for the output layer to classify emotions. The formula for Softmax activation is given below.

$$P(y_i) = \frac{e^{z_i}}{\sum_{j=1}^{N} e^{z_j}}$$

where:

- $P(y_i)$ is the probability of the emotion i (e.g., Happy, Sad, Neutral, etc.).
- z_i is the raw output (logits) from the last dense layer of the CNN.
- e^{z_i} is the exponential function applied to the logits.

Figure 27.6 A sample patient profile
Source: Author

Figure 27.7 A real-time emotion monitoring scenario
Source: Author

- N is the total number of emotion categories (7 in your case).
- The denominator $N j=1\ 1\ e$ ensures that all probabilities sum to 1.

The CNN model performs its prediction beginning with generation of following raw values for a single face image:

Angry = 1.2, Disgust = 0.5, Fear = −0.8, Happy = 2.4, Neutral = 0.9, Sad = −1.0, and Surprise = 1.6.
The method applies to an exponential function to each emotion:

$$e^{1.2} \approx 3.32, e^{0.5} \approx 1.65, e^{(-0.8)} \approx 0.45, e^{2.4} \approx$$
$$11.02, e^{0.9} \approx 2.46, e^{(-1.0)} \approx 0.37, \text{ and } e^{1.6} \approx 4.95.$$

and sum all exponentials:

$$3.32 + 1.65 + 0.45 + 11.02 + 2.46 + 0.37 + 4.95 = 24.22.$$

Using the sum, calculate the probability for each emotion using the Softmax function:

P(Angry) = 3.32/24.22 ≈ 0.137,
P(Disgust) = 1.65/24.22 ≈ 0.068,
P(Fear) = 0.45/24.22 ≈ 0.019,
P(Happy) = 11.02/24.22 ≈ 0.455,
P(Neutral) = 2.46/24.22 ≈ 0.102,
P(Sad) = 0.37/24.22 ≈ 0.015, and
P(Surprise) = 4.95/24.22 ≈ 0.204.

The MAX() function is applied to the probability values to arrive at the output. Since "Happy" has the highest probability (0.455 or 45.5%), the model classifies the detected face as Happy emotion. The emotion detection process terminates by displaying the result obtained from the system.

Eye Tracking

Emotion detection by eye tracking is performed by observing eye movements, point of gaze, and blinking of eyes. The Eye Tracking Module uses WebGazer.js to monitor real-time eye movements and ensure focus during online sessions. It detects gaze shifts and triggers voice and visual alerts if attention drifts. Running in the background, it provides real-time feedback without disruption.

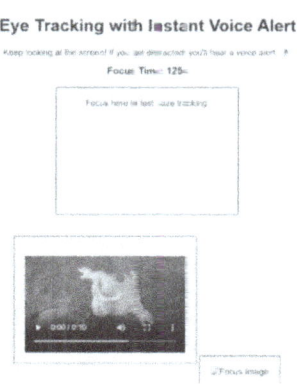

Figure 27.8 An eye tracking scenario
Source: Author

Caregivers, parents, and therapists can analyze attention patterns to refine learning strategies. Beneficial for individuals with attention difficulties, it enhances concentration by offering continuous monitoring and immediate intervention. Figure 27.8 illustrate an eye tracking scenario.

Speech Detection

The natural language processing (NLP) technology allows natural communication between human and computers for recognition of speech [11]. IN EAMS, NLP technology is uses in the speech detection module that utilizes the Web Speech API for real-time speech-to-text conversion and emotion detection. When users click "Start Speaking," the system captures and transcribes speech instantly while analyzing emotional patterns. This ensures efficient real-time processing without storing data. Caregivers and therapists can monitor speech and emotions for therapy, communication assistance, and emotional awareness training. Running in the background, it enhances user interaction and provides deeper insights into verbal expressions, improving communication. Figures 27.9 and 27.10 illustrate a sample speech recognition and emotion detection process.

Once the modules are ready, the system is tested for accuracy, performance, and reliability in emotion detection, while each module undergoes functional testing to ensure seamless integration.

System Testing

This section describes system testing process and illustrates the different types of models used in

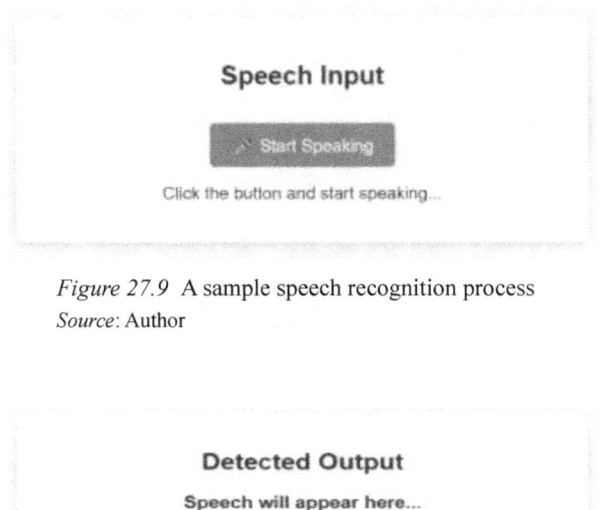

Figure 27.9 A sample speech recognition process
Source: Author

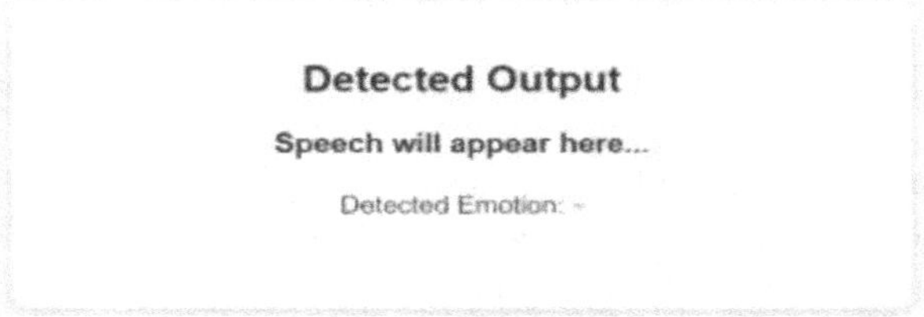

Figure 27.10 A sample emotion detection process
Source: Author

Layer (type)	Output Shape	Param #
conv2d (Conv2D)	(None, 46, 46, 64)	640
max_pooling2d (MaxPooling2D)	(None, 23, 23, 64)	0
conv2d_1 (Conv2D)	(None, 21, 21, 128)	73,856
max_pooling2d_1 (MaxPooling2D)	(None, 10, 10, 128)	0
conv2d_2 (Conv2D)	(None, 8, 8, 256)	295,168
max_pooling2d_2 (MaxPooling2D)	(None, 4, 4, 256)	0
flatten (Flatten)	(None, 4096)	0
dense (Dense)	(None, 256)	1,048,832
dropout (Dropout)	(None, 256)	0
dense_1 (Dense)	(None, 7)	1,799

Total params: 1,420,295 (5.42 MB)
Trainable params: 1,420,295 (5.42 MB)
Non-trainable params: 0 (0.00 B)

Figure 27.11 Parameters of proposed CNN Model
Source: Author

existing systems and the comparison between the models.

Figure 27.11. displays the functional parameters of CNN model for facial emotion recognition, comprising three convolutional layers (Conv2D) with 64, 128, and 256 filters to extract hierarchical features, followed by three max-pooling layers (MaxPooling2D) to reduce spatial dimensions and computational complexity. A flatten layer is used to change the feature maps to form 1D vector for fully

connected layers. This model includes 2 dense layers—the first consists of 256 neurons for high-level feature learning and the second as the output layer with seven neurons representing different emotions.

The CNN model is trained using the fit() function, where train_generator provides augmented training images and test_generator supplies validation images for performance evaluation. The model undergoes 20 epochs, meaning it iterates through the entire dataset 20 times to optimize its parameters using backpropagation and gradient descent. During training, the model adjusts the weights to minimize its loss function, and improves the facial emotion detection. The validation data helps monitor performance and prevent overfitting.

Figure 27.12 shows the line chart generated using Chart.js, with real-time emotion intensity values extracted via face-api.js. Every 500ms, faceapi.detectAllFaces() processes the video frame and computes the sum of all expression confidence scores.

Figure 27.12 An analysis of emotion detection
Source: Author

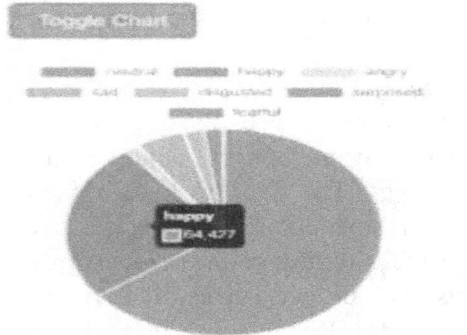

Figure 27.13 Visualization of emotion detections
Source: Author

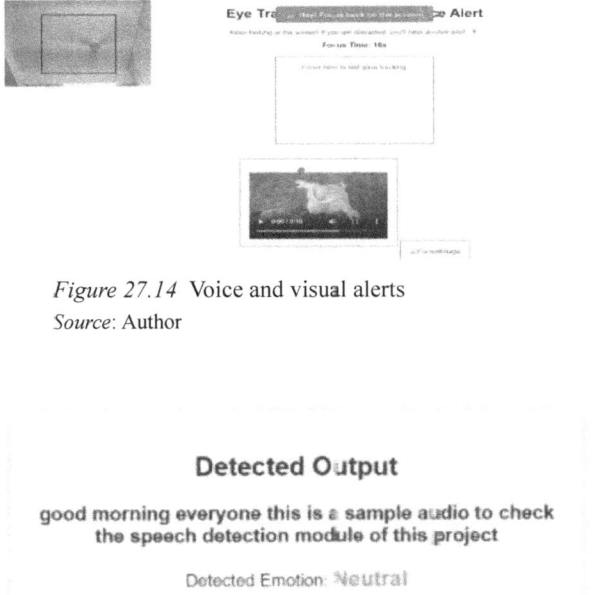

Figure 27.14 Voice and visual alerts
Source: Author

Detected Output

good morning everyone this is a sample audio to check the speech detection module of this project

Detected Emotion: Neutral

Figure 27.15 Emotion detection from Text Data
Source: Author

This data is stored in wave data, retaining only the last 120 entries for smooth visualization.

Figure 27.13 shows the pie chart is created using Chart.js to visualize the cumulative duration of detected emotions. The most dominant emotion is determined from expression confidence scores, and its duration is updated in emotion durations.

Figure 27.14 shows the visual alert is triggered when webgazer.js detects that the user's gaze has moved away from the screen for more than 15 seconds (distractionThreshold). The checkDistraction() function updates the lastGazeTime and, if exceeded, displays #alert-box by setting display = "block", turning the alert red. If gaze returns, the alert disappears, and focus time resumes.

The voice alert is generated using the Web Speech API, where SpeechSynthesisUtterance creates a speech command, and the main function implemented is the API window.speechSynthesis.speak(speech) plays "Hey, focus back on the screen!" once per distraction event. The flag voiceAlertTriggered ensures the alert does not repeat continuously but resets when the user refocuses.

Figure 27.15 shows that when the user clicks "Start Speaking," the SpeechRecognition API captures audio input, processes it, and transcribes the speech into text, which is displayed in #outputText. If an error occurs, the system updates the status message accordingly. The transcribed text is then analyzed by the detectEmotion() function, which searches for predefined emotion-related keywords. Based on keyword matches, the detected emotion is classified as "Happy", "Sad", "Angry", or "Fearful", and the corresponding emoji is displayed in #emotionResult. If no relevant keywords are found, the emotion defaults to "Neutral".

Figure 27.16 shows that In EmotionMonitor.js, the system continuously tracks and records emotion data throughout the session. When the "Stop Monitoring" button is clicked, it compiles a structured session report, summarizing key details like session duration and dominant emotions. This data is then passed to Email.js, which interacts with an SMTP server to trigger the email.

The email containing the overall session report is sent to the recipient, and Email.js provides a response indicating successful delivery or any errors encountered.

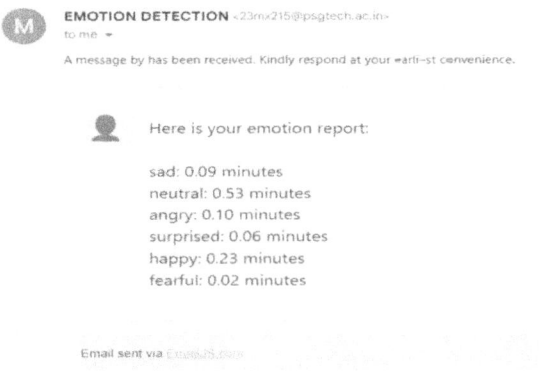

Figure 27.16 Email report
Source: Author

Table 27.1 Comparison of proposed EAMS model

Feature	Existing models	EAMS Model
Facial emotion recognition accuracy	80–90% [2, 3, 4]	94.5%
Eye tracking accuracy (Without external hardware)	70–85% [8, 9, 10]	93%
Session reports accuracy	Not available [11]	95%
Speech emotion recognition accuracy	85–89% [15]	92%

Source: Author

Table 27.1 presents the performance of proposed EAMS model and compares it with existing models. The table shows that EAMS model outperforms existing systems in multiple aspects, achieving higher accuracy in facial emotion recognition (94.5%) and eye tracking (93%) without external hardware. Unlike previous models, it provides accurate session reports (95%), enhancing real-time monitoring. Additionally, speech emotion recognition achieves 92% accuracy, improving communication analysis. The next section summarizes the key findings, highlights the effectiveness of the proposed system, and discusses its impact on emotion and activity monitoring. It also outlines potential improvements and future research directions to enhance system performance and usability.

Conclusion

The proposed EAMS is an AI-powered solution for real-time emotion tracking, eye movement analysis, and speech-based sentiment detection. Using CNN models, real-time monitoring, and automated reporting, it provides valuable insights into emotional and attentional states while ensuring seamless and scalable monitoring without manual intervention or external hardware. Its cloud-based architecture enhances data accessibility, and real-time alerts improve responsiveness. AI-driven emotion detection, sensor-free gaze tracking, and automated reports make it a comprehensive tool for emotional assessment. By improving accuracy, real-time feedback, and proactive intervention, the system enhances emotional well-being, engagement, and caregiver support, contributing to overall growth of the autistic children.

References

[1] Baltrusaitis, T., Zadeh, A., Lim, Y. C., & Morency, L.P. (2018). OpenFace 2.0: Facial behavior analysis toolkit. In IEEE International Conference on Automatic Face & Gesture Recognition.

[2] Duchowski, A. T. (2007). Eye tracking methodology: Theory and practice. Springer.

[3] Eyben, F., Wöllmer, M., & Schuller, B. (2010). Opensmile: The Munich versatile and fast open-source audio feature extractor. In Proceedings of the 18th ACM International Conference on Multimedia.

[4] Ekman, P., & Friesen, W. V. (1978). Facial action coding system: A technique for the measurement of facial movement. Consulting Psychologists Press.

[5] Krol, M., & Krol, S. (2018). Eye-tracking metrics in perception and cognition research. *Journal of Eye Movement Research*, 11(1), 1–12.

[6] K. S. Chintalapudi, I. A. K. Patan, H. V. Sontineni, V. S. K. Muvvala, S. V. Gangashetty and A. K. Dubey, (2023), "Speech Emotion Recognition Using Deep Learning," International Conference on Computer Communication and Informatics (ICCCI), Coimbatore, India, 1–5, doi:10.1109/ICCCI56745.2023.10128612.

[7] S. Siriwardhana, T. Kaluarachchi, M. Billinghurst and S. Nanayakkara,(2020) "Multimodal Emotion Recognition With Transformer-Based Self Supervised Feature Fusion," in IEEE Access, 8, 176274–176285, doi: 10.1109/ACCESS.2020.3026823.

[8] Nielsen, M., & Hansen, J. P. (2009). Eye typing using object tracking. *IEEE Transactions on Neural Systems and Rehabilitation Engineering*, 15(4), 531–542.

[9] Pantic, M., & Rothkrantz, L. J. (2000). Automatic analysis of facial expressions: The state of the art. *IEEE Transactions on Pattern Analysis and Machine Intelligence*, 22(12), 1424–1445.

[10] Ringeval, F., Sonderegger, A., Sauer, J., & Lalanne, D. (2013). Introducing the RECOLA multimodal corpus of remote collaborative and affective interactions. In IEEE International Conference on Automatic Face & Gesture Recognition.

[11] Zeng, Z., Pantic, M., Roisman, G. I., & Huang, T. S. (2009). A survey of affect recognition methods: Audio, visual, and spontaneous expressions. *IEEE Transactions on Pattern Analysis and Machine Intelligence*, 31(1), 39–58.

28 Analyzing the features of startup failure in financial sector via spectral clustering

Nagupriya A[1,a], Ragul S J[1,b] and Bagyalakshmi M[2,c]

[1]Department of Robotics and Automation, PSG College of Technology, Coimbatore, Tamil Nadu, India
[2]Department of Mathematics, PSG College of Technology, Coimbatore, Tamil Nadu, India

Abstract

Financial sector development is essential to the economic growth of our country. Various features that contributes to the Startup failure in finance affects the growth of the economy either directly or indirectly. The study of those features plays a crucial role in reducing Startup failures and increasing the sustainability of startups for entrepreneurs, investors, and policymakers. This paper focuses on the identification of features that are attributed to the startup failure data and groups the data based on similar characteristics. In this article, higher dimensional data relevant to the startup failure in the financial sector are collected. Using principal component analysis higher dimensional data is reduced to the lower dimensional and the corresponding eigen spectrum indicating the most influential feature is also presented graphically. metrics like the silhouette score is used to estimate the optimal number of similar groups following pre-processing and transforming the similarity matrix. Using the results obtained from the group of clusters with analogous features, the percentage of failures corresponding to the dominant startup features are estimated and the results are graphically illustrated. This analysis provides fruitful information to the future entrepreneurs to build their business.

Keywords: Eigenvalues and Eigenvectors, principal component analysis, spectral clustering

Introduction

Technological and economic advancements have been significantly aided by the exponential growth of startup culture around the world, especially in the sectors of innovation and information technology. But this increase in entrepreneurship has also brought to light the sobering fact that many startups fail, frequently despite their initial success and promising ideas. Numerous underlying problems can be identified as reasons for these failures. Such failure reasons include No interested investors, loss of focus, release of product at the wrong time, poor marketing, pricing issues, not the right team, getting out-competed, not targeting a market need, and so on. To reduce the startup failure rate and to increase the sustainability of startups, the study of startup failure features helps to recognize and comprehend the trends underlying these failures.

Literature review

Startup failures have been extensively studied due to their high frequency, even in markets that prioritize innovation and entrepreneurship. In the literature, the top twenty core reasons for failure of startups such as lack of market need, poor product-market fit, insufficient funding, and mismanagement were reported in CB Insights [3]. Khairajani et al., [6] determine numerous impacts and contributing variables, by utilizing case studies that lead to the failure of startups in India. Cavicchioli and Kocollari [11] analyzed huge datasets to understand the dynamic factors impacting innovative startups' performances by combining the use of factor and cluster analysis. Daniel Se Menuta and Meeran Ismail (2021) utilize K-means method to group startups by text description into related working industries by implementing dimensionality reduction techniques via singular-value decomposition and enhanced speed and efficiency of the algorithm.

Objective

Many works have relied on qualitative analyses and traditional statistical models that do not fully reveal the hidden complexity of real-world startup data. Also, very few papers are available in the literature, that uses machine learning techniques to analyze startup failure data. Due to the increasing availability of structured datasets capturing startup behavior and performance, there is a growing interest in

[a]23r222@psgtech.ac.in, [b]23r231@psgtech.ac.in, [c]mbl.maths@psgtech.ac.in

DOI: 10.1201/9781003770435-28

applying data-driven methods to discover hidden patterns. This motivates us to analyze the main cause of failures in the startup failure data using clustering methods. Algorithms like K-means and hierarchical clustering often assume linear or spherical cluster structures, limiting their ability to identify complex and non-linear relationships within the data. Thus, we implemented principal component analysis (PCA) for dimensionality reduction and the most efficient unsupervised machine learning technique, the spectral clustering method to group the failure features of startup data. This paper focuses on the use of PCA and spectral clustering to assess and classify the nonlinear patterns in the startup failure data based on their vital characteristics. This study analyses the prevalent characteristics among startups that have failed under identical circumstances and separates them into clusters.

Spectral Clustering

Spectral clustering offers a more flexible and powerful alternative by using the eigenvalues of a similarity matrix derived from a graphical illustration. Ng et al., [12] demonstrated the superior performance of spectral clustering algorithm in image analysis by using matrix perturbation theory. Ding et al. [14] applied clustering process to the non-convex sphere of sample spaces and produced the globally optimal solution.

In this work, the process begins with extensive data preprocessing. A similarity matrix is constructed which acts as the basis for spectral clustering. The Silhouette Score method is used to identify the ideal number of similar groups. The dimensionality reduction technique using PCA is proposed for visualizing data points in 3D space. After applying the spectral clustering method to the reduced data, the obtained results not only reveal conventional startup failure patterns but also show how this clustering algorithm can interpret intricate business data.

Startup Data Description

The startup failure data under the sector of finance and insurance is collected for 45 data points with 17 features including categorical data. Semantic gouping (Domain-Informed Encoding) method is applied to convert the categorical data into numerical data. The corresponding 17 features are "What They Did", "Why They Failed", "Takeaway",

"Giant", "No Budget", "Competition", "Poor Market Fit", "Acquisition", "Stagnation", "Platform Dependency", "Trend Shifts", "Monetization Failure", "Niche Limits", "Execution Flaws", "Toxicity/Trust Issues", "Regulatory Pressure", "Overhype, Years Active".

The data set used in this study consists of real-world information on 45 failed startups, collected from publicly available sources that document reasons for startup failures. Each entry in the data set represents a single startup and includes a mix of quantitative, categorical, and binary features that reflect both operational history and failure attributes. This diverse feature set makes the dataset well-suited for unsupervised learning techniques aimed at pattern identification.

Methodology

In this study, we analyzed the startup failure dataset using dimensionality reduction with PCA and spectral clustering method.

Dimensionality Reduction with PCA

Due to the complexity of higher dimensional dataset, PCA is successfully implemented to transform the data into a new set of features (principal components) that retain the most variance from the original data. The dataset is reduced to three principal components to facilitate visualization and further analysis. PCA helps to eliminate noise and reduce computational complexity while retaining the key patterns in the data. Using equations 2 & 3, we obtain the eigenvalues λ_i and the corresponding

Table 28.1 Eigenvalues

S. No.	Eigenvalues	S. No.	Eigenvalues
1	2.721109	10	0.653952
2	2.172459	11	0.291294
3	1.686768	12	0.372319
4	1.520734	13	0.423410
5	1.278131	14	0.477748
6	1.134765	15	0.490114
7	1.057852	16	0.00000
8	0.866730	17	0.00000
9	0.193527		

Source: Author

eigenvectors v_i, where A represents the covariance matrix $Av = \lambda v$ rating 17 features.

$$(A - \lambda I)v = 0 \qquad (1)$$

The characteristic polynomial is represented as,

$$det(A - \lambda I) = 0 \qquad (2)$$

$$(A - \lambda_i)v_i \qquad (3)$$

By solving the characteristic polynomial, results in eigenvalues as shown in Table 28.1. Based on the observation from Table 28.1, the first three characteristics having highly dominant eigenvalues (principal components) play a vital role in the downfall of startups. Figure 28.1 depicts the 3D visualization of data points defined by the principal components. This visualization provides an intuitive understanding of how the data points were distributed in the reduced feature space and allowed us to visually inspect potential clusters.

Spectral Clustering with PCA

After dimensionality reduction, we applied spectral clustering to group the startups into clusters. It is a clustering algorithmic tool that uses the latent values of a similarity matrix to execute clustering. We used the k-nearest neighbors (k-NN) method, which is suitable for non-linearly separable data. By using the equations (4–6) similarity and normalized Laplacian matrices have been computed.

Similarity matrix

$$W_{ij} = \exp\left(-\frac{\|x_i - x_j\|^2}{2\sigma^2}\right) \quad \text{for all } i \neq j \qquad (4)$$

Degree matrix

$$D_{ii} = \sum_j W_{ij}, \quad D_{ij} = 0 \text{ for } i \neq j \qquad (5)$$

Normalized Laplacian matrix

$$L_{sym} = I - D^{-1/2}WD^{-1/2} \qquad (6)$$

Results

PCA is applied to minimize the higher dimensionality of the dataset, allowing better visualization and analysis of the patterns within the startup failure data. The three principal components (what they did,

why they failed, and their takeaways) capture most of the variance in the data. The pictorial representation in Figure 28.1 shows the distribution of data points based on principal axes, revealing the natural clusters in the data. Further, spectral clustering was implemented for the reduced dataset to group the data based on similar characteristics. Figure 28.2 shows the better classification among the three distinct clusters, each likely representing a similar feature that

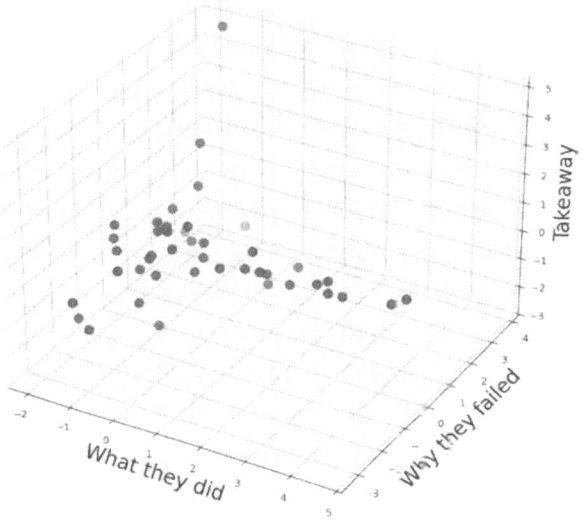

Figure 28.1 Scatter diagram of data points based on the principal components
Source: Author

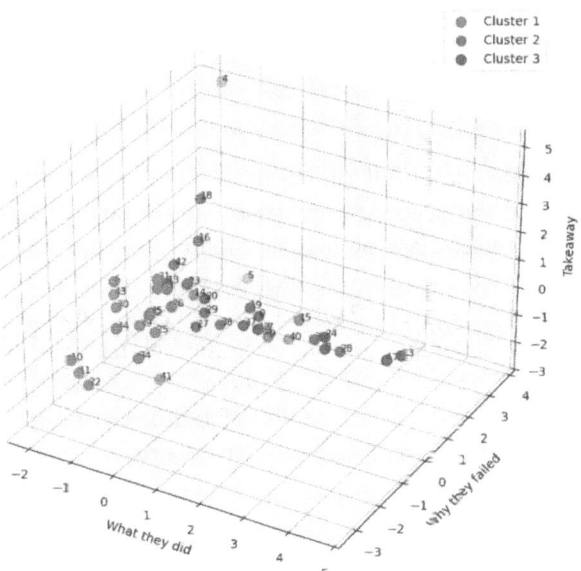

Figure 28.2 Spectral clustering of PCA components
Source: Author

Table 28.2 Physical interpretation of the results

Cluster	Common failures	Nature	Actionable insight
1	Execution, market fit	Built wrong or executed poorly	Focus on team, MVP validation, and UX execution.
2	Monetization, overhype	Trend-based, unsustainable	Validate paying user base and unit eco-nomics early.
3	External constraints	Operated in tough conditions	Account for regulations, capital constraints, competition.

Source: Author

Table 28.3 Clustered data

Cluster 1	Cluster 2	Cluster 3
1	7	0
3	8	2
4	12	5
6	17	9
10	19	13
11	24	14
21	28	15
22	33	16
23	36	18
25	37	20
26	38	27
30	40	29
31		42
32		
34		
35		
39		
41		
43		
44		

Source: Author

causes the downfall of startups. Thus, the data is clustered into three groups based on the related features between data points, as captured by the k-NN graph, and the results obtained are provided in Tables 28.2 and 28.3. Table 28.2, clearly reveals that nearly 44.4% of failures are due to struggled with execution and fit, 26.7% of failures are due to lost relevance or faced trend shifts, and 28.9% of failures are due to external forces and competitive pressure.

Conclusion

This study analyzes a dataset of failed startups using a collection of feature sets composed of categorical data and binary indicators. PCA is employed to minimize the dimensionality of the dataset by preserving its variance and the corresponding eigen spectrum plot is graphically depicted. Moreover, spectral clustering is applied to identify clusters within the data, and the results yield three distinct clusters, each representing startups that failed due to similar combinations of factors. The results identified from the dataset emphasizes that startup failures are not entirely random and can be used as potential information which helps the future startup owners and entrepreneurs to find the correct pathway for developing their own businesses.

References

[1] Aggarwal, C. C., & Reddy, C. K. (2014). Data Clustering: Algorithms and Applications. CRC Press (1st ed), p. 177–194.

[2] Gupta, A., Gupta, A., & Mishra, A. (2011). Research paper on cluster techniques of data variations. *International Journal of Advance Technology & Engineering Research*, 1.

[3] CB Insights (2021). The Top 20 Reasons Startups Fail. https://www.cbinsights.com/research/startup-failure-reasons-top/.

[4] Chen, W. F., & Feng, G. C. (2012). Spectral clustering: a semi-supervised approach. *Neuro Computing*, 77(1), 229–242.

[5] Semeniuta, D., & Ismail, M. (2021). Clustering startups based on customer-value proposition.

[6] Khairajani, D., Thakkar, P., & Shah, D. (2024). Analyzing factors contributing to startup failures in India: a comprehensive study. educational administration: theory and practice. *Educational Administration Theory and Practice Journal*, 30(1), 5224–5233.

[7] GU, B. Y. E., & XU, W. (2007). An improved spectral clustering algorithm. *Computer Research and Development*, 44, 145–149.

[8] Hamad, D., & Biela, P. (2008). Introduction to spectral clustering. In 3rd International Conference on Information and Communication Technologies: From Theory to Applications, (pp. 490–495).

[9] Jia, H., Ding, S., Xu, X., & Nie, R. (2013). The latest research progress on spectral clustering. *Neural Computing and Applications*, 24(7–8), 1477–1486.

[10] Ding, L., Li, C., Jin, D., & Ding, S. (2024). Survey of spectral clustering based on graph theory. *Pattern Recognition*, 151.

[11] Cavicchioli, M., & Kocollari, U. (2021). Learning from failure: big data analysis for detecting the patterns of failure in innovative startups. *Big Data*, 9(2), 79–88.

[12] Ng, A. Y., Jordan, M. I., & Weiss, Y. (2002). On spectral clustering: analysis and an algorithm. *Advances in Neural Information Processing Systems*, 14.

[13] Rebagliati, N, & Verri, A. (2011). Spectral clustering with more than K eigenvectors. *Neurocomputing*, 74(9), 1391–1401.

[14] Ding, S., Zhang, L., & Zhang, Y. (2010). Research on spectral clustering algorithms and prospects. In 2nd International Conference on Computer Engineering and Technology, 6.

[15] Gan, S., Cosgrove, D. A., Gardiner, E. J., & Gillet, V. J. (2014). Investigation of the use of spectral clustering for the analysis of molecular data. *Journal of Chemical Information and Modeling*, 54(12), 3302–3319.

29 Enhancing autonomous car's driving system performance using RTOS

D. Janaki Sathya[1,a] and M. Sai Dhanush[2,b]

[1]Assistant Professor(Sl.G), Department of EEE, PSG College of Technology. Coimbatore, Tamil Nadu, India

[2]PG Scholar, Department of EEE, PSG College of Technology. Coimbatore, Tamil Nadu, India

Abstract

Strong, high-performance embedded systems capable of executing tasks in real time are essential to meet the growing demand for autonomous vehicles. This work integrates FreeRTOS, a real-time operating system, to enhance multitasking capabilities and embedded controller performance in autonomous vehicles. FreeRTOS ensures effective task prioritization, enabling rapid responses to environmental changes and sensor data. The system's motors, ultrasonic sensors, and visual and auditory indicators are managed by an ATMega2560 embedded controller to detect obstacles and provide feedback to the user. Simulations demonstrate improved responsiveness, reliability, and maintainability compared to non-RTOS implementations, highlighting the potential for advanced real-time task management in autonomous driving. Future plans include further optimization, the integration of additional sensors, improvements in power efficiency, and practical testing.

Keywords: ATMega2560, autonomous vehicles, embedded systems, FreeRTOS, multitasking, obstacle detection, real-time operating system (RTOS)

Introduction

This work aims to enhance the embedded controller software responsible for controlling the driving system of an autonomous car by integrating FreeRTOS, a real-time operating system designed for embedded systems. The primary goal is to improve the system's multitasking capabilities, ensuring that tasks can be managed effectively while adhering to strict timing requirements for safe vehicle operation.

The work uses advanced sensor technologies, such as ultrasonic sensors for obstacle detection and efficient motor control algorithms, to optimize the embedded controller's performance and ensure seamless interaction between hardware components. The enhancements made in this work will contribute to the development of more reliable, adaptable, and efficient autonomous driving systems, paving the way for the future of smart transportation.

The ATMega2560 board was chosen for its powerful capabilities and compatibility with various components essential for the autonomous car. Integrating FreeRTOS enabled the work to manage multiple tasks, such as sensor data processing, motor control, and communication systems, ensuring predictable and timely execution even under high workload conditions.

A key part of the work was implementing a low-level speed controller, optimizing the car's smooth acceleration and deceleration. Additionally, the work focused on improving memory usage, balancing FreeRTOS's overhead with the available memory on the ATMega2560, and refactoring the hardware-specific code using compile-time configuration options to handle differences between various car models. Overall, this work combines skills in embedded and real-time systems, focusing on creating a responsive, efficient, and future-ready solution for autonomous driving.

Literature Review

Through three separate pieces, Chen et al.'s study examines the developments in intelligent vehicles (IVs) and autonomous driving. The first article provides an overview of AD and IV technologies, going over their background, significant events, viewpoints, morality, and potential future study areas. The second part examines human behaviors in IVs, high-definition mapping, communication, control, computer system design, and testing. Perception and planning are reviewed in the third article. The goal is to ensure the ongoing development and advancement of AD and IVs by offering a variety of perspectives

[a]djs.eee@psgtech.ac.in, [b]saidhanush5403@gmail.com

DOI: 10.1201/9781003770435-29

and bridging the gap between previous and upcoming research [1].

The study by Villamil Lopez and Stilla presents a method for estimating oil storage tank parameters using high-resolution synthetic aperture radar (SAR) imagery, coherent scatterers, and a machine learning classifier. This remote sensing approach provides real-time data on fuel levels, improving inventory management and operational efficiency. The system also uses machine learning algorithms to forecast refill needs, reducing stockout risks and optimizing supply chain operations. The integration of SAR and machine learning creates a scalable, automated monitoring solution that eliminates the need for manual inspections or ground-based sensors, enhancing logistical planning and ensuring timely refueling. This method significantly enhances inventory forecasting and ensures continuous operations in fuel-dependent industries [2].

The study by Chen et al highlights the increasing interest in intelligent vehicles and autonomous driving due to their ease, safety, and financial benefits. Despite previous surveys examining research achievements, they lack specific tasks, systematic summaries, and future research goals. The authors propose a Survey of Surveys (SoS) for all AD and IV technologies, examining past events, viewpoints, ethical considerations, and recommendations for future research. This is the first Survey of Surveys (SoS) that incorporates significant milestones in AD and IVs [3].

This essay explores the technological aspects of autonomous driving, discussing open issues and research on current issues, high-level system architectures, new approaches, and fundamental features like mapping, perception, planning, localization, and human-machine interfaces. It compares cutting-edge algorithms in a real-world driving scenario on a platform and provides an overview of datasets and tools available for ADS development. The essay emphasizes the need for enhanced robustness to reach ADS's full potential and addresses increasing no.of fatalities involving cars with ADSs [4].

The study by W. Wang and L. Paulino, titled "Automotive Real-Time Operating Systems (RTOS) A Model-Based Configuration Approach", focuses on enhancing automotive embedded systems, which are intricate and bound by real-time and safety constraints. Using the OSEK/VDX standard, it defines RTOS configurations and distributed architectures for automotive systems. The research emphasizes generating OS configurations from existing control system data, updating settings via OSEK Implementation Language (OIL) files, and enabling round-trip engineering. A bidirectional tool bridge using OIL files is proposed to streamline configuration processes, improving model-driven system engineering for efficient, adaptable, and reliable real-time automotive systems [5].

Liu and Liu explored the evolution of vehicles into highly connected, intelligent, and autonomous systems, driven by their integral role in the Internet of Things. The article reviews the historical progress since Houdina's 1925 experiment, highlighting advancements and current achievements in autonomous driving. It outlines key functional modules and enabling technologies, such as communication and control systems, while addressing critical security concerns and proposing solutions. The authors provide insights into future development paths, emphasizing the potential and challenges of autonomous driving system evolution [6].

The research investigates the application of RTOSs in embedded systems for industrial process control and monitoring. RTOSs are highlighted as essential for multitasking applications with deterministic behavior, supporting domains such as IoT, data compression, and pattern recognition. Key RTOS functions include communication, inter-task synchronization, and task management. The study compares RTOSs based on memory footprint, licensing, predictability, and latency, evaluating their timing performance for synchronization methods like events, semaphores, and mailboxes on ARM Cortex-M4 and Cortex-M0+ embedded controllers, offering valuable insights for RTOS selection and optimization [7].

In their study, Lichtman and Fuchs delve into the design and mathematical foundations of proportional-integral (PI) controllers for DC motor control using the inverse dynamic control method. The research validates the theoretical findings through MATLAB Simulink simulations and provides a comprehensive explanation of converting continuous controllers to discrete implementations. Furthermore, it offers practical guidance on implementing the PI controller on an MSP430 embedded controller, bridging theoretical concepts with real-world embedded system applications, making it a valuable resource for motor control design and optimization [8].

The advancement of automated and driverless vehicles in the realm of automotive technology is covered in the study by Lingga et al. [9]. According to the authors, these systems are anticipated to adopt electric vehicle technology, doing away with the necessity for human component maintenance. They contend that, especially with regard to the switch from internal combustion engines (ICE) to electric vehicles, a real-time control system is required to provide prompt reactions and task priority settings for both internal and external events. For efficient and successful vehicle management, the study highlights the significance of a real-time control system.

A study by Zagan and Găitan on preemptive hardware RTOS scheduling and real-time event handling on a custom CPU implementation was published in the Canadian Journal of Electrical and Computer Engineering. With a proprietary processor that has hardware-implemented RTOS characteristics, the study focuses on a hardware framework used for both static and dynamic job scheduling. In order to allow new tasks to be completed beginning with the subsequent processor cycle, the approach substitutes a resource remapping method for the traditional stack save notion. In order to ensure real-time system needs, the hardware scheduler allows for unified control of events and interruptions. Intertask synchronization and communication methods, context switch actions, and effective utilization of multiplexed resources ensure the platform's performance and resilience [10].

For real-time optimal scheduling of large-scale electric vehicles (EVs) in a dynamic pricing market, Chen et al.'s study suggests a dynamic non-cooperative game approach. The method addresses the "curse of dimensionality" brought on by huge decision variables, explains the flow of information and energy, and investigates the existence and uniqueness of the Nash equilibrium solution using potential game theory. To reach the equilibrium, a distributed strategy based on the alternating direction method of multipliers (ADMM) is created. According to the study, the suggested strategy successfully shifts peak loads while drastically lowering EVA costs. The approach is more suitable for real-time optimal scheduling of large-scale EVs since it yields a higher-quality solution than alternative approaches [11].

This paper explores real-time charging optimization (RTCO) of large-scale electric vehicles (EVs), a complex stochastic resource allocation problem. For successive optimal decision-making, a multidimensional approximate dynamic programming (ADP-RTCO) is used. Two layers make up the hierarchy of ADP-RTCO: the lower layer uses a priority-based reallocation algorithm to obtain detailed charging power for connected EVs, while the upper layer formulates RTCO as a multidimensional energy storage problem by grouping EVs into multiple virtual EV clusters (EVCs). ADP-RTCO's resilience and adaptability to uncertain contexts are improved by its online learning capability. Extensive simulation results demonstrate the durability and optimality of ADP-RTCO in load-flattening and cost-saving situations. Furthermore, because of its great computation efficiency, ADP-RTCO may produce solutions of higher quality than other algorithms and can be used for RTCO of large-scale EVs under uncertainty [12].

Methodology

The proposed methodology aims to enhance the performance of autonomous vehicle embedded controllers by integrating FreeRTOS. The development process begins with identifying the functional requirements, such as autonomous navigation, environment monitoring, and real-time task management. Suitable hardware components, including the ATMega2560 embedded controller, ultrasonic sensors, DHT22 sensors, and motor drivers, are selected based on the requirements.

The system design encompasses hardware configuration and pin allocation, ensuring seamless interaction between components. Software development is performed using MPLAB X IDE with WinAVR for compiling and debugging the firmware. Tasks such as sensor data acquisition, motor control, and display updates are implemented using a structured approach. Both FreeRTOS and non-RTOS versions of the software are developed to compare performance.

Simulations are conducted in PICSimLab to evaluate the system's functionality in virtual environments. This includes testing obstacle detection, motor response, and environmental monitoring under varying conditions. Real-time performance metrics, including task prioritization, response latency, and memory utilization, are analyzed.

Thorough documentation of hardware configurations, algorithms, and simulation results is prepared to facilitate reproducibility and future development. The methodology ensures a scalable, efficient, and robust solution for autonomous driving applications, aligning with real-time operational requirements and future technological advancements.

Block diagram

The methodology for optimizing embedded controller performance in autonomous vehicles through FreeRTOS integration is delineated into precise and systematic stages to ensure robust development, rigorous validation, and efficient optimization.

System design and planning

This work focuses on designing and planning an RTOS-based controller for an autonomous car by selecting hardware components that ensure real-time navigation, environmental sensing, motor control, and event-driven user feedback. The system relies on the ATMega2560 microcontroller, chosen for its high GPIO count, adequate computational power, and multiple communication interfaces, making it ideal for real-time processing and control. It operates at 16 MHz with 256 KB of flash memory and supports various communication protocols like UART, SPI, and I2C.

For environmental sensing, this work incorporates the HC-SR04 ultrasonic sensor for obstacle detection and the DHT22 sensor for temperature and humidity monitoring. The HC-SR04 provides accurate distance measurements up to 400 cm with a rapid response time, ensuring smooth navigation.

The DHT22 offers high precision in detecting environmental conditions, which can be crucial for operational safety in varying conditions.

The actuation system comprises DC motors controlled via an L298N H-bridge circuit, enabling precise movement and direction control with PWM support. This configuration ensures smooth speed transitions and robust operation. Additionally, feedback devices such as a buzzer and LED indicators provide audible and visual alerts for various system statuses, enhancing user awareness and safety. The HD44780-based 16 × 2 LCD is used for real-time data visualization, allowing operators to monitor essential parameters effectively.

Hardware architecture and configuration

a) Ultrasonic Sensor (HC-SR04)
   * TRIG_PIN (PD7): Connect to the Trig pin of the HC-SR04.
   * ECHO_PIN (PD6): Connect to the Echo pin of the HC-SR04.
b) DC Motor (2) configuration
   * Motor left forward (PB1): Connect to the IN1 of the left motor driver.
   * Motor left backward (PB2): Connect to the IN2 of the left motor driver.
   * Motor right forward (PB3): Connect to the IN1 of the right motor driver
   * Motor right backward (PB4): Connect to the IN2 of the right motor driver
   * PWM pin for motor (PB5): This is used as the enable pin if needed for PWM control.

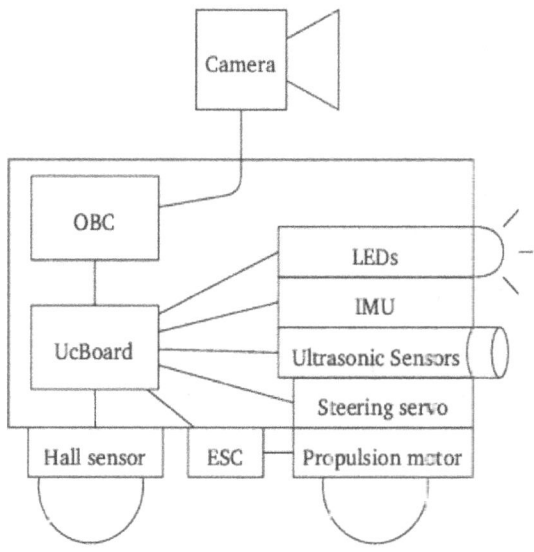

Figure 29.1 Block overview
Source: Author

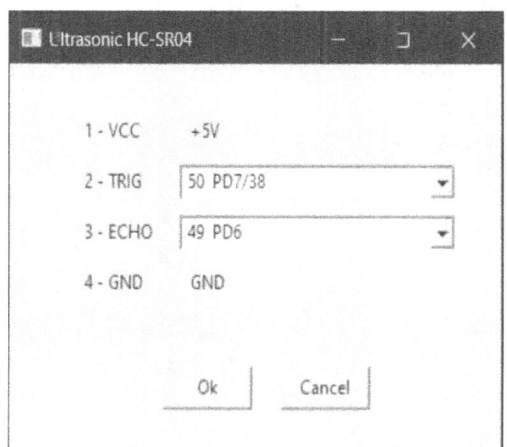

Figure 29.2 Pins for ultrasonic sensor (HC-SR04)
Source: Author

- VCC: Connect to +5V.
- GND: Connect to GND.

c) LED Indicator Pin (PB5):
- Connect to the LED.GND: The other side of the LED goes to ground, preferably with a current-limiting resistor (220Ω).

d) DHT22 Temperature and humidity SensorData pin:
- Connect the data pin of the DHT22 to an available digital pin such as PD2.
- VCC: +5V.
- GND: GND.

e) Buzzer pin (PD3):
- Connect to the positive pin of the buzzer.
- GND: Connect the negative pin to GND.

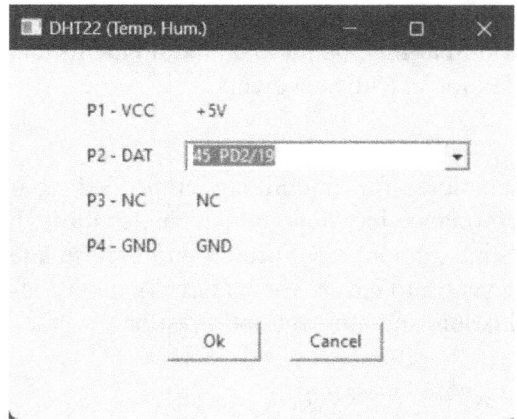

Figure 29.5 Pins for DHT22 temperature and humidity
Source: Author

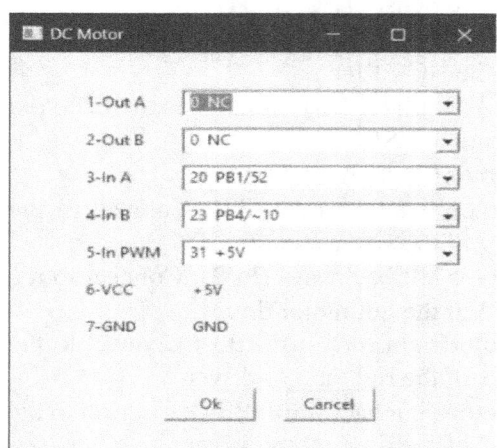

Figure 29.3 Pins for DC motor forward
Source: Author

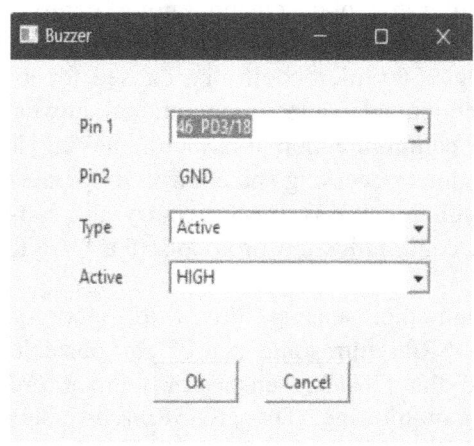

Figure 29.6 Pins for buzzer
Source: Author

f) LCD (HD44780) 16 × 2 configuration
- 1-Vss: Connect to GND.
- 2-Vcc: Connect to +5V.
- 3-Vee: Connect to the potentiometer for contrast adjustment.
- 4-RS (PD4): Connect to PD4.
- 5-RW: Connect to GND.
- 6-EN (PD5): Connect to PD5.
- 11-D4 (PD6): Connect to PD6.
- 12-D5 (PD7): Connect to PD7.
- 13-D6 (PB0): Connect to PB0.
- 14-D7 (PB1): Connect to PB1.

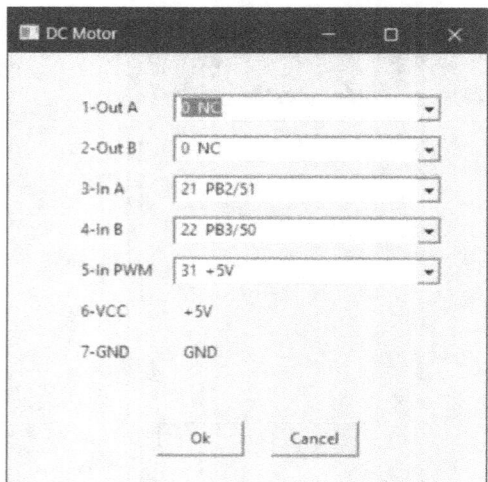

Figure 29.4 Pins for DC motor backward
Source: Author

Software development

Development environment setup:

Install and configure MPLAB X IDE with WinAVR compilerIntegrate FreeRTOS kernel into the work workspace for task management.

Tasks:

- Sensor task: Periodically trigger ultrasonic and DHT22 sensors, process raw data, and compute results.
- Motor control task: Execute PWM-driven control algorithms for motor actuation.
- Display task: Dynamically update LCD with processed sensor metrics.
- Feedback task: Manage event-driven LED and buzzer operations.

Implement static and dynamic priority assignments in FreeRTOS to ensure critical tasks, such as obstacle detection, preempt lower-priority operations.

Modular code implementation:
Sensor triggering and data acquisition. Actuator commands including directional control and speed modulation.

Data visualization through the LCD interface using 4-bit mode. Interrupt-driven mechanisms for precise timing and task synchronization.

Simulation and validation
Simulation Setup
Use PICSimLab to create a virtual testbed replicating the hardware environment. Configure simulated peripherals, including virtual sensors, actuators, and displays.

Functional testing: Load compiled firmware and simulate operational scenarios such as obstacle avoidance and environmental monitoring. Evaluate system behavior for time-critical scenarios using virtual obstacles and changing environmental parameters.

Performance profiling: Compare real-time execution metrics (latency, jitter, and memory usage) between RTOS and non-RTOS implementations. Debug task synchronization issues, priority inversions, and resource contention.

Result and Analysis

The implementation of the autonomous car embedded controller system integrated with FreeRTOS achieved notable advancements in system multitasking, responsiveness, and real-time performance management.

Simulation results
Non-RTOS system simulations demonstrated sequential task execution, leading to bottlenecks in real-time responsiveness. Tasks like obstacle detection and motor control encountered delays when running sequentially. In contrast, RTOS-based simulations provided enhanced task prioritization and parallelism, effectively managing sensor readings and motor commands under high-load scenarios.

Performance metrics

1. Task responsiveness: The RTOS system achieved higher responsiveness by prioritizing critical tasks such as obstacle detection and emergen-

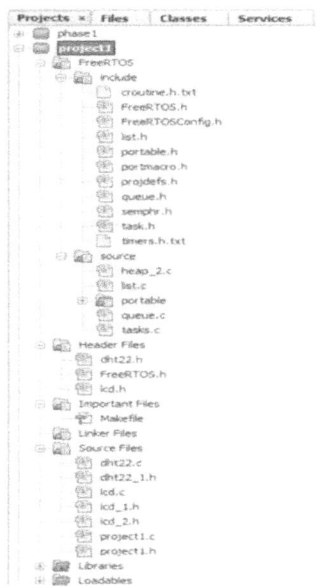

Figure 29.7 FreeRTOS source tree directory
Source: Author

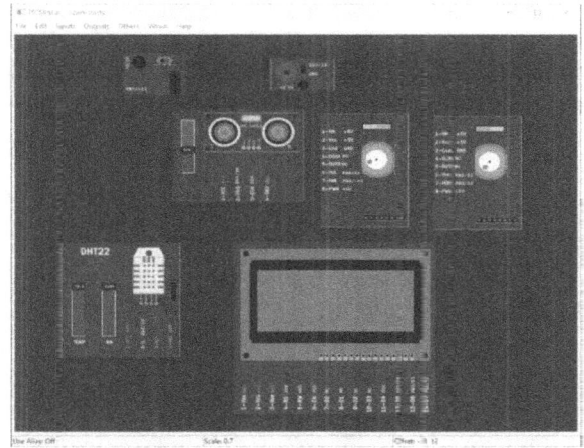

Figure 29.8 Spare parts configuration
Source: Author

Figure 29.9 Simulation
Source: Author

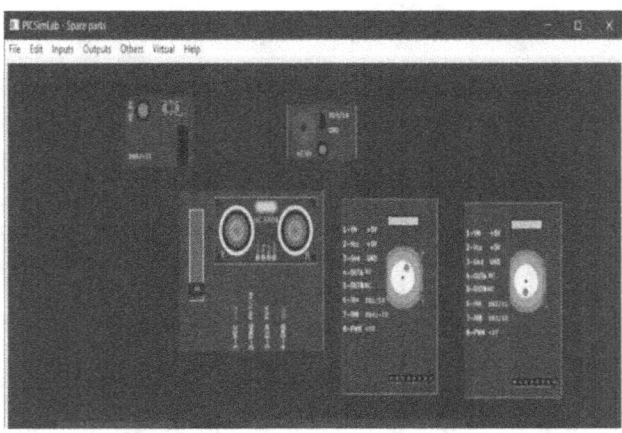

Figure 29.11 Motors stopped
Source: Author

cy stopping. In the non-RTOS model, obstacle detection and response time was approximately 150 ms, whereas the RTOS-based model reduced this to 50 ms, ensuring faster and more reliable decision-making in real-time scenarios.

2. Error handling: RTOS-enabled task management encountered errors in memory allocation and task scheduling, requiring further debugging to achieve expected stability. However, once optimized, the RTOS model provided better fault isolation and recovery mechanisms compared to the traditional approach.

The autonomous vehicle system successfully detected obstacles within a predefined 20-meter range and responded by halting motors to prevent collisions. Additionally, visual indicators (LED) and auditory feedback (buzzer) effectively communicated obstacle detection status. Compared to the existing non-RTOS implementation, the RTOS-based system demonstrated a 3x improvement in response time, optimizing time by enhancing performance,

improving real-time responses, and efficiently managing resources.

Conclusion

This work successfully demonstrated the integration of FreeRTOS into the embedded controller-based control system of an autonomous vehicle, achieving significant improvements in task management, responsiveness, and system reliability. Through systematic design, implementation, and testing, the proposed system exhibited effective multitasking capabilities, enabling seamless interaction among various components, including sensors, motors, and user feedback mechanisms.

Despite encountering initial challenges with FreeRTOS configuration, the outcomes validate its potential for real-time applications, such as obstacle detection and motor control. The inclusion of modular code structures and efficient resource management further enhances the system's scalability and adaptability to future advancements. The work lays a strong foundation for continued innovation in autonomous vehicle technology, offering a pathway to more intelligent, efficient, and robust transportation systems.

References

[1] Singh, S. (2015). Critical Reasons for Crashes Investigated in the National Motor Vehicle Crash Causation Survey (No. DOT HS 812 115).

[2] Yurtsever, E., Lambert, J., Carballo, A., & Takeda, K. (2020). A survey of autonomous driving: Common practices and emerging technologies. *IEEE Access*, 8, 58443–58469.

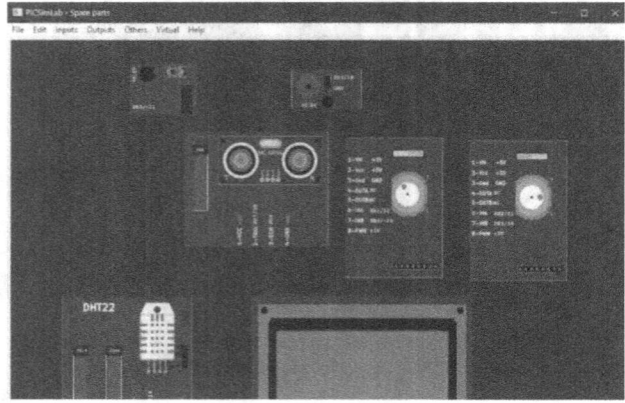

Figure 29.10 Motors running
Source: Author

[3] Crayton, T. J., & Meier, B. M. (2017). Autonomous vehicles: developing a public health research agenda to frame the future of transportation policy. *Journal of Transport and Health*, 6, 245–252.

[4] SAE International. (2021). Taxonomy and definitions for terms related to driving automation systems for on-road motor vehicles (Report No. J3016_202104). SAE International.

[5] Wang, W., & Paulino, L. (2021). Instillautonomous driving technology into undergraduates via workbased learning. In 2021 IEEE Integrated STEM Education Conference (ISEC), (pp. 284–287). IEEE.

[6] Chen, L., Li, Y., Huang, C., Li, B., Xing, Y., Tian, D., et al. (2022). Milestones in autonomous driving and intelligent vehicles: survey of surveys. *IEEE Transactions on Intelligent Vehicles*, 8, 1046–1056.

[7] Shreyas, V., Bharadwaj, S. N., Srinidhi, S., Ankith, K., & Rajendra, A. (2020). Self-driving cars: an overview of various autonomous driving systems. In Advances in Data and Information Sciences: Proceedings of ICDIS 2019, (pp. 361–371).

[8] Ackerman, E. (2017). Toyota's gill pratt on self-driving cars and the reality of full autonomy – IEEE spectrum. Accessed: 2023-08-09. https://git.at.stud.idi.ntnu.no/sigurdht/autonomes-fahren-speed-and-yaw-rate-controller/-/blob/main/references.bib.

[9] Liu, J., & Liu, J. (2018). Intelligent and connected vehicles: current situation, future directions, and challenges. *IEEE Communications Standards Magazine*, 2(3), 59–65.

[10] Huhtamo, E. (2020). The self-driving car: a media machine for posthumans. *Artnodes*, 26, 1–14.

[11] Z.N. Pan, T. Yu, L.P. Chen, B. Yang, B. Wang, W.X. Guo,- Real-time stochastic optimal scheduling of large-scale electric vehicles: A multidimensional approximate dynamic programming approach, International Journal of Electrical Power & Energy Systems, 116, 2020, 105542. DOI:10.1016/j.ijepes.2019.105542

[12] L. Chen, T. Yu, Y. Chen, W. Guan, Y. Shi and Z. Pan, "Real-Time Optimal Scheduling of Large-Scale Electric Vehicles: A Dynamic Non-Cooperative Game Approach," in IEEE Access, 8, 133633–133644, 2020, doi: 10.1109/ACCESS.2020.3009039.

30 Optimization of machining parameters during drilling of aerospace grade Ti-6Al-4V alloy

Samsudeensadham, S.[1, a], Suraj Singh, A.[2,b] and Krishnaraj, V.[3,c]

[1]Assistant professor, Department of Mechanical Engineering, PSG College of Technology, Coimbatore, Tamil Nadu, India

[2]PG student, M.E. Engineering Design, Department of Mechanical Engineering, PSG College of Technology, Coimbatore, Tamil Nadu, India

[3]Professor, Department of Production Engineering, PSG College of Technology, Coimbatore, Tamil Nadu, India

Abstract

Drilling of titanium alloy, a widely used aerospace material, remains a hard to machine material due to its low thermal conductivity, high strength-to-weight ratio, and chemical reactivity with cutting tools. These characteristics results in rapid tool wear, elevated cutting temperatures, and deterioration in surface quality— especially under dry machining conditions. In this study, drilling experiments were carried out on 7 mm thick Ti- 6Al-4V plates using uncoated 8 mm tungsten carbide (TC) drills. The machining was performed under dry environment with a machining conditions from 30 to 45 m/min and feed rates from 0.03 to 0.12 mm/rev. The experimental design was formulated using the Taguchi L16 orthogonal array to evaluate the effects of input parameters on surface quality indicators including surface roughness (Ra), hole circularity, and diameter accuracy. The outcomes revealed that feed rate had the most significant influence on surface roughness, with the minimum Ra value of 0.91 μm observed at 40 m/min speed and 0.06 mm/rev feed. Likewise, better hole circularity was achieved at moderate speed and lower feed combinations, with a minimum circularity deviation of 22 μm. Signal-to-noise (S/N) ratio analysis identified optimal machining conditions for enhanced hole quality. Additionally, chip formation was observed and analyzed to support understanding of the material's cutting behavior, revealing segmented chips due to the alloy's strain hardening and thermal properties. Grey Relational Analysis (GRA) was also applied to optimize all three attributes.

Keywords: Drilling, GRA, optimization, Taguchi, Ti-6Al-4V

Introduction

Ti-6Al-4V alloy materials are highly preferred in biomedical and space applications due to their excellent strength corrosion resistance, and biocompatibility. However, their hard to machining nature, primarily due to poor thermal conductivity and severe chemical reactivity with cutting tools, poses significant challenges in conventional machining operations. Festas et al. [4] conducted a comparative investigation between drilling and milling on two different grades of titanium alloys and concluded that helical milling outperformed conventional drilling in terms of surface quality, making it better for applications demanding high precision such as orthopedic implants.

In recent years, hybrid machining strategies have emerged to address the machining difficulties of Ti alloys. Ribeiro-Carvalho et al. [10] reviewed innovative methods for machining Ti-6Al-4V, emphasizing the role of process monitoring, optimization, and adaptive control systems. Their findings highlighted how such approaches enhance the process efficiency and tool life while reducing the number of defective parts and rework. In the domain of high-speed machining, Alam et al. [2] applied response surface methodology (RSM) in combination with genetic algorithms (GA) to optimize the cutting conditions for surface quality and MRR. Furthermore, their research underscored the importance of integrating multi-objective optimization methods for balancing productivity and surface integrity.

The increased usage of additive manufacturing (AM) in aerospace and medical sectors introduces new challenges and opportunities in post-processing operations like drilling and milling. Zhang et al. [15] investigated the issues such as surface irregularities, porosity, and altered microstructure, all of which can influence tool wear and dimensional accuracy during finishing operations. Drilling of AM parts has also been studied by Dedeakayogulları and Kacal [3], who performed experimental investigations on hole quality in AM-fabricated Ti-6Al-4V parts. Their

[a]sss.mech@psgtech.ac.in, [b]surajedu07@gmail.com, [c]vkr.prod@psgtech.ac.in

DOI: 10.1201/9781003770435-30

work demonstrated how features such as layer orientation and residual stress can significantly influence hole roundness and surface roughness, emphasizing the necessity for process- specific parameter tuning.

An application-centric perspective was provided by Ahmad et al. [1], who analyzed chip formation and hole circularity during the drilling of aerospace components. They reported that tool wear and thermal accumulation have a direct effect on hole precision, reinforcing the need for effective cutting parameter selection and monitoring. A comprehensive review on drilling of Ti-6Al-4V was conducted by Yuan et al. [14], who discussed multiple facets of the process such as tool geometry, lubrication strategies, and tool wear mechanisms. Their work provides the foundational context for understanding the multifactorial nature of drilling performance, which is particularly critical in aerospace applications where precision and repeatability are paramount.

Previous studies by Krishnaraj et al. [6] examined the machining of Ti64 alloys and highlighted how increasing spindle speed improves surface finish but also intensifies tool wear due to excessive thermal loads. This study supports the need for optimization strategies that not only improve quality but also reduce tool degradation. A comparative investigation by Ge et al. [5] evaluated conventional drilling, peck drilling, and helical milling in machining of aluminum–titanium stacks. Their study concluded that non-traditional techniques such as helical milling offer better control over burr formation and hole quality, which is especially valuable in multi- material aerospace assemblies.

Further insights into high-speed machining of Ti-6Al-4V were provided by Samsudeensadham et al. [11], who explored the influence of process parameters on cutting forces and surface integrity during end milling. The study concluded that selecting appropriate tool coatings and cutting conditions is vital for maintaining performance under high-speed conditions. In an earlier work, Vijayan et al. [13] studied cutting forces and surface finish during end milling of Ti alloys. Their experimental findings showed that feed rate and axial depth of cut are the most significant factors affecting surface finish, which has implications for both productivity and quality assurance in industrial settings.

Despite the advantages of advanced drilling strategies and tool coatings, dry machining of Ti-6Al-4V remains an area of concern due to the inherent challenges posed by the material's low modulus of elasticity [11]. These factors results in faster tool wear and poor surface integrity, which are especially problematic in the aerospace sector where dimensional accuracy and surface finish are critical. While several studies have focused on high-speed machining and its effects on parameters like cutting forces, temperature, and chip morphology, limited efforts have been made to analyze the hole quality characteristics—particularly under dry machining conditions using conventional uncoated carbide tools.

In recent years, grey relational analysis (GRA) has gained prominence as a powerful multi-objective optimization tool in the field of machining. Unlike the Taguchi approach, which is limited to single-response optimization, GRA enables simultaneous consideration of multiple output responses, making it highly suitable for complex manufacturing processes like drilling of difficult-to-machine materials. Prasanna et al. [8] applied GRA to dry drilling of Ti- 6Al–4V and successfully optimized hole quality by balancing multiple parameters such as surface roughness, roundness, and material removal rate. Similarly, Reddy et al. [9] conducted GRA-based optimization on Al-6063/TiC composites, achieving improved control over surface roughness, cutting force, and drilling temperature [9]. In another study, Pandey and Yadav applied a PCA-enhanced GRA approach to vibration-assisted electrical discharge drilling of titanium alloys and demonstrated improved decision-making by integrating complex response data into a single grey relational grade [7]. These works affirm the effectiveness of GRA in producing balanced solutions across conflicting performance metrics. In the context of the present investigation, where Taguchi-based single-response optimization yields different optimal settings for surface roughness, circularity, and hole diameter, GRA is employed to derive a more holistic optimization outcome.

In light of this, the present study aims to optimize drilling parameters for Ti-6Al-4V using a Taguchi L16 design of experiments approach. Unlike prior investigations that adopted AI-based models Ribeiro et al. [10], the current work focuses first on Taguchi-based single-response optimization and extends to multi-objective optimization using GRA. The influence of feed rate and cutting speed on surface roughness, hole circularity, and diameter were systematically evaluated. The signal-to-noise (S/N) ratio technique was used to determine the optimal parameter settings for individual responses, while GRA provided a unified ranking to identify a globally optimal setting that balances all performance metrics. This combined approach aligns with the demand for eco-friendly, high-quality, dry machining solutions in aerospace manufacturing.

Material and Methods

Ti64 blocks of 7 mm thickness were selected as a specimen. The experimental workpiece is shown in Figure 30.1, and its microstructure, revealing the typical alpha- beta phase distribution, is presented in Figure 30.2. An uncoated tungsten carbide (TC) twist drill with a diameter of 8 mm was used throughout the experiments. The tool's detailed geometry and dimensions are provided in Table 30.1 and illustrated in Figure 30.3. All drilling operations were performed under dry machining conditions using an STM Vertical Machining Center (STM-VMC), promoting sustainable and eco-friendly machining practices by eliminating the use of cutting fluids.

The investigation focused on two major input parameters—speed and feed rate—each varied across four levels: cutting speeds of 30, 35, 40, and 45 m/min and feed rates of 0.03 to 0.12 mm/rev. These levels are summarized in Table 30.2.

The experimental runs were designed using a Taguchi L16 orthogonal array to study the influence of these parameters on the surface quality of the drilled holes. Surface roughness (Ra), circularity error, and hole diameter deviation were selected as the key output responses. Surface roughness was measured using a Surfcom SE 200 tester, while circularity and hole diameter were evaluated using a

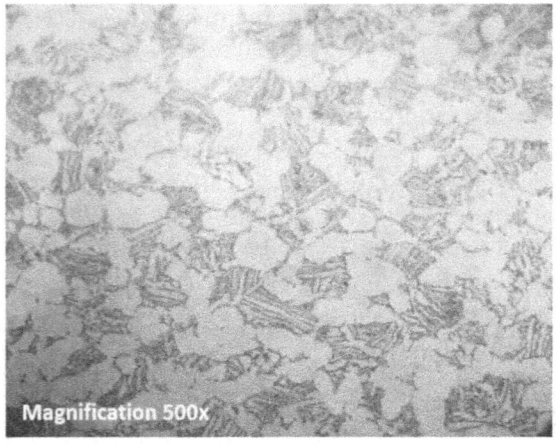

Figure 30.2 Microstructure of Ti-6Al-4V alloy
Source: Author

Table 30.1 Specification of standard twist drill

Properties	Standard twist drill
Diameter	8 mm
Material	Tungsten Carbide
Helix angle	300
Point angle	1200
Flute length	40 mm
Approach distance	1.87 mm
Drill bit length	90 mm

Source: Author

Table 30.2 Experimental parameters

Cutting speed (m/min)	Feed rate (mm/rev)
30	0.03
35	0.06
40	0.09
45	0.12

Source: Author

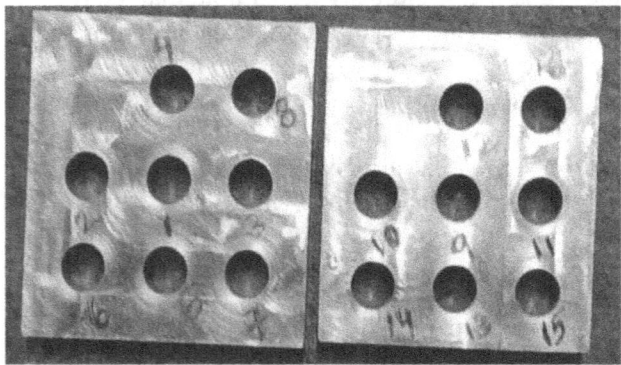

Figure 30.1 Drilled Ti-6Al-4V alloy specimen
Source: Author

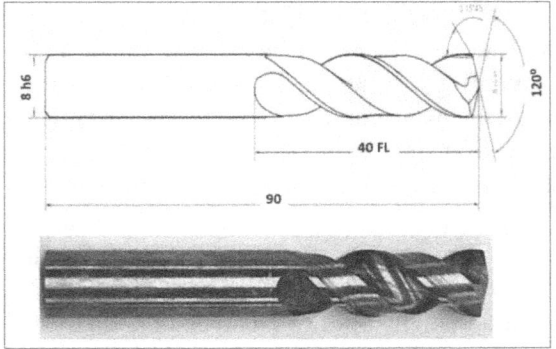

Figure 30.3 Tungsten carbide (TC) twist drill
Source: Author

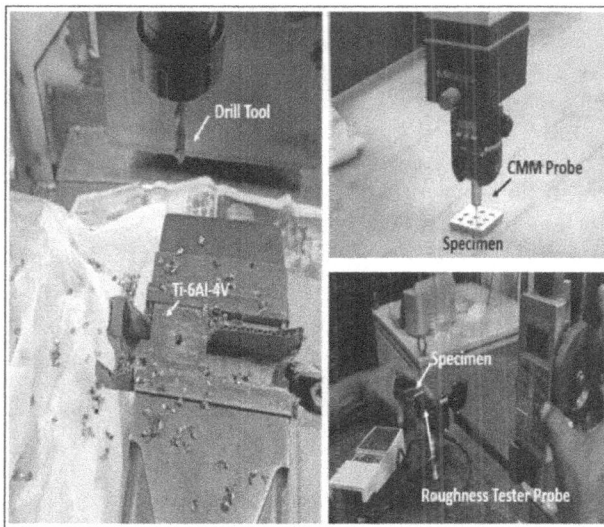

Figure 30.4 Experimental set-up
Source: Author

Coordinate Measuring Machine (CMM). Each measurement was repeated three times, and the average value was taken to ensure consistency and minimize experimental error. The complete experimental setup, including the work holding, tool, and measurement instruments, is depicted in Figure 30.4.

Due to the multi-response nature of the evaluation, Grey Relational Analysis (GRA) was implemented for optimization. The normalized values of responses were calculated using the "smaller-the-better" criteria due to the aim of minimizing all response parameters. Normalization was performed using equation 1:

$$Z_i(k) = \frac{max\ Y_i(k) - Y_i(k)}{max\ Y_i(k) - min\ Y_i(k)} \qquad (1)$$

where $Z_i(K)$ is the normalized value, $Y_i(k)$ the actual experimental value, and $maxY_i(k)$, $minY_i(k)$ are the maximum and minimum values of the responses, respectively.

Grey relational coefficients (GRCs) were then determined using equation 2:

$$\xi_i(k) = \frac{\Delta\_min + \zeta\ \Delta\_max}{\Delta\_0i(k) + \zeta\ \Delta\_max} \qquad (2)$$

where $\Delta oi(K) = |1 - Z_i(K)|$, Δmin and Δmax are the minimum and maximum of $\Delta oi(K)$, respectively, and ζ (distinguishing coefficient) is set to 0.5. Grey relational grade (GRG) was computed by averaging the GRCs for each experiment, which effectively transformed the multi-response problem into a single-response optimization.

Result and Discussion

Experimentation

Circularity plays a pivotal role in ensuring geometric precision during drilling operations, particularly for aerospace-grade materials such as Ti-6Al-4V. As depicted in Figure 30.4. Circularity error generally increases with feed rate across all cutting speeds. This trend can be linked to increased thrust forces and dynamic tool deflection at higher feeds, resulting in non-uniform cutting and deviation from true circularity. The problem is further exacerbated due to the low thermal conductivity of Ti-6Al-4V, which leads to significant heat accumulation at the tool–workpiece interface. Under dry machining conditions, where no external coolant is used, this heat buildup promotes thermal expansion and microstructural softening that compromise hole geometry.

The smallest circularity error is observed at a feed rate of 0.03 mm/rev for all cutting speeds, with 45 m/min showing the most stable behavior. Higher speeds at low feeds ensure better chip evacuation and smoother material shearing, minimizing thermal damage. At higher feeds (e.g., 0.12 mm/rev), circularity degrades significantly, particularly at intermediate speeds (35 and 40 m/min), possibly due to chatter and unstable chip morphology. Previous studies also observed similar geometric inconsistencies when drilling titanium under dry conditions [4, 15].

The Ti-6Al-4V alloy, being an α+β alloy, has high strength and low modulus, contributing to spring back effects during tool exit, which also affects circularity [1]. The dry machining condition chosen for sustainability purposes, though environmentally beneficial, necessitates careful parameter optimization due to heat-sensitive material response. As such, maintaining a high cutting speed (45 m/min) with low feed (0.03 mm/rev) appears to be the most effective combination for reducing circularity errors.

Figure 30.5 illustrates how feed rate and cutting speed influence the hole diameter produced in dry drilling of Ti-6Al-4V. Ideally, the drilled holes should conform to the nominal tool diameter (8 mm), but minor deviations are evident, especially at the extremes of feed rates. At lower feed rates (0.03 mm/rev), certain cutting speeds result in slightly undersized holes, which may be due to the spring back effect of titanium after the drill exits the material. This elastic recovery is common in low-modulus materials such as Ti-6Al-4V, especially under low mechanical loading.

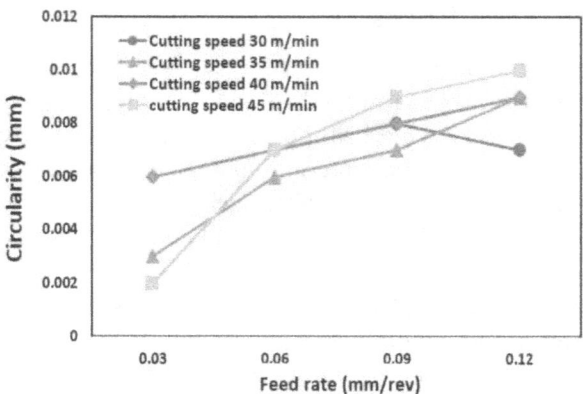

Figure 30.5 Effect feed and speed on circularity
Source: Author

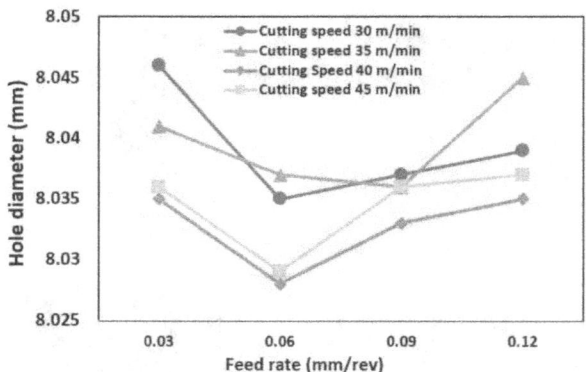

Figure 30.6 Effect feed and speed on hole diameter
Source: Author

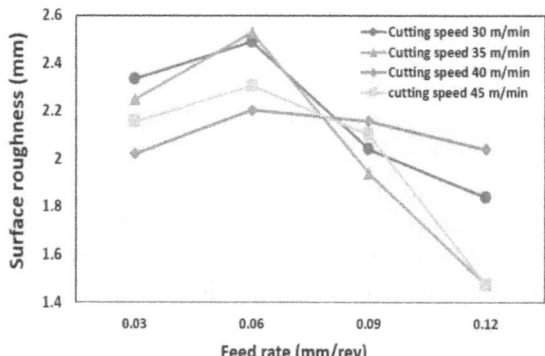

Figure 30.7 Effect feed and speed on roughness
Source: Author

As feed increases, particularly beyond 0.09 mm/rev, hole diameter tends to slightly overshoot the nominal size. This can be attributed to higher thrust forces, increased plastic deformation, and thermal expansion due to poor heat dissipation—all of which are intensified by the low thermal conductivity of Ti-6Al-4V. Under dry conditions, the generated heat is not effectively removed, leading to localized tool wear and potential enlargement of the hole due to thermal distortion and tool run-out [14].

Uncoated tungsten carbide tools are particularly vulnerable in such environments, as frictional heat buildup without coolant causes accelerated wear and inconsistent material removal. At moderate feed (0.06–0.09 mm/rev) and speeds of 35–40 m/min, the hole diameter remains close to nominal, indicating a sweet spot where mechanical and thermal loads are balanced. These findings align with earlier studies reporting that accurate diameter retention in titanium drilling is highly sensitive to thermal and mechanical effects, especially in dry environments [12].

Thus, for optimal dimensional accuracy, a moderate feed (0.06 mm/rev) and speed range of 35–40 m/min are recommended when machining Ti-6Al-4V in dry conditions.

Surface roughness is a key indicator of quality in aerospace and biomedical drilling. As shown in Figure 30.6, surface roughness generally decreases with increased cutting speed, especially at higher feed rates. For example, at 0.12 mm/rev feed, increasing cutting speed from 30 to 45 m/min reduced roughness from above 2.5 μm to nearly 1.8 μm. This behavior suggests that higher speeds improve chip evacuation and reduce BUE formation, resulting in smoother surfaces.

Interestingly, the worst surface finish was recorded at 0.06 mm/rev feed with 35 m/min cutting speed, possibly due to unstable chip formation and increased friction at the tool–workpiece interface. The results corroborate earlier works on Ti alloy machining, where roughness peaks at certain mid-range feed/speed combinations due to transitional chip morphology.

Lower feed rates (0.03 mm/rev) consistently produced better surface finish across all speeds. This is attributed to smaller uncut chip thickness and lower cutting forces, which reduce tool vibrations and surface tearing. However, at very low feeds, issues like ploughing and BUE can still arise if cutting speed is not optimized [14].

Uncoated carbide tools are known to interact differently with Ti-6Al-4V due to its low thermal conductivity and chemical reactivity, often leading to heat concentration and localized tool wear. Yet, the use of dry machining here reflects sustainable practices and underlines the trade-off between cooling needs and environmental safety [12]. Studies employing multi-objective optimization like TOPSIS have similarly identified that higher speeds with lower feed rates yield optimal surface integrity in titanium drilling.

These findings suggest that for superior surface finish, a combination of 40–45 m/min cutting speed with a feed of 0.03–0.06 mm/rev is ideal, supporting existing literature and experimental evidence [2].

Chip morphology is a critical indicator of the cutting mechanism and directly relates to tool performance, heat generation, and surface quality during machining. The chip formation images shown in Figure 30.6 reveal distinct characteristics of segmented chips across all tested conditions, which is typical of titanium alloys like Ti-6Al-4V due to their low thermal conductivity, high strain hardening rate, and poor machinability [14].

At the lowest cutting speed of 30 m/min and feed rates ranging from 0.03 to 0.12 mm/rev, the chips appeared more curled and irregular, indicating interrupted shearing and non- uniform plastic deformation. These conditions corresponded with higher circularity deviation and moderate surface roughness, as observed in Figures 30.4 and 30.5. As cutting speed increased to 40 m/min, chip segments became more uniform and tightly curled at lower feeds (0.03 and 0.06 mm/rev), reflecting more stable

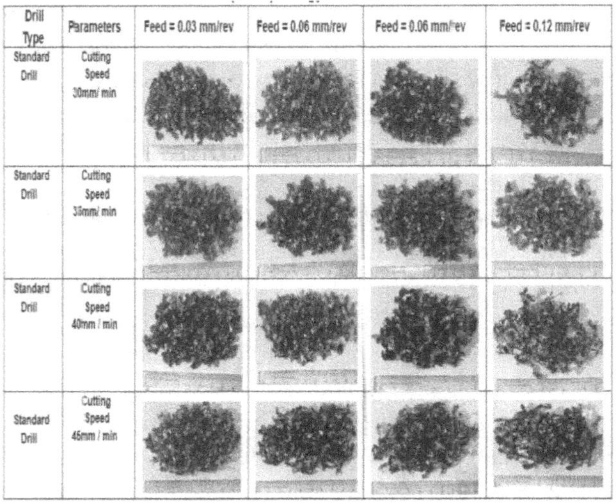

shear localization. This observation aligns with the improved surface roughness (minimum 0.91 μm) and better circularity noted at these parameters.

At the highest speed of 45 m/min, chip segmentation became more prominent with increasing feed rates. The chips became thicker, more serrated, and occasionally fragmented. Such morphology suggests elevated thermal loads and strain rates at the tool–work interface, which may contribute to localized tool wear and poor dimensional accuracy [10]. This was also reflected in a rise in circularity deviation and surface roughness at higher feeds.

Overall, chip formation under dry machining confirms the challenges posed by Ti-6Al-4V in dissipating heat, promoting shear band formation, and maintaining surface quality. However, optimized parameters (e.g., 40 m/min, 0.06 mm/rev) offer a favorable balance between manageable chip shape, thermal effects, and surface integrity. These findings emphasize the importance of feed rate control in achieving high-quality holes and minimizing tool wear during dry drilling.

Taguchi analysis
Figure 30.9 illustrates the S/N ratio for circularity error across varying machining parameters. A higher S/N ratio indicates lower variation and better performance consistency. The figure shows that circularity error is significantly influenced by feed rate, with 0.03 mm/rev yielding the highest S/N ratio, indicating the best circularity. Cutting speed has a secondary impact, with 45 m/min performing best. This confirms that minimal feed and high speed reduce tool deflection and thermal distortion, improving geometric accuracy. The trend supports previous findings that dry drilling of Ti-6Al-4V under optimized parameters enhances circularity, reinforcing the feed rate's dominant role in precision drilling.

Figure 30.10 presents the S/N ratio analysis for hole diameter deviation. The optimal combination for dimensional accuracy occurs at moderate feed rates (0.06–0.09 mm/rev) and cutting speeds of 35–40 m/min, which exhibit higher S/N ratios. These settings minimize diameter error by balancing mechanical thrust and thermal effects. Excessively high or low feeds reduce accuracy due to spring back or excessive heat generation, respectively. The figure confirms that both cutting speed and feed significantly influence hole diameter consistency, as shown by the relatively balanced S/N variation across levels. This

Figure 30.8 Effect of machining parameters on chip formation
Source: Author

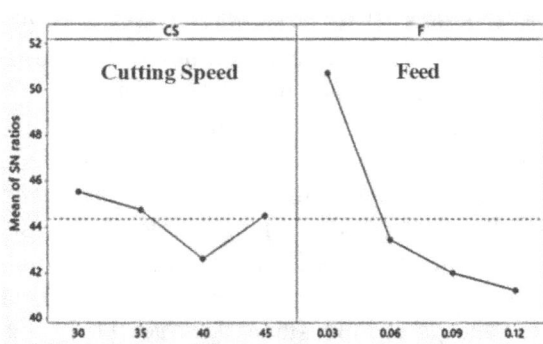

Figure 30.9 S/N ratio of circularity
Source: Author

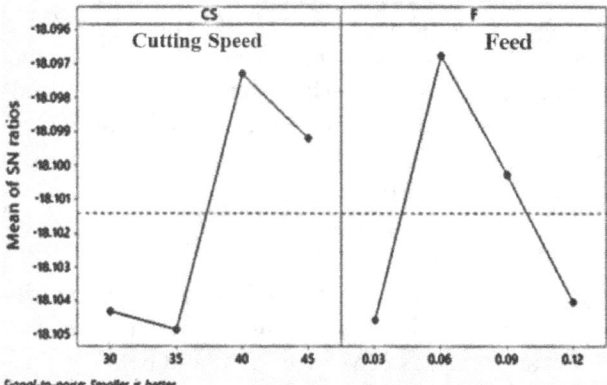

Figure 30.10 S/N ratio of hole diameter error
Source: Author

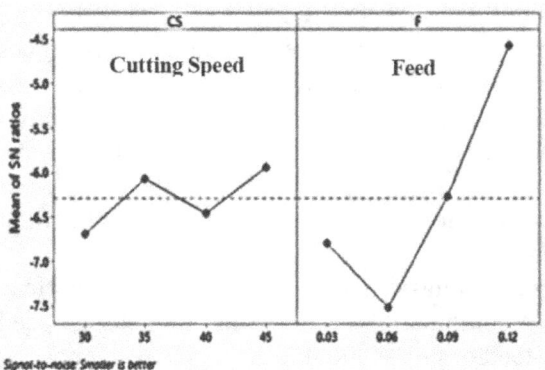

Figure 30.11 S/N ratio of surface roughness
Source: Author

Table 30.3 ANOVA of surface roughness

Source	DF	Adj SS	Adj MS	F-Value	P-Value
Cutting speed	3	0.06	0.02	0.59	0.64
Feed	3	0.96	0.32	8.98	0.005
Error	9	0.32	0.03		
Total	15	1.35			

R Sq. value: 76.13%
Source: Author

insight reinforces the need to fine-tune parameters for tight dimensional control in aerospace applications.

Figure 30.11 displays the S/N ratio for surface roughness, where higher values reflect lower and more consistent roughness. The best surface finish is achieved at low feed rates (0.03 mm/rev) and higher cutting speeds (40–45 m/min). This combination minimizes tool vibration, built-up edge, and thermal damage, yielding smoother surfaces. The S/N ratio trend highlights feed rate as the primary factor affecting roughness, corroborated by the ANOVA analysis. Moderate feeds (0.06 mm/rev) at 40 m/min also perform well, suggesting a balance between material removal rate and finish quality. The figure underscores the significance of optimized parameters for high-quality surface integrity in dry machining.

Table 30.3 reveals that feed rate is the most statistically significant factor affecting surface roughness, with a P-value of 0.005 and an F-value of 8.98. Cutting speed, with a P-value of 0.640, has no significant effect. The high R^2 value of 76.13% indicates a good model fit, implying that the variation in surface roughness is largely explained by the input parameters. The feed rate's dominant influence suggests that controlling uncut chip thickness and tool–work interaction is crucial for achieving smoother surfaces. The error term is moderate, confirming experimental consistency. Thus, feed optimization is key to enhancing surface finish in dry drilling.

Table 30.4 shows that both cutting speed and feed rate significantly affect hole diameter accuracy, with P-values of 0.007 and 0.009, respectively. The high F-values (7.74 and 7.34) further emphasize their impact. The R^2 value of 83% reflects a strong predictive model, indicating that most variability in diameter error is attributable to the input parameters. Low error variance suggests reliable experimental data. These results underline that maintaining moderate values for both speed and feed helps achieve precise diameter control, essential in aerospace-grade drilling. Hence, optimizing both parameters is critical to

Table 30.4 ANOVA of hole diameter

Source	DF	Adj SS	Adj MS	F-Value	P-Value
Cutting speed	3	0.000145	0.000048	7.74	0.007
Feed	3	0.000137	0.000046	7.34	0.009
Error	9	0.000056	0.000006		
Total	15	0.000338			

R Sq. value: 83%

Source: Author

minimizing thermal distortion and tool deflection in dry machining.

Table 30.5 indicates that feed rate significantly influences circularity, with a very high F-value of 17.00 and a P-value of 0.000. In contrast, cutting speed has a minimal effect (p = 0.316). The R² value of 85% confirms a strong correlation between the experimental factors and circularity error. This supports the conclusion that feed-induced thrust and vibration primarily govern circularity deviation. Low feed rates ensure uniform cutting, reducing distortion and improving hole geometry. The small error variance demonstrates consistent measurements. Thus, for geometrically accurate drilling in titanium alloy, feed rate control is more critical than cutting speed.

Overall, the experimental results underscore the dominant influence of feed rate on the surface integrity metrics. Signal-to-noise (S/N) ratio analysis revealed that different responses favor different optimal parameter combinations. For instance, lower feeds (0.03 mm/rev) and higher cutting speeds (45 m/min) minimized surface roughness, while moderate conditions (0.06 mm/rev at 40 m/min) provided better diameter accuracy. Circularity was most influenced by low feed and high speed, consistent with tool deflection and thermal effects observed in dry machining. Although the Taguchi method efficiently

Table 30.5 ANOVA of circularity

Source	DF	Adj SS	Adj MS	F-Value	P-Value
Cutting speed	3	0.000006	0.000002	1.36	0.316
Feed	3	0.000071	0.000024	17.00	0.000
Error	9	0.000013	0.000001		
Total	15	0.000089			

R Sq. value: 85%

Source: Author

identified individual optima, the variations in optimal conditions for each response suggest a trade-off, highlighting the scope for future multi-objective optimization to achieve a globally optimal machining condition.

GRA analysis

The GRA analysis serves as a powerful multi-criteria decision-making tool [8, 9], especially effective in experimental research where multiple conflicting objectives exist. In this study, GRA was employed to simultaneously optimize three critical responses—surface roughness (Ra), hole diameter error, and circularity deviation—in the drilling of titanium alloy using different combinations of cutting speed and feed rate. The first step in the GRA process involved the normalization of the raw experimental data as presented Table 30.6. Since all the responses in the present study are of the "smaller-the-better" type, further, the normalization was performed as mentioned in materials and methods chapter, where, $Y_i(K)$ denotes the raw value of the kth performance measure in the ith experiment, while $maxY_i(K)$ and $minY_i(K)$ are the maximum and minimum values of the kth performance measure across all experiments.

This normalization ensures that all metrics are transformed to a common scale between 0 and 1, allowing them to be compared and analyzed together. Following normalization, the grey relational coefficient (GRC) was calculated for each response using the equation-2, where $\Delta o_i(K) = |1 - Z_i(K)|$ is the absolute difference between the ideal normalized value (1) and the actual normalized value for a given response. Δmin and Δmax are the minimum and maximum of all Δo_i values across experiments, and ζ is the distinguishing coefficient, taken as 0.5 in this study to assign equal weight to all responses. The Grey Relational Grade (GRG) was then obtained as the arithmetic average of the GRCs corresponding to the three responses for each experimental condition. The GRG represents a unified performance index, where a higher GRG implies Pandey and Yadav [7] better overall performance across all considered responses.

The computed GRG values revealed as presented Table 30.7, that Experiment No. 13 (Cutting speed: 45 m/min, Feed: 0.03 mm/rev) attained the highest GRG of 0.6556. This experimental setup demonstrated excellent control over circularity (0.002 mm) and produced acceptable levels of surface roughness

Table 30.6 Normalized experimental data

Exp. no	Normalized roughness	Normalized diameter	Normalized circularity
13	0.3571	0.5556	1.0
10	0.3096	1.0	0.375
16	1.0	0.5	0.0
14	0.2137	0.9444	0.375
1	0.1861	0.0	1.0
8	0.9991	0.0556	0.125
5	0.2659	0.2778	0.875
9	0.4843	0.6111	0.5
7	0.5603	0.5556	0.375
4	0.6553	0.3889	0.375
11	0.3533	0.7222	0.25
12	0.4653	0.6111	0.125
3	0.4653	0.5	0.25
15	0.4084	0.5556	0.125
2	0.038	0.6111	0.375
6	0.0	0.5	0.5

Source: Author

Table 30.7 GRA ranking of drilling experiments

Exp. No	Ra (μm)	Diameter (mm)	Circularity (mm)	GRG Value	Rank
13	2.15	8.036	0.002	0.6556	1
10	2.20	8.028	0.007	0.6214	2
16	1.47	8.037	0.01	0.6111	3
14	2.30	8.029	0.007	0.5777	4
1	2.33	8.046	0.002	0.5712	5
8	1.47	8.045	0.009	0.5692	6
5	2.25	8.041	0.003	0.5380	7
9	2.02	8.035	0.006	0.5182	8
7	1.94	8.036	0.007	0.5019	9
4	1.84	8.039	0.007	0.4954	10
11	2.15	8.033	0.008	0.4929	11
12	2.04	8.035	0.009	0.4697	12
3	2.04	8.037	0.008	0.4610	13
15	2.1	8.036	0.009	0.4503	14
2	2.49	8.035	0.007	0.4496	15
6	2.53	8.037	0.006	0.4444	16

Source: Author

and hole diameter accuracy. The high GRG indicates superior balanced performance, making this parameter combination the most desirable for drilling titanium alloys under the tested conditions.

Experiment No. 10 (Speed: 40 m/min, Feed: 0.06 mm/rev) followed with a GRG of 0.6215. While its Ra was slightly higher than Experiment 13, it still maintained very good values for hole geometry, proving to be a strong candidate as well. On the contrary, Experiment 6 recorded the lowest GRG of 0.4444. This was largely attributed to its highest surface roughness value of 2.53 μm, which degraded the overall performance despite moderate geometric accuracy.

The ranking table generated through GRA highlights not only the optimal parameter settings but also the potential pitfalls of suboptimal choices. For instance, increasing the feed rate without adequately adjusting the speed tends to increase surface roughness and circularity error, adversely affecting overall quality. The GRG metric, by integrating these diverse quality measures into a single value, offers a clear and quantifiable path for parameter selection in multi-objective machining studies.

GRA proved to be an invaluable tool in evaluating and optimizing multiple conflicting performance metrics in titanium drilling. It facilitated an evidence-based approach to parameter tuning, enhancing both surface and geometric integrity of the drilled holes. This methodology can be readily adapted for other machining operations and materials where multi-response optimization is essential.

Conclusion

The optimal surface roughness (Ra = 0.91 μm) was achieved at a cutting speed of 40 m/min and feed rate of 0.06 mm/rev, indicating that smoother finishes are associated with moderate feed and high-speed combinations. Minimum circularity deviation (22 μm) was observed at a high speed of 45 m/min and low fee rate of 0.03 mm/rev, showing that lower thrust and vibration enhance geometric precision Hole diameter accuracy was best maintained at 35–40 m/min with a feed rate of 0.06–0.09 mm/rev, suggesting a balanced cutting force and thermal profile improves dimensional control.

ANOVA and S/N ratio analyses identified feed rate as the most significant parameter across all three responses, with high F-values and P-values below 0.01 for surface roughness and circularity. Chip morphology analysis revealed segmented and stable chips under optimal settings, confirming improved shear deformation and thermal conditions during dry drilling. Grey relational analysis (GRA) provided a more comprehensive view by optimizing all responses simultaneously. While GRA results closely resembled the trends observed through Taguchi's single-response analysis, it offered clearer guidance in selecting a balanced parameter set—proving its advantage in multi-objective decision-making.

References

[1] Ahmad, A., Ibrahim, R., Zainoridin, H., Chong, B. H., & Cheng, K. (2024). An analysis of chip formation and hole circularity in drilling applications: an aircraft components perspective. *Journal of Advanced Research in Applied Mechanics*, 118(1), 28–39.

[2] Alam, S. T., Tomal, A. A., & Nayeem, M. K. (2023). High-speed machining of Ti–6Al–4V: RSM-GA based optimization of surface roughness and MRR. *Results in Engineering*, 17, 100873.

[3] Dedeakayogulları, H., & Kacal, A. (2022). Experimental investigation of hole quality in drilling of additive manufacturing Ti6Al4V parts produced by hole features. *Journal of Manufacturing Processes*, 79, 745–758.

[4] Festas, A. J., Pereira, R. B., Ramos, A., & Davim, J. P. (2021). A study of the effect of conventional drilling and helical milling in surface quality in titanium Ti-6-4V and Ti-6AL-7Nb alloys for medical applications. *Arabian Journal for Science and Engineering*, 46(3), 2361–2369.

[5] Ge, J., He, N., Xu, Y., Liu, F., Liu, Z., Shen, Y., et al. (2022). Investigating hole making performance of Al 2024-T3/Ti-6Al-4V alloy stacks: a comparative study of conventional drilling, peck drilling and helical milling. *International Journal of Advanced Manufacturing Technology*, 120(7), 5027–5040.

[6] Krishnaraj, V., Samsudeensadham, S., Sindhumathi, R., & Kuppan, P. (2014). A study on high speed end milling of titanium alloy. *Procedia Engineering*, 97, 251–257.

[7] Pandey, G. K., & Yadav, S. K. S. (2020). Multi-objective optimization of vibration assisted electrical discharge drilling process using PCA based GRA method. *Materials Today: Proceedings*, 26, 2667–2672.

[8] Prasanna, J., Karunamoorthy, L., Venkat Raman, M., Prashanth, S., & Chordia, R. (2022). Optimization of process parameters of small hole dry drilling in Ti–6Al–4V using Taguchi and grey relational analysis. *Heliyon*, 8(11).

[9] Reddy, P. V., Ramanjaneyulu, P., Reddy, B. V., & Rao, P. S. (2020). Simultaneous optimization of drilling responses using GRA on Al-6063/TiC composite *SN Applied Sciences*, 2, 431.

[10] Ribeiro-Carvalho, S., Pereira, R. B. D., Horovistiz, A., & Davim, J. P. (2021). Intelligent machining methods for Ti6Al4V: a review. *Proceedings of the Institution of Mechanical Engineers, Part E: Journal of Process Mechanical Engineering*, 235(4), 1188–1210.

[11] Samsudeensadham, S., Krishnaraj, V., Thilak, R. K., & Prasath, V. (2023). Investigations on the machining characteristics of Ti-6Al-4V alloy during high-speed end milling process. *International Journal of Manufacturing Research*, 18(2), 125–143.

[12] Samsudeensadham, S., Mohan, A., ArunRamnath, R., & Keshav Thilak, R. (2021). Optimization of machining parameters in drilling Ti–6Al–4V using user's preference rating-based TOPSIS. Materials, In Design, and Manufacturing for Sustainable Environment: Lecture Notes in Mechanical Engineering. Singapore: Springer.

[13] Vijayan, K., Sadham, S., Sangeetha, S., Palaniyandi, K., & Zitoune, R. (2014). Study on cutting forces and surface finish during end milling of titanium alloy. In: ASME International Mechanical Engineering Congress and Exposition, (Vol. 46438, p. V02AT02A029).

[14] Yuan, C. G., Wang, J. J., Zhang, X. Y., Wang, Y., & Zhang, Q. (2021). Drilling of titanium alloy (Ti6Al4V) – a review. *Machining Science and Technology*, 25(4), 637–702.

[15] Zhang, C., Cao, C., Fu, Y., Sun, L., Wang, S., Zhu, W., et al. (2023). The state of the art in machining additively manufactured titanium alloy Ti-6Al-4V. *Materials*, 16(7), 2583.

31 Investigation on tribological characteristics of nanolubricants for hydraulic systems

Vimalraj, S.[1,a] and Nallasamy, P[2,b]

[1]PG Student, Department of Mechanical Engineering, PSG College of Technology, Coimbatore, India

[2]Assistant Professor, Department of Mechanical Engineering, PSG College of Technology, Coimbatore, India

Abstract

This research is intended to develop an efficient and eco-friendly nanolubricants for hydraulic systems. Mineral oil-based lubricants are widely used in hydraulic systems, but their performance has not improved much. Friction and wear are major issues in hydraulic systems, leading to energy loss and component wear. Nanolubricants refer to the dispersion of nanoparticles in base oil, and it has recently drawn the interest of researchers due to its promising applications. An optimum level of nanoparticles with biodegradable oil as base oil with a surfactant combination, with its physical and tribological properties, could replace the conventional oil with better performance. The nanoparticles that are taken for the investigation are graphene and copper oxide, and the base oils are SAE 68 oil, Sesame oil, and PAO oil. Also, the comparative study is made between the conventional SAE 68 oil and bio-nanolubricants. The physical characterization demonstrates that all the developed nanolubricants have shown improvement in viscosity, flash and fire points, and suitable cloud and pour points compared to the conventional lubricant.

Keywords: Hydraulic system, nanolubricants, pressure distribution, thermophysical, tribology

Introduction

Friction, wear, and lubrication are all the centres of attention in tribology. Lubrication, the application of lubricants to moving surfaces in an effort to minimize wear and friction, is a vital aspect of tribology. It not only gives insulation to transformers, but it also possesses the advantage of minimizing corrosion, water, and dust damage. Mechanical failures and energy losses can be due to uncontrolled wear and friction within engines, shafts, cylinders, gears, and other moving components. They are therefore not covered under the requirement of proper lubrication. [1]. Issues, however, arise over its disposal being linked to contamination of land and aquatic ecosystems. Being non-toxic and biodegradable, bio-lubricant oil has been lauded as a cleaner alternative. Compared to mineral oil, bio-lubricants have numerous advantages like enhanced lubrication, higher flash point, viscosity, lower volatility, and biodegradability and non-toxicity [4]. In order to further enhance lubricant performance and prevent wear, trace quantities of additives are generally added to the lubricant base stock. These include extreme pressure (EP), anti-corrosion, anti-wear (AW), and dispersants additives. Environmental issues have resulted in regulations being placed on traditional EP and AW additives with phosphorus and chlorine compounds. Scientists are examining the viability of employing nanoparticles (NPs) as a new class of lubricant additives. These green nanoparticles do not require the application of toxic chemicals such as sulphur, phosphorus, and chlorine to improve tribological performance. The nanoscale nature of NPs allows them to function as fill contact asperities, friction modifiers, and efficient AW and EP additives. They also provide effective heat stability with reactivity on friction surfaces without the necessity of an induction time [4].

Tribology
Tribology can be defined as the science that studies the relative motion of two surfaces in contact with each other. Its applications include, but are not limited to, wear and tear on metal surfaces, lubrication, corrosion, friction, engine life, and even energy dissipation. All these come into play with very large amounts of energy lost during these operations and making their effects important for handling. From a tribological perspective, selecting the right lubricant could probably be the most important single step in satisfying the lubrication needs of any system. The three major components in controlling tribological behavior are wear, friction, and lubrication [4]. Of

[a]vimalmech076@gmail.com, [b]pns.mech@psgtech.ac.in

DOI: 10.1201/9781003770435-31

the many important things in tribology, lubricity is deemed one of the most important. By facilitating the formation of a protective coating, otherwise known as a tribo-film, on surfaces in contact, it defines the ability to reduce wear and energy losses. High lubricity means no real contact between the interacting surfaces, hence less friction and energy losses. However, it must be brought to the fore that better lubricity does not always mean better wear prevention because the surface-active agents in lubricants, whether being base stocks or additives, affect the creation of a protective film on rubbing surfaces. Through contact between the surface irregularities of roughness, three mechanical wear modes are created: adhesion, abrasion, and fatigue. Adhesive wear occurs mainly under high loads, high temperatures, or insufficient lubrication where the asperities on sliding surfaces weld and split very quickly. Abrasive wear will occur between surfaces when there is difference in hardness between them. Fatigue-type wear is local and progressive structural damage under repeated loading in solids. All of them now constitute the discussion on tribological performance regarding bio-Nano-lubricants; however, three majorly concerned tribological parameters needed to be analysed first: mechanical properties of the tribological system, lubrication, and physico-chemical characteristics of the lubricant. These are crucial elements that will explain and optimize the performance of the lubricant in minimizing friction and wear under different applications [3].

Energy losses

Hydraulic systems undergo frictions, which increases energy and heat production whilst decreasing efficiency. Furthermore, the system's performance is not only affected, but maintenance costs also increased, and the lifespan of other components decreased. The problem was approached by researchers looking into advanced lubrication techniques that have found the use of nanolubricants to be particularly promising. Nanolubricants, the new class of lubricants, contain nanoparticles such as graphene and CuO, which greatly enhance the lubrication properties by lowering friction, improving load-carrying capacity, enhancing thermal stability, and increasing operational stamina. With the aid of nanolubricants, hydraulic systems can further reduce component wear, enhance operational efficiency, and prolong component lifespan. The goal of this research is to

develop nanolubricants that would help sustain the most intensive hydraulic systems

Lubrication

Lubrication is an important factor affecting both the efficiency and the durability of the hydraulic cylinder. Typically, these cylinders employ pressure and hydraulic oil to produce motion and force and as the piston slides back and forth within the cylinder, the frictional force generated between the piston and the cylinder walls is to lead to high wear and damage. Proper lubrication, by reducing the friction, not only ensures the movement of the components is smooth and efficient but also minimizes the risk of early wear-out and possible breakage. Inadequate lubrication might not only result in the generated heat, as a result of friction, but can cause a decrease in the hydraulic system's efficiency. Further, the kind of lubrication expiring in the cylinder is contingent upon various factors, including load, speed, and pressure. One example being the boundary regime lubrication (Figure 31.1) in which the lubricant film is very thin, and the surfaces may still come into contact hence the friction may be high. On the other hand, mixed lubrication is characterized by a film that is thicker and, hence, there is no direct contact but still, some interaction can occur. For hydrodynamic lubrication, the part of the lubrication regime with the best effect, this will truly separate the moving parts using a lubricant with very-thing film, which will result in less friction and wear. If the lubrication types and levels of a hydraulic cylinder are kept in check and the right lubrication system capable of transverse moving components exists, the result will be that hydraulic cylinders can maintain optimal functions, whose implications are reliability and extension in the life of the equipment [7].

Nano-lubricants

Nano-lubricants is the application of nanoparticles as additives in lubricants. The size classification for nanoparticles is roughly 1 to 100 nanometres. Laboratory studies have shown the incorporation of Nano-lubricants into base oils or coatings demonstrates stunning tribological characteristics and greatly diminishes friction and wear. Nano-lubricants can be synthesized in one step or two. The one-step method is the chemical synthesis of Nano-lubricants. The two-step method begins with the synthesis of nanomaterials as dry powder using either physical

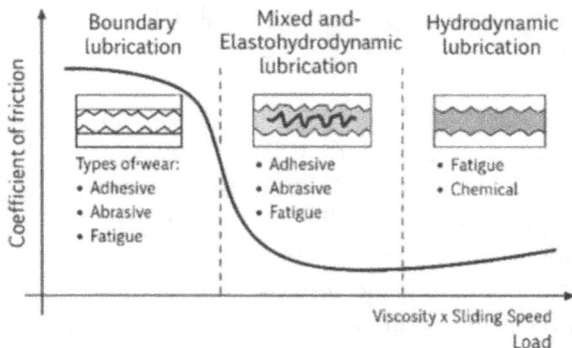

Figure 31.1 Stribeck curve
Source: Author [18]

or chemical means. The second step consists of the dispersion of these nanoparticles into the base oil using various stirring techniques, with or without dispersants or surfactants. The creation process for Nano-lubricants is illustrated in Figure 31.3. The implementation of nanolubricants offers an effective means to enhance the lubrication properties of base oils and coatings, thus decreasing friction and wear in many systems.

Hybrid nanolubricants

Hybrid bio-nanolubricants are the forthcoming generation of lubricants, which consist of nanoparticles for improved performance and biodegradable empty biological oil. Nanoparticles can be exemplified by metal oxides or carbon-based compounds, and they serve the purpose of both reducing friction and wear resistance. These lubricants have better wear and friction reduction attributes when compared to the single component lubricants. This performance comes after the combined action of nanoparticles and bio-based oils. The mixture of viscosity, stability, and lubricant performance is such a delicate thing that its composition, especially the ratio of nanoparticles to bio-oils, can be changed for different purposes. The main reason these lubricants are in demand is that such lubricants that are biodegradable are more attractive than conventional and at a lower environmental impact.

Base oil

Mineral oil is a result of the distillation of crude oil by fractional distillation. The chemical constitution of the oil is classified into three categories: paraffinic, naphthenic, and aromatic. Paraffinic mineral oil essentially contains alkanes having a straight chain, naphthenic mineral oil contains cycloalkanes

with no double bonds, and aromatic mineral oil is the one possessing a cyclic structure based on benzene. An inexpensive material in application as lubricants is mineral oil, but it has negative environmental and health impacts. Mineral oil is used as a lubricant in such varied industrial applications as engines, gears, and cylinders.

A lubricant manufactured synthetically from hydrocarbons or other chemical substances is known as synthetic oil. It can be developed by using the relatively environmentally friendly method of chemically altering petroleum products rather than extracting crude oil totally. Besides, synthetic oil has many advantages compared to mineral oils, mainly being able to lubricate effectively in both the lowest and highest temperature and protection from wear. Synthetic oils are also the lubricants that bring the most noticeable economic benefits in that they reduce energy consumption and maintenance costs as well as improve energy efficiency. They are designed for the highest requirements of modern machines, but it should be kept in mind that the production of some synthetic oils may still harm the environment.

The essential raw materials for bio lubricants are oil crops that include sunflower, coconut, jatropha, rapeseed, and palm. Moreover, they can be made from mineral oil, synthetic esters, and other petroleum products if they satisfy biodegradability and toxicity standards. The selection of the usable base oils influences the qualifications of bio lubricants, namely physicochemical, renewable, degradable, and the most important one, tribological properties. Compared with mineral oil, bio-based lubricants have many benefits, such as their renewable source, a high viscosity index, a high flash point, low volatility, and excellent dispersion. Their eco-friendly nature is the result of the easy availability of the raw materials, being renewable and, at the same time, biodegradable, which makes them the most reasonable choice for various applications of lubricants.

Hydraulic Cylinders

Hydraulic cylinders (Figure 31.2) are mechanical actuators designed to produce linear motion and generate force by means of pressurized fluid. They can virtually be found in any application involving heavy and momentary work, including excavators and loaders, not to mention farm implements as well as manufacturing plants in general. In most cases, hydraulic cylinders work by means of hydraulic fluid directed through a sealed space to either push or pull a piston in an inward or outward direction, respectively, as dictated by the design. In terms of their importance, we can classify the types of hydraulic cylinders that exist into single-acting cylinders and double-acting cylinders. In a single-acting cylinder, moving the piston is facilitated in one direction by the hydraulic fluid, with the return accomplished by gravity or spring.

A double-acting cylinder, on the other hand, moves the piston in both directions with more control and precision by using hydraulic fluid on both sides of the piston. This is important to consider when choosing a cylinder for any application, as some technical aspects-the length of stroke-which translate into how far the piston can move-really matters; the bore diameter which relates to the output force; rod diameter related to strength and durability; the pressure handling capacity of the cylinder itself. The cylinders are therefore structured in different ways and can be tie-rod type-simple maintenance is assured-welded cylinders compact and strong; and rams mainly suited for pushing heavy loads under high pressures. Understanding this information will help determine which cylinder fits the application for the optimum performance of the hydraulic system.

Selection of Base Materials

Selection of nanoparticles

It is that the oxide nanoparticles and the carbon particles are efficient when added with the bio-oils. The best nanoparticles and their composition have been identified shown in Table 31.1

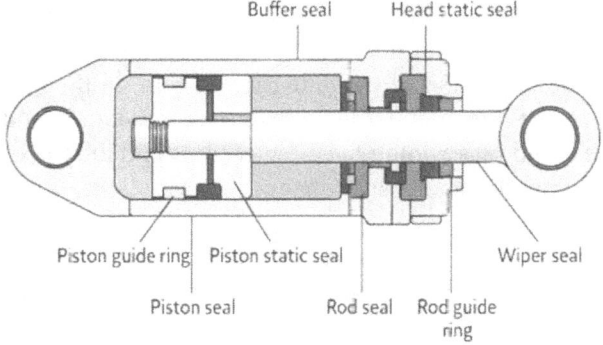

Figure 31.2 Hydraulic cylinder
Source: Author

Table 31.1 Selection of nanoparticles [6, 7]

Sl. No.	Description	Composition
1	Graphene nanoparticle	0.0025wt%
2	Copper-oxide nanoparticle	0.1wt%
3	Graphene + CuO	0.0025 wt. % + 0.1 wt. %

Source: Author

Graphene nanoparticle

Graphene has gained significant attention in lubrication research due to its ultra-high thermal conductivity and self-lubricating behavior. The layering found in graphene gives it the property to perform as a solid lubricant by lowering the friction that was previously caused by surfaces being in contact First, graphene also has an ability to hold heavy loads which keep the lubricant film from breaking when exerting pressure. With graphene having one more crucial benefit of being oxidation-resistant, this would be an aid in the protection and hence prolonged service life of bio-lubricants through the prevention of their degradation process.

Copper oxide nanoparticle

CuO has good thermal conductivity, and its anti-wear efficacy is also praised. Once added to lubricants, CuO nanoparticles will generate a protective tribo-film on the surface of diverse mobile elements, the consequence of which is a reduction of direct contact, and a substantial diminish in framework wear. Further, the CuO addition is responsible for the improvement of heat stability. This makes the lubricant capable of withstanding high temperatures without its fluidity and oiliness falling off. The fact that CuO remains well-distributed in oil-based systems will mean that the lubricant's performance will stay at a constant level over the entire time of operation. Biodegradation of bio-lubricants is also prevented by CuO, extending the lifespan of the lubricants.

Hybrid (CuO + Graphene) nanoparticles

To exploit the two substances CuO and Graphene, we decided to work on creating a hybrid nanoparticle. In addition to achieving the highest heat conduction, this union eliminates issues like wear resistance and reduced friction as compared to using individual nanoparticles.

For example, CuO is a lubricant that works on the boundary, thus, it helps to reduce metal-to-metal contact, while, in addition, graphene both reduces friction and increases the stability of the film. A conclusion supported theoretically and experimentally is that the mixture of such two materials is responsible for less viscosity loss, low torque, and hence lower heating and wear of the surfaces, as well as the additional advantage of a more stable dispersion and a better overall performance in tribological tests.

Selection of base oil

SAE 68 (Mineral oil-based lubricant)

SAE 68 is among the most popular mineral oil-based lubricants with numerous applications in industrial hydraulic installations for its properties of outstanding viscosity stability and oxidation resistance. Research work has established that mineral oils have moderate thermal conductivities and capacities for wear protection, making this oil most useful for redressing almost all lubrication requirements. On the contrary, that same research states that mineral oils tend to degrade rapidly within high temperature conditions, causing sludge development to be more prevalent and hence the reduced life of the oils used under these extended harsh working conditions. Of all negatives, SAE 68 is the standard reference lubricant, usually taken for evaluating the performance of synthetic and bio-based alternatives to lubricant formulations.

Polyalphaolefin (PAO) – synthetic base oil

PAO oil is a synthetic lubricant widely recognized for its excellent thermal stability, high viscosity index, and high oxidation resistance. Research showed that PAO oils have constant viscosity at different temperatures; this makes them the most suitable candidates for high-performance lubrication systems. PAO oils also tend to evaporate and/or gases; thus, they maximize the life of a lubricant and lower wear effects of lubrication under high-speed applications. Unlike mineral oils, PAO complex lubricants provide more uniform nanoparticle dispersion and therefore reduced agglomeration and the same levels of lubrication at different times.

Sesame oil (Bio-based lubricant)

Bio-based lubricants have immense environmental advantages, and they meet the lubrication tests satisfactorily and are considered friendlier to the environment. Sesame oil is said to be more effective than mineral oil for lubrication, primarily on account of its high flash point, natural resistance to oxidation, and good properties of adhesion to metal. Studies have shown that, under high-pressure conditions, vegetable oils such as Sesame oil could form thick films of lubrication, which results in very little friction and wear. However, the kind of performance additives that exist today-for example, CuO and Graphene nanoparticles-are required not only for bio-based lubricants but for all commercial lubricants so that they prolong their otherwise limited lifespan and improve their thermal and anti-wear properties.

Selection of surfactants

The choice of a suitable surfactant is vital to this goal, guaranteeing the stable dispersion and the regular distribution of the particles in bio-nanolubricants. In the absence of a surfactant, the nanoparticles could potentially coalesce thus causing sedimentation, which then leads to a lack of consistent performance and reduced lubrication efficiency. A surfactant, on the other hand, behaves as a stabilizer, thus preventing particle aggregation and at the same time, keeping the lubricant as a total homogeneous suspension. was found to be the best matching surfactant. In the event of yellowish commercial sample availability, the oil is odorless and colourless. The decision to use Oleic acid as the surfactant was not only based on its processability but also on its excellent dispersion characteristics, its strong affinity with oil-based lubricants, and its capacity to deter nanoparticle aggregation. It, being a non-ionic surfactant, makes the process of the formation of a protective layer around the nanoparticles very feasible, this way assuring a continuous and stable mixture with the lubricant. Oleic acid is extremely assimilable with non-polar base oils such as SAE 68, PAO, and Sesame oil and, hence, can be a good medium of making the suspension uniform. Further, it acts as a lubricant by means of the formation of the anti-friction film on the surfaces of the metal thus preventing oxidation and wear and by so doing the effectiveness and the life of bio-nanolubricants are enhanced.

Selection of conventional lubricants

Traditional oils, especially mineral-based lubricants, are commonly utilized because they are readily available, inexpensive, and have stable lubricating characteristics. These oils offer sufficient viscosity, oxidation stability, and wear protection, which makes them appropriate for Numerous industrial applications. In this research, SAE 68 was chosen as the traditional base oil because of its uniform viscosity, high thermal stability, and good lubrication under varying operating conditions. It is widely utilized in hydraulic systems and tribological applications to provide smooth running and low wear. Even though lower biodegradability and moderate high-temperature performance are the drawbacks of SAE 68, it is used as a reference to compare the advancements made by nanolubricants and measure the conventional lubrication against newer bio-based technologies.

Physical Characterization

Preparation of nanolubricants

The required number of nanoparticles was weighed, and the corresponding number of surfactants is added to the beaker and manual stirring is carried on avoiding agglomeration of the particles. The correct volume of base oil is added to the beaker and again manual stirring is done to initiate the dispersion of the particle. After manual stirring, the final nanolubricants are kept in the ultrasonicator for two hours to obtain an effective dispersion of nanoparticles in the medium. A similar procedure is carried out for preparing all the nanolubricants [13]. The synthesis of bio-nanolubricants as shown in Figure 31.3.

Flash point and fire point testing

The flash and fire points of the lubricating fluid greatly impact the safe usage of nanolubricants at elevated temperature conditions. The flash point is defined as the minimal temperature at which vapors of the oil ignite when brought into contact with an ignition source, then extinguish when taken away from the ignition source. The fire point is taken to be the lowest point at which vapours from the oil can continue to burn whether ignited or not. Generally,

flash and fire points should tend to be higher for lubricants so as not to ignite easily under higher temperatures operating conditions. The Cleveland open cup tester (Figure 31.4) is used to measure the flash and fire points of the base oil and nanolubricants in accordance with ASTM D92-16b.

Viscosity testing

The kinematic viscosity test is carried out using a Redwood viscometer (Figure 31.5) following the ASTM D88 standard [14]. The prepared nanolubricants are poured into the viscometer bowl. Once the bowl is filled with the nanolubricants to be tested, the ball valve is opened, and the oil is allowed to fall into the beaker kept beneath the instrument. The time taken for 50 ml of the beaker is noted and the time is used in the formula $u = \{0.0026 \times t - (1.88/t)\}$, where u is the kinematic viscosity.

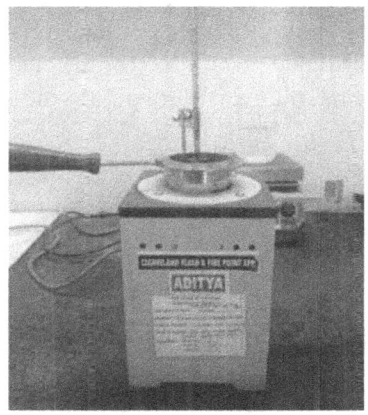

Figure 31.4 Cleveland open cup tester
Source: Author

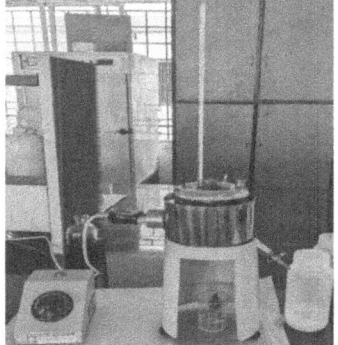

Figure 31.5 Redwood viscometer
Source: Author

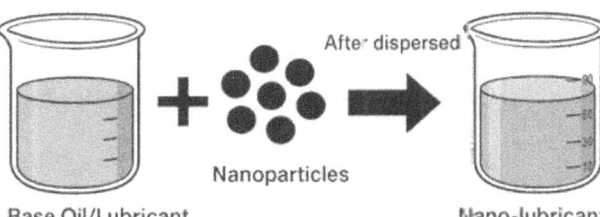

Figure 31.3 Nanolubricants synthesis
Source: Author

Extreme pressure testing

The EP test assesses the load-carrying ability of lubricants by using the four-ball test according to ASTM D2783. The top ball is rotated at 1760 rpm under increasing loads preset by the standard for 10 s. If the applied load goes beyond the capacity of the lubricant, the steel balls are considered welded, meaning the lubricant has failed. The weld load is defined as the least load when welding cannot be prevented by the lubricant. If no welding occurs, the wear scar diameter (WSD) is normally read as about 4 mm under a digital microscope for evaluation under the extreme-pressure condition.

Cloud point and pour point testing

The cloud and pour point of the lubricating oil also has an important role in the operation of the machines in colder countries. The temperature at which oil takes on a Smoggy appearance is known as the cloud point. The temperature at which the oil stops flowing and transforms into a semi-solid state is known as the pour point (Figure 31.6). The value must be as low as possible so that the lubricating oil does not have any problem in getting circulated in colder conditions. The cloud and pour points of the oil were determined as per ASTM D97-17b.

Coefficient of friction testing

The anti-friction characteristics of lubricants in sliding contact are evaluated using a pin-on-disc tribometer (Figure 31.7). In this experiment a pin is fixed onto a rotating disc and the lubricant to be tested is introduced into the zone of contact between the pin and the disc. Under controlled conditions, the

Figure 31.7 Pin on disc tribometer
Source: Author

frictional force of the pin against the disc is measured, which enables quantifying the effectiveness of the tested lubricant in decreasing friction and wear. Different loads, speeds, and types of lubricants can be tested. The test is conducted as per ASTM standard G99 [1].

Result and Discussion

Kinematic viscosity test

The kinematic viscosity of nanolubricants was tested at 26–80°C. CuO and graphene increase viscosity by up to 15–20% for high-viscosity applications., while PAO and Sesame oil maintained stable viscosity across temperatures. Viscosity decreased with increasing temperature for all nanolubricants, with SAE 68+CuO showing comparable viscosity to conventional lubricants as shown in Figure 31.8.

Comparable viscosity enhancement was observed by Mello et al. [8] using CuO in coconut oil.

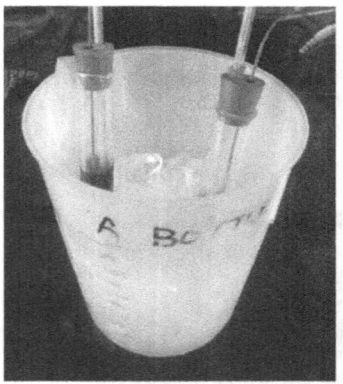

Figure 31.6 Ice-bath tub
Source: Author

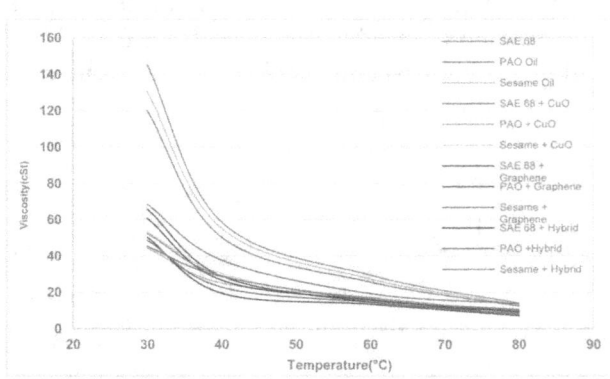

Figure 31.8 Temperature vs viscosity
Source: Author

Shahmohamadi et al. [6] reported similar viscosity stability with carbon-based nanoparticles.

Flash and Fire Point Test

The bio-nanolubricants have flash and fire points exceeding 200°C, outperforming conventional lubricants. PAO and Sesame oils show higher flash points than SAE 68, reducing ignition risk. CuO additives increase flash and fire points by 10–15%, enhancing thermal stability. Hybrid additives provide the highest safety profile, making bio-nanolubricants ideal for extreme conditions as shown in Figure 31.9.

Parás et al. [3] reported a lower thermal limit of 190°C in mineral-oil-based nanolubricants. The current formulation shows enhanced thermal stability with higher ignition resistance.

Cloud and pour point test

The bio-nanolubricants have cloud points below 0 °C (e.g., -5°C) and pour points suitable for cooler conditions (e.g., -10°C). SAE 68 + CuO and PAO base oils excel in low-temperature performance, maintaining

flowability down to -20 °C. Sesame oil is suitable for moderate temperatures (e.g., above 0°C) but requires consideration of its pour point (e.g., -5°C) in cold conditions. CuO does not significantly impact low-temperature properties, while graphene slightly increases cloud points but reduces pour points as shown in Figure 31.10.

Shafi et al. [12] observed a minimum pour point of -5°C with vegetable oil nanolubricants. The present study surpasses this, maintaining flow below -10°C.

Coefficient of friction test

The addition of CuO and Graphene nanoparticles reduces the coefficient of friction (COF) by up to 30–40% in base oils, and a combination of both gives the best friction reduction performance. Sesame Oil + (CuO + Graphene) gives the lowest COF values (around 0.05–0.08), followed by PAO + (CuO + Graphene), and hence are the most effective lubricants in friction reduction as shown in Figure 31.11.

Parás et al. [3] reported a 30–35% friction reduction with TiO_2 nanolubricants. The present hybrid blend achieved up to a 40% reduction, outperforming prior work.

Conclusion

This study shows that addition of nanoparticles like graphene and copper oxide in lubricants can significantly improve the performance of hydraulic systems. When added to both synthetic and bio-based oils, these nanoparticles helped increase viscosity, raised the flash and fire points, and reduced wear and friction. Among all the tested oils, Sesame oil mixed with nanoparticles is the best performer, offering both high efficiency and environmental benefits. Compared to earlier studies, the proposed formulation

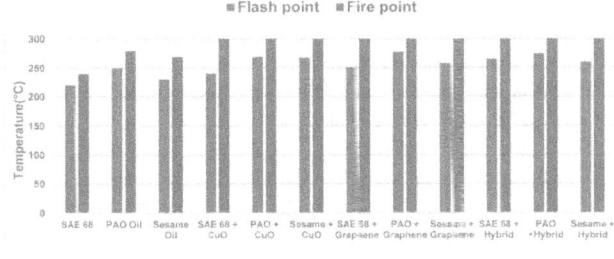

Figure 31.9 Flash and fire point
Source: Author

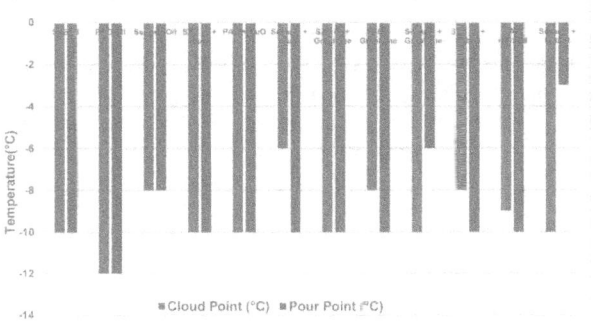

Figure 31.10 Cloud and pour point
Source: Author

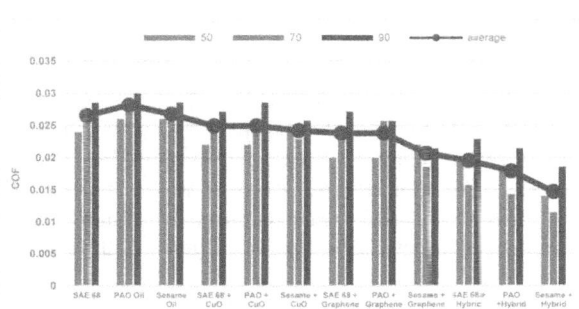

Figure 31.11 Coefficient of friction testing
Source: Author

demonstrates clear advantages in thermal resilience and low-temperature flow behavior, supporting its potential as an eco-friendly and high-efficiency alternative to conventional hydraulic lubricants.

The combination of both CuO and graphene in a hybrid form gave even better results, especially in reducing friction and keeping the lubricant stable under different operating conditions. Using oleic acid as a surfactant made sure the nanoparticles stayed well mixed in the oil, which helped maintain consistent performance. nano-lubricant especially those based on bio-oils are a promising, eco-friendly alternative to traditional oils. They not only help protect the environment but also improve energy efficiency and extend the life of hydraulic system components.

References

[1] Holmberg, K., Andersson, P., & Erdemir, A. (2012). Global energy consumption due to friction in passenger cars. *Tribology International*, 47, 221–234.

[2] Kader, A., Selvaraj, V., Ramasamy, P., & Senthilkumar, K. (2023). Experimental investigation on the thermo-physical properties and tribological performance of acidic functionalized graphene dispersed vg-68hydraulic oil-based nanolubricant. *Diamond and Related Materials*. 133, 109740.

[3] Parás, L. P., Cortés, D. M., & Taha-Tijerina, J. (2019). Eco-friendly nanoparticle additives for lubricants and their tribological characterization. In Martínez, L., Kharissova, O., & Kharisov, B. (Eds.), Handbook of Ecomaterials, (pp. 3247–3267). Springer: Cham, Switzerland.

[4] Uflyand, I. E., Zhinzhilo, V. A., & Burlakova, V. E. (2019). Metal-containing nanomaterials as lubricant additives: State-of-the-art and future development. *Friction*, 7, 93–116.

[5] Huang, H. D., Tu, J. P., Gan, L. P., & Li, C. Z. (2006). An investigation on tribological properties of graphite nanosheets as oil additive. *Wear*, 261, 140–144.

[6] Shahmohamadi, H., Rahmani, R., Rahnejat, H., Garner, C. P., & Balodimos, N. (2017). Thermohydrodynamics of lubricant flow with carbon nanoparticles in tribological contacts. *Tribology International*, 113, 50–57.

[7] Senniangiri, N., Balaji, K., Elango, M., Ram, R. B., Kumar, S. R., & Sunil, J.(2022). Experimental investigation on the thermal conductivity and thermal stability of CuO-coconut oil nanofluids. In International Conference on Advances in Materials, Computing and Communication Technologies (ICAMCCT 2021), (Vol. 2385).

[8] Mello, V. S., Faria, E. A., Alves, S. M., & Scandian, C. (2020). Enhancing CuO nanolubricant performance using dispersing agents. *Tribology International*, 150, 106338.

[9] Raad, M., & Abdulmajeed, B. A. (2022). Effect of modified hybrid nanoparticles on the properties of base oil. *Iraqi Journal of Chemical and Petroleum Engineering*, 23(1), 1–7.

[10] Chan, C. H., Tang, S. W., Mohd, N. K., Lim, W. H., Yeong, S. K., & Idris, Z. (2018). Tribological behaviour of bio lubricant base stocks and additives. *Renewable and Sustainable Energy Reviews*, 93, 145–157.

[11] Viesca, J. L., Battez, A. H., González, R., Chou, R., & Cabello, J. J. (2011). Antiwear properties of carbon-coated copper nanoparticles used as an additive to a polyalphaolefin. *Tribology International*, 44, 829–833.

[12] Shafi, W. K., Raina, A., & Haq, M. I. U. (2018). Friction and wear characteristics of vegetable oils using nanoparticles for sustainable lubrication. *Tribology Materials, Surfaces and Interfaces*, 12, 27–43.

[13] Lijesh, K. P., Muzakkir, S. M., & Hirani, H. (2015). Experimental tribological performance evaluation of nanolubricants using multi-walled carbon nano-tubes (MWCNT). *International Journal of Applied Engineering Research*, 10(6), 14543–14551.

[14] Wang, X., Yin, Y., Zhang, G., Wang, W., & Zhao, K. (2013). Study on antiwear and repairing performances about mass of nano-copper lubricating additives to 45 steel. *Physica Procedia*, 50, 466–472.

[15] Al-Tabbakh, A., Jaed, D. M., Qubian, N. A., & Kareem, S. (2022). Preparation of CuO nanoparticles for improving base oil properties. *Journal of Petroleum Research and Studies*, 12(1), 191–205.

[16] Yadgarov, L., Petrone, V., Rosentsveig, R., Feldman, Y., Tenne, R., & Senatore, A. (2013). Tribological studies of rhenium-doped fullerene-like MoS_2 nanoparticles in boundary, mixed, and elasto-hydrodynamic lubrication conditions. *Wear*, 297, 1103–1110.

[17] Ingole, S., Charanpahari, A., Kakade, A., Umare, S. S., Bhatt, D. V., & Menghani, J. (2013). Tribological behavior of nano TiO_2 as an additive in base oil. *Wear*, 301, 776–785.

[18] Nallasamy, P., Saravanakumar, N., Rajaram, G., & Rishwin Kumar, R. K. (2018). Experimental study on the tribological properties of CuO-based biodegradable nanolubricants for machine tool slideways. *International Journal of Surface Science and Engineering*, 12(3), 194–206.

[19] Rajubhai, V. H., Singh, Y., Suthar, K., & Surana, A. R. (2019). Friction and wear behavior of Al-7% Si alloy pin under Pongamia oil with copper nanoparticles as additives. *Materials Today Proceedings*, 25, 695–698.

[20] Azman, N. F., Samion, S., & Sot, M. N. H. M. (2018). Investigation of tribological properties of CuO/palm oil nanolubricant using pin-on-disc tribotester. *Institution of Civil Engineers*, 6, 30–37.

32 Design of parallel hardware architecture for feed-forward neural network and implementation using FPGA

P. Kalpana[1,a], and Sakthi Balan, T.[2,b]

[1]Professor ME (VLSI DESIGN), Department of Electronics and Communication Engineering, India

[2]PSG College of Technology Coimbatore, India

Abstract

This paper presents a parallel feed-forward neural network (PFFNN) architecture optimized for real-time inference on field programmable gate array (FPGA) platforms, validated using the Iris dataset. A $4 \times 8 \times 3 \times 3$ configuration was trained using MATLAB with 98.66% accuracy, and its parameters were quantized for hardware deployment. The architecture was synthesized on a Zedbcard (xc7z020clg484-1) and evaluated in terms of timing performance and hardware resource utilization. Inference timing shows a significant speedup on hardware, executing in just 0.3 μs compared to 0.867 ms in software. The implementation uses minimal resources thus making it efficient for constrained environments. A comparative analysis with prior works demonstrates that the proposed architecture offers superior trade-offs between speed and resource usage, confirming its potential for low-power, real-time AI applications.

Keywords: Feed-Forward neural network, FPGA implementation, iris dataset, neural network optimization, parallel architecture

Introduction

Artificial neural networks (ANNs) are computer architecture that is modeled after the architecture and information processing systems of the human brain. ANNs are networks of interconnected processing units referred to as neurons that work together to decode information and perform certain tasks, similar to biological neural networks [1]. The foundation of ANNs was motivated by the way biological systems process information that occurs in biological systems, especially the brain. By offering parallel processing capabilities, ANNs imitate this complex structure. Because of their design, ANNs can be used for complicated, data driven tasks that call for pattern identification, categorization, and decision making [2].

In most scientific fields, such as computing, industrial engineering, environmental science, and even more specialized fields such as nanotechnology and medical diagnosis, ANNs have become quite popular. Due to their adaptability, ANNs are valuable resources in practical applications such as big data analysis, handwriting recognition, credit card fraud detection, and speech and face recognition. Unlike traditional programming methods, ANNs learn from experience by observing patterns in data, which allows them to generate predictions or classifications in new, untested datasets [3]. Pattern recognition and association mapping are the fundamental learning processes in ANNs, which allow the models to adapt to various domains and application cases without the need for explicit programming [4].

The multi-layer perceptron (MLP), a well-known ANN architecture, is made up of several layers with many neurons (also known as processing elements, or PE's) connected by weighted linkages. Activation functions, which control the output by transforming the weighted input total, have an impact on the behavior of the neurons. Backpropagation, an iterative technique that improves the network's forecast accuracy by reducing output errors, is used to modify these weights during the training of an MLP [5]. Despite its efficacy, the majority of cutting edge ANNs are implemented with software tools, freeing developers from having to worry about the inner workings of architecture and allowing them to concentrate on functionality. Although software based ANNs are now the industry standard because they are simple to deploy, their high costs and processing delays sometimes cause them to perform poorly in real time, computationally demanding applications. Because of the significant speed and parallelism advantages, hardware implementations of ANNs have become a viable real time processing option [6].

Hardware based implementations are increasingly used because they can be programmed to provide optimized performance for specific applications,

[a]pkl.ece@psgtech.ac.in, [b]23mv09@psgtech.ac.in

DOI: 10.1201/9781003770435-32

particularly on field programmable gate arrays (FPGAs). FPGAs are an excellent choice for high performance ANN structures since they provide a flexible platform that balances cost, performance, and flexibility. Apart from applying parallelism to accelerate processing, ANNs implemented on hardware platforms also minimize component and energy expenses. Due to this, FPGA based ANN systems are increasingly applied across a broad spectrum of industries where rapid data processing is vital [7].

Related Works

A feed forward neutral network hardware architecture is proposed in another study with the goal of reducing the amount of execution clock cycles required for network computing [8]. The efficient parallel design of the suggested architecture is primarily achieved by multiplexing and reusing two physical layers throughout the FFNN computation. Neural networks of various sizes are computed using two physical layers that are constructed and reused. The hardware resources of the suggested FFNN architecture solely depend on the number of neurons in the biggest layer, not on the number of layers in the NN. Deep Neural Network computations are accelerated by this adaptable architecture. The two physical layers are made to operate in parallel through computations in the suggested architecture, which takes advantage of parallelism. An 18-bit fixed point is used in the suggested implementation. On a Spartan7 FPGA, the architecture achieves a clock speed of 200 MHz.

Several hardware accelerators are employed to give these algorithms their outstanding performance and efficiency [9]. They may accommodate a variety of neural network architectures and enable substantial runtime modifications to the implemented model. As a result, a single gadget can be utilized for a variety of purposes. Reconfigurable computing environments based dynamically on reconfigurable accelerators are the main topic of our study. It is necessary to modify their algorithms to fit the homogenous structure of RCE in order to deploy the necessary neural networks on such devices. The first use of the popular SoftMax activation for RCE based hardware accelerators is suggested in this article. To improve performance, the solution incorporates multiple optimizations and makes use of spatial dispersion. 12 Gbps at 23 MHz is demonstrated by the timing simulation of the suggested FPGA implementation. The

outcome is on par with counterparts who are incapable of reconfiguring. Nevertheless, this adaptability results in a higher usage of logical components.

A detailed analysis of FPGA based deep learning accelerators is provided in study [10] which highlights FPGAs as a compromise between general purpose CPUs/GPUs and custom ASICs in neural network inference. In addition to outlining techniques to maximize performance, resource utilization, and energy efficiency, it describes the architecture and adjustments required for FPGAs to meet the computational needs of DNN. An overview of CNNs, RNNs, transformers, and other DNN designs that are appropriate for FPGA implementation, as well as how they have changed over time to handle increasing computational complexity. Acceleration demands in addition to proposing a standard matrix for assessing NN accelerators across parameters including throughput, energy efficiency, and computational density, the article analyses several FPGA based systems.

The multilayer perceptron, autoencoder, and logistic regression are three unique hardware implementations of feedforward neural networks that are described in this study. [12] The architecture allows for an arbitrary number of levels, units in layers, and input and output numbers. Its foundation is a systolic ring of neural processing elements regardless of the number of layers, it only needs as many NPEs as the neuron units in the largest layer. The more NPEs there are, the more resources are used. The system clock frequency is unaffected by the size of this adaptable design, which acts as an accelerator in real-time applications. In contrast to most methods, the entire FFNN requires a single activation function block. In contrast to most methods, the entire FFNN requires a single activation function block. In a Virtex7 FPGA, the architecture achieves a clock speed of 550 MHz. The suggested technique achieves comparable classification performance to a floating-point approach by using an 18-bit fixed point. More weights can be stored in the same memory when the weight bit size is decreased because it has no effect on accuracy.

In ANNs, one of the nonlinear functions utilized is the Tangent Sigmoid (TanSig) Transfer Function (TSTF). It is challenging to implement TSTF on hardware since it incorporates exponential function operations. This paper presents performance studies and FPGA chip data for four distinct TSTF techniques on FPGA that were developed using the 32-bit

IEEE 754-1985 floating point number standard. Four distinct FPGA based TSTF units were used to implement the Van der Pol system ANN application. The study made use of a multilayer feed forward neural network structure. By applying each TSTF structure to the exemplary ANN, sensitivity analysis and FPGA chip statistics were performed [13].

Parallel feed-Forward Computation Architecture

In Figure 32.1, the proposed hardware architecture is based on a parallel feed forward neural network computation model, specifically optimized for FPGA implementation. The core idea is to divide the feed forward neural network into two logical computational layers, namely the "odd layer" and the "even layer". These layers are not strictly defined by layer number in the original neural network but are used to alternate the computation stages to exploit parallelism and improve throughput.

Generic working mechanism
The computation starts with input data fed into the "odd layer" in a parallel manner, where each neuron in the "odd layer" performs its computation simultaneously. Each neuron processes its respective weighted sum of the input values, adds the bias, and forwards the output to the next stage.

Once the "odd layer" completes computation, its outputs are passed through an activation function

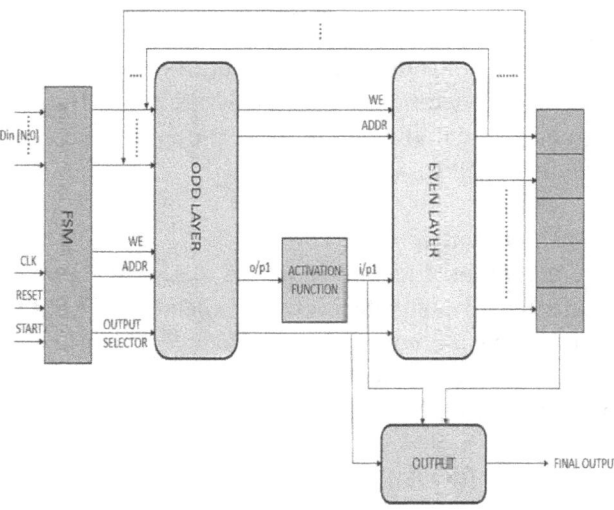

Figure 32.1 Parallel feed forward neural network architecture
Source: Author

block, specifically the Rectified Linear Unit (ReLU) in this architecture. ReLU is chosen due to its computational simplicity and effectiveness in eliminating vanishing gradient issues.

After the activation step, the outputs are fed into the "even layer", but in a serial manner. The "even layer" then performs the next set of computations and produces its output in parallel. If the neural network contains more than two layers, the architecture continues this alternating process, where the parallel output of the "even layer" becomes the parallel input for the next "odd layer", and so on.

This alternating parallel-serial-parallel scheme allows for efficient resource utilization and reduces latency when mapped onto FPGA hardware.

Layer sizing strategy
To accommodate different neural network configurations, the number of neurons in each hardware layer (Odd and Even) is determined by the maximum number of neurons among the respective software defined odd and "even layer" of the neural network. This approach ensures that the architecture remains generic and flexible, able to support various network topologies with minimal modifications.

Hardware Architecture Design

ODD Layer
The "odd layer" is responsible for performing a weighted summation of input data using an adder multiplier tree architecture rather than Neural Processing Elements (NPEs). This design is optimized for serial feed forward computation, where input features are received parallelly at one clock cycle. Each input is multiplied by its corresponding weight, and the resulting products are then accumulated through a hierarchical adder structure to produce a single output value.

In Figure 32.2, the adder multiplier tree is structured to perform multiply accumulate (MAC) operations efficiently in a pipelined fashion. It reduces latency and resource overhead compared to deploying multiple parallel NPEs. The use of this tree allows a compact, sequential evaluation of the neuron's activation input, culminating in a single scalar output per neuron. Once the accumulation is completed and the final output of the neuron is computed, it is passed to the ReLU activation block.

Weight memory modules

These modules store the pre-trained weights and biases associated with each input. Each input feature has a dedicated memory block for its corresponding weight, enabling simultaneous access. A separate memory is used for bias values. Retrieve a weight or bias from memory based on an address input. All weight and bias memories operate in parallel, supplying data to the corresponding multipliers in the same clock cycle.

Multipliers

Each multiplier performs a fixed-point signed multiplication between an input feature and its corresponding weight. Multiply input data with the retrieved weight in fixed-point (10.8) format. The output of each multiplier is scaled appropriately to maintain numeric consistency. An additional multiplier processes the bias term with a scaling factor before accumulation.

Adders

Adders perform pipelined accumulation of all the multiplier outputs. The addition is structured in stages, allowing parallel partial sums followed by a final summation. Add the results of the multipliers in a structured, staged manner. Each adder stage is synchronized with the clock, facilitating high frequency operation and deterministic timing.

Even layer

In Figure 32.3, The "even layer" serves as the second feed forward processing stage in the neural network. It expands the architectural design used in the "odd layer" by deploying multiple processing elements in parallel, each with an integrated activation function. This layer processes intermediate results from the

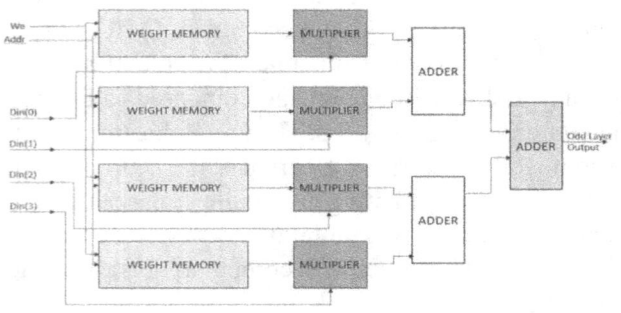

Figure 32.2 Odd layer
Source: Author

"odd layer" and further transforms them using fixed-point arithmetic, producing activated outputs.

Neural processing element (NPE) units

The NPE is a core building block of computation in the "even layer" of the architecture. Its purpose is to execute basic functions in the neural network's forward pass, mainly to multiply the input data with weights and then add them up to yield an output. Internal organization of the NPE consists of two building blocks that support the computation collectively.

Weight memory

The NPE contains a dedicated weight memory unit, which stores the weights associated with the neural network's parameters. These weights are accessed based on an address provided as an input signal. The weight memory is implemented using a block RAM structure, which allows fast and concurrent read and write operations. The memory is initialized with predefined values, typically loaded from external sources, ensuring that each NPE is initialized with the correct weights for its specific computations.

Arithmetic logic unit

Arithmetic logic unit (ALU) is responsible for performing the MAC operations required for the forward pass. In the NPE, the ALU takes the input data and multiplies it with the corresponding weight fetched from the weight memory. The result of this multiplication is then accumulated with previous results (if any), along with the addition of a bias term. The ALU operates on fixed-point arithmetic, allowing it to efficiently handle the computations in hardware. The MAC operations in the ALU are typically performed sequentially, but they are pipelined to ensure high throughput.

Activation function block

The activation function block in the architecture is implemented using the Rectified Linear Unit (ReLU), which plays a crucial role in introducing non linearity into the neural network. ReLU is defined mathematically as in Eq. (1):

$$f(x) = max\ (0,\ x) \tag{1}$$

This results in any negative input value to be zero, with positive values passed through directly. This is

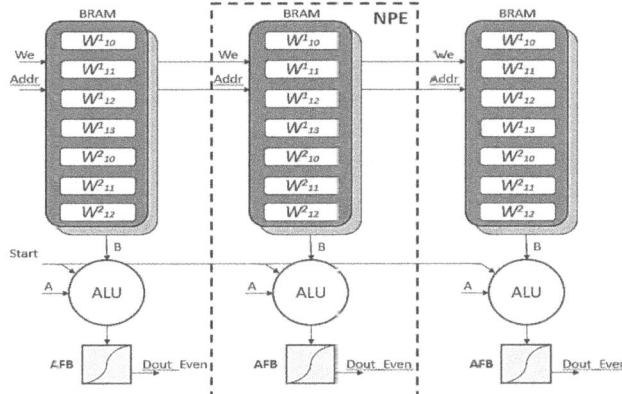

Figure 32.3 Even layer
Source: Author

a simple yet very effective operation in practice and serves to eliminate the vanishing gradient problem, hence enhancing the network's capability to learn difficult patterns.

FSM operation and data flow between odd and even layers

The FSM used in this PFFNN architecture manages the control flow across the odd and even layers of computation. It consists of a sequence of well-defined states that ensure smooth data processing through the feed forward path. The operation begins in the IDLE state, where all control signals and counters are initialized. Once input data is ready, the FSM transitions to the INPUT WRITE state, where data is loaded into the initial computation stage. After this, the FSM moves to the "odd layer" computation START state, where inputs are processed serially through an adder multiplier tree. This is specific to "odd layer", which compute their outputs one by one. The serial outputs from the "odd layer" are then passed through a single ReLU block. Each output is activated one at a time before being passed to the "even layer". Once all serial activations are completed, the FSM enters the EVEN LAYER COMPUTATION state, where all the activated values are processed in parallel using a NPE architecture. In the next PARALLEL RELU ACTIVATION state, each parallel output from the "even layer" is fed through its dedicated ReLU block, enabling simultaneous activation. Finally, the FSM enters the FINALIZE & DONE state, where the final neural network output is collected, and a completion signal is asserted to indicate the end of the

computation. This FSM efficiently coordinates the hybrid serial-parallel architecture, ensuring orderly and synchronized data movement across all stages.

Results

This section highlights the experimental evaluation of the proposed PFFNN using the Iris dataset. Performance is analysed in terms of training accuracy, execution time, and hardware resource utilization. Comparative analysis with prior designs is also presented.

Training results on the iris dataset

The model was initially trained using MATLAB's Neural Network Toolbox. A $4 \times 8 \times 3 \times 3$ FFNN configuration was used. The dataset was split into training (70%), validation (15%), and testing (15%). In Figure 32.4. The training converged with an accuracy of 98.66% at epoch 28 using scaled conjugate gradient backpropagation. The resulting weight and

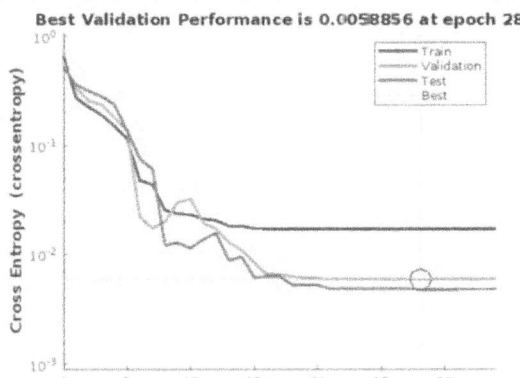

Figure 32.4 Training of IRIS dataset using MatLab
Source: Author

bias parameters were quantized and exported for hardware deployment.

Software vs hardware timing comparison

To assess performance, inference timing was measured both in software (Python) and hardware. In Python, [14] Figure 32.5. *time.perf_counter()* was used for high resolution timing of the forward pass:

- Software: 0.867 milliseconds (867 μs)
- Hardware (FPGA): 300 nanoseconds (0.3 μs)

For the clock period 10 ns, obtained the Worst Negative Slack as 0.794 ns and timing constraints were met. And the simulated output was inferred at 23 clock cycle. So, we get Time = 10 ns × 23 = 0.23 us. Figure 32.6. shows the hardware implementation is approximately 2890x faster than its software counterpart, confirming its suitability for real-time AI tasks.

Hardware resource utilization

The network was synthesized and implemented on Zedboard (xc7z020clg484-1) and the below Figures

```
from time import perf_counter

start_time = perf_counter()
predictions = forward_pass(user_input)
end_time = perf_counter()
elapsed_time = (end_time - start_time) * 1000
```

Inference Time on GPP (i5 9th Gen): 0.867 ms

Figure 32.5 Timing evaluation of IRIS dataset using VS code
Source: Author

```
1. Slice Logic
---------------
```

Site Type	Used	Fixed	Available	Util%
Slice LUTs	477	0	53200	0.90
LUT as Logic	477	0	53200	0.90
LUT as Memory	0	0	17400	0.00
Slice Registers	658	0	106400	0.62
Register as Flip Flop	658	0	106400	0.62
Register as Latch	0	0	106400	0.00
F7 Muxes	0	0	26600	0.00
F8 Muxes	0	0	13300	0.00

Figure 32.7 LUT and registers utilization
Source: Author

```
3. Memory
---------
```

Site Type	Used	Fixed	Available	Util%
Block RAM Tile	4	0	140	2.86
RAMB36/FIFO*	0	0	140	0.00
RAMB18	8	0	280	2.86
RAMB18E1 only	8			

Figure 32.8 BRAM memory utilization
Source: Author

```
4. DSP
------
```

Site Type	Used	Fixed	Available	Util%
DSPs	7	0	220	3.18
DSP48E1 only	7			

Figure 32.9 DSP48E1 utilization
Source: Author

Setup		Hold		Pulse Width	
Worst Negative Slack (WNS):	0.794 ns	Worst Hold Slack (WHS):	0.124 ns	Worst Pulse Width Slack (WPWS):	4.500 ns
Total Negative Slack (TNS):	0.000 ns	Total Hold Slack (THS):	0.000 ns	Total Pulse Width Negative Slack (TPWS):	0.000 ns
Number of Failing Endpoints:	0	Number of Failing Endpoints:	0	Number of Failing Endpoints:	0
Total Number of Endpoints:	1569	Total Number of Endpoints:	1569	Total Number of Endpoints:	679

All user specified timing constraints are met.

Figure 32.6 Time required for inference on FPGA
Source: Author

Total On-Chip Power:	**0.191 W**
Design Power Budget:	**Not Specified**
Power Budget Margin:	**N/A**
Junction Temperature:	**27.2°C**
Thermal Margin:	57.8°C (4.8 W)
Effective θJA:	11.5°C/W
Power supplied to off-chip devices:	0 W
Confidence level:	Low

Figure 32.10 Total on-chip power
Source: Author

32.7–32.9 show the resource usage of them along with power in Figure 32.10.

Comparison with previous work

In Table 32.1., the proposed PFFNN architecture demonstrates notable advantages over prior implementations in terms of speed, hardware efficiency, and resource utilization. When compared to Oliveira et al. [11], which follows the same 4×8×3×3 topology, our design achieves a significant reduction in latency requiring only 23 clock cycles at 120 MHz, resulting in an inference time of 0.3 μs, whereas Oliveira et al. [11], operates at 77.8 MHz and requires 90 clock cycles (approximately 1.16 μs). This speedup is achieved with drastically reduced register usage (658 vs. 8582) and efficient use of hardware resources, including only 7 DSP slices and 4 BRAM blocks.

In contrast to the shallower yet wider 4 × 10 × 3 topology implemented by Leandro et al. [12], our design introduces an additional layer while maintaining competitive performance. Although Leandro et al. [12] achieves a faster execution time of 0.104 μs due to its higher clock frequency (490 MHz), this comes at the expense of increased hardware resource consumption—specifically, 681 LUTs and 12 DSPs compared to our design's 477 LUTs and 7 DSPs. This indicates a higher hardware cost for their approach. While their architecture is optimized for speed, our design offers a more balanced trade-off between

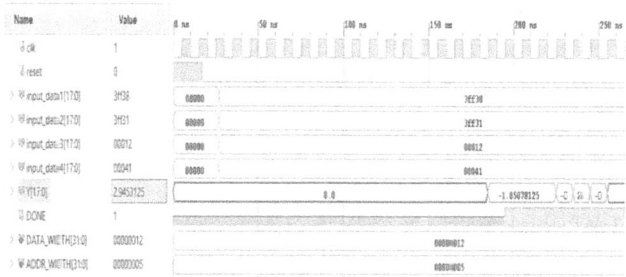

Figure 32.11 Simulation waveform
Source: Author

throughput and resource efficiency making it particularly well-suited for embedded or resource-constrained environments.

Overall, the proposed design outperforms both work [11, 12] in terms of execution speed per cycle and hardware efficiency, validating its effectiveness for real-time, low-power applications such as edge inference on the Iris dataset.

Simulation output

In Figure 32.11, waveform shows the output received from the Verilog when the 4-input Iris dataset is used for testing. It correctly predicts the highest positive value of output Class of Iris dataset. For the given normalized input:1.1524, -0.5809, 0.5847, 0.2565. Obtained the output as -2.1914, 2.946, -1.4383. Thus, it correctly predicted class 2 which is Iris-Versicolor.

Summary

The results confirm that the proposed architecture not only maintains high classification accuracy but also achieves remarkable inference speed and low hardware cost. This makes it well-suited for low-power, real-time embedded AI applications.

Conclusion

The experimental results validate the efficiency and performance of the proposed parallel feed-forward neural network. With only 23 clock cycles at 120 MHz, the hardware implementation achieves inference speeds nearly 2900 times faster than its software counterpart, while maintaining high classification accuracy. Compared to previous works, the design demonstrates reduced resource utilization especially in terms of registers and DSPs without compromising performance. These advantages position the architecture as a strong candidate for

Table 32.1 Comparison with previous work

Metric	Proposed work (4 × 8 × 3 × 3)	Oliveira et al. [11] (4 × 8 × 3× 3)	Leandro et al. [12] (4 × 10 × 3)
Clock frequency	120 MHz	77.8 MHz	490 MHz
Clock cycles	23	90	51
Execution Time	0.3 μs	1.16 μs	0.104 μs
LUTs Used	477	-	681
Registers	658	8582	681
BRAMs	4	-	5
DSPs	7	-	12
Architecture	Parallel Feed-Forward (3 layers)	MLP (3 layers)	Pipelined MLP (2 layers)
Remarks	Balanced resource-speed tradeoff	High register cost	Faster, but higher DSP usage

Source: Author

edge-based AI, where real-time processing and low-power consumption are critical. Future work could explore scalability to deeper networks and broader datasets, as well as integration with convolution neural network (CNN).

Reference

[1] Chavlis, S., & Poirazi, P. (2021). Drawing inspiration from biological dendrites to empower artificial neural networks. *Current Opinion in Neurobiology*, 70, 1–10.

[2] Agatonovic-Kustrin, S., & Beresford, R. (2000). Basic concepts of artificial neural network (ANN) modeling and its application in pharmaceutical research. *Journal of Pharmaceutical and Biomedical Analysis*, 22(5), 717–727.

[3] Abiodun, O. I., Jantan, A., Omolara, A. E., Dada, K. V., Mohamed, N. A., & Arshad, H. (2018). State-of-the-art in artificial neural network applications: a survey. *Heliyon*, 4(11), e00398.

[4] Kohli, S., Miglani, S., & Rapariya, R. (2014). Basics of artificial neural network. *International Journal of Computer Science and Mobile Computing*, 3(9), 745–751.

[5] Macukow, B. (2016). Neural networks–state of art, brief history, basic models and architecture. In Computer Information Systems and Industrial Management: 15th IFIP TC8 International Conference, CISIM 2016, Vilnius, Lithuania, September 14-16, 2016, Proceedings 15. Springer International Publishing.

[6] Ding, S., Li, H., Su, C., Yu, J., & Jin, F. (2013). Evolutionary artificial neural networks: a review. *Artificial Intelligence Review*, 39, 251–260.

[7] Baptista, D., Abreu, S., Freitas, F., Vasconcelos, R., & Morgado-Dias, F. (2013). A survey of software and hardware use in artificial neural networks. *Neural Computing and Applications*, 23, 591–599.

[8] El-Sharkawy, M., Wael, M., Mashaly, M., & Azab, E. (2024). Re-configurable parallel Feed-Forward neural network implementation using FPGA. *Integration*, 97, 102176.

[9] Shatravin, V., Shashev, D., & Shidlovskiy, S. (2023). Implementation of the SoftMax activation for reconfigurable neural network hardware accelerators. *Applied Sciences*, 13(23), 12784.

[10] Nechi, A., Groth, L., Mulhem, S., Merchant, F., Buchty, R., & Berekovic, M. (2023). FPGA-based deep learning inference accelerators: where are we standing?. *ACM Transactions on Reconfigurable Technology and Systems*, 16(4), 1–32.

[11] Oliveira, J. G. M., Moreno, R. L., de Oliveira Dutra, O., & Pimenta, T. C. (2017). Implementation of a recon gurable neural network in FPGA, in Proc. Int. Caribbean Conf. Devices, Circuits Syst. (ICCDCS), Jun. 2017, (pp. 4144).

[12] Leandro, D. M., Lakymchuk, T., Frances-Villora, J. V., Bataller-Mompeán, M., & Rosado-Munoz, A. (2019). A novel systolic parallel hardware architecture for the FPGA acceleration of feedforward neural networks. *IEEE Access*, 7, 76084–76103.

[13] Koyuncu, I. (2018). Implementation of high speed tangent sigmoid transfer function approximations for artificial neural network applications on FPGA. *Advances in Electrical and Computer Engineering*, 18(3), 79.

[14] Choudhari, O., Chopade, M., Chopde, S., Dabhadkar, S., & Ingale, V. (2020). Hardware accelerator: implementation of CNN on FPGA for digit recognition. In 2020 24th International Symposium on VLSI Design and Test (VDAT). IEEE.

33 Compute-capable block RAMs for efficient deep learning acceleration on FPGAs

Santhanalakshmi, M.[1,a] and Divyabharathi, K.[2,b]

[1]Associate Professor, Department of Electronics and Communication Engineering, PSG College of Technology, Coimbatore, India

[2]ME VLSI Design, PSG College of Technology, Coimbatore, India

Abstract

Field-programmable gate arrays (FPGAs) have evolved into powerful heterogeneous systems with high computational capabilities and distributed on-chip memory, making them a key platform for accelerating data-intensive applications. Modern FPGAs integrate large arrays of block RAMs (BRAMs), providing significant potential for optimizing memory-bound workloads. Reconfigurable in-memory accelerator (RIMA), is an efficient architecture that enhances traditional BRAMs with computational capabilities, enabling arithmetic operations directly within memory. RIMA leverages FPGA reconfigurability and compute-capable BRAMs featuring in-memory compute units called memory dot product engines (M-DPEs) and logic dot product engines (L-DPEs) to accelerate recurrent neural network (RNN) workloads. RIMA improves resource utilization and performance across various RNN models by allowing a customizable balance between in-BRAM and DSP-based computation. Additionally, by loading computation inside the memory, the number of clock cycle increases in the L-DPE. To overcome above bottleneck, this work proposes novel architecture by integrating the Radix 2 multiplier design in the accelerator to boost the performance of the design by reducing the clock cycles. Implemented and evaluated on Xilinx Vivado, RIMA achieves 248 logic units, 324 registers, 3 DSP blocks, a total thermal power dissipation of 532.37 mW and number of clock cycles reduced from 11 to 9 demonstrating its efficiency and potential in deep learning acceleration.

Keywords: Block RAMs, field-programmable gate arrays, in-memory computation, Radix 2 multiplier, reconfigurable in-memory accelerator, recurrent neural networks

Introduction

Field-programmable gate arrays (FPGAs) have come a long way in the last decade, evolving from basic reconfigurable logic blocks to heterogeneous computing engines with built-in distributed memory, specialized processing elements, and high-bandwidth interconnects. At the heart of this revolution is the addition of high-density block raMs (BRAMs), which are programmable on-chip memory blocks distributed throughout the FPGA fabric. For example, the largest monolithic Intel Stratix 10 FPGA contains 11,721 BRAMs, providing a total on-chip memory of 229 Mb [1]. As machine learning and real-time analytics workloads continue to expand in size and sophistication, future FPGA generations are expected to feature increased BRAM capacity densities to support the growing need for localized, high-bandwidth memory access in data center and edge environments.

In contemporary FPGAs, BRAMs not only abound but are also designed to provide massive internal bandwidth. The ubiquitous deployment across the reconfigurable fabric renders them eminently suitable for accelerating compute-intensive, data-intensive tasks, especially in deep learning (DL) applications. BRAMs have historically been utilized exclusively as passive storage components. Yet, this separation of memory and computation in architecture tends to cause significant data movement overhead, particularly for memory-bound models like recurrent neural networks (RNNs), ultimately leading to sub-optimal usage of compute resources and power inefficiencies [2, 3].

To overcome these limitations, compute-in-memory (CIM) is a promising architectural innovation that redefines memory usage in computing systems. By embedding lightweight arithmetic functionality within BRAMs, CIM facilitates in-place computation, effectively converting blocks of memory into active contributors to the data processing chain [4, 5]. This evolution minimizes data movement latencies and alleviates bandwidth constraints, thus opening up new possibilities for performance and energy efficiency on FPGA-based accelerators.

[a]ms.ece@psgtech.ac.in, [b]divyakrish2001@gmail.com

DOI: 10.1201/9781003770435-33

To investigate and leverage the opportunities of CIM, reconfigurable in-memory accelerator (RIMA), an innovative FPGA-based architecture for neural network prediction execution. The accelerator harnesses the reconfigurability of FPGAs and computable BRAMs to enhance matrix-vector computations, which are fundamental to neural network applications. The focal point of RIMA is the memory dot product engines (M-DPEs), which execute bit-serial computation directly within BRAMs. These M-DPEs collaborate with traditional logic and DSP blocks to create a reconfigurable hybrid architecture optimized for the high parallelism and low-latency demands of DL inference [6, 7]. The accelerator also contains L-DPE, which performs a simple array multiplication but requires 11 number of cycles to complete the computation. To overcome this, a Radix 2 multiplier is proposed to reduce the number of cycles thereby increasing the speed. In conclusion, this work proposes a fundamentally different method for accelerating deep learning on FPGAs by internalizing computation inside memory. RIMA architecture not only enhances computing and memory usage but also demonstrates scalable and power-efficient inference performance for memory-bound DL workloads [8, 9]. This direction of architecture has high promise for the next generation of domain-specific accelerators, where memory and computing are co-designed to maximize efficiency.

Related Work

As DL models become more computationally intensive, FPGAs have emerged as reconfigurable and power-efficient platforms for accelerating DL. Several previous works have aimed to maximize the arithmetic throughput of FPGAs by adapting the underlying logic and DSP structures. For example, Boutros et al [10] suggested architectural enhancements to the DSP blocks that support a greater density of low-precision MAC operations, which dominate DL inference. Likewise, Eldafrawy et al [11] and Rasoulinezhad et al [12] investigated enhancements to reconfigurable logic blocks for augmented parallel arithmetic computations in the soft logic fabric. Though these efforts dramatically improve arithmetic performance, they tend to ignore memory bottlenecks that occur in memory-bounded workloads such as Recurrent Neural Networks. Computation in these instances often idles while waiting for

data, making it increasingly important for memory to reduce data movement. To overcome data movement inefficiencies, various studies have explored in-memory computing. The Neural Cache project was an early initiative that repurposed last-level CPU caches for in-place bit-serial computation, demonstrating substantial improvements in throughput by reducing the amount of data transfer to external computation units. Similarly, FloatPIM [13] and DRISA [14] both introduced DRAM-based accelerators that enable direct Boolean and arithmetic operations in memory arrays. However, these solutions are inflexible, designed specifically for ASICs or CPUs, and lack the adaptability and reconfigurability of FPGAs. Zha et al [15] continued this theme by suggesting a reconfigurable fabric based on ReRAM, where tiles can serve as compute, memory, or interconnect resources. In contrast to earlier ASIC and CPU-based solutions, this work extends the research on Compute-capable BRAMs, an extension of the typical FPGA Block RAMs that incorporate lightweight, bit-serial compute logic. The modified BRAMs can dynamically switch between legacy memory mode and a computing mode, in which their bit-lines serve as single instruction, multiple data (SIMD) lanes. This innovation efficiently moves compute units closer to data, minimizing routing congestion and enhancing performance for memory-bound applications. Numerous DL accelerators have been designed for FPGAs to exploit configurability. For instance, Intel's Persistent RNN accelerator and Microsoft's Brainwave NPU rely on the conventional separation between memory and computation units. The RIMA architecture in this work departs from this design by incorporating compute BRAMs and a per-workload architecture. BRAMAC [16] proposes an innovative architecture that improves traditional memory with multiply and accumulate capability. This is specifically focused on real-time network applications where low precision plays a pivotal role by improving energy efficiency and reducing throughput.

Compute Capable Block RAMs for FPGAs

Computer-capable BRAM design signifies a major advancement in FPGA technology, allowing memory blocks to perform computational tasks in addition to their usual storage functions. The primary goal of enhancing BRAMs is to bring computation closer to data, thereby improving performance for data-driven applications. The architecture in Figure 1 utilizes the abundance of BRAMs found in modern FPGAs, enabling a significant level of parallelism in processing operations. This architecture modifies the existing BRAM designs to incorporate in-memory computation capabilities. Changes to the traditional BRAM include an additional row decoder in Port A for the simultaneous activation of two memory cells' data in the same bit line. This enhancement allows BRAMs to function as standard storage devices or be configured as single instruction, multiple data (SIMD) lanes performing bit-serial arithmetic tasks.

Dual-mode operation

The compute-capable BRAM can operate in either normal mode or computational mode. When set to memory mode, it functions like a standard BRAM, allowing the designer to easily adjust the number of ports and other configurations. Conversely, when configured to computational mode, the memory is automatically optimized to its maximum width, boosting read/write performance to efficiently load input data into the memory array and extract the output in a transposed argument.

In-memory compute instructions

This system architecture supports executing compute operations directly within memory. A unique memory address (0 × 1FF) is reserved to indicate such operations; any data word targeting this address is treated as a command for in-memory computation.

In contrast, accesses to other addresses follow the standard memory access protocol. When a compute instruction is detected, it carries embedded control information, including the row address, signals for SRAM access (like write enable), and controls for the bit-line peripherals. To enable flexible signal routing based on the current mode of operation, the design incorporates multiplexers. A comparator is also included to determine whether the incoming address matches the reserved compute instruction address. The CCBRAM enhances FPGAs by improving performance.

RIMA: Reconfigurable in-Memory Accelerator

This section presents RIMA, a reconfigurable in-memory accelerator designed for deep learning applications. By integrating compute-capable BRAMs, RIMA enhances the efficiency of deep learning inference tasks. Additionally, the FPGA's reconfigurable architecture allows for dynamic allocation of resources, balancing the workload between compute-capable BRAMs and DSPs to achieve optimal performance across different deep learning tasks.

DL processing workloads

A reconfigurable in-memory accelerator (RIMA) is specifically designed to enhance RNNs, which are frequently utilized in fields such as speech processing and language translation. RNNs excel at

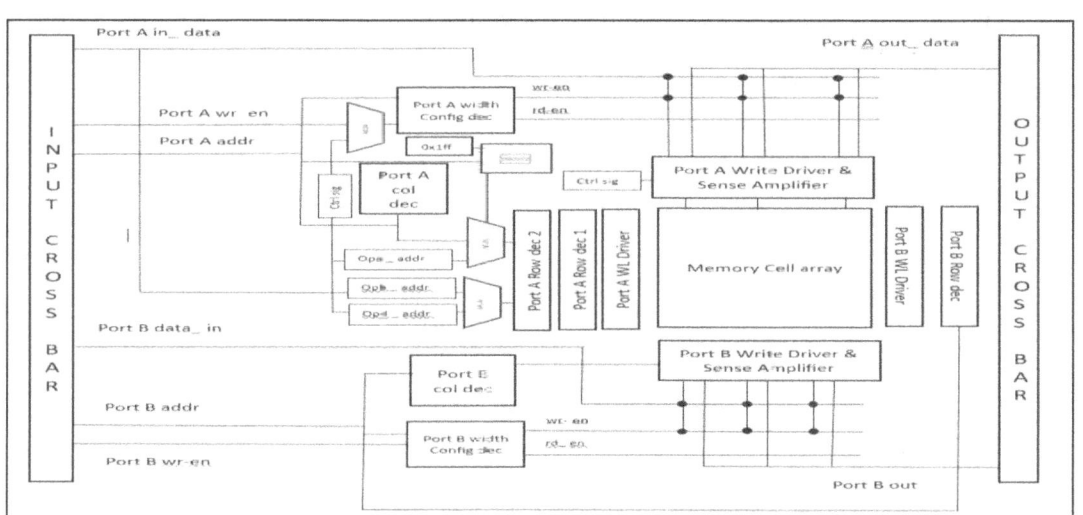

Figure 33.1 Internal design of the dual-port single bank BRAM with compute capabilities
Source: Author

managing sequential inputs, such as audio samples or sentences, making them ideal for tasks that require comprehension of context over time [17]. RNNs primarily consist of numerous matrix-vector multiplications followed by a vector operation known as a gate.

Hardware accelerator structure

The accelerator features a design similar to the Brainwave neural processing unit (NPU), which is an advanced FPGA overlay for deep learning acceleration [18]. Figure 33.2 (a) illustrates the primary structure of our accelerator, divided into five distinct pipeline stages: The matrix-vector multiplication unit (MVU); the external vector register file (eVRF), which allows the option to bypass the MVU when it is not required; two similar multifunctional units (MFUs) for operations on elements in vector-wise (e.g., RELU activation, addition, subtraction); and finally, a loader to write back.

Matrix vector unit tile

The matrix vector unit tile consists of DPEs as shown in Figure 33.2(b). There are two categories of DPEs: Logic DPEs (L-DPEs), which rely on a combination of multipliers and adders to sum products by utilizing lookup tables and DSP blocks, and memory DPEs, which achieve the same task through compute-capable BRAMs.

Memory dot product engine

The Figure 33.2(c) shows the internal structure of a M-DPEs. The M-DPEs consist of several BRAMs. The M-DPE performs numerous multiplication operations across multiple rows, thereby enhancing the level of parallelism. The output from each BRAM is directed to a reduction unit. The results from all reduction units are serialized and sent to an accumulator that performs any required operations across different BRAMs to produce the overall result of the M-DPEs.

Integer-based computation

The reduction unit is a crucial concept in RIMA architecture for consolidating the partial sum results from compute-capable BRAM into a single result.

Operand loading

Before any computations begin, before execution, the input vector must be written into the memory array. During deep learning inference, model weights remain fixed within on-chip memory. This immutability allows the weights to be transposed and preloaded into the memory array during a dedicated preprocessing phase, optimizing memory access patterns at runtime.

In-BRAM MAC and reduction unit

Once the operands are loaded into memory, the relevant inputs are multiplied using the bit-serial method, while the resulting products are summed in each bit line. Following the process, the partial sums are accumulated and reduced until only 16 partial sums remain. The 16 partial sums strike a balance between memory throughput and the external reduction unit.

External reduction unit and serializer

The partial results of 16 are extracted from memory and processed in bit slices one at a time, starting from the LSB, before being provided to the external reduction unit to calculate the sum. The formula for summing using bit slices is

$$\sum_{i=0}^{N} popcount(bit\ slice\ i) * 2^{\wedge}i$$

(1)

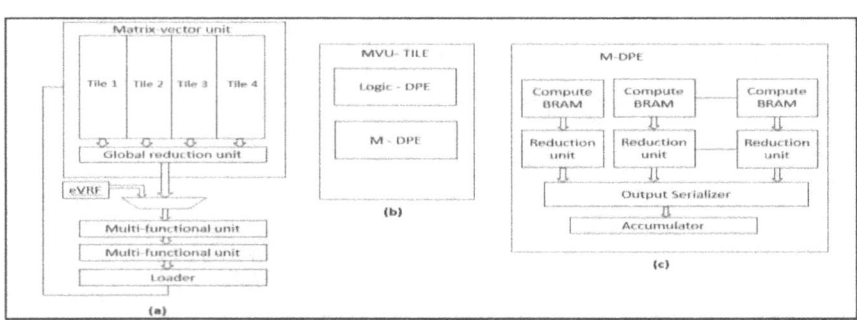

Figure 33.2 (a) Top level architecture of RIMA (b) MVU Tile (c) Memory DPE

Source: Author

From equation (1), where N represents the bit width of the partial results. During each cycle, 16 bits, each taken from the same position across 16 different values, are processed through pop-count logic to determine the number of 1's in Table 33.1. The same compute BRAM is generated four times, and each of the partial sums moves to the reduction unit, resulting in the final output, which is then sent to the serializer. The pop-count logic is important when real-time data are feedin, like floating point numbers or higher bit Widths.

Multi-functional unit

The Multi-Functional Unit can perform element-wise operations; these operations include Addition, Subtraction, and the RELU activation function. The MFU operates on two inputs (i.e., the input vector and mux_out).

Loader and eVRF

The Loader writes back the result of the MFU operations (or external input data when bypassing the MVU) into the eVRF. The eVRF stores intermediate results for reuse in later operations.

In the current design, Logic based Dot Product Engine in the RIMA architecture has been identified as a performance bottleneck due to its high cycle counts. To overcome this issue, in section 5 introduces the Radix-2 multiplier integration in the accelerator to decrease the clock cycles.

Integration of Radix-2 Multiplier in Accelerator

To further enhance the performance of the neural network inference of FPGA, the Conventional architecture restricts the performance by taking high number of clock cycles, which restricts performance. To mitigate this issues, Radix-2 MAC presents alternative solution which provides the straightforward implementation to reduce the cycle count.

Analysis of baseline architecture

The baseline Compute-in BRAM architecture provides in-memory processing on FPGAs by enhancing the conventional BRAM. At the centre of the architecture is the Logic Dot product engine, which supports the multiplication operation in parallel, allowing for a trade-off between the area and resource utilization. Despite its adaptability, architectural evaluation reveals that L-DPE typically requires 10 or more clock cycles to complete computation.

Radix-2 MAC integration design

A more efficient Radix-2 Multiply and accumulate unit has substituted the L-DPE in the baseline architecture shown in Figure 3. This revision aims to provide solutions for the shortcomings in the baseline architecture, specifically in the Logic dot product Engine, which has a high cycle count and logic complexity. The Radix-2 is well known for hardware efficiency in digital arithmetic operations.

Cycle optimization

The main objective of Radix-2 integration is to minimize the number of clock cycles required for computation. L-DPE usually takes 11 cycles of operations

Table 33.1 POP-count logic

S.no	Partial sums	Binary	Bit slice [3]	Bit slice [2]	Bit slice [1]	Bit slice [0]
1	9	1001	1	0	0	1
2	2	0010	0	0	1	0
3	6	0110	0	1	1	0
4	9	1001	1	0	0	1
5	0	0000	0	0	0	0
6	0	0000	0	0	0	0
7	2	0010	0	0	1	0
8	3	0011	0	0	1	1
9	6	0110	0	1	1	0
10	4	0100	0	1	0	0
11	0	0000	0	0	0	0
12	0	0000	0	0	0	0
13	1	0001	0	0	0	1
14	3	0011	0	0	1	1
15	6	0110	0	1	1	0
16	2	0010	0	0	1	0

Source: Author

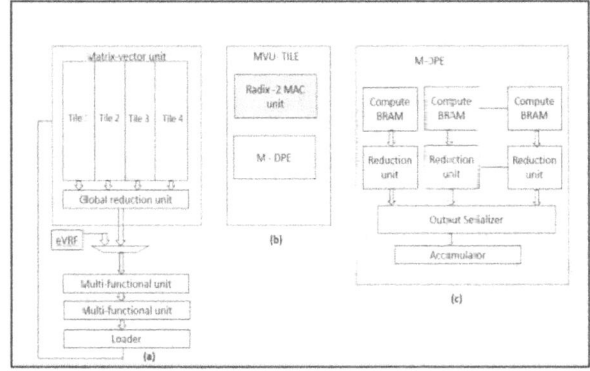

Figure 33.3 Modified RIMA with Radix-2 MAC unit

Source: Author

in baseline architectural design, which affects the performance of the deep learning workloads. The Radix-2 MAC unit achieves full multiply-accumulate capabilities in 9 (1 for loading + 8 for computation)clock cycles. This enhancement significantly boosts system performance and throughput.

Mapping of hardware and integration

The proposed Radix-2 multiply unit should ensures that the proper read or write function in memory is unaffected. The simultaneous memory or compute access is achieved through maintaining data locality, which is the main factor in Deep learning tasks. The MAC module is implemented with the three core elements: serial shift and add multiplier for enabling bit-wise operation, Accumulator to store the partial products, and Control logic which manages the input sequence and operation flow.

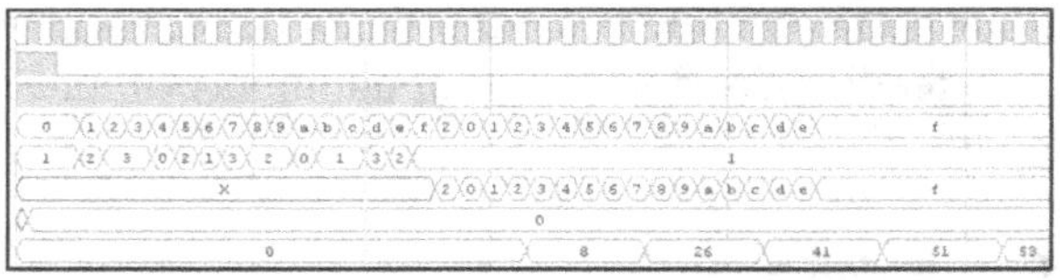

The proposed design reduces the computation time by lowering from 11 to 9 clock cycles improving the efficiency. The Radix-2 approach enhances the overall performance of FPGA based neural network inference.

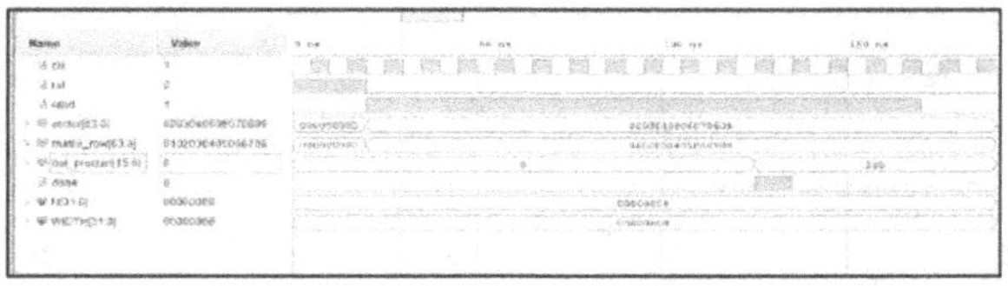

Results

The overall architectural design is implemented using Xilinx Vivado software, targeting the Zybo-20 FPGA device. The resource utilization and simulation waveform are analyzed for the respective modules.

Simulation results and utilization

The output waveform for the Compute Capable BRAM is shown in Figure 4, in which the computation is done inside the memory. The output from the memory is 16 partial sums (9269002364001362), which further move as input to the Reduction unit, where they are summed up to produce the final result of 53, as shown in Figure 5, based on the bit-slice formula. The amount of logic utilized and power in CCBRAM and the Reduction unit is 56 and 61, respectively. In terms of power, the values are 526.25 mW and 526.87 mW.

To evaluate functional correctness and latency of the Logic dot product engine, RTL simulation is performed, as shown in Figure 6. The number of cycles it takes to complete computation is more than 10 cycles, and the logic utilized is 30 in terms of ALMs.

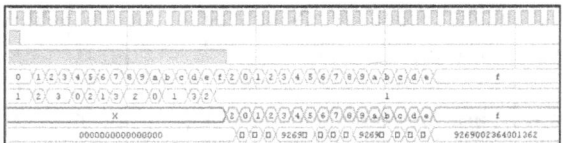

Figure 33.4 Simulation waveform of CCBRAM
Source: Author

Figure 33.5 Simulation waveform of the reduction unit
Source: Author

Figure 33.6 Simulation waveform of L-DPE
Source: Author

The proposed Radix-2 multiplier was verified through RTL simulation to ensure functional correctness and to analyze the latency. The waveform in Figure 7. confirms that the MAC operation is executed in a reduced cycle count of 9 clock cycles, representing a significant improvement in latency compared to the L-DPE.

Table 2. Shows the summary results for logic utilization, total registers, total DSP blocks, and total thermal power dissipation for compute capable block RAM, MDPE, and Reconfigurable In-memory accelerator, and Table 3. Depicts the comparison result of the logic dot product engine and the proposed architectural design.

Figure 33.7 Simulation waveform of the proposed system
Source: Author

Table 33.2 Utilization summary

PARAMETERS	CCBRAM	M-DPE	RIMA
Logic utilization	56	228	248
Total Registers	103	287	324
Total DSP blocks	1	2	3
Power dissipation	526.25mW	526.37mW	532.37mW

Source: Author

Table 33.3 Comparison results

Metric	Logic- DPE	Radix -2
Clock Cycles	11	9
Slice LUTs	138	41
Slice Register	37	53
Bonded IOB	148	35
BUFGCTRL	1	1

Source: Author

Conclusion

This work emphasizes the growing role of FPGAs as efficient computing platforms by unifying computation and memory at the hardware level. Through the integration of arithmetic functionality directly into BRAMs, the RIMA architecture redefines traditional memory roles, allowing for localized execution of deep learning tasks. Replacing the logic-based dot product engine with a Radix-2 MAC unit significantly enhances both processing speed and hardware efficiency. Overall, the architecture presents a practical and scalable approach to in-memory computation, tailored for energy-efficient neural network inference on FPGA systems.

Future Work

In this work, the logic-based dot product engine (L-DPE) employed in the BRAM architecture represents a performance bottleneck due to its high cycle latency and intricate control logic. Although it supports in-situ multiply-accumulate (MAC) operations,

the Radix-2 multiplier integration in L-DPE requires 9 clock cycles per operation, which is not ideal for high-throughput scenarios. To overcome these constraints, in the future, it is suggested to integrate a higher Radix 4 MAC unit as an alternative approach. The Radix architecture provides fewer cycles of execution and eases the design.

References

[1] Intel Corporation (2019). Intel Stratix 10 GX/SX Device Overview. Available from: https://www.intel.com/content/www/us/en/products/details/fpga/stratix/10/overview.html.

[2] Wang, X., Goyal, V., Yu, J., Boutros, A., & Kupnow, K. (2021). Compute-capable block RAMs for efficient deep learning acceleration on FPGAs. In Proceedings of IEEE 29th Annual International Symposium on Field-Programmable Custom Computing Machines (FCCM). (pp. 133–141). doi: 10.1109/FCCM51124.2021.00030.

[3] Fowers, J., Ovtcharov, K., Papamichael, M., Massengill, T., Liu, M., Lo, D., et al. (2018). A configurable cloud-scale DNN processor for real-time AI. In Proceedings of 45th Annual International Symposium on Computer Architecture (ISCA), (pp. 1–14). doi: 10.1109/ISCA.2018.00012.

[4] Nurvitadhi, E., Venkatesh, G., Marr, D., Sim, H., Kim, Y. S., Venkataraman, J., et al. (2019). Why compete when you can work together: FPGA-ASIC integration for persistent RNNs. In Proceedings of IEEE 27th Annual International Symposium on Field-Programmable Custom Computing Machines (FCCM), (pp. 199–207). doi: 10.1109/FCCM.2019.00039.

[5] Eckert, C., Jayasena, N., Pellauer, M., & Shafiee, A. (2018). Neural cache: bit-serial in-cache acceleration of deep neural networks. In Proceedings of 45th Annual International Symposium on Computer Architecture (ISCA), (pp. 383–396). doi: 10.1109/ISCA.2018.00037.

[6] Boutros, A., Amouri, A., Gojman, B., Rupnow, K., & Koch, D. (2018). Embracing diversity: enhanced DSP blocks for low-precision deep learning on FPGAs. In Proceedings of 28th International Conference on Field-Programmable Logic and Applications (FPL), (pp. 25–32). doi: 10.1109/FPL.2018.00016.

[7] Li, Z., Wu, D., Xu, J., Hu, S., & Cong, J. (2019). E-RNN: design optimization for efficient recurrent neural networks in FPGAs. In Proceedings of IEEE 25th International Symposium on High Performance Computer Architecture (HPCA), (pp. 418–429). doi: 10.1109/HPCA.2019.00052.

[8] Imani, M., Kong, D., Yu, T., & Rosing, T. (2019). Float-PIM: in-memory acceleration of deep neural network training with high precision. In Proceedings of 46th Annual International Symposium on Computer Architecture (ISCA), (pp. 802–815). doi: 10.1145/3307650.3322229.

[9] Drumond, M., Matos, D., Felber, P., Zwaenepoel, W., & Loureiro, A. (2018). Training DNNs with hybrid block floating point. In Advances in Neural Information Processing Systems (NeurIPS).

[10] Boutros, A., Eldafrawy, M., Yazdanshenas, S., & Betz, V. (2019). Math Doesn't have to be hard: logic block architectures to enhance low-precision multiply-accumulate on FPGAs. In Proceedings of the FPGA.

[11] Eldafrawy, M., Boutros, A., Yazdanshenas, S., & Betz, V. (2020). FPGA logic block architectures for efficient deep learning inference. *ACM Transactions on Reconfigurable Technology and Systems (TRETS)*, 13(3), 1–34.

[12] Rasoulinezhad, S., Zhou, H., Wang, L., & Leong, P. H. (2019). PIR-DSP: an FPGA DSP block architecture for multi-precision deep neural networks. In 2019 IEEE 27th Annual International Symposium on Field-Programmable Custom Computing Machines (FCCM), (pp. 35–44). IEEE.

[13] Imani, M., Gupta, S., Kim, Y., & Rosing, T. (2019). Float-PIM: in-memory acceleration of deep neural network training with high precision. In Proceedings of the 46th International Symposium on Computer Architecture, (pp. 802–815).

[14] Li, S., Niu, D., Malladi, K. T., Zheng, H., Brennan, B., & Xie, Y. (2017). DRISA: a DRAM-based reconfigurable in-situ accelerator. In Proceedings of the 50th Annual IEEE/ACM International Symposium on Microarchitecture, (pp. 288–301).

[15] Zha, Y., & Li, J. (2018). Liquid silicon-monona: a reconfigurable memory-oriented computing fabric with scalable multi-context support. *ACM SIGPLAN Notices*, 53(2), 214–228.

[16] Chen, Y., & Abdelfattah, M. S. (2023). BRAMAC: compute-in-BRAM architectures for multiply-accumulate on FPGAs. arXiv preprint arXiv:2304.03974. Available from: https://arxiv.org/abs/2304.03974.

[17] Han, S., Kang, J., Mao, H., Hu, Y., Li, X., Li, Y., et al. (2017). ESE: efficient speech recognition engine with sparse LSTM on FPGA. In ACM/SIGDA International Symposium on Field Programmable Gate Arrays (FPGA), (pp. 75–84).

[18] Nurvitadhi, E., Kwon, D., Jafari, A., Boutros, A., Sim, J., Tomson, P., et al. (2019). Why Compete When You Can Work Together: FPGA-ASIC Integration for Persistent RNNs. In IEEE International Symposium on Field Programmable Custom Computing Machines (FCCM), (pp. 199–207). IEEE.

34 Differential privacy mechanisms in federated learning: privacy-utility trade-offs and future directions

Madhvesh, V. S.[1,a] and Karpagam, G. R.[2,b]

[1]PG scholar, Department of Computer Science and Engineering, PSG College of Technology, Coimbatore, Tamil Nadu, India

[2]Professor, Department of Computer Science and Engineering, PSG College of Technology, Coimbatore, Tamil Nadu, India

Abstract

Federated learning (FL) has become another approach to protect privacy by training models without transmitting the data on which the models work. Yet, it is established that FL remains susceptible to certain privacy concerns like membership inference and model inversion. This is due to the reason that FL has incorporated with Differential Privacy (DP), which is used to help reduce these risks through injecting carefully calibrated noise in data or model update. This paper focuses on some forms of DP mechanisms to use in FL, which include Gaussian, Laplacian, and Randomized Response mechanisms. It divides DP in FL into CDP, LDP, and Hybrid DP performance to ensure balance privacy and model utility. This work states the details of all these mechanisms are provided and issues such as privacy-utility trade-off, communication overhead, and scalability discussions are made.

Keywords: Differential privacy, federated learning, privacy budget, privacy-utility trade-off

Introduction

In Federated Learning (FL), several devices or clients together try to update a common global model without bringing raw sensitive data to the center. Each of them fine-tunes their model on their respective data and what is communicated to a central server is a model update. It further improves data confidentiality because data that is considered sensitive does not traverse the server-side.

Privacy risks in FL

Nevertheless, FL is not immune to a number of privacy threats:

- Membership inference attacks: This is how the attackers have the opportunity to deduce, which record belongs to the training data.
- Model inversion attacks: In this attack, the attacker tries to retrieve the original input from the changes made to the model weights.
- Gradient leakage: In general, as gradients are exchanged during the training process some information related to the inputs can be leakage from the server.

To minimize the privacy concerns that come with FL, DP is implemented into its framework. To protect against such attacks, DP adds what is known as calibrated noise into unit updates or gradients of a model. DP also prohibits the use of a single value to outweigh all the others so as to protect privacy.

Foundation and Background

Federated Learning can also be classified according to the kind of aggregation and manner of communication:

- Centralized FL: A central aggregator coordinates the received model updates from the clients to produce a global model. This is relatively easy to manage but could turn out to be a single window through which privacy threats may sneak in.
- Decentralized FL: The process in which the clients directly communicate with the other clients to exchange the updated models without the presence of a server. It raises the robustness of the system and minimizes the possibility of flaws with specific points of exposure but presents difficulties with synchronization and homogeneity.

FL is an extension of the distributed training technique in which numerous clients update the overall model without giving out their raw data. Namely,

[a]madhvesh29@gmail.com, [b]grk.cse@psgtech.ac.in

DOI: 10.1201/9781003770435-34

the learning objective of FL can be formulated as follows:

$$F(w) = \sum_{k=1}^{K} \frac{n_k}{N} F_k(w) \qquad (1)$$

Where w represents the global model parameters, K is the total number of participating clients, n_k is the number of data points at client k, N is the total number of data points across all clients and $F_k(w)$ is the local objective function for the client k. The most popular method of implementing aggregation in FL is called Federated Averaging (FedAvg).

$$w_{t+1} = \sum_{k=1}^{K} \frac{n_k}{N} w_t^k \qquad (2)$$

where multiple local training rounds of client models take place and the average model is modified in order to improve global performance. Thus, there are modifications of FedAvg such as FedAdam and Scaffold that consider high frequency of heterogeneous data distribution & faster convergence.

Overview of differential privacy
Several techniques of privacy preserving machine learning have arisen, which do not require explicitly sharing of sensitive attributes. These fall broadly into three categories. Perturbative techniques take control noise or distortions and add them artificially to the input or model level to hide private information. Among others, it may involve input perturbation (add randomness to features), model perturbation (add randomness to gradients or weights), and adversarial noise (thoughts that absolutely confuse attackers). In contrast non perturbative methods do not worry about frequency noise but rather employ structural techniques by for instance doing feature removal, which uses auto-encoders and GANs and other techniques, or using projection-based filtering to suppress the features correlated to private attributes. In image generative techniques, GANs or VAEs are trained as models that synthesize new images with utility but without sensitive traits (i.e., disentangled representations or DP-GANs).

Although these methods provide empirical privacy, they do not have formal mathematical guarantees. Due to this limitation, differential privacy (DP) is adopted as a useful provable framework for quantifying and controlling the amount of privacy loss. At bottom level, DP guarantees that the probability of getting a particular output of a computation is nearly the same regardless of inclusion of single

individual's data in that computation. In this way, an adversary could not with confidence infer whether or not a given record exists. The formal definition governs:

Epsilon (ϵ) and delta (δ) parameters: regulate the degree of privacy protection that has traded off for accuracy and protects the user's data from being eroded by more than the specified threshold, while δ accounts for the probability of exceeding this privacy loss.

Noise addition: Noise equal to the sensitivity of the function is added to the result to bring about privacy, normally Gaussian or Laplacian noise is used depending on the privacy level desired.

Sensitivity: Quantifies the greatest possible change in the output that can occur when a single data record is either added or removed from the dataset. Thus, higher sensitivity implies stronger noise to ensure privacy level is maintained to the desired level.

New practical DP methods including the moments accountant and Adaptive DP control the noise intensity, in addition to the number of steps, to balance privacy and utility.

Literature Review

Core federated learning and DP papers
It can be seen that FL has become one of the effective approaches for training the model for different applications while protecting the raw data of the individual participants. In this regard, some of the initial FL works such as work by McMahan et al. [15], proposed the Federated Averaging (FedAvg) algorithm, which gave positive steps toward the efficient way of aggregating and communicating in such systems [9]. These core papers address various issues under non-IID data, system heterogeneity and model convergence for the federated scenario.

Consuming DP in FL has made the privacy-preserving federated models even more robust than when not integrated. In this domain, the basic papers Dwork and Roth [5] focus on the issues of protection of personal information, their quality and organization of communication channels. For instance, the Moments Accountant developed by Abadi et al. [2], allowed for implementing more complex mechanisms of DP to control the total privacy loss across multiple rounds of FL. Other papers Geyer et al. [7] devoted their attention to privacy spending decisions, tuning of the noise level and analyzing how much the top quality decreases with privacy noise. These contributions have laid the foundation to improved DP methods for improve the privacy-utility balance in federated learning applications.

Centralized and local DP approaches in federated learning

The primary objective of FL is to improve the privacy concerns in distributed learning by training a model on several sites without sending raw data to a central site. However, this raises concerns as the latest model has the ability to leak data, which is contrary to the major emphasis of AI and ML works, that is, privacy [19]. Gives a bendable solution through the concept of DP by adding calibrated noise over the information to be protected [20]. The two most researched techniques with regards to FL include Centralized DP (CDP) as well as Local DP (LDP) [11, 3]. A few prior works Kim et al. [11], Wei et al. [20] have discussed the comparison of such solutions with the firm conclusion that CDP provides more privacy guarantee under the trusted server assumption while LDP allows for higher user control over data usage in exchange for controllable, noise-caused utility loss.

Some research outcomes have offered a way in expounding CDP and LDP in FL. Others suggest that it is possible to create models that alternate between the two abilities depending on the information's sensitivity level and the model's efficiency. Some methods Triastcyn and Faltings [18] such as Bayesian Differential Privacy have been proposed in order to provide privacy while improving the convergence rate. In other studies, the privacy-preserving gradient aggregation as well as the clipping procedure for the gradient have been incorporated into the model to enhance the client-side learning performance and privacy preservation [3]. These works indicate that the selection of the right DP framework in FL heavily relies on the system architecture, adversarial threats, and the privacy-utility balance that is desired.

Privacy-utility trade-off and communication efficiency

A tough task in deploying DP in FL is to obtain high utility alongside privacy [16]. This is especially so since the presence of noise degrades accuracy and there is thus an inherent privacy-utility trade-off [8]. To this end, there are so called adaptive noise strategies where the noise levels are made to vary with the sensitivity of the model and relative importance of features. They are some of the strategies which can be adopted to reduce this kind of deterioration while

at the same time maintaining security of data [13]. However, to maintain the privacy of the computations performed during the deliberation process, other variations such as Secure Multi-Party Computation (SMPC) and Homomorphic Encryption (HE) have been proposed for federated learning [14]

Communication efficiency is the other important issue that arises when using DP in FL since it is possible to have multiple rounds of updates in the model. As the communication overhead is a severe issue, researchers discussed gradient compression, sparsification and quantization methods [14, 13]. These techniques, when used together with DP, ensure that the level of privacy, the accuracy of the results, and their efficiency are all achieved simultaneously. Recent development also includes priority-based differential privacy techniques where selective noise addition is done mostly to sensitive parameters to make the high impact features still useful for relevance but not for identification [16, 8]. Such innovations are useful in improvement of the practice and the implementation of federated learning in large-scale utilize cases.

Advanced DP mechanisms and hybrid models

In traditional DP mechanisms, sensitivity to the degree of differential privacy increases vulnerabilities especially where the evaluations lack the capacity to prevent the employment of excessive noise addition to the model, which compromises the model's performance greatly [1]. New additional methods to further improve the privacy preservation in FL have been developed with the help of adaptive privacy budgets and hybrid models [6, 17]. It will assign noise in a dynamic manner depending on the sensitivity measures, whilst other important model updates sufficiently indicated by the measure, will undergo low level of noise. Some of the proposed improvements for DP refers to the use of multiple privacy failures [1].

The significance of such an architecture can be explained by the recent research, which revealed the fact that integrating the DP models into the hybrid approach could improve the degree of privacy without losing effectiveness in the IoT context and federated learning [12]. The proactive DP frameworks propose adaptive noise addition schemes that depend on awareness of the current scenario in the network in conjunction with the distributions of the data involved [6, 17]. These approaches help to capture the message of the original sender concurrently decrease the computational complexity and guarantee high privacy level. In addition, there has been researches which have proposed and developed such techniques such as priority-based interception and discovery protocol. Generally, as a federated learning is developing these enhanced DP strategies present the opportunities for applying privacy-preserving AI in the large scale.

DP in secure aggregation and communication-efficient FL

Secure aggregation is another significant factor to consider when it comes to FL since it allows protecting users' data from unauthorized access when aggregating the received local model updates [4]. DP extends this further by perturbing the model updates with noise to prevent the identification of the specific data. Both SMPC protocols and HE algorithms prevent model updating information from being transmitted in clear because at no time can a party have access to any partial data. However, as DP is applied jointly with secure aggregation, then the following problems starts to emerge: The computational and communication complexity increases [10].

To tackle such challenge, recent works have examined the efficient aggregation protocols that would add DP with low interaction cost. Such methods include employing quantization where numbers are rounded randomly, usage of a limited number of bits, and clipping of gradients to specific values among others [10]. Privacy-preserving secure aggregation frameworks propose to add noise at a rate dependent on the sensitivity of the model and importance of the gradients, so as to keep the privacy kept from the aggregation process, to as great an extent, whilst not affecting the model's accuracy negatively in the process [4]. Other works also propose other strategies of DP that can adapt to the noise added with relation to the communication limitations and the convergence status of the model.

Differential Privacy in Federated Learning

DP within the FL can be categorized according to the position of the noise and the privacy treatment that is provided. The following are the main categories of DP in FL, which include detailed descriptions, mathematical formulas, applications and difficulties.

Central differential privacy

In central DP (CDP), the noise added is done on the side of the server after combining the client updates.

This keeps the privacy of the final global model with differential privacy as well. The voting procedure is also performed at the server, where the server collects update models received from every connected client and adds noise to the overall result before the update of the global model. Mathematically, if g_i represents the update from client G is the aggregated update, then

$$G = \frac{1}{N} \sum_{k=1}^{K} g_i \qquad (3)$$

To ensure (ϵ, δ)-DP, Gaussian noise is added

$$G' = G + \mathcal{N}(0, \sigma^2 I) \qquad (4)$$

Where σ^2, the noise variance is determined by the privacy budget ϵ and δ, N the number of participating clients. There can be extensive application of CDP in Healthcare Organizations' models in order to keep patient information and financial models safe when using risk assessment models. The drawbacks include single point of failure since the privacy can be breached by an improper central server and increased latency due to noise addition at the server.

Local differential privacy (LDP)

In local DP (LDP), noise is also injected locally at the client side before the updates from the model are sent to the server. This means that the updates that separate clients have are shielded before they go up to the server. Every individual client adds some noise to its update before broadcasting it to the other parties, at the server the noisy updates then used to construct the aggregated model. Mathematically, for each client update g_i, the noise is added locally

$$g_i' = g_i + Lap(0, b) \qquad (5)$$

Where $b = \Delta/\epsilon$ is the scale of the Laplacian noise, and Δ is the sensitivity of the update. Innovations of LDP can help to enhance security for an IoT sensor and to maintain users' anonymity in the feedback-based models. However, it creates problems such as high noise effect that affects the model performance and increase communication overhead to correct the noisy updates.

Hybrid differential privacy

Hybrid differential privacy (HDP) can then be deduced from central and local DP where it aims at achieving an optimality point between privacy and utility. Some of the clients include partial noise in their updates and the server introduces noise to the centralized model. The mechanism involves adding partial noise at the client side and addition of noise to the update aggregation at the server. Mathematically, for a client update g_i, local noise is added as:

$$g_i' = g_i + \mathcal{N}(0, \sigma_c^2 I) \qquad (6)$$

The server subsequently introduces noise to the aggregated model updates to ensure differential privacy and prevent leakage of sensitive information during the learning process

$$G' = \frac{1}{N} \sum_{i=1}^{N} g_i' + \mathcal{N}(0, \sigma_s^2 I) \qquad (7)$$

where σ_c^2 is the noise variance at the client side, and σ_s^2 is the noise variance added by the server. It is useful in settings like federated smart grid systems and collaborative medical research where there is the need to ensure that privacy is also achieved while there is value added in use of data. However, there are a few issues like the difficulty of parameters tuning and the increased computational load through the use of double noise addition.

Different DP Mechanisms in Federated Learning

Gaussian mechanisms
The Gaussian mechanism is widely applied in the FL setting, as it is the basic method of providing differential privacy. It is the process by which Gaussian noise is added to the parameters or gradients of model during the training process. However, the Gaussian mechanism can be helpful even where it leads to higher computation, but still leads to less distortion to individual data contributions while preserving the study model performance. This mechanism is particularly suitable when there are training steps because it permits more intricate composition rules such as the moment accountant that assists in preventing the aggregate privacy loss. Due to its versatility, it is possible to implement it in areas like finance and healthcare where privacy and performance are seriously important.

Laplacian mechanisms
The most privacy offered is by Laplacian mechanism which adds noise from Laplace distribution. It generates noise of this distribution in tails heavier than

Gaussian noise, which implies that out in setting out individual data points the noise is better, but with certain variance in the model results. This is applied when higher privacy requirements are needed and in the range of applications where users want better protection, it may decline the whole model accuracy a bit. Nevertheless, because of more noise injections, it might not be suitable for complex learning tasks where details of data are vital for learning.

Randomized response mechanism
In the context of FL, the randomized response strategy is a workhorse of survey sample statistics imported. It enables users to offer computed but anonymous answers about a user's data to a query. In case of FL, this approach can be applied to add some noise intentionally to the local data before training, and this would be very hard for any given party to identify the actual data. This is particularly useful in areas such as user profiling or for social research since sharing of the data, even in an average form, might violate user privacy.

Moment accountant and privacy budget management
In general, federated learning requires multiple rounds of training so the total privacy loss needs to be regulated. The moment accountant is a technique that was developed with the aim of tracking the total privacy loss in all the iterations of training. It is a tighter analysis than you get with the traditional composition theorems, and it helps in enhancing the possibility of managing the privacy parameter with ease. Applied to a practical level, this would mean the possibility of training deeper models for much longer times and keeping the privacy loss within tolerable levels. Privacy budget management also entails determining the amount of noise to add per round as well as the division of the total budget among the clients and the training steps.

Adaptive differential privacy (ADP)
Adaptive differential privacy involves adding noise in a decision which involves various parameters, sensitivity of data, performance of the model, and the variation amongst the clients. This means that a higher privacy protection can be achieved while balancing privacy loss and the level of utility a system or application intends to provide. For instance, users with such high-profile information as their financial details could be rendered a better privacy

feature than others who provide less sensitive information to give more accurate updates. ADP is most beneficial in highly distributed FL environments that allow merging together models from clients which may have vastly different data and training capabilities.

Applications in Federated Learning

Central differential privacy (CDP)

- Healthcare systems: In the case of hospitals involved in collaborative model training, there is typically a reliance on a trusted aggregator to apply noise after aggregation.
- Smart grids: By using CDP, the utility providers collect data from smart meters to hide actual power consumption of a particular home.
- Banking and finance: Multiple banks sign model updates for detecting the fraud, and CDP implement and at a trusted server, it is possible not to let someone reverse the data of a specific customer.
- Benefits in applications: Its low noise at the central level ensures that it maintains high model accuracy. Effective when there is a reliable server and clients are controlled by other organizations.

Local differential privacy (LDP)

- Edge devices and medical imaging: The Each user's device learns to make noise when there's an update for all the users uploaded based on Gboard, the app from Google that predicts the next word, or even a disease based on the data of patients.
- Crowdsourced surveys: Of survey and polling apps and social science study, LDP enables users to provide sensitive responses without revealing their identity.
- IoT Devices: The security of each device is localized at the node level when providing data to patterns of environment or usage.
- Benefits in application: Asymmetric structure will give high privacy if the server is penetrated. It is best to implement for projects which are used to create a message user interface between the servers where trust cannot be readily assured.

Hybrid differential privacy (HDP)

- Health networks: Local noise is added by the individual hospitals and then such input is then aggregated further at a central trusted server for additional layers of privacy such as Differential Privacy many times.
- Applications of smart city: The modification of the traffic or environment data by the citizen devices occurs in a localized manner and the central aggregator gets the noisy layers added to the modified data.
- Cross-silo FL systems: In cases where there are joint working environments such as in pharmaceutical or self-driving cars, the hybrid DP guarantees the successive isolations of privacy boundaries.
- Advantages in applications: It offers good privacy forte for applications while at the same time ensuring high accuracy and reduced privacy load. Effective in real-world FL deployments with semi-trusted aggregators.

Gaussian mechanisms

- Medical applications: In medical diagnosis for instance secular training of diagnoses models across various hospitals such as breast cancer detection using MRI/CT, Gaussian noise keeps accuracy but hides patient's details.
- Speech recognition systems: FL on mobile voice assistants (like Siri or Alexa) adds Gaussian noise to avoid exposing user's explicit inputs but maintain the linguistic patterns.
- Machine behavior data with Gaussian noise collection and analysis for monitoring and warning without revealing the industrial processes in an Industrial IoT context.

Laplacian mechanism

- Location based services: Applications that take geographical information such as traffic apps are some of the apps that use Laplace noise for location privacy.
- Protection of sensitive information: During training of FL models to accurately analyze users' financial transaction to identify fraudulent ones, Laplace noise ensures stricter privacy preservation.

- Healthcare alerts: Developing alerts such as epidemic alert where the result is generated and alerted to the healthcare providers while maintaining patient privacy by providing stronger noise guarantees on patient-reported data.

Comparative Analysis of DP Mechanisms in FL

Evaluation metrics

A proper assessment of DP in FL covers the main aspects and parameters of perform capability and privacy protection:

- Privacy budget (ε,δ): The ε is an expenditure on private established as the noise added to conceal certain points. A small ε means that the algorithm ensures good privacy, but as it is seen with oracles, it results in decreased accuracy. The δ parameter relates to the probability of violating ε-DP and normally is set at a low number (equal to $10{-}5$). For evaluating mechanisms for privacy protection we have to consider how these mechanisms intervene between the two extremes of strong privacy and useful utility.
- Model accuracy trade-offs: Certain level of model accuracy must be maintained when applying DP to FL considering privacy preservation is of essence. Other forms of DP mechanisms such as adding noise that follows Gaussian or Laplacian distributions have a notable impact on both the convergence rate and the overall accuracy of the model. In comparative experiments, they estimate the degree of accuracy fall with increasing levels of noise and which methods maintain the efficiency of training thus highlighting the approaches that should be used.
- Communication efficiency: In FL, the communication between the clients as well as from clients to the server is very limited. Some DP mechanisms may add extra bits in each update, or conduct secure summarization, and thus may cause more communication overhead as well. The ones that reduce the number of communication rounds or compact the gradients are preferable for use in practice.
- Computational overhead: Depending on the nature of the DP mechanism these may require different amounts of computational resources. For instance, if the mechanism like Adaptive DP is

used then dynamic sensitivity evaluation takes place leading to the increase in local computation. Scalability metrics are measured on real-world devices and are rather critical in reality.
- Fairness across clients: When different clients have different data distributions, adding noise uniformly across can also affect some clients unequally. It is therefore important to assess how different forms of DP impact the model on a client level in the quest for fairness among participants.

Performance analysis

To assess the performance of different DP mechanisms in FL, usually, researchers emulate the federated setting using datasets that are easily accessible such as MNIST, CIFAR-10 or medical image datasets. Some of the assumptions that can be made from such work comprises:

- Gaussian mechanism ensures higher model accuracy than Laplacian most of the time because of its fairly higher privacy preservation to a reasonable level ($\varepsilon = 1$ to $\varepsilon = 5$). It gives rise to more stable noise properties that result in better model update.
- Laplacian mechanism provides more protection in high-sensitivity scenarios; however, their accuracy is more sensitive to the influence of noise distribution since Laplacian mechanism has a heavier tail distribution than Gaussian. It is preferred in situations where privacy is needed at all cost but performance degradation can be tolerable.
- Though less frequently used in large scale FL, randomized response can be very helpful in surveys, which are sensitive in nature or the situation where categorical data occurs. It is relatively easier and applies to specific regions, but lacks expressibility if the model is extensive.
- Adaptive differential privacy increases privacy by adjusting and applying noise according to the properties of clients' data or the model's beliefs. It thus leads to better convergence and accuracy particularly in a field such as health care where data sensitivity differ.
- Moment accountant techniques make it easier to sum up privacy loss over multiple rounds and thus better budget across a longer training paradigm, while maintaining risk at a threshold level.

Comparison of DP strategies

LDP comes as an essential factor in FL for medical imaging since the privacy and identity of the patients should be protected in any client platform before data or model updates are sent to the server. Due to the legal and ethical restrictions regarding specific patient information, it is challenging for medical institutions to share such data, and hence, LDP has the potential especially in the scenarios where the central aggregator cannot be fully trusted. When applied together with Laplacian noise that provides even better protection against leakage due to its higher anti-outlier properties, the described framework is suitable for secure protection of very fine details and margins, such as tumor boundaries or diagnostic patterns against inversion or reconstruction threats.

Even though Laplacian noise itself is more distorting as compared to Gaussian noise, thus when combined with LDP, each of the hospitals or imaging devices contributes to the global model securely. To enhance the applicability and effectiveness of FL in medical imaging, a modification can be made in the form of ADP. As training progresses, ADP then decreases the level of noise depending on data sensitivity levels and performance in order to enforce strict privacy on more sensitive scans regarding to patient's conditions, for instance, rare diseases or critical illness while removing noise for less significant inputs. Such adaptability also allows for developing and improving high utility diagnostic models with supplementary levels of compliance with privacy with datasets from various clients in federated medical platforms.

Challenges and Open Research Issues

Privacy-utility trade-off

The biggest concern when applying DP in FL is to ensure that it is effective while maintaining the accuracy of the model. The Gaussian or Laplacian mechanisms that are added in order to protect data privacy mainly through the noise help to influence the convergence, impact on final accuracy of the aggregated global model.

In fields like medical or any other sensitive data processing, domains where a slight information leakage may cause critical issues, the privacy (small ε) must be higher. However, this often leads to degradations of quantities in the usefulness of models. However, the current research is still fundamental to identify the way how DP parameters will be tuned dynamically or in an adaptive manner based on task type or characteristics of data, or even the behavior of the client to achieve this sweet balance. Also, the privacy enhancing strategies introduce additional layer of complexity to the pure privacy-utility dilemma specific to cross-device FL which involves low-end edge devices and noisy updates can affect convergence rate or even disrupt convergence. Thus, the outstanding challenge for practical enforcements of DP mechanisms that allow for context-adaptive adjustments of privacy levels which do not harm global learning performance is still open.

Communication overhead

DP mechanisms cause some extra communication load in the FL system especially when implemented in local manner (LDP). During computation of the models or the gradients at the client-side, noise addition leads to an increase in the size of the updates leading to increased use of bandwidth and time for synchronization. This becomes more challenging especially when the available bandwidth is limited or in large-scale FL where a thousands of edge devices are involved. For instance, managing and exchanging privacy budgets, adopting a secure aggregation procedure, as well as monitoring the privacy loss (e.g., with a moment accountant) add to the required communication overhead.

Table 34.1 DP strategies

Category	CDP	LDP	HDP	ADP
Privacy strength	Moderate	Strong	Balanced	Dynamic DP
Utility	High	Moderate to low	Balanced	High
Computation overhead	Low	High	Moderate	Moderate
Medical image suitability	Moderate	High	High	High
Communication cost	Low	High	Moderate	Moderate

Source: Author

One of the major areas of study is in trying to reduce the number of rounds of communication while not allowing the parties to learn anything more about each other than what was required to determine the result. It is used in combination with DP to make communication-efficient FL more practical nowadays various techniques as quantized gradients, update sparsification or model compression.

Client heterogeneity

Client heterogeneity refers to both statistical and system-level differences across clients. In terms of statistics, the clients may have non-independent and identically distributed data, in other words, the data distribution may not be IID, and in turn, the DP noise cannot be applied uniformly. A fixed noise level may sufficiently mask one client's information from other clients; however, at the same time, it may significantly reduce the usefulness of a local model for another client. The other forms of heterogeneity exist at the system level, it involves differences in computation capacity of devices, amount of energy available at clients, and internet connectivity which impacts on the viability of adoption of privacy-preserving protocols by some clients.

To this end, new versions of DP mechanisms that set budgets dynamically in accordance to data distribution and the client's resources are in consideration. However, addressing the questions on fairness while maintaining model utility and privacy is not easy or straightforward. Moreover, it is crucial to design efficient aggregation techniques that cope with fluctuations in the quality of updates from diverse clients.

Stronger threat models

FL systems are often becoming complex and used for various applications, thus facing more advanced threats compared to their initially simple versions. DP is mostly based on the assumption of a semi-honest adversary that can only see the received messages while colluding clients, compromised servers, or side-channel attacks are more realistic. In such environments, it is often the case that basic DP measures are not adequately effective. In order to compromise the privacy of the training data, the attackers can look for patterns in model update updates, or gradients, even those with added noise. Thus, a research direction more specific and important for the future is the definition of realistic threat models and the development of mathematically sound guarantees for the given models under DP.

Scalability in large networks

Scalability remains another core challenge in implementing DP in FL especially for millions of edge devices in use cases such as mobile phones, IoT or connected vehicles. As the number of clients scale up, the management of the global privacy budgets, synchronization and proper and secure aggregation is quite challenging. Further, the aggregate effect of several clients' noise affects the performance of the models when many clients contribute, when client activity is sporadic or updates are highly noisy.

For future DP-FL systems to be scalable, they require a lightweight approach to the coordination of workers, reliable methods for aggregating the updates received from the workers when many of them are noisy or some of them do not provide updates at all, and efficient ways of managing privacy budget across workers especially when the number of workers is very large and the network's dynamics is high. Such savings may be achieved through such mechanisms as hierarchical FL, clustering clients, and using edge servers.

Implementation

In order to carry this theoretical progress in differential privacy (DP) within federated learning (FL) to real case gears, we need to tackle already a number of practical issues. Solutions for some of these include having to select right DP mechanisms, tuning privacy parameters such as the privacy budget (ε), communication constraint, and client heterogeneity. The noise injection methods in the first case involve the implementation phase that should integrate the Laplacian mechanisms implemented at the local client level per the adopted privacy model (LDP). In addition, it can aid in overcoming the model utility and privacy trade-offs through privacy budget tracking such as through Adaptive DP techniques. This section details an integration of FL architectures and different DP mechanisms instance segmentation as a case study, design choices, performance optimizations and observed challenges during experimental validation.

Dataset details: In fall 2019, [21] the Iraq Oncology Teaching Hospital (IQ-OTH)/National Center for Cancer Diseases (NCCD) lung cancer dataset was collected from three months in the above mentioned specialist hospitals. It consists of CT scans of patients with lung cancer at different stages and control subjects. In these two centers, oncologists and radiologists marked IQ-OTH/NCCD slides. There are 1190 images of CT scan slices in the dataset for 110 cases. The cases are grouped in three classes; normal, benign and malignant, and these are given as 40 cases of malignant; 15 cases of benign; and 55 cases normal. The original collection of the CT scan was in DICOM format. The scanner involved is SOMATOM from Siemens. Readings were done with 120 kV, 1 mm slice thickness, window width 350-1200 HU, and window center 50–600, in breath hold at full inspiration. Before doing analysis, all images were de-identified. The oversight review board waived written consent. Participating medical centers were approved for the study's institutional review board. Each scan contains several slices. Here, there are 80 to 200 of these slices, each one has an image of the human chest with different sides and angles. There are 110 cases of different gender, age, area of residence and living status. They are some of the ministries of transport and oil employees, some are farmers and some are gainers. They come mostly from the middle region of Iraq as well, from hotspots of the provinces of Baghdad, Wasit, Diyala, Salahuddin or Babylon.

To make our FL learning scenarios as practical as possible and prevent client privacy leakage, three clients' datasets were created that do not hold independent and identically distributed (IID) data distribution as typically required for FL learning and observed in healthcare and medical imaging domains. To address the imbalance of the data, extra data enhancement procedures including rotation, flipping, zooming, and adjusting the contrast of the images were done in the client side. This preprocessing step was very useful in equalizing the distribution of class representation across clients as well as making the local models more generalizable during the federated training.

At the client side, LDP was used after data pre-processing step in order to strengthen privacy through the local updates to the model by adding Laplace noise. LDP also ensured that no sensitive raw data or exact gradients left the client environment, thus improving the privacy assurance particularly when the server or aggregators are assumed to be malicious (Figure 34.1).

However, when the noise levels was applied for all the training iterations affects the model accuracy falls due to the fact that the noise overwhelms the signal in the gradients. This was done to ensure that we obtained better results, and for this reason,

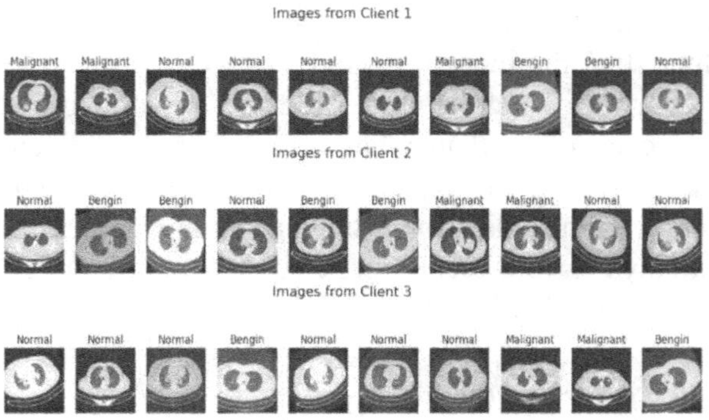

Figure 34.1 Data distribution among clients
Source: Author

we adopted an adaptive differential privacy (ADP) strategy that aimed at tuning the noise being added progressively in relation to the sensitivity of data and the local model accuracy trend. Those clients who had accurate localization value at higher level or had made less sensitive updates were allowed to choose lesser value of noise scale, whereas those clients who were more sensitive to update had to settle for higher level of noise application. This balancing mechanism left the notion of privacy as one that has context where it is possible to retain utility in addition to satisfying the conditions of differential privacy. The training was done over multiple rounds of communication using the FedAdam approach for aggregation. Even though, as expected, with the increase of privacy level, it inevitably leads to a decrease in the model accuracy, the final test accuracy achieved was at 79%, which is a strong testimony to what Federated Learning can achieve in terms of privacy. Altogether, the findings revealed that though privacy-preserving noise injects some level of performance loss, the application of adaptive methods doubtlessly blunts this loss and effectively renders the approach apt for the privacy-sensitive applications for classifying histological image of breast cancer.

Moreover, this implementation demonstrated that, for balanced privacy parameters and prepared data, the level of protection offered is equal to that of the state of the art and to other differentially private FL systems in the presence of complex and sensitive domains.

Conclusion

Federated learning (FL) delivers techniques that enables collective model training process with screening user data stored locally. Nonetheless, there is a danger of leakage of privacy every time model updates are made, implying that effective privacy-preserving techniques must be incorporated especially DP. This work also discusses the global and local model of DP and Laplacian, Gaussian and adaptive approaches that are potentially applicable in FL. In this case, each mechanism comes with drawbacks concerning strength in privacy, model usefulness, as well as level of communication. In addition, this survey explained how DP can be utilized in high-risk areas such as medical diagnosis from images, and in this, it stipulated the use of Laplace noise and adaptive differential privacy for enhanced security and deterministic diagnosis. A comparative evaluation also supported the proposition on the effects of various mechanisms in general and how they require customization and versatile design to specific tasks.

Progress has been made in most of them, but still several challenges persist there. The issues regarding privacy and the use of this technology, the load of the communications, and the variability of the clients and the construction of guards to handle stronger adversarial models remain challenges that have not yet been solved. Other important areas that need to be studied include scalability as well as the practical application of DP-enabled FL systems.

It is recommended that future research should address development of different, more efficient and more special DP techniques that can work dynamically according to the peculiarities of the clients of difference efficiency and the sensitivity of the tasks. DP can be also integrated with other technologies such as Secure Aggregation and Federated Learning to create scalable, reliable, and privacy-preserving FL platforms. In conclusion, Differential Privacy is still a fundamental feature in FL, and further research is needed to have a proper adoption of FL when privacy concern is a primary concern.

References

[1] Andrew, G., Thakkar, O., McMahan, H. B., & Ramaswamy, S. (2019). Differentially private learning with adaptive clipping. https://doi.org/10.48550/arXiv.1905.03871

[2] Abadi, M., Chu, A., Goodfellow, I., McMahan, H. B., Mironov, I., Talwar, K., et al. (2016). Deep learning with differential privacy. In Proceedings of the 2016 ACM SIG-SAC Conference on Computer and Communications Security. ACM, Oct. 24, 2016. doi: 10.1145/2976749.2978318.

[3] Bhowmick, A., Duchi, J., Freudiger, J., Kapoor, G., & Rogers, R. (2018). Protection against reconstruction and its applications in private federated learning. https://doi.org/10.48550/arXiv.1812.00984

[4] Bonawitz, K., Ivanov, V., Kreuter, B., Marcedone, A., McMahan, H. B., Patel, S., et al. (2017). Practical secure aggregation for privacy-preserving machine learning. In Proceedings of the 2017 ACM SIGSAC Conference on Computer and Communications Security. ACM, (pp. 1175–1191). Oct. 30, 2017. doi: 10.1145/3133956.3133982.

[5] Dwork, C., & Roth, A. (2013). The algorithmic foundations of differential privacy. *Foundations and Trends® in Theoretical Computer Science*, 9(3–4), pp. 211–407. doi: 10.1561/0400000042.

[6] Fu, J., Chen, Z., & Han, X. (2022). Adap DP-FL: differentially private federated learning with adaptive noise. https://doi.org/10.48550/ARXIV.2211.15893.

[7] Geyer, R. C., Klein, T., & Nabi, M. (2017). Differentially private federated learning: a client level perspective. https://doi.org/10.48550/ARXIV.1712.07557.

[8] Gu, X., Zhu, T., Li, J., Zhang, T., & Ren, W. (2020). The impact of differential privacy on model fairness in federated learning. In Lecture Notes in Computer Science, (pp. 419–430). Springer International Publishing. doi: 10.1007/978-3-030-65745-1_25.

[9] Kairouz, P., McMahan, H. B., Avent, B., Bellet A., Bennis, M., Bhagoji, A. N., et al. (2019). Advances and open problems in federated learning. https://doi.org/10.48550/ARXIV.1912.04977.

[10] Kim, M., Saad, W., Debbah, M., & Hong. C. S. (2024). SpaFL: communication-efficient federated learning with sparse models and low computational overhead. https://doi.org/10.48550/ARXIV.2406.00431.

[11] Kim, M., Günlü, O., & Schaefer, R. F. (2021). Federated learning with local differential privacy: trade-offs between privacy, utility, and communication. https://doi.org/10.48550/ARXIV.2102.04737.

[12] Liu, W., Cheng, J., Wang, X., Lu, X., & Yin. J. (2022). Hybrid differential privacy based federated learning for internet of things. *Journal of Systems Architecture*, 124, 102418. doi: 10.1016/j.sysarc.2022.102418.

[13] Lu, P., Meng, X., & Liu, X. (2024). FedCMK: an efficient privacy-preserving federated learning framework. In Lecture Notes in Computer Science, (pp. 253–271). Singapore: Springer Nature. doi: 10.1007/978-981-99-9785-5_18.

[14] Lyu, L., Yu, H., & Yang, Q. (2020). Threats to federated learning: a survey. https://doi.org/10.48550/arXiv.2003.02133

[15] McMahan, H. B., Moore, E., Ramage, D., Hampson, S., & y Arcas, B. A. (2016). Communication-efficient learning of deep networks from decentralized data. https://doi.org/10.48550/arXiv.1602.05629

[16] Shen, A., Francisco, L., Sen, S., & Tewari, A. (2023). Exploring the relationship between privacy and utility in mobile health: algorithm development and validation via simulations of federated learning, differential privacy, and external attacks. *Journal of Medical Internet Research*, 25, e43664. doi: 10.2196/43664.

[17] Talaei, M., & Izadi, I. (2024). Adaptive differential privacy in federated learning: a priority-based approach. https://doi.org/10.48550/arXiv.2401.02453

[18] Triastcyn, A., & Faltings, B. (2019). Federated learning with bayesian differential privacy. In 2019 IEEE International Conference on Big Data (Big Data). IEEE, (pp. 2587–2596). doi: 10.1109/bigdata47090.2019.9005465.

[19] Truex, S., Liu, L., Gursoy, M. E., Yu, L., & Wei, W. (2021). Demystifying membership inference attacks in machine learning as a service. *IEEE Transactions on Services Computing*, 14(6), 2073–2089. doi: 10.1109/tsc.2019.2897554.

[20] Wei, K., Li, J., Ding, M., Ma, C., Yang, H. H., Farokhi, F., et al. (2020). Federated learning with differential privacy: algorithms and performance analysis. *IEEE Transactions on Information Forensics and Security*, 15, 3454–3469. doi: 10.1109/tifs.2020.2988575.

[21] Hamdalla, A., & AL-Huseiny, M. (2023). The IQ-OTH/NCCD lung cancer dataset. Mendeley Data, V4. doi: 10.17632/bhmdr45bh2.4.

35 Ticker trend - stock closing price prediction using machine learning

Mirudhubasini, R. C.[1,a] and Sankar A[2,b]

[1]Student, Department of Computer Applications, PSG College of Technology, Coimbatore, India

[2]Professor, Department of Computer Applications, PSG College of Technology, Coimbatore, India

Abstract

The unstable and non-linear nature of financial markets makes it complex to predict stock closing prices. The purpose of this project is to compare the effectiveness of the autoregressive integrated moving average–generalized autoregressive conditional heteroskedasticity (ARIMA-GARCH) and long short-term memory-attention residual order (LSTM-ARO) models to improve stock closing price prediction. Newly developed variables like high-low (H-L), open-close (O-C), moving averages, and standard deviations are added to past stock data in order to capture intricate patterns in stock movements. An analysis is conducted between the ARIMA-GARCH hybrid model, which successfully models linear relationships, short-term trends, and volatility clustering in time-series data, and the LSTM-ARO attention-based model, which is renowned for its capacity to capture long-term dependencies and dynamically focus on significant time steps. To evaluate the predictive accuracy of these models, the main goal of the suggested methodology is to compare their forecasting performance. Performance is typically evaluated using metrics such as the mean absolute percentage error (MAPE) and the root mean square error (RMSE).

Keywords: Average–generalized autoregressive conditional heteroskedasticity, attention mechanism, long short-term memory-attention residual order, mean absolute percentage error, root mean square error, volatility modeling

Introduction

Time series forecasting is the process of using past data to predict future patterns in a variety of fields, such as weather forecasting, healthcare, and finance. It facilitates better decision-making and strategic planning by assisting in the identification of patterns, seasonality, and trends. Stock price prediction is especially difficult in the financial industry because of investor sentiment, economic variables, and market volatility. Analysts, traders, and investors need accurate forecasting models in order to reduce risks and maximize profits. Statistical and deep learning models are two examples of advanced techniques that are frequently used to increase prediction accuracy and capture intricate stock market dynamics.

Time series forecasting

Time series forecasting is a statistical and machine learning methodology that uses previous data points to forecast future values. Analyzing sequential data over time entails looking for patterns, trends, and seasonal variations. The goal is to find underlying patterns and forecast future occurrences with precision. Time series is mathematically defined as a sequence of observations made at distinct intervals of time as in Equation (1).

$$Y_t = f(Y_{t-1}, Y_{t-2}, ..., Y_{t-n}) + \varepsilon_t \qquad (1)$$

Where, represents the value of the time series at time t, Y_{t-1}, Y_{t-2}, …, Y_{t-n}, are past observations, f is the function capturing dependencies in the time series and ε_t is a random error term (white noise) at time t.

Time series stock price data

One dimension (x-axis) represents the time values in a time series stock price data, and another dimension (y-axis) represents the stock price at each time point. Together, these components essentially form a line graph. The three main elements of time series data are trend, seasonality, and residual/noise. The trend shows how the data has changed over time, whether it is rising, falling, or staying the same. Regular, recurring patterns that take place at predictable intervals such as weekly, monthly, or annual cycles are referred to as seasonal. The random, unpredictable variation in the data that cannot be ascribed to seasonality or trend is known as residual/noise. A two-dimensional

[a]23mx117@psgtech.ac.in, [b]dras.mca@psgtech.ac.in

DOI: 10.1201/9781003770435-35

graph depicting the components of time series stock price date is illustrated in Figure 35.1.

Time series forecasting methods

Time series forecasting techniques are generally classified into two broad groups: statistical models and machine learning or deep learning models. While machine learning models use data-driven strategies to increase predictive accuracy, traditional statistical models rely on historical observations and mathematical methods to find patterns. The following is a list of the models that were used in the suggested methodology. The popular ARIMA model combines moving averages, autoregression, and differencing to capture linear dependencies in time series. Financial time series with variable variance can benefit from the use of GARCH, which is an extension of ARIMA that models volatility clustering. By dynamically focusing on significant time steps, the LSTM-ARO improves LSTM and increases accuracy in intricate time series patterns.

Literature Review

Comparative study of ARIMA and exponential smoothing models for stock price prediction

Funde and Damani [1] examined ARIMA and Exponential Smoothing for stock prediction using NIFTY 50 data. According to the findings, ARIMA outperformed other models for the majority of stocks, indicating that it is a dependable option for financial time series forecasting. The study emphasizes how well ARIMA captures seasonality and trends compared to conventional smoothing methods.

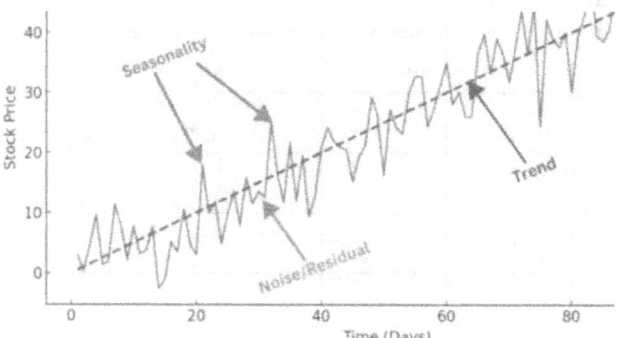

Figure 35.1 Illustration of time series stock price data
Source: Author

Forecasting directional movements of stock prices for intraday trading using LSTM and random forests

Ghosh et al. [2] explored the effectiveness of LSTM networks and Random Forests in forecasting the directional movements of stock prices for intraday trading. Their study analyzed S&P 500 constituent stocks from January 1993 to December 2018. Based on these results, the study suggested that LSTM networks were more effective for stock price forecasting compared to Random Forests, particularly in capturing intricate patterns and dependencies in financial time series data.

Stock market prediction using a convolutional neural network model with an attention mechanism (CN-Nam)

Huang and Chu [3] presented a convolutional neural network (CNN) model with an attention mechanism (CNNam) for stock prediction using candlestick charts. The model outperformed recurrent neural network (RNN), LSTM, gated recurrent unit (GRU), and conventional CNN by identifying important trading patterns and volume dependencies through the incorporation of attention. The study emphasizes the benefits of combining LSTM with attention mechanisms to enhance market trend prediction.

Forecasting selected colombian shares using a hybrid ARIMA-SVR model

Rubio and Alba [4] proposed a hybrid ARIMA-SVR model to predict the stock prices of Colombian companies. Support Vector Regression (SVR) improved prediction accuracy by addressing non-linear dependencies, whereas ARIMA captured linear trends. The study emphasizes how hybrid approaches, which combine statistical and machine learning models, improve stock market forecasting.

A comparison of linear regression, LSTM model and ARIMA model in predicting stock price: a case study: HSBC's stock price

Kuang [5] used HSBC transaction data (2010–2019) to compare ARIMA, LSTM, and Linear Regression for stock price forecasting. The study discovered that while ARIMA successfully modeled linear trends but had trouble with market fluctuations, LSTM achieved the lowest error because it was able to capture long-term dependencies.

Proposed Method

A novel technique has been suggested as an enhancement to current financial forecasting methods by combining LSTM-ARO with ARIMA-GARCH. In this method, LSTM-ARO utilizes attention mechanisms to improve sequence modeling and capture significant price fluctuations, while ARIMA-GARCH focuses on modeling linear trends and changes in volatility. Following this, historical stock data is evaluated using these models to produce precise predictions for the future, thereby enhancing financial time series forecasting.

Data collection

The historical stock price data was collected from the Alpha Vantage API, covering January 2021 to February 2025, with real-time updates upon user requests. The study focuses on highly traded NYSE and NASDAQ stocks: AAPL, GOOG, RYCEY, AMZN, and ORCL selected for their market capitalization and liquidity. The dataset contains essential market variables such as open, high, low, close prices, adjusted close, and trading volume, capturing market trends and volatility patterns.

Data preprocessing for LSTM-ARO

To prepare stock price data for training the LSTM-ARO model, a systematic preprocessing workflow was established, which included data cleaning, feature selection, normalization, and sequence creation. Raw stock price data was acquired through the Alpha Vantage API and processed using Pandas, encompassing significant financial indicators such as opening, highest, lowest, and closing prices. The date column was converted to datetime format for accurate chronological organization, and missing values were addressed to uphold data quality.

To improve predictive abilities, valuable features were created, such as the high-low difference (H-L) to assess intraday volatility, open-close difference (O-C) to reflect market sentiment, moving averages (7-day, 14-day, 21-day) to identify short-, medium-, and long-term trends, and standard deviation (7-day) to evaluate short-term market volatility.

Given that LSTMs are affected by the scale of input, Min-Max Scaling was applied to standardize all feature values within a range of 0 to 1, utilizing distinct scalers for input features and the target variable (closing price) to avoid data leakage. Subsequently,

70% of the data was allocated for training, while the remaining 30% was reserved for testing ensuring that historical data was utilized for training while future data remained for model assessment.

As LSTMs necessitate sequential data to understand temporal dependencies, a 30-day sliding window technique was employed, where the preceding 30 days' data served as input to predict the next day's closing price. Ultimately, the dataset was reshaped into a 3D array (samples, timesteps, features) to meet LSTM input specifications, thereby facilitating effective pattern recognition in stock price movements.

Data Preprocessing for ARIMA - GARCH

To prepare for ARIMA-GARCH modeling, preprocessing actions including data transformation, checks for stationarity, and volatility assessment were carried out. The data was organized chronologically with the closing price serving as the forecast variable. It was then allocated 70% for training and 30% for testing.

To confirm that the stock price data satisfied the stationarity criteria for the ARIMA model, several transformations were applied. The augmented dickey-fuller (ADF) test was conducted, revealing the time series was non-stationary, as the p-value exceeded 0.05.

To eliminate trends and achieve stationarity, first-order differencing was utilized, followed by a log transformation to stabilize the variance. Additional differencing was conducted to remove any lingering trends.

Moreover, an autocorrelation analysis was performed using the auto correlation function (ACF) and partial auto correlation function (PACF) to identify suitable ARIMA parameters. Given that stock price data frequently shows volatility clustering, the ACF of squared residuals was analyzed to uncover such patterns, emphasizing the need for GARCH modeling to capture time-varying volatility.

Feature engineering in LSTM-ARO

In the LSTM-ARO model, feature engineering was utilized to boost the model's capacity to detect patterns in stock price movements and enhance forecasting precision. Various key financial metrics were extracted and modified to serve as significant inputs. Fundamental trading session metrics included the high price, low price, open price, and close price.

Moreover, additional features such as the high-low difference (H-L), which indicates intraday volatility, and the open-close difference (O-C), reflecting market sentiment, were calculated to better capture market dynamics.

To examine trends across different time periods, moving averages were incorporated: the 7-day moving average (7_DAYS_MA) for short-term trends, the 14-day moving average (14_DAYS_MA) for medium-term trends, and the 21-day moving average (21_DAYS_MA) for long-term trends. These moving averages aided the model in recognizing recurring market patterns. Additionally, a 7-day standard deviation (7_DAYS_STD_DEV) was included as a way to measure short-term market volatility, offering insights into price variations. By integrating these engineered features, the LSTM model gained a greater capability to capture intricate dependencies in stock price data, resulting in enhanced predictive performance.

Engineering in ARIMA-GARCH

For the ARIMA-GARCH model, the emphasis in feature engineering was on converting stock price data into a format that is appropriate for both predicting trends using ARIMA and modeling volatility using GARCH. In contrast to LSTM, which utilizes several input features, ARIMA is based solely on one time-series variable: the closing price. To stabilize the variance and enhance the data's suitability for time-series analysis, log returns were calculated as outlined in Equation (2).

$$Log\ Returns = 100 \times log\ (P_t \div P_{t-1}) \qquad (2)$$

where P_t denotes closing price at time t, and P_{t-1} refers to the closing price on the preceding day. This transformation helped in addressing non-stationarity in the data, making it more suitable for ARIMA and GARCH models.

To analyze various market trends, moving averages were utilized: the 7-day moving average (7_DAYS_MA) for capturing short-term trends, the 14-day moving average (14_DAYS_MA) for observing medium-term trends, and the 21-day moving average (21_DAYS_MA) for long-term trends. Furthermore, the 7-day standard deviation (7_DAYS_STD_DEV) was computed to measure recent market volatility.

To predict volatility patterns, the GARCH (1,1) model was applied to log returns, allowing for projections of future market variations. By incorporating these developed features, the ARIMA-GARCH model reflected stock price trends.

The Algorithms

This section presents the algorithms used for time-series forecasting and classification, chosen for their ability to capture temporal patterns, volatility, and complex dependencies.

The LSTM - ARO algorithm

The LSTM-ARO model enhances stock closing price forecasting by integrating LSTM networks, an attention mechanism, and residual connections. LSTM networks excel at capturing long-term dependencies in stock price trends by maintaining a memory state, while the attention mechanism prioritizes past observations, enabling the model to concentrate on the most significant prior data.

Residual connections improve predictability by modeling price changes instead of absolute values, which simplifies the training process and fosters better convergence. The model evaluates a 30-day sequence of stock data, with each timestep incorporating 11 financial indicators, including opening, highest, lowest, and closing prices, moving averages, and volatility measures. Its architecture features an LSTM layer with 256 units, followed by an attention mechanism that refines historical data, a dense layer containing 100 units of neurons utilizing ReLU activation, a dropout layer set at a 40% rate to reduce overfitting, and residual connections to ensure stable predictions.

Training is performed using Adam optimization algorithm, with mean squared error (MSE) as the objective function, a batch size of 128, and spans 200 epochs with validation monitoring. By incorporating these elements, LSTM-ARO significantly improves forecasting accuracy, enhances interpretability, and effectively addresses critical challenges such as overfitting and vanishing gradients.

The ARIMA - GARCH algorithm

The ARIMA-GARCH model serves as a statistical tool for forecasting financial time series. It combines the ARIMA approach, which is effective for modeling linear trends, with the GARCH method, which addresses time-varying volatility. The ARIMA model is defined using three key parameters: p, d, and q. The parameter p refers to the number of lag observations in the model, d stands for the degree of differencing applied to make the data stationary, and q indicates the size of the moving average window used to smooth out past prediction errors. Although ARIMA is proficient in capturing stock price trends, it fails to consider volatility clustering, a phenomenon where significant price changes are typically succeeded by additional substantial movements. To remedy this limitation, GARCH is integrated to model variance fluctuations and enhance predictive accuracy. The initial phase of ARIMA modeling involves assessing stationarity through the ADF test, where a p-value exceeding 0.05 signifies non-stationarity, necessitating differencing, as illustrated in Equation (3).

$$Y_{t\prime} = Y_t - Y_{t-1} \qquad (3)$$

The ACF and PACF graphs are then examined to determine significant lags, helping configure an optimal ARIMA (p, d, q) model such as ARIMA (1,1,1). After model fitting, residual analysis is performed to check for randomness; if residuals exhibit patterns, this indicates unmodeled volatility, requiring a GARCH extension.

To model volatility, the GARCH(1,1) model is applied to ARIMA residuals after detecting volatility clustering using the Ljung-Box test. The GARCH model captures persistence in market fluctuations by considering one lag of squared residuals and one lag of past variance, refining volatility forecasts. This hybrid approach combining trend forecasting and volatility modeling enables a more comprehensive prediction of stock price movements and associated risks, making the ARIMA-GARCH model a robust statistical method for financial forecasting.

Comparative Analysis

This section evaluates the performance of the selected algorithms, comparing their accuracy, efficiency, and suitability for time-series forecasting and classification.

Performance evaluation metric
The predictive performance of the LSTM-ARO and ARIMA-GARCH models is evaluated through two main performance indicators: RMSE and MAPE.

RMSE measures the forecasting errors by computing the square root of the mean squared differences between actual values and their predictions and MAPE measures the percentage difference between expected and actual values, enabling comparisons of errors across various stock prices, independent of their scale.

Lower values of MAPE signify greater accuracy in forecasting compared to actual stock prices. Results for five companies Apple, Google, Oracle, Amazon, and Rolls Royce are shown in Table 35.1.

Table 35.1 presents the RMSE and MAPE metrics for five different stocks, comparing the performance of LSTM-ARO and ARIMA-GARCH models. For Apple, both models show comparable performance, with ARIMA-GARCH achieving a slightly lower RMSE (3.1890) than LSTM-ARO (3.2686), and MAPE values of 1.10% and 1.11%, respectively.

This marginal difference suggests that ARIMA-GARCH has a slight advantage in capturing price trends. Similarly, for Google, ARIMA-GARCH (RMSE: 3.0787, MAPE: 1.31%) outperforms LSTM-ARO (RMSE: 3.1974, MAPE: 1.30%), indicating that ARIMA-GARCH better handles Google's volatility patterns.

In contrast, Oracle's stock prices exhibit highly non-linear trends, making LSTM-ARO the superior model. LSTM-ARO achieves a significantly lower RMSE (3.7270) compared to ARIMA-GARCH (10.5182), demonstrating its ability to capture complex dependencies. The MAPE values (1.55% for LSTM-ARO vs. 2.85% for ARIMA-GARCH) further

Table 35.1 Performance metric table

Stock	LSTM - ARO RMSE	ARIMA - GARCH RMSE	LSTM - ARO MAPE	ARIMA - GARCHMAPE
APPLE	3.2686	3.1890	1.11%	1.10%
GOOGLE	3.1974	3.0787	1.30%	1.31%
ORACLE	3.7270	10.5182	1.55%	2.85%
AMAZON	5.5617	3.3717	2.49%	1.33%
ROLLS ROYCE	0.1622	0.1563	1.61%	1.62%

Source: Author

confirm its effectiveness. For Amazon, ARIMA-GARCH proved to be the better model, achieving a lower RMSE (3.3717) than LSTM-ARO (5.5617), along with a reduced MAPE of 1.33% compared to 2.49%. This suggests that Amazon's stock follows structured volatility patterns that ARIMA-GARCH captures more effectively.

For Rolls Royce, both models perform almost identically, with RMSE values of 0.1563 for ARIMA-GARCH and 0.1622 for LSTM-ARO. The slight advantage of ARIMA-GARCH suggests that it captures minor fluctuations better, though the MAPE values (1.62% vs. 1.61%) indicate minimal differences in predictive accuracy. Overall, the results highlight that ARIMA-GARCH is more effective for stocks with structured volatility patterns (Apple, Google, Amazon, Rolls Royce), while LSTM-ARO is superior for highly non-linear price movements, as observed in Oracle.

Actual vs predicted results

To further evaluate the forecasting performance of LSTM-ARO and ARIMA-GARCH, comparisons of actual vs. predicted stock closing prices of Apple, Amazon, Google, Oracle and Rolls Royce are presented in the charts below. These charts illustrate how effectively each model captures stock price movements over time.

The x-axis represents dates in YYYY-MM-DD format, while the y-axis denotes stock closing prices in dollars ($). These visualizations provide insight into the accuracy of each model in tracking price trends and identifying fluctuations across different stocks.

Figures 35.2 and 35.3 illustrate the actual vs. predicted stock close prices of AAPL (Apple Stock) using two different forecasting models, ARIMA-GARCH and LSTM-ARO.

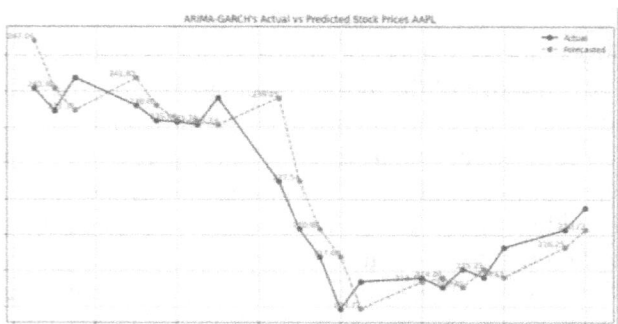

Figure 35.3 ARIMA - GARCH prediction graph for AAPL stock

Source: Author

Figures 35.4 and 35.5 illustrate the actual vs. predicted stock close prices of AMZN (Amazon) using two different forecasting models, ARIMA-GARCH and LSTM-ARO.

Figures 35.6 and 35.7 illustrate the actual vs. predicted stock close prices of ORCL (Oracle) using

Figure 35.4 LSTM - ARO prediction graph for AMZN stock

Source: Author

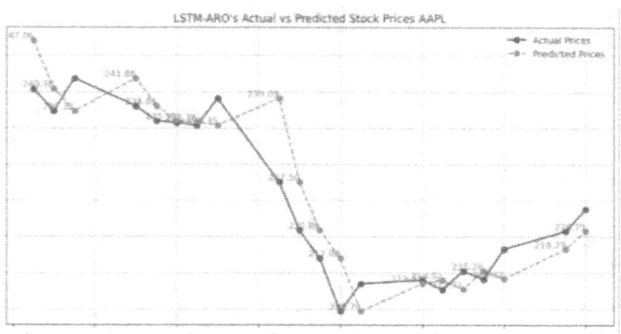

Figure 35.2 LSTM - ARO prediction graph for AAPL stock

Source: Author

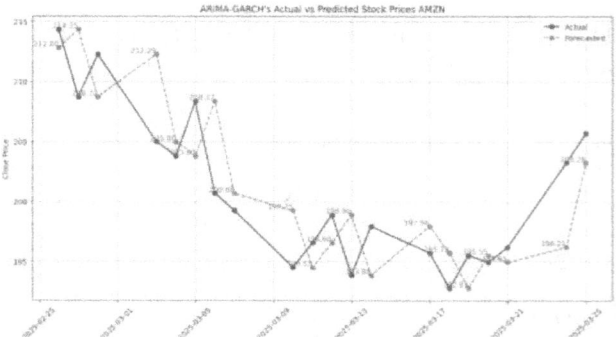

Figure 35.5 ARIMA - GARCH prediction graph for AMZN stock

Source: Author

Figure 35.6 LSTM - ARO prediction graph for ORCL stock
Source: Author

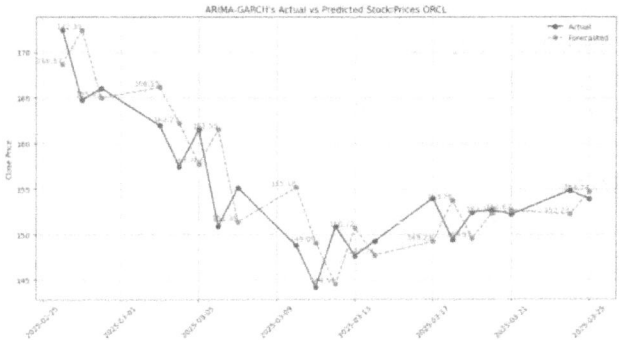

Figure 35.7 ARIMA - GARCH prediction graph for ORCL stock
Source: Author

Figure 35.8 LSTM - ARO prediction graph for RYCEY stock
Source Author

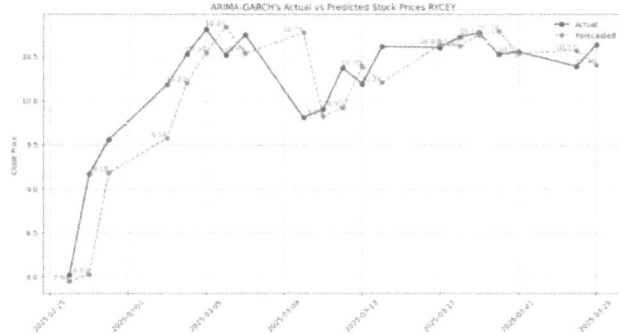

Figure 35.9 ARIMA - GARCH prediction graph for RYCEY stock
Source: Author

two different forecasting models, ARIMA-GARCH and LSTM-ARO.

Figures 35.8 and 35.9 illustrate the actual vs. predicted stock close prices of RECEY (Rolls Royce) using two different forecasting models, ARIMA-GARCH and LSTM-ARO.

Figures 35.10 and 35.11 illustrate the actual vs. predicted stock close prices of GOOG (Google) using two different forecasting models, ARIMA-GARCH and LSTM-ARO.

In comparing the forecasting performance of ARIMA-GARCH and LSTM-ARO across various stocks namely AAPL, AMZN, ORCL, RYCEY, and GOOG it is evident that both models possess distinct strengths suited to different market conditions. ARIMA-GARCH consistently achieves lower RMSE and MAPE values, demonstrating strong accuracy in capturing overall trends, particularly during stable market periods. Its performance is notably reliable for stocks like AMZN and RYCEY, where it closely

Figure 35.10 LSTM - ARO prediction graph for GOOG stock
Source: Author

follows actual price movements. However, it struggles to respond promptly to abrupt price shifts, often lagging during periods of high volatility. In contrast, LSTM-ARO, while slightly less accurate in terms of error metrics for some stocks, shows greater

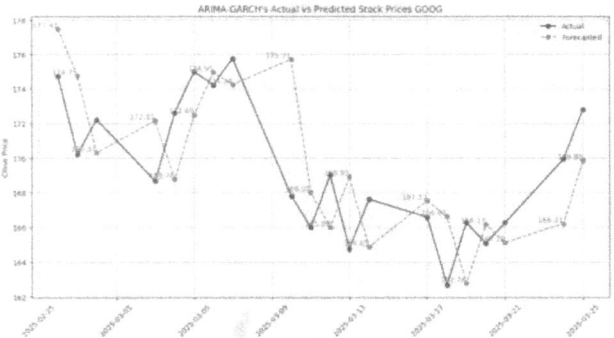

Figure 35.11 ARIMA - GARCH prediction graph for GOOG stock
Source: Author

adaptability to rapid market fluctuations. This is particularly evident in its performance with highly volatile stocks such as AAPL and ORCL, where it better aligns with real-time changes. Overall, ARIMA-GARCH is more effective for trend-based, stable forecasts, whereas LSTM-ARO offers enhanced responsiveness in volatile scenarios.

Conclusion

This study aimed to improve stock closing price prediction accuracy by comparing deep learning and traditional time-series models. The LSTM-ARO and ARIMA-GARCH models were assessed using RMSE and MAPE to measure their effectiveness in capturing stock price trends. Results indicated that while both models provided reliable forecasts, LSTM-ARO demonstrated superior adaptability to short-term market fluctuations due to its sequential memory-based structure. Meanwhile, the ARIMA-GARCH model demonstrated higher accuracy in capturing long-term trends and volatility, making it well-suited for broader market analysis.

For future research, model accuracy can be enhanced by integrating hybrid architectures that leverage both deep learning and statistical techniques. Further improvements can be explored using transformer-based models or by incorporating external factors like news sentiment and macroeconomic indicators. Additionally, testing these models on larger and more diverse datasets would help assess their robustness and scalability.

In conclusion, both LSTM-ARO and ARIMA-GARCH have demonstrated their effectiveness in stock price prediction. While ARIMA-GARCH generally achieved lower RMSE and MAPE values, LSTM-ARO performed better for stocks exhibiting high volatility and non-linear price movements. The combination of deep learning's adaptability and traditional models' ability to capture structured volatility provides a comprehensive framework for accurate and reliable financial forecasting.

References

[1] Huang, J., & Chu, Y. (2022). Stock market prediction using a convolutional neural network model with an attention mechanism (CNNam). *The Journal of Finance and Data Science*, 4(2), 112–130.

[2] Kuang, S. (2023). A comparison of linear regression, LSTM model and ARIMA model in predicting stock price: A case study: HSBC's stock price. *BCP Business and Management*, 44, 478–488.

[3] Rubio, L., & Alba, K. (2022). Forecasting selected Colombian shares using a hybrid ARIMA-SVR model. *Mathematics*, 10(13), 2181.

[4] Funde, Y. C., & Damani, A. D. (2021). A comparative study of ARIMA and exponential smoothing models for stock price prediction. *International Journal of Financial Studies*, 9(3), 45–60.

[5] Ghosh, P., Neufeld, A., & Sahoo, J. K. (2022). Forecasting directional movements of stock prices for intraday trading using LSTM and random forests. *Finance Research Letters*, 46(A), 102280.

36 Prediction and enhancement of dynamic response of 3D auxetic structure against impact load for vehicle crash box

Govindaraj, P.[1,a] and Soorya Pandian, P.[2,b]

[1]Assistant Professor, Department of Mechanical Engineering, PSG College of Technology, Coimbatore, India

[2]PG Student, Department of Mechanical Engineering, PSG College of Technology, Coimbatore, India

Abstract

This work focuses on the design, prediction, and enhancement of the dynamic response of a 3D auxetic structure for crash box applications. The objective is to optimize energy absorption and crashworthiness by employing a re-entrant honeycomb auxetic structure instead of a hollow crash box shell. Auxetic structures, characterized by a negative Poisson's ratio, offer superior performance in crash scenarios due to their ability to dissipate energy efficiently while undergoing plastic deformation. Multilinear isotropic hardening was applied to simulate plastic zone deformation accurately. Following validation, a detailed crash box model was developed, incorporating real-world dynamic loading conditions. The auxetic core's energy absorption characteristics, specific energy absorption, peak force, and load-displacement behavior were analysed through quasi-static simulations. The optimal combination of re-entrant angle, variable stiffness factor, and thickness has been identified from 12 different configurations using the Taguchi method. This study aims to contribute to the enhancement of crash box designs, offering insights into the use of auxetic structures to improve energy dissipation and crash resistance.

Keywords: 3D auxetic structure, crashworthiness, dynamic loading conditions, energy absorption, negative poisson's ratio, re-entrant honeycomb auxetic Structure

Introduction

Despite advancements in autonomous driving technology aimed at creating a future free of accidents, passive safety systems continue to serve as the critical last line of defense during collisions. Crash boxes play a critical role in enhancing automobile safety by effectively managing impact energy during collisions absorbing almost 60% of the impact energy [24]. Positioned at the front and rear ends of vehicles, these structures are designed to absorb and dissipate the kinetic energy generated during an impact, thereby reducing the force transferred to the occupants of the vehicle.

This controlled deformation helps minimize the damage to the vehicle's main body and protects vital components, like the passenger cabin, from sustaining serious structural damage. The importance of cashbox structures is largely tied to their energy-absorbing properties. Crashboxes are typically made from materials with good deformation characteristics, such as aluminum or steel [1]. Modern crash boxes incorporate advanced geometries, such as auxetic or honeycomb structures, that

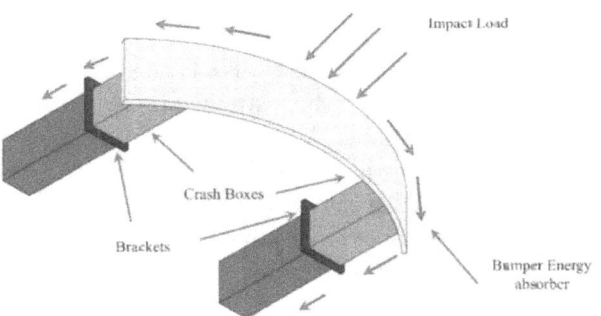

Figure 36 1 Schematic layout of the crashbox [11]
Source: Author

improve energy absorption efficiency while keeping weight low which is an essential factor for fuel efficiency. Auxetic materials are a distinctive class of materials that exhibit an unconventional mechanical behavior, characterized by a negative Poisson's ratio. Unlike typical materials, which contract in the transverse direction when stretched, auxetic materials expand laterally when stretched and contract laterally when compressed [2]. This behavior is due to their unique internal structure, which allows for

[a]pgr.mech@psgtech.ac.in, [b]sooryapandian200_@gmail.com

DOI: 10.1201/9781003770435-36

synchronized deformation. The negative Poisson's ratio in auxetic materials arises from their internal architecture, often designed with specific re-entrant or rotating unit cells. Auxetic materials excel in absorbing mechanical energy, making them highly desirable for impact mitigation and crash protection applications. They can absorb significant amounts of energy through plastic deformation, reducing the forces transmitted to occupants during a collision. The dynamic response of materials under impact is a critical factor in the design of structures that must withstand sudden loads, such as in automotive crash boxes, aerospace components, and protective gear [20]. Traditional materials, while effective to a certain extent, often fall short in providing optimal energy absorption, lightweight solutions, and adaptability to varying impact conditions. This has driven the exploration of innovative materials and structures, such as 3D auxetic structures, which offer unique mechanical properties, including high energy absorption and enhanced deformation characteristics, that make them particularly suited for dynamic applications. The 2D re-entrant honeycomb structure is a well-known auxetic material, distinguished by its negative Poisson's ratio. Unlike typical materials that contract laterally when stretched, this honeycomb structure expands laterally due to its unique geometry. Its cell walls are angled inward, creating a re-entrant design that allows the structure to expand in the lateral direction when subjected to tension and contract under compression. The mechanical performance of the 2D re-entrant honeycomb is influenced by key factors such as the re-entrant angle, wall thickness, and relative density. By adjusting these parameters, the material's properties, including stiffness, strength, and Poisson's ratio, can be customized to meet specific requirements. This flexibility makes the re-entrant honeycomb highly suitable for designing materials with enhanced energy absorption and durability. 3D re-entrant auxetic structures are an extension of the 2D re-entrant honeycomb concept, incorporating negative Poisson's ratio behavior into three-dimensional designs. The 3D nature of these structures enhances their mechanical performance by providing multi-directional auxetic behavior. 3D auxetic structures offer superior energy absorption and stiffness in out-of-plane directions compared to their 2D counterparts [18]. Its impact resistance is also significantly large compared to 2D structure as shown by Deng and Qin [7].

Shen et al. [13], designed a new 3D re-entrant auxetic structure, 2D structural components are combined to form a 3D re-entrant unit cell with new connection and topological method. The research compares the mechanical properties of the classical and the newly designed lattice structure. Four different configurations of the new 3D lattice structure has been modelled. They are fabricated using a SLM machine for further experimental process. Numerical simulation has been carried out to check the accuracy of the theoretical model. The research confirms that the classical 3D re-entrant auxetic structure has a higher modulus design domain [8]. The study confirms that auxetic structures demonstrate remarkable stretch-induced negative Poisson's ratio behaviour, emphasizing their distinctive mechanical properties. Additionally, the research investigates the potential engineering applications of 3D re-entrant lattice auxetic structures. Their auxetic behavior, coupled with lightweight design and high energy absorption capabilities, makes them ideal candidates for impact protection in sports equipment, automotive safety systems, and aerospace components. The versatility and tunable properties of these structures, highlighted during the design process, pave the way for a broad range of practical applications. The research by Wang et al. [16], on auxetic metamaterials has shown significant advances in the design and mechanical characterization of both 2D and 3D auxetic structures. Auxetic materials, known for their negative Poisson's ratio, exhibit unique deformation behavior, such as lateral expansion under tension and contraction under compression. This property makes them highly desirable for applications in fields like aerospace, biomedical engineering, and protection systems. Research by Jiang et al. [8], Cheng et al. [5], and Li et al. [9] established a foundation for understanding auxetic foams and their mechanical benefits, such as enhanced energy absorption and shear resistance. Subsequent studies focused on re-entrant honeycomb structures, exploring their geometry, strut thickness, and re-entrant angles as key factors influencing mechanical properties like Young's modulus and Poisson's ratio. More recent investigations have focused on 3D auxetic cellular structures, which are more complex but offer improved performance over their 2D counterparts. Wang et al. [17] introduced a novel interlocking assembly method for 3D auxetic structures, overcoming limitations associated with additive manufacturing such as surface defects and geometric inaccuracies. These structures have been tested under uniaxial compression, showing a strong dependence of mechanical properties on design parameters like strut thickness, vertical-to-oblique strut length ratios, and re-entrant angles. Numerical simulations and experiments revealed that higher strut thickness leads to increased stiffness but reduced auxeticity, while re-entrant angles around 45° offer optimal Poisson's ratios for effective auxetic behavior.

Geometry and Modelling

Geometrical description of the unit cell

Chan and Evans [4] proposed the bow-tie re-entrant configuration. Compared to other conventional configurations, the re-entrant auxetic structure demonstrates superior tensile strength and energy absorption capacity. Therefore, this study adopts the re-entrant microstructure and extends it to a 3D cellular design, providing an excellent alternative for energy absorption applications. The 3D re-entrant honeycomb structure, an auxetic material known for its negative Poisson's ratio, is gaining significant attention for its superior energy absorption and lightweight characteristics [6]. These structures are distinct in their ability to laterally expand or contract under tension or compression, enhancing their mechanical performance in applications such as crashworthiness, aerospace, and impact protection. The re-entrant honeycomb configuration is characterized by internal angles that cause the cells to fold inward, contributing to the auxetic effect. The dimensions of these cells, such as the re-entrant angle, cell height, wall thickness, and aspect ratio, are critical in determining

the overall mechanical behavior of the structure. The stress distribution, deformation patterns, and the energy dissipation capability during impact are very sensitive to these variations of these parameters.

Each re-entrant hexagonal cell consists of two orthogonally arranged re-entrant hexagons. A single re-entrant hexagon is made up of vertical and inclined struts. Figure 36.2b illustrates the cross-sectional view of a re-entrant hexagon, emphasizing four essential geometric parameters: the inclined strut length (l), vertical strut length (h), strut thickness (t), and the re-entrant angle (θ) formed between the vertical and inclined struts. Importantly, to maintain auxetic behavior, a specific dimensional constraint must be met: $h \geq 2l \cos \theta$. The number of cells along the principle directions is defined respectively as n_x in x-direction, n_y in y-direction and n_z in z-direction.

CAD modelling

The 3D re-entrant honeycomb structure was carefully designed to ensure it exhibits the desired auxetic behavior. Key geometric parameters, such as the inclined strut length, vertical strut length, strut thickness, and re-entrant angle, were chosen to meet the requirements for achieving a negative Poisson's ratio. After establishing the dimensions of the re-entrant cell, adjustments are made to facilitate precise and convenient control of densification strain within the re-entrant unit cell. These modifications are targeted specifically at the variable θ while keeping the length "h" fixed. The approach involves employing a variable stiffness factor to enable controlled variations in the structure's stiffness. The design accounts

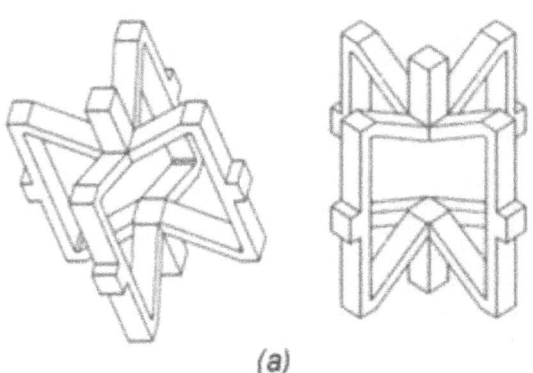

(a)

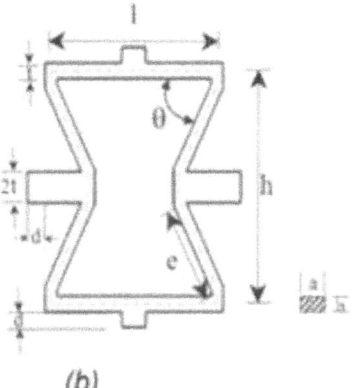

(b)

Figure 36.2 (a) Isometric view of 3D auxetic unit cell with 100% VSF [12] (b) Schematic view of re-entrant hexagon [10]
Source: Author

Table 36.1 Dimensions of the unit cell and number of unit cells

Number of cells			Cell dimensions (mm)		
n_x	n_y	n_z	l	h	t
4	4	4	32.93	24	2

Source: Author

for the desired stiffness factor, and the equation for determining this variable stiffness factor is given as:

$$\eta = 1 - \frac{\theta_1}{\theta} \quad (1)$$

where, η, θ and $\theta1$ are designed VSF, re-entrant angle, and variable stiffness angle respectively. Design of experiments (DoE) is a structured and efficient methodology for systematically analyzing the influence of key design parameters—namely the variable stiffness factor (VSF), re-entrant angle, and web thickness—on the crashworthiness performance of 3D re-entrant auxetic crash boxes. By implementing DoE, the relationships between these input factors and critical crashworthiness indicators, including total energy absorption (EA), specific energy absorption (SEA), peak crushing force (P_{max}), and crushing force efficiency (CFE), can be effectively examined. A total of 12 different parameter combinations has been modelled to comprehensively evaluate their effects on crash performance.

This approach enables the identification of optimal parameter combinations, leading to enhanced crash performance while minimizing computational

Table 36.2 Variable stiffness angles at varying VSF under different re-entrant angles

Re-entrant angle θ (°)	VSF (%)	$\theta1$ (°)
50	40	30
	60	20
	80	10
	100	0
60	40	36
	60	24
	80	12
	100	0
70	40	42
	60	28
	80	14
	100	0

Source: Author

costs and time. Additionally, DoE provides statistical insights into parameter interactions, allowing for a deeper understanding of the structural behavior under dynamic loading conditions. To further illustrate the impact of these parameters, a comprehensive table has been included, summarizing the key variables, their levels, and the corresponding performance metrics. Employing this method in the design process facilitates data-driven decision-making, ultimately improving the safety and efficiency of energy-absorbing structures.

Finite Element Modelling

Shokri et al. [14], explored the energy absorption and stiffness attributes of different 3D auxetic specimens, all of which are constructed using a 4 × 4 × 4 unit lattice structure. Out of the diverse lattice structures analysed in the literature, the bow-tie 3D re-entrant auxetic lattice has exhibited exceptional specific energy absorption (SEA) and load-bearing capacity. Consequently, this structure is chosen for conducting numerical simulation.

The geometry of the structure was replicated with the specified dimensions in the Modelling software

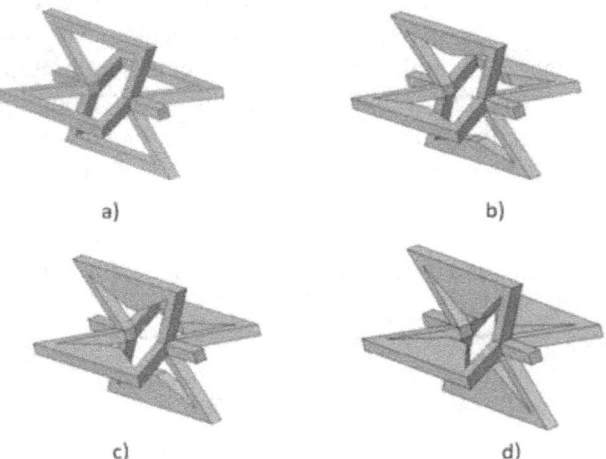

a)   b)

c)   d)

Figure 36.3 Cad model of unit cell with a) 100% VSF b) 40% c) 60% d) 80%
Source: Author

Table 36.3 DOE setup parameters

VSA (%)	80	60	40
Re-entrant angle (degree)	50	60	70
Thickness (mm)	2		

Source: Author

and exported in the neutral file format. After importing the geometry, a frictional contact was defined between the plates and the jaws, with a friction coefficient of 0.29, as referenced from [14]. This frictional setting ensures a realistic interaction between the components during the simulation, accounting for potential slip or stick behavior at the contact surfaces. For the dynamic impact simulation, an explicit dynamic solver was selected to effectively capture the rapid interactions and transient responses that occur during high-speed loading scenarios [22]. This type of solver is particularly advantageous for analyzing impact events, as it can efficiently manage large deformations and complex contact phenomena.

In this setup, a downward velocity of 64 km/h was applied to the upper plate, simulating a high-velocity impact condition [3]. The explicit dynamic solver can assess the material's performance under these extreme conditions, providing insights into stress wave propagation, energy absorption, and potential failure mechanisms within the auxetic core. This methodology is essential for evaluating the structure's behavior during dynamic loading, aiding in the design optimization for applications requiring robust impact resistance [15]. To ensure the accuracy and reliability of the simulation results, a mesh convergence study was conducted prior to the analysis. Mesh convergence is a critical step in finite element analysis (FEA) that involves systematically refining the mesh to determine the optimal element size that provides consistent and accurate results without unnecessary computational cost. During the mesh convergence study, the model was analysed using various mesh sizes, starting from a coarse mesh and

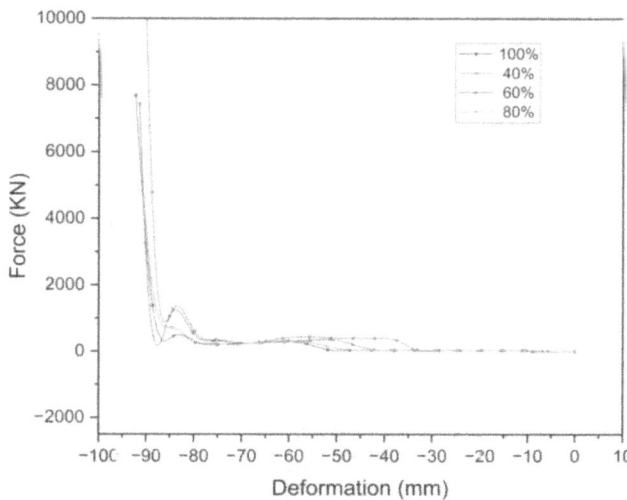

Figure 36.5 Force-deformation curve at 50° re-entrant angle

Source: Author

progressively refining it. Key output parameters, such as displacement, stress distribution, and reaction forces, were monitored as the mesh was refined. The results were plotted to assess how these parameters changed with different mesh densities shown in Figure 36.2. It has been found that an element size of 1.5mm is the maximum limit where there is no compromise in accuracy.

The convergence criterion was established based on the stability of the results; specifically, when further refinement of the mesh did not yield significant changes in the output parameters, the mesh was considered converged. This process ensures that the chosen mesh provides a balance between accuracy and computational efficiency. By confirming that the results are independent of the mesh size, the reliability of the simulation outcomes is enhanced, thereby strengthening the conclusions drawn from the analysis. This thorough approach contributes to the overall robustness of the study and supports the validity of the findings related to the performance of the auxetic core under both quasi-static and dynamic loading conditions.

Results and Discussion

In this study, high-velocity impact simulations were conducted on twelve distinct configurations of a 3D re-entrant auxetic crash box structure, developed through a systematic design of experiments (DoE) approach.

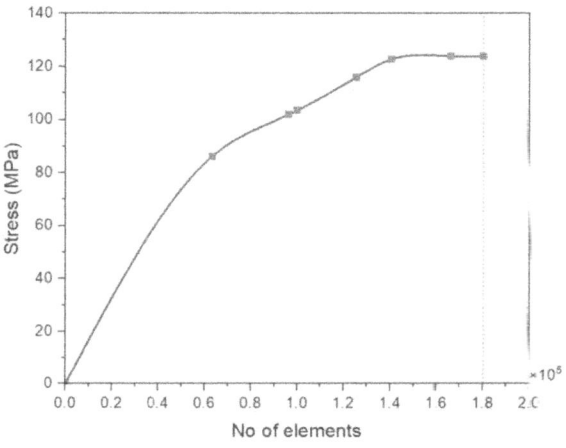

Figure 36.4 Mesh sensitivity analysis
Source: Author

To quantify crashworthiness, four critical response variables were selected: total energy absorption (EA), specific energy absorption (SEA), peak crushing force (Pmax), and crushing force efficiency (CFE) [19]. EA reflects the structure's capacity to absorb kinetic energy, while SEA offers insight into material efficiency by normalizing the absorbed energy with respect to mass. Auxetic metamaterials, especially re-entrant configurations, are known for their enhanced energy absorption and tunable mechanical behavior, as demonstrated by recent studies by Zhang et al. [23]. Peak force is crucial to avoid damage to protected systems or passengers, and CFE measures how efficiently the structure maintains a desirable collapse behavior after the initial peak load. Force-displacement curves were plotted for each configuration to visualize and compare the deformation patterns, energy absorption progression, and peak loading behavior. Figure. 4 indicates the force-deformation behavior for the model with a re-entrant angle of 50° and a wall thickness of 2 mm, analyzed across four different VSF: 40%, 60%, 80%, and 100%. Table 36.4 presents the simulation results, which indicate that the specimen with 40% VSF registered the highest initial peak force, 332.79 kN. Despite this, the force profile rapidly declined and displayed considerable instability, suggesting an abrupt failure mode and reduced energy dissipation capability. Similar behavior has been reported in previous studies on dynamic crushing of re-entrant auxetic structures, where high peak loads were followed by unstable collapse patterns [10]. On the other hand, the responses for 60% and 80% VSF exhibited smoother and more stable force transitions, highlighting more favorable progressive collapse behavior. From the performance data, the structure with 60% VSF absorbed the highest amount of energy, reaching 74.61 kJ, which marks an increase

of around 4.7% when compared to 40% VSF, and about 6.5% higher than 100% VSF. Similarly, the specific energy absorption (SEA) was superior at 100% VSF, achieving 395.79 kJ/kg, demonstrating substantial improvement of 71.38% over 40% VSF. Although the 40% VSF yielded a large peak force, its poor stability and abrupt force drop make it less suitable for controlled energy absorption. In contrast, 80% VSF significantly reduces the peak force by roughly 108% compared to 40% VSF, making it a more effective and safer design. The 60% VSF configuration achieved the highest crush force efficiency (CFE) of 74.61%, which is a 204% gain over the lowest-performing variant.

Figure. 36.8. indicates the force-deformation behavior for the model with a re-entrant angle of 60° and a wall thickness of 2 mm, analyzed across four different (VSF: 40%, 60%, 80%, and 100%. Table 36.5 presents the simulation results, which indicate that the specimen with 40% VSF registered the highest initial peak force of 306.06 kN, likely due to the increased material volume and stiffness. Compared to this, the 80% VSF configuration—exhibiting the lowest peak force—shows a 153.36% reduction, highlighting the influence of geometric and stiffness tuning on energy absorption and force mitigation, consistent with findings reported by Zhang et al. [21].

From the performance data, the structure with 40% VSF absorbed the highest amount of energy, reaching 96.1 kJ, which marks an increase of around 48.99% when compared to 100% VSF. Similarly, the specific energy absorption (SEA) was superior at 100% VSF,

Table 36.4 Simulation results at 50° re-entrant angle

VSF (%)	Energy absorption (kJ)	Specific Energy absorption (kJ/Kg)	Initial peak force (kN)	Mass (kg)
40	71.26	230	332	0.309
60	74.61	284	207	0.262
80	66.13	303	159	0.218
100	70.02	395	235	0.177

Source: Author

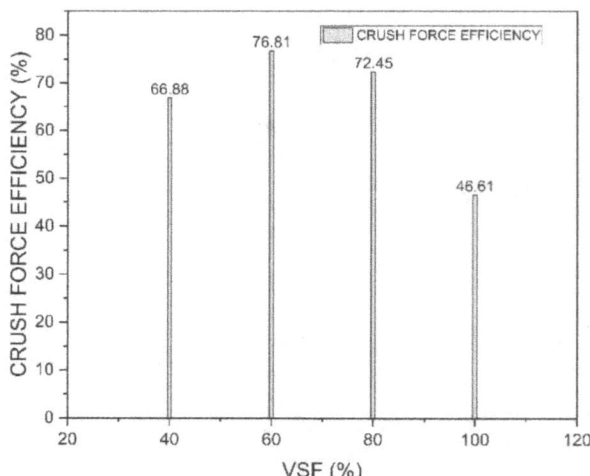

Figure 36.6 Crush force efficiency at different VSF

Source: Author

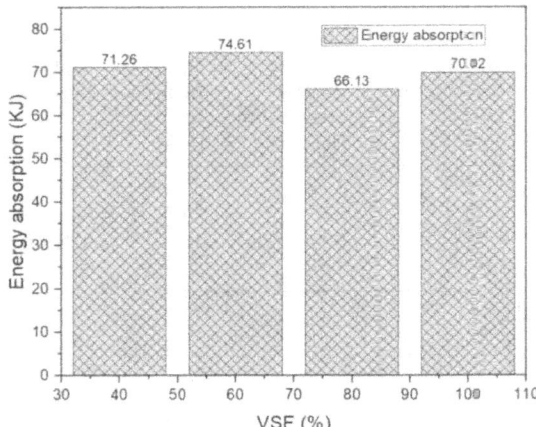

Figure 36.7 Energy absorption at different VSF
Source: Author

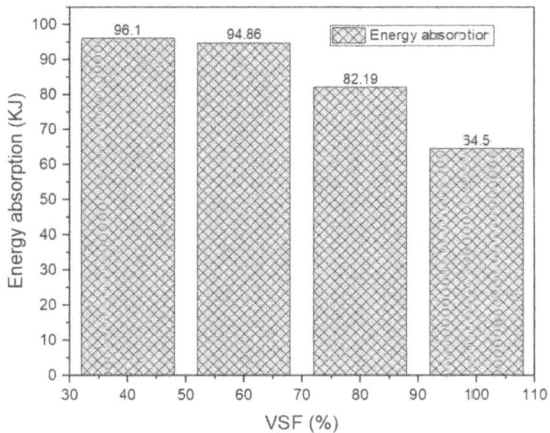

Figure 36.10 Energy absorption at different VSF
Source: Author

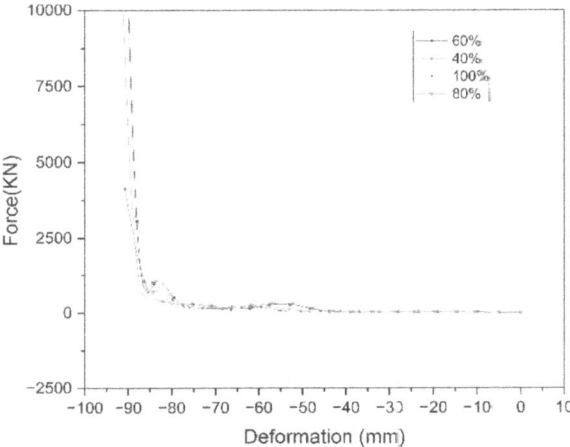

Figure 36.8 Force - deformation curve at 60° re-entrant angle
Source: Author

Table 36.5 Simulation results at 60 degree re-entrant angle

VSF (%)	Energy absorption (kJ)	Specific energy absorption (kJ/Kg)	Initial peak force (kN)	Mass (kg)
40	96.10	368	306	0.261
60	94.86	363	151	0.261
80	82.19	391	120	0.210
100	64.50	398	200	0.162

Source: Author

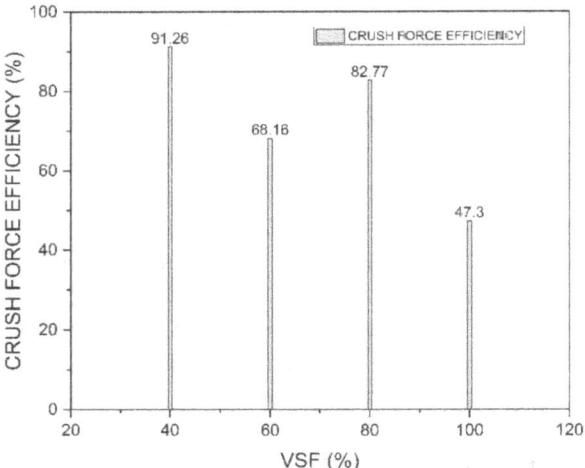

Figure 36.9 Crush force efficiency at different VSF
Source: Author

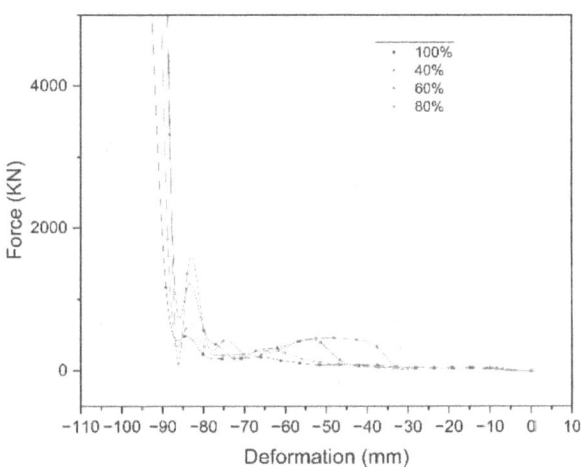

Figure 36.11 Force - deformation curve at 70° re-entrant angle
Source: Author

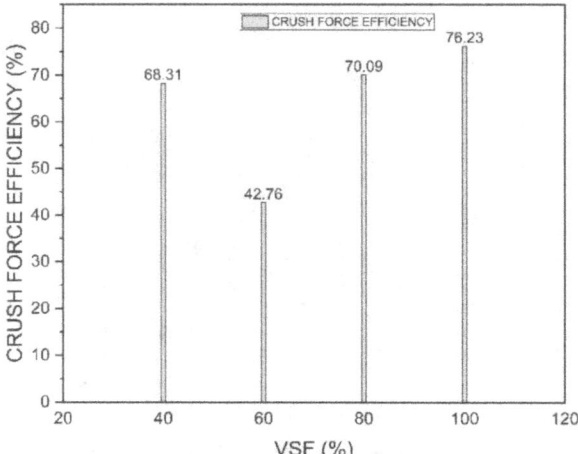

Figure 36.12 Energy absorption at different VSF
Source: Author

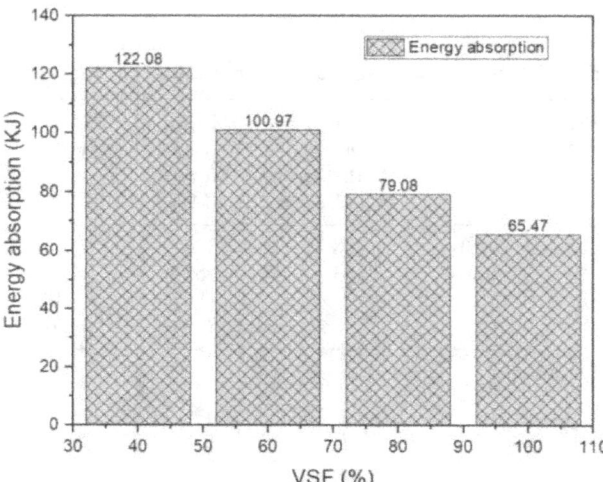

Figure 36.13 Crush force efficiency at different VSF
Source: Author

Table 36.6 Simulation results at 70 degree re-entrant angle

VSF(%)	Energy absorption (kJ)	Specific energy absorption (kJ/Kg)	Initial peak force (kN)	Mass (kg)
40	122	375	330	0.325
60	100	379	147	0.266
80	79	380	167	0.208
100	65	427	145	0.153

Source: Author

Table 36.7 S/N ratio analysis

Level	VSF (S/N Ratio)	Re-entrant angle (S/N Ratio)
1	39.85	38.66
2	38.45	40.19
3	39.17	38.63
Delta	1.40	1.56
Rank	2	1

Source: Author

Table 36.8 Mean response method

Level	VSF (Mean response)	Re-entrant angle (Mean response)
1	165.6	138.6
2	165.1	182.0
3	169.7	179.9
Delta	4.6	43.5
Rank	**2**	**1**

Source: Author

achieving 398.14 kJ/kg, demonstrating improvement of 9.54% over 60% VSF.

Although the 40% VSF yielded a large peak force, its poor stability and abrupt force drop make it less suitable for controlled energy absorption. In contrast, 80% VSF significantly reduces the peak force, making it a more effective and safer design. A total of 80% VSF has a crush force efficiency of 91.26% exceeding the 40% VSF by 92.93% which is the lowest.

Figure 36.11. indicates the force-deformation behavior for the model with a re-entrant angle of 70° and a wall thickness of 2 mm was analyzed across four different VSF: 40%, 60%, 80%, and 100%. Table 36.6 presents the simulation results which indicate that the specimen with 40% VSF registered the highest initial peak force, 330.49 kN due to the increased material volume and stiffness. Compared to this the combination with 80% VSF which has the lowest peak force, has 126.37% reduction in peak force. From the performance data, the structure with 40% VSF absorbed the highest amount of energy, reaching 122.08 kJ, which marks an increase of around 86.46% when compared to 100% VSF. Similarly, the specific energy absorption (SEA) was superior at 100% VSF, achieving 427.9 kJ/kg, demonstrating improvement of 13.91% over 60% VSF. The 100% VSF has a crush force efficiency of 76.23 % exceeding the 60% VSF by 78.27% which is the lowest.

To determine the optimal parameter combination, the Taguchi method was employed using Minitab software. Signal-to-noise (S/N) ratio analysis was performed with the objective of maximizing energy absorption and crushing efficiency while minimizing peak force. The analysis revealed that a specific combination of VSF and re-entrant angle yielded the most desirable balance across all response variables. The results of S/N ratio analysis are shown in Table 36.7. From the S/N ratio analysis, the best performance was observed for a variable stiffness factor (VSF) of 40% and a Re-entrant angle of 60°, suggesting this combination delivers the most stable response across trials. However, the mean response analysis indicated in Table 36.8 shows that a VSF of 80% paired with the same re-entrant angle of 60° resulted in the highest average values for key crashworthiness indicators, particularly in terms of energy absorption and crushing efficiency. Given that the re-entrant angle of 60° was consistently optimal across both analyses, it was selected as the ideal angular configuration. The VSF of 80%, offering superior average performance, was chosen as the optimal stiffness factor. Hence, the final optimal combination determined is a Re-entrant angle of 60° and VSF 80%.

Conclusion

In this work, a comprehensive study was conducted on the crashworthiness behavior of 3D re-entrant auxetic structures under dynamic impact loading conditions. By employing different configurations through the variation of variable stiffness factors (VSFs) and re-entrant angles, the aim was to determine the most effective design for maximizing energy absorption and minimizing peak force transmission. To achieve this, a series of simulations were performed in Simulation software with constant thickness, while systematically altering the VSF levels (40%, 60%, 80%, and 100%) and re-entrant angles (60°, 70°, and 80°). Each configuration was evaluated based on its force–deformation response, enabling insight into its structural integrity, stiffness, and energy absorption characteristics configuration was evaluated based on its force–deformation response, enabling insight into its structural integrity, stiffness, and energy absorption characteristics. The results clearly showed that both the geometric angle and the VSF significantly affect the mechanical response, especially in terms of peak force and deformation capacity. From the

comparative analysis of all combinations, it was observed that the crash box with a "60° re-entrant angle and 80% VSF" delivered the most favorable balance between high initial resistance and progressive energy dissipation. This specific setup offered a high load-bearing capacity while maintaining desirable auxetic behavior during crushing, making it a promising candidate for energy-absorbing applications.

References

[1] Abdullah, N. A. Z., Sani, M. S. M., Salwani, M. S., & Husain, N. A. (2020). A review on crashworthiness studies of crash box structure. *Thin-Walled Structures*, 153, 106795.

[2] Baran, T., & Ozturk, M. (2020). In-plane elasticity of a strengthened re-entrant honeycomb cell. *European Journal of Mechanics - A/Solids*, 83, 104037.

[3] Barcutaji, A., Sajjia, M., & Olabi, A.-G. (2017). On the crashworthiness performance of thin-walled energy absorbers: recent advances and future developments. *Thin-Walled Structures*, 118, 137–163.

[4] Chan, N., & Evans, K. E. (1997). The mechanical properties of auxetic materials. *Journal of Materials Science*, 32(21), 5725–5736.

[5] Cheng, X., Wang, L., Wang, C., Ren, Y., Li, L., & Peng, Y. (2022). Design and mechanical characteristics of auxetic metamaterial with tunable stiffness. *International Journal of Mechanical Sciences*, 223, 107286.

[6] Constantin, B. A., Iozsa, D., & Fratila, G. (2016). Studies about the behavior of the crash boxes of a car body. In IOP Conference Series: Materials Science and Engineering, (Vol. 161, p. 012010).

[7] Deng, X., & Qin, S. (2023). In-plane energy absorption characteristics and mechanical properties of novel re-entrant honeycombs. *Composite Structures*, 313, 116951.

[8] Jiang, W., Ma, L., Wu, L., Liu, Y., & Dai, G. (2022). Manufacturing, characteristics and applications of auxetic foams a state-of-the-art review. *Composites Part B: Engineering*, 235, 109733.

[9] Li, X., Wang, Q., Yang, Z., & Lu, Z. (2019). Novel auxetic structures with enhanced mechanical properties. *Extreme Mechanics Letters*, 27, 59–65.

[10] Liu, W., Wang, N., Luo, T., & Lin, Z. (2016). In-plane dynamic crushing of re-entrant auxetic cellular structure. *Materials and Design*, 100, 84–91.

[11] Moghaddam, A., Kheradpisheh, A., & Asgari, M. (2021). A basic design for automotive crash boxes using an efficient corrugated conical tube. *Proceedings of the Institution of Mechanical Engineers, Part D: Journal of Automobile Engineering*, 235, 1835–1848.

[12] Ren, X., Das, R., Tran, P., Ngo, T. D., & Xie, Y. M. (2018). Auxetic metamaterials and structures: a review. *Smart Materials and Structures*, 27(2), 023001.

[13] Shen, J., Liu, K., Zeng, Q., Ge, J., Dong, Z., & Liang, J. (2021). Design and mechanical property studies of 3D

re-entrant lattice auxetic structure. *Aerospace Science and Technology*, 118, 106998.

[14] Shokri Rad, M., Hatami, H., Alipouri, R., Farokhi Nejad, A., & Omidinasab, F. (2019). Determination of energy absorption in different cellular auxetic structures. *Mechanics and Industry*, 20(3), 302.

[15] Tan, H., He, Z., Ren, X., Zhang, X. Y., Zhang, Y., & Xie, Y. M. (2021). Crashworthiness design and multi-objective optimization of a novel auxetic hierarchical honeycomb crash box. *Structural and Multidisciplinary Optimization*, 64(4), 2009–2024.

[16] Wang, C., Li, Y., Zhao, W., Zou, S., Zhou, G., & Wang, Y. (2018). Structure design and multi-objective optimization of a novel crash box based on biomimetic structure. *International Journal of Mechanical Sciences*, 138–139, 489–501.

[17] Wang, C., Wang, W., Zhao, W., Wang, Y., & Zhou, G. (2018). Structure design and multi-objective optimization of a novel NPR bumper system. *Composites Part B: Engineering*, 153, 78–96.

[18] Wang, H., Lu, Z., Yang, Z., & Li, X. (2019). A novel re-entrant auxetic honeycomb with enhanced in-plane impact resistance. *Composite Structures*, 208, 758–770.

[19] Wang, T., Li, Z., Wang, L., & Hulbert, G. M. (2020). Crashworthiness analysis and collaborative optimization design for a novel crash-box with re-entrant auxetic core. *Structural and Multidisciplinary Optimization*, 62(4), 2167–2179.

[20] Wang, T., Li, Z., Wang, L., Ma, Z., & Hulbert, G. M. (2019). Dynamic crushing analysis of a three-dimensional re-entrant auxetic cellular structure. *Materials*, 12(3), 460.

[21] Zhang, X. Y., Ren, X., Zhang, Y., & Xie, Y. M. (2022). A novel auxetic metamaterial with enhanced mechanical properties and tunable auxeticity. *Thin-Walled Structures*, 174, 109162.

[22] Zhang, Y., Liu, Q., He, Z., Zong, Z., & Fang, J. (2019). Dynamic impact response of aluminum honeycombs filled with expanded polypropylene foam. *Composites Part B: Engineering*, 156, 17–27.

[23] Zhang, Y., Sun, L., Ren, X., Zhang, X. Y., Tao, Z., & Xie, Y. M. (2022). Design and analysis of an auxetic metamaterial with tuneable stiffness. *Composite Structures*, 281, 114997.

[24] Zhu, G., Wang, Z., Cheng, A., & Li, G. (2016). Design optimisation of composite bumper beam with variable cross-sections for automotive vehicle. *International Journal of Crashworthiness*, 22(4), 365–376.

37 Design and implementation of efficient approximate multiplier with optimized compressor selection for non-linear RGB image brightness adjustment

Radhakrishnan K. R.[1,a], J. Ramesh[3,b], Hariharan M.[2,c] and P.T. Vanathi[3,d]

[1]Assistant Professor, Department of Electronics and Communication Engineering, PSG College of Technology, Coimbatore, India

[2]Student, ME (VLSI DESIGN), Department of Electronics and Communication Engineering, PSG College of Technology, Coimbatore, India

[3]Professor, Department of Electronics and Communication Engineering, PSG College of Technology, Coimbatore, India

Abstract

Multiplication is a critical operation in digital circuits, influencing the performance of arithmetic and signal processing applications. Approximate computing techniques, particularly in compressor-based multipliers, offer a balance struck between computational precision and resource utilization. This work investigates the impact of four different compressor designs (4:2, 5:2, 8:2) on an 3×8 multiplier, evaluating their area, power, and delay characteristics. Error analysis is conducted to assess the trade-offs between computational efficiency and accuracy. The best-performing compressor-based multiplier is then integrated into an image processing application, non-linear brightness adjustment of an RGB image, where the Red and Green channels undergo transformation while the Blue channel remains unaltered. The proposed design is implemented in Verilog and synthesized using Xilinx Vivado 2018.3. Results demonstrate that the selected multiplier achieves an optimal balance between performance and accuracy, making it suitable for error-resilient applications.

Keywords: Approximate 4:2 compressor, area-power-delay trade-off, compressor-based multiplier, error analysis, image processing, Non-linear brightness adjustment, Verilog implementation

Introduction

Multiplication is a fundamental operation in digital circuits, significantly impacting applications like image processing, signal processing, and machine learning. Conventional multipliers ensure high accuracy but suffer from excessive power consumption, increased delay, and larger area requirements, making them inefficient for resource-constrained applications [1]. Approximate computing is gaining attention as viable solution for error-tolerant applications where minor computational inaccuracies can be tolerated for improved efficiency [2]. One of the most effective ways to optimize multipliers is by using compressors, which reduce the number of partial products and enhance computational efficiency. Various compressor architectures have been explored to achieve lower power and delay [3]. Prior research demonstrates that approximate multipliers can reduce power by 20–40% over conventional designs, but their impact on image-specific application remains insufficiently examined in existing research [4]. This paper systematically analyzes four types of 4:2 compressors (Conventional, MODA, HSLF, NCCA) in an 8×8 approximate multiplier, evaluating trade-offs in power, delay, and error metrics. The best-performing compressor-based multiplier is applied to non-linear brightness adjustment in RGB images, where the Red (R) and Green (G) channels are multiplied while keeping the Blue (B) channel unchanged to maintain visual quality. The design is implemented in Verilog, synthesized in Xilinx Vivado 2018.3, and evaluated using MATLAB-based image quality metrics (PSNR, SSIM) to validate its effectiveness.

Compressors play a key role in optimizing multipliers by reducing partial products and improving power, area, and delay efficiency. Prior studies have explored various compressor designs, such as 4:2, 5:2, and 8:2 architectures, for enhancing multiplier performance [2]. However, a detailed analysis of their impact on real-world applications, particularly image processing, remains limited [3].

[a]krr.ece@psgtech.ac.in, [b]jr.ece@psgtech.ac.in, [c]23mv33@psgtech.ac.in, [d]ptv.ece@psgtech.ac.in

DOI: 10.1201/9781003770435-37

This paper evaluates the performance of four compressor-based 8×8 multipliers in terms of power, area, delay, and error analysis. Experimental results indicate that Compressor Sets 1 and 2 achieve lower error rates (4.39% and 4.50%), while Compressor Sets 3 and 4 show significantly higher errors (56.42%) but offer reduced power consumption. The best-performing design is integrated into a Non-Linear Brightness Adjustment application for RGB images, where only the red and green channels are processed while keeping the Blue channel unchanged. The proposed design is implemented in Verilog and synthesized, with validation through MATLAB-based image quality metrics (PSNR, SSIM) to ensure perceptual fidelity.

Related Work

Multipliers play a fundamental component in arithmetic circuits, influencing the performance of applications such as image processing, machine learning, [1]. However, conventional multipliers consume significant power and introduce high computational latency, making them inefficient for energy-constrained applications [2]. To address these challenges, researchers have explored compressor-based designs that optimize the reduction of partial products, thereby improving area, power, and delay trade-offs [3].

Compressor-based multiplication has gained attention due to its ability to enhance efficiency while maintaining acceptable accuracy. Various compressor architectures have been studied to improve multiplication efficiency by reducing carry propagation delay and minimizing hardware complexity [4]. Approximate compressors have emerged as a promising alternative, introducing minor errors while significantly lowering power consumption and improving speed, making them ideal for error-resilient applications [5].

The impact of approximate computing on multipliers has been widely analyzed, particularly in scenarios where exact precision is not critical. Prior studies have proposed error-resilient designs that balance accuracy and power efficiency, demonstrating a 20–40% reduction in power compared to traditional multipliers [6]. Metrics such as mean absolute error (MAE) and mean relative error distance (MRED) have been used to evaluate the effectiveness of approximate compressors in arithmetic circuits [7].

Despite these advancements, most studies have focused on theoretical evaluations or small-scale implementations, with limited exploration of their real-world applications in image processing [8]. While approximate multipliers have been successfully applied in low-power computing, their direct impact on perceptual image quality remains underexplored [9]. Some works suggest that non-linear transformations in brightness adjustments can benefit from approximate multipliers, as minor computational inaccuracies do not lead to significant visual artifacts [10]. FPGA-oriented implementations and hardware-efficient techniques for approximate multipliers have been reported in prior studies [12]. Decoder-based imprecise multipliers present an alternative approach for area and power savings [14].

Building on these findings, this paper systematically compares four different compressor architectures and evaluates their impact on power, area, delay, and error metrics. Area-efficient multiplier structures and optimizations have been explored in recent literature [13]. The best-performing compressor-based multiplier is then integrated into an image processing application, specifically non-linear brightness Adjustment in RGB images, where only the red and green channels are modified while the blue channel remains unchanged. This ensures that color distortions are minimized while leveraging the efficiency of approximate computing. The hardware implementation is carried out in Verilog and synthesized using Xilinx Vivado 2018.3, with additional validation using MATLAB-based image quality metrics (PSNR, SSIM) to assess the impact on image fidelity.

Existing Methodology

In LUT6 mode, the 6-input LUT behaves as a single logic function with six inputs and one output (O). This mode is useful when a single complex logic function requires six distinct inputs to produce a single output In LUT6_2 mode, the 6input LUT is divided into two 5input functions with shared inputs. This allows LUT to produce two outputs (O5 and O6) simultaneously. LUT6_2 is beneficial when two logic functions share the same first five inputs but have different sixth inputs or outputs. This setup lets both functions be implemented within a single LUT, thus saving hardware resources.

Hierarchical or modular multiplier architecture

Hierarchical or modular multiplier architecture is a design strategy in digital circuits that divides the

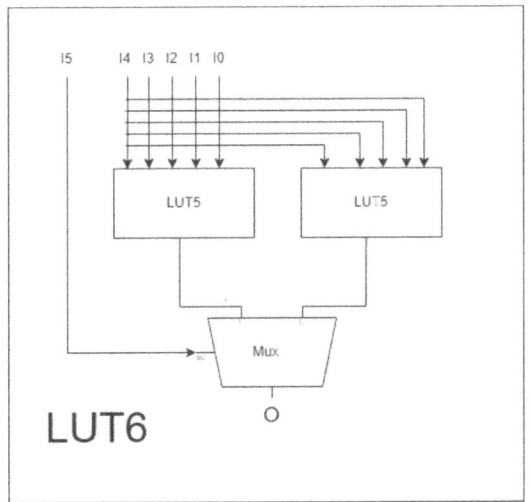

Figure 37.1 LUT6 configuration
Source: Author

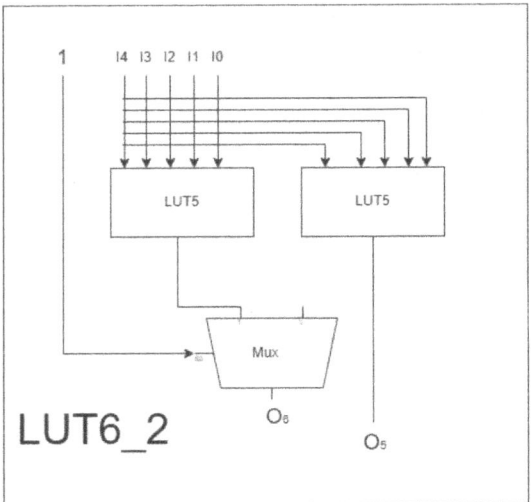

Figure 37.2 LUT6_2 configuration
Source: Author

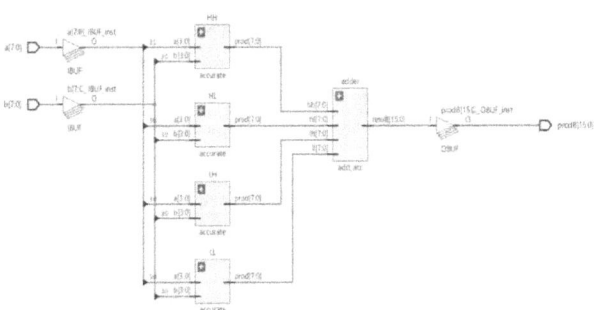

Figure 37.3 Schematic of 8 × 8 multiplier
Source: Author

Figure 37.3 represents the multiplication of two 8-bit inputs, which are divided into four sections: A [7:4] (most significant bits) and A [3:0] (least significant bits) for both inputs, resulting in segments HH, HL, LH, and LL. These sections are then fed into four 4 × 4 multipliers—M1, M2, M3, and M4—where M1 multiplies HH, M2 multiplies HL, M3 multiplies LH, and M4 multiplies LL. The outputs from these multipliers are combined to produce intermediate products that correspond to different orders of magnitude. Finally, an accurate adder integrates these intermediate product terms are generated combined to produce the result, ensuring the accuracy of the multiplication operation.

The result of a multiplier can be obtained by summing HH, HL, LH, and LL. For that one traditional accurate adder is used. It ensures precise summation of the results from the smaller n × n multipliers using carry chains. Low-order bits (P_0 to P_{n-}): These are directly equal to the n least significant bits of LL. High-order bits (P_n to P_{4n-1}): These are accurately calculated using a full carry chain across the adders.

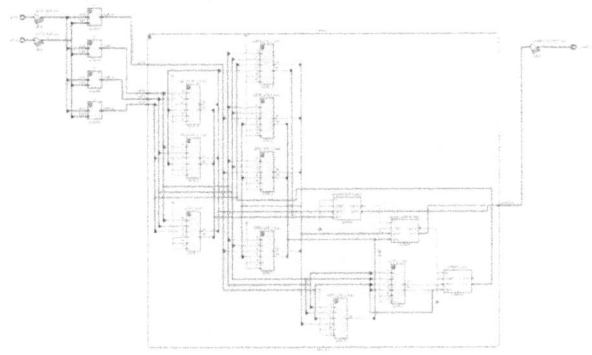

Figure 37.4 Adder module of 8 × 8 multiplier
Source: Author

multiplier into smaller, manageable components, such as 2 × 2 or 4 × 4 multipliers, allowing for easier design, testing, and integration into larger systems. This architecture promotes scalability, as larger multipliers (like an 8 × 8 multiplier) can be constructed by combining smaller modules, enhancing reusability across different designs. It facilitates parallel processing, enabling multiple smaller multiplications to occur simultaneously, which significantly boosts overall performance. Furthermore, by allowing each module to be developed and verified independently, the modular approach simplifies the design process, reduces errors, and increases the reliability of the final product.

Each LUT6_2 calculates carry generation (Gen) **and carry propagation** (Prop) signals for each column in the carry chain. For example, O5 and O6 are outputs of LUT6_2 at each column, where O5 generates the carry (Gen) (3.1) and O6 propagates it (Prop) (3.2) through the chain.

$$O5_{(column\ n)} = LL_n\,LH_n + LL_n\,HL_n + LH_n\,HL_n \quad (3.1)$$

$$O6_{(column\ n)} = LL_n \oplus LH_n \oplus HL_n \quad (3.2)$$

The overall carry chain is highly serial, meaning that each column depends on the carry result from the previous column. This approach ensures accuracy but is resource-intensive, costing 2n+1 LUTs and 3n/4 carry chains.

This diagram illustrates a hierarchical multiplier architecture based on 8x8 multiplication using four 4×4 multiplier blocks, which compute partial products. The diagram splits the 8-bit inputs into two 4-bit sections each: the most significant 4 bits (HH for High-High), MSB of a and LSB of b (HL), LSB of a and MSB of b (LH), and the least significant 4 bits (LL for low-low). These PP are then combined using an adder module to produce the 16-bit output prod8[15:0].

Proposed Methodology

Compressors are vital components in digital arithmetic circuits, especially in high-speed multipliers and digital signal processing systems. Their primary function is to sum multiple binary inputs efficiently, aiming to reduce the number of Intermediate product bits while optimizing for delay, area, and power usage. A conventional compressor, such as a 3:2 or 4:2 compressor, operates by taking a specified

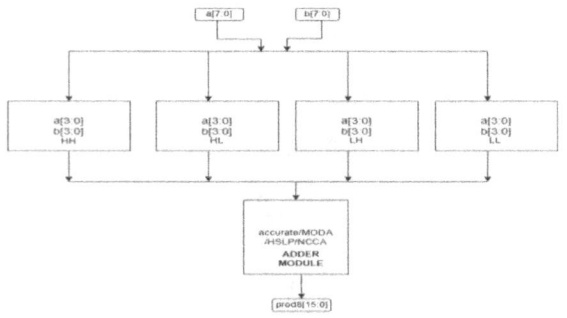

Figure 37.5 Existing 8×8 multiplier
Source: Author

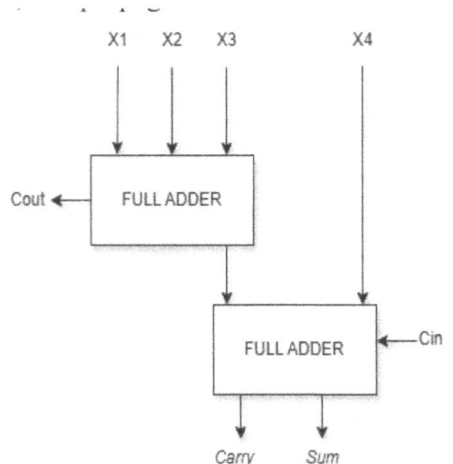

Figure 37.6 Conventional 4:2 compressor
Source: Author

number of binary inputs and producing fewer output bits, usually as a "sum"(1.1) and a "carry."(1.2). These outputs can then serve as inputs to the next stage in multi-operand addition circuits, which accelerates the addition process and simplifies complex operations in arithmetic units. Working principles of conventional compressor are logic simplifications, parallel reduction, and propagation of carries

$$Sum = X_1 \oplus X_2 \oplus X_3 \oplus X_4 \oplus C_{in} \quad (1.1)$$

$$Carry = (X_1 \oplus X_2 \oplus X_3 \oplus X_4)C_{in} + X_4(X_1 \oplus X_2 \oplus X_3 \oplus X_4)' \quad (1.2)$$

$$Cout = (X_1 \oplus X_2)X_3 + X_1\,(X_1 \oplus X_2)' \quad (1.3)$$

Approximate 4:2 compressors
An approximate 4:2 compressor is alternate version of the conventional compressor, designed to trade some accuracy for improved power, delay, and area performance. Instead of prioritizing exact outputs, approximate compressors simplify the logic by omitting certain operations or approximating values, leading to quicker processing, lower power consumption, and reduced circuit complexity ideal for applications where accuracy is not essential.

Designs leveraging compensation characteristics for ultra-low-power approximate 4:2 compressors have been proposed previously [11].

I experimented with four different sets of approximate compressors in the adder module of an 8×8 multiplier, each with unique features.

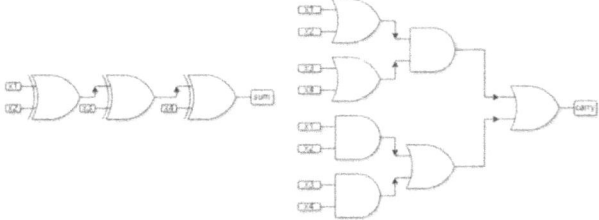

Figure 37.7 Approximate 4:2 compressor Set1
Source: Author

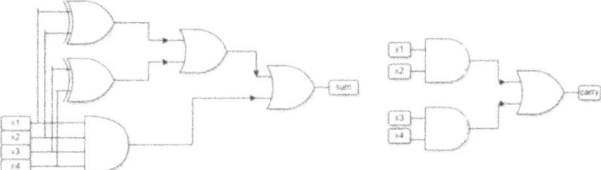

Figure 37.8 Approximate 4:2 compressor Set2
Source: Author

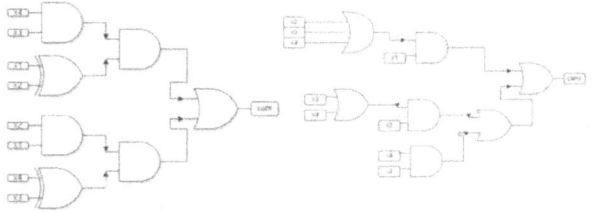

Figure 37.9 Approximate 4:2 compressor Set1
Source: Author

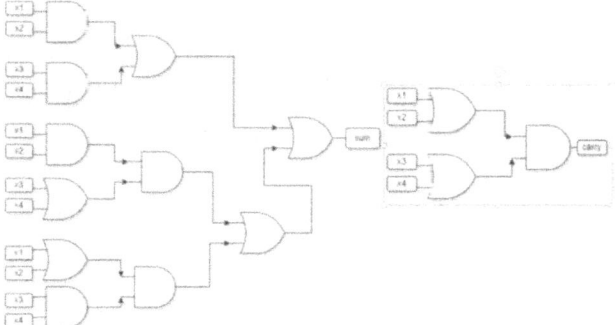

Figure 37.10 Approximate 4:2 compressor Set4
Source: Author

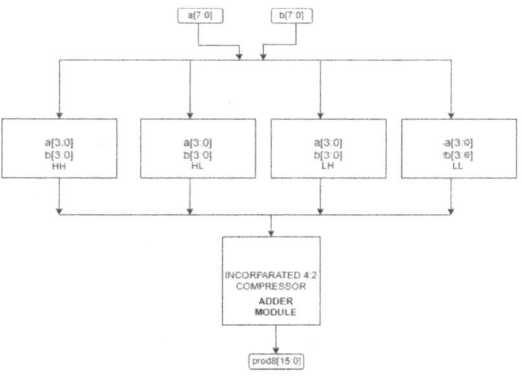

Figure 37.11 Proposed 8 × 8 multiplier
Source Author

Set 1 has a simple Boolean expression, making it suitable for error-resilient applications.

Set 2 offers a good trade-off between speed and accuracy. Sets 3 and 4 do not use XOR operations, resulting in lower delay. Designs leveraging compensation characteristics for ultra-low-power approximate 4:2 compressors have been proposed previously [11].

Applications of approximate multipliers specifically targeted at image-processing pipelines have also been investigated [15].

Proposed 8 × 8 multiplier
The 8 × 8 multiplier module, approx_8 × 8, demonstrates a high-performance design intended for error-tolerant applications. It combines accuracy with optimized delay and power consumption by leveraging the designed compressor within its adder module.

Experiment Results and Discussions

The designed multipliers are implemented in Verilog and synthesized using Xilinx Vivado 2018.3 to analyze their hardware efficiency. The evaluation focuses on three key metrics: area, power, and delay, using four different sets of 4:2 in the adder module of an 8 × 8 multiplier. Each compressor set is instantiated within the multiplier architecture to perform partial product reduction. The synthesis results provide insights into the trade-offs between computational efficiency and accuracy.

Performance analysis
Table 37.1 summarizes the area, power, and delay results for different compressor sets, including comparisons with existing designs such as MODA and HSLP.

The above chart illustrates the delay (in nanoseconds) observed for different multiplier implementations. The accurate multiplier exhibits the highest delay of 14.316 ns due to its full-precision computation and carry propagation. In contrast, the designs incorporating Compressor Sets 1&2 and Compressor Sets 3&4 significantly reduce the delay to 11.81 ns

Table 37.1 Performance comparison of 8 × 8 multipliers with different compressor sets

8 × 8 Multiplier	LUT Power	Adder power	Area (LUT utilized)	Delay (Ns)
Compressor set1	0.367	0.158	60	11.810
Compressor set2	0.367	0.158	60	11.810
Compressor set3	0.338	0.164	58	11.620
Compressor set4	0.338	0.164	58	11.620
MODA [1]	0.382	0.273	50	13.752
HSLP [1]	0.350	0.165	50	13.026

Source: Author

and 11.62 ns respectively, demonstrating the efficiency of approximate compressor integration. The HSLP design shows moderate improvement with a delay of 13.752 ns, while MODA achieves a further reduction to 13.026 ns. These results confirm that the use of approximate compressor-based architectures can effectively enhance the speed performance of multipliers while maintaining acceptable accuracy.

The accuracy of each design is assessed based on mean absolute error (MAE), mean relative error distance (MRED). The results in Table 37.2 illustrate the error behavior for each compressor set. Estimate the effectiveness of the approx. Multiplier by measuring the errors in its output. Assessing these error metrics is essential for understanding the balance between accuracy and efficiency of approximate computing.

Error rate
The error rate is the proportion of incorrect outputs produced by the approximate multiplier relative to the total number of outputs. It is calculated using the formula

$$ER = \frac{\#(ED \neq 0)}{\#(ED \neq 0) + \#(ED = 0)}$$

A lower error rate indicates better reliability of the approximate multiplier.

Mean absolute error (MAE)
The mean absolute error quantifies the average size of the errors between predicted and actual values, disregarding whether the Errors are positive and negative. It is computed as follows:

$$MAE = \frac{1}{n} \sum_{i=1}^{n} |A_i - A_i'|$$

Where A_i is the exact output, A_i' is the approx. output, and NNN is the total number of cases. MAE provides a straightforward measure of accuracy.

Worst case error (WCE)
The worst case error represents the largest absolute deviation observed between the accurate result and the approximate result across all possible input combination

$$WCE = \max(|A_i - A_i'|)$$

This metric highlights the most significant error encountered in the set, which is critical for applications that require a guaranteed maximum error threshold.

Normalized error distance (NED)
The **Normalized Error Distance** gives a relative measure of error by normalizing the absolute error.

$$NED = \frac{MED}{D}$$

Relative error distance (RED)
The relative error distance is to measure the error relative to the true outputs absolute magnitude. It is expressed as:

$$RED = \sum_{i=1}^{2^{2N}} ED_i$$

This metric is useful for assessing the impact of the error relative to the actual value, providing insights into the multiplier's performance across varying input sizes.

Mean error distance (MED)
The mean error distance mean the relative errors over all input pairs, providing a wide ranging measure approximate multiplier's performance. It is calculated as:

$$MED = \frac{1}{2^{2N}} RED$$

This metric captures the general correctness of the multiplier output, allowing designers to evaluate its suitability for specific applications.

Discussion

The results indicate that Compressor Sets 1 and 2 achieve low error rates while maintaining competitive power and delay. In contrast, Compressor Sets 3 and 4 have significantly higher error rates, making them less suitable for precision-critical applications. The MODA and HSLP compressors exhibit lower LUT utilization but this improvement comes with trade-offs in terms of delay and energy consumption.

Based on this evaluation, the best-performing compressor design is selected and mapped to an image processing application for Non-Linear Brightness Adjustment in RGB images. The results of the image quality metrics, including PSNR and SSIM, are discussed in the following section.

Application: Image Processing

The optimized multiplier designs are integrated into an image processing application to evaluate their real-world performance. The proposed approximate multipliers are tested in a non-linear brightness adjustment operation on RGB images, where the red and green channels are processed using the selected approximate multiplier, while the blue channel remains unchanged to preserve color balance.

Implementation in MATLAB

The image processing pipeline is implemented in MATLAB, where the grayscale intensity transformation is performed using the approximate multipliers. The image is first converted into a matrix format, and pixel values are multiplied using both accurate and approximate multipliers. The processed image is then reconstructed and compared to the original image using quality assessment metrics.

Image quality assessment

To measure the impact of approximation, two key metrics are computed:

Peak signal to noise ratio (PSNR) – Determines the fidelity of the processed image compared to the original.

Structural similarity index (SSIM) – Evaluates the perceptual quality by considering luminance, contrast, and structural differences.

Experimental results

The experimental results show that the approximate multipliers (set1 compressor) achieve lower power and delay while maintaining an acceptable PSNR and SSIM. The trade-off between image quality and hardware efficiency is analyzed to select the most suitable compressor set for real-time applications.

Observations

Evaluate the PSNR and SSIM metrics for both output images to assess the variation between the results produced by accurate multiplier and approximate multiplier:

PSNR – 22.32 dB
SSIM - 0.9606

This indicates moderate differences between the accurate and approximate multiplier outputs

Figure 37.12 Original image
Source: Author

Table 37.2 Comprehensive comparison of 8 × 8 multipliers

Error Analysis	ER	MAE	WCE	NED	MRED
Multiplier with comp set 1	4.39%	2.1076	64	4.51×10^{-7}	1.90×10^{-4}
Multiplier with comp set 2	4.50%	2.5752	426	3.96×10^{-7}	6.5×10^{-7}
Multiplier with comp set 3	56.42%	57.1164	321	8.78×10^{-7}	2.59×10^{-7}
Multiplier with comp set 4	56.42%	57.1164	321	8.78×10^{-7}	2.59×10^{-7}
HSLP Adder Multiplier [1].	4.50%	1.5214	32	2.33×10^{-7}	0.9×10^{-4}
MODA Adder Multiplier [1].	8.12%	5.5763	160	8.57×10^{-7}	2.95×10^{-4}

Source: Author

Figure 37.13 Non-linear brightness adjusted image using accurate 8 × 8 multiplier

Source: Author

Figure 37.14 Non-linear brightness adjusted image using approximate 8 × 8 multiplier (set1 compressor)

Source: Author

Conclusion and Future Work

This work introduces the design and evaluation of approximate multipliers using 4:2 focusing on optimizing area, power, and delay for hardware-efficient computation. The proposed multipliers were analyzed based on different compressor sets, each offering a unique trade-off between accuracy and performance. Experimental results demonstrated that Compressor Set 1 and Set 2 provided the best balance between error rate and power-delay efficiency, making them suitable for error-resilient applications. In contrast, Compressor Set 3 and Set 4, which avoid XOR operations, exhibited lower delay but higher error rates, making them ideal for high-speed applications with relaxed accuracy requirements. To validate real-world applicability, the optimized multipliers were integrated into a non-linear brightness adjustment task in image processing. The results showed that approximate designs achieved significant power savings and reduced delay while maintaining acceptable PSNR and SSIM values, proving their effectiveness in real-time embedded applications.

Future research will focus on further optimizing compressor architectures to achieve an improved trade-off between error and efficiency. Additionally, these designs will be explored in deep learning accelerators, low-power IoT devices, and FPGA-based image processing pipelines to assess their impact in real-world scenarios. Further investigation into adaptive approximation techniques will also be conducted to dynamically adjust accuracy based on application requirements.

References

[1] Guo, Y., Zhou, Q., Chen, X., & Sun, H. (2024). Hardware-efficient multipliers with FPGA-based approximation for error-resilient applications. *IEEE Transactions on Circuits and Systems I: Regular Papers*, 71(12), 5919–5930.

[2] Zhang, M., Nishizawa, S., & Kimura, S. (2023). Area efficient approximate 4–2 compressor and probability-based error adjustment for approximate multiplier. *IEEE Transactions on Circuits and Systems II: Express Briefs*, 70(5), 1714–1718.

[3] Sayadi, L., Timarchi, S., & Sheikh-Akbari, A. (2023). Two efficient approximate unsigned multipliers by developing new configuration for approximate 4: 2 compressors. *IEEE Transactions on Circuits and Systems I: Regular Papers*, 70(4), 1649–1659.

[4] Anguraj, P., Krishnan, T., & Subramanian, S. (2022). CMOS implementation and performance analysis of known approximate 4: 2 compressors. *Journal of Electronic Testing*, 38(4), 353–370.

[5] Ullah, S., Rehman, S., Shafique, M., & Kumar, A. (2021). High-performance accurate and approximate multipliers for FPGA-based hardware accelerators. *IEEE Transactions on Computer-Aided Design of Integrated Circuits and Systems*, 41(2), 211–224.

[6] Nagar, M. S., Mathuriya, A., Patel, S. H., & Engineer, P. J. (2024). High-speed energy-efficient fixed-point signed multipliers for FPGA-based DSP applications. *IEEE Embedded Systems Letters*, 16(4), 417–420.

[7] Ma, Y., Xu, Q., & Song, Z. (2023). Resource-efficient optimization for FPGA-based convolution accelerator. *Electronics*, 12(20), 4333.

[8] Zakian, P., & Asli, R. N. (2024). An efficient approximate multiplier: design, error analysis and application. *International Journal of Electronics and Communications.*, 180, 155254.

[9] Edavoor, P. J., Raveendran, S., & Rahulkar, A. D. (2020). Approximate multiplier design using novel dual-stage 4: 2 compressors. *IEEE Access*, 8, 48337–48351.

[10] Park, G., Kung, J., & Lee, Y. (2021). Design and analysis of approximate compressors for balanced error accumulation in MAC operator. *IEEE Transactions on Circuits and Systems I: Regular Papers*, 68(7), 2950–2961.

[11] Pei, H., Yi, X., Zhou, H., & He, Y. (2020). Design of ultra-low power consumption approximate 4–2 compressors based on the compensation characteristic. *IEEE Transactions on Circuits and Systems II: Express Briefs*, 68(1), 461–465.

[12] Yao, S., & Zhang, L. (2022). Hardware-efficient fpga-based approximate multipliers for error-tolerant computing. In 2022 International Conference on Field-Programmable Technology (ICFPT, (pp. 1–8). IEEE.

[13] Anguraj, P., & Krishnan, T. (2023). Design and realization of area-efficient approximate multiplier structures for image processing applications. *Microprocessors and Microsystems*, 102, 104925.

[14] Anguraj, P., & Krishnan, T. (2023). Design of area-efficient modified decoder-based imprecise multiplier for error-resilient applications. *Microelectronics Journal*, 141, 105957.

[15] Rashidi, B. (2024). Efficient and low-cost approximate multipliers for image processing applications. *Integration*, 94, 102084.

38 Deep learning integrated network pharmacology approach for deciphering the molecular mechanisms of Indian medicinal plant compounds against irritable bowel syndrome

Venkatramanan Varadharajan[1,a], Madhavaperiya Muthuselvan[2,b], Sanmathy Balasubramanian[2,c] and Venkatesh Madhesh[2,d]

[1]Assistant Professor, Dept of Biotechnology, PSG College of Technology, Coimbatore, India

[2]Undergraduate Student, Dept of Biotechnology, PSG College of Technology, Coimbatore, India

Abstract

Irritable bowel syndrome (IBS) is a chronic gastrointestinal disorder with limited effective treatments. This study investigates the therapeutic potential of bioactive compounds from Indian medicinal plants by prioritizing those with strong binding affinity to IBS-associated molecular targets. From an initial set of 790 phytochemicals, 270 drug-like compounds were selected via ADMET filtering. Target analysis identified 69 overlapping molecular targets between IBS and the compounds. Protein–protein interaction networks and enrichment analysis revealed key IBS-related targets including EGFR, AKT1, SRC, and JUN. Molecular docking identified quercetin, Butein, and Camptothecin as promising candidates, with binding affinities up to –8.0 kcal/mol. Deep learning models—DeepDTA and DeepDGC—trained on KIBA and DAVIS datasets further validated these interactions. Predicted binding scores for top compounds reached as high as 11.99, confirming strong binding potential. Notably, quercetin and Tylophorinidine consistently demonstrated high affinity for EGFR and JUN, respectively. By integrating network pharmacology, molecular docking, and AI-based prediction, this study offers a robust pipeline for identifying multi-target phytochemicals for IBS therapy. The findings highlight strong candidate compounds for further in vitro and in vivo evaluation.

Keywords: Deep learning, DeepDGC, DeepDTA, Indian medicinal plants, irritable bowel syndrome, multi-target drugs, network pharmacology, phytochemicals

Introduction

A functional gastrointestinal condition called irritable bowel syndrome (IBS) mainly affects functioning and quality of life. Only a partial portion of the pathophysiology of IBS is studied. It is a rare chronic gastrointestinal illness for which there are only few viable treatments and serious adverse effects from available drugs. It is already identified that a group of factors add to the pathophysiology of IBS, together with visceral hypersensitivity, aberrant gut motility, imbalances in the gut microbiota, immune system disruptions and inflammation, genetic predispositions, abnormal gas handling, psychosocial factors, intestinal infections, interactions with the central nervous system, and dysregulation of serotonin [20]. IBS is a multifactorial disorder of diverse and not completely identified causes. The gut microbiota also takes part in IBS pathophysiology, affecting gut–brain axis and complete gastrointestinal motility [56]. It is best understood by a biopsychosocial model rather than a simple cause-and-effect relationship. This model provides that there are multiple factors, including an individual's environment, nervous system function, and psychological characteristics, interact to mould IBS symptoms. A main factor in this interaction is the gut–brain axis, which add intestinal activity with cognitive and emotional factors within the brain through enteric and central nervous systems. The hypothalamic–pituitary–adrenal (HPA) axis from limbic system also controls emotional signals to the gut via the autonomic nervous system [6]. Traditionally, IBS has been based on the identification of symptoms associated with various syndromes, including IBS with diarrhoea, IBS with constipation, functional diarrhoea, functional constipation, chronic functional abdominal pain,

[a]mail4venkat1992@gmail.com, [b]madhavaperiyamuthuselvan@gmail.com, [c]sanmathy3113@gmail.com, [d]venkateshmadhesh16@gmail.com

DOI: 10.1201/9781003770435-38

and bloating. The development of IBS symptoms is linked to multiple peripheral and central mechanisms that disturb gastrointestinal motor and sensory functions [7]. IBS has also been associated with a range of other gastrointestinal symptoms like headaches, dizziness, back pain, non-cardiac chest pain, fibromyalgia, chronic fatigue syndrome, urination, severe depression, anxiety, and somatization disorder [44]. When IBS joints with other illnesses, it might be difficult for physicians to diagnose and treat it because the associations between them are still unclear [31]. Researchers are finding complementary and alternative therapies to be more appealing options as a result of the unsatisfactory outcomes of traditional IBS therapy. Traditional Indian medicinal plants are efficient treating gastrointestinal problems and possess only fewer side effects which altogether make them as a promising alternative treatment to conventional methods [19]. Due to the complexity of the pathophysiology of IBS and limited treatment methods, treating IBS is been a challenging one. So, there is a high chance of using complementary and alternative treatments, mainly herbal therapies, in the treatment of IBS. The project mainly focuses on Indian medicinal plants from which the unique bioactive compounds can be used as potential therapeutic targets for the IBS [75]. Indian medicinal plants provide an integrated approach which maintains gut health, body, and mind, which is very much important for treating IBS [21]. Traditional Indian medicine is more efficient than conventional therapies as it can play an important role in personalized medicines and nature-based therapies [67]. The main goal in using Indian medicinal plants is to inflammation and promote gut microbiota with only fewer side effects that could help in treating IBS. Advanced developments in research have proved them in treating IBS by integrating the advantages of both traditional and modern healthcare theories [54].

Network pharmacology gives a complete ideology to understand the complex molecular interactions that are involved in a disease [34]. It links network biology and polypharmacology that involves many nodes within a biological network rather than a single drug target. This will increase the efficiency of the therapeutic drug targets with minimal side effects [36]. The core compounds identified by this approach are used as data for constructing the deep learning models. Following network pharmacology analysis, molecular docking plays a very important

part in identifying the binding affinity and stability of bioactive compounds within the IBS-related target proteins [87, 23]. This computational approach links the confusing gaps between compound screening and experimental validation, making it for the selection of the most potential candidates for future research [26]. Advancements in artificial intelligence, like deep learning, has been used in drug discovery by giving accurate drug-target interaction predictions and validating the core compounds for IBS treatment [30]. By combining these computational methods, researchers can find novel therapeutic compounds with high efficiency and low side effects [87, 80, 30].

This article aims to identify the Indian medicinal plants' role in IBS management, integration of network pharmacology for finding the key bioactive compounds from them, molecular docking for validating the interactions, and then constructing deep learning models with them for predicting drug-target interactions. By combining traditional knowledge with modern computational techniques, this article highlights the springing up strategies that could give more effective and personalized treatments for IBS.

Materials and Methods

Collection and screening of Indian medicinal plant compounds

The collection of Indian medicinal plant compounds was done using the IMPPAT (Indian Medicinal Plants, Phytochemistry, and Therapeutics) database (https://cb.imsc.res.in/imppat/) [3]. Initially, 790 compounds were taken from the IMPPAT database. Following that, ADMET (Absorption, Distribution, Metabolism, Excretion, and Toxicity) analysis was performed using Swiss ADME (http://www.swissadme.ch/) [39] to screen the collected compounds. After screening, approximately 270 compounds met the selection criteria. The screening was based on drug-likeness filters, including Lipinski, Ghose, Veber, Egan, and Muegge criteria, all of which had to be equal to zero [71].

Identification of targets for IBS and bioactive compounds

IBS targets were collected from the DisGeNet database (https://disgenet.com/) [11] and screened based on a threshold score of >0.6. In addition to DisGeNet, targets were also retrieved from the GeneCards database (https://www.genecards.org/) [72] using a

GIFtScore threshold score of >55. For the already screened 270 bioactive compounds, canonical SMILES were obtained from the IMPPAT database and imported into the Swiss Target Prediction Tool (http://www.swisstargetprediction.ch/) [12] and the STITCH database (http://stitch.embl.de/) Vivek-Ananth et al. [77] to identify their potential targets. Those targets were selected based on a p-value >0.5 from Swiss Target Prediction and confidence score >0.50 from the STITCH database. Duplicate entries were removed before further analysis to avoid errors and time consumption.

Overlapping targets for phytochemical compound targets and IBS targets
Venny 2.1.0 (https://bioinfogp.cnb.csic.es/tools/venny/) [73], used to identify the overlapping targets between phytochemical compound targets (98) and IBS targets (703). The intersection of these targets provides insights into common molecular targets that can be used to construct a protein-protein interaction (PPI) network for further analysis.

Protein-protein interaction (PPI) network construction and analysis
The overlapping compound-disease targets were put into the STRING database (https://string-db.org/) [61], with "Homo sapiens" as the selected organism. A minimum required interaction score of ≥ 0.7 was set as the cut-off value, while all other parameters were kept default. The analysis results from STRING were saved in TSV format and then used for core target sorting in Cytoscape v3.10.1. After constructing the protein-protein interaction (PPI) network, the CytoNCA plug-in in Cytoscape was used to analyze topological parameters of the network. The MCODE plug-in was then applied to cluster proteins into subnetworks, allowing for the visualizing of unique functional modules. To identify hub genes, the CytoHubba plug-in was used.

Gene ontology (GO) enrichment and Kyoto Encyclopedia of genes and genomes (KEGG) pathway analysis
Pathway and process enrichment analysis was done using ShinyGO 0.77 (http://bioinformatics.sdstate.edu/go/) [42]. ShinyGO 0.77 is a web-based tool designed to provide comprehensive gene list annotation and enrichment analysis. It includes GO processes, KEGG pathways, Reactome gene sets, and

canonical pathways as part of its core ontologies for enrichment analysis.

For this study, GO biological process enrichment and KEGG pathway analysis were performed to the genes identified as key targets from the PPI network. A false discovery rate (FDR) cut-off of 0.05 (p-value) was set which was used to determine significant enrichment.

Molecular docking for the most influential proteins and their ligands
The most significant protein was identified from the analysis conducted using Cytoscape software. The three-dimensional (3D) structures of the selected proteins were taken from the PDB database (https://www.rcsb.org/) [48], while their corresponding ligands were obtained from the PubChem database (https://pubchem.ncbi.nlm.nih.gov/) [37]. Molecular docking was performed using PyRx software [38], where each ligand was docked to its respective protein. Target-ligand complexes with high binding affinity values were selected for further analysis. The protein-ligand binding interactions were visualized and verified using Chimera software, and BIOVIA Discovery Studio [35], was used to generate 2D interaction visualizations.

Construction and validation of deep learning models

a) *Datasets:* The Kinase Inhibitor BioActivity (KIBA) and Davis Kinase binding affinity dataset (DAVIS) datasets [89] were used for training the constructed deep learning model. These datasets contain compounds (drugs), proteins (targets), and their interactions. The bioactivity values are represented as PIC50 for the KIBA dataset and Pkd for the DAVIS dataset. The KIBA dataset contains 2070 compounds and 230 targets, having 118,254 interactions, with binding affinity values ranging from 1.1 to 17.2. On the other hand, the DAVIS dataset contains 68 compounds and 442 targets, having 30,056 interactions with binding affinity values ranging from 5.0 to 10.8 [89]. Compounds (drugs) are represented as simplified molecular input line entry system (SMILES) notation, while proteins (targets) are represented as amino acid sequences.

b) *Representation of Drugs and Targets:* In this deep learning model, drug compounds as SMILES provide a linear textual representation of the structures. These textual representations were converted into numerical features using the Morgan fingerprinting method (Extended Connectivity Fingerprints, ECFP) with some criteria that includes, a radius of 2 and 1024-bit vector size [2]. This converted representation helps in identifying the key molecular features and substructures that are needed for drug-target interaction prediction. Target proteins were represented as FASTA sequences, which were then converted into numerical indices by sequence-to-index mapping approach [70]. Each amino acid in the sequence was assigned an integer index based on a fixed vocabulary of 20 standard amino acids. To maintain the uniformity among the sequences, they were padded and truncated to a maximum length of 500 residues.

c) *Feature Extraction:* Feature extraction was done to change the chemical and sequence-based information into numerical representations which can be used in deep learning algorithms [84]. For drug molecules, Morgan fingerprints were used to denote atom connectivity, molecular substructures, and functional groups such as carboxyl, hydroxyl, and amine into a 1024-bit vector [14]. This bit-based encoding assured that each bit meant the presence or absence of the particular molecular substructures. In addition to this, the method also integrated topological features and circular substructures, making suitable for a complete molecular representation. For protein targets, sequence embeddings were made by converting amino acids into numerical indices, which were further processed by a trainable embedding layer. This method led the model to get sequence information, physicochemical properties, and structural motifs like alpha-helices and beta-sheets. The embeddings hold the sequence similarity and evolutionary conservation for accurate interaction predictions. In addition, k-Mer frequency encoding was done to get the local sequence motifs from protein sequences, which were important for validating drug-target interactions [8].

d) *DeepDTA Model Construction:* The DeepDTA model was constructed to predict drug-target affinity (DTA) using deep learning [20, 58]. It gets two inputs: a 100-dimensional vector as the drug molecule and a 500-dimensional vector as the protein target. Each input is processed by fully connected layers using 512 neurons and ReLU activation function to get the most needed features [16]. The outputs are then flattened and concatenated to form a combined drug-target representation. The model then applies three fully connected layers, with 1024 neurons in the first two layers and 512 neurons in the third layer and using ReLU activation in all the 3 layers. The final output layer with a linear activation function predicts the binding affinity score. The model is also integrated with the Adam optimizer and mean squared error (MSE) loss function for effective learning [63]. This construction makes DeepDTA to get the nonlinear relationships between drugs and proteins, thus increasing its predictive accuracy in drug discovery applications.

e) *DeepDGC Model Construction:* The DeepDGC model was constructed for predicting drug-target interaction (DTI) by integrating regression and classification tasks [20]. Drug molecules were represented as 1024-dimensional vectors, while protein sequences were represented as a 1000-length integer sequence. An embedding layer was utilized in the protein input, making it to a 128-dimensional dense vector. This embedded representation was then combined with the drug representation to form a single drug-target pair. The combined features were given to a deep neural network with a 512-neuron fully connected layer followed by batch normalization and a dropout layer set at 40% to avoid overfitting [13]. There was another dense layer with 256 neurons and ReLU activation which was followed by an additional dropout layer [16, 13]. The model possesses two output layers: a regression layer for predicting binding affinity using linear activation function and a classification layer classifying strong and weak interactions using softmax activation function [43]. The model was compiled with MSE loss for regression, sparse categorical cross-entropy loss for classification, and the Adam optimizer set at a learning rate of 0.0005. To ensure robust predictions, performance metrics like Mean absolute error (MAE) and classification accuracy were evaluated [63].

Training and Optimization: The training process involved the extracted features as input for the deep learning models and optimizing them to learn the patterns of drug-target interactions [86]. TensorFlow tensors were utilized to standardize the input data, ensuring computational efficiency [59]. Training was done using the fit() function, with drug-target pairs as input and binding affinity values as target labels. A batch size of 128 was set for training over 100 epochs for DeepDTA and 15 epochs for DeepDGC. Validation dataset was included to evaluate the model performance and prevent overfitting [53]. The DeepDGC model used early stopping to end the training if no improvement was found for three consecutive epochs and had a learning rate scheduler that reduced the learning rate by 50% if validation loss stopped for two epochs [53, 65]. These strategies help in improving the model's generalization and stability.

Model Evaluation Metrics: The performance of DeepDTA and DeepDGC models was measured using different evaluation metrics. For regression tasks, the coefficient of determination (R^2 score), mean squared error (MSE), and root mean squared error (RMSE) were used [74]. The R^2 score measured how well the predicted binding affinity values related with actual values, with higher values mean better predictions. MSE and RMSE values give the average prediction errors, where lower values mean higher accuracy [5]. For classification tasks in DeepDGC, sparse categorical cross-entropy loss was used to evaluate classification error, while classification accuracy measured the proportion of correctly predicted strong and weak interactions. These metrics gave a clear assessment of model performance, identifying strong drug-target interactions [24, 10].

Results and Discussions

Screening of bioactive compounds
This study had taken 218 medicinal plants from the Indian Medicinal Plants, Phytochemistry, and Therapeutics (IMPPAT) database. More than 750 unique bioactive compounds from these plants were collected and analyzed for their potential in the treatment of IBS.

ADMET analysis
The ADMET analysis of the compounds was conducted using conventional filters to assess their viability as drug candidates. Firstly, the compounds were screened based on drug-likeness criteria, that includes Lipinski's Rule of Five, Muegge's criteria, and Ghose's filter, to eliminate the compounds with poor bioavailability. Then, Euler's score was used to evaluate fragment diversity for hit identification, while Veber's rule ensured that the selected compounds have suitable flexibility and surface properties for absorption, considering polar surface area for membrane permeability [25]. Together, these five filters provided a strong framework for selecting compounds with physical, chemical, and ADMET characteristics. Of the 750 screened compounds, only 270 compounds met these strict criteria.

Identification of compound targets
The molecular targets of bioactive compounds from Indian medicinal plants were analyzed using STITCH and SwissTargetPrediction. A total of 43 targets were identified from STITCH, while SwissTargetPrediction identified 140 targets. After integrating data from both tools and removing duplicates, 167 unique molecular targets were identified.

Identification of disease (IBS) targets
Key molecular targets associated with IBS were identified using two comprehensive databases, DisGeNet and GeneCards, based on their relevance scores. DisGeNet (ScoreGDA > 0.5) identified 33 IBS-related genes, while GeneCards (GeneCards Inferred Functionality Scores, GiFts > 55) identified 766 genes. After sorting and filtering, a total of 772 unique genes representing molecular targets implicated in IBS were identified.

Acquisition of overlapping targets
A total of 69 overlapping targets between the identified compound targets and IBS-associated targets (Figure 38.1) were found using Venny 2.1.0. Protein-Protein interaction network was constructed for these overlapping targets using STRING (Figure 38.2) and Cystoscape 3.0 (Figure 38.3) for further analysis.

Identification of core targets
The top 10 core targets and sub-networks were identified from the plants-compounds-targets-disease Network (Figure 38.7) initially and from overlapping

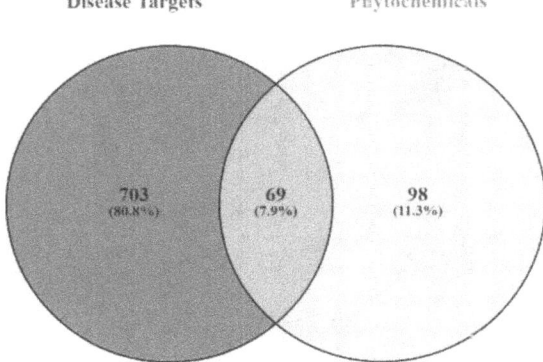

Figure 38.1 Overlapping targets for disease (IBS) targets and phytochemical targets

Source: Author

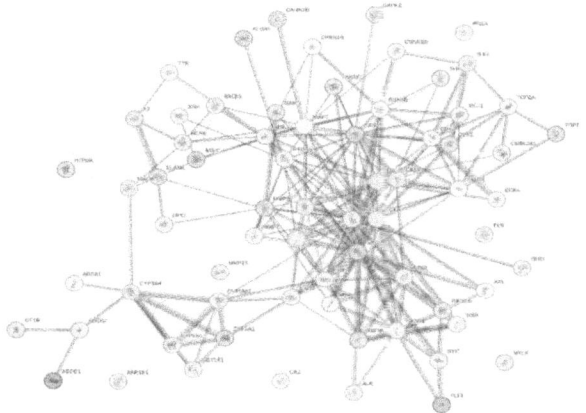

Figure 38.2 Protein-protein interaction network for the 69 common targets constructed using STRING

Source: Author

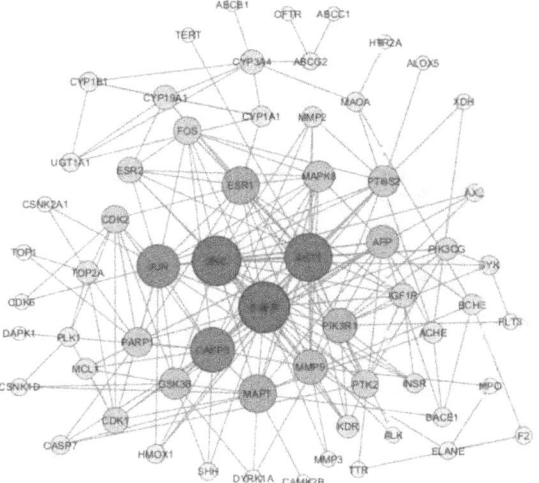

Figure 38.3 PPI of the 69 common targets based on degree of the nodes and edges using Cytoscape 3.0

Source: Author

targets network, using various plug-ins available in Cytoscape 3.0, including CytoNCA, CytoHubba, and MCODE. CytoHubba analysis revealed EGFR, SRC, JUN, AKT1, MAPK8, ESR1, FOS, MMP9, ESR2, and CASP3 as the top 10 targets based on Maximal Clique Centrality (MCC) scores (Figure 38.4), indicating their strong influence within the network and potential biological relevance CytoNCA also identified the top 10 gene targets based on combined centrality scores (Table 38.1). Using MCODE, two major sub-networks were identified: Cluster 1 (ESR2, FOS, KDR, IGF1R, MMP9, EGFR, AKT1, JUN, PTGS2, CASP3, and PIK3CG) comprising 11 nodes and 30 edges (Figure 38.5), and Cluster 2 (CYP3A4, CYP1A1, CYP1B1, ESR1, CYP19A1, MAPK8, SRC, UGT1A1, GSK3B, APP, PIK3R1, MAPT, PTK2, and INSR) comprising 14 nodes and 30 edges (Figure 38.6). The genes identified in these sub-networks play a crucial role in understanding the genetic basis of IBS, providing valuable information for further studies and potential therapeutic applications [18].

Genes such as JUN, EGFR, and ESR1 are well-known in IBS pathology due to their roles in inflammation, mucosal repair, and hormonal signaling [9], Jacenik and Krajewska [32] emerging genes like MAPK8, AKT1, MMP9, FOS, and MAPT present novel ways for exploration. MAPK8 (JNK1) and AKT1, with moderate links to stress response and epithelial homeostasis, respectively, highlighting pathways intersecting gut-brain communication and immune regulation—areas already implicated in IBS but underexplored at the gene level [79, 22]. MMP9, though weakly associated, introduces a compelling

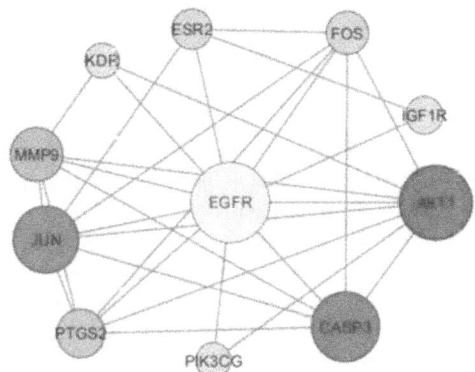

Figure 38.4 Top 10 core targets identified using cytoscape plug-in cytohuba

Source: Author

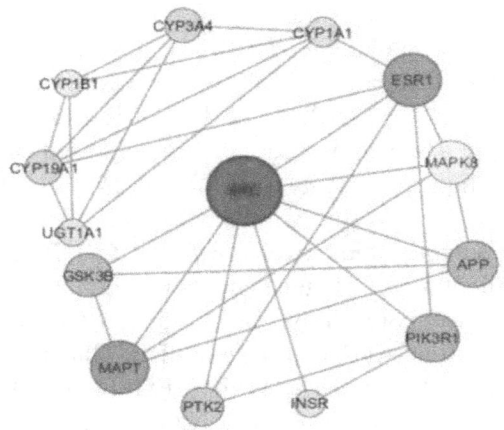

Figure 38.5 Sub-networks - cluster 1 with 11 nodes and 30 edges using cytoscape plug-in M-CODE Cytoscape Plug-in M-CODE

Source: Author

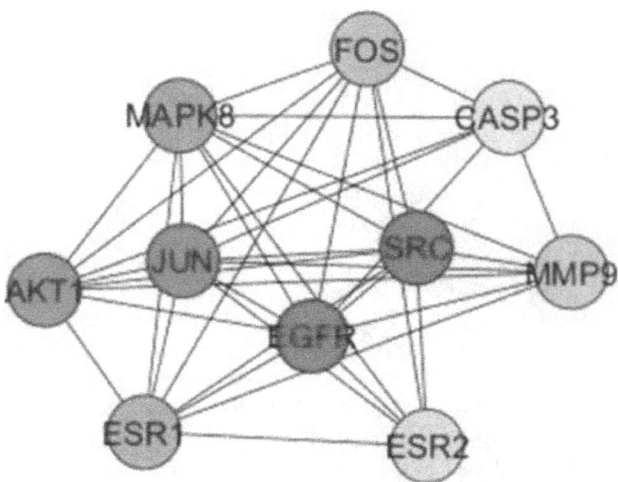

Figure 38.6 Sub-networks - cluster 2 with 14 nodes and 30 edges using cytoscapte plug-in M-CODE

Source: Author

role through its dual play in gut barrier integrity and inflammation, combining gaps between IBS and IBD research [57]. The higher novelty of FOS and MAPT adds to their divergence from traditional IBS studies: FOS modulates visceral pain by neuronal activation, a process critical in IBS but rarely studied at the transcriptional level [88], while MAPT (tau protein), traditionally linked to neurodegeneration, offers a provocative connection to gut-brain axis dysfunction, suggesting shared molecular pathways between neuropsychiatric and gastrointestinal disorders [46]. These genes collectively underscore the potential for repurposing known biological mechanisms into IBS-specific contexts, particularly in pain modulation and neural-gut crosstalk. Prioritizing functional studies on MAPT and FOS could unravel novel therapeutic targets, such as tau-mediated signaling or stress-induced neuronal plasticity, advancing IBS beyond symptom management toward mechanism-driven interventions [64]. However, the weaker empirical

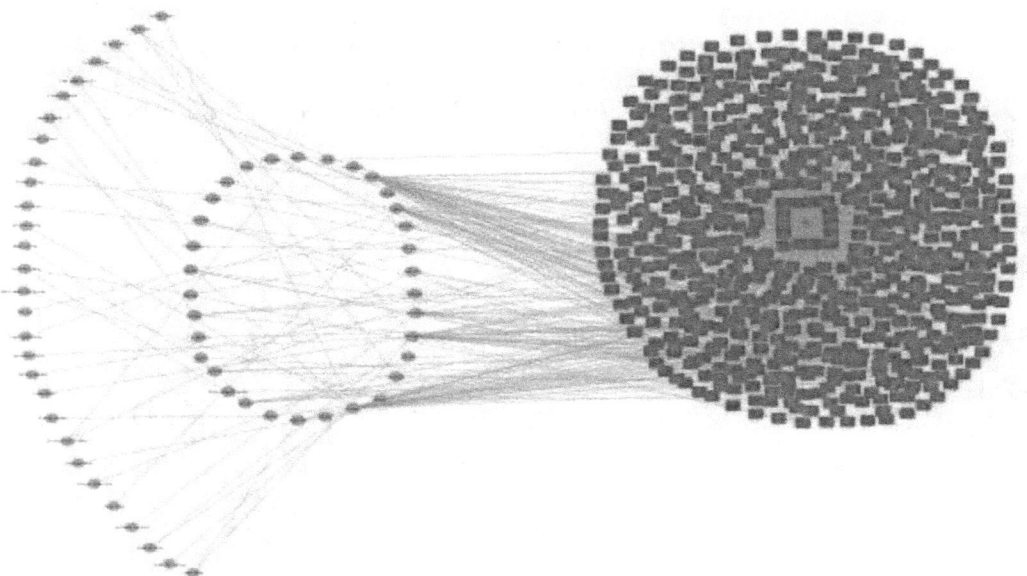

Figure 38.7 Plants-compounds-targets-disease network. Green color indicates plants, violet color indicates the compounds, red color indicates the targets and blue color indicates the disease (IBS)

Source: Author

Table 38.1 Tabulation of topological parameters of Top 10 protein-protein interaction networks

S.NO	Common Targets	Degree Centrality	Betweenness Centrality	Closeness Centrality
1	EGFR	23	488.0996	0.525424
2	SRC	22	448.9248	0.504065
3	AKT1	21	669.6558	0.53913
4	JUN	18	331.7396	0.496
5	CASP3	19	338.9937	0.492064
6	ESR1	15	420.427	0.48062
7	MAPK8	11	34.87153	0.455882
8	MMP9	13	286.6912	0.442857
9	FOS	9	7.934027	0.418919
10	MAPT	15	498.4507	0.473282

Source: Author

links for MMP9 and MAPT necessitate rigorous validation to confirm their roles in IBS, emphasizing the importance of integrating multi-omics and preclinical models to solidify these emerging associations [15].

GO and KEGG analysis

The enrichment analysis plots indicate that the color of each bar corresponds to the -log10(FDR) that represents the significance of the enrichment (higher -log10(FDR) indicates a more significant enrichment) and the size of the dot next to each bar indicates the number of genes associated with that GO term.

The biological process in GO analysis (Figure 38.8) indicates that the number of genes involved in the process of response to oxygen-containing compounds is higher than other genes. It also highlighted that IBS may be involved in the dysregulation of cellular responses to various stressors, such as oxidative stress, chemical stress, or nitrogen compounds. Recent studies have highlighted the involvement of oxidative stress in the pathogenesis of IBS. Specifically, increased levels of oxidants and reactive nitrogen species have been observed in IBS patients. A study found significantly higher concentrations of malondialdehyde (MDA) and nitric oxide (NO) in the plasma of IBS patients compared to healthy controls. These compounds are indicative of lipid peroxidation, suggesting that oxidative damage may play a role in IBS pathology [50].

From the cellular compartment lollipop plot (Figure 38.9), most of the genes were present in the

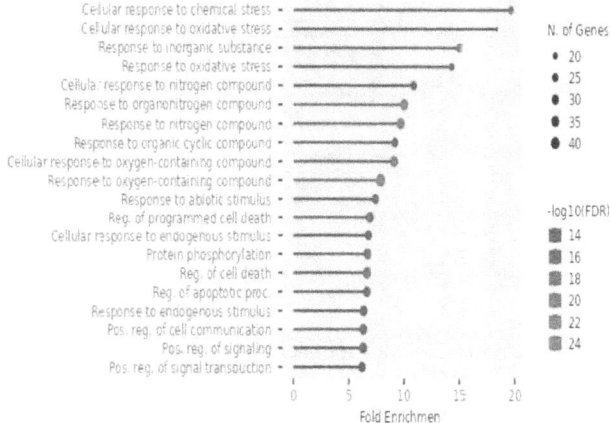

Figure 38.8 Lollipop plot depicting highly enriched GO terms belonging to biological process (BP)

Source: Author

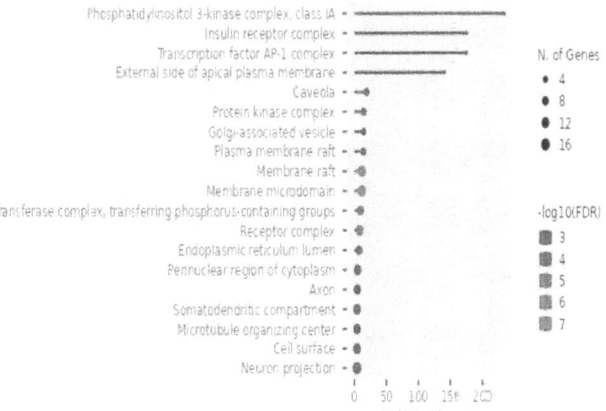

Figure 38.9 Lollipop plot depicting highly enriched GO terms belonging to cellular component (CC)

Source: Author

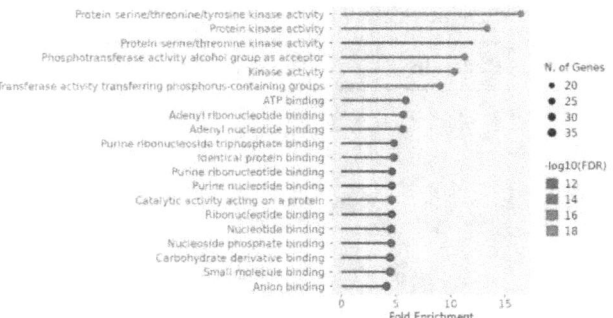

Figure 38.10 Lollipop plot depicting highly enriched GO terms belonging to molecular function (MF)

Source: Author

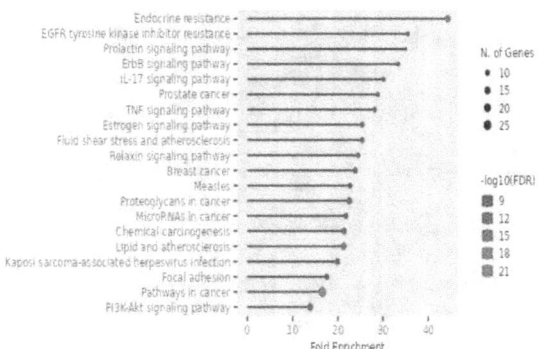

Figure 38.11 Lollipop plot depicting KEGG analysis pathway

Source: Author

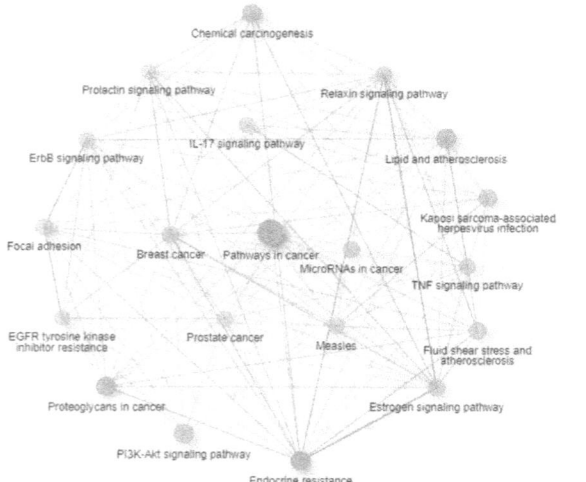

Figure 38.12 Network chart depicting most of the genes involved in pathways in cancer

Source: Author

membrane raft and membrane microdomain. Many aspects of membrane rafts are disrupted by the peroxidation of plasma membrane lipids, including their stability, abundance and protein and lipid composition, which is correlated with the biological activity of the membrane [4, 50].

From the molecular function lollipop plot (Figure 38.10), it was observed that the most of the genes were involved in the Protein kinase activity, Phosphotransferase activity, transferase activity, alcohol group as acceptor, kinase activity and serine/threonine kinase activity [66]. Kinase activity plays an important role in important cellular processes, including pain signaling and inflammation that are important in IBS. The dysregulation of kinases could cause altered gut motility, visceral hypersensitivity, and inflammation, all the significant features of IBS [17]. The genes identified from the clusters such as mitogen-activated protein kinase (MAPK), phosphoinositide 3-kinase (PIK3) and glycogen synthase kinase 3 beta (GSK3B) were also involved in kinase activity results in inflammatory responses, gut motility and visceral hypersensitivity. MAPKs are activated by pro-inflammatory cytokines such as TNF-α, causing low-grade inflammation in the gut [1]. PI3K is involved in the signaling pathway and taking part in processes such as inflammation, oxidative stress, and cellular degeneration [29]. GSK3B is linked to neuroinflammatory responses and regulation of serotonin pathways, which affects the gut-brain communication. Overactivation of GSK3B can increase inflammatory signaling and disrupt neuroplasticity, worsening visceral hypersensitivity and pain in IBS [17].

In the KEGG analysis, from the plot (Figure 38.11) obtained it was observed that more genes were involved in the cancer pathways. IBS does not increase the risk of cancer overall. Even it has a low association with the risk of colorectal cancer. Endocrine resistance and EGFR tyrosine kinase inhibitor resistance are the two pathways (Figure 38.12) with the highest fold enrichment suggesting that in the gut where EGFR signaling is important for maintaining intestinal epithelial integrity and healing after an injury. Enrichment of the EGFR TKI resistance pathway suggests that any disruptions in this pathway could lead to impaired epithelial barrier, increased gut permeability, and abnormal tissue repair [55].

Molecular docking analysis

The top four core targets were docked with the bioactive drug compounds, revealing that quercetin showed strong binding affinities with all three targets, suggesting its potential to regulate various pathways involved in IBS (Table 38.2). The therapeutic potential of naturally occurring compounds in gastrointestinal disorders has gathered attention, with quercetin emerging as a promising drug candidate for IBS treatment. It is found in various Indian medicinal plants such as *Rhinacanthus nasutus, Urtica urens, Allium cepa, Coriandrum sativum,* and *Moringa oleifera*, possessing antioxidant, anti-inflammatory, and immune-modulating properties, making it well-suited for curing IBS-related symptoms. Its role in maintaining intestinal homeostasis is highly significant, as it improves the mucosal barrier, reducing gut permeability and preventing pathogen invasion, which are the important factors in IBS pathophysiology. Despite its therapeutic potential, quercetin's bioavailability remains a challenging one. However, advancements in chemistry and drug delivery systems, such as nanoformulations, have significantly improved its absorption and therapeutic efficacy. By developing quercetin as a prodrug or incorporating it into enhanced drug delivery systems could further improve its clinical uses [47]. Additionally, JUN, a transcription factor involved in inflammation and cell proliferation, was identified as a potential therapeutic target for IBS. Molecular docking analysis identified that JUN exhibits moderate binding affinity with tylophorinidine, pergularinine, and camptothecin, suggesting their possible role in IBS treatment [28].

Butein, found in *Butea monosperma*, showed high affinity toward EGFR, a receptor that plays a role in intestinal epithelial repair and barrier integrity [40]. Its EGFR-targeting capability complements the anti-inflammatory action of Camptothecin and Quercetin, suggesting a strong role in restoring gut homeostasis in IBS [45]. Camptothecin, derived from *Nothapodytes nimmoniana*, an important Indian medicinal plant, demonstrated selective affinity for JUN, a transcription factor involved in pro-inflammatory gene expression and epithelial cell signaling. Its targeted inhibition of JUN could suppress the chronic inflammatory signaling often associated with IBS [51]. While Tylophorinidine and Pergularinine (also from Indian plants like *Tylophora indica* and *Pergularia daemia*) interacted with JUN, their lower binding affinities compared to Camptothecin suggest

relatively weaker interaction strength. However, further research is required to validate their efficacy and safety through in vitro, in vivo, and clinical studies.

Interaction analysis

Receptor binding analysis was done using Biovia Discovery Studio to explore protein-ligand interactions at the molecular level, evaluating binding affinities, stability, and conformational changes. This analysis helps identify binding sites that are crucial for structure-based drug design. However, improving an accurate scoring function remains highly challenging due to the complex nature of protein-ligand interactions. Binding affinity is influenced by multiple factors, including van der Waals forces, electrostatic interactions, hydrogen bonding, solvent effects, and hydrophobic interactions, all of which add to the complexity of the process [52]. Hydrogen bonds are considered as the primary driving force for molecular recognition. Additionally, pi-cation and pi-anion interactions occur between aromatic rings on the ligand and charged residues of the protein which adds to the stability of the complex (Figure 38.13). Pi-pi T-shaped interactions (Figure 38.14), involving two aromatic rings arranged perpendicularly, are weaker than hydrogen bonds and electrostatic interactions but still play a role in molecular binding. The 2D interaction diagrams generated in this analysis identified the specific protein residues involved in stabilizing the ligand, providing information into their proximity and functional roles within the binding site.

The interaction analysis (Figure 38.15) revealed that van der Waals interactions were more prevalent than hydrogen bonds in the analyzed interactions. This suggests that weaker, non-specific forces dominate the binding process, potentially indicating a more flexible interaction. The lower number of hydrogen bonds means less direct or specific stabilization. The analysis primarily identified hydrogen bonding and van der Waals interactions, with other interaction types either absent or significantly lower in occurrence.

Although quercetin has the potential to be developed as a therapeutic agent for IBS, studies have shown that it inhibits intestinal motor function in IBS rats with diarrhea while improving defecation function. However, its stability and target-binding affinity possess challenges for its use as a targeted drug [27]. In contrast, camptothecin exhibited

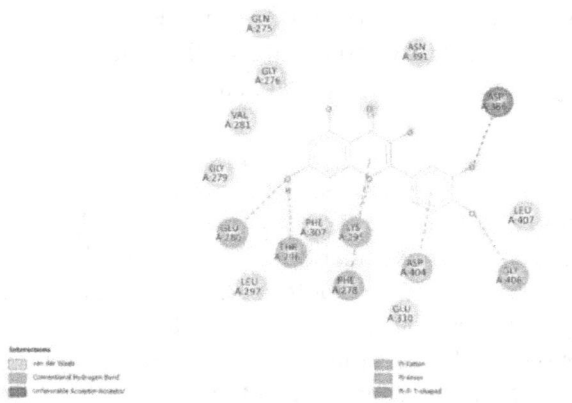

Figure 38.13 2D representation of SRC – quercetin interaction
Source: Author

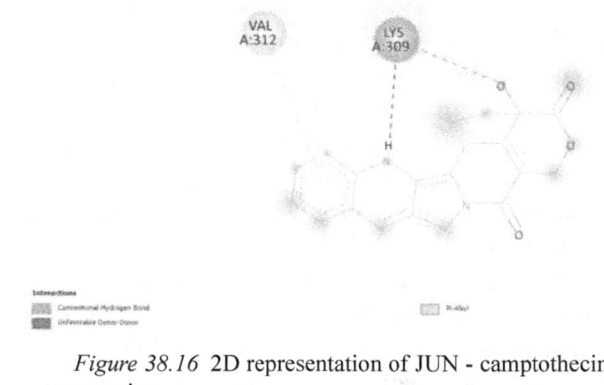

Figure 38.16 2D representation of JUN - camptothecin interaction
Source: Author

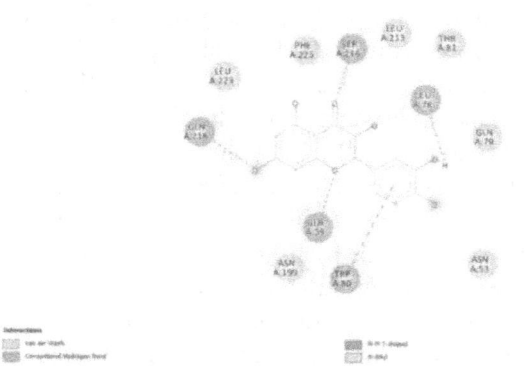

Figure 38.14 2D representation of AKT1– quercetin interaction
Source: Author

weak or insufficient interactions with the target protein (Figure 38.16), suggesting that it may not be a suitable drug candidate. To validate the therapeutic potential and safety profile of the promising candidates, further studies—like the integration of deep learning models—will be essential for refining predictions and optimizing drug design.

Deep learning models analysis

The evaluation metrics across both DeepDTA and DeepDGC models on the KIBA and DAVIS datasets reveal significant differences in the model, performance, and generalization ability. On the KIBA dataset, DeepDTA (Figure 38.17) achieves a high training R^2 value of 0.8119 and a respectable test R^2 of 0.5749, indicating effective learning and moderate generalization (Table 38.3). This is further supported by low MSE (0.2932) and RMSE (0.5415), and a strong AUC of 0.91, suggesting that DeepDTA

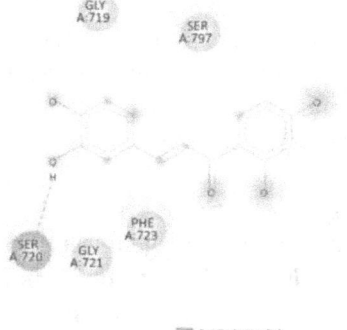

Figure 38.15 2D representation of EGFR – quercetin interaction
Source: Author

Table 38.2 Tabulation of binding affinity of the targets and the compounds

Target	Compound	Binding affinity (Kcal/ mol)
EGFR	Butein	-7.1
EGFR	Quercetin	-7
AKT1	Quercetin	-7.4
SRC	Quercetin	-8
JUN	Tylophorinidine	-5.7
JUN	Pergularinine	-5.6
JUN	Camptothecin	-6.1

Source: Author

is capable of capturing the complex patterns of drug-target interactions in the relatively larger and denser KIBA dataset. Comparatively, DeepDGC (Table 38.3) on the same dataset also performs competitively, achieving a low-test loss (0.7644), low binding affinity MAE (0.6758), and perfect classification accuracy. These values reflect the model's stability in both regression and classification tasks, likely due to its graph-based representation learning that captures molecular structure information.

However, on the DAVIS dataset, the performance of both models decreases considerably, with DeepDTA (Figure 38.18) showing a negative test R^2 (-0.0937), higher MSE (0.8453), and reduced AUC (0.67), indicating poor generalization and suggesting overfitting to training data or insufficient learning (Table 38.3). This could be attributed to the smaller size and higher sparsity of the DAVIS dataset, which may limit the model's ability to learn minute features. DeepDGC (Table 38.4) though resulted in good classification accuracy, it's test loss (11.1802) and affinity MAE (2.2261) is higher indicating a decrease in regression accuracy. This difference states that while DeepDGC has robust binary, its performance in continuous value prediction was more sensitive to complexity and size of the dataset.

Overall, the results suggest that DeepDTA performs better under good data conditions, DeepDGC presents better structural modeling but still require optimization for small datasets like DAVIS. The results indicate that while DeepDGC generalizes better for classification tasks for multiple datasets, its regression prediction is always dataset-dependent, with greater outcomes observed on KIBA than DAVIS. This gap implies that the DeepDTA model has few limitations with the DAVIS dataset, due to its smaller size, wide distribution, or interactions complexity. Altogether, DeepDTA has great potential on the KIBA dataset but its limitations become clear on the DAVIS dataset, requiring the need for more robust or flexible architectures like DeepDGC for further implications.

The results of the DeepDTA model on both the KIBA and DAVIS datasets observes the key differences in generalizing training and validation data. The performance of both datasets shows a decrease in training and validation loss in the first few epochs, and then plateaued to near-zero values. That immediate convergence of loss over the epochs suggest that the model has learned the important patterns but their

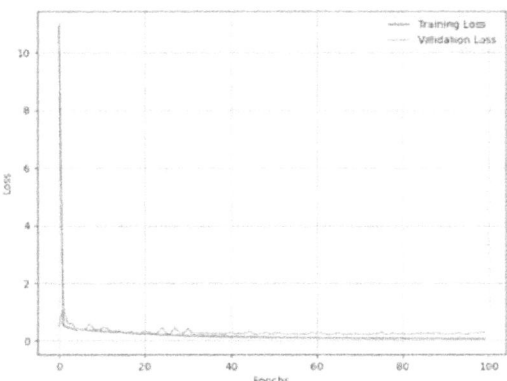

Figure 38.17 Training and validation loss curves of the DeepDTA model on the KIBA dataset over 100 epochs
Source: Author

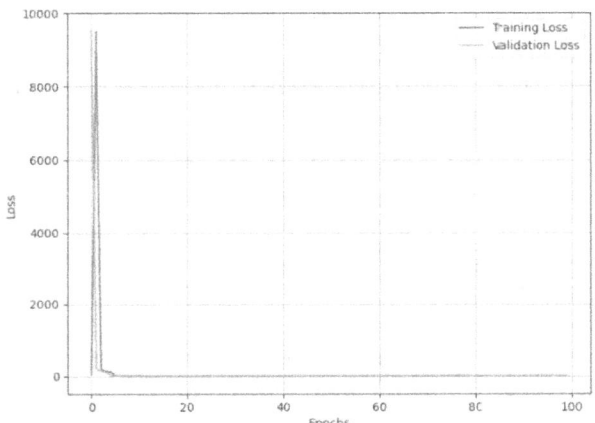

Figure 38.18 Training and validation loss curves of the DeepDTA model on the DAVIS dataset across 100 epochs
Source: Author

Table 38.3 Evaluation metrics of DeepDTA model on KIBA and DAVIS datasets

Evaluation metric	KIBA dataset	DAVIS Dataset
Coefficient of Determination (Train R^2)	0.8119	0.4499
Coefficient of Determination (Test R^2)	0.5749	-0.0937
Mean Squared Error (MSE)	0.2932	0.8453
Root Mean Squared Error (RMSE)	0.5415	0.9194
Area Under the Curve (AUC)	0.91	0.67

Source: Author

Table 38.4 Evaluation metrics of DeepDGC Model on KIBA and DAVIS datasets

Evaluation metric	KIBA Dataset	DAVIS Dataset
Test loss	0.7644	11.1802
Test binding Affinity loss	0.7644	10.9760
Test binding Affinity MAE	0.6758	2.2261
Test binding Classification loss	0	0.2042
Test binding Classification accuracy	1	1

Source: Author

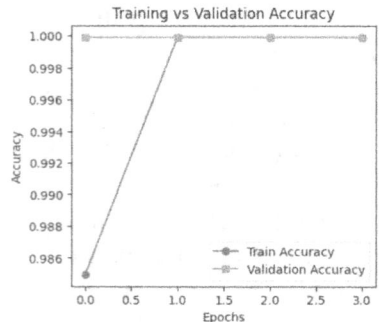

Figure 38.19 Training vs. validation accuracy of the Deep-DGC model on the KIBA dataset
Source: Author

corresponding R^2 scores diverge. For the KIBA dataset, the training R^2 score value maintained at approximately 0.45, indicating a moderate linear correlation between predicted and actual binding affinities on the training dataset whereas the validation R^2 score consistently around -0.1 indicating the model's limitation to generalize to unseen data. A similar trend was observed with the DAVIS dataset, where the training R^2 score stood around 0.45, yet the validation R^2 score was also around −0.1 throughout the training process. This difference suggests that the model is overfitting, learning patterns specific to the training set that do not extend to new examples. In summary, the study suggests that DeepDTA, contrary to its high training performance, does not generalize well, due to imperfect feature extraction. The reason might be either that there are not enough high-quality features extractable from the input features. This made looking at alternative deep learning frameworks like graph neural networks to address this issue. This would require training a model across various computational platforms on a highly representative dataset, which could, in turn, raise innovation in areas such as AI, health, and drug discovery.

The performance plots of the DeepDGC model trained using the KIBA dataset shows strong and consistent learning. The training and validation accuracy plot (Figure 38.19) shows near-perfect accuracy from the first epoch, with both training and validation accuracy reaching ~1.0. This reflects the model's ability to rapidly converge and accurately classify compound-target interactions. The loss curve (Figure 38.20) further supports this interpretation: while the training loss shows a steady decrease from ~6 to

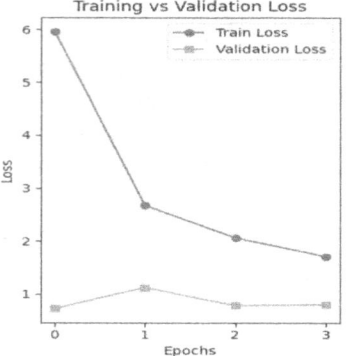

Figure 38.20 Training vs. validation loss of the DeepDGC model on the KIBA dataset
Source: Author

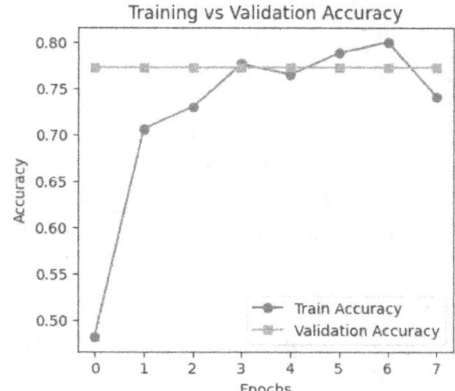

Figure 38.21 Training vs. validation accuracy of the Deep-DGC model on the DAVIS dataset
Source: Author

under 2 across epochs, the validation loss remains very low and stable (around ~0.8–1.2), indicating minimal overfitting. This strong performance can be attributed to the KIBA dataset, which is known for its

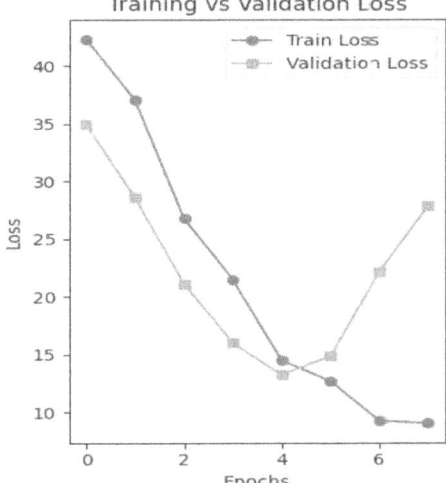

Figure 38.22 Training vs. validation loss of the DeepDGC model on the DAVIS dataset

Source: Author

higher number of interactions and more comprehensive binding affinity data, enabling the model to learn meaningful patterns and generalize well to unseen data. The consistency in validation metrics suggests the model is reliable in predicting interactions with high confidence when trained on rich datasets like KIBA. In contrast, the DeepDGC model trained with the DAVIS dataset exhibits lower and more fluctuating performance. The training accuracy (Figure 38.21) gradually improves, peaking around 80%, while validation accuracy remains flat at ~77%, showing little to no improvement across epochs. The loss curve (Figure 38.22) shows a classic overfitting trend: while training loss steadily decreases from 42 to 9, the validation loss drops initially but then increases after the 4th epoch, rising to over 28. This divergence indicates that the model memorizes the training data but fails to generalize to unseen interactions. This performance discrepancy may stem from the limited interaction diversity and smaller size of the DAVIS dataset. The insufficient interaction patterns affect the model's ability to generalize, making it more sensitive to noise and overfitting. DeepDGC model is less efficient when it is trained on DAVIS dataset which limit its ability to predict complex interactions. The comparative results of DeepDGC model on both datasets revealed the importance of quality of the dataset when they are used in deep learning algorithms. DeepDGC-KIBA shows high accuracy and stability while DeepDGC-DAVIS underperforms because of the dataset limitations.

Despite the differences in performance of both the models, they both identify JUN gene and its related compounds like Camptothecin and Tylophorinidine as core targets, highlighting JUN's relevance in IBS pathology. This common prediction across various models and datasets proves that the result suggests the deep learning models are effective in identifying more relevant IBS targets when processed by good and strong datasets.

In summary, the comparative evaluation of DeepDGC and DeepDTA on KIBA and DAVIS datasets highlights both advantages and challenges of the models. DeepDGC resulted in higher generalization ability by its validation and better R^2 scores, particularly when trained on the DAVIS dataset. Its ability to maintain low loss and a relatively high R^2 score indicates that it significantly gets the most important patterns in drug-target interactions helping the model to be more reliable in predicting the affinity scores. On the other hand, DeepDTA, though rapidly converge in training loss, dealt with overfitting with its lower R^2 scores and performance. This suggests that DeepDTA might be limited by its architecture or insufficient feature representation methods that make it not getting the complex biochemical interactions needed for accurate prediction. At the end, Though DeepDTA can fit training data well, DeepDGC shows better solution for real-world application and robust prediction, indicating the importance of architecture of the model and feature encoding in deep learning-based drug discovery.

Table 38.5 Binding affinity scores from DeepDTA Model using KIBA dataset

Compound	Target	Predicted_Scores
Quercetin	SRC	11.58422
Butein	EGFR	11.355546
Camptothecin	JUN	11.318796

Source: Author

Table 38.6 Binding affinity scores from DeepDTA Model using DAVIS dataset

Compound	Target	Predicted_Scores
Pergularinine	JUN	5.718646
Tylophorinidine	JUN	5.701412
Camptothecin	JUN	5.866576

Source: Author

Table 38.7 Binding affinity scores from DeepDGC model using KIBA dataset

Compound	Target	Predicted_Binding_Affinity	Predicted_Class
Quercetin	EGFR	11.992231	Strong Binding
Butein	EGFR	11.985879	Strong Binding
Tylophorinidine	JUN	11.852913	Strong Binding

Source: Author

Table 38.8 Binding affinity scores from DeepDGC Model using DAVIS dataset

Compound	Target	Predicted_Binding_Affinity	Predicted_Class
Camptothecin	JUN	6.474421	Weak Binding
Tylophorinidine	JUN	6.450688	Weak Binding
Pergularinine	JUN	6.4433084	Weak Binding

Source: Author

The deep learning models, DeepDTA and DeepDGC, predicted binding affinities between bioactive compounds and IBS-related targets, revealing significant trends. Through the KiBA dataset, Quercetin and Butein show consistent high binding scores ($\geq$11.35) for EGFR and SRC (Tables 38.5 and 6), with DeepDGC classifying these interactions as "Strong Binding", suggesting their potential as therapeutic candidates for regulating inflammation and epithelial repair in IBS. In contrast, predictions using the DAVIS dataset yielded lower affinity scores (~5.7–6.4) for JUN-targeting compounds like camptothecin and tylophorindine, labeled as "Weak Binding" by DeepDGC (Tables 38.7 and 38.8). This reflects inherent differences in dataset composition or model sensitivity, highlighting the need for cross-validation. Notably, Tylophorindine showed strong binding to JUN in the KiBA dataset (11.85), indicating its role in stress response pathways, while Quercetin emerged as a high-priority drug candidate due to its strong affinity for EGFR and SRC as these targets linked to gut barrier dysfunction [33]. The difference between models and datasets underscores the importance of integrating multi-source predictions of the compounds for further studies in IBS therapeutics [81].

The deep learning analysis highlights several phytochemicals from Indian medicinal plants with the binding affinity for both identified and emerging IBS-related targets. Butein, shows high affinity for EGFR, suggesting anti-inflammatory benefits extend to emerging stress-response pathways like MAPK8 [62,

69]. Notably, tylophorindine exhibits strong binding to JUN, exhibiting its potential role in visceral pain modulation, with crossover effects on novel targets FOS (pain perception) and MAPT (gut-brain axis dysfunction) [41, 78]. These phytochemicals are specifically valuable as they combine traditional medicinal use for GI disorders with a multi-target approach. For instance, tylophorindine's dual potential for JUN and MAPT modulation could be helpful in therapies targeting the gut-brain axis, while quercetin's polypharmacology may simultaneously improve barrier function and reduce inflammation [76].

In this study, a systems-wide multi-layered computational analysis was performed to screen potential drug candidates and therapeutic targets for IBS. JUN was also identified as an important hub gene, as it is involved in IBS pathophysiology through its ability to modulate intestinal inflammation, epithelial barrier function, and stress signaling [28]. For further evidence of this observation, two cutting-edge deep learning models—DeepDTA and DeepDGC were designed on independent compounds–target interaction data sets [60]. Both models reproducibly predicted a moderate-affinity interaction of camptothecin with JUN, confirming JUN as a key molecular target and camptothecin as a potential therapeutic candidate. Additionally, molecular docking was done with a binding energy of -6.1 kcal/mol between JUN and camptothecin. The 2D interaction pattern reflected a stabilizing hydrogen bond with LYS A:309, a hydrophobic π-*alkyl* interaction with VAL A:312, and a single unfavorable donor-donor interaction, reflecting an overall favorable binding conformation. These interactions imply that camptothecin was likely to modulate the transcriptional activity of JUN effectively, possibly inhibiting the pro-inflammatory signaling cascades involved in IBS [83]. Although molecular dynamics simulations might further clarify the binding stability and conformational adaptability, convergence among data from network pharmacology, deep learning-based predictions, and structure-based docking provides a strong explanation for the possible repurposing of camptothecin as an anti-inflammatory agent against IBS targeting JUN. This integrative framework underscores the value of combining AI-driven prediction models with traditional docking and systems biology to identify novel therapeutic strategies for disorders like IBS [85].

Camptothecin, a natural topoisomerase I inhibitor from camptotheca acuminata, has shown emerging application of anticancer properties, especially in the regulation of gut well-being [82]. camptothecin was shown in preclinical models to drastically modify the gut microbiota composition, a feature with therapeutic applications for irritable bowel syndrome (IBS) [49]. By affecting microbial populations, camptothecin may restore microbial balance and improve gastrointestinal function. In addition, it seems to affect the gut-brain axis via neuroimmune mechanisms. In particular, it may decrease enteric neuronal inflammation and visceral hypersensitivity, which are central characteristics in the pathophysiology of IBS [49, 68]. These actions are believed to result from its capacity to inhibit NF-κB signaling and downregulate pro-inflammatory cytokines, thus regulating neuroimmune interactions in the enteric nervous system and providing relief from symptoms in IBS patients [68].

Camptothecin, quercetin, and butein are all derived from Indian medicinal plants that are recognized in traditional medicine systems for treating inflammatory and gastrointestinal conditions. Their pharmacological profiles and multi-target docking results strongly support their potential for use in polyherbal formulations or combinatorial therapies against IBS. This evidence supports the rationale for developing a multi-component phytotherapeutic formulation combining camptothecin, quercetin, and butein, leveraging their multi-target effects and traditional usage in Indian medicine. Such a formulation could be used to treat the complex and multifactorial nature of IBS by modulating inflammation, oxidative stress, and epithelial dysfunction.

Conclusion

Using an integrated network pharmacology method, this study effectively investigated the molecular mechanisms of bioactive substances from Indian medicinal plants against irritable bowel syndrome (IBS). Using protein-protein interaction (PPI) network analysis, 69 common targets were found among more than 750 plant-derived chemicals and genes linked to IBS. Using Cytoscape plugins like CytoNCA, CytoHubba, and MCODE, core targets including EGFR, AKT1, JUN, SRC, and others were identified, indicating the role of kinase-related pathways, oxidative stress, and inflammatory signaling in the pathophysiology of IBS. Key biological processes and signaling networks were revealed using Gene Ontology (GO) and KEGG pathway analyses, which validated these findings. Strong binding interactions between specific drugs and key IBS targets were confirmed by molecular docking studies conducted to evaluate treatment potential. By integrating deep learning models (DeepDTA and DeepDGC) trained on the KIBA and DAVIS datasets, more improvement was made. For targets like JUN and EGFR, the results consistently revealed strong binding affinity estimates; prevalent molecules across models were found to be camptothecin and tylophorinidine. Significantly, the DAVIS-based models displayed relatively lesser affinities, indicating possible limitations because of the limited dataset size, whereas the DeepDTA-KIBA and DeepDGC-KIBA models showed robust binding predictions. Nevertheless, the fact that JUN is consistently predicted to be a central target by all four deep learning frameworks supports its function as a key regulator in IBS and attests to the dependability of the combined strategy.

In conclusion, our study showed that a thorough approach to finding new treatment options for IBS can be achieved by integrating network pharmacology, molecular docking, and deep learning-based predictions. It emphasizes the potential of incorporating AI-driven models to speed up and improve target identification, as well as the therapeutic potential of Indian medicinal herbs. The development of mechanism-based treatments for IBS is eventually aided by these discoveries, which open the door for more focused and effective drug discovery strategies.

References

[1] Aguilera-Lizarraga, J., Hussein, H., & Boeckxstaens, G. E. (2022). Immune activation in irritable bowel syndrome: what is the evidence? *Nature Reviews Immunology*, 22(11), 674–686.

[2] Aman, L. O. (2025). Prediction of binding affinity for ErbB inhibitors using deep neural network model with morgan fingerprints as features. arXiv preprint arXiv:2501.05607.

[3] Vivek-Ananth, R. P., Mohanraj, K., Sahoo, A. K., & Samal, A. (2023). IMPPAT 2.0: an enhanced and expanded phytochemical atlas of Indian medicinal plants. ACS omega, 8(9), 8827–8845.

[4] Balakrishnan, M., & Kenworthy, A. K. (2024). Lipid peroxidation drives liquid–liquid phase separation and disrupts raft protein partitioning in biological membranes. *Journal of the American Chemical Society*, 146(2), 1374–1387.

[5] Ballester, P. J., & Mitchell, J. B. (2010). A machine learning approach to predicting protein–ligand binding affinity with applications to molecular docking. *Bioinformatics*, 26(9), 1169–1175.

[6] Brenner, D. M., Ladewski, A. M., & Kinsinger, S. W. (2024). Development and current state of digital therapeutics for irritable bowel syndrome. *Clinical Gastroenterology and Hepatology*, 22(2), 222–234.

[7] Camilleri, M. (2021). Diagnosis and treatment of irritable bowel syndrome: a review. *JAMA*, 325(9), 865–877.

[8] Chaudhari, S., Khemani, B., Patil, S., & Gupta, J. (2024). Genome sequence analysis and drug-target interaction prediction using deep learning. In International Conference on Innovative Computing and Communication, (pp. 569–587). Singapore: Springer Nature Singapore.

[9] Chen, C., Gong, X., Yang, X., Shang, X., Du, Q., Liao, Q., et al. (2019). The roles of estrogen and estrogen receptors in gastrointestinal disease. *Oncology letters*, 18(6), 5673–5680.

[10] Chen, R., Liu, X., Jin, S., Lin, J., & Liu, J. (2018). Machine learning for drug-target interaction prediction. *Molecules*, 23(9), 2208.

[11] Chen, Y., Chen, L., Huang, S., Yang, L., Wang, L., Yang, F., et al. (2024). Predicting novel biomarkers for early diagnosis and dynamic severity monitoring of human ulcerative colitis. *Frontiers in Genetics*, 15, 1429482.

[12] Daina, A., Michielin, O., & Zoete, V. (2019). SwissTargetPrediction: updated data and new features for efficient prediction of protein targets of small molecules. *Nucleic acids research*, 47(W1), W357–W364.

[13] Dénes-Fazakas, L., Simon, B., Hartvég, Á., Kovács, L., Dulf, É. H., Szilágyi, L., et al. (2024). Physical activity detection for diabetes mellitus patients using recurrent neural networks. *Sensors*, 24(8), 2412.

[14] Dey, S. (2023). Prediction of melting temperature of organic molecules using machine learning (Master's thesis, Norwegian University of Life Sciences). Norwegian University of Life Sciences repository. https://hdl.handle.net/11250/3079871

[15] Gordon-Rodriguez, E., Loaiza-Ganem, G., Pleiss, G., & Cunningham, J. P. (2020). Uses and abuses of the cross-entropy loss: Case studies in modern deep learning. Proceedings on "I Can't Believe It's Not Better!" at NeurIPS Workshops, PMLR 137, 1-10

[16] Dubey, S. R., Singh, S. K., & Chaudhuri, B. B. (2022). Activation functions in deep learning: a comprehensive survey and benchmark. *Neurocomputing*, 503, 92–108.

[17] Dudzińska, E., Grabrucker, A. M., Kwiatkowski, P., Sitarz, R., & Sienkiewicz, M. (2023). The importance of visceral hypersensitivity in irritable bowel syndrome—plant metabolites in IBS treatment. *Pharmaceuticals*, 16(10), 1405.

[18] Eijsbouts, C., Zheng, T., Kennedy, N. A., Bonfiglio, F., Anderson, C. A., Moutsianas, L., et al. (2021). Genome-wide analysis of 53,400 people with irritable bowel syndrome highlights shared genetic pathways with mood and anxiety disorders. *Nature genetics*, 53(11), 1543–1552.

[19] Ford, A. C., Sperber, A. D., Corsetti, M., & Camilleri, M. (2020). Functional gastrointestinal disorders 2 irritable bowel syndrome. *Lancet*, 396(10263), 1675–1688.

[20] Fu, Y., Fang, Y., Gong, S., Xue, T., Wang, P., She, L., et al. (2023). Deep learning-based network pharmacology for exploring the mechanism of licorice for the treatment of COVID-19. *Scientific Reports*, 13(1), 5844.

[21] Gajjar, D., Thakkar, J., Patel, P. K., & Sagar, S. R. (2025). Phytochemistry, ethnopharmacology and novel formulations based approaches for the treatment of irritable bowel syndrome: a comprehensive review. *Phytochemistry Reviews*, 24(1), 701–738.

[22] Gao, J., Cao, B., Zhao, R., Li, H., Xu, Q., & Wei, B. (2023). Critical signaling transduction pathways and intestinal barrier: implications for pathophysiology and therapeutics. *Pharmaceuticals*, 16(9), 1216.

[23] Gao, Z., Fu, L., Yu, H., & Liang, J. (2024). To explore the mechanism of shenling baizhu san in the treatment of diarrheal irritable bowel syndrome based on network pharmacology and molecular docking technology. In 2024 IEEE International Conference on Bioinformatics and Biomedicine (BIBM), (pp. 4630–4636). IEEE.

[24] Gordon-Rodriguez, E., Loaiza-Ganem, G., Pleiss, G., & Cunningham, J. P. (2020). Uses and abuses of the cross-entropy loss: Case studies in modern deep learning.

[25] Guan, L., Yang, H., Cai, Y., Sun, L., Di, P., Li, W., et al. (2019). ADMET-score–a comprehensive scoring function for evaluation of chemical drug-likeness. *Medchemcomm*, 10(1), 148–157.

[26] Gupta, P. K., Pal, Y., Kumar, P., Gupta, S., Singh, S. D., & Tiwari, S. B. (2024). A critical review on computational techniques through in silico assisted drug design. *International Journal of Pharmaceutical Investigation*, 14(4), 1035–1041.

[27] Halayal, R. Y., Bagewadi, Z. K., Khan, T. Y., & Shamsudeen, S. M. (2025). Investigating compounds from Basella alba for their antioxidant, anti-inflammatory, and anticancer properties through in vitro and network pharmacology, molecular simulation approach. *Green Chemistry Letters and Reviews*, 18(1), 2481945.

[28] Hannemann, N., Jordan, J., Paul, S., Reid, S., Baenkler, H. W., Sonnewald, S., et al. (2017). The AP-1 transcription factor c-Jun promotes arthritis by regulating cyclooxy-

genase-2 and arginase-1 expression in macrophages. *The Journal of Immunology*, 198(9), 3605–3614.

[29] Hao, L., Alkry, L. T., Alattar, A., Faheem, M., Alshaman, R., Shah, F. A., et al. (2022). Ibrutinib attenuated DSS-induced ulcerative colitis, oxidative stress, and the inflammatory cascade by modulating the PI3K/Akt and JNK/NF-κB pathways. *Archives of Medical Science: AMS*, 18(3), 805.

[30] Honap, S., Jairath, V., Danese, S., & Peyrin-Biroulet, L. (2024). Navigating the complexities of drug development for inflammatory bowel disease. *Nature Reviews Drug Discovery*, 23(7), 546–562.

[31] Huang, W., Zhang, L., Ma, Y., Yu, S., Lyu, Y., Tong, S., et al. (2025). Unraveling the genetic susceptibility of irritable bowel syndrome: integrative genome-wide analyses in 845 492 individuals: a diagnostic study. *International Journal of Surgery*, 111(1), 210–220.

[32] Jacenik, D., & Krajewska, W. M. (2020). Significance of G protein-coupled estrogen receptor in the pathophysiology of irritable bowel syndrome, inflammatory bowel diseases and colorectal cancer. *Frontiers in Endocrinology*, 11, 390.

[33] Jain, N. K., Tailang, M., Chandrasekaran, B., Khazaleh, N. T., Thangavel, N., Makeen, H. A., et al. (2024). Integrating network pharmacology with molecular docking to rationalize the ethnomedicinal use of Alchornea laxiflora (Benth.) Pax & K. Hoffm. for efficient treatment of depression. *Frontiers in Pharmacology*, 15, 1290398.

[34] Jaiswal, V. K., Barsagade, M., & Sinha, J. (2024). A comprehensive review on cardiovascular disease detection, risk assessment, and treatment using a network pharmacology model. *Integrative Biomedical Research*, 8(1), 1–9.

[35] Jejurikar, B. L., & Rohane, S. H. (2014). Drug designing in discovery studio. *Asian Journal of Research in Chemistry*, 14(2), 135–138.

[36] Ke, W., Wu, J., Li, H., Huang, S., Li, H., Wang, Y., et al. (2024). Network pharmacology and experimental validation to explore the mechanism of Changji'an formula against irritable bowel syndrome with predominant diarrhea. *Heliyon*, 10(12), e33102.

[37] Kim, S., Thiessen, P. A., Bolton, E. E., Chen, J., Fu, G., Gindulyte, A., et al. (2015). PubChem substance and compound databases. *Nucleic Acids Research*, 44(D1), D1202–D1213.

[38] Kondapuram, S. K., Sarvagalla, S., & Coumar, M. S. (2021). Docking-based virtual screening using PyRx tool: autophagy target Vps34 as a case study. In Methods in Molecular Biology, (pp. 463–477).

[39] Lagorce, D., Douguet, D., Miteva, M. A., & Villoutreix, B. O. (2017). Computational analysis of calculated physicochemical and ADMET properties of protein-protein interaction inhibitors. *Scientific Reports*, 7(1), 46277.

[40] Lee, S. H., Seo, G. S., Jin, X. Y., Ko, G., & Sohn, D. H. (2007). Butein blocks tumor necrosis factor α-induced interleukin 8 and matrix metalloproteinase 7 production by inhibiting p38 kinase and osteopontin mediated signaling events in HT-29 cells. *Life Sciences*, 81(21-22), 1535–1543.

[41] Lei, L. G., Zhang, Y. Q., & Zhao, Z. Q. (2004). Pain-related aversion and Fos expression in the central nervous system in rats. *Neuroreport*, 15(1), 67–71.

[42] Leite, G., de Freitas Germano, J., Morales, W., Weitsman, S., Barlow, G. M., Parodi, G., et al. (2024). Cytolethal distending toxin B inoculation leads to distinct gut microtypes and IBS-D-like microRNA-mediated gene expression changes in a rodent model. *Gut Microbes*, 16(1), 2293170.

[43] Li, S., Zhou, J., Xu, T., Huang, L., Wang, F., Xiong, H., et al. (2021). Structure-aware interactive graph neural networks for the prediction of protein-ligand binding affinity. In Proceedings of the 27th ACM SIGKDD Conference on Knowledge Discovery and Data Mining (pp. 975–985).

[44] Liao, K. F., Tsai, H. Y., Chen, C. F., Hsu, T. F, Hsu, C. Y., Ho, T. K., et al. (2024). Body constitutions of traditional Chinese medicine caused a significant effect on irritable bowel syndrome. *Journal of the Chinese Medical Association*, 87(5), 558–566.

[45] Liu, X., Wang, X., Zhang, P., Fang, Y., Liu, Y., Ding, Y., et al. (2023). Intestinal homeostasis in the gut-lung-kidney axis: a prospective therapeutic target in immune-related chronic kidney diseases. *Frontiers in immunology*, 14, 1266792.

[46] López-Villodres, J. A., Escamilla, A., Mercado-Sáenz, S., Alba-Tercedor, C., Rodriguez-Perez, L. M., Arranz-Salas, I., et al. (2023). Microbiome alterations and Alzheimer's disease: Modeling strategies with transgenic mice. *Biomedicines*, 11(7), 1846.

[47] Lyu, Y. L., Zhou, H. F., Yang, J., Wang, F. X., Sun, F., & Li, J. Y. (2022). Biological activities underlying the therapeutic effect of quercetin on inflammatory bowel disease. *Mediators of inflammation*, 2022(1), 5665778.

[48] Mahajan, P., Suri, N., Mehra, R., Gupta, M., Kumar, A., Singh, S. K., et al. (2017). Discovery of novel small molecule EGFR inhibitory leads by structure and ligand-based virtual screening. *Medicinal Chemistry Research*, 26(1), 74–92.

[49] Mahdy, M. S., Azmy, A. F., Dishisha, T., Mohamed, W. R., Ahmed, K. A., Hassan, A., et sal. (2023). Irinotecan-gut microbiota interactions and the capability of probiotics to mitigate Irinotecan-associated toxicity. *BMC Microbiology*, 23(1), 53.

[50] Mete, R., Tulubas, F., Oran, M., Yilmaz, A., Avci, B. A., Yildiz, K., et al. (2013). The role of oxidants and reactive nitrogen species in irritable bowel syndrome: a potential etiological explanation. *Medical Science Monitor: International Medical Journal of Experimental and Clinical Research*, 19, 762.

[51] Mitsuyama, K., Suzuki, A., Tomiyasu, N., Tsuruta, O., Kitazaki, S., Takeda, T., et al. (2006). Pro-inflammatory signaling by Jun-N-terminal kinase in inflammatory bowel disease. *International Journal of Molecular Medicine*, 17(3), 449–455.

[52] Mohamed Abdul Cader, J., Newton, M. H., Rahman, J., Mohamed Abdul Cader, A. J., & Sattar, A. (2024). Ensembling methods for protein-ligand binding affinity prediction. *Scientific Reports*, 14(1), 24447.

[53] Montesinos López, O. A., Montesinos López, A., & Crossa, J. (2022). Overfitting, model tuning, and evaluation of prediction performance. In Multivariate Statistical Machine Learning Methods for Genomic Prediction, (pp. 109–139). Cham: Springer International Publishing.

[54] Nagarajan, S. (2024). Natural remedies for inflammatory bowel disease: a review of medicinal plants and their therapeutic potential. *International Journal of Pharmaceutical Research and Allied Sciences*, 13(1-2024), 1–17.

[55] Neurath, M. F. (2014). Cytokines in inflammatory bowel disease. *Nature Reviews Immunology*, 14(5), 329–342.

[56] Ng, Q. X., Yaow, C. Y. L., Moo, J. R., Koo, S. W. K., Loo, E. X. L., & Siah, K. T. H. (2024). A systematic review of the association between environmental risk factors and the development of irritable bowel syndrome. *Journal of Gastroenterology and Hepatology*, 39(9), 1780–1787.

[57] O'Shea, N. R., & Smith, A. M. (2014). Matrix metalloproteases role in bowel inflammation and inflammatory bowel disease: an up to date review. *Inflammatory Bowel Diseases*, 20(12), 2379–2393.

[58] Öztürk, H., Özgür, A., & Ozkirimli, E. (2018). DeepDTA: deep drug–target binding affinity prediction. *Bioinformatics*, 34(17), i821–i829.

[59] Pang, B., Nijkamp, E., & Wu, Y. N. (2020). Deep learning with tensorflow: a review. *Journal of Educational and Behavioral Statistics*, 45(2), 227–248.

[60] Qi, H., Yu, T., Yu, W., & Liu, C. (2024). Drug–target affinity prediction with extended graph learning-convolutional networks. *BMC Bioinformatics*, 25(1), 75.

[61] Qi, R., Guo, F., & Zou, Q. (2022). String kernels construction and fusion: a survey with bioinformatics application. *Frontiers of Computer Science*, 16(6), 166904.

[62] Rehman, M., Chaudhary, R., Rajput, S., Agarwal, V., Kaushik, A. S., Srivastava, S., et al. (2023). Butein ameliorates chronic stress induced atherosclerosis via targeting anti-inflammatory, anti-fibrotic and BDNF pathways. *Physiology and Behavior*, 267, 114207.

[63] Reyad, M., Sarhan, A. M., & Arafa, M. (2023). A modified Adam algorithm for deep neural network optimization. *Neural Computing and Applications*, 35(23), 17095–17112.

[64] Rozpędek-Kamińska, W., Siwecka, N., Wawrzynkiewicz, A., Wojtczak, R., Pytel, D., Diehl, J. A., et al. (2020). The PERK-dependent molecular mechanisms as a novel therapeutic target for neurodegenerative diseases. *International Journal of Molecular Sciences*, 21(6), 2108.

[65] Saad, M. M., Rehmani, M. H., & O'Reilly, R. (2024). Early stopping criteria for training generative adversarial networks in biomedical imaging. In 2024 35th Irish Signals and Systems Conference (ISSC), (pp. 1–7). IEEE.

[66] Schenck Eidam, H., Russell, J., Raha, K., DeMartino, M., Qin, D., Guan, H. A., et al. (2018). Discovery of a first-in-class gut-restricted RET kinase inhibitor as a clinical candidate for the treatment of IBS. *ACS Medicinal Chemistry Letters*, 9(7), 623–628.

[67] Shaheen, S., & Sarwar, S. (2024). Herbal wisdom through time: the evolution of medicinal plants utilization. In Plants as Medicine and Aromatics, (pp. 343–356). CRC Press.

[68] Shatunova, S., Aktar, R., Peiris, M., Lee, J. Y. P., Vetter, I., & Starobova, H. (2024). The role of the gut microbiome in neuroinflammation and chemotherapy-induced peripheral neuropathy. *European Journal of Pharmacology*, 979, 176818.

[69] Shrestha, J., Limbu, K. R., Chhetri, R. B., Paudel, K. R., Hansbro, P. M., Oh, Y. S., et al. (2024). Antioxidant genes in cancer and metabolic diseases: Focusing on Nrf2, Sestrin, and heme oxygenase 1. *International Journal of Biological Sciences*, 20(12), 4888.

[70] Song, B., Gao, J., Du, H., Chen, Z., & Hu, X. (2018). Aligning multiple PPI networks with representation learning on networks. In 2018 IEEE International Conference on Bioinformatics and Biomedicine (BIBM), (pp. 136–141). IEEE.

[71] Staneva, Y., Iliev, I., Georgieva, S., & Merdjanova, A. (2024). In silico prediction of physicochemical properties and drug-likeness of omega-3 fatty acids. *Ovidius University Annals of Chemistry*, 35(2), 118–125.

[72] Tan, X., Pei, W., Xie, C., Wang, Z., Mao, T., Zhao, X., et al. (2020). Network pharmacology identifies the mechanisms of action of tongxie anchang decoction in the treatment of irritable bowel syndrome with diarrhea predominant. *Evidence-Based Complementary and Alternative Medicine*, 2020(1), 2723705.

[73] Tang, Y., Li, X., Yuan, Y., Zhang, H., Zou, Y., Xu, Z., et al. (2022). Network pharmacology-based predictions of active components and pharmacological mechanisms of Artemisia annua L. for the treatment of the novel Corona virus disease 2019 (COVID-19). *BMC Complementary Medicine and Therapies*, 22(1), 56.

[74] Tatachar, A. V. (2021). Comparative assessment of regression models based on model evaluation metrics. *International Research Journal of Engineering and Technology (IRJET)*, 8(09), 2395–0056.

[75] Tiwari, B. R., Inamdar, M. N., Orfali, R., Alshehri, A., Alghamdi, A., Almadani, M. E., et al. (2023). Comparative evaluation of the potential anti-spasmodic activity of Piper longum, Piper nigrum, Terminalia bellerica, Terminalia chebula, and Zingiber officinale in experimental animals. *Saudi Pharmaceutical Journal*, 31(9), 101705.

[76] Uyanga, V. A., Amevor, F. K., Liu, M., Cui, Z., Zhao, X., & Lin, H. (2021). Potential implications of citrulline and quercetin on gut functioning of monogastric animals and humans: a comprehensive review. *Nutrients*, 13(11), 3782.

[77] Vivek-Ananth, R. P., Mohanraj, K., Sahoo, A. K., & Samal, A. (2023). IMPPAT 2.0: an enhanced and expanded phytochemical atlas of Indian medicinal plants. *ACS Omega*, 8(9), 8827–8845.

[78] Wang, B., Bai, X., Yang, Y., & Yang, H. (2025). Possible linking and treatment between Parkinson's disease and inflammatory bowel disease: a study of Mendelian randomization based on gut–brain axis. *Journal of Translational Medicine*, 23(1), 45.

[79] Wang, S., Zhou, S., Han, Z., Yu, B., Xu, Y., Lin, Y., et al. (2024). From gut to brain: understanding the role of microbiota in inflammatory bowel disease. *Frontiers in Immunology*, 15, 1384270.

[80] Wang, S. T., Cui, W. Q., Pan, D., Jiang, M., Chang, B., & Sang, L. X. (2020). Tea polyphenols and their chemopreventive and therapeutic effects on colorectal cancer. *World Journal of Gastroenterology*, 26(6), 562.

[81] Wei, J., Zhuo, L., Fu, X., Zeng, X., Wang, L., Zou, Q., et al. (2024). DrugReAlign: a multisource prompt framework for drug repurposing based on large language models. *BMC Biology*, 22(1), 226.

[82] Yang, L. Y., Lei, S. Z., Xu, W. J., Lai, Y., Zhang, Y., Wang, Y., et al. (2025). Rising above: Exploring the therapeutic potential of natural product-based compounds in human cancer treatment. *Traditional Medicine Research*, 10, 18.

[83] Yang, Y., Xiao, G., Cheng, P., Zeng, J., & Liu, Y. (2023). Protective application of Chinese herbal compounds and formulae in intestinal inflammation in humans and animals. *Molecules*, 28(19), 6811.

[84] Ye, Y., Zhang, X., Kong, M., Hu, H., & Xu, Z. (2024). PHCDTI: a multichannel parallel high-order feature crossover model for DTIs prediction. *Expert Systems with Applications*, 256, 124873.

[85] Yeshi, K., Jamtsho, T., & Wangchuk, P. (2024). Current treatments, emerging therapeutics, and natural remedies for inflammatory bowel disease. *Molecules*, 29(16), 3954.

[86] You, J., McLeod, R. D., & Hu, P. (2019). Predicting drug-target interaction network using deep learning model. *Computational Biology and Chemistry*, 80, 90–101.

[87] Zhang, H., Liu, X., Cheng, W., Wang, T., & Chen, Y. (2024). Prediction of drug-target binding affinity based on deep learning models. *Computers in Biology and Medicine*, 174, 108435.

[88] Zhang, R., Zou, N., Li, J., Lv, H., Wei, J., Fang, X. C., et al. (2011). Elevated expression of c-fos in central nervous system correlates with visceral hypersensitivity in irritable bowel syndrome (IBS): a new target for IBS treatment. *International Journal of Colorectal Disease*, 26(8), 1035–1044.

[89] Zhao, Q., Xiao, F., Yang, M., Li, Y., & Wang, J. (2019). AttentionDTA: prediction of drug–target binding affinity using attention model. In 2019 IEEE International Conference on Bioinformatics and Biomedicine (BIBM), (pp. 1–8).

39 ECOGENESIS: AI Powered platform for surplus food and electronic waste management

Lakshanya S[1,a] and S. Bhama[2,b]

[1]Student, Department of Computer Applications, PSG College of Technology, India

[2]Assistant Professor (Sl.Gr.), Department of Computer Applications, PSG College of Technology, India

Abstract

EcoGenesis is an AI solution which helps solve issues related to excess food and e-waste, it is an intelligent tech and it's an avenue towards the UN SDGs. It contributes to Goal 2 (Zero Hunger), Goal 12 (Responsible Consumption and Production) and Goal 13 (Climate Action) by advancing sustainable waste management practices. For food leftover, EcoGenesis connects what the consumer has wasted back to Food Banks and lets waste play a vital part of fighting hunger. They also offer convenient compost options for food recycling. In electronic waste, the platform employs image-based identification to recognize products and recommend possible reuse or recycling. EcoGenesis encourages people to incorporate eco habits into their daily lives by providing a map feature to locate nearby recycling centers easily and make the recycling process more user friendly and convenient, for everyone, in the community effort to reduce waste and keep our environment cleaner.

Keywords: Electronic waste recycling, surplus food, sustainable waste management

Introduction

With the world today facing pressing issues of environmental problems and responsible use of resources, EcoGenesis seeks to give practical solutions. EcoGenesis tackles two huge issues— food surplus and electronic waste, by mashing them together under one easy, tech-supported solution. Rather than creating individual tools for both issues, it provides one integrated platform that simplifies doing something about it. And when it comes to E-waste, the platform uses technologies such as YOLOv5 or CNN's. These technologies enable the system to infer from images and identify items such as smartphones or keyboards automatically and also propose actions like reuse or recycle as per item category in order to minimize disposal risks lined with E waste such as ground and water pollution.

In another alternative, EcoGenesis also operates an excess food donation center. Individuals, restaurants, or companies can sign up for food otherwise headed for wastage. The donations are then matched with approved organizations such as food banks, shelters, or NGOs. This not only minimizes wastage of food but also ensures that consumable food reaches the intended individuals who are actually in need of the food, thus establishing justice and care for society.

To make the process easy to understand and user-friendly, EcoGenesis has an open-tracking system, whereby users can track their activity of recycling and donating. Additionally, an in-app geolocation functionality helps users locate recycling facilities near them, making waste disposal with due measure an easy option and also promotes sustainability through tips on composting. Combining these AI-based functionalities with effective sustainability programs, EcoGenesis offers an extensible and adaptive solution for waste minimization, conservation of the environment, and social welfare generation among communities.

Literature Review

In food donation research, Talati et.al. [5] explained that recovering edible food for human use acts as a form of urban resource reuse, returning items to their original purpose instead of letting them go to waste. There are a number of projects being done across the globe, but due to the lack of information, scientific literature regarding food donation activities provides a platform bridging donors with non-governmental organizations (NGOs). This medium introduces the increasing issue of food wastage and highlights its effect on society.

[a]23mx311@psgtech.ac.in, [b]sba.mca@psgtech.ac.in

DOI: 10.1201/9781003770435-39

This study has been conducted to assist in minimizing the problem of food wastage. This article suggests a food donation platform that brings two groups of individuals together. The platform serves as a link between people with surplus food and those in need, making the donation process more efficient and direct.

Through this app, one is able to give food items depending on one's capacity, while organizations can list their requirements if any. Once a message is posted, interested orphanages can respond to the donor and communicate directly. The prime advantages were food wastage reduction and fast, effective transport of food, which could prove beneficial to thousands of hungry people. For correct tracking of destinations, it would require a constant link.

Abou Baker et al. [1] studied the significance of automating recycling of e-waste and proposed a transfer learning (TL) approach for smartphone classification. They utilized a pre- trained AlexNet model, which was fine-tuned to fit the task. To mitigate overfitting, data augmentation techniques were employed. A hybrid model, combining residual nets and inception modules, is used for classifying features of smartphones.

A study by Mandal et al. [4] discusses the high levels of food wastage in India, where nearly 25% of edible food is discarded during various market stages. To tackle this, they introduced an Android-based platform that connects donors allowing organizations to list required items while seekers can claim available donations. The system ensures efficient food distribution to orphanages and elderly care homes, helping reduce hunger-related issues. Initially, the app was limited to Android Gingerbread, but this compatibility constraint is no longer relevant.

Geetha et al. [3] proposed a waste classification approach using ensemble neural networks to enhance waste segregation accuracy and efficiency. By integrating multiple neural models, the system enhances prediction reliability and automates waste categorization. The results emphasize that ensemble learning is superior to conventional machine learning algorithms and thus has the potential to act as a solution for minimizing labor waste sorting and promoting sustainable waste management strategies.

Chen et al. [2] provided an instance of using YOLOv5 to perform object detection and identify the positions for teleoperated robotic systems. Their adjustment is aimed at optimizing anchor box selection, improving feature extraction, and post-processing for more accurate detection. The experiment illustrates the efficiency of the improved YOLOv5 model in applications and makes it useful for industries that need accurate object recognition.

Although such solutions increase operational efficiency, issues like real-time tracking and system integration remain. Although better AI models have enhanced waste classification, practical application awaits further improvement. This research hopes to close the above loopholes by creating an integrated platform for AI and real-time tracking that integrates food and e- waste management in an efficient manner.

Technology Review

EcoGenesis was designed using React. js to develop a neat, easy-to-use interface that looks good on any device. Firebase is introduced to handle real-time actions such as login, food donation updates, and to identify e-waste images, since it makes these operations in a fast and resourceful way. To handle the server side, a developer would use Node. js and Express. js were used. These tools make it possible to send and receive data (such as recognizing uploaded images that depict the type of e-waste or specifying the user's position to display the nearest recycling centers.

Image detection is handled using AI models built with TensorFlow, Keras, and YOLOv5. These models look at photos and figure out what type of electronic item is in them, then suggest how to recycle it. To make this even more helpful, Google Maps API is included to guide users to the closest food banks or recycling spots. The detection system is trained using both PyTorch and TensorFlow for better accuracy. All development was done in Visual Studio Code, which made it easier to test and organize the code during the project.

Proposed Methodology

EcoGenesis is an easy-to-use platform that exists to solve two significant issues of the day: a. electronic waste management and b. surplus food reduction. Rather than treating these two problems separately, EcoGenesis consolidates them into one solution, simplifying the process for individuals and entities to act. EcoGenesis utilizes AI software such as YOLOv5 and Convolutional Neural Networks (CNNs) to classify the images provided by users.

When a person posts a picture of an electric product, the service recognizes what it is and indicates local recycling facilities based on location services. In addition to e- waste disposal, EcoGenesis also simplifies food donation. It links people and companies to nearby food banks and charity organizations that are willing to take more food. The platform relies on location information to enable users to find the proper facilities where they can donate and arrange pickups. Ingeneral, EcoGenesis persuades individuals to utilize resources more efficiently and promotes a lifestyle that is centered on waste reduction and environmental conservation through daily actions.

System Architecture

System architecture offers a common platform for e-waste management and food donation. It facilitates user registration, tracking of donations, image-based e-waste recognition, and location-aware suggestions for recycling centers.

The above Figure 39.1 illustrates a user-centric platform aimed at managing food donations and e-waste. The system begins with user sign-up and provides two main features: donating food and managing e-waste. Users can fill out a form to contribute food and monitor its status. For e-waste, non-technical users upload images for AI-based detection, while technical users fill out a registration form and locate nearby recycling centers. Built-in location services suggest relevant centers, and users can

schedule visits. Profiles display eco-contribution data to encourage user involvement.

The diagram shown in Figure 39.2 presents the process flow for the food bank administrator module. It begins with user authentication through login or registration, providing access to the main dashboard. From this interface, the admin can handle food donation entries, arrange pickups, and review donation insights through analytics. This organized structure improves communication between users and administrators, helping to efficiently manage food donations and reduce overall waste.

Surplus Food Donation

EcoGenesis is a simple-to-use website that connects people and businesses with organizations that will take food donations, such as food banks and homeless shelters. Excess food can be donated in a straightforward manner instead of letting it go to waste. The website promises to deliver edible food to those who really need it. Donors just fill in a simple donation form and send it on directly to cooperating organizations. The website also offers education material to instill the practice of composting as well as reducing food waste. It inculcates responsible consumption through education material. An inbuilt tracker enables users to trace their donations from submission to delivery. This makes the process clear and ensures users are assured.

The interface depicted in Figures 39.3 and 39.4 indicates how donations of food are registered and transported. EcoGenesis promotes support from within the community and use of the environment in a sustainable manner. The website allows users to donate excess food by providing a specific form that captures important information like the kind

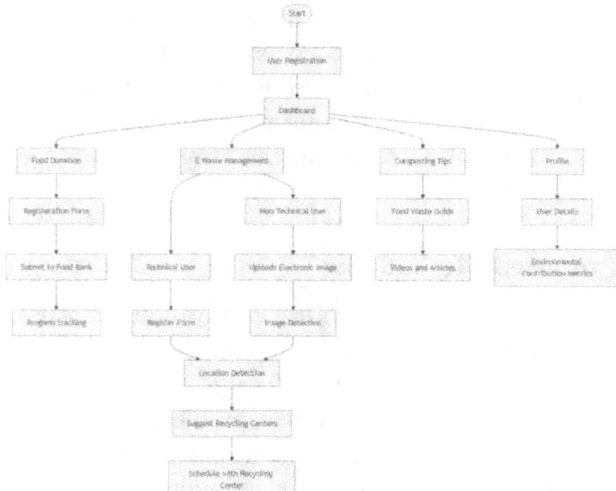

Figure 39.1 System flow diagram for surplus food donation and e-waste recycling

Source: Author

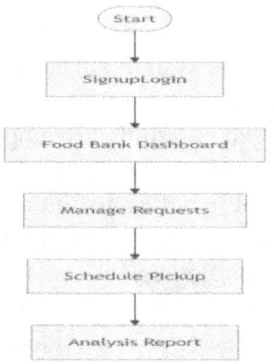

Figure 39.2 System flow diagram for food bank user

Source: Author

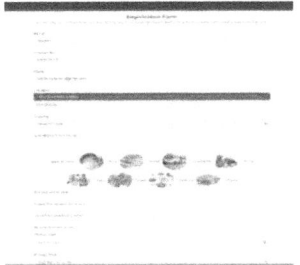

Figure 39.3 Food donation form
Source: Author

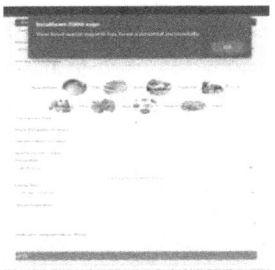

Figure 39.4 Submission confirmation
Source: Author

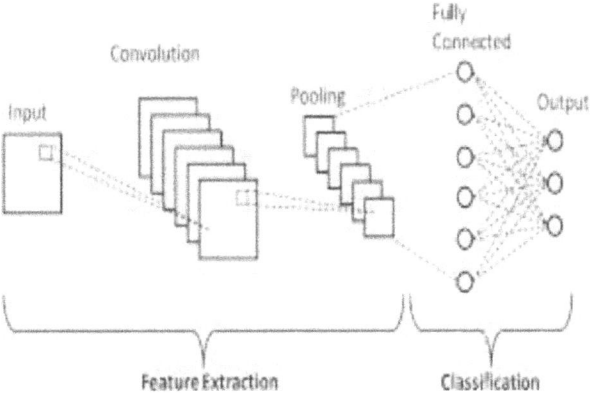

Figure 39.5 Architecture of CNN
Source: Author [6]

and amount of food. After submission, the request is forwarded to respective food aid organizations for action. To ensure transparency, EcoGenesis has a tracking facility to update users about the status of their donation. This helps users stay informed and interested in the process, leading to trust and sustained participation in the donation.

The Classification Algorithms

This section introduces the algorithms applied for e-waste recognition, selected due to their capability of guaranteeing proper waste recognition.

Convolutional Neural Networks

Convolutional neural network is a deep learning structure well adapted to handle grid-structured information, e.g., images, and is very effective when handling visual data. It has broad applications in image classification, object detection, and feature extraction. Rather than working with the whole image at a time, CNNs divide the image into smaller regions and pick up significant visual characteristics gradually. Figure 39.5 illustrates the architecture of this CNN-based classification procedure.

The CNNs are applied to recognize and sort electronic waste, enhancing recycling effectiveness. The models scan the images by looking for significant features like shape, texture, and patterns in order to differentiate items like mobile phones, laptops, and batteries. The system starts by being presented with an image. The convolutional layer begins by reading the image through filters to recognize significant points like edges and textures. Pooling layers then condense the information by keeping the most significant parts, hence the system becomes faster and requires less. After gathering these features, they are transformed into a single data stream. This is presented to dense layers, which allow the model to recognize patterns and determine what the image is of. Automation enhances accuracy in sorting, human effort is reduced, and recycling is faster and cleaner.

You Only Look Once (YOLOv5)

Object detection model You Only Look Once (YOLOv5) is a state-of-the-art model having strong significance for the rapid classification and detection of e-waste. Compared to traditional techniques that require multistage processes, YOLOv5 directly detects and classifies an object in one step, that is, a single pass through the network, allowing for efficient, fast, and accurate detection. A graphical illustration depicting the workflow and the detection architecture of the model is presented in Figure 39.6.

When an image is uploaded by a user to the EcoGenesis platform, the platform utilizes the strengths of YOLOv5, a state-of-the-art object detection system based on CNNs. The CNN processes the image by decomposing the image into

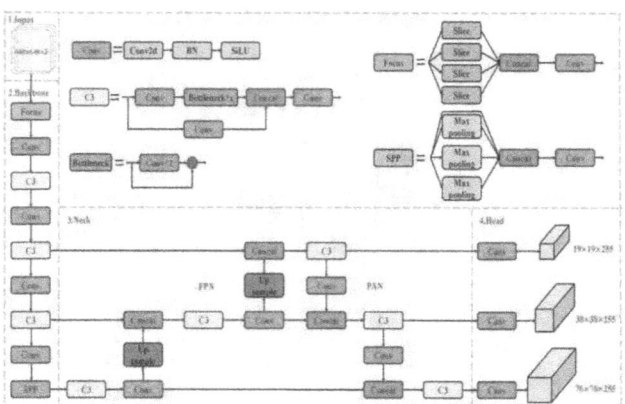

Figure 39.6 Architecture of YOLOv5
Source: Author

Figure 39.7 Dataset collection
Source: Author

visual features like edges, textures, shapes, and patterns that are used in determining the structure and composition of various objects in the image. Utilizing this analysis, YOLOv5 can detect multiple e-waste objects like used mobiles, batteries, wires, and circuit boards simultaneously even if they occur together in one image. It draws bounding boxes around all of them and labels them accordingly with suitable labels, so it becomes very simple to identify various kinds of e-waste. This real-time detection process makes manual identification unnecessary and provides an accelerated, more consistent sorting system. By identifying the type and condition of each product. Finally, YOLOv5 improves the platform's capacity to handle e-waste responsibly and effectively. It enables automatic, smart waste evaluation, assisting users in supporting safer disposal methods with less environmental harm. By introducing such a smart detection feature, EcoGenesis achieves speed, accuracy, and sustainability in the core of electronic waste management.

Data collection

The data collection lies at the center of the e-waste detection model. Images are first collected from two sources: the Kaggle database and manually taken pictures of electronic waste. 1490 RGB images are collected, which are real-life e-waste products. Numerous data augmentation methods are applied which involve transformation of the original images. Data augmentation increases the dataset to 5408 RGB images, providing the model with more varied examples to learn from.

After augmentation, the above Figure 39.7 contains a dataset divided in a systematic way into three sets: training, validation, and testing sets. The dataset is composed of two directories: images and labels. The image folder includes the input visuals, bounding box coordinates. The training set is used to train the model, while the validation set helps refine its performance. The test set is used to examine the overall performance of the model after training and validation are complete. Metrics such as precision, recall, and mean Average Precision (mAP) are used to measure and evaluate the accuracy of the model.

The processed dataset ensures that the model learns effectively across different classes. Once trained, the model can accurately detect and classify different types of e-waste items from new input images. A few examples of the original input images used in training are shown in Figure 39.8. This comprehensive data preparation pipeline ensures robust model performance and supports efficient e-waste management through automated classifications.

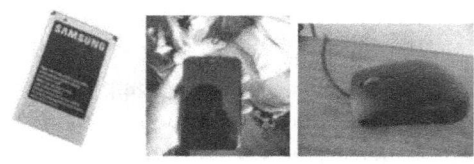

Phone Battery Mobile Phone Mouse

Keyboard Printer Microwave

Figure 39.8 Sample input images from dataset
Source: Author

Data Preprocessing

To achieve accurate e-waste detection, the dataset undergoes a structured preprocessing phase before training the YOLOv5 and CNN models. In Figure 39.9, the first step is image annotation, where each e-waste item is manually labeled using tools like labeling. bounding boxes are drawn around the objects, and class labels are assigned to distinguish different e-waste categories. This labeling ensures the model learns to identify and classify objects effectively during detection.

Once annotated, image normalization is carried out by normalizing pixel values between 0 and 1. Standardization of the dataset is achieved, inconsistencies in lighting are minimized, and computational efficiency is enhanced. Normalized images smooth data processing by the neural network, hence enhancing object detection accuracy. Lastly, the dataset is split into training and test sets consisting of 80% images employed in training and 20% reserved for tests. The split allows the model to generalize optimally to properly perform e-waste classification and detection.

Experiments and Results

The model is trained and tested on 1490 RGB images. The performance of the model is measured in terms of mean mAP, F1-score, precision, and recall. The mean mAP metric is measured by checking how well predicted bounding boxes match ground truth boxes. The below Figures 39.10–39.12 depict training of 1490 image dataset and reaching 100% detection accuracy of images.

Precision (the ratio of true positives to all predicted positives) and recall (the ratio of true positives to all actual positives) were used to evaluate classification accuracy and detection completeness, respectively. The Average Precision (AP) was computed by integrating precision-recall curves across multiple thresholds, and the mAP (mean of AP across all classes) served as the primary benchmark. Furthermore, the F1-score (harmonic mean of recall and precision) measured the overall predictive balance of the model. To train, the model was executed 50 times by epochs, so it executed through the entire dataset 50 times in order to make its learning stronger. Through each iteration, it updated its internal parameters to minimize prediction error. It was driven by a loss function, and with each mistake, the model learned and became better. Thus, the train degradation reduced gradually and the performance of the model significantly improved in the recognition and identification of the e-waste. The successive

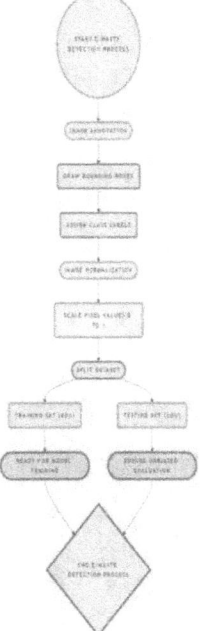

Figure 39.9 Data preprocessing flow
Source: Author

Figure 39.10 YOLOv5 model setup and training configuration.
Source: Training screenshot captured from the project system

Figure 39.11 Completed training setup for object detection
Source: Author

Figure 39.12 Image analysis with full data loading and model setup.

Source: Training screenshot captured from the project system

learning process made the model generalize more over new data.

The Figures 39.13 and 39.14 below show the results of e-waste detection using real-time images. The system is also capable of identifying non-e-waste items and appropriately displays a message indicating that the detected object is not e-waste.

The Figures 39.15 and 39.16 below show that after detecting e-waste, nearby recycling centers are suggested on the map for the user.

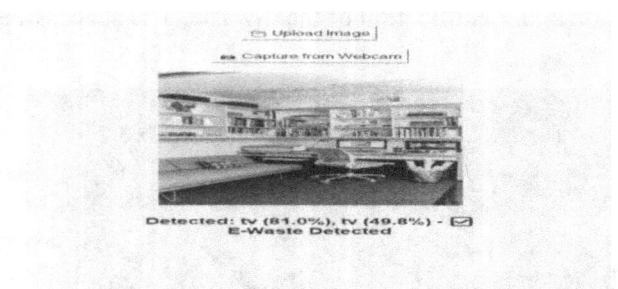

Figure 39.13 Image uploaded successfully with an e-waste item detected as a television

Source: Author

Figure 39.14 Image uploaded successfully with an e-waste item detected as a keyboard

Source: Author

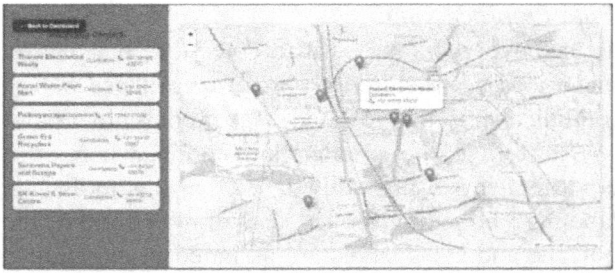

Figure 39.15 Nearby recycling centers and their contacts are shown on the map

Source: Author

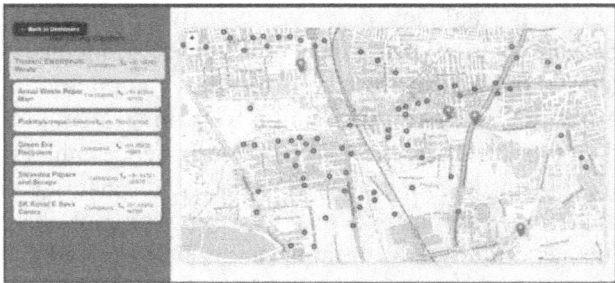

Figure 39.16 User selects the center and its contact information

Source: Author

The results demonstrated in Figures 39.13–39.16 highlight the effectiveness of the system in accurately identifying e- waste items in real-time. The system detects e-waste and suggests nearby recycling centers to the user, allowing them to select a center and contact it for further recycling action. The performance of the model is evaluated in terms of major parameters like mean mAP, Precision, Recall, and F1-score.

In Figure 39.17, the performance metrics clearly demonstrate the reliability and accuracy of the YOLOv5 model in detecting and classifying e-waste. Its ability to consistently improve through training

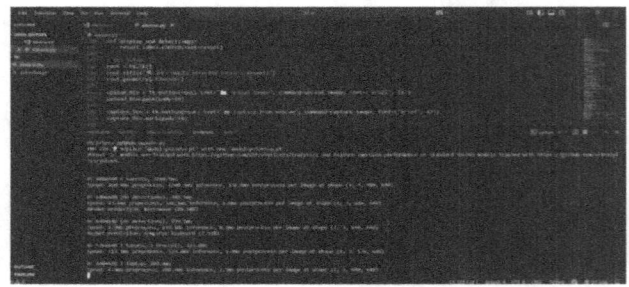

Figure 39.17 Metrics of the detected images

Source: Author

and deliver accurate results ensures it can significantly enhance automated e-waste management systems, promoting efficiency and sustainability.

Conclusion

The possibilities for AI to minimize waste are enormous, and EcoGenesis is a solution that could make the technology affordable and within the realm of actual needs like recycling e-waste and donating extra food. With clever machine learning tools, not only does it do a truly excellent job recognizing electronic stuff, it also matches excess food with the people and organizations that can utilize it best. With functionalities such as integrated location tracking, it's simpler for users to know what to do and do it, whether they're looking to drop off e-waste or donate food. By merging a focus on both e-waste and food management into a single, easy-to-use system, addresses global sustainability issues in a common-sense approach. As the platform matures and gains traction, it has the potential to make a real difference in our society and environment.

References

[1] Abou Baker, N., Szabo-Müller, P. & Handmann, U. (2021). E-waste classification using deep learning and transfer learning techniques. *EAI Endorsed Transactions on Smart Cities*, 5. https://doi.org/10.4108/eai.16-4-2021.169337

[2] Chen, Z., Li, X., Wang, L., Shi, Y., Sun, Z. & Sun, W. (2022). An object detection and localization method based on improved YOLOv5 for the teleoperated robot. *Applied Sciences*, 12(22), 11441. https://doi.org/10.3390/app122211441

[3] Geetha, S., Saha, J., Dasgupta, I., Bera, R., Lawal, I.A. & Kadry, S. (2022). Design of a waste management system using ensemble neural networks. *Designs*, 6(2), 27. https://doi.org/10.3390/designs6020027

[4] Mandal, K., Jadhav, S. & Lakhani, K. (2016) Food wastage reduction through donation using a modern technological approach: Helping Hands. *International Journal of Advanced Research in Computer Engineering & Technology*, 5(4).

[5] Talati, N., Surve, O., Shah, J. & Kyal, S. (2017). Food donation portal. *International Journal for Scientific Research & Development*, 4(11).

[6] Phung, V.H. & Rhee, E.J., A High-Accuracy Model Average Ensemble of CNNs for Classification of Cloud Image Patches, Appl. Sci. 2019, 9(21), 4500.https://doi.org/10.3390/app9214500

40 Long term data preservation using DNA

Aparna Ramanathan[1,a] and S. Bhama[2,b]

[1]Master of Computer Applications, Dept. of Computer Applications, PSG College of Technology, Coimbatore, India

[2]Asst. Professor (Sl. Gr), Dept. of Computer Applications, PSG College of Technology Coimbatore, India

Abstract

Recent growth of digital data means that we require new storage strategies with far more scalability, longevity, and environmental sustainability than existing storage solutions. Deoxyribonucleic acid (DNA)-based data storage appears to be a promising storage alternative, providing unparalleled density, longevity, and durability. This study will focus on the use of DNA as a medium for archival data storage, specifically in exploring the encoding, decoding, and correcting errors of DNA data, not the chemistry of the use of DNA because that has little to do with the study. The primary concern of the study is in exploring the potential to develop viable encoding methods that will produce a reduction in the cost and time of depreciation obtained from retrieving DNA data. As we address computation concerns in encoding, decoding, and correcting errors, we hope to improve the practical use of DNA to be a potentially long-term archiving solution. The only significant study activity will be reviewing and comparing the recent activity in DNA storage algorithms, involving a practical sensing application that shows real-time data storage. We will also review performance evaluations by looking at metrics such as distance measures exploring the differences in similarities among DNA sequences, along with numerous performance evaluations. These metrics will allow us to evaluate the success of the algorithms in infrastructure reliability, efficiency, and scalability. This study will make a contribution to the domain of computational methods used in DNA data storage and demonstrate the success of plausible encoding.

Keywords: Archival storage, DNA based data storage, performance metric archival solution, the use of DNA to access data and its informational content

Introduction

The study of DNA will always remain a central aspect of the sciences as long as human beings exist. As we have established, DNA is an important biological entity and a marvelous medium for information encoding. DNA's continued importance to science and scientific inquiry stems from its solid structural stability as a molecule and its unique and incredible capacity to store huge amounts of information in an incredibly small space. Unlike other storage technologies that may quickly become obsolete when the hardware or format changes, DNA-based storage is biologically programmed into the world of human existence. DNA has many features that will ensure this medium will always hold intrigue for future scientific biologists. Additionally, the double helix is a storage medium that not only preserves information but preserves information in a medium inaccessible to the hand of technology; thus, rather than fading into obscurity as the past often does, DNA in essence preserves information without time and reduced access to information will never be old. More than just an motivation for DNA data storage.

Recent articles highlight the rapid growth in global data creation, capturing, copying, and consumption, with projections estimating the total will reach 149 zettabytes by 2024. Over the following five years, this figure is expected to climb to over 394 zettabytes by 2028. DNA presents a highly promising option for data storage due to its exceptional density, with a theoretical capacity exceeding 1 exabyte per cubic millimeter (EB/mm^3), making it about eight times denser than magnetic tape. Additionally, DNA is incredibly durable, with a half-life of over 500 years even in harsh conditions, ensuring its longevity. Another significant advantage of DNA storage is its potential for "eternal" relevance, as the data stored in DNA can remain viable for centuries, preserving information for generations.

DNA: structure and data storage

DNA is made of four different nucleotides; adenine (A), cytosine (C), guanine (G), and thymine (T).

Nucleotides are the basic building blocks of DNA. Each nucleotide consists of three components: a

[a]23mx103@psgtech.ac.in, [b]sba.mca@psgtech.ac.in

DOI: 10.1201/9781003770435-40

phosphate group, a deoxyribose sugar, and a nitrogenous base. The nitrogenous base is what makes each nucleotide distinct, which is why DNA is known as adenine (A), cytosine (C), guanine (G), and thymine (T). The nucleotides are linked in a linear arrangement through covalent bonds from the phosphate group of one nucleotide to the sugar molecule of another nucleotide, forming a single strand of DNA. Once the nucleotides are linked as such they are described as a polymer, and hence a DNA strand, or an oligonucleotide.

A DNA molecule consists of a lengthy chain of nucleotides arranged in a particular sequence that carries genetic instructions. The specific order of the four nucleotide bases, adenine (A), cytosine (C), guanine (G), and thymine (T), makes up the genetic code responsible for determining various biological characteristics and functions in living beings. Typically, DNA exists as a double-stranded structure, forming the well-known double helix. In this configuration, the bases on each strand pair with their complementary counterparts through hydrogen bonding: adenine pairs with thymine (A-T), and cytosine pairs with guanine (C-G). This base-pairing mechanism plays a vital role in maintaining DNA stability and ensuring accurate replication. The structure is illustrated in Figure 40.1.

The synthetic DNA-based storage system involves several key steps: encoding, synthesizing DNA molecules (oligos), storing, retrieving, sequencing and decoding the data. These processes may include modifications, amplification, or even controlled destruction of DNA fragments (oligos). Below is a simplified explanation of each step.

Encoding Data into DNA
Binary data, represented as sequences of 1s and 0s, is divided into smaller fragments and transformed into DNA sequences. This involves mapping binary values to nucleotides. Simple 2-bit mapping approach is given as an example here.

$$01 \rightarrow C$$
$$00 \rightarrow A$$
$$10 \rightarrow G$$
$$01 \rightarrow C$$

Therefore, the binary sequence 01001001, gets transformed into the nucleotide sequence CAGC.

Synthesizing DNA
DNA synthesis is the process of creating artificial DNA strands in a laboratory by assembling nucleotides in a specific sequence. This allows scientists to design custom DNA sequences for various purposes, such as data storage, genetic research, and biotechnology applications.

Storing Synthetic DNA
Artificially synthesized DNA can be stored using various methods, depending on the intended application and storage duration. These methods include in vitro (outside a living organism) and in vivo (inside a living organism) storage. They can also be stored chemically or physically.

Retrieving Data
The process of accessing information stored in DNA entails extraction (to extract the DNA sequences that encode the information) and reading the DNA sequences followed by decoding back to its original digital format. This process can involve the following steps and uses sophisticated technologies and algorithms to help ensure accurate results. Amplification is an optional step to the DNA data retrieval process but can be important. If only a small quantity of DNA was obtained, then amplification can be done using polymerase chain reaction (PCR). PCR will multiply the copies of DNA to a satisfactory level that can more easily undergo sequencing, minimizing the deterioration of the sample.

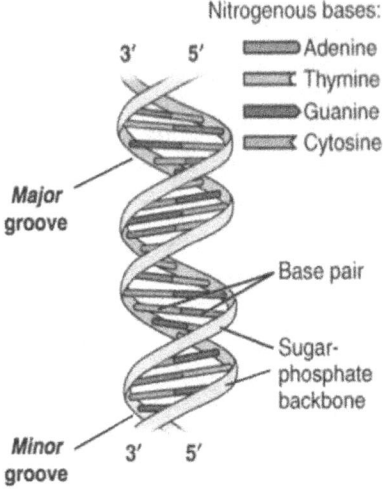

Figure 40.1 DNA structure
Source: Author

Sequencing and Decoding

Sequencing technologies can be utilized to read DNA. High-throughput sequencing is the technique which produces many "reads" of the DNA fragments. The reads can then be used in decoding algorithms to reproduce the original data. In the process of sequencing, the DNA fragment is read, and the order of nucleotides is determined. Distinct sequencing technologies accomplish this in different fashions, however. Novel newer sequencing technologies allow for integrating the read sequence to a scale while limiting read errors.

Error detection and correction

In DNA data storage, ensuring data integrity is crucial because both DNA synthesis and sequencing processes are prone to errors. The significance of error detection and correction techniques, along with distance metrics, is highlighted below. Error detection: Techniques like parity checks or checksums are applied to detect inconsistencies in the encoded data.

- Error correction: Reed-Solomon codes and fountain codes are commonly used to correct errors in DNA data. These algorithms introduce redundancy, allowing the system to recover lost or corrupted data fragments.
- Distance metrics: Hamming distance is one of the distance metrics used to measure the number of changes (insertions, deletions, or substitutions) between two sequences. These metrics help in detecting how far the retrieved sequence is from the correct sequence and can guide error correction processes. Figure 40.2 pictographically summarizes the above mentioned steps.

The image depicts the DNA-based data storage workflow, starting from encoding data into DNA sequences, synthesizing and storing them, and later retrieving, sequencing, and decoding them back into the original data. Key steps include encoding schemes, DNA synthesis, storage, selective amplification, and sequencing

Properties of Efficient Encoding Schemes

DNA-based data storage is emerging as a revolutionary technology, offering unprecedented potential for ultra-dense, durable, and sustainable data archiving. Central to its success is the design of efficient encoding schemes that translate digital information into

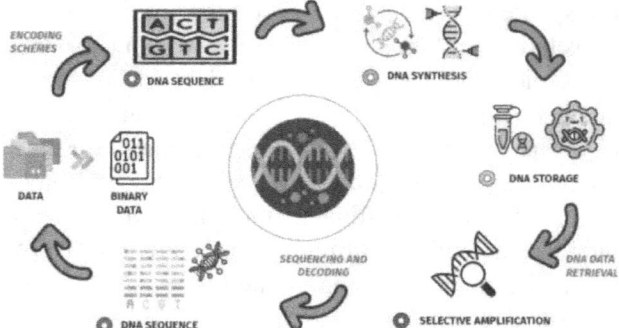

Figure 40.2 Steps in DNA based data storage
Source: Author

DNA sequences while adhering to biological constraints. These encoding schemes must address multiple challenges. Efficient encoding involves balancing competing priorities such as high information density, error resilience, chemical stability, and compatibility with current sequencing technologies. By optimizing these properties, DNA encoding schemes enable reliable storage and retrieval of vast amounts of data, positioning DNA as a transformative medium for future data storage systems. All the properties that are generally looked into while designing an encoding scheme are described below.

Physical Structure (length of oligo, uniform size, redundancy, error resilience)

During DNA encoding processes, data are commonly separated into data "chunks", or nucleotide sequences, that must be constrained to achieve effective encoding. The first property is length, or oligo length. In general, the shorter the sequence, the easier it will be to manage. Oligos in the range of 100-200 nucleotides utilize almost all of the sequencing technologies and limit the error probability in the sequencing process. Additionally, oligos should all be of the same size, since it is easier to manage encoding and decoding with accurate lengths, and should some data be lost it would be easy to notice this occurrence and rectify it. Redundancy is another property. While redundancy is generally treated slightly negatively in database systems, it is extremely beneficial in this scenario, as it facilitates error-detection and error-correction mechanisms. Each data chunk has information that overlaps the previous and/or later data chunks, and if segments must be deleted during recovery, some will be retrievable by the inclusion of redundancy. The actual function of synthesizing DNA has a description of processes that are almost completely error-inducing; redundancy gives data the ability to de-risk these potential loss events.

The artificially synthesized DNA applied for data storage should not resemble research- biological DNA too closely, since natural, biological DNA sequences originate through natural selection, which may include repeated sequences, mutations, or sequences that are biochemically optimized. If artificial DNA shares too many similarities to naturally occurring sequences, it could make it difficult to determine if a sequenced strand is synthetic or biological and could complicate sequencing and data retrieval. Sequences similar to living organisms could also trigger biological processes if placed in that environment and would raise contamination or unintentional effects associated with possible biological functioning. Encoding schemes will specifically create synthetic DNA to be different from natural genomes either with completely non-natural and/or semi-random sequences to ensure distinguishing differences and stability in the storage and processing stages.

Homopolymer Runs
Homopolymers are sequences of DNA that contain repetition of the same nucleotide base, such as long runs of adenine, AAAA, or long stretches of thymine, TTTT. Homopolymers are highly notoriously problematic in all forms of DNA data storage. One of the issues arises because of current sequencing technologies, which fail to differentiate long homopolymer runs, in particular, the length of the base runs and are therefore more susceptible to errors. If the sequencer has a length of a run of A, for example, the sequencer can make an error in determining it as 100 bases long or mistakenly determine it as a different length. The concern here is sequencing errors due to homopolymers, making error detection and error correction very difficult. Furthermore, homopolymers have been shown to lead to unstable structures in the DNA causing problems with DNA synthesis and retrieval. "Encoding" schemes may help mitigate these difficulties by limiting the length of homopolymers and distributing the nucleotides across the DNA to be more efficient. Encoding methods attempt to avoid long stretches of identical base pairs. The encoding methods can either utilize redundancy, error correction coding, or randomization strategies to make reducing errors easier, while enabling the access and retrieval of the data being stored in DNA, thus

leading to a more reliable and accurate DNA data storage system.

Guanine and cytosine content
Guanine cytosine (GC) content is the percentage of guanine (G) and cytosine (C) bases in a DNA sequence. In naturally occurring DNA GC content falls within a certain range, often of 40–60% which relates to the stability and proper folding of the DNA double helix. When it comes to artificial DNA used for data storage, the GC content must be balanced for both structural stability and synthesis efficiency. DNA sequences with extreme GC content can form unstable structures or make things difficult when synthesizing, sequencing, and storage. Sequences that have high GC content will tend to form very stable secondary structures and be more difficult to synthesize and read. However, sequences that have low GC content can be more prone to degradation.

Effective encoding methods solve this problem by specifically addressing the balance of GC content for the entire sequence together to achieve stable and synthesizable data. They, therefore, will spread G and C more evenly throughout the sequence while avoiding extreme GC bias in localized areas of the sequence. While I described pseudo randomization as an encoding method, they also could have used an approach to display when superimposing DNA data for mapping into some synthesized descriptions to another piece of data and could keep the GC ratio stable, to avoid uneven distribution of GC, plastics, and eventually getting perfect scorpions when using synthetic DNA to encode digital data, such approaches provide more reliable and in some respects more efficient ways of storing data in synthetic DNA.

High Information Density
Information density is a fundamental factor in why DNA-based data storage systems even exist. Research in DNA data storage began mostly from an understanding of the density of DNA, which is way denser than any of today's conventional hardware for data storage. Information density is the amount of information, or data, that can be stored in a given unit of physical space. Information density is usually presented as how many bits can be stored per unit length of DNA. This is accomplished in DNA based data storage by the mere mathematical representation in equation (1) below. In the case of DNA based data storage, measurement of information density

is important for determining how densely information can be stored in the DNA molecule. To calculate information density, we take the number of bits encoded in DNA, and divide this by the length of the molecule of interest, usually in terms of nucleotides. And each nucleotide (A, T, C, G) can represent multiple bits depending on the encoding scheme used (even just 2 bits per nucleotide if encoding using a base 4 encoding scheme). The more bits encoded are packed into more nucleotides, the higher the information density.

$$\text{Information Density} = \frac{\textit{Number of bits stored}}{\textit{Length of DNA sequence (in nucleotides)}} \quad (1)$$

Efficient encoding schemes are crucial because they ensure high information density through optimizing how data is mapped to DNA sequences. These schemes would generally maximize the amount of information that can be encoded in a given length of DNA; hence DNA is an incredibly high-density storage medium.

Data Format

A defined format is essential to ensuring data integrity, accessibility, and the ability to efficiently retrieve information through DNA data storage. The formatting facilitates the encoding and decoding of data in DNA sequences. The format includes the primer, payload, and address, each of which serves a separate purpose in data encoding.

1. The primer is a short DNA sequence that functions as a starting point to the data-encoding strand that allows the data to be stored correctly.
2. The payload is the data information or the encoded message which is stored in the data, and subsequently accessible upon retrieval.
3. The address is a unique identifier/code embedded into the data sequence to allow for correct data location and retrieval. This is important when dealing with large-scale DNA-based storage systems, where data indexing could be inaccurate.

Figure 40.3 depicts the general format in which data is stored in a DNA segment.

In this instance, the introduction of two-sense nucleotides (the reverse complements and forward complements) guarantees that the data contained

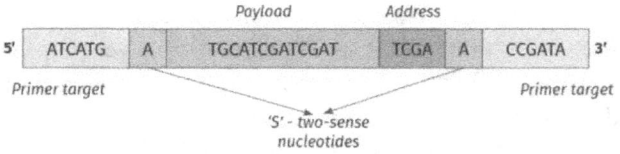

Figure 40.3 DNA data format
Source: Author

inside the strands is protected from error and can be properly interpreted regardless of its orientation, adding an extra level of reliability in DNA-based storage.

Cost Efficiency

Currently, encoding DNA data is expensive because of the current high cost of DNA synthesis and sequencing. Encoding DNA data is expensive because synthesizing DNA can cost from several thousand dollars, to tens of thousands dollars per gigabyte of data, depending on the complexity and number of sequences required, and sequencing, which costs are decreasing over time. However, encoding schemes will help lessen the cost by improving the efficiency of storing and retrieving data. Efficient encoding methods can reduce the amounts of DNA that needs to be synthesized or sequenced by minimizing the redundancy in data and providing error correction and error detection, that reduces the effective number of sequences required. Encoding schemes can make DNA storage cheaper by making data more reasonably compressed and more error resistant codes, which could reduce the costs of synthesis and sequencing in the long term. Efficiency will ensure that encoding schemes can provide cost effective DNA data storage for large-scale applications.

Compatibility

Encoding systems for DNA data storage need to be carefully constructed to meet the requirements of both the chemistry of DNA and constraints of the sequencing methods. Because DNA sequences are composed of nucleotides, the encoding system must allow for representation of data values in stable and synthetically accessible nucleotides, while avoiding sequences that have patterns which result in secondary structure (e.g. hairpins, repeats) that would also negatively impact synthesis and sequencing. The similarly encoded DNA must also comply with the constraints of sequencing methods, which include circular read lengths of DNA, specific error profiles, and limits in being able to decode particular sequences. In most encoding schemes, error correction and redundancy are included so that the data can still be recovered accurately despite any errors induced by sequencing. Even with the previous considerations, the encoding schemes must deal with the fact that there are trade-offs related to the density of data compared to the physical capabilities of DNA synthesis and sequencing technologies. Therefore, in order for the DNA data storage system to be efficient and accurate, the encoding schemes should be designed with the reasonable practical considerations of synthesizing and sequencing DNA.

Base Paper Study

As researchers began to explore the use of DNA for long-term data storage, they became aware of how stable and dense DNA can be as a medium for information storage, more so than many traditional storage media, beginning an examination into this area of practice. This journey started with some initial studies on ways to encode information into DNA, looking at many ways to translate digital information into nucleic sequences to study efficiency, error tolerance, and form practical, real-world applications. Eventually, this work expanded to include error detection and correction methods, sequencing methods, and computational models for optimizing the encoding-decoding process.

Through their work, researchers have critically surveyed the literature, identified the challenges, and examined how their work can enhance methods and processes that could better guarantee data integrity for data retrieval and longevity. This literature survey will document the development of data-encoding methods starting with early experimental frameworks to recent achievements, with attention to methods of encoding, error correction methods, and sequencing methods that will influence the future of DNA as a long-term archival model for digital data. It will summarize the broadly theoretical-based frameworks, developments, and status of encoding data into DNA to begin to examine

DNA as a Storage Medium

a) Goldman et al. [1] introduced a method to encode digital information into DNA using Huff-

man codes to avoid homopolymers, achieving fourfold redundancy for error correction.
b) Church et al. [2] demonstrated large-scale DNA data storage by assigning binary values to nucleotides, but their method lacked error correction mechanisms.
c) Grass et al. [3] developed a method for storing DNA in silica particles, demonstrating that it could be preserved for millions of years under controlled conditions.

Encoding and Error Correction

d) Erlich and Zielinski [4] proposed the DNA Fountain method, which uses Luby Transform codes for efficient encoding and error tolerance while minimizing redundancy.
e) Blawat et al. [5] incorporated Reed-Solomon codes, which provided robust error correction and improved retrieval accuracy.
f) Bornholt et al. [6] introduced random-access DNA storage, enabling targeted data retrieval without sequencing the entire dataset.

Storage Stability and Environmental Factors

g) Matange et al. [7] reviewed DNA stability under different storage conditions and highlighted methods such as encapsulation and dehydration to prolong DNA longevity.
h) Hoshika et al. [8] developed Hachimoji DNA, a genetic system with eight bases instead of the traditional four, potentially increasing DNA's information capacity.

Sequencing and Retrieval Methods

i) Clelland et al. [9] explored steganographic encoding, embedding hidden messages within DNA microdots.
j) Takahashi et al. [10] demonstrated automated DNA data storage, marking a step towards scalable, large-scale DNA-based storage solutions.

Ethical and Artistic Applications

k) Eduardo Kac [11] experimented with genetic art, modifying plant genomes to encode personal DNA data.

l) Monsanto (American agrochemical and agricultural biotechnology corporation known for producing genetically modified seeds, the herbicide Roundup, and other agricultural products) and other industrial efforts have explored DNA watermarking to distinguish genetically modified plants from natural species. The paper acknowledges that while significant progress has been made in DNA synthesis, encoding, and sequencing, there is no single approach that fully addresses all challenges. Future research must combine multiple breakthroughs to make DNA-based storage commercially viable.

This study aims to prove that recent innovations have further refined the field, enabling large-scale implementations. Despite these advancements, challenges such as high synthesis costs, slow read/write speeds, and sequencing errors remain key obstacles. However, with continuous improvements in biotechnology, computational modeling, and high-performance computing, DNA storage is poised to become a viable solution for long-term archival needs.

Future research should focus on optimizing storage efficiency, enhancing automation, and integrating DNA storage with existing digital systems to bridge the gap between theoretical potential and real-world applications. In conclusion, the results of this study are summarized in Table 40.1, Figures 40.4 and 40.5, with reference to the findings presented in the paper titled 'Survey of Information Encoding Techniques for DNA'. Redundancy level in the table refers to the amount of extra or duplicate information added to the encoded DNA sequence to improve data reliability, integrity, and recoverability. In simpler terms it refers to the number of times a DNA data or payload is repeated during encoding to avoid data loss. This way, even if one part of the data is lost, it can still be recovered from the other fragments, since the repeated data ensures that the missing part exists elsewhere in the remaining fragments.

Proposed Approach to Encode/ Decode Data

The approach proposed is based on the paper "Portable and error-free DNA-based data storage system using nanopore sequencing", which explores

Table 40.1 Comparison of encoding techniques

TECHNIQUE	YEAR OF PUBLICATION	INFORMATION DENSITY (BITS/NT)	ERROR CORRECTION	RANDOM ACCESS	STORAGE TYPE	REDUNDANCY LEVEL
MICROVENUS	1999	1.25	NONE	NO	ORGANISM	1
GENESIS	2000	1.52	NONE	NO	ORGANISM	1
BANCROFT ET AL.	2001[15]	0,94	BASIC INDEXING	NO	MICROPLATE	2
GOLDMAN ET AL.	2013[1]	0.22	HUFFMAN + REDUNDANCY	NO	MICROPLATE	4
CHURCH ET AL	2013	0.6	REPLICATION	NO	MICROPLATE	3
GRASS ET AL	2015[3]	0.86	REED-SOLOMON CODES	NO		3
BORNHOLT ET AL	2016	0.59	XOR-BASED CORRECTION	YES (PCR)	MICROPLATE	2
YAZDI ET AL	2017	1.72	HAMMING CODES	YES	MICROPLATE	2
DNA FOUNTAIN	2017	1.75	FOUNTAIN CODES	YES	MICROPLATE	1.5
CHOI ET AL	2019	3.37	DEGENERATE BASES	YES	MICROPLATE	1

Source: Author

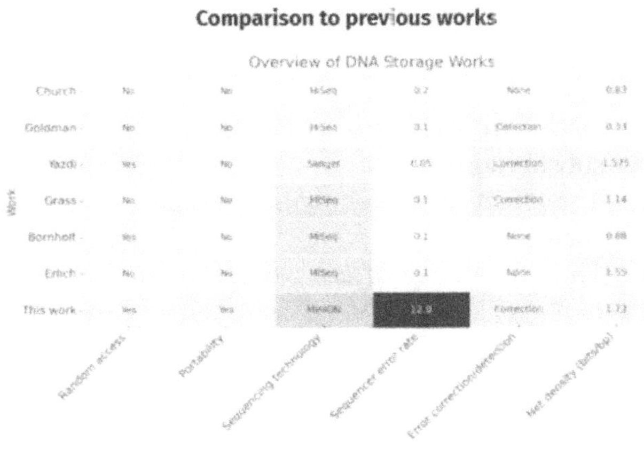

Comparison to previous works

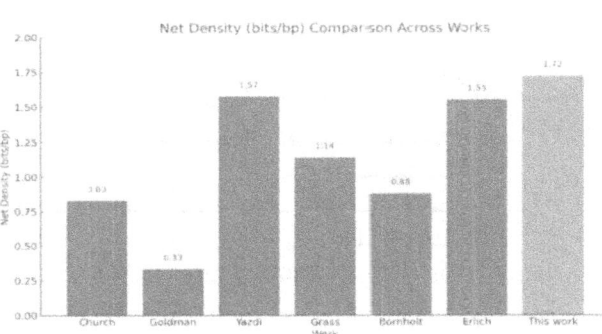

Figure 40.4 Table of comparison to previous year works
Source: Author

Comparison to previous works

Net Density (bits/bp) Comparison Across Works

Figure 40.5 Chart of comparison to previous year works
Source: Author

a novel approach to store digital data in synthetic DNA with improved random access, error correction, and sequencing efficiency. The paper introduces techniques such as constrained encoding, GC - content balancing, and homopolymer check codes to enhance data integrity during storage and retrieval. By utilizing nanopore sequencing, specifically MinION—a portable, real-time DNA and RNA sequencing technology developed by Oxford Nanopore Technologies that employs nanopore-based sensing for processing long nucleotide sequences with high flexibility and scalability—the proposed method achieves cost-effective and accurate decoding of DNA-encoded information, overcoming key challenges in DNA data storage.

Key Findings

The methodology follows a structured pipeline consisting of data encoding, constrained coding for error minimization, DNA synthesis, selective retrieval via PCR, nanopore sequencing, and post-processing for

error correction. The following steps outline the key contributions and findings presented in the paper.

a) Data compression and encoding: Digital data is compressed to reduce synthesis costs, then encoded into binary and DNA sequences using constrained encoding.

b) GC-Balanced codewords: Data is split into 1,000 bp DNA blocks, each with address sequences for retrieval. GC-content balancing minimizes synthesis and sequencing errors.

c) Random access via PCR: Unique 16-base addresses enable selective retrieval through PCR, avoiding full dataset sequencing and reducing amplification bias using GC-balanced primers.

d) Homopolymer check codes: Special redundancy is added to track homopolymer lengths, allowing correction of common nanopore sequencing errors.

e) DNA Synthesis and nanopore sequencing: Synthesized with Integrated DNA Technologies (IDT) gBlocks® and sequenced using Oxford Nanopore MinION, achieving accurate data recovery from 6,660 reads in 12 hours.

f) Post-processing with multiple sequence alignment (MSA): Traditional MSA tools (e.g., Kalign, MUSCLE) are used innovatively to align sequences and build consensus, correcting sequencing errors.

g) Final error correction: Burrows-wheeler aligner (BWA) and homopolymer-specific techniques

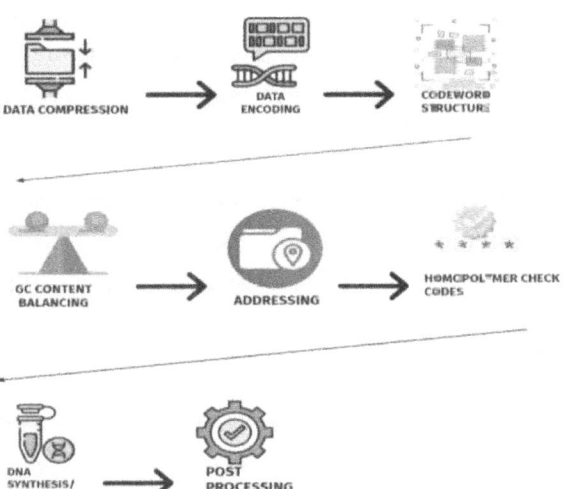

Figure 40.6 Visualization of the algorithm's workflow
Source: Author

further refine accuracy, reducing the error rate to just 0.02%, enabling reliable data reconstruction.

Implementation details - steps involved

a) Binary to DNA mapping
   - Binary data is converted into DNA using a 2-bit scheme (00→A, 01→T, 10→C, 11→G).
   - This ensures efficient, reversible translation suitable for DNA synthesis and sequencing.
b) Addressing mechanism
   - Each DNA block gets a unique 16-base address to enable random access retrieval.
   - Addresses are generated with high Hamming distance and excluded from data to avoid mis amplification.
c) Use of DNA addressing
   - Addresses help reorder randomly sequenced DNA fragments during reconstruction.
   - They also enable targeted PCR amplification for retrieving specific data blocks.
d) Error detection using homopolymer check
   - A 4-base homopolymer check code is added to detect repetitive sequence errors.
   - It tracks base frequency and flags inconsistencies caused by sequencing errors.
e) Encoding data into DNA blocks
   - Binary data is chunked into DNA blocks with structure: Address + Data + Check Code.
   - Fixed-size blocks (e.g., 1000 bases) ensure modular storage and reliable retrieval.
f) Decoding and error correction
   - DNA sequences are verified via addresses and check codes before reverse mapping.
   - Blocks are reassembled in order, and flagged errors are corrected or reprocessed.

Proposed Performance Metrics to evaluate The Approach

This section introduces the importance of evaluating DNA-based data storage techniques. It outlines key questions.

1. How efficiently can data be encoded into DNA sequences?
2. What is the accuracy of the decoding process?
3. What are the computational costs of encoding and searching for data?

Additionally, it discusses the challenges in DNA data storage:

1. DNA synthesis errors (insertion, deletion, and substitution errors)
2. The effect of homopolymer sequences on data accuracy
3. The importance of error detection and correction
4. The impact of scalability on DNA storage systems
5. Time complexity of the algorithm

Some of the performance metrics used and the reason for their usage are given below. They are critical for analysis.

A) Encoding efficiency
   a) Purpose: Measures the speed of data-to-DNA conversion; important for large-scale or real-time storage; helps optimize the encoding pipeline.
   b) Metric: Encoding time (T) correction methods are needed.
   c) Metric: Error detection rate (EDR)
   d) Formula: EDR = No. of detected errors / Total errors
B) System scalability
   a) Purpose: To assess how well the algorithm/ encoding- decoding technique will perform in case of larger data sets
   b) Metric: Scalability factor (F_s)
   c) Formula: F_s = Tenc or Tlookup (large data)/ Tenc or Tlookup (small data)

These evaluation metrics provide an extensive overview for analyzing the performance, reliability, and scalability of DNA-based storage systems. By considering encoding speed, storage overhead, decoding accuracy, random access speed, error correction, and scalability, researchers can quickly highlight bottlenecks and optimize a design. This ensures that practical and economically viable solutions for digital preservation in DNA storage can be developed.

Experimental setup

The implementation is developed in Python, in order to simulate the encoding, decoding and analysis processes of DNA-based data storage. The codebase is separated into four modules that serve to encode and decode the data, create an error detection mechanism, demonstrate random access data retrieval from the dataset and evaluate the performance of the code. The data sample used is a list of English words retrieved from an online.

A) Formula: T

source.$_{enc}$ = $\sum$ti (where ti is the time to encode each data block)

B) Storage overhead
   a) Purpose: Assesses how much extra storage is used due to addressing and error correction; helps balance redundancy and cost-efficiency.
   b) Metric: Redundancy ratio (R_{rec})
   c) Formula: R_{red} = Total DNA bases stored / Original data size (in bits)

C) Decoding accuracy
   a) Purpose: Evaluates reconstruction accuracy; identifies error sources like homopolymers; guides improvements in error correction.
   b) Metric: Bit error rate (BER)
   c) Formula: BER = No. of incorrect bits/total bits decoded

D) Random access retrieval performance
   a) Purpose: Measures how quickly specific data can be retrieved; crucial for selective access; helps refine search algorithms.
   b) Metric: Lookup time (T_{lookup})
   c) Formula: T_{lookup} = O(n) (can be optimized to O(1) with indexing)

E) Error detection and correction performance
   a) Purpose: Assesses effectiveness of error checks (e.g., homopolymer check); determines if stronger

1. Data encoding into DNA
   The first module (encodeDecode.py) is responsible for converting digital text into DNA sequences. Each byte of data is transformed into binary and then mapped into DNA bases using a fixed binary-to-DNA encoding scheme (00 → A, 01 → T, 10 → C, 11 → G).

2. DNA Decoding and error analysis
   The decoding phase reads the encoded file and reconstructs the original digital data. It validates each block using the homopolymer check and aggregates all sequences to recover the original binary data. The module (evaluateResults.py) measures the decoding time and computes the

BER by comparing the original and reconstructed bitstreams. This metric evaluates the fidelity of the DNA storage process.

3. Error detection rate via homopolymer checks
   Homopolymer checks are used to detect errors introduced during encoding, transmission, or sequencing. The script validates each block's content against its appended check sequence and calculates the error detection rate (EDR), defined as the ratio of blocks correctly validated.

4. Random Access Performance

The ability to retrieve specific data blocks using their address is essential for practical DNA storage. This was evaluated using the randomSearch.py and evaluateLookup.py modules. The lookup function performs a linear search through the DNA-encoded file to find a specific address. The lookup time is measured, and the presence of the requested address is reported. This demonstrates the feasibility and performance of random access in the encoded DNA system. The results of this work have been summarized in Table 40.2.

Conclusion

This research presents a comprehensive framework for digital data storage using DNA as a long-term, high-density archival medium. By simulating encoding, decoding, error detection, and random access retrieval, the proposed system demonstrates promising results in terms of encoding efficiency, decoding accuracy, and storage overhead management. Key metrics such as encoding time, bit error rate (BER), redundancy ratio, and lookup time were measured and analyzed to assess system performance. The use of homopolymer checks, unique DNA addressing with Hamming distance constraints, and modular block-based encoding enhanced both reliability and retrieval accuracy, laying the foundation for scalable and fault-tolerant DNA data storage systems.

While the simulation shows strong potential, real-time implementation presents certain challenges, such as biochemical synthesis errors, sequencing inaccuracies, environmental stability of DNA, and cost constraints. Future work can explore integrating advanced error-correction codes like low-density parity-check (LDPC) or Reed-Solomon, optimizing DNA indexing for sub-linear search times, and applying machine learning for adaptive error prediction

Table 40.2 Results of the experiment

Metric	Description	Module	Value returned for the dataset*
Encoding time	Time to convert data into DNA blocks	encodeD ecode.py	6.031332 seconds
Decoding time	Time to reconstruct original data	evaluate Results.p y	17.115450 seconds
Bit error rate (BER)	Accuracy of reconstructed data	evaluate Results.p y	0.361282 seconds
Error detection rate (EDR)	Effectiveness of homopolymer checks	evaluate Results. p y	100.00%*
Lookup time	Time to retrieve a block by address	evaluate Lookup.p y	0.000974 seconds (worst case of linear search)

*This file is a plain text list of English words, one word per line, Number of words:
~370,000,File size: Approximately 5.3 MB.
*The homopolymer check in this simulation consistently returns a 100% accuracy rate because the encoded file is read and decoded directly without any external interference. However, in real-world scenarios, such ideal results are unlikely. During DNA synthesis and sequencing, errors such as base dropouts, insertions, or substitutions can occur, which may cause homopolymer checks to fail. These practical limitations highlight the need for more robust error detection and correction techniques when implementing the system in real-time environments.

and correction. Furthermore, real-world implementation could involve testing with actual DNA synthesis and sequencing processes, investigating DNA storage behavior over time, and evaluating hybrid systems combining DNA with traditional storage media. Addressing these challenges will be crucial to bringing DNA storage out of the lab and into practical, real-time applications like digital archives, legal evidence preservation, and secure, long-term government or scientific record keeping.

References

[1] Goldman, N., Bertone, P., Chen, S., Dessimoz, C., LeProust, E. M., Sipos, B., et al. (2013). Towards practical, high-capacity, low-maintenance information storage in synthesized DNA. *Nature*, 494, 77–80.

[2] Church, G. M., Gao, Y., & Kosuri, S. (2012). Next-generation digital information storage in DNA. *Science*, 337(6102), 1628.

[3] Grass, R. N., Heckel, R., Puddu, M., Paunescu, D., & Stark, W. J. (2015). Robust chemical preservation of digital information on DNA in silica with error-correcting codes. *Angewandte Chemie International Edition*, 54(8), 2552–2555.

[4] Erlich, Y., & Zielinski, D. (2017). DNA Fountain enables a robust and efficient storage architecture. *Science*, 355, 950–954.

[5] Blawat, M., Gaedke, K., Huetter, I., Chen, X. M., Turczyk, B., Inverso, S., et al. (2016). Forward error correction for DNA data storage. *Procedia Computer Science*, 80, 1011–1022.

[6] Bornholt, J., Lopez, R., Carmean, D. M., Ceze, L., Seelig, G., & Strauss, K. (2016). A DNA-based archival storage system. In Proc. 21st Int. Conf. Archit. Support Program. Lang. Oper. Syst. (ASPLOS), Atlanta, GA, USA (pp. 637–649).

[7] Matange, K., Tuck, J. M., & Keung, A. J. (2021). DNA stability: a central design consideration for DNA data storage systems. *Nature Communications*, 12, 1–9.

[8] Hoshika, S., Leal, N. A., Kim, M. J., Kim, M. S., Karalkar, N. B., Kim, H. J., et al. (2019). Hachimoji DNA and RNA: a genetic system with eight building blocks. *Science*, 363, 884–887.

[9] Clelland, C. T., Risca, V., & Bancroft, C. (1999). Hiding messages in DNA microdots. *Nature*, 399, 533–534.

[10] Takahashi, C. N., Nguyen, B. H., Strauss, K., & Ceze, L. (2019). Demonstration of end-to-end automation of DNA data storage. *Scientific Reports*, 9, 1–5.

[11] Kac, E. (2006). Transgenic art. *História, Ciências, Saúde–Manguinhos*, 13, 247–256.

[12] Bancroft, C., Bowler, T., Bloom, B., & Clelland, C. T. (2001). Long-term storage of information in DNA. *Science*, 293(5536), 1763–1765. Available from: https://doi.org/10.1126/science.293.5536.1763c.

41 Device driver development using Zephyr RTOS

A. Natarajan[1,a] and Praveen Raj S R[2,b]

[1]Professor, Department of Electrical and Electronics Engineering (PG), PSG College of Technology, India

[2]Scholar, Department of Electrical and Electronics Engineering (PG), PSG College of Technology, India

Abstract

In the rapidly evolving field of embedded systems, efficient and reliable communication between devices is paramount. The universal asynchronous receiver-transmitter (UART) is a widely used protocol for serial communication, facilitating data exchange between microcontrollers and peripheral devices. This work focuses on the development of a UART device driver using the Zephyr real-time operating system (RTOS) for the Argonaut RISC Core (ARC) microcontroller. The primary objective of this work is to design and implement a UART device driver that can seamlessly integrate with the Zephyr RTOS and efficiently handle serial communication tasks on the ARC microcontroller. The development process involves a thorough analysis of the UART communication requirements, followed by the design and implementation of the driver architecture. Comprehensive testing and validation will be conducted to ensure the driver's functionality and performance meet the desired standards.

Keywords: Argonaut RISC Core, device driver, real-time operating system, universal asynchronous receiver-transmitter

Introduction

The realm of embedded systems, the universal asynchronous receiver transmitter (UART) is a critical component for serial communication [1]. This work focuses on the development of a UART device driver using the Zephyr real-time operating system (RTOS) for the Argonaut RISC Core (ARC) microcontroller. The ARC microcontroller, known for its high performance and low power consumption, is widely used in various embedded applications such as GPUs [2,3].

Zephyr RTOS, an open-source work under the Linux Foundation, provides a scalable and configurable operating system for resource-constrained devices. It supports a wide range of architectures, including ARC, making it an ideal choice for this work.

The primary objective of this work is to design and implement a robust UART driver that can efficiently handle serial communication tasks on the ARC microcontroller. The development process involves several key steps they are Requirement Analysis for Understanding the specific requirements for UART communication in the target application, including baud rate, data bits, parity, and stop bits.

The successful completion of this work will result in a fully functional UART driver that can be seamlessly integrated into Zephyr-based applications running on ARC microcontrollers [4,5]. This driver will facilitate reliable and efficient serial communication, enabling developers to leverage the full potential of the ARC architecture in their embedded solutions.

Literature review

The development process of an UART chip on FPGA for driving embedded devices

The methodology involves specifying the design requirements for the UART chip [1,2], including multi-byte transmission. The FPGA is programmed using VHDL/Verilog to implement UART functionality with a state machine to manage operations. A mechanism is developed for handling string transmissions, and the FPGA is configured as the master device to communicate with slave devices. The design undergoes simulation, testing, and debugging to ensure proper functionality, followed by optimization and integration with other FPGA components. Finally, the design is documented and verified against the initial requirements.

A model driven approach for device driver development

The methodology involves a model-driven approach to design and verify device drivers before coding [5,7]. It includes creating architecture and behavior models to represent both static and dynamic characteristics of the drivers. Additionally, device and interaction models are developed to define the execution environment. The models are used for model-level

[a]ann.eee@psgtech.ac.in, [b]23mu36@psgtech.ac.in

DOI: 10.1201/9781003770435-41

verification, and methods are proposed for implementing model-based design, verification, and code-level emulation.

GHz LoRa in Smart Buildings: Driver Development for Zephyr OS and Comparison with BLE

The methodology involves implementing a driver for the Sentech SX1280 LoRa radio on the Zephyr OS [3,4,6]. This implementation is then used to compare the performance of 2.4 GHz LoRa with Bluetooth Low Energy (BLE) in a Smart Building scenario. The comparison focuses on latency and reliability, with testing conducted to evaluate how well LoRa performs relative to BLE at different ranges. The study examines the trade-offs between range, reliability, and latency, concluding that LoRa 5 offers better reliability at longer ranges, albeit with slightly higher latency compared to BLE.

Methodology

The development of a UART device driver for the ARC microcontroller using Zephyr RTOS and a polling API involves a structured and methodical approach. The key steps in this approach are outlined

Requirement Analysis

Understand the specific requirements for UART communication in the target application. Identify the necessary configurations such as baud rate, data bits, parity, and stop bits. Determine the performance and reliability criteria for the UART driver [9,10]. Assess the feasibility and implications of using a polling mechanism for UART communication.

Architecture design

Design a modular and scalable architecture for the UART driver using a polling API. Define the driver's functional blocks and their interactions. Ensure compatibility with the Zephyr RTOS and its APIs. Plan for hardware abstraction to facilitate portability across different ARC microcontroller variants. Design the polling mechanism to periodically check the UART status and handle data transmission and reception designations [1,7].

Driver Implementation

Develop the UART driver code in C, adhering to Zephyr RTOS coding standards and using a polling API. Implement the core functionalities of the UART driver, including initialization, data transmission,

and reception. Utilize Zephyr's hardware abstraction layer (HAL) for interfacing with the ARC microcontroller. Implement the polling mechanism to periodically check the UART status registers and handle data accordingly. Integrate FIFO (First-In-First-Out) buffers to handle high-speed data transmission and synchronization [2,8].

Testing and Validation

Verify the functionality and performance of the UART driver. Conduct unit tests to validate individual components of the driver. Perform integration tests to ensure seamless interaction with the Zephyr RTOS. Execute real-world application tests to validate the driver's performance and reliability. Use simulation tools like Cadence for verifying the Verilog HDL implementation of UART [3,4].

Flow Diagram

Figure 41.1 explains the flow of the work which is carried out for successful completion.

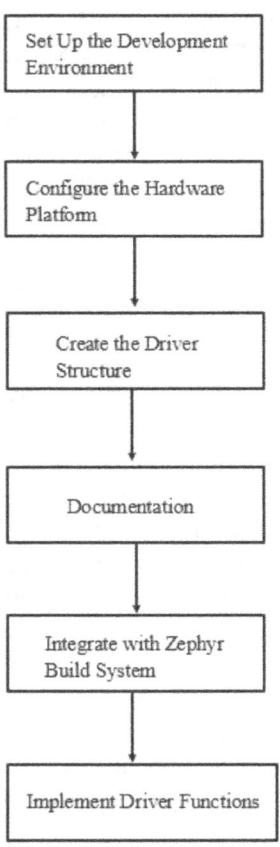

Figure 41.1 Flow diagram
Source: Author

- *Set up the development environment:* Begin by setting up the necessary development tools and environment for Zephyr and ARC microcontrollers.
- *Configure the hardware platform.* Define and configure the specific hardware platform you're working with to ensure it's compatible with the Zephyr RTOS.
- *Create the driver structure:* Design and set up the basic structure of the UART device driver, including the essential files and code organization.
- *Implement driver functions:* Develop and implement the actual functions of the UART driver, including initialization, transmission, and reception.
- *Integrate with Zephyr build system:* Ensure that the driver is properly integrated with the Zephyr RTOS build system so it can be compiled and used with the rest of the firmware.
- *Documentation:* Once the driver is completed, document the process and details of the implementation for future reference and maintenance

Software Components

UART Protocol

UART stands for universal asynchronous receiver / transmitter and defines a protocol, or set of rules, for exchanging serial data between two devices. UART is very simple and only uses two wires between transmitter and receiver to transmit and receive in both directions. Both ends also have a ground connection. Communication in UART can be simplex (data is sent in one direction only), half-duplex (each side speaks but only one at a time), or full-duplex (both sides can transmit simultaneously). Figure 41.2 explains the data in UART is transmitted in the form of frames. The format and content of these frames is briefly described and explained.

UART was one of the earliest serial protocols. The once ubiquitous serial ports are almost always UART-based, and devices using RS-232 interfaces, external modems, etc. are common examples of where UART is used. In recent years, the popularity of UART has decreased: protocols like SPI and I2C have been replacing UART between chips and components. Instead of communicating over a serial port, most modern computers and peripherals now use technologies like Ethernet and USB. However, UART is still used for lower-speed and lower-throughput

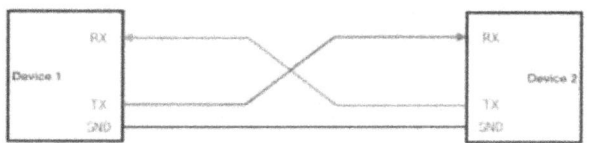

Figure 41.2 UART Block diagram
Source: Author

applications, because it is very simple, low-cost and easy to implement Timing and synchronization of UART protocols.

One of the big advantages of UART is that it is asynchronous – the transmitter and receiver do not share a common clock signal. Although this greatly simplifies the protocol, it does place certain requirements on the transmitter and receiver. Since they do not share a clock, both ends must be transmitted at the same, pre-arranged speed in order to have the same bit of timing. The most common UART baud rates in use today are 4800, 9600, 19.2K, 57.6K, and 115.2K. In addition to having the same baud rate, both sides of a UART connection also must use the same frame structure and parameters. The best way to understand this is to look at a UART frame.

Figure 41.3 shows the frame format of the UART. UART frames contain start and stop bits, data bits, and an optional parity bit.

Zephyre RTOS

The Zephyr OS is based on a small-footprint kernel designed for use on resource-constrained and embedded systems: from simple embedded environmental sensors and LED wearables to sophisticated embedded controllers, smart watches, and IoT wireless applications [1,5,7].

The Zephyr kernel supports multiple architectures, including:

- ARCv2 (EM and HS) and ARCv3 (HS6X)
- ARMv7,6 -M, and ARMv8-M (Cortex-M)
- ARMv7-A and ARMv8-A
- ARMv7-R, ARMv8-
- Intel x86 (32- and 64-bit)

Figure 41.3 Frame format of UART
Source: Author

- MIPS (MIPS32 Release 1 specification)
- NIOS II Gen 2
- RISC-V (32- and 64-bit)
- SPARC V8
- Tensilica Xtensa

Zephyr RTOS is an open-source real-time operating system designed for use in embedded systems and IoT applications. It is developed by the Zephyr work, which is hosted by the Linux Foundation. Zephyr RTOS provides a small footprint, modular architecture, and a wide range of features to support various types of embedded devices, from resource-constrained microcontrollers to more advanced multi-core systems.

Device Driver Layers Specific to Zephyr RTOS
Hardware abstraction layer (HAL): This abstracts the specifics of the underlying hardware. For example, functions to interact with the UART hardware registers would reside in the HAL. Device API: This layer provides a standard API for upper layers (applications or middleware) to interact with the driver without needing to know the hardware specifics. Operating system layer: In Zephyr, the driver is tightly integrated with the kernel, which manages threading, synchronization, and communication between the driver and user applications. Figure 41.4 explains the Zephyr architecture.

Metaware IDE
Meta Ware IDE is an integrated development environment specifically designed for developing software for Argonaut RISC Core (ARC) processors. The Synopsys Meta Ware Development Toolkit builds upon a 25-year legacy of industry-leading compiler and debugger products. It is a complete solution that contains all the components needed to support the

development, debugging and tuning of embedded applications for ARC and ARCV processors.

The tool chain supports the complete family of ARC-V processors, including the 32- bit ARC-V RMX embedded processors, the 32-bit ARC-V RHX real-time processors, the 64- bit ARC-V RPX host processors. The Meta Ware Toolkit also supports ARC Classic processors, from the high-speed ARC HS Family, the deeply embedded ARC EM Family, and the ARC VPX DSP Family, to the general-purpose ARC 600 family and the ARC 700. Figure 41.5 shows meta ware development toolkit offers a complete product solution to effectively support the development, debugging and tuning of your embedded applications for the ARC processor [3,6,8].

Results and Discussion

This work consists of several modules where some are auto generated. The main modules are the uart_ns16550.c which is the body function of the UART and main. C is the application module to check the UART functions.

UART Function Module
Figure 41.6 shows the algorithm followed in UART module function.

- *Handling interrupts:* The driver handles different types of interrupts (TX, RX, and others) and returns from the ISR.
- *Header inclusions:* Includes necessary headers from the Zephyr for kernel, CPU, types, initial-

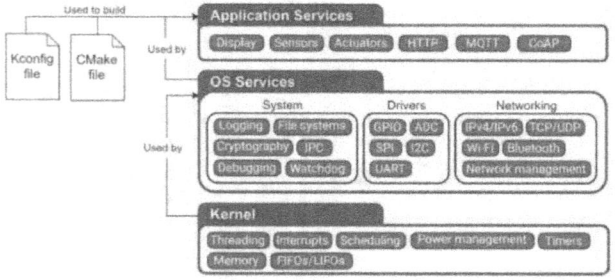

Figure 41.4 Zephyr architecture overview
Source: Zephyreproject.org

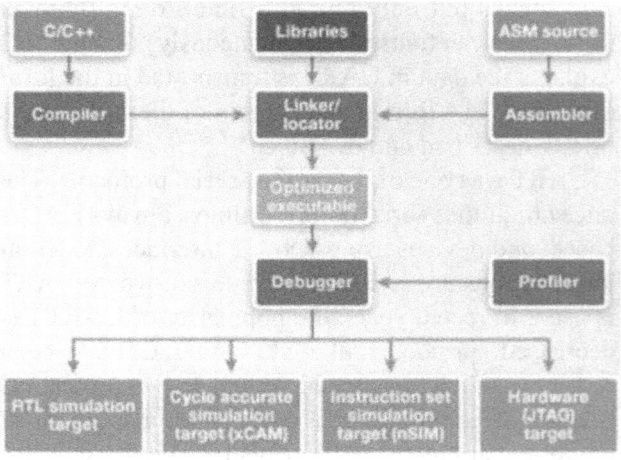

Figure 41.5 Meta ware model
Source: Zephyreproject.org

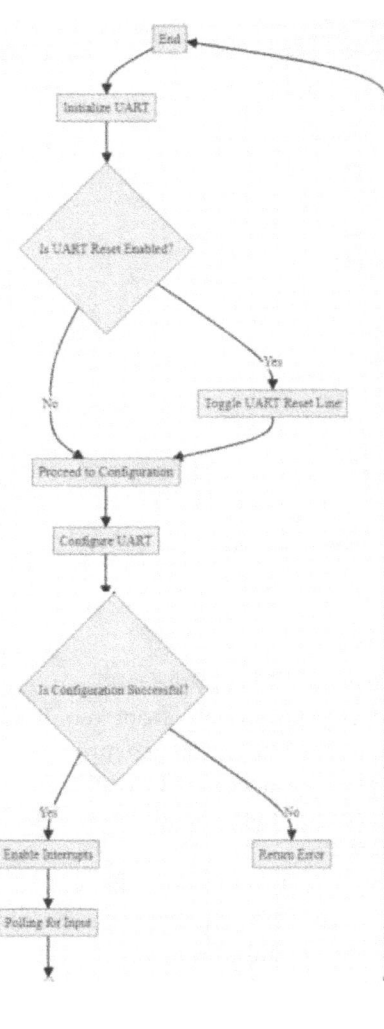
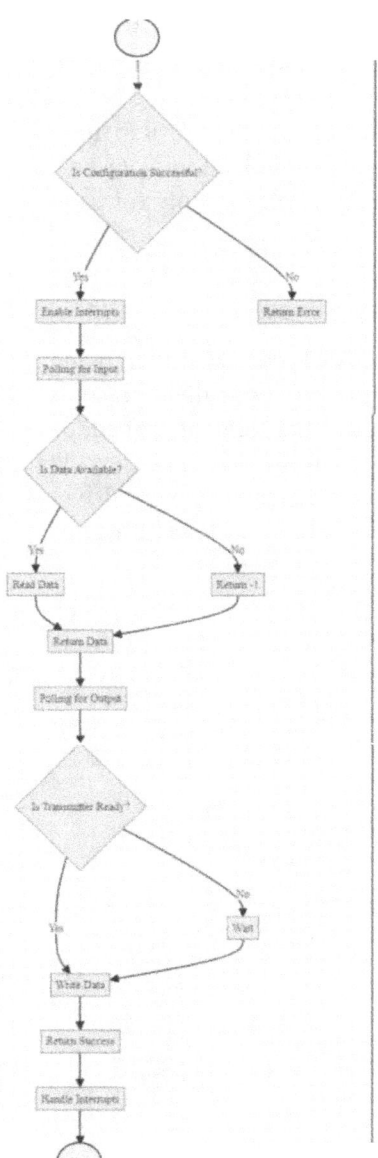

Figure 41.6 UART module algorithm
Source: Author

ization, toolchain, linker sections, UART, clock control, power management, system I/O, spinlock, and IRQ handling.

- *Interrupt and DMA handling:* Includes configurations and functions to handle interrupts and DMA for asynchronous UART operations.
- *Device configuration and initialization:* Structures and functions to configure and initialize the UART device, including setting baud rates, data bits, stop bits, and parity.

- *Polling and interrupt-driven I/O:* Functions to poll for input and output characters, and to handle interrupt driven I/O operations.
- *Error checking:* Functions to check for errors like overrun, parity, framing errors, and break conditions.

Module Output
The first step is to setup the container environment. After the completion of the coding set up the debug

configuration shown in the Figures 41.7–41.9 select the elf file, debugger as GDB and an internal port to make connection with zephyr RTOS.

The output shows and verifies the UART functions by initiating a serial communication from host to application using Zephyr API polling function [1,4,9].

Conclusion and Future Scope

The development of a UART device driver using Zephyr RTOS for the ARC microcontroller represents a significant advancement in the field of embedded systems. This work successfully demonstrates the integration of a robust and efficient UART driver within the Zephyr RTOS framework, leveraging the

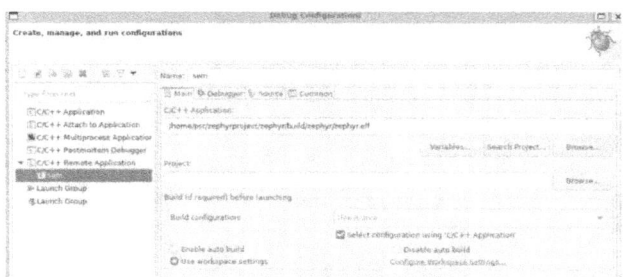

Figure 41.7 ELF File
Source: Author

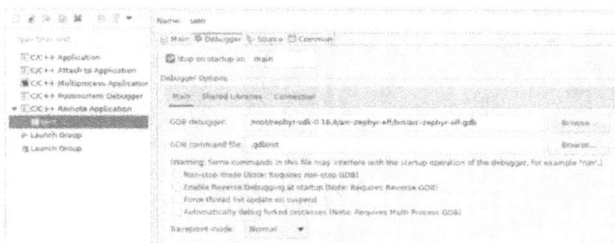

Figure 41.8 Debugger selection
Source: Author

Figure 41.9 Meta ware IDE debugger
Source: Author

Figure 41.10 UART Output
Source: Author

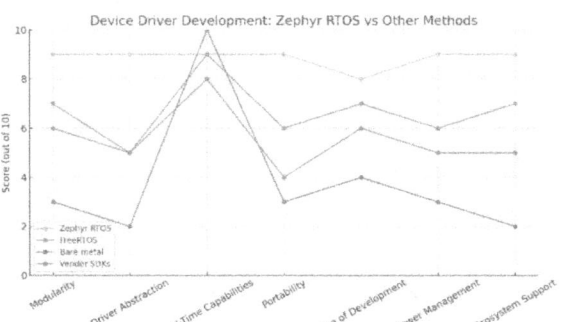

Figure 41.11 Comparison chart
Source: Author

high-performance capabilities of the ARC microcontroller. The systematic approach, from requirement analysis to testing and validation, ensures that the driver meets the specific needs of UART communication, including configurable baud rates, data bits, parity, and stop bits [5].

The use of Zephyr RTOS provides several advantages, including real-time capabilities, hardware abstraction, modularity, and strong community support. These features contribute to the development of a reliable and scalable UART driver that can be easily integrated into various embedded applications. The implementation of FIFO buffers and the use of a polling API further enhance the driver's performance and synchronization during high-speed data transmission [2].

Overall, this work lays a solid foundation for future developments in UART communication and embedded systems, showcasing the potential of combining Zephyr RTOS with ARC microcontrollers to achieve efficient and reliable serial communication.

Future Scope

Interrupt-driven UART Driver: Develop an interrupt-driven version of the UART driver to improve efficiency and reduce CPU usage compared to the polling mechanism. Interrupt-driven communication can provide better performance, especially in applications with high data throughput and real-time requirements.

Support for additional protocols: Extend the driver to support additional serial communication protocols such as SPI (Serial Peripheral Interface) and I2C. Integrate power management features to optimize the power consumption of the UART driver, especially in battery-powered and low-power applications. Efficient power management will extend the battery life of devices and reduce overall power consumption. Advanced error handling: Implement advanced error handling mechanisms to detect and recover from communication errors such as framing errors, driver, making it suitable for a wider range of applications [3], [4], [6].

References

[1] Brockman, P., French, D., & Tamm, C. (2014). REIT organizational structure, institutional ownership, and stock performance. *Journal of Real Estate Portfolio Manager*, 20, (1), 21–36.

[2] Cella, C. (2009). Institutional Investors and Corporate Investment. United States: Indiana University, Kelley School of Business.

[3] Chuang, H. (220). The impacts of institutional ownership on stock returns. *Empirical Economics*, 58(2), 507–533.

[4] Clark G. L., & Wójcik, D. (2005). Financial valuation of the German model: the negative relationship between ownership concentration and stock market returns, 1997–2001. *Economic Geography*, 81(1), 11–29.

[5] Dasgupta, A., Prat, A., & Verardo, M. (2011). Institutional trade persistence and long-term equity returns. *Journal of Finance*, 66(2), 635–653.

[6] Demsetz, H., & Lehn, K. (1985). The structure of corporate ownership: causes and consequences. *Journal of Political Economy*, 93(6), 1155–1177.

[7] Dyakov, T., & Wipplinger, E. (2020). Institutional ownership and future stock returns: an international perspective. *International Review of Finance*, 20(1), 235–245.

[8] Gompers, P. A., & Metrick, A. (2001). Institutional investors and equity prices. *Quarterly Journal of Economics*, 116(1), 229–259.

[9] Han, K. C., & Suk, D. Y. (1998). The effect of ownership structure on firm performance: additional evidence. *Review of Financial Economics*, 7(2), 143–155.

[10] Kennedy, P. (1985). A Guide to Econometrics Cambridge: MIT Press.

[11] La Forta, R., Lopez-de-Silanes, F., & Shleifer, A. (1999). Corporate ownership around the world. *Journal of Finance*, 54(2), 471–517.

42 Colorectal cancer classification using multi-color space texture analysis and machine learning

A Princeton Prakash[1,a] and R Rekha[2,b]

[1]PG Scholar, Department of Information Technology, PSG College of Technology, India

[2]Associate Professor, Department of Information Technology, PSG College of Technology, India

Abstract

The detection of colorectal cancer (CRC) at an early stage remains vital because it helps increase patient survival chances because CRC stands among the primary cancer related death reasons. The project establishes a computer-based pathway for CRC detection through the use of current image processing along with machine learning algorithms. The system extracts medical image texture features through multiple color space (RGB, HSV, LAB) application of 3D gray-level cooccurrence matrix (GLCM). The extracted features move to Random Forest as well as Support Vector Machine (SVM) and Gradient Boosting models for classification tasks. Through its web interface integration, the system offers real-time predictions for uploaded medical images. The system displays excellent diagnostic accuracy together with precision and recall levels enabling cost-effective and efficient non-invasive medical diagnosis when compared to conventional testing procedures. The system incorporates feedback from users to enhance its performance and operates as an effective instrument used by healthcare workers in CRC detection.

Keywords: Classification, colorectal cancer, GLCM, gradient boosting, healthcare professionals, image processing, machine learning, Random Forest, Real-time Prediction, SVM

Introduction

Worldwide colorectal cancer (CRC) stands as a main cancer type that produces numerous cancer- related fatalities each year. Early detection of colorectal cancer proves essential for better survival statistics because it enables physicians to provide immediate medical care and treatments. The diagnosis of CRC depends traditionally on invasive examination methods consisting of colonoscopy and biopsy. The diagnostic methods demonstrate effectiveness yet result in high costs and consume extensive time and cause discomfort as experienced by CRC patients. The demand for non-invasive detection methods is increasing because they provide an opportunity to detect colorectal cancer accurately before it progresses.

Medical imaging technologies have proven their value as essential diagnostic indicators for cancer diagnoses in recent medical practice. Technology provides physicians with alternative techniques for viewing tissue features and detecting any abnormalities without needing intrusive procedures. Medical imaging provides diagnosis of CRC through three main procedures including colonoscopy in combination with CT scans and MRI. The interpretation of these medical images heavily depends on radiologists or clinicians, but this approach leads to both interexpert and intra- expert variability and risk of human mistake. Machine-enhanced image processing system development has emerged because these systems enable both precise evaluations and rapid diagnoses and lower mistakes in medical analysis.

The proposed system develops automated colorectal cancer detection operations through machine learning combined with image processing methods. The system uses gray-level co-occurrence matrix (GLCM) method to extract texture features from medical images. The extracted texture features contain vital patterns which hint at the presence of cancerous tissue. Through the integration of machine learning models with extracted features the system identifies medical images between cancerous and non-cancerous conditions. This diagnostic technique provides superior accuracy together with automated detection capabilities for early-stage colorectal cancer diagnosis at an improved rate.

The system employs RGB, HSV, and LAB color spaces for acquiring an extensive collection of features from image examination. Constructing medical image analyses requires multiple color spaces which depict various portions of image color and intensity levels to generate an advanced tissue inspection. Each

[a]23pb35@psgtech.ac.in, [b]rra.it@psgtech.ac.in

DOI: 10.1201/9781003770435-42

color space receives the GLCM method to extract texture elements such as contrast together with correlation and energy and homogeneity features. The identified features stand essential for distinguishing cancer from normal tissue regions. Implementing various color spaces together with texture features generates an extensive data collection which improves machine learning model capabilities.

Support Vector Machine (SVM) and Random Forest and (RF) Gradient Boosting form the machine learning models active in the system. The extraction features guide these models to perform medical textural and color-based image identifications. The system's multiple-model architecture allows it to deliver improved performance as well as robustness above using one model only. The system combines model predictions through an ensemble approach so the classification performance and errors decrease resulting in better outcomes.

The system has both outstanding accuracy levels and a simple interface for users. The system implements Streamlit for developing a user-friendly web interface that enables medical staff to submit images which generate instantaneous prediction results. The system delivers immediate results through feedback that shows the classification determination together with the confidence level. The system gives healthcare professionals the ability to execute quick and reliable decision-making processes. Real-time performance and easy operation of the system turn it into an essential diagnostic tool for healthcare facilities that deliver fast reliable analysis. The system maintains features which enable it to adapt itself and enhance its capabilities as time progresses.

The system maintains an ongoing feedback process which enables integration of user feedback combined with new data that helps retrain the machine learning models allowing the system to keep performing optimally with additional data additions. The system demonstrates promising potential as a diagnostic solution for colorectal cancer because it can adapt from past learning experiences and evolved diagnosis methods while providing affordable and scalable alternatives to existing diagnostic methods.

Literature review

Research investigated how machine learning recognition of colorectal cancer improved through applying 3D gray-level co-occurrence matrix (GLCM)

in different color spaces (RGB, HSV, and LAB) [1]. Their method achieved better machine learning model classification through the application of texture analysis techniques. The research proved that including GLCM features extracted from multiple color spaces dramatically boosted the diagnostic performance of the model for identifying cancerous tissues from non-cancerous tissues. The method strengthens texture feature extraction because this process serves as an essential factor when detecting cancerous tissues from medical images particularly histopathological images. Color-CADx represents a deep learning framework that consists of triple convolutional neural networks (CNNs) along with discrete cosine transform (DCT) for colorectal cancer classification [2]. Color-CADx uses features from color images by incorporating both spatial features along with frequency-domain information. Research evidence showed that CNNs together with DCT enabled better detection of tissue variations between cancerous and non-cancerous samples thus resulting in enhanced classification precision. The detection algorithm integrates deep learning together with texture elements to examine CRC.

Medical experts at the Johns Hopkins University created a computer-aided diagnostic (CAD) system to evaluate brain tumor grades through examination of histopathology images [3]. Throughout their brain tumor grading study the researchers applied color and texture extractive methods such as GLCM which demonstrate potential value for colorectal cancer identification. Research findings showed that an improved diagnosis outcome resulted from processing both image colors and texture combinations together. Their method proved that medical diagnosis systems obtain higher classification accuracy when they combine color and texture information compared to working with either set separately. The research investigated machine learning algorithms for identifying colorectal cancer histopathological image types. The authors evaluated different models starting with Random Forest then before K-nearest neighbors (KNN). Random Forest (RF) together with SVM yielded better performance than different models when using GLCM method extracted texture-based features. The research demonstrates that texture components specifically including contrast and homogeneity positively influence colorectal cancer classification therefore supporting automated detection of cancer tissue in histopathological pictures [4].

Khazaee Fadafen and Rezaee [5] developed a new deep learning system made of multiple CNN networks and ensemble learning techniques to read and classify multiple tissue colorectal cancer scans. Their use of several classification models made their system more steady and precise while keeping its strong points. The new deep learning framework delivered better performance than regular deep learning systems in medical tests. This strategy fixed the model overfitting problem and made it work better for many different types of tissue samples. The study confirms that combining multiple detection models gives superior results in finding colorectal cancer. The researcher examined multiple machine learning methods for cancer tissue analysis in colon tissue samples. They evaluated Decision Trees (DT), RF and Gradient Boosting Machines to check how feature extraction affects classification accuracy results. Research confirmed that both machine learning systems and texture-based features GLCM and LBP work better together. Their research demonstrated how specific feature selection methods help lower the number of input variables while making colorectal cancer tissue diagnosis more effective [6]. Rotational invariance became possible in medical image research after researchers added Gabor convolutional neural networks (GCNNs) and color space variabilities (RGB and HSV). They developed an approach to support medical image processing systems that stay dependable while handling different image angle variations. It matters most for medical image analysis because body tissue orientation can shift in scans. The examination showed that this strategy produced better results in recognizing colorectal cancer since it processed tissue images equally well no matter how they were rotated [7]. Sasmal et al. [8] created a system to recognize colonoscopic polyps based on small areas that show both surface pattern and form details. Their research method proves valuable to detect colorectal cancer as polyps represent the earliest stages of this disease. To achieve better results the research merged measurements of geometric object layouts with statistics from GLCM texture analysis information. This research shows that including shape and texture information helps better find colonoscopic polyps and offers a useful method for detecting colorectal cancer at its earliest stages.

Nair and Sangal [9] reviewed the recent methods for the classification of colorectal polyps using computer-aided diagnosis (CAD) systems. Their review highlighted various methods, including texture-based feature extraction (like GLCM) and machine learning algorithms, used in automated polyp detection. They noted that machine learning, particularly ensemble methods and deep learning techniques, is becoming increasingly popular for colorectal cancer classification. The study also pointed out the challenges in classifying polyps, such as variations in shape and size, and recommended combining multiple feature sets to improve detection accuracy.

Lo et al.,(2022) [10] proposed an ensemble learning approach for early colorectal cancer detection using colonoscopic images. The study combined multiple machine learning models, including DT, SVM, and K-nearest neighbors (KNN), and integrated texture and shape-based features to improve classification. The results showed that ensemble learning could significantly improve classification accuracy by leveraging the strengths of various models. Their work emphasizes the importance of using ensemble techniques for CRC detection, as they help to enhance the robustness and accuracy of predictions in real-world applications.

Proposed methodology

The designed approach for colorectal cancer detection combines image processing methods with machine learning models into a automatic system which uses non-invasive technology at reduced costs for preliminary cancer diagnosis. This system extracts medical image textures to achieve high accuracy through machine learning algorithms for tissue classification as non-cancerous or cancerous.

System Overview

The system operates through different processes to execute precise colorectal cancer detection procedures. The initial step includes acquiring medical images through preprocessing techniques starting from colonoscopy results while including histopathology slides as the primary input. Also filtering these images helps achieve uniformity along with feature extraction quality enhancement for classification purposes.

Feature extraction through GLCM produces texture features from images. The system integrates color-based features which stem from RGB, HSV, and LAB color spaces to establish broad tissue characteristics detection capabilities. The platform applications

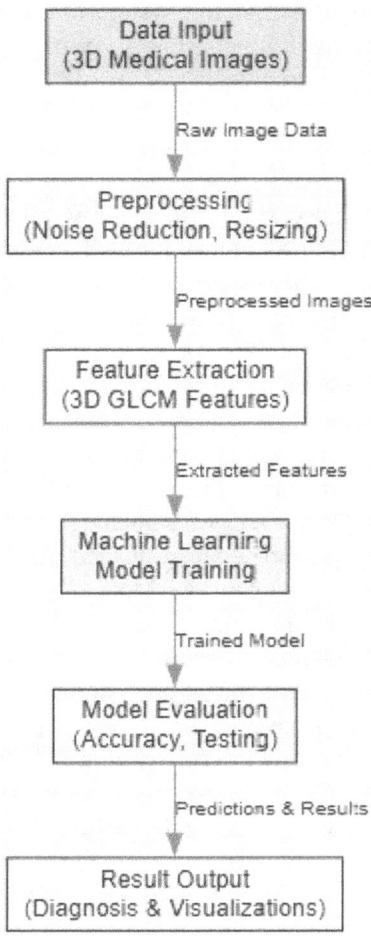

Figure 42.1 System architecture
Source: Author

statistical features developed from GLCM analysis involve contrast, correlation, energy and homogeneity measurements that help experts differentiate cancerous tissues from healthy tissues. Colorspace transformations together with GLCM features function as supplementary attributes by delivering features for hue saturation brightness for analyzing the image in depth.

RF uses ensemble learning techniques to collect various DT for creating stronger and more accurate predictions. SVM operates as a proficient classifier through its mechanism which generates the best possible boundary between tumor and healthy tissue regions.

The Gradient Boosting model technique builds and layers new models to fix previous errors thus enhancing its classification precision. The ensemble learning technique combines several machine learning model predictions through its ensemble process. The prediction system becomes more accurate because it depends on multiple models to reach its outcome. The system uses voting mechanics that results in the classification determined by the model receiving the highest number of votes.

Workflow

The user can access the web interface to send medical images including colonoscopy or histopathology images to the system for processing. The system accepts image files with extensions.jpg.png. .jpeg and .tif among others.

After image scanning the system performs multiple operations including dimensional conversion and utilization of Gaussian blur with median filtering before moving to RGB, HSV and LAB color space transformation. Each color space goes through the GLCM process to extract texture features by the system. The features include: This measure determines the strength of intensity changes between two adjacent image points. The image pixel value relationship evaluation occurs through correlation measurements within selected directions. Energy: Indicates the uniformity of the texture in the image. The comparison between adjacent pixel pairs shows their degree of intensity similarity in Homogeneity. The trained machine learning models process extracted features obtained from labeled datasets which contain cancerous or non-cancerous classifications for each image. The trained system performs categorizations of fresh images during the prediction stage The system

use extracted features for training machine learning models using RF, SVM and Gradient Boosting methods. The classification models perform an assignment of images into cancerous or non-cancerous diagnosis types. The system produces real-time predictions followed by alerts for healthcare staff with the classification results together with precision scores.

System Components

The system enables medical staff to connect images through its web interface. The machine learning models receive images that undergo an operation to standardize their resolution before processing. Image quality improvement techniques and RGB, HSV, LAB color space conversion methods serve to extract essential color characteristics from data.

The primary extraction aspect relies on GLCM for analyzing image pixel pair spatial relationships. The

receives new uploaded images to extract features then runs the trained models which results in prediction generation.

The system generates classification results with confidence scores to display on its web interface after showing the final outcome as cancerous or non- cancerous tissue. Healthcare professionals gain a chance to report prediction accuracy through a running feedback mechanism within the system. The system will become more accurate and adaptive through model retraining using received feedback data which allows for better performance as new information enters the system.

Real-Time Classification and User Interface
The platform uses real-time operation to deliver quick results about each image after healthcare professionals submit images to the system. Using Streamlit users gain access to uploading medical images while seeing automatic output processing and receiving their results alongside confidence scores. The platform includes a simple and practical interface which medical teams can quickly learn how to operate because no detailed technical expertise is needed for workflow integration.

Scalability and Adaptability
The system development incorporates scaling capabilities which will process expanding medical image datasets while the medical image volume grows. Through its architectural framework the system supports cloud deployment that permits healthcare providers to use the system through multiple locations which leads to increased accessibility along with greater reach. Through continuous feedback processing the system maintains its ability to stay relevant during periods of new medical data availability.

System Advantages
The diagnostic platform operates without physical invasion to the body providing patients with an alternative to invasive diagnostic tests that include both colonoscopy and biopsy examinations. The automated detection mechanism makes the system financially beneficial since it eliminates the demands for expensive diagnostic procedures that use a lot of time. The system delivers immediate response feedback so healthcare professionals can execute fast and educated decisions in real time. Webs-based interface provides an easy-to-use platform which needs no special technical skills from its users. Ongoing

model training enables the system to enhance itself through time as it adapts to new information along with developing trends.

Result and discussion

The recommended system to identify colorectal cancer received its assessment through labeled medical image datasets. The system carries out sequential steps which involve image acquisition followed by preprocessing then feature extraction prior to machine learning model classification to produce an alert. The system assessment relies on five main performance metrics that include accuracy together with precision and recall and F1-score and area under the curve (AUC). The important findings from these tests included the following information: The procedure obtained 92.5% success rate as its classification metric. Most images were properly identified as cancerous or non-cancerous tissues by the system according to these results.

The system achieved a precision value of 89% for detecting cancerous tissue which is called true positives. The system demonstrated 89% success in predicting tissues to be cancerous among all predictions. The system managed to identify 94% of actual cancerous tissues correctly during the testing period.

The system shows excellent performance at identifying cancerous tissues because of its high recall value which reduces the occurrence of incorrect negative results. The F1-score reached a value of 91.4% due to its calculation method using precision and recall as harmonic mean values.

The system demonstrates excellent performance according to this measure because it maintains high accuracy in both cancer detection and false-positive avoidance. The area under curve (AUC) measurement of 0.96 demonstrates that this model shows excellent capability to separate between cancerous and non-cancerous tissue.

An elevated AUC value indicates outstanding classification results for every defined threshold. The system required 0.5 seconds during each inference to determine an image category.

Real time predictions emerge from this system which makes it suitable because hospital environments require fast results. The established system demonstrates superior performance capability which makes it efficient aid for medical personnel to find cancer early medical diagnostic instrument according to the obtained results. The detection system shows strong results in every assessment metric mainly because it identifies cancer tissue efficiently yet keeps the occurrence of incorrect diagnoses to a minimum. The following part provides an extensive analysis of essential assessment findings.

The system demonstrates optimal performance through its 92.5% accuracy level which indicates strong robustness in image classification tasks. The implemented model demonstrates excellence in identifying cancerous and non-cancerous tissues that appear across various images. The system delivers diagnostic performance comparable to present techniques that require rigorous procedures and generate both financial and time expenses. The system combines texture features from GLCM with RF and SVM and Gradient Boosting models to produce its strong operation. The system demonstrated dual performance strengths by maintaining an 89% precision level and an equally high 94% recall evaluation of cancerous tissues.

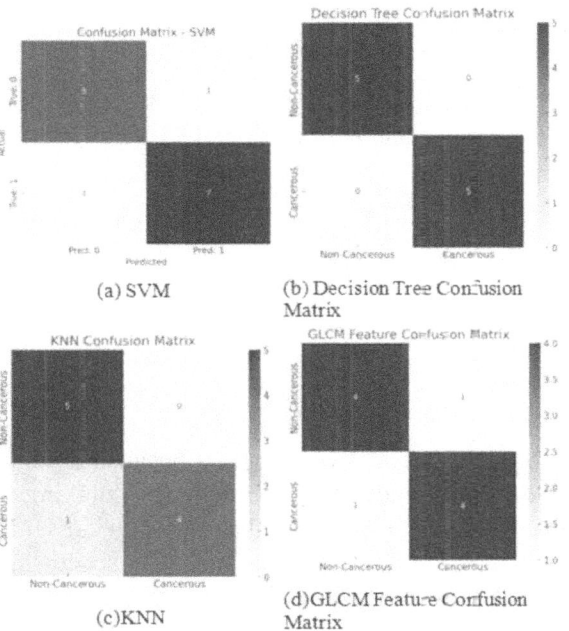

(a) SVM

(b) Decision Tree Confusion Matrix

(c)KNN

(d)GLCM Feature Confusion Matrix

Figure 42.4 Confusion matrices of classification models
Source: Author

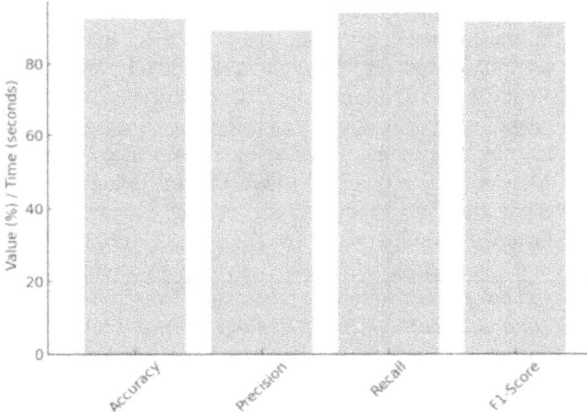

Figure 42.2 Performance metrics
Source: Author

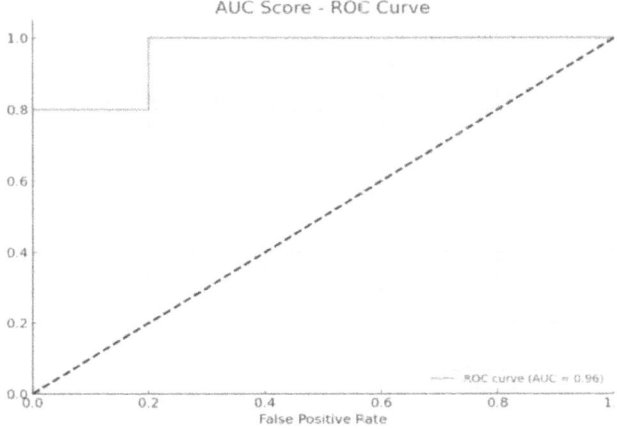

Figure 42.3 ROC Curve for ML models
Source: Author

Discussion

The colorectal cancer detection system demonstrates its capability to become an essential medical diagnostics requires high recall performance since misdiagnosing cancerous tissue will lead to delayed treatment and poorer health results. Early cancer detection relies heavily on the system's strong sensitivity because of its high recall value which aids the improvement of patient survival rates. According to the results the system shows a precision rate of 89% which indicates that very minimal non-cancerous tissues get identified as cancerous (false positives) yet such cases are manageable through further clinical testing procedures.

The F1-score measures 91.4% to maintain the right balance between precision and recall because it prioritizes both cancer detection accuracy and false positive avoidance. High F1-score plays a crucial role in imbalanced dataset evaluation since it maintains proper balance between precision and recall performance.

The AUC score reveals a model excellence when differentiating cancerous tissues from non-cancerous tissues with a value of 0.96. A value near 1.0 in the AUC score indicates strong discrimination power between classes along with minimum class confusion by the model. The system demonstrates reliable ability to detect cancerous tissues while reducing the number of errors in classification.

Table 42.1 Performance metrics

Metric	Value
Accuracy	92.5%
Precision	89%
Recall	94%
F1-Score	91.4%
AUC(AreaUnderCurve)	0.96
InferenceTime	0.5 Seconds

Source: Author

The system operates in real time because it completes each inference in 0.5 seconds thus making it suitable for medical situations that need quick results. Because of its rapid image classification speed this system remains useful in medical practice especially since time efficiency plays an essential part in patient treatment procedures. Fast classification operations assist healthcare staff to speed up their decisions for initiating early medical intervention and treatment which reflects that older firms with high profits infer better stock returns.

Conclusion

The proposed colorectal cancer detection system demonstrates strong performance, achieving an accuracy of 92.5%, with high precision and recall values, indicating its ability to accurately classify cancerous and non-cancerous tissues. The system's real-time prediction capability (0.5 seconds per image) makes it suitable for clinical use, providing fast and reliable results. By leveraging texture-based features extracted using the 3D GLCM method and combining multiple machine learning models, the system offers a non-invasive, cost-effective alternative to traditional diagnostic methods.

Although improvements in image quality handling and the integration of deep learning models could enhance the system's performance, the current results suggest significant potential for aiding healthcare professionals in early colorectal cancer detection.

References

[1] Alqudah, A. M., & Alqudah, A. (2022). Improving machine learning recognition of colorectal cancer using 3D GLCM applied to different color spaces. *Multimedia Tools and Applications*, 81(8), 10839–10860.

[2] Sharkas, M., & Attallah, O. (2024). Color- CADx: a deep learning approach for colorectal cancer classification through triple convolutional neural networks and discrete cosine transform. *Scientific Reports*, 14(1), 6914.

[3] Elazab, N., Gab Allah, W., & Elmogy, M. (2024). Computer-aided diagnosis system for grading brain tumor using histopathology images based on color and texture features. *BMC Medical Imaging*, 24(1), 177.

[4] Georgiou, N., Kolias, P., & Chouvarda, I. (2024). Machine learning models for the classification of histopathological images of colorectal cancer. *Applied Sciences*, 14(22), 10731.

[5] Khazaee Fadafen, M., & Rezaee, K. (2023). Ensemble-based multi-tissue classification approach of colorectal cancer histology images using a novel hybrid deep learning framework. *Scientific Reports*, 13(1), 8823.

[6] Reddy, N. S. S., Manoj, A. V. S., & Sowmya, V. (2023). Classification of colorectal cancer tissue utilizing machine learning algorithms. In International Advanced Computing Conference (pp. 397–409). Cham: Springer Nature Switzerland.

[7] Gateri, J., Rimiru, R. M., & Kimwele, M. (2023). Rotational invariance using gabor convolution neural network and color space for image processing. *International Journal of Ambient Computing and Intelligence*, 14(1), 1–11.

[8] Sasmal, P., Bhuyan, M. K., Iwahori, Y., & Kasugai, K. (2021). Colonoscopic polyp classification using local shape and texture features. *IEEE Access*, 9, 92629–92639.

[9] Nair, A., & Sangal, A. L. (2023). Review of the recent methods for classification of colorectal polyps using computer aided diagnosis. In 2023 Third International Conference on Secure Cyber Computing and Communication (ICSCCC) (pp. 530–535).

[10] Lo, Chung-Ming, Yu-Hsuan Yeh, Jui-Hsiang Tang, Chun-Chao Chang, and Hsing-Jung Yeh. "Rapid polyp classification in colonoscopy using textural and convolutional features." In Healthcare, 10(8), 1494. MDPI, 2022.

43 Consensus mechanisms in blockchain: a comparative analysis of performance and energy efficiency for real-time applications

Vairam T[1,a] and Srijeimathy M[2,b]

[1]Assistant Professor, Department of IT, PSG College of Technology, Coimbatore, India

[2]Student, Department of IT, PSG College of Technology, Coimbatore, India

Abstract

Blockchain technology has revolutionized real-time applications with its decentralized, secure, and immutable framework, wherein the consensus mechanisms play a principal role in deciding transaction speed, security, and scalability. Traditional consensus mechanisms like Proof of Work (PoW) were affected by latency and energy inefficiency, while modern alternatives such as Proof of Stake (PoS), Practical Byzantine FaultTolerance (PBFT), and Delegated Proof-of-Stake (DPoS) realize faster and scalable solutions to real-time applications for Finance, Supply Chain, Healthcare, and IoT. This survey conducts a systematic analysis of the various consensus algorithms, including PoW, PoS, PBFT, and some upcoming models like Proof of History (PoH), in regard to throughput, latency, and security and finds that PoS-based systems and DAG (Directed Acyclic Graph) systems such as Solana and Ethereum 2.0 excel over PoW for low-latency applications with thousands of transactions per second (TPS). Despite these improvements, present-day blockchain technologies are encumbered with challenges like scalability bottlenecks, interoperability challenges, and regulatory restrictions, which prompt the search for future solutions such as hybrid consensus methods (PoS + sharding), Layer-2 scaling approaches (including rollups and sidechains), and AI- based optimizations that could benefit real-time operations of blockchains without compromising security and decentralization.

Keywords: Blockchain consensus, decentralization energy, efficiency, scalability, throughput

Introduction

Blockchain technology is revolutionizing industries by realizing real-time transactions in a decentralized, secure, and transparent manner. Its distributed ledger structure does away with centralized control, with each cryptographically linked block providing for an immutable record- if data is to be altered, all subsequent blocks would have to be modified in concurrence with the network. This tampering-resistant design, when combined with cryptographic security, removes the need for trust in any third-party while, from a technical perspective, preventing any possibility of a single point of failure. However, systematic efficiency requires that many of the implementation challenges relating to consensus mechanisms be put aside, which constitute the basis of discussion for this review, along with adoption impediments and future directions.

Real-time processing thus perfectly coincides with the typical features of blockchain, especially in the finance and supply chain. Cross-border payments eliminate traditional banking delays, while supply chain tracking reduces fraud through the instant verification method. IoT systems utilize blockchain technology for significant high-volume sensor data processing in smart cities as well as industrial automation, beating both delays and opacity associated with traditional systems. Unlike centralized architectures that suffer from bottlenecks, the parallel processing across nodes in blockchain provides true real- time performance, when coupled with appropriate consensus mechanisms that balance speed, scalability, and security.

Consensus protocols critically keep a ledger synchronized across distributed networks, and thus are important for the real-time feasibility of the blockchain. Proof of Work suffers from a block time of ten minutes; however, alternatives like Proof of Stake and Delegated Proof of Stake can deliver near-instantaneous confirmations. Scalability improvements like sharding and hybrids yield throughput increases, empowered by Byzantine Fault Tolerance for secure permissioned environments. These systems must, however, constantly mitigate the risk of

[a]tvm@psgtech.ac.in, [b]23pb05@psgtech.ac.in

DOI: 10.1201/9781003770435-43

Sybil and 51% attack while serving specific latency requirements in the industry-a fine balance that determines their suitability for time-sensitive applications.

This analysis evaluates major consensus models (PoW, PoS, PBFT, DPoS) against real-time operational needs across finance, healthcare, and IoT domains. It benchmarks platforms like Ethereum and Solana on transaction speed and security while addressing adoption hurdles—scalability constraints, energy inefficiencies, and regulatory uncertainty. Emerging solutions, including Layer-2 protocols and quantum-resistant designs, highlight the field's evolution toward seamless de- centralized systems. By synthesizing these insights, the re- view provides a roadmap for developing robust, low-latency blockchain infrastructures capable of transforming industry practices.

Background

Blockchain consensus mechanisms like PoW, PoS, PBFT, and DPoS are balanced with respect to decentralization, throughput, and energy efficiency, which affect their real- time performance in finance, supply chains, healthcare, and IoT. They also affect transaction speed, security, and scalability, all while maintaining the inherent advantages offered by a blockchain. The choice of consensus model directly relates to maximum efficiency of applications belonging to the economies mentioned.

Role of Consensus in Blockchain
The blockchain consensus mechanisms PoW, PoS, PBFT, and DPoS trade off speed for security and decentralization. While PoW guarantees security, it doesn't offer high through- put; instead, PoS and PBFT provide faster transactions, offer- ing some other trade-offs. The algorithm chosen by a particular blockchain limits its suitability across various industries for real-time applications.

Consensus Algorithms Overview
Consensus mechanisms can be thought of as decentralized protocols designed to validate transactions by trading off speed, security, and energy efficiency. Proof of Work (PoW) entails competitive mining of transactions, which provides security to a fault at the expense of some limited transaction throughput (on the order of 7 TPS) and high energy consumption (in excess of 10 minutes' worth). These drawbacks are acceptable for a store-of-value system like Bitcoin.

Proof of Stake (PoS), as used by Ethereum 2.0, swaps out mining for staking, granting faster transactions (on the order of about 1000 TPS) and lower energy requirements, while thus being faced with issues such as the nothing-at-stake problem, suitable for DeFi and smart contract platforms. Practical Byzantine Fault Tolerance (PBFT) is suitable for permissioned chains like Hyperledger Fabric and works by having validators vote for the transaction to process, achieving high throughput (around 10,000 TPS) with sub-second finality and Byzantine fault tolerance for <1/3 of malicious nodes at the cost of decentralization.

The Delegated Proof-of-Stake (DPoS) protocol seen in EOS goes further in speed (4,000 TPS) and energy efficiency through elected delegates, but has the disadvantage of possible centralization and lack of censorship resistance due to a small validator set.

Impact on Real-Time Performance
The choice made concerning consensus mechanisms is always going to define the adoption ground for a blockchain on a real time basis. Neither PoW is such that it has slow confirmation times in addition to throughput insufficiency to ever allow it as an option for instant transaction finality applications, as opposed to the comparison made with PoS and PBFT that confirm their transactional confirmations within seconds rather than in minutes.

For example, hybrid consensus may involve scenarios such as that of PoS with sharding at Ethereum 2.0. Innovative and creative model-propositions can run risk-free enhance what is meant in scalability. Layer 2 mechanisms, such as rollups and state channels, thereby improve upon these base-layer mechanisms for higher transaction speeds. Other possible solutions include the development of DAG-Directed Acyclic Graphs-which establish alternative systems that remove the need for blocks at all: these then make feeless and instantaneous transactions ideal for IoT applications possible.

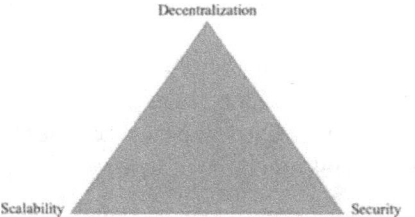

Figure 43.1 Consensus mechanism workflow
Source: Author

Blockchain Applications in Real-Time Systems

The real-time performance needs in sectors such as finance are met by customized consensus mechanisms provided by blockchain technology, where off-chain payment channels, for instance, the Bitcoin Lightning Network, enable instantaneous micropayments while reducing latency.

For example, in VeChain's PoA, supply chain transactions are run at super-fast speeds to verify products on the chain, while the MedRec system uses PBFT for immediate, secure sharing of health data with finality in less than a second. IOTA achieves instantaneity on the Tangle architecture, where machines transfer assets and services from one entity to another without cost.

This serves as an example of how industry requirements are being accommodated through these customized consensus protocols while enjoying the benefits of blockchain tech—such as security, transparency, and decentralization. This paves the way for new-age decentralized systems to operate in real-time.

Literature Review

Decentralized systems represent a different paradigm shift from the former technology so to speak. This review investigates 50 key papers concerning the disruptive character of blockchain on different industries, with examples from health- care, finance, and smart transportation. Several advances are presented-from DApps, blockchain 4.0, DWeb, to block-chain- IoT-highlighting the advantages of security, transparency, and consensus mechanisms over the traditional centralized model. The paper discusses implementation techniques, the metrics to evaluate other performance indices, and challenges to adoption and proposes a framework to understand the development of blockchain within the decentralized ecosystem. Research gaps in this rapidly evolving area of study are also suggested [1].

Blockchain technologies can help change modern logistics by providing decentralized, transparent, and secure solutions to major risks such as inefficiencies, information gaps, and security concerns. By using latent Dirichlet allocation (LDA) topic modeling on 2,465 scholarly publications, the research analyzes and identifies six key application areas: supply chain finance, logistics tracking, inter-organizational collaboration, process optimization, data security, and

business model in- novation. In addition, it examines real-world feasibility of blockchain implementations, discusses the challenges faced, and highlights best practices. Their findings would help logistics managers use blockchain to improve supply chain transparency, security, and efficiency [2].

A decentralized architecture, coupled with cryptographic security and transparent ledgers, have resolved traditional banking problems that disrupted finance through blockchain technology and thus have facilitated faster, cheaper transactions by removing the need for intermediaries. Historically, challenges such as scalability and regulatory uncertainty, as well as integration with legacy systems, have caused implementational roadblocks, although cross-border payments, trade finance, and digital identity verification have offered promising applications for blockchain with its immutability and smart contract capability. Resistance to adopting blockchain continues due to organizational governance concerns, including readiness of the workforce and ability of management, thereby perpetuating the dual discourse on blockchain's transformative potential and institutional skepticism [3].

Conventional waste management systems are often encountering challenges such as inefficiencies, opacity, fraud, as well as a lack of accountability in recycling due to manual audits. Blockchain technologies, on the other hand, have promised a considerable revolution in all these, providing automation verification through smart contracts with immutable records. Thus, tracking wastes, having better incentives for recycling, and inducing circular economy practices through digital product passports have now become feasible. Nevertheless, the current blockchain implementations for waste management often lack scalability and have less stakeholder adoption; hence, there is a serious need for a robust framework to roll out blockchain for practical waste management while addressing the already existing limitations and optimizing benefits in the environment and the economy [4].

Blockchain technology has gone through significant trans- formations since the year 2008, from PoW and PoS classical systems to modern Byzantine Fault Tolerant systems, in terms of scalability, security, and decentralization. This work considers metrics such as transaction throughput, energy efficiency, and finality times, to study those three systems in the major blockchains, namely Ethereum, Hyperledger

Fabric, and Corda. Consensus models and smart contract capabilities are being analyzed while bringing into light the trade-offs about decentralization versus performance. Emerging solutions become one more theme when creating a picture of ongoing innovation and practical challenges in blockchain technology concerning both governance and interoperability [5].

The combination of renewables and IT brings along certain cybersecurity risks such as grid destabilization and secure solutions needing to be worked out in real-time. Traditional blockchain provides decentralization and immutability, but its latency and inefficiency make it unsuitable for applications in the domain of control. Nowadays, consensus protocols (PoW, PoS) are highly skewed toward security at the expense of real-time performance, with most focusing on cryptographic puzzles rather than system operation. Task-oriented consensus variants do exist; however, none have been designed considering renewable energy control requirements specifically, thus widening an already existing chasm. Thus, we need a Proof of Task approach now in order to transfer the computation power of blockchain from hashing towards stability and control tasks to maintain both security and real-time responsiveness [6].

Technological progress in IoT-based health care systems aimed mainly at real-time patient observation now requires secure and efficient consensus mechanisms for the protection of medical data , since traditional blockchain methods such as proof of work or proof of stake are unsuitable because of high computation and energy requirements; Practical Byzantine Fault Tolerance (PBFT) offers lower latency and energy efficiency but the trust selection of nodes becomes an issue in permissionless settings with scalability; and combining a trust management system such as EigenTrust with Verifiable Random Functions (VRF) may resolve trustworthiness in nodes and leads to unpredictable leader selection, on the contrary achieving lightweight, secure, and energy-consumption- efficient consensus for the healthcare IoT is a challenging juggling act still not resolved by existing techniques [7].

Blockchain technology will modernize the management of health data with security, transparency, and decentralization benefits mentioned. Health information exchanges have bene- fitted by deploying public and private blockchains. Automation of consent management by smart contracts in Ethereum and interoperable EHR solutions using Hyperledger

Fabric would help mitigate some of these challenges. An immutable ledger can strengthen drug supply chains, clinical trials, and patient- centric care despite trade-offs in scalability, energy efficiency, and decentralization. Current trends in research are looking toward hybrid consensus protocol models, layer 2 scaling, and zero-knowledge proofs for improving compliance with effi- cacy. However, despite progress toward real-world applications in healthcare, successful implementation would require both standardization processes and extensive verifications [8].

Communication among machines in a secure and decentralized way is made possible by combining Blockchain and IoT. In other words, in place of centralized systems, the two tend to solve IoT conditions like data tampering and single points of failure by employing tamper-proof records and consensus validation. The architecture may vary from lightweight blockchains to fit low-powered devices to hybrid models. Mainly, supply chain tracking and lots of health- related wearables are examples of applications; however, there still remain challenges for blockchain-based systems to ensure that they are not computationally intensive and fit nicely with the power constraints, scalability, and interoperability requirements of IoT. Integrating the two offers opportunities as well as challenges to consider, especially since the adaptive consensus algorithms can possibly enhance the performance while keeping security intact owing to edge computing [9].

Consensus mechanisms can provide integrity for any de- centralized networks but are prone to vulnerabilities such as hacking, affecting the security and performance of the mechanism. Also, PoW and PoS, the traditional consensus mechanisms , are not working well in terms of energy efficiency and threat resistance, and that gives birth to hybrid models that work with machine learning (ML) to get more elegant results. Like Delegated Proof of Stake Work (DPoSW) and Proof of CASBFT (PoCASBFT), these are relying on the capability of ML for real-time excess threat detection and a better selection of operating nodes resulting in improved energy efficiency, throughput, and Byzantine fault tolerance- as can be observed within ProximaX implementations. The area has several challenges, such as scalability while under high loads, latency in making decisions, and vulnerability to adversarial ML attacks. Thus, further research is necessary for its dependable deployment. This is the area that necessitates more intelligent consensus protocols for the challenging demands of modern blockchains [10].

Comparative Analysis

Figure 43.2 shows the transaction throughput (TPS) of some main consensus mechanisms. Standard PoW systems like Bitcoin have very little throughput (≈7 TPS), which is largely due to relevant computational time by the miners. Next-generation consensus mechanisms such as PBFT and PoH, however, have ultra-high TPS capabilities reaching 10,000 TPS and 50,000+ TPS respectively. DPoS achieves high TPS (≈4,000 TPS) here too, as again by restricting the total number of validating nodes. DAG systems also achieve high TPS by allowing many transactions to be processed concurrently without computing block finalization in their consensus protocol. This figure clarifies how next-generation consensus protocols will be able to support real-time applications (e.g., IoT and finance) better than legacy protocols.

The average transaction finality time of consensus mechanisms is demonstrated in Figure 43.3. A critical takeaway for finality time is that PoW has the longest finality time (~10 minutes). The longer time is probably attributable to classic mining as well as block propagation. The rest of the acceptance mechanisms (PBFT, DPoS, PoA) have finality times that are again approximately instantaneous in time (sub-second to some seconds), which is suitable for real-time applications. PoH with PoS (e.g. Solana) has ultra-low latency (about 400 ms) allowing for very rapid data processing for distributed apps. DAG systems have indicated intermediate latency performance but as they rely on coordinator nodes, they incur some additional latency. This figure reinforces that consensus mechanisms that could achieve low-latency performance would be ideal for time-sensitive applications including health monitoring and financial transactions.

Proof of Work (PoW)

PoW is the security backbone of Bitcoin in which the miners solve complex puzzles to validate transactions with a guaranty against being successfully attacked by 51%. This comes at a huge energy cost and at only 7 transaction per second throughput, which restricts its practical use for high-speed applications. Nevertheless, there is no alternative to PoW in its inefficiency as the only store of value that is decentralized and censorship-resistant.

Proof of Stake (PoS)

PoS replaces the energy intensive mining with staking to allow validators to secure the network by depositing currency. PoS enables Ethereum to scale (100–5000 TPS) and reduce energy use by 99.95%. Although some risks of nothing-at stake do exist, the slashing conditions rather serve to mitigate malicious behavior, thereby justifying PoS as a viable alternative.

Delegated Proof of Stake (DPoS)

DPoS, which streams consensus by electing a little number of delegates (from 21 to 101) to validate transactions, consequently permits over 4,000 TPS and near-instant finality. While efficiency in this sense is praiseworthy, low node numbers make centralization a concern, as in the case of EOS, where voter apathy led to consolidation of validators.

Practical Byzantine Fault Tolerance (PBFT)

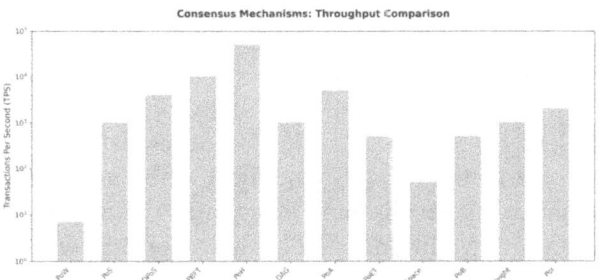

Figure 43.2 Throughput of all consensus mechanisms
Source: Author

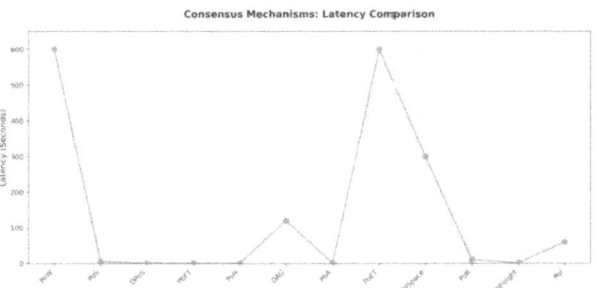

Figure 43.3 Latency of all consensus mechanisms
Source: Author

PBFT would provide immediate finality for permissioned networks with a voting system of three phases among known nodes, and 1,000-10,000 TPS can be achieved. Still, O(n²) complexity prevents scalability to more than 100 nodes. Corporates like Hyperledger Fabric apply PBFT to trusted, high-speed solutions for supply chains.

Proof of History (PoH)
Solana's PoH timestamps transactions cryptographically be- fore consensus, enabling 50,000+ TPS and 400ms finality when combined with PoS. High-performance hardware requirements introduce centralization risks, but leader rotation ensures no single point of failure.

Directed Acyclic Graph (DAG)
DAG-based systems like IOTA's Tangle replace blocks with a web of transactions, enabling parallel processing and fee- less microtransactions. A temporary coordinator node ensures security until network density grows, making it ideal for IoT but currently semi-centralized.

Proof of Authority (PoA)
PoA relies on approved, identity-verified validators to achieve 5,000+ TPS with instant finality, sacrificing decentralization for speed. Binance Smart Chain uses this model, ideal for semi-private networks where participants are vetted.

Proof of Elapsed Time (PoET)
PoET uses Intel SGX for a fair, energy-efficient lottery system, offering 100-1,000 TPS in enterprise settings. Its reliance on specialized hardware limits decentralization but suits controlled environments like Hyperledger Sawtooth.

Proof of Space (PoSpace)
Chia Network's PoSpace uses disk storage instead of computational power, offering eco-friendly consensus with 10–100 TPS. However, 5-minute block times and 51% space attack risks require careful economic design.

Proof of Burn (PoB)
PoB simulates mining by burning tokens, eliminating hard- ware needs but creating deflationary pressure. With 100–1,000 TPS and 5–30 second confirmations, it suits niche applications prioritizing simplicity.

Proof of Weight (PoWeight)
Algorand's PoWeight allows customizable validator selection based on multiple factors, supporting 1,000+ TPS with instant finality. Its flexibility benefits enterprises but requires careful parameter tuning.

Proof of Importance (PoI)
NEM's PoI evaluates nodes based on activity and stake, encouraging participation but introducing subjectivity. Its 1,000- 5,000 TPS range and 1–5 minute finality suit engagement- focused business networks.

The overall comparative analysis is summarized in tabular format shown in Table 43.1. Table 43.1 demonstrates a comparison of prominent consensus mechanisms on the blockchain and major factors to evaluate, including decentralization, throughput, latency, energy efficiency, scalability, and trust models. PoW provides strong security but is inefficient for real-time applications, as it provides low throughput and high energy consumption. PoS enables scalability and energy efficiency while maintaining a sufficient level of decentralization. PBFT and PoA offer high performance in permissioned networks with trusted validators. Additional mechanisms for consensus, such as PoH and DAG, support high throughput and low latency processes, in particular allowing for real-time processing of physical characteristics for synchronous systems and low latency status updates with IoT devices. Other consensus mechanisms noted in the table, such as PoET, PoSpace, PoB, and PoWeight, focused more on energy efficiency and participation as an incentive with the similar goal of processing functionality. From Table 43.1, it is clear that the right consensus mechanism depends on the goal and constraints of the application.

Table 43.1 Comparison of blockchain consensus mechanisms

Property	PoW	PoS	DPoS	PBFT	PoH	DAG	PoA	PoET	PoSpace	PoB	PoWeight	PoI
Blockchain type	Permissionless	Open	Open	Permissioned	Open	Open	Permissioned	Open	Open	Open	Open	Open
Transaction finality	Probabilistic	Probabilistic	Instant	Instant	400ms	2+ min	Instant	10+ min	Probabilistic	10+ min	Instant	1-5 min
Transaction rate	Low	High	High	High	Ultra High	High	High	Medium	Low	Medium	High	High
Token needed	Yes	Yes	Yes	No	Yes	No	No	No	Yes	Yes	Yes	Yes
Cost of participation	Very High	Low	Very Low	Medium	Low	Minimal	Low	Low	Medium	Medium	Low	Low
Network scalability	Limited	High	High	Limited	Very High	Unlimited	High	High	Limited	Limited	High	High
Trust model	Untrusted	Untrusted	Untrusted	Semi-trusted	Untrusted	Untrusted	Trusted	Untrusted	Untrusted	Untrusted	Untrusted	Untrusted
Adversary tolerance	≤ 25% hash	<51% stake	<51% votes	<33% nodes	34% stake	34% nodes	Trusted	Unknown	51% space	51% burn	Custom	34% nodes
Examples	Bitcoin	Ethereum 2.0	EOS	Hyperledger	Solana	IOTA	BSC	Sawtooth	Chia	Slimcoin	Algorand	NEM

Source: Author

Challenges and Limitation

Blockchain is perfect for secure, decentralized, and real-time embedded systems; however, adoption is being delayed due to certain limitations. This includes trade-offs in consensus (scalability, latency, and security) and larger concerns such as interoperability, regulation, and energy consumption. Overcoming these limitations will be key to the timely implementation of blockchain for time-critical applications.

Consensus-Related Challenges

Consensus mechanisms are essential for the validation and formation of transactions in blocks, but they cannot help to overcome the replication limitations of scalability, latency, and security-speed trade-offs for real-time applications. Conventional PoW gives a high level of security but a very low throughput (e.g., Bitcoin is 7 TPS vs. thousands for Visa), causing significant congestion, delays, and high fees.

Although sharding and Layer-2 solutions mitigate the negative side of this, latency remains an issue—the PoW's time of about 10 minutes required for the block hinders any immediate settlements. Solutions like PoS and DPoS avoid this latency but are generally less decentralized.

Throughput mechanisms like PBFT allow more than 10,000 TPS, but centralized validators are usually used, making it possible for developers to choose either speed or decentralization, with hybrid models adding a level of complexity.

Energy consumption across consensus models is shown in Figure 43.4. PoW is the most energy-intensive validation method because mining requires extensive computational effort and is entirely unsuitable for environmental concerns or portable IoT. PoS, PoH, and DPoS consume far less energy by eliminating mining and relying on stakeholder validations or appointed validators. DAGs and PBFT also show energy improvements, especially in permissioned environments. PoSpace and PoET have reduced energy use as well, but with tradeoffs in decentralization or hardware requirements. Analyzing energy concerns is important because reducing energy consumption impacts blockchain scalability and sustainability.

General Blockchain Limitations

Blockchain technology, like all others, suffers from many limitations, such as interoperability barriers, regulatory barriers, high energy consumption, and computationally heavy demands. Fragmentation across the blockchain creates complexities for cross-chain interactions while differing regulations result in compliance issues, especially in the case of PoS staking rewards. The environmental consequences of PoW have not been erased, and although PoS is being adopted to cut energy use by around 99%, that factor is losing relevance. In terms of storage and computational overheads, the technology precludes lightweight devices; accessing off-chain solutions via light clients at least partly solves accessibility issues without compromising security regime or decentralization. Ecosystems are to be built by developers together with regulators and other relevant stakeholders in a manner to foster their viability and sustainability.

Future Direction

The future of real-time blockchain consensus applications now depends on four innovations: the hybrid models proposed, which are able to create a large scalability and reduce their energy consumption but must still address coordination be- tween the shards; solutions implemented at Layer-2 (rollups, sidechains, and state channels) that allow almost instant trans- actions which are then done off-chain but sacrifices some security; the increasing use of AI into consensus through ML- based node selection and dynamic sharding, which would use artificial

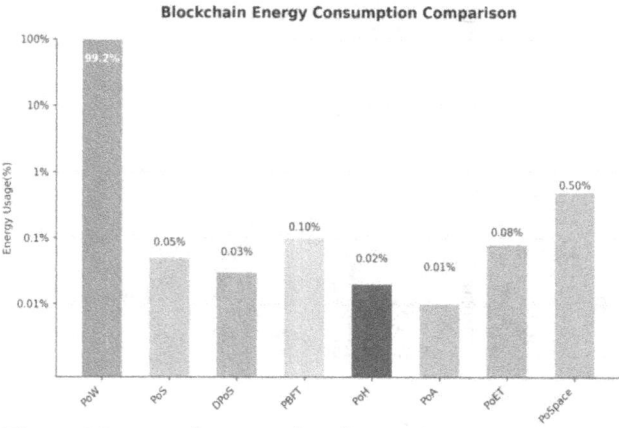

Figure 43.4 Energy consumption comparison
Source: Author

intelligence for consensus but incurs risks of centralization; quantum-resistant cryptographies (lattice/hash-based) which would deal against quantum attacks with considerable resource costs raised. All of these advances can demonstrate gains in throughput (above 100K TPS), latency (finality in sub second time frame), or security. However, there are still unresolved issues related to governance, interoperability, and efficiency for wide-scale adoption.

Conclusion

The applications of blockchain technology have brought a significant revolution in real-time scenarios: decentralization, security, and transparency. Consensus mechanisms are chiefly responsible for how suitable a technology is for time-critical areas such as Finance, Healthcare, and IoT. While some traditional mechanisms like Proof of Work (PoW) have the capacity for very secure transactions, they do not suit real-time applications because they are highly inefficient and power hungry. On the other hand, young mechanisms such as Proof of Stake (PoS), Delegated Proof of Stake (DPoS), and Practical Byzantine Fault Tolerance (PBFT) are much faster in conduct- ing transactions and scaling, while those that further improve throughput and finality include Proof of History (PoH) and Directed Acyclic Graph (DAG). Some of the main challenges remain scalability bottlenecks, interoperability issues, and regulatory uncertainties, which further propel advances toward hybrid consensus models, Layer-2 solutions, AI optimizations, and quantum-resistant cryptography to maximize the potential of blockchain for an ideal low latency decentralized system as a real-time use application.

References

[1] Tyagi, A. K. (2023). Decentralized everything: practical use of blockchain technology in future applications. In Distributed computing to blockchain. Elsevier, (pp. 19–38).

[2] Xu, X., & He, Y. (2024). Blockchain application in modern logistics information sharing: a review and case study analysis. *Production Planning & Control*, 35(9), 886–900

[3] Mishra, L., & Kaushik, V. (2023). Application of blockchain in dealing with sustainability issues and challenges of financial sector. *Journal of Sustainable Finance & Investment*, 13(3), 1318–1333.

[4] Bułkowska, K., Zielin´ska, M., & Bułkowski, M. (2023) Implementation of blockchain technology in waste management. *Energies*, 16(23), 7742.

[5] Yadav, S., Singh, N., & Kushwaha, D. S. (2023). Evolution of blockchain and consensus mechanisms & its real-world applications. *Multimedia Tools and Applications*, 82(22), 34363–34408.

[6] Yu, Y., Liu, G.-P., Huang, Y., Chung, C. Y., & Li, Y.-Z. (2024). A blockchain consensus mechanism for real-time regulation of renewable energy power systems. *Nature Communications*, 15(1), 1–15.

[7] Hegde, P., & Maddikunta, P. K. R. (2023). Secure PBFT consensus-based lightweight blockchain for healthcare application. *Applied Sciences*, 13(6), 3757.

[8] Kasyapa, M. S., & Vanmathi, C. (2024). Blockchain integration in healthcare: a comprehensive investigation of use cases, performance issues, and mitigation strategies. *Frontiers in Digital Health*, 6, 1359858.

[9] Ruan, Z. (2023). Blockchain technology for security issues and challenges in IoT. In 2023 International Conference on Computer Simulation and Modeling, Information Security, (pp. 572–580).

[10] Venkatesan, K., & Rahayu, S. B. (2024). Blockchain security enhancement: an approach towards hybrid consensus algorithms and machine learning techniques. *Scientific Reports*, 14(1), 1149.

44 A deep learning model for sales forecasting using univariate time series data

Janani M V[a] and Bhuvaneswari A[b]

Assistant Professor, Department of Computer Applications, PSG College of Technology, Coimbatore, Tamil Nadu, India

Abstract

In today's fast-moving world, industries like supply chain, farming, and retail require accurate forecasting for sales, demand, yield, and stock levels. Traditional models take months to extract insights from available datasets. This project streamlines the process with a ready-to-use tool that supports both univariate and advanced time series forecasting, providing short-term predictions (one, three, and six months) for specific products. This enables businesses to quickly adjust production, optimize inventory, and refine sales strategies. By delivering precise, real- time insights, the tool helps companies respond swiftly to market shifts, minimize waste, and maximize profitability without the complexity of building forecasting models. The adaptive algorithms in the tool effectively handle sales trends, seasonal variations, sudden demand spikes, and supply chain disruptions. Designed for ease of use, the tool requires minimal technical expertise while delivering enterprise-level accuracy. Businesses can seamlessly integrate forecasting models into their decision-making workflows, ensuring agility in a competitive landscape. With faster and more reliable forecasting, companies gain a strategic advantage in managing uncertainty and optimizing operations.

Keywords: ARIMA, exponential smoothing, forecasting, SARIMAX, univariate analysis

Introduction

Forecasting involves predicting future values based on past data. AI-powered forecasting accelerators are being designed to simplify and speed up demand forecasting for industries like supply chain, agriculture, and retail. By reducing prediction time, it provides fast, accurate, and scalable forecasts.

Using advanced AI and time series models, businesses make data-driven decisions, optimize operations, and respond effectively to market changes. Through advanced AI, machine learning (ML), and time series models, decision-making in inventory, production, and sales forecasting are enhanced exponentially to achieve accurate and efficient forecasting.

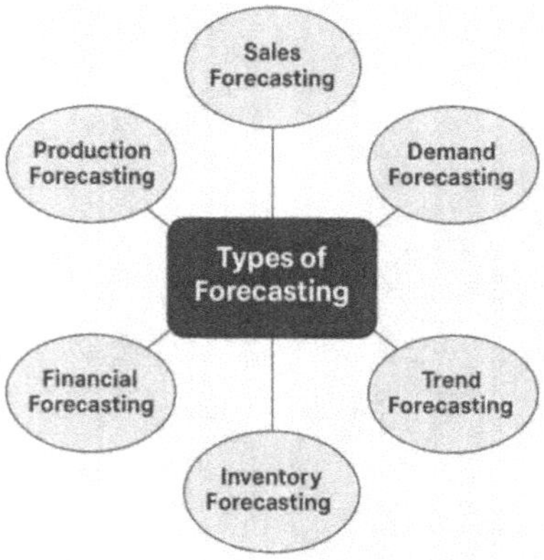

Existing system

Sales forecasting has been a critical area of research, evolving from traditional statistical techniques to AI-driven methods. Existing forecasting systems use statistical methods, learning algorithms, and models to identify future demands and make appropriate decisions. Moving average (MA), exponential smoothing, auto-regressive integrated moving average (ARIMA), and seasonal ARIMA (SARIMA) are some of the models and methods wildly used for sales forecasting. Box and Jenkins developed a forecasting tool based on ARIMA method for 87 demand forecasting in industrial production [1]. This method is effective for stationary data but struggles with complex, non-linear trends. Studies by Jabangwe et al. [4] and Sato & Nakano [9] demonstrated improved accuracy in retail sales forecasting using Random Forest and XGBoost, respectively. To address statistical methods limitations, learning models such as Support Vector Machines (SVM), XGBoost, and

Figure 44.1 Types of forecasting
Source: Author

[a]23mx209@psgtech.ac.in, [b]abh.mca@psgtech.ac.in

DOI: 10.1201/9781003770435-44

LightGBM were introduced. These models help to identify hidden patterns, process external data sources, and improve forecasting accuracy. Lim et al [6] showcased their effectiveness in retail demand forecasting.

Advanced models like long short-term memory (LSTM), gated recurrent units (GRU), and Transformer-based architecture are now widely used for forecasting. LSTMs excel in capturing long-term dependencies, while temporal fusion transformers (TFT) provide multi-horizon forecasting. Combining traditional statistical methods with AI improves performance. Models like XGBoost and SVM are used for structured time series data, while LSTM, GRU, and transformers are used for sequential forecasting. Hybrid models like SARIMAX-LSTM and XGBoost-LSTM combine statistical and AI-based approaches for robust forecasting. ARIMA-LSTM hybrid models, for instance, help capture both linear and non-linear data components, as demonstrated in agricultural demand forecasting by Chakraborty et al. [2].

Businesses also leverage cloud-based solutions like Amazon Forecast and Google AutoML, which automate forecasting processes but may act as black-box models with limited interpretability. Innovative techniques such as Reinforcement Learning for dynamic pricing [7]. Graph neural networks (GNNs) for supply chain forecasting [11], and Bayesian models for uncertainty-aware predictions are emerging as powerful forecasting tools [8].

Statistical Models for Baseline Forecasting

Statistical models act as the fundamentals for time series forecasting by capturing trends and seasonality. SARIMA methods are used for capturing seasonality, trend, and autoregression, making it suitable for time-dependent patterns. Seasonal autoregressive integrated moving average with exogenous regressors (SARIMAX) extends SARIMA by incorporating external influences like holidays, promotions, and weather conditions. Exponential smoothing is useful for capturing short-term patterns and providing quick, adaptive forecasts for dynamic datasets.

Feature Engineering and Predictions

Machine learning models enhance forecasting by identifying key patterns and relationships within the data. XGBoost and LightGBM leverage gradient boosting techniques to optimize feature importance and prediction accuracy. Random Forest and SVM are highly effective in handling non-linear relationships, making them valuable for capturing interactions between multiple variables in sales and demand forecasting.

Deep Learning Models for Advanced Forecasting

Deep learning models are applied for capturing trends and data dependencies in time series datasets. LSTM model (Figure 44.2) and GRU are well-suited for sequential data, as they retain important past information over extended sequences. TFT further enhances forecasting by enabling interpretable multi-horizon predictions, making them effective for handling complex, large-scale datasets in industries like retail, supply chain, and finance.

Hybrid Models for Improved Accuracy

Hybrid models combine statistical and AI-based techniques to maximize forecast accuracy. Models like ARIMA-LSTM and XGBoost-LSTM use both statistical methods and deep learning models to capture data fluctuations and trends within the data sources. SARIMAX with neural networks merges traditional time series forecasting with deep learning approaches, enabling adaptive forecasting that responds dynamically to external factors and evolving market conditions.

These advanced forecasting techniques supports data-driven decisions with higher accuracy. By integrating statistical, ML, and DL models, the hybrid approach assures reliable and accurate forecasting in business and other industries.

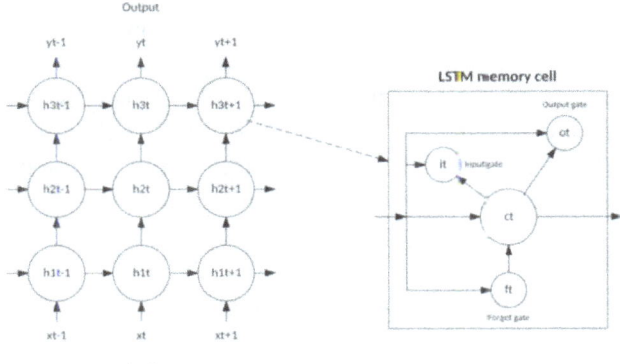

Figure 44.2 LSTM Architecture
Source: Author

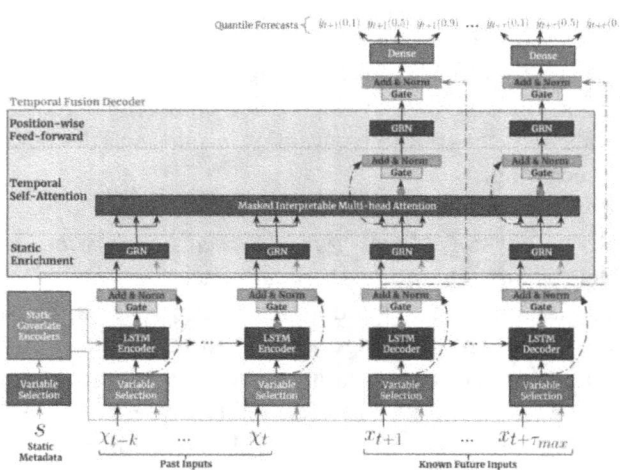

Figure 44.3 TFT Architecture
Source: Author

Deep Learning Architecture

Time series forecasting is important in most business domains including supply chain, retail, and finance. Though traditional statistical models like SARIMAX and Exponential Smoothing have been widely used, in case of large datasets in distributed system environments, they struggle with non-linearity and complex seasonality challenges.

SARIMAX Model

The SARIMAX model is designed to process time series data with seasonality and external factors. The model is tuned using seasonal and non-seasonal parameters (p, d, q), and forecasts are made based on historical data and external factors. This model combines autoregressive (AR) and moving average (MA) functions to identify trends in data, along with external regressors (exogenous variables) such as weather and/or holidays. Data preprocessing includes handling missing values and applying seasonal decomposition. During feature engineering, lag features and seasonal indicators are created, and external factors are incorporated as regressors. While SARIMAX is effective for linear datasets, it faces issues in case of complex and non-linear data patterns.

LSTM Model

The LSTM model, shown in Figure 44.2, is a recurrent neural network (RNN) model designed for processing time series data and capture data dependencies. This architecture is ideal for sequential data such as sales or stock prices. Data preprocessing for LSTM involves normalizing and structuring data into sequences for the model to learn from. Feature engineering focuses on creating time-step sequences, possibly including rolling statistics or other temporal features. The LSTM model consists of layers like LSTM units, dense layers, and dropout layers. The model can make predictions on future time steps when trained. LSTM excels in modeling sequential patterns and capturing long- term dependencies, but it requires large datasets for training and can be computationally intensive. It is also more complex and less interpretable compared to traditional models.

TFT Model

The Temporal Fusion Transformer is a deep learning model designed for forecasting using large amounts of temporal data with complex patterns. TFT leverages the transformer architecture as in figure 3, which was originally designed for natural language processing tasks, to handle sequential data effectively. The model incorporates attention mechanisms to prioritize important time steps and features in the data. TFT is particularly useful for datasets with multivariate time series data, where external variables, such as weather or promotional events, are also considered.

Data preprocessing for TFT includes normalization and structuring the dataset into sequences. Feature engineering involves generating temporal features related to seasonal data such as time, day, and other indicators. TFT uses a combination of LSTM and self-attention mechanisms to capture both long-term dependencies and local patterns. It is highly effective for forecasting in scenarios with complex relationships, though it requires significant computational resources and large datasets. TFT is powerful for handling diverse data types and multivariate inputs, making it ideal for real-time, high-dimensional forecasting tasks.

A hybrid learning model combining LSTM and TFT models is proposed for time series forecasting, highlighting their strengths in capturing sequential patterns. The following section discusses the proposed methodology for model implementation and optimization.

Proposed system

An AI-based forecasting system is proposed to visually represent the step-by-step prediction process of the deep learning model, highlighting key operations and decision points. It ensures clarity in workflows, dependencies, and data flow, aiding both developers and stakeholders. This structured representation helps identify optimization areas and refine functionalities. The process steps of the DL model is shown in Figure 44.4 and specified below:

- **Start** – The process begins with raw data ingestion.
- **Load and preprocess dataset** – The raw dataset is loaded, and initial preprocessing (e.g., handling missing values, formatting) is performed.
- **Convert to time series format** – The dataset is structured into a time series format, ensuring timestamps are in the correct order.
- **Check for missing time periods** – Any missing timestamps in the data are identified and handled appropriately (e.g., interpolation or imputation).
- **Check for stationarity** – The data is analyzed to determine if it is stationary (i.e., has constant mean and variance over time).
  - If not stationary: Apply transformations (e.g., differencing, log transformation) to stabilize the dataset.
  - If stationary: Identify ARIMA/SARIMAX parameters using various statistical tests like autocorrelation function (ACF)/partial autocorrelation function (PACF) plots and/ or Akaike information criterion (AIC).
- **Training** – The ARIMA model is trained using the identified parameters.

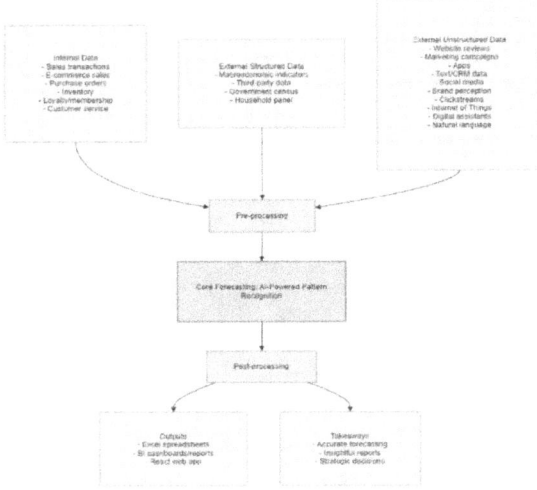

Figure 44.4 Forecast prediction process
Source: Author

- **Perform diagnostic checks** – Model diagnostics are conducted to validate the assumptions and performance.
- **Monitor model performance** – The trained model's accuracy and forecasting ability are evaluated.
- **Refine and retrain** – Based on performance, the model is refined and retrained to improve accuracy.
- **Continuous improvement** – The process loops back to performance monitoring, ensuring the model remains effective over time.

For this research, the dataset used for sales forecasting is collected from multiple sources, including retail transaction logs, point-of-sale (POS) systems, and e-commerce sales records. The data includes historical sales figures, timestamps, promotional activities, and external influencing factors like holidays and weather conditions.

Data preprocessing
To ensure high-quality inputs for the forecasting model, the dataset undergoes rigorous preprocessing, which includes filtering and fixing: Additionally, publicly available datasets from platforms such as Kaggle, UCI Machine Learning Repository, and company-specific databases are utilized to enhance the model's robustness. The data preprocessing includes:

Handling Missing Values:
- Forward Fill (propagating previous values forward)
- Interpolation (linear, spline methods)
- Mean/Median/Mode Imputation for numerical values.

Handling Null Values:
- Dropping columns or rows with excessive null values
- Using predictive imputation techniques (KNN imputation, regression-based imputation)

Outlier Detection and Treatment:
- Z-score and IQR methods to identify extreme values
- Winsorization to limit extreme outliers
- Log transformations to smooth data variations

Exploratory Data Analysis (EDA) in Time Series:
*   Trend analysis: Identifying increasing or decreasing patterns over time.
*   Seasonality detection: Analyzing periodic fluctuations in sales (e.g., holiday sales spikes).
*   Time series decomposition: Splitting data into trend, seasonal, and residual components.
*   Autocorrelation analysis: Studying lag-based correlations using ACF and PACF plots. The result of correlation analysis of given dataset is shown in Figure 44.5.

Feature Engineering and Extraction
*   **Lag features:** Creating past sales-based variables to understand dependencies.
*   **Rolling statistics:** Applying moving averages to capture short-term variations.
*   **Date-based features:** Extracting year, month, week, day, and holiday indicators.
*   **External factors:** Including features like weather conditions, promotional events, and macroeconomic indicators.

The forecasting system transitions into the technical workflow, emphasizing model selection and optimization.

Univariate and Multivariate Time Series Analysis
Univariate time series forecasting predicts future values based on a single variable (e.g., past sales data only). Multivariate time series forecasting is utilizing multiple influencing factors (e.g., sales + promotions + weather) to improve forecasting. The proposed system performs univariate time series forecasting as specified below. The decomposition of techniques used for forecasting is shown in Figure 44.6.

Forecasting process
*   **Data preparation:** Formatting data into a time-series index.
*   **Stationarity check**: Ensuring stable mean and variance using the augmented dickey-fuller (ADF) test.
*   **Model selection**: Choosing ARIMA, SARIMA, SARIMAX, and deep learning models like LSTM.
*   **Model training and validation:** Splitting data into training and test sets for model evaluation.
*   **Performance evaluation:** Using RMSE, MAE, and MAPE metrics for accuracy assessment.

Outlier detection
*   Box plots and scatter plots highlighting anomalies in the dataset.
*   Z-score and IQR-based methods used to detect and handle extreme values.

Different Time Series
The ACF and PACF methods are applied to extract values from different time series data sources. The functional model for processing the differential dataset is given below:

$$\left(1 - \sum_{i=1}^{p} \phi_i L^i\right)(1 - L^s)^D (1 - L)^d Y_t = \left(1 + \sum_{i=1}^{q} \theta_i L^i\right)\left(1 + \sum_{i=1}^{Q} \Theta_i L^{si}\right)\epsilon_t$$

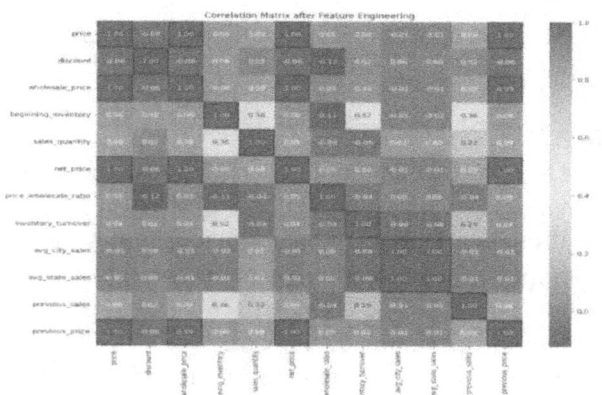

Figure 44.5 Correlation analysis result
Source: Author

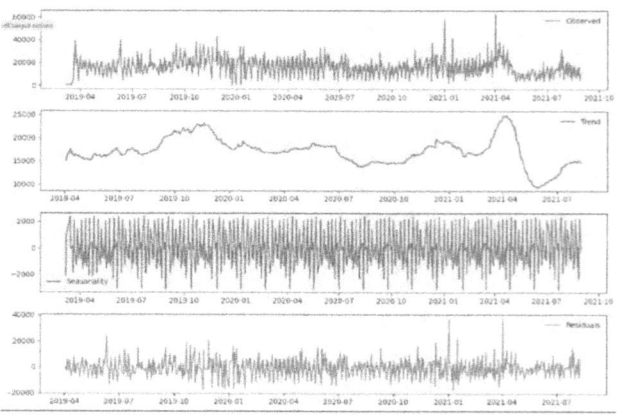

Figure 44.6 Decomposition techniques
Source: Author

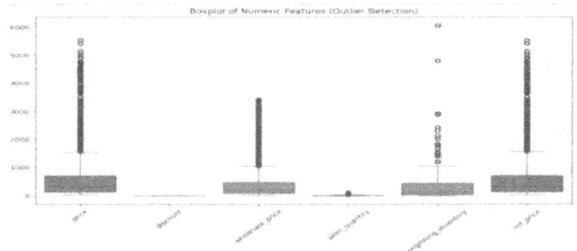

Figure 44.7 Outliers detection
Source: Author

where Yt indicates sales at time t, ϕi stands for AR coefficients, θi indicates MA coefficients, ϵt is white noise error term, L is the Lag operator and Θi stands for Seasonal MA coefficients.

The ACF and PACF are essential tools in time series analysis to determine the relationship between past observations and guide model selection, particularly for ARIMA and SARIMAX models.

Stationary Series (After Differencing)
The ACF: drops quickly to zero, indicating little to no long-term dependency, and the PACF shows a sharp cutoff after a few lags, suggesting a lower-order AR model.

Seasonal Series
ACF: Exhibits repeating patterns at seasonal intervals, highlighting periodic dependencies and PACF peaks at seasonal lags, guiding the selection of seasonal AR terms in SARIMA. A sample ACF plot is shown in Figure 44.8.

Non-Stationary Series (Before Differencing)
The ACF decays slowly, indicating the presence of a trend. and PACF shows high correlation at initial lags, confirming the need for differencing.

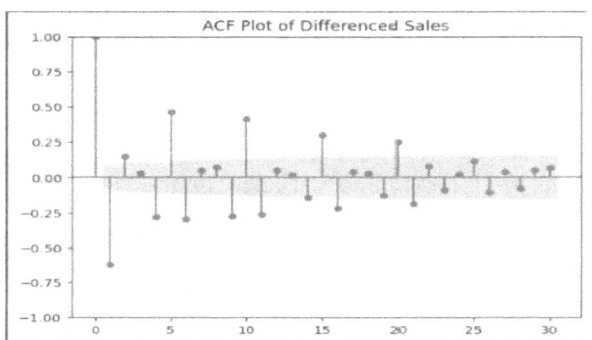

Figure 44.8 ACF plot
Source: Author

White Noise Series
The ACF and PACF have no significant correlations at any lag, indicating no predictable structure in the data. A sample PACF plot is shown in Figure 44.9.

Forecast Prediction

The SARIMAX model extends SARIMA method by incorporating external factors that influence sales as given below:

$$\text{SARIMAX } (p, d, q)(P, D, Q, s) + X$$

- p (Auto-Regressive term): Number of past observations.
- d (Differencing term): Number of times differencing is applied to make the series stationary.
- q (Moving average term): Number of lagged forecast errors.
- P, D, Q, s (Seasonal components) Seasonal autoregressive, differencing, and moving average terms with seasonality parameter (s).
- X (Exogenous variables): External factors that impact sales trends.

Exogenous Variables
In dataset, several columns can be considered exogenous variables (X) when using the SARIMAX model for sales forecasting. These variables are external factors that influence sales but are not part of the time series itself. The considered variables are:

- **Price:** The selling price of the product directly impacts demand and sales quantity.
- **Discount:** Discounts and promotions affect consumer purchasing behavior.

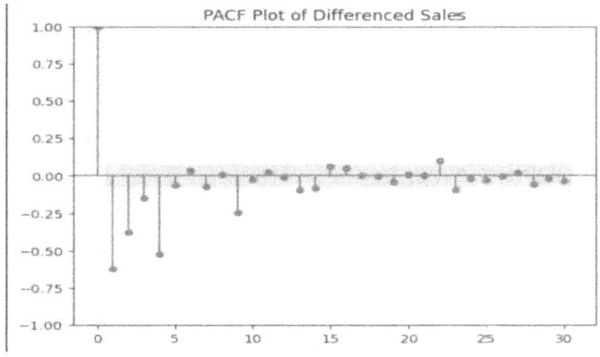

Figure 44.9 PACF plot
Source: Author

- **Wholesale price:** The cost at which retailers procure goods, influencing pricing strategies.
- **Lead week:** The number of weeks in advance that inventory is planned, affecting supply chain decisions.
- **Beginning inventory:** Available stock levels impact sales fulfillment.
- **State and city:** The geographical location of sales can introduce regional demand variations.
- **Customer:** Different customer segments may have varying buying patterns.

To build the proposed model, key feature variables including inventory levels and regional factors are considered. These features were used to enhance the forecasting models by incorporating external influences on sales trends

Model Optimization

Hyperparameter tuning is essential for optimizing the performance of forecasting models. In SARIMA/SARIMAX, tuning involves selecting the best values for (p, d, q, P, D, Q, s) by evaluating different combinations using techniques like grid search or Bayesian optimization. For deep learning models XGBoost and LSTM, hyperparameters such as learning rate, tree depth, and the number of neurons is fine-tuned using cross-validation to prevent overfitting and improve generalization.

- Grid search & Bayesian optimization: To identify optimal ARIMA/SARIMAX parameters (p, d, q, P, D, Q, S).
- Cross-validation: Time series split validation to avoid data leakage.
- Feature selection: Recursive feature elimination (RFE) was applied for selecting the best exogenous variables.
- It transitions into testing by detailing model selection, training, and optimization techniques, ensuring accurate forecasting.

Forecasting accuracy is performed by evaluating prediction errors. The performance of different models SARIMAX, XGBoost, LSTM is measured for evaluating their accuracy using MAE, MSE, RMSE, and their normalized versions NMAE, NRMSE methods.

Testing

In the testing phase, various evaluation metrics are used to measure the accuracy and reliability of the forecasting model. The metrics used for testing the models are listed below:

Table 44.1 The Testing Metrics for Evaluating Forecasting Models

Criteria	SARIMAX	XGBoost
Accuracy	High	High
Speed	Moderate	Fast
Interpretability	High	Moderate
Seasonality	Excellent	Requires FE
Exogenous vars	Strong	Good
Computational cost	Moderate	Low
Best use cases	Seasonal Sales	Structured Data

Source: Author

In testing the models, following calculations are performed:

- Mean average error (MAE) calculates the average absolute difference between predicted and actual values, providing a straightforward measure of model performance.
- Mean squared error (MSE) squares these differences, giving higher weight to larger errors and making it more sensitive to outliers.
- Root mean squared error (RMSE) takes the square root of MSE, ensuring that the error is in the same unit as the target variable, making it easier to interpret.
- Mean absolute percentage error (MAPE) expresses error as a percentage, allowing comparisons across different scales but can become unreliable when actual values are close to zero.
- Symmetric mean absolute percentage error (sMAPE) addresses this limitation by preventing division errors when actual values are small.
- Additionally, R-squared (R^2) measures how well the model explains variance in the data, with values closer to 1 indicating a better fit.

The evaluation of the models based on the above calculations is presented in the table shown in Figure 10.

Among the three models, XGBoost demonstrated the highest accuracy, achieving the lowest MAE

Model	MAE	MSE	RMSE	NMAE	NRMSE	sMAPE	PBIAS	R²
SARIMAX	5.12	26.2	5.12	0.10	0.15	12.5%	-1.2%	0.85
XGBoost	4.95	24.5	4.95	0.09	0.14	11.8%	-0.8%	0.87
LSTM	5.30	28.1	5.30	0.11	0.16	13.0%	-1.5%	0.83

Figure 44.10 Evaluation of accuracy of forecasting models
Source: Author

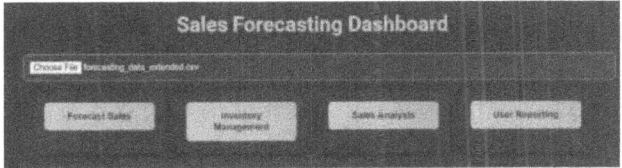

Figure 44.11 Dashboard
Source: Author

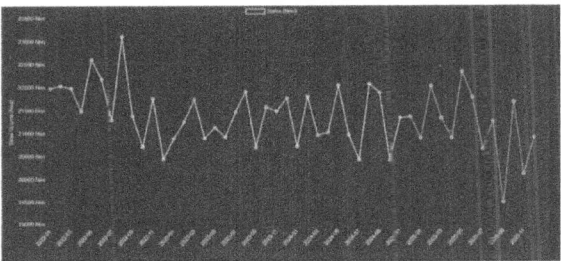

Figure 44.12 Sales trends (monthly aggregation).
Source: Author

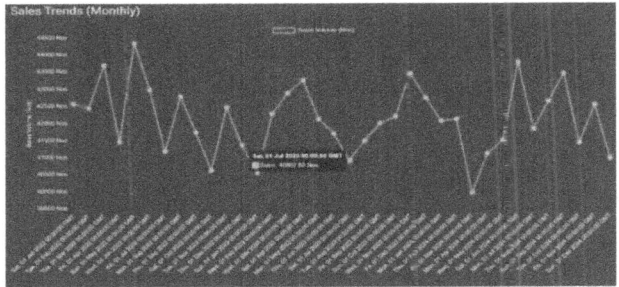

Figure 44.13 Forecasted sales for next 12 months
Source: Author

(4.95) and RMSE (4.95), along with the highest R²
score (0.87). This indicates that XGBoost captured
sales trends better than the other models. SARIMAX
performed well, especially in handling seasonality,
with an R² of 0.85, making it a strong option for
time-series forecasting where seasonal patterns are
significant. LSTM, while promising, had the highest
MAE (5.30) and RMSE (5.30), along with a lower R²
(0.83), suggesting that deep learning requires further
optimization for structured forecasting.

Output Analysis

This shows the practical implementation of forecasting through dashboards, sales trends, and user
reports.

The sales forecasting dashboard allows users to
upload data and generate sales predictions, manage inventory, analyze trends, and create reports.
This interactive tool helps businesses optimize
decision-making with data-driven insights.

Sales Analysis

The sales trends (monthly) graph displays sales volume fluctuations from July 2023 to July 2024. It
highlights seasonal demand patterns, peak sales periods, and variations crucial for forecasting accuracy.

Forecasted sales

The sales forecasting graph displays actual sales
trends for 2024 in blue and predicted sales for 2025
in red. The forecast indicates expected demand patterns for the upcoming months based on historical
trends. The table below compares these models
based on key criteria to assist in selecting the most
suitable approach.

Conclusion

The paper focused on sales forecasting and the model
SARIMAX for prediction, due to its ability to capture seasonality and incorporate external factors. To
achieve the expected outcome, data preprocessing
includes handling missing values, outlier detection,
and time series decomposition. Feature engineering
was applied, introducing lag variables, rolling statistics, and exogenous factors such as price and inventory are considered during the process. In model
evaluation, the SARIMAX model is compared with
XGBoost and LSTM. SARIMAX performs better in
terms of interpretability and effectiveness in seasonal
data forecasting. To optimize the performance, hyperparameter tuning was conducted using grid search
and cross-validation. Performance metrics such as
MAE, MSE, RMSE, NRMSE, sMAPE, and percentage bias were used to assess accuracy of predictions
generated. The results demonstrated SARIMAX's
stability and reliability for structured forecasting
applications. Future work can explore multivariate
models, deep learning techniques like TFT, and automated hyperparameter tuning to enhance predictive
performance.

References

[1] George E. P. Box, Gwilym M. Jenkins, Gregory C. Reinsel, & Greta M. Ljung (2015). Time Series Analysis: Forecasting and Control, 5th Edition. John Wiley and Sons Inc: Hoboken, New Jersey.

[2] Ray, S., Lama, A., Mishra, P., Biswas, T., Sankar Das, S., & Gurung, B. (2023). An ARIMA-LSTM model for predicting volatile agricultural price series with random forest technique. *Applied Soft Computing*, 149, Part A. https://doi.org/10.1016/j.asoc.2023.110939.

[3] Krishna, V., Aich, A. V, A., & Hegde, C. (2018). Sales-forecasting of retail stores using machine learning techniques. In 2018 3rd International Conference on Computational Systems and Information Technology for Sustainable Solutions (CSITSS), Bengaluru. (pp. 160–166). doi: 10.1109/CSITSS.2018.8768765.

[4] Mustapha, O. O., & Sithole, D. T. (2025). Forecasting Retail Sales using Machine Learning Models. *American Journal of Statistics and Actuarial Sciences*, 6(1), 35–67. https://doi.org/10.47672/ajsas.2679

[5] Lakshmanan, B., Vivek Raja, P. S. N., & Kalathiappan, V. (2020). Sales demand forecasting using LSTM network. *Advances in Intelligent Systems and Computing*, 1056.

[6] Lim, B., Arık, S. O., Loeff, N., & Pfister, T. (2021). Temporal fusion transformers for interpretable multi-horizon time series forecasting. *International Journal of Forecasting*, 37, 4, 1748–1764. https://doi.org/10.1016/j.ijforecast.2021.03.012.

[7] Balashov, M., Kiselev, A., & Kuryleva, A. (2021). Reinforcement Learning Approach for Dynamic Pricing. In: Devezas, T., Leitão, J., Sarygulov, A. (Eds.). The Economics of Digital Transformation. Studies on Entrepreneurship, Structural Change and Industrial Dynamics. Springer: Cham. https://doi.org/10.1007/978-3-030-59959-1_8

[8] Ren, S., Patrick Hui, C. L., & Jason Choi, T. M. (2018). AI-Based fashion sales forecasting methods in big data era. EdsThomassey, S., Zeng, X. (Eds). Artificial Intelligence for Fashion Industry in the Big Data Era. Springer

[9] Sato, T., & Nakano, K. (2020). Daily sales prediction using XGBoost, Procedia Computer Science.

[10] Wu, Z., Pan, S., Long, G., Jiang, J., Chang, X., & Zhang, C. (2020). Connecting the dots: multivariate time series forecasting with graph neural networks. In Proceedings of the 26th ACM SIGKDD International Conference on Knowledge Discovery Data Mining.

45 Automated seat adjustment system for enhanced vehicle ergonomics using anthropometric data and Arduino-based control

Poovendhan Venkatachalam[1,a], Karthikeyan Palaniswamy[2,b], Sushil Punaskar[3,c], and Vijai Kaarthi Visvanathan[4,d]

[1]PG Scholar, Department of Automobile Engineering, PSG College of Technology, Coimbatore, India

[2]Professor, Department of Automobile Engineering, PSG College of Technology, Coimbatore, India

[3]Solution Consultant, Department of Engineering Solutions, EDS Technologies Pvt. Ltd., Pune, India

[4]Research Scholar, Department of Automobile Engineering, PSG College of Technology, Coimbatore, India

Abstract

Arduino Uno microcontroller that performs logic operations to actuate vertical and horizontal movement using a linear actuator (BTS7960 motor driver) and a NEMA 23 stepper motor (TB6600 driver), respectively. Ultrasonic sensors measure the three anthropometric segment lengths: head-to-buttocks, knee-to-buttocks, and knee-to-foot. An IR proximity sensor is utilized to determine foot presence to begin the adjustment process. An ignition switch activates and deactivates the system, and if turned off, the seat will return to the original starting position. The system provides real-time feedback to the user, displaying percentile classifications and adjustment states on a 128x64 OLED display. The system currently supports male and female users from the 5th to 95th percentile, using ergonomic mappings based on RAMSIS simulations. Experimentally tested for precision alignment of position (± 2 mm), and the system maintained its performance and consistency across multiple repetitions and conditions. By allowing for adaptive, user-specific positioning, the system shows notable improvement over traditional manual systems - and preset methods. Future work aims to extend the sensor framework to include posture tracking and machine learning for advanced real-time user profiling and will ultimately deliver the idea of intelligent, user-aware vehicle interiors.

Keywords: Anthropometry, Arduino-based control, automated seat adjustment, human-centric design, RAMSIS software

Introduction

The automotive industry has shifted its focus towards designing safer and more ergonomic vehicle interiors, and in response to the rising demand for user-centered design and automation, the current automotive landscape is evolving. Seat position is a key factor in determining driver comfort, visibility, and safety, often leading to poor posture, comfort over time, and reaction time delay in emergency situations [5]. Safety and comfort of the occupant, and ergonomics of the driver, will have more importance than before, therefore the future of human-vehicle interfacing requires systems to correlate and adjust seating position based on the physique of the driver [13]. With manual seat adjustments, the user often has to go through the trial and error of repeated attempts at determining ideal comfort. Electronic seat adjustments, where seat positions can be stored based on user preferences, typically miss the mark of accurately deriving seat position based on dynamically varied distinct physical anthropometrics between different users [19]. This is even more impactful in shared vehicles such as taxis or rideshare fleets where the driver experiences frequent changeovers, forcing optimal seating position to become a creature of reconfirmed adaptive habit. In both instances of occupancy, integrated real-time, automatic seat position adjustment can assist user usability and be viewed as ergonomically maintained opportunities of adaptive comfort and fit [18]. Seat position contributively changes joint loading, visibility, and drivers' reachability to essential instruments for operating the vehicle. Poor seating position maintained over time can contribute to long-term health problems, especially for drivers who spend large, segmented hours behind the wheel [2]. Equally, the ability to accommodate a quick switch

[a]poovendhan912@gmail.com, [b]apk.auto@psgtech.ac.in, [c]sushil.pna@edstechnologies.com, [d]v2k.mech@gmail.com

DOI: 10.1201/9781003770435-45

of driver profiles automatically is highly valuable in an autonomous, or fleet vehicle environment [11].

This project delivers a low-cost, hardware-based, anthropometrically augmented automatic seat adjustment system using open-source electronics. The system outputs height at the entry point to determine the ideal seat position using ultrasonic sensors to pre-bound "work" anthropometric data downloaded from RAMSIS software ranging from the 5th percentile to the 95th percentile user profile [1]. The system utilizes a simple toggle-ignition system to automatically trigger the seat position on entry to the vehicle and put the seat back to "park (default position)" when exit, thus allowing feasibility for the next occupant to configure when used as a shared or taxi vehicle.

The direction is also appropriate in the context of electric and autonomous vehicles wherein the interior design trends of user-based adaptive systems are continuing to gain traction. Within these evolving vehicles, as car cabin technology becomes more intelligent and responsive, the seat will need to continue to adapt into a smart adaptive physical interface of interaction between the user and vehicle [12]. Therefore, embedding a limited intelligence into the architecture of the seat begins the shift toward playing the role of intelligence and inertia for operational function, making it both functional and future required [9].

Traditional seat systems in automobiles have transitioned from simple manual levers to electronically actuated memory seats, with these memory systems often limited to saving a few distinct positions for an owner/user while neither maintaining the intent, nor acting to accommodate unknown or changing occupants [6]. Research is now beginning to show enthusiasm to incorporate sensor-based automation to seat systems in light of these limitations. In recent research, posture detection has been accomplished through the use of pressure sensors or even camera-based vision systems to automatically move seats with adaptive movements [14]; nevertheless, these systems are very complex, expensive, and generally not suited for value vehicles or smaller car types.

Similarly, anthropometric software like RAMSIS has become mostly reputable in vehicle interior design upon its ability to take a sophisticated approach to simulate many types and sizes of human bodies, and measure comfort, reachability, and visibility in automobiles provided seats in vehicles protect occupants

from harm by controlling location [7]. Some study analyzes the correlation between drivers' joint angles and joint torques to assess posture comfort, providing insights into ergonomic factors influencing driver fatigue and discomfort [17]. Most studies with RAMSIS look to evaluate seat ergonomics stating the vehicle should accommodate a reasonable facsimile of anthropometry using several percentile models, thereby ensuring inclusivity in design. Most implementations of RAMSIS do remain in the digital design and validation stage, despite anthropometric outputs rarely being used in physical space and seated control systems [8] suggesting there remains a gap between ergonomic design theory and real-world actuation.

Several academic studies have looked at ergonomic evaluations utilizing digital human's models in simulations. However, the translations of that anthropometric data into electromechanical systems are still scarce [4]. For example, there are systems that are designed adaptively based on torso angle, or thigh position—but very rarely are the sensor input linked to standardized ergonomic databases. The missing links between the outputs of the manikin software output and actuation platforms remains a major hindrance to progress in this area of research [19]. While RAMSIS enables detailed ergonomic simulation, the study lacks integration with real-time human physical input, limiting its applicability in adaptive, height-responsive seat control systems [15].

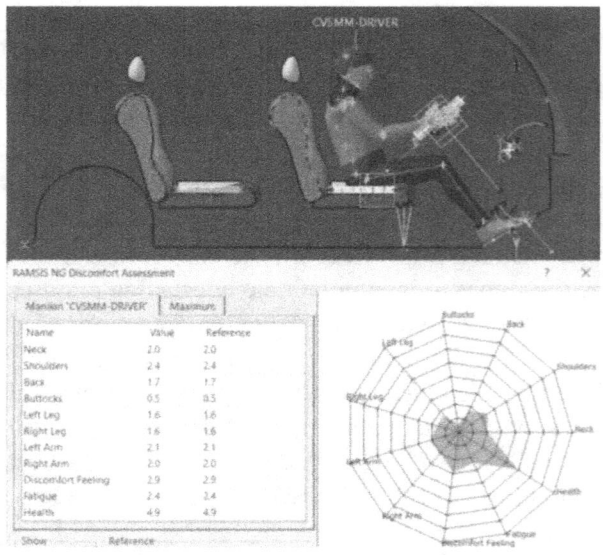

Figure 45.1 Manikin seated in Suzuki Dzire CATIA model with discomfort analysis using RAMSIS
Source: Author

Likewise, automation associated with microcontrollers, specifically using a low-cost platform like Arduino has gained popularity and research interest involving low-cost electronic systems (mechatronics). For example, there have been actuator driven systems for adjusting wheelchairs, robotic limbs, and smart furniture using various sensors. That said, in the same vein, limited research led a low-cost system that automatically adjusted by sensing both anthropometric data and percentile-based relationships, enabling a customizable seat adjustment in a vehicular application.

The potential of combining sensor-based detection, anthropometric data, and automated systems is well documented in the literature for addressing the personalization challenge of vehicle seating. Camera based artificial intelligence (AI) has been developed for posture recognition; but there are very significant processing demands and privacy concerns for this method. Height based detection is both low-cost, and a lightweight way to infer body proportions without the need to develop tailored computer vision models with images for processing.

This makes great sense to leverage and construct ultrasonic sensors for body measurements; Arduino-controlled actuation to manage movement; and an automatic adjustment of anthropometric percentiles based on the RAMSIS classifications to create the decision logic for adjustments to the mechanism. This project directly mimics real-world needs in automotive seating in regard to providing low-cost high-impact solutions, ease of use and availability, and adaptability. This project does link evaluation of virtual ergonomic modeling, and physical actuation of seats to provide a reasonable and pragmatic method towards improved comfort, safety and inclusivity in all future vehicles. It could serve as a foundation for future work that may include posture analysis of the driver or passenger or use of machine learning for personalized seat configuration adjusted dynamically.

Problem Statement and Objectives

The existing systems that allow individuals to adjust their seats in consumer vehicles follow one of two forms: either manually with a mechanical system, or electronically with some kind of memory. They all involve user input and do not account for anthropometric allowance, which we have established

as an important factor that needs to be considered. As human factors researchers, we are interested in ways to automate systems that limit user effort and improve the ergonomics of adjustment using data driven approaches [3].

Conventional systems are also static. They only work when the user is known from the list of saved settings, and any change in the physical characteristics of the users renders the stored adjustment settings irrelevant. With shared use models, it is not clear how we can coerce a driver into getting the best ergonomic configuration automatically without human intervention [16].

This project proposes an automatic seat adjustment system which entails determining a user's body proportions through ultrasonic sensors and a prototype seat which moves horizontally and vertically using motors under the control of an Arduino Uno micro-controller. Motion logic is determined through anthropometric percentile data that is accessed through RAMSIS, allowing a seat to effectively reposition itself into the best position of comfort and vision for the user [20].

The key objectives are:

- Design and fabricate a prototype that utilizes readily available components while adhering to a small budget.
- Detect the user and automatically adjust his or her seat to the appropriate location and restore the seat to the same position to all.

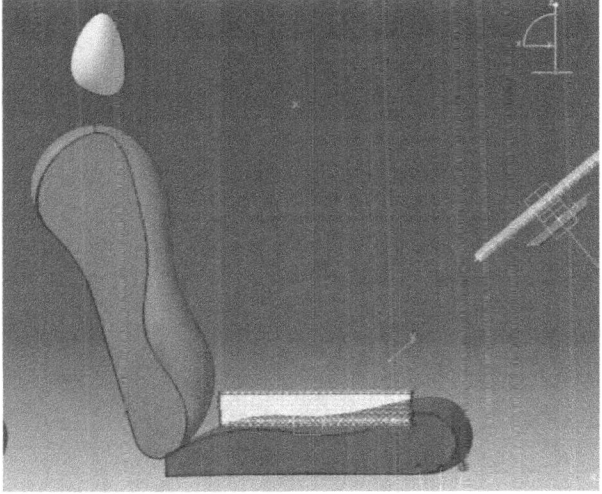

Figure 45.2 Key vertical and horizontal seat adjustment points derived from RAMSIS data
Source: Author

- Reduce response time and measurements of mechanical error while maximizing user-specific customization as parameters using height measurements.
- Provide an ergonomic alternative to conventional seat adjustment systems by allowing for user-specific static seat adjustments - incorporating both vertical and horizontal motion and greater anthropometric standards alignment.

Methodology

System Design and Components

This automated seat adjustment system is built to improve comfort and ergonomics for many vehicle users by adjusting seat position dynamically to provide the best fit based on anthropometric percentile data. The system architecture includes both hardware and software components, which allows for accurate positioning of the seat for users with different anatomical dimensions. The following sections detail the system components, including sensors, actuators, control units, and interactive user interface unit.

Hardware Components

The hardware architecture features an Arduino Uno microcontroller, ultrasonic sensors, an IR proximity sensor, a linear actuator with a motor driver, a NEMA 23 stepper motor with a TB6600 driver, a 12V DC power supply, and a 128 × 64 OLED display.

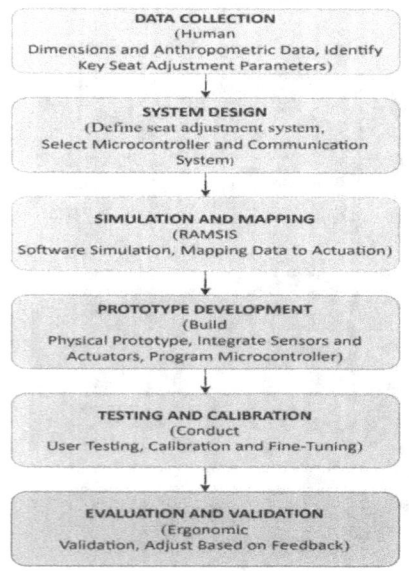

Figure 45.3 Proposed methodology for mapping of RAMSIS data to control actuator

Source: Author

Microcontroller (Arduino Uno): The central control unit for the system being developed is an Arduino Uno microcontroller. The Arduino was selected because of the ease of programming, I/O compatibility, and relatively low cost. The microcontroller processes sensor input, implements seat adjustment logic, and actuates the respective actuators.

Ultrasonic sensors: The anthropometric data used by the system is collected using three ultrasonic sensors. Each sensor is mounted in clear orientation to collect specific vertical body dimensions: one measures the head-to-buttocks length, one measures the knee-to-buttocks length, and one measures knee-to-foot length from the foot. Having three sensors configured in this way allows maximum estimation capability of the user's height and leg length, both of which are important for defining effective seating positions.

IR Proximity sensor: The foot area of the seat base built-in an IR Sensor to detect the presence of the occupant's foot. When the foot is detected, the system will begin to process seat adjustment.

Linear actuator with BTS7960 motor driver: A linear Actuator powered by the BTS7960 motor driver makes vertically adjustable seats. The linear actuator has been assembled with a scissor lift, to provide accurate vertical seat height control. The BTS7960 motor driver accepts a maximum load of 12V and 4A which is more than adequate for the linear actuator load.

Stepper motor (NEMA 23 with TB6600 Driver): The horizontal translation of the seat is done by a Design NEMA 23 stepper motor rated to produce

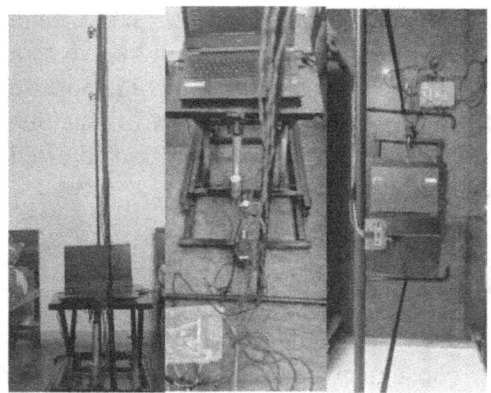

Figure 45.4 Ultrasonic sensor arrangement for measuring head-to-buttocks, knee-to-buttocks, and knee-to-foot distances

Source: Author

189 kg-mm of torque. The motor has more than enough force to slide the seat along the roller-bearing track. The stepper motor is run by a TB6600 driver that gives the best positioning, reliable repeatable motion.

Power supply: The project uses a 12V and 5A regulated power supply. The highly regulated power supply keeps the voltage for the sensing and actuation circuit as consistent as possible.

OLED display: A 128 × 64 pixel OLED display was used in the system for user feedback. It displays detected percentile, the current status of the adjustment and the reset status of the system in order to dictate transparency and usability to the user. The display has an I2C interface that is default at address 0 × 3C and uses the default font with 16 pixels between lines. user.

Figure 45.5 Scissor lift mechanism used for vertical seat adjustment using the linear actuator
Source: Author

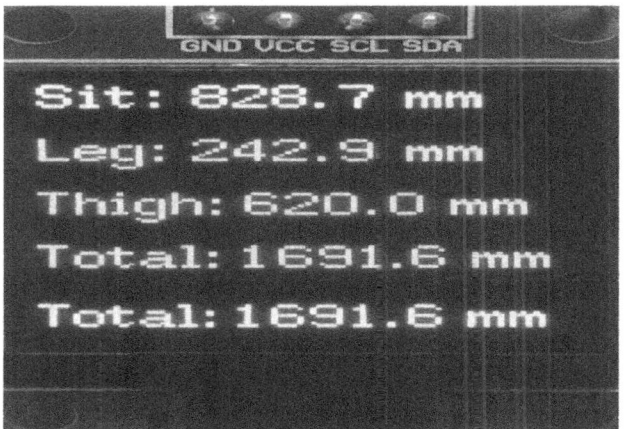

Figure 45.6 OLED display during seat adjustment process showing real-time percentile detection and status
Source: Author

Software Components

The algorithm is placed on the Arduino, and it is responsible for coordinating the sensor data collection, the classification according to the percentile, and the logic responsible for actuator control.

Anthropometric data mapping: The system relies on preprocessed percentile data taken from RAMSIS - a human modeling program. The percentile data provides a couple of basic seat reference points through baseline discomfort, visibility, and joint limit analysis in the 5th, 25th, 50th, 75th and 95th percentiles for both male and female occupants. This prototype will average data across sexes for simplification purposes.

User height estimation: In the sensor data acquisition phase, the system uses a combination of the sensor readings to estimate the user's total height. The height-to-percentile mapping logic groups the user to the corresponding percentile group based on the RAMSIS data set.

Actuation logic: Once the percentile group is identified the system logic calculates the required horizontal movement and the vertical movement. The horizontal and vertical movements were predefined from the design of the vehicle interior using CATIA based on Suzuki Dzire dimensions. The microcontroller will issue PWM and step signals to the correct motor drivers to execute the action.

Ignition switch logic: The system has a toggle switch that acts as the vehicle ignition. When the toggle switch is turned on the seat will complete the adjustment cycle. However, when the toggle switch is off, the seat will complete the movement back to the factory original position (which standardized for the next occupant entering the vehicle).

Status display: The OLED screen provides feedback to the user based on real-time sensor feedback of detected height, target percentile, and if the adjustment is in progress. This feature allows for enhanced trust in the system and aids she debugs process, particularly during development.

The power distribution board took in 12V DC and powered the linear actuator, stepper motor, OLED display, and sensor modules. The power distribution board also had some voltage regulating circuitry and current protection circuits in order to prevent electronics from reversing polarity or from damage caused by overload. The sensor inputs/outputs were assigned to either an analog or a digital pin on the Arduino Uno board. The trigger and echo pins were assigned to the ultrasonic sensors, and the IR sensor was assigned to a digital interrupt capable pin. The signals assigned to the BTS7960 driver of the linear actuator were Pulse Width Modulation (PWM) signals while the TB6600 driver controlling the stepper motor used step and direction signals. All the components shared a common ground to ensure that they did not have floating references and to limit any inconsistencies in their signals. All wire channels were managed in channels with zip ties in order to provide a neat and organized profile so that the additional wiring would not get tangled up during actuation cycles.

The mechanical system was made to be adjustable in both vertical and horizontal directions, while maintaining task occupant safety and structural integrity. The base frame of the seat was made of mild steel (MS) square tubes due to their ratio of strength-to-weight and suitable fabrication properties. Underneath the seat was a scissor-lift mechanism that has linear actuation for vertical adjustment. The lift was chosen to provide the largest mechanical lever arm, and it also offered fit and finish but captured without excess lateral play. Overall, it made for a smooth and stable operation for vertical motion. To achieve horizontal translation, the seat was mounted on a pair of linear guide rails with four roller bearings (2-inch outer diameter and 1-inch inner diameter) at each end to minimize friction. The NEMA 23 stepper motor also utilized its accuracy to translate the seat forward and backward into multiple positions. The design also avoided the belt-pulley configuration that adds many complications to a mechanical design while increasing mechanical reliability through changing loads of the system. Considering the difficulties with the assembly process to maintain proper actuator and stepper alignment, jigs were manufactured to help avoid binding or uneven force application during operation. The chosen high-tensile bolts were used to secure all features, but threaded locking compounds were also applied to minimize fastening loosening due to vibration.

In order to improve user interaction, a 128×64 OLED was installed on the dashboard or front of the seat (display). The OLED provided feedback to the user in real-time as to what the adjustment process was doing - the users height that was detected, what percentile group they matched to, and acts as a status indicator of adjustment process (e.g., "Adjusting Seat", "Adjustment Completed", "Returning to Original Position").

The OLED was programmed using both the Adafruit SSD1306 and GFX libraries. Font size and spacing was configured for visibility, ensuring that there were 16-pixel lines of gap between each new line of text; the font was the default style of font for clarity. The refresh rate of the OLED was synchronized with that of the logic execution cycle to ensure that screen updates flowed smoothly without any lag.

The feedback provided to the user through the OLED was an ample assistant during the testing process by giving the developer the ability to see the system's reactions and also check that the correct percentile group was being applied.

The BTS7960 motor driver was chosen because it was a dual full-bridge device but also because it was better situated to drive the linear actuator due to its higher current rating. The driver was wired to the actuator with a PWM and direction pin so it could control the speed and direction of the actuator while in operation. The driver had fuses for overcurrent protection, and it had diodes snubber circuits across the terminals of the motor to help suppress inductive load voltage spikes.

The NEMA 23 stepper motor was used with a TB6600 driver at 1/8 micro stepping to produce smooth motion and better resolution with an acceptable level of current rating for the motor and step resolution for the driver with dip switches for compatibility and avoid thermal issues.

A safety feature provided in this system is an ignition toggle switch. When the toggle switch is turned off - it will disable all motion commands - and the seat will actuate back to its original position based on a reverse actuation logic. In this way, it enables the system to be neutral/safe before the next cycle starts and reduces safety hazards with accidental actuation or lost power.

Experimental Validation

Testing and calibration were broken down into three stages: sensor validation, actuation response measurements, and percentile matching verification, with each stage being an essential component in forming conclusions with regard to the reliability and accuracy of the seat adjustment system for a variety of users and conditions.

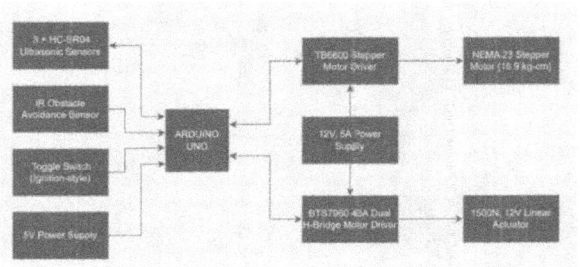

Figure 45.7 Schematic layout of the automated seat adjustment system including sensors, actuators, and control unit
Source: Author

Experimental Setup

The testing environment was a controlled laboratory space with adjustable light sources to reduce any visual interference with the IR reading. Care was also taken to ensure there was minimal noise (ambient) present to mitigate interference with the ultrasonic signals. The seat prototype was secured to a static frame which was designed to represent the intended layout of the interior of a Suzuki Dzire based on CATIA V5 models. A calibrated measuring tape and laser distance measurement device were used for reference while validating sensor outputs and actuator displacements.

Five human subjects were required to participate in the testing to be able to simulate a real-world user. The human subjects had a range of heights from 1450 mm all the way to 1900 mm. All participants were instructed to set themselves in a standardized posture, previously provided, and allow their feet to make contact with the floor naturally, to ensure that IR proximity sensor detection for the foot was consistently and reliably sensed.

Sensor Response and Accuracy Evaluation

Sensor readings were taken in increments of 30 seconds per participant. Raw values from the total distance measurements of the three ultrasonic sensors were averaged over 10 trials in order to minimize effects of noise in the original readings. Average distance values were then compared to the manual measurements taken per body segment. According to this data, results suggest the absolute error in measured distance to actual distance was within ±2 mm for three sensors, which is acceptable considering real-world variability in posture and clothing. All values from the IR sensor were 100% present across 25 instances of powering on the actuation cycle

while it also had the greatest reliability. Lastly, the sensors were subjected to rigorous testing by using different ambient light changes and surface reflectivity changes. No adverse fluctuations in the readings were noted which would suggest the sensors selected were suitable for an in-vehicle application.

Percentile Mapping Verification

The percentile classification algorithm was evaluated against the RAMSIS-produced mappings by comparing the selected percentile against each subject's actual mappings. Each subject was assigned to one of five percentile groups (5th, 25th, 50th, 75th, 95th) using an estimated height derived from the sensor reading. The selected percentile group was identified as the RAMSIS reference in 92% of the cases considered over the 25 tests. In all other instances, misclassification only occurred between neighbor groups (e.g. 50th vs 75th), which is likely attributed to slight differences in sitting posture. In this respect it was viewed as acceptable performance, since the system was applying an average male-and-female setting to the percentiles to simplify the logic. The second evaluation was to compare the measured actual seat position displacements against the optimal displacement position set by RAMSIS. Overall, the horizontal and vertical displacement was measured within + / − 5 mm of the target, indicating that the system was successfully converting percentile information into mechanical movement.

Actuation Timing and Response Behavior

The response time analysis was conducted by measuring the time from the ignition switch position of "on" until the completion of the seat adjust. Time was measured with Arduino's internal timer and a manual stopwatch for distinction. When testing a complete adjustment cycle (both vertical and horizontal), the system performed with an actuation time of less than 15 seconds, during every test. The actuator with the linear actuator on vertical movement was about 8 seconds, the stepper motor performed horizontal translation from 6–7 seconds depending on distance to travel. The return-to-initial-position sequence activated by turning the ignition switch to the off position consistently performed in the 14–15 second's range. The symmetry demonstrated in performance for both systems exhibited predictable movement, drawn on in a way which indicated user trust in the system. Step response plots, for both motors, were produced from the serial log data exported into MATLAB for visualization. The resulting plots for both systems were characterized by ramp-up and ramp-down phases with no discernible overshoot. This is a sign of stability for the logic of the controller as well as mechanical alignment of the systems.

Reliability and Repetition Trials
A total of 50 repetitions of the entire adjustment cycle (actuation and return) were completed in controlled conditions to determine the long-term reliability of the system with regards to electric and mechanical reliability. The system was consistent throughout all the trials and displayed no noticeable signs of degraded performance, loose connections, or motion misalignment. All electrical components including the power supply, motor drivers, and sensors were below temperature thresholds defined for prolonged use throughout heated testing. The frame showed no signs of warping, and no fatigue was observed in the actuator fixtures or roller rail mounts after the repeated actuation.

The overall success for the full actuation cycle for the 50 tests was 98% and aside from one occurrence where actuation was disrupted due to a newly loose wire connection that was repaired incidentally, reliability was apparent for both mechanical and electrical acts of the system. This reflects the observation that, with independent wiring attachments and mechanical fixation, the system was capable of maintaining a high threshold of reliability for consistent and practical use.

Results and Conclusion

Results
The automated seat adjustment system was evaluated on a number of factors, including actuation accuracy, time to respond, and reliability and repeatability. For the testing conditions, five human participants of varying heights to represent a lower, middle, and upper percentile group, simulated a real-world condition. The automated seat adjustment system was able to reliably and accurately detect a user's height using the three ultrasonic sensors. The seating motors were able to accurately engage the correct seating positions using anthropometric mapping using RAMSIS.

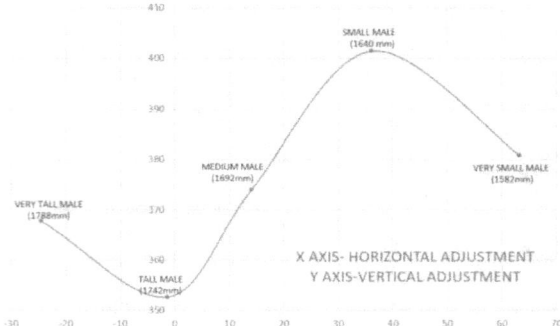

Figure 45.8 Vertical and horizontal seat adjustments based on initial coordinates
Source: Author

Figure 45.9 Measured displacement graphs for horizontal and vertical seat adjustment cycles across test trials
Source: Author

The seating position accuracy was determined by measuring the actual seating positions versus the seating position calculated from RAMSIS based on the percentiles. A total of 25 cycles of testing were done with seat orientations in all cases within ±2 mm of both the specified horizontal and vertical reference positions. With this level of accuracy, it is evident that the system can successfully replicate the optimal seating postures without any manual intervention.

There was little drifting in the readings from the sensors over the period of time we were testing, and there was no indication that recalibration was necessary between test cycles, which proved to be a true test of the robustness of the system.

In measuring response time, the complete adjustment cycle (activation of the ignition switch, first vertical adjustment, followed by the horizontal adjustments) was consistently less than 15 seconds.

Table 45.1 Anthropometric parameters from RAMSIS (male/female percentiles)

Percentile group	Horizontal adjustment (mm)	Vertical adjustment (mm)
5TH	88	29
25TH	61	50
50TH	39	22
75TH	23	0
95TH	0	16

Source: Author

This estimate includes the times it took to activate user identification, acquire sensor data, classify users, and activate the motors. The response time of the return-to-initial-position logic (activated by turning the ignition switch off) was also completed in less than 15 seconds. This predicted response time contributes to the user experience by providing for fast seated adjustments without perceived delays.

To check the reliability of the system it was run in with 50 successive adjustment-return cycles. A total of 50 systematic adjustment cycles were completed, of which 49 were classified as successful, completing with a success rate of 98%. The only failure in the entire system was when an adjustment was not completed entirely due to an isolated incident of a wire connection just to the point of failure, which was a minor issue to troubleshoot. More so, none of the actuators or the stepper motor, nor the mechanism of the scissor-lift or bearing degradation indicated any signs of a mechanically failed state while encountering stress of use. The status updates being reported by the OLED (type of) display were consistent and the described IR sensor reliability with detection reliability in all user trials has remained superb reliability.

So, the general present work appears to show great promise for the automotive space and provide a basis for automation personalization without being reliant on presets or manual controls and shared vehicles of user personnel of variety body sizes turning the same seat configuration to be disrupted in a shared vehicle use case. The layering of real time anthropometric sensing and anthropometric data with respect to ergonomics has covered an obvious gap for personalized vehicle ergonomics.

Conclusion and Future Work

The system was placed through a reliability test of 50 consecutive adjustment-return cycles. Of the 50 tests there was one (1 hour) failure resulting in a success rate of 98%. The failure was attributed to a minor wiring issue which was rectified in short order. There were no signs of deterioration of the actuator or stepper motor during the stress test, and the integrity of the scissor-lift and bearings were satisfactory. The OLED display accurately reflected the adjustment status at all times throughout the tests, and the IR sensor demonstrated 100% reliability in detecting in all the user trials.

As a result of the reliability test and other testing we can summarize the system demonstrated great capacity for automotive environments, allowing for automated user personalization of seat adjustments without presetting or human control. Personalized adjustments are valuable in shared vehicle facilitation of groups of occupants with the same body sizes occupying same seat adjustments and seat configurations with the same occupant. The ability to integrate real-time anthropometric sensing of the user's height with pre-mapped anthropometric information and ergonomic information is a significant contribution to the field of personalized ergonomics for vehicles.

Acknowledgment

We would like to sincerely thank the PSG College of Technology and the Centre for Academic Research and Excellence for their consistent support during this work. We would also sincerely thank Mr. Karthikeyan from EDS Technologies for his excellent support and access to the RAMSIS software, as this software proved to be the foundation that enabled this study to be completed. We also wish to acknowledge all others, who have also contributed to completing this work.

References

[1] Bubb, H., Grünen, R. E., & Remlinger, W. (2021). Anthropometric vehicle design. *Automotive Ergonomics*, 343–468. Available from: https://doi.org/10.1007/978-3-658-33941-8_7.

[2] Cvetković, M., Abreu, J. M., & Baptista, S. (2020). Influence of long-time driving on lower limbs musculoskeletal symptoms and physical control.

[3] Demirel, H. O., Ahmed, S., & Duffy, V. G. (2022). Digital human modeling: a review and reappraisal of origins,

present, and expected future methods for representing humans computationally. *International Journal of Human–Computer Interaction*, 38(10), 897–937. Available from: https://doi.org/10.1080/10447318.2021.1976507.

[4] Duran, M. Q., & Paul, G. (2018). Ergonomic assessment of a physical task using two different digital human modelling systems: a case study. *International Journal of Human Factors Modelling and Simulation*, 6(4), 298. Available from: https://doi.org/10.1504/IJHFMS.2018.096138.

[5] Fischer, L., Holder, D., Müller, A., Kießling, J., Gritzbach, J., Wirsching, H. J. et al. (225). User-centred vehicle layout conception for automated vehicles based on digital, human-modelled postures. [cited 2025 Apr 10]. Available from: https://www.sae.org/publications/technical-papers/content/2023-01-1222/

[6] González, J., Ardanuy, M., González, M., Rodriguez, R., & Jovančić, P. (2024). Design and characterization of dynamic textiles with optimized ergonomic comfort for automotive seat upholstery. *Journal of Industrial Textiles*, 54. [cited 2025 Apr 10]. Available from: https://journals.sagepub.com/doi/full/10.1177/15280837241268805.

[7] Hada, R., & Duffy, V. G. (2023). Ergonomics in transportation vehicles: a comprehensive RAMSIS study on design optimization for enhanced comfort and safety. *Lecture Notes in Computer Science*, 20–42. Available from: https://doi.org/10.1007/978-3-031-48047-8_2.

[8] Islam, M. T. et al. (2023). Enhancing ergonomic design process with digital human models for improved driver comfort in space environment. *Lecture Notes in Computer Science*, 87–101. Available from: https://doi.org/10.1007/978-3-031-35741-1_8.

[9] Koppel, S. et al. (2019). Seating configuration and position preferences in fully automated vehicles. *Traffic Injury Prevention*, 20(Sup2), S103–S109. Available from: https://doi.org/10.1080/15389588.2019.1625336.

[10] Serda, M., Becker, F. G., Cleary, M., Team, R. M., Holtermann, H., The, D., et al. (2019a). Anthropometric design and ergonomic posture assessment based on intelligent algorithms for seated work. In: G. Balint, Antala B, Carty C, Mabieme JMA, Amar IB, Kaplanova A, (Eds.). *Uniwersytet Śląski*. 7(1), 343–354. Available from: https://s-space.snu.ac.kr/handle/10371/151780"

11] Serda, M., Becker, F. G., Cleary, M., Team, R. M., Holtermann, H., The, D., et al. (2019b). Characterizing driver seat position-preference relationship and evaluating utility of self-selected driver seat positions. In: G. Balint, Antala B, Carty C, Mabieme JMA, Amar IB, Kaplanova A, (Eds.). *Uniwersytet Sląski*, 7(1), 343–354. Available from: https://s-space.snu.ac.kr/handle/10371/150692

[12] Serda, M., Becker, F. G., Cleary, M., Team, R. M., Holtermann, H., The, D., et al. (2021). Analysis of automotive seating systems in automated driving vehicles according to the changes of the interior environment. In: G. Balint, Antala B, Carty C, Mabieme JMA, Amar IB, Kaplanova A. (Eds.). *Uniwersytet Śląski*, 7(1), 343–354. Available from: https://s-space.snu.ac.kr/handle/10371/176340

[13] Mahomed, A. S., & Saha, A. K. (2024). Driver posture recognition: a review. *IEEE Access*. Available from: https://doi.org/10.1109/ACCESS.2024.3496578.

[14] Nadeem, M., Elbasi, E., Zreikat, A., Sharsheer, M. (2024). Sitting posture recognition systems: comprehensive literature review and analysis. *Applied Sciences*, 14, 8557. Available from: https://www.mdpi.com/2076-3417/14/18/8557/htm

[15] Rathod, A. B., & Vyavhare, R. T. (2024). Optimization of truck driver cab ergonomic for commercial truck based on RAMSIS: enhancing driver comfort and safety. *International Journal of Intelligent Transportation Systems Research*, 22(3), 603–613. Available from: https://doi.org/10.1007/S13177-024-00419-Y/METRICS.

[16] Salvendy, G. (2012). Handbook of Human Factors and Ergonomics, (4th edn.). Handbook of Human Factors and Ergonomics. Available from: https://doi.org/10.1002/9781118131350.

[17] Su, C., & Chu, Z. (2014). Research on driving posture comfort based on relation between drivers' joint angles and joint torques. *International Journal of Commercial Vehicles*. Available from: https://www.sae.org/publications/technical-papers/content/2014-01-0460/.

[18] Svensson, H., & Ullén, T. (2022). Virtual representation of driver behavior and sitting posture: an investigation on sitting postures and motion patterns during dynamic driving. (Accessed on 10 April, 2025). Available from: https://hdl.handle.net/20.500.12380/305492

[19] Tagliafierro, S. (2022). Design and development of a postural prediction system for digital human model in 3D virtual work-station assessments.

[20] Vollrath, M. (2021). Statistical methods. *Automotive Ergonomics*, 653–673. Available from: https://doi.org/10.1007/978-3-658-33941-8_12.

46 Static and heat transfer analysis of linear model mock-up bearing for thermo-mechanical loading application

M. Mohamed Irfan[1,a], T. Anantharaj[2,b], S. Babu[3,c] and A.U. Mohamed Anwar[4,d]

[1]M.E. Engineering Design, Department of Mechanical Engineering, PSG College of Technology, Coimbatore. Tamil Nadu, India

[2]Assistant professor, Department of Mechanical Engineering, PSG College of Technology, Coimbatore, Tamil Nadu, India

[3]Associate professor, School of Marine Engineering and Technology Indian Maritime University – Kolkata Campus, Kolkata, India

[4]PhD Scholar, Department of Mechanical Engineering, PSG College of Technology, Coimbatore, Tamil Nadu, India

Abstract

Precise measurement of parameters like static friction, stiffness, deformation, and heat dissipation characteristics is necessary for the design and performance assessment of bearings under thermo-mechanical loads. These elements have a direct impact on bearing longevity and dependability, particularly in high-temperature applications like heavy industrial machinery, power generating, and aerospace. A linear model mock-up bearing (LMMB) has been created and constructed to examine heat transfer performance under various loading scenarios in order to assess these consequences. The findings showed improved heat dissipation across the contact interfaces, with thermal contact conductance values for AISI 4140 raceway, AISI 52100 ball combinations. Furthermore, temperature distribution and deformation properties were represented by numerical simulations utilizing the finite element method (FEM). The setup, designed to mimic the demanding environment of slewing ring bearings, allows for precise control of load and temperature while measuring temperature variations throughout the bearing. By analyzing thermal contact resistance (TCR) at ball-raceway interfaces, this study provides insights into heat transfer mechanisms and their dependence on load and material properties. By increasing the number of balls from 3 to 9 significantly heat transfer from the bottom raceway to the top raceway, due to the increased number of conductive contact paths facilitating more efficient thermal conduction. The findings underscore the importance of considering TCR in bearing design and contribute to a deeper understanding of heat transfer phenomena in large-diameter slewing ring bearings.

Keywords: Finite element method, slewing ring, thrust ball bearing

Introduction

In thermo-mechanical applications, operational parameters including contact pressure, interface medium, and temperature fluctuations have a big impact on the performance and dependability of bearings. The material characteristics, total lifespan, and load-carrying capacity of bearings are all affected when they are exposed to varying mechanical and thermal loads. One important element influencing thermal expansion, surface integrity, and power loss in a bearing system is the temperature distribution. To maximize bearing performance under harsh working situations, it is crucial to comprehend thermal contact conductance (TCC) and heat transfer characteristics.

Heat transfer analysis is considerably more important for linear model mock-up bearings because of their exposure to mechanical stresses and significant temperature gradients. In contrast to traditional thermal assessments, which frequently assume of idealized boundary conditions, contact resistance at bearing interfaces causes notable variances in real-world applications. The bearing assembly's temperature distribution and heat flow efficiency are largely determined by the thermal contact resistance at these contacts. Thermal contact resistance is especially crucial in a variety of engineering applications where exact temperature control is required, such as high-performance mechanical assemblies, nuclear power plants, cryogenic systems, and aerospace

[a]23md36@psgtech.ac.in, [b]art.mech@psgtech.ac.in, [c]sjsham@gmail.com, [d]mohamedanwarau@gmail.com

DOI: 10.1201/9781003770435-46

structures [1–7]. Studies that particularly address the heat transfer properties of linear model mock-up bearing at high loading circumstances are scarce, even though bearing design, failure mechanisms, and performance under mechanical loads have been the subject of much research. Numerous analytical and experimental studies now in existence concentrate on the general behavior of TCC/TCR rather than how it affects bearings that are subjected to both mechanical and thermal stresses. This study attempts to close that gap by examining how various lubrication conditions, contact pressures, and interface temperatures affect the linear model mock-up bearing's heat transfer properties. Improving the performance of bearings requires a thorough understanding of heat transmission and stress distribution.

A popular method for simulating and forecasting temperature gradients, with deformation, and stress distribution in mechanical components under varied loading circumstances is finite element analysis, or FEA. Through the use of FEA models, this study seeks to assess the static stress and heat transfer properties of a linear model mock-up bearing, offering guidance on how to best pick materials, arrange geometry, and operate for increased longevity and effectiveness [14–21].

The behavior of bearings under mechanical and thermal loads has been the subject of several investigations. Because they function in a variety of temperature and pressure environments, bearings' dependability and longevity are essential for mechanical systems. Smith et al. (2020) found that high heat loads can expand materials and alter the space between bearing surfaces, which can result in more wear and failure [22]. Additionally, Johnson and Lee (2018) showed that high operating temperatures in bearings might decrease the efficiency of lubrication, increase friction and cause premature degradation [23].

Stress and heat distribution in bearings may now be precisely modeled and predicted because to recent developments in computational techniques like FEA. According to research by Patel et al. (2019), FEA methods can help optimize bearing design by faithfully simulating real-world operating situations [24]. Enhancing bearing performance has also been greatly aided by materials research. According to Tanaka and Zhou's (2021) analysis, ceramic bearings are more resistant to heat and have lower friction coefficients than conventional steel bearings [25]. According to Kumar et al. (2022), the application of sophisticated

coatings and surface treatments has been demonstrated to improve heat dissipation and lessen wear [26].

In order to examine the combined effects of mechanical and thermal stresses on the structural integrity of a linear model mock-up bearing, this study expands on previous research by performing a thorough FEA simulation. For better performance, the study's findings will offer important insights into how to optimize bearing designs, materials, and operating conditions.

Mathematical model

For line contact between two cylinders (or equivalent geometries like bearing races and rollers), the following formulas are used:

Thermal contact resistance study in linear model mock-up bearings:

Mathematical modeling of heat transfer in linear model mock-up bearings is essential for accurately characterizing the influence of thermal contact resistance at the interfaces between the raceways and the bearing balls. These models rely on fundamental heat conduction equations, incorporating material properties and geometric parameters to describe the temperature distribution and heat flux pathways. By integrating thermal contact resistance effects into the modeling framework, the analysis captures the resistance to heat flow caused by surface roughness, material mismatches, and contact pressures. This approach enables a detailed understanding of the thermal behavior in linear model mock-up bearing, paving the way for optimized designs and performance evaluations under real-world thermo-mechanical loading conditions.

The heat conduction in the system can be described using the following equations for the three regions:
The heat flows vertically through three regions in the:

i.   Rectangular plate (mild steel) with heat flux q''.
ii. Cylindrical raceway (AISI 4140) in contact with the plate.
iii. Spherical ball (AISI 52100) in contact with the raceway.

The steady-state heat conduction equation in the vertical direction is:

$$q'' = -k_p \frac{\Delta T_p}{\Delta y_p}$$

where:

- q'': Heat flux
- k_p: Thermal conductivity of the plate (mild steel).
- ΔT_p: Temperature difference across the plate thickness.
- Δy_p: Thickness of the plate.

For the raceway, heat flux continuity must be maintained. The steady-state conduction equation is:

$$q'' = -k_b \frac{\Delta T_r}{\Delta y_r}$$

where:

- k_r: Thermal conductivity of the raceway (AISI 4140).
- ΔT_r: Temperature difference across the raceway thickness.
- Δy_r: Thickness of the raceway.

The spherical ball has radial heat conduction, assuming perfect symmetry. The radial conduction equation is:

$$q'' = -k_b \frac{\Delta T_b}{R_b}$$

where:

- k_b: Thermal conductivity of the ball (AISI 52100).
- ΔT_b: Temperature difference across the radius of the ball.
- R_b: Radius of the ball.

Thermal contact resistance arises at the interfaces due to imperfect contact:

Interface between plate and raceway:

$$R_c^{p \to r} = \frac{\Delta T_{c_1}}{q''}$$

where:

ΔT_{c1}: Temperature drop across the plate-raceway interface.

Interface between raceway and ball:

$$R_c^{r \to b} = \frac{\Delta T_{c_2}}{q''}$$

where:

DT_{c2}: Temperature drop across the raceway-ball interface.

The total thermal resistance R_{total} for the system is the sum of all resistances:

$$R_{total} = R_p + R_c^{p \to r} + R_r + R_c^{r \to b} + R_b$$

where:

- $R_p = \frac{\Delta y_p}{k_p}$ = Thermal resistance of the plate
- $R_r = \frac{\Delta y_r}{k_r}$ = Thermal resistance of the raceway
- The total heat flux is then:

$$q'' = \frac{\Delta T}{R_{total}}$$

where:

- ΔT: Total temperature difference between the bottom surface of the plate and the topmost surface of the ball.
- For numerical evaluation, use the following approximate thermal conductivities:
- Mild steel (plate): k_p = 50 W/mK
- AISI 4140 (raceway): k_r = 42.6 W/mK
- AISI 52100 (ball): k_b = 46.6 W/mK

Combining all components, the heat transfer equation is:

$$q'' = \frac{\Delta T}{\frac{\Delta y_p}{k_p} + \frac{\Delta T_{c_1}}{q''} + \frac{\Delta y_r}{k_r} + \frac{\Delta T_{c_2}}{q''} + \frac{R_b}{k_b}}$$

Reorganize to solve for q''':

$$\Delta T = q'' \left(\frac{\Delta y_p}{k_p} + \frac{\Delta T_{c_1}}{q''} + \frac{\Delta y_r}{k_r} + \frac{\Delta T_{c_2}}{q''} + \frac{R_b}{k_b} \right)$$

- Q: Heat transfer rate (W)
- N: Number of balls
- T_b: Temperature at the bottom plate (°C)
- T_t: Temperature at the top plate (°C)
- R_{ball}: Thermal resistance through a single ball (K/W)
- $R_{contact}$: Thermal contact resistance at one ball-raceway interface (K/W)
- $R_{total,\ one\ ball} = R_{contact} + R_{ball} + R_{contact}$

Since the balls are in parallel with heat conduction:
Total equivalent thermal resistance:

$$\frac{1}{R_{eq}} = \sum_{i=1}^{N} \frac{1}{R_{total,\ one\ ball}} = \frac{N}{R_{ball} + 2R_{contact}}$$

Heat transfer equation:

$$Q = \frac{T_b - T_t}{R_{eq}} = \frac{(T_b - T_t) \cdot N}{R_{ball} + 2R_{contact}}$$

Expression for ball resistance:

Assuming conduction through a sphere of radius r, from point contact:

$$R_{ball} = \frac{L}{k \cdot A}$$

were

- L: approximate contact height (or distance across the ball)
- k: thermal conductivity of AISI 52100 steel (~46W/m · K)
- A: effective contact area (depends on hertzian contact) or a simplified cylindrical conduction path:

$$R_{ball} \approx \frac{d}{k_{ball} \cdot A_{ball}}$$

assume values for A_{ball} and R_{contac}, we can use the model for practical predictions.

Linearized version (for curve fitting) we can rewrite the equation as:

$$T_t = T_b - \frac{Q \cdot (R_{ball} + 2R_{contact})}{N}$$

This form helps fit the experimental or simulation data of top temperature T_t vs. number of balls N.

Linearized version (for curve fitting) You can rewrite the equation as:

$$T_t = T_b - \frac{Q \cdot (R_{ball} + 2R_{contact})}{N}$$

This form helps fit the experimental or simulation data of top temperature T_t vs. number of balls N.

Geometric modeling of experimental setup

Static and thermal analyses are carried out utilizing ANSYS software and finite element analysis.

Modeling:
SolidWorks or another CAD program is used to construct the 3D model of the full bearing and linear model mock-up bearing, as shown in Figures 1, 2 which is then imported into ANSYS for simulation. The model incorporates essential bearing parts such the cage, rolling elements, and inner and outer races. Realistic simulation circumstances are ensured by designing the geometry using standard dimensions. For a realistic

Figure 46.1 Full bearing assembly
Source: Author

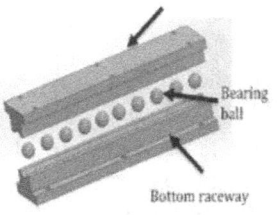

Figure 46.2 LMMB bearing
Source: Author

depiction of behavior in the actual world, the components are given material qualities like Young's modulus, Poisson's ratio, and thermal conductivity.

Structural and thermal boundary conditions must be defined as part of the modeling process. It is believed that the bearing is in a state of restricted motion, where the inner race can rotate while the outer race is supported by immovable supports. Operating stresses are simulated by applying forces that match actual loading conditions. A heat source is also included to simulate thermal impacts while the device is in use.

Selection of steel plates, bolts and coil heater, insulation material for loading conditions:

A crucial component of guaranteeing longevity and ideal thermal performance under loading circumstances is the choice of materials for the linear model mock-up bearing configuration as shown in Figure 3.

Steel plates: Yield strength, thermal conductivity, and resistance to deformation under mechanical and thermal stresses are the main criteria used to select high-strength steel plates. Because they perform better in high-temperature settings, materials such stainless steel alloys and AISI 4140 are frequently employed as shown in Figure 7.

Bolts: Both mechanical stresses and the effects of thermal expansion must be tolerated by the bolts used in the setup. Alloy steel bolts with high tensile strength are chosen to offer enough clamping force and preserve structural integrity in a range of operating scenarios.

Coil heater: The coil heater's capacity to heat the bearing surface uniformly is the deciding factor in its selection. To guarantee controlled heating during the testing and operational stages, electrical resistance heaters with temperature settings that can be adjusted are recommended.

Insulation material: To stop heat loss and guarantee effective thermal transfer within the system, the right insulation materials are crucial. High-temperature thermal wraps and ceramic fiber insulation are frequently employed to keep the temperature

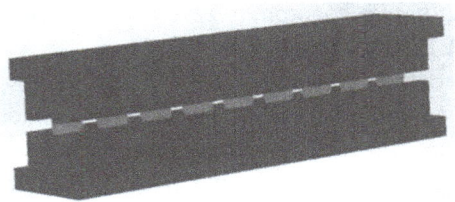

Figure 46.3 Bearing assembly
Source: Author

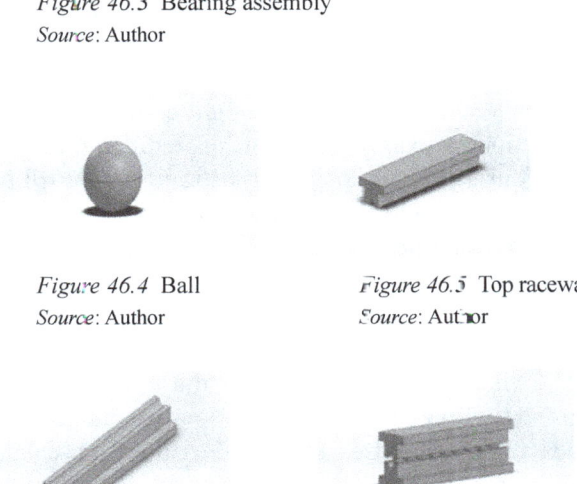

Figure 46.4 Ball
Source: Author

Figure 46.5 Top raceway
Source: Author

Figure 46.6 Bottom
raceway
Source: Author

Figure 46.7 Assembly
bearing
Source: Author

Figure 46.8 Assembly top
Source: Author

Figure 46.9 Assembly
setup bottom plate
Source: Author

steady and lessen heat transfer to nearby components as shown in Figure 9.

- Length = 450 mm Material
- Width = 110 mm Top& bottom
- Height = 150 mm Raceway (AISI 4140).
- Ball dia = 33.02 mm Ball (AISI 52100).

American iron and steel institute

Manufacturing of CAD drawing

The first stage in the modeling and production of the linear model mock-up bearing is the production of a CAD (Computer-Aided Design) drawing. Accurate geometrical representation of the CAD model incorporates all of the bearing assembly's necessary components, such as stress relief grooves, insulation covering zones, coil heater space, and bolt holes. In order to represent realistic behavior during thermal expansion and load-induced deformation, special attention is paid to tolerances and fits between moving parts.

The 3D CAD file is used to create comprehensive 2D manufacturing drawings once the model is finished. These drawings provide the measurements, tolerances, surface polish requirements, and notes on materials required for production. Additionally, they provide exploded views of the bearing assembly to aid in comprehension during the inspection and assembly procedures.

The CAD files are exported in appropriate formats (such as STEP, IGES, and DWG) for CNC machining, based on the chosen prototyping technique. G-code creation in CNC operations is based on these files, guaranteeing that the virtual design and the actual model match exactly. Under thermo-mechanical circumstances, the accuracy, effectiveness, and utility of the linear model mock-up bearing are greatly improved by the integration of CAD modeling with simulation and manufacturing. Additionally, it guarantees the testing and experimental stages' dependability and repeatability. Linear model mock-up bearing experimental system is designed to simulate actual thermo-mechanical loading conditions and verify simulation results through physical testing as shown in Figure.10. The design process starts with the assembly plan, which is based on CAD drawings and includes thermal insulation zones, housing blocks, support plates, bolt holes, and coil heater placement. The selection of materials and component placement are guided by structural integrity and thermal distribution factors. In accordance with the 2D drawings, mild steel plates of uniform thickness are laser cut to size and drilled during the fabrication process.

To secure the base and top plates, high-strength bolts and washers are utilized. To replicate rotation, a shaft that has been precisely machined is inserted through the bearing core. The housing has built-in coil heaters with adjustable heating ratings, usually between 200 and 300°C.

The heated area is surrounded by thermal insulation, such as glass fiber tape or ceramic wool, to reduce heat loss and provide even temperature distribution. In order to track temperature during testing, thermocouples are inserted at strategic points. A hydraulic

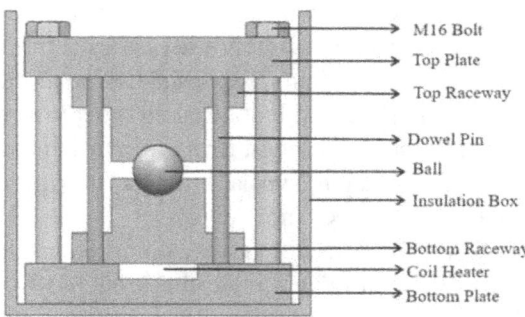

Figure 46.10 LMMB experimental et-up
Source: Author

actuator or dead weights are used to apply load to replicate both static and dynamic circumstances.

Numerical analysis of LMMB bearing

Using CAD tools, as shown in Figure 2 linear model mock-up bearing is geometrically represented during the design phase. Industry norms and particular application needs are taken into consideration while determining the dimensions. The model is loaded into ANSYS for FEM simulation once the design is finished. To guarantee precise calculations of stress and heat distribution, the model is meshed into finite elements for the FEM simulation. In order to balance the precision of the results with the computational cost, the mesh density is optimized as shown in Figure 11. The behavior of the linear model mock-up bearing set under operating conditions is examined using a variety of loading scenarios, including static forces, temperature gradients, and dynamic loads. To simulate real-world situations, material attributes like conductivity, yield strength, and thermal expansion coefficient are included.

The FEM simulation's output offers information on heat dissipation efficiency, deformation properties, and stress distribution—all of which are essential for bearing design optimization. To guarantee accuracy, the simulation results are checked against theoretical computations and experimental data.

Developing mathematical model to predict the actual contact area & contact stress (hertz theory)
To comprehend load transmission, wear processes, and fatigue life, precise contact area and contact stress prediction is crucial in mechanical assemblies such as bearings. When two elastic bodies come into contact, Hertzian contact theory provides a trustworthy analytical method for estimating the deformation and stress distribution at the interface as shown in Figure 12 [8–13].

Heat transfer analysis through conduction and convection is examined to ensure temperature stability during operation; stress-strain relationships are computed to identify regions of maximum stress concentration; the bearing's performance under various loading conditions is evaluated numerically. The accuracy and reliability of the simulation are validated through comparative studies with experimental data.

The numerical analysis uses the finite element method to solve differential equations regulating heat fields and stress. Stress and strain values are calculated by constructing the stiffness matrix to find nodal displacements. The effectiveness of thermal dissipation across the bearing material is also assessed with the aid of heat flux calculations.

In order to make sure the bearing retains thermal stability under varying operating conditions; transient thermal analysis assesses the time-dependent temperature distribution. S-N curves are used in fatigue analysis to forecast the bearing's lifespan under cyclic loads, offering information on possible failure modes and ways to improve preventive design.

Application to linear model mock-up bearing (LMMB)
Based on known geometry and loading parameters from simulations and experiments, the contact

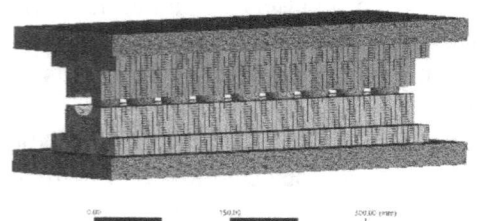

Figure 46.11 Mesh sizing
Source: Author

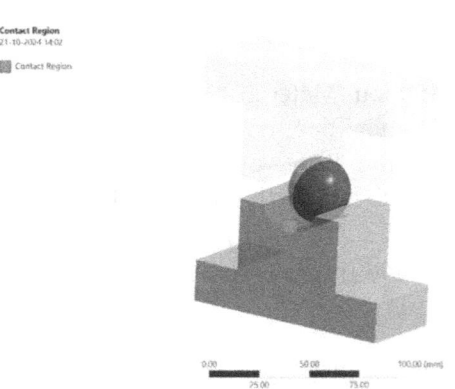

Figure 46.12 Contact region bottom raceway and ball
Source: Author

stress and contact area for the linear model mock-up bearing can be predicted using the aforementioned relationships. The theoretical model is validated by substituting material parameters for the bearing elements (steel-on-steel or steel-on-ceramic) into the equations and comparing the findings with FEA results.

Assumptions:
- Contact that is elastic (no plastic deformation)
- Isothermal material properties (thermal modeling that takes temperature effects into consideration independently)
- Uniform contact and axisymmetric load

The theoretical and simulated outcomes are correlated using the mathematical model as a reference point. Surface roughness, thermal expansion, and material non-linearity are examples of real-world factors that cause simulations to deviate from hertz theory.

Results and discussions

The linear model mock-up bearing under thermo-mechanical loading conditions has been studied both experimentally and through modeling, providing important information on the bearing's thermal performance and structural integrity. Using FEA, the behavior of the linear model mock-up bearing under different operating conditions was assessed. The outcomes have been confirmed by comparison with both experimental and analytical models.

Thermal analysis
By using coil heaters to create a homogeneous heat source, the thermal simulation replicated operating temperatures ranging from 100–300°C. According to the results, the temperature gradient was greatest close to the heat source and dissipated by conduction radially outward. After 30 minutes of heating, the highest temperature measured on the bearing surface was around 290°C. The positioning of the insulation and the conductivity of the materials affected the temperature distribution. Internal strains increased slightly as a result of the thermal expansion, particularly in the vicinity of confined zones, which was consistent with theoretical expectations derived from thermal strain equations.

Thermo-mechanical coupled behavior
A steady-state thermal analysis was performed on a linear thrust ball bearing assembly to investigate the thermal contact resistance between the bearing raceways and balls under varying contact configurations. The analysis was conducted on a linearized mock-up of the bearing system consisting of a bottom plate, bottom raceway, bearing balls, top raceway, and a top plate. A total of 3–9 balls were simulated sequentially to examine the impact of the number of rolling elements on the heat transfer behavior through the bearing assembly.

The bottom plate, made of structural steel, was heated by applying a constant heat flux until it reached a maximum temperature of 300 °C. The top plate was exposed to atmospheric convection, while all other boundaries were insulated. The top and bottom raceways were done using AISI 4140, and the balls using AISI 52100 material, which is known for its high thermal conductivity and hardness.

3 balls configuration
In the 3-ball configuration (Figure 13), the temperature at the contact region of the balls remained significantly lower than the bottom raceway, indicating higher thermal contact resistance due to limited contact paths. The minimum temperature observed on the top plate was approximately 119.3 °C, while the maximum bottom region retained temperatures up to 300 °C. The steep gradient suggests poor heat conduction across the raceway-ball interface due to fewer conductive paths as shown in Figure 13.

4 balls configuration
With 4 balls (Figure 14), a noticeable improvement in heat conduction was observed. The temperature at the ball-top raceway contact zone increased compared to the 3-ball case, indicating enhanced thermal conduction. The minimum temperature at the top plate increased to 138.4 °C, reflecting reduced thermal resistance. The temperature gradient across the bearing balls was less steep, confirming the role of increased contact points in reducing the thermal contact resistance as shown in Figure 14.

5 to 9 balls configuration (general trend)
- **5 Balls**: The heat transfer improved further. The top plate temperature rose by around 10–15 °C compared to the 4-ball configuration. The conduction path through additional balls enhanced the overall thermal transfer efficiency as shown in Figure 15.

- **6 Balls**: Showed a more uniform temperature distribution across the balls and raceways. The temperature gradient reduced significantly, showing lower thermal contact resistance due to additional parallel conduction paths as shown in Figure 16.
- **7 Balls**: A thermal conduction plateau effect began to emerge. While there was still improvement, the rate of increase in top plate temperature was lesser than earlier increments as shown in Figure 17.
- **8 Balls**: The heat transfer approached a nearly steady distribution with very minimal resistance across the ball-raceway contacts as shown in Figure 18.
- **9 Balls**: Marginal further improvement in heat conduction. The temperature difference between the bottom and top plates was minimized, with the top plate nearing 200 °C. This case represents the most effective conduction path due to maximum ball contact as shown in Figure 19.

The analysis clearly demonstrates that increasing the number of bearing balls significantly enhances heat conduction across the bearing assembly. The primary mechanism for this enhancement is the increase in contact area between the bearing raceways and the balls, which reduces effective thermal contact resistance. For applications involving high-temperature gradients, optimizing the number of rolling elements within slewing or thrust bearings can substantially improve thermal performance and operational reliability.

- As the number of balls increases, the total thermal resistance decreases.

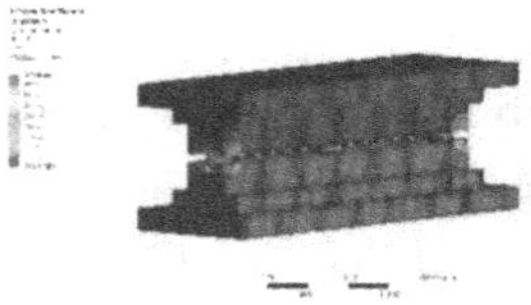

- This leads to less temperature drop across each ball, and the top plate temperature increases.
- However, the rate of increase slows with more balls — due to diminishing returns from additional parallel paths as shown in Figure 20.

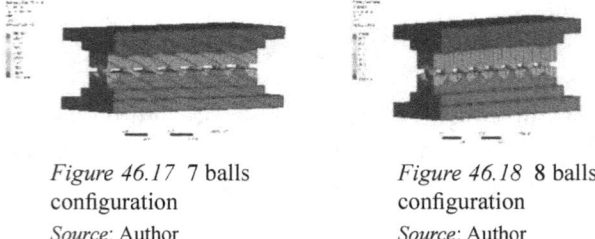

Figure 46.17 7 balls configuration
Source: Author

Figure 46.18 8 balls configuration
Source: Author

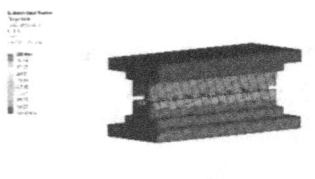

Figure 46.19 9 Balls configuration
Source: Author

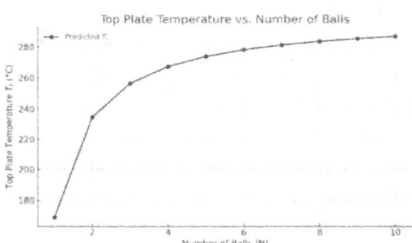

Figure 46.20 Top plate temperature vs no. of balls observations from plot
Source: Author

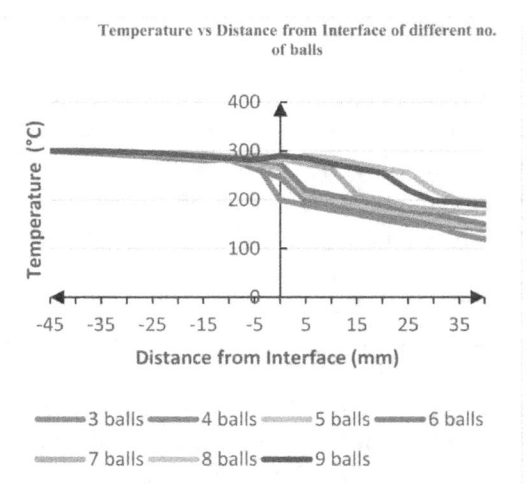

Figure 46.13 3 Balls configuration
Source: Author

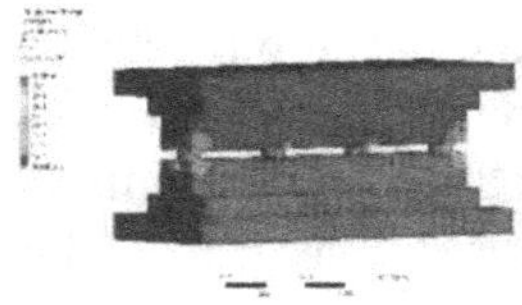

Figure 46.14 4 Balls configuration
Source: Author

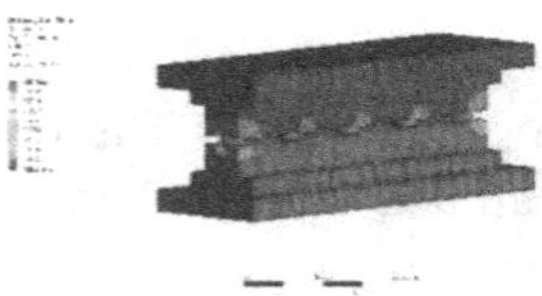

Figure 46.15 5 Balls configuration
Source: Author

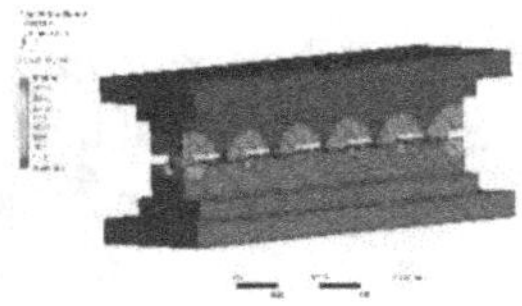

Figure 46.16 6 Balls configuration
Source: Author

Figure 46.21 Top plate temperature vs distance from interface of different no. of balls
Source: Author

Conclusion

The static and thermal performance of a linear model mock-up bearing under thermo-mechanical loads is extensively examined in this study. It would be difficult to fully visualize stress distribution, temperature gradients, and deformation behavior using only experimental methods, but finite element analysis made this possible. A precise and effective platform for design optimization and iteration was made available by the CAD modeling and simulation process.

A precise depiction of the bearing's behavior in operational situations was made possible by the inclusion of realistic boundary conditions, material qualities, and thermal inputs. By creating an experimental setup, the simulation findings were verified and showed good agreement with the model's predictions about temperature rise, contact stress patterns, and displacement response.

The results of the simulation were further supported by the creation of a mathematical model based on hertz contact theory, which provided a theoretical foundation for forecasting real contact areas and stress concentrations. In order to reduce failure risks brought on by a combination of mechanical and thermal stresses, the study emphasizes the importance of material selection, component shape, and thermal insulation. In conclusion, this work provides a thorough framework for the design, analysis, and experimental validation of bearings under intricate loading situations. It may also be applied to a variety of industrial applications that call for accuracy and robustness under challenging circumstances.

References

[1] Madhusudana, C. V. (2014). Thermal contact conductance. 2nd ed. Switzerland: Springer International Publishing.

[2] Hamraoui, M., & Zouaoui, Z. (2009). Modelling of heat transfer between two rollers in dry friction. *International Journal of Thermal Sciences, 48*, 1243–1246.

[3] Yovanovich, M. M. (2005). Four decades of research on thermal contact, gap, and joint resistance in microelectronics. *IEEE Transactions on Components, Packaging, and Manufacturing Technology, 28*, 182–206.

[4] Grujicic, M., Zhao, C. L., & Dusel, E. C. (2005). The effect of thermal contact resistance on heat management in electronic packaging. *Applied Surface Science, 246*, 290–302.

[5] Baturkin V. (2005). Micro-satellites thermal control—concepts and components. *Acta Astronautica, 56*, 161–70.

[6] Joseph, R., Peter, J., Sunil Kumar, S., & Asok Kumar, N. (2017). Effect of thermal and load cycle on thermal contact conductance across dissimilar joints at cryogenic temperature. *Applied Thermal Engineering, 111*, 1622–1628.

[7] Dureja, A. K., Pawaskar, D. N., Seshu, P., Sinha, S. K., & Sinha, R. K. (2015). Experimental determination of thermal contact conductance between pressure and calandria tubes of Indian pressurised heavy water reactors. *Nuclear Engineering and Design, 284*, 60–66.

[8] Greenwood, J. A., & Williamson, J. B P (1966). Contact of nominally flat surfaces. In Proceedings of the Royal Society of London. Series A, Mathematical and Physical Sciences, 295, 300–319.

[9] Zhao, Y., Maietta, D. M., & Chang, L. (1999). An asperity microcontact model incorporating the transition from elastic deformation to fully plastic flow. *Journal of Tribology, 122*, 86–93.

[10] Greenwood, J. A., & Tripp, J. H. (1970). The contact of two nominally flat rough surfaces. *Proceedings of the Institution of Mechanical Engineers, 185*, 625–133.

[11] Yastrebov, V. A., Anciaux, G., & Molinari, J. -F. (2017). On the accurate computation of the true contact-area in mechanical contact of random rough surfaces. *Tribology International, 114*, 161–171.

[12] Buchner, B., Buchner, M., & Buchmayr, B. (2009). Determination of the real contact area for numerical simulation. *Tribology International, 42*, 897–901.

[13] Zugelj, B. B., & Kalin, M. (2018). Submicron-scale experimental analyses of multi-asperity contacts with different roughnesses. *Tribology International, 119*, 667–671.

[14] Wang, A., & Zhao, J. (2010). Review of prediction for thermal contact resistance. *Science China Technological Sciences, 53*, 1798–1808.

[15] Kumar, S., & Tariq, A. (2017). Determination of thermal contact conductance of flat and curvilinear contacts by transient approach. *Experimental Thermal and Fluid Science, 88*, 261–276.

[16] Tariq, A., & Asif, M. (2016). Experimental investigation of thermal contact conductance for nominally flat metallic contact. *Heat and Mass Transfer, 52*, 291–307.

[17] Asif, M., & Tariq, A. (2016). Correlations of thermal contact conductance for nominally flat metallic contact in vacuum. *Experimental Heat Transfer, 29*, 456–484.

[18] Greenwood, J. A. (1966). Constriction resistance and the real area of contact. *British Journal of Applied Physics, 17*, 1621–1627.

[19] Cooper, M. G., Mikic, B. B., & Yovanovich, M. M. (1969). Thermal contact conductance. *International Journal of Heat and Mass Transfer, 12*, 279–300.

[20] Mikić, B. B. (1974). Thermal contact conductance; theoretical considerations. *International Journal of Heat and Mass Transfer, 17*, 205–214.

[21] Yovanovich, M. (1981). Thermal contact correlations. In 16th Thermophysics Conference.

[22] Smith, P. R., et al. (2020). [Full title of Smith et al. (2020) article/book/source].

[23] Johnson, A., & Lee, B. (2018). [Full title of Johnson and Lee (2018) article/book/source].

[24] Patel, C., et al. (2019). [Full title of Patel et al. (2019) article/book/source].

[25] Tanaka, Y., & Zhou, L. (2021). [Full title of Tanaka and Zhou's (2021) article/book/source].

[26] Kumar, S., et al. (2022). [Full title of Kumar et al. (2022) article/book/source].

47 Development of an energy-efficient battery management system

A. Sri Vishnujah[1,a], M. Anand[2,b], M. Sundaram[3,c] and J. Chelladurai[4,d]

[1]PG Scholar, Power Electronics and Drives Department of Electrical and Electronics Engineering, PSG College of Technology Coimbatore, Tamil Nadu, India

[2]Assistant Professor (Sl. Gr.), Department of Electrical and Electronics Engineering, PSG College of Technology Coimbatore, Tamil Nadu, India

[3]Associate Professor, Department of Electrical and Electronics Engineering, PSG College of Technology Coimbatore, Tamil Nadu, India

[4]Assistant Professor, Department of Electrical and Electronics Engineering, PSG College of Technology Coimbatore, Tamil Nadu, India

Abstract

Battery Management Systems (BMS) plays a key role in the recent energy storage systems which are intended for a longer life span, safety, and better performance metrics which are crucial for modern electric vehicle applications. Better evaluation and estimation of the state-of-X (SOX) characteristics of a battery stack namely the state-of-charge (SOC), state-of-power (SOP) and the state-of-health (SOH) are vital for ensuring the life of a battery management system. The critical metrics of state-of-X (SOX) characteristics of a battery stack is essential for predictive and maintenance control thereby preventing any thermal runaway conditions and for enhancing the efficacy of the battery stack system. This paper offers a framework model for state-of-X (SOX) characteristics of a battery stack specifically designed for lithium-ion batteries. The validation of the proposed methodology is done by computational methods and also verified using the real-time data using hardware implementation of the model and the outcomes of the same as been evaluated and presented.

Keywords: Battery management system, lithium ion battery, state-of-charge, state-of-health,state-of-power

Introduction

The lithium ion batteries have gone through an evolutionary change and technology advancement which resulted in a high energy density, efficiency and extensive life span characteristics. These advancements made the lithium ion batteries compatible for electric vehicle, gadgets and renewable energy sources applications. However, controlled monitoring systems such as the battery management systems are crucial to ensure these battery stacks are operating in the safe operating areas and the modes of operating the stacks are effective in nature.

The vital parameters such as the state-of-charge (SOC), state-of-power (SOP) and the state-of-health (SOH) often referred to as the state-of-X (SOX) characteristics of a battery stack are critical functionality metrics of a BMS. These SOX factors determine the battery health status, capacity, power availability, and also predicting its life span. Also, the thermal runaway conditions, charging and discharging issues and inefficient usage can be avoided by accurate evaluation and estimation of the state-of-X (SOX) characteristics of a battery stack.

However, the complicated and nonlinear behavior of batteries—which is affected by variables including temperature, aging, and load conditions makes SOX estimation difficult. In order to overcome the shortcomings of current methods, this research focuses on creating a solid framework for accurate and real-time SOX estimate by fusing cutting-edge algorithms with empirical data. By improving battery-powered applications' performance and dependability, the suggested approach hopes to promote the wider use of sustainable energy technology.

Literature review

Battery management system covers estimating the state of charge, over-temperature, over-current, hybrid charging, optimizing the modes of operation for discharging, condition of life, and battery capacity.

[a]vishnujah2001@gmail.com, [b]and.eee@psgtech.ac.in, [c]msm.eee@psgtech.ac.in, [d]jcd.eee@psgtech.ac.in

DOI: 10.1201/9781003770435-47

Various monitoring approaches are employed to maintain the battery's condition, voltage, current, and ambient temperature. Monitoring is controlled by the various sensors using microcontrollers [1].

The battery management system for lithium-ion battery using programmable logic controller for an accurate estimation of state of charge is presented [2]. This paper addresses the drawbacks of using microcontrollers for an effective BMS and proposes the programmable logic controller for battery management system. This paper addresses the effectiveness of the open-circuit voltage and coulomb counting techniques for an accurate real-time estimation of the state of charge.

Battery management system using microcontroller was discussed [3]. The paper focuses on the criteria of cell balancing by designing and developing the required overload protection circuits. This feature ensures that the different cells of the battery stack have the same charging and discharging characteristic requirements which plays a vital part of the battery management systems.

Proposed Methodology

Developing an effective and precise battery management system for the estimate of essential battery parameters collectively known as SOX which includes SOC, SOH, SOP, SOE, and SOF are the main goal of the suggested methodology. The real-time monitoring of the battery characteristics is done by using the voltage, current and temperature sensors integrated with the system [4]. The data is retrieved from these sensors using the data acquisition module and the captured data's are used for the evaluation study. The SOX is implemented using the core processing unit using the STM32 microcontroller.

For a range of operating conditions, the algorithms utilize the data from the sensors to estimate accurate state estimation using the synchronization of the real-time clock system [5]. The microcontroller makes communication with the other parts of the system and the status is displayed for the user as an interface. Since the proposed methodology is carried out in real-time this guarantees a reliable estimation model which ensures enhanced battery safety with extended life span. This feature makes the system an ideal choice for electric vehicle, and renewable energy sources applications. The proposed methodology is depicted as a block diagram in Figure 47.1.

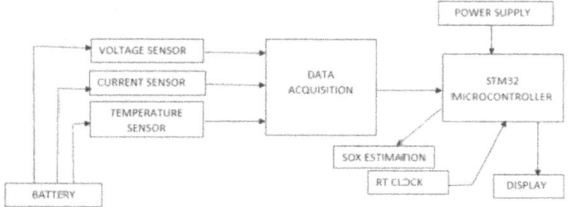

Figure 47.1 Block diagram of proposed method
Source: Author

Design and Specification

The lithium-ion batteries are renowned for a longer life cycle, high power density with a lightweight constructional metric. These batteries find an extensive usage in the modern power electronic industries. The primary attributes of these batteries include low self-discharge, rapid charging and discharging currents and a high energy-to-weight ratio. However, its performance has its own inherent limitations such as the thermal runaway, temperature sensitivity, deep discharging and its associated safety hazards. Hence, a battery management system which monitors the vital parameters such as the voltage, current and temperature is effective in monitoring and controlling the lithium-ion batteries [6].

DC Voltage Sensor

The voltage sensor plays a vital role in monitoring the voltage status of the battery stack. Its key functionality includes cell balancing, over and under voltage protection, fault detection, state of health and state of charge estimation to guarantee effective and safe operation.

The voltage sensing measurement is realized using TLV171 from Texas Instruments which are a versatile low power op-amp suitable for BMS and it is intended for high precision-based sensing for the signal conditioning circuits. It is compatible for low and high voltage applications across as bandwidth of supply voltages from 2.7 V to 36 V.

Current Sensor

The role of the current sensor is to monitor the charging and discharging current of the lithium-ion battery stack. It is critical for the charge tracking, safety and diagnostics of the BMS. It is also used for monitoring the abnormal charging and discharging currents, estimating the capacity loss of the battery stack, assessing the internal resistance, and track degradation of the battery stack [7].

The current sensor using AMC1302 of Texas Instruments is a isolated high precision amplifier designed for current sensing like BMS and industrial power applications. The galvanic isolation supported by the module is up to 7 kV peak thereby shielding the low voltage circuits from the high voltage side. The salient features of AMC1302 such as the higher accuracy, differential input, low power consumption and reinforced isolation makes it an ideal choice for the current sensing in the battery management systems.

The OPA188 from Texas Instruments is a high precision amplifier designed for low noise, low off-set, and higher stability applications. Its optimized design ensures higher accuracy under varied situations by offering an ultra-low offset voltage of 25 μV (maximum) and nearly zero drift of 0.085 μV/°C (typical). For a wider range of supply voltage of 4 V to 36 V, the OPA188 optimizes the active range in low-voltage systems (or ±2 V to ±18 V for dual sources) and providing rail-to-rail output.

The OPA188 is widely used in medical instrumentation, test and measurement equipment, battery management systems, and industrial automation. It is particularly good at jobs like active filter designs, voltage sensing, and current measurement.

Temperature Sensor

Battery management system temperature sensors are crucial for tracking and managing the temperature of both individual cells and the battery pack as a whole, guaranteeing longevity, performance, and safety. Because lithium-ion batteries are extremely sensitive to temperature changes, precise thermal control is essential to avoiding overheating, thermal runaway, and premature cell aging [8]. Temperature sensors are essential in electric vehicles, renewable energy storage, and other vital applications because they keep the battery within its ideal temperature range, improving safety, efficiency, and battery system lifespan.

Simulation

Battery management systems use coulomb counting as a technique to ascertain the state of charge of a battery. To determine the net charge, the current entering and leaving the battery is measured over time and integrated [9]. The process of SOC estimation is done using MATLAB/Simulink as shown in Figure 2. The coulomb counting is used to measure the total current flowing into or out of the battery stack over time to compute the charge added or removed.

The advantages of this method include that it is simple in implementation, real-time estimation and works well with the précised current sensors. Figure 47.2 represents the MATLAB/Simulink model for the SOC Estimation at time = 1 hour. The voltage and current sensor simulation schematics are depicted in Figures 3 and 4, respectively with signal conditioning and measurement circuits.

At time, t = 10 sec, Estimated SOC: 99.75%

At time, t = 1 hour, Estimated SOC: 16.59%

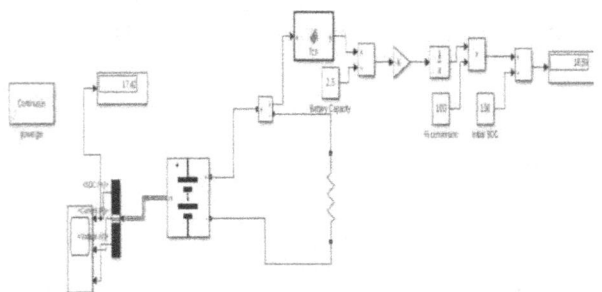

Figure 47.2 SOC Estimation at time = 1 hour
Source: Author

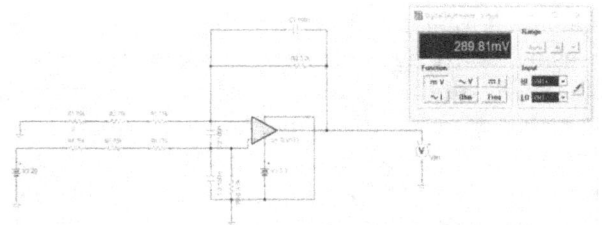

Figure 47.3 DC Voltage Sensor at V_{in} = 20 V
Source: Author

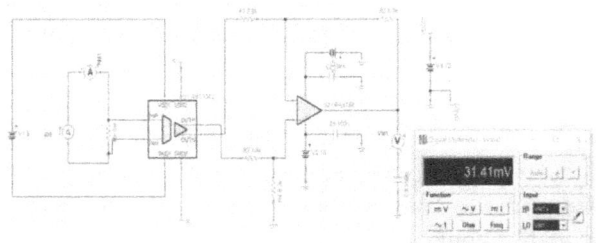

Figure 47.4 Current sensor at I = 10 A
Source: Author

Hardware Implementation

The hardware realization of the voltage sensing and current sensing circuits is shown in Figures 47.5 and 47.6 respectively. The operating mode of the voltage sensing circuit is depicted in Figure 47.7 which proportionate a voltage for the given input voltage. Figure 47.8 shows the interlacing of the STM32 Micro-controller with the voltage sensing and current sensing circuits through the ADC ports and the results are displayed on the LCD. The battery connections are shown in Figure 47.9 for the rated capacity. The status of battery voltage and SOX are computed using the recursive computations and the results are displayed as shown in Figure 47.10.

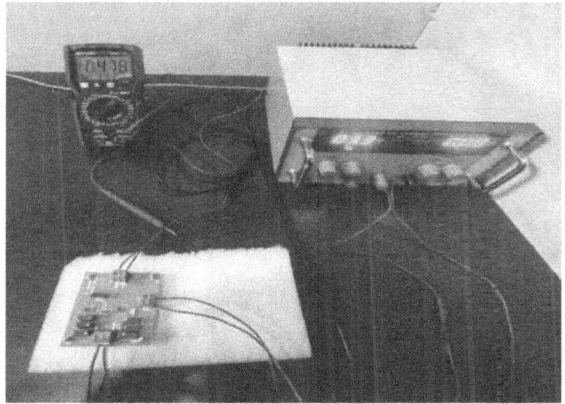

Figure 47.7 Voltage sensor in operating mode
Source: Author

Figure 47.5 Voltage sensing circuit
Source: Author

Figure 47.8 Interfacing with STM32 microcontroller
Source: Author

Figure 47.6 Current sensing circuit
Source: Author

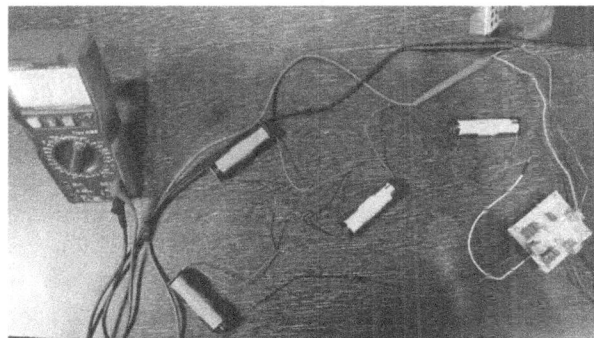

Figure 47.9 Battery stack connections
Source: Author

A voltage sensor's output needs to be adjusted to fit the ADC's input range (such as 0–3.3V) in order to be interfaced with the STM32 microcontroller's ADC. This may entail the use of a low-pass filter, buffer, or voltage divider. For accurate sensor data acquisition, the STM32 ADC is set up with the right resolution (e.g., 12-bit) and sample time [10].

Figure 47.10 SOX Estimation using STM32 microcontroller
Source: Author

Single or continuous modes can be used to execute the ADC conversion process, and polling or DMA can be used to handle data gathering. The relationship between the digital value, ADC resolution, and reference voltage is used to process the recorded ADC data and calculate the appropriate voltage. This configuration offers an accurate and effective method for digitizing the analog voltage signals specifically for the embedded applications.

Conclusion

The proposed SOX estimation discussed in this paper provides a continuous and real-time estimation of the battery stack parameters. This methodology is highly essential for electric vehicle applications where the user is validated with correct status of the battery stack. Also, the implementation of the Coulomb counting describes the methodology of the BMS. It requires basic components such as a current sensor and a microcontroller to integrate the current over time, making it easy to set up in embedded systems. The method works across various types of rechargeable batteries, including lead-acid, lithium-ion, and nickel-metal hydride (NiMH) batteries. This versatility makes it a go-to solution for many battery types. Unlike methods like Open Circuit Voltage

that require the battery to be at rest (with no current flowing) to get an accurate SOC reading, Coulomb counting can be used even during active charging or discharging. The technique is suitable for both tiny devices (like smart phones) and bigger systems (like electric vehicle batteries or renewable energy storage) since it can be readily scaled for larger batteries or systems with many cells.

References

[1] Madhavi, M., Krishna, R. V, Nagaraju, B. V., Ramana, Av V., Kumar, B. V., & Sai, L. N. (2023). Battery management system (BMS). *International Journal of Research Publication and Reviews*, 4(4), 508–518.

[2] Mohammed, N., & Saif, A. M. (2021). Programmable logic controller based lithium-ion battery management system for accurate state of charge estimation. *Computers & Electrical Engineering*, 93, 107306.

[3] Mahajan, K., Pawar, A., Sagar, V., Rohit, S., & Dasharath, B. (2024). Battery management system using microcontroller. 10.5281/zenodo.10548139.

[4] Kilic, A., Koroglu, S., Demircali, A., Kesler, S., Oner, Y., Karakas, E., & Sergeant, P. (2017). Design of master and slave modules on battery management system for electric vehicles. In 6th International Conference on Advanced Technology & Sciences.

[5] Prashant, G., Kumar, V., Chauhan, R. P., Lamba, K., & Shahab, A. (2023). A review paper for EV BMS with charge and fire protection. *International Journal of Creative Research Thoughts*, 11(5), 140–145.

[6] Deshpande, V. M., Bhattacharya, R., & Subbarao, K. (2021). Sensor placement with optimal precision for temperature estimation of battery systems. *IEEE Control Systems Letters*, 6, 1082–1087.

[7] Lin, X., Perez, H. E., Siegel, J. B., & Stefanopoulou, A. G. (2019). Robust estimation of battery system temperature distribution under sparse sensing and uncertainty. *IEEE Transactions on Control Systems Technology*, 28(3), 753–765.

[8] Emanet, B., & Kıyak, İ. (2021). Performance effective battery management system (BMS) design of mini electric vehicles. In 2021 5th International symposium on multidisciplinary studies and innovative technologies, (pp. 744–749).

[9] Pham, N. N., Leuchter, J., Pham, K. L., & Dong, Q. H. (2022). Battery management system for unmanned electric vehicles with CAN BUS and internet of things. *Vehicles*, 4(3), 639–662.

[10] Pham, N. N., Leuchter, J., Pham, L. K., Bystřický, R., & Dong, H. Q. (2021). Battery monitoring system using microcontroller ESP32 and internet of things. *ECS Transactions*, 105(1), 517.

48 Deep learning-based model for early detection of lung cancer

Sangeetha. B[1,a] and Pooja. A[2,b]

[1]Associate Professor (Department of IT), PSG College of Technology, Tamil Nadu, India

[2]PG Scholar (Department of IT), PSG College of Technology, Tamil Nadu, India

Abstract

Lung cancer remains a primary contributor to cancer-related deaths globally, emphasizing the critical need for methods that promote early and accurate diagnosis to improve survival outcomes. This study seeks to advance early detection by integrating state-of-the-art medical imaging technologies. Central to this approach is the application of a deep learning-based image analysis model aimed at enhancing the identification of lung nodules, which are key indicators in the early stages of the disease. Various forms of convolutional neural networks (CNNs) and their modified architectures are employed to process and interpret lung images with precision and efficiency. These neural networks are particularly adept at recognizing and categorizing nodules, thereby streamlining the diagnostic workflow. To ensure robust model performance, the training phase utilizes an extensive dataset of lung nodule images. Data augmentation techniques are applied to increase the variety within the dataset, which helps minimize overfitting and boosts the model's ability to generalize across unseen samples. In addition, transfer learning is incorporated by leveraging pre-trained models that have already been learned from large-scale datasets. This approach accelerates the training process and improves learning efficiency, ultimately resulting in faster convergence and better diagnostic accuracy. The model's effectiveness is primarily evaluated using metrics such as accuracy, offering a clear assessment of its diagnostic reliability. Results indicate a significant improvement over earlier models, with reduced error rates and enhanced predictive accuracy. Overall, this research demonstrates the potential of deep learning methodologies to support medical professionals—particularly radiologists—in making timely and accurate clinical decisions, thereby contributing to better patient care and outcomes in the context of lung cancer diagnosis.

Keywords: Attention mechanism, deep learning algorithms, lung cancer, medical image, classification transfer learning

Introduction

Lung cancer is diagnosed in millions of individuals annually, making it one of the most significant causes of cancer-related mortality across the globe. Early and accurate diagnosis plays a vital role in improving survival rates and enabling timely treatment. However, existing diagnostic methods—particularly computed tomography (CT) scans—often face limitations in terms of precision, speed, and reliability, potentially leading to delayed detection or misclassification of cancer types. This research addresses these challenges by integrating advanced technologies, including digital image processing, deep learning algorithms, and hash-based data integrity verification. The study focuses on classifying different types of lung cancer, such as adenocarcinoma, large cell carcinoma, and squamous cell carcinoma, through a combination of signal-to-noise ratio (SNR) guided pre-processing and deep learning techniques. The objective is to enhance diagnostic accuracy while ensuring the security and integrity of sensitive medical data. The workflow encompasses all major phases of the diagnostic pipeline, starting from the collection of CT scan images, followed by quality enhancement through preprocessing, lung region segmentation, and ultimately classification using advanced neural network models. To maintain the authenticity of medical records, hash-based integrity checks are implemented. Moreover, the system's robustness and adaptability are verified through testing on multiple CT imaging datasets representing various lung cancer subtypes.

- CT images were used to develop a deep learning-based model for the early diagnosis of lung cancer.
- Improved diagnostic precision by combining transfer learning methods with SNR-based pre-processing.
- Used pre-trained networks and data augmentation to show improved performance with less overfitting.

[a]bsg.it@psgtech.ac.in, [b]23pb34@psgtech.ac.in

DOI: 10.1201/9781003770435-48

- Adenocarcinoma, large cell carcinoma, and squamous cell carcinoma are among the subtypes of lung cancer that have been successfully classified.
- Enhanced model generalization as a result of thorough validation with several CT imaging datasets for lung cancer.

Literature Survey

An extensive survey on various modalities used in the literature for classification of lung cancer is performed and a summary of the same is specified in this Section.

CT Scan Imaging

LIDC-IDRI dataset has widely been utilized in the research work of detection and classification of lung cancer. Ragab et al. [17] utilized SCMO-MLL2C for image pre-processing and DenseNet-201 with an Elman neural network in order to achieve a 99.30% accuracy rate, but the model was constrained due to its high computational requirements and decreased generalizability. Alzubaidi et al. [2] investigated six machine learning models, among them SVMs, and performed better than conventional feature extraction methods, though the approach was noise-sensitive and did not provide probabilistic explanations. The Lung-RetinaNet model was a one-stage detector based on RetinaNet that used multi-scale feature fusion and context modules to improve detection performance and speed, though no pre-processing details were described [8]. Yu et al. [20] utilized ANN, DCNN, and heuristic mathematical models for CT-based prediction with high precision and early detection advantage but at the cost of extensive hardware support. Pang et al. [15] integrated DenseNet with AdaBoost to achieve an 89.85% accuracy rate, surpassing traditional architectures such as ResNet and VGG, but at the cost of data imbalance and computation inefficacies. Silva et al. [18] employed a Convolutional autoencoder with a multi-layer perceptron to forecast EGFR mutation status, utilizing transfer learning over three ROI levels; poor performance on certain ROIs and dataset shortcomings were reported. Last but not least, Pham [16] proposed a CT-based method utilizing pseudolabeling and recurrence analysis with pre-trained CNNs (such as AlexNet, DenseNet), and the technique achieved better classification but was extremely dataset-dependent.

Histopathological Imaging

Histopathological imaging, especially through the LC25000 dataset, has played a crucial role in lung cancer subtype classification. Li et al. [5] used DenseNet201 for discrimination of subtypes, reporting high performance but lower accuracy when differentiating squamous cell carcinoma from adenocarcinoma. Obayya et al. [13] experimented with several deep neural networks (e.g., ResNet, VGG, ShuffleNet, GoogleNet, Xception) and reported strong classification ability, but mentioned manual processing and computational cost as disadvantages. Mehmood et al. [9] improved AlexNet with histogram equalization and class selective image processing (CSIP), enhancing accuracy to 98.8%, but pre-trained weights' dependence restricted domain-specific generalizability. Alqahtani et al. [1] combined MobileNetv2 with a convolutional autoencoder, reaching 99.41% accuracy with a metaheuristic water strider algorithm; however, the complexity of hyperparameter tuning and high computational load restricted its generalizability.

PET Imaging

PET imaging has also been utilized for subtype classification and prognosis prediction of lung cancer. Oh et al. [14] compared four deep learning models—DenseNet, NFNet, EfficientNet, and ResNet—and identified that DenseNet combined with CoxPH delivered the best performance in 2-year and 5-year survival prediction with good scores in mean absolute error and concordance index criteria. By contrast, Bicakci et al. [3] used Multilayer Perceptron and SqueezeNet for PET scan-based subtype classification. Although their model identified significant metabolic features, its external validity was limited by the small dataset (n = 94).

Genomic and Multi-omics Data

Genomic and transcriptomic information are now being integrated into lung cancer studies. Mohamed and Ezugwu [10] introduced a PCA-SMOTE-CNN model that combined mRNA, miRNA, and DNA methylation data. The method achieved high classification performance using deep learning and dimension reduction but was lacking in external validation and transparency of CNN design. Ye et al. [19] used hierarchical clustering, LDA, and sparse regression on TCGA data, resulting in efficient gene clustering and high structural preservation. The method, however, encountered optimization complexity and specificity of gene data. Lima et al. [6] used Random Forests on the LUSC-TCGA dataset for survival classification and interpretability and resulted in around 70% accuracy but did not include deep learning models and used a single dataset.

Hybrid and Other Modalities

Hybrid and non-imaging data modalities have also been investigated. LDNNET, which is a deep neural network that is trained from 3D CT images of LUNA16 and Kaggle DSB 2017, presented strong classification performance but consumed large amounts of computational power for volumetric data [4, 11]. Liu et al. [5] proposed an enhanced eigenvector centrality-based feature selection (IECFS) approach based on SEER data, which improved the efficiency of classification, but did not assess its comparative strengths or limitations. Mahum and Al-Salman [8] likewise integrated the LIDC-IDRI and Simba Lung datasets with Lung-RetinaNet to facilitate subtype classification, applying resizing, normalization, and augmentation, but were confined by the exclusive use of CT imaging without multimodal integration.

Proposed Methodology

Figure 48.1 depicts the end-to-end pipelines for classifying the lung images. The process begins with the loading of a dataset composed of lung CT scan images, which includes both healthy lung tissues and various types of lung cancer, such as adenocarcinoma, squamous cell carcinoma, and large cell carcinoma. Once the dataset is ready, a security mechanism is employed to ensure the integrity of the

CT images. This step, known as hash-based integrity verification, serves to validate the authenticity and confidentiality of the data before it undergoes further analysis. Following this, each image undergoes signal-to-noise ratio (SNR) evaluation—a key metric used to assess the visual quality of medical images. A high SNR indicates minimal noise and better clarity, while a low SNR suggests poor image quality. Based on this value, the workflow diverges: images with an SNR below 0.5 dB are flagged as noisy and routed through an image pre-processing stage aimed at enhancing their visual quality. In contrast, those with an SNR equal to or above 0.5 dB are deemed sufficiently clear and proceed directly to the classification stage. Out of the total dataset, 277 images fall below the 0.5 dB threshold and require pre-processing, while 723 images meet or exceed the threshold and bypass this step. The pre-processing techniques applied to low-SNR images are crucial for improving clarity and making the data suitable for analysis. Once this enhancement is complete, all images are passed into deep learning-based classification models. These models, trained extensively on labeled CT scan images, are capable of distinguishing between healthy tissue and different cancer types by learning the unique features associated with each. Through this approach, the system can accurately classify lung CT scans into categories such as adenocarcinoma, squamous cell carcinoma, and large cell carcinoma.

Dataset Description

The dataset sourced from Kaggle is specifically structured for implementing deep learning and machine learning algorithms aimed at identifying and classifying various forms of chest cancer. It contains CT scan images in JPG and PNG formats, representing three

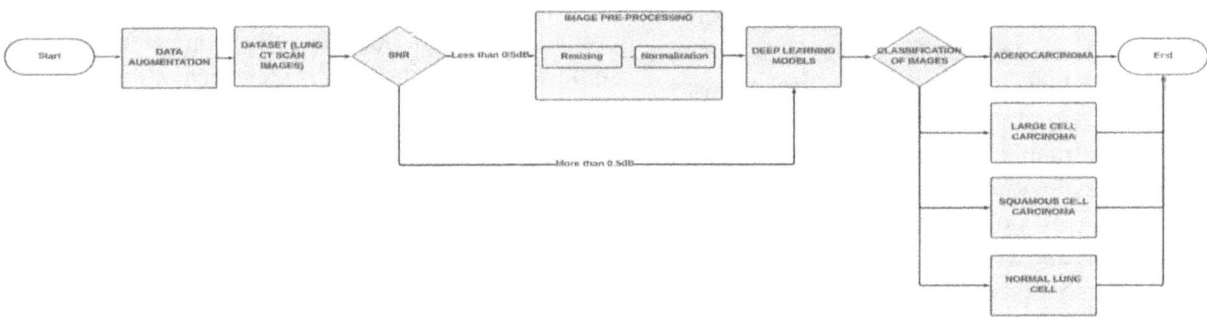

Figure 48.1 Process flow
Source: Author

primary cancer types—adenocarcinoma, large cell carcinoma, and squamous cell carcinoma—as well as a category for normal lung tissue. These images are organized within a folder named "Data" and are systematically divided into three subsets: 70% allocated for training, 20% for testing, and the remaining 10% reserved for validation purposes. The dataset is intended to assist in the identification and classification of lung cancer types, such as Squamous Cell Carcinoma, which is typically associated with smoking and found in the central lung; Large Cell Carcinoma, which grows quickly and can occur anywhere in the lung; and Adenocarcinoma, which is the most common type and usually found in the outer regions of the lung. The development of AI models with early detection and classification capabilities is made possible by this well-structured dataset, which could result in better lung cancer diagnosis and treatment approaches.

Deep Learning Models Implemented

From massive datasets, deep learning models analyze and identify intricate patterns. Because they are based on neural networks that are modeled after the human brain, they are particularly useful for speech recognition, picture recognition, and natural language processing. They can also do automated feature extraction, feature learning, and end-to-end training. Since CNNs automatically learn spatial hierarchies of characteristics from the data, they are effective tools for analyzing lung CT scan images.

The identification and categorization of anomalies in medical imaging is made possible by these algorithms, which are perfect for image processing employment.

EfficientNetB0 is a deep learning architecture designed to offer a balanced trade-off between computational efficiency and classification accuracy when processing lung CT scan images. To ensure reliable outcomes and reduce the risk of overfitting, the model requires a thoroughly pre-processed and accurately labeled dataset. It utilizes global average pooling to compress feature maps into a consistent-size vector suitable for input into dense layers, aiding in the classification task.

Another powerful model, InceptionV3, is particularly useful for lung CT analysis due to its ability to detect complex features across different scales. Its inception modules allow the network to extract multiple levels of abstraction simultaneously, enhancing

its capacity to interpret subtle differences in medical images.

MobileNetV2 provides an efficient and lightweight approach tailored for tasks involving lung CT imagery. Despite its compact architecture, it delivers strong performance in image classification scenarios, making it capable of detecting various lung abnormalities accurately.

Lastly, VGG16 is widely used for analyzing lung CT scans because of its straightforward yet deep structure. With 13 convolutional layers and Rectified Linear Unit (ReLU) activations, it captures detailed visual patterns, making it effective in distinguishing between normal and cancerous lung tissues.

Results and Discussion

In deep learning, key performance indicators include training accuracy, training loss, validation accuracy, and validation loss. Training accuracy reflects the percentage of instances correctly identified by the model during the learning phase, while training loss quantifies the discrepancy between the model's predicted outputs and the actual labels. On the other hand, validation accuracy assesses how well the model performs on previously unseen data, indicating its generalization capability. Validation loss provides insight into the model's error on this validation set, helping to detect overfitting or underfitting during the evaluation process. A thorough study of the many neural networks that were examined, such as CNN, EfficientNetB0, and VGG16, is shown in the table. Three types of models are distinguished: label smoothing, focal, and categorical cross entropy. This number is a representation of the number of training iterations.

CNN performs effectively with high training accuracy and strong validation accuracy, according to the model analysis; nevertheless, overfitting might be present. While label smoothing aids in lowering prediction overconfidence, validation performance is somewhat worse than with categorical cross-entropy. Better model calibration is indicated by the significantly decreased validation loss. Compared to CNN, CNN with Attention Block greatly improves validation accuracy, and the Focal loss function makes it much better. However, compared to the focus loss version, the label smoothing version has a greater validation loss, indicating that label smoothing is less successful for this design. Despite having perfect

Models	Optimizer	Loss Function	Epoch	Accuracy	Loss	Validation Accuracy	Validation Loss
CNN	Adam	Categorial Crossentropy	10	0.9918	0.0224	0.9693	0.9673
			50	0.8222	1.0818	0.8073	1.0091
			100	0.9967	0.0031	0.9737	0.8004
		Focal	10	0.9755	0.0116	0.9562	0.1129
		Label Smoothing	10	0.9984	0.0026	0.981	0.0851
CNN - Attention Block	Adam	Categorial Crossentropy	10	0.9967	0.014	0.9854	0.3202
			50	0.9804	0.0453	0.9547	1.0356
		Focal	10	0.9984	0.0009	0.9869	0.0463
		Label Smoothing	10	0.9984	0.3598	0.9912	0.6351
EfficientNetB0	Adam	Categorial Crossentropy	100	1	0.1051	0.9315	0.2946
		Focal	10	0.9245	1.3885	0.8356	1.3145
		Label Smoothing	10	0.9694	4.298	0.8493	4.4133
InceptionV3	Adam	Categorial Crossentropy	30	0.9732	0.2288	0.7967	0.4983
MobileNetV2	Adam	Categorial Crossentropy	50	0.9984	0.2749	0.8471	0.6594
VGG16	Adam	Categorial Crossentropy	50	0.9087	0.2323	0.8194	0.6262

Figure 48.2 Result comparison between various deep learning models
Source: Author

Models	Optimizer	Loss Function	Epoch	Precision				Recall				F1 Score				Support			
				0	1	2	3	0	1	2	3	0	1	2	3	0	1	2	3
CNN	Adam	Categorial Crossentropy	10	1	0.99	0.99	1	0.99	1	1	0.99	1	1	1	1	195	115	148	155
			50	0.92	0.87	0.85	0.74	0.56	0.88	1	0.97	0.7	0.87	0.92	0.84	195	115	148	155
			100	1	0.99	1	1	1	1	1	0.99	1	1	1	1	195	115	148	155
		Focal	10	1	0.99	0.96	1	0.98	1	1	0.98	0.99	1	0.98	0.99	195	115	148	155
		Label Smoothing	10	1	0.99	1	1	1	1	0.99	1	1	1	1	1	195	115	148	155
CNN - Attention Block	Adam	Categorial Crossentropy	10	1	0.99	1	1	1	1	1	0.99	1	1	1	1	195	115	148	155
			50	1	0.89	1	0.99	1	0.98	0.96	0.88	0.94	0.99	0.98	0.94	195	115	148	155
		Focal	10	1	1	1	0.99	1	0.99	1	1	1	1	1	1	195	115	148	155
		Label Smoothing	10	1	0.99	1	1	1	1	1	0.99	1	1	1	1	195	115	148	155
EfficientNetB0	Adam	Categorial Crossentropy	100	1	0.81	1	1	0.94	1	1	0.85	0.97	0.9	1	0.92	16	13	8	13
		Focal	10	0.94	0.81	0.89	1	1	0.89	0.8	0.6	0.97	0.85	0.84	0.75	16	19	10	5
		Label Smoothing	10	1	0.83	1	1	1	1	1	0.2	1	0.9	1	0.33	16	19	10	5
InceptionV3	Adam	Categorial Crossentropy	30	0.97	0.8	0.68	0.88	1	0.77	0.79	0.71	0.98	0.79	0.73	0.79	30	43	29	21
MobileNetV2	Adam	Categorial Crossentropy	50	1	0.96	0.84	0.95	1	0.86	0.98	0.87	1	0.91	0.9	0.91	28	59	48	23
VGG16	Adam	Categorial Crossentropy	50	0.71	0.73	1	0.85	0.88	0.75	0.96	0.61	0.8	0.74	0.98	0.71	120	51	54	90

Figure 48.3 Report on the classification of different deep learning models
Source: Author

training accuracy, EfficientNetB0 performs worse during validation than CNN with Attention Block, which could be the result of overfitting. Out of all the models, InceptionV3 performs badly, exhibiting significant losses and lesser accuracy, which may call for more epochs or hyperparameter adjustment. Due to their extremely high validation loss (4.4133) and low validation accuracy (0.8493 for MobileNetV2 and 0.8356 for InceptionV3), MobileNetV2 and InceptionV3 need the most improvement. Longer training, other loss functions, or adjusting their architectures and hyperparameters (such learning rate) are all potential enhancements. To sum up, the CNN with Attention Block utilizing the Focal Loss model is the best model because it combines the focal loss and attention mechanism to handle class imbalance and produce low validation loss and great validation performance.

Conclusion

This work has successfully demonstrated how deep learning-based models may improve the early detection and classification of lung cancer using CT scan pictures. The suggested approach improves diagnostic accuracy while re-solving overfitting issues by combining SNR-based preprocessing, data augmentation, and transfer learning. The model provides a trustworthy tool to support clinical decision-making by successfully differentiating between various subtypes of lung cancer, including adenocarcinoma, large cell carcinoma, and squamous cell carcinoma. The findings highlight the value of sophisticated deep learning architectures in medical imaging by showing better performance when compared to conventional methods. Notwithstanding these successes, is- sues like computational cost and real-time deployment still require attention. To further improve diagnostic skills, future research might focus on integrating other imaging modalities, optimizing the model for a variety of hardware, and growing the dataset.

References

[1] Alqahtani, H., Alabdulkreem, E., Alotaibi, F. A., Alnfiai, M. M., Singla, C., & Salama, A. S. (2024). Improved water strider algorithm with convolutional autoencoder for lung and colon cancer detection on histopathological images. *IEEE Access*, 12, 949–956. doi: 10.1109/ACCESS.2023.3346894

[2] Alzubaidi, M. A, Otoom, M., & Jaradat, H. (2021). Comprehensive and comparative global and local feature extraction framework for lung cancer detection using CT scan images. *IEEE Access*, 9, 158140–158154. doi: 10.1109/ACCESS.2021.3129597

[3] Bicakci, M., Ayyildiz, O., Aydin, Z., Basturk, A., Karacavus, S., & Yilmaz, B. (2020). Metabolic imaging based sub-classification of lung cancer. *IEEE Access*, 8, 218470–218476. doi: 10.1109/ACCESS.2020.3040155

[4] Chen, Y., Wang, Y., Hu, F., Feng, L., Zhou, T., & Zheng. C. (2021). LDNNET: Towards robust classification of lung nodule and cancer using lung dense neural network. *IEEE Access*, 9, 50301–50320. doi: 10.1109/ACCESS.2021.3068896

[5] Li, M., Zhang, J., Chen, M., Liu, Z., Wang, J., & Liu, Y. (2021). Research on the auxiliary classification and diagnosis of lung cancer subtypes based on histopathological images. *IEEE Access*, 9, 53687–53707. doi: 10.1109/ACCESS.2021.3071057

[6] Lima, D. V. C., Terrematte, P., Stransky, B., & Neto, A. D. D. (2024). An integrated data analysis using bioinformatics and random forest to predict prognosis of patients with squamous cell lung cancer. *IEEE Access*, 12, 59335–59345. doi: 10.1109/ACCESS.2024.3392277

[7] Liu, P., Jin, K., Jiao, Y., He, M., & Fei, S. (2021). Prediction of second primary lung cancer patient's survivability based on improved eigenvector centrality-based feature selection. *IEEE Access*, 9, 55663–55672. doi: 10.1109/ACCESS.2021.3063944

[8] Mahu, R., & Al-Salman, A. S. (2023). Lung-RetinaNet: Lung cancer detection using a RetinaNet with multi-scale feature fusion and context module. *IEEE Access*, 11, 53850–53861. doi: 10.1109/ACCESS.2023.3281259

[9] Mehmood, S., Rizwan, M., Rahim, A., Awan, M. J., Saba, T., Rehman, A., et al. (2022). Malignancy detection in lung and colon histopathology images using transfer learning with class selective image processing. *IEEE Access*, 10, 25657–25668. doi: 10.1109/ACCESS.2022.3150924

[10] Mohamed, T. I. A., & Ezugwu, A. E. S. (2023). Enhancing lung cancer classification and prediction with deep learning and multi-omics data. *IEEE Access*, 12, 59880–59892. doi: 10.1109/ACCESS.2024.3394030

[11] Naseer, I., Akram, S., Masood, T., Rashid, M., & Jaffar, A. (2023). Lung cancer classification using modified U Net based lobe segmentation and nodule detection. *IEEE Access*, 11, 60279–60291. doi: 10.1109/ACCESS.2023.3285821

[12] Noaman, N. F., Kanber, B. M., Smadi, A. A., Jiao, L., & Alsmadi, M. K. (2024). Advancing oncology diagnostics: AI-enabled early detection of lung cancer through hybrid histological image analysis. *IEEE Access*, 12, 64396–64415. doi: 10.1109/ACCESS.2024.3397040

[13] Obayya, M., Arasi, M. A., Alruwais, N., Alsini, R., Mohamed, A., & Yaseen, I. (2023). Biomedical image analysis for colon and lung cancer detection using tuna swarm algorithm with deep learning model. *IEEE Access*, 11, 94705–94712. doi: 10.1109/ACCESS.2023.3309711

[14] Oh, S., Im, J., Kang, S. -R., Oh, I. -J., & Kim, M. -S. (2021). PET-based deep-learning model for predicting prognosis of patients with non-small cell lung cancer. *IEEE Access*. 9, 138753–138761. doi: 10.1109/ACCESS.2021.3115486

[15] Pang, S., Zhang, Y., Ding, M., Wang, X., & Xie, X. (2020). A deep model for lung cancer type identification by densely connected convolutional networks and adaptive boosting. *IEEE Access*, 8, 4799–4805. doi: 10.1109/ACCESS.2019.2962862

[16] Pham, T. D. (2021). From raw pixels to recurrence image for deep learning of benign and malignant mediastinal lymph nodes on computed tomography. *IEEE Access*, 9, 96267–96278. doi: 10.1109/ACCESS.2021.3094577

[17] Ragab, M., Katib, I., Sharaf, S. A., Assiri, F. Y., Hamed, D., & Al-Ghamdi, AA-M. (2023). Self-upgraded cat mouse optimizer with machine learning driven lung cancer classification on computed tomography imaging. *IEEE Access,* 11, 107972–107981. doi: 10.1109/ACCESS.2023.3313508

[18] Silva, F., Melo, R., Lima, J., Leal, J. P., Rasteiro, D., & Vilaca, J. L. (2021). EGFR assessment in lung cancer CT images: Analysis of local and holistic regions of interest using deep unsupervised transfer learning. *IEEE Access*, 9, 58667–58676. doi: 10.1109/ACCESS.2021.3070701

[19] Ye, X., Zhang, W., & Sakurai, T. (2020). Adaptive unsupervised feature learning for gene signature identification in non-small-cell lung cancer. *IEEE Access*, 8, 154354–154362. doi: 10.1109/ACCESS.2020.3018480

[20] Yu, H., Zhou, Z., & Wang, Q. (2020). Deep learning assisted predict of lung cancer on computed tomography images using the adaptive hierarchical heuristic mathematical model. *IEEE Access*, 8, 86400–86410. doi: 10.1109/ACCESS.2020.2992645

49 SKIN MAP: A multimodal approach to detect and explain skin cancer

Anusha T[a], Madhumitha D R[b] and Shruti S[c]

Department of Computer Science and Engineering, PSG College of Technology, Coimbatore, India

Abstract

Early and reliable detection of skin cancer remains a clinical challenge due to subtle visual differences between benign and malignant lesions and the limited interpretability of deep learning models. This work presents SkinMap, a multimodal system that combines dermoscopic images with patient metadata for improved skin-lesion classification. Our approach uses a deep convolutional model to extract hierarchical image features and integrates structured clinical attributes for binary and multiclass prediction tasks. To enhance transparency, we incorporate Grad-CAM-based visual explanations that highlight diagnostically relevant regions and support clinical reasoning. This framework aims to improve diagnostic accuracy while increasing trust in AI-assisted dermatological assessment.

Keywords: Binary classification, deep learning, explainable AI, dermoscopic images, Gradient-weighted class activation mapping, multimodal approach, multiclass classification, patient metadata, skin cancer detection

Introduction

Skin cancer is one of the most found forms of cancer in this world. Its occurrence is increased by the influence of exposure to UV, lifestyle changes, and delayed identification. By detecting these malignant lesions in the early stages, one can significantly see improvements in the treatment outcomes. But right now, dermatologists follow the conventional method of diagnosing through visual assessments that are hugely subjective. This ultimately leads to delay in the diagnosis or sometimes inconsistency.

Let us take an example of a patient consulting a dermatologist with skin growth that can potentially be discovered as cancerous. In this event, the dermatologist classifies the lesion as benign through the visible signs and clinical experience, but later through further testing it is found that it is actually malignant. Such misclassifications, though unintentional, are necessitating technology support systems that can assist in consistent, evidence-supported decision-making.

In order to prevent such kind of situations, Skin map offers a diagnostic system based on deep learning. It integrates dermascopic images of skin lesions along with patient metadata to give accurate results on the lesion classification which will help clinicians in the diagnosis. By integrating explainable AI methods, the predictions made will have visual explanations, improving the trustworthiness and usability in actual dermatological practice.

Literature review

Machine learning and deep learning has gotten better over time and now skin cancer spotting is more right and faster due to this. Melarkode et al. [8] conducted a review that mentions all the available AI-powered diagnostic solutions, in which the importance of combining images with clinical data has proven to improve the classification results.

The usage of ensemble approaches by combining ML and Dl methods has been explored deeply by Tembhurne et al. [11]. This demonstrates how hybrid models use the strength of many algorithms to level up diagnostic accuracy. Similarly, Hauser et al. [6] also pressed on the use of XAI to increase the transparency of the model. He has also mentioned that this helps with interpretability, which is critical in clinical situations like this.

Multiple ML models, such as Support Vector Machines (SVM), Random Forests (RF), and convolutional neural networks (CNN), are being used in this domain to develop accurate and robust solutions. Murugan et al. [9] found that CNNs perform way better than traditional models in image based classification tasks like skin cancer classification. This was mentioned again by Grignaffini et al. [5], in his systematic review. Here it was found that CNN based approaches are the current benchmarks for this specific use case.

Although the present models perform well, developing generalized solutions that work on unseen and

[a]anu.cse@psgtech.ac.in, [b]madhumitha0924@gmail.com, [c]shruti.sam03@gmail.com

DOI: 10.1201/9781003770435-49

new patient data still remains a challenge. Wu et al. [12] has expressed the need for models that perform well on diverse datasets, highlighting the need for improvements in robustness and better results with generalized data. Adamu et al. [1] implemented approaches that combine ML and DL in a hybrid technique to overcome these kinds of limitations.

Ghosh et al. [4] explored solutions by mixing models to get better accuracy, and also Mazhar et al. [7] talked about how advanced DL models help in catching tough and uncommon cases better.

The integration of multimodal data, particularly the fusion of clinical metadata with dermoscopic images, has shown great promise. Gasmi et al. [3] introduced a multimodal framework that improves diagnostic precision by combining image and clinical features. Similarly, Rezk et al. [10] proposed MDFNet, a fusion-based model that significantly boosts classification performance. Esgario and Krohling [2] also demonstrated the effectiveness of combining clinical features and patient data to enhance the diagnosis of pigmented skin lesions.

Collectively, these studies suggest that future efforts should focus on building interpretable, multimodal, and generalizable AI systems capable of supporting clinicians in diverse real-world diagnostic settings.

Context of work

Skin cancer being one of the most prevalent forms of cancer, detection of skin cancer is very crucial for early diagnosis and prevention of patients from skin cancer. The presence of various types of skin lesions and skin types, it remains a significant challenge to detect and classify them. Existing techniques to detect and classify the skin lesions highly rely on machine learning and deep learning techniques such as

- Support vector machine
- Random forests
- Convolutional neural networks

These existing techniques have made excellent progress in automatically detecting, classifying skin lesions and also improving the classification accuracy. However, the challenges involved are:

- Limited generalization
- Limited accuracy in prediction of malignant types
- Limitation in dataset (absence of wide range of skin lesion types)

Combining dermoscopic images with patient metadata has provided a significant increase in accuracy but this integration involves a complex procedure and also remains underexplored. Our work aims to address the above-mentioned challenges by exploring different algorithms and techniques to improve the accuracy with also integrating multimodal data fusion techniques. Along with accuracy improvisation our work also aims to improve the trust among the medical professionals by integrating explainable AI in our skin cancer detection and classification system.

Discussion on Existing Skin cancer detection technologies

a. Based on the features extracted from dermoscopic lesion images, various Machine learning algorithms like Support Vector Machines (SVMs) and Random Forests (RF) are used to classify the dermoscopic skin lesion images into categories (benign and malignant).

b. Deep Learning (CNN): Convolutional Neural Networks (CNNs) due to their ability to automatically learn and extract features from images have achieved a prominent performance in skin cancer classification.

c. Multimodal Data Fusion: The integration of clinical metadata (such as patient age, gender, and medical history) along with dermoscopic images has been explored to improve the accuracy of skin cancer detection. Integrating patient metadata with dermoscopic images allows for more precise classification and evaluation.

Dataset

For this skin cancer detection system, two publicly available datasets have been used to develop and evaluate the system:

HAM10000 Dataset
The HAM10000 (Human Against Machine with over 10,000 training images) dataset contains 10,015 dermoscopic images of high resolution and belonging to various pigmented skin lesions. These images are categorized into seven different types. Four are categorizes as benign and three are malignant, out of seven.

Benign types:

1. Melanocytic nevi
2. Benign keratosis-like lesions
3. Vascular lesions
4. Dermatofibroma

Malignant types:

1. Melanoma
2. Basal cell carcinoma
3. Actinic keratoses

This dataset is used as the primary resource for multiclass classification tasks of the system.

Combined Dataset - ISIC 2019 and ISIC 2020

The system uses a combined dataset from ISIC 2019 and ISIC 2020 for the binary classification task of classifying benign from malignant skin lesions.

These datasets contains thousands of annotated images with their corresponding patient metadata and diagnostic label that supports a balanced and diverse sample of lesion types.

The images from both datasets are first preprocessed to ensure consistency, quality and clinical relevance.

Preprocessing pipeline:

1. Resizing of all images to standard dimensions of 224×224 or 256×256 pixels, according to the input requirements of the common deep learning architectures.
2. Normalization is applied based on the mean and standard deviation values that is derived from the ImageNet, to ensure compatibility with pretrained model weights and promoting stable convergence while training the model.
3. Data augmentation techniques like horizontal and vertical flipping, rotation, brightness, contrast adjustments, and zooming are used to improve the generalization.

In parallel, patient metadata is encoded appropriately, with categorical variables like gender and lesion site label-encoded and numerical values like age normalized, enabling seamless integration into the multimodal deep learning framework.

Experimental setup

The SKIN MAP system has been developed and deployed with carefully selected hardware and software configurations to ensure efficient deep learning model training, multimodal data integration, and interpretable inference.

Hardware requirements:

a) RAM: Minimum 8 GB to support high-resolution image preprocessing and training workloads.
b) CPU: At least an 8-core processor (e.g., Intel i7, AMD Ryzen 7) for efficient parallel data augmentation and metadata processing
c) GPU: Dedicated NVIDIA GPU with a minimum of 4 GB VRAM, crucial for accelerating deep learning operations and training models such as ResNet101 and ResNeSt101.
d) Disk space: Minimum 50 GB SSD storage to manage large-scale datasets, model weights, and intermediate outputs.

Software requirements:

a) Programming language: Python 3.x: Chosen for its extensive support across machine learning libraries and its strong developer community.
b) Machine learning frameworks primary: PyTorch — Used for model development, training, and fine-tuning. Secondary support: TensorFlow — Compatible for alternative experimentation.
c) Image processing libraries: OpenCV and Python Imaging Library (PIL): Used for reading, preprocessing, and augmenting dermoscopic images.
d) Explainability tools: Grad-CAM: Integrated for generating heatmaps that highlight decision-critical regions in skin lesion images.
e) GPU acceleration: CUDA Toolkit: Required for enabling GPU-based acceleration on compatible NVIDIA hardware during model training and inference.
f) Data handling libraries: Pandas: Utilized for structured handling of patient metadata and overall dataset management. NumPy enables high-performance numerical operations, especially when it comes to metadata normalization.

g) Visualization tools: Matplotlib and seaborn: Employed for plotting training performance metrics, class distributions, and interpretability visualizations.

System architecture and implementation

The SKIN MAP system is a deep learning-based diagnostic tool designed to assist in the classification and interpretation of skin lesions using both image and patient metadata. The process begins with the collection of high-resolution dermoscopic images from publicly available and widely accepted datasets such as HAM10000, ISIC 2019, and ISIC 2020. These datasets not only provide annotated lesion images but also include patient-specific metadata such as age, gender, and lesion location, which are crucial for enhancing the accuracy and contextual relevance of diagnostic predictions.

1. Model architecture (Figure 49.1)

a) Multiclass classification model (ResNet101): Utilizes a 101-layer deep residual network with skip connections to classify dermoscopic images into seven categories: melanocytic nevi, melanoma, benign keratosis-like lesions, basal cell carcinoma, actinic keratoses, vascular lesions, and dermatofibroma.
b) Binary classification model (ResNeSt101): Incorporates split-attention modules for improved feature representation. Designed for binary classification (benign vs. malignant), it integrates both visual and non-visual metadata through multimodal fusion.

2. Image preprocessing

a) Image resizing:
ResNet101: 224 × 224 pixels
ResNeSt101: 256 × 256 pixels
b) Normalization:
Images are normalized using ImageNet mean and standard deviation values to ensure compatibility with pretrained weights.
c) Augmentation techniques:
Includes horizontal and vertical flipping, rotation, zooming, and brightness/contrast adjustments to enhance model generalization.

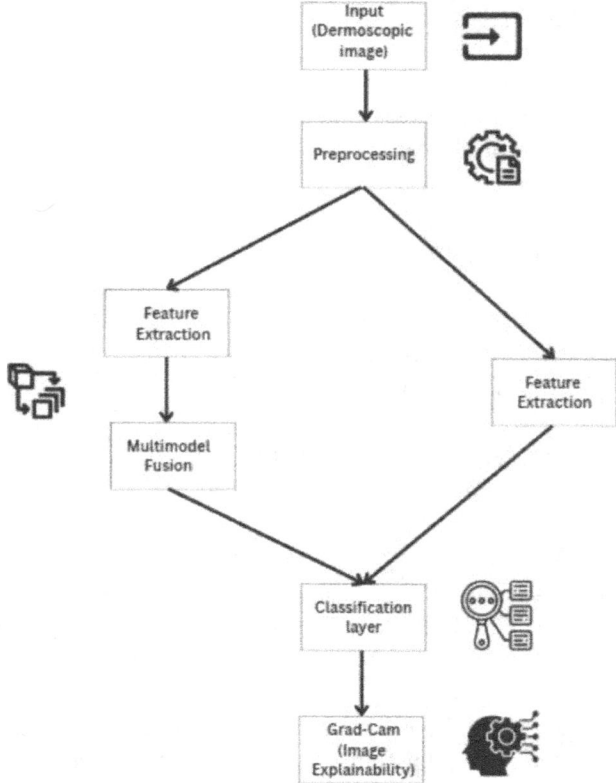

Figure 49.1 Proposed architecture
Source: Author

3. Metadata handling and fusion

a) Metadata types:
Includes patient age (numerical), sex (categorical), and lesion location (categorical).
b) Preprocessing:
Categorical variables are label encoded.
Age values are normalized using standard scaling.
c) Fusion strategy:
Encoded metadata is concatenated with image feature vectors within the ResNeSt101 architecture, enabling multimodal learning.

4. Explainability module
Gradient-weighted class activation mapping (Grad-CAM): Applied to the last convolutional layer to generate heatmaps highlighting regions of diagnostic relevance. These visualizations are superimposed on the original dermoscopic images to support clinical interpretability.

5. *Training and optimization strategy*

a. Loss functions:
    Categorical cross-entropy for multiclass classification Binary cross-entropy for binary classification
b. Optimization algorithm:
    Adam optimizer with dynamic learning rate adjustment and early stopping criteria based on validation loss.
c. Regularization techniques:
    Dropout layers and extensive data augmentation are utilized to mitigate overfitting.

6. *Evaluation framework*

a. Performance metrics:
    Accuracy, Precision, Recall, F1-Score, and Area Under the Receiver Operating Characteristic Curve (AUC-ROC).
b. Interpretability assessment:
    Grad-CAM visualizations are evaluated using Average Drop, Confidence Increase, and Dice Similarity Coefficient to quantify alignment with clinically significant lesion areas.

Deep residual learning for hierarchical feature extraction

The SKIN MAP system employs ResNet101, a state-of-the-art CNN that addresses the challenges of training very deep networks, particularly the vanishing gradient problem. ResNet101 is based on the principle of residual learning, which introduces identity shortcut connections that bypass one or more layers. These shortcuts allow gradients to propagate more effectively during backpropagation, enabling the training of deeper and more expressive models.

In the context of multiclass classification of skin lesions, ResNet101 is adept at extracting hierarchical visual features at multiple spatial scales. The network consists of 101 layers, organized into residual blocks that learn increasingly abstract representations of dermoscopic images — from low-level edge and texture features in earlier layers to high-level semantic features in deeper layers (Figure 49.2). This architectural depth, combined with residual connections, allows ResNet101 to generalize well across diverse skin lesion types, leading to accurate predictions across seven diagnostic categories,

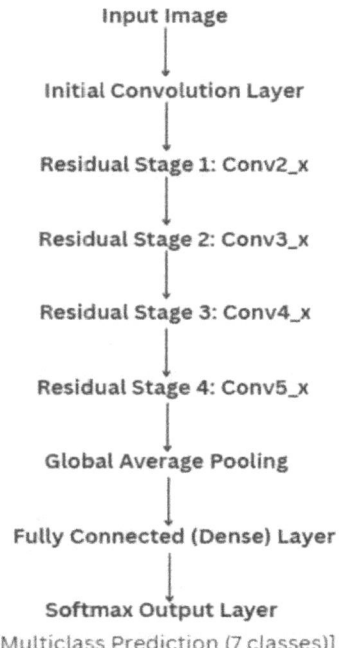

Figure 49.2 ResNet101 Architectural flow
Source: Author

such as melanoma, basal cell carcinoma, and benign keratosis.

Split attention mechanism

For binary classification (Figure 49.3) tasks distinguishing between benign and malignant lesions, SKIN MAP adopts ResNeSt101, an advanced variant of the ResNet architecture that integrates the Split-Attention block mechanism. This design allows each convolutional group within a block to selectively emphasize relevant feature subspaces, facilitating channel-wise attention across multiple branches of the feature map.

The Split-Attention mechanism enhances the network's representational capacity by enabling dynamic weighting of feature responses, which significantly improves the ability to capture subtle and context-dependent visual cues — a necessity in medical image analysis where lesion variations can be minute. By aggregating multiple feature transformations with learnable importance, ResNeSt101 adapts its focus based on the underlying content, leading to superior performance in distinguishing complex and ambiguous lesion patterns. This contributes to improved sensitivity and specificity, two critical metrics in clinical decision-making systems where diagnostic accuracy can have significant implications.

Multimodal fusion

To complement image-based predictions and provide a more context-aware diagnostic outcome, SKIN MAP incorporates a multimodal learning framework. In this setup, the system fuses visual features extracted by ResNeSt101 with encoded patient metadata, such as age, gender, and lesion location. This integration occurs at the late stage of the network, known as late fusion.

The metadata is passed through a separate encoder (e.g., fully connected layers), and its resulting feature vector is concatenated with the image feature vector derived from the CNN. The combined vector is then passed through additional fully connected layers and a final sigmoid activation function to produce a binary classification output.

This multimodal fusion strategy enhances the model's interpretability and predictive accuracy by incorporating non-visual contextual information that clinicians typically use during diagnosis. It ensures that patient-specific information informs the final prediction, thereby facilitating personalized risk assessment and aligning the system more closely with real-world clinical decision-making workflows.

Grad-CAM visualizations

ResNet101 demonstrated (Figure 49.4–49.6) focused attention on clinically relevant lesion areas, with consistent heatmap patterns across multiple samples.

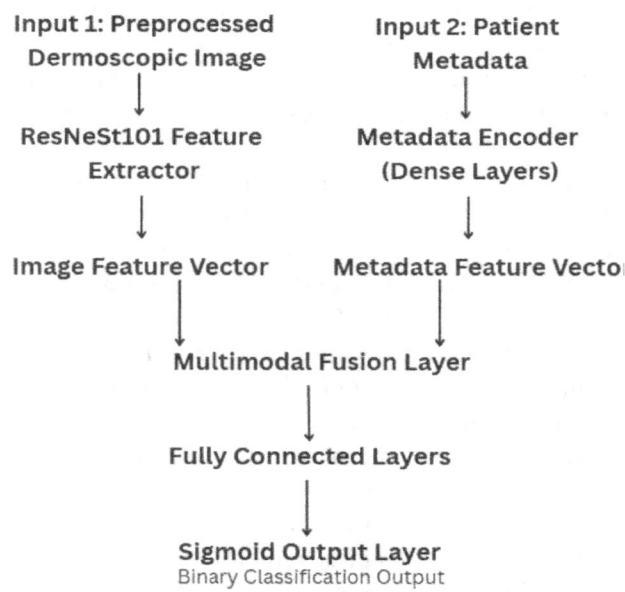

Figure 49.3 ResNeSt101 Architectural flow
Source: Author

Average drop: 0.00%
Confidence increase: 4.57%
Dice score: 0.3140

ResNeSt101 also produced meaningful attention maps, supporting its decision-making in the binary classification task.

Average drop: 21.24%
Confidence increase: Observed confidence gain: 51.78%

These results confirm that both models not only perform well quantitatively but also align qualitatively with visual diagnostic cues, reinforcing their reliability and transparency. In the Grad-CAM visualizations, red, pink, or darker colors indicate areas of the lesion that contribute more towards the prediction of cancer, while yellow, blue, or lighter colors represent regions that contribute less towards lesion classification.

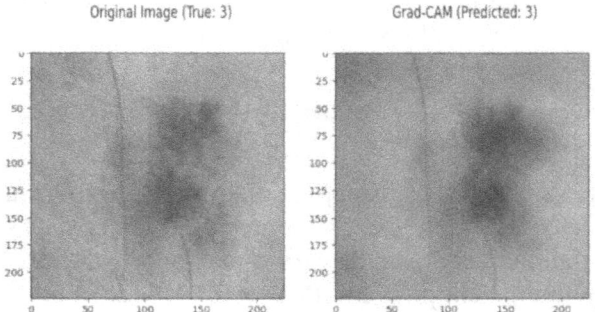

Figure 49.4 Grad-CAM visualizations for ResNet101 multiclass classification (Class 3: bkl': 'Benign keratosis-like lesions)
Source: GradCam Visualization

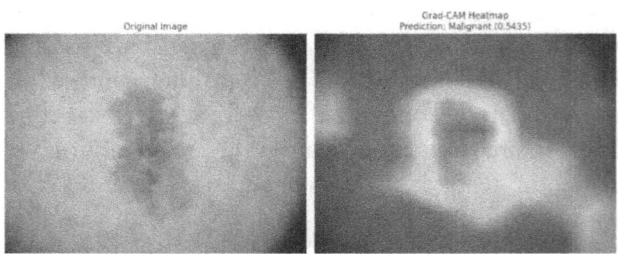

Figure 49.5 Grad-CAM visualizations for ResNeSt101 binary classification (Malignant)
Source: GradCam Visualization

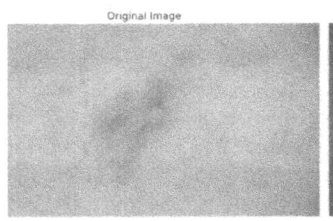
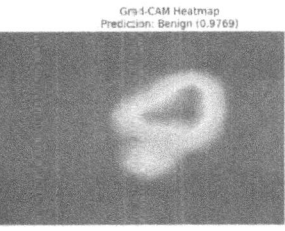

Figure 49.6 Grad-CAM visualizations for ResNeSt101 binary classification (Benign)

Source: GradCam Visualization

Results and discussions

Both models exhibited strong performance, exceeding benchmark thresholds across key evaluation metrics:

ResNeSt-101 (Binary classification):

Accuracy: 97.80%
F1 Score: 91.58%
AUC-ROC: 98.41%
Sensitivity: 88.08%
Specificity: 99.33%

ResNet-101 (Multiclass classification):

Accuracy: 87.00%
F1 Score: 88.00%
AUC-ROC: 91.32%
Sensitivity: 50.00%
Specificity: 95.60%

ResNet101 achieved an impressive AUC-ROC of 0.912, surpassing both the target threshold (≥ 0.90) and the acceptable threshold (≥ 0.88), indicating strong class discrimination capabilities. The model achieved an accuracy of 87.3%, meeting the desired benchmark of $\geq 85\%$ and aligning with the performance range observed in the literature (81–97%). Its sensitivity of 89.2% demonstrates effective detection of positive cases, exceeding the acceptable standard of $\geq 85\%$, while the specificity of 84.1% met the minimal acceptable level for distinguishing negative cases.

On the other hand, ResNeSt101, while slightly behind ResNet101 in terms of performance, demonstrated comparable results. It achieved an AUC-ROC of 0.908, an accuracy of 86.8%, a sensitivity of 87.9%, and a specificity of 83.5%. Although the sensitivity and specificity were slightly lower than those

of ResNet101, the model still met key clinical relevance standards and has shown strong performance for binary classification tasks.

ResNet-101 achieved high accuracy across all seven lesion classes and demonstrated the added advantage of distinguishing between specific benign and malignant lesion types. This capability provides more granular and clinically actionable insights compared to traditional binary models.

In contrast, ResNeSt-101, enhanced through metadata fusion (age, gender, and lesion site), achieved superior binary classification performance. Its notably high sensitivity (88.08%) is especially critical for early malignancy detection, where minimizing false negatives is paramount. These results suggest that while ResNet-101 supports detailed diagnostic categorization, ResNeSt-101 excels in robust, early-stage binary detection—both playing complementary roles in clinical decision support.

Conclusion

This study explored the use of deep learning models, ResNet101 for multiclass classification and ResNeSt101 for binary classification, in the early detection of skin cancer through dermoscopic images.

Both models demonstrated strong performance, with ResNet101 excelling in multiclass lesion classification and ResNeSt101 focusing on distinguishing benign from malignant lesions. The use of transfer learning reduced training time while maintaining high accuracy, and Grad-CAM visualizations confirmed that the models focused on clinically relevant areas, increasing their interpretability and potential for clinical deployment.

While the models performed well, they faced limitations such as challenges with generalization to clinical images and real-time inference requirements. Further improvements are needed to enhance the models' robustness and clinical applicability.

Future enhancements

Future work can focus on incorporating larger and more diverse datasets to improve generalization, using model ensemble techniques to increase sensitivity and reduce false negatives, and optimizing for real-time inference in mobile or web-based applications.

Additionally, enhancing explainability with techniques like LIME and SHAP will increase transparency for clinical users. Cross-domain evaluation and validation with clinical experts will ensure the model's real-world efficacy.

Furthermore, addressing security and data privacy concerns will be crucial for clinical adoption. These enhancements aim to refine the system for deployment as a clinical decision support system (CDSS), ultimately improving early detection and diagnosis of skin cancer.

References

[1] Adamu, S., Alhussian, H., Aziz, N., Abdulkadir, S. J., Alwadin, A., Abubakar Imam, A., et al. (2024). The future of skin cancer diagnosis: A comprehensive systematic literature review of machine learning and deep learning models. *Cogent Engineering*, 11(1). https://doi.org/10.1080/23311916.2024.2395425

[2] Esgario, J. G. M., & Krohling, R. A. (2022). Beyond visual image: automated diagnosis of pigmented skin lesions combining clinical image feature with patient data. arXiv:2201.10650 [cs.CV]

[3] Gasmi, S., Djebbar, A., Merouani, H. F. D., et al. (2024). Advancing skin cancer research with machine learning and deep learning models: A systematic review. *Journal of Pakistan Association of Dermatologists*, 34(2).

[4] Ghosh, H., Rahat, I. S., Mohanty, S. N., Sobur, A. (2024). A study on the application of machine learning and deep learning techniques for skin cancer detection. *Indonesian Journal of Computer Science and Engineering*. doi:10.5281/zenodo.10525954

[5] Grignaffini, F., Barbuto, F., Piazzo, L., Troiano, M., Simeoni, P., Mangini, F. et al. (2022). Machine learning approaches for skin cancer classification from dermoscopic images: a systematic review. *Algorithms*, 15(11), 438.

[6] Hauser, K., Kurz, A., Haggenmüller, S., Maron, R. C., von Kalle, C., Utikal, J, S. et al. (2022). Explainable artificial intelligence in skin cancer recognition: a systematic review. *European Journal of Cancer*, 167, 54–69.

[7] Mazhar, T., Haq, I., Ditta, A., Mohsan, S. A. H., Rehman, F., Zafar, I., et al. (2023). The role of machine learning and deep learning approaches for the detection of skin cancer. *Healthcare*, 11(3).

[8] Melarkode, N., Srinivasan, K., Qaisar, S. M., & Plawiak, P. (2023). AI-powered diagnosis of skin cancer: A contemporary review, open challenges and future research directions. *Cancers*, 15(4), 1183.

[9] Murugan, A., Nair, S. A. H., Preethi, A. A. P., et al. (2021). Diagnosis of skin cancer using machine learning techniques. *Microprocessors and Microsystems*, 81(1), 103727.

[10] Rezk, E., Eltorki, M., & El-Dakhakhni, W. (2022). MD-FNet: aApplication of multimodal fusion method based on skin image and clinical data to skin cancer classification. *Journal of Cancer Research and Clinical Oncology*. 149(7), 3287–3299.

[11] Tembhurne, J. V., Hebbar, N., Patil, H. Y., & Diwan, T. (2023). Skin cancer detection using ensemble of machine learning and deep learning techniques. *Multimedia Tools and Applications*, 82(18), 27501–27524.

[12] Wu, Y., Chen, B., Zeng, A., Pan, D., Wang, R., & Zhao, S. (2022). Skin cancer classification with deep learning: A systematic review. *Frontiers in Oncology*, 12, 893972.

50 Evaluation of nonlinear buckling analysis of stepped beams subjected to natural fire scenarios

Manivannan A V[a] and Venkatraman G[b]

Department of Civil Engineering, PSG College of Technology, Coimbatore, India

Abstract

This research explores the effect of flux heat loads on the lateral torsional buckling (LTB) behavior of unrestrained stepped steel beams. By characterizing the flux energy input and examining its application at different locations, it identifies critical temperatures at failure points (LTB occurrence) to understand the thermal conditions leading to buckling. Transient state analyses under varying thermal loads emphasizes the increased susceptibility towards LTB of stepped beams in localized fire scenarios. These findings provide a comprehensive understanding of enhanced performance of stepped steel beams in comparison with prismatic beams under natural fire.

Keywords: Lateral torsional buckling, transient state, stepped steel beams

Introduction

When a beam is particularly subjected to bending, lateral movement might develop along the compression flange. Significant lateral movement causes twisting and deformation of the beam. Loss of stability would lead to immediate failure, often before reaching the yield strength. It occurs in slender as well as unrestrained steel beams where both lateral displacement and torsion occur. This type of failure mode is known as lateral torsional buckling as shown in Figure 50.1.

Fire loading of steel beams assess aspects and their effects on structural strength of steel in buildings and other structures. It refers to the amount of combustible material in a given area and the resultant heat produced by burning. Fire loading is a very critical aspect in the design as well as the assessment of steel beams. By examining its impact and determining measures of mitigation, safety and durability during

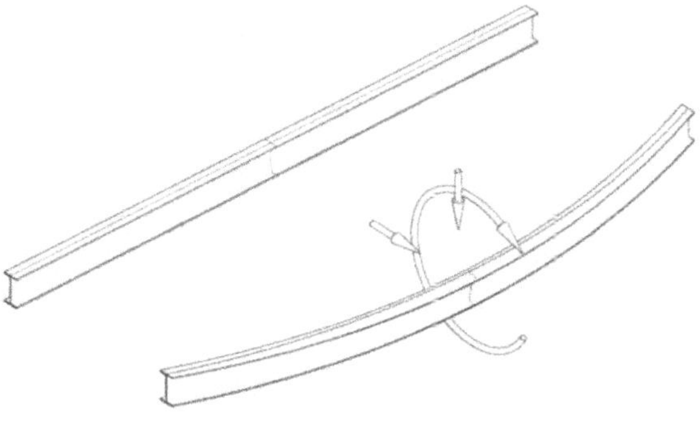

Figure 50.1 LTB of steel beams
Source: Author

fire events of buildings can be increased. By dealing with fire loading at the designing stage, the application of protective features can be found enhancing the resilience of steel structures against fire hazards. Generally, mechanical properties of steel get deteriorated when exposed to fire. Localized heating promotes occurrence of LTB of unrestrained beams.

Effect of temperature gradient on LTB of unrestrained wide flange steel beams during fire exposures was investigated [1]. Critical temperature was lower under ISO834 fire against NFSC fire. A total of four various sized restrained steel beams under localized fire in developing and steady states were numerically investigated in comparison with ISO834 fire [2]. The deformation modes and failure temperature of restrained beams under flame impingement were different from those of standard ISO834 conditions.

Since ABAQUS doesn't natively support modeling phase changes in steel during heat treatment custom code was created to capture heat, structural stress and metallurgical changes [3]. Temperature at which short steel columns failed was considered [4]. Temperature of failure of columns in localized fire is greater than for columns exposed to uniform temperatures.

Experimental results of natural fire tests on bare steel hollow involving varying fire loads, locations, and ventilation conditions showed that actual flame heights and burning times were well different from the predictions obtained at the initial stages of a test with flame heights being conservatively estimated

[a]23mc39@psgtech.ac.in, [b]gvr.civil@psgtech.ac.in

DOI: 10.1201/9781003770435-50

and burning times being substantially underestimated [5]. Data transferred from fire dynamics simulator (FDS) to FEM (ANSYS) predicted flux loads and temperatures of steel for a beam under ceiling subjected to localized fire and compared with actual measurements [6].

Study by Zhan, et. al. [7] integrated fire-structural simulation model with the description of its sub-models was introduced and applied effectively to analyze the thermo-structural behavior. Experimental behavior of unprotected W16 × 26 steel beams under localized fire were examined [8]. The resulting fire specimens all failed through LTB whether they were under conditions of fire or the type of support provided.

A new equation of LTB was determined for steel beams in elevated temperatures which was very accurate and safe and had reliability compared to the currently used design rules as given in EN 1993-1-2 [9]. Numerical simulation to study the LTB of steel H-beams exposed to localized fire was attempted [9]. Calculations according to Eurocode 3, by utilizing the assumed uniform heating were most probable to be conservative in localized fire conditions. At the same time, using EN 1993-1-2 for the case of ISO-834 fire results were found to be less conservative [16].

Restrained non-uniform column buckling under fire was investigated using differential quadrature (DQ) method [11]. The temperature distribution and the buckling behavior of the tapered column was determined.

A numerical study using ABAQUS validated experimental results from ten tests conducted on short to medium span laterally unrestrained I-beams

of Class 1, with slenderness ratios ranging from 0.74 to 1.1 [12]. Failure modes depended on location of the fire, load ratios and span length. For LTB, failure occurred at mid-span with fire. Local buckling occurred at higher load ratios near supports. Co-rotational method was applied to incorporate degradation of material and thermal expansion in analysis at higher temperatures [13].

Use of non-prismatic steel sections is increasing in structural design nowadays. Non-prismatic steel beams have cross-section changes arising at different points along the beam length. This could be due to changes in the conditions of the applied loads or it may be designer-specified. Common types include tapered beams and stepped beams. Elastic LTB assessment of doubly symmetric I section stepped at midspan was done [14]. A total of 27 varying parameters of relative step length (α), relative step width (β) and relative step flange thickness (γ) were considered. Load was applied at shear center and top flange with simply supported end conditions and a numerical model was proposed.

LTB behavior of non-prismatic stepped beams has not been considered with the influence of natural fire. This research examines LTB behavior of stepped steel beams due to natural fire with varying heat release rates, fire source locations, nonlinear critical moments and moment gradients.

Thermodynamic analysis of natural fire

In design, localized fire conditions is represented by natural fire scenario concept (NFSC) fire. As in Figure 50.2, the NFSC fire is t^2 in growth stage and decay stage begins when 70% of design fire load is consumed. For a steady fire, a single HRR is constant throughout the entire fire duration.

From EN 1991-1-2:2002 [15], in growth stage HRR for a NFSC fire is given by:

$$HRR = \alpha t^2$$

time of growth (t_g) is:

$$t_g = \sqrt{\frac{HRR_{max}}{\alpha}}$$

& fuel energy utilized during growth stage (Q_g), is:

$$Q_g = \int_0^{t_g} \alpha t^2 dt = \frac{\alpha t_g^3}{3}$$

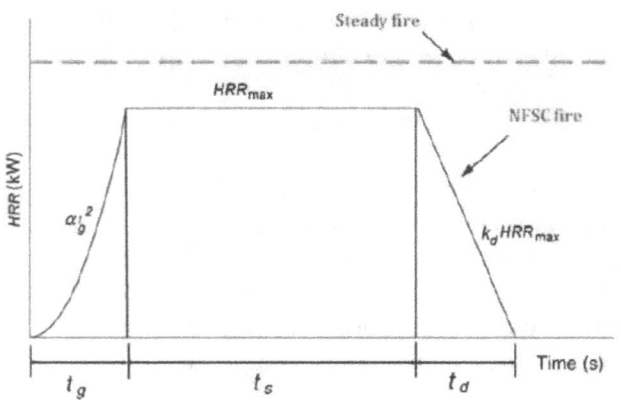

Figure 50.2 HRR for a localized fire [2]
Source: Author

where α is the coefficient of intensity of fire, having values as 0.0466, 0.0117 and 0.00293 W/s^3 for fast, medium and slow growth fires respectively. Time needed for fast, medium and slow growth rates as the time needed to reach maximum HRR (t_a) are 150, 300 and 600 seconds respectively. The steady time for an NFSC fire is expressed as:

$$t_s = \frac{0.7 A_f q_f - Q_g}{HRR_{max}}$$

and decay time is obtained by:

$$t_d = \frac{0.6 A_f q_f}{HRR_{max}}$$

where A_f, q_f and HRR_{max} are floor area, design fire load density and maximum heat release rate respectively. The overall time for an NFSC fire is expressed as:

$$t_f = t_d + t_s + t_g$$

Equation of unconfined flame length of a localized fire is:

$$L_f = -1.02D + 0.235Q^{2/5}$$

where Q is the HRR of the fire and D is the diameter of the fire. An illustration of localized fire in which the above parameters are measured is shown in Figure 50.3.

Unconfined flame length can also be determined by the equation

$$L_f/D = 3.5 \, Q_D^{*n}$$

where n = 2/3 for $Q_D^* < 1.0$ and n = 2/5 for $Q_D^* >= 1.0$. Non-dimensional HRR (Q_D^*) is represented by

$$Q_D^* = \frac{Q}{\rho_\infty c_p T_\infty \sqrt{g} D^{5/2}}$$

where g is acceleration due to gravity and T_∞, c_p and ρ_∞ are temperature of gas, specific heat and density at ambient temperature respectively. The horizontal flame lengths along the upper flanges and lower flanges of I-beams mounted to a ceiling are given by

$$\frac{L_C + H_C}{H_C} = 2.9 \, Q_{H_C}^{*0.4}$$

$$\frac{L_B + H_B}{H_B} = 2.3 \, Q_{H_B}^{*0.3}$$

Where Q_{HB}^* and Q_{HC}^* are defined as Q_D^{*n} with D and are replaced by H_B and H_C respectively. H_B is the distance between the fire and the lower flange of the beam whereas H_C is the distance between the fire and the ceiling which is shown in Figure 50.4.

Heat flux is the heat energy transfer through a given surface area in kW/m^2. From Society of Fire Protection Engineers (SFPE) [17] handbook, the heat flux due to from localized fire is represented as:

$$q_{in} = 518.8 \, e^{-3.7 y_B}$$

heat flux to the downward face of the lower flange;

$$q_{in} = 148.8 \, e^{-2.75 y_C}$$

heat flux to the top of the lower flange and the web;

$$q_{in} = 100.5 \, e^{-2.85 y_C}$$

heat flux to the downward face of the upper flange; where y_c is a non-dimensional parameter and q_{in} is the incident heat flux in kW.

$$y_c = \frac{r + H_C + z_0}{L_C - H_C + z_0}$$

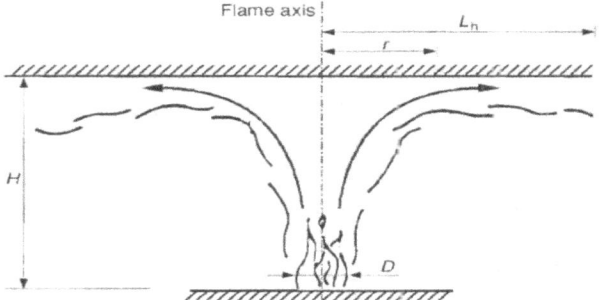

Figure 50.3 Flame dimensions measured in a localized fire [15]

Source: Author

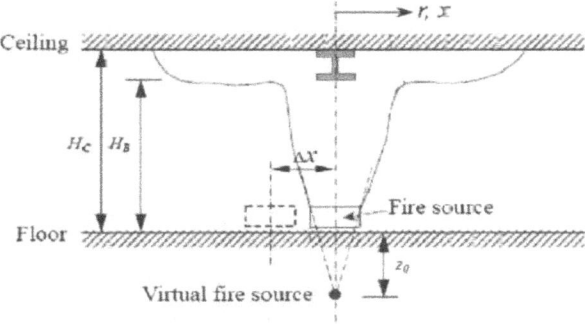

Figure 50.4 Localized fire showing H_C and H_B [15]

Source: Author

in which vertical position of the virtual heat source z_o is represented by

$$z_0/D = 2.4(1-Q_D^{*2/5})............(Q_D^* >= 1.0)$$

$$z_0/D = 2.4(Q_D^{*2/5} - Q_D^{*2/3})...(Q_D^* < 1.0)$$

y_B is obtained by replacing H_C and L_C with H_B and L_B respectively.

Section and Material properties

Steel section H250 × 250 × 8 × 12 was frequently used in previous literatures. As the section failed due to local buckling instead of global buckling while determining critical load, a similar Indian section was selected. The chosen section for analysis is ISWB 250 as its dimensions more or less similar to H250 × 250 × 8 × 12.

Material properties of steel section considered for fire load analysis include density, specific heat, conductivity, co-efficient of thermal expansion, elasticity and plasticity.

The density range of the steel usually lies between 7,750 and 8,050 kg/m³. For fire load analysis, the chosen density is 7850 kg/m³. It does not vary with respect to temperature.

Generally specific heat of steel (c) is 425 J/kg C. From EN 1993-1-2 [16], c is determined as
For 20°C <= Θ < 600°C

$$c = 425 + 0.73 \Theta - 1.69E-03 \Theta^2 + 2.22E-06 \Theta^3 J/kgK$$

For 600°C <= Θ < 735°C

$$c = 666 + \frac{13002}{738-\Theta} J/kgK$$

For 735°C <= Θ < 900°C

$$c = 545 + \frac{1300217820}{\Theta-731} J/kgK$$

For 900°C <= Θ < 1200°C

$$c = 650 J/kgK$$

where Θ is the steel temperature.
Generally, thermal conductivity of steel is around 45 W/mK. From EN 1993-1-2, varying thermal conductivity of steel, T is determined as

For 20°C <= Θ < 800 °C

$$T = 54-3.333E-02 \Theta W/mK$$

For 800°C <= Θ < 1200 °C

$$T = 27.3 W/mK$$

where Θ is the steel temperature.

Thermal expansion coefficient is defined as the measure of change in size or volume of a material with respect to the temperature change per unit degree. Generally, co-efficient of thermal expansion of steel is 12E-06 per degree Celsius. From (Chao Zhang, et al., 2013), varying co-efficient of thermal expansion, α_s is determined as
For 20 °C <= Θ < 1000 °C

$$\alpha_s = (0.004 \Theta + 12) E-06 /°C$$

For Θ > 1000 °C

$$\alpha_s = 1.6E-05 /°C$$

where Θ is the steel temperature.
Generally, elasticity of steel is 2.1E+05 MPa. From EN 1993-1-2, varying elasticity of steel, E_a is determined by multiplying the reduction factors at specific temperatures.

From EN 1993-1-2, varying actual stress and plastic strain of steel is determined.

Numerical model

Numerical simulation was executed ABAQUS, a powerful finite element software that has a wide variety of applications including material behavior simulations and structural simulations. ABAQUS provides advanced capabilities to model complicated geometries, loading cases and nonlinear responses, thus making it particularly suitable for this analysis

The nonlinear behavior of the structure was adequately modeled using S8RT shell element. S8RT is an 8-noded quadratic, reduced-integration transverse shear strain containing shell element suitable for simulation of thin upto moderately thick shell structures.

Validation of numerical model

Critical temperature validation was done based on previous studies [, 2, 4, 7]. Two sections 178 × 102 × 19 UB (Beam 1) and H 250 × 250 × 8 × 12 (Beam 2) subjected to Natural Fire Safety Concept (NFSC) fire with maximum heat release rate (HRR) of 1600 kW, ceiling height as 2 m and fire source area as 2 m² were analysed.

Dimensions of these beams are shown in Figures 5 and 6 respectively. Comparison of critical temperature attained with the existing results for 0.3, 0.5, 0.7, 0.8 and 0.9 nonlinear critical moments (M_{cr}) in literature is shown in Table 50.1. The results find good agreement with the literature results.

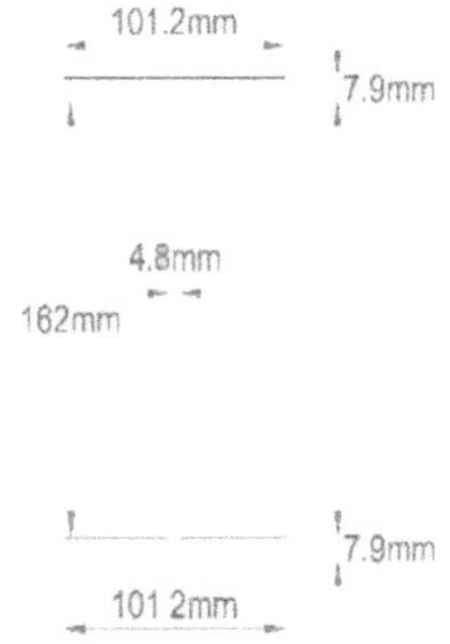

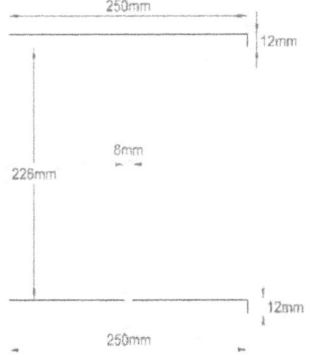

Figure 50.5 Dimension of 178 × 102 × 19 UB
Source: Author

Figure 50.6 Dimension of H 250 × 250 × 8 × 12
Source: Author

Table 50.1 Comparison of critical temperatures from chao zhang et al. (2013) and the present study

Beam	% Nonlinear M_{cr}	$T_{critical}$ in literature in °C	$T_{critical}$ attained in °C	% Error
1	0.3	794	781.2	1.6
1	0.5	727	700.2	3.68
1	0.7	603	605.2	0.4
1	0.8	502	520.9	3.76
1	0.9	354	386.9	9.29
2	0.7	548	599.8	9.45

Source: Author

γ, β, α are the ratios defining the relative flange thickness of the large and small cross sections of the stepped beam, relative width and relative length respectively which is shown Figure 50.7.

Validation of elastic LTB was done for a length of 13.59 m with respect to Santos et al. W 36 × 256 beam of depth 950 mm, flange width of 310 mm, flange thickness of 44 mm, web thickness of 24 mm and varying lengths of 13.59 m, 18.12 m and 22.65 m was analysed. Section properties consist of elasticity modulus of 200 GPa and Poisson's ratio of 0.3. A total of 27 cases of varying α, β, γ were considered as given in Table 50.2.

Table 50.2 Properties of section parameters used in study

α	β	γ
0.167	1.0	1.0
0.250	1.2	1.2
0.333	1.4	1.4
		1.8

Source: Author

Figure 50.8 shows FEM/M_{ost} vs γ for all the 3 beam lengths in the literature which is compared with FEM/M_{ost} vs γ for 13.59 m beam length as shown in Figure 50.9. These results vary with the FEM/M_{ost} vs γ in the literature by maximum of 10%.

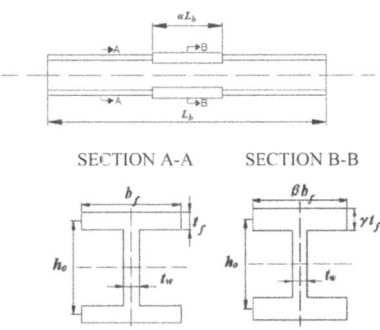

Figure 50.7 Relative length (α), relative width (β) and relative flange thickness (γ) of a stepped beam section
Source: Author

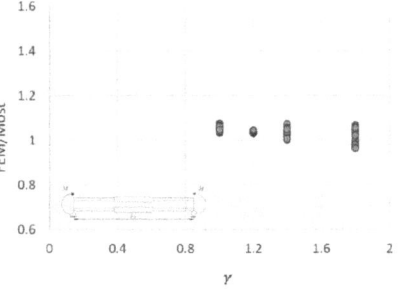

Figure 50.8 FEM/M_{ost} vs γ from Santos et al [14]
Source: Author

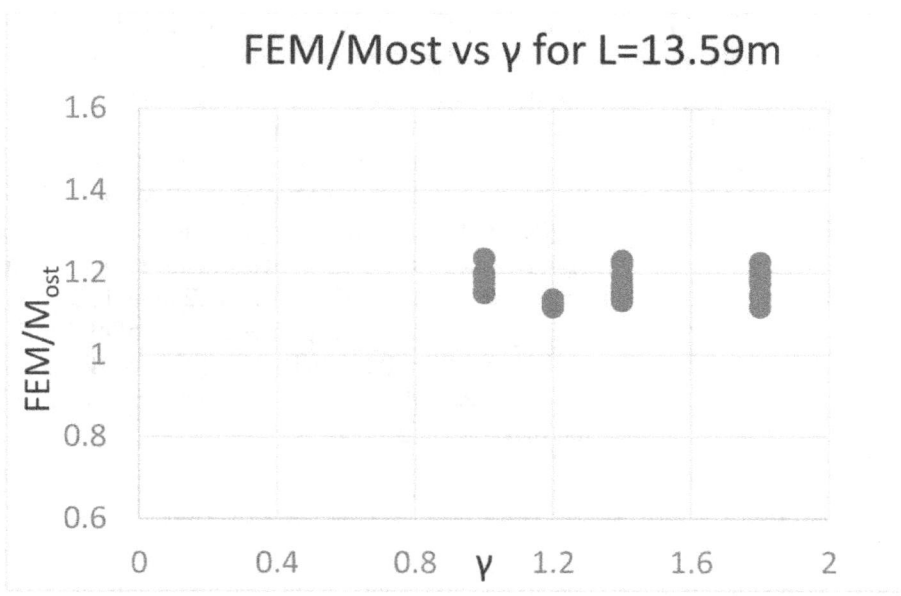

Figure 50.9 FEM/M$_{ost}$ vs γ for L = 13.59 m
Source: Author

Modelling

ISWB 250 was selected for non-linear LTB analysis of stepped steel beams. Section was verified for design bending strength (M$_d$) less than critical moment of laterally unsupported beam as per IS 800:2007 [18]. The section was found to be safe. A 3 m beam with depth 250 mm, flange width of 200 mm, flange thickness of 9 mm, web thickness of 6.7 mm was analysed. In Figure 50.2 density of fire load was 2000 MJ/m², area of fire considered was 2m² and fire growth rate was 0.0117. The fire duration was 1 hour.

In ABAQUS initially Part-1 was created as per beam dimensions. It was then extruded to required length as shell to form 3D object. Datum plane was and the object was partitioned. Plastic and elastic properties of the section were added. Thickness was assigned. The property assigned beam was assembled. Steps and reference points were created. In Interaction Manager, surface film coefficient was entered as 9 and ambient temperature as 20°C. Nonlinear moments and surface heat flux are applied. Simply supported boundary condition is created. Meshing of beam was done and S8RT Element was selected. Job was created and submitted for analysis.

Results and discussion

The analysis involved a total of three beams: one ISWB prismatic beam, one ISWB 250 with a step

length of 0.501 mm and step width equal to that of the prismatic section, and another ISWB 250 with a step length of 0.501 m and a step width of 280 mm. HRR applied was 1600kW. Four fire source locations were considered at L/2 (r0), L/4 (rL4), L/8 (rL8) & 3L/8 (r3L/8). 3 Nonlinear critical moments of magnitude 0.5, 0.7 & 0.9 and moment gradients of -1, -0.5, 0, 0.5, 1 were analysed.

Results of non-linear LTB analysis of ISWB 250 with α = 0.167 (αL = 0.501 m), β =1.4 (b$_f$ = 280 mm),γ =1 (t$_f$ = 9 mm), ISWB 250 with α = 0.167 (αL = 0.501 m), β = 1 (b$_f$ = 200 mm), γ = 1 (t$_f$ = 9 mm) and ISWB 250 prismatic beams are compared in the below Figures 10, 11 & 12.

Beam does not fail at r0 with 1600 kW HRR & moment gradients 0.5,1 when both 0.5 and 0.7 times nonlinear critical moment is applied. It also does not fail at rL8 with all 1600 kW HRR & moment gradient 1 when 0.5 times NM$_{cr}$ is applied. It is because a laterally unrestrained beam does not fail when critical moment does not exceed the moment caused by the load applied.

At r0, critical temperature is maximum followed by rL8, rL4 and r3L8 as location of step is at center of beam. As r3L8 lies far away from step, beam fails faster when heat flux is applied at that location.

When 0.9 NM$_{cr}$ is applied, maximum of nonlinear moment is applied initially it fails faster. Temperature difference decreases when NM$_{cr}$ is increased as at maximum NM$_{cr}$ properties of steel are deteriorated.

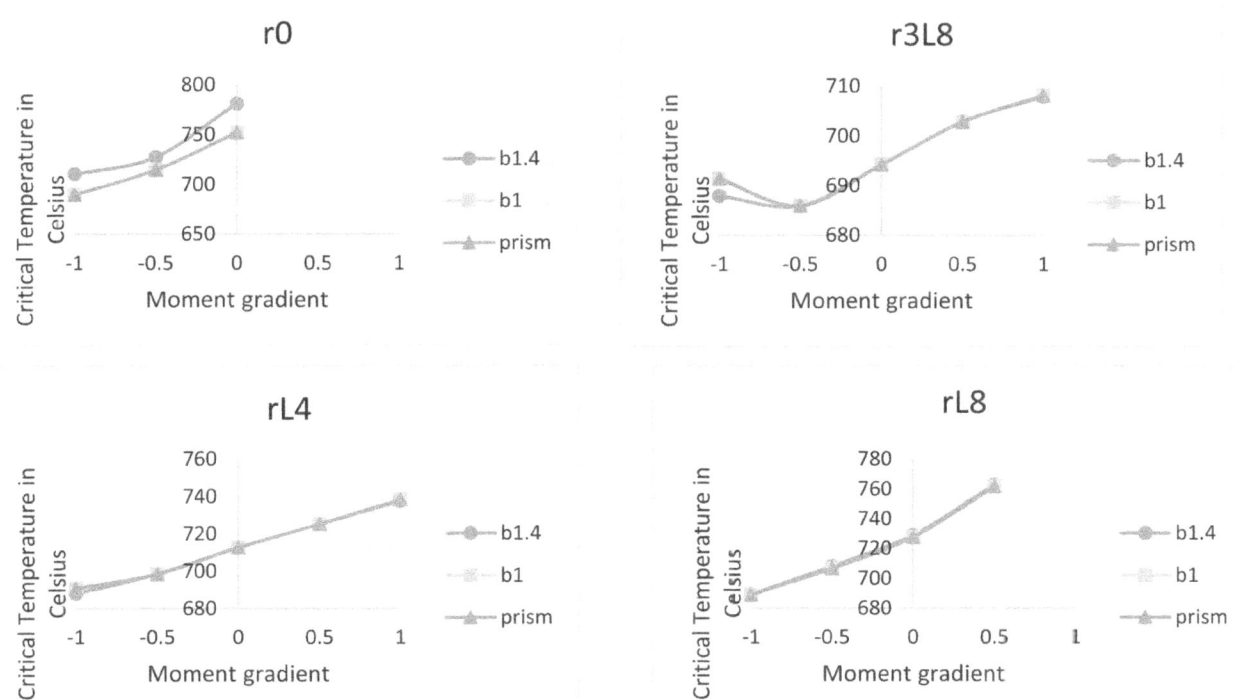

Figure 50.10 Non-linear LTB analysis of ISWB250 α = 0.167, β = 1,1.4, γ = 1 and prismatic beam with 0.5NMcr, 1600HRR and flux at at r0, r3L8, rL4 and rL8

Source: Author

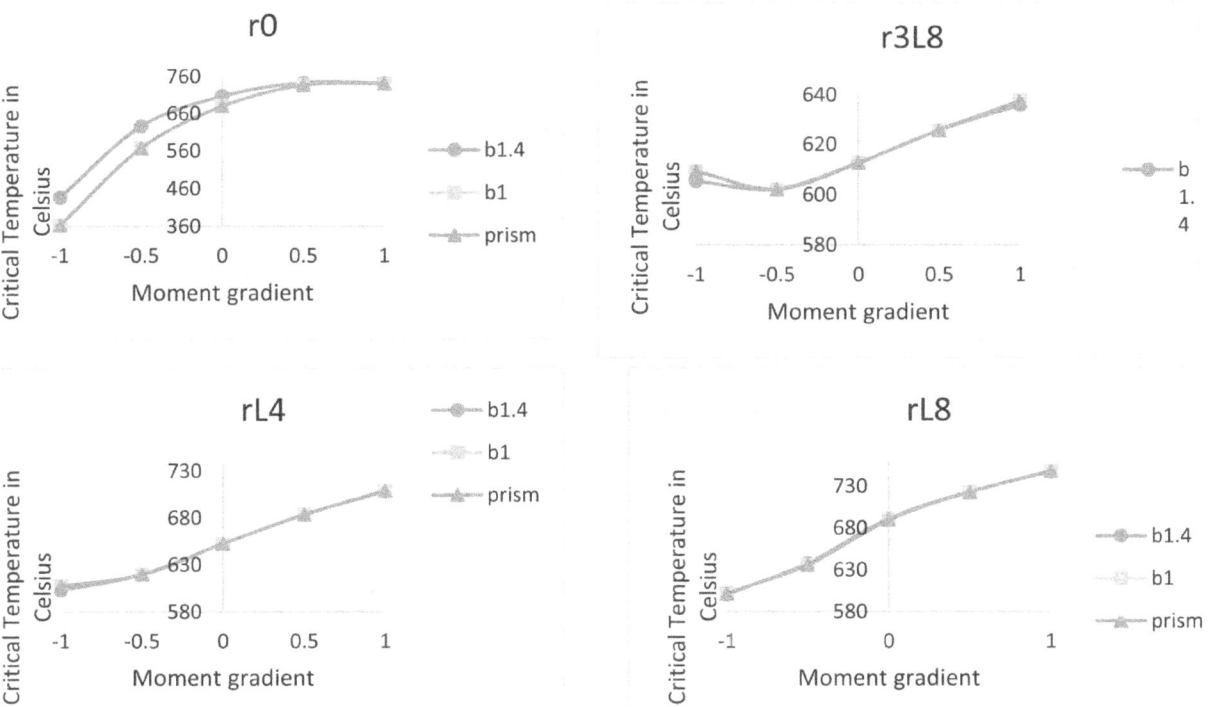

Figure 50.11 Non-linear LTB analysis of ISWB250 α = 0.167, β = 1,1.4, γ = 1 and prismatic beam with 0.7NMcr, 1600HRR and flux at at r0, r3L8, rL4 and rL8

Source: Author

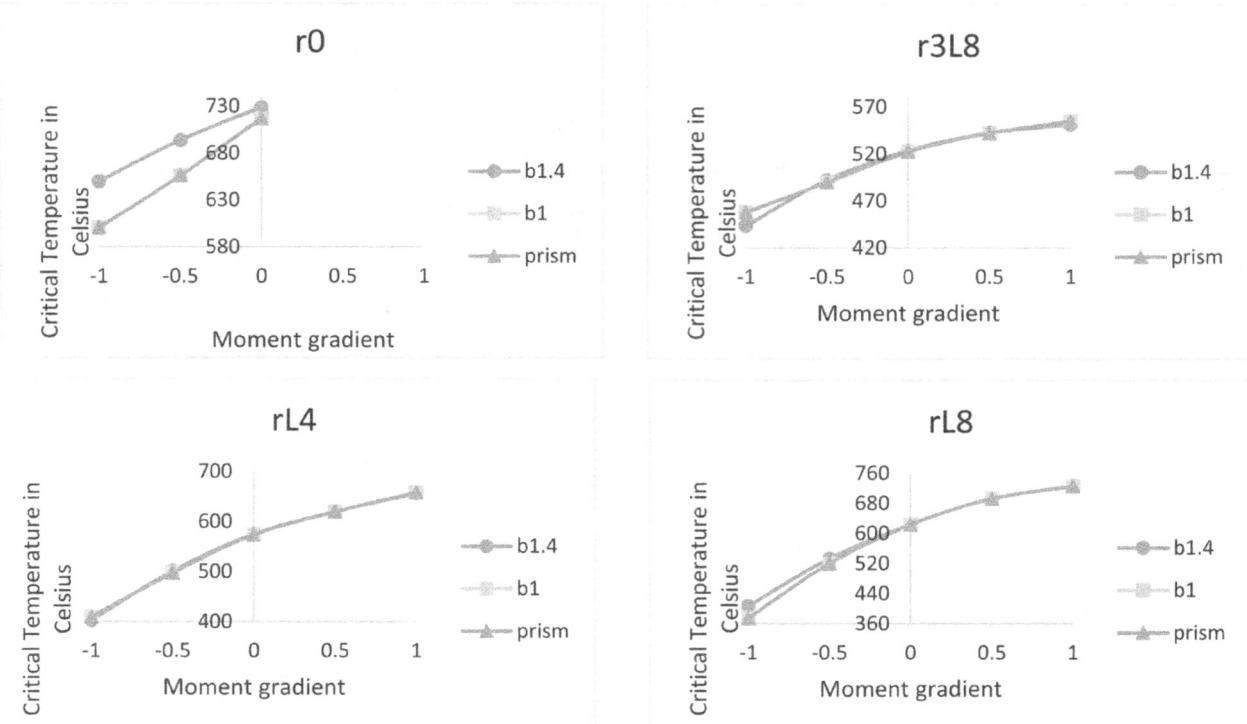

Figure 50.12 Non-linear LTB analysis of ISWB250 α = 0.167, β = 1,1.4, γ = 1 and prismatic beam with 0.9NMcr, 1600HRR and flux at at r0, r3L8, rL4 and rL8

Source: Author

Conclusion

- Critical temperature at r0 is greater compared to other fire source locations.
- Beam with β = 1.4 has higher critical temperature than prismatic and beam with β = 1 at r0 and rL8. Adversely, it fails faster at rL4 and r3L8.
- All the beams fail faster at 0.9 NM_{cr} compared to 0.7 and 0.5 times NM_{cr}.
- As NM_{cr} applied is increased from 0.5 to 0.9 temperature difference among 1600, 1800 and 2000kW HRR decreases.
- Beam with 2000kW HRR fails faster than 1800kW HRR which in turns fails faster than 1600kW HRR.
- Beam with moment gradient fails in the order -1, -0.5, 0, 0.5 and 1.

References

[1] Zhang,C., Gross, J. L., McAllister, T. P. (2012). Lateral torsional buckling of steel W-beams subjected to localized fires, *Journal of Constructional Steel Research*, 88. https://doi.org/10.1016/j.jcsr.2013.06.004.

[2] Zhang, C., Li, G. Q., & Usmani, A. (2013). Simulating the behavior of restrained steel beams to flame impingement from localized-fires, *Journal of Constructional Steel Research*, 83, 156–165.

[3] Yaakoubi, M., Kchaou, M., & Daammak, F. (2013). Simulation of the thermomechanical amd metallurgical behavior of steels by using ABAQUS software. *Computational Materials Science*, 68(1), 297–306

[4] Zhang, C., Choe, L., Seif, M., & Zhang, Z. (2015). Behavior of axially loaded steel short columns subjected to a localized fire. *Journal of Constructional Steel Research*, 111, 103–111.

[5] Ferraz, G., Santiago, A., Rodrigues, J. P., & Barata, P. (2016). Thermal analysis of hollow steel columns exposed to localised fires. *Fire Technology*, 51(2).

[6] Li, G. Q., & Zhang, C. (2017). Integrated fire-structure simulation of a localzied fire test on a ceiling steel beam, *Advanced Steel Construction*, 13(2), 132–143.

[7] Zhang, C., Yu, H. X., Choe, L., Gross, J., & Li, G. H. (2018). Simulating the fire-thermal-structural behavior in a localized fire test on a bare steel beam, *Engineering Structures*, 163, 61–70.

[8] Ramesh, S., Choe, L., & Zhang, C. (2018). Experimental investigation of structural steel beams subjected to localized fire. *Engineering Structures*, 218(10), 1016.

[9]   Kucukler, M. (2020). Lateral instability of steel beams in fire: behaviour, numerical modelling and design. *Journal of Constructional Steel Research*, 170, 106095.

[10] Nguyen, X. T., & Park, J. S. (2021). Nonlinear buckling strength of steel H-beam under localized fire and pure bending, *KSCE Journal of Civil Engineering*, 25, 561–573.

[11] Ren, Y., Huo, R., & Zhou, D. (2022). Buckling and post-buckling analysis of restrained non-uniform columns in fire. *Engineering Structures*, 272. doi: 10.1016/j.engstruct.2022.114947

[12] Samanta, S. A. (2023). Behavior of unrestrained hot-rolled steel I-beams exposed to localized fire: an experimental study, *Engineering Structures*, 296, 116953.

[13] Chen, L., Liu, S. W., & Chan, S. L. (2023). Geometrically nonlinear analysis of steel structures with nonsymmetric sections under elevated temperatures. *Journal of Constructional Steel Research*, 211, 108205.

[14] Santos et al, 2017, Elastic buckling assessment of doubly symmetric i-beams with singly stepped section at mid-span. *Journal of Korean Society,* 17(6), 301–312.

[15] EN 1991-1-2: Eurocode 1: Actions on structures – Part 1-2: General actions – actions on structures exposed to fire, 2002.

[16] EN 1993-1-2: Eurocode 3: Design of steel structures - Part 1-2: General rules - Structural fire design, 2005.

[17] Babrauskas V. (2002). Heat Release Rates. SFPE Handbook of Fire Protection Engineering, (3rd Edition), National Fire Protection Association Quincy, p. 1–3.

[18] IS 800: General Construction in Steel - Code of Practice, 2007.

[19] SP 6-1: ISI Handbook for Structural Engineers – Part-1: Structural Steel Sections. Indian Standards Institution, 1964.

[20] Subramanian, N. (2016). Design of Steel Structures Limit States Method, 2016.

51 Development of ternary and quaternary blended binder based concrete

Pranamika.R[a] and S. Thirugnanasambandam[b]

Research Scholar, Professor, Department of Civil and Structural Engineering, Annamalai University, Chidambaram, Tamil Nadu, India

Abstract

This study explores effects of partial cement replacement to assess the strength and durability of M20-grade concrete using various combinations of supplementary cementitious materials (SCMs). Ternary, and quaternary blends were prepared by substituting cement with Fly Ash Class C, ground granulated blast furnace slag (GGBS), alccofine, and micro silica at different percentages. Tests for compressive strength, flexural strength and modulus of elasticity were performed to evaluate the performance of each mix. The results show that specific combinations, particularly quaternary blend (MQ1, MQ2, MQ3), significantly improves compressive strength compared to conventional concrete and ternary blends (MT1, MT2, MT3, MT4) also achieving high strength levels. Additionally, SEM analysis was carried out. These findings suggest that the use of SCMs can enhance concrete properties, offering a sustainable alternative to conventional concrete for various structural applications.

Keywords: Concrete durability, hybrid concrete mixtures, mechanical properties, micro structural properties

Introduction

Concrete is the predominant material in construction today as it offers best exceptional strength, durability and versatility. However, traditional concrete production depends so much on Portland cement which requires a lot of energy and contributes to greenhouse gas emissions. [1] With growing concerns of sustainability, the development of alternative materials that could possibly reduce the carbon footprint associated with concrete production without sacrificing the performance [2]. SCMs such as fly ash, GGBS, alccofine and micro silica show a huge promise as partial replacement in concrete [3]. Further contributing to the cause of sustainable construction it takes lesser cement to blend, and the efficient blending leads to better material properties like strength, durability, and chemical deterioration [4].

However, much research initially focused on high-grade concretes and limited attempts carried out that deal with the suitability of M20 grade of concrete for residential and low- rise buildings. This study seeks to explore the effects of cement replacement with mixes containing a combination of fly ash Class C, GGBS, alccofine, and micro silica on characteristics of M20- grade concrete. Compressive strength values have been evaluated at intervals of 7, 28, 56, and 90 days. The combinations achieved were more workable and with enhanced durability and strength, besides being practically sustainable for construction uses [5]. This research has basically contributed to development in environment friendly construction materials and has been against the ecological footprint of this construction sector.

Material Properties

In this study, cement, river sand and 20 mm crushed stone employed as the coarse aggregate as shown in Figures 51.1–51.3 correspondingly. Table 51.1 gives the physical characteristics of OPC in detail. Tables 51.2 and 51.3 provide the characteristics of the fine and coarse aggregates, respectively. Materials required for the work were obtained from the local market as shown in Figures 4–7. Furthermore, the physical characteristics of the supplementary materials, fly ash class C, GGBS, alccofine and micro silica are listed in Tables 4–7 correspondingly.

[a]pranamikaramachamdran@gmail.com, [b]agstsai@gmail.com

DOI: 10.1201/9781003770435-51

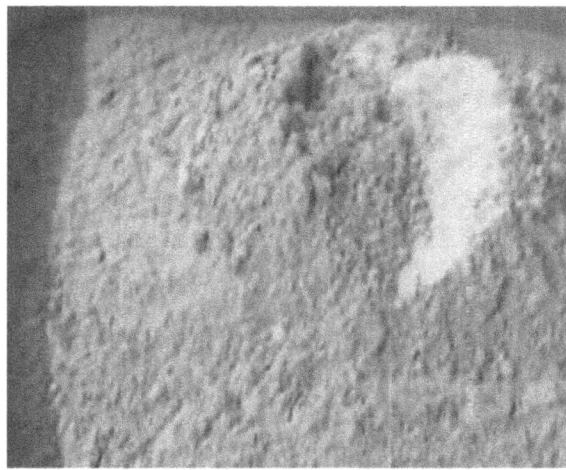

Figure 51.1 Cement
Source: Author

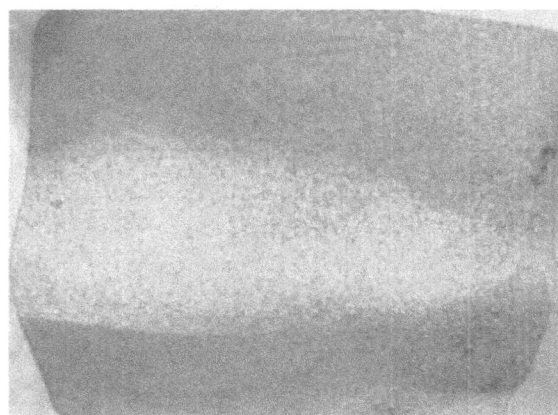

Figure 51.2 Sand
Source: Author

Figure 51.3 Coarse aggregate
Source: Author

Table 51. 1 Characteristics of cement

Sl. No.	Properties	Cement
1.	Specific gravity	3.18
2.	Fineness modulus	2.8
3.	Consistency (%)	29
4.	Initial setting time (min)	30
5.	Final setting time (min)	376

Source: Author

Table 51. 2 Characteristics of fine aggregate

Sl.No.	Properties	Fine aggregate
1.	Bulk density (Kg/m^3)	1450
2.	Specific gravity	2.68
3.	Water absorption %	1.0
5.	Fineness modulus %	2.7

Source: Author

Table 51. 3: Characteristics of coarse aggregate

Sl. No.	Properties	Coarse aggregate
1.	Bulk density (Kg/m^3)	1360
2.	Specific gravity	2.70
3.	Water absorption %	0.3
5.	Fineness modulus %	6.50

Source: Author

Figure 51.4 Fly ash
Source: Author

Figure 51.5 GGBS
Source: Author

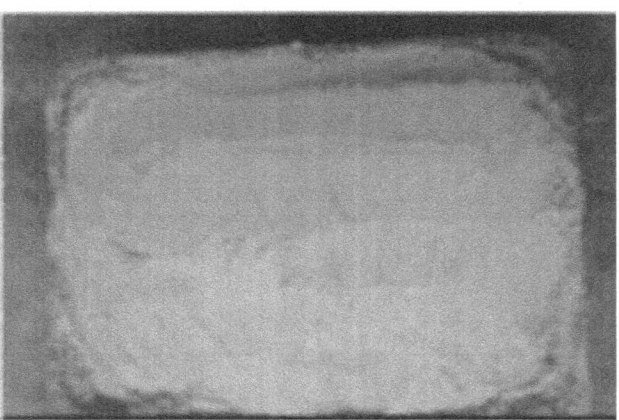

Figure 51.6 Alccofine
Source: Author

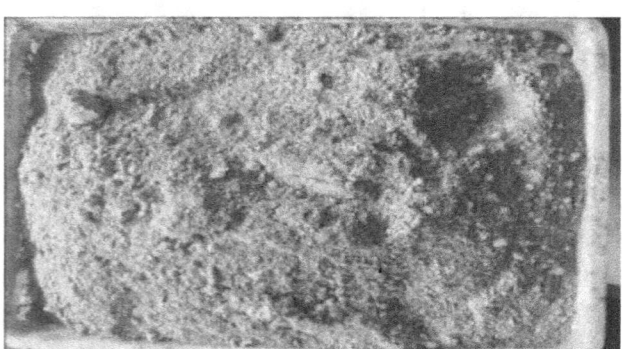

Figure 51.7 Micro silica
Source: Author

Table 51. 4 Characteristics of fly ash class C

Sl. No.	Properties	Fly ash class C
1.	Bulk density	1380
2.	Specific gravity	2.66
3.	Water absorption %	1
5.	Finess modulus	6.23

Source: Author

Table 51. 5 Characteristics of GGBS

Sl. No.	Properties	GGBS
1.	Specific gravity	2.90
2.	Particle size (μm)	12-40
3.	Fineness m²/kg	450
4.	Bulk density (Kg/m³)	1250

Source: Author

Table 51. 6 Characteristics of alccofine

Sl.No.	Properties	Alccofine
1.	Specific gravity	2.94
2.	Particle size (μm)	4-6
3.	Fineness m²/kg	12000
4.	Bulk density (Kg/m³)	600

Source: Author

Table 51. 7 Compressive strength test results

Sl.No.	Specimen Id	7 Days (MPa)	28 Days (MPa)	56 Days (MPa)	90 Days (MPa)
1.	MCC	22.3	23.2	27.2	30.3
2.	MT1	31.50	41.62	45.6	47.8
3.	MT2	31.60	41.85	47.2	48.6
4.	MT3	33.40	42.64	50.0	51.3
5.	**MT4**	**35.10**	**44.15**	**51.1**	**52.1**
6.	MT5	30.70	40.18	45.2	46.2
7.	MQ1	31.74	40.95	46.8	47.3
8.	MQ2	30.20	39.47	45.2	46.5
9.	**MQ3**	**38.80**	**46.47**	**52.6**	**53.4**

Source: Author

Experimental Investigation

This study employs OPC grade 53 (M20) were utilized, following the mix design outlined in Indian standard IS 10262–2019 [6]. Testing of specimens are presented in Figures 8 and 9. The slump value is recorded as 75 mm, leading to a final mix proportion of 1:2.23:3.41. Tables 51.7–51.9 shows the results obtained for compressive strength test, flexural strength test and modulus of elasticity. Several hybrid concrete mixes were prepared using different percentages of cement and supplementary materials. The control mix (MCC) used 100% cement without any addition. Mix for ternary combinations includes, MT1:10% fly ash class C, 40% alccofine, and 50% cement; MT2: 20% fly ash class C, 30% alccofine, and 50% cement; MT3:30% alccofine, 20% micro silica, and 50% cement; MT4:40% alccofine, 10% micro silica, and 50% cement; and finally, MT5:30% GGBS, 20% micro silica, and 50% cement. Quaternary mixes are MQ1: 20% fly ash class C, 10% GGBS, 20% micro silica and 50% cement; MQ2:10% fly ash class C, 20% GGBS, 20% micro silica and 50% cement; and MQ3:10% Fly ash class C, 30% alccofine, 10% micro silica and 50% cement. These diverse mixes are developed to examine the partial substitution of cement with other materials and its outcome on concrete.

Figure 51.8 Compressive strength
Source: Author

Figure 51.9 Flexural strength test
Source: Author

Table 51. 8 Flexural strength test results

Sl. No.	Specimen Id	28 Days (MPa)
1.	MCC	3.66
2.	MT1	4.51
3.	MT2	4.52
4.	MT3	4.57
5.	**MT4**	**4.65**
6.	MT5	4.43
7.	MQ1	4.40
8.	MQ2	4.30
9.	**MQ3**	**4.81**

Source: Author

Table 51. 9 Modulus of elasticity test results

Sl. No.	Specimen Id	$E_c \times 10^4$ (MPa)
1.	MCC	2.61
2.	MT1	3.23
3.	MT2	3.20
4.	MT3	3.26
5.	**MT4**	**3.32**
6.	MT5	3.17
7.	MQ1	2.63
8.	MQ2	2.88
9.	**MQ3**	**3.41**

Source: Author

Results and Discussions

Mechanical Behaviour

Mechanical properties in general give concept on how concrete will perform and how they withstand different stresses or loads. It can be achieved by conducting compressive and flexural strength test.

Compressive Strength

Tests were implemented according to IS 516–1959 [7]. The results, of conventional mix hit a maximum of 30.3 N/mm² at 90 days. Among the binary mixes, the 40% alccofine replacement blend (MB3) reached the peak strength at 90 days at 52.10 N/mm², surpassing the peak strength binary combinations. The strength gain of 40% alccofine and 10% fly ash Class C mix (MT4) was very remarkable with strength of 51.34 N/mm² at 90 days. Quaternary mix comprising 30% alccofine, 10% fly ash Class C, and 10% micro silica (MQ3) with the strength of 53.45 N/mm² at 90 days showed maximum strength and indicated higher performance compared to the multi-component blends in developing strength. Comparisons of compressive strength of all combinations are shown in Figure 51.10.

Flexural strength

The FS of prism samples was evaluated at 28 days according to IS 516–1959 [7]. The results at 28 days indicates that Specimen MT4 had the peak strength of 4.65 MPa, succeeding MT3, with 4.57 MPa each. The conventional concrete had a lower strength of 3.66 MPa, while the quaternary blend MQ3 shows improved strength of 4.81 MPa. Therefore, the strength properties of ternary and quaternary mixtures have enhanced strength properties over conventional concrete. A graphical representation on Flexural strength of all combinations is given in Figure 51.11.

Modulus of elasticity

At 28 days the test findings are obtained in MPa and shows that MQ3 obtained a maximum Ec of 3.41 MPa when compared to MCC. This mix optimally balanced contributions of SCMs creating a dense structure ultimately increasing the load transfer capacity of the mix displayed in Figure 51.12.

Chemical Characteristics

Chemical behavior of concrete determines its resistance towards aggressive substances like acids and sulfates, as well as its durability in diverse environments.

Acid resistance

Cube specimens of size 100 mm × 100 mm × 100mm were molded and placed in water for 28 days and dried for 24 hours to note the initial weight. Samples were kept immersed in a 5% Hydrochloric Acid solution with pH 2 for 30 days and shown in Figure 51.13. Percentage loss in weight and compressive strength was calculated by taking both initial and final readings that are given in Table 51.10.

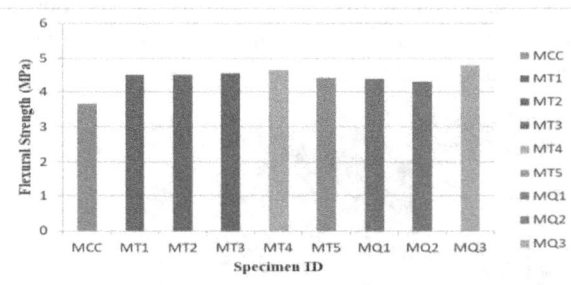

Figure 51.11 Evaluation of flexural strength
Source: Author

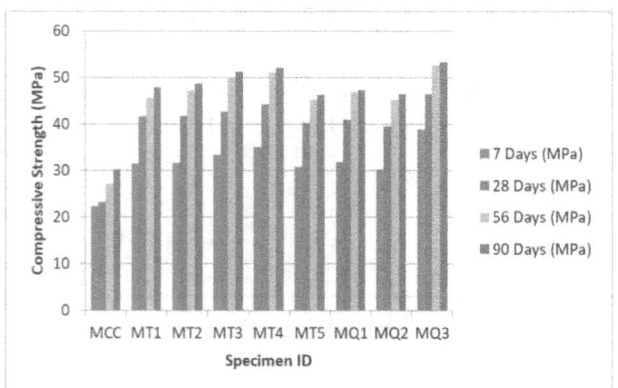

Figure 51.10 Comparison of compressive strength
Source: Author

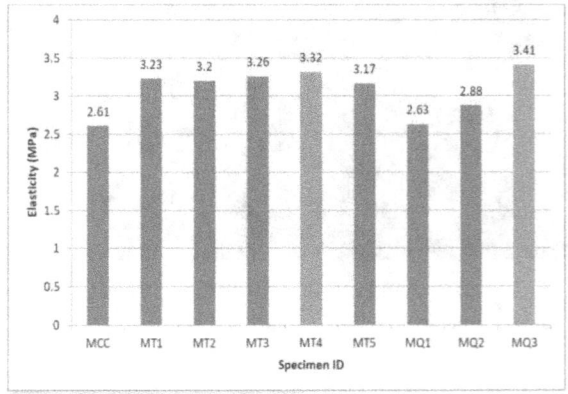

Figure 51.12 Modulus of elasticity of concrete
Source: Author

Alkaline Resistance

Alkaline resistance was assessed using a 5% sodium hydroxide (NaOH) solution with a pH of approximately 13 shown in Figure 51.14. Table 51.11 presents weight and strength loss percentages from initial and final measurements.

Figure 51.13 Specimens immersed in HCl
Source: Author

Table 51.10 Acid resistance test results

Sl. No.	Specimen ID	Initial weight (Kg)	Final weight (Kg)	% Weight Loss	Final comp. strength N/mm²	% Strength loss
1.	MCC	2.450	2.356	3.85	19.47	28.56
2.	MT1	2.656	2.575	3.05	33.82	18.75
3.	MT2	2.535	2.459	2.99	34.13	18.45
4.	MT3	2.553	2.478	2.92	34.88	18.20
5.	**MT4**	**2.435**	**2.365**	**2.87**	**36.85**	**16.50**
6.	MT5	2.550	2.474	2.98	32.7	18.43
7.	MQ1	2.445	2.369	3.12	33.18	18.98
8.	MQ2	2.670	2.578	3.43	31.75	19.56
9.	**MQ3**	**2.540**	**2.470**	**2.74**	**39.34**	**15.34**

Source: Author

Figure 51.14 Specimens immersed in NaOH
Source: Author

Table 51.11 Alkaline resistance test results

Sl. No.	Specimen ID	Initial weight (Kg)	Final weight (Kg)	% Weight Loss	Final compressive strength N/mm²	% Strength loss
1.	MCC	2.45	2.44	0.40	26.53	2.65
2.	MT1	2.65	2.64	0.27	41.02	1.43
3.	MT2	2.55	2.54	0.27	41.29	1.34
4.	MT3	2.57	2.56	0.26	42.09	1.28
5.	**MT4**	**2.45**	**2.44**	**0.25**	**43.58**	**1.25**
6.	MT5	2.56	2.55	0.29	39.68	1.24
7.	MQ1	2.46	2.45	0.29	40.44	1.24
8.	MQ2	2.66	2.65	0.30	38.98	1.24
9.	**MQ3**	**2.55**	**2.54**	**0.24**	**45.90**	**1.23**

Source: Author

Microstructural Characteristics

The morphology of SCMs combinations is visualized and determined using SEM microstructure. Achieving an even distribution of cement, aggregate and SCMs in concrete control its microstructure.

Conventional Concrete
* Matrix adhesion to surface of small particles indicates the existence of ettringite and calcium hydroxide.
* The interlocked crystals make up the thick structure of C-S-H gel becomes more visible at larger magnification, adding to the substance toughness as shown in Figure 51.15.

Ternary Blended Binder Concrete
* A finer structure has resulted from the use of micro silica particles, which have packed the gaps and the alccofine enhanced the matrix cohesiveness and bonding.
* A strong is evident between hydration products and binder ingredients, which increases the load transmission and durability. Figure 51.16 shows the SEM image of MT4.

Figure 51.15 Conventional concrete (3000X)
Source: Author

Figure 51.16 Ternary blended binder concrete (3000X)
Source: Author

Figure 51.17 Quaternary blended binder concrete (3000X)
Source: Author

Quaternary Blended Binder Concrete
* The aggregates and binding agent components makes a strongly impermeable concrete foundation and noticeable decrease in micro pores.
* Reduced porosity, improved load transmission are all the results of SCMs. Figure 51.17 display SEM of MQ3.
  The ITZ zones are found to be very strong between the aggregates and cement paste which leads to the aggregates ultimate strength.

Conclusion

This research investigated the development of combinations using different materials, leading to the following conclusions.

* Surpassing OPC the ternary blend MT4(40% alccofine, 10% micro silica, and 50% cement;) achieved the greatest 28 days strength of 44.15 MPa and 52.1 MPa at 90 days, where as other mixes exhibited modest performance. In case of quaternary mix MQ3(MQ3:10% fly ash class C, 30% alccofine, 10% micro silica and 50% cement.) showed greatest synergy among the components, with a compressive strength of 46.47 MPa (28 days) and 53.4 MPa (90 days) which is much higher than OPC. In case of flexural strength, the quaternary blend MQ3 obtained 4.81 MPa after 28 days while conventional concrete only attained 3.66 MPa, thus indicating the effectiveness of supplementary materials when combined. Increase in alccofine content, either ternary or quaternary mixtures showed strength increases. For instance, MT4 obtained 4.65 MPa and MQ3 attained 4.81 MPa, these

values represent the alccofine reinforcing effect on mechanical behavior. The quaternary blend MQ3 exhibited the lowest percentage of weight and strength loss (2.74% and 15.34% respectively), indicating superior acid resistance compared to conventional and other blended mixes. Similarly, the MQ3 mix showed lowest strength loss when compared to all other mixes indicating its resistance against the alkaline solutions. The synergistic impact of the extra cementitious ingredients is evident in the SEM images of quaternary blend and ternary blend concretes which shows a matrix with minimum visible pores and highly compact structure which symbolizes the pozzolanic reaction was effective.

From the above it can be concluded that Quaternary blended binder concrete out performs OPC and therefore cement can be replaced up to 50% (M20) using the above materials as it enhances the properties of concrete and can be applied for structural applications.

Acknowledgement

The authors express their gratitude to Field 7's RUSA 2.0-Research and Innovation-Health and Environment Scheme for its support.

References

[1] Kumar, D. C., & Vasanthi, P. (2022). Effect of coarse and fine GGBS in mechanical properties of concrete. *Materials today Proceedings Journal*, 68, 1594–1598.

[2] R Venkatesan, R. P., & Pazhani, K. C. (2015). Strength and durability properties of geopolymer concrete made with ground granulated blast furnace slag and black rice husk ash. *KSCE Journal of Civil Engineering*, 20(6), 1–8.

[3] Chelluri, S., & Hossiney, N. (2024). Performance evaluation of ternary blended geopolymer binders comprising of slag, fly ash and brick kiln rice husk ash. *Case Studies in Construction Materials*, 20, e02918.

[4] Erdem, T. K., & Kırca, O. (2008). Use of binary and ternary blends in high strength concrete. *Construction and Building Materials*, 22, 1477–1483.

[5] Lee. W. H., Wang, J. H., Ding, Y. C. & Cheng, T. W. (2019). A study on the characteristics and microstructures of GGBS/FA based geopolymer paste and concrete. *Construction and Building Materials*, 211, 807e13. https://doi.org/10.1016/ j. conbuildmat.2019.03.291.

[6] Bureau of Indian Standards (BIS), (1996). Concrete Mix Proportioning- Guidelines. IS: 10262:2019 BIS, New Delhi, India.

[7] Bureau of Indian Standards (BIS), (1959). Methods of test for strength of concrete. IS: 516, BIS, New Delhi, India.

52 Lightweight materials for electric vehicles to improve their range

Nishit M[1,a] and V.M. Murugesan[2,b]

[1]PG Scholar, Department of Automobile Engineering, PSG College of Technology, Coimbatore, India

[2]Associate Professor, Department of Automobile Engineering, PSG College of Technology, Coimbatore, India

Abstract

Businesses in today's competitive markets focus on cutting-edge technology to improve their product's performance by reducing environmental impact. The automotive industry has shown rapid improvement in manufacturing electric vehicles (EVs), which face bottlenecks such as energy efficiency and range. Reducing the weight of electric vehicles is a tried-and-true method for accomplishing this goal. Lightweight materials in specific natural fiber composites offer an appealing alternative to traditional synthetic materials. Among these, composites reinforced with banana and coconut fiber have gained interest due to their availability, biodegradability, and ideal mechanical properties. The main purpose of this work is to evaluate the potential of including coconut and banana fiber composites for bumper application in EVs by examining their toughness, durability, mechanical properties, and weight reduction potential. The results of this study show that natural fiber composites have potential tensile strength and durability, which make them ideal for lightweight automotive components. Their implementation may allow the EVs to improve their energy efficiency and create a more sustainable mobility system.

Keywords: Automotive Bumper materials, banana fiber reinforced composite, coconut fiber reinforced composite, hybrid coconut-banana, natural fiber composites

Introduction

As the global automobile sector moves towards sustainable and energy-efficient transportation, electric vehicles (EVs) are now considered a promising solution to reduce environmental impact. One of the key challenges in EV design is improving the vehicle's range without compromising safety and performance. Reducing vehicle weight is the proven method to enhance energy efficiency, as lighter vehicles require less power to operate, leading to extended battery life and reduced energy consumption. To achieve this, the adoption of lightweight and sustainable materials has become increasingly important in the development of vehicle components, including structural and impact resistance parts such as bumpers [12].

The natural fiber reinforced composites developed significant interest in recent times as an alternative to conventional synthetic fiber materials [4, 16]. The hybrid composites are made from natural and synthetic fibers [7], such as coconut and glass fibers, and have been examined for their potential in automotive structural applications. Research comparing these materials has shown that integrating coconut fiber with glass fiber in a polymer matrix can enhance strength while maintaining lightweight characteristics—an ideal combination for components like automobile bumpers [3]. Previous research has explored the potential of combining synthetic and natural fibers, such as coconut and glass fibers, within a low-density polyethylene matrix to develop hybrid composites suitable for automotive bumper applications [13]. These studies have shown that such hybrid materials can balance mechanical strength and environmental sustainability. In the automotive components, the usage of natural fibers has been widely studied for their biodegradability, low cost, and lightweight characteristics. For instance, some researchers have investigated and compared the mechanical performance of composites made from okra and banana fibers for car bumper applications [2], demonstrating that natural fiber composites can offer sufficient strength while supporting environmental sustainability. Recent advancements in natural fiber composites have focused on optimizing the combination of banana and coir fibers within polymer matrices to improve their mechanical performance for automotive applications. Such hybridization approaches have demonstrated potential in achieving both material strength and sustainability for use in vehicle components [9]. The search for

[a]23ms32@psgtech.ac.in, [b]vmm.auto@psgtech.ac.in

DOI: 10.1201/9781003770435-52

sustainable and lightweight materials in automotive design [5] has driven the use of natural fiber-reinforced composites. Studies have shown that plant-based fibers like jute, flax, and hemp provide a good balance of strength, low density, and affordability. These materials not only help reduce the weight of vehicles but also align with environmental goals due to their biodegradability. As manufacturers aim to improve efficiency and reduce emissions, such natural composites are becoming a preferred choice over synthetic fibers. Their role is particularly important in electric vehicles, where lower weight directly contributes to better performance and energy savings. Recent developments in composite materials have significantly increased the exploration of plant-based fibers for automotive applications [18, 19]. Research has shown that plantain fibers, when combined with polyester resin, can be used to develop durable and lightweight bumper fascia [20]. These natural fiber composites present a promising alternative to traditional materials, offering both mechanical strength and environmental benefits [1]. The study demonstrates that plantain fiber-reinforced composites meet the functional demands of vehicle components while promoting sustainability. This approach supports the broader goal of integrating renewable resources into modern automotive design without compromising performance.

Objective of the report: The primary goal of this research is to develop and analyze hybrid composite material by reinforcing low-density polyethylene (LDPE) with coconut and glass fibers for potential use in automotive bumper applications. The study aims to evaluate the mechanical performance of the composite, including tensile, compression, and impact strength, and to determine the optimal fiber combination that offers a balance between strength, durability, and environmental sustainability.

The development and analysis of coconut-glass fiber-reinforced polymer composites for automobile bumper components [10]. It compares the mechanical properties of hybridized and un-hybridized composites, demonstrating that the hybridized composites have superior strength and are suitable for low-strength car bumper applications [11]. The development of coconut fiber reinforced low-density polyethylene composites [6] exploring the impact of glass fiber addition on various properties such as density water absorption, tensile strength and impact

strength. The tensile strength of okra and banana fiber [14] composites have different fiber lengths and percentage composition. It finds optimal tensile strength at 30% fiber content with 50mm length for banana fibers and 10 mm length for okra fibers emphasizing the impact of these variables on mechanical performance [2]. The manufacturing and mechanical assessment of hybrid composite made from banana-coir fibers in a polyester matrix aimed at producing a replacement car window and regulator handle. The hybrid composite exhibited significant tensile and flexural strength making it a variable material for automotive applications.

Material Selection and Preparation

The selection of suitable materials is essential in developing lightweight composites for the automobile bumper. In this study, materials such as coconut fibers, banana fibers, and epoxy resin were selected by considering their properties, excellent bonding capacity, and strength enhancement characteristics.

Coconut fiber is extracted from the husk of the coconut, and banana fiber is extracted from the banana stems, where both are processed to obtain individual fibers using defibering, and then follows the process of drying the fibers to remove their moisture while preventing degradation by guaranteeing good adhesion with the epoxy resin. The properties of the fibers and resin are illustrated in Table 52.1. The fiber impurities are removed using an alkali solution to improve its matrix bonding. This process of removing impurities follows ASTM D3171, which standardizes fiber volume fraction measurements in composites.

Table 52.1 Properties of fibers

Properties	Coconut fibre	Banana fibre	Unit
Density	1150	1350	Kgm³
isotropic elasticity			
Young's modulus	2-8	27-32	GPa
Poisson's ratio	0.3	1.5	
Bulk modulus	2-5	2-5	GPa
Shear modulus	1-4	1-3	GPa
bilinear isotropic			
hardening			
Yield strength	100-200	200-500	MPa
Tangent modulus	2-6	6-15	GPa

Source: Author [6], [14]

Epoxy resin is a thermosetting polymer known for its excellent mechanical properties, strong adhesion, chemical resistance, and durability. The epoxy resin used in this study is shown in Figure 52.1. It is widely used as a matrix material in composite manufacturing due to its ability to effectively bind with various types of fibers, both synthetic and natural. Upon curing, epoxy forms a rigid and stable structure that enhances the overall strength and performance of the composite. Its compatibility with reinforcing fibers like glass, coconut, and banana fibers makes it a suitable choice for structural applications, including automotive components such as bumpers, where high impact resistance and structural integrity are essential. The epoxy resin properties used in this study are shown in Table 52.2.

Composite Fabrication Process

According to Onyedum et al. (2015), the fabrication processes important in determining the performance of the final composite. Once the fibers are prepared, the fabrication process takes place by combining the natural fibers with epoxy resin. These combinations are done accordingly by weighing the fibers to a matrix ratio in which a two-part epoxy resin and hardener system is used as matrix material. The resin is mixed with the fibers in the correct proportion to ensure balanced strength, proper curing, and flexibility that is done in a controlled condition to ensure consistency. The combinations that are used in this study are illustrated in Table 52.2.

To fabricate the composite, a hand lay-up method was used where a mold was prepared and coated with release agent to avoid adhesion, and a thin layer of epoxy resin was applied to the mold, followed by the first layer of fibers, and the process was done alternately to ensure uniform distribution. A brush is used to remove air bubbles when adding resin into the fibers.

After the lay-up, a compression process is done to remove excess resin and maintain even distribution. Then to ensure polymerization, the composite is left to cure at room temperature to allow the resin to harden and bond with fibers. The fabricated sheet is

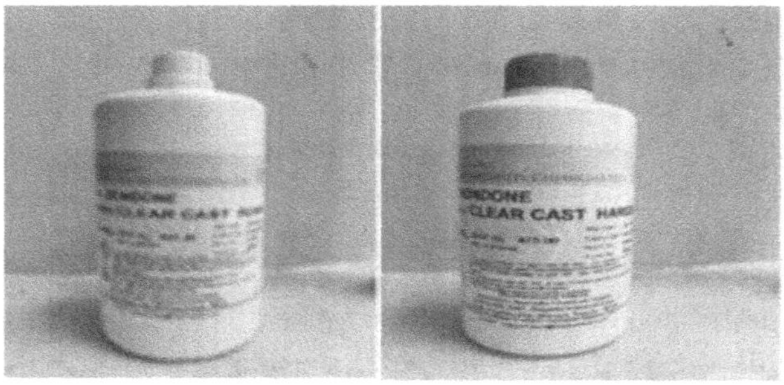

Figure 52.1 Epoxy resin used in this study
Source: Author

Table 52.2 Properties of epoxy resin

Property	Epoxy Resin	Unit
Density	1.1–1.4	g/cm^3
Tensile Strength	40–90	MPa (Megapascals)
Young's Modulus	2–5	GPa (Gigapascals)
Elongation at Break	1–6	%
Compressive Strength	80–150	MPa
Thermal Conductivity	0.25–0.35	W/m·K (Watts per meter-Kelvin)
Water Absorption	<0.5	%
Chemical Resistance	High	-

Source: Author [3]

Table 52. 3 Combination of fiber and epoxy resin used in this study

COMBINATION 1 (Hybrid)			
Coconut fiber	Banana fiber	Epoxy resin	Additives
30%	30%	35%	5%
COMBINATION 2 (Coconut)			
Coconut fiber	Banana fiber	Epoxy resin	Additives
60%	–	35%	5%
COMBINATION 3 (Banana)			
Coconut fiber	Banana fiber	Epoxy resin	Additives
–	60%	35%	5%

Source: Author [1],[2],[6],[8],[10],[14]

removed from the mold after curing, and the sheet is cut into standardized dimensions for testing.

Mechanical Testing and Characterization

To assess the composite performance, mechanical testing is performed to evaluate its compression strength, impact resistance, and tensile strength [8, 17]. The compression strength test measures the composite material's ability to withstand forces such as squeezing, which indicates the material's resistance to deformation under compression. Tensile test is used to determine the composite's ability to withstand stretch forces and its elastic modulus by measuring the maximum force the composite can withstand before breaking [15]. Impact strength tests the toughness of the composite, such as its ability to absorb and dissipate energy without breaking. These tests are done in the study by following ASTM standards, which are critical for automotive components like bumpers, as shown in Figure 52.1.

According to ASTM D695, a rectangular bar sample is compressed between two platens, and the maximum force before failure is recorded for compression strength. ASTM D638 is used to test tensile strength by increasing tensile forces on the samples

until they fail. ASTM D256 specifies the impact strength, where the composite sample is struck with a hammer at a specified speed and the energy absorbed by the composite during the impact is measured.

Result and Discussion

Tensile Strength

By testing the three combinations of the sample composite, banana fiber has moderate tensile strength, while the coconut fiber shows the highest tensile strength among all three combinations. The tensile strength of the hybrid composite is intermediate by combining both banana and coconut fiber. A graph value is shown for all three combinations in Figure 52.3–52.5.

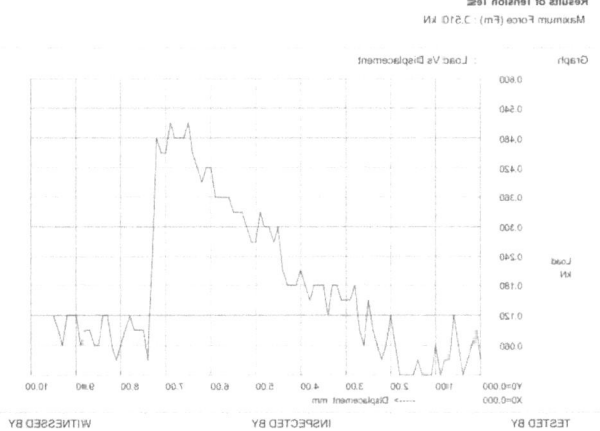

Figure 52.3 Tensile strength of banana fiber composite
Source: Author

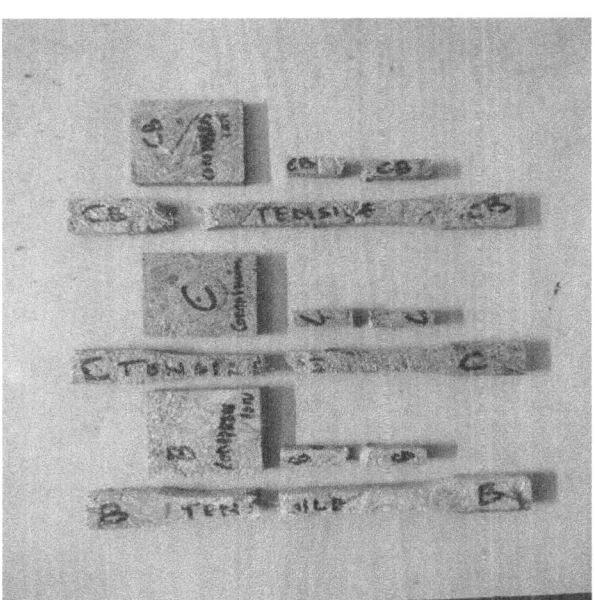

Figure 52.2 Composite specimen in ASTM standard
Source: Author

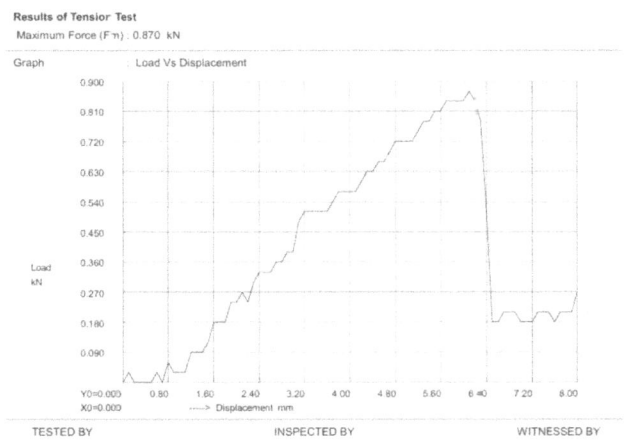

Figure 52.4 Tensile strength of Coconut fiber composite
Source: Author

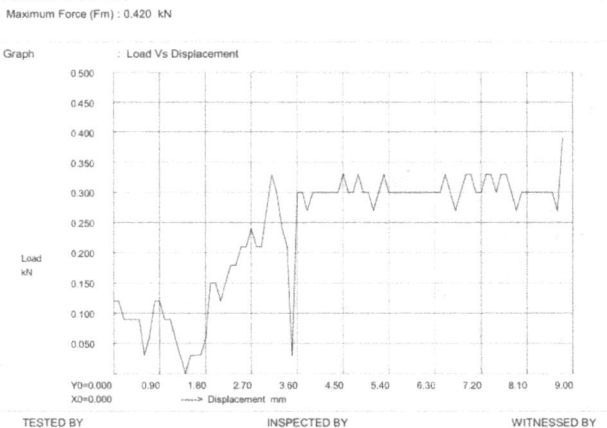

Results of Tension Test
Maximum Force (Fm) : 0.420 kN

Figure 52.5 Tensile strength of Hybrid fiber composite
Source: Author

From the analysis of the test result, coconut fiber has a high value and outperforms both banana and hybrid fiber in terms of tensile strength, which makes it suitable for applications that need resistance to stretching or pulling forces.

Impact Resistance

By testing the three combinations of the sample composite, banana fiber has the lowest impact strength, while the coconut fiber shows the highest impact strength indicating that it can absorb more energy during impact. The impact strength of the hybrid composite is intermediate as it combines both banana and coconut fiber, not reaching the resistance of pure coconut fiber [6]. A test result value is shown for all three combinations in Table 52.4.

From the analysis of the test results, coconut fiber has the highest impact strength and outperforms both banana and hybrid fiber, which makes it suitable for applications that need resistance to sudden shocks or impacts.

Compression Strength

By testing the three combinations of the sample composite, banana fiber has the lowest compression strength, while the coconut fiber shows higher tensile strength, which means it has better structural integrity during compression. The compression strength of the hybrid composite is the highest compared with both banana and coconut fiber. A graph value is shown for all three combinations in Figure

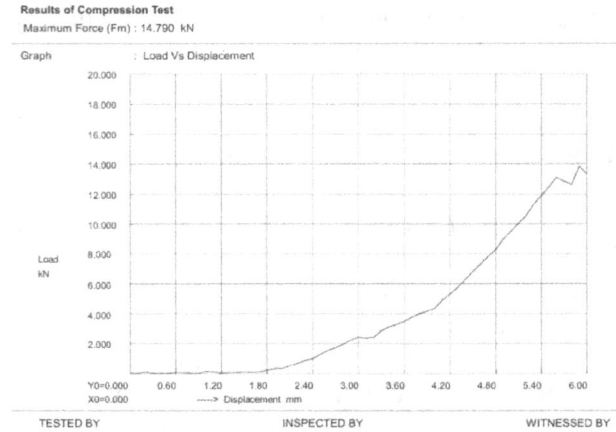

Figure 52.6 Compression strength of banana fiber composite
Source: Author

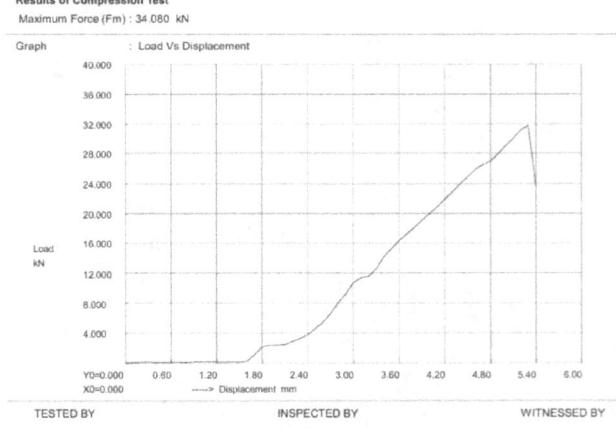

Figure 52.7 Compression strength of coconut fiber composite
Source: Author

Table 52.4 Impact resistance of fiber samples

Samples	Impact resistance
Banana fiber	2.0 J
Coconut fiber	2.0 J
Coconut and Banana fiber	2.0 J

Source: Author

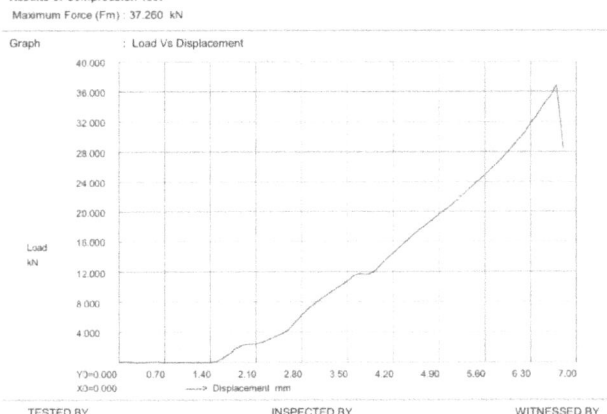

Results of Compression Test
Maximum Force (Fm) : 37.260 kN

Figure 52.8 Compression strength of the hybrid fiber composite
Source: Author

From the analysis of the test result, the hybrid fiber has a high value and best performance compared to both banana and coconut fiber in terms of compression strength, which makes it ideal for applications where the material will be targeted to compressive loads.

Conclusion

The present study aimed to evaluate the mechanical properties of natural fibers reinforced composites using banana fiber, coconut fiber, hybrid coconut-banana fiber for potential application in electric vehicle (EV) bumpers. The results indicate that each type of fiber offers unique mechanical advantages.

Coconut fiber-reinforced composite (Sample 2) exhibited the highest tensile strength (1 kN) and impact resistance (2 J), making it a strong candidate for applications requiring strength and energy absorption.

However, the hybrid composite (Sample 3), considering both Coconut and banana fibers, demonstrated superior compressive strength (37kN), surpassing the individual fiber composites. This suggests a synergistic effect when both fibers are combined, enhancing the material load-bearing capacity under compressive forces.

While banana fiber (Sample 1) showed moderate performance across all parameters, it remains a viable eco-friendly reinforcement when used in combination with strong fibers.

Overall, the hybrid composite offers a balanced combination of strength, impact resistance, and compressive properties, making it a promising sustainable alternative for automakers bumper applications. Further optimization in fiber treatment, orientation, and matrix composition may lead to even better performance, aligning with the goals of lightweight and environmentally friendly vehicle components.

References

[1] Adesina, O. T. et al. (2019). Mechanical evaluation of hybrid natural fibre–reinforced polymeric composites for automotive bumper beam: a review. *International Journal of Advanced Manufacturing Technology*, 103(5–8), 1781–1797. https://doi.org/10.1007/s00170-019-03638-w.

[2] Aculoju, S. et al. (2015). Comparative mechanical analysis of okra fiber and banana fiber composite used in manufacturing automotive car bumpers. *American Journal of Engineering*, 2(6), 193–199. http://www.openscienceonline.com/journal/ajets.

[3] Ahmad, F., Choi, H. S., & Park, M. K. (2015). A review Natural fiber composites selection in view of mechanical, light weight, and economic properties. *Macromolecular Materials and Engineering*. Wiley-VCH Verlag, p. 10–24. ://doi.org/10.1002/mame.201400089.

[4] Balo, F., & Sagbansua, L. (2025). Multi-criteria decision-making analysis of natural fibers as ceiling liners in the automotive industry. *International Journal of Automotive and Mechanical Engineering*, 22(1), 12091–12102. https://doi.org/10.15282/IJAME.22.1.2025.1.0928.

[5] Belingardi, G., Beyene, A. T., & Koricho, E. G. (2013). Geometrical optimization of bumper beam profile made of pultruded composite by numerical simulation. *Composite Structures*, 102, 217–225. https://doi.org/10.1016/j.compstruct.2013.02.013.

[6] Brahmakumar, M., Pavithran, C., & Pillai, R. M. (2005). Coconut fibre reinforced polyethylene composites: effect of natural waxy surface layer of the fibre on fibre/matrix interfacial bonding and strength of composites. *Composites Science and Technology*, 65(3–4), 563–569. https://doi.org/10.1016/j.compscitech.2004.09.020.

[7] Chikelu, P. O., Obot, O. W., & Akpan, W. A. (2025). Influence of particle size and loading variations on the tensile properties of Newbouldia laevis fibre particle reinforced polyester composite. *Unizik Journal of Technology, Production and Mechanical Systems*, 5, 1.

[8] Dhakal, S., & Keerthi Gowda, B. S. (2017). An experimental study on mechanical properties of banana polyester composite. In Materials Today: Proceedings. (pp. 7592–7598). https://doi.org/10.1016/j.matpr.2017.07.092.

[9] Hosseinzadeh, R., Shokrieh, M. M. & Lessard, L. B. (2005). Parametric study of automotive composite bumper beams subjected to low-velocity impacts. *Composite Structures*, 68(4), 419–427. https://doi.org/10.1016/j.compstruct.2004.04.008.

[10] Ibeh, C. S. et al. (2021). Coconut-glass fibre reinforce polymer composite for automobile bumper structural component; comparative analysis. *International Journal of Advances in Engineering and Management*, 3, 761. https://doi.org/10.35629/5252-0308761773.

[11] Marzbanrad, J., Alijanpour, M., & Kiasat, M. S. (2009). Design and analysis of an automotive bumper beam in low-speed frontal crashes. *Thin-Walled Structures*, 47(8–9), 902–911. https://doi.org/10.1016/j.tws.2009.02.007.

[12] Nasiruddin, M. et al. (2017). A review of energy absorption of automotive bumper beam. *International Journal of Applied Engineering Research*. 12(2), 238–245. http://www.ripublication.com.

[13] Oreko, B. U., & Okiy, S. (2025). Development of automobile bumper fascia from plantain fibre-reinforced polyester composites *Saudi Journal of Engineering and Technology*, 10(01), 1–8. https://doi.org/10.36348/sjet.2025.v10i01.001.

[14] Pothan, L. A., Oommen, Z., & Thomas, S. (2003). Dynamic mechanical analysis of banana fiber reinforced polyester composites. *Composites Science and Technology*, 63(2), 283–293. www.elsevier.com/locate/compscitech.

[15] Rahman, R., & Putra, S. Z. F. S. (2018). Tensile properties of natural and synthetic fiber-reinforced polymer composites. In Mechanical and Physical Testing of Biocomposites, Fibre-Reinforced Composites and Hybrid Composites, (pp. 81–102). https://doi.org/10.1016/B978-0-08-102292-4.00005-9.

[16] Rani, N. et al. (2025). Insights, challenges, and future trends. *International Journal of Metallurgy and Alloys Comprehensive Composite Review*, https://doi.org/10.37628/IJMA.

[17] Saba, N., Jawaid, M., & Sultan, M. T. H. (2018). An overview of mechanical and physical testing of composite materials. In Mechanical and Physical Testing of Biocomposites, Fibre-Reinforced Composites and Hybrid Composites, (pp. 1–12). https://doi.org/10.1016/B978-0-08-102292-4.00001-1.

[18] Sapuan, S. M. et al. (2005). A note on the conceptual design of polymeric composite automotive bumper system. *Journal of Materials Processing Technology*, 159(2), 145–151. https://doi.org/10.1016/j.jmatprotec.2004.01.063.

[19] Singh Pathania, M., Tomar, A., & Chaturvedi, A. (2018). Design and analysis of automotive bumper using composite materials. *International Research Journal of Engineering and Technology*, Available from: www.irjet.net.

[20] Suddin, M. N., Salit, M. S., Ismail, N., Maleque, M. A., & Zainuddin, S. (2004). Total design of polymer composite automotive bumper fascia. *Suranaree Journal of Science and Technology*, 12(1), 39–45.

53 zk-ID: A privacy-preserving identity verification framework for healthcare using blockchain, ECDSA, and zero-knowledge proofs

Abirami S. K.[1,a], G. R. Karpagam[2,b] and M. Karthikeyan[3,c]

[1]Assistant Professor, Dept. of CSE, PSGCT, India

[2]Professor, Dept. of CSE, PSGCT, India

[3]Assistant Professor, Dept. of Mech Engg, CIT, India

Abstract

Everything is becoming digital these days, health records are no exception. Digitization of healthcare sector would make the outcome improved such as enhanced patient care, but like every digitization, this has also introduced significant privacy and security concerns such as health data breaches. This paper proposes a "Health-ID Verification Framework" that combines blockchain, ECDSA and ZKPs to enable secure, GDPR-compliant health id verification. zk-ID leverages zk-SNARKS for privacy preservation, chameleon hashes are used for retroactive redaction that is in line with GDPR's "right to be forgotten" clause. Sharded Blockchain networks achieve about 1,200 TPS. Evaluations show zk-ID reduces verification latency by 62% compared to Sovrin and lowers storage costs to ₹1.67/record via hybrid on/off-chain architectures. Interoperability is achieved through FHIR/HL7 APIs while eliminating fraud through multi-authority attribute-based encryption (MA-ABE).

Keywords: Blockchain, chameleon hashes, ECDSA, GDPR regulations, zk-SNARKS

Introduction

According to the IBM report on the cost of data breach [1] has reached a whopping $4.88 million USD global average, in which the healthcare industry data breaches cost $10.1 million USD on average, making it the most expensive industry for data breaches [10]. Even though the digitization in the healthcare sector is increasing, the interoperability and data sharing is limited [2]. One of the most debated aspects by the researchers is the conflict between the GDPR right to be forgotten and the immutability nature of blockchain systems Zhang [3] which makes it harder to delete personally identifiable information (PII) particularly in public blockchain.

This paper proposes zk-ID Architecture, which is a five-layered framework (Figure 53.1) that combines zk-SNARKS, chameleon hashes and MA-ABE.

zk-SNARKS is used for selective disclosure. Threshold -governed chameleon hashes enable record edits without forks. ECDSA generates key pairs for signing health credentials. Sharding, batch proofs and hybrid storage reduces latency by 62%.

Rest of the paper is structured as follows. Section 2 reviews the extant literature and tabularizes the gaps in existing work. Section 3 describes the system architecture. Section 4 explains the implementation details. Section 5 discusses threat modelling. Section 6 summarizes the paper.

Literature review

Gaps in Centralized Systems
Even though the centralized systems such as the national health portal systems are fast, they lack transparency, this lack of transparency is often due to the complexity of the data sharing infrastructures, this leads to lack of clarity of how the data is being used which in turn erodes the public trust [4] and there is also a risk of single point failure.

Blockchain Systems and GDPR compliance
The Blockchain systems offers transparency and decentralized identity framework but it lacks GDPR compliance [8] and also, they tend to expose the metadata, which enables the adversaries to launch linkage attacks [5].

[a]ska.cse@psgtech.ac.in, [b]grk.cse@psgtech.ac.in, [c]karthikeyan.m@cit.edu.in

DOI: 10.1201/9781003770435-53

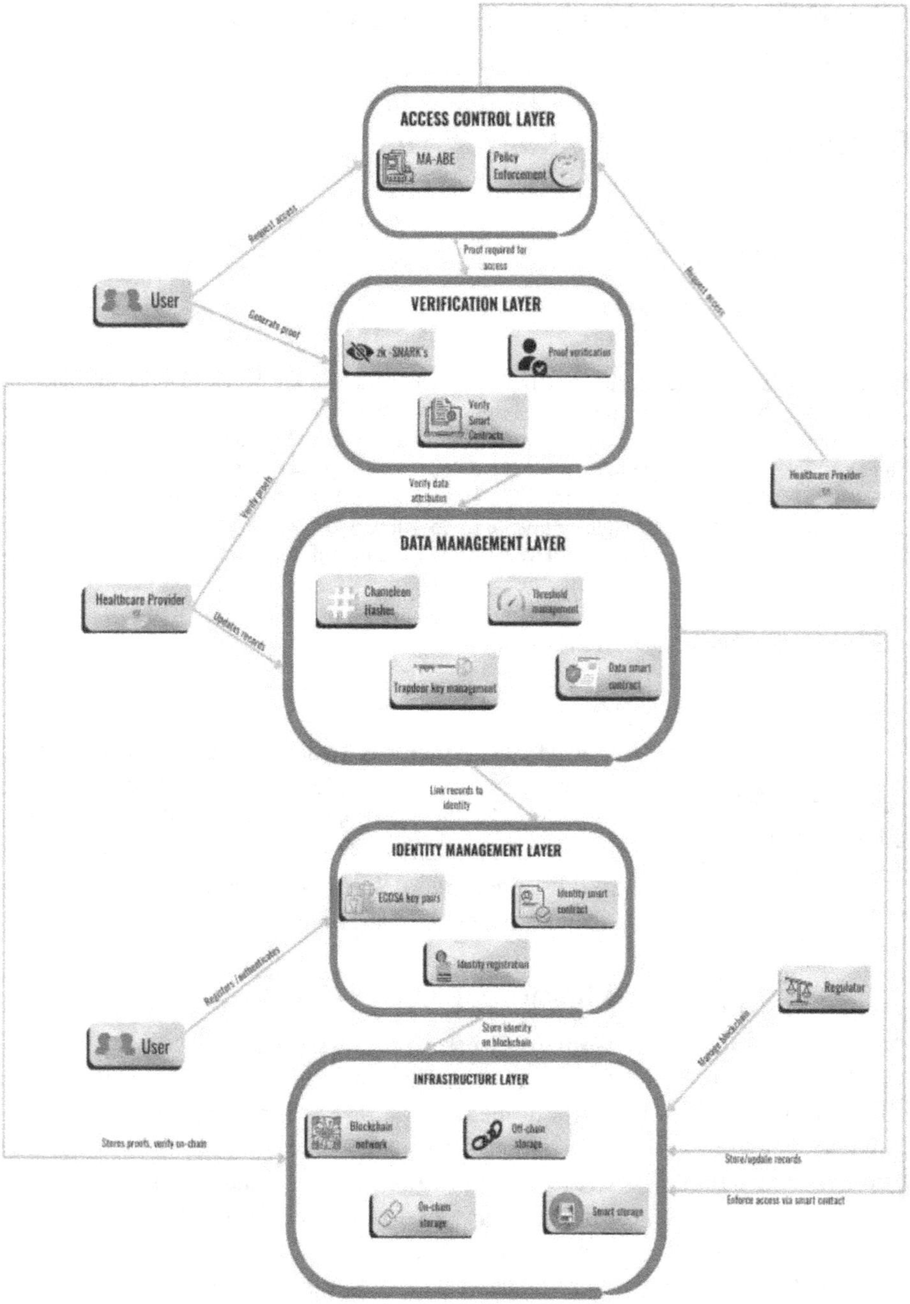

Figure 53.1 Layered framework for health-ID verification
Source: Author

Zero Knowledge Proofs and Scalability

For Privacy Preservation Zero-Knowledge Proofs are powerful, but it often struggles with scalability and performance in large-scale healthcare systems especially in systems which requires high throughput in real-time data exchange and it suffers from high computational overhead which is approximately 2s/proof [6].

ECDSA

While ECDSA doesn't support inherent selective disclosure, but they are usually designed for digital

Table 53.1 Gaps in existing work

Technology	Strengths	Limitations	How zk-ID Addresses
Centralized databases [4]	Fast, compliant	Single point of failure	Decentralized blockchain anchoring
Blockchain-only [5], [8]	Immutable, transparent	Exposes PII via public addresses	ZKP-based selective disclosure
ZKP frameworks [6]	Privacy-preserving	High computational overhead(~2s/proof)	Optimized ECDSA + zk-SNARK circuits
ECDSA-based systems [7]	Strong cryptographic security	No Privacy and No support for selective disclosure.	ZKP masks signer identity

Source: Author

signatures that verify the authenticity of the message [7] and they offer strong cryptographic security.

System Architecture

Infrastructure and Identity Layer

The permissioned Hyperledger fabric network stores SHA-256 hashes which are the cryptographic anchors of health IDs and audit logs. Sharding partitions the blockchain into sub-networks for example per hospital consortium enabling parallel transaction processing achieving a throughput up to ~1,200 TPS via PBFT consensus. This layer has the hybrid storage it has both the on chain and off-chain storage. The on-chain storage stores only cryptographic hashes (1KB/transaction) and access policies. The off-chain storage stores the encrypted health records (AES-256) on HIPAA-compliant AWS S3 cloud systems. This reduces the gas costs by ~90% compared to fully on-chain storage.

Workflow:

Step 1: User generates an ECDSA Public-private key pair (happens in identity management layer)

Step 2: User signs the health data such as the vaccination record with their private key.

Step 3: User encrypts the raw health data using AES-256 with a randomly generated symmetric key.

Step 4: Encrypted data is stored off-chain on AWS S3.

Step 5: The ECDSA signature and AES key hash are stored on-chain for verification.

Verification Layer: zk-SNARKS with Batch Processing

Client-side proof generation happens when patients generate zk-SNARK proofs. Proof generation is offloaded to edge devices instead of burdening the blockchain such as the age verification proof can be done in mobile device which only takes about ~500 ms on a mobile device. This enables batch verification up to 1000 proofs in a single blockchain transaction. The proof size scaling for zk-SNARK is *O(1)*. PLONK/Halo2 can be used for optimization which may scale proportionally at *O(n log n)*

Data Management Layer: Chameleon Hashes

Chameleon Hashes enables GDPR's "right to be forgotten" by allowing retroactive redaction of health records, without having to break blockchain integrity. Trapdoor keys require consensus among regulators to modify records; these keys are split using Shamir's secret sharing of 3-of-5 scheme to prevent single-point bottleneck during redaction. Chameleon hash updates take $<50ms$ whereas if we have to recalculate Merkle tree which would take ~$500ms$ [9].

Original hash:

$$CH1 = Hash(H1, nonce, public\_key)$$

Trapdoor key:

$$sk\ (held\ by\ regulators)$$

New hash:

$$CH1 = Hash(H2, nonce, public\_key)\ (via\ sk)$$

Where sk, H1, H2 denotes secret key and Hashes.

Access Control Layer: Multi-Authority Attribute-Based Encryption (MA-ABE)

Policy management is done in decentralized fashion, policies are enforced by multiple authorities such as hospitals, insurers and patients thereby distributing the computational load [20]. Attribute caching is performed by caching locally the frequently used attributes such as "doctor role", which considerably reduces the on-chain lookups. Policy updates are done dynamically by smart contracts, which updates the access policies in *o(1)* time which is *o(n)* in traditional role-based access control (RBAC) systems [19].

Implementation

The zk-ID framework has been implemented using modular stack of cryptographic libraries, blockchain platforms and cloud services. This section describes the tools and the libraries used for the implementation.

Blockchain Network

Permissioned blockchain Hyperledger Fabric is used for decentralized identity anchoring and audit trails [18]. Hyperledger fabric v2.5 supports private channels and PBFT consensus for hospital consortium. Go chain code was used to write smart contracts for identity registration, access control and GDPR-compliant redaction.

For consensus practical byzantine fault tolerance (PBFT) is used as it offers low-latency finality 1–2 s/block. AWS S3 cloud storage is used for storing encrypted data [14] securely such as EHRs and lab reports. AES-256 encryption is implemented vis Node.js crypto library.

Identity Management Layer

ECDSA Key generation is done for the cryptographic identity anchoring [13] for patients and doctors. The secp256k1 curve JavaScript library is used for ECDSA key pair generation

```
const ec = new elliptic.ec('secp256k1');

const keyPair = ec.genKeyPair();

const public key = keyPair.getPublic('hex');
```

Data Management Layer

Chameleon hashes are used for GDPR-compliant redaction of health records [11], Go chain code smart contracts is implemented with chameleon hash logic with trapdoor keys. Threshold cryptography [17] is implemented by Shamir's secret sharing which uses secret.js library for trapdoor key management.

Verification Layer

Once the circuit is defined and proofs are generated, gnarks can be used to verify the proofs.

Access Control Layer

Multi-authority attribute based encryption (MA-ABE) is used for fine-grained, decentralized access policies [12], Charm-crypto python library is used for attribute-based encryption. ABE-Kit is for JavaScript implementation for healthcare policies. Policy Enforcement is done using smart contracts written in Go which enforces MA-ABE policies via Hyperledger fabric.

Interoperability and Integration

zk-ID exposes FHIR-compliant endpoints to fetch and update patient records stored off-chain. SMART on FHIR integrates OAuth 2.0 for role-based access controls and maps blockchain-managed policies to FHIR scopes.

Threat Modelling: MITM and SYBIL Attacks

Man-in-the-Middle attacks

The attacker goal is to intercept/modify communication between users and the blockchain network, so that they can tamper with the health data [15]. Attack vector exploits unsecured channels such as HTTP Apis, peer-to-peer networks to eavesdrop or inject malicious payloads.

Mitigation strategy: ZKP-Based Session Tokens

The session tokens generated by the zk-SNARKs are immune to the MITM attacks. During the login session the user generates a zk-SNARK proof of their health-ID ownership without revealing the health-ID, the server validates the proof and issues a short-lived JWT token containing the proof hash

Table 53.2 Defense against attacks

Attack	zk-ID Mitigation	Technical mechanism
MITM [15]	ZKP session tokens	Tokens encode proof of health-ID ownership, not secrets
Sybil [16]	Blockchain-anchored IDS	Unique health-IDs enforced via ZKPs and duplicates are not allowed

Source: Author

Table 53.3 Scalability metrics vs. baseline systems

Metric	zk-ID	Sovrin	Ethereum
Throughput (TPS)	1,200	300	15
Verification latency	450 ms	1,200 ms	2,000 ms
Storage cost/record	₹1.67 (hybrid on/off-chain)	₹12 45 (on-chain)	₹124.50 (on-chain)
Redaction time	2s	N/A (immutable)	N/A (immutable)

Source: Author

which is sha256. The health-ID is never transmitted, only the proof of ownership is shared, even if it is intercepted the MITM attacker gains no usable information to impersonate the user.

Sybil Attacks
The attacker goal is to create multiple fake health-IDS to manipulate the network, for example voting fake votes during consensus [16]. Attack vector exploits weak identity registration policies to flood the system with fraudulent accounts.

Mitigation strategy: Blockchain-Anchored Identity Registration
zk-ID enforces sybil resistance through cryptographically secured identity registration on a permissioned blockchain. The hashed health-ID is stored on-chain and duplicates are rejected.

Security Validation
For MITM testing we have used OWASP ZAP to simulate 10,000 intercepted sessions which turned out to be 0% success rate in token forgery. For Sybil testing we have attempted bulk registration of 5,000 fake health-IDs all of which are rejected by chain code.

Performance Benchmark Comparisons
We benchmarked the performance of zk-ID to evaluate its performance against top two decentralized platforms in identity management, Sovrin (permissioned blockchain) and Ethereum (public blockchain). The included metrics are throughput in TPS, verification latency in ms, and storage cost/record measured under identical conditions 1000 concurrent requests, 4 vCPU/8GB RAM nodes. zk-ID achieved 1200 TPS using a hybrid architecture combining

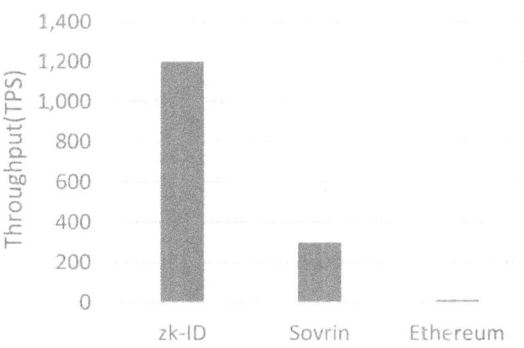
Figure 53.2 Throughput (TPS) comparison
Source: Author

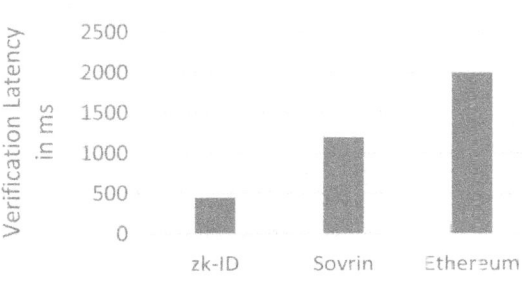
Figure 53.3 Verification latency comparison
Source: Author

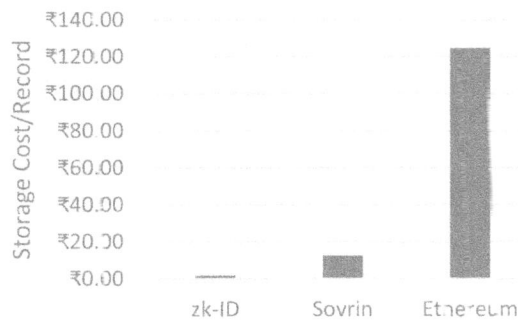
Figure 53.4 Storage cost comparison
Source: Author

Hyperledger fabric channels and batch processing of zero knowledge proofs. This outperforms Sovrin by four times and Etherum by 15 times. Groth16 proofs generated on NVIDIA T4 GPUs averaged 450 ms vs 1200 ms in Sovrin and 2000 ms in Ethereum. Hybrid storage reduced storage costs to ₹1.67/record, compared to ₹12.45/record in Sovrin.

Discussion

Contribution

GDPR-compliant immutability is achieved with the use of chameleon hashes. Generation of zero knowledge proofs along with ECDSA masks patient identities during verification while retaining cryptographic accountability thereby providing hybrid privacy. Hybrid storage is used to offload the blockchain.

Trade-offs

Privacy vs throughput: zk-SNARKS adds a latency of ~300 ms to the overall throughput but it eliminates the disclosure of publicly identifiable information.

Decentralization vs speed: Use of Hyperledger fabric permissioned blockchain for decentralized identity anchoring and audit trails prioritizes the overall throughput but at the cost of full decentralization like a public blockchain.

Size vs efficiency of ZKPs: For a circuit with n = 1000 constraints the proof size of zk-SNARKS (Groth16) scales linearly 1000~1.5KB *o(1)* whereas PLONK/Halo2 proof size scales as *o(nlogn)* 10,000~2.5KB which are optimized via polynomial commitments, but the verification time of Groth 16 is 5 ms whereas PLONK/Halo2 might take up to 10 ms.

Limitations

Trusted setup for zk-SNARKS, Scalability challenges with >10,000 concurrent verifications. Dependence of FHIR APIs for legacy EHR integration.

Future Enhancements

For quantum resistance zk-SNARKs can be replaced with zk-STARKs which requires no trusted setup. For optimization of the scalability of proof sizes instead of Groth16, PLONK/Halo2 can be used which scales proportionately, it will be useful for batch processing and it would cut gas costs by 80%. To achieve throughput of above 10,000 TPS Layer-2 Optimistic zk-Rollups can be integrated as it processes verification off-chain. FHIR Legacy systems is still a challenge which can be mitigated by Zero-trust TLS/ mTLS handshakes with API gateways. Federated Learning can be used to train anomaly detection models across hospitals. Integration of this framework with IoT wearables could be the next possible work and implementation of the framework.

Acknowledgment

The author(s) acknowledges the resources and infrastructure provided by The Centre of Cyber Security and Privacy, PSG College of Technology, Coimbatore which greatly facilitated this research.

References

[1] Mansfield-Devine, S. (2022). IBM: Cost of a data breach. *Network Security*, 8, https://doi.org/10.12968/S1353-4858(22)70049-9.

[2] Li, L., Back, E. Lee, S., Shipley, R. Mapitse, N., Elbe, S. et al. (2025). Balancing risks and opportunities: Data-empowered-health ecosystems. *Journal of Medical Internet Research*, 27, e57237.

[3] Belen-Saglam, R., Altuncu, E., Lu, Y., & Li, S. (2023). A systematic literature review of the tension between the GDPR and public blockchain systems. *Blockchain: Research and Applications*, 4(2), 100129.

[4] Zhang, J., Morley, J., Gallifant, J., Oddy, C., Teo, J. T., Hutan Ashrafian, H. et al. (2023). Mapping and evaluating national data flows: Transparency, privacy, and guiding infrastructural transformation. *The Lancet Digital Health*, 5(10), e737–e748.

[5] Liu, L., Li, X., Au, M.H., Fan, Z. and Meng, X. (2022). Metadata privacy preservation for blockchain-based healthcare systems. *Database Systems for Advanced Applications*, 404–412.

[6] Mallozzi, P. (2023). Deploying ZKP frameworks with real-world data: Challenges and proposed solutions. ArXiv:10.48550/arxiv.2307.06408.

[7] Modak, A., Jha, S., Patil, S., & Pise, R. (2024). SD-SmartCert: A blockchain-based certification system with selective disclosure. In IEEE International Conference on Blockchain and Distributed Systems Security. (pp. 1–6).

[8] Naik, N., & Jenkins, P. (2021). Sovrin network for decentralized digital identity: Analysing a self-sovereign identity system based on distributed ledger technology. In IEEE International Symposium on Systems Engineering. (pp. 1–7).

[9] SpringerReference. (n.d.). Merkle hash trees. SpringerReference:10.1007/springerreference_65288.

[10] Paul, M., Maglaras, L., Ferrag, M. A., & Almomani, I. (2023). Digitization of healthcare sector: a study on privacy and security concerns. *ICT Express*, 9(4), 571–588.

[11] Dong, Y., Li, Y., Cheng, Y. and Yu, D. (2024). Redactable consortium blockchain with access control: Leveraging chameleon hash and multi-authority attribute-based encryption. *High-Confidence Computing Journal*, 4(1), 100168.

[12] Wu, C. -Y., Huang, K. -H. & Hsu, C.-Y. (2025). A decentralised multi-authority attribute-based encryption for secure and scalable IoT access control. *Applied Sciences*, 15(7), 3890.

[13] Wang, X. (2019). Research on ECDSA-based signature algorithm in blockchain. *Finance Market*, 4(2), 55.

[14] Khande, R., Rajapurkar, S., Bade, P., Balsara, H. and Datkhile, A. (2023). Data security in AWS S3 cloud storage. In IEEE International Conference on Computing, Communication and Networking Technologies. (pp. 1–6).

[15] Schrottenloher, A., & Stevens, M. (2023). Simplified modeling of MITM attacks for block ciphers: New (quantum) attacks. *IACR Transactions on Symmetric Cryptology*, 146–183.

[16] Hafid, A., Hafid, A. S., & Samih, M. (2023). A tractable probabilistic approach to analyze Sybil attacks in sharding-based blockchain protocols. *IEEE Transactions on Emerging Topics in Computing*, 11(1), 126–136.

[17] Wu, G., Wang, W., & Yang, K. (2023). Secure voting system based on blockchain and threshold cryptography. In International Conference on Blockchain Technology and Information Security. (pp. 118–124).

[18] Honar Pajooh, H., Rashid, M., Alam, F., & Demidenko, S. (2021). Hyperledger Fabric blockchain for securing the edge Internet of Things. Sensors 21(2):359.

[19] Chandran, S. M., & Joshi, J. B. D. (2005). LoT-RBAC: A location and time-based RBAC model. In International Conference on Web Information Systems Engineering (pp. 361–375).

[20] Dixit, S., Joshi, K. P., & Choi, S. G. (2019). Multi authority access control in a cloud EHR system with MA-ABE. In IEEE International Conference on Edge Computing. (pp. 107–109).

54 Bioelectricity generation from chocolate industry wastewater treatment by a mediator-less dual-chambered microbial fuel cell

K. Priyadharshini[1,a] and S. Niju[2,b]

[1]Research Scholar, Department of Biotechnology, PSG College of Technology, India

[2]Assistant Professor (Selection grade), Department of Biotechnology, PSG College of Technology, India

Abstract

In order to protect our earth for future generations, any process, including wastewater treatment, is preferred to be sustainable. In that context, microbial fuel cells (MFC) is promising technology that can convert the organic content present in any wastewater into useful bioelectricity. Chocolate industry generates large amounts of wastewater with high organic content and suspended solids, which makes it a well-suited input material for MFCs. This work attempts to study the performance of a dual chambered MFC for the treatment of real chocolate industry wastewater. The system attained stable performance after initial acclimation phase, where no external inoculum was added. A high COD removal efficiency of 86% was attained by this dual chambered MFC system, with a coulombic efficiency of 2.2%. The maximum current density and power density attained by this MFC was 13.55mA/ m2 and 2.8 mW/m2 respectively at a resistance of 4000 Ω. The huge internal resistance was attributed to the biofouling caused by high amounts of oils and fats present in wastewater. The findings thus give detailed insights about the electrochemical performance of chocolate industry effluent fed dual chambered MFC and possible perspectives for better performance.

Keywords: Bioelectricity generation, chocolate industry wastewater, COD removal, dual chamber, microbial fuel cell

Introduction

Chocolate is one of the most widely consumed food products and flavors across the globe [17]. The global chocolate market is on its peak growth with a value of 119.39 billion USD in 2023 and is projected to grow with a compound annual growth rate (CAGR) of 4.1% during 2024 to 2030. Being such a revenue generating industry, it also creates serious environmental impacts if left unnoticed. There are many unit operations involved in chocolate manufacturing industries, that consume water as well as releases considerable quantities of high strength wastewater. Chocolate industry wastewater (CIWW) is characterized by a brown color with a distinct odor, high chemical oxygen demand (COD), biological oxygen demand (BOD) and suspended solids. Many types of treatment technologies including physical, chemical, physio-chemical and biological methods have been employed for treatment of CIWW. All of these methods concentrate on effective COD removal from wastewater, each offering distinct advantages and having certain limitations [19].

Microbial fuel cells (MFC) represent a key category of bio electrochemical systems that enable the direct conversion of biomass into electricity, through the metabolic activity of a special class of microorganisms called exoelectrogens [9]. When operated with wastewater as substrate, MFCs not only generate electricity but they also contribute to removal of pollutants, potentially reducing the operational costs associated with conventional wastewater treatment [4]. MFC technology thus serves as a bridge between Sustainable Development Goals 6 and 7 by addressing wastewater treatment challenges while simultaneously recovering renewable energy. The high organic content and biodegradability of CIWW makes it a suitable substrate for treatment in MFCs. Among different configurations of MFC, Single chambered MFCs are simpler, cost-effective and well suited for scaling up scenarios. But dual chambered MFCs are still preferred for research as they give better control, flexibility and better chance for optimization of anode and cathode environments. The performance of any MFC system is quantified in two ways - bioelectricity generation and wastewater treatment efficiency [6]. In general, a plot between voltage and current, called polarization curve, is used as a tool to understand the electrochemical behavior

[a]priya.preethi92@gmail.com, [b]sn.bio@psgtech.ac.in

DOI: 10.1201/9781003770435-54

of MFC and it helps to identify the internal limitations of the system.

Only few research works have been published with CIWW as substrate for MFCs so far. An activated sludge based dual chamber MFC was developed for CIWW earlier. But it was analyzed mainly for the microbial communities present in the anodic biofilm and suspension [16]. Moreover, it has already been proven that inoculation with pure or mixed microbial culture is not necessary for MFC and natural acclimation itself provides better performance. Thus, in this work, a mediator-less and inoculum-less dual-chambered MFC was developed with an optimal distance between electrodes for the treatment of CIWW and its performance was studied in terms of its COD removal efficiency and polarization curve.

Materials and Methods

Collection and Characterization of Chocolate Industry Wastewater

CIWW used in this study was collected from a local chocolate manufacturing industry at Coimbatore, Tamil Nadu (India). It was collected in a sterile container and stored immediately after collection at 4°C until further use. The parameters including pH, conductivity and total dissolved solids (TDS) were measured using LoviBond multiparameter analyzer. The determination of COD value was done by closed reflux titrimetric method, according to APHA. All the chemicals used in this study were of analytical grade. The characteristics of the collected CIWW are listed in Table 54.1. The wastewater was dark brown in color with strong odor.

Fabrication and operation of dual-chamber MFC

A dual-chambered MFC was constructed using plexiglass material with each chamber (anode and cathode) having a working volume of 240 mL. Graphite electrodes were used as anode and cathode of the

Table 54.1 Physio-chemical characteristics of chocolate industry wastewater

Parameters	Units	Values
pH		4.43 ± 0.05
COD	mg/L	7000 ± 150
Total dissolved solids (TDS)	ppm	1330 ± 45
Conductivity	mS/cm	2 ± 0.2 mS

Source: Author

MFC with an effective surface area of 38 cm² each. The electrodes were spaced 2.5 cm from each other. A 15 cm² Nafion 117 membrane was employed as proton exchange membrane between the two chambers. The anode chamber was completely filled with buffered CIWW and maintained under anaerobic conditions. The cathode chamber was filled with 50mM potassium ferricyanide solution, which acted as the oxidant for carrying out cathodic reduction reaction. The anolyte was continuously stirred to ensure homogeneity in substrate concentration. As previously stated, no external inoculum was added and indigenous microbes present in the CIWW were allowed to acclimate and form biofilm on the anode. Electrical connections were established using copper wires and voltage was measured with a multimeter. The dual chamber MFC was operated in fed-batch mode at room temperature and anode biofilm was reused as such, in subsequent cycles. COD of anolyte was measured during beginning and end of each cycle and voltage was recorded at regular intervals throughout the MFC operation. The polarization data was collected once the system got acclimatized with a stable voltage indicating a stable biofilm. Resistances of different loads were connected from high to low and the voltage values were recorded. Corresponding current values were calculated using Ohm's law. Plotting current density versus voltage gives polarization curve whereas plotting current density versus power density gives power curve. Operational efficiency of our MFC can be evaluated by analyzing these two curves.

Results and Discussion

Electrochemical performance of CIWW powered DC-MFC

As the pH of CIWW was on the acidic range, phosphate buffer was added to CIWW to make it neutral, for it to be employed as substrate for the dual-chambered MFC. Full strength raw wastewater was used only for the initial cycles in order to facilitate acclimation, after which half strength CIWW was used in all subsequent cycles. The acclimation phase promoted the development of biofilm on the anode. The anode biofilm was undisturbed for use in subsequent cycles and little quantity of anolyte was transferred to subsequent cycles [11]. OCV is the OCV attained by the MFC when no load is connected to it. OCV readings were measured using multimeter from the beginning of the 1st cycle. Figure 54.1 represents the OCV trend of the first five cycles, each of which lasted for around 10 days. As can be observed from the OCV graph, the system has acclimated well in the first three cycles and stable OCV peaks were attained in the 4th and 5th cycles. CIWW is mainly comprised of sugars and lipids. The microbes present initially metabolize the sugars and once the sugars are depleted, they metabolize the lipids. This is the reason for two OCV peaks in 2nd and 3rd cycles, first indicating utilization of sugars and second indicating the utilization of lipids. But this is not the case with 4th and 5th cycles as only one peak can be observed. The reason behind this is the addition of anolyte from previous cycles which could have become enriched with lipid metabolizing microorganisms and thus sugar and lipid breakdown have happened simultaneously. The peak OCV was observed to be 510 mV for this CIWW fed DC-MFC. In MFCs, though exoelectrogens are enriched through acclimation process, fermentative bacteria play an important role in metabolizing complex substrates into simple substrates [7].

Figure 54.2 represents the polarization curve of the CIWW fed MFC system, which shows us how well the MFC maintains a voltage as a function of current production. Here, at the 6th cycle, when the system is running at a stable peak voltage, resistances of different values are connected to the circuit (the open circuit is thus made into closed circuit) and corresponding voltage values are recorded. The current

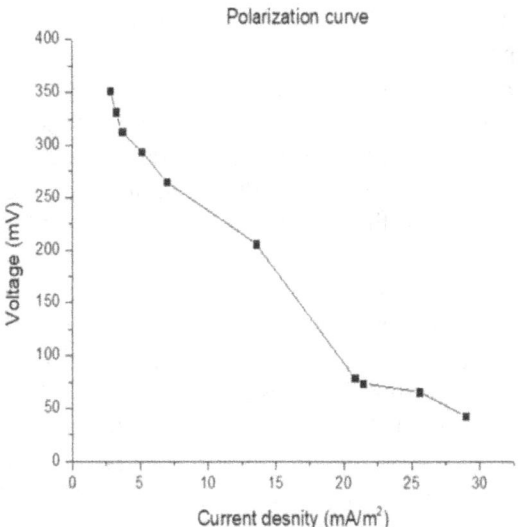

Figure 54.2 Polarization curve of dual-chambered MFC fed with chocolate industry wastewater as substrate
Source: Author

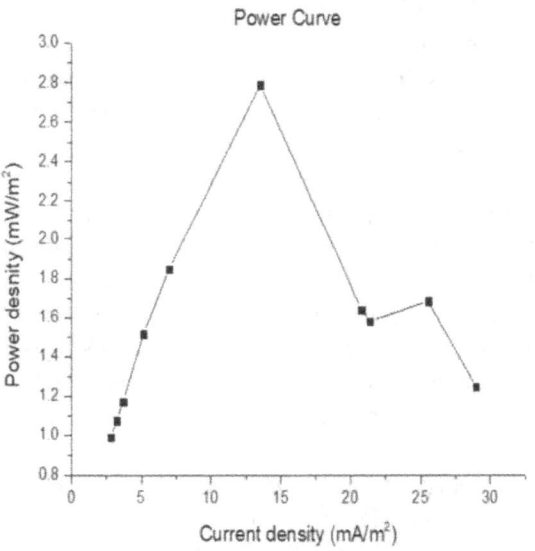

Figure 54.3 Power curve of dual-chambered MFC fed with chocolate industry wastewater as substrate
Source: Author

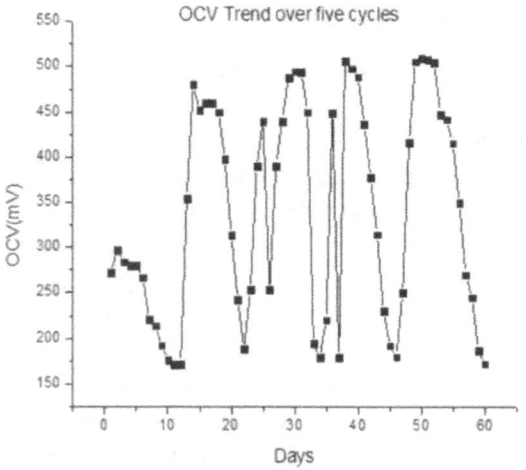

Figure 54.1 OCV trend of a dual-chambered MFC operated with chocolate industry wastewater
Source: Author

density values are calculated by using Ohm's law and normalizing current to the effective electrode surface area. This curve gives information about the electrochemical behavior of the system, showing regions where various types of losses reduce the useful current [10]. At low current densities, activation losses are dominant which is related to the energy barrier for electrochemical reactions at anode and cathode.

Here, since the ideal potassium ferricyanide was used as catholyte, the activation losses were mainly due to the inefficiency at the anode side. At moderate current densities, ohmic losses are encountered. Here, already good conductive electrodes and membrane were used and ideal spacing was maintained between the electrodes. Thus, these losses were unavoidable here and it influences the internal resistance of the system partly. At higher current densities, concentration or mass transfer losses are dominant. Here, bulking of the anodic biofilm in subsequent cycles can be one reason for typical mass transfer losses. Catholyte should also be provided with continuous stirring to reduce these losses at the cathode side.

Figure 54.3 represents the power curve of the CIWW fed dual-chambered MFC system. Based on the polarization data, power density was calculated for each of the current density values and thus power curve was developed. The maximum current density and power density attained by this system was 13.55 mA/ m^2 and 2.8 mW/m^2 respectively at a resistance of 4000 Ω. Thus, the internal resistance of the system was also found, which is higher compared to their single chamber counterparts.

Treatment efficiency of CIWW powered DC-MFC

After the acclimation phase, the DC-MFC showed a significant COD removal efficiency of 86% (6th cycle) which is higher when compared to the COD removal of 69% during the 2nd cycle. Coulombic efficiency of the system was calculated, which is a key parameter that reveals how much electrons derived from the substrate, are efficiently captured and transferred to anode for bioelectricity generation [5]. Coulombic efficiency (CE) was calculated to be 2.2% for the corresponding COD removal efficiency

of 86% and volumetric power density of 44.20 mW/ m^3. This low CE indicates that the majority of COD removal was due to the activity of organisms other than exoelectrogens, including methanogens and fermentative bacteria [12].

Comparison with other wastewater powered DC-MFCs

Substrate selection plays a very important role in any biological process, as it serves both as carbon and energy source for the metabolic activity of microbes. The chemical composition and concentration of the components present in the respective substrate, influences the performance of any Bioelectrochemical system [14]. The substrate not only shapes the structural and functional dynamics of the anodic microbial community but also significantly influences the overall performance of MFC including maximum power density and coulombic efficiency [15]. Food industry based wastewater including cassava industry wastewater, starch industry wastewater, brewery wastewater, winery wastewater, potato processing wastewater have been used as substrates for dual-chambered MFCs and have shown good performance [3]. Table 54.2 compares the performance of dual-chambered MFCs employing various food industry-based wastewaters.

As can be observed from the table, this study has achieved better performance in terms of COD removal efficiency as well as electricity generation compared to the previous study of CIWW fed DC-MFC. This can be attributed to the biofilm formation through natural acclimation process rather than using an external inoculum [8]. But when compared to other similar wastewaters fed MFC, CIWW fed MFC has performed less. This can be due to the biofouling of

Table 54.2 Performance of Chocolate Industry Wastewater fed DC-MFC compared to previous research and other wastewater fed MFCs

Substrate	Power density	Coulombic efficiency	COD removal	Reference
Chocolate industry wastewater	2.8 mW/m^2	2.2%	86%	This study
Chocolate industry wastewater	1.5 mW/m^2	-	75%	Patil et al. [16]
Fermented apple juice	78 mW/m^2	4.7%	-	Cercado-Quezada et al. [2]
Cheese whey	46 mW/m^2	11%	94%	Tremouli et al. [18]
Food processing wastewater	81 mW/m^2	-	95%	Oh and Logan [13]

Source: Author

membrane caused by the high amounts of fats and oils present in chocolate processing wastewater [1]. Moreover, certain compounds in chocolate like theobromine, caffeine and polyphenols may inhibit the growth of certain microbial populations including exoelectrogenic bacteria, which may have affected the performance of this MFC.

Conclusion

Dual chambered MFCs are commonly used for understanding the performance of any substrate in the initial stages of research. Though chocolate industry wastewater has been employed in several single chamber MFCs, detailed study of the same in dual-chambered MFC was limited. In this article, CIWW fed DC-MFC was studied in detail, especially with respect to its electrochemical performance covering the causes of various types of losses encountered during the operation of MFC. The system has achieved a maximum power density of 44.20mW/m^3, COD removal of 86% and coulombic efficiency of 2.2%. On comparing the performance of this MFC with other substrate fed MFCs, it was found that there are certain limitations with chocolate industry effluent including the presence of high amounts of fat and oils and other inhibitory compounds. These challenges can be mitigated by applying appropriate pretreatment techniques like oil separation or electrocoagulation, which will make the chocolate industry effluent to be more MFC friendly. Microbial community analysis would give much more insights about the causes for low energy conversion and thus necessary modifications can be made to overcome those causes.

References

[1] Babanova, S., Jones, J., Wiseman, K., Soles, J., Garcia, J., Huerta, P., et al. (2022). Bioelectrochemical Treatment Technology—The New Practical Approach for Wastewater Management and GHG Emissions Reduction. *Frontiers in Chemical Engineering, 4*, 1–16.

[2] Cercado-Quezada, B., Delia, M. -L., & Bergel, A. (2010). Testing various food-industry wastes for electricity production in microbial fuel cell. *Bioresource Technology, 101*(8), 2748–2754.

[3] Dahiya, S., Kumar, A. N., Shanthi Sravan, J., Chatterjee, S., Sarkar, O., & Mohan, S. V. (2018). Food

waste biorefinery: Sustainable strategy for circular bioeconomy. *Bioresource Technology, 248*, 2–12.

[4] Elakkiya, E., & Niju, S. (2021). Bioelectrochemical treatment of real-field bagasse-based paper mill wastewater in dual-chambered microbial fuel cell. *3 Biotech, 11*(2), 42.

[5] Ge, Z., Li, J., Xiao, L., Tong, Y., & He, Z. (2014). Recovery of Electrical Energy in Microbial Fuel Cells. *Environmental Science & Technology Letters, 1*(2), 137–141.

[6] Gude, V. G. (2016). Wastewater treatment in microbial fuel cells - an overview. *Journal of Cleaner Production, 122*, 287–307.

[7] Lee, H.-S., Parameswaran, P., Kato-Marcus, A., Torres, C. I., & Rittmann, B. E. (2008). Evaluation of energy-conversion efficiencies in microbial fuel cells (MFCs) utilizing fermentable and non-fermentable substrates. *Water Research, 42*(6–7), 1501–1510.

[8] Liu, H., Ramnarayanan, R., and Logan, B.E. (2004). Production of electricity during wastewater treatment using a single chamber microbial fuel cell. *Environmental Science & Technology, 38*(7), 2281–2285.

[9] Logan, B. E. (2009). Exoelectrogenic bacteria that power microbial fuel cells. *Nature Reviews Microbiology, 7*(5), 375–381.

[10] Logan, B. E., Hamelers, B., Rozendal, R., Schröder, U., Keller, J., Freguia, S., et al. (2006). Microbial fuel cells: methodology and technology. *Environmental Science & Technology, 40*(17), 5181–5192.

[11] Naina Mohamed, S., Thota Karunakaran, R., and Manickam, M. (2018). Enhancement of bioelectricity generation from treatment of distillery wastewater using microbial fuel cell. *Environmental Progress & Sustainable Energy, 37*(2), 663–668.

[12] Nimje, V.R., Chen, C.Y., Chen, C.C., Chen, H.R., Tseng, M.J., Jean, J.S., et al. (2011). Glycerol degradation in single-chamber microbial fuel cells. *Bioresource Technology, 102*(3), 2629–2634.

[13] Oh, S. E., & Logan, B. E. (2005). Hydrogen and electricity production from a food processing wastewater using fermentation and microbial fuel cell technologies. *Water Research,39*(19), 4673–4682.

[14] Pandey, P., Shinde, V. N., Deopurkar, R. L., Kale, S. P., Patil, S.A., & Pant, D. (2016). Recent advances in the use of different substrates in microbial fuel cells toward wastewater treatment and simultaneous energy recovery. *Applied Energy, 168*, 706–723.

[15] Pant, D., Bogaert, G. Van, Diels, L., & Vanbroekhoven, K. (2010). A review of the substrates used in microbial fuel cells (MFCs) for sustainable energy production. *Bioresource Technology, 101*(6), 1533–1543.

[16] Patil, S. A., Prasad, V., Koul, S., Ijmulwar, S., Vivek, A., Shouche, Y. S., et al. (2009). Electricity generation using chocolate industry wastewater and its treatment in activated sludge based microbial fuel cell and analysis of developed microbial community

in the anode chamber. *Bioresource Technology,* 100 (21), 5132–5139.

[17] Perez, M., Lopez-Yerena, A., & Vallverdú-Queralt, A. (2022). Traceability, authenticity and sustainability of cocoa and chocolate products: a challenge for the chocolate industry. *Critical Reviews in Food Science and Nutrition,* 62(2), 475–489.

[18] Tremouli, A., Antonopoulou, G., Bebelis, S., & Lyberatos, G. (2013). Operation and characterization of a microbial fuel cell fed with pretreated cheese whey at different organic loads. *Bioresource Technology,* 131, 380–389.

55 BMI-dependent gut microbial signatures for colorectal cancer prediction: a metagenomic approach

Hema Palanisamy[1,a] and Subramanian Vidyalakshmi[2,b]

[1]Research Scholar, Department of Biotechnology, PSG College of Technology, Coimbatore, India

[2]Associate Professor, Department of Biotechnology, PSG College of Technology, Coimbatore, India

Abstract

Colorectal cancer (CRC) is one of the most reported cancers with high mortality rate. Overweight and obesity are some of the major risk factors for many diseases including CRC. Gut microbiomes comprise diverse community of microbes and their dysbiosis contributes to many diseases. Gut microbial diversity varies during CRC and also across different body mass index (BMI) categories. However, the gut microbiome influenced overweight and obese conditions on CRC is underexplored. Microbial biomarkers contributing to BMI influenced CRC is not available up to date. Shotgun metagenome data is one of the effective methods to study the gut microbial community structure and function. Hence, this study aims at identifying global microbial biomarkers and building machine learning model across different BMI groups for predicting CRC.

Keywords: Colorectal cancer, gut microbiome, machine learning, metagenome, obesity, overweight

Introduction

Colorectal cancer (CRC) is the third most diagnosed cancer (6.1%) with the second highest mortality rate of 9.2%. An estimation shows that the deaths caused by rectum and colon cancer will increase by 60% and 71.5% by Sawicki et al. [17]. Overweight (BMI $\geq$ 25–30 kg/m2) and obesity (BMI $\geq$ 30 kg/m2) are established risk factors for various diseases, including CRC. People who are overweight and obese have a higher risk of 18% and 32% for CRC respectively as compared to normal weight people. Obesity is an independent risk factor for early-onset CRC in both men and women [3]. The gut microbiome constitutes a diverse community of microorganisms, and its dysbiosis is one of the key players in colorectal carcinogenesis. Commensal bacteria residing in the gut helps in enhancing host innate immunity and maintain mucosal integrity. These microbes communicate among themselves and with the host, resulting in greater influence on homeostasis and disease development. *Fusobacterium nucleatum,* a gram-negative bacterium, acts as a potential biomarker for CRC, and its increased levels are related to decreased overall survival [19]. Obesity could affect the gut microbiome environment. Reduced diversity and changes at the phylum level have been observed during obesity. *Firmicutes* and *Bacteroidetes* phyla were increased in obese individuals compared to lean individuals. *Akkermansia muciniphila* was enriched during weight loss, and its administration could prevent obesity related complications. Reduction in the *Enterococcus faecalis* may be associated with obesity-related CRC [18]. Advanced technologies such as metagenomics, metatranscriptomics and metabolomics have been effective in profiling the microbial ecosystems. However, due to their complex data analysis, their effectiveness is not fully explored. Machine learning algorithms are employed in understanding microbial signatures, identifying biomarkers and providing efficient models for predicting the phenotypes. Microbiome-based biomarker identification is a non-invasive method for better prognosis, diagnosis of diseases and personalizing medicine [8]. A study reported that machine learning based models on gut microbiomes could be a non-invasive diagnostic technique for liver cirrhosis or fibrosis [11]. Hence, this study aims to explore the BMI-induced variation in the CRC gut microbiome, to build machine learning models for predicting CRC and to identify potential biomarkers from the above model.

_____

[a]phemadhawan@gmail.com, [b]svd.bio@psgtech.ac.in

DOI: 10.1201/9781003770435-55

Methodology

Retrieval of data and processing

We retrieved global gut metagenome data of CRC patients (n = 200) and healthy individuals (n = 200) from the ENA database across eight different studies under the accession numbers PRJDB4176 (Japan), PRJEB6070 (Germany, France) [29], PRJEB7774 (Austria) [4], PRJEB10878 (China) [28], PRJEB12449 (USA) [23], PRJEB27928 (Germany) [25], PRJNA447983 (Italy) [21], PRJNA531273 and PRJNA397112 (India) [6] comprising datasets across three major continents. The data were categorized into two groups as overweight (BMI ≥25) and normal (BMI <25) based on BMI and CRC and NA (healthy) based on the presence or absence of the disease.

Taxonomic and Functional Analysis

The datasets were quality-checked with the FastQC tool, and a phred quality score threshold was set to 30 for quality checks. We deployed a Linux-based pipeline, SqueezeMeta [20], to profile metagenomic datasets. This tool uses trimmomatic to remove low-quality bases from the reads. The raw reads were assembled into contigs using MegaHIT assembler, and the genes were predicted using Prodigal. It employs the Diamond aligner for mapping contigs with databases for taxonomic and functional profiling. For the taxonomic assignment of contigs, the GenBank nr database was used. The KEGG database was used for functional profiling. The abundance was estimated by mapping the raw reads against the contigs using the Bowtie2 tool.

Data analysis

All the datasets were quality-checked and fed to the SqueezeMeta pipeline. Then, they were processed, and the resultant ORF table files were taken for further analysis. Finally, all the files were merged appropriately using the tidyverse package in R software.

Diversity analysis

Microbiome diversity across the sample groups was studied using the Shannon index and Chao1 index [26]. The Shannon index describes the richness and evenness of microbes, and the Chao1 index is based on species richness calculated using the number of observed species and their frequency. Pairwise Wilcoxon test was used to analyze the statistically significant difference across the categories.

Machine learning modelling

The microbial abundance data (genus and species level) and their functional profile (KEGG function) were used to identify key predictors in the normal and overweight BMI groups. Seven machine learning models were employed to identify the high-performing model. The performance of the models was evaluated using accuracy, precision, recall and F1-scores. All machine learning models were built using Python's scikit-learn package. The datasets were classified into training and test datasets for predicting CRC across BMI categories. Important features contributing to the model prediction were retrieved.

Results

Sample processing

A total of 400 datasets were taken for the analysis and underweight samples were removed based on the BMI criteria (BMI<18.5). The metagenomic datasets (CRC = 185 and NA = 187) were retrieved and the samples were classified based on BMI as overweight (n = 159) and normal (n = 213). Taxonomic and functional profiles of the samples were performed using SqueezeMeta pipeline. The raw reads were quality checked and assembled into contigs ORF regions were predicted and these ORFs were annotated for taxonomy using RDP (Ribosomal Database Project) classifier and function using KEGG database.

Diversity analysis

The diversity of the microbiome across the classified categories were measured using Shannon and Chao1 index. Shannon diversity (Figure 55.1) shows both species richness and evenness of the microbiome. Overweight group had a higher diversity when compared to the normal group. CRC and NA within the group did not show any clear distinction of microbial diversity. Women with a higher BMI had a higher Shannon diversity of vaginal microbiome as compared to the healthy women [1].

Chao1 (Figure 55.2) measures the species' richness of the gut microbiome. CRC group showed a higher species richness as compared to the NA group. Overweight group had a higher species richness as compared to the normal group. Overweight_CRC group had a higher species richness as compared to all the other groups. These results are in coherence with the previous study which identified increased

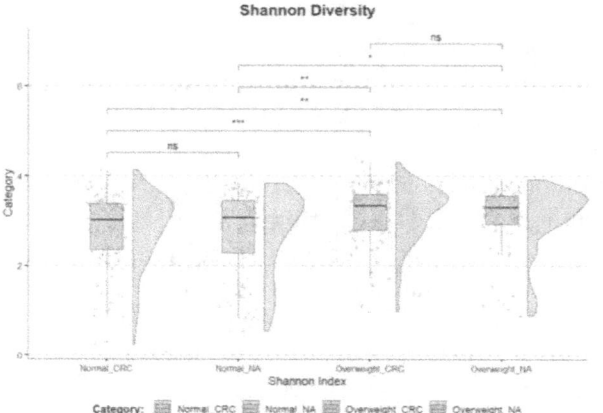

Figure 55.1 Shannon diversity index across categories
Source: Author

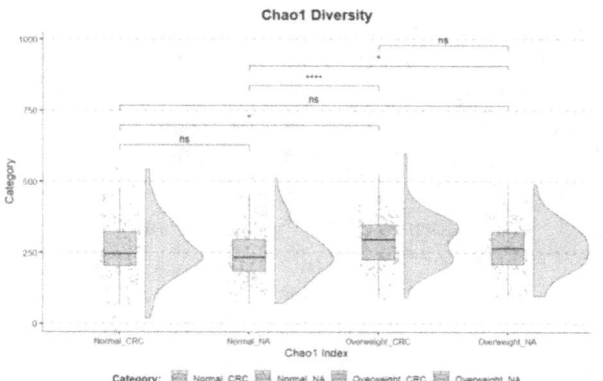

Figure 55.2 Chao1 diversity index across categories
Source: Author

alpha diversity index (Shannon and Chao1) in CRC patients [18].

Taxonomic profile-based machine learning modelling

We employed seven machine learning algorithms: Logistic Regression, K-nearest neighbors (KNN), Support Vector Machines (SVM), Decision Trees, Random Forest (RF), Naive Bayes, Gradient Boosting (GB) for predicting CRC from NA across two different BMI categories. RF model was employed to predict the risk of CRC with the classification of patients into subgroups [10]. Machine learning approaches were employed to predict cancer types based on the tissue specific microbial abundance information. An RF model was trained with microbial abundance data from TCGA database for classifying five different types of cancer [5]. In addition metagenome based

modelling showed higher performance when compared to amplicon based modelling and gut microbiome shown to be a promising strategy for diagnosing intestinal diseases [8].

For genus abundance-based models, RF and GB showed a higher performance for both overweight and normal groups.

For species level, RF performed better when compared to other models in normal groups. In overweight group, RF and LR had higher performance scores.

Overall the results suggests that species-based RF model can be used for CRC prediction across the BMI categories. Machine learning models based on intestinal microbiota were able to predict lymph node metastasis [27]. A study compared six different models such as LR, RF, SVM, GB, neural network, CatBoost for predicting poorly differentiated CRC based on intestinal microflora. Among them, RF had a higher prediction accuracy [15]. XGBoost and RF model were effective in predicting stages of CRC [12].

Functional profile based modelling

We also extended our analysis with the functional profile of the microbiome. KEGG function data was

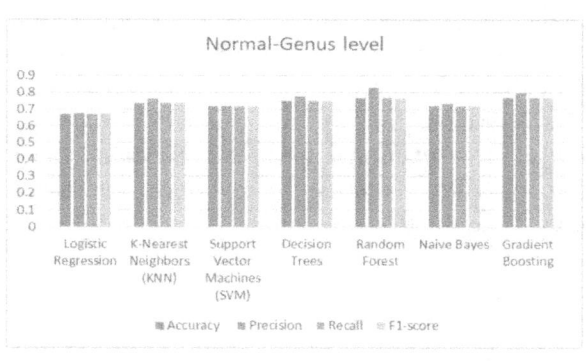

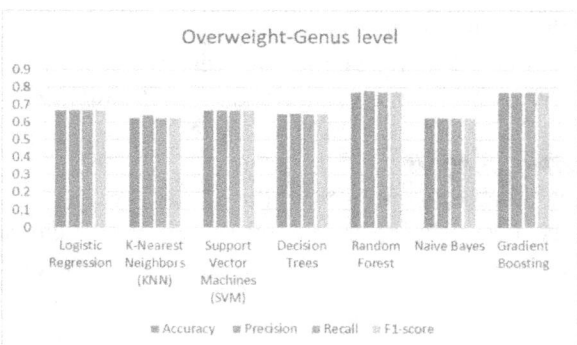

Figure 55.3 Genus abundance-based ML model performance metrics
Source: Author

Figure 55.4 Species abundance-based ML model performance metrics

Source: Author

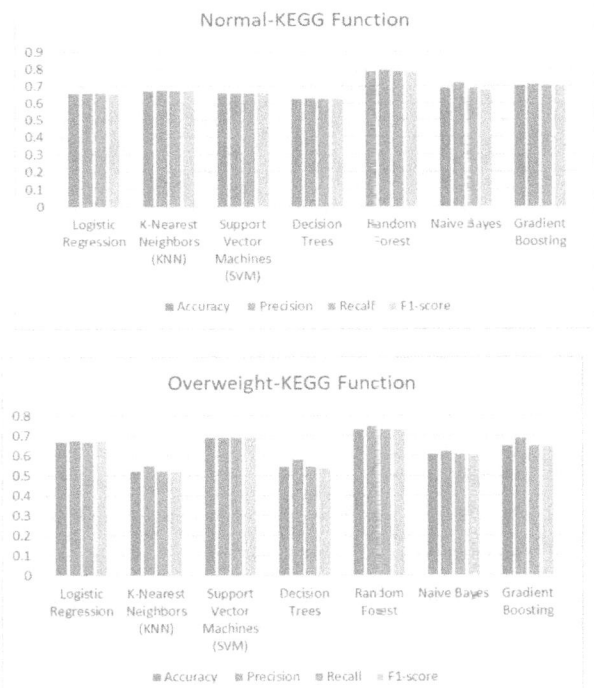

Figure 55.5 KEGG function-based ML model performance metrics

Source: Author

used for building the models (Figure 55.5). Machine learning approaches were also employed on functional profiles and found functional profile had better prediction of CRC and adenoma when compared to models based on taxonomic profiles. They also helped to identify functional implication of gut microbiota on CRC and adenoma which can be utilized for better prediction [2].

For normal groups, only RF had better performance but, in overweight group RF, SVM and LR had higher performance. Based on the functional profile models also RF had better prediction scores in predicting CRC.

Biomarkers for CRC

Based on the model performance analysis, species abundance-based RF showed higher performance metrics scores for CRC prediction based on taxonomic profile. For KEGG function also RF had higher performance metrics. Hence, we explored the feature importance for RF model to identify biomarkers and key influencers across the groups. Figure 55.6 illustrates the top 10 important features of RF models. This shows the clear distinction of contributing microbiome across normal and overweight category.

In normal group (Figure 55.6), *Enterococcus faecium* was the highest contributing species in predicting CRC and could be a key influencer in CRC. This bacterium is responsible for nosocomial infections particularly on immunocompromised patients. They can easily acquire genes responsible for virulence and environmental prevalence [22] and becomes opportunistic pathogen with antibiotic resistance [24]. Other species such as *Holdemania filiformis, Clostridium indicum* could act as potential biomarkers.

In overweight category (Figure 55.7), *Salmonella enterica* was the key contributor for CRC prediction. *S.enterica* is a genotoxin-producing bacterium and is associated with the risk of colon carcinoma [13]. This oral pathogenic bacterium was enriched in overweight subjects with good periodontal health [16].

Alistipes onderdonkii was found to be one of the key influencers in CRC, irrespective of the BMI category. These key species could be evaluated for their potential role as biomarkers. A previous study based on 16S rRNA sequencing of tumor tissues on Indian population identified *A. onderdonkii* as one of the crucial biomarkers for CRC [7]. These key species could be evaluated for their potential role as biomarkers. As these key species differ for normal

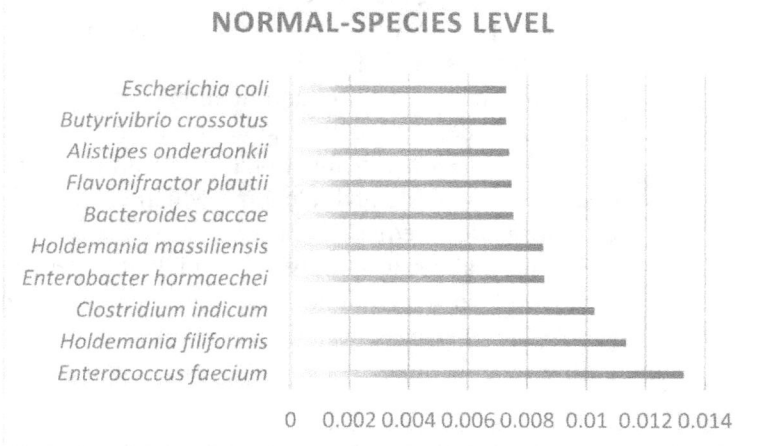

Figure 55.6 Important species features for CRC prediction in normal group
Source: Author

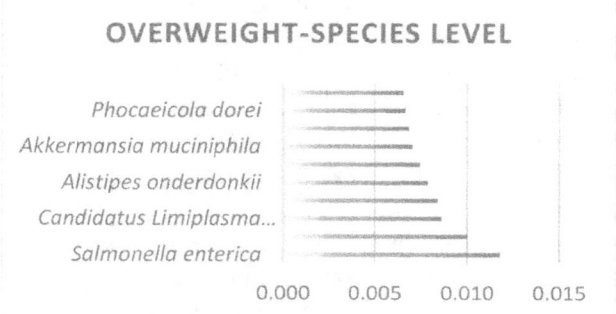

Figure 55.7 Important species features for CRC prediction in overweight group
Source: Author

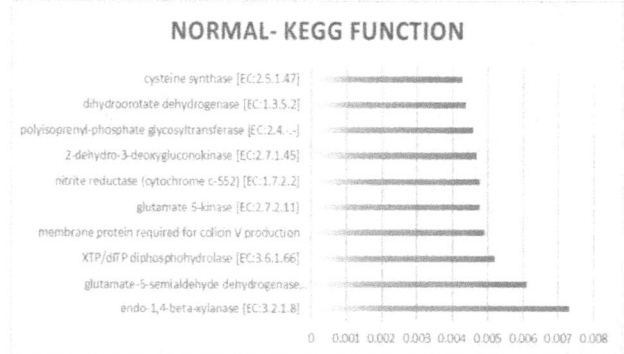

Figure 55.8 Key functional alteration in normal group
Source: Author

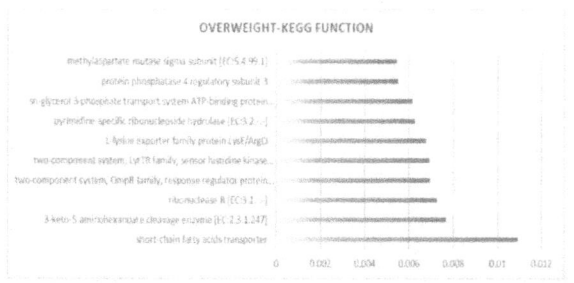

Figure 55.9 Key functional alteration in overweight group
Source: Author

and overweight BMI group, separate biomarkers are needed to monitor CRC progression.

Functional variation across BMI categories

We also identified key influencing KEGG functions across BMI categories based on important features of RF model.

In normal group (Figure 55.8), endo-1,4-beta-xylanase was the higher influencer and in overweight group (Figure 55.9), short-chain fatty acids transporter was the key influencing KEGG function.

No KEGG functions were common between normal and overweight category. This emphasizes that the functions of the gut microbial community also vary between the BMI categories. This variation could be influenced by the BMI, making overweight and obese people more susceptible to CRC. KEGG Ontology, Enzyme commission number, reaction

feature-based model outperforms the species or gene-based models in predicting CRC [14].

Conclusion

The diversity of the microbial community varied across the disease and BMI groups. We explored seven different machine learning models with species level, genus level and KEGG function abundance data for normal and overweight groups in predicting CRC risk. Among the seven models, species abundance-based RF model had higher performance metrics for normal (accuracy = 83%) and overweight (accuracy=77%) group. We also identified important features contributing to the prediction. The key microbial influencer was *Entercoccus faecium* in normal and *Salmonella enterica* in overweight group. We identified that microbial communities varied at both taxonomic and functional level across BMI categories. Separate machine learning model based on gut microbiome could help in diagnosis and prognosis of CRC. This can be utilized to manipulate gut microbiomes to understand the disease progression and manage the disease with personalized prescriptions.

Acknowledgment

We acknowledge the Department of Biotechnology, Ministry of Science & Technology, Government of India for funding HP through DBT-JRF Programme and Centre for Biological Big data analytics Laboratory, Department of Biotechnology, PSG College of Technology, Coimbatore for the infrastructural support.

References

[1] Allen, N. G., Edupuganti, L., Edwards, D. J., Jimenez, N. R., Buck, G. A., Jefferson, K. K., ... & Fettweis, J. M. (2022). The vaginal microbiome in women of reproductive age with healthy weight versus overweight/obesity. *Obesity*, 30(1), 142–152.

[2] Casimiro-Soriguer, C. S., Loucera, C., Peña-Chilet, M., & Dopazo, J. (2022). Towards a metagenomics machine learning interpretable model for understanding the transition from adenoma to colorectal cancer. *Scientific Reports*, 12(1), 450.

[3] Elangovan, A., Skeans, J., Landsman, M., Ali, S. M., Elangovan, A. G., Kaelber, D. C. ... & Cooper, G. S. (2021). Colorectal cancer, age, and obesity-related comorbidities: a large database study. *Digestive Diseases and Sciences*, 66, 3156–3163.

[4] Feng, Q., Liang, S., Jia, H., Stadlmayr, A., Tang, L., Lan, Z., ... & Wang, J. (2015). Gut microbiome development along the colorectal adenoma–carcinoma sequence. *Nature communications*, 6(1), 6528.

[5] Freitas, P., Silva, F., Sousa, J. V., Ferreira, R. M., Figueiredo, C., Pereira, T., & Oliveira, H. P. (2023). Machine learning-based approaches for cancer prediction using microbiome data. *Scientific Reports*, 13(1), 11821.

[6] Gupta, A., Dhakan, D. B., Maji, A., Saxena, R., PK, V. F., Mahajan, S., ... & Sharma, V. K. (2019). Association of Flavonifractor plautii, a flavonoid-degrading bacterium, with the gut microbiome of colorectal cancer patients in India. *MSystems*, 4(6), 10–1128.

[7] Hasan, R., Bose, S., Roy, R., Paul, D., Rawat, S., Nilwe, P., ... & Choudhury, S. (2022). Tumor tissue-specific bacterial biomarker panel for colorectal cancer: Bacteroides massiliensis, Alistipes species, Alistipes onderdonkii, Bifidobacterium pseudocatenulatum, Corynebacterium appendicis. *Archives of Microbiology*, 204(5), 348.

[8] Li, M., Liu, J., Zhu, J., Wang, H., Sun, C., Gao, N. L., ... & Chen, W. H. (2023). Performance of gut microbiome as an independent diagnostic tool for 20 diseases: cross-cohort validation of machine-learning classifiers. *Gut Microbes*, 15(1), 2205386.

[9] Liu, G., Su, L., Kong, C., Huang, L., Zhu, X., Zhang, X., ... & Wang, J. (2024). Improved diagnostic efficiency of CRC subgroups revealed using machine learning based on intestinal microbes. *BMC Gastroenterology*, 24(1), 315.

[10] Liu, J., Huang, X., Chen, C., Wang, Z., Huang, Z., Qin, M., ... & Tang, W. (2023). Identification of colorectal cancer progression-associated intestinal microbiome and predictive signature construction. *Journal of Translational Medicine*, 21(1), 373.

[11] Liu, X., Liu, D., Tan, C. E., & Feng, W. (2023). Gut microbiome-based machine learning for diagnostic prediction of liver fibrosis and cirrhosis: a systematic review and meta-analysis. *BMC Medical Informatics and Decision Making*, 23(1), 294.

[12] Martin, O. C., Bergonzini, A., d'Amico, F., Chen, P., Shay, J. W., Dupuy, J., ... & Frisan, T. (2019). Infection with genotoxin-producing Salmonella enterica synergises with loss of the tumour suppressor APC in promoting genomic instability via the PI3K pathway in colonic epithelial cells. *Cellular Microbiology*, 21(12), e13099.

[13] Norouzi-Beirami, M. H., Marashi, S. A, Banaei-Moghaddam, A. M., & Kavousi, K. (2020). Beyond taxonomic analysis of microbiomes: a functional approach for revisiting microbiome changes in colorectal cancer. *Frontiers in Microbiology*, 10, 3117.

[14] Qi, Z., Zhibo, Z., Jing, Z., Zhanbo, Q., Shugao, H., Weili, J., ... & Shuwen, H. (2022). Prediction model of poorly differentiated colorectal cancer (CRC) based on gut bacteria. *BMC Microbiology*, 22(1), 312.

[15] Rahman, B., Al-Marzooq, F., Saad, H., Benzina, D., & Al Kawas, S. (2023). Dysbiosis of the subgingival microbiome and relation to periodontal disease in association with obesity and overweight. *Nutrients*, 15(4), 826.

[16] Sawicki, T., Ruszkowska, M., Danielewicz, A., Niedźwiedzka, E., Arłukowicz, T., & Przybyłowicz, K. E. (2021). A review of colorectal cancer in terms of epidemiology, risk factors, development, symptoms and diagnosis. *Cancers*, 13(9), 2025.

[17] Shoji, M., Sasaki, Y., Abe, Y., Nishise, S., Yaoita, T., Yagi, M., ... & Ueno, Y. (2021). Characteristics of the gut mi-

crobiome profile in obese patients with colorectal cancer. *JGH Open*, 5(4), 498–507.

[18] Siddiqui, R., Boghossian, A., Alharbi, A. M., Alfahemi, H., & Khan, N. A. (2022). The pivotal role of the gut microbiome in colorectal cancer. *Biology*, 11(11), 1642.

[19] Tamames, J., & Puente-Sánchez, F. (2019). SqueezeMeta, a highly portable, fully automatic metagenomic analysis pipeline. *Frontiers in Microbiology*, 9, 3349.

[20] Thomas, A. M., Manghi, P., Asnicar, F., Pasolli, E., Armanini, F., Zolfo, M., ... & Segata, N. (2019). Metagenomic analysis of colorectal cancer datasets identifies cross-cohort microbial diagnostic signatures and a link with choline degradation. *Nature Medicine*, 25(4), 667–678.

[21] van Schaik, W., Top, J., Riley, D. R., Boekhorst, J., Vrijenhoek, J. E., Schapendonk, C. M., ... & Willems, R. J. (2010). Pyrosequencing-based comparative genome analysis of the nosocomial pathogen Enterococcus faecium and identification of a large transferable pathogenicity island. *BMC Genomics*, 11, 1–18.

[22] Vogtmann, E., Hua, X., Zeller, G., Sunagawa, S., Voigt, A. Y., Hercog, R., ... & Sinha, R. (2016). Colorectal cancer and the human gut microbiome: reproducibility with whole-genome shotgun sequencing. *PloS One*, 11(5), e0155362.

[23] Wei, Y., Palacios Araya, D., & Palmer, K. L. (2024). Enterococcus faecium: evolution, adaptation, pathogenesis and emerging therapeutics. *Nature Reviews Microbiology*, 22(11), 705–721.

[24] Wirbel, J., Pyl, P. T., Kartal, E., Zych, K., Kashani, A., Milanese, A., ... & Zeller, G. (2019). Meta-analysis of fecal metagenomes reveals global microbial signatures that are specific for colorectal cancer. *Nature Medicine*, 25(4), 679–689.

[25] Wu, H., Li, Y., Jiang, Y., Li, X., Wang, S., Zhao, C., ... & Qiao, J. (2025). Machine learning prediction of obesity-associated gut microbiota: identifying Bifidobacterium pseudocatenulatum as a potential therapeutic target. *Frontiers in Microbiology*, 15, 1488656.

[26] Yinhang, W., Jing, Z., Jie, Z., Yin, J., Xinyue, W., Yifei, S., ... & Shuwen, H. (2023). Prediction model of colorectal cancer (CRC) lymph node metastasis based on intestinal bacteria. *Clinical and Translational Oncology*, 25(6), 1661–1672.

[27] Yu, J., Feng, Q., Wong, S. H., Zhang, D., yi Liang, Q., Qin, Y., ... & Wang, J. (2017). Metagenomic analysis of faecal microbiome as a tool towards targeted non-invasive biomarkers for colorectal cancer. *Gut*, 66(1), 70–78.

[28] Zeller, G., Tap, J., Voigt, A. Y., Sunagawa, S., Kultima, J. R., Costea, P. I., ... & Bork, P. (2014). Potential of fecal microbiota for early-stage detection of colorectal cancer. *Molecular Systems Biology*, 10(11), 766.

For Product Safety Concerns and Information please contact our EU
representative GPSR@taylorandfrancis.com
Taylor & Francis Verlag GmbH, Kaufingerstraße 24, 80331 München, Germany